Engaging. Trackable. Affordable.

CourseMate brings course concepts to life with interactive learning, study, and exam preparation tools that support ADJUST.

INCLUDES:

Integrated eBook, **interactive teaching and learning tools,** and **Engagement Tracker**, a first-of-its-kind tool that monitors student engagement in the course.

ON THE WEB

ADJUST

ONLINE RESOURCES INCLUDED!

STUDENT RESOURCES:

- Interactive eBook
- Flashcards
- Self-Assessments
- Self-Reflections
- Practice Quizzing
- Videos
- Virtual Psychology Labs

Students sign in at **www.cengagebrain.com**

INSTRUCTOR RESOURCES:

- All Student Resources
- Engagement Tracker
- First Day of Class Instructions
- LMS Integration
- Instructor's Manual
- Test Bank
- PowerPoint® Slides

Instructors sign-in at **www.cengage.com/login**

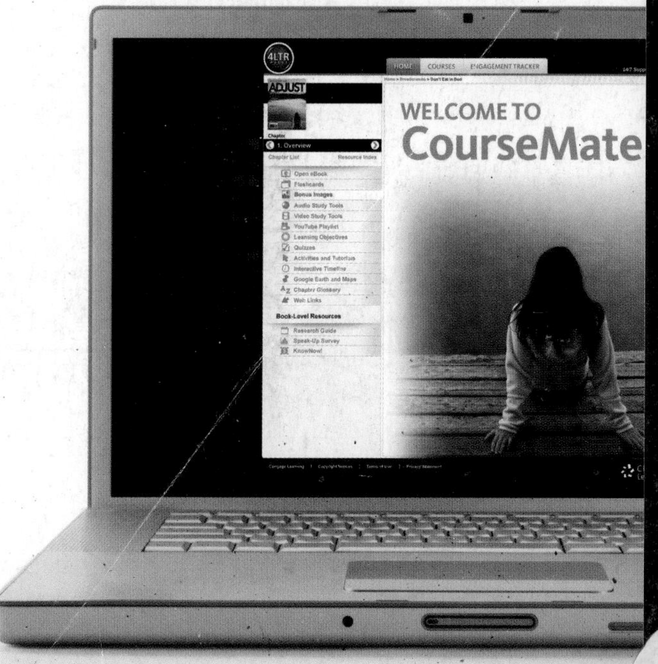

ADJUST: Applying Psychology to Life
Wayne Weiten, Elizabeth Hammer, Dana Dunn

Publisher: Jon-David Hague

Acquisitions Editor: Timothy Matray

Developmental Editor: Kristin Makarewycz, Trina McManus

Assistant Editor: Casey Lozier

Editorial Assistant: Nicole Richards

Media Editor: Jasmin Tokatlian

Brand Manager: Elisabeth Rhoden

Market Development Manager: Christine Sosa

Product Development Manager, 4LTR Press: Steven Joos

Content Project Manager: Jennifer Risden

Art Director: Jennifer Wahi

Manufacturing Planner: Karen Hunt

Rights Acquisitions Specialist: Dean Dauphinais

Production Service and Layout: Joan Keyes, Dovetail Publishing Services

Photo Researcher: Terri Wright

Text Researcher: Terri Wright

Copy Editor: Jackie Estrada

Illustrator: Carol Zuber-Mallison

Text Designer: Ke Design

Cover Designer: Ke Design

Front Cover Image: © Dan Barnes/iStockphoto

Inside Cover/Back Cover/Gatefold/Page i Images: active woman holding water and magazine: © sdominick/iStockphoto; pile of dollars: © alexsl/iStockphoto; college hangout vector image: © A-Digit/iStockphoto; laptop isolated: © CostinT/iStockphoto; A+ with a circle: © photovideostock/iStockphoto; forty-three separate people in a crowd vector image: © Leontura/iStockphoto; laptop in use: © René Mansi/iStockphoto; open magazine: © brebca/iStockphoto; desktops vector image: © A-Digit/iStockphoto; group of people vector image: © mustafahacalak/iStockphoto; study: © A-Digit/iStockphoto; friends studying: © A-Digit/iStockphoto

Compositor: Graphic World, Inc.

Library of Congress Control Number: 2012953801

ISBN-13: 978-1-133-59498-7
ISBN-10: 1-133-59498-0

Wadsworth
20 Davis Drive
Belmont, CA 94002-3098
USA

Cengage Learning is a leading provider of customized learning solutions with office locations around the globe, including Singapore, the United Kingdom, Australia, Mexico, Brazil, and Japan. Locate your local office at **www.cengage.com/global.**

Cengage Learning products are represented in Canada by Nelson Education, Ltd.

To learn more about Wadsworth, visit **www.cengage.com/wadsworth.**

Purchase any of our products at your local college store or at our preferred online store **www.cengagebrain.com.**

Printed in the United States of America
2 3 4 5 6 7 17 16 15 14 13

ADJUST BRIEF CONTENTS

© Zurijeta/Shutterstock.com

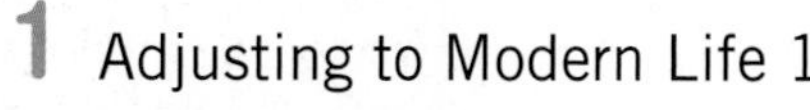
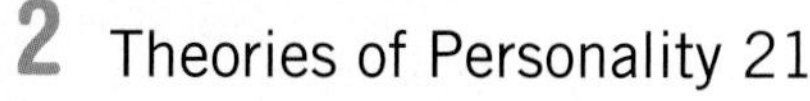

© OtnaYdur/Shutterstock.com

© Bruce Rolff/Shutterstock.com

ADJUST | CONTENTS

© Blend Images/Ariel Skelley/Getty Images

© EIGHTFISH/Getty Images

3 STRESS AND ITS EFFECTS 47

4 COPING PROCESSES 69

© Cultura RM/Masterfile

© Masterfile/Royalty-Free

7 SOCIAL THINKING AND SOCIAL INFLUENCE 137

© KL Services/Masterfile

© Diane Diederich/Getty Images

8 INTERPERSONAL COMMUNICATION 161

© Rayes/Getty Images

9 FRIENDSHIP AND LOVE 183

10 MARRIAGE AND INTIMATE RELATIONSHIPS 205

© Masterfile

© Bruno Ehrs/Corbis

11 GENDER AND BEHAVIOR 227

12 DEVELOPMENT AND EXPRESSION OF SEXUALITY 251

© Dewayne Flowers/Shutterstock

© Masterfile/Royalty-Free

© biffspandex/iStockphoto

15 PSYCHOTHERAPY 319

© Toltek/iStockphoto

© Blend Images/Ariel Skelley/Getty Images

LEARNING OBJECTIVES

1-1 Provide examples of people's search for direction in their lives, and analyze the value of self-help books.

1-2 Describe the two key facets of psychology, and explain the concept of adjustment.

1-3 Explain the nature of experimental and correlational research, and evaluate the advantages of each approach.

1-4 Review information on the factors that are and are not predictive of subjective well-being.

1-5 Discuss some strategies for improving study habits, note taking, reading comprehension, and memory.

STUDY TOOLS ▶ After you have read the chapter, you can Test Yourself and learn about other Study Tools on page 19.

CHAPTER 1

Adjusting to MODERN LIFE

© Photo_Concepts/iStockphoto

1-1 The Search for Direction

We are the children of technology. In many respects, we live in a time of unparalleled progress. Modern societies have made extraordinary strides in transportation, energy, communication, agriculture, and medicine. Yet despite our technological advances, social problems and personal difficulties seem more prevalent than ever before. Indeed, many social critics argue that the quality of our lives and our sense of personal fulfillment have declined rather than increased. This is the paradox of progress.

What is the cause of this paradox? Many explanations have been offered. Erich Fromm (1981) has argued that the progress we value so much has scrambled our value systems and undermined our traditional sources of emotional security, such as family, community, and religion. Alvin Toffler (1980) attributes our collective alienation and distress to our being overwhelmed by rapidly accelerating cultural change. Tim Kasser (2002) speculates that excessive materialism weakens the social ties that bind us, stokes the fires of insecurity, and undermines our collective sense of well-being. Whatever the explanation, many theorists, working from varied perspectives, agree that *the basic challenge of modern life has become the search for meaning, a sense of direction, and a personal philosophy*. This daunting search, which sometimes goes awry, manifests itself in many ways.

For example, we could discuss how hundreds of thousands of Americans have invested large sums of money to enroll in "self-realization" programs such as Scientology, Silva Mind Control, John Gray's Mars and Venus relationship seminars, and Tony Robbins's Life Mastery seminars. These programs typically promise to provide profound enlightenment and to quickly turn one's life around. Many participants claim that the programs have revolutionized their lives. However, most experts characterize such programs as intellectually bankrupt, and book and magazine exposés reveal them as simply lucrative money-making schemes (Behar, 1991; Pressman, 1993). In a particularly scathing analysis of these programs, Steve Salerno (2005) outlines the enormous financial benefits reaped by their inventors, such as Tony Robbins ($80 million in annual income) and John Gray ($50,000 per speech). In his critique, Salerno also attacks the hypocrisy and inflated credentials of many leading self-help gurus. For example, he asserts that John Gray's doctorate came from a nonaccredited correspondence college and that radio therapist Dr. Laura, who does not have a degree in psychology or psychiatry, is "a critic of premarital and extramarital sex who's indulged in both" (p. 44). More than anything else, the enormous success of these self-help gurus and self-realization programs demonstrates just how desperate some people are for a sense of purpose in their lives.

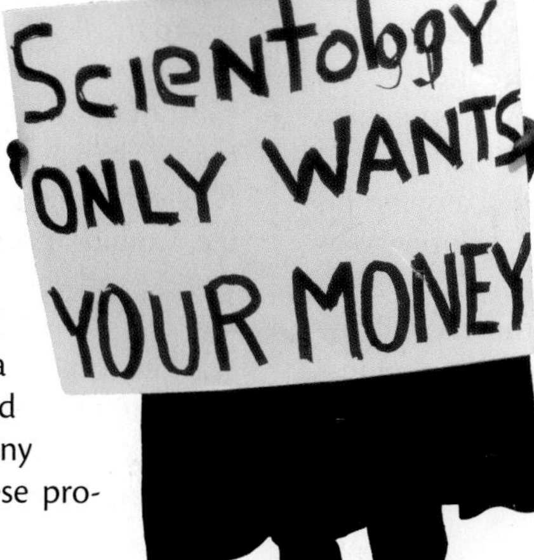

© Sergei Bachlakov/Shutterstock.com

For the most part, self-realization programs are harmless scams that appear to give some participants an illusory sense of direction or a temporary boost in self-confidence. But in some cases they probably lead people down ill-advised pathways that prove harmful. The ultimate example of the potential for harm unfolded in October 2009 in Sedona, Arizona, where three people died and eighteen others were hospitalized, many with serious injuries, after participating in a "spiritual warrior" retreat that required them to spend hours in a makeshift sweat lodge (Harris & Wagner, 2009). The retreat was run by James Ray, a self-help guru whose website promised to teach people "how to trigger your Unconscious Mind to automatically increase your level of wealth and fulfillment." Ray, who has written several inspirational books and appeared on major national TV talk shows, had built a $9-million-a-year self-help empire. The fifty to sixty people who participated in his ill-fated retreat paid over $9,000 apiece for the privilege. After spending 36 hours fasting in the desert on a "vision quest," they were led into a tarp-covered sweat lodge for an endurance challenge that was supposed to show them that they could gain confidence by conquering physical discomfort.

Unfortunately, the sweat lodge turned out to be poorly ventilated and overheated, so that within an hour people began vomiting, gasping for air, and collapsing. Undaunted, Ray, urged his followers to persevere, telling them that the vomiting was good for them and saying, "You have to go through this barrier" (Doughtery, 2009). No one was physically forced to stay (and a few did leave), but Ray was an intimidating presence who strongly exhorted everyone to remain, so they could prove that they were stronger than their bodies. Tragically, he pushed their bodies too far; by the end of the ceremony many of the participants were seriously ill. Yet, according to one account, "At the conclusion, seemingly unaware of the bodies of the unconscious lying around him, Ray emerged triumphantly, witnesses said, pumping his fist because he had passed his own endurance test" (Whelan, 2009).

Some of the aftermath of this event has also proven revealing. Consistent with the assertion that it really is all about the money, Ray provided a *partial* refund to the family of Kirby Brown, a participant who *died* in the sweat lodge (Martinez, 2009). And the reactions of some of Ray's followers after the sweat lodge tragedy have been illuminating. You might think that, after recklessly leading people "over a cliff," Ray might be discredited in the eyes of his followers. But think again. Reporters working on this horrific story had no trouble finding Ray advocates who continued to enthusiastically champion his vision for self-improvement (Kraft, 2009). This unwavering faith in Ray's teachings provides a remarkable testimonial to the persuasive power of the charismatic leaders who promote self-realization programs. Nonetheless, in 2011 an Arizona jury deliberated for less than 12 hours before convicting Ray on three counts of negligent homicide (Riccardi, 2011).

We could also discuss how a number of unorthodox religious groups—commonly called *cults*—have attracted countless converts who voluntarily embrace a life of regimentation, obedience, and zealous ideology. It is difficult to get good data, but one study suggested that more than 2 million young adults are involved with cults in the United States (Robinson, Frye, & Bradley, 1997). It is widely believed that cults use brainwashing and mind control to seduce lonely outsiders. In reality, converts are a diverse array of normal people who are swayed by ordinary—albeit sophisticated—social influence strategies (Singer, 2003). According to Philip Zimbardo (1992), people join cults because these groups appear to provide simple solutions to complex problems, a sense of purpose, and a structured lifestyle that reduces feelings of uncertainty.

Although we might choose to examine any of these examples of people's search for a sense of direction, we will reserve our in-depth analysis for a manifestation of this search that is even more germane to our focus on everyday adjustment: the spectacular success of best-selling "self-help" books.

1-1a SELF-HELP BOOKS

Americans spend roughly $650 million annually on "self-help books" that offer do-it-yourself treatments for common personal problems (Arkowitz & Lilienfeld, 2006). This fascination with self-improvement is nothing new. For decades, American readers have displayed a voracious appetite for self-help books such as *I'm OK—You're OK* (Harris, 1967), *The Seven Habits of Highly Effective People* (Covey, 1989), *Don't Sweat the Small Stuff . . . and It's All Small Stuff* (Carlson, 1997), *The Purpose Driven Life* (Warren, 2002), *The Secret* (Byrne, 2006), and *Become a Better You: Seven Keys to Improving Your Life Every Day* (Osteen, 2009).

If the consumption of these literary narcotics were even remotely as helpful as their publishers claim, we would be a nation of serene, happy, well-adjusted people.

With their simple recipes for achieving happiness, most of these books have not been timid about promising to change the quality of the reader's life. Unfortunately, merely reading a book is not likely to turn your life around. If only it were that easy! If only someone could hand you a book that would solve all your problems! If the consumption of these literary narcotics were even remotely as helpful as their publishers claim, we would be a nation of serene, happy, well-adjusted people. It is clear, however, that serenity is not the dominant national mood. Quite the contrary, in recent decades Americans' average anxiety level has moved upward (Twenge, 2000), and the prevalence of depression has increased as well (Kessler, 2002). The multitude of self-help books that crowd bookstore shelves represent just one more symptom of our collective distress and our search for the elusive secret of happiness.

© Wayne Weiten

The Value of Self-Help Books

It is somewhat unfair to lump all self-help books together for a critique, because they vary widely in quality. Surveys exploring psychotherapists' opinions of self-help books suggest that there are indeed some excellent books that offer authentic insights and sound advice (Starker, 1990). Many therapists encourage their patients to read carefully selected self-help books (Campbell & Smith, 2003). Thus, it would be foolish to dismiss all these books as shallow drivel. Unfortunately, however, the gems are easily lost in the mountains of rubbish. A great many self-help books offer little of real value to the reader. Generally, they suffer from four fundamental shortcomings.

First, they are dominated by "psychobabble." The term *psychobabble*, coined by R. D. Rosen (1977), seems appropriate to describe the "hip" but hopelessly vague language used in many of these books. Statements such as "It's beautiful if you're unhappy," "You've got to get in touch with yourself," and "You gotta be you 'cause you're you" are typical examples of this language. At best, such terminology is ill-defined; at worst, it is meaningless. Clarity is sacrificed in favor of a jargon that prevents, rather than enhances, effective communication.

A second problem is that self-help books tend to place more emphasis on sales than on scientific soundness. The advice offered in these books is far too rarely based on solid, scientific research (Paul, 2001; Rosen, 1993). Instead, the ideas are frequently based on the authors' intuitive analyses, which may be highly speculative. Even when books are based on well-researched therapeutic programs, interventions that are effective in clinical settings with professional supervision may not be effective when self-administered without professional guidance (Rosen, Glasgow, & Moore, 2003).

The third shortcoming is that self-help books don't usually provide explicit directions about how to change your behavior. These books tend to be smoothly written and "touchingly human" in tone. They often strike responsive chords in the reader by aptly describing a common problem that many of us experience. The reader says, "Yes, that's me!" Unfortunately, when the book focuses on how to deal with the problem, it usually provides only a vague distillation of simple common sense, which could be covered in two rather than two-hundred pages.

Fourth, many of these books encourage a remarkably self-centered, narcissistic approach to life (Justman, 2005). ***Narcissism* is a personality trait marked by an inflated sense of importance, a need for attention and admiration, a sense of entitlement, and a tendency to exploit others.** The term is based on the Greek myth of Narcissus, an attractive young man in search of love who sees himself reflected in water and falls in love with his own image. Although there are plenty of exceptions, the basic message in many self-help books is "Do whatever you feel like doing, and don't worry about the consequences for other people." This "me first" philosophy emphasizes self-admiration, an entitlement to special treatment, and an exploitive approach to interpersonal relationships. Interestingly, research suggests that narcissism levels have increased among recent generations of college students (Twenge & Campbell, 2009). It is hard to say how much popular self-help books have fueled this rise in narcissism, but surely they have contributed.

© Thinkstock

What to Look for in Self-Help Books

Because self-help books vary so widely in quality, it seems a good idea to provide you with some guidelines about what to look for in seeking genuinely helpful books. The following thoughts give you some criteria for judging books of this type.

1. This may sound backward, but look for books that do not promise too much in the way of immediate change. The truly useful books tend to be appropriately cautious in their promises and realistic about the challenge of altering your behavior. As Arkowitz and Lilienfeld (2006, p. 79) put it, "Be wary of books that make promises that they obviously cannot keep, such as curing a phobia in five minutes or fixing a failing marriage in a week."

2. Try to check out the credentials of the author or authors. Book jackets will often exaggerate the expertise of authors, but these days a quick Internet search can often yield more objective biographical information and perhaps some perceptive reviews of the book.

3. Try to select books that mention, at least briefly, the theoretical or research basis for the program they advocate. It is understandable that you may not be interested in a detailed summary of research that supports a particular piece of advice. However, you should be interested in whether the advice is based on published research, widely accepted theory, anecdotal evidence, clinical interactions with patients, or pure speculation by the author. Books that are based on more than personal anecdotes and speculation should have a list of references in the back (or at the end of each chapter).

4. Look for books that provide detailed, explicit directions about how to alter your behavior. Generally, these directions represent the crucial core of the book. If they are inadequate in detail, you have been shortchanged.

5. More often than not, books that focus on a particular kind of problem, such as overeating, loneliness, or marital difficulties, deliver more than those that promise to cure all of life's problems with a few simple ideas. Books that cover everything are usually superficial and disappointing. Books that devote a great deal of thought to a particular topic tend to be written by authors with genuine expertise on that topic. Such books are more likely to pay off for you.

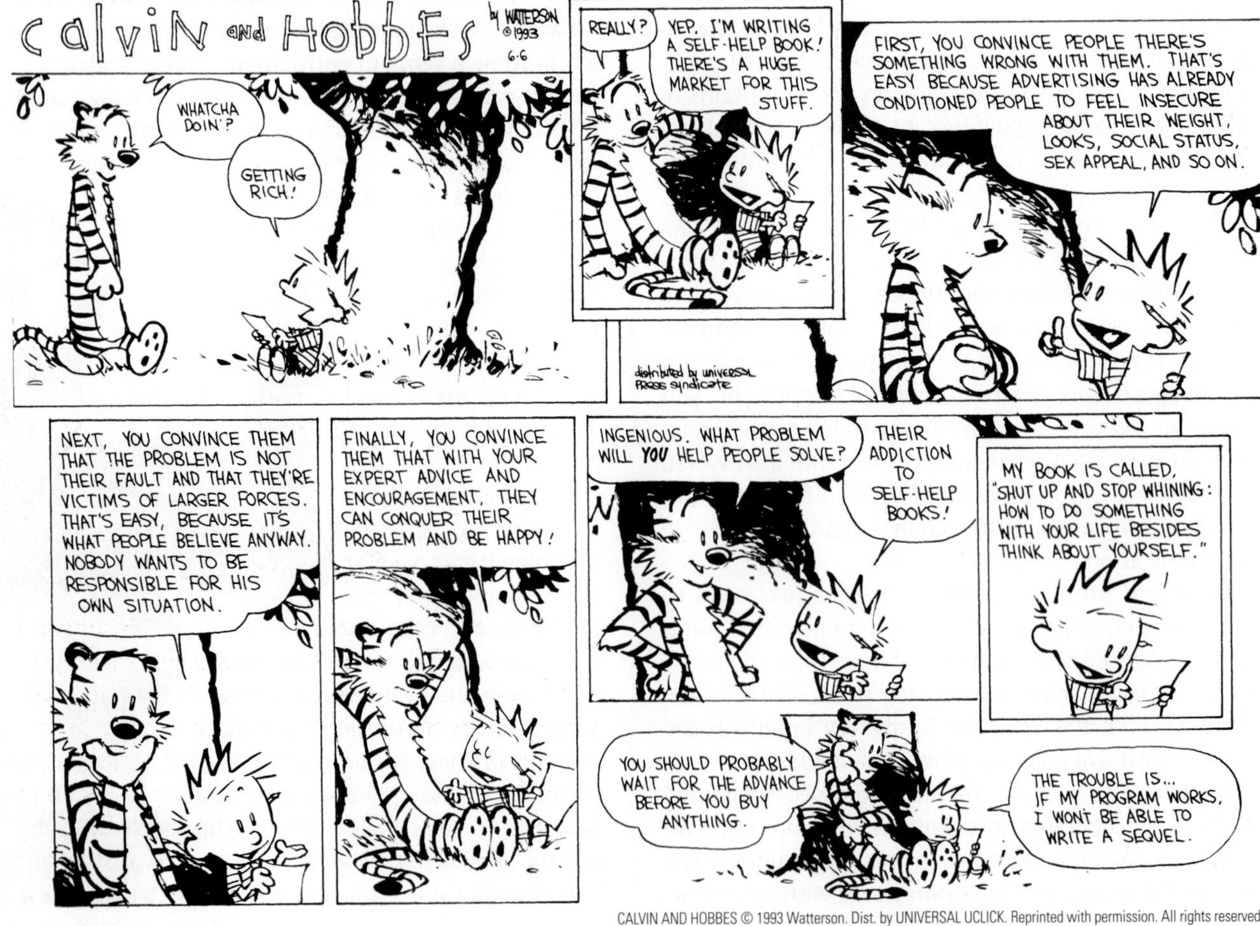

1-1b THE APPROACH OF THIS TEXTBOOK

Clearly, living in our complex, modern world is a formidable challenge. This book is about that challenge. It is about you. It is about life. Specifically, it summarizes for you the scientific research on human behavior that appears relevant to the challenge of living effectively in contemporary society. It draws primarily, but not exclusively, from the science we call psychology.

This text deals with the same kinds of problems addressed by self-help books and self-realization programs: anxiety, stress, interpersonal relationships, frustration, loneliness, depression, self-control. However, it makes no boldly seductive promises about solving your personal problems, turning your life around, or helping you achieve tranquillity. Such promises simply aren't realistic. Psychologists have long recognized that changing a person's behavior is a difficult challenge, fraught with frustration and failure. Troubled individuals sometimes spend years in therapy without resolving their problems.

This reality does not mean that you should be pessimistic about your potential for personal growth. You most certainly can change your behavior. Moreover, you can often change it on your own without consulting a professional psychologist. We would not be writing this text if we did not believe it could be potentially beneficial to our readers. But it is important that you have realistic expectations. Reading this book will not be a revelatory experience. No mysterious secrets are about to be unveiled. All this book can do is give you some useful information and point you in some potentially beneficial directions. The rest is up to you.

1-2 The Psychology of Adjustment

Now that we have spelled out our approach in writing this text, it is time to turn to the task of introducing you to some basic concepts. In this section, we'll discuss the nature of psychology and the concept of adjustment.

1-2a WHAT IS PSYCHOLOGY?

***Psychology* is the science that studies behavior and the physiological and mental processes that underlie it, and it is the profession that applies the accumulated knowledge of this science to practical problems.** Psychology leads a complex dual existence as both a *science* and a *profession*. Let's examine the science first. Psychology is an area of scientific study, much like biology or physics. Whereas biology focuses on life processes and physics focuses on matter and energy, psychology focuses on *behavior* and *related mental and physiological processes*.

***Behavior* is any overt (observable) response or activity by an organism.** Psychology does *not* confine itself to the study of human behavior. Many psychologists believe that the principles of behavior are much the same for all animals, including humans. As a result, these psychologists often prefer to study animals—mainly because they can exert more control over the factors influencing the animals' behavior.

Psychology is also interested in the mental processes—the thoughts, feelings, and wishes—that accompany behavior. Mental processes are more difficult to study than behavior because they are private and not directly observable. However, they exert critical influence over human behavior, so psychologists have strived to improve their ability to "look inside the mind" to analyze decision making, problem solving, and memory. Finally, psychology includes the study of the physiological processes that underlie behavior. Thus, some psychologists try to figure out how bodily processes such as neural impulses, hormonal secretions, and genetic coding regulate behavior.

Photo: © Levent Konuk/Shutterstock.com ; Graphic: © Thomas Bethge/Shutterstock.com

The other facet of psychology is its highly practical side, represented by the many psychologists who provide a variety of professional services to the public. Although the profession of psychology is quite prominent today, this aspect of psychology was actually slow to develop. Until the 1950s psychologists were found almost exclusively in the halls of academia, teaching and doing research. However, the demands of World War II stimulated rapid growth in psychology's first

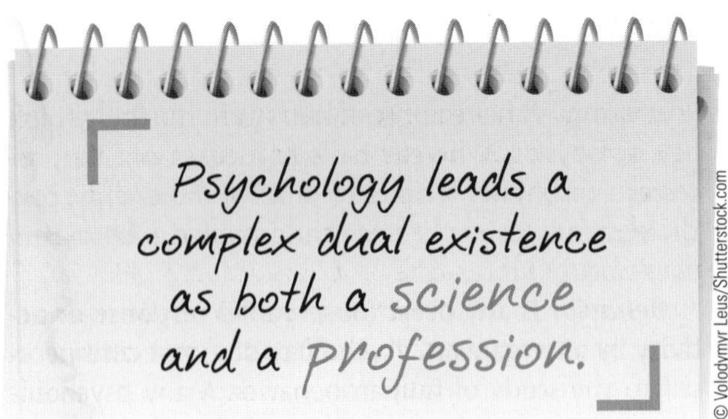
Psychology leads a complex dual existence as both a science and a profession.
© Volodymyr Leus/Shutterstock.com

professional specialty: clinical psychology. ***Clinical psychology* is the branch of psychology concerned with the diagnosis and treatment of psychological problems and disorders.** During World War II, a multitude of academic psychologists were pressed into service as clinicians to screen military recruits and treat soldiers suffering from trauma. Many found their clinical work interesting and returned from the war to set up training programs to meet the continued high demand for clinical services. Within a couple of decades, over half of the new Ph.D.'s in psychology were specializing in clinical work, and the discipline of psychology had come of age as a profession.

1-2b WHAT IS ADJUSTMENT?

We have used the term *adjustment* several times without clarifying its exact meaning. The concept of adjustment was originally borrowed from biology. It was modeled after the biological term *adaptation*, which refers to efforts by a species to adjust to changes in its environment. Just as a field mouse has to adapt to an unusually brutal winter, a person has to adjust to changes in circumstances such as a new job, a financial setback, or the loss of a loved one. Thus, ***adjustment* refers to the psychological processes through which people manage or cope with the demands and challenges of everyday life.**

The demands of daily life are diverse, so in studying the process of adjustment we will encounter a broad variety of topics. In our early chapters we discuss general issues, such as how personality affects people's patterns of adjustment, how individuals are affected by stress, and how people use coping strategies to deal with stress. From there we move on to chapters that examine adjustment in an interpersonal context. We discuss topics such as impression formation, social pressure, interpersonal communication, friendship, love, marriage, divorce, gender roles, career development, and sexuality. Finally, toward the end of the book we discuss how the process of adjustment influences a person's mental health, and we look at therapeutic interventions for psychological disorders. Before we begin considering these topics in earnest, however, we need to take a closer look at psychology's approach to investigating behavior—the scientific method.

1-3 The Scientific Approach to Behavior

We all expend a great deal of effort in trying to understand our own behavior as well as the behavior of others. We wonder about any number of behavioral questions: Why am I so anxious when I interact with new people? Why is Sam always trying to be the center of attention at the office? Why does Juanita cheat on her wonderful husband? Are extraverts happier than introverts? Is depression more common during the Christmas holidays?

Given that psychologists' principal goal is to explain behavior, how are their efforts different from everyone else's? The key difference is that psychology is a *science*, committed to *empiricism*. ***Empiricism* is the premise that knowledge should be acquired through observation.** When we say that scientific psychology is empirical, we mean that its conclusions are based on systematic observation rather than on reasoning, speculation, traditional beliefs, or common sense. Scientists are not content with having ideas that sound plausible; they must conduct research to *test* their hypotheses. There are two main types of research methods in psychology: *experimental methods* and *correlational methods*. We discuss them separately because an important distinction exists between them.

1-3a EXPERIMENTAL RESEARCH: LOOKING FOR CAUSES

Does misery love company? This question intrigued social psychologist Stanley Schachter. When people feel anxious, do they want to be left alone, or do they prefer to have others around? Schachter hypothesized that increases in anxiety would cause increases in the desire to be with others, which psychologists call the *need for affiliation*. To test this hypothesis, Schachter (1959) designed a clever experiment. **The *experiment* is a research method in which the investigator manipulates one (independent) variable under carefully controlled conditions and observes whether any changes occur in a second (dependent) variable as a result.** Psychologists depend on this method more than any other.

Independent and Dependent Variables

An experiment is designed to find out whether changes in one variable (let's call it *x*) cause changes in another variable (let's call it *y*). To put it more concisely, we want to know how *x* affects *y*. In this formulation, we refer to *x* as the independent variable, and we call *y* the dependent variable. **An *independent variable* is a condition or event that an experimenter varies in order to see its impact on another variable.** The independent variable is the variable that the experimenter controls or manipulates. It is hypothesized to have some effect on the dependent variable. The experiment is conducted to verify this effect. **The *dependent variable* is the variable that is thought to be affected by the manipulations of the independent variable.** In psychology studies, the dependent variable usually is a measurement of some aspect of the subjects' behavior.

In Schachter's experiment, *the independent variable was the participants' anxiety level,* which he manipulated in the following way. Subjects assembled in his laboratory were told by a Dr. Zilstein that they would be participating in a study on the physiological effects of electric shock and that they would receive a series of shocks. Half of the participants were warned that the shocks would be very painful. They made up the *high-anxiety* group. The other half of the participants, assigned to the *low-anxiety* group, were told that the shocks would be mild and painless. These procedures were simply intended to evoke different levels of anxiety. In reality, no one was actually shocked at any time. Instead, the experimenter indicated that there would be a delay while he prepared the shock apparatus for use. The participants were asked whether they would prefer to wait alone or in the company of others. *This measure of the subjects' desire to affiliate with others was the dependent variable.*

Experimental and Control Groups

To conduct an experiment, an investigator typically assembles two groups of participants who are treated differently in regard to the independent variable. We call these groups the experimental and control groups. **The *experimental group* consists of the subjects who receive some special treatment in regard to the independent variable. The *control group* consists of similar subjects who do not receive the special treatment given to the experimental group.**

Let's return to the Schachter study to illustrate. In this experiment, the participants in the high-anxiety condition were the experimental group. They received a special treatment designed to create an unusually high level of anxiety. The participants in the low-anxiety condition were the control group.

It is crucial that the experimental and control groups be similar except for the different treatment they receive in regard to the independent variable. This stipulation brings us to the logic that underlies the experimental method. If the two groups are alike in all respects *except for the variation created by the manipulation of the independent variable,* then any differences between the two groups on the dependent variable *must be due to this manipulation of the independent variable.* In this way researchers isolate the effect of the independent variable on the dependent variable. In his experiment, Schachter isolated the impact of anxiety on need for affiliation. What did he find? As predicted, he found that increased anxiety led to increased affiliation. The percentage of people who wanted to wait with others was nearly twice as high in the high-anxiety group as in the low-anxiety group.

The logic of the experimental method rests heavily on the assumption that the experimental and control groups are alike in all important matters except for their different treatment with regard to the independent variable. Any other differences between the two groups cloud the situation and make it difficult to draw solid conclusions about the relationship between the independent variable and the dependent variable. To summarize our discussion of the experimental method, Figure 1.1 on the next page provides an overview of the various elements in an experiment, using Schachter's study as an example.

Advantages and Disadvantages

The experiment is a powerful research method. Its principal advantage is that it allows scientists to draw conclusions about cause-and-effect relationships between variables. Researchers can draw these conclusions about causation because the precise control available in the experiment permits them to isolate the relationship between the independent variable and the dependent variable. No other research method can duplicate this advantage.

For all its power, however, the experimental method has its limitations. One disadvantage is that researchers are often interested in the effects of variables that cannot be manipulated (as independent variables) because of ethical concerns or practical realities. For instance, you might be interested in whether a nutritionally poor diet during pregnancy increases the likelihood of birth defects. This clearly is a significant issue. However, you obviously cannot

FIGURE 1.1 The basic elements of an experiment

This diagram provides an overview of the key features of the experimental method, as illustrated by Schachter's study of anxiety and affiliation. The logic of the experiment rests on treating the experimental and control groups alike except for the manipulation of the independent variable.

HYPOTHESIS:
Anxiety increases desire to affiliate
Choice of subjects
College students
Assignment to groups
Experimental
Control
Standardized (similar) conditions
Laboratory setting with Dr. Zilstein
Manipulation of independent variable
"Shocks will be very painful . . ." (high anxiety)
"Shocks will be mild and painless . . ." (low anxiety)
Measurement of dependent variable
"Would you prefer to wait alone or with others?" (desire to affiliate)
Results
High-anxiety group wanted to wait with others more than low-anxiety group did
CONCLUSION:
Anxiety does increase desire to affiliate

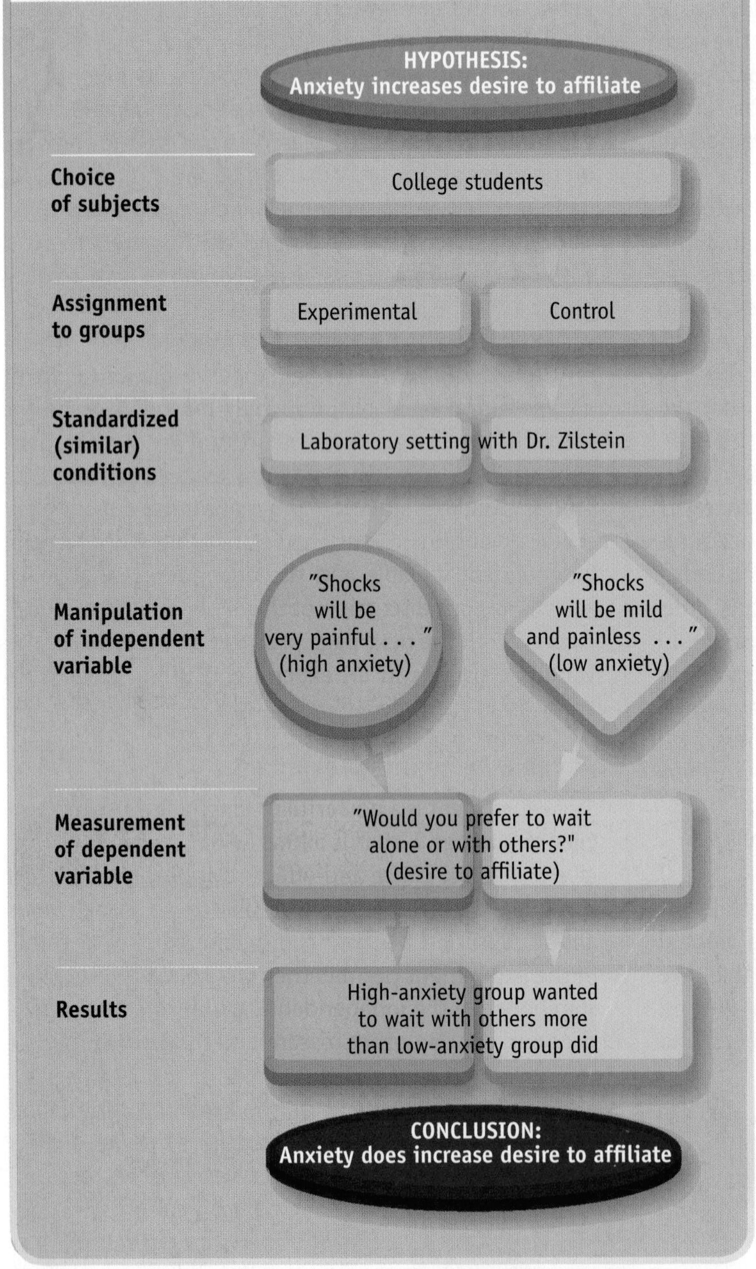

select one hundred pregnant women and assign fifty of them to a condition in which they consume an inadequate diet. The potential risk to the health of the women and their unborn children would make this research strategy unethical. To explore this question, you would have to use correlational research methods, which we turn to next.

1-3b CORRELATIONAL RESEARCH: LOOKING FOR LINKS

As we just noted, in some cases psychologists cannot exert experimental control over the variables they want to study. In such situations, all a researcher can do is make systematic observations to see whether a link or association exists between the variables of interest. Such an association is called a correlation. A *correlation* exists when two variables are related to each other. The definitive aspect of correlational studies is that the researchers cannot control the variables under study.

Measuring Correlation

The results of correlational research are often summarized with a statistic called the *correlation coefficient.* We'll be referring to this widely used statistic frequently as we discuss studies throughout the remainder of this text. **A *correlation coefficient* is a numerical index of the degree of relationship that exists between two variables.** A correlation coefficient indicates (1) how strongly related two variables are and (2) the direction (positive or negative) of the relationship.

Two kinds of relationships can be described by a correlation. A *positive* correlation indicates that two variables co-vary in the same direction. This means that high scores on variable *x* are associated with high scores on variable *y* and that low scores on variable *x* are associated with low scores on variable *y.* For example, there is a positive correlation between high school grade point average (GPA) and subsequent college GPA. That is, people who do well in high school tend to do well in college, and those who perform poorly in high school tend to perform poorly in college (see Figure 1.2).

In contrast, a *negative* correlation indicates that two variables co-vary in the opposite direction. This means that people who score high on variable *x* tend to score low on variable *y*, whereas those who score low on *x* tend to score high on *y*. For example, in most college courses, there is a negative correlation between how frequently a student is absent and how well the student performs on exams. Students who have a high number of absences

FIGURE 1.2 | Positive and negative correlations

Variables are positively correlated if they tend to increase and decrease together, and they are negatively correlated if one variable tends to increase when the other decreases. Hence, the terms *positive correlation* and *negative correlation* refer to the *direction* of the relationship between two variables.

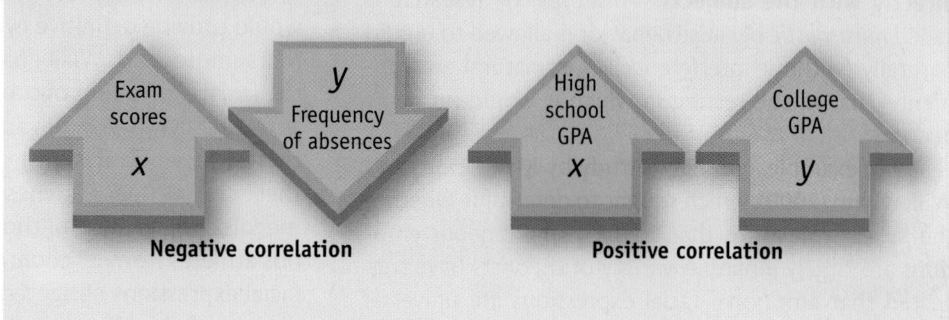

tend to earn low exam scores, while students who have a low number of absences tend to get higher exam scores (see Figure 1.2).

While the positive or negative sign indicates whether an association is direct or inverse, the *size* of the coefficient indicates the *strength* of the association between two variables. A correlation coefficient can vary between 0 and +1.00 (if positive) or between 0 and −1.00 (if negative). A coefficient near zero tells us there is no relationship between the variables. The closer the correlation to either −1.00 or +1.00, the stronger the relationship. Thus, a correlation of +.90 represents a stronger tendency for variables to be associated than a correlation of +.40 does (see Figure 1.3). Likewise, a correlation of −.75 represents a stronger relationship than a correlation of −.45. Keep in mind that the *strength* of a correlation depends only on the size of the coefficient. The positive or negative sign simply shows whether the correlation is direct or inverse. Therefore, a correlation of −.60 reflects a stronger relationship than a correlation of +.30.

Correlational research methods comprise a number of approaches, including naturalistic observation, case studies, and surveys. Let's examine each of these to see how researchers use them to detect associations between variables.

FIGURE 1.3 | Interpreting correlation coefficients

The magnitude of a correlation coefficient indicates the strength of the relationship between two variables. The closer a correlation is to either +1.00 or −1.00, the stronger the relationship between the variables. The square of a correlation, which is called the *coefficient of determination,* is an index of a correlation's strength and predictive power. This graph shows how the coefficient of determination and predictive power go up as the magnitude of a correlation increases.

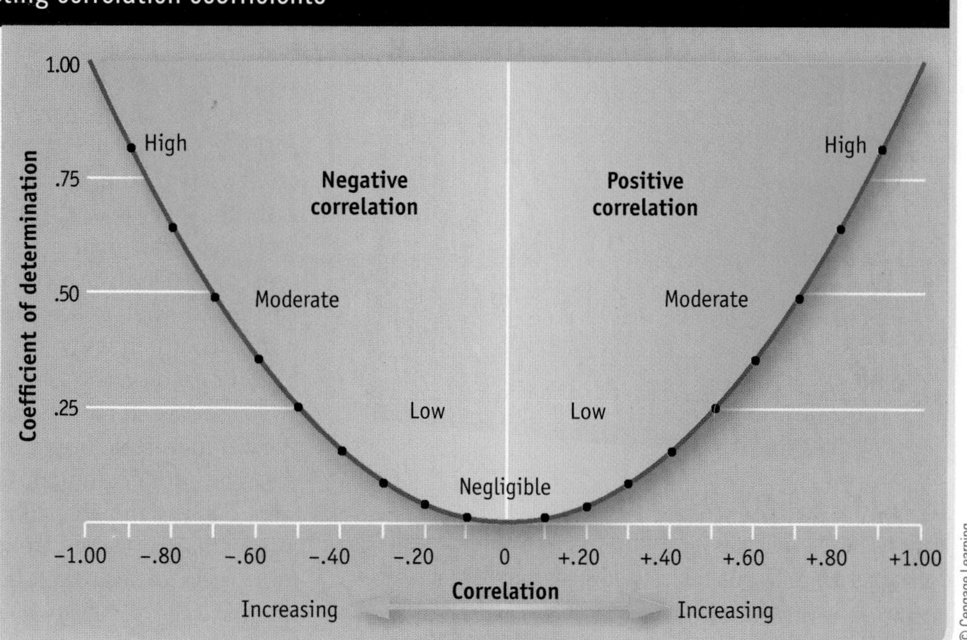

Naturalistic Observation

In *naturalistic observation* a researcher engages in careful observation of behavior without intervening directly with the subjects. This type of research is called *naturalistic* because behavior is allowed to unfold naturally (without interference) in its natural environment—that is, the setting in which it would normally occur.

As an example, consider a study by Matsumoto and Willingham (2009), which sought to determine whether the facial expressions that go with spontaneous emotions are largely innate. A variety of theorists have suggested that emotional facial expressions are universal across cultures and biologically built-in by-products of evolutionary forces (Izard, 1994). Yet it has proven difficult to clearly demonstrate that emotional facial expressions are not influenced by learning. However, Matsumoto and Willingham came up with an ingenious way to investigate the issue by using naturalistic observation: They compared the facial expressions of congenitally blind athletes with sighted athletes. Learning could not be a source of influence on the facial expressions of congenitally blind individuals, so if the blind athletes' facial expressions turned out to be indistinguishable from those of sighted athletes, this finding would provide definitive evidence on the matter. Thus, Matsumoto and Willingham carefully photographed the facial expressions of congenitally blind judo athletes in the Paralympic Games and of sighted judo athletes in the Olympic Games, just after they had won or lost their crucial final matches (for gold, silver, or bronze medals). The analysis of thousands of photos of numerous athletes from 23 countries yielded clear results: the facial expressions of sighted and blind athletes were indistinguishable. These findings provide strong support for the hypothesis that the facial expressions that go with emotions are wired into the human brain.

In a creative application of naturalistic observation, Matsumoto and Willingham (2009) shot photos of the award ceremonies for congenitally blind and sighted athletes to gain insight into whether facial expressions of emotion are innate.

Case Studies

A *case study* is an in-depth investigation of an individual subject. Psychologists typically assemble case studies in clinical settings where an effort is being made to diagnose and treat some psychological problem. To achieve an understanding of an individual, a clinician may use a variety of procedures, including interviewing the person, interviewing others who know the individual, direct observation, examination of records, and psychological testing. Usually, a single case study does not provide much basis for deriving general laws of behavior. If researchers have a number of case studies available, however, they can look for threads of consistency among them, and they may be able to draw some general conclusions.

This was the strategy used by a research team in Finland that wanted to explore the psychological characteristics of people who take their own lives (Henriksson et al., 1993; Isometsa et al., 1995). Their sample consisted of all the known suicides in Finland for an entire year. The investigators conducted thorough interviews with the families of the suicide victims and with the health care professionals who had treated them. The researchers also examined the suicide victims' medical, psychiatric, and social agency records, as well as relevant police investigations and forensic reports. Comprehensive case reports were then assembled for each person who committed suicide.

These case studies revealed that in 93% of the suicides the victim suffered from a significant psychological disorder. The most common diagnoses, by a large margin, were depression and alcohol dependence. In 571 cases, victims had a health care appointment during the last four weeks of their lives, but only 22% of these people discussed the possibility of suicide during their final visit.

Even more surprising, the sample included 100 people who saw a health professional on the *same day* they killed themselves, yet only 21% of these individuals raised the issue of suicide. The investigators concluded that mental illness is a contributing factor in virtually all completed suicides and that the vast majority of suicidal people do not spontaneously reveal their intentions to health care professionals.

Surveys

***Surveys* are structured questionnaires designed to solicit information about specific aspects of participants' behavior.** They are sometimes used to measure dependent variables in experiments, but they are mainly used in correlational research. Surveys are commonly used to gather data on people's attitudes and on aspects of behavior that are difficult to observe directly (marital interactions, for instance).

As an example, consider a study by David Schmitt and colleagues (2003) that set out to determine whether gender differences in desire for sexual variety transcend culture. Previous research in the United States had found a significant gender gap in the number of sex partners people reported they would like to have over the course of their lives (Buss & Schmitt, 1993). To find out whether these differences would replicate in other cultures, Schmitt and his associates surveyed 16,288 people from six continents, thirteen islands, and fifty-two nations. Their survey, which was translated into a variety of languages, asked participants how many sexual partners they ideally would like to have over time periods ranging from 1 month to 30 years. In the statistical analysis, the data from the fifty-two nations was grouped into 10 world regions. In all ten regions men reported that they were interested in having substantially more sex partners than women did. The authors conclude that sex differences in the desire for sexual variety "are cross-culturally universal," and they go on to discuss the possible evolutionary significance of this gender gap.

© Frantisek Czanner/ Shutterstock.com

"Correlation is no assurance of causation."

© desuza.communications/iStockphoto

Advantages and Disadvantages

Correlational research methods give psychologists a way to explore questions that they could not examine with experimental procedures. Thus, *correlational research broadens the scope of phenomena that psychologists can study.* Unfortunately, correlational methods have one major disadvantage. The investigator does not have the opportunity to control events to isolate cause and effect. *Consequently, correlational research cannot demonstrate conclusively that two variables are causally related.* The crux of the problem is that correlation is no assurance of causation.

When we find that variables *x* and *y* are correlated, we can safely conclude only that *x* and *y* are related. We do not know *how x* and *y* are related. We do not know whether *x* causes *y*, whether *y* causes *x*, or whether both are caused by a third variable. For example, survey studies show a positive correlation between relationship satisfaction and sexual satisfaction (Schwartz & Young, 2009). Although it's clear that good sex and a healthy intimate relationship go hand in hand, it's hard to tell what's causing what. We don't know whether healthy relationships promote good sex or whether good sex promotes healthy relationships. Moreover, we can't rule out the possibility that both are caused by a third variable. Perhaps sexual satisfaction and relationship satisfaction are both caused by compatibility in values. The plausible causal relationships in this case are diagrammed for you in Figure 1.4 on the next page, which illustrates the "third-variable problem" in interpreting correlations. This problem occurs often in correlational research. Indeed, it will surface in the next section, where we review the empirical research on the correlates of happiness.

1-4 The Roots of Happiness: An Empirical Analysis

What exactly makes a person happy? This question has been the subject of much speculation. Commonsense hypotheses about the roots of happiness abound. For example, you have no doubt heard that money cannot buy happiness. But do you believe it? A television

FIGURE 1.4 Possible causal relations between correlated variables

When two variables are correlated, there are several possible explanations. It could be that *x* causes *y*, that *y* causes *x*, or that a third variable, *z*, causes changes in both *x* and *y*. As the correlation between relationship satisfaction and sexual satisfaction illustrates, the correlation itself does not provide the answer. This conundrum is sometimes referred to as the "third variable problem."

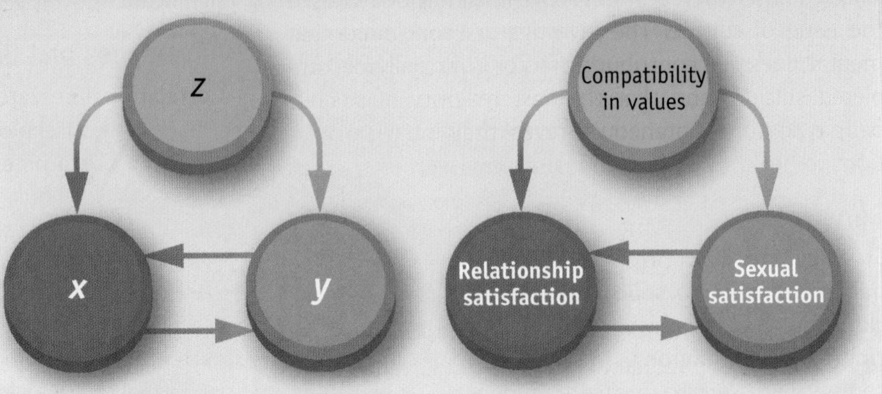

commercial says, "If you've got your health, you've got just about everything." Is health indeed the key? We often hear about the joys of parenthood, the joys of youth, and the joys of the simple, rural life. Are these the factors that promote happiness?

In recent years, social scientists have begun putting these and other hypotheses to empirical test. Quite a number of survey studies have been conducted to explore the determinants of ***subjective well-being*—individuals' personal assessments of their overall happiness or life satisfaction.** The findings of these studies are quite interesting. We review this research because it is central to the topic of adjustment and because it illustrates the value of collecting data and putting ideas to an empirical test. As you will see, many commonsense notions about happiness appear to be inaccurate.

The first of these ideas is the apparently widespread assumption that most people are relatively unhappy. Writers, social scientists, and the general public seem to believe that people around the world are predominantly dissatisfied, yet empirical surveys consistently find that the vast majority of respondents—even those who are poor or disabled—characterize themselves as fairly happy. When people are asked to rate their happiness, only a small minority place themselves below the neutral point on the various scales used (see Figure 1.5). When the average subjective well-being of entire nations is computed, based on almost 1000 surveys, the means cluster strongly toward the positive end of the scale (Tov & Diener, 2007). That's not to say that everyone is equally happy. Researchers have found substantial and thought-provoking disparities among people in subjective well-being, which we will analyze momentarily. But the overall picture seems rosier than anticipated.

FIGURE 1.5 Measuring happiness with a nonverbal scale

Researchers have used a variety of methods to estimate the distribution of happiness. For example, in one study in the United States, respondents were asked to examine the seven facial expressions shown and to select the one that "comes closest to expressing how you feel about your life as a whole." As you can see, the vast majority of participants chose happy faces. (Data adapted from Myers, 1992)

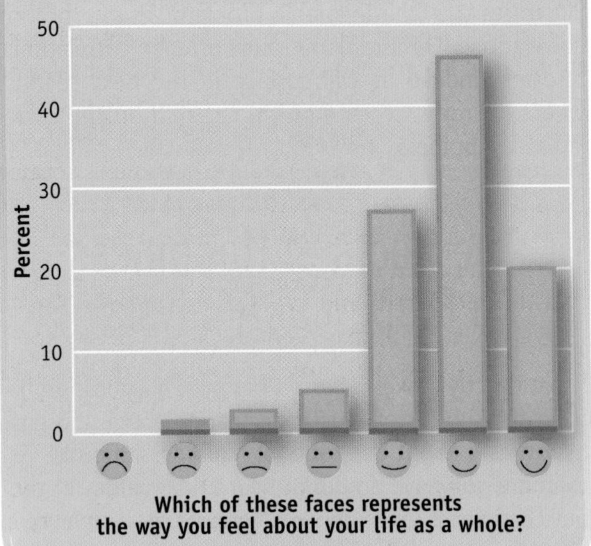

1-4a WHAT ISN'T VERY IMPORTANT?

Let us begin our discussion of individual differences in happiness by highlighting those things that turn out to be relatively unimportant determinants of subjective well-being. Quite a number of factors that one might expect to be influential appear to bear little or no relationship to general happiness.

Money. Most people think that if they had more money, they would be happier. There *is* a positive correlation between income and feelings of happiness, but the association is surprisingly weak. For example, one study found a correlation of just .12 between income and happiness in the United States (Johnson & Krueger, 2006). Admittedly, being very poor can contribute to unhappiness. Yet, once people ascend above a certain level of income, additional wealth does not seem to foster greater happiness. One recent study in the United States estimated that once people exceed an income of around $75,000, little relation is seen between wealth and subjective well-being (Kahneman & Deaton, 2010). Why isn't income a better predictor of happiness? One reason is that a disconnect seems to exist between actual income and how people feel about their financial situation. Research (Johnson & Krueger, 2006) suggests that the correlation between actual wealth and people's subjective perceptions of whether they have enough money is surprisingly modest (around .30).

Another problem with money is that in this era of voracious consumption, rising income contributes to escalating material desires (Kasser et al., 2004). When these desires outstrip what people can afford, dissatisfaction is likely. Thus, complaints about not having enough money are routine even among people who earn hefty six-figure incomes. Interestingly, there is some evidence that people who place an especially strong emphasis on the pursuit of wealth and materialistic goals tend to be somewhat less happy than others (Van Boven, 2005). Perhaps they are so focused on financial success that they derive less satisfaction from other aspects of their lives (Nickerson et al, 2003). Consistent with this view, one study found that higher income was associated with working longer hours and allocating fewer hours to leisure pursuits (Kahneman et al., 2006). The results of another recent study suggested that wealthy people become jaded in a way that undermines their ability to savor positive experiences (Quoidback et al., 2010).

Age. Age and happiness are consistently found to be unrelated. Age accounts for less than 1% of the variation in people's happiness (Myers & Diener, 1997). The key factors influencing subjective well-being may shift some as people grow older—work becomes less important, health more so—but people's average level of happiness tends to remain remarkably stable over the life span.

Once people ascend above a certain level of income, additional wealth does not seem to foster greater happiness.

Parenthood. Children can be a tremendous source of joy and fulfillment, but they can also be a tremendous source of headaches and hassles. Apparently, the good and bad aspects of parenthood balance each other out, because the evidence indicates that people who have children are neither more nor less happy than people without children (Argyle, 2001).

Intelligence and attractiveness. Intelligence and physical attractiveness are highly valued traits in modern society. But researchers have *not* found an association between either characteristic and happiness (Diener, Kesebir & Tov, 2009; Diener, Wolsic, & Fujita, 1995).

1-4b WHAT IS SOMEWHAT IMPORTANT?

Research has identified three facets of life that appear to have a moderate impact on subjective well-being: health, social activity, and religious belief.

Health. Good physical health would seem to be an essential requirement for happiness, but people adapt to health problems. Research reveals that individuals who develop serious, disabling health conditions aren't as unhappy as one might guess (Riis et al., 2005). Good health may not, by itself, produce happiness, because people tend to take good health for granted. Such considerations may help explain why researchers find only a moderate positive correlation (average = .32) between health status and subjective well-being (Argyle, 1999). While health may promote happiness to a moderate degree, happiness may also foster better health, as research has found a positive correlation between happiness and longevity (Veenhoven, 2008).

Social activity. Humans are social animals, and people's interpersonal relations *do* appear to contribute to their happiness. People who are satisfied with their friendship networks and who are socially active report above-average levels of happiness (Diener & Seligman, 2004). One recent study that periodically recorded participants' daily conversations found that those who had more deep, substantive conversations were happier than those who mostly engaged in small talk (Mehl et al., 2010). This finding is not all that surprising, in that one would expect people with richer social networks to have more deep conversations.

Religion. The link between religiosity and subjective well-being is modest, but a number of surveys suggest that people with heartfelt religious convictions are more likely to be happy than people who characterize themselves as nonreligious (Myers, 2008). Researchers aren't sure how religious faith fosters happiness, but there is some interesting conjecture. Among other things, religion can give people a sense of purpose and meaning in their lives, help them accept their setbacks gracefully, connect them to a caring, supportive community, and comfort them by putting their ultimate mortality in perspective.

© bikeriderlondon/Shutterstock.com; Frame: © Vitaly Korovin/Shutterstock.com

1-4c WHAT IS VERY IMPORTANT?

The list of factors that turn out to be very important ingredients of happiness is surprisingly short. Only a few variables are strongly related to overall happiness.

Love, marriage, and relationship satisfaction. Romantic relationships can be stressful, but people consistently rate being in love as one of the most critical ingredients of happiness. Furthermore, although people complain a lot about their marriages, the evidence indicates that marital status is a key correlate of happiness. Among both men and women, married people are happier than people who are single or divorced, and this disparity holds around the world in widely different cultures (Diener et al., 2000). Furthermore, among married people, marital satisfaction predicts personal well-being (Proulx, Helms, & Buehler, 2007). The research in this area generally has used marital status as a crude but easily measured marker of relationship satisfaction. In all likelihood, it is relationship satisfaction that fosters happiness. In other words, one does not have to be married to be happy. Relationship satisfaction probably has the same association with happiness in cohabiting heterosexual couples and gay couples.

Work. Given the way people often complain about their jobs, we might not expect work to be a key source of happiness, but it is. Although less critical than relationship satisfaction, job satisfaction is strongly associated with general happiness (Judge & Klinger, 2008). Studies also show that unemployment has strong negative effects on subjective well-being (Lucas et al., 2004). It is difficult to sort out whether job satisfaction causes happiness or vice versa, but evidence suggests that causation flows both ways.

Genetics and personality. The best predictor of individuals' future happiness is their past happiness (Lucas & Diener, 2008). Some people seem destined to be happy and others unhappy, regardless of their triumphs or setbacks. Evidence suggests that happiness does not depend on external circumstances—buying a nice house, getting promoted—as much as on internal factors, such as one's outlook on life (Lyubomirsky, Sheldon, & Schkade, 2005). With this finding in mind, researchers have investigated whether a hereditary basis might exist for variations in happiness. These studies suggest that people's genetic predispositions account for a substantial portion of the variance in happiness, perhaps as much as 50% (Lyubomirsky et al., 2005). How can one's genes influence one's happiness? Presumably, by shaping one's temperament and personality, which are known to be highly heritable. Hence, researchers have begun to look for links

Photo: © INSADCO Photography/Alamy; Graphic: © L_amica/Shutterstock.com

between personality and subjective well-being, and they have found some relatively strong correlations. For example, *extraversion* is one of the better predictors of happiness (Lucas & Diener, 2008). People who are outgoing, upbeat, and sociable tend to be happier than others. Additional personality correlates of happiness include conscientiousness, agreeableness, self-esteem, and optimism (Lucas, 2008).

1-4d CONCLUSIONS

We must be cautious in drawing inferences about the *causes* of happiness, because the available data are correlational (see Figure 1.6). Nonetheless, the empirical findings suggest a number of worthwhile insights about the roots of happiness.

First, research on happiness demonstrates that the determinants of subjective well-being are precisely that: subjective. *Objective realities are not as important as subjective feelings.* In other words, your health, your wealth, your job, and your age are not as influential as how you *feel* about your health, wealth, job, and age.

FIGURE 1.6 | Possible causal relations among the correlates of happiness

Although we have considerable data on the correlates of happiness, it is difficult to untangle the possible causal relationships. For example, we know that a moderate positive correlation exists between social activity and happiness, but we can't say for sure whether high social activity causes happiness or whether happiness causes people to be more socially active. Moreover, in light of the finding that a third variable—extraversion—correlates with both variables, we have to consider the possibility that extraversion causes both greater social activity and greater happiness.

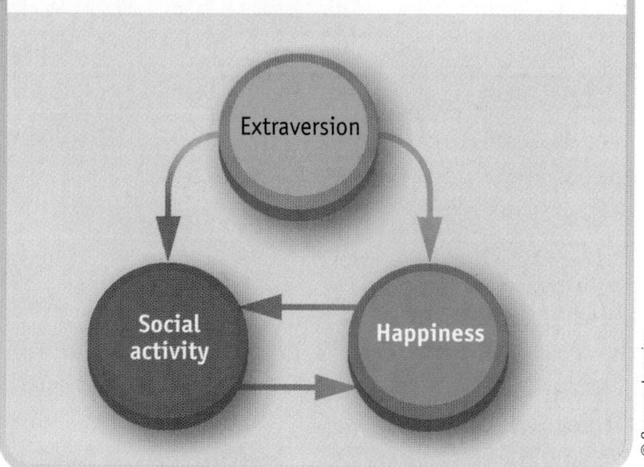

Second, *when it comes to happiness, everything is relative.* In other words, you evaluate what you have relative to what the people around you have. Thus, people who are wealthy assess what they have by comparing themselves to their wealthy friends and neighbors, and their *relative* standing is crucial (Boyce, Brown, & Moore, 2010). This is one reason for the low correlation between wealth and happiness. You might have a lovely home, but if it sits next to a neighbor's palatial mansion, this situation might be a source of more dissatisfaction than happiness.

Third, *research on happiness has shown that people are surprisingly bad at predicting what will make them happy.* We assume that we know what is best for us. But research on ***affective forecasting*—efforts to predict one's emotional reactions to future events**—suggests otherwise (Wilson & Gilbert, 2005). People routinely overestimate the pleasure that they will derive from buying an expensive automobile, taking an exotic vacation, earning an important promotion, moving to a beautiful coastal city, or building their dream home. Likewise, people tend to overestimate the misery and regret that they will experience if they have a romantic breakup, don't get into the college they want, fail to get a promotion, or develop a serious illness. Thus, the roadmap to happiness is less clearly marked than widely assumed.

Fourth, *research on subjective well-being indicates that people often adapt to their circumstances.* This adaptation effect is one reason that an increase in income doesn't necessarily bring an increase in happiness. Thus, ***hedonic adaptation* occurs when the mental scale that people use to judge the pleasantness-unpleasantness of their experiences shifts so that their neutral point, or baseline for comparison, is changed** (*hedonic* means related to pleasure). Unfortunately, when people's experiences improve, hedonic adaptation may *sometimes* put them on a *hedonic treadmill*—their baseline moves upward, so that the improvements yield no real benefits (Kahneman, 1999). However, when people have to grapple with major setbacks, hedonic adaptation probably helps protect their mental and physical health. For example, people who are sent to prison and people who develop debilitating diseases are not as unhappy as one might assume, because they adapt to their changed situations and evaluate events from a new perspective (Frederick & Loewenstein, 1999). That's not to say that hedonic adaptation in the face of life's difficulties is inevitable or complete, but people adapt to setbacks much better than widely assumed (Lucas, 2007).

We turn next to an example of how psychological research can be applied to everyday problems. In our first application section, we will review research evidence related to the challenge of being a successful student.

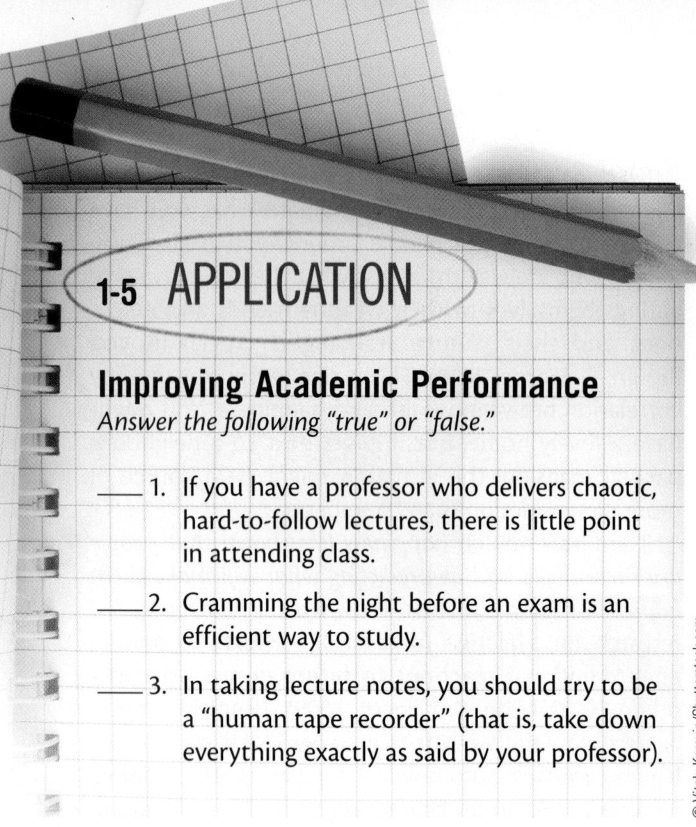

1-5 APPLICATION

Improving Academic Performance

Answer the following "true" or "false."

____ 1. If you have a professor who delivers chaotic, hard-to-follow lectures, there is little point in attending class.

____ 2. Cramming the night before an exam is an efficient way to study.

____ 3. In taking lecture notes, you should try to be a "human tape recorder" (that is, take down everything exactly as said by your professor).

As you will soon learn, all of these statements are false. If you answered them all correctly, you may already have acquired the kinds of skills and habits that lead to academic success. If so, however, you are not typical. Today, a huge number of students enter college with remarkably poor study skills and habits—and it's not entirely their fault. The U.S. educational system generally does not provide much in the way of formal instruction on good study techniques. So, in this first Application, we'll start with the basics and try to remedy this deficiency to some extent by sharing some insights that psychology can provide on how to improve your academic performance.

1-5a DEVELOPING SOUND STUDY HABITS

Learning can be immensely gratifying, but studying usually involves hard work. The first step toward effective study habits is to face this reality. You don't have to feel guilty if you don't look forward to studying. Most students don't. Once you accept the premise that studying doesn't come naturally, it should be clear that you need to set up an organized program to promote adequate study. Such a program should include the following three considerations.

Set up a schedule for studying. Research on the differences between successful and unsuccessful college students suggests that successful students monitor and regulate their use of time more effectively (Allgood et al., 2000). If you wait until the urge to study hits you, you may still be waiting when the exam rolls around. Thus, it is important to allocate definite times to study. Review your time obligations (work, housekeeping, and so on) and figure out in advance when you can study. In allotting certain times to studying, keep in mind that you need to be wide awake and alert.

It's important to write down your study schedule. Doing so serves as a reminder and increases your commitment to the schedule. As shown in Figure 1.7, you should begin by setting up a general schedule for the quarter or semester. Then, at the beginning of each week, plan the specific assignments that you intend to work on during each study session. This approach should help you avoid cramming for exams at the last minute. Cramming is an ineffective strategy for most students (Wong, 2006). It will strain your memorization capabilities, can tax your energy level, and may stoke the fires of test anxiety.

In planning your weekly schedule, try to avoid the tendency to put off working on major tasks such as term papers and reports. Time management experts point out that many of us tend to tackle simple, routine tasks first, saving larger tasks for later, when we supposedly will have more time. This common tendency leads

FIGURE 1.7 Example of an activity schedule

One student's general activity schedule for a semester is shown here. Each week the student fills in the specific assignments to work on during the upcoming study sessions.

	Mon	Tues	Wed	Thurs	Fri	Sat	Sun
8 A.M.						Work	
9 A.M.	History	Study	History	Study	History	Work	
10 A.M.	Psych	French ↓	Psych	French ↓	Psych	Work	
11 A.M.	Study		Study		Study	Work	
Noon	Math	Study	Math	Study	Math	Work	Study
1 P.M.							Study
2 P.M.	Study	English ↓	Study	English ↓	Study		Study
3 P.M.	Study		Study		Study		Study
4 P.M.							
5 P.M.							
6 P.M.	Work	Study	Work				Study
7 P.M.	Work	Study	Work				Study
8 P.M.	Work	Study	Work				Study
9 P.M.	Work	Study	Work				Study
10 P.M.	Work		Work				

many of us to delay working on major assignments until it's too late to do a good job. You can avoid this trap by breaking major assignments into smaller component tasks that you schedule individually.

Find a place to study where you can concentrate. Where you study is also important. The key is to find a place where distractions are likely to be minimal. Most people cannot study effectively while watching TV, listening to loud music, or overhearing conversations. Don't depend on willpower to carry you through these distractions. It's much easier to plan ahead and avoid the distractions altogether.

Reward your studying. One of the reasons it is so difficult to motivate oneself to study regularly is that the payoffs for studying often lie in the distant future. Even short-term rewards, such as an A in the course, may be weeks or months off. To combat this problem, it helps to give yourself immediate rewards for studying. It is easier to motivate yourself to study if you reward yourself with a tangible payoff, such as a snack, TV show, or phone call to a friend, when you finish. Thus, you should set realistic study goals and then reward yourself when you meet them.

1-5b IMPROVING YOUR READING

Much of your study time is spent reading and absorbing information. The keys to improving reading comprehension are to preview reading assignments section by section, work hard to actively process the meaning of the information, strive to identify the key ideas of each paragraph, and carefully review these key ideas after each section. Modern textbooks often contain a variety of learning aids that you can use to improve your reading. If a book provides study aids such as a chapter outline, chapter review, or learning objectives, don't ignore them. They can help you recognize the important points in the chapter.

Another issue related to textbook reading is whether and how to mark up one's reading assignments. Many students deceive themselves into thinking that they are studying by running a marker through a few sentences here and there in their text. If they do so without thoughtful selectivity, they are simply turning a textbook into a coloring book. This reality probably explains why some professors are skeptical about the value of highlighting textbooks. Nonetheless, research suggests that highlighting textbook material *is* a useful strategy—if students are reasonably effective in focusing on the main ideas in the material and if they subsequently review what they have highlighted (Caverly, Orlando, & Mullen, 2000).

When executed effectively, highlighting can foster active reading, improve reading comprehension, and reduce the amount of material that one has to review later (Van Blerkom, 2006). The key to effective text marking is to identify (and highlight) only the main ideas, key supporting details, and technical terms. Text marking is a delicate balancing act. If you highlight too little of the content, you are not identifying enough of the key ideas. But if you highlight too much of the content, you are not going to succeed in condensing what you have to review to a manageable size.

© Olga Danylenko/Shutterstock.com

1-5c GETTING MORE OUT OF LECTURES

Although lectures are sometimes boring and tedious, it is a simple fact that poor class attendance is associated with poor grades. For example, Lindgren (1969) found that absences from class were much more common among "unsuccessful" students (grade average of C– or below) than among "successful" students (grade average of B or above), as shown in Figure 1.8. Even when you have an instructor who delivers hard-to-follow lectures from which you learn virtually nothing, it is still

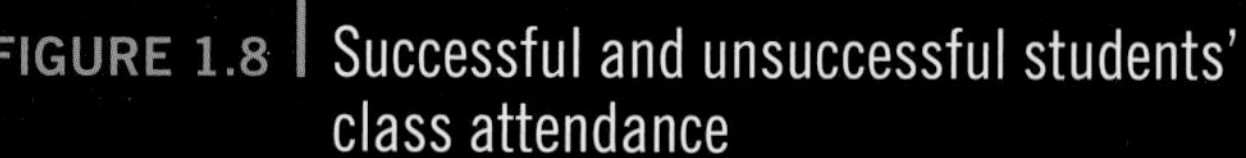

FIGURE 1.8 Successful and unsuccessful students' class attendance

Lindgren (1969) found that attendance was much better among successful students than unsuccessful students.

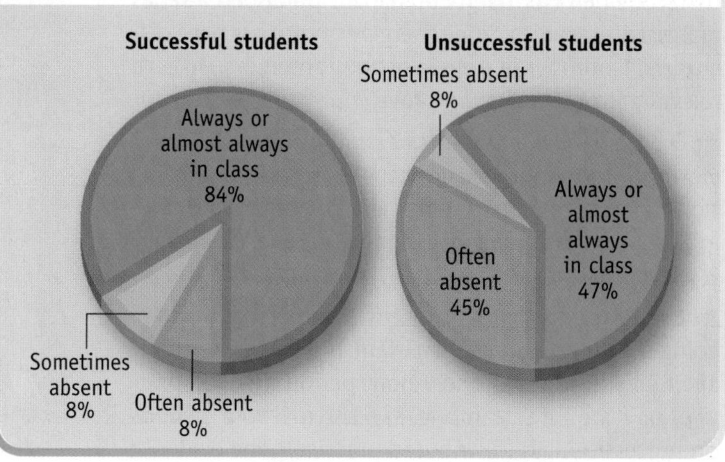

© Cengage Learning

important to go to class. If nothing else, you'll get a feel for how the instructor thinks. Doing so can help you anticipate the content of exams and respond in the manner your professor expects.

Studies indicate that attentive note taking *is* associated with enhanced learning and performance in college classes (Titsworth & Kiewra, 2004). Books on study skills (Longman & Atkinson, 2005; McWhorter, 2007) offer a number of suggestions on how to take good-quality lecture notes. These suggestions include:

- *Use active listening procedures.* With active listening, you focus full attention on the speaker. Try to anticipate what's coming and search for deeper meanings. Pay attention to nonverbal signals that may serve to further clarify the lecturer's intent or meaning.
- *Prepare for lectures by reading ahead on the scheduled subject.* If you review the text, you have less information to digest that is brand new. This strategy is especially important when course material is complex and difficult.
- *Write down lecturers' thoughts in your own words.* Don't try to be a human tape recorder. Translating the lecture into your own words forces you to organize the ideas in a way that makes sense to you.
- *Look for subtle and not-so-subtle clues about what the instructor considers to be important.* These clues may range from simply repeating main points to saying things like "You'll run into this again."
- *Ask questions during lectures.* Doing so keeps you actively involved and allows you to clarify points you may have misunderstood. Many students are more bashful about asking questions than they should be. They don't realize that most professors welcome questions.

1-5d APPLYING MEMORY PRINCIPLES

Scientific investigation of memory processes dates back to 1885, when Hermann Ebbinghaus published a series of insightful studies. Since then, psychologists have discovered a number of principles about memory that are relevant to helping you improve your study skills.

- *Engage in adequate practice (study).* Repeatedly reviewing information usually leads to improved retention. Continued rehearsal may also pay off by improving your *understanding* of assigned material (Bromage & Mayer, 1986).
- *Use distributed practice.* Let's assume that you are going to study 9 hours for an exam. Is it better to "cram" all of your study into one 9-hour period (massed practice) or distribute it among, say, three 3-hour periods on successive days (distributed practice)? The evidence indicates that retention tends to be greater after distributed practice than massed practice (Rohrer & Taylor, 2006).
- *Organize information.* Retention tends to be greater when information is well organized (Einstein & McDaniel, 2004). Hierarchical organization is particularly helpful when it is applicable. Thus, it may be a good idea to *outline* reading assignments for school.
- *Emphasize deep processing.* One line of research suggests that how *often* you go over material is less critical than the *depth* of processing that you engage in. Thus, if you expect to remember what you read, you have to wrestle fully with its meaning (Einstein & McDaniel, 2004). When you read your textbooks, try to relate information to your own life and experience.
- *Test yourself.* It is a good idea to informally test yourself on information that you think you have mastered before confronting a real test. In addition to checking your mastery, recent research suggests that testing actually enhances retention, a phenomenon dubbed the *testing effect* (Karpicke & Roediger, 2008). Studies have shown that taking a test on material increases performance on a subsequent test even more than studying for an equal amount of time.

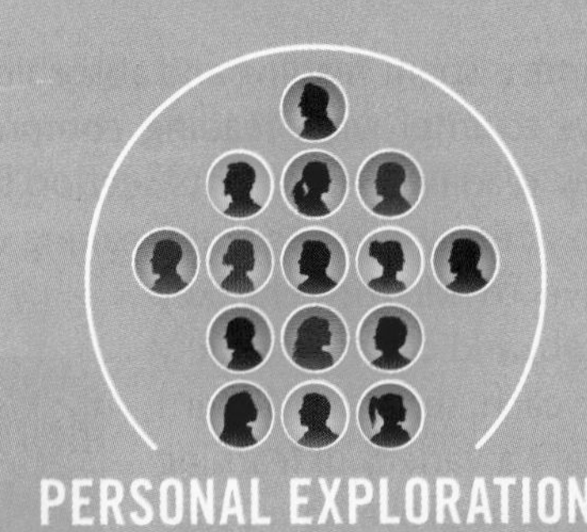

PERSONAL EXPLORATION TOOLS

Curious about yourself? To learn more about how topics in this chapter relate to you, go online to CourseMate at www.cengagebrain.com where you can:

- Complete a **Self-Reflection** exercise that will help you think about your personal experiences in relation to topics in the chapter.
- Take a **Self-Assessment** scale that will show you how you score on a research instrument that measures personality traits or attitudes.
- Explore **Recommended Readings** that will provide brief overviews of useful self-help books.

STUDY TOOLS ▸ 1

Ready to study? In your book you can:

- **Test Yourself** with a multiple-choice quiz (below)
- Rip out the **Chapter Review card** (in the back of the book) to refresh yourself on the chapter's Key Ideas and Key Terms

Or you can go online to CourseMate at www.cengagebrain.com where you can:

- Take additional Practice Quizzes to prepare for your exam
- Review Key Terms with flash cards and a crossword puzzle
- View videos that expand on selected concepts

TEST YOURSELF

1. **Which of the following is *not* offered in the text as a criticism of self-help books?**
   a. They are infrequently based on solid research.
   b. Most don't provide explicit directions for changing behavior.
   c. The topics they cover are often quite narrow.
   d. Many are dominated by psychobabble.

2. **The field of psychology is:**
   a. a scientific discipline.
   b. a profession that delivers services to the public.
   c. both a science and a profession.
   d. neither a science or a profession.

3. **The adaptation of animals when their environments change is similar to _______________ in humans.**
   a. orientation
   b. assimilation
   c. evolution
   d. adjustment

4. **An experiment is a research method in which the investigator manipulates the _______________ variable and observes whether changes occur in a (an) _______________ variable as a result.**
   a. independent; dependent
   b. control; experimental
   c. experimental; control
   d. dependent; independent

5. **A researcher wants to determine whether a certain diet causes children to learn better in school. In the study, the independent variable is**
   a. the type of diet.
   b. a measure of learning performance.
   c. the age or grade level of the children.
   d. the intelligence level of the children.

6. **A psychologist collected background information about a psychopathic killer, talked to him and people who knew him, and gave him psychological tests. Which research method was she using?**
   a. Case study
   b. Naturalistic observation
   c. Survey
   d. Experiment

7. **The principal advantage of experimental research is that**
   a. experiments are convincing to people.
   b. experiments replicate real-life situations.
   c. an experiment can be designed for any research problem.
   d. it allows the researcher to draw cause-and-effect conclusions.

8. **Research has shown that which of the following is moderately correlated with happiness?**
   a. Income
   b. Intelligence
   c. Parenthood
   d. Social activity

9. **Which of the following is *not* one of the conclusions drawn about the determinants of happiness?**
   a. Objective realities are not as important as subjective feelings.
   b. When it comes to happiness, everything is relative.
   c. Research has shown that people are pretty good at predicting what will make them happy.
   d. Research indicates that people often adapt to their circumstances.

10. **A good reason for taking notes in your own words, rather than verbatim, is that**
    a. most lecturers are quite wordy.
    b. "translating" on the spot is good mental exercise.
    c. it reduces the likelihood that you'll later engage in plagiarism.
    d. it forces you to assimilate the information in a way that makes sense to you.

Answers: 1. c, pages 3–4; 2. c, pages 5–6; 3. d, page 6; 4. a, pages 6–7; 5. a, page 7, 6. a, pages 10–11; 7. d, page 7; 8. d, pages 13–14; 9. c, page 15; 10. d, page 18

© EIGHTFISH/Getty Images

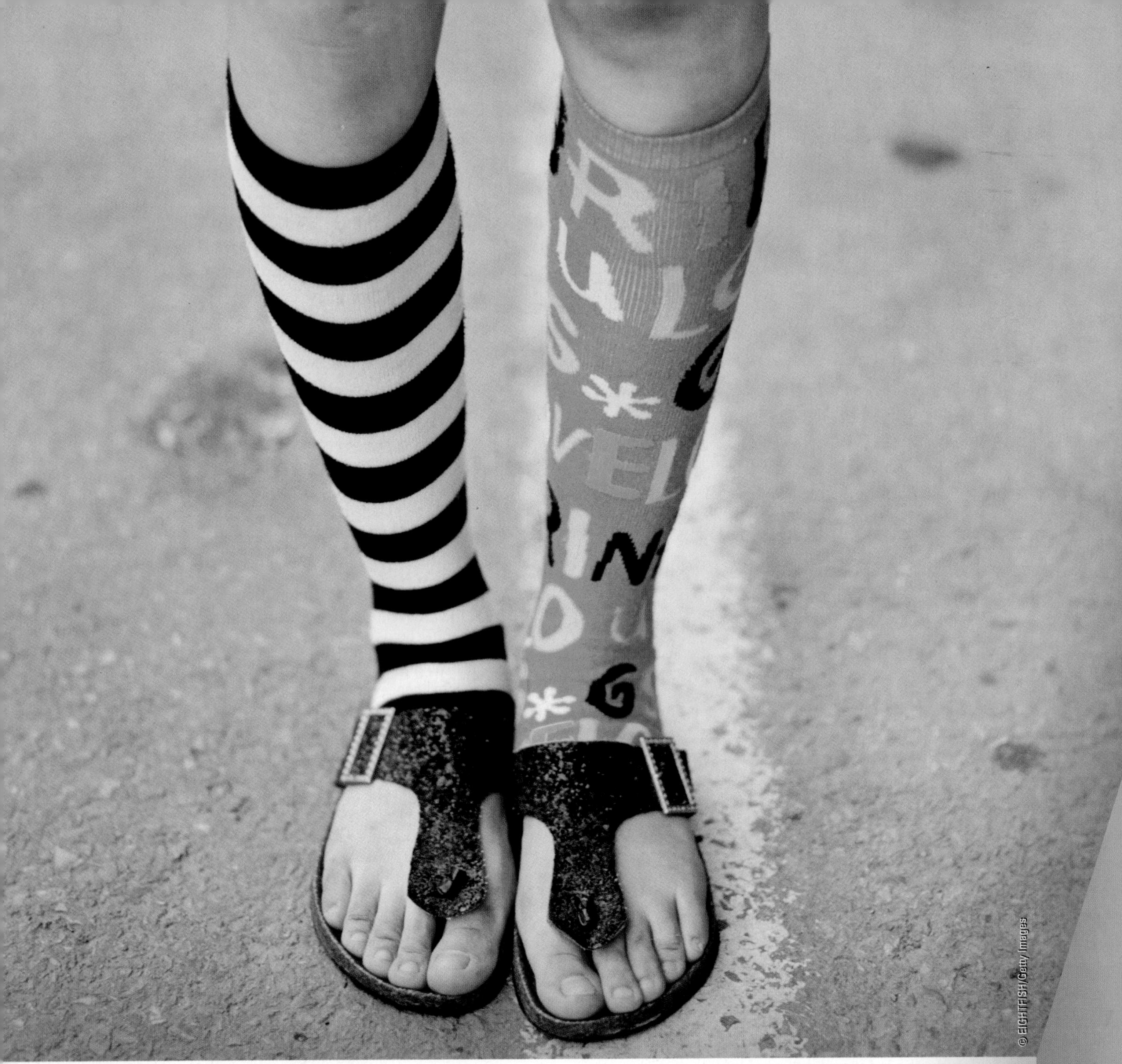

LEARNING OBJECTIVES

2-1 Explain the concept of personality traits, and describe the five-factor model of personality.

2-2 Outline Freud's theory of personality and psychosexual development.

2-3 Understand how classical conditioning, operant conditioning, and observational learning help shape personality.

2-4 Describe Rogers's views on self-concept development and Maslow's hieracrchy of needs.

2-5 Discuss the genetic and evolutionary roots of personality.

2-6 Explain how researchers have found both cross-cultural similarities and differences in personality.

2-7 Describe the nature, value, and limitations of personality tests.

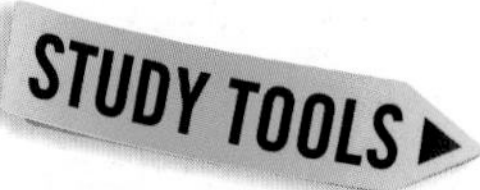

STUDY TOOLS ▶ After you have read the chapter, you can Test Yourself and learn about other Study Tools on page 44.

CHAPTER 2

Theories of PERSONALITY

© Photo_Concepts/iStockphoto

© George Doyle/Photos.com

Imagine that you are hurtling upward in an elevator with other people when suddenly a power blackout brings the elevator to a halt 45 stories above the ground. Your companions might adjust to this predicament differently. One might crack jokes to relieve tension. Another might make ominous predictions that "we'll never get out of here." A third might calmly think about how to escape from the elevator. These varied ways of coping with the same stressful situation occur because each person has a different personality. Personality differences significantly influence people's patterns of adjustment. Thus, theories intended to explain personality can contribute to our effort to understand adjustment processes. In this chapter, we introduce you to various theories that attempt to explain the structure and development of personality.

2-1 What Is Personality?

What does it mean if you say that a friend has an optimistic personality? Your statement suggests that the person has a fairly *consistent tendency* to behave in a cheerful, hopeful, enthusiastic way, looking at the bright side of things, across a wide variety of situations. Although no one is entirely consistent in his or her behavior, this quality of *consistency across situations* lies at the core of the concept of personality. *Distinctiveness* is also central to the concept of personality. Everyone has traits seen in other people, but each individual has her or his own distinctive *set* of personality traits. Thus, as illustrated by our elevator scenario, the concept of personality helps explain why people don't all act alike in the same situation. In sum, *personality refers to an individual's unique constellation of consistent behavioral traits*. Let's look more closely at the concept of traits.

We all make remarks like "Melanie is very *shrewd*" or "Doug is too *timid* to succeed in that job." When we attempt to describe an individual's personality, we usually do so in terms of specific aspects of personality, called traits. **A *personality trait* is a durable disposition to behave in a particular way in a variety of situations.** Adjectives such as *honest, dependable, moody, impulsive, suspicious, anxious, excitable, domineering*, and *friendly* describe dispositions that represent personality traits.

Most trait theories of personality assume that some traits are more basic than others. According to this notion, a small number of fundamental traits determine other, more superficial traits. For example, a person's tendency to be impulsive, restless, irritable, boisterous, and impatient might all derive from a more basic tendency to be excitable.

A number of psychologists have taken on the challenge of identifying the basic traits that form the core of personality. In recent decades, the most influential theory has been the *five-factor model* developed by Robert McCrae and Paul Costa (1997, 2008a, 2008b). They argue that the vast majority of personality traits derive from just five higher-order traits that have come to be known as the "Big Five": extraversion, neuroticism, openness to experience, agreeableness, and conscientiousness (see Figure 2.1 on the next page). Let's take a closer look at these traits:

1. *Extraversion.* People who score high in extraversion are characterized as outgoing, sociable, upbeat, friendly, assertive, and gregarious. Extraverts have a more positive outlook on life than others and are highly motivated to pursue social contact, intimacy, and interdependence (Wilt & Revelle, 2009).

Trait models attempt to break down personality into its basic dimensions. McCrae and Costa (1987, 2003) maintain that personality can be described adequately with the five higher-order traits identified here, widely known as the Big Five traits.

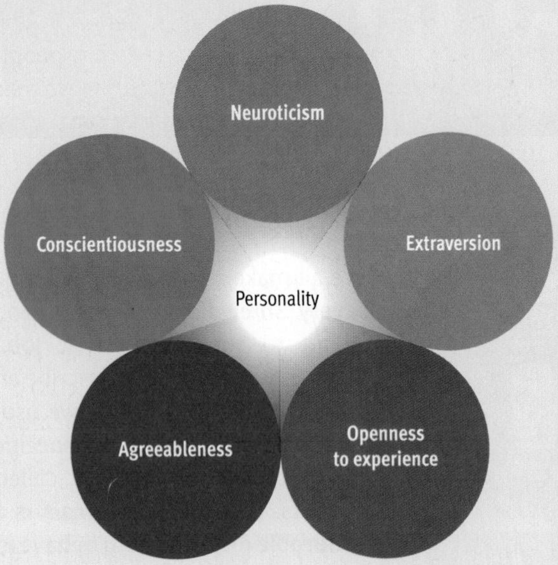

Factor	Characteristics
Neuroticism	Worried versus calm Insecure versus secure Self-pitying versus self-satisfied
Extraversion	Sociable versus retiring Fun-loving versus sober Affectionate versus reserved
Openness to experience	Imaginative versus down-to-earth Preference for variety versus preference for routine Independent versus conforming
Agreeableness	Softhearted versus ruthless Trusting versus suspicious Helpful versus uncooperative
Conscientiousness	Well organized versus disorganized Careful versus careless Self-disciplined versus weak willed

Source: Trait descriptions from McCrae, R. R., & Costa, P. T. (1986). Clinical assessment can benefit from recent advances in personality psychology. *American Psychologist, 41*, 1001–1003. Adapted with permission.

2. *Neuroticism*. People high in neuroticism tend to be anxious, hostile, self-conscious, insecure, and vulnerable. They tend to overreact more in response to stress than others. They also tend to exhibit impulsiveness and emotional instability (Widiger, 2009).

3. *Openness to experience*. Openness is associated with curiosity, flexibility, vivid fantasy, imaginativeness, artistic sensitivity, and unconventional attitudes. People who are high in openness tend to be tolerant of ambiguity and have less need for closure on issues than others (McCrae & Sutin, 2009). Evidence also suggests that openness to experience is associated with relatively low levels of prejudice against minorities (Flynn, 2005).

4. *Agreeableness*. Those who score high in agreeableness tend to be sympathetic, trusting, cooperative, modest, and straightforward. People who score at the opposite end of this personality dimension are characterized as suspicious, antagonistic, and aggressive. Agreeableness is associated with empathy and helping behavior (Graziano & Tobin, 2009).

5. *Conscientiousness*. Conscientious people tend to be diligent, disciplined, well organized, punctual, and dependable. Conscientiousness is associated with strong self-discipline and the ability to regulate oneself effectively (Roberts et al., 2009). Studies have also shown that conscientiousness fosters diligence and dependability in the workplace (Lund et al., 2007).

Correlations have been found between the Big Five traits and quite a variety of important life outcomes. For instance, certain Big Five traits are associated with career success. Conscientiousness is a positive predictor of occupational attainment (Miller Burke & Attridge, 2011), whereas neuroticism is a negative predictor (Roberts, Caspi, & Moffitt, 2003). The likelihood of divorce can also be predicted by personality traits, as neuroticism elevates the probability of divorce, whereas agreeableness and conscientiousness reduce it (Roberts et al., 2007). Finally, neuroticism is associated with an elevated prevalence of virtually all of the major mental disorders, not to mention a number of physical illnesses (Widiger, 2009). In contrast, conscientiousness is correlated with the experience of less illness and with reduced mortality (Martin, Friedman, & Schwartz, 2007).

2-2 Psychodynamic Perspectives

Psychodynamic theories include all the diverse theories descended from the work of Sigmund Freud that focus on unconscious mental forces. Freud inspired many brilliant scholars who followed in his intellectual footsteps. Some of these followers simply refined and updated Freud's theory. Others veered off in new directions and established independent, albeit related, schools of thought. Today, the psychodynamic umbrella covers a large collection of related theories. In this section, we'll examine Freud's ideas in some detail and then take a brief look at the work of two of his most significant followers, Carl Jung and Alfred Adler.

2-2a FREUD'S PSYCHOANALYTIC THEORY

Sigmund Freud was a physician specializing in neurology when he began his medical practice in Vienna near the end of the 19th century. Like other neurologists in his era, he often treated people troubled by nervous problems such as irrational fears, obsessions, and anxieties. Eventually he devoted himself to the treatment of mental disorders using an innovative procedure he developed, called *psychoanalysis,* that required lengthy verbal interactions in which Freud probed deeply into patients' lives. Decades of experience with his patients provided much of the inspiration for Freud's theory of personality.

Photo: © Peter Aprahamian/Corbis; Frame: © Thomas Bethge/Shutterstock.com

National Library of Medicine

Freud's psychoanalytic theory was based on decades of clinical work. He treated a great many patients in the consulting room pictured here. The room contains numerous artifacts from other cultures—and the original psychoanalytic couch.

Although Freud's theory gradually gained prominence, most of his contemporaries were uncomfortable with it, for at least three reasons. First, he argued that unconscious forces govern human behavior. This idea was disturbing because it suggested that people are not masters of their own minds. Second, he claimed that childhood experiences strongly determine adult personality. This notion distressed many, because it suggested that people are not masters of their own destinies. Third, he said that individuals' personalities are shaped by how they cope with their sexual urges. This assertion offended the conservative, Victorian values of his time. Thus, Freud endured a great deal of criticism, condemnation, and outright ridicule, even after his work began to attract more favorable attention. Let's look at the ideas that generated so much controversy.

Structure of Personality

Freud (1901, 1920) divided personality structure into three components: the id, the ego, and the superego. He saw a person's behavior as the outcome of interactions among these three elements.

The *id* is the primitive, instinctive component of personality that operates according to the pleasure principle. Freud referred to the id as the reservoir of psychic energy. By this he meant that the id houses the raw biological urges (to eat, sleep, defecate, copulate, and so on) that energize human behavior. The id operates according to the *pleasure principle,* which demands immediate gratification of its urges. The id engages in *primary process thinking,* which is primitive, illogical, irrational, and fantasy oriented.

The *ego* is the decision-making component of personality that operates according to the reality principle. The ego mediates between the id, with its forceful desires for immediate satisfaction, and the external social world, with its expectations and norms regarding suitable behavior. The ego considers social realities—society's norms, etiquette, rules, and customs—in deciding how to behave. The ego is guided by the *reality principle,* which seeks to delay gratification of the id's urges until appropriate outlets and situations can be found. In short, to stay out of trouble, the ego often works to tame the unbridled desires of the id.

In the long run, the ego wants to maximize gratification, just like the id. However, the ego engages in *secondary process thinking,* which is relatively rational, realistic, and oriented toward problem solving. Thus, the ego strives to avoid negative consequences from society and its representatives (for example, punishment by parents or teachers) by behaving "properly." It also attempts to achieve long-range goals that sometimes require putting off gratification.

While the ego concerns itself with practical realities, **the *superego* is the moral component of personality that incorporates social standards about what represents right and wrong.** Throughout their lives, but especially during childhood, individuals receive training about what constitutes good and bad behavior. Eventually they internalize many of these social norms, meaning that they truly *accept* certain moral principles. Then *they* put pressure on *themselves* to live up to these standards. The superego emerges out of the ego at around 3 to 5 years of age. In some people, the superego can become irrationally demanding in its striving for moral perfection. Such people are plagued by excessive guilt.

According to Freud, the id, ego, and superego are distributed across three levels of awareness. He contrasted the unconscious with the conscious and preconscious (see Figure 2.2). **The *conscious* consists of whatever one is aware of at a particular point in time.** For example, at this moment your conscious may include the current train of thought in this text and a dim awareness in the back of your mind that your eyes are getting tired and you're beginning to get hungry. **The *preconscious* contains material just beneath the surface of awareness that can be easily retrieved.** Examples might include your middle name, what you had for supper last night, or an argument you had with a friend yesterday. **The *unconscious* contains thoughts, memories, and desires that are well below the surface of conscious awareness but that nonetheless exert great influence on one's behavior.** Examples of material that might be found in your unconscious would include a forgotten trauma from childhood or hidden feelings of hostility toward a parent.

Conflict and Defense Mechanisms

Freud assumed that behavior is the outcome of an ongoing series of internal conflicts. Battles among the id, ego, and superego are routine. Why? Because the id wants to gratify its urges immediately, but the norms of civilized society frequently dictate otherwise. For example, your id might feel an urge to clobber a co-worker who constantly irritates you. However, society frowns on such behavior, so your ego would try to hold this urge in check, and you would find yourself in a conflict. Freud believed that internal conflicts are a routine part of people's lives.

Freud asserted that conflicts centering on sexual and aggressive impulses are especially likely to have far-reaching consequences. Why did he emphasize sex and aggression? Two reasons were prominent in his thinking. First, Freud thought that sex and aggression are subject to more complex and ambiguous social controls than other basic motives. Thus, people often get mixed messages about what is appropriate. Second, Freud noted that sexual and aggressive drives are thwarted more regularly than other basic biological urges.

FIGURE 2.2 Freud's model of personality structure

Freud theorized that people have three levels of awareness: the conscious, the preconscious, and the unconscious. To dramatize the size of the unconscious, it has often been compared to the portion of an iceberg that lies beneath the water's surface. Freud also divided personality structure into three components—id, ego, and superego—that operate according to different principles and exhibit different modes of thinking. In Freud's model, the id is entirely unconscious, but the ego and superego operate at all three levels of awareness.

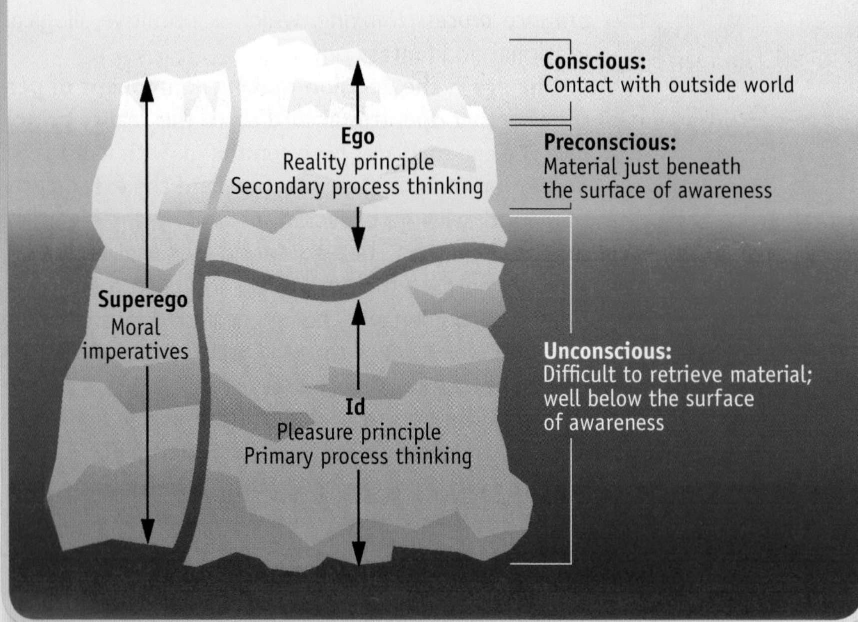

"ALL I WANT FROM THEM IS A SIMPLE MAJORITY ON THINGS."

ScienceCartoonsPlus.com © 1999 by Sidney Harris

Most psychic conflicts are trivial and are quickly resolved one way or the other. Occasionally, however, a conflict will linger for days, months, and even years, creating internal tension. Indeed, Freud believed that lingering conflicts rooted in childhood experiences cause most personality disturbances. More often than not, these prolonged and troublesome conflicts involve sexual and aggressive impulses that society wants to tame. These conflicts are often played out entirely in the unconscious. Although you may not be aware of these unconscious battles, they can produce *anxiety* that slips to the surface of conscious awareness. This anxiety is attributable to your ego worrying about the id getting out of control and doing something terrible.

The arousal of anxiety is a crucial event in Freud's theory of personality functioning (see Figure 2.3). Anxiety is distressing, so people try to rid themselves of this unpleasant emotion any way they can. This effort to ward off anxiety often involves the use of defense mechanisms. ***Defense mechanisms* are largely unconscious reactions that protect a person from painful emotions such as anxiety and guilt.** Typically, they are mental maneuvers that work through self-deception. A common example is ***rationalization,* which involves creating false but plausible excuses to justify unacceptable behavior.** You would be rationalizing if, after cheating someone in a business transaction, you tried to reduce your guilt by explaining that "everyone does it."

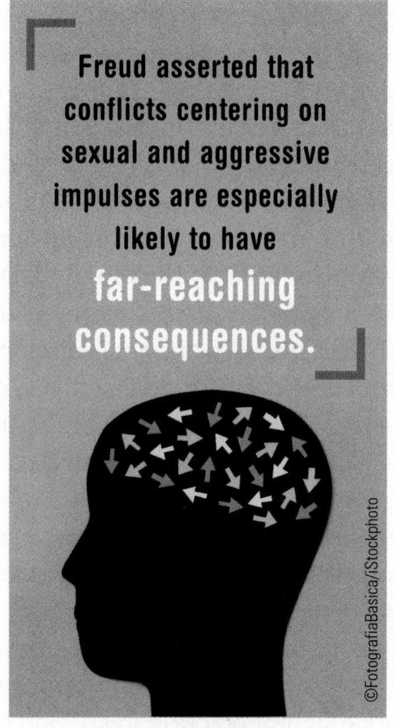

©FotografiaBasica/iStockphoto

Repression is the most basic and widely used defense mechanism. ***Repression* involves keeping distressing thoughts and feelings buried in the unconscious.** People tend to repress desires that make them feel guilty, conflicts that make them anxious, and memories that are painful. Repression is "motivated forgetting." If you forget a dental appointment or the name of someone you don't like, repression may be at work.

FIGURE 2.3 Freud's model of personality dynamics

According to Freud, unconscious conflicts between the id, ego, and superego sometimes lead to anxiety. This discomfort may lead to the use of defense mechanisms, which may temporarily relieve anxiety.

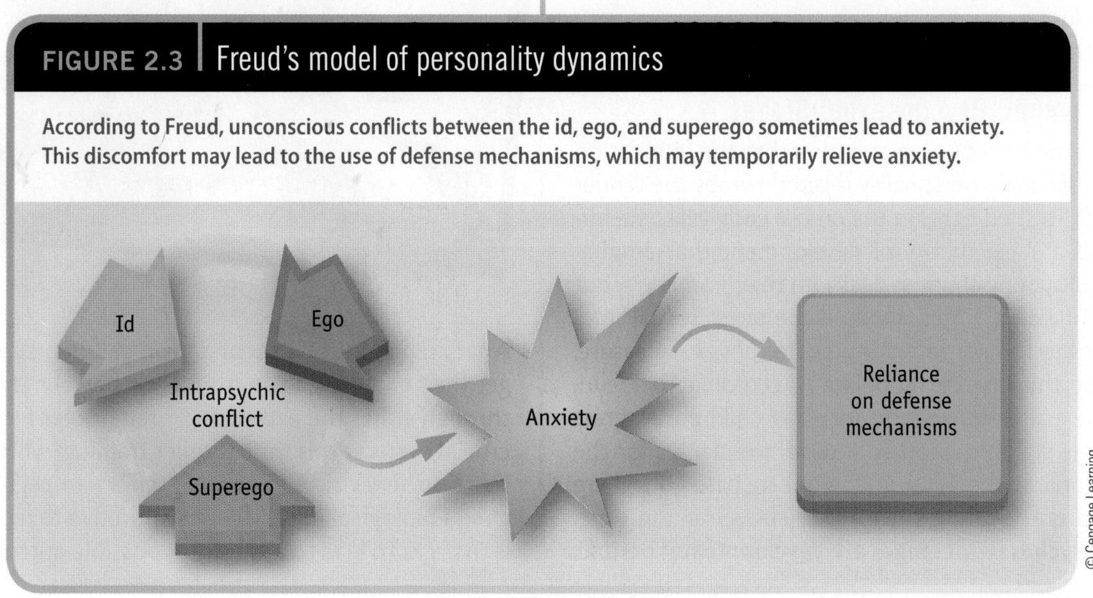

© Cengage Learning

Self-deception can also be seen in the mechanisms of projection and displacement. ***Projection*** **involves attributing one's own thoughts, feelings, or motives to another.** For example, if your lust for a co-worker makes you feel guilty, you might attribute any latent sexual tension between the two of you to the *other person's* desire to seduce you. ***Displacement*** **involves diverting emotional feelings (usually anger) from their original source to a substitute target.** If your boss gives you a hard time at work and you come home and slam the door, yell at your dog, and lash out at your spouse, you are displacing your anger onto irrelevant targets.

Other prominent defense mechanisms include reaction formation, regression, and identification. ***Reaction formation*** **involves behaving in a way that is the opposite of one's true feelings.** Guilt about sexual desires often leads to reaction formation. Freud theorized that many males who ridicule homosexuals are defending against their own latent homosexual impulses. The telltale sign of reaction formation is the exaggerated quality of the opposite behavior.

Regression **involves a reversion to immature patterns of behavior.** When anxious about their self-worth, some adults respond with childish boasting and bragging (as opposed to subtle efforts to impress others). For example, a fired executive having difficulty finding a new job might start making ridiculous statements about his incomparable talents and achievements. Such bragging is regressive when it is marked by massive exaggerations that anyone can see through.

Identification **involves bolstering self-esteem by forming an imaginary or real alliance with some person or group.** For example, youngsters often shore up precarious feelings of self-worth by identifying with rock stars, movie stars, or famous athletes. Adults may join exclusive country clubs or civic organizations with which they identify.

Development: Psychosexual Stages

Freud made the startling assertion that the foundation of an individual's personality is laid down by the tender age of 5! To shed light on the crucial early years, he formulated a stage theory of development that emphasized how young children deal with their immature, but powerful, sexual urges (he used the term "sexual" in a general way to refer to many urges for physical pleasure, not just the urge to copulate). According to Freud, these sexual urges shift in focus as children progress from one stage to another. Indeed, the names for the stages (oral, anal, genital, and so on) are based on where children are focusing their erotic energy at the time. Thus, ***psychosexual stages*** **are developmental periods with a characteristic sexual focus that leave their mark on adult personality.**

Freud theorized that each psychosexual stage has its own unique developmental challenges or tasks. The way these challenges are handled supposedly shapes personality. The notion of *fixation* plays an important role in this process. *Fixation* is a failure to move forward from one stage to another as expected. Essentially, the child's development stalls for a while. Fixation is caused by *excessive gratification* of needs at a particular stage or by *excessive frustration* of those needs. Either way, fixations left over from childhood affect adult personality. Generally, fixation leads to an overemphasis on the psychosexual needs that were prominent during the fixated stage. Freud described a series of five psychosexual stages. Let's examine some of the major features of each stage.

Oral stage. During this stage, which usually encompasses the first year of life, the main source of erotic stimulation is the mouth (in biting, sucking, chewing, and so on). How caretakers handle the child's feeding experiences is supposed to be crucial to subsequent development. Freud attributed considerable importance to the manner in which the child is weaned from the breast or the bottle. According to Freud, fixation at the oral stage could form the basis for obsessive eating or smoking later in life (among many other things).

Anal stage. In their second year, children supposedly get their erotic pleasure from their bowel movements, through either the expulsion or retention of feces. The crucial event at this time is toilet training, which represents society's first systematic effort to regulate the child's biological urges. Severely punitive toilet training is thought to lead to a variety of possible outcomes. For example, excessive punishment might produce a latent feeling of hostility toward the "trainer," who usually is the mother. This hostility might generalize to women in general. Another possibility is that heavy reliance on punitive measures might lead to an association between genital concerns and the anxiety that the punishment arouses. This genital anxiety from severe toilet training could evolve into anxiety about sexual activities later in life.

Phallic stage. Around age 4, the genitals become the focus for the child's erotic energy, largely through self-stimulation. During this pivotal stage, the *Oedipal complex* emerges. Little boys develop an erotically tinged preference for their mother. They also feel hostility toward their father, whom they view as a competitor for mom's affection. Little girls develop a special attachment to their father. At about the same time, they learn that their genitals are very different from those of little boys, and they supposedly develop *penis envy.* According to Freud, girls feel hostile toward their mother because they blame her for their anatomical "deficiency."

To summarize, in the *Oedipal complex* children manifest erotically tinged desires for their other-sex parent, accompanied by feelings of hostility toward their same-sex parent. The name for this syndrome was taken from the Greek myth of Oedipus, who was separated from his parents at birth. Not knowing the identity of his real parents, he inadvertently killed his father and married his mother.

According to Freud, the way parents and children deal with the sexual and aggressive conflicts inherent in the Oedipal complex is of paramount importance. The child has to resolve the dilemma by giving up the sexual longings for the other-sex parent and the hostility toward the same-sex parent. Healthy psychosexual development is supposed to hinge on the resolution of the Oedipal conflict. Why? Because continued hostile relations with the same-sex parent may prevent the child from identifying adequately with that parent. Without such identification, Freudian theory predicts that many aspects of the child's development won't progress as they should.

© Zurijeta/Shutterstock.com

Latency and genital stages. Freud believed that from age 6 through puberty, the child's sexuality is suppressed—it becomes "latent." Important events during this *latency stage* center on expanding social contacts beyond the family. With the advent of puberty, the child evolves into the *genital stage.* Sexual urges reappear and focus on the genitals once again. At this point the sexual energy is normally channeled toward peers of the other sex, rather than toward oneself, as in the phallic stage.

In arguing that the early years shape personality, Freud did not mean that personality development comes to an abrupt halt in middle childhood. However, he did believe that the foundation for one's adult personality is solidly entrenched by this time. He maintained that future developments are rooted in early, formative experiences and that significant conflicts in later years are replays of crises from childhood.

In fact, Freud believed that unconscious sexual conflicts rooted in childhood experiences cause most personality disturbances. His steadfast belief in the psychosexual origins of psychological disorders eventually led to bitter theoretical disputes with two of his most brilliant colleagues: Carl Jung and Alfred Adler. Jung and Adler both argued that Freud overemphasized sexuality. Freud summarily rejected their ideas, so Jung and Adler felt compelled to go their own ways, developing their own psychodynamic theories of personality.

2-2b OTHER PSYCHODYNAMIC APPROACHES

Carl Jung called his new approach *analytical psychology.* Like Freud, Jung (1933) emphasized the unconscious determinants of personality. However, he proposed that the unconscious consists of two layers. The first layer, called the *personal unconscious,* is essentially the same as Freud's version of the unconscious. In addition, Jung theorized the existence of a deeper layer he called the collective unconscious. **The *collective unconscious* is a storehouse of latent memory traces inherited from people's ancestral past that is shared with the entire human race.** Jung called these ancestral memories *archetypes.* They are not memories of actual, personal experiences. Instead, archetypes are emotionally charged images and thought forms that have universal meaning. These archetypal images and ideas show up frequently in dreams and are often manifested in a culture's use of symbols in art, literature, and religion. Jung felt that an understanding of archetypal symbols helped him make sense of his patients' dreams.

Alfred Adler called his psychoanalytic approach *individual psychology.* Adler (1927) argued that the foremost human drive is not sexuality, but a *striving for superiority.* Adler viewed such striving as a universal drive to adapt, improve oneself, and master life's challenges. He asserted that everyone has to work to overcome some feelings of inferiority. ***Compensation* involves efforts to overcome imagined or real inferiorities by developing one's abilities.** Adler believed that compensation is entirely normal. However, in some people inferiority feelings can become excessive, resulting in what is widely known today as an *inferiority complex*—exaggerated feelings of weakness and inadequacy. Adler explained personality disturbances by noting that an inferiority complex can distort the normal process of striving for superiority. He maintained that some people engage in *overcompensation* in order to conceal, even from themselves, their feelings of inferiority. People with an inferiority complex work to achieve status, gain power over others, and acquire the trappings of success (fancy clothes, impressive cars, or whatever seems important to them). They tend to flaunt their success in an effort to cover up their underlying inferiority complex. The problem is that such people engage in unconscious self-deception, worrying more about *appearances* than *reality.*

Photo: © Michael N. Paras/Corbis; Graphic: © L_amica/Shutterstock.com

2-2c EVALUATING PSYCHODYNAMIC PERSPECTIVES

The psychodynamic approach has given us a number of far-reaching theories of personality. These theories yielded some bold new insights for their time. Psychodynamic theory and research have demonstrated that (1) unconscious forces can influence behavior, (2) internal conflict often plays a key role in generating psychological distress, (3) early childhood experiences can exert considerable influence over adult personality, and (4) people do rely on defense mechanisms to reduce their experience of unpleasant emotions (Porcerelli et al., 2010; Westen, Gabbard, & Ortigo, 2008).

In a more negative vein, psychodynamic formulations have been criticized on several grounds, (Crews, 2006; Kramer, 2006; Torrey, 1992). First, some critics maintain that psychodynamic theories have often been too vague to permit a clear scientific test. Concepts such as the superego, the preconscious, and collective unconscious are difficult to measure. Second, the empirical evidence on psychodynamic theories has often been characterized as inadequate. Insofar as researchers have accumulated evidence on psychodynamic theories, it has provided only modest support for the central hypotheses. Third, many critics have argued that psychodynamic theories have generally provided a rather male-centered, even sexist, view of personality.

2-3 Behavioral Perspectives

Behaviorism is a theoretical orientation based on the premise that scientific psychology should study observable behavior. Behaviorism has been a major school of thought in psychology since 1913, when John B. Watson published an influential article. Watson argued that psychology should abandon its earlier focus on the mind and mental processes and focus exclusively on overt behavior. He contended that psychology cannot study mental processes in a scientific manner because these processes are private and not accessible to outside observation.

In completely rejecting mental processes as a suitable subject for scientific study, Watson took an extreme position that is no longer dominant among modern behaviorists. Nonetheless, his influence was enormous, as psychology changed its primary focus from the study of the mind to the study of behavior.

The behaviorists have shown little interest in internal personality structures such as Freud's id, ego, and superego, because such structures can't be observed. They prefer to think in terms of "response tendencies," which *can* be observed. Thus, most behaviorists view an individual's personality as a *collection of response tendencies that are tied to various stimulus situations.* A specific situation may be associated with a number of response tendencies that vary in strength, depending on an individual's past experience (see Figure 2.4).

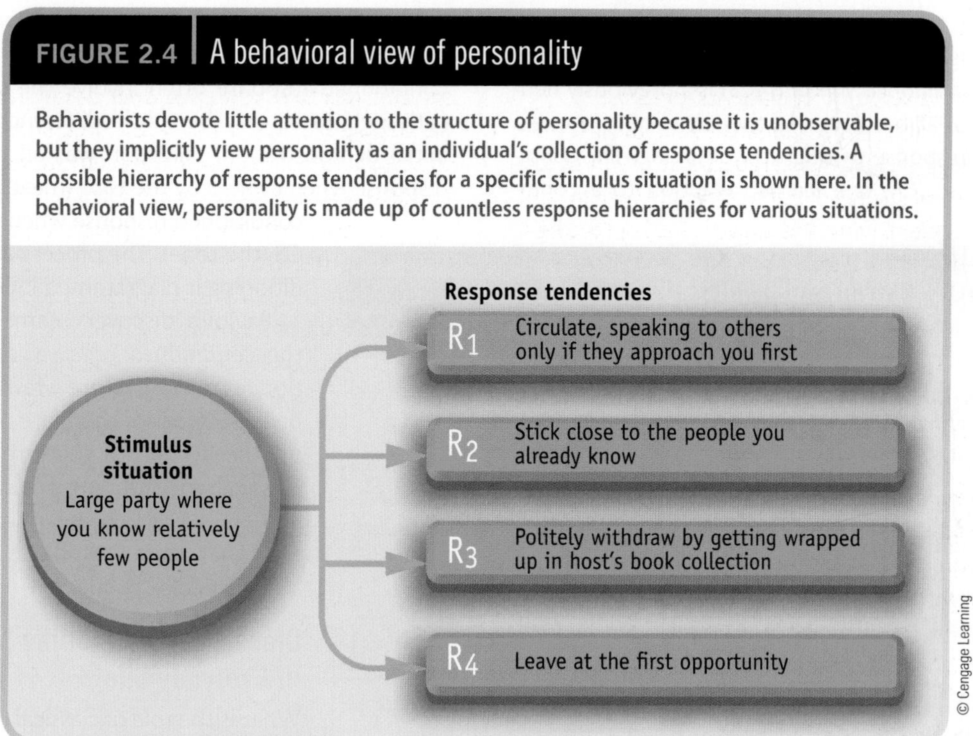

FIGURE 2.4 | A behavioral view of personality

Behaviorists devote little attention to the structure of personality because it is unobservable, but they implicitly view personality as an individual's collection of response tendencies. A possible hierarchy of response tendencies for a specific stimulus situation is shown here. In the behavioral view, personality is made up of countless response hierarchies for various situations.

Although behaviorists have shown relatively little interest in personality structure, they have focused extensively on personality *development*. They explain development the same way they explain everything else—through learning. Specifically, they focus on how children's response tendencies are shaped through classical conditioning, operant conditioning, and observational learning. Let's look at these processes.

2-3a PAVLOV'S CLASSICAL CONDITIONING

Do you go weak in the knees when you get a note at work that tells you to go see your boss? Do you get anxious when you're around important people? If so, you probably acquired these common responses through classical conditioning. ***Classical conditioning* is a type of learning in which a neutral stimulus acquires the capacity to evoke a response that was originally evoked by another stimulus.** This process was first described back in the early 1900s by Ivan Pavlov, a prominent Russian physiologist who did Nobel Prize–winning research on digestion.

© brian guest/Age fotostock

The Conditioned Reflex

Pavlov (1906) was studying digestive processes in dogs when he discovered that the dogs could be trained to salivate in response to the sound of a tone. What was so significant about a dog salivating when a tone was sounded? The key was that the tone started out as a *neutral* stimulus; that is, originally it did not produce the response of salivation (after all, why should it?). However, Pavlov managed to change that by pairing the tone with a stimulus (meat powder) that did produce the salivation response. Through this process, the tone acquired the capacity to trigger the response of salivation. What Pavlov had demonstrated was *how learned reflexes are acquired.*

At this point we need to introduce the special vocabulary of classical conditioning. In Pavlov's experiment the bond between the meat powder and salivation was a natural association that was not created through conditioning. In unconditioned bonds, the *unconditioned stimulus (UCS)* is a stimulus that evokes an unconditioned response without previous conditioning. The *unconditioned response (UCR)* is an unlearned reaction to an unconditioned stimulus that occurs without previous conditioning.

In contrast, the link between the tone and salivation was established through conditioning. In conditioned bonds, the *conditioned stimulus (CS)* is a previously neutral stimulus that has acquired the capacity to evoke a conditioned response through conditioning. The *conditioned response (CR)* is a learned reaction to a conditioned stimulus that occurs because of previous conditioning. Note that the unconditioned response and conditioned response often involve the same behavior (although there may be subtle differences). In Pavlov's initial demonstration, salivation was an unconditioned response when evoked by the UCS (meat powder) and a conditioned response when evoked by the CS (the tone). The process of classical conditioning is diagrammed in Figure 2.5.

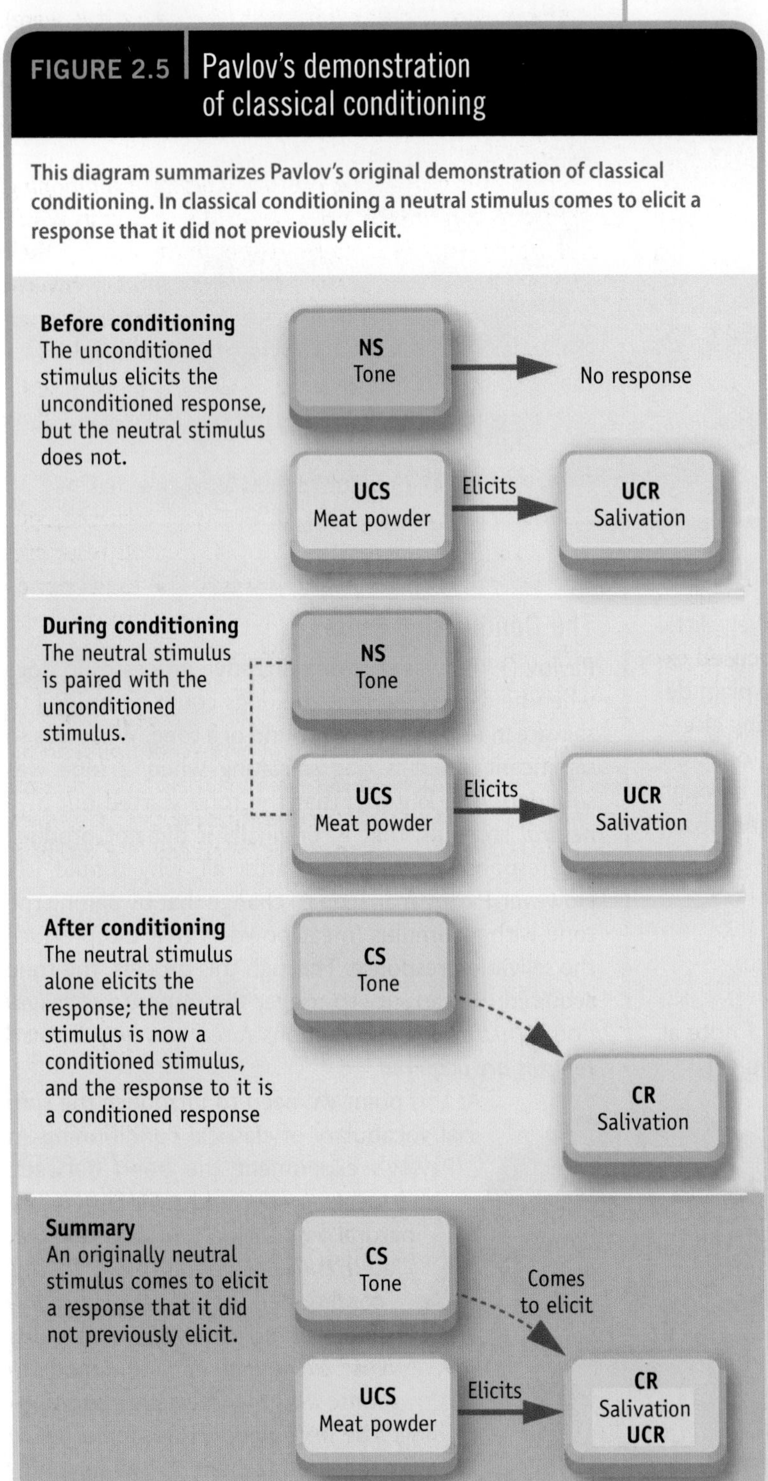

Before conditioning
The unconditioned stimulus elicits the unconditioned response, but the neutral stimulus does not.
NS
Tone
No response
UCS
Meat powder
Elicits
UCR
Salivation
During conditioning
The neutral stimulus is paired with the unconditioned stimulus.
NS
Tone
UCS
Meat powder
Elicits
UCR
Salivation
After conditioning
The neutral stimulus alone elicits the response; the neutral stimulus is now a conditioned stimulus, and the response to it is a conditioned response
CS
Tone
CR
Salivation
Summary
An originally neutral stimulus comes to elicit a response that it did not previously elicit.
CS
Tone
Comes to elicit
UCS
Meat powder
Elicits
CR
Salivation
UCR

FIGURE 2.5 Pavlov's demonstration of classical conditioning

This diagram summarizes Pavlov's original demonstration of classical conditioning. In classical conditioning a neutral stimulus comes to elicit a response that it did not previously elicit.

Pavlov's discovery came to be called the *conditioned reflex.* Classically conditioned responses are viewed as reflexes because most of them are relatively involuntary. Responses that are a product of classical conditioning are said to be *elicited.* This word is meant to convey the idea that these responses are triggered automatically.

Classical Conditioning in Everyday Life

What is the role of classical conditioning in shaping personality in everyday life? Among other things, it contributes to the acquisition of emotional responses, such as anxieties, fears, and phobias (Mineka & Zinbarg, 2006). This is a relatively small but important class of responses, as maladaptive emotional reactions underlie many adjustment problems. For example, one middle-aged woman reported being troubled by a bridge phobia so severe that she couldn't drive on interstate highways because of all the viaducts she would have to cross. She was able to pinpoint the source of her phobia. Back in her childhood, whenever her family would drive to visit her grandmother, they had to cross a little-used, rickety, dilapidated bridge out in the countryside. Her father, in a misguided attempt at humor, made a major production out of these crossings. He would stop short of the bridge and carry on about the enormous danger of the crossing. Obviously, he thought the bridge was safe or he wouldn't have driven across it. However, the naive young girl was terrified by her father's scare tactics, and the bridge became a conditioned stimulus eliciting great fear. Unfortunately, the fear spilled over to all bridges, and 40 years later she was still carrying the burden of this phobia.

FIGURE 2.6 Classical conditioning of anxiety

A stimulus (in this case, a newsroom) that is frequently paired with anxiety-arousing events (reprimands and criticism) may come to elicit anxiety by itself, through classical conditioning.

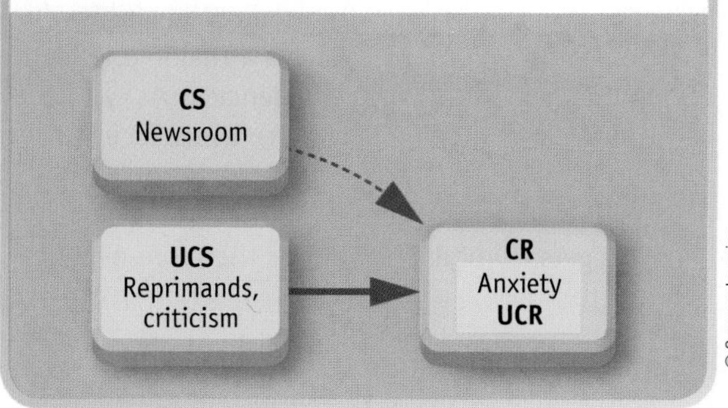

Classical conditioning also appears to account for more realistic and moderate anxiety responses. For example, imagine a news reporter in a high-pressure job where he consistently gets negative feedback about his work from his bosses. The negative comments from his supervisors function as a UCS eliciting anxiety. These reprimands are paired with the noise and sight of the newsroom, so that the newsroom becomes a CS triggering anxiety, even when his supervisors are absent (see Figure 2.6).

Fortunately, not every frightening experience leaves a conditioned fear in its wake. A variety of factors influence whether a conditioned response is acquired in a particular situation. Furthermore, a newly formed stimulus-response bond does not necessarily last indefinitely. The right circumstances can lead to ***extinction*—the gradual weakening and disappearance of a conditioned response tendency.** What leads to extinction in classical conditioning? It is the consistent presentation of the CS *alone*, without the UCS. For example, when Pavlov consistently presented *only* the tone to a previously conditioned dog, the tone gradually stopped eliciting the response of salivation. How long it takes to extinguish a conditioned response depends on many factors. Foremost among them is the strength of the conditioned bond when extinction begins. Some conditioned responses extinguish quickly, while others are difficult to weaken.

Positive reinforcement motivates much of everyday behavior.

2-3b SKINNER'S OPERANT CONDITIONING

Classical conditioning best explains reflexive responding controlled by stimuli that *precede* the response. However, both animals and humans make many responses that don't fit this description. Consider the response you are engaging in right now—studying. It is definitely not a reflex (life might be easier if it were). The stimuli that govern it (exams and grades) do not precede it. Instead, your studying response is mainly influenced by events that follow it—specifically, its *consequences.*

This kind of learning is called *operant conditioning.* ***Operant conditioning* is a form of learning in which voluntary responses come to be controlled by their consequences.** Operant conditioning probably governs a larger share of human behavior than classical conditioning, since most human responses are voluntary rather than reflexive. Because they are voluntary, operant responses are said to be *emitted* rather than *elicited.*

The study of operant conditioning was led by B. F. Skinner (1953, 1974), a Harvard University psychologist who spent most of his career studying simple responses made by laboratory rats and pigeons. The fundamental principle of operant conditioning is uncommonly simple. Skinner demonstrated that *organisms tend to repeat those responses that are followed by favorable consequences, and they tend not to repeat those responses that are followed by neutral or unfavorable consequences.* In Skinner's scheme, favorable, neutral, and unfavorable consequences involve reinforcement, extinction, and punishment, respectively. We'll look at each of these concepts in turn.

The Power of Reinforcement

According to Skinner, reinforcement can occur in two ways, which he called *positive reinforcement* and *negative reinforcement.* ***Positive reinforcement* occurs when a response is strengthened (increases in frequency) because it is followed by the arrival of a (presumably) pleasant stimulus.** Positive reinforcement is roughly synonymous with the concept of reward. Notice, however, that reinforcement is defined *after the fact,* in terms of its effect on behavior. Why? Because reinforcement is subjective. Something that serves as a reinforcer for one person may not function as a reinforcer for another. For example, peer approval is a potent reinforcer for most people, but not all.

Positive reinforcement motivates much of everyday behavior. You study hard because good grades are likely to follow as a result. You go to work because this behavior produces paychecks. Perhaps you work extra hard in the hope of winning a promotion or a pay raise. In each of these examples, certain responses occur because they have led to positive outcomes in the past. Positive reinforcement influences personality development in a straightforward way. Responses followed by pleasant outcomes are strengthened and tend to become habitual patterns of behavior. For example, a youngster might clown around in class and gain appreciative comments and smiles from schoolmates. This social approval will probably reinforce clowning-around behavior (see Figure 2.7). If such behavior is reinforced with some regularity, it will gradually become an integral element of the youth's personality.

Negative reinforcement **occurs when a response is strengthened (increases in frequency) because it is followed by the removal of a (presumably) unpleasant stimulus.** Don't let the word *negative* here confuse you. Negative reinforcement *is* reinforcement. Like positive reinforcement, it strengthens a response. However, this strengthening occurs because the response gets rid of an aversive stimulus (see Figure 2.7). Consider a few examples: You rush home in the winter to get out of the cold. You clean your house to get rid of a mess. Parents give in to their child's begging to halt his whining. Negative reinforcement plays a major role in the development of avoidance tendencies. As you may have noticed, many people tend to avoid facing up to awkward situations and sticky personal problems. This personality trait typically develops because avoidance behavior gets rid of anxiety and is therefore negatively reinforced.

FIGURE 2.7 Positive and negative reinforcement in operant conditioning

Positive reinforcement occurs when a response is followed by a favorable outcome, so that the response is strengthened. In negative reinforcement, the removal (symbolized here by the "No" sign) of an aversive stimulus serves as a reinforcer. Negative reinforcement produces the same result as positive reinforcement: The person's tendency to emit the reinforced response is strengthened (the response becomes more frequent).

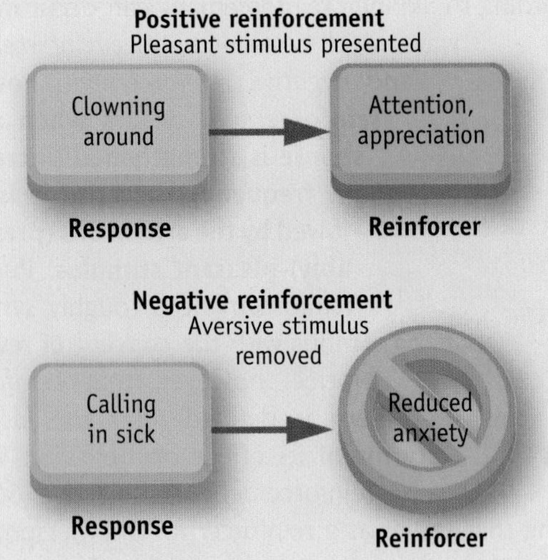

Extinction and Punishment

Like the effects of classical conditioning, the effects of operant conditioning may not last forever. In both types of conditioning, *extinction* refers to the gradual weakening and disappearance of a response. In operant conditioning, extinction begins when a previously reinforced response stops producing positive consequences. As extinction progresses, the response typically becomes less and less frequent and eventually disappears. Thus, the response tendencies that make up one's personality are not necessarily permanent. For example, the youngster who found that his classmates reinforced clowning around in grade school might find that his attempts at comedy earn nothing but indifferent stares in high school. This termination of reinforcement would probably lead to the gradual extinction of the clowning-around behavior.

Some responses may be weakened by punishment. In Skinner's scheme, ***punishment*** **occurs when a response is weakened (decreases in frequency) because it is followed by the arrival of a (presumably) unpleasant stimulus.** The concept of punishment in operant conditioning confuses many students on two counts. First, it is often mixed up with negative reinforcement because both involve aversive (unpleasant) stimuli. Please note, however, that they are altogether different events with opposite outcomes! In negative reinforcement, a response leads to the *removal* of something aversive, and this response is *strengthened*. In punishment, a response leads to the *arrival* of something aversive, and this response tends to be *weakened*.

The second source of confusion involves the tendency to view punishment as only a disciplinary procedure used by parents, teachers, and other authority figures. In the operant model, punishment occurs

© auremar/Shutterstock.com

whenever a response leads to negative consequences. Defined in this way, the concept goes far beyond actions such as parents spanking children or teachers handing out detentions. For example, if you wear a new outfit and your friends make fun of it and hurt your feelings, your tendency to wear this clothing will probably decline—because of punishment.

The impact of punishment on personality development is just the opposite of reinforcement. Generally speaking, those patterns of behavior that lead to punishing (that is, negative) consequences tend to be weakened. For instance, if your impulsive decisions always backfire, your tendency to be impulsive should decline.

2-3c BANDURA'S OBSERVATIONAL LEARNING

Albert Bandura is one of several theorists who have added a cognitive flavor to behaviorism since the 1960s. Bandura refers to his model as *social cognitive theory.* Bandura (1986, 1999) agrees with the basic thrust of behaviorism in that he believes that personality is largely shaped through learning. However, he contends that conditioning is not a mechanical process in which people are passive participants. Instead, he maintains that individuals actively seek out and process information about their environment in order to maximize their favorable outcomes.

Bandura's foremost theoretical contribution has been his description of observational learning. ***Observational learning*** **occurs when an organism's responding is influenced by the observation of others, who are called models.** Bandura does not view observational learning as entirely separate from classical and operant conditioning. Instead, he asserts that both classical and operant conditioning can take place indirectly when one person observes another's conditioning.

To illustrate, suppose you observe a friend behaving assertively with a car salesman. Let's say that his assertiveness is reinforced by the exceptionally good buy he gets on the car. Your own tendency to behave assertively with salespeople might well be strengthened as a result. Notice that the favorable consequence is experienced by your friend, not you. Your friend's tendency to bargain assertively should be reinforced directly, but your tendency to bargain assertively may also be strengthened indirectly (see Figure 2.8).

The theories of Skinner and Pavlov make no allowance for this type of indirect learning. After all, observational learning requires that you pay *attention* to your friend's behavior, that you *understand* its consequences, and that you store this *information* in *memory.* Obviously, attention, understanding, information, and memory involve cognition, which behaviorists used to ignore.

As social cognitive theory has been refined, it has become apparent that some role models tend to be more influential than others (Bandura, 1986). Both children and adults tend to imitate people they like or respect more so than people they don't. People are also especially prone to imitate the behavior of those they consider attractive or powerful (such as celebrities). In addition, imitation is more likely when individuals see similarity between the model and themselves. Above all else, people are more likely to copy a model if they see the model's behavior lead to positive outcomes (reinforcement).

FIGURE 2.8 | Observational learning

In observational learning, an observer attends to and stores a mental representation of a model's behavior (for example, assertive bargaining) and its consequences (such as a good buy on a car). According to social cognitive theory, many of our characteristic responses are acquired through observation of others' behavior.

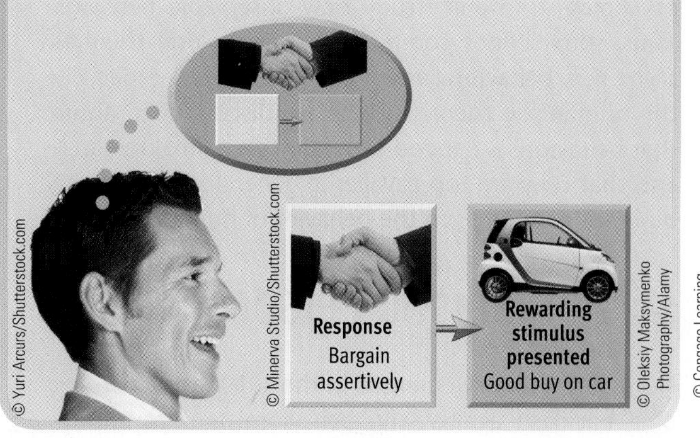

> Your self-concept may not be entirely consistent with your actual experiences. To put it more bluntly, your self-concept **may be inaccurate.**

© Angela Waye/Shutterstock.com

2-3d EVALUATING BEHAVIORAL PERSPECTIVES

Behavioral theories are firmly rooted in empirical research rather than clinical intuition. Pavlov's model has shed light on how conditioning can account for people's sometimes troublesome emotional responses. Skinner's work has demonstrated how personality is shaped by the consequences of behavior. Bandura has shown how observational learning can help mold people's characteristic behavior.

Behaviorists, in particular Walter Mischel (1990), have also provided the most thorough account of why people are only moderately consistent in their behavior. For example, a person who is shy in one context might be quite outgoing in another. Other models of personality largely ignore this inconsistency. The behaviorists have shown that it occurs because people behave in ways they think will lead to reinforcement in the situation at hand. In other words, situational factors are important determinants of behavior. Thus, a major contribution of the behavioral perspective has been its demonstration that personality factors and situational factors jointly shape behavior (Fleeson, 2004).

Of course, each theoretical approach has its shortcomings, and the behavioral approach is no exception (Pervin & John, 2001). The behaviorists used to be criticized because they neglected cognitive processes. The rise of social cognitive theory blunted this criticism. However, social cognitive theory undermines the foundation on which behaviorism was built—the idea that psychologists should study only observable behavior. Thus, some critics complain that behavioral theories aren't very behavioral anymore. Other critics, especially the humanistic theorists, who we discuss next, argue that behaviorists depend too much on animal research and that they are too cavalier in generalizing from the behavior of animals to the behavior of humans.

2-4 Humanistic Perspectives

Humanistic theory emerged in the 1950s as something of a backlash against the behavioral and psychodynamic theories. Freudian theory was criticized for its belief that primitive, animalistic drives (sex and aggression) dominate behavior. Behaviorism was criticized for its preoccupation with animal research. Critics argued that both schools view people as helpless pawns controlled by their environment and their past. Many of these critics blended into a loose alliance that came to be known as "humanism" because of its exclusive interest in human behavior. *Humanism* is a theoretical orientation that emphasizes the unique qualities of humans, especially their free will and their potential for personal growth. Humanistic psychologists do not believe that we can learn anything of significance about the human condition from animal research.

Humanistic theorists take an optimistic view of human nature. In contrast to most psychodynamic and behavioral theorists, humanistic theorists believe that (1) human nature includes an innate drive toward personal growth, (2) individuals have the freedom to chart their courses of action and are not pawns of their environment, and (3) humans are largely conscious and rational beings who are not dominated by unconscious, irrational needs and conflicts.

The humanistic approach clearly provides a different perspective on personality than either the psychodynamic or behavioral approach. In this section we'll review the ideas of the two most influential humanistic theorists, Carl Rogers and Abraham Maslow.

2-4a ROGERS'S PERSON-CENTERED THEORY

Carl Rogers (1951, 1961) was one of the founders of the human potential movement, which emphasizes personal growth through sensitivity training, encounter groups, and other exercises intended to help people get in touch with their true selves. Like Freud, Rogers based his personality theory on his extensive therapeutic interactions with many clients. Rogers called his approach a *person-centered theory.*

Rogers viewed personality structure in terms of just one construct. He called this construct the *self,* although it is more widely known today as the *self-concept.* **A *self-concept* is a collection of beliefs about one's own nature, unique qualities, and typical behavior.** Your self-concept is your mental picture of yourself. It is a collection of self-perceptions. For example, a self-concept might include such beliefs as "I am easygoing" or "I am pretty" or "I am hardworking."

Rogers stressed the subjective nature of the self-concept. Your self-concept may not be entirely consistent with your actual experiences. To put it more bluntly, your self-concept may be inaccurate. Most people are prone to distort their experiences to some extent to promote a relatively favorable self-concept. For example, you may believe that you are quite bright academically, but your grade transcript might suggest otherwise. Rogers used the term ***incongruence* to refer to the disparity between one's self-concept and one's actual experience.** In contrast, if a person's self-concept is reasonably accurate, it is said to be *congruent* with reality. Everyone experiences *some* incongruence; the crucial issue is how much (see Figure 2.9). Rogers maintained that a great deal of incongruence undermines a person's psychological well-being.

In terms of personality development, Rogers was concerned with how childhood experiences promote congruence or incongruence. According to Rogers, everyone has a strong need for affection, love, and acceptance from others. Early in life, parents provide most of this affection. Rogers maintained that some parents make their affection *conditional.* That is, they make it depend on the child's behaving well and living up to expectations. When parental love seems conditional, children often distort and block out of their memory those experiences that make them feel unworthy of love. At the other end of the spectrum, Rogers asserted that some parents make their affection *unconditional.* Their children have less need to block out unworthy experiences because they have been assured that they are worthy of affection no matter what they do.

Rogers believed that unconditional love from parents fosters congruence and that conditional love fosters incongruence. He further theorized that individuals who grow up believing that affection from others (besides their parents) is conditional go on to distort more and more of their experiences to feel worthy of acceptance from a wider and wider array of people, making the incongruence grow.

"Just remember, son, it doesn't matter whether you win or lose—unless you want Daddy's love."

FIGURE 2.9 Rogers's view of personality structure

In Rogers's model, the self-concept is the only important structural construct. However, Rogers acknowledged that one's self-concept may not jell with the realities of one's actual experience—a condition called incongruence. Different people have varied amounts of incongruence between their self-concept and reality.

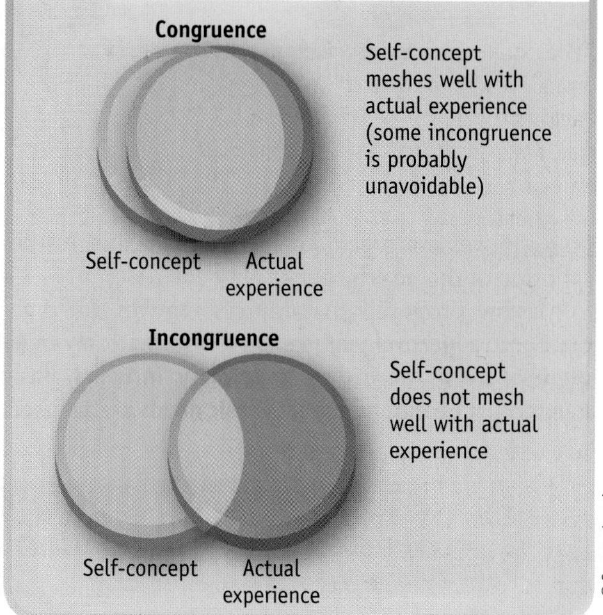

According to Rogers, experiences that threaten people's personal views of themselves are the principal cause of troublesome anxiety. Thus, people with highly incongruent self-concepts are especially likely to be plagued by recurrent anxiety (see Figure 2.10 on the next page). To ward off this anxiety, such people often behave defensively. That is, they ignore, deny, and distort reality to protect their inaccurate self-concept.

2-4b MASLOW'S THEORY OF SELF-ACTUALIZATION

Abraham Maslow (1970) was a prominent humanistic theorist who argued that psychology should take a greater interest in the nature of the healthy personality, instead of dwelling on the causes of disorders. "To oversimplify the matter somewhat," he said, "it is as if Freud supplied to us the sick half of psychology and we must now fill it out with the healthy half" (Maslow, 1968, p. 5). Maslow's key contributions were his analysis of

FIGURE 2.10 | Rogers's view of personality development and dynamics

Rogers's theory of development posits that conditional love leads to a need to distort experiences, which fosters an incongruent self-concept. Incongruence makes one prone to recurrent anxiety, which triggers defensive behavior, which fuels more incongruence.

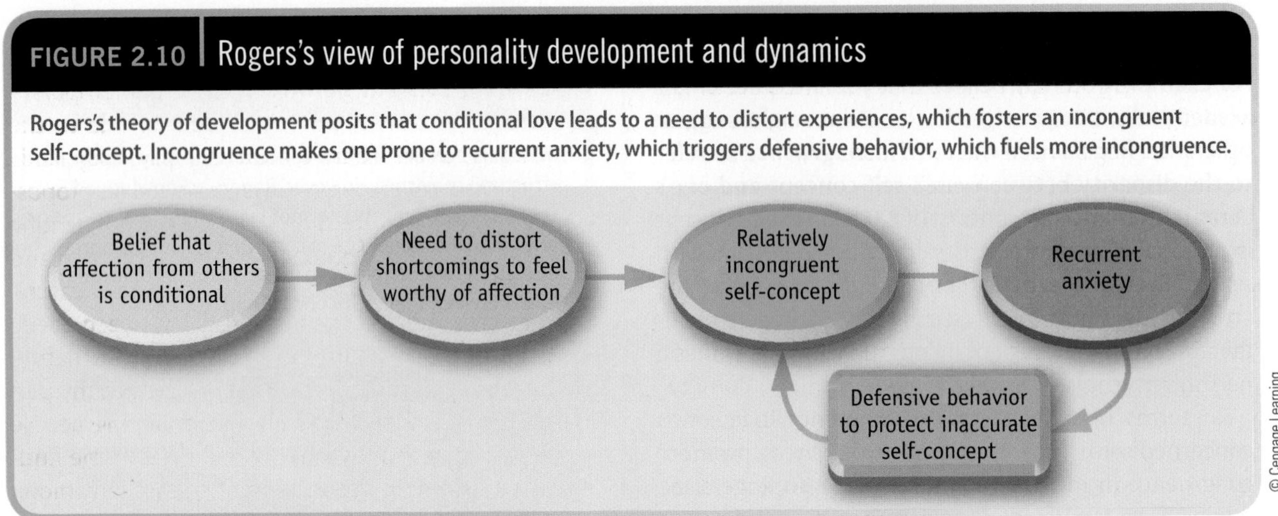

how motives are organized hierarchically and his description of the healthy personality.

Maslow proposed that human motives are organized into a ***hierarchy of needs*—a systematic arrangement of needs, according to priority, in which basic needs must be met before less basic needs are aroused.** This hierarchical arrangement is usually portrayed as a pyramid (see Figure 2.11). The needs toward the bottom of the pyramid, such as physiological or security needs, are the most basic. Higher levels in the pyramid consist of progressively less basic needs. When a person manages to satisfy a level of needs reasonably well

FIGURE 2.11 | Maslow's hierarchy of needs

According to Maslow, human needs are arranged in a hierarchy, and individuals must satisfy their basic needs first, before progressing to higher needs. In the diagram, higher levels in the pyramid represent progressively less basic needs. People progress upward in the hierarchy when lower needs are satisfied reasonably well, but they may regress back to lower levels if basic needs cease to be satisfied.

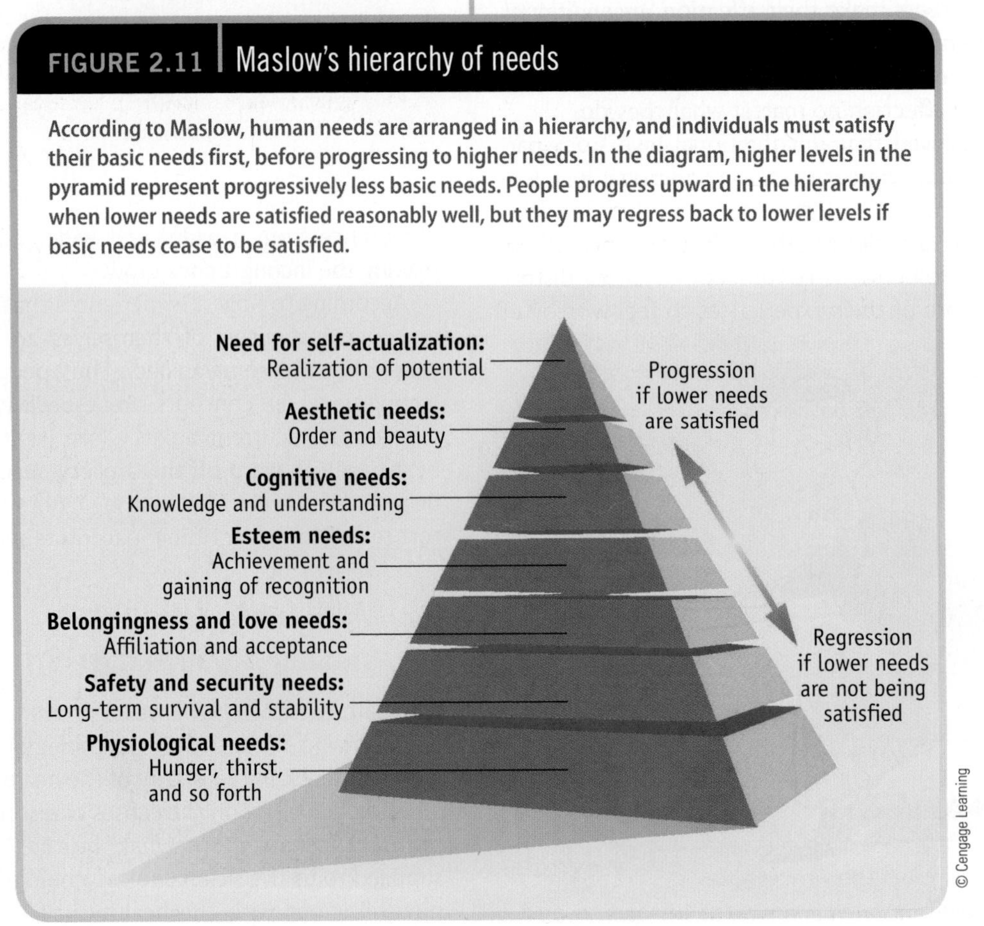

(complete satisfaction is not necessary), *this satisfaction activates needs at the next level.*

Maslow argued that humans have an innate drive toward personal growth—that is, evolution toward a higher state of being. Thus, he described the needs in the uppermost reaches of his hierarchy as *growth needs*. These include the needs for knowledge, understanding, order, and aesthetic beauty. Foremost among the growth needs is the ***need for self-actualization*, which is the need to fulfill one's potential;** it is the highest need in Maslow's motivational hierarchy. Maslow summarized this concept with a simple statement: "What a man *can* be, he *must* be." According to Maslow, people will be frustrated if they are unable to fully utilize their talents or pursue their true interests. For example, if you have great musical talent but must work as an accountant, or if you have scholarly interests but must work as a sales clerk, your need for self-actualization will be thwarted. Maslow's pyramid has penetrated popular culture to a remarkable degree. For example, Peterson and Park (2010) note that a Google search located over 766,000 images of Maslow's pyramid on the Internet—a figure that topped the number of images for the *Mona Lisa* and *The Last Supper*!

Because of his interest in self-actualization, Maslow conducted research to analyze the nature of the healthy personality. He called people with exceptionally healthy personalities *self-actualizing persons* because of their commitment to continued personal growth. He identified various traits characteristic of self-actualizing people, which are listed in Figure 2.12. In brief, Maslow found that self-actualizers are accurately tuned in to reality and are at peace with themselves. He found that they are open and spontaneous and that they retain a fresh appreciation of the world around them. Socially, they are sensitive to others' needs and enjoy rewarding interpersonal relations. However, they are not dependent on others for approval, nor are they uncomfortable with solitude. They thrive on their work, and they enjoy their sense of humor. Finally, he found that they strike a nice balance between many polarities in personality, in that they can be both childlike and mature, rational and intuitive, conforming and rebellious.

2-4c EVALUATING HUMANISTIC PERSPECTIVES

The humanistic approach deserves credit for making the self-concept a widely used construct in psychology and for highlighting the importance of psychological health. One could also argue that the humanists' optimistic, growth-oriented approach laid the foundation for the emergence of the positive psychology movement that is increasingly influential in contemporary psychology. Of course, there is a negative side to the balance sheet as well (Burger, 2008). Like psychodynamic theorists, the humanists have been criticized for proposing hypotheses that are difficult to put to a scientific test. Humanistic concepts such as personal growth and self-actualization are difficult to define and measure. Critics also charge that the humanists have been overly optimistic in their assumptions about human nature and unrealistic in their descriptions of the healthy personality. For instance, Maslow's self-actualizing people sound *perfect.* In reality, Maslow had a hard time finding self-actualizing persons. When he searched among the living, the results were so disappointing that he turned to the study of historical figures. Thus, humanistic portraits of psychological health are perhaps a bit unrealistic.

FIGURE 2.12 | Maslow's view of the healthy personality

Humanistic theorists emphasize psychological health instead of maladjustment. Maslow's sketch of the self-actualizing person provides a provocative picture of the healthy personality.

CHARACTERISTICS OF SELF-ACTUALIZING PEOPLE

- Clear, efficient perception of reality and comfortable relations with it
- Spontaneity, simplicity, and naturalness
- Problem centering (having something outside themselves they "must" do as a mission)
- Detachment and need for privacy
- Autonomy, independence of culture and environment
- Continued freshness of appreciation
- Mystical and peak experiences
- Feelings of kinship and identification with the human race
- Strong friendships, but limited in number
- Democratic character structure
- Ethical discrimination between means and ends, between good and evil
- Philosophical, unhostile sense of humor
- Balance between polarities in personality

2-5 Biological Perspectives

Could personality be a matter of genetic inheritance? This possibility was largely ignored for many decades of personality research until Hans Eysenck made a case for genetic influence in the 1960s. In this section, we'll discuss Eysenck's theory and look at more recent behavioral genetics research on the heritability of personality. We'll also examine evolutionary perspectives on personality.

2-5a EYSENCK'S THEORY

Hans Eysenck was born in Germany but fled to London during the era of Nazi rule. He went on to become one of Britain's most prominent psychologists. According to Eysenck, personality is largely shaped by a person's genes. How is heredity linked to personality in Eysenck's model? In part, through conditioning concepts borrowed from behavioral theory. Eysenck (1967, 1982) theorizes that some people can be conditioned more readily than others because of inherited differences in their physiological functioning (specifically, their level of arousal). These variations in "conditionability" are assumed to influence the personality traits that people acquire through conditioning.

Eysenck views personality structure as a hierarchy of traits. Numerous superficial traits are derived from a smaller number of more basic traits, which are derived from a handful of fundamental higher-order traits. Eysenck has shown a special interest in explaining variations in *extraversion-introversion*. He has proposed that introverts tend to have higher levels of physiological arousal, or perhaps higher "arousability." This makes them more easily conditioned than extraverts. According to Eysenck, people who condition easily acquire more conditioned inhibitions than others. These inhibitions make them more bashful, tentative, and uneasy in social situations. This social discomfort leads them to turn inward. Hence, they become introverted.

2-5b RECENT RESEARCH IN BEHAVIORAL GENETICS

Recent twin studies have provided impressive support for Eysenck's hypothesis that personality is largely inherited. **In *twin studies* researchers assess hereditary influence by comparing the resemblance of identical twins and fraternal twins on a trait.** The logic underlying this comparison is as follows. *Identical twins* emerge from one egg that splits, so that their genetic makeup is exactly the same (100% overlap). *Fraternal twins* result when two eggs are fertilized simultaneously; their genetic overlap is only 50%. Both types of twins *usually* grow up in the same home, at the same time, exposed to the same relatives, neighbors, peers, teachers, events, and so forth. Thus, both kinds of twins normally develop under similar environmental conditions, but identical twins share more genetic kinship. Hence, if sets of identical twins exhibit more personality resemblance than sets of fraternal twins, this greater similarity is probably attributable to heredity rather than to environment. The results of twin studies can be used to estimate the heritability of personality traits and other characteristics. **A *heritability ratio* is an estimate of the proportion of trait variability in a population that is determined by variations in genetic inheritance.** Heritability can be estimated for any trait. For example, the heritability of height is estimated to be around 80% (Johnson, 2010), whereas the heritability of intelligence appears to be about 50%–70% (Petrill, 2005).

© Kenneth Sponsler/Shutterstock.com

© John Schwegel/Shutterstock.com

The accumulating evidence from twin studies suggests that heredity exerts considerable influence over many personality traits. For instance, in research on the Big Five personality traits, identical twins have been found to be much more similar than fraternal twins on all five traits (Plomin et al., 2008). This is true even when the identical twins are reared in different homes. Overall, five decades of research on the determinants of the Big Five traits suggests that the heritability of each trait is in the vicinity of 50% (Krueger & Johnson, 2008).

2-5c THE EVOLUTIONARY APPROACH TO PERSONALITY

In the realm of biological approaches to personality, the most recent development has been the emergence of an evolutionary perspective. Evolutionary psychologists assert that the patterns of behavior seen in a species are products of evolution in the same way that anatomical characteristics are. *Evolutionary psychology* examines behavioral processes in terms of their adaptive value for members of a species over the course of many generations. The basic premise of evolutionary psychology is that natural selection favors behaviors that enhance organisms' reproductive success—that is, passing on genes to the next generation. Evolutionary theorists assert that personality has a biological basis because natural selection has favored certain personality traits over the course of human history (Figueredo et al., 2009). Thus, evolutionary analyses of personality focus on how various traits—and the ability to recognize these traits in others—may have contributed to reproductive fitness in ancestral human populations.

Evolutionary theorists assert that personality has a biological basis because natural selection has favored certain personality traits over the course of human history.

For example, David Buss (1991, 1997) has argued that the Big Five personality traits stand out as important dimensions of personality across a variety of cultures because those traits have had significant adaptive implications. Buss points out that humans have historically depended heavily on groups, which afford protection from predators or enemies, opportunities for sharing food, and a diverse array of other benefits. In the context of these group interactions, people have had to make difficult but crucial judgments about the characteristics of others, asking such questions as: Who will make a good member of my coalition? Who can I depend on when in need? Who will share their resources? Thus, Buss argues that the Big Five emerge as fundamental dimensions of personality because humans have evolved special sensitivity to variations in the ability to bond with others (extraversion), the willingness to cooperate and collaborate (agreeableness), the tendency to be reliable and ethical (conscientiousness), the capacity to be an innovative problem solver (openness to experience), and the ability to handle stress (low neuroticism). In a nutshell, Buss argues that the Big Five reflect the most salient features of people's adaptive behavior over the course of evolutionary history.

2-5d EVALUATING BIOLOGICAL PERSPECTIVES

Recent research in behavioral genetics has provided convincing evidence that hereditary factors help shape personality. Evolutionary theorists have developed thought-provoking hypotheses about how natural selection may have sculpted the basic architecture of personality. Nonetheless, we must take note of some weaknesses in biological approaches to personality. Some critics argue that efforts to carve personality into genetic and environmental components are ultimately artificial. The effects of heredity and environment are twisted together in complicated interactions that can't be separated cleanly (Funder, 2001; Rutter, 2007). Other critics note that *hindsight bias*—the common tendency to mold one's interpretation of the past to fit how events actually turned out—presents thorny problems for evolutionary theorists (Cornell, 1997). The assertion that the Big Five traits had major adaptive implications over the course of human history seems plausible, but what would have happened if other traits, such as dominance or shrewdness, had shown up in the Big Five? With the luxury of hindsight, evolutionary theorists surely could have constructed plausible explanations for how these traits promoted reproductive success in the distant past. Thus, some critics have argued that evolutionary explanations are post hoc, speculative accounts contaminated by hindsight bias.

2-6 Culture and Personality

Are there connections between culture and personality? In recent decades psychology has become more interested in cultural factors, sparking a renaissance in culture-personality research (Church, 2010). This research has sought to determine whether Western personality constructs are relevant to other cultures and whether cultural differences can be seen in the prevalence of specific personality traits. As with cross-cultural research in other areas of psychology, these studies have found evidence of both continuity and variability across cultures.

For the most part, continuity has been apparent in cross-cultural comparisons of the *trait structure* of personality. When English-language personality scales

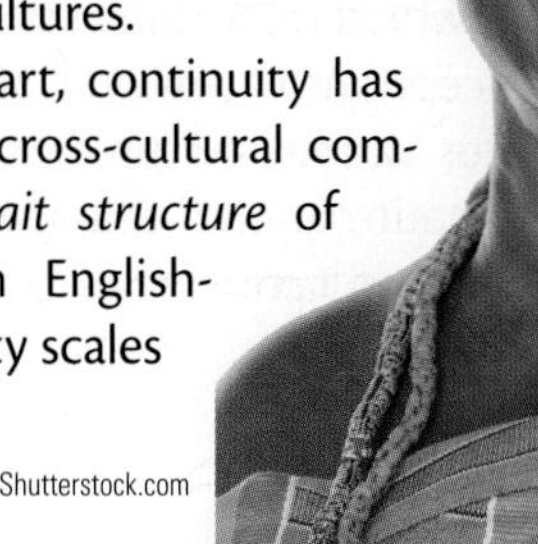

have been translated and administered in other cultures, the predicted dimensions of personality have emerged from the statistical analyses (Chiu, Kim, & Wan, 2008). For example, when scales that tap the Big Five personality traits have been administered and subjected to analysis in other cultures, the usual five traits have typically emerged (McCrae & Costa, 2008a). Thus, research tentatively suggests that the basic dimensions of personality trait structure may be universal.

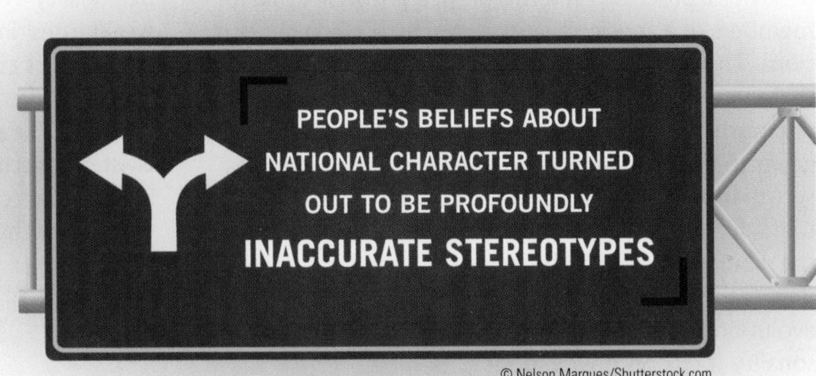

On the other hand, some cross-cultural variability is seen when researchers compare the average trait scores of samples from various cultural groups. For example, in a study comparing 51 cultures, McCrae et al. (2005) found that Brazilians scored relatively high in neuroticism, Australians in extraversion, Germans in openness to experience, Czechs in agreeableness, and Malaysians in conscientiousness, to give but a handful of examples. These findings should be viewed as very preliminary, as a variety of methodological problems make it difficult to ensure that samples from different cultures are comparable (Heine, Buchtel, & Norenzayan, 2008). Nonetheless, the findings suggest that genuine cultural differences may exist in some personality traits. That said, the observed cultural disparities in average trait scores were modest in size.

The availability of the data from the McCrae et al. (2005) study allowed Terracciano et al. (2005) to evaluate the concept of *national character*—the idea that various cultures have widely recognized prototype personalities. Terracciano and his colleagues asked subjects from many cultures to describe the *typical* member of *their* culture on rating forms guided by the five-factor model. Generally, subjects displayed substantial agreement on these ratings of what was typical for their culture. The averaged ratings, which served as the measures of each culture's national character, were then correlated with the actual mean trait scores for various cultures compiled in the McCrae et al. (2005) study. The results were definitive—the vast majority of the correlations were extremely low and often even negative. In other words, there was little or no relationship between perceptions of national character and actual trait scores for various cultures (see Figure 2.13). People's beliefs about national character, which often fuel cultural prejudices, turned out to be profoundly inaccurate stereotypes.

FIGURE 2.13 | An example of inaccurate perceptions of national character

Terracciano et al. (2006) found that perceptions of national character (the prototype or typical personality for a particular culture) are largely inaccurate. The data shown here for one culture—Canadians—illustrates this inaccuracy. Mean scores on the Big Five traits for a sample of real individuals from Canada are graphed in red. Averaged perceptions of national character for Canadians are graphed in blue. The discrepancy between perception and reality is obvious. Terracciano et al. found similar disparities between views of national character and actual trait scores for a majority of the cultues they studied. (Adapted from McCrae & Terracciano, 2005)

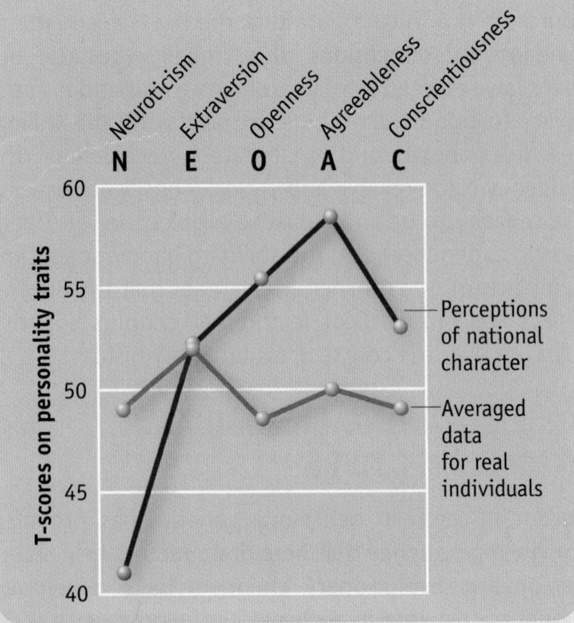

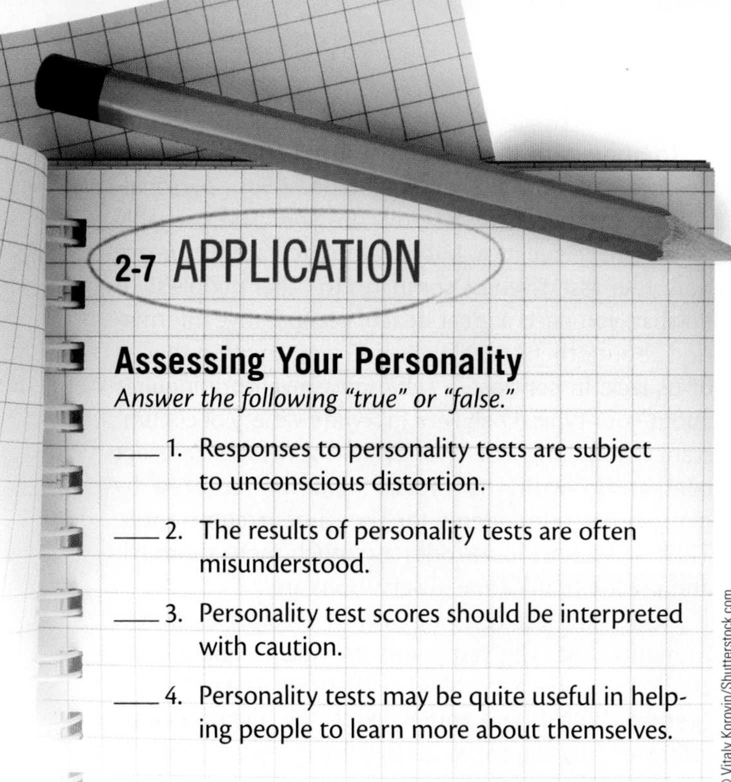

2-7 APPLICATION

Assessing Your Personality

Answer the following "true" or "false."

___ 1. Responses to personality tests are subject to unconscious distortion.

___ 2. The results of personality tests are often misunderstood.

___ 3. Personality test scores should be interpreted with caution.

___ 4. Personality tests may be quite useful in helping people to learn more about themselves.

© Vitaly Korovin/Shutterstock.com

If you answered "true" to all four questions, you earned a perfect score. Yes, personality tests are subject to distortion. Admittedly, test results are often misunderstood, and they should be interpreted cautiously. In spite of these problems, however, psychological tests can be very useful. The chief value of psychological tests lies in their ability to help people form a realistic picture of their personal qualities.

2-7a KEY CONCEPTS IN PSYCHOLOGICAL TESTING

A *psychological test* is a standardized measure of a sample of a person's behavior. Psychological tests are measurement instruments. They are used to measure abilities, aptitudes, and personality traits. Note that your responses to a psychological test represent a *sample* of your behavior. This fact should alert you to one of the key limitations of psychological tests: It's always possible that a particular behavior sample is not representative of your characteristic behavior. We all have our bad days. A stomachache, a fight with a friend, a problem with your car—all might affect your responses to a particular test on a particular day. Because of the limitations of the sampling process, test scores should always be interpreted *cautiously*.

Standardization and Norms

Psychological tests are *standardized* measures of behavior. ***Standardization* refers to the uniform procedures used to administer and score a test.** All subjects get the same instructions, the same questions, the same time limits, and so on, so that their scores can be compared meaningfully.

The standardization of a test's scoring system includes the development of test norms. ***Test norms* provide information about where a score on a psychological test ranks in relation to other scores on that test.** Why do we need test norms? Because in psychological testing, everything is relative. Psychological tests tell you how you score *relative to other people.* They tell you, for instance, that you are average in impulsiveness, or slightly above average in assertiveness, or far below average in anxiety. These interpretations are derived from the test norms.

Reliability and Validity

Any kind of measuring device, whether it's a tire gauge, a stopwatch, or a psychological test, should be reasonably consistent. That is, repeated measurements should yield reasonably similar results. To appreciate the importance of reliability, think about how you would react if a tire pressure gauge gave you several very different readings for the same tire. You would probably conclude that the gauge was broken and toss it into the garbage, because you know that consistency in measurement is essential to accuracy.

***Reliability* refers to the measurement consistency of a test.** A reliable test is one that yields similar results upon repetition of the test. Like most other types of measuring devices, psychological tests are not perfectly reliable. They usually do not yield the exact same score when repeated. A certain amount of inconsistency is unavoidable because human behavior is variable. Personality tests tend to have lower reliability than mental ability tests because daily fluctuations in mood influence how people respond to such tests.

Even if a test is quite reliable, we still need to be concerned about its validity. ***Validity* refers to the ability of a test to measure what it was designed to measure.** If we develop a new test of assertiveness, we have to provide some evidence that it really measures assertiveness. Validity can be demonstrated in a variety of ways. Most of them involve correlating scores on a test with other measures of the same trait, or with related traits.

2-7b SELF-REPORT INVENTORIES

The vast majority of personality tests are self-report inventories. *Self-report inventories* are personality scales that ask individuals to answer a series of questions about their characteristic behavior. When you respond to a self-report personality scale, you endorse statements as true or false as applied to you, you indicate how often you behave in a particular way, or you rate yourself with respect to certain qualities. For example, on the Minnesota Multiphasic Personality Inventory, people respond "true," "false," or "cannot say" to 567 statements such as the following:

I get a fair deal from most people.
I have the time of my life at parties.
I am glad that I am alive.
Several people are following me everywhere.

The logic underlying this approach is simple: Who knows you better than you do? Who has known you longer? Who has more access to your private feelings?

The entire range of personality traits can be measured with self-report inventories. Some scales measure just one trait dimension, such as the Narcissistic Personality Scale, a 40-item test that assesses the trait of narcissism. Others simultaneously assess a multitude of traits. The Sixteen Personality Factor Questionnaire (16PF), developed by Raymond Cattell and his colleagues, is a representative example of a multitrait inventory. The 16PF is a 187-item scale that measures sixteen basic dimensions of personality, called source traits, which are shown in Figure 2.14.

As we noted earlier, some theorists believe that only five trait dimensions are required to provide a full description of personality. The five-factor model led to the creation of the NEO Personality Inventory. Developed by Paul Costa and Robert McCrae (1992), the NEO Inventory is designed to measure the Big Five traits: neuroticism, extraversion, openness to experience, agreeableness, and conscientiousness. The NEO Inventory is widely used in research and clinical work, and updated revisions of the scale have been released (Costa & McCrae, 2008).

To appreciate the strengths of self-report inventories, consider how else you might assess your personality. For instance, how assertive are you? You probably have some vague idea, but can you accurately estimate how your assertiveness compares to other people's? To do that, you need a great deal of comparative information about others' usual behavior—information that all of us lack. In contrast, a self-report inventory inquires about your typical behavior in a wide variety of circumstances requiring assertiveness and generates an exact comparison with the typical behavior reported by many other respondents for the same circumstances. Thus, self-report inventories are much more thorough and precise than casual observations are.

However, these tests are only as accurate as the information that the test-takers provide. Deliberate deception can be a problem with these tests (Rees & Metcalfe, 2003), and some people are unconsciously influenced by the social desirability or acceptability of

FIGURE 2.14 The Sixteen Personality Factor Questionnaire (16PF)

Cattell's 16PF is designed to assess sixteen basic dimensions of personality. The pairs of traits listed across from each other in the figure define the sixteen factors measured by this self-report inventory. The profile shown is the average profile seen among a group of airline pilots who took the test.

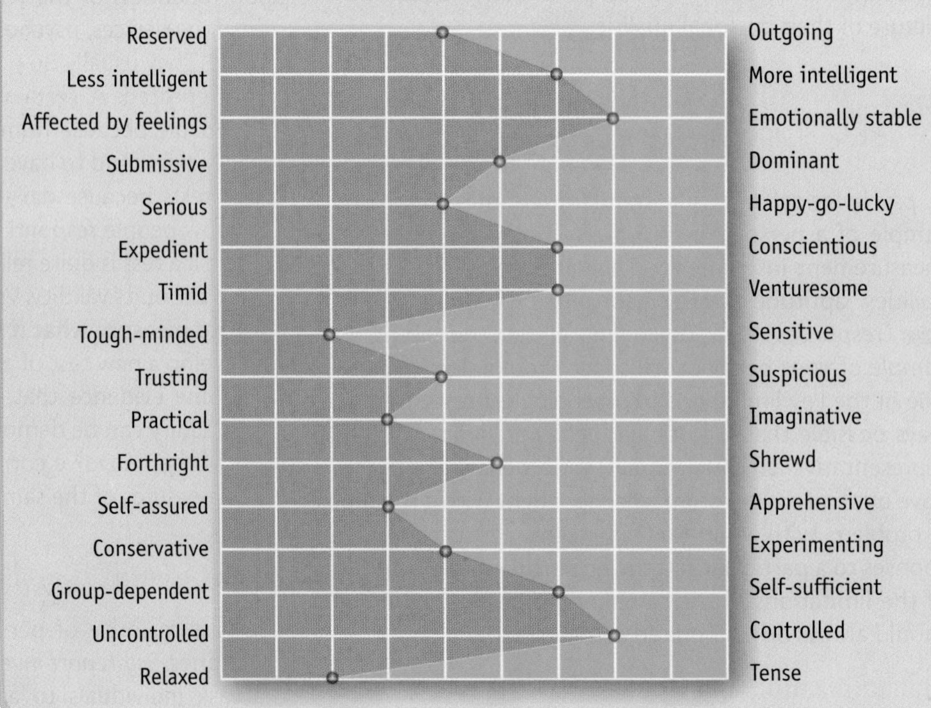

Source: Adapted from Cattell, R. B. (1973, July). Personality pinned down. *Psychology Today,* 40–46. Reprinted by permission of Psychology Today Magazine. Copyright © 1973 Sussex Publishers, Inc.

the statements (Kline, 1995). Without realizing it, they endorse only those statements that make them look good. This problem provides another reason why personality test results should always be regarded as suggestive.

2-7c PROJECTIVE TESTS

Projective tests, which all take a rather indirect approach to the assessment of personality, are used extensively in clinical work. *Projective tests* ask people to respond to vague, ambiguous stimuli in ways that may reveal the respondents' needs, feelings, and personality traits. The Rorschach test, for example, consists of a series of ten inkblots. Respondents are asked to describe what they see in the blots. In the Thematic Apperception Test (TAT), a series of pictures of simple scenes is presented to subjects who are asked to tell stories about what is happening in the scenes and what the characters are feeling. For instance, one TAT card shows a young boy contemplating a violin resting on a table in front of him.

> Ambiguous materials can serve as a blank screen onto which people project their concerns, conflicts, and desires.

The assumption underlying projective testing is that ambiguous materials can serve as a blank screen onto which people project their characteristic concerns, conflicts, and desires. Thus, a competitive person who is shown the TAT card of the boy at the table with the violin might concoct a story about how the boy is contemplating an upcoming musical competition at which he hopes to excel. The same card shown to a person high in impulsiveness might elicit a story about how the boy is planning to sneak out the door to go dirt-bike riding with friends.

Unfortunately, the scientific evidence on projective measures is unimpressive. In a thorough review of the relevant research, Lillienfeld, Wood, and Garb (2000) conclude that projective tests tend to be plagued by inconsistent scoring, low reliability, inadequate test norms, cultural bias, and poor validity estimates. They also assert that, contrary to advocates' claims, projective tests are susceptible to some types of intentional deception (primarily, faking poor mental health). Based on their analysis, Lillienfeld and his colleagues argue that projective tests should be referred to as projective "techniques" or "instruments" rather than tests because "most of these techniques as used in daily clinical practice do not fulfill the traditional criteria for psychological tests" (p. 29). Although the questionable scientific status of these techniques is a very real problem, their continued popularity suggests that they yield subjective information that many clinicians find useful (Viglione & Rivera, 2003).

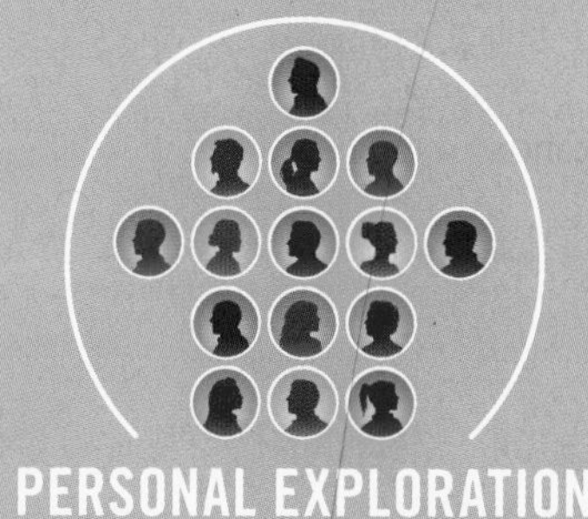

PERSONAL EXPLORATION TOOLS

Curious about yourself? To learn more about how topics in this chapter relate to you, go online to CourseMate at www.cengagebrain.com where you can:

- Complete a **Self-Reflection** exercise that will help you think about your personal experiences in relation to topics in the chapter.
- Take a **Self-Assessment** scale that will show you how you score on a research instrument that measures personality traits or attitudes.
- Explore **Recommended Readings** that will provide brief overviews of useful self-help books.

STUDY TOOLS ▶ 2

Ready to study? In your book you can:

- **Test Yourself** with a multiple-choice quiz (below)
- Rip out the **Chapter Review card** (in the back of the book) to refresh yourself on the chapter's Key Ideas and Key Terms

Or you can go online to CourseMate at www.cengagebrain.com where you can:

- Take additional Practice Quizzes to prepare for your exam
- Review Key Terms with flash cards and a crossword puzzle
- View videos that expand on selected concepts

TEST YOURSELF

1. Which of the following is *not* included in McCrae and Costa's five-factor model of personality?
   a. Neuroticism
   b. Extraversion
   c. Conscientiousness
   d. Authoritarianism

2. Harvey Hedonist has devoted his life to the search for physical pleasure and immediate need gratification. Freud would say that Harvey is dominated by
   a. his ego.
   b. his superego.
   c. his id.
   d. Bacchus.

3. You're feeling guilty after your third bowl of ice cream. You tell yourself it's all right because yesterday you skipped lunch. Which defense mechanism is at work?
   a. Conceptualization
   b. Displacement
   c. Rationalization
   d. Identification

4. According to Adler, __________ is a universal drive to adapt, improve oneself, and master life's challenges.
   a. compensation
   b. striving for superiority
   c. avoiding inferiority
   d. social interest

5. The strengthening of a response tendency by virtue of the fact that the response leads to the removal of an unpleasant stimulus is
   a. positive reinforcement.
   b. negative reinforcement.
   c. primary reinforcement.
   d. punishment.

6. According to Rogers, disparity between one's self-concept and actual experience is referred to as
   a. a delusional system.
   b. dissonance.
   c. conflict.
   d. incongruence.

7. According to Maslow, which of the following is *not* characteristic of self-actualizing persons?
   a. Accurate perception of reality
   b. Being spontaneous and natural
   c. Being uncomfortable with solitude
   d. Sensitivity to others' needs

8. If identical twins exhibit more personality resemblance than fraternal twins, it's probably due mostly to
   a. similar treatment from parents.
   b. their greater genetic overlap.
   c. their strong identification with each other.
   d. others' expectations that they should be similar.

9. When English-language personality scales have been translated and administered in other cultures:
   a. the trait structure of personality has turned out to be dramatically different.
   b. the usual Big Five traits have emerged from the statistical analyses.
   c. the personality scales have proven useless.
   d. a seven-trait solution has usually emerged from the statistical analyses.

10. In psychological testing, consistency of results over repeated measurements refers to
   a. standardization.
   b. validity.
   c. statistical significance.
   d. reliability.

Answers: 1. d, pages 21–22; 2. c, page 23; 3. c, page 25; 4. b, page 28; 5. b, page 32; 6. d, page 35; 7. c, page 37; 8. b, page 38; 9. b, pages 39–40; 10. d, page 41

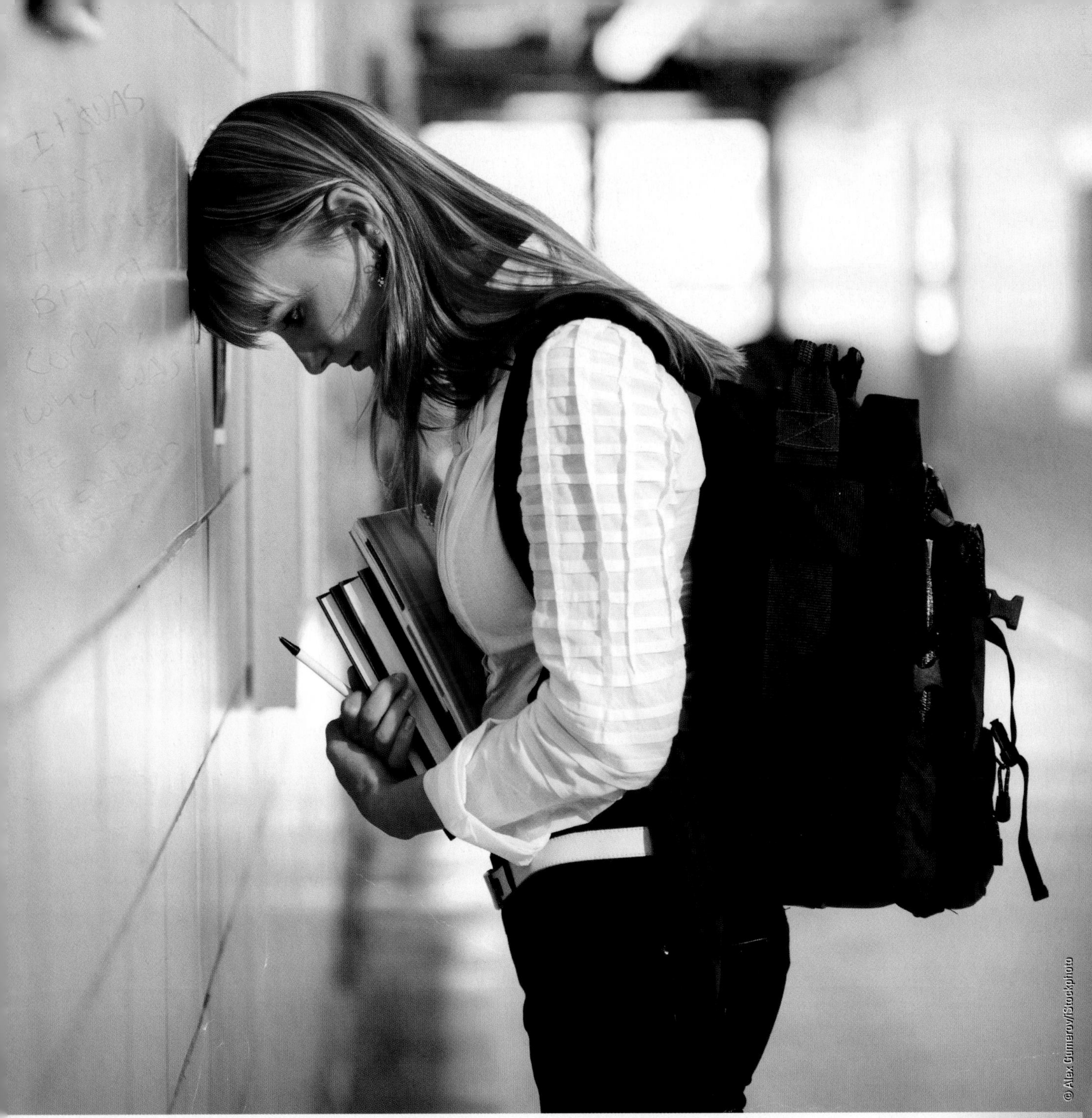

LEARNING OBJECTIVES

3-1 Understand how one's appraisals, environment, and culture can influence the experience of stress.

3-2 Describe the four major sources of stress in modern life.

3-3 Discuss some of the typical emotional, physiological, and behavioral responses to stress.

3-4 Describe some of the potential effects of stress, both positive and negative.

3-5 Identify three moderating variables that influence one's stress tolerance.

3-6 Explain how one might reduce stress through behavior modification.

After you have read the chapter, you can Test Yourself and learn about other Study Tools on page 66.

CHAPTER 3

STRESS and ITS EFFECTS

© Photo_Concepts/iStockphoto

You're in your car headed home from school. Traffic is barely moving. You groan as the radio reports that the traffic jam is only going to get worse. Another motorist nearly hits you trying to cut into your lane. Your pulse quickens as you shout insults at the driver. Your stomach knots up as you think about the term paper that you have to work on tonight. Suddenly you remember that you promised the person you're dating that the two of you would get together tonight. There's no way. Your heartbeat quickens as you contemplate the fight that looms on the horizon.

As this example shows, stress comes in all sorts of packages: large and small, pretty and ugly, simple and complex. In this chapter, we analyze the nature of stress, outline the major sources of stress, and discuss how people respond to stressful events at several levels.

3-1 The Nature of Stress

Over the years, the term *stress* has been used in different ways. Some theorists have viewed stress as a *stimulus* event that presents difficult demands (getting fired, for instance), while others have viewed stress as the *response* of physiological arousal elicited by a troublesome event. The emerging consensus among contemporary researchers is that stress is neither a stimulus nor a response but rather a special stimulus-response transaction in which one feels threatened or experiences loss or harm (Carver, 2007). Hence, we will define ***stress* as any circumstances that threaten or are perceived to threaten one's well-being and thereby tax one's coping abilities.** The threat may be to one's immediate physical safety, long-range security, self-esteem, reputation, or peace of mind.

3-1a STRESS IS AN EVERYDAY EVENT

Stress is a part of everyday life. Indeed, a 2010 poll by the American Psychological Association showed that, for many of us, stress levels are high and on the rise. The majority of Americans surveyed reported moderate or high levels of stress with financial worries topping the list of concerns. It seems that being "stressed out" has become a hallmark of modern life.

Undeniably, stress is associated with overwhelming, traumatic crises such as floods, earthquakes, and nuclear accidents. Studies conducted in the aftermath of such disasters typically find elevated rates of psychological problems and physical illness in the affected communities (Raphael & Dobson, 2000). However,

BABY BLUES

© CORBIS/Age fotostock

these infrequent events represent the tip of the iceberg. Many everyday events, such as waiting in line, having car trouble, misplacing your keys, and staring at bills you can't pay, are also stressful. Of course, major and minor stressors are not entirely independent. A major stressful event, such as going through a divorce, can trigger a cascade of minor stressors, such as looking for an attorney, taking on new household responsibilities, and so forth.

You might guess that minor stressors would produce minor effects, but that isn't necessarily true. Routine hassles may have significant negative effects on a person's mental and physical health. In fact, researchers found that scores on a scale measuring daily hassles were more strongly related to participants' mental health than were the scores on a scale measuring major life events (Kanner et al., 1981). Why would minor hassles be more strongly related to mental health than major stressful events? Many theorists believe that stressful events can have a *cumulative* or *additive* impact (Seta, Seta, & McElroy, 2002). In other words, stress can add up. Routine stresses at home, at school, and at work might be fairly benign individually, but collectively they can create great strain.

3-1b STRESS LIES IN THE EYE OF THE BEHOLDER

Not everyone becomes overwhelmed by stress from daily hassles. The experience of feeling threatened depends on what events you notice and how you choose to interpret or *appraise* them. Events that are stressful for one person may be routine for another. For example, many people find flying in an airplane quite stressful, but frequent fliers may not even raise an eyebrow. Some people enjoy the excitement of going out on a date with someone new; others find the uncertainty terrifying.

In discussing appraisals of stress, Richard Lazarus and Susan Folkman (1984) distinguish between primary and secondary appraisal (see Figure 3.1). ***Primary appraisal*** **is an initial evaluation of whether an event is (1) irrelevant to you, (2) relevant but not threatening, or (3) stressful.** When you view an event as stressful, you are likely to make a ***secondary appraisal,*** **which is an evaluation of your coping resources and options for dealing with the stress.** For instance, your primary appraisal would determine whether you saw an upcoming job interview as stressful. Your secondary appraisal would determine how stressful the interview appeared, in light of your ability to deal with the event.

It should come as no surprise that people's appraisals of stressful events alter the impact of the events themselves. Negative interpretations of events are often associated with increased distress surrounding these events. In fact, when studying a sample of children after the 9/11 terrorist attacks, Lengua and her colleagues (2006) found that children's appraisals of the event predicted their stress symptoms as much as their coping styles or pre-attack stress loads did.

People are rarely objective in their appraisals of potentially stressful events. A classic study of hospitalized patients awaiting surgery showed only a slight correlation between the objective seriousness of a person's upcoming surgery and the amount of fear the person

FIGURE 3.1 Primary and secondary appraisal of stress

Primary appraisal is an initial evaluation of whether an event is (1) irrelevant to you, (2) relevant but not threatening, or (3) stressful. When you view an event as stressful, you are likely to make a *secondary appraisal,* which is an evaluation of your coping resources and options for dealing with the stress. (Based on Lazarus & Folkman, 1984)

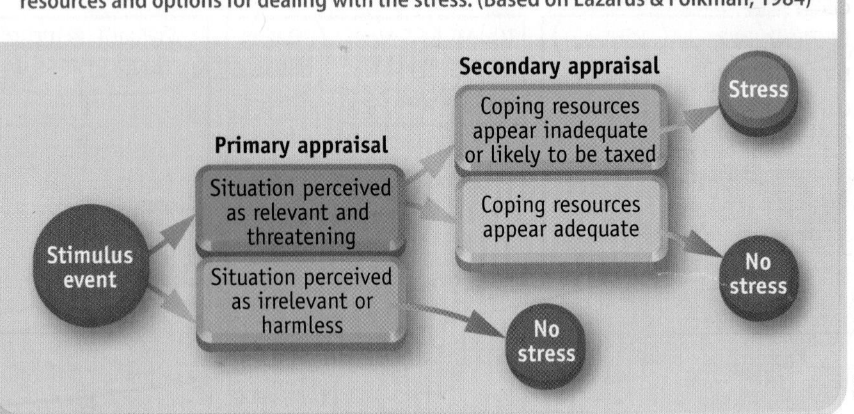

© Cengage Learning

experienced (Janis, 1958). Clearly, some people are more prone to feel threatened by life's difficulties than others are. Thus, stress often lies in the eye (actually, the mind) of the beholder.

3-1c STRESS MAY BE EMBEDDED IN THE ENVIRONMENT

Although the perception of stress is a highly personal matter, many kinds of stress come from the environmental circumstances that individuals share with others. ***Ambient stress*** **consists of chronic environmental conditions that, although not urgent, are negatively valued and place adaptive demands on people.** Features of the environment such as excessive noise, traffic, and crowding can threaten well-being and leave their mark on mental and physical health. For example, investigators have found an association between chronic exposure to high levels of noise and elevated blood pressure among children attending school near Los Angeles International Airport (Cohen et al., 1980). Studies also suggest an association between high residential density and increased physiological arousal, psychological distress, and social withdrawal (Evans, 2001). Even temporary experiences of crowding, such as being packed into a passenger train for a crowded commute, can be stressful (Evans & Wener, 2007).

3-1d STRESS IS INFLUENCED BY CULTURE

Although certain types of events (such as the loss of a loved one) are probably viewed as stressful in virtually all human societies, cultures vary greatly in the predominant forms of stress people experience. Even within the modern, Western world, disparities can be found in the constellation of stressors experienced by specific cultural groups (Mino, Profit, & Pierce, 2000). In recent years, social scientists have explored the effects of ethnicity-related sources of stress and have documented that racial discrimination negatively affects mental health and well-being (Brondolo et al., 2011). In one study of 520 African Americans, 96% of the respondents reported experiencing some type of racial discrimination in the most recent year—and 95% of these subjects indicated that they found this discrimination to be stressful (Klonoff & Landrine, 1999). For immigrants, ***acculturation,*** **or changing to adapt to a new culture,** is a major source of stress related to reduced well-being (Ying & Han, 2006). Scientists are still exploring the degree to which ethnicity-related stress may have detrimental effects on individuals' mental and physical health.

© drbimages/iStockphoto

3-2 Major Sources of Stress

An enormous variety of events can be stressful for one person or another. To achieve a better understanding of stress, theorists have tried to analyze the nature of stressful events by differentiating between *acute stressors* and *chronic stressors* (Dougall & Baum, 2001). ***Acute stressors*** **are threatening events that have a relatively short duration and a clear endpoint.** Examples would include having a difficult encounter with a belligerent drunk, waiting for the results of a medical test, or having your home threatened by severe flooding. ***Chronic stressors*** **are threatening events that have a relatively long duration and no readily apparent time limit.** Examples would include persistent financial strains produced by huge credit card debts, ongoing pressures from a hostile boss at work, or the demands of caring for a sick family member over a period of years. Of course, this distinction is far from perfect. It is hard to decide where to draw the line between a short-lived versus lengthy stressor, and even brief stressors can have long-lasting effects. Whether acute or chronic, stressors come from all aspects of our lives. Let's take a look at four major sources of stress: frustration, conflict, change, and pressure.

3-2a FRUSTRATION

"It is very frustrating to watch the deterioration of my parents' relationship. They argue constantly and refuse to seek any professional help. I feel very helpless and sometimes even very angry, not at them, but at the whole situation."

This scenario illustrates frustration. As psychologists use the term, ***frustration*** **occurs in any situation in which the pursuit of some goal is thwarted.** In essence, you experience frustration when you want something and you can't have it. Everyone has to deal with frustration virtually every day. Traffic jams, long daily commutes, and annoying drivers, for instance, are routine sources of frustration that can increase stress levels. Some frustrations, such as *failures* and *losses*, can be sources of significant stress. Fortunately, most frustrations are brief and insignificant. You may be quite upset when you go to the auto shop to pick up your car and find that it hasn't been fixed as promised. However, a few days later you'll probably have your precious car back, and all will be forgotten.

3-2b INTERNAL CONFLICT

"Should I or shouldn't I? My fiancé surprised me with an engagement ring. I knew if I refused the ring he would be terribly hurt and our relationship would suffer. However, I don't really know whether or not I want to marry him. On the other hand, I don't want to lose him either."

Like frustration, internal conflict is an unavoidable feature of everyday life. That perplexing question "Should I or shouldn't I?" comes up countless times on a daily basis. ***Internal conflict*** **occurs when two or more incompatible motivations or behavioral impulses compete for expression.** As we discussed in Chapter 2, Sigmund Freud proposed over a century ago that internal conflicts generate considerable psychological distress. This conflict sometimes reflects a choice between two attractive goals (Do I want to order the pizza or the spaghetti?), sometimes a choice between two unattractive goals (Should I stay in an unhappy relationship or be alone?), and sometimes a choice about whether to pursue a single goal that has both attractive and unattractive aspects (Should I take that high paying job in a city I hate?). Higher levels of internal conflict are associated with higher levels of psychological distress (King & Emmons, 1990).

3-2c CHANGE

"After graduation, I landed my dream job and moved to another state. For the first time, I am living alone, far away from my friends and family. Everything is different. I am learning how to do my new job, trying to make friends, and navigating my way around my new city. I love my job, but it's difficult dealing with all these changes at once."

Life changes represent a key source of stress. ***Life changes*** **are any noticeable alterations in one's living circumstances that require readjustment.** According to Holmes and Rahe (1967), changes in personal relationships, changes at work, changes in finances, and so forth can be stressful even when the changes are welcomed. Based on this analysis, Holmes and Rahe developed the Social Readjustment Rating Scale (SRRS) to measure life change as a form of stress. The scale assigns numerical values to forty-three major life events that are supposed to reflect the magnitude of the readjustment required by each change (see Figure 3.2). Respondents are asked to indicate how often they experienced any of these forty-three events during a certain time period (typically, the past year). The person then adds up the numbers associated with each event checked. The total is an index of the amount of change-related stress the person has recently experienced.

Overall, people with higher scores on the SRRS tend to be more vulnerable to many kinds of physical illness—and many types of psychological problems as well (Rahe et al., 2000). However, experts have criticized this research, citing problems with the methods used and raising questions about the meaning of the findings (Monroe & McQuaid, 1994). The scale is dominated by negative events; perhaps it's the frustration caused by the negative events, rather than the change per se, that creates most of the stress assessed by the scale. In fact, when taking into account the desirability and undesirability of respondents' life changes, findings clearly indicated that life change is *not* the crucial dimension measured by the SRRS and that negative life events cause much of the stress tapped by the scale (Turner & Wheaton, 1995). Should we discard the notion that change is stressful? Not entirely. It is quite plausible that change constitutes a major source of stress in people's lives. However, we have little reason to believe that change is *inherently* or *inevitably* stressful.

3-2d PRESSURE

"My father questioned me at dinner about some things I did not want to talk about. I know he doesn't want to hear my answers, at least not the truth. I've spent my life trying to live up to his expectations. Recently, this has made our relationship very strained and painful."

At one time or another, most of us have probably remarked that we were "under pressure." What does that expression mean? ***Pressure*** **involves expectations or demands that one behave in a certain way.** Pressure can be

FIGURE 3.2 | Social Readjustment Rating Scale (SRRS)

Devised by Holmes and Rahe (1967), this scale is designed to measure the change-related stress in one's life. The numbers on the right are supposed to reflect the average amount of stress (readjustment) produced by each event. Respondents check off the events that have happened to them recently and add up the associated numbers to arrive at their stress scores.

SOCIAL READJUSTMENT RATING SCALE

Life event	Mean value	Life event	Mean value
Death of a spouse	100	Son or daughter leaving home	29
Divorce	73	Trouble with in-laws	29
Marital separation	65	Outstanding personal achievement	28
Jail term	63	Spouse begins or stops work	26
Death of close family member	63	Begin or end school	26
Personal injury or illness	53	Change in living conditions	25
Marriage	50	Revision of personal habits	24
Fired at work	47	Trouble with boss	23
Marital reconciliation	45	Change in work hours or conditions	20
Retirement	45	Change in residence	20
Change in health of family member	44	Change in school	20
Pregnancy	40	Change in recreation	19
Sex difficulties	39	Change in church activities	19
Gain of a new family member	39	Change in social activities	18
Business readjustment	39	Loan for lesser purchase (car, TV, etc.)	17
Change in financial state	38	Change in sleeping habits	16
Death of a close friend	37	Change in number of family get-togethers	15
Change to a different line of work	36	Change in eating habits	15
Change in number of arguments with spouse	35	Vacation	13
Mortgage or loan for major purpose	31	Christmas	12
Foreclosure of mortgage or loan	30	Minor violations of the law	11
Change in responsiblities at work	29		

Source: Adapted from Holmes, T. H., & Rahe, R. (1967). The Social Readjustment Rating Scale. *Journal of Psychosomatic Research, 11,* 213–218. Copyright © 1967 by Elsevier Science Publishing Co. Reprinted by permission.

divided into two subtypes: the pressure to *perform* and the pressure to *conform.* You are under pressure to perform when you are expected to execute tasks and responsibilities quickly, efficiently, and successfully. For example, salespeople are usually under pressure to move lots of merchandise. Students are under pressure to get good grades. Pressures to conform to others' expectations are also common. Suburban homeowners are expected to keep their lawns well manicured. Teenagers are expected to adhere to their parents' values and rules.

Studies have found a strong relationship between pressure and a variety of psychological symptoms and problems (Weiten, 1998). In fact, pressure has turned out to be more strongly related to measures of mental health than the SRRS and other established measures of stress. Academic pressures, common for students worldwide, are related to increased anxiety and depression and affect student motivation and concentration

(Andrews & Hejdenberg, 2007). Research suggests that stress resulting from academic pressure may actually impede academic performance and lead to problematic behaviors such as drinking (Kieffer, Cronin, & Gawet, 2006). Interestingly, studies of high school and college students find that pressure is often self-imposed (Misra & Castillo, 2004). By setting realistic expectations for ourselves, we might have more control over our stress than we realize.

3-3 Responding to Stress

The human response to stress is complex and multidimensional. Stress affects people on several levels. Consider again the chapter's opening scenario, in which you're driving home in heavy traffic, thinking about overdue papers and relationship conflicts. Let's look at some of the reactions we mentioned. When you groan in reaction to the traffic report, you're experiencing an *emotional response* to stress—in this case, annoyance and anger. When your pulse quickens and your stomach knots up, you're exhibiting *physiological responses* to stress. When you shout insults at another driver, your verbal aggression is a *behavioral response* to the stress at hand. Thus, we can analyze people's reactions to stress at three levels: (1) their emotional responses, (2) their physiological responses, and (3) their behavioral responses. Figure 3.3 depicts these three levels of response.

3-3a EMOTIONAL RESPONSES

Psychologists debate how to define emotion, and many conflicting theories purport to explain emotion. However, everyone has a good idea of what it means to be anxious, elated, gloomy, jealous, disgusted, excited, guilty, or nervous. So rather than pursue the technical debates about emotion, we'll rely on your familiarity with the concept and simply note that ***emotions* are powerful, largely uncontrollable feelings, accompanied by physiological changes.** More often than not, stress tends to elicit unpleasant emotions. For example, in studying one of the most severe disasters of modern times, the Indian Ocean tsunami of 2004, researchers found that almost 84% of survivors showed signs of severe emotional distress, including depression and anxiety (Souza et al., 2007).

Negative Emotions

There are no simple one-to-one connections between certain *types* of stressful events and particular emotions, but researchers have begun to uncover some strong links between specific *cognitive reactions* to stress and specific emotions. For example, self-blame tends to lead to guilt, helplessness to sadness, and so forth. Although stressful events can evoke many negative emotions, some are certainly more likely than others. According to Richard Lazarus (1993), common negative emotional responses to stress include the following:

FIGURE 3.3 The multidimensional response to stress

A potentially stressful event, such as a major exam, will elicit a subjective cognitive appraisal of how threatening the event is. If the event is viewed with alarm, the stress may trigger emotional, physiological, and behavioral reactions. The human response to stress is multidimensional.

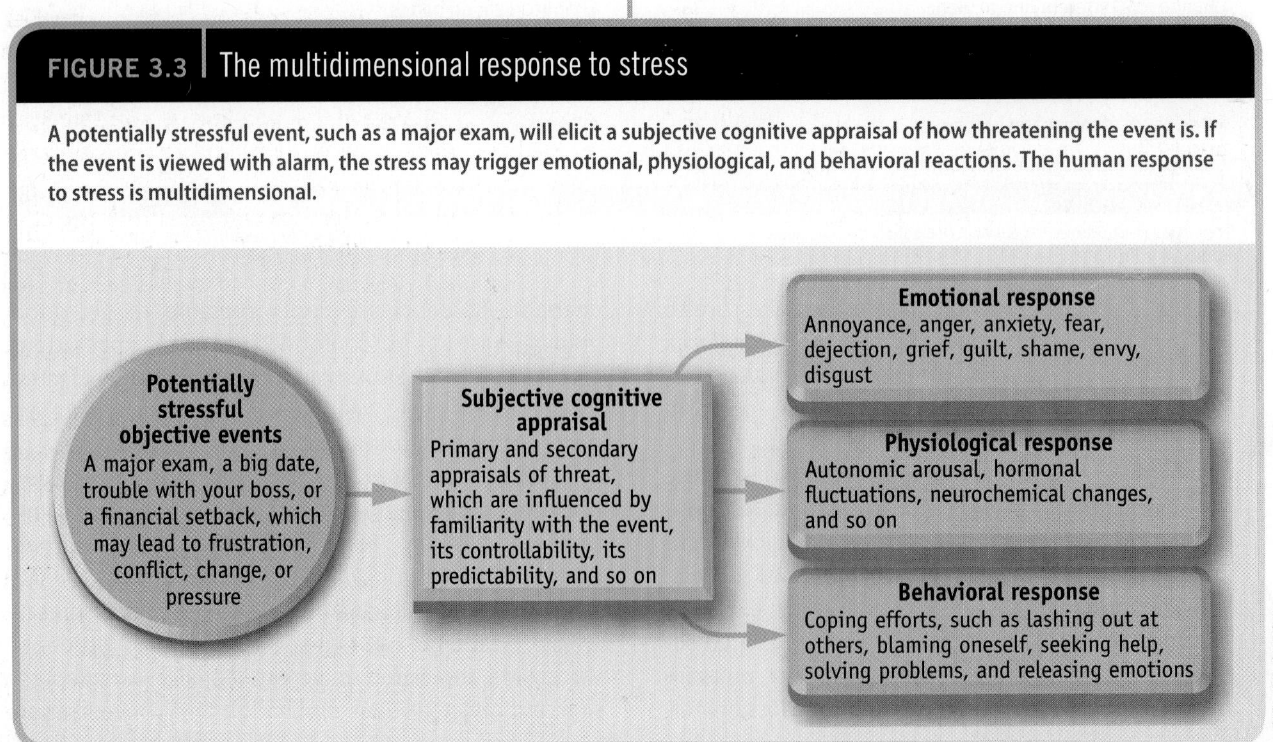

Potentially stressful objective events
A major exam, a big date, trouble with your boss, or a financial setback, which may lead to frustration, conflict, change, or pressure
Subjective cognitive appraisal
Primary and secondary appraisals of threat, which are influenced by familiarity with the event, its controllability, its predictability, and so on
Emotional response
Annoyance, anger, anxiety, fear, dejection, grief, guilt, shame, envy, disgust
Physiological response
Autonomic arousal, hormonal fluctuations, neurochemical changes, and so on
Behavioral response
Coping efforts, such as lashing out at others, blaming oneself, seeking help, solving problems, and releasing emotions

- *Annoyance, anger, and rage.* Stress often produces feelings of anger ranging in intensity from mild annoyance to uncontrollable rage. Frustration is particularly likely to generate anger.
- *Apprehension, anxiety, and fear.* Stress probably evokes anxiety and fear more frequently than any other emotions. Anxiety can be elicited by the threat of impending frustration, internal conflicts, the uncertainty associated with change, or the pressure to perform.
- *Dejection, sadness, and grief.* Sometimes stress—especially frustration—simply brings one down. Routine setbacks, such as traffic tickets and poor grades, often produce feelings of dejection. More profound setbacks, such as deaths and divorces, typically leave one grief-stricken.

By setting realistic expectations for ourselves, we might have more control over our stress than we realize.

©FotografiaBasica/iStockphoto

Of course, the above list is not exhaustive. In his insightful analyses of stress-emotion relations, Lazarus (1993) mentions other negative emotions that often figure prominently in reactions to stress, including guilt, shame, envy, jealousy, and disgust.

Positive Emotions

Although investigators have tended to focus heavily on the connection between stress and negative emotions, research by Susan Folkman (2008) has shown that positive emotions also occur during periods of stress. This finding may seem counterintuitive, but researchers have found that people experience a diverse array of pleasant emotions even while enduring the most dire of circumstances. Consider, for example, the results of a five-year study of coping patterns in 253 caregiving partners of men with AIDS (Folkman et al., 1997). Surprisingly, over the course of the study the caregivers reported experiencing positive emotions about as often as they experienced negative ones—except during the time immediately surrounding the death of their partners.

Other studies have replicated these findings. For instance, Fredrickson and colleagues (2003) examined participants' emotional functioning early in 2001 and then again in the weeks following the 9/11 terrorist attacks in the United States. Like most U.S. citizens, these participants reported many negative emotions in the aftermath of 9/11, including anger, sadness, and fear. However, within this "dense cloud of anguish," positive emotions also emerged. For example, people felt gratitude for the safety of their loved ones, many took stock and counted their blessings, and quite a few reported renewed love for their friends and family. Fredrickson et al. (2003) also found that the frequency of pleasant emotions correlated positively with a measure of subjects' resilience, whereas unpleasant emotions correlated negatively with resilience. Similar results were found for survivors of the 2001 El Salvador earthquake (Vazquez et al., 2005).

Thus, contrary to common sense, positive emotions do *not* vanish during times of severe stress. Moreover, these positive emotions appear to play a key role in helping people bounce back from the negative emotions associated with stress (Zautra & Reich, 2011). In fact, the benefits of positive emotions are so strong that Fredrickson (2006) argues that people should "cultivate positive emotions in themselves and in those around them as means to achieving psychological growth and improved psychological and physical well-being over time" (p. 85).

Effects of Emotional Arousal

Emotional responses are a natural and normal part of life. Even unpleasant emotions serve important purposes. Like physical pain, painful emotions can serve as warnings that one needs to take action. However, strong emotional arousal can also hamper efforts to cope with stress. For example, research has found that high emotional arousal can sometimes interfere with attention and memory retrieval and can impair judgment and decision making (Janis, 1993).

However, such interference isn't *necessarily* the case. The *inverted-U hypothesis* predicts that task performance should improve with increased emotional arousal—up to a point, after which further increases in arousal become disruptive and performance deteriorates (Mandler, 1993). This idea is referred to as the inverted-U hypothesis because plotting performance as a function of arousal results in graphs that approximate an upside-down U (see Figure 3.4 on the next page). In these graphs, the level of arousal at which performance peaks is characterized as the *optimal level of arousal* for a task. This optimal level of arousal appears to depend in part on the complexity of the task at hand. The conventional wisdom is that *as tasks become more complex, the optimal level of arousal (for peak performance) tends to decrease.* As you can see, a fairly high level of arousal should be optimal on simple tasks (such as

FIGURE 3.4 | Arousal and performance

Graphs of the relationship between emotional arousal and task performance tend to resemble an inverted U, as increased arousal is associated with improved performance up to a point, after which higher arousal leads to poorer performance. The optimal level of arousal for a task depends on the complexity of the task. On complex tasks, a relatively low level of arousal tends to be optimal. On simple tasks, however, performance may peak at a much higher arousal level.

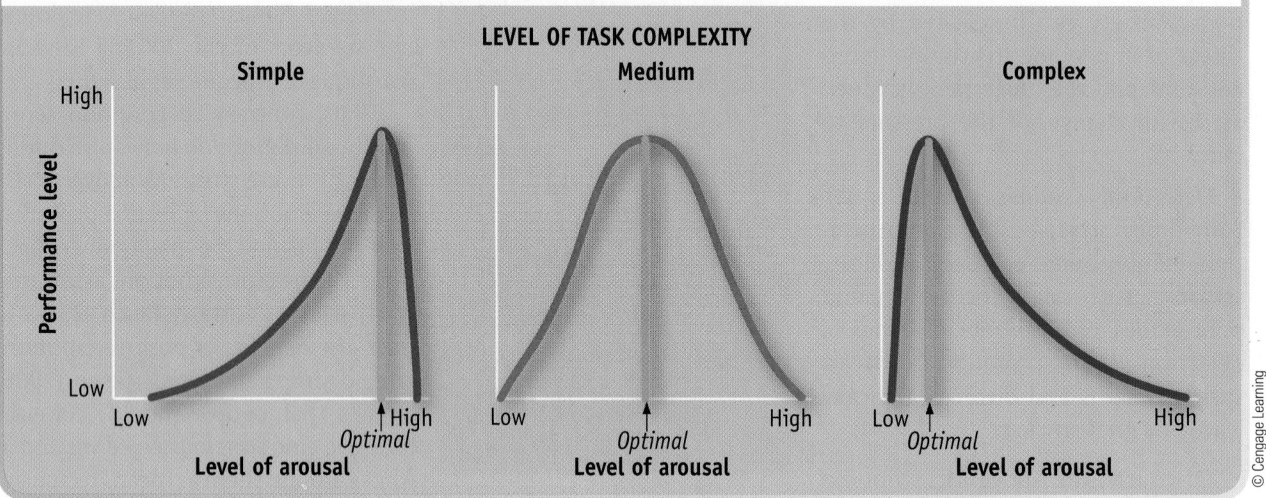

driving 8 hours to help a friend in a crisis). However, performance should peak at a lower level of arousal on complex tasks (such as taking a difficult exam).

3-3b PHYSIOLOGICAL RESPONSES

As we have seen, stress frequently elicits strong emotional responses. These emotions bring about important physiological changes. Even in cases of moderate stress, you may notice that your heart has started beating faster, you have begun to breathe harder, and you are perspiring more than usual. How does all this (and much more) happen? Let's see.

The "Fight-or-Flight" Response

Even though he did not refer to it as stress, Walter Cannon (1929) was a pioneer in stress research with his work on the fight-or-flight response. **The *fight-or-flight response* is a physiological reaction to threat that mobilizes an organism for attacking (fight) or fleeing (flight) an enemy.** For instance, if you see a threatening figure, typically your heart rate increases, blood pressure rises, respiration increases, digestion slows—all things that prepare you to act and that are adaptive from an evolutionary viewpoint. These responses occur in the body's autonomic nervous system. **The *autonomic nervous system (ANS)* is made up of the nerves that connect to the heart, blood vessels, smooth muscles, and glands.** As its name hints, the autonomic nervous system is somewhat *autonomous*. That is, it controls involuntary, visceral functions that people don't normally think about, such as heart rate, digestion, and perspiration.

The autonomic nervous system can be broken into two divisions (see Figure 3.5). The fight-or-flight response is mediated by the *sympathetic division* of the autonomic nervous system, which mobilizes bodily resources for emergencies. The *parasympathetic division* of the ANS generally conserves bodily resources. For instance, it slows heart rate and promotes digestion to help the body save and store energy.

The fight-or-flight response is seen in many species. In humans, this automatic reaction is widely viewed as a leftover from our evolutionary past. This response was probably quite adaptive for ancestral humans who routinely had to deal with threats to their physical safety. But in our modern world, where most stressors cannot be handled simply through fight or flight, this response appears less adaptive. Work pressures, relationship problems, and financial difficulties require far more complex responses. Moreover, these chronic stressors often continue for lengthy periods of time, so that the fight-or-flight response leaves one in a state of enduring physiological arousal. Hans Selye, a Canadian scientist who conducted extensive research on stress, first voiced concern about the effects of such prolonged arousal.

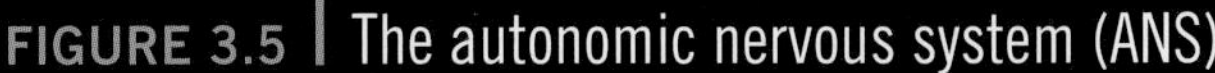

FIGURE 3.5 The autonomic nervous system (ANS)

The ANS is composed of the nerves that connect to the heart, blood vessels, smooth muscles, and glands. The ANS is subdivided into the *sympathetic division,* which mobilizes bodily resources in times of need, and the *parasympathetic division,* which conserves bodily resources. Some of the key functions controlled by each division of the ANS are summarized in this diagram.

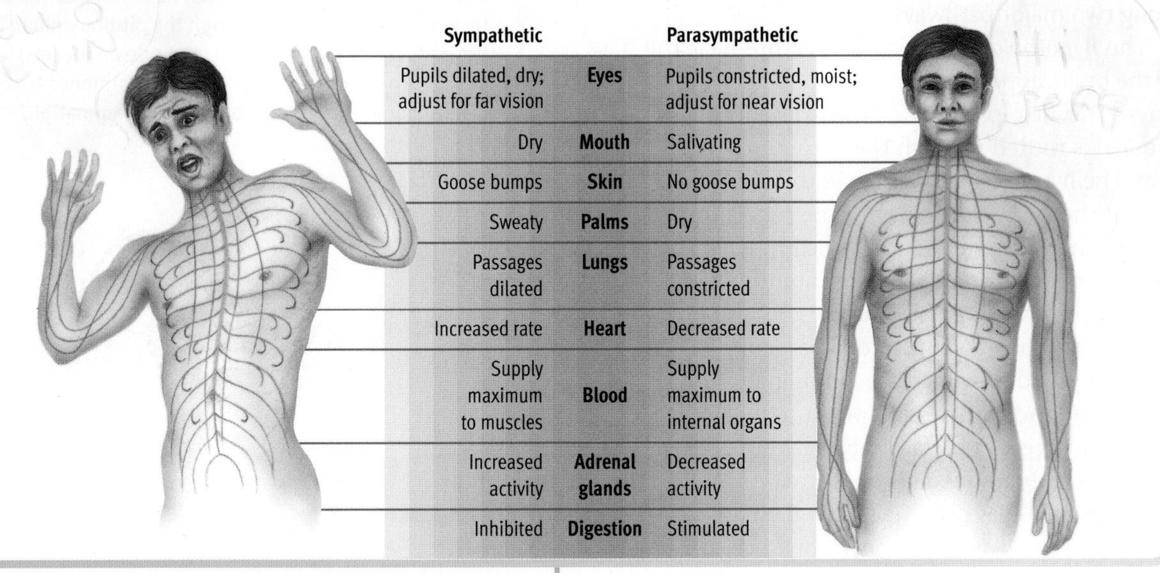

Sympathetic
Parasympathetic
Pupils dilated, dry; adjust for far vision
Eyes
Pupils constricted, moist; adjust for near vision
Dry
Mouth
Salivating
Goose bumps
Skin
No goose bumps
Sweaty
Palms
Dry
Passages dilated
Lungs
Passages constricted
Increased rate
Heart
Decreased rate
Supply maximum to muscles
Blood
Supply maximum to internal organs
Increased activity
Adrenal glands
Decreased activity
Inhibited
Digestion
Stimulated

The General Adaptation Syndrome

The concept of stress was popularized in both scientific and lay circles by Hans Selye (1936). Beginning in the 1930s, Selye exposed laboratory animals to a diverse array of unpleasant stimuli (heat, cold, pain, mild shock, restraint, and so on). The patterns of physiological arousal he observed in the animals were largely the same, regardless of which unpleasant stimulus elicited them. Thus, Selye concluded that stress reactions are *nonspecific.* In other words, they do not vary according to the specific type of circumstances encountered. Initially, Selye wasn't sure what to call this nonspecific response to a variety of noxious agents. In the 1940s, he decided to call it *stress,* and his influential writings gradually helped make the word part of our everyday vocabulary (Cooper & Dewe, 2004).

To capture the general pattern all species exhibit when responding to stress, Selye (1956) formulated a seminal theory called the general adaptation syndrome. **The *general adaptation syndrome* is a model of the body's stress response, consisting of three stages: alarm, resistance, and exhaustion.** In the first stage of the general adaptation syndrome, an *alarm reaction* occurs when an organism recognizes the existence of a threat (whether a predator or a big deadline). Physiological arousal increases as the body musters its resources to combat the challenge. Selye's alarm reaction is essentially the fight-or-flight response originally described by Cannon. If stress continues, the organism may progress to the second phase of the general adaptation syndrome, called the *stage of resistance.* During this phase, physiological changes stabilize as coping efforts get under way. Typically, physiological arousal continues to be higher than normal, although it may level off somewhat as the organism becomes accustomed to the threat.

If the stress continues over a substantial period of time, the organism may enter the third stage, called the *stage of exhaustion.* According to Selye, the body's resources for fighting stress are limited. If the stress cannot be overcome, the body's resources may be depleted, and physiological arousal will decrease. Eventually, the individual may collapse from exhaustion. During this phase, the organism's resistance declines. This reduced resistance may lead to what Selye called "diseases of adaptation," such as ulcers, high blood pressure, or other stress-related illnesses. His model provided guidance for generations of researchers who worked out the details of how stress reverberates throughout the body. Let's look at some of those details.

STRESS

© Stephen Coburn/Shutterstock.com

Brain-Body Pathways

The *endocrine system* consists of glands that secrete chemicals called hormones into the bloodstream. The major endocrine glands include the pituitary, pineal, thyroid, and adrenal glands. When you experience stress, your brain sends signals to the endocrine system along two major pathways.

The *hypothalamus*, a small structure near the base of the brain, appears to initiate action along both pathways. The first pathway (shown on the right in Figure 3.6) is routed through the autonomic nervous system. The hypothalamus activates the sympathetic division of the ANS. A key part of this activation involves stimulating the central part of the *adrenal glands* (the adrenal medulla) to release large amounts of *catecholamines* into the bloodstream. These hormones radiate throughout your body to mobilize it for action. Heart rate and blood flow increase, pumping more blood to your brain and muscles. Respiration and oxygen consumption speed up, facilitating alertness. Digestive processes are inhibited to conserve your energy. The pupils of your eyes dilate, increasing visual sensitivity.

The second pathway (shown on the left in Figure 3.6) involves more direct communication between the brain and the endocrine system. The hypothalamus sends signals to the so-called master gland of the endocrine system, the *pituitary*. The pituitary secretes a hormone (ACTH) that stimulates the outer part of the adrenal glands (the adrenal cortex) to release another important set of hormones—*corticosteroids*. These hormones play an important role in the response to stress. They stimulate the release of chemicals that help increase your energy and help inhibit tissue inflammation in case of injury (Munck, 2000).

Both sets of stress hormones (catecholamines and corticosteroids) appear to contribute to suppression of the immune system. Your immune system provides you with resistance to infections. However, evidence indicates that stress can suppress certain aspects of the multifaceted immune response, reducing its overall effectiveness in repelling invasions by infectious agents (Dhabhar, 2011). It is becoming clear that physiological responses to stress extend into every corner of the body. Moreover, some of these responses may persist long after a stressful event has ended.

FIGURE 3.6 Brain-body pathways in stress

In times of stress, the brain sends signals along two pathways. The pathway through the autonomic nervous system (shown in blue on the right) controls the release of catecholamine hormones that help mobilize the body for action. The pathway through the pituitary gland and the endocrine system (shown in purple on the left) controls the release of corticosteroid hormones that increase energy and ward off tissue inflammation.

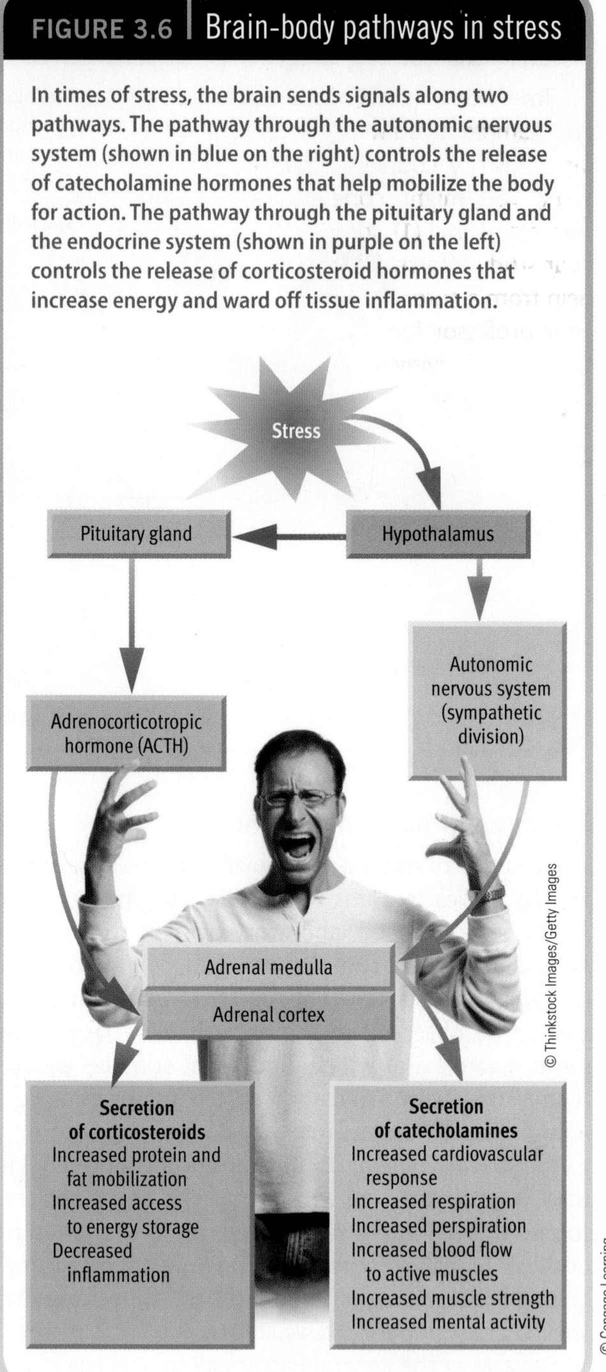

3-3c BEHAVIORAL RESPONSES

Although people respond to stress at several levels, their behavior is the crucial dimension of these reactions. Emotional and physiological responses to stress—which are often undesirable—tend to be largely automatic. However, dealing effectively with stress at the behavioral level may shut down these potentially harmful emotional and physiological reactions.

Most behavioral responses to stress involve coping. ***Coping* refers to active efforts to master, reduce, or tolerate the demands created by stress.** The popular use of the term often implies that coping is inherently healthy. When we say that someone "coped with her problems," we imply that she handled them effectively. In reality, coping responses may be either healthy or unhealthy. For example, if you were flunking a history course at midterm, you might cope with this stress by (1) increasing your study efforts, (2) seeking help from a tutor, (3) blaming your professor for your poor grade, or (4) giving up on the class. Clearly, the first two coping responses would more likely lead to a positive outcome than the second two would.

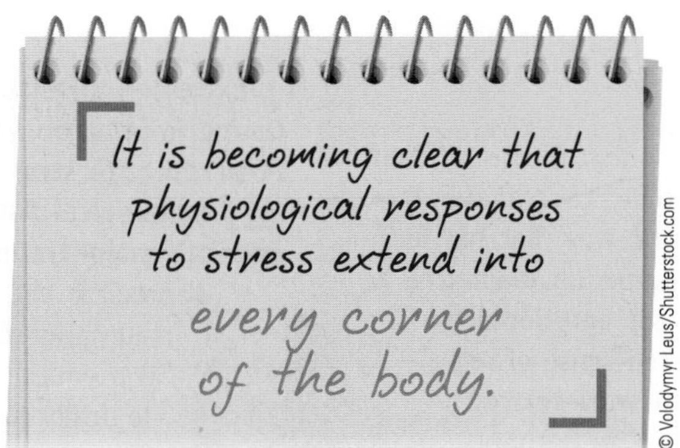
It is becoming clear that physiological responses to stress extend into every corner of the body.
© Volodymyr Leus/Shutterstock.com

Because of the complexity and importance of coping processes, we devote all of the next chapter to ways of coping. At this point, it is sufficient to note that coping strategies help determine whether stress has any positive or negative effects on an individual. In the next section, you'll see what some of those effects can be.

3-4 The Potential Effects of Stress

People struggle with stressors every day, most of which come and go without leaving an enduring imprint. However, when stress is severe or when demands pile up, stress may have long-lasting effects. These effects, often called "adaptational outcomes," are relatively long-lasting (though not necessarily permanent) consequences of exposure to stress. Although stress can have beneficial effects, research has focused mainly on possible negative outcomes, so you'll find our coverage slanted in that direction. Note that we will discuss *reducing* the effects of stress (through effective coping) in the next chapter.

3-4a IMPAIRED TASK PERFORMANCE

Frequently, stress takes its toll on the ability to perform effectively on a task at hand. For instance, Roy Baumeister (1984) theorized that pressure to perform often makes people self-conscious and that this elevated self-consciousness disrupts their attention, thereby interfering with performance. He theorizes that attention may be distorted in two ways. First, elevated self-consciousness may divert attention from the demands of the task, creating distractions. Second, on well-learned tasks that should be executed almost automatically, the self-conscious person may focus *too* much attention on the task. Thus, the person thinks too much about what he or she is doing and "chokes" under pressure.

Baumeister found support for his theory in a series of laboratory experiments in which he manipulated the pressure to perform on a simple perceptual-motor task. His theory also garnered some support in a pair of studies of the past performance of professional sports teams in championship contests (Baumeister, 1995). These findings were particularly impressive in that gifted professional athletes are probably less likely to choke under pressure than most other samples one might assemble. Laboratory research on "normal" subjects is more pertinent to the issue, and it also suggests that choking under pressure is fairly common (Butler & Baumeister, 1998).

3-4b DISRUPTION OF COGNITIVE FUNCTIONING

The effects of stress on task performance often result from disruptions in thinking or in cognitive functioning. In a study of stress and decision making, Keinan (1987) measured participants' attention under stressful and nonstressful conditions and found that stress disrupted two specific aspects of attention. First, it increased participants' tendency to jump to a conclusion too quickly without considering all their options. Second, it increased their tendency to do an unsystematic, poorly organized review of their available options. Brandes et al. (2002) examined trauma survivors within days of their experience and found that those with severe stress levels had poorer attention than those with few distress symptoms. Brandes speculates that poor attention might play an important role in actually shaping one's memory for a traumatic event.

The results of studies also suggest that stress can have detrimental effects on certain aspects of memory functioning. Stress can reduce the efficiency of the "working memory" system that allows people to juggle information on the spot (Beilock et al., 2004). In stressful situations, people may not be able to process, manipulate, or integrate new information as effectively as normal. Ironically, simply being in a situation where you need cognitive resources the most (studying for a final exam, traveling in a foreign country) can produce this resource-sapping stress effect. Researchers note, however, that stress has a complicated relationship with memory in that short-term, mild-to-moderate stressors can actually enhance memory, especially for emotional aspects of events (Sapolsky, 2004).

3-4c BURNOUT

Burnout is an overused buzzword that means different things to different people. Nonetheless, researchers have described burnout in a systematic way that has facilitated scientific study of the phenomenon. ***Burnout*** **is a syndrome involving physical and emotional exhaustion, cynicism, and a lowered sense of self-efficacy that is attributable to work-related stress.** Exhaustion, which is central to burnout, includes chronic fatigue, weakness, and low energy. Cynicism is manifested in highly negative attitudes toward oneself, one's work, and life in general. Reduced self-efficacy involves declining feelings of competence at work that give way to feelings of hopelessness and helplessness.

What causes burnout? According to Maslach and Leiter (2007), "Burnout is a cumulative stress reaction to ongoing occupational stressors" (p. 368). Factors in the workplace that appear to promote burnout include work overload, interpersonal conflicts at work, lack of control over responsibilities and outcomes, and inadequate recognition for one's work (see Figure 3.7). As you might expect, burnout is associated with increased absenteeism and reduced productivity, as well as increased vulnerability to a variety of health problems.

3-4d PSYCHOLOGICAL PROBLEMS AND DISORDERS

On the basis of clinical impressions, psychologists have long suspected that chronic stress might contribute to many types of psychological problems and mental disorders. Since the late 1960s, advances in the measurement of stress have allowed researchers to verify these suspicions in empirical studies. In the domain of common psychological problems, studies indicate that stress may contribute to insomnia and other sleep disturbances (Akerstedt, Kecklund, & Axelsson, 2007), sexual difficulties (Slowinski, 2007), alcohol abuse (Colder, 2001), and drug abuse (Goeders, 2004).

Beyond these problems, research reveals that stress often contributes to the onset of full-fledged psychological disorders, including depression (Rehm, Wagner, & Ivens-Tyndal, 2001), schizophrenia (McGlashan & Hoffman, 2000), anxiety disorders (Falsetti & Ballenger, 1998), and eating disorders (Cooper, 1995).

Extremely stressful, traumatic incidents can leave a lasting imprint on victims' psychological functioning. ***Posttraumatic stress disorder (PTSD)*** **involves enduring psychological disturbance attributed to the experience of a major traumatic event.** Researchers began to appreciate the frequency and severity of posttraumatic stress disorder after the Vietnam war ended in 1975 and a great many psychologically scarred veterans returned home. These veterans displayed a diverse array of psychological problems and symptoms that in many cases lingered much longer than expected. Studies suggest that nearly a half million Vietnam veterans were still suffering from PTSD over a decade after the end of the war (Schlenger et al., 1992). PTSD did not become an official psychological diagnosis until 1980, and since that time researchers have studied the disorder extensively to better understand the long-term impact of exposure to trauma (Yehuda, 2003).

© gualtiero boffi/Shutterstock.com

Although PTSD is widely associated with the experiences of veterans, it is frequently seen after a rape, a serious automobile accident, a robbery or assault, or the witnessing of someone's death. PTSD is also common in the wake of major disasters, such as floods, hurricanes, earthquakes, fires, and so forth (Koopman, Classen, & Spiegel, 1994).

Research suggests that approximately 9% of people have suffered from PTSD at some point in their lives, and it is twice as common in women as in men (Feeny, Stines, & Foa, 2007). PTSD is seen in children as well as adults, and children's symptoms often show up in their play or drawings (La Greca, 2007). In some instances, PTSD does not surface until many months or years after a person's exposure to severe stress. Although PTSD is not unusual in the wake of traumatic events, it is important to note that the vast majority of people who experience such events do *not* develop PTSD (Ozer & Weiss, 2004). Individuals who have especially intense emotional reactions during or immediately after the traumatic event are more vulnerable to developing to PTSD.

3-4e PHYSICAL ILLNESS

Stress can also have an impact on one's physical health. Although there is room for debate on some specific diseases, stress may influence the onset and course of

FIGURE 3.7 | The antecedents, components, and consequences of burnout

Christina Maslach and Michael Leiter have developed a systematic model of burnout that specifies its antecedents, components, and consequences. The burnout syndrome itself consists of the three components shown in the center of the diagram. (Based on Leiter & Maslach, 2001)

Antecedents of burnout: Work overload; Lack of social support; Lack of control, autonomy; Inadequate recognition, rewards

Components of burnout: Exhaustion; Cynicism; Lowered self-efficacy

Consequences of burnout: Increased physical illness; Increased absenteeism, turnover; Decreased commitment to job; Reduced productivity

heart disease, stroke, gastrointestinal disorders, tuberculosis, multiple sclerosis, arthritis, diabetes, leukemia, cancer, various types of infectious disease, and probably many other types of illnesses. Chapter 5 goes into greater detail, but suffice it to say that modern evidence continues to demonstrate that numerous diseases are influenced by stress.

Of course, stress is only one of many factors that may contribute to the development of physical illness. Some of the physical effects of stress might be exacerbated by the risky behaviors that people are more likely to exhibit when stressed. For example, stress appears to be related to increases in substance abuse, including problematic drinking (Veenstra et al., 2007), chronic marijuana use (Preston, 2006), and cigarette smoking (Wills, 1986). Obviously, these behaviors come with their own health hazards. Add stress to the mix and one becomes even more vulnerable to disease and illness.

3-4f POSITIVE EFFECTS

The effects of stress are not exclusively negative. Recent years have brought increased interest in positive aspects of the stress process, including favorable outcomes that follow in the wake of stress. To some extent, the new focus on the possible benefits of stress reflects a new emphasis on "positive psychology." Some influential theorists have argued that the field of psychology has historically devoted too much attention to pathology, weakness, and damage and how to heal suffering (Seligman, 2003a). Although this approach has yielded valuable insights and progress, it has also resulted in an unfortunate neglect of the forces that make life worth living. The positive psychology movement seeks to shift the field's focus away from negative experiences. Advocates of positive psychology argue for increased research on well-being, contentment, hope, courage, perseverance, nurturance, tolerance, and other human strengths and virtues (Peterson & Seligman, 2004). One of these strengths is resilience in the face of stress.

The beneficial effects of stress may prove more difficult to pinpoint than the harmful effects because they may be more subtle. However, there appear to be at

DILBERT

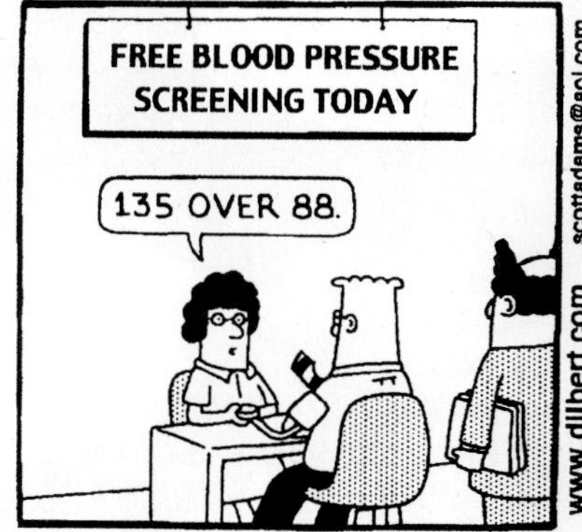

least three ways in which stress can have positive effects. First, stress can promote positive psychological change, or what Tedeschi and Calhoun (1996) call *posttraumatic growth.* Stressful events sometimes force people to develop new skills, reevaluate priorities, learn new insights, and acquire new strengths. In other words, the adaptation process initiated by stress may lead to personal changes for the better. For example, a breakup with a boyfriend or a girlfriend may lead individuals to change aspects of their behavior that they find unsatisfactory. Experiences of posttraumatic growth are now well documented, and it appears that this phenomenon is evident in people facing a variety of stressful circumstances, including bereavement, cancer, sexual assault, and combat (Tedeschi & Calhoun, 2004).

Second, stressful events help satisfy the need for stimulation and challenge. Studies suggest that most people prefer an intermediate level of stimulation and challenge in their lives (Sutherland, 2000). Although we think of stress in terms of stimulus overload, underload can be stressful as well. Thus, most people would experience a suffocating level of boredom if they lived a stress-free existence. In a sense, then, stress fulfills a basic need of the human organism.

Third, today's stress can inoculate and psychologically prepare individuals so that they are less affected by tomorrow's stress. Some studies suggest that exposure to stress can increase stress tolerance—as long as the stress isn't overwhelming (Meichenbaum, 1993). Thus, a woman who has previously endured business setbacks may be much better prepared than most people to deal with a bank foreclosure on her home.

3-5 Factors Influencing Stress Tolerance

Some people seem to be able to withstand the ravages of stress better than others. Why? Because a number of *moderator variables* can soften the impact of stress on physical and mental health. To shed light on differences in how well people tolerate stress, we'll look at a number of key moderator variables, including social support, hardiness, and optimism. As you'll see, these factors influence people's emotional, physical, and behavioral responses to stress. These complexities are diagrammed in Figure 3.8, which builds on Figure 3.3 to provide a more complete overview of the factors involved in individuals' reactions to stress.

3-5a SOCIAL SUPPORT

Friends may be good for your health! This startling conclusion emerges from studies on social support as a moderator of stress. ***Social support* refers to various types of aid and succor provided by members of one's social networks.** A vast body of literature has found evidence that social support is favorably related to physical health. For example, Jemmott and Magloire (1988) examined the effect of social support on immune response in a group of students going through the stress of final exams. They found that students who reported stronger social support had higher levels of an antibody that plays a key role in warding off respiratory infections.

Social support seems to be good medicine for the mind as well as the body, as most studies also find a positive association between social support and mental health (Sarason, Pierce, & Sarason, 1994). It appears that social support serves as a protective buffer during times of high stress, reducing the negative impact of stressful events—and that social support has its own positive effects on health, which may be apparent even when people aren't under great stress. With regard to more severe stress, social support appears to be a key factor in reducing the likelihood of PTSD among Vietnam veterans (King et al., 1998) and in increasing the likelihood of posttraumatic growth (Prati & Pietrantoni, 2009). Additionally, studies suggest that *providing* social support to others can also have both psychological benefits (less depression and perceived stress) and

FIGURE 3.8 | Overview of the stress process

This diagram builds on Figure 3.3 (the multidimensional response to stress) to provide a more complete overview of the factors involved in stress. This diagram adds the potential effects of stress (seen on the far right) by listing some of the positive and negative adaptational outcomes that may result from stress. It also completes the picture by showing moderating variables (seen at the top) that can influence the effects of stress (including some variables not covered in the chapter).

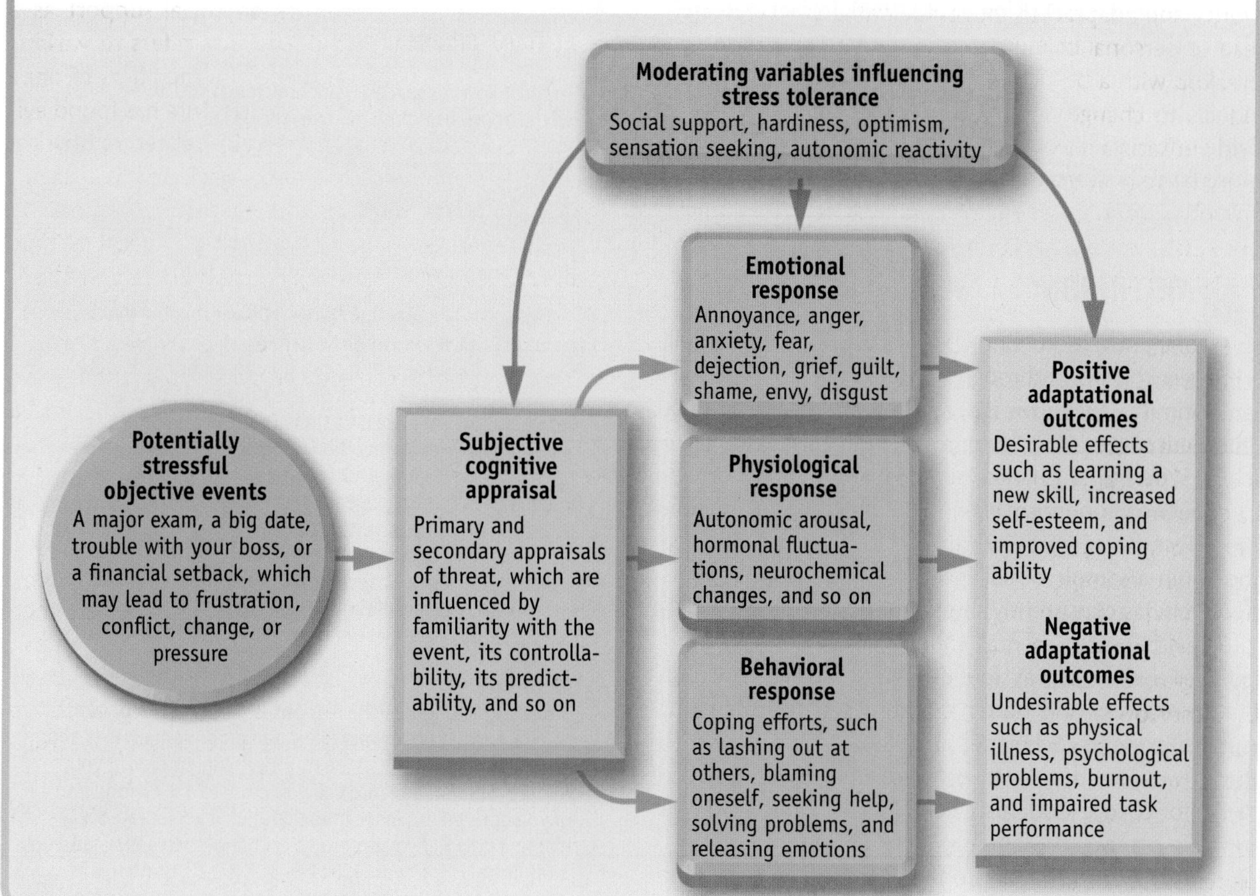

Moderating variables influencing stress tolerance
Social support, hardiness, optimism, sensation seeking, autonomic reactivity
Potentially stressful objective events
A major exam, a big date, trouble with your boss, or a financial setback, which may lead to frustration, conflict, change, or pressure
Subjective cognitive appraisal
Primary and secondary appraisals of threat, which are influenced by familiarity with the event, its controllability, its predictability, and so on
Emotional response
Annoyance, anger, anxiety, fear, dejection, grief, guilt, shame, envy, disgust
Physiological response
Autonomic arousal, hormonal fluctuations, neurochemical changes, and so on
Behavioral response
Coping efforts, such as lashing out at others, blaming oneself, seeking help, solving problems, and releasing emotions
Positive adaptational outcomes
Desirable effects such as learning a new skill, increased self-esteem, and improved coping ability
Negative adaptational outcomes
Undesirable effects such as physical illness, psychological problems, burnout, and impaired task performance

physical benefits (lower blood pressure) (Brown et al., 2003).

Although the benefits outweigh the costs, social support networks can have their drawbacks. It is only recently that researchers have begun to examine some of the negative aspects of social support (conflict, insincerity, dependency), a research area that bears watching in the near future.

3-5b HARDINESS

Another line of research indicates that an attribute called *hardiness* may moderate the impact of stressful events (Eschleman, Bowling, & Alarcon, 2010). Suzanne (Kobasa) Ouellette reasoned that if stress affects some people less than others, some people must be *hardier* than others. Hence, she set out to determine what factors might be the key to these differences in hardiness.

Kobasa (1979) used a modified version of the Holmes and Rahe (1967) stress scale (SRRS) to measure the amount of stress experienced by a group of executives. As in most other studies, she found a modest correlation between stress and the incidence of physical illness. However, she carried her investigation one step further than previous studies. She compared the high-stress executives who exhibited the expected high incidence of illness against the high-stress executives who stayed healthy. She administered a battery of psychological tests and found that the hardier executives "were more committed, felt more in control, and had bigger appetites for challenge" (Kobasa, 1984, p. 70).

These traits have also shown up in many other studies of hardiness.

Thus, ***hardiness* is a disposition marked by commitment, challenge, and control that is associated with strong stress resistance.** The benefits of hardiness showed up in a study of Vietnam veterans, which found that higher hardiness was related to a lower likelihood of developing PTSD (King et al., 1998). In fact, research shows that hardiness is a good predictor of success in high-stress occupations such as the military (Bartone et al., 2008). Fortunately, it appears that hardiness can be learned, and it often comes from strong social support and encouragement from friends and family (Maddi, 2007).

3-5c OPTIMISM

Everyone knows someone whose glass is always half full, who sees the world through rose-colored glasses, who is an optimist. ***Optimism* is a general tendency to expect good outcomes.** Pioneering research in this area by Michael Scheier and Charles Carver (1985) found a correlation between optimism as measured by the Life Orientation Test (see Figure 3.9) and relatively good physical health in a sample of college students. Since that time, research has consistently shown that optimism is associated with better mental and physical health. For instance, optimism was found to be associated with a faster recovery and better postsurgery adjustment for surgical patients (Scheier et al., 1989). Additionally, optimism was found to be inversely related to PTSD symptoms for college students who knew a victim of the 9/11 terrorist attacks (Ai, Santangelo, & Cascio, 2006).

Why does optimism promote a variety of desirable outcomes? Above all else, research suggests that optimists cope with stress in more adaptive ways than pessimists do (Carver & Scheier, 2002). Optimists are more likely to engage in action-oriented, problem-focused, carefully planned coping and are more willing than pessimists to seek social support. By comparison, pessimists are more likely to deal with stress by avoiding it, giving up, or engaging in denial. We will be discussing specific types of coping styles in the next chapter.

Although the benefits are clear, psychologists are currently debating whether optimism is *always* beneficial. What about times when a rosy outlook is inaccurate and unrealistic? Does it really help an employee to be optimistic about that promotion if there isn't much chance she'll get it? Additionally, being optimistic can lead to risky behaviors if one holds an "it-can't-happen-to-me" attitude. Research has demonstrated that women with an optimistic bias toward their risk for breast cancer are less likely to go in for screening (Clarke at al., 2000). And optimistic smokers are more likely to endorse myths such as "All lung cancer is cured" and "There is no risk of lung cancer if you only smoke for a few years" (Dillard, McCaul, & Klein, 2006). Gillham and Reivich (2007) argue that, when it comes to optimism, what is most adaptive is some sort of middle ground where one displays "optimism that is closely tied to the strength of wisdom" (p. 320).

FIGURE 3.9 Measuring Optimism

The personality trait of optimism can be measured by the Life Orientation Test (LOT) developed by Scheier and Carver (1985). Follow the instructions for this scale to obtain an estimate of your own optimism.

THE LIFE ORIENTATION TEST (LOT)

In the following spaces, mark how much you agree with each of the items, using the following scale:

4 = strongly agree
3 = agree
2 = neutral
1 = disagree
0 = strongly disagree

______ **1.** In uncertain times, I usually expect the best.
______ **2.** It's easy for me to relax.
______ **3.** If something can go wrong for me, it will.
______ **4.** I always look on the bright side of things.
______ **5.** I'm always optimistic about my future.
______ **6.** I enjoy my friends a lot.
______ **7.** It's important for me to keep busy.
______ **8.** I hardly ever expect things to go my way.
______ **9.** Things never work out the way I want them to.
______ **10.** I don't get upset too easily.
______ **11.** I'm a believer in the idea that "every cloud has a silver lining."
______ **12.** I rarely count on good things happening to me.

Scoring

Cross out and ignore the responses you entered for items 2, 6, 7, and 10, which are "filler" items. For items 3, 8, 9, and 12, you need to reverse the numbers you entered. If you entered a 4, change it to 0. If you entered a 3, change it to 1. If you entered a 2, leave it unchanged. If you entered a 1, change it to 3. If you entered a 0, change it to 4. Now add up the numbers for items 1, 3, 4, 5, 8, 9, 11, 12, using the new numbers for the reversed items. This sum is your score on the Life Orientation Test. For college students, approximate norms are as follows: High score (25–32), intermediate score (18–24), low score (0–17).

Source: Adapted from Scheier, M. F., & Carver, C. S. (1985). Optimism, coping, and health: Assessment and implications of generalized outcome expectancies. *Health Psychology, 4*, 219–247. Copyright 1985 by American Psychological Association. Adapted with permission.

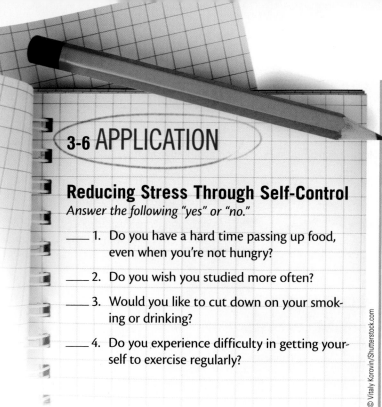

3-6 APPLICATION

Reducing Stress Through Self-Control

Answer the following "yes" or "no."

____ 1. Do you have a hard time passing up food, even when you're not hungry?

____ 2. Do you wish you studied more often?

____ 3. Would you like to cut down on your smoking or drinking?

____ 4. Do you experience difficulty in getting yourself to exercise regularly?

© Vitaly Korovin/Shutterstock.com

If you answered "yes" to any of these questions, you have struggled with the challenge of self-control. This Application discusses how you can use the techniques of behavior modification to improve your self-control. If you stop to think about it, self-control—or rather a lack of it—underlies many of the stressors that people struggle with in everyday life.

Behavior modification **is a systematic approach to changing behavior through the application of the principles of conditioning.** Advocates of behavior modification assume that behavior is a product of learning, conditioning, and environmental control. They further assume that *what is learned can be unlearned.* Thus, they set out to "recondition" people to produce more desirable patterns of behavior. Behavior modification techniques have proven particularly valuable in efforts to improve self-control. Our discussion will borrow liberally from an excellent book on self-modification by David Watson and Roland Tharp (2007). We will discuss five steps in the process of self-modification.

3-6a SPECIFYING YOUR TARGET BEHAVIOR

The first step in a self-modification program is to specify the target behavior(s) that you want to change. Behavior modification can only be applied to a clearly defined behavior, yet many people tend to describe their problems in terms of unobservable personality *traits* rather than overt behaviors. For example, asked what behavior he would like to change, a man might say, "I'm too irritable." That may be true, but it is of little help in designing a self-modification program. To identify target behaviors, you need to closely observe your behavior and list specific *examples* of responses that lead to the trait description. For instance, the man who regards himself as "too irritable" might identify two overly frequent responses, such as arguing with his wife and snapping at his children. These are specific behaviors for which he could design a self-modification program.

3-6b GATHERING BASELINE DATA

The second step in a self-modification program is to gather baseline data. You need to systematically observe your target behavior for a period of time (usually a week or two) before you work out the details of your program. After all, you can't tell whether your program is working effectively unless you have a baseline for comparison. In most cases, you would simply keep track of how often the target response occurs in a certain time interval. Thus, if studying is your target behavior, you will probably monitor hours of study. If you want to modify your eating, you will probably keep track of how many calories you consume. You should keep permanent written records, preferably in the form of a chart or graph (see Figure 3.10 on the next page).

Smoking is just one of the many maladaptive habits that can be reduced or eliminated through self-modification techniques.

© Christian J. Stewart/Photos.com

You should also monitor the antecedents of your target behavior. ***Antecedents*** **are events that typically precede the target response.** Often these events play a major role in evoking your target behavior. For example, if your target is overeating, you might discover that the bulk of your overeating occurs late in the evening while you watch TV. If you can pinpoint this kind of antecedent-response connection, you may be able to design your program to break the link.

Finally, you need to monitor the typical consequences of your target behavior. Try to identify the reinforcers that are maintaining an undesirable target behavior or the unfavorable outcomes that are suppressing a desirable target behavior. In trying to identify reinforcers, remember that avoidance behavior is usually maintained by negative reinforcement (see Chapter 2). That is, the payoff for avoidance is usually the removal of something aversive, such as anxiety or a threat to self-esteem.

FIGURE 3.10 Example of record keeping in a self-modification program for losing weight

Graphic records are ideal for tracking progress in behavior modification efforts.

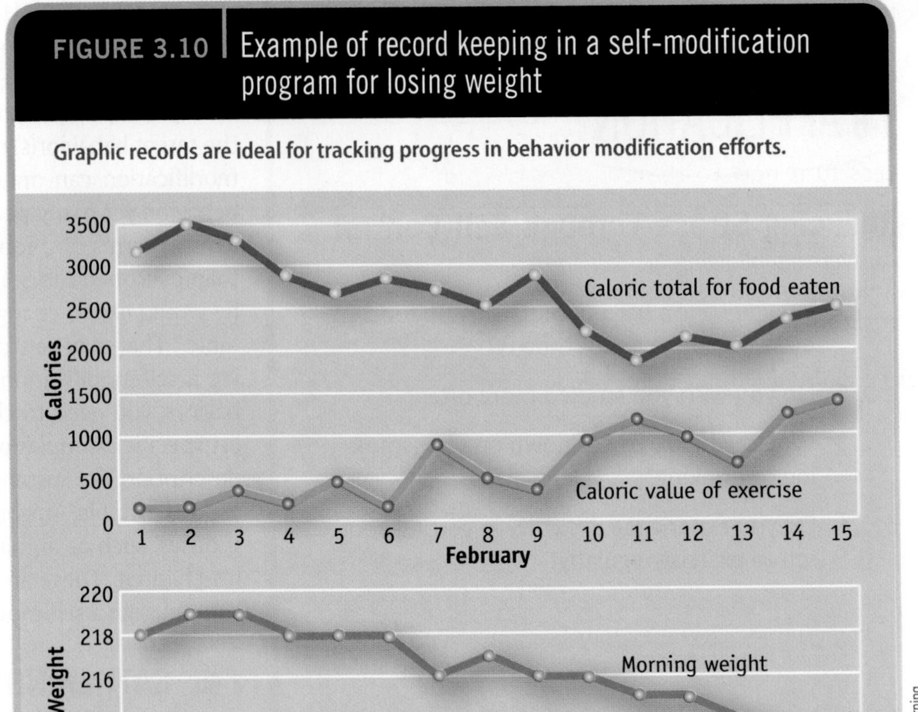

3-6c DESIGNING YOUR PROGRAM

Once you have selected a target behavior and gathered adequate baseline data, it is time to plan your intervention program. Generally speaking, your program will be designed either to increase or to decrease the frequency of a target behavior.

Increasing Response Strength

Efforts to increase the frequency of a target behavior depend largely on the use of positive reinforcement. In other words, you reward yourself for behaving properly. Although the basic strategy is quite simple, doing it skillfully involves a number of considerations.

Selecting a reinforcer. To use positive reinforcement, you need to find a reward that will be effective for you. Be sure to be realistic and choose a reinforcer that is really available to you. Making yourself earn rewards that you previously took for granted is often a useful strategy in a self-modification program. For example, if you normally watch your favorite television show on Thursday nights, you might make this viewing contingent on studying a certain number of hours during the week. Avoid doling out too much reinforcement, as doing so can undermine the motivational power of your reinforcers.

Arranging the contingencies. Once you have chosen your reinforcer, you have to set up reinforcement contingencies. These contingencies will describe the exact behavioral goals that must be met and the reinforcement that may then be awarded. For example, in a program to increase exercise, you might make spending $40 on clothes (the reinforcer) contingent on having jogged 15 miles during the week (the target behavior).

In some cases, you may want to reinforce a target response that you are not currently capable of making, such as jogging 8 miles a day. This situation calls for ***shaping,*** **which is accomplished by reinforcing closer and closer approximations of the desired response.** Thus, you might start jogging two miles a day and add a half-mile each week until you reach your goal. Try to set behavioral goals that are both challenging and realistic. You want your goals to be challenging so that they lead to improvement in your behavior. However, setting unrealistically high goals—a common mistake in self-modification—often leads to unnecessary discouragement.

Decreasing Response Strength

Let's turn now to the challenge of reducing the frequency of an undesirable response. You can go about this task in a number of ways.

Reinforcement. Reinforcers can be used in an indirect way to decrease the frequency of a response. This may sound paradoxical, since you have learned that reinforcement strengthens a response. The trick lies in how you define the target behavior. For example, in the case of overeating you might define your target behavior as eating *more* than 1600 calories a day (a response that you want to decrease) or, alternatively as eating *less* than 1600 calories a day (a response that you want to increase). If you choose the latter definition, you can reinforce yourself whenever you eat less than 1600 calories in a day, which ultimately decreases your overeating.

Control of antecedents. A worthwhile strategy for decreasing the occurrence of an undesirable response may be to identify its antecedents and avoid exposure to them. In the case of overeating, for instance, the easiest way to resist temptation is to avoid having to face it. Thus, you might stay away from favorite restaurants or avoid purchasing unhealthy snack food.

Punishment. The strategy of decreasing unwanted behavior by punishing yourself for that behavior is an obvious option that people tend to overuse. The biggest problem with punishment in a self-modification effort is the difficulty in following through and punishing oneself. If you're going to use punishment, keep two guidelines in mind. First, do not use punishment alone. Use it in conjunction with positive reinforcement. If you set up a program in which you can earn only negative consequences, you probably won't stick to it. Second, use a relatively mild punishment so that you will actually be able to administer it to yourself.

3-6d EXECUTING AND EVALUATING YOUR PROGRAM

Once you have carefully designed your program, the next step is to implement it. You need to continue to accurately record the frequency of your target behavior so you can evaluate your progress. The success of your program depends on your not "cheating," such as giving yourself a reward when you have not actually earned it.

You can reduce the likelihood of cheating by constructing a ***behavioral contract*****—a written agreement outlining a promise to adhere to the contingencies of a behavior modification program.** The formality of signing such a contract in front of friends or family seems to make many people take their program more seriously. You can further reduce the likelihood of cheating by having someone other than yourself dole out the reinforcers and punishments. Behavior modification programs often require some fine-tuning, so don't be surprised if you need to make a few adjustments.

3-6e ENDING YOUR PROGRAM

Ending you program involves setting terminal goals such as reaching a certain weight, studying with a certain regularity, or going without cigarettes for a certain length of time. Often, it is a good idea to phase out your program by planning a gradual reduction in the frequency or potency of your reinforcement for appropriate behavior. You should always be prepared to reinstitute the program if you find yourself slipping back to your old patterns of behavior. Ironically, it can be the very stress you are trying to reduce that drives you back into old, unhealthy habits.

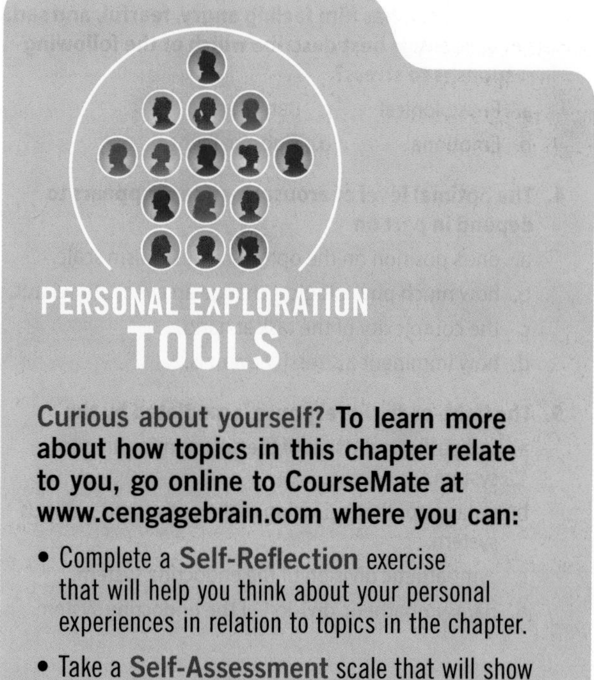

PERSONAL EXPLORATION
TOOLS
Curious about yourself? To learn more about how topics in this chapter relate to you, go online to CourseMate at www.cengagebrain.com where you can:
• Complete a Self-Reflection exercise that will help you think about your personal experiences in relation to topics in the chapter.
• Take a Self-Assessment scale that will show you how you score on a research instrument that measures personality traits or attitudes.
• Explore Recommended Readings that will provide brief overviews of useful self-help books.

© edge69/iStockphoto

STUDY TOOLS ▶ 3

Ready to study? In your book you can:

- **Test Yourself** with a multiple-choice quiz (below)
- Rip out the **Chapter Review card** (in the back of the book) to refresh yourself on the chapter's Key Ideas and Key Terms

Or you can go online to CourseMate at www.cengagebrain.com where you can:

- Take additional Practice Quizzes to prepare for your exam
- Review Key Terms with flash cards and a crossword puzzle
- View videos that expand on selected concepts

TEST YOURSELF

1. Secondary appraisal refers to

a. second thoughts about what to do in a stressful situation.
b. second thoughts about whether an event is genuinely threatening.
c. initial evaluation of an event's relevance, threat, and stressfulness.
d. evaluation of coping resources and options for dealing with a stressful event.

2. Juan just completed writing a 10-page report. When he tried to save it, his computer crashed and he lost all his work. What type of stress is Juan experiencing?

a. Frustration
b. Conflict
c. Life change
d. Pressure

3. Jamal has recently gone through a stressful divorce. The situation has him feeling angry, fearful, and sad. These feelings best describe which of the following responses to stress?

a. Physiological
b. Emotional
c. Behavioral
d. Fight-or-flight

4. The optimal level of arousal for a task appears to depend in part on

a. one's position on the optimism/pessimism scale.
b. how much physiological change an event stimulates.
c. the complexity of the task at hand.
d. how imminent a stressful event is.

5. The fight-or-flight response is mediated by the

a. sympathetic division of the autonomic nervous system.
b. parasympathetic division of the autonomic nervous system.
c. sympathetic division of the endocrine system.
d. parasympathetic division of the endocrine system.

6. Selye exposed lab animals to various stressors and found that

a. each type of stress caused a particular physiological response.
b. each type of animal responded to stress differently.
c. patterns of physiological arousal were similar, regardless of the type of stress.
d. patterns of physiological arousal were different, even when stressors were similar.

7. Salvador works as an art director at an advertising agency. His boss overloads him with responsibility but never gives him any credit for all his hard work. He feels worn down, disillusioned, and helpless at work. Salvador is probably experiencing

a. an alarm reaction.
b. burnout.
c. PSTD.
d. ambient stress.

8. Stress can __________ the functioning of the immune system.

a. stimulate
b. destroy
c. suppress
d. enhance

9. Joan has a personal disposition marked by commitment, challenge, and control. Further, she handles stress well. This disposition is referred to as

a. hardiness.
b. optimism.
c. courage.
d. conscientiousness.

10. Peggy is planning a behavior modification program to lose weight. Her first step in this process should be to

a. gather baseline data about her eating habits.
b. specify the target behavior she wants to change.
c. select a reinforcer that will be personally rewarding.
d. sign a behavioral contract in front of her friends.

Answers: 1. d, page 48; 2. a, pages 49–50; 3. b, pages 52–53; 4. c, pages 53–54; 5. a, page 54; 6. c, page 55; 7. b, page 58; 8. c, pages 58–59; 9. a, pages 61–62; 10. b, page 63

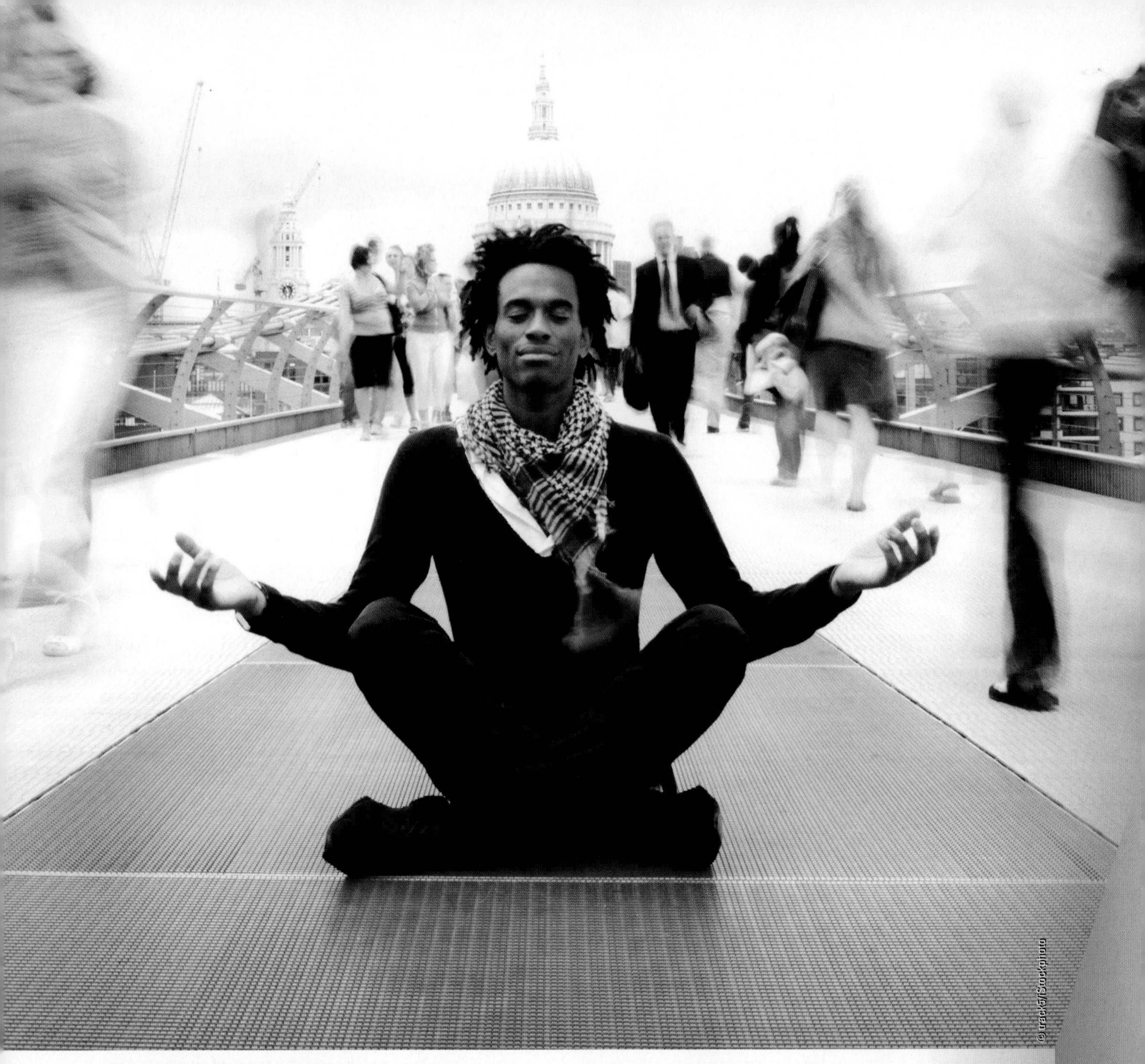

LEARNING OBJECTIVES

4-1 Identify some common responses to stress that tend to be maladaptive.

4-2 Describe the characteristics of constructive coping, and distinguish among the three categories of coping techniques.

4-3 Understand the merits of appraisal-focused constructive coping strategies, including rational thinking, humor, and positive reinterpretation.

4-4 Discuss the adaptive value of problem-focused coping strategies, including systematic problem solving, seeking help, and improving time management.

4-5 Summarize evidence on the merits of emotion-focused coping techniques, such as cultivating emotional intelligence, expressing emotions, managing hostility, forgiving others, and meditating.

4-6 Identify the causes of wasted time and procrastination, and describe strategies for managing time effectively.

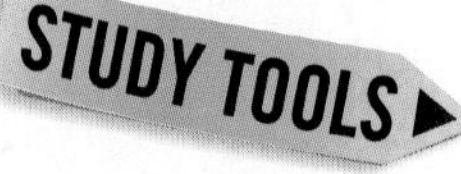

STUDY TOOLS ▶ After you have read the chapter, you can Test Yourself and learn about other Study Tools on page 89.

CHAPTER 4

COPING Processes

© Photo_Concepts/iStockphoto

"I have begun to believe that I have intellectually and emotionally outgrown my husband. However, I'm not really sure what this means or what I should do. Maybe this feeling is normal and I should ignore it and continue my present relationship. This seems to be the safest route. Maybe I should seek a lover while continuing with my husband. Then again, maybe I should start anew and hope for a beautiful ending with or without a better mate."

© Yuri Arcurs/Shutterstock.com

The woman quoted above is in the throes of a conflict. Although it is hard to tell just how much emotional turmoil she is experiencing, it's clear that she is under substantial stress. What should she do? Is it psychologically healthy to remain in an emotionally hollow marriage? Is seeking a secret relationship a reasonable way to cope with this unfortunate situation? Should she just strike out on her own and let the chips fall where they may? These questions have no simple answers. As you'll soon see, decisions about how to cope with life's difficulties can be incredibly complex. Further, a person's mental and physical health depends, in part, on his or her ability to cope effectively with stress. ***Coping* refers to efforts to master, reduce, or tolerate the demands created by stress.**

People cope with stress in many ways, selecting their coping tactics from a large and varied menu of options, some of which are healthier than others. In this chapter we start by reviewing some common coping patterns that tend to have relatively little value. After discussing these ill-advised coping techniques, we offer an overview of what it means to engage in more effective, "constructive" coping. The most adaptive approach is to use a variety of coping strategies. We hope our discussion provides you with some new ideas about how to deal with the stresses of modern life.

4-1 Common Coping Patterns of Limited Value

In everyday terms, when we say that someone "coped with her problems," we imply that she handled them effectively. In reality, however, all strategies are not created equal. Coping processes range from the helpful to the counterproductive. For example, coping with the disappointment of not getting a good grade by plotting to sabotage your professor's computer would clearly be a problematic way of coping. Hence, we distinguish between coping patterns that tend to be helpful and those that tend to be maladaptive. Bear in mind, however, that our generalizations about the adaptive value of various coping strategies are based on trends or tendencies identified by researchers. Unlike what many self-help books and talk show hosts would have you believe, no coping strategy can guarantee a successful outcome. Furthermore, the adaptive value of a coping technique depends on the exact nature of the situation. As you'll see in this section, even ill-advised coping tactics may be helpful in certain circumstances, but more often than not, they are counterproductive.

4-1a GIVING UP

When confronted with stress, people sometimes simply give up and withdraw from the battle. Martin Seligman (1992) has developed a model of this giving-up syndrome that sheds light on its causes. In Seligman's original research, animals were subjected to electric shocks they could not escape. The animals were then given an opportunity to learn a response that would allow them to escape the shock. However, many of the animals became so apathetic and listless that they didn't even try to learn the escape response. When researchers made similar manipulations with *human* subjects using inescapable noise (rather than shock) as the stressor, they observed parallel results (Hiroto & Seligman, 1975). This syndrome is referred to as learned helplessness. ***Learned helplessness* is passive behavior produced by exposure to unavoidable aversive events.** Unfortunately, this tendency to give up may be transferred to situations in which one is not really helpless. Hence, some people routinely respond to stress with fatalism and resignation, passively accepting setbacks that might be dealt with effectively. In adolescents, learned helplessness is associated with disengagement in academics and an increase in depression (Maatta, Nurmi, & Stattin, 2007).

Seligman originally viewed learned helplessness as a product of conditioning. However, research with human participants has led Seligman and his colleagues to revise their theory. Their current model proposes that people's *cognitive interpretation* of aversive events determines whether they develop learned helplessness. Specifically, helplessness seems to occur when individuals come to believe that events are beyond their control. This belief is particularly likely to emerge in people who exhibit what Seligman calls a *pessimistic explanatory style*. Among other things, such people tend to attribute setbacks to personal inadequacies instead of situational factors (Seligman, 1990).

Overall, giving up is not a highly regarded method of coping. Carver and his colleagues (1993) have studied this coping strategy, which they refer to as *behavioral disengagement*, and found that it is associated with increased rather than decreased distress. However, giving up could be adaptive in some instances. For example, if you are thrown into a job that you are not equipped to handle, it might be better to quit rather than face constant pressure and diminishing self-esteem. There is something to be said for recognizing one's limitations, avoiding unrealistic goals, and minimizing self-imposed stress.

4-1b ACTING AGGRESSIVELY

Tragic incidents of highway violence—so-called "road rage"—exemplify maladaptive ways in which drivers cope with the stress, anxiety, and hostility experienced while driving. Such incidents have unfortunately become common enough that some professionals are calling for road rage to become an official psychiatric diagnosis (Ayar, 2006). The U.S. cities with the most (and least) reports of road rage are listed in Figure 4.1. Road rage vividly illustrates that people often respond to stressful events by acting aggressively. ***Aggression* is**

FIGURE 4.1 | Road rage survey

In 2009, AutoVantage, a national auto club, conducted its annual road rage survey. The ten best and worst U.S. cities for road rage are shown here. When asked to identify the major causes of road rage, survey participants commonly listed bad driving, traffic problems, stress, and frustration.

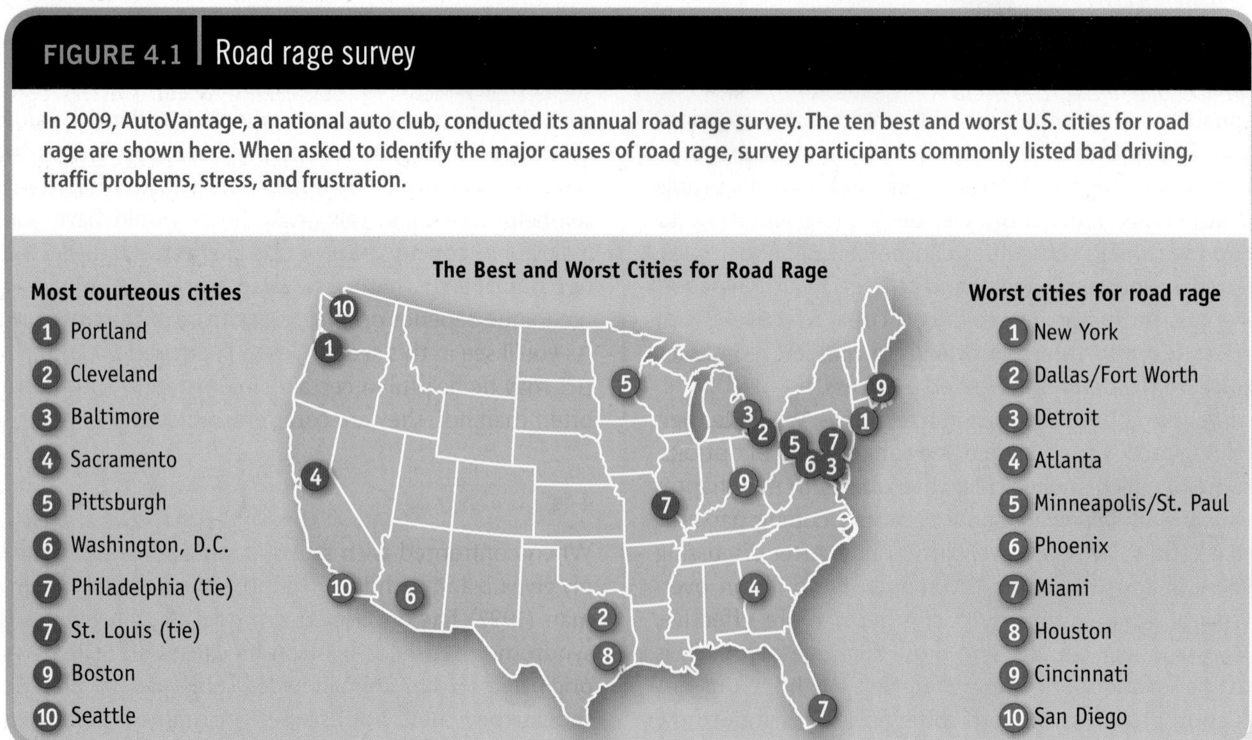

Source: From Affinion Group. (2009, June 16). *AutoVantage road rage survey reveals best, worst cities* [Press release]. Retrieved from http://www.affiniongroupmedia.com/themes/site_themes/affinionassests/releases/autovantage/Road_Rage_09/media/National_Rls.pdf.

any behavior intended to hurt someone, either physically or verbally. Snarls, curses, and insults are much more common than shootings or fistfights, but aggression of any kind can be problematic.

Frustration frequently elicits aggression. People often lash out aggressively at others who had nothing to do with their frustration, especially when they can't vent their anger at the real source of their frustration. For instance, you'll probably suppress your anger rather than lash out verbally at a police officer who gives you a speeding ticket. Twenty minutes later, however, you might be downright brutal in rebuking a waiter who is slow in serving your lunch. As we discussed in Chapter 2, Sigmund Freud noticed this diversion of anger to a substitute target long ago; he called it *displacement*. Unfortunately, research suggests that when someone is provoked, displaced aggression is a common response (Hoobler & Brass, 2006).

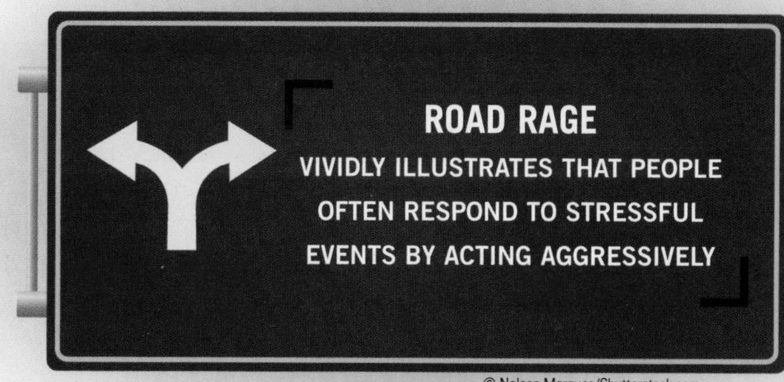
ROAD RAGE
VIVIDLY ILLUSTRATES THAT PEOPLE OFTEN RESPOND TO STRESSFUL EVENTS BY ACTING AGGRESSIVELY
© Nelson Marques/Shutterstock.com

Freud theorized that behaving aggressively could get pent-up emotion out of one's system and thus be adaptive. He coined the term ***catharsis* to refer to this release of emotional tension.** The Freudian notion that it is a good idea to vent anger has become widely disseminated and accepted in modern society. Books, magazines, and self-appointed experts routinely advise that it is healthy to "blow off steam" by playing a violent video game or watching an aggressive sporting event, thereby releasing and reducing anger. However, experimental research generally has *not* supported the catharsis hypothesis. Indeed, *most studies find just the opposite: Behaving in an aggressive manner tends to fuel more anger and aggression* (Bushman, 2002).

For instance, Craig Anderson and Brad Bushman (2001) conducted a groundbreaking review of the research on violent video games and found that playing these games was related to increased aggression and aggressive thoughts. In fact, they found that the relationship between media violence and aggressive behavior was almost as strong as the relationship between smoking and cancer (see Figure 4.2 on the next page). Exposure to media violence not only desensitizes people to violent acts, it encourages automatic aggressive responses (Uhlmann & Swanson, 2004) and increases feelings of hostility (Arriaga et al., 2006a).

© Yuri Arcurs/Shutterstock.com

Is there an up side to anger and aggression? As a coping strategy, acting aggressively has little value. Carol Tavris (1982) points out that aggressive behavior usually backfires because it elicits aggressive responses from others that generate more anger. She asserts, "Aggressive catharses are almost impossible to find in continuing relationships because parents, children, spouses, and bosses usually feel obliged to aggress back at you" (1982, p. 131). In fact, the interpersonal conflicts that often emerge from aggressive behavior actually induce additional stress.

4-1c INDULGING YOURSELF

Stress sometimes leads to reduced impulse control, or *self-indulgence* (Tice, Bratslavsky, & Baumeister, 2001). For instance, after an exceptionally stressful day, some people head for their kitchen, a grocery store, or a restaurant in pursuit of something sweet. Others cope with stress by making a beeline for the nearest shopping mall for a spending spree. Still others respond to stress by indulging in injudicious patterns of drinking, smoking, gambling, and drug use.

Moos and Billings (1982) identified *developing alternative rewards* as a common response to stress. It makes sense that when things are going poorly in one area of your life, you may try to compensate by pursuing substitute forms of satisfaction. Thus, it is not surprising that there is evidence of stress-induced eating (Wardle & Gibson, 2007), smoking (McClernon & Gilbert, 2007), gambling (Wood & Griffiths, 2007), and alcohol and drug use (Goeders, 2004). In fact, psychologists speculate that the general relationship

FIGURE 4.2 Comparison of the relationship between media violence and aggression to other correlations

Many studies have found a correlation between exposure to media violence and aggression. However, some critics have argued that the correlation is too weak to have any practical significance in the real world. In a rebuttal of this criticism, Bushman and Anderson (2001) note that the average correlation in studies of media violence and aggression is .31. They argue that this association is almost as strong as the correlation between smoking and the probability of developing lung cancer, which is viewed as relevant to real-world issues, and notably stronger than a variety of other correlations shown here that are assumed to have practical importance.

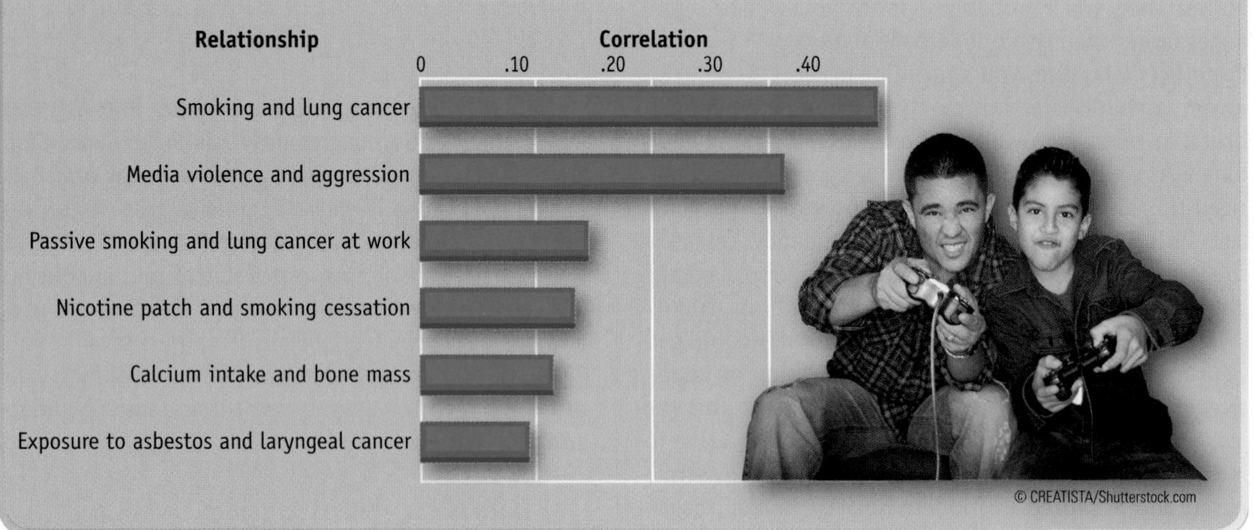

© Cengage Learning

Source: Adapted from Bushman, B. J., & Anderson, C. A. (2001). Media violence and the American public: Scientific facts versus media misinformation. *American Psychologist, 56*(6–7), 477–489. (Figure 2). Copyright © 2001 American Psychological Association. Reprinted with permission.

between stress and poor physical health might be attributable in part to these unhealthy behaviors (Carver, 2011).

There is nothing inherently maladaptive about indulging oneself as a way of coping with life's stresses. If a hot fudge sundae or some new clothes can calm your nerves after a major setback, who can argue? However, if a person consistently responds to stress with excessive self-indulgence, obvious problems are likely to develop. Stress-induced eating is typically unhealthy (one rarely craves broccoli or grapefruit after a hard day) and may result in poor nutrition or obesity. Excesses in drinking and drug use may endanger one's health and affect work or relationship quality. Additionally, these indulgences can cause emotional ambivalence as immediate pleasure gives way to regret, guilt, or embarrassment. Given the risks associated with self-indulgence, it has rather marginal adaptive value.

© Ariwasabi/Shutterstock.com

4-1d BLAMING YOURSELF

In a postgame interview after a tough defeat, a prominent football coach was brutally critical of himself. He said that he had been outcoached, that he had made poor decisions, and that his game plan was faulty. He almost eagerly assumed all the blame for the loss himself. In reality, he had taken some reasonable risks that didn't go his way and had suffered the effects of poor execution by his players. Looking at it objectively, the loss was attributable to the collective failures of fifty or so players and coaches. However, the coach's unrealistically negative self-evaluation was a fairly typical response to stress. When confronted by stress (especially frustration and pressure), people often become highly self-critical.

CATHY

The tendency to engage in "negative self-talk" in response to stress has been noted by a number of influential theorists. As we will discuss in greater detail later in this chapter, Albert Ellis (1973) calls this phenomenon "catastrophic thinking" and focuses on how it is rooted in irrational assumptions. According to Ellis, catastrophic thinking causes, aggravates, and perpetuates emotional reactions to stress that are often problematic. Along more serious lines, researchers have found that self-blame is associated with increased distress and depression for individuals who have experienced traumas such as sexual assault, war, and natural disasters. For victims of sexual assault specifically, self-blame is associated with heightened PTSD symptoms and greater feelings of shame (Ullman et al., 2007). Likewise, blaming oneself is related to increased depression and anxiety for those dealing with serious health issues (Anson & Ponsford, 2006). Although being realistic and recognizing one's weaknesses has value, especially when engaging in problem solving, self-blame as a coping strategy can be enormously counterproductive.

4-1e USING DEFENSIVE COPING

Defensive coping is a common response to stress. We noted in Chapter 2 that the concept of defense mechanisms was originally developed by Sigmund Freud. Though rooted in the psychoanalytic tradition, this concept has gained acceptance from psychologists of most persuasions.

The Nature of Defense Mechanisms

***Defense mechanisms* are largely unconscious reactions that protect a person from unpleasant emotions such as anxiety and guilt.** Figure 4.3 on the next page describes some of the common defense mechanisms that people use with some regularity. Although widely discussed in the popular press, defense mechanisms are often misunderstood. Let's explore them more deeply in the hopes of clearing up any misconceptions.

What do defense mechanisms defend against? Above all else, defense mechanisms shield the individual from the *emotional discomfort* elicited by stress. Their main purpose is to ward off unwelcome emotions or to reduce their intensity. Foremost among the emotions guarded against is anxiety. People are especially defensive when the anxiety is the result of some threat to their self-esteem. Guilt and dejection are two other emotions that people often try to evade through defensive maneuvers.

How do they work? Defense mechanisms work through *self-deception*. They accomplish their goals by distorting reality so it does not appear so threatening (Aldwin, 2007). Let's say you're doing poorly in school and are in danger of flunking out. Initially, you might use *repression* to block awareness of the possibility that you could fail. This tactic might temporarily fend off feelings of anxiety. If it becomes difficult to avoid the obvious, you might resort to *rationalization*, telling yourself that additional study would not accomplish anything, when the objective fact is that you could still salvage your grades in some of your classes. Thus, defense mechanisms work their magic by bending reality in self-serving ways (Bowins, 2004).

Are they conscious or unconscious? Mainstream Freudian theory originally assumed that defenses operate entirely at an unconscious level. However, the concept of defense mechanisms has been broadened to include maneuvers people may be aware of. Thus, defense mechanisms can be conscious or unconscious (Erdelyi, 2001).

FIGURE 4.3 Common defense mechanisms

According to Freud, people use a variety of defense mechanisms to protect themselves from painful emotions. Definitions of seven common defense mechanisms introduced in Chapter 2 are shown on the left, along with examples of each on the right.

DEFENSE MECHANISMS, WITH EXAMPLES

Definition	Example
Repression involves keeping distressing thoughts and feelings buried in the unconscious.	A traumatized soldier has no recollection of the details of a close brush with death.
Projection involves attributing one's own thoughts, feelings, or motives to another person.	A woman who dislikes her boss thinks she likes her boss but feels that the boss doesn't like her.
Displacement involves diverting emotional feelings (usually anger) from their original source to a substitute target.	After a parental scolding, a young girl takes her anger out on her little brother.
Reaction formation involves behaving in a way that is exactly the opposite of one's true feelings.	A parent who unconsciously resents a child spoils the child with outlandish gifts.
Regression involves a reversion to immature patterns of behavior.	An adult has a temper tantrum when he doesn't get his way.
Rationalization involves the creation of false but plausible excuses to justify unacceptable behavior.	A student watches TV instead of studying, saying that "additional study wouldn't do any good anyway."
Identification involves bolstering self-esteem by forming an imaginary or real alliance with some person or group.	An insecure young man joins a fraternity to boost his self-esteem.

Are they normal? Definitely. Most people use defense mechanisms on a fairly regular basis (Thobaben, 2005). They are entirely normal patterns of coping. The notion that only neurotic people use defense mechanisms is inaccurate.

Can Defense Mechanisms Ever Be Healthy?

This is a critical and complicated question. More often than not, the answer is no. In fact, defensive coping has been linked to increased negative emotions, depression, and suicide risk (Hovanesian, Isakov, & Cervellione, 2009). In general, defense mechanisms are poor ways of coping, for a number of reasons. First, defensive coping is an avoidance strategy, and avoidance rarely provides a genuine solution to our problems. Second, defenses such as rationalization and projection often represent "wishful thinking," which is likely to accomplish little. Third, a defensive coping style has been related to poor health, in part because it often leads people to delay facing up to their problems (Weinberger, 1990). For example, if you were to block out obvious warning signs of cancer or diabetes and failed to obtain needed medical care, your defensive behavior could be fatal. Although illusions may protect us from anxiety in the short term, they can create serious problems in the long term.

Given the obvious problems associated with illusions, most theorists used to regard accurate contact with reality as the hallmark of sound mental health. However, in landmark research, Shelley Taylor and Jonathon Brown (1994) reviewed several lines of evidence suggesting that defensive illusions may be adaptive for mental health and well-being. First, they note that "normal" (that is, nondepressed) people tend to have overly favorable self-images. In contrast, depressed people exhibit less favorable—but more realistic—self-concepts. Second, normal participants overestimate the degree to which they control chance events. In comparison, depressed participants are less prone to this illusion of control. Third, normal individuals are more likely than their depressed counterparts to display unrealistic optimism in making projections about the future.

As you might guess, critics have expressed considerable skepticism about the idea that illusions are adaptive. One possible resolution to this debate is Roy Baumeister's (1989) theory that it's all a matter of degree and that there is an "optimal margin of illusion." According to Baumeister, extreme self-deception is maladaptive, but small illusions may often be beneficial.

4-2 The Nature of Constructive Coping

Our discussion thus far has focused on coping strategies that tend to be less than ideal. Of course, people also exhibit many healthy strategies for dealing with stress. We will use the term ***constructive coping* to refer to efforts to deal with stressful events that are judged to be relatively healthful.** Keep in mind that even the healthiest coping responses may turn out to be ineffective in some cases. Thus, the concept of constructive coping is simply meant to convey a healthy, positive connotation, without promising success.

In labeling certain coping responses consructive or healthy, psychologists are making value judgments.

What makes a coping strategy constructive? Frankly, in labeling certain coping responses constructive or healthy, psychologists are making value judgments. It's a gray area in which opinions will vary to some extent. Nonetheless, some consensus emerges from the burgeoning research on coping and stress management. Key themes in this literature include the following (Kleinke, 2007):

1. Constructive coping involves confronting problems directly. It is task relevant and action oriented. It involves a conscious attempt to rationally evaluate your options in an effort to solve your problems.

2. Constructive coping takes effort. Using such strategies to reduce stress is an active process that involves planning.

3. Constructive coping is based on reasonably realistic appraisals of your stress and coping resources. A little self-deception may sometimes be adaptive, but excessive self-deception and highly unrealistic negative thinking are not.

4. Constructive coping involves learning to recognize and manage potentially disruptive emotional reactions to stress.

5. Constructive coping involves learning to exert some control over potentially harmful or destructive habitual behaviors. It requires the acquisition of some behavioral self-control.

These points should give you a general idea of what we mean by constructive coping. To organize our discussion, we will use a classification scheme proposed by Moos and Billings (1982) to divide constructive coping techniques into three broad categories: *appraisal-focused coping* (aimed at changing one's interpretation of stressful events), *problem-focused coping* (aimed at altering the stressful situation itself), and *emotion-focused coping* (aimed at managing potential emotional distress). Figure 4.4 shows common coping strategies that fall into each category.

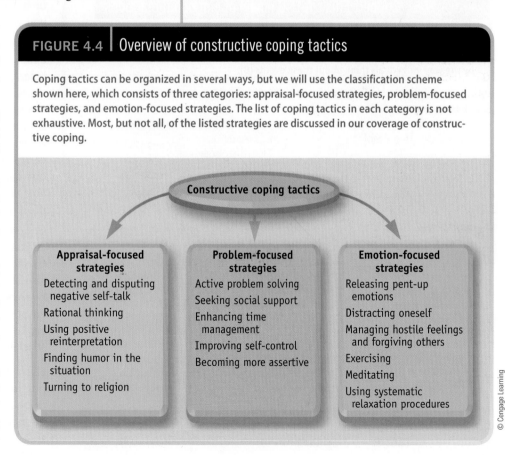

FIGURE 4.4 Overview of constructive coping tactics

Coping tactics can be organized in several ways, but we will use the classification scheme shown here, which consists of three categories: appraisal-focused strategies, problem-focused strategies, and emotion-focused strategies. The list of coping tactics in each category is not exhaustive. Most, but not all, of the listed strategies are discussed in our coverage of constructive coping.

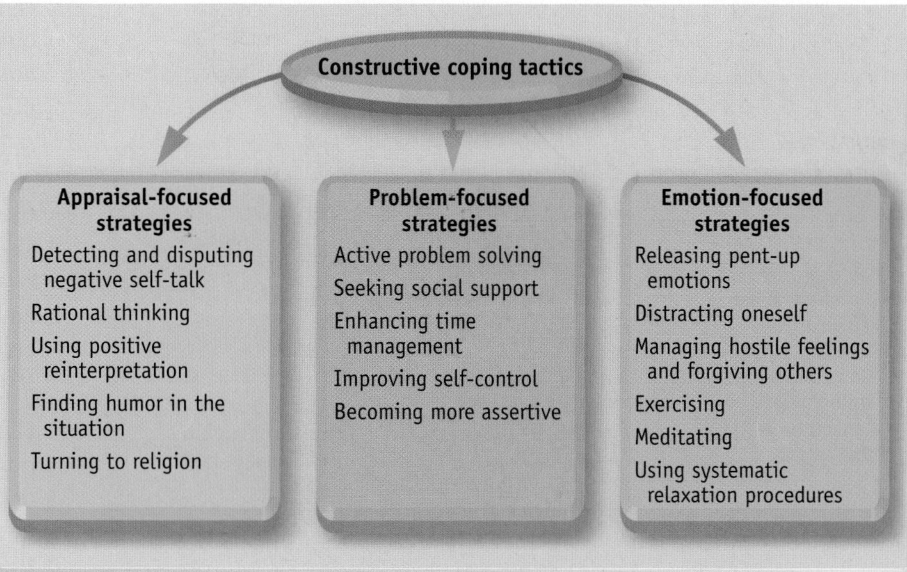

Constructive coping tactics

Appraisal-focused strategies	Problem-focused strategies	Emotion-focused strategies
Detecting and disputing negative self-talk	Active problem solving	Releasing pent-up emotions
Rational thinking	Seeking social support	Distracting oneself
Using positive reinterpretation	Enhancing time management	Managing hostile feelings and forgiving others
Finding humor in the situation	Improving self-control	Exercising
Turning to religion	Becoming more assertive	Meditating
		Using systematic relaxation procedures

It is important to note that many strategies could fall under more than one of these broad categories. For instance, one could seek social support for practical purposes (problem-focused) or emotional purposes (emotion-focused).

4-3 Appraisal-Focused Constructive Coping

As we've seen, the experience of stress depends on how one interprets or appraises threatening events. People often underestimate the importance of the appraisal phase in the stress process. They fail to appreciate the highly subjective feelings that color the perception of threat to one's well-being. In fact, a useful way to deal with stress is to alter your appraisal of threatening events. In this section, we'll examine Albert Ellis's ideas about reappraisal and discuss the value of using humor and positive reinterpretation to cope with stress.

4-3a ENGAGING IN RATIONAL THINKING

Albert Ellis (1977) was a prominent and influential theorist who died in 2007 at the age of 93. He believed that people could short-circuit their emotional reactions to stress by altering their appraisals of stressful events. Ellis's insights about stress appraisal are the foundation for his widely used system of therapy. ***Rational-emotive behavior therapy* is an approach to therapy that focuses on altering clients' patterns of irrational thinking to reduce maladaptive emotions and behavior.**

Ellis maintained that *you feel the way you think.* He argued that problematic emotional reactions are caused by negative self-talk, which, as we mentioned earlier, he called catastrophic thinking. ***Catastrophic thinking* involves unrealistic appraisals of stress that exaggerate the magnitude of one's problems.** Ellis used a simple A-B-C sequence to explain his ideas (see Figure 4.5):

A. *Activating event.* The A in Ellis's system stands for the activating event that produces the stress. The activating event may be any potentially stressful transaction. Examples might include an automobile accident, the cancellation of a date, a delay while waiting in line at the bank, or a failure to get a promotion you were expecting.

B. *Belief system.* B stands for your belief about the event, which represents your appraisal of the stress. According to Ellis, people often view minor setbacks as disasters, engaging in catastrophic thinking: "How awful this is. I can't stand it!" "Things never turn out fairly for me." "I'll be in this line forever." "I'll never get promoted."

C. *Consequence.* C stands for the consequence of your negative thinking. When your appraisals of stressful events are highly negative, the consequence tends to be emotional distress. Thus, you feel angry, outraged, anxious, panic stricken, disgusted, or dejected.

Ellis asserts that most people do not understand the importance of phase B in this three-stage sequence. They unwittingly believe that the activating event (A) *causes* the consequent emotional

FIGURE 4.5 Albert Ellis's A-B-C model of emotional reactions

Most people tend to attribute their negative emotional reactions (C) directly to stressful events (A). However, Ellis argues that emotional reactions are really caused by the way individuals think about these events (B).

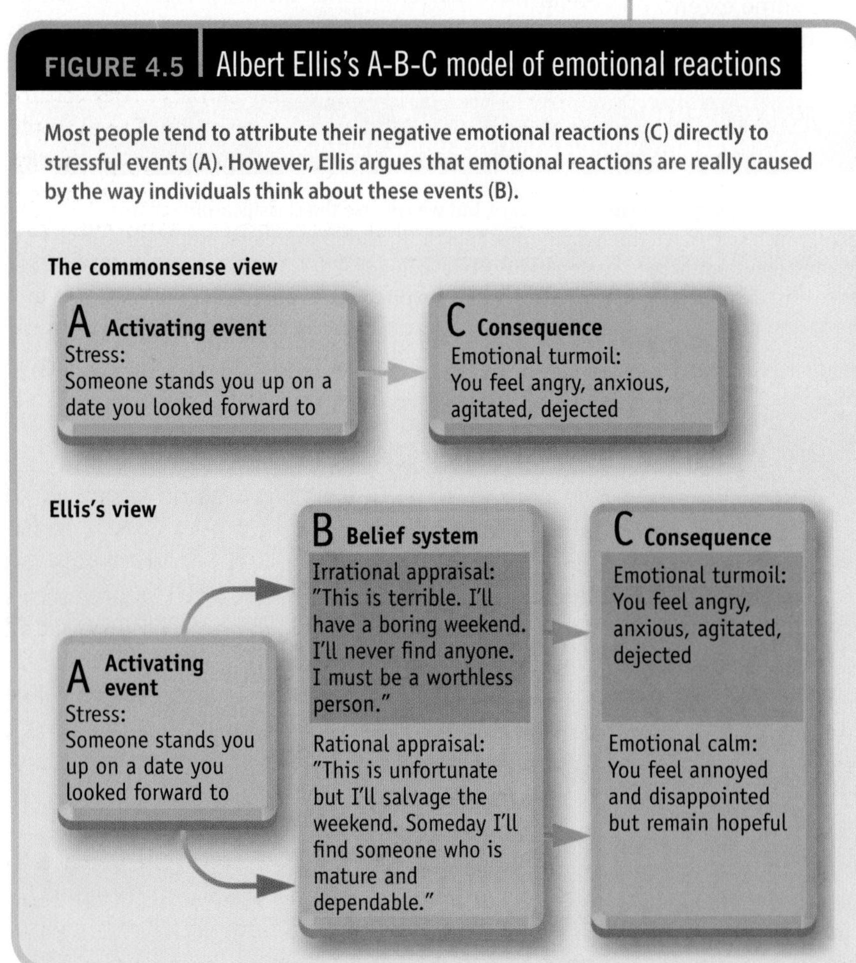
The commonsense view
A Activating event
Stress:
Someone stands you up on a date you looked forward to
C Consequence
Emotional turmoil:
You feel angry, anxious, agitated, dejected
Ellis's view
A Activating event
Stress:
Someone stands you up on a date you looked forward to
B Belief system
Irrational appraisal:
"This is terrible. I'll have a boring weekend. I'll never find anyone. I must be a worthless person."
Rational appraisal:
"This is unfortunate but I'll salvage the weekend. Someday I'll find someone who is mature and dependable."
C Consequence
Emotional turmoil:
You feel angry, anxious, agitated, dejected
Emotional calm:
You feel annoyed and disappointed but remain hopeful

turmoil (C). However, Ellis maintains that A does *not* cause C. It only appears to do so. Instead, Ellis asserts that B causes C. Emotional distress is actually caused by one's catastrophic thinking in appraising stressful events.

According to Ellis, it is common for people to turn inconvenience into disaster and make "mountains out of molehills." For instance, imagine that someone stands you up on a date you were eagerly looking forward to. You might think, "Oh, this is terrible. I'm going to have another boring weekend. People always mistreat me. I'll never find anyone to fall in love with. I must be an ugly, worthless person." Ellis would argue that such thoughts are irrational. He would point out that it does not follow logically from being stood up that you (1) must have a lousy weekend, (2) will never fall in love, or (3) are a worthless person. Thinking this way does nothing but increase distress.

People often underestimate the importance of the **appraisal phase** in the stress process.

©FotografiaBasica/iStockphoto

The Roots of Catastrophic Thinking

Ellis (1995) theorized that unrealistic appraisals of stress are derived from the irrational assumptions that people hold. He maintained that if you scrutinize your catastrophic thinking, you will find that your reasoning is based on an unreasonable premise, such as "I must have approval from everyone" or "I must perform well in all endeavors." These faulty assumptions, which most people hold unconsciously, generate catastrophic thinking and emotional turmoil. To facilitate emotional self-control, it is important to learn to spot irrational assumptions and the unhealthy patterns of thought that they generate. Here are four particularly common irrational assumptions:

1. *I must have love and affection from certain people.* Everyone wants to be liked and loved. There is nothing wrong with that. However, many people foolishly believe that they should be liked by everyone they come into contact with. If you stop to think about it, that's clearly unrealistic. Once individuals fall in love, they tend to believe that their future happiness depends absolutely on the continuation of that one, special relationship. They believe that if their current love relationship were to end, they would never again be able to achieve a comparable one. This is an unrealistic view of the future. Such views make the person anxious during a relationship and severely depressed if it comes to an end.

2. *I must perform well in all endeavors.* We live in a highly competitive society. We are taught that victory brings happiness. Consequently, we feel that we must always win. For example, many athletes are never satisfied unless they perform at their best level. However, by definition, their best level is not their typical level, and they set themselves up for inevitable frustration.

3. *Other people should always behave competently and be considerate of me.* People are often angered by others' stupidity and selfishness. For example, you may become outraged when a mechanic fails to fix your car properly or when a salesperson treats you rudely. It would be nice if others were always competent and considerate, but you know better—they are not. Yet many people go through life unrealistically expecting others' efficiency and kindness in every situation.

4. *Events should always go the way I like.* Some people simply won't tolerate any kind of setback. They assume that things should always go their way. For example, some commuters become tense and angry each time they get stuck in rush-hour traffic. They seem to believe that they are entitled to coast home easily every day, even though they know that rush hour rarely is a breeze. Such expectations are clearly unrealistic and doomed to be violated. Yet few people recognize the obvious irrationality of the assumption that underlies their anger unless it is pointed out to them.

Reducing Catastrophic Thinking

How can you reduce your unrealistic appraisals of stress? Ellis asserts that you must learn (1) how to detect catastrophic thinking and (2) how to dispute the irrational assumptions that cause it. Detection involves acquiring the ability to spot unrealistic pessimism and wild exaggeration in your thinking. Examine your self-talk closely. Ask yourself why you're getting upset. Force yourself to verbalize your concerns, covertly or out loud. Look for key words that often show up in catastrophic thinking, such as *should, ought, always, never,* and *must.*

Disputing your irrational assumptions requires subjecting your entire reasoning process to scrutiny. Try to root out the assumptions from which your conclusions are derived. Most people are unaware of their assumptions. Once these thoughts are unearthed, their irrationality may be quite obvious. If your assumptions seem reasonable, ask yourself whether your conclusions follow logically. Try to replace your catastrophic thinking with more low-key, rational analyses. Such strategies should help you redefine stressful situations in ways that are less threatening. Challenging one's assumptions isn't the only appraisal-based coping strategy; another way to defuse such situations is to turn to humor.

4-3b USING HUMOR AS A STRESS REDUCER

In a New Orleans suburb in the aftermath of Hurricane Katrina, "the grimy residue of receded floodwater covered the blue Chevrolet pickup parked outside a shattered two-story house, but the offer spray-painted on the vehicle in white overflowed with enthusiasm: 'For Sale. Like New. Runs Great'" (Associated Press, 2005). Obviously, the hurricane didn't destroy this victim's sense of humor. When the going gets tough, finding some humor in the situation is not uncommon and is usually beneficial. In a study of coping styles, McCrae (1984) found that 40% of his participants reported using humor to deal with stress.

Empirical evidence showing that humor moderates the impact of stress has been accumulating over the last 25 years. For instance, in one influential study, Martin and Lefcourt (1983) found that a good sense of humor functioned as a buffer to lessen the negative impact of stress on mood. Their results showed that high-humor participants were less affected by stress than their low-humor counterparts.

It appears that some types of humor are more effective than others in reducing stress. Chen and Martin (2007) found that humor that is affiliative (used to engage or amuse others) or self-enhancing (maintaining a humorous perspective in the face of adversity) is related to better mental health. In contrast, coping through humor that is self-defeating (used at one's own expense) or aggressive (criticizing or ridiculing others) is related to poorer mental health. Likewise, using a lot of self-defeating humor and very little self-enhancing or affiliative humor is associated with increased depression (Frewen et al., 2008).

How does humor help reduce the effects of stress and promote wellness? Several explanations have been proposed (see Figure 4.6). One possibility is that humor affects appraisals of stressful events. Jokes can help people put a less-threatening spin on their trials and tribulations. Kuiper, Martin, and Olinger (1993) demonstrated that students who used coping humor were able to appraise a stressful exam as a positive challenge, which in turn lowered their perceived stress levels. Another possibility is that humor increases the experience of positive emotions. In a study of laughter in the workplace, participants who practiced laughing 15 minutes a day for three weeks showed significant increases in positive emotions, even 90 days after the study was over (Beckman, Regier, & Young, 2007).

Another hypothesis is that a good sense of humor buffers the effects of stress by facilitating positive social interactions, which promote social support. In a study of Vietnam prisoners of war, Henman (2001) found that

FIGURE 4.6 Possible explanations for the link between humor and wellness

Research suggests that a good sense of humor buffers the effects of stress and promotes wellness. Four hypothesized explanations for the link between humor and wellness are outlined in the middle column of this diagram. As you can see, humor may have a variety of beneficial effects.

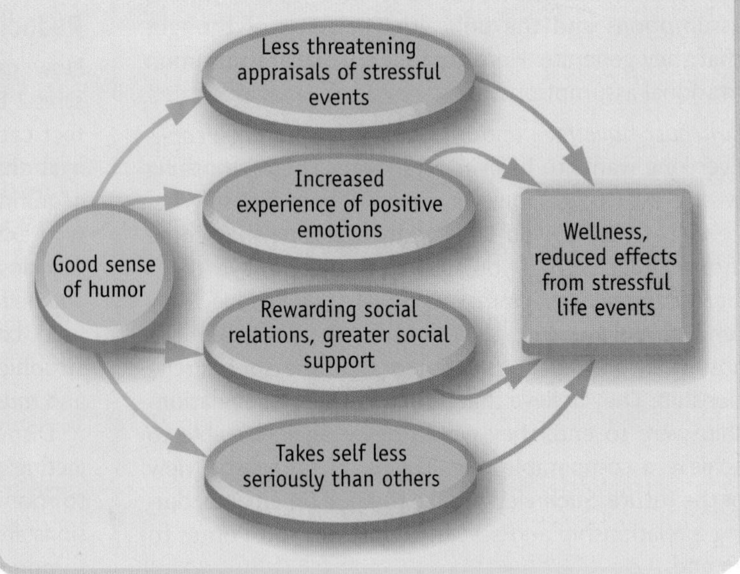

using humor to build connections "contributed to the survival and resilience of these men" (p. 83). Finally, Lefcourt and colleagues (1995) argue that high-humor people may benefit from not taking themselves as seriously as low-humor people do. As they put it, "If persons do not regard themselves too seriously and do not have an inflated sense of self-importance, then defeats, embarrassments, and even tragedies should have less pervasive emotional consequences for them" (p. 375). Thus, humor is a rather versatile coping strategy that may have many benefits when used properly.

4-3c RELYING ON POSITIVE REINTERPRETATIONS

When you are feeling overwhelmed by life's difficulties, you might try the commonsense strategy of recognizing that "things could be worse." No matter how terrible your problems seem, you probably know someone who has even bigger troubles. That is not to say that you should derive satisfaction from others' misfortune, but rather that comparing your own plight with others' even tougher struggles can help you put your problems in perspective. Research suggests that this strategy of making positive comparisons with others is a common coping mechanism that can result in improved mood and self-esteem (Wills & Sandy, 2001). Moreover, this strategy does not depend on knowing others who are clearly worse off. You can simply imagine yourself in a similar situation with an even worse outcome (example: two broken legs after a horseback-riding accident instead of just one). One healthy aspect of positive reinterpretation is that it can facilitate calming reappraisals of stress without the necessity of distorting reality. Over time this perspective can decrease the stress of the situation.

Another way to engage in positive reinterpretation is to search for something good in a bad experience. Distressing though they may be, many setbacks have positive elements. After experiencing divorces, illnesses, layoffs, and the like, many people remark that "I came out of the experience better than I went in," or "I grew as a person." Studies of victims of natural disasters, heart attacks, and bereavement have found an association between this type of *benefit finding* under duress and relatively sound psychological and physical health (Lechner, Tennen, & Affleck, 2009). Of course, the positive aspects of a personal setback may be easy to see after the stressful event is behind you. The challenge is to recognize these positive aspects while you are still struggling with the setback, so that it becomes less stressful.

off the mark.com by Mark Parisi
I CAN DEAL WITH IT... I'VE BEEN EATEN BY A SNAKE, BUT I'LL JUST GO ON WITH MY LIFE... I'M OKAY!
LEWIS TESTS THE LIMITS OF POSITIVE THINKING.
offthemark.com

Mark Panisi/Atlantic Features © 1992/offthemark.com

4-4 Problem-Focused Constructive Coping

Problem-focused coping includes efforts to remedy or conquer the stress-producing problem itself. This type of coping is associated with positive outcomes such as emotional growth in times of stress. In this section, we'll discuss systematic problem solving, the importance of seeking help, and effective time management.

4-4a USING SYSTEMATIC PROBLEM SOLVING

In dealing with life's problems, the most obvious (and often most effective) course of action is to tackle them head-on. In fact, problem solving has been linked to better psychological adjustment, lower levels of depression, reduced alcohol use, and fewer health complaints (Heppner & Lee, 2005). Obviously, people vary in their problem-solving skills. However, evidence suggests that these skills can be enhanced through training. With this thought in mind, we will sketch a general outline of how to engage in more systematic problem solving. The plan described here is a synthesis of observations by various experts, especially Mahoney (1979), Miller (1978), and Chang and Kelly (1993).

Social support can be a powerful force that helps buffer the deleterious effects of stress.

© Angela Waye/Shutterstock.com

Clarify the Problem

You can't tackle a problem if you're not sure what it is. Therefore, the first step in any systematic problem-solving effort is to clarify the nature of the problem. Sometimes the problem will be all too obvious. At other times the source of trouble may be quite difficult to pin down. In any case, you need to arrive at a specific concrete definition of your problem.

Two common tendencies typically hinder people's efforts to get a clear picture of their problems. First, they often describe their problems in vague generalities ("My life isn't going anywhere" or "I never have enough time"). Second, they tend to focus too much on negative feelings, thereby confusing the consequences of problems ("I'm so depressed all the time" or "I'm so nervous I can't concentrate") with the problems themselves ("I don't have any friends at my new school" or "I have taken on more responsibilities that I can realistically handle").

Generate Alternative Courses of Action

The second step in systematic problem solving is to generate alternative courses of action. Notice that we did not call these alternative *solutions*. Many problems do not have a readily available solution that will completely resolve the problem. If you think in terms of searching for complete solutions, you may prevent yourself from considering many worthwhile courses of action. Instead, it is more realistic to search for alternatives that may produce some kind of improvement in your situation.

Besides avoiding the tendency to insist on solutions, you need to avoid the temptation to go with the first alternative that comes to mind. Many people are a little trigger-happy. They thoughtlessly try to follow through on the first response that occurs to them. Various lines of evidence suggest that it is wiser to engage in brainstorming about a problem. ***Brainstorming*** **is generating as many ideas as possible while withholding criticism and evaluation.** In other words, you generate alternatives without paying any attention to their apparent practicality. This approach facilitates creative expression of ideas and can lead to more alternative courses of action from which to choose.

Evaluate Your Alternatives and Select a Course of Action

Once you generate as many alternatives as you can, you need to start evaluating the possibilities. There are no simple criteria for judging the relative merits of your alternatives. However, you will probably want to address three general issues. First, ask yourself whether each alternative is realistic. In other words, what is the probability that you can successfully execute the intended course of action? Try to think of any obstacles you may have failed to anticipate. In making this assessment, it is important to try to avoid both foolish optimism and unnecessary pessimism.

Second, consider any costs or risks associated with each alternative. The "solution" to a problem can be worse than the problem itself. Assuming you can successfully implement your intended course of action, what are the possible negative consequences? Third, compare the desirability of the probable outcomes of each alternative. In making your decision, you have to ask yourself, "What is important to me? Which outcomes do I value the most?" Through careful evaluation you can select the best course of action.

Take Action While Maintaining Flexibility

You can plan your course of action as thoughtfully and intentionally as possible, but no plan works if you don't follow through and implement it. In so doing, try to maintain flexibility. Do not get locked into a particular plan. Few choices are truly irreversible. You need to monitor results closely and be willing to revise your strategy.

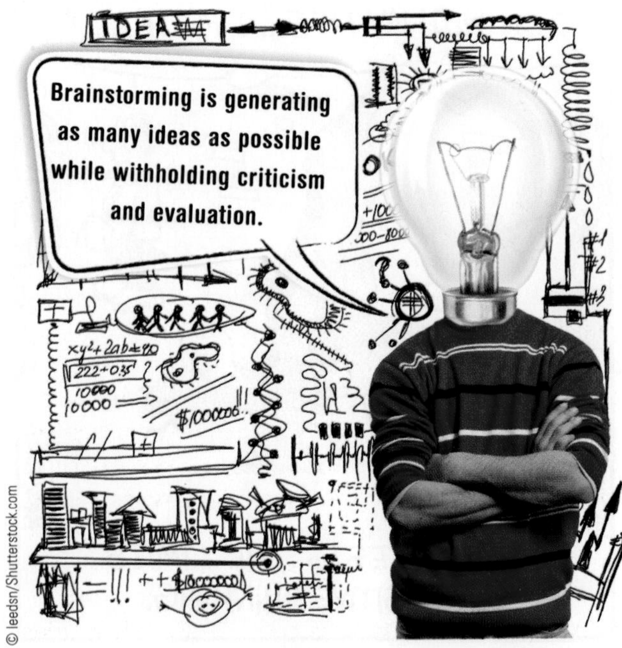
IDEA
Brainstorming is generating as many ideas as possible while withholding criticism and evaluation.

© leedsn/Shutterstock.com

In evaluating your course of action, try to avoid the simplistic success/failure dichotomy. You should simply look for improvement of any kind. If your plan doesn't work out too well, consider whether it was undermined by any circumstances that you could not have anticipated. Finally, remember that you can learn from your failures. Even if things did not work out, you may now have new information that will facilitate a new attack on the problem.

4-4b SEEKING HELP

In Chapter 3, we saw that social support can be a powerful force that helps buffer the deleterious effects of stress and has positive effects of its own (Taylor, 2007). In trying to tackle problems directly, it pays to keep in mind the value of seeking aid from friends, family, coworkers, and neighbors. So far, we have discussed social support as if it were a stable, external resource available to different people in varying degrees. In reality, social support fluctuates over time and evolves out of one's interactions with others. Some people have more support than others because they have personal characteristics that attract more support or because they make more effort to seek support. Keep in mind that support that is perceived to be insincere or inappropriate can actually decrease one's sense of self-worth and overall well-being (Rook, August, & Sorkin, 2011).

Interestingly, cultural factors, often overlooked by researchers, seem to play an important role in what individuals see as problems and how they solve them. This is especially true with regard to who seeks social support. Taylor and colleagues (2004) found that Asians and Asian Americans are less likely to seek social support in times of stress than European Americans are. When examined closely, this difference appears to be rooted in cultural concerns about relationships. That is, individuals from cultures high in collectivism (discussed in Chapter 6) don't want to risk straining relationships or disrupting group harmony by calling on others for help in times of stress (Kim et al., 2006). When using social support for coping, Asian Americans tend to benefit more from support that does not involve disclosure of personal distress—that is, support that doesn't emotionally burden the other person (Kim, Sherman, & Taylor, 2008). Of course, broad similarities exist in how people from different cultures *react* to stress. For example, individuals from both collectivistic and individualistic cultures view receiving comfort as an effective coping strategy. There appear to be cultural differences, however, in actively *seeking* help (Mortenson, 2006). Given that social support is such an important resource, researchers will no doubt continue to examine it within a cultural context.

Photo: © OtnaYdur/Shutterstock.com; Frame: © Vitaly Korovin/Shutterstock.com

4-4c IMPROVING TIME MANAGEMENT

Talk to the average person and you will discover that many of the stressors of modern life result from a lack of time. Individuals vary in their time perspectives. Some people are *future oriented*, able to see the consequences of immediate behavior for future goals, whereas others are *present oriented*, focused on immediate events and not worried about consequences. These orientations influence how people manage their time and meet their time-related commitments. Future-oriented individuals, for example, are less likely to procrastinate and are more reliable in meeting their commitments (Harber, Zimbardo, & Boyd, 2003). Regardless of orientation, most people could benefit from managing their time more effectively. Because it is such a crucial coping strategy, we devote the entire application at the end of this chapter to time management.

4-5 Emotion-Focused Constructive Coping

Let's be realistic: There are going to be occasions when appraisal-focused coping and problem-focused coping are not successful in warding off emotional turmoil. Some problems are too serious to be whittled down much by reappraisal, and others simply can't be "solved." Moreover, even well-executed coping strategies may take time to work before emotional tensions begin to subside. In these cases, recognizing and regulating one's emotions can be a useful skill (Stanton, 2011). In this section, we will discuss a variety of coping abilities and strategies that relate mainly to the regulation of emotions.

4-5a ENHANCING EMOTIONAL INTELLIGENCE

According to some theorists, *emotional intelligence* is the key to being resilient in the face of stress. The concept of emotional intelligence was originally formulated by Peter Salovey and John Mayer (1990). ***Emotional intelligence*** **consists of the ability to perceive and express emotion, use emotions to facilitate thought, understand and reason with emotion, and regulate emotion.** Emotional intelligence includes four essential components (Salovey, Mayer, & Caruso, 2005). First, people need to be able to accurately perceive emotions in themselves and in others and to have the ability to express their own emotions effectively. Second, people need to be aware of how their emotions shape their thinking, decision making, and coping with stress. Third, people need to be able to understand and analyze their emotions, which may often be complex and contradictory. Fourth, people need to be able to regulate their emotions so that they can dampen negative emotions and make effective use of positive ones.

Researchers continue to study emotional intelligence in relation to coping. Pashang and Singh (2008) found that those high in emotional intelligence were more likely to use problem-solving strategies to deal with anxiety, while those with lower levels used more distraction and denial. Low emotional intelligence has also been linked to increased worry and avoidance (Matthews et al., 2006). At work, low emotional intelligence is related to increased burnout (Xie, 2011). Because this construct appears to be important for general well-being, investigators are exploring ways to cultivate emotional intelligence in classrooms, workplaces, and counseling settings. One study found that positive emotional expression can lead to an increase in emotional intelligence (Wing, Schutte, & Byrne, 2006). That leads us to our next topic.

4-5b EXPRESSING EMOTIONS

Try as you might to redefine or resolve stressful situations, you no doubt still go through times when you feel wired with stress-induced tension. When this happens, there's merit in the commonsense notion that

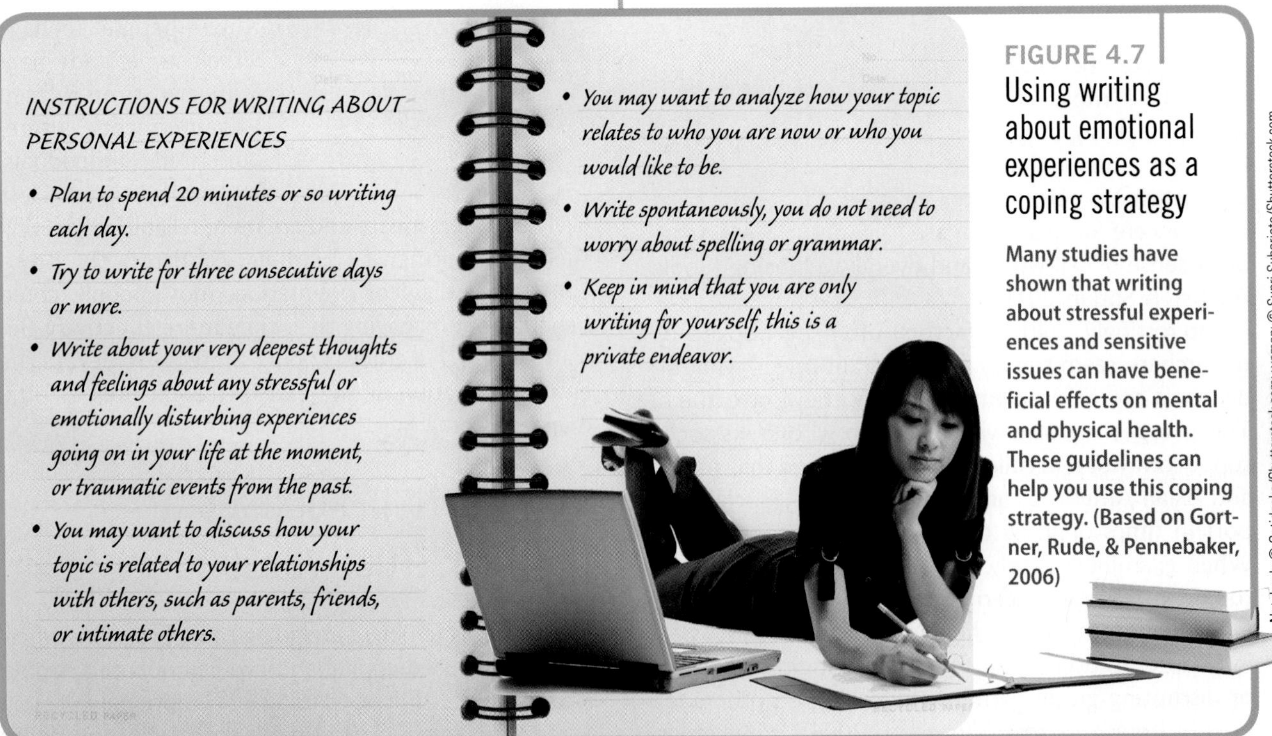

INSTRUCTIONS FOR WRITING ABOUT PERSONAL EXPERIENCES
• Plan to spend 20 minutes or so writing each day.
• Try to write for three consecutive days or more.
• Write about your very deepest thoughts and feelings about any stressful or emotionally disturbing experiences going on in your life at the moment, or traumatic events from the past.
• You may want to discuss how your topic is related to your relationships with others, such as parents, friends, or intimate others.
• You may want to analyze how your topic relates to who you are now or who you would like to be.
• Write spontaneously, you do not need to worry about spelling or grammar.
• Keep in mind that you are only writing for yourself; this is a private endeavor.

FIGURE 4.7 Using writing about emotional experiences as a coping strategy

Many studies have shown that writing about stressful experiences and sensitive issues can have beneficial effects on mental and physical health. These guidelines can help you use this coping strategy. (Based on Gortner, Rude, & Pennebaker, 2006)

you should try to release the emotions welling up inside. Why? Because the physiological arousal that accompanies emotions can become problematic. For example, research suggests that people who inhibit the expression of anger and other emotions are somewhat more likely than others to have elevated blood pressure (Jorgensen et al., 1996). Moreover, research suggests that efforts to actively suppress emotions result in increased stress and autonomic arousal (Gross, 2001). Note that such findings do not mean you should act aggressively (a coping strategy of limited value discussed earlier in the chapter). Instead, we are focusing on appropriate, healthy expression of emotions.

James Pennebaker and his colleagues have shown that emotional expression through talking or writing about stressful personal issues can have beneficial effects. For example, in one study of college students, half the subjects were asked to write three essays about their difficulties in adjusting to college. The other half wrote three essays about superficial topics. The participants who wrote about their personal problems and traumas enjoyed better health in the following months than the other participants did (Pennebaker, Colder, & Sharp, 1990). Additionally, emotional disclosure, or "opening up," is associated with improved mood, more positive self-perceptions, fewer visits to physicians, and enhanced immune functioning (Niederhoffer & Pennebaker, 2005). Smyth and Pennebaker (1999) assert that "when people put their emotional upheavals into words, their physical and mental health seems to improve markedly." They conclude that "the act of disclosure itself is a powerful therapeutic agent" (p. 70). Figure 4.7 summarizes some guidelines for writing about personal issues and trauma that should make this coping strategy more effective for you.

4-5c MANAGING HOSTILITY AND FORGIVING OTHERS

Scientists have compiled quite a bit of evidence that hostility is related to increased risk for heart attacks and other types of illness. So how can individuals effectively regulate negative emotions that include anger and hostility? The goal of hostility management is not merely to suppress the overt expression of hostility that may continue to seethe beneath the surface, but to actually reduce the frequency and intensity of one's hostile feelings. The first step toward this goal is to learn to quickly recognize one's anger. A variety of strategies can be used to decrease hostility, including reinterpretation of annoying events, distraction, and the kind of rational self-talk advocated by Ellis (Williams & Williams, 1993). Efforts to increase empathy and tolerance can also contribute to hostility management, as can forgiveness, which has become the focus of a contemporary line of research in psychology.

People tend to experience hostility and other negative emotions when they feel "wronged"—that is, when they believe that the actions of another person were harmful, immoral, or unjust. People's natural inclination is either to seek revenge or to avoid further contact with the offender (McCullough & Witvliet, 2005). Although there is debate among researchers about the exact definition, ***forgiveness*** **involves counteracting the natural tendencies to seek vengeance or avoid an offender, thereby releasing this person from further liability for his or her transgression.** Research suggests that forgiving is an effective emotion-focused coping strategy that is associated with better adjustment and

In September 1994, Reg and Maggie Green were vacationing in Italy when their seven-year-old son, Nicholas, was shot and killed during a highway robbery. In an act of forgiveness that stunned Europe, the Greens chose to donate their son's organs, which went to seven Italians. The Greens, shown here five years after the incident, have weathered their horrific loss better than most, perhaps in part because of their willingness to forgive.

well-being (Worthington et al., 2007). For example, in one study of divorced or permanently separated women, the extent to which the women had forgiven their former husbands was positively related to several measures of well-being and was inversely related to measures of anxiety and depression (McCullough, 2001). Forgiveness not only decreases one's own psychological distress, it also increases one's empathy and positive regard for the offending person (Williamson & Gonzales, 2007). Interestingly, researchers are beginning to explore some of the potential negative aspects of forgiveness (McNulty, 2011). For instance, could forgiveness relieve an offender of his guilt to the extent that it makes it more likely he will offend again? Although there is more work to be done in this area, findings to date suggest that it may be healthy for people to learn to forgive others more readily.

© Randy Glasbergen

"I'm learning how to relax, doctor—
but I want to relax *better* and *faster*!
I want to be on the cutting edge of relaxation!"

4-5d LEARNING TO MEDITATE AND RELAX

Recent years have seen an increased interest in meditation as a method for regulating negative emotions caused by stress. ***Meditation*** **refers to a family of mental exercises in which a conscious attempt is made to focus attention in a nonanalytical way.** There are many approaches to meditation. In the United States, the most widely practiced approaches are those associated with yoga, Zen, and transcendental meditation (TM).

What are the immediate *physical* effects of going into a meditative state? Most studies find decreases in participants' heart rate, respiration rate, oxygen consumption, and carbon dioxide elimination (Whitehouse, Orne, & Orne, 2007). Taken together, these physical changes suggest that meditation can lead to a potentially beneficial physiological state characterized by relaxation and suppression of arousal.

What about the long-term *psychological* benefits that have been claimed for meditation? Research suggests that meditation may have some value in reducing the effects of stress. In particular, regular meditation is associated with lower levels of some stress hormones (Infante et al., 2001). Research also suggests that meditation can improve mental health while reducing anxiety and drug abuse (Alexander et al., 1994). Other studies report that meditation may have beneficial effects on blood pressure (Barnes, Treiber, & Davis, 2001), self-esteem (Emavardhana & Tori, 1997), mood and one's sense of control (Easterlin & Cardena, 1999), happiness (Smith, Compton, & West, 1995), and overall physical health and well-being (Reibel et al., 2001).

At first glance these results are impressive, but they need to be viewed with some caution. Critics wonder whether placebo effects, sampling bias, and other methodological problems may contribute to some of the reported benefits of meditation (Shapiro et al., 2005). In addition, at least some of these beneficial effects may be just as attainable through other mental focusing procedures, such as systematic relaxation (Shapiro, 1984). Indeed, ample evidence suggests that relaxation procedures can soothe emotional turmoil and reduce stress-induced physiological arousal (Smyth et al., 2001). And one controlled experiment comparing meditation and relaxation found that they decrease distress and increase positive moods equally well (Jain et al., 2007). Thus, simply learning to relax can be a useful strategy for dealing with stress.

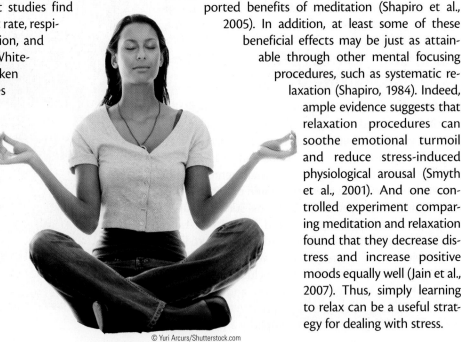

© Yuri Arcurs/Shutterstock.com

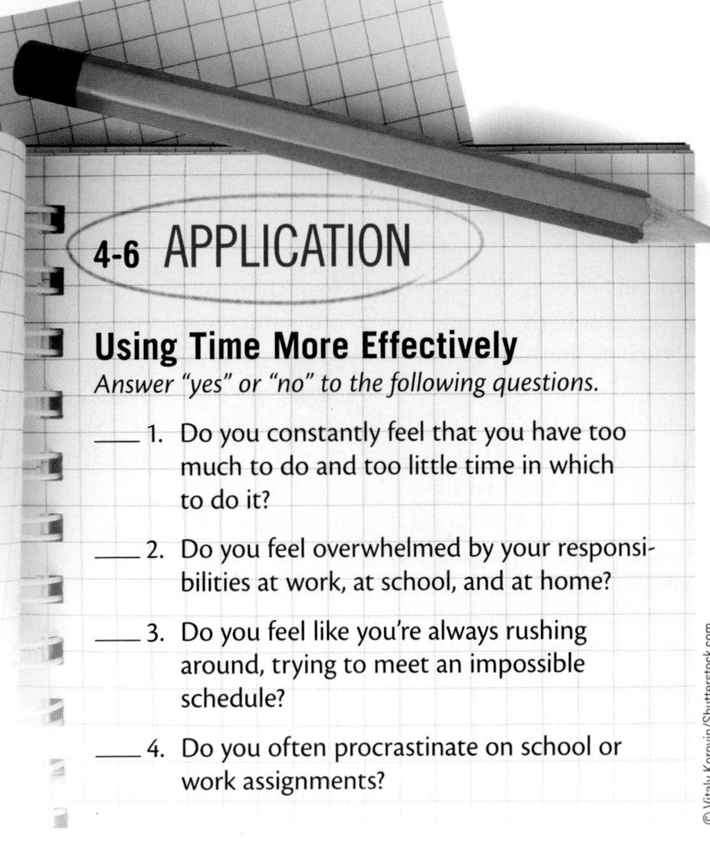

4-6 APPLICATION

Using Time More Effectively

Answer "yes" or "no" to the following questions.

____ 1. Do you constantly feel that you have too much to do and too little time in which to do it?

____ 2. Do you feel overwhelmed by your responsibilities at work, at school, and at home?

____ 3. Do you feel like you're always rushing around, trying to meet an impossible schedule?

____ 4. Do you often procrastinate on school or work assignments?

If you answered yes to the majority of these questions, you're struggling with time pressure, a huge source of stress in modern life. You can estimate how well you manage time by responding to the brief questionnaire in Figure 4.8. If the results suggest that your time is out of your control, you may be able to make your life less stressful by learning sound time-management strategies.

A prominent time-management researcher, R. Alec Mackenzie (1997), points out that time is a nonrenewable resource. It can't be stockpiled like money, food, or other precious resources. You can't turn back the clock. Furthermore, everyone, whether rich or poor, gets an equal share of time—24 hours per day, 7 days a week. Although time is our most equitably distributed resource, some people spend it much more wisely than others. Let's look at some of the ways in which people let time slip through their fingers without accomplishing much.

4-6a THE CAUSES OF WASTED TIME

When people complain about "wasted time," they're usually upset because they haven't accomplished what they really wanted to do with their time. Wasted time is time devoted to unnecessary, unimportant, or unenjoyable activities. There are many reasons people waste time on such activities.

Inability to set or stick to priorities. Time consultant Alan Lakein (1996) emphasizes that it's often tempting

FIGURE 4.8 Assessing your time management

The brief questionnaire shown here is designed to evaluate the quality of one's time management. Although it is geared more for working adults than college students, it should allow you to get a rough handle on how well you manage your time.

HOW WELL DO YOU MANAGE YOUR TIME?

Listed below are ten statements that reflect generally accepted principles of good time management. Answer these items by circling the response most characteristic of how you perform your job. Please be honest. No one will know your answers except you.

1. Each day I set aside a small amount of time for planning and thinking about my job.
0. Almost never 1. Sometimes 2. Often 3. Almost always

2. I set specific, written goals and put deadlines on them.
0. Almost never 1. Sometimes 2. Often 3. Almost always

3. I make a daily "to do list," arrange items in order of importance, and try to get the important items done as soon as possible.
0. Almost never 1. Sometimes 2. Often 3. Almost always

4. I am aware of the 80/20 rule and use it in doing my job. (The 80/20 rule states that 80 percent of your effectiveness will generally come from achieving only 20 percent of your goals.)
0. Almost never 1. Sometimes 2. Often 3. Almost always

5. I keep a loose schedule to allow for crises and the unexpected.
0. Almost never 1. Sometimes 2. Often 3. Almost always

6. I delegate everything I can to others.
0. Almost never 1. Sometimes 2. Often 3. Almost always

7. I try to handle each piece of paper only once.
0. Almost never 1. Sometimes 2. Often 3. Almost always

8. I eat a light lunch so I don't get sleepy in the afternoon.
0. Almost never 1. Sometimes 2. Often 3. Almost always

9. I make an active effort to keep common interruptions (visitors, meetings, telephone calls) from continually disrupting my work day.
0. Almost never 1. Sometimes 2. Often 3. Almost always

10. I am able to say no to others' requests for my time that would prevent my completing important tasks.
0. Almost never 1. Sometimes 2. Often 3. Almost always

To get your score, give yourself

3 points for each "almost always"
2 points for each "often"
1 point for each "sometimes"
0 points for each "almost never"

Add up your points to get your total score. If you scored

0–15 Better give some thought to managing your time.
15–20 You're doing OK, but there's room for improvement.
20–25 Very good.
25–30 You cheated!

Source: From Le Boeuf, M. (1980, February). Managing time means managing yourself. *Business Horizons Magazine, 24*(1), pp. 41–46. Copyright 1980, reprinted with permission from Elsevier.

to deal with routine, trivial tasks ahead of larger and more difficult tasks. Thus, students working on a major paper often check Facebook, fold the laundry, or reorganize their desk instead of concentrating on the paper. Why? Routine tasks are easy, and working on them allows people to rationalize their avoidance of more important tasks. Unfortunately, many of us spend too much time on trivial pursuits, leaving our more important tasks undone.

Inability to say no. Other people are constantly making demands on our time. They want us to exchange gossip in the hallway, go out to dinner on Friday night, cover their hours at work, help with a project, listen to their sales pitch on the phone, join a committee, or coach Little League. Clearly, we can't do everything that everyone wants us to. However, some people just can't say no to others' requests for their time. Such people end up fulfilling others' priorities instead of their own. Thus, McDougle (1987) concludes, "Perhaps the most successful way to prevent yourself from wasting time is by saying *no*" (p. 112).

Inability to delegate responsibility. Some tasks should be delegated to others—assistants, subordinates, fellow committee members, partners, spouses, children, and so on. However, many people have difficulty delegating work. Barriers to delegation include unwillingness to give up any control, lack of confidence in subordinates, fear of being disliked, the need to feel needed, and the attitude that "I can do it better myself" (Mitchell, 1987). The problem, of course, is that people who can't delegate waste a lot of time on others' work.

Inability to throw things away. Some people are pack rats who can't throw anything into the wastebasket. Their desks are cluttered with piles of mail, newspapers, magazines, reports, and books. At home, their kitchen drawers bulge with rarely used utensils and their closets bulge with old clothes that are never worn. Pack rats lose time looking for things that have disappeared among all the chaos and end up reshuffling the same paper, rereading the same mail, resorting the same files, and so on. According to Mackenzie (1997), they would be better off if they made more use of their wastebaskets.

© Ablestock.com/Photos.com

Inability to accept anything less than perfection. High standards are admirable, but some people have difficulty finishing projects because they expect them to be flawless. They dwell on minor problems and keep making microscopic changes in their papers, projects, and proposals. They are caught in what Emanuel (1987) calls the "paralysis of perfection." They end up spinning their wheels, redoing the same work over and over instead of moving on to the next task. Additionally, perfectionism has been linked to procrastination, which we turn to next.

4-6b THE PROBLEM OF PROCRASTINATION

***Procrastination* is the tendency to delay tackling tasks until the last minute.** Almost everyone procrastinates on occasion. However, research suggests that about 20% of adults are chronic procrastinators (Ferrari, 2001). Not just a U.S. phenomenon, this trend appears to apply to a number of cultures (Ferrari et al., 2007). Procrastination is more likely when people have to work on aversive tasks or when they are worried about their performance being evaluated (Senecal, Lavoie, & Koestner, 1997).

Why do people procrastinate? In a review of the literature, Steel (2007) found that procrastination was strongly related to low self-efficacy, low conscientiousness, lack of self-control, poor organization, low achievement motivation, and high distractibility. In addition, perfectionism and the type of irrational thinking described by Albert Ellis seem to foster procrastination (Bridges & Roig, 1997).

Other factors besides personality can affect procrastination. Schraw and colleagues (2007) identified six general principles related to academic procrastination, including these three:

1. *Desire to minimize time on a task.* As you know, for the mod-

ern student, time is at a premium. Sometimes delaying as much academic work as possible seems to be a way to safeguard some personal time. As one student reported, "The truth is, I just don't have time *not* to procrastinate. If I did everything the way it could be done, I wouldn't have a life" (Schraw et al., 2007, p. 21).

2. *Desire to optimize efficiency.* Procrastination can be viewed as allowing one to be optimally efficient, concentrating academic work into focused time frames. Students reported that being pressed for time means that there is less opportunity for busywork, boredom, or false starts.

3. *Close proximity to reward.* Students often procrastinate because they are rewarded for it. By putting off academic work until the last minute, students not only get more immediate feedback (the grade), but they also get a sudden release of stress. In this way, procrastination is similar to other thrill-seeking behaviors.

Although these principles seem reasonable and many people rationalize their delaying tactics by claiming that "I work best under pressure" (Ferrari, 1992), the empirical evidence suggests otherwise. Studies show that procrastination tends to have a negative impact on the quality of task performance (Ferrari, Johnson, & McCown, 1995). In fact, Britton and Tesser (1991) found that time management was a better predictor of college GPA than SAT scores! Another consideration is that waiting until the last minute may make a task more stressful—and while the release of this built-up stress might be exciting, performance often declines under conditions of high stress (as we saw in Chapter 3). Moreover, work quality may not be the only thing that suffers when people procrastinate. Studies indicate that as a deadline looms, procrastinators tend to experience elevated anxiety and increased health problems (Tice & Baumeister, 1997). To avoid these pitfalls, let's discuss some effective ways to manage your time.

4-6c TIME-MANAGEMENT TECHNIQUES

What's the key to better time management? Most people assume that it's increased *efficiency*—that is, learning to perform tasks more quickly. Improved efficiency may help a little, but time-management experts maintain that efficiency is overrated. They emphasize that the key to better time management is increased *effectiveness*—that is, learning to allocate time to your most important tasks. This distinction is captured by a widely quoted slogan in the time-management literature: "Efficiency is doing the job right, while effectiveness is doing the right job." Here are some suggestions for using your time more effectively (based on Lakein, 1996; Mackenzie, 1997; Morgenstern, 2000):

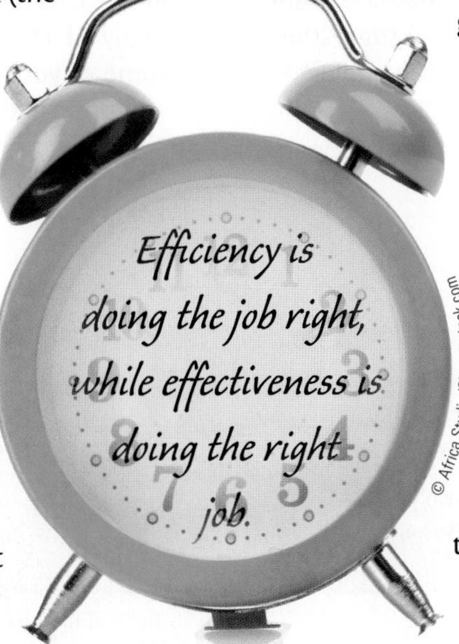
Efficiency is doing the job right, while effectiveness is doing the right job.

© Africa Studio/Shutterstock.com

1. *Monitor your use of time.* The first step toward better time management is to monitor your use of time to see where it all goes. Doing so requires keeping a written record of your daily activities. At the end of a week, you should analyze exactly how your time was allocated. Two weeks of recordkeeping should allow you to draw some conclusions about where your time goes. Your records will help you make informed decisions about reallocating your time. When you begin your time-management program, these records will also give you a baseline for comparison, so that you can see whether your program is working.

2. *Clarify your goals.* You can't wisely allocate your time unless you decide what you want to accomplish. Lakein (1996) suggests that you ask yourself, "What are my lifetime goals?" Write down all the goals you can think of, even relatively frivolous things like going deep-sea fishing or becoming a wine expert. Some of your goals will be in conflict. For instance, you can't become a vice president at your company in Wichita and still move to the West Coast. Thus, the tough part comes next. You have to wrestle with your goal conflicts. Figure out which goals are most important to you, and order them in terms of priority. These priorities should guide you as you plan your activities on a daily, weekly, and monthly basis.

3. *Plan your activities using a schedule.* People resist planning because it takes time, but in the long run planning saves time. Thorough planning is essential to effective time management. At the beginning of each week, you should make a list of short-term goals. This list should be translated into daily "to do" lists of planned activities. To avoid the tendency to put off larger projects, break them into smaller, manageable components, and set deadlines for completing the components. Your planned activities should be allocated to various time slots on a written schedule. Schedule your most

important activities into the time periods when you tend to be most energetic and productive.

4. *Protect your prime time.* The best-laid plans can quickly go awry because of interruptions. There isn't any foolproof way to eliminate interruptions, but you may be able to shift most of them into certain time slots while protecting your most productive time. The trick is to announce to your family, friends, and co-workers that you're blocking off certain periods of "quiet time" when visitors and phone calls will be turned away. Of course, you also have to block off periods of "available time" when you're ready to deal with everyone's problems.

5. *Increase your efficiency.* Although efficiency is not the key to better time management, it's not irrelevant. Time-management experts do offer some suggestions for improving efficiency, including the following (Klassen, 1987; Schilit, 1987):

- *Handle paper once.* When e-mails, letters, reports, and such cross your desk, they should not be stashed away to be read again and again before you deal with them. Most paperwork can and should be dealt with immediately.
- *Tackle one task at a time.* Jumping from one problem to another is inefficient. As much as possible, stick with a task until it's done. In scheduling your activities, try to allow enough time to complete tasks.
- *Group similar tasks together.* It's a good idea to bunch up small tasks that are similar. This strategy is useful when you're paying bills, replying to e-mails, returning phone calls, and so forth.
- *Make use of your down time.* Most of us endure a lot of "down time," waiting in doctors' offices, sitting in needless meetings, or riding on buses and trains. In many of these situations, you may be able to get some of your easier work done—if you think ahead and bring it along.

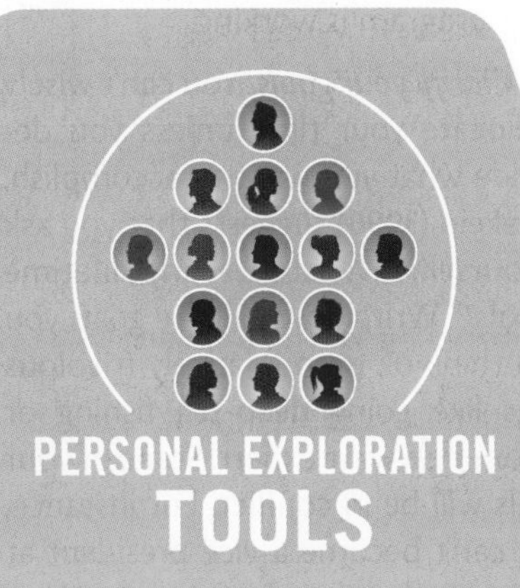

PERSONAL EXPLORATION TOOLS

Curious about yourself? To learn more about how topics in this chapter relate to you, go online to CourseMate at www.cengagebrain.com where you can:

- Complete a **Self-Reflection** exercise that will help you think about your personal experiences in relation to topics in the chapter.
- Take a **Self-Assessment** scale that will show you how you score on a research instrument that measures personality traits or attitudes.
- Explore **Recommended Readings** that will provide brief overviews of useful self-help books.

© edge69/iStockphoto

STUDY TOOLS ▶ 4

Ready to study? In your book you can:

- **Test Yourself** with a multiple-choice quiz (below)
- Rip out the **Chapter Review card** (in the back of the book) to refresh yourself on the chapter's Key Ideas and Key Terms

Or you can go online to CourseMate at www.cengagebrain.com where you can:

- Take additional Practice Quizzes to prepare for your exam
- Review Key Terms with flash cards and a crossword puzzle
- View videos that expand on selected concepts

TEST YOURSELF

1. Suzie responds to stress with fatalism and resignation. She passively accepts setbacks instead of trying to deal with them effectively. She is exhibiting

a. self-indulgence.
b. learned helplessness.
c. displacement.
d. catastrophic thinking.

2. Which of the following assertions is supported by research on the cathartic effects of media violence?

a. Playing violent video games releases pent-up hostility.
b. Playing violent video games is related to increased prosocial behavior.
c. Exposure to media violence desensitizes individuals to violent acts.
d. Exposure to media violence discourages aggressive responses.

3. Richard feels sure that he failed his calculus exam and that he will have to retake the course. He is very upset. When he gets home, he orders a jumbo-size pizza and drinks two six-packs of beer. Richard's behavior illustrates which of the following coping strategies?

a. Self-indulgence
b. Catastrophic thinking
c. Defensive coping
d. Positive reinterpretation

4. Defense mechanisms involve the use of ____________ to guard against negative ________________.

a. self-deception, behaviors
b. self-deception, emotions
c. self-denial, behaviors
d. self-denial, emotions

5. Taylor and Brown found that nondepressed people's self-images tend to be ________________; depressed people's tend to be ________________.

a. accurate, inaccurate
b. less favorable, more favorable
c. overly favorable, more realistic
d. more realistic, overly favorable

6. According to Albert Ellis, people's emotional reactions to life events result mainly from

a. their arousal level at the time.
b. their beliefs about events.
c. congruence between events and expectations.
d. the consequences following events.

7. Wanda works at a software firm. Today her boss unfairly blamed her for the fact that a new program is behind schedule. The unjustified public criticism really had an impact on Wanda. That evening, she went to a meditation class to get her anger under control. Wanda is engaging in which category of coping?

a. Self-focused coping
b. Appraisal-focused coping
c. Problem-focused coping
d. Emotion-focused coping

8. Ken and Connie are trying to solve a financial problem. Together they generate as many ideas as possible while withholding criticism and evaluation. They are engaging in

a. brainstorming
b. emotional intelligence
c. positive reinterpretation
d. emotion-focused coping

9. Research by James Pennebaker and his colleagues suggests that wellness is promoted by

a. depending on more mature defense mechanisms.
b. strong self-criticism.
c. writing about one's traumatic experiences.
d. inhibiting the expression of anger.

10. Which of the following is discussed in your text as a cause of wasted time?

a. Inability to procrastinate
b. Inability to work diligently
c. Inability to dwell on minor problems
d. Inability to throw things away

Answers: 1. b, page 70; 2. c, page 71; 3. a, pages 71–72; 4. b, pages 73–74; 5. c, page 74; 6. b, pages 76–77; 7. d, page 84; 8. a, page 80; 9. c, page 82; 10. d, pages 85–86

© Cultura RM/Masterfile

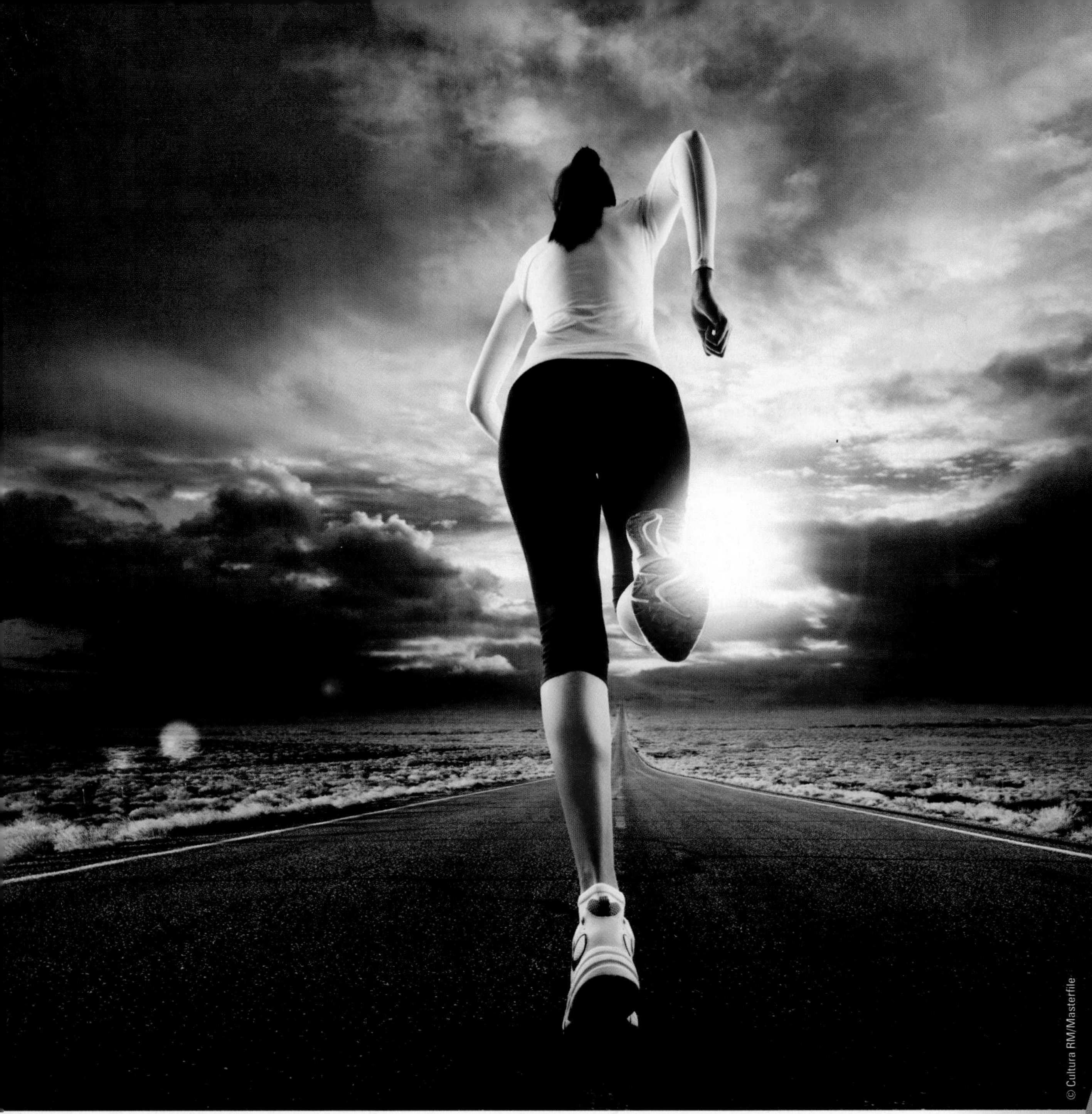

LEARNING OBJECTIVES

5-1 Explain how stressful events and certain personality traits can promote either health or disease.

5-2 Describe ways that people's good habits can foster well-being and bad habits can compromise health.

5-3 Discuss the distinct psychological effects of various recreational drugs, as well as their physical and psychological risks.

5-4 Identify factors influencing decisions to seek medical treatment, the quality of doctor-patient communication, and compliance with medical recommendations.

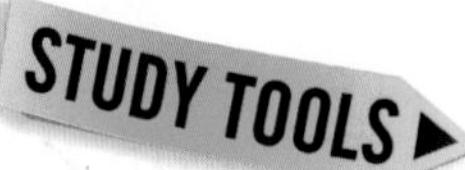

STUDY TOOLS ▶ After you have read the chapter, you can Test Yourself and learn about other Study Tools on page 113.

CHAPTER 5

Psychology and PHYSICAL HEALTH

© Photo_Concepts/iStockphoto

© GeoM/Shutterstock.com

Janet carries a full course load, works a part-time job, and plans to pursue a challenging career in nursing. She hopes to work in a hospital for a few years before enrolling in graduate school. Right now, however, her life is regulated by work: homework, her job, and course-related work in the wards of a teaching hospital. In a typical semester, Janet feels in control for the first few weeks, but then her work piles up: tests, papers, reading, appointments, labs, and so on. Instead of getting eight full hours of sleep, she often does with much less. Fast food becomes a familiar and necessary comfort. She can't jog or get to the gym as much as she'd like. On the rare occasion she does take a break, it tends to involve watching television, catching up with friends on Facebook, or texting with her boyfriend, who attends another school. By the end of the term, she is anxious, stressed, tired, and run down. In fact, she usually celebrates the end of the semester by getting sick instead of having relaxing times with her friends and family. This unfortunate cycle repeats itself the next semester.

Are you at all like Janet? How often do you become ill in a typical semester? Do you begin strong and healthy but feel worn out and frayed by the end? If you are like many students, your lifestyle has a close connection to your health and well-being.

More than any other time in history, people's health is likely to be compromised by *chronic diseases*—conditions that develop across many years—rather than by *contagious diseases*, those caused by specific infectious agents (such as measles, flu, or tuberculosis). Moreover, lifestyle and stress play a much larger role in the development of chronic diseases than they do in contagious diseases. Today, the three leading chronic diseases (heart disease, cancer, and stroke) account for almost 54% of all deaths in the United States, and these mortality statistics reveal only the tip of the iceberg. Psychological and social factors also contribute to many other, less serious maladies, such as headaches, insomnia, backaches, skin disorders, asthma, and ulcers.

Traditionally, illness has been thought of as a purely biological phenomenon produced by an infectious agent or some internal physical breakdown in the body. In contrast, the ***biopsychosocial* model holds that physical illness is caused by a complex interaction of biological, psychological, and sociocultural factors.** This model does not suggest that biological factors are unimportant. Rather, it simply asserts that biological factors operate in a psychosocial context that can also be highly influential. Medical and psychological professionals who adhere to the biopsychosocial model also focus on other factors, including cultural values. Figure 5.1 on the next page illustrates how the three sets of factors in the biospsychosocial model affect one another and, in turn, health.

The growing recognition that psychological factors influence physical health led to the development of a new specialty within psychology. ***Health psychology* is concerned with how psychosocial factors relate to the promotion and maintenance of health and with the causation, prevention, and treatment of illness.** In this chapter we focus on the rapidly growing domain of health psychology. The chapter's first section analyzes how stress and personality are related to health and illness. The second section examines common health-impairing habits, such as smoking and overeating. The third section expands on one particular type of health-impairing habit: the use of recreational drugs. The Application discusses how people's reactions to illness can affect their health.

FIGURE 5.1 | The biopsychosocial model

Whether one's health is good or bad, the biopsychosocial model assumes that health is not just the result of biological processes. According to this increasingly influential view, one's physical health depends on interactions between biolgical factors, psychological factors, and social system factors. Some key factors in each category are depicted here.

5-1 Stress, Personality, and Illness

What does it mean to say that personality can affect wellness? A guiding assumption is that a person's characteristic demeanor can influence his or her physical health. As noted in Chapter 2, personality is made up of the unique grouping of behavioral traits that a person exhibits consistently across situations. Thus, an individual who is chronically grumpy, often hostile toward others, and routinely frustrated is more likely to develop an illness and perhaps even to die earlier than someone who is emotionally open, is friendly, and leads a balanced life (Friedman, 2007). Of course, the link between personality and disease is somewhat more complex but nonetheless real. We begin with a look at heart disease, far and away the leading cause of death in North America.

5-1a PERSONALITY, EMOTIONS, AND HEART DISEASE

Heart disease accounts for nearly 25% of the deaths in the United States every year. ***Coronary heart disease*** **results from a reduction in blood flow through the coronary arteries, which supply the heart with blood.** This type of heart disease causes about 90% of heart-related deaths. Atherosclerosis is the principal cause of coronary disease (Giannoglou et al., 2008). ***Atherosclerosis*** **is a gradual narrowing of the coronary arteries,** usually caused by a buildup of fatty deposits and other debris on the inner walls (see Figure 5.2). Narrowed coronary arteries may eventually lead to situations in which the heart is temporarily deprived of adequate blood flow, causing a condition known as *myocardial ischemia.* This ischemia may be accompanied by brief chest pain, called *angina.* If a coronary artery is blocked completely (by a blood clot, for instance), the abrupt interruption of blood flow can produce a full-fledged heart attack, or *myocardial infarction.* Established risk factors for coronary disease include smoking, diabetes, high cholesterol levels, and high blood pressure (Greenland et al., 2003).

Contrary to public perception, cardiovascular diseases kill women just as much as men (Liewer et al., 2008), but these diseases tend to emerge in women about 10 years later than in men. Interestingly, when women reach menopause—usually around age 50—they have a higher risk of heart disease than men (Mattar et al., 2008).

Hostility and Coronary Risk

In the 1960s and 1970s a pair of cardiologists, Meyer Friedman and Ray Rosenman (1974), were investigating the causes of coronary disease. Originally, they were interested in the usual factors thought to produce a high risk of heart attack: smoking, obesity, physical inactivity, and so forth. Although they found these factors to be important, they eventually recognized that a piece of the puzzle was missing. Many people who smoked constantly, got little exercise, and were severely overweight still managed to avoid the ravages of heart disease. Meanwhile, others who seemed to be in much better shape with regard to these risk factors experienced the misfortune of a heart attack. What was their explanation for these perplexing findings? Stress!

FIGURE 5.2 Atherosclerosis

Atherosclerosis, a narrowing of the coronary arteries, is the principal cause of coronary disease. (a) A normal artery. (b) Fatty deposits, cholesterol, and cellular debris on the walls of the artery have narrowed the path for blood flow. (c) Advanced atherosclerosis. In this situation, a blood clot might suddenly block the flow of blood through the artery.

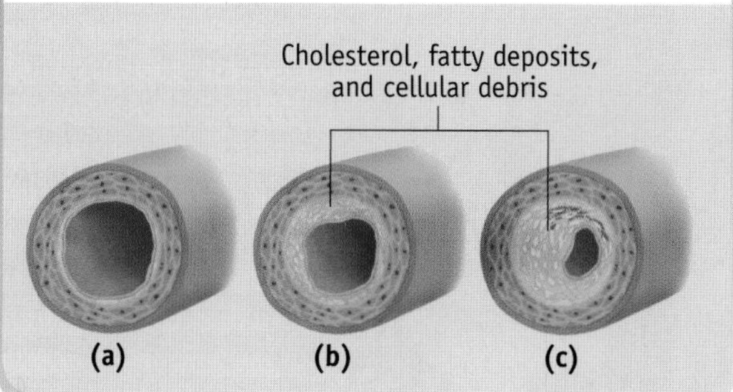

© Cengage Learning

FIGURE 5.3 Anger and coronary risk

Working with a large sample of healthy men and women who were followed for a median of 4.5 years, Williams et al. (2000) found an association between trait anger and the likelihood of a coronary event. Among subjects who displayed normal blood pressure at the study's beginning, a moderate anger level was associated with a 36% increase in coronary attacks, and a high level of anger nearly tripled participants' risk for coronary disease.

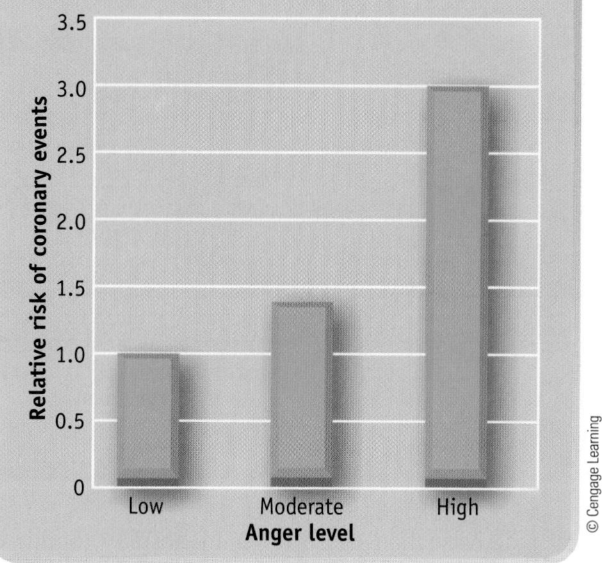

© Cengage Learning

Specifically, they identified an apparent connection between coronary risk and a pattern of behavior they called the *Type A personality,* which involves self-imposed stress and intense reactions to stress (Allan, 2011).

Friedman and Rosenman divided people into two basic types. **The *Type A personality* includes three elements: (1) a strong competitive orientation, (2) impatience and time urgency, and (3) anger and hostility.** In contrast, **the *Type B personality* is marked by relatively relaxed, patient, easygoing, amicable behavior.** Type A's are ambitious, hard-driving perfectionists who are exceedingly time conscious. They routinely try to do several things at once. They fidget frantically over the briefest delays, are concerned with numbers, and often focus on the acquisition of material objects. Easily aggravated and quick to anger, they tend to be highly competitive, achievement-oriented workaholics who drive themselves with many deadlines. In contrast, Type B's are less hurried, less competitive, and less easily angered than Type A's.

Decades of research uncovered a tantalizingly modest correlation between Type A behavior and increased coronary risk. However, in recent years, researchers have found a stronger link between personality and coronary risk by focusing on a specific component of the Type A personality: anger and hostility (Myrtek, 2007). ***Hostility* refers to a persistent negative attitude marked by cynical, mistrusting thoughts, feelings of anger, and overtly aggressive actions.** In one study of almost 13,000 men and women who had no prior history of heart disease (Williams et al., 2000), investigators found an elevated incidence of heart attacks among participants who exhibited an angry temperament. The participants, who were followed for a median period of 4.5 years, were classified as being low (37.1%), moderate (55.2%), or high (7.7%) in anger. Among participants with normal blood pressure, the high-anger subjects experienced almost three times as many coronary events as the low-anger subjects (see Figure 5.3).

Why are anger and hostility associated with coronary risk? Research suggests a number of possible explanations (see Figure 5.4 on the next page). First, anger-prone individuals appear to exhibit greater physiologi-

© Alex James Bramwell/Shutterstock.com

FIGURE 5.4 Mechanisms that may link hostility and anger to heart disease

Explanations for the apparent link between cynical hostility and heart disease are many and varied. Four widely discussed possibilities are summarized in the middle column of this diagram.

Cynical hostility and anger

Greater physiological reactivity in response to stress may cause wear and tear in cardiovascular system.

Exposure to self-imposed stress may be high because hostility and anger lead to interpersonal difficulties.

Hostility may undermine social support from others that might buffer the effects of stress.

Cynicism might lead to poor health habits, such as lack of exercise, excessive consumption of fast foods, or denial of symptoms.

Increased incidence of coronary heart disease

cal reactivity than those lower in hostility (Smith & Gallo, 1999). The frequent ups and downs in heart rate and blood pressure may create wear and tear in their cardiovascular systems.

Second, hostile people probably create additional stress for themselves (Smith, 2006). For example, their quick anger may provoke many arguments and conflicts with others. Consistent with this line of thinking, Smith and colleagues (1988) found that subjects high in hostility reported more hassles, more negative life events, more marital conflict, and more work-related stress than subjects who were lower in hostility.

Third, thanks to their antagonistic ways of relating to others, hostile individuals tend to have less social support than others (Chen, Gilligan, & Coups, 2005). Williams (1996), for example, found that single people or those who had no close friend to share private thoughts and concerns with were three times more likely to die in a five-year period after their original heart attack than those who had either a spouse or a close friend.

Fourth, perhaps because of their cynicism, people high in anger and hostility seem to exhibit a higher prevalence of poor health habits that may contribute to the development of cardiovascular disease. People high in hostility are more likely to smoke, drink alcohol and coffee, and be overweight than others (Everson et al., 1997).

Emotional Reactions and Heart Disease

Although work on personality risk factors has dominated research on how psychological functioning contributes to heart disease, recent studies suggest that emotional reactions may also be critical. *One line of research has supported the hypothesis that transient mental stress and the resulting emotions that people experience can tax the heart.* Laboratory experiments with cardiology patients have shown that brief periods of mental stress can trigger acute symptoms of heart disease, such as myocardial ischemia and angina (Gottdiener et al., 1994). Related research considers the impact of holding back or suppressing emotions, particularly anger. Ironically, perhaps, keeping negative emotions to oneself is potentially more harmful than expressing anger toward others (Jorgensen & Kolodziej, 2007). Learning to recognize one's impending emotional state, such as feeling angry, but then expressing the emotion as calmly and rationally as possible may be a healthier response (Siegman, 1994),

Depression and Heart Disease

Another line of research has recently implicated depression as a major risk factor for heart disease. *Depressive disorders*, which are characterized by persistent feelings of sadness and despair, are a fairly common form of psychological disorder (see Chapter 14). Many studies have found elevated rates of depression among patients with heart disease, but most theorists have explained this correlation by asserting that being diagnosed with heart disease makes people depressed. However, some

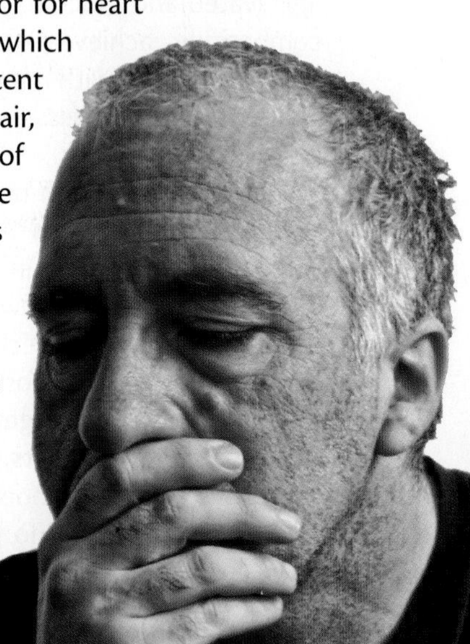

studies suggest that the causal relation may also flow in the opposite direction—*that the emotional dysfunction of depression may cause heart disease.* For example, Pratt and colleagues (1996) examined people 13 years after they were screened for depression. Participants who had been depressed at the time of the original study were four times more likely than others to experience a heart attack during the intervening 13 years. Because the participants' depressive disorders preceded their heart attacks, one cannot argue that heart disease caused their depression. Overall, studies suggest that depression roughly doubles one's chances of developing heart disease (Lett et al., 2004).

5-1b STRESS AND CANCER

People generally view *cancer* as the most sinister, tragic, frightening, and unbearable of diseases. In reality, cancer is actually a *collection* of over 200 related diseases that vary in their characteristics and amenability to treatment (Nezu et al., 2003). ***Cancer* refers to malignant cell growth, which may occur in many organ systems in the body.** The core problem in cancer is that cells begin to reproduce in a rapid, disorganized fashion. As this reproduction process lurches out of control, the teeming new cells clump together to form tumors. If this wild growth continues unabated, the spreading tumors cause tissue damage and begin to interfere with normal functioning in the affected organ systems.

Although the findings are complicated, evidence indicates that stress and cancer are connected (Baum, Trevino, & Dougall 2011). A careful meta-analysis of 165 independent studies revealed unequivocally that stress-related psychosocial variables are associated with cancer (Chida et al., 2008). The study demonstrated that higher stress predicted higher rates of the disease in initially healthy populations, lower survival rates among individuals diagnosed with cancer, and higher cancer mortality in general.

Although research has linked psychological factors to the *onset* of cancer, there is even more evidence that stress and personality influence the *course* of the disease. Patients typically have to grapple with fear of the unknown; difficult and aversive treatment regimens; nausea, fatigue, and other treatment side effects; interruptions in intimate relationships; career disruptions; job discrimination; and financial worries. Moreover, depression can become a problem among cancer patients during active treatment (Reich, Lesur, & Perdrizet-Chevallier, 2008. The impact of all this stress may depend in part on one's personality. Research suggests that mortality rates are somewhat higher among patients who respond with depression, repressive coping, and other negative emotions (Friedman, 1991). In contrast, prospects appear to be better for patients who can maintain their emotional stability and enthusiasm. Of course, all the data linking psychosocial factors to cancer are correlational. and there is some debate about the causal processes at work (Tez & Tez, 2008).

5-1c STRESS AND OTHER DISEASES

The development of questionnaires to measure life stress has allowed researchers to look for correlations between stress and a variety of diseases. Among infectious diseases, stress has been clearly implicated in development of the common cold (Cohen, 2005). The typical research paradigm is to intentionally inoculate healthy volunteers with cold viruses, keep them under quarantine (in separate hotel rooms), and then observe who comes down with a cold. People reporting higher levels of stress are more likely to become ill. What about more chronic diseases? Zautra and Smith (2001) found an association between life stress and the course of rheumatoid arthritis. Other researchers have connected stress to lower back pain (Lampe et al., 1998), the occurrence of asthmatic reactions (Chen & Miller, 2007), periodontal disease (Marcenes & Sheiham, 1992), irritable bowel syndrome (Blanchard & Keefer, 2003), and peptic ulcers (Levenstein, 2002).

Why should stress increase the risk for so many kinds of illness? A partial answer may lie in immune functioning.

5-1d STRESS AND IMMUNE FUNCTIONING

The apparent link between stress and many types of illness probably reflects the fact that stress can undermine the body's immune functioning. **The *immune response* is the body's defensive reaction to invasion by bacteria, viral agents, or other foreign substances.**

The human immune response works to protect the body from many forms of disease.

Studies have related stress to suppressed immune activity in humans. In one study, medical students provided researchers with blood samples so that their immune response could be assessed at various points (Kiecolt-Glaser et al., 1984). The students provided the baseline sample a month before final exams and contributed the "high-stress" sample on the first day of their finals. The subjects also responded to the Social Readjustment Rating Scale (SRRS; see Chapter 3) as a measure of recent stress. Reduced levels of immune activity were found during the extremely stressful finals week. Reduced immune activity was also correlated with higher scores on the SRRS.

Chronic illnesses can have a negative impact on immune function (Nelson et al., 2008), and the presence of stress can undermine people's ability to deal with these illnesses (Fang et al., 2008). In a thorough review of 30 years of research on stress and immunity, Segerstrom and Miller (2004) conclude that chronic stress can reduce both *cellular immune responses* (which attack intracellular pathogens, such as viruses) and *humoral immune responses* (which attack extracellular pathogens, such as bacteria). They also report that the *duration* of a stressful event is a key factor determining its impact on immune function. Long-lasting stressors, such as caring for a seriously ill spouse or enduring unemployment for months, are associated with greater immune suppression than relatively brief stressors (Cohen et al., 1998). Unfortunately, too, evidence suggests that in the face of stress, people's immune systems do not fight off illness as well as they grow older (Graham, Christian, & Kiecolt-Glaser, 2006).

5-1e CONCLUSIONS

A wealth of evidence suggests that stress influences physical health. However, virtually all of the relevant research is correlational, so it cannot demonstrate conclusively that stress *causes* illness (Smith & Gallo, 2001). The association between stress and illness could be due to a third variable. Perhaps some aspect of personality or some type of physiological predisposition makes people overly prone to interpret events as stressful *and* overly prone to interpret unpleasant physical sensations as symptoms of illness (see Figure 5.5). Moreover, critics of this research note that many of the studies used research designs that may have inflated the apparent link between stress and illness (Schwarzer & Schulz, 2003). Alternatively, stress may simply alter health-related behaviors, increasing the incidence of "bad habits"—such as smoking, drinking alcohol, using illegal drugs, and ignoring sleep needs—all of which increase people's risk for diseases and disrupt their immunity (Segerstrom & Miller, 2004).

FIGURE 5.5 | The stress/illness correlation

Based on the evidence as a whole, most health psychologists would probably accept the assertion that stress often contributes to the causation of illness. However, some critics argue that the stress-illness correlation could reflect other causal processes. One or more aspects of personality, physiology, or memory might contribute to the correlation between high stress and a high incidence of illness.

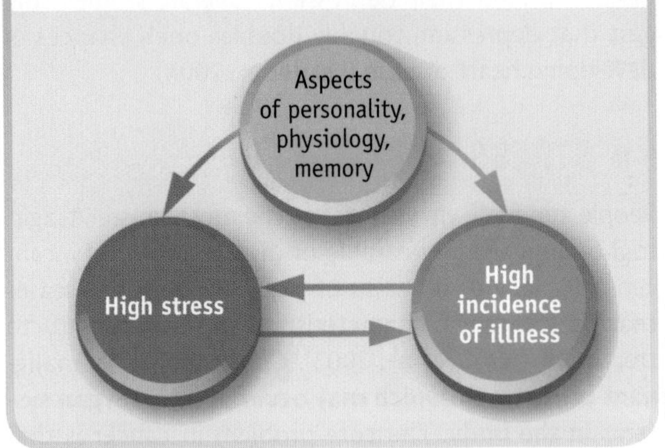

Despite methodological problems favoring inflated correlations, the research in this area consistently indicates that the *strength* of the relationship between stress and health is modest. The correlations typically fall in the .20s and .30s (Cohen, Kessler, & Gordon, 1995). Clearly, stress is not an irresistible force that produces inevitable effects on health. A complex network of biopsychosocial factors influence health, including genetic endowment, exposure to infectious agents and environmental toxins, and the choices people make in daily life. In the next section we look at some of these factors as we examine health-impairing habits and lifestyles.

5-2 Habits, Lifestyles, and Health

Some people seem determined to dig an early grave for themselves. They do precisely those things they have been warned are particularly bad for their health. For example, some people drink heavily even though they know they're corroding their liver. Others eat all the wrong foods even though they know they're increasing their risk for a heart attack. Unfortunately, health-impairing habits contribute to far more deaths than most people realize. In a recent analysis of the causes of death in the United States, Mokdad and colleagues (2004) estimate that unhealthy behaviors are responsible for about half of all deaths each year. The habits that account for the most premature mortality, by far, are smoking, poor diet, and physical inactivity. Other leading behavioral causes of death include alcohol consumption, unsafe driving, sexually transmitted diseases, and illicit drug use.

It may seem puzzling that people behave in self-destructive ways. Why do they do it? Several factors are involved. First, many health-impairing habits creep up on people slowly. For instance, drug use may grow imperceptibly over years, or exercise habits may decline ever so gradually. Second, many health-impairing habits involve activities that are quite pleasant at the time. Actions such as eating favorite foods, smoking cigarettes, and getting "high" are potent reinforcing events. Third, the risks associated with most health-impairing habits are chronic diseases such as cancer that usually take 10, 20, or 30 years to develop. It is relatively easy to ignore risks that lie in the distant future.

People have a tendency to underestimate the risks associated with their own health-impairing habits while viewing the risks associated with others' self-destructive behaviors much more accurately.

©FotografiaBasica/iStockphoto

Fourth, it appears that *people have a tendency to underestimate the risks associated with their own health-impairing habits* while viewing the risks associated with others' self-destructive behaviors much more accurately (Weinstein, 2003). In other words, most people are aware of the dangers associated with certain habits, but they often engage in *denial* when it is time to apply this information to themselves. Thus, some people exhibit ***unrealistic optimism*** **wherein they are aware that certain health-related behaviors are dangerous, but they erroneously view those dangers as risks for others rather than themselves.** In effect, they say to themselves "bad things may well happen to other people, but not to me" (Gold, 2008). In the context of taking health risks and engaging in unwise behavior, unrealistic optimism may prevent people from taking appropriate precautions to protect their physical and mental well-being (Waters et al., 2011).

Yet another problem is that people are exposed to a great deal of conflicting information about what's healthy and what isn't. It seems like every week a report in the media claims that yesterday's standard health advice has been contradicted by new research. This apparent inconsistency confuses people and undermines their motivation to pursue healthy habits. Sometimes it seems that health and happiness are more a matter of luck than anything else. In reality, the actions individuals take and the self-control they exercise can matter a great deal.

In this section we discuss how health is affected by smoking, drinking, overeating and obesity, and lack of exercise. We also look at behavioral factors that relate to AIDS. The health risks of recreational drug use are covered in the next section.

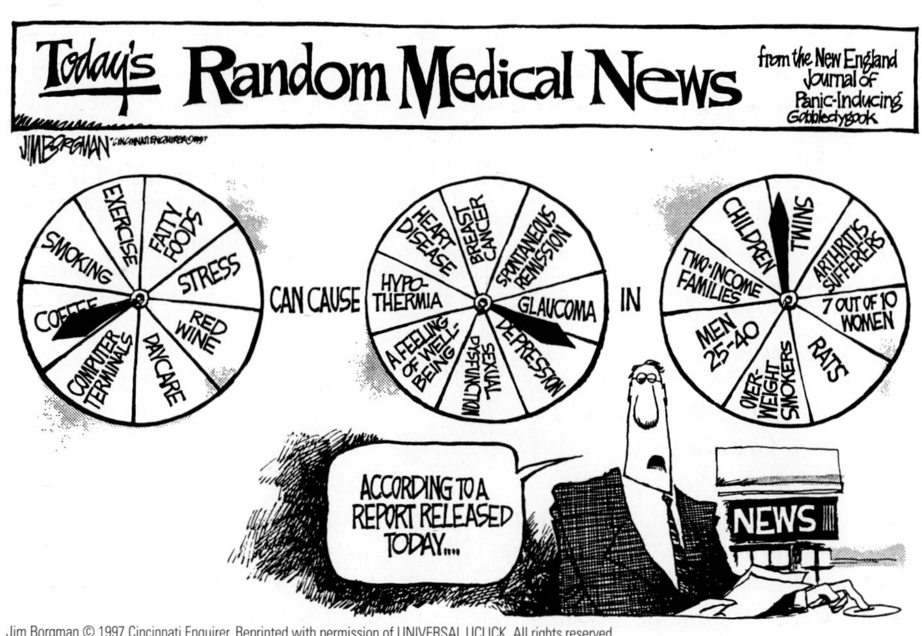

5-2a SMOKING

Why do people smoke? Smokers claim that cigarettes elevate their mood, suppress hunger pangs (which they believe helps them stay thin), and enhances alertness and attention. The percentage of people who smoke has declined noticeably since the mid-1960s. Nonetheless, about 24% of adult men and 18% of adult women in the United States continue to smoke regularly. Smoking among college-aged students has dropped from close to 30% to just under 20% (Harris, Schwartz, & Thompson, 2008). Unfortunately, smoking is even more common in many other countries.

Health Effects

Accumulating evidence clearly shows that smokers face a much greater risk of premature death than nonsmokers. For example, the average smoker has an estimated life expectancy *13–14 years shorter* than that of a similar nonsmoker (Schmitz & Delaune, 2005). The overall risk is positively correlated with the number of cigarettes smoked and their tar and nicotine content. Cigar smoking, which has increased dramatically in recent years, elevates health risks almost as much as cigarette smoking (Baker et al., 2000).

Why are mortality rates higher for smokers? Smoking increases the likelihood of developing a surprisingly large range of diseases, as you can see in Figure 5.6 (Schmitz & Delaune, 2005). Lung cancer and heart disease kill the largest number of smokers; in fact, smokers are almost twice as likely to succumb to cardiovascular disease as nonsmokers are. Smokers also have an elevated risk for oral, bladder, and kidney cancer, as well as cancers of the larynx, esophagus, and pancreas; for atherosclerosis, hypertension, stroke, and other cardiovascular diseases; and for bronchitis, emphysema, and other pulmonary diseases (U.S. Department of Health and Human Services, 2004). Most smokers know about the risks associated with tobacco use, but they tend to underestimate the actual risks as applied to themselves. At the same time, they overestimate the likelihood they can quit smoking when they want to (Weinstein, Slovic, & Gibson, 2004).

Giving Up Smoking

Studies show that if people can give up smoking, their health risks decline reasonably quickly (Kenfield et al., 2008). Five years after people stop smoking, their health risk is already noticeably lower than that for people who continue to smoke. The health risks for people who give up tobacco continue to decline until they reach a normal level after about 15 years. Evidence suggests that 70% of smokers would like to quit, but they are reluctant to give up a major source of pleasure and worry about craving cigarettes, gaining weight, becoming anxious and irritable, and feeling less able to cope with stress (Grunberg, Faraday, & Rahman, 2001).

Research shows that long-term success rates for efforts to quit smoking

FIGURE 5.6 Health risks associated with smoking

This figure provides an overview of the various diseases that are more common among smokers than nonsmokers. As you can see, tobacco elevates one's vulnerability to a remarkably diverse array of diseases, including the three leading causes of death in the modern world: heart attack, cancer, and stroke.

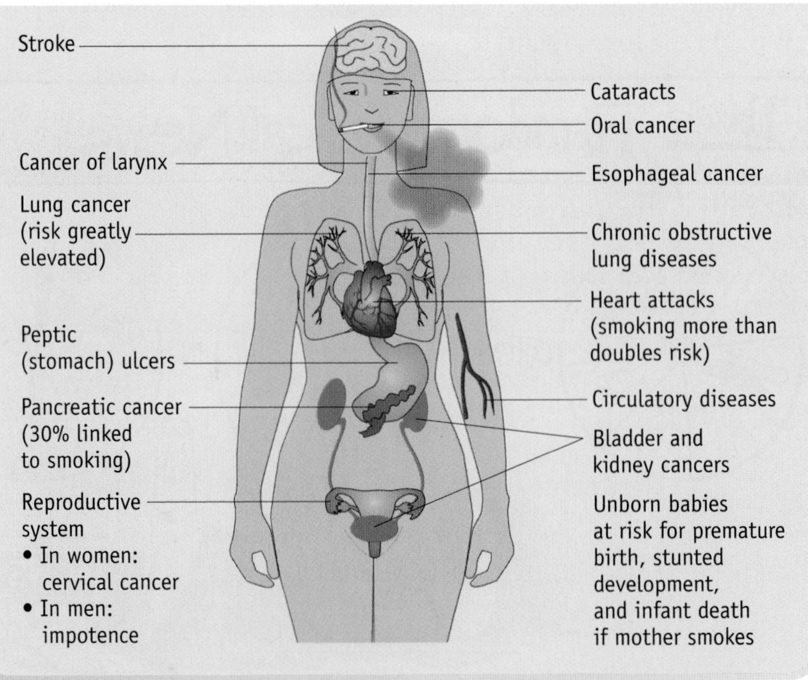

Source: From Hoeger, W. W. K., and Hafen, B. Q. (1998). *Wellness* (2nd ed.). Belmont, CA: Wadsworth. © 1998 Cengage Learning.

are in the vicinity of only 25% (Cohen et al., 1989). Discouragingly, people who enroll in formal smoking cessation programs are only slightly more successful than people who try to quit on their own (Swan, Hudman, & Khroyan, 2003). In fact, it is estimated that the vast majority of people who successfully give up smoking quit on their own, without professional help (Niaura & Abrams, 2002).

In recent years attention has focused on the potential value of *nicotine substitutes,* which can be delivered via gum, pills like Chantix, skin patches, nasal sprays, or inhalers. The rationale for nicotine substitutes is that insofar as nicotine is addictive, using a substitute might be helpful during the period when the person is trying to give up cigarettes. Controlled studies have demonstrated that nicotine substitutes increase long-term rates of quitting in comparison to placebos (Swan, Hudman, & Khroyan, 2003). However, the increases are modest, and the success rates are still discouragingly low.

5-2b DRINKING

Alcohol rivals tobacco as one of the leading causes of health problems in North America. Alcohol encompasses a variety of beverages containing ethyl alcohol, such as beers, wines, and distilled spirits. The concentration of alcohol in these drinks varies from about 4% in most beers up to 40% in 80-proof liquor (or more in higher-proof liquors). Survey data indicate that about half of adults in the United States drink. Figure 5.7 shows the percentage of adults in the United States who are regular, infrequent, or former drinkers.

Drinking is particularly prevalent on college campuses. When researchers from the Harvard School of Public Health surveyed nearly 11,000 undergraduates at 119 schools, they found that 81% of the students drank (Wechsler et al., 2002). Moreover, 49% of the men and 41% of the women reported that they engage in binge drinking with the intention of getting drunk, and 40% of college students report drinking five or more alcoholic drinks at one sitting at least monthly (Johnston et al., 2009). Perhaps most telling, college students spend far more money on alcohol ($5.5 billion annually) than they do on their books.

Alcohol rivals tobacco as one of the leading causes of health problems in North America.

©stockcam/iStockphoto

FIGURE 5.7 Types of adult drinkers in the United States

Just over 60% of adults in the United States categorize themselves as current drinkers. About one-quarter of all adults are lifelong abstainers.

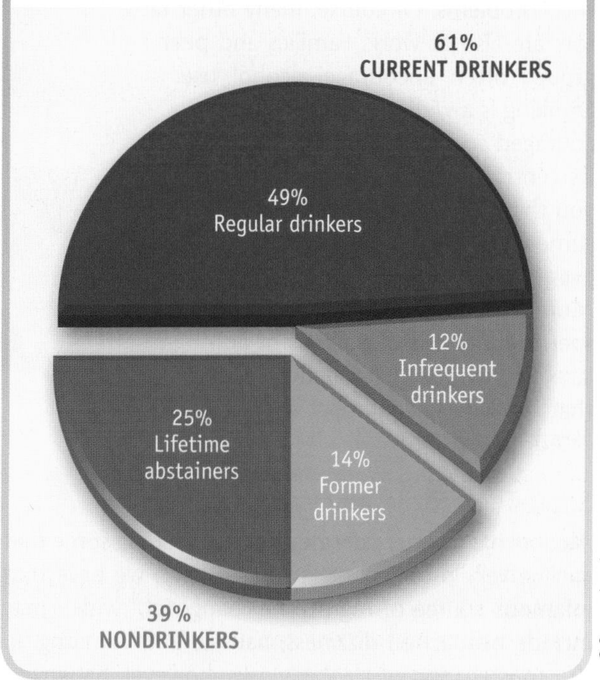

© Cengage Learning

Source: Adapted from *Healthy United States, 2007* (Table 68), 2007, by National Center for Health Statistics, Hyattsville, MD: U.S. Government Printing Office.

Why Do People Drink?

The effects of alcohol are influenced by the user's experience, relative size and weight, gender, motivation, and mood, as well as by the presence of food in the stomach, the proof of the beverage, and the rate of drinking. Thus, we see great variability in how alcohol affects different people on different occasions. Nonetheless, the central effect is a "Who cares?" brand of euphoria that

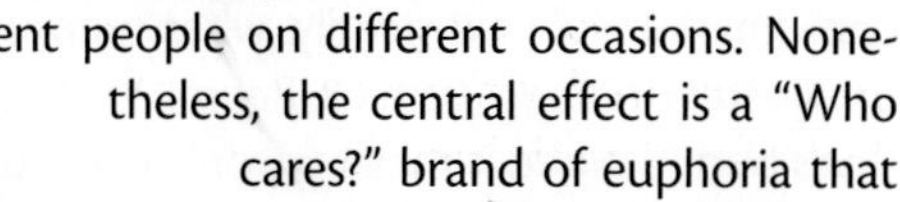

© Yuri Arcurs/Shutterstock.com

temporarily boosts self-esteem as one's problems melt away. Negative emotions such as tension, worry, anxiety, and depression are dulled, and inhibitions may be loosened (Johnson & Ait-Daoud, 2005). Thus, when first-year college students are asked why they drink, they say it's to relax, to feel less tense in social situations, to keep friends company, and to forget their problems. Of course, many other factors are also at work. Families and peer groups often encourage alcohol use. Drinking is a widely endorsed and encouraged social ritual in our culture. Its central role is readily apparent if you think about all the alcohol consumed at weddings, reunions, sports events, holiday parties, and so forth. Moreover, the alcohol industry spends hundreds of millions of dollars on advertising to convince us that drinking is cool, sexy, sophisticated, and harmless.

© DmitriMaruta/Shutterstock

Short-Term Risks and Problems

Alcohol has a variety of side effects, including some that can be very problematic. To begin with, we have that infamous source of regret, the "hangover," which may include headaches, dizziness, nausea, and vomiting. In the constellation of alcohol's risks, however, hangovers are downright trivial. For instance, life-threatening overdoses are more common than most people realize. Although it's possible to overdose with alcohol alone, a more common problem is overdosing on combinations of alcohol and sedative or narcotic drugs.

In substantial amounts, alcohol has a decidedly negative effect on intellectual functioning and perceptual-motor coordination. The resulting combination of tainted judgment, slowed reaction time, and reduced coordination can be deadly when people attempt to drive after drinking (Gmel & Rehm, 2003). Depending on one's body weight, it may take only a few drinks for driving to be impaired. It's estimated that alcohol contributes to 40% of all automobile fatalities in the United States (Yi et al., 2006). Drunk driving is a major social problem and the leading cause of death in young adults.

With their inhibitions released, some drinkers become argumentative and prone to aggression. In the Harvard survey of undergraduates from 119 schools, 29% of the students who did *not* engage in binge drinking reported that they had been insulted or humiliated by a drunken student; 19% had experienced serious arguments; 9% had been pushed, hit, or assaulted; and 19.5% had been the target of unwanted sexual advances (Wechsler et al., 2002). Worse yet, alcohol appears to contribute to about

FIGURE 5.8 | Detecting a drinking problem

Facing the reality that one has a problem with alcohol is always difficult. This list of the chief warning signs associated with problem drinking is intended to help with this process.

IDENTIFYING AN ALCOHOL PROBLEM

You may have a drinking problem if:

- You drink in secret.
- You feel worried about your drinking.
- You routinely consume more alcohol than you expected.
- You experience "black outs" so that you forget what you did or said while drinking.
- You hear concern expressed by family and friends about your drinking.
- You cover up or lie about how often, and how much, you drink alcohol.
- You feel ashamed about your drinking.
- You get into arguments with those close to you about your drinking.

You may be abusing alcohol if:

- You frequently consume alcohol to deal with stress or worry.
- You know your drinking is harming your personal relationships, but you continue to drink anyway.
- Your drinking is causing you to neglect your responsibilities at home, at school, or at work.
- Your behavior is illegal and dangerous to others (e.g., you drink and drive).
- You want to stop drinking but you cannot seem to do it.
- You find yourself dropping other activities (e.g., exercise, hobbies, spending time with friends or family) because you need to have a drink.

Based on http://www.helpguide.org/mental/alcohol_abuse_alcoholism_signs_effects_treatments.htm; http://www.med.unc.edu/alcohol/prevention/signs.html; http://www.webmd.com/mental-health/alcohol-abuse/alcohol-abuse-and-dependence-symptoms

90% of student rapes and 95% of violent crime on campus.

Long-Term Health Effects

Alcohol's long-term health risks are mostly (but not exclusively) associated with chronic, heavy consumption of alcohol. Estimates of the number of people at risk vary considerably. According to Schuckit (2000) approximately 5%–10% of American men and women engage in chronic alcohol abuse and another 10% of men and 3%–5% of women probably suffer from *alcohol dependence*, or *alcoholism*. ***Alcohol dependence (alcoholism)* is a chronic, progressive disorder marked by a growing compulsion to drink and impaired control over drinking that eventually interferes with health and social behavior.** Whether alcoholism is best viewed as a disease or as a self-control problem is the source of considerable debate, but experts have reached a reasonable consensus about the warning signs of alcoholism. These signs include preoccupation with alcohol, drinking to relieve uncomfortable feelings, gulping drinks, clandestine drinking, and the other indicators listed in Figure 5.8.

FIGURE 5.9 Health risks associated with drinking

This figure provides an overview of the various diseases more common among drinkers than abstainers. As you can see, alcohol elevates one's vulnerability to a remarkably diverse array of diseases.

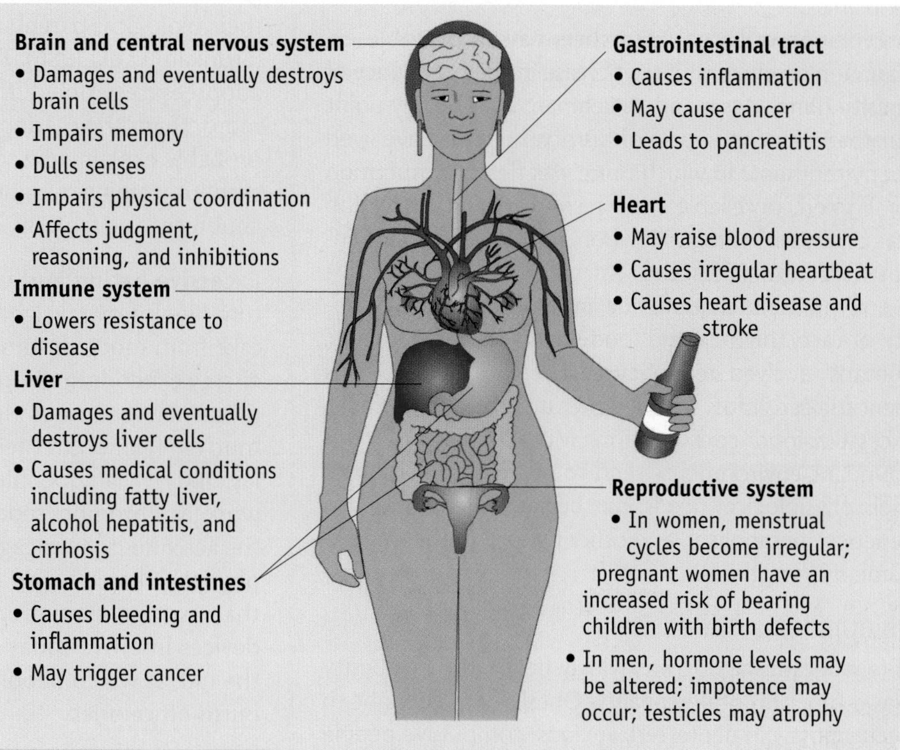

Brain and central nervous system
• Damages and eventually destroys brain cells
• Impairs memory
• Dulls senses
• Impairs physical coordination
• Affects judgment, reasoning, and inhibitions
Immune system
• Lowers resistance to disease
Liver
• Damages and eventually destroys liver cells
• Causes medical conditions including fatty liver, alcohol hepatitis, and cirrhosis
Stomach and intestines
• Causes bleeding and inflammation
• May trigger cancer
Gastrointestinal tract
• Causes inflammation
• May cause cancer
• Leads to pancreatitis
Heart
• May raise blood pressure
• Causes irregular heartbeat
• Causes heart disease and stroke
Reproductive system
• In women, menstrual cycles become irregular; pregnant women have an increased risk of bearing children with birth defects
• In men, hormone levels may be altered; impotence may occur; testicles may atrophy

Source: From Hoeger, W. W. K., and Hafen, B. Q. (1998). *Wellness* (2nd ed.). Belmont, CA: Wadsworth. © 1998 Cengage Learning.

Alcoholism and problem drinking are associated with an elevated risk for a wide range of serious health problems, which are summarized in Figure 5.9 (Mack, Franklin, & Frances, 2003). Although there is some thought-provoking evidence that moderate drinking may reduce one's risk for coronary disease, it is clear that heavy drinking increases the risk for heart disease, hypertension, and stroke. Excessive drinking is also correlated with an elevated risk for various types of cancer, including oral, stomach, pancreatic, colon, and rectal cancer. Moreover, serious drinking problems can lead to cirrhosis of the liver, malnutrition, pregnancy complications, brain damage, and neurological disorders. Finally, alcoholism can produce severe psychotic states, characterized by delirium, disorientation, and hallucinations.

5-2c OVEREATING

Obesity is a common health problem. The criteria for obesity vary somewhat. One simple, intermediate criterion is to classify people as obese if their weight exceeds their ideal body weight by 20%. If this criterion is used, 31% of men and 35% of women in the United States qualify as obese (Brownell & Wadden, 2000). Obesity is an immediate and growing problem: As recently as the 1980s, only 13% of adult Americans were considered to be obese (Ogden, Carroll, & Flegal, 2008).

Many experts prefer to assess obesity in terms of ***body mass index (BMI)*—weight (in kilograms) divided by height (in meters) squared (kg/m^2).** This increasingly used index of weight controls for variations in height. A BMI of 25.0–29.9 is typically regarded as overweight, and a BMI over 30 is considered obese. If a BMI over 25 is used as the cutoff, almost two-thirds of American adults are struggling with weight problems (Sarwer, Foster, & Wadden, 2004).

Obesity is a significant health problem that elevates one's mortality risk. In fact, obesity is probably responsible for the early deaths of well over a quarter of a million people in North America each year (DeAngelis, 2004). Overweight people are more vulnerable than others to heart disease, diabetes, hypertension, respiratory problems, gallbladder disease, stroke, arthritis, some cancers, muscle and joint pain, and back problems.

Evolution-oriented researchers have a plausible explanation for the dramatic increase in the prevalence of obesity (Pinel, Assanand, & Lehman, 2000). They point out that over the course of history, humans have lived in environments in which there was fierce competition for limited, unreliable food resources, and starvation was a very real threat. However, in today's modern, industrialized societies, the vast majority of humans live in environments that provide an abundant, reliable supply of tasty, high-calorie food. In these environments, humans' evolved tendency to overeat when food is plentiful leads most people down a pathway of chronic, excessive food consumption. Most people in food-abundant environments tend to overeat in relation to their physiological needs, but because of variations in genetics, metabolism, and other factors, only some become overweight.

Determinants of Obesity

A few decades ago it was widely believed that obesity was a function of personality. Obesity was thought to occur mostly in depressed, anxious, compulsive people who overeat to deal with their negative emotions or in individuals who are lazy and undisciplined. However, research eventually showed that there is no such thing as an "obese personality" (Rodin, Schank, & Striegel-Moore, 1989), although some traits are associated with weight fluctuation (Sutin et al., 2011). Instead, research indicated that a complex network of interacting factors—biological, social, and psychological—determine whether people develop weight problems (Berthoud & Morrison, 2008).

Heredity. Chief among the factors contributing to obesity is *genetic predisposition*. In one influential study, adults raised by foster parents were compared with their biological parents in regard to body mass index (Stunkard et al., 1986). The investigators found that the adoptees resembled their biological parents much more than their adoptive parents. Genetic factors probably explain why some people can eat constantly without gaining weight whereas other people grow chubby eating far less.

Excessive eating and inadequate exercise. The bottom line for overweight people is that their energy intake from food consumption chronically exceeds their energy expenditure from physical activities and resting metabolic processes. In other words, they eat too much in relation to their level of exercise (Wing & Polley, 2001). Many people's private lives as well as their work lives promote sedentary comfort, so that many of the activities they engage in daily are more mental than physical. People work and play less with their bodies than past generations, and a number of labor-saving devices improve today's quality of life while reducing the rate at which people obtain "natural" exercise that burns off calories.

Set point. People who lose weight on a diet have a rather strong (and depressing) tendency to gain back all the weight they lose. The reverse is also true. People who have to work to put weight on often have trouble keeping it on (Leibel, Rosenbaum, & Hirsch, 1995). These observations suggest that your body may have a *set point*, or a natural point of stability in body weight. When fat stores slip below a crucial set point, the body supposedly begins to compensate for this change (Keesey, 1993). Thus, *settling-point theory* (Pinel et al., 2000) proposes that weight tends to drift around the level at which the constellation of factors that determine food consumption and energy expenditure achieve an equilibrium. According to this view, weight tends to remain stable as long as there are no durable changes in any of the factors that influence it.

Losing Weight

Whether out of concern about their health or just old-fashioned vanity, an ever-increasing number of people are trying to lose weight. One study found that at any given time, about 21% of men and 39% of women are dieting (Hill, 2002). Research has provided some good

© David Sipress/The New Yorker Collection/www.cartoonbank.com

news for those who need to lose weight. Studies have demonstrated that relatively modest weight reductions (e.g., 10%) can significantly diminish many of the health risks associated with obesity. Thus, the traditional objective of obesity treatment—reducing to one's ideal weight—has been replaced by more modest and realistic goals (Sarwer et al., 2004).

While many factors may contribute to obesity, there is only one way to lose weight. Individuals must change their ratio of energy intake (food consumption) to energy output (physical activities). To lose 1 pound a person needs to burn up 3,500 more calories than he or she consumes. Those wanting to shed pounds have three options: (1) sharply reduce food consumption, (2) sharply increase exercise output, or (3) simultaneously decrease food intake and step up exercise output in more moderate ways. Virtually all experts recommend the third option, as exercise seems especially important for *maintaining* reduced weight, just as it is the single best predictor of long-term weight loss (Curioni & Lourenco, 2005).

© Volodymyr Leus/Shutterstock.com

Some people have surgery to reduce their weight, an option generally reserved for individuals who are seriously obese or who have other weight problems that warrant drastic action to cause weight loss quickly. One popular form of surgery shrinks the size of the stomach by placing what is known as a gastric band around it, while another surgical approach is a gastric bypass, where food is rerouted around the bulk of the stomach and a portion of the intestines. Both procedures involve risks and are life-altering; patients must usually take nutritional supplements while carefully watching their food consumption for the rest of their lives (Tucker, Szomstetin, & Rosenthal, 2007).

Finally, self-modification techniques can be helpful in achieving gradual weight loss. Overall, the evidence on weight-loss programs suggests that they are moderately successful in the short term (the first 6 months), but in the long run the vast majority of people regain most of the weight that they lose (Jeffery et al., 2000).

5-2d LACK OF EXERCISE

A great deal of evidence suggests that there is a link between exercise and health. Research indicates that regular exercise is associated with increased longevity (Lee & Skerrett, 2001). Moreover, you don't have to be a dedicated athlete to benefit from exercise. Even a moderate level of reasonably regular physical activity is associated with lower mortality rates (Richardson et al., 2004; see Figure 5.10 on the next page). Unfortunately, only 25% of American adults get an adequate amount of regular exercise (Dubbert et al., 2004).

Benefits of Exercise

Exercise is correlated with greater longevity because it promotes a diverse array of specific benefits. First, an appropriate exercise program can enhance cardiovascular fitness and thereby reduce one's susceptibility to cardiovascular problems (Schlicht, Kanning, & Bös, 2007). Second, regular physical activity can contribute to the avoidance of obesity (Hill & Wyatt, 2005), reducing one's risk for related health problems, including diabetes, respiratory difficulties, arthritis, and back pain. Third, some studies suggest that physical fitness is also associated with a decreased risk for colon cancer and for breast and reproductive cancer in women (Thune & Furberg, 2001). The apparent link between exercise and

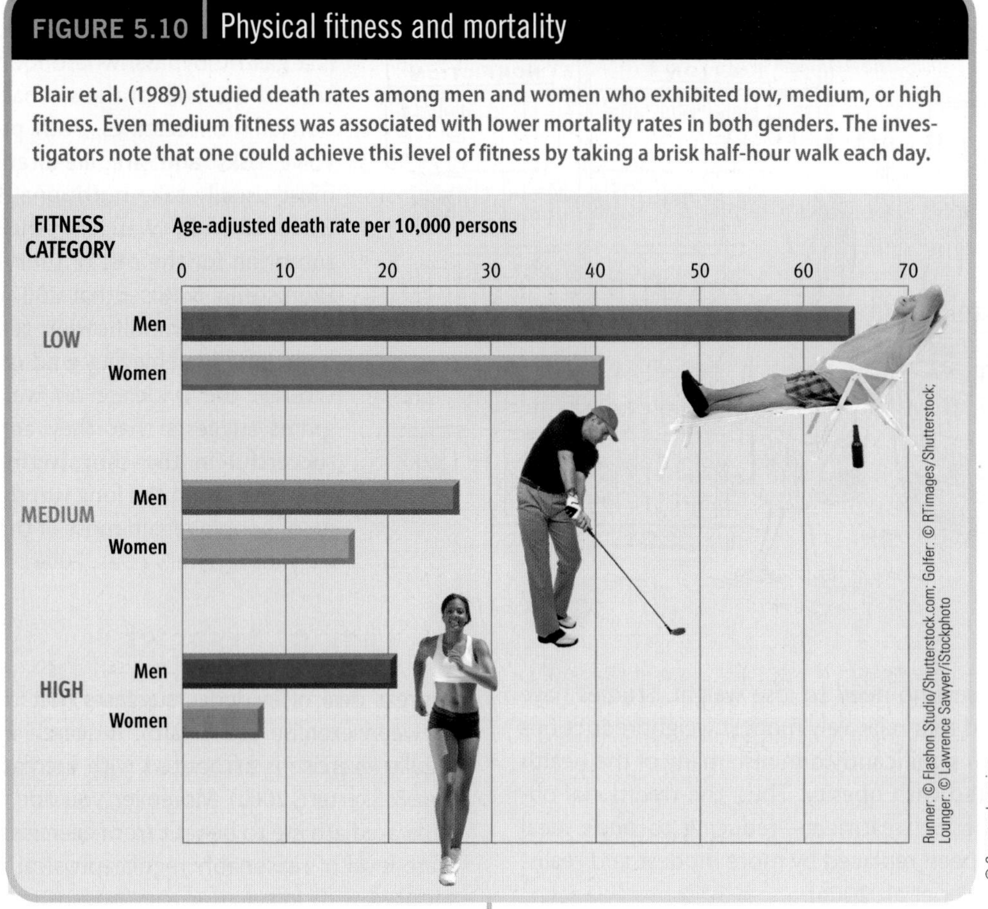

FIGURE 5.10 | Physical fitness and mortality

Blair et al. (1989) studied death rates among men and women who exhibited low, medium, or high fitness. Even medium fitness was associated with lower mortality rates in both genders. The investigators note that one could achieve this level of fitness by taking a brisk half-hour walk each day.

reduced cancer risk has been a pleasant surprise for scientists, who are now scrambling to replicate the findings and figure out the physiological mechanisms underlying this association (Rogers et al., 2008).

Fourth, exercise may serve as a buffer that reduces the potentially damaging effects of stress (Plante, Caputo, & Chizmar, 2000). Fifth, exercise may have a favorable impact on mental health, which in turn may have positive effects on physical health. Sixth, successful participation in an exercise program can produce desirable personality changes that may promote physical wellness. Research suggests that fitness training can lead to improvements in one's mood, self-esteem, and work efficiency, as well as reductions in tension and anxiety (Dunn, Trivedi, & O'Neal, 2001).

Devising an Exercise Program

Putting together a good exercise program is difficult for many people. Exercise is time consuming, and if you're out of shape, your initial attempts may be painful, aversive, and discouraging. People who do not get enough exercise cite lack of time, lack of convenience, and lack of enjoyment as the reasons (Jakicic & Gallagher, 2002). To circumvent these problems, it is wise to heed the following advice:

1. *Look for an activity that you will find enjoyable.* Shop around for a physical activity that you find intrinsically enjoyable. Doing so will make it much easier for you to exercise regularly.

2. *Exercise regularly without overdoing it.* Sporadic exercise will not improve your fitness. At the other extreme, an overzealous approach can lead to frustration, not to mention injury.

3. *Increase the amount of time you exercise gradually.* Don't rush it. Start slowly and build up gradually, as any amount of exercise is apt to be better than no exercise.

© auremar/Shutterstock.com

4. *Reinforce yourself for your participation.* To offset the inconvenience or pain that may be associated with exercise, it is a good idea to reinforce yourself for your participation.

5. *It's never too late to begin an exercise regimen.* Even modest regular exercise has pronounced health benefits, as has been shown in studies with participants well into their 70s, 80s, and 90s.

5-2e BEHAVIOR AND AIDS

At present, some of the most problematic links between behavior and health may be those related to AIDS, a pandemic, or worldwide epidemic. AIDS stands for ***acquired immune deficiency syndrome*, a disorder in which the immune system is gradually weakened and eventually disabled by the human immunodeficiency virus (HIV).** Being infected with the HIV virus is *not* equivalent to having AIDS. AIDS is the final stage of the HIV infection process, typically manifested about 7–10 years after the original infection (Carey & Vanable, 2003). With the onset of AIDS, one is left virtually defenseless against a number of opportunistic infectious agents. Prior to 1996–1997, the average length of survival for people after the onset of the AIDS syndrome was about 18 to 24 months. Encouraging advances in the treatment of AIDS with drug regimens referred to as *highly active antiretroviral therapy* hold out promise for *substantially* longer survival (Anthony & Bell, 2008).

Transmission

The HIV virus is transmitted through person-to-person contact involving the exchange of bodily fluids, primarily semen and blood. The two principal modes of transmission in the United States have been sexual contact and the sharing of needles by intravenous (IV) drug users. In the United States, sexual transmission has occurred primarily among gay and bisexual men, but heterosexual transmission has increased in recent years (Centers for Disease Control, 2006). In the world as a whole, infection through heterosexual relations has been more common.

Misconceptions

Misconceptions about AIDS are widespread. Ironically, the people who hold these misconceptions fall into two polarized camps. On the one hand, a great many people have unrealistic fears that AIDS can be readily transmitted through casual contact with infected individuals. These people worry unnecessarily about contracting AIDS from a handshake, a sneeze, or an eating utensil. They tend to be paranoid about interacting with homosexuals, thus fueling discrimination against gays. Some people also believe that it is dangerous to donate blood when, in fact, blood donors are at no risk whatsoever. On the other hand, many young heterosexuals who are sexually active with a variety of partners foolishly downplay their risk for HIV, naively assuming that they are safe as long as they avoid IV drug use and sexual relations with gay or bisexual men. They greatly underestimate the probability that their sexual partners may have previously used IV drugs or had unprotected sex with an infected individual. They don't understand, for instance, that most bisexual men do not disclose their bisexuality to their female partners (Kalichman et al., 1998). In sum, many myths about AIDS persist, despite extensive efforts to educate the public about this complex and controversial disease.

Prevention

The behavioral changes that minimize the risk of developing AIDS are fairly straightforward, although making the changes is often easier said than done. In all groups, the more sexual partners a person has, the higher the risk that he or she will be exposed to the HIV virus. Thus, people can reduce their risk by having sexual contacts with fewer partners and by using condoms to control the exchange of semen. It is also important to curtail certain sexual practices (in particular, anal sex) that increase the probability of semen/blood mixing.

5-3 Understanding the Effects of Drugs

This section focuses on the use of drugs for their pleasurable effects, commonly referred to as *drug abuse* or *recreational drug use.* Drug abuse reaches into every corner of our society and is a problematic health-impairing habit. Although small declines appear to have occurred in the overall abuse of drugs in recent years, survey data show that illicit drug use has mostly been increasing since the 1960s (Winick & Norman, 2005).

Recreational drug use involves personal, moral, political, and legal, as well as occasionally religious, issues that are not matters for science to resolve. However, the more knowledgeable you are about drugs, the more informed your decisions and opinions about them will be. Accordingly, in this section we will try to provide you with nonjudgmental, realistic coverage of issues related to recreational drug use. We begin by reviewing key drug-related concepts and then examine the effects and risks of five types of widely abused drugs: narcotics, sedatives, stimulants, hallucinogens, and marijuana.

5-3a DRUG-RELATED CONCEPTS

The principal types of recreational drugs are described in Figure 5.11. This table lists representative drugs in each of the five categories and indicates how the drugs are taken, their principal medical uses, their desired effects, and their common side effects.

Most drugs produce tolerance effects. ***Tolerance* is a progressive decrease in a person's responsiveness to a drug with continued use.** Tolerance effects usually lead people to consume larger and larger doses of a drug to attain the effects they desire. Tolerance builds more rapidly to some drugs than to others. The first column in Figure 5.12 (which lists the risks associated with drug abuse) indicates whether various categories of drugs tend to produce rapid or gradual tolerance.

In evaluating the potential problems associated with the use of specific drugs, a key consideration is the likelihood of either physical or psychological dependence. Although both forms of drug dependence have a physiological basis, important differences exist between the two syndromes. ***Physical dependence* exists when a person must continue to take a drug to avoid withdrawal illness (which occurs when drug use is terminated).** The symptoms of *withdrawal illness* (also called *abstinence syndrome*) vary depending on the drug. Withdrawal from heroin and barbiturates can produce fever, chills, tremors, convulsions, seizures, vomiting,

FIGURE 5.11 | Major categories of abused drugs

This chart summarizes the methods of ingestion, chief medical uses, and principal effects of five major types of recreational drugs. (Based on Julien, 2008; Levinthal, 2008; Lowinson, et al., 2005)

COMPARISON OF MAJOR CATEGORIES OF ABUSED DRUGS

Drugs	Methods of administration	Principal medical uses	Desired effects	Short-term side effects
Narcotics (opiates) Morphine Heroin	Injected, smoked, oral	Pain relief	Euphoria, relaxation, anxiety reduction, pain relief	Lethargy, drowsiness, nausea, impaired coordination, impaired mental functioning, constipation
Sedatives Barbiturates (e.g., Seconal) Nonbarbiturates (e.g., Quaalude)	Oral, injected	Sleeping pill, anticonvulsant	Euphoria, relaxation, anxiety reduction, reduced inhibitions	Lethargy, drowsiness, severely impaired coordination, impaired mental functioning, emotional swings, dejection
Stimulants Amphetamines Cocaine	Oral, sniffed, injected, freebased, smoked	Treatment of hyperactivity and narcolepsy; local anesthetic (cocaine only)	Elation, excitement, increased alertness, increased energy, reduced fatigue	Increased blood pressure and heart rate, increased talkativeness, restlessness, irritability, insomnia, reduced appetite, increased sweating and urination, anxiety, paranoia, increased aggressiveness, panic
Hallucinogens LSD Mescaline Psilocybin	Oral		Increased sensory awareness, euphoria, altered perceptions, hallucinations, insightful experiences	Dilated pupils, nausea, emotional swings, paranoia, jumbled thought processes, impaired judgment, anxiety, panic reaction
Cannabis Marijuana Hashish THC	Smoked, oral	Treatment of glaucoma; other uses under study	Mild euphoria, relaxation, altered perceptions, enhanced awareness	Bloodshot eyes, dry mouth, reduced memory, sluggish motor coordination, sluggish mental functioning, anxiety

cramps, diarrhea, and severe aches and pains. The agony of withdrawal from these drugs virtually compels addicts to continue using them. Withdrawal from stimulants leads to a different and somewhat milder syndrome dominated by fatigue, apathy, irritability, depression, and disorientation.

Psychological dependence **exists when a person must continue to take a drug to satisfy intense mental and emotional craving for it.** Psychological dependence is more subtle than physical dependence, as it is not marked by a clear withdrawal reaction. However, psychological dependence can create a powerful, overwhelming need for a drug. The two types of dependence often coexist—that is, many people manifest both psychological and physical dependence on a specific drug. Both types of dependence are established gradually with repeated use of a drug. However, specific drugs vary greatly in their potential for creating dependence. The second and third columns in Figure 5.12 provide estimates of the risk of each kind of dependence for the drugs covered in our discussion.

An *overdose* is an excessive dose of a drug that can seriously threaten one's life. Any drug can be fatal if a person takes enough of it, but some drugs carry more risk of overdose than others. In Figure 5.12, column 5 estimates the risk of accidentally consuming a lethal overdose of various drugs. Drugs that are central nervous system (CNS) depressants—narcotics and sedatives—carry the greatest risk of overdose. It's important to understand that the effects of these drugs are additive. Many overdoses involve lethal *combinations* of CNS depressants. What happens when people overdose on these drugs? Their respiratory system usually grinds to a halt, producing coma, brain damage, and death within a brief period. In contrast, fatal overdoses with CNS stimulants (cocaine and amphetamines) usually involve a heart attack, stroke, or cortical seizure.

© Angela Waye/Shutterstock.com

In evaluating the potential problems associated with the use of specific drugs, a key consideration is the likelihood of either physical or psychological dependence.

Now that our basic vocabulary is spelled out, we can begin to examine the effects and risks of major recreational drugs. Of course, we'll be describing the *typical* effects of each drug. Please bear in mind that the effects of any drug depend on the user's age, body weight, physiology, personality, mood, expectations, and previous experience with the drug. The dose and potency of the drug, the method of administration, and the setting in which the drug is taken also influence its effects (Leavitt, 1995).

5-3b NARCOTICS

© Gaja/Shutterstock.com

Narcotics **(or opiates) are drugs derived from opium that are capable of relieving pain.** In government regulations, the term *narcotic* is used in a haphazard way to refer to a variety of drugs besides opiates. The most widely abused opiates are heroin, morphine, and a relatively new painkiller called Oxycontin (oxycodone). However, less potent opiates, such as codeine, Demerol, and Vicodin, are also subject to misuse.

Effects

The most significant narcotics problem in modern, Western society is the use of heroin. Most users inject this drug intravenously with a hypodermic needle. The main effect is an overwhelming sense of euphoria. This "Who cares?" feeling makes the heroin

FIGURE 5.12 Specific risks for various categories of drugs

This chart shows the estimated risk potential for tolerance, dependence, and overdose for the five major categories of drugs discussed in this section.

RISKS ASSOCIATED WITH ABUSED DRUGS

Drugs	Tolerance	Risk of physical dependence	Risk of psychological dependence	Fatal overdose potential
Narcotics (opiates)	Rapid	High	High	High
Sedatives	Rapid	High	High	High
Stimulants	Rapid	Moderate	High	Moderate to high
Hallucinogens	Gradual	None	Very low	Very low
Cannabis	Gradual	None	Low to moderate	Very low

© Cengage Learning

high an attractive escape from reality. Common side effects include nausea, lethargy, drowsiness, constipation, and slowed respiration.

Risks

Narcotics carry a high risk for both *psychological and physical dependence.* It is estimated that there are about 600,000 heroin addicts in the United States (Winick & Norman, 2005). Although heroin withdrawal usually isn't life threatening, it can be terribly unpleasant, so that "junkies" have a desperate need to continue their drug use. Once dependence is entrenched, users tend to develop a *drug-centered lifestyle* that revolves around the need to procure more heroin. Heroin use in the U.S. has leveled off since the 1990s (Johnston et al., 2008). Still, heroin is blamed for over 4,000 deaths annually in the United States, so *overdose* is a very real danger. The effects of opiates are additive with those of other CNS depressants, and most narcotic overdoses occur in combination with the use of sedatives or alcohol. Junkies also risk *contracting an infectious disease* (hepatitis, AIDS) because they often share hypodermic needles and tend to be sloppy about sterilizing them.

Although the dangers of hallucinogens have probably been exaggerated in the popular press, there are some significant risks.
©FotografiaBasica/iStockphoto

5-3c SEDATIVES

© troy/ Shutterstock.com

***Sedatives* are sleep-inducing drugs that tend to decrease central nervous system and behavioral activity.** In street jargon, they are often called "downers." Over the years, the most widely abused sedatives have been the barbiturates, which are compounds derived from barbituric acid. However, barbiturates have gradually become medically obsolete and diminished in availability, so sedative abusers have had to turn to drugs in the benzodiazepine family, such as Valium (Wesson et al., 2005).

Effects

People abusing sedatives generally consume larger doses than are prescribed for medical purposes. These overly large doses have a euphoric effect similar to that produced by drinking large amounts of alcohol. Feelings of tension, anxiety, and depression are temporarily replaced by a relaxed, pleasant state of intoxication, in which inhibitions may be loosened. Sedatives carry a truckload of dangerous side effects. Motor coordination suffers badly, producing slurred speech and a staggering walk, among other things. Intellectual functioning also becomes sluggish, and judgment is impaired. The person's emotional tone may become unstable, with feelings of dejection often intruding on the intended euphoric mood.

Risks

Sedatives have the potential to produce *both psychological and physical dependence.* They are also among the leading causes of *overdoses* in the United States because of their additive interactions with other CNS depressants (especially alcohol) and because of the degree to which they impair judgment. In their drug-induced haze, sedative abusers are likely to take doses they would ordinarily recognize as dangerous. Sedative users also elevate their risk for *accidental injuries* because these drugs can have significant effects on motor coordination.

5-3d STIMULANTS

© Christopher Elwell/ Shutterstock.com

***Stimulants* are drugs that tend to increase central nervous system and behavioral activity.** They range from mild, widely available forms, such as caffeine and nicotine, to stronger, carefully regulated stimulants, such as cocaine and amphetamines ("speed"). Here we focus on the latter two drugs.

Cocaine, an organic substance extracted from the coca shrub, is usually consumed as a crystalline powder that is snorted through the nasal cavities, although it can be consumed orally or intravenously. "Crack" is a processed variant of cocaine, consisting of little chips of cocaine that are usually smoked. Smoking crack tends to be more dangerous than snorting cocaine powder because smoking leads to a more rapid absorption of the drug into the bloodstream and more concentrated delivery of the drug to the brain. That said, all the forms of cocaine and all the routes of administration can deliver highly toxic amounts of the drug to the brain (Repetto & Gold, 2005). Synthesized in a pharmaceutical laboratory, amphetamines are usually consumed orally. However, speed is also sold as a crystalline powder (called "crank" or "crystal meth") that may be snorted or injected intravenously. A smokable form of methamphetamine, called "ice," is seen in some regions.

Effects

Amphetamines and cocaine have almost indistinguishable effects, except that cocaine produces a very brief high (20–30 minutes unless more is taken), while a speed high can last many hours. Stimulants produce a euphoria very different from that created by narcotics or sedatives. They produce a buoyant, elated, enthusiastic, energetic, "I can conquer the world!" feeling accompanied by increased alertness. Common side effects include increased blood pressure, muscle tension, sweating, and restlessness. Some users experience unpleasant feelings of irritability, anxiety, and paranoia.

© Olaf Speier/Shutterstock.com

Risks

Stimulants can cause physical dependence, but the physical distress caused by stimulant withdrawal is mild compared to that caused by narcotic or sedative withdrawal. Psychological dependence on stimulants is a more common problem. Cocaine can create an exceptionally *powerful psychological dependence* that compels the user to pursue the drug with a fervor normally seen only when physical dependence exists (Gold & Jacobs, 2005).

Both cocaine and amphetamines can suppress appetite and disrupt sleep. Thus, heavy use of stimulants may lead to poor eating, poor sleeping, and ultimately, a *deterioration in physical health.* Furthermore, stimulant use increases one's risk for stroke, heart attack, and other forms of cardiovascular disease, and crack smoking is associated with a variety of respiratory problems (Gourevitch & Arnsten, 2005). All of the risks associated with stimulant use increase when more potent forms of the drugs (crack and ice) are used. Overdoses on stimulants used to be relatively infrequent. However, in recent years, *cocaine overdoses have increased sharply* as more people experiment with more dangerous modes of ingestion.

5-3e HALLUCINOGENS

© Arie v.d. Wolde/Shutterstock.com

Hallucinogens **are a diverse group of drugs that have powerful effects on mental and emotional functioning, marked most prominently by distortions in sensory and perceptual experience.** The principal hallucinogens are LSD, mescaline, and psilocybin, which have similar effects, although they vary in potency. Mescaline comes from the peyote plant, psilocybin comes from a particular type of mushroom, and LSD is a synthetic drug. Common street names for hallucinogens include "acid," "mushrooms," "fry," and "blotter."

Effects

Hallucinogens intensify and distort perception in ways that are difficult to describe, and they temporarily impair intellectual functioning, as thought processes become meteoric and jumbled. These drugs can produce awesome feelings of euphoria that sometimes include an almost mystical sense of "oneness" with the human race, which is why they have been used in religious ceremonies in various cultures. Unfortunately, at the other end of the emotional spectrum, they can also produce nightmarish feelings of anxiety, fear, and paranoia, commonly called a "bad trip."

Risks

There is no potential for physical dependence on hallucinogens, and no deaths attributable to overdose are known to have occurred. Psychological dependence has been reported but appears to be rare. Reports that LSD increases chromosome breakage were based on poor research methodology (Dishotsky et al., 1971). However, like most drugs, hallucinogens may be harmful to a fetus if taken by a pregnant woman.

Although the dangers of hallucinogens have probably been exaggerated in the popular press, there are some significant risks (Pechnick & Ungerleider, 2005). Emotion is highly volatile with these drugs, so users can never be sure they won't experience *acute panic* from a terrifying bad trip. Generally, this disorientation subsides within a few hours, leaving no permanent emotional scars. However, in such a severe state of disorientation, *accidents and suicide* are possible. *Flashbacks* are vivid hallucinogenic experiences occurring long after the original drug ingestion. They do not appear to be a common problem, but repetitious flashbacks have proved troublesome for some individuals. In a small minority of users, hallucinogens may contribute to the emergence of a *variety of psychological disorders* (psychoses, depressive reactions, paranoid states) that may be partially attributable to the drug (Pechnick & Ungerleider, 2005).

5-3f MARIJUANA

© Ju-Lee/Photos.com

Cannabis **is the hemp plant from which marijuana, hashish, and THC are derived.** Marijuana (often called "pot," "weed," "reefer," or "grass") is a mixture of dried leaves, flowers, stems, and seeds taken from the plant, while hashish comes from the plant's resin.

Effects

When smoked, cannabis has an almost immediate impact that may last several hours, depending on the user's expectations and experience with it, the drug's potency, and the amount smoked. The drug has subtle effects on emotion, perception, and cognition (Grinspoon, Bakalar, & Russo, 2005). Emotionally, the drug tends to create a mild, relaxed state of euphoria. Perceptually, it enhances the impact of incoming stimulation, thus making music sound better, food taste better, and so on. Cannabis tends to produce a slight impairment in cognitive functioning (especially short-term memory) and perceptual-motor coordination while the user is high. However, there are huge variations among users.

Risks

Overdose and physical dependence are not problems with marijuana, but as with any other drug that produces pleasant feelings, it has the potential to produce *psychological dependence.* Marijuana can also cause *transient problems with anxiety and depression* in some people. Of greater concern is recent research suggesting that marijuana use during adolescence *may help to precipitate schizophrenia* in young people who have a genetic vulnerability to the disorder (Compton, Goulding, & Walker, 2007; see Chapter 14). Studies also suggest that cannabis may have a more *negative effect on driving* than has been widely believed (Ramaekers, Robbe, & O'Hanlon, 2000). Indeed, people often make riskier decisions under the influence of marijuana, which may account for its link to increased risk for injuries (Kalant, 2004). Like tobacco smoke, marijuana smoke carries carcinogens and impurities into the lungs, thus increasing one's chances for *respiratory and pulmonary diseases, and probably lung cancer* (Kalant, 2004). However, the evidence on other widely publicized risks remains controversial. Here is a brief overview of the evidence on some of these controversies:

- *Does marijuana reduce one's immune response?* Probably not, as infectious diseases do not appear to be more common among marijuana smokers than among nonsmokers (Klein, Friedman, & Specter, 1998).
- *Does marijuana lead to impotence and sterility in men?* Available evidence suggests that marijuana has little lasting impact on male smokers' fertility or sexual functioning (Grinspoon, Bakalar, & Russo, 2005).
- *Does marijuana have long-term negative effects on cognitive functioning?* An association has been found between chronic, heavy marijuana use and measureable impairments in attention and memory that shows up when users are not high (Solowij et al., 2002). However, the cognitive deficits are modest and certainly not disabling, and one study found that the deficits vanished after a month of marijuana abstinence (Pope, Gruber, & Yurgelun-Todd, 2001).

Photo: © kolosigor/Shutterstock.com; graphic frame: © L_amica/Shutterstock.com

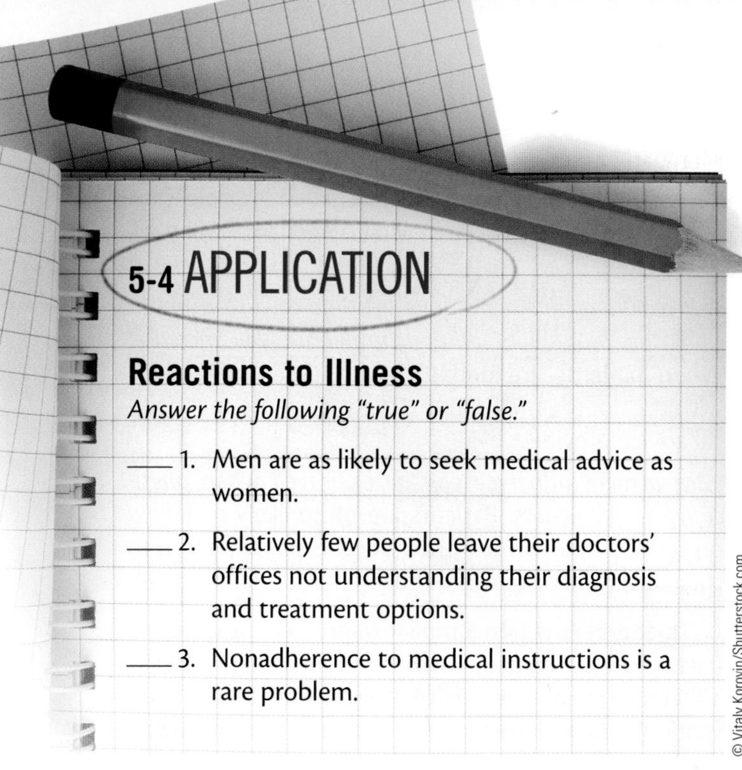

5-4 APPLICATION

Reactions to Illness

Answer the following "true" or "false."

____ 1. Men are as likely to seek medical advice as women.

____ 2. Relatively few people leave their doctors' offices not understanding their diagnosis and treatment options.

____ 3. Nonadherence to medical instructions is a rare problem.

© Vitaly Korovin/Shutterstock.com

As you will learn in this Application, all of these statements are false. If you answered all of them accurately, you may already be well informed about how people respond to illness. If not, you *should* be. Intelligent decisions about when to seek medical treatment require an understanding of the common pitfalls people fall prey to where their health is concerned.

So far we have emphasized the psychosocial aspects of maintaining health and minimizing the risk of illness. Health is also affected by how individuals respond to physical symptoms and illnesses. Some people engage in denial and ignore early-warning signs of developing diseases. Others engage in active coping efforts to conquer their diseases. In this Application, we discuss the decision to seek medical treatment, communication with health providers, and compliance with medical advice.

5-4a THE DECISION TO SEEK TREATMENT

Have you ever experienced nausea, diarrhea, stiffness, headaches, cramps, chest pains, or sinus problems? Of course you have; everyone experiences some of these problems periodically. However, whether you view these sensations as *symptoms* is a matter of individual interpretation, and the level of symptoms is what prompts people to seek medical advice (Ringström et al., 2007). When two persons experience the same unpleasant sensations, one may shrug them off as a nuisance, while the other may rush to a physician. Studies suggest that those who are relatively high in anxiety and neuroticism tend to report more symptoms of illness than others do (Feldman et al., 1999). Those who are extremely attentive to bodily sensations and health concerns also report more symptoms than the average person (Barsky, 1988).

© Jeff Banke/Shutterstock.com

Variations in the perception of symptoms help explain why people vary so much in their readiness to seek medical treatment (Cameron, Leventhal, & Leventhal, 1993). Generally, people are more likely to seek medical care when their symptoms are unfamiliar, appear to be serious, last longer than expected, or disrupt their work or social activities (Martin et al., 2003). Social class matters, too. Higher socioeconomic groups report having fewer symptoms and better health, but when sickness occurs, member of these groups are more likely to seek medical care than lower-income people are (Grzywacz et al., 2004). Medical consultation is much more likely when friends and family view symptoms as serious and encourage the person to seek medical care, although nagging a person about seeking care can sometimes backfire (Martin et al., 2003). Gender also influences decisions to seek treatment, as women are much more likely than men to utilize medical services (Galdas, Cheater, & Marshall, 2005).

The process of seeking medical treatment can be divided into three stages of active, complex problem solving (Martin et al., 2003). First, people have to decide that their physical sensations *are* symptoms—that they are indicative of illness. Second, they have to decide that their apparent illness warrants medical attention. Third, they have to go to the trouble to make the actual arrangements for medical care, which can be complicated and time consuming. Small wonder then, that the biggest problem in regard to treatment seeking is the tendency of many people to delay the pursuit of needed professional consultation. Delays in seeking medical help can be important, because early diagnosis and quick intervention can facilitate more effective treatment of many health problems.

5-4b COMMUNICATING WITH HEALTH PROVIDERS

When people seek help from physicians and other health care providers, many factors can undermine effective communication. A large portion of medical patients leave their doctors' offices not understanding what they have been told and what they are supposed to do (Johnson & Carlson, 2004). This situation is unfortunate, because good communication is a crucial requirement for sound medical decisions, informed choices about treatment, and appropriate follow-through by patients.

There are many barriers to effective provider-patient communication (DiMatteo, 1997). Economic realities dictate that medical visits be generally quite brief, allowing little time for discussion. Illness and pain are subjective matters that may be difficult to describe. Many providers use too much medical jargon and overestimate their patients' understanding of technical terms. Some providers are uncomfortable being questioned and discourage their patients' information seeking. Patients who are upset and worried about their illness may simply forget to report some symptoms or to ask questions they meant to ask. Other patients are evasive about their real concerns because they fear a serious diagnosis. Many patients are reluctant to challenge doctors' authority and are too passive in their interactions with providers. Doctors and nurses often believe their explanations are clear; however, patient misunderstanding can be a common phenomenon, one posing particular problems for individuals whose instructions regarding diagnosis, treatment, and medication are complex (Parker, 2000).

5-4c ADHERENCE TO MEDICAL ADVICE

Many patients fail to adhere to the instructions they receive from physicians and other health care professionals. The evidence suggests that noncompliance with medical advice may occur 30% of the time when short-term treatments are prescribed for acute conditions and 50% of the time when long-term treatments are needed for chronic illness (Johnson & Carlson, 2004). Nonadherence takes many forms. Patients may fail to begin a treatment regimen, may stop the regimen early, may reduce or increase the levels of treatment that were prescribed, or may be inconsistent and unreliable in following treatment procedures (Clifford, Barber, & Horn, 2008). Nonadherence is a major problem that has been linked to increased sickness, treatment failures, and higher mortality. Moreover, nonadherence wastes expensive medical visits and medications and increases hospital admissions, leading to enormous economic costs. In the United States alone, nonadherence may be a $300-billion-a-year drain on the health care system (DiMatteo, 2004).

Here are some considerations that influence the likelihood of adherence (Johnson & Carlson, 2004):

1. *Frequently, noncompliance occurs because patients simply forget instructions or fail to understand the instructions as given.* Medical professionals often forget that what seems obvious and simple to them may be obscure and complicated to many of their patients.

2. *Another key factor is how aversive or difficult the treatments are.* If the prescribed regimen is unpleasant or disruptive to routine behavior, compliance will tend to decrease.

3. *If a patient has a negative attitude toward a physician, the probability of noncompliance will increase.* When patients are unhappy with their interactions with the doctor, they're more likely to ignore the medical advice provided.

4. *Treatment adherece can be improved when physicians do follow-ups.* Patients are more likely to follow prescribed treatments if their doctors pay attention to them after the diagnosis has been made (Llorca, 2008).

To address the noncompliance problem, researchers have investigated many methods of increasing patients' adherence to medical advice (Martin et al., 2010). Interventions have included simplifying instructions, providing more rationale for instructions, reducing the complexity of treatment regimens, helping patients with emotional distress that undermines adherence, and training patients in the use of behavior modification strategies. All of these interventions can improve adherence, although their effects tend to be modest (Christensen & Johnson, 2002).

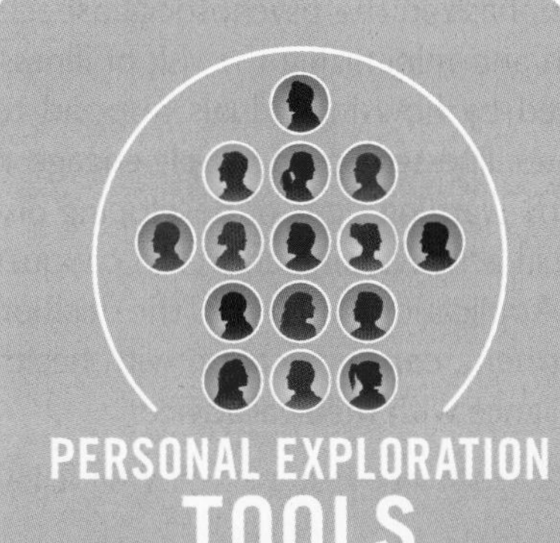

PERSONAL EXPLORATION TOOLS

Curious about yourself? To learn more about how topics in this chapter relate to you, go online to CourseMate at www.cengagebrain.com where you can:

- Complete a **Self-Reflection** exercise that will help you think about your personal experiences in relation to topics in the chapter.
- Take a **Self-Assessment** scale that will show you how you score on a research instrument that measures personality traits or attitudes.
- Explore **Recommended Readings** that will provide brief overviews of useful self-help books.

STUDY TOOLS ▶ 5

Ready to study? In your book you can:

- **Test Yourself** with a multiple-choice quiz (below)
- Rip out the **Chapter Review card** (in the back of the book) to refresh yourself on the chapter's Key Ideas and Key Terms

Or you can go online to CourseMate at www.cengagebrain.com where you can:

- Take additional Practice Quizzes to prepare for your exam
- Review Key Terms with flash cards and a crossword puzzle
- View videos that expand on selected concepts

TEST YOURSELF

1. The greatest threats to health in our society today are

a. environmental toxins.
b. accidents.
c. chronic diseases.
d. contagious diseases caused by specific infectious agents.

2. Which of the following is *not* associated with elevated coronary risk?

a. Cynical hostility
b. Strong emotional reactions to transient mental stress
c. Obsessive-compulsive disorder
d. Depression

3. Why do people tend to act in self-destructive ways?

a. Many health-impairing habits creep up on them.
b. Many health-impairing habits involve activities that are quite pleasant at the time.
c. The risks tend to lie in the distant future.
d. All of the above are the case.

4. Some short-term risks of alcohol consumption include all but which of the following?

a. Hangovers and life-threatening overdoses in combination with other drugs
b. Poor perceptual coordination and driving drunk
c. Increased aggressiveness and argumentativeness
d. Transient anxiety from endorphin-induced flashbacks

5. Heredity's relationship to obesity is that

a. genetic factors have little impact on people's weight.
b. heredity has scant influence on BMI but does influence weight.
c. genetic predisposition accounts for much of the variation in people's weight.
d. heredity is responsible for severe, morbid obesity but has little influence over the weight of normal people.

6. Which of the following has *not* been found to be a mode of transmission for AIDS?

a. Sexual contact among homosexual men
b. The sharing of needles by intravenous drug users
c. Sexual contact among heterosexuals
d. Sharing food

7. Which of the following risks is *not* typically associated with narcotics use?

a. Overdose
c. Physical dependence
b. Infectious disease
d. Flashbacks

8. The use of sedatives may result in personal injury because they

a. cause motor coordination to deteriorate.
b. enhance motor coordination too much, making people overconfident about their abilities.
c. suppress pain warnings of physical harm.
d. trigger hallucinations such as flying.

9. Regarding the seeking of medical treatment, the biggest problem is

a. the tendency of many people to delay seeking treatment.
b. the tendency of many people to rush too quickly for medical care for minor problems.
c. not having enough doctors to cover people's needs.
d. the tendency of people in higher socioeconomic categories to exaggerate their symptoms.

10. In which of the following cases are people most likely to follow the instructions they receive from health care professionals?

a. When the instructions are complex and punctuated with impressive medical jargon
b. When they do not fully understand the instructions but still feel the need to do something
c. When they like and understand the health care professional
d. All of the above

Answers: 1. c, page 91; 2. c, pages 92–95; 3. d, page 97; 4. d, page 100; 5. c, page 102; 6. d, page 105; 7. d, page 108; 8. a, page 108; 9. a, pages 111–112; 10. c, page 112

© Masterfile/Royalty-Free

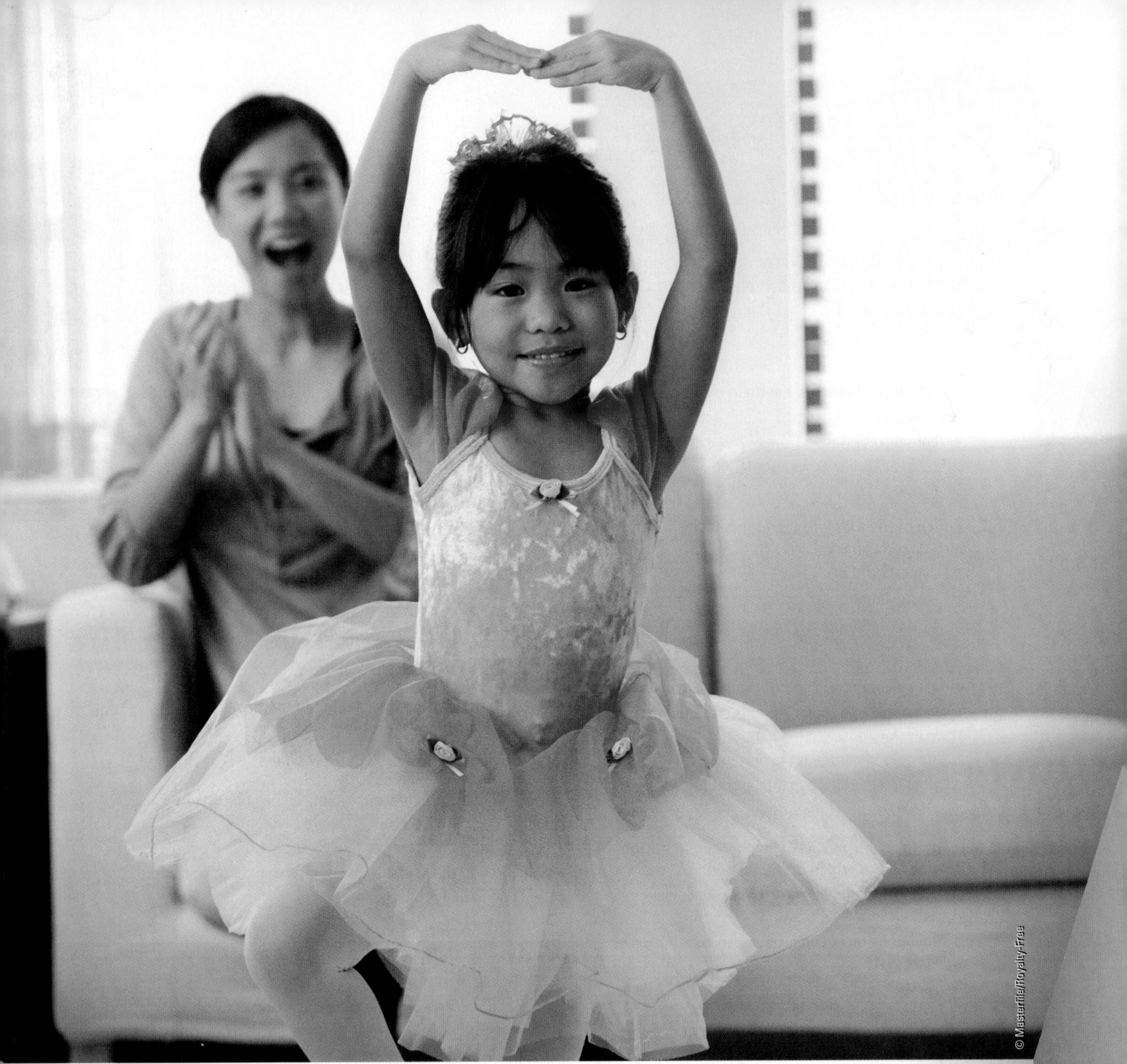

LEARNING OBJECTIVES

6-1 Describe the nature of the self-concept and factors that shape it.

6-2 Explain the importance of self-esteem, its relation to adjustment, and how it develops.

6-3 Discuss self-attributions, motives for self-understanding, and the process of self-enhancement.

6-4 Define self-regulation, its psychological benefits, and its challenges.

6-5 Discuss why and how people engage in impression management, and describe strategies for creating favorable impressions.

6-6 List seven ways to build self-esteem.

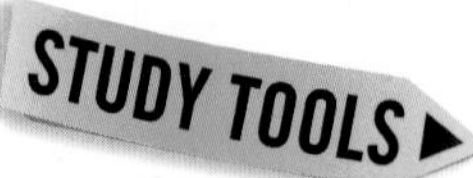

STUDY TOOLS ▶ After you have read the chapter, you can Test Yourself and learn about other Study Tools on page 135.

CHAPTER 6

The SELF

© Tyler Olson/Shutterstock.com

© Photo_Concepts/iStockphoto

Today is your first official day of college and psychology is your first class. You arrive early. You take a seat near the front of the lecture hall and immediately feel conspicuous. You don't know anyone in the class; in fact, you suddenly realize you don't know anyone at the university except for your roommate, who is still more or less a stranger. Many students seem to know one another. They are laughing, talking, and catching up while you just sit there, quiet and alone. They seem friendly, so why won't they talk to you? Should you speak to them first? Are you dressed okay—what about your hair? You begin to question yourself: Will you ever make any friends in this class or at the university? Oh, here comes the professor. She seems nice enough, but you wonder what she expects. Will this class be difficult? Wait a minute: What if the professor calls on you in front of all these strangers who already know each other? Will you sound intelligent or look foolish? As the professor begins to take the class roll, your mind is racing. You feel tense and your stomach gets a little queasy as she gets closer in the alphabet to your name.

This scenario demonstrates the process of self-perception and the effects it can have on emotion, motivation, and goal setting. People engage in this sort of self-reflection constantly, especially when they are trying to understand the causes of their own behavior.

In this chapter, we highlight the self and its important role in adjustment. We begin by looking at two major components of the self: self-concept and self-esteem. Then we review some key principles of the self-perception process. Next, we turn to the important topic of self-regulation. Finally, we focus on how people present themselves to others. In this chapter's Application, we offer some suggestions for building self-esteem.

6-1 Self-Concept: Your Picture of Yourself

If you were asked to describe yourself, what would you say? You'd probably start off with some physical attributes such as "I'm tall," "I'm of average weight," or "I'm blonde." Soon you'd move on to psychological characteristics: "I'm friendly," "I'm honest," "I'm reasonably intelligent," and so forth. People usually identify whatever makes them unique in a particular situation. These distinctive qualities fit into their self-definitions. You probably do the same thing. How did you develop these beliefs about yourself? Have your self-views changed over time? Read on.

6-1a THE NATURE OF THE SELF-CONCEPT

Although the self-concept is usually talked about as a single entity, it is actually a multifaceted structure (Mischel & Morf, 2003). **The *self-concept* is an organized collection of beliefs about the self.** These beliefs, also called *self-schemas*, shape social perception, are developed from past experience, and are concerned with one's personality traits, abilities, physical features, values, goals, and social roles. People have self-schemas on dimensions that are important to them, including both strengths and weaknesses. Figure 6.1 on the next page depicts the self-concepts of two hypothetical individuals. Each self-schema is characterized by relatively distinct thoughts and feelings. For instance, you might have considerable information about your social skills and feel quite self-assured about them but have limited information and less confidence about your physical skills.

Beliefs about the self influence not only current behavior but also future behavior. ***Possible selves* are one's conceptions about the kind of person one might become in the future**. If you have narrowed your career choices to personnel manager and psychologist, they would represent two possible selves in the career realm. Possible selves are developed from past experiences, current behavior, and future expectations. They make people attentive to goal-related information and role models and mindful of the need to practice goal-related skills. As such, they help individuals not only to envision desired future goals but also to achieve them (McElwee & Haugh, 2010). Sometimes, however, possible selves are negative and represent what you fear you might become—such as an alcoholic like Uncle George or a recluse lacking intimate relationships like your next-door neighbor. In these cases, possible selves function as images to be avoided (Lee & Oyserman, 2009).

© olly/Shutterstock.com

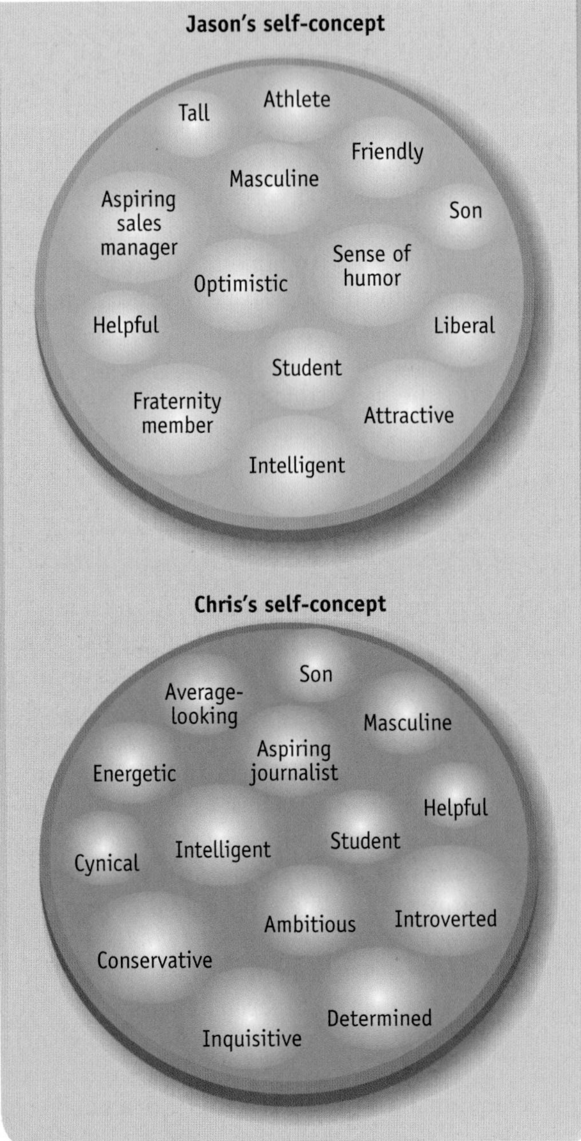

FIGURE 6.1 | The self-concept and self-schemas

The self-concept is composed of various self-schemas, or beliefs about the self. Jason and Chris have different self-concepts in part because they have different self-schemas.

© Cengage Learning

Individuals' beliefs about themselves are not set in concrete—but neither are they easily changed. People are strongly motivated to maintain a consistent view of the self across time and situations. Thus, once the self-concept is established, the individual has a tendency to preserve and defend it. In the context of this stability, however, self-beliefs do have a certain dynamic quality. Self-concepts seem to be most susceptible to change when people shift from an important and familiar social setting to an unfamiliar one, such as when they go off to college or to a new city for their first "real" job. This flexibility clearly underscores the social foundations of the self-concept.

6-1b FACTORS SHAPING THE SELF-CONCEPT

A variety of sources influence one's self-concept. Chief among them are one's own observations, feedback from others, and cultural values.

One's Own Observations

Individuals begin observing their own behavior and drawing conclusions about themselves early in life. Children will make statements about who is the tallest, who can run fastest, or who can swing the highest. Leon Festinger's (1954) ***social comparison theory* proposes that individuals compare themselves with others in order to assess their abilities and opinions.** People compare themselves to others to determine how attractive they are, how they did on the history exam, how their social skills stack up, and so forth (Dijkstra, Gibbons, & Buunk, 2010).

Although Festinger's original theory claimed that people engage in social comparison for the purpose of accurately assessing their abilities, research suggests that they also engage in social comparison to improve their skills and to maintain their self-image (Wheeler & Suls, 2005). Sometimes social comparison is self-focused, such as when a successful professional woman compares her "current self" to the passive, withdrawn "past self" of high school. Generally, however, people compare themselves against others with particular qualities. **A *reference group* is a set of people who are used as a gauge in making social comparisons.** People choose their reference groups strategically. For example, if you want to know how you did on your first test in social psychology (ability appraisal), your reference group would likely be the entire class.

What happens when people compare themselves to others who are better or worse off than them? For instance, if you want to improve your tennis game (skill development), your reference group should be limited to superior players, whose skills give you a goal to pursue. Such *upward social comparisons* can motivate you and direct your future efforts (Blanton et al., 1999). On the other hand, if your self-esteem needs bolstering, you will probably make a *downward social comparison,* looking to those whom you perceive to be worse off, thereby enabling you to feel better about yourself (Aspinwall & Taylor, 1993).

People's observations of their own behavior are not entirely objective. Indeed, the general tendency is to distort reality in a positive direction. In other words, most people tend to evaluate themselves in a more positive light than they really merit (Taylor & Brown, 1988). The strength of this tendency was highlighted in a large survey of high school seniors conducted as part of the SAT (Myers, 1980). By definition, 50% of students must be "above average" and 50% "below average" on specific questions. However, 100% of the respondents saw themselves as above average in "ability to get along with others." And 25% of the respondents thought that they belonged in the top 1%! This better-than-average effect seems to be a common phenomenon.

© Bruce Rolff/Shutterstock.com

Feedback from Others

Individuals' self-concept is shaped significantly by the feedback they get from important people in their lives. Early on, parents and other family members play a dominant role. Parents give their children a great deal of direct feedback, saying such things as "We're so proud of you" or "If you just tried harder, you could do a lot better in math." Most people, especially when young, take this sort of feedback to heart. Thus, it comes as no surprise that studies find a link between parents' views of a child and the child's self-concept (Burhans & Dweck, 1995). There is even stronger evidence for a relationship between children's *perceptions* of their parents' attitudes toward them and their own self-views (Felson, 1992).

Whether positive or negative, feedback from others plays an important role in shaping a youngster's self-concept.

© Yuri Arcurs/Shutterstock.com

Teachers, Little League coaches, Scout leaders, classmates, and friends also provide feedback during childhood. In later childhood and adolescence, parents and classmates are particularly important sources of feedback and support (Harter, 2003). Later in life, feedback from close friends and marriage partners assumes importance.

Keep in mind that people filter feedback from others through their existing self-perceptions. That is, individuals don't see themselves exactly as others see them but rather as they *believe* others see them (Baumeister & Twenge, 2003). Thus, feedback from others usually reinforces people's self-views. When feedback about the self conflicts with a person's central self-conceptions, he or she is quite capable of selectively forgetting it; yet the person can recall it when motivated toward self-improvement, including the way he or she regulates close relationships with others (Green et al., 2009).

Cultural Values

Self-concept is also shaped by cultural values. Among other things, the society in which one is reared defines what is desirable and undesirable in personality and behavior. For example, American culture puts a high premium on individuality, competitive success, strength, and skill. When individuals meet cultural expectations, they feel good about themselves and experience increases in self-esteem (Cross & Gore, 2003).

Cross-cultural studies suggest that different cultures shape different conceptions of the self. One important way cultures differ is on the dimension of individualism versus collectivism (e.g., Triandis, 2001). ***Individualism* involves putting personal goals ahead of group goals and defining one's identity in terms of personal attributes rather than group memberships.** In contrast, ***collectivism* involves putting group goals ahead of personal goals and defining one's identity in terms of the groups one belongs to** (such as family, tribe, work group, social class, caste, and so on). Although it's tempting to think of these perspectives in either-or terms, it is more appropriate to view them as qualities that vary in degree and that can be assessed (Fischer et al., 2009). Thus, it is more accurate to say that certain cultures are more or less individualistic (or collectivist) than others rather than see them as either one or the other.

Individuals reared in individualistic cultures usually have an *independent view of the self*, perceiving themselves as unique, self-contained, and distinct from others. In contrast, individuals reared in collectivist cultures typically have an *interdependent view of the self*. They see themselves as inextricably connected to others and believe that harmonious relationships with others are of utmost importance. Thus, in describing herself, a person living in an individualistic culture might say, "I am kind," whereas someone in a collectivist culture might respond, "My family thinks I am kind" (Triandis, 2001). Figure 6.2 depicts the self-conceptions of individuals representative of these contrasting worldviews.

Researchers have noted parallels between the self-views promoted by individualistic and collectivist cultures and the self-views of some groups. For example, women usually have more interdependent self-views than men (Cross & Madson, 1997). But don't take this finding to mean that men are less social than women; rather, it means that men and women get their social needs met in different ways. Thus women are usually involved in close relationships involving intimate friends and family members (*relational* interdependence), while men tend to interact in social groups such as clubs and sports teams (*collective* interdependence) (Gabriel & Gardner, 1999). These gender differences in self-views may explain other observed gender differences, such as women being more likely than men to share their feelings and thoughts with others.

6-2 Self-Esteem: Gauging Your Worth

One of the functions of the self-concept is to evaluate the self; the result of this evaluation is termed *self-esteem*. ***Self-esteem* refers to one's overall assessment of one's worth as a person.** Do you think of yourself in primarily positive or negative terms? Self-esteem is a global self-evaluation that blends many specific evaluations about one's adequacy as a student, an athlete, a worker, a spouse, a parent, or whatever is personally

FIGURE 6.2 Independent and interdendent views of the self

(a) Individuals in cultures that support an independent view perceive the self as clearly separated from significant others. (b) Individuals in cultures that support an interdependent view perceive the self as inextricably connected to others.

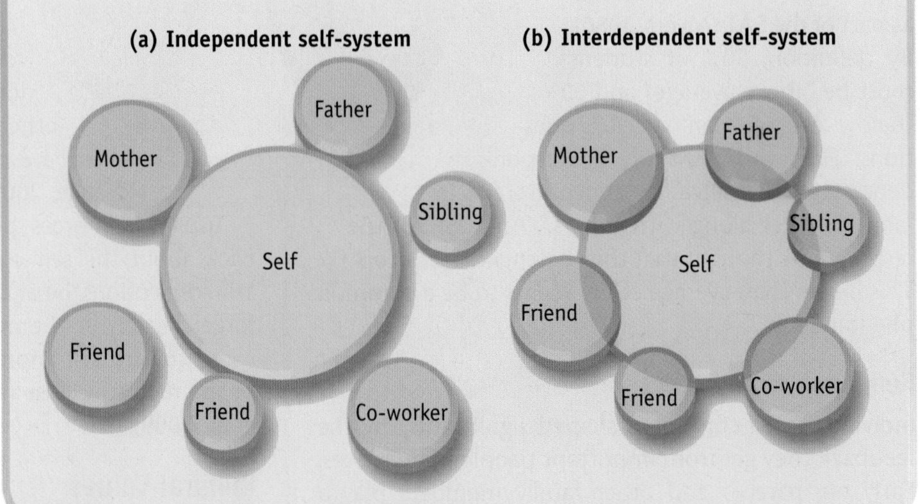

Source: Adapted from Markus, H. R., & Kitayama, S. (1991). Culture and the self: Implications for cognition, emotion, and motivation. *Psychological Review, 98*, 224–253. Copyright 1991 by American Psychological Association. Adapted with permission.

relevant. Figure 6.3 shows how specific elements of the self-concept may contribute to self-esteem. If you feel basically good about yourself, you probably have high self-esteem.

People with high self-esteem are confident, taking credit for their successes in various ways while seeking venues for demonstrating their skills (Baumeister, 1998). Compared to individuals with low self-esteem, they are also relatively sure of who they are (Campbell, 1990). In reality, the self-views of people with low self-esteem are not more negative; rather, they are more confused and tentative (Campbell & Lavallee, 1993). In other words, their self-concepts seem to be less clear, less complete, more self-contradictory, and more susceptible to short-term fluctuations than the self-views of high-self-esteem individuals. According to Roy Baumeister (1998), an eminent authority on the self, this "self-concept confusion" means that individuals with low self-esteem simply don't know themselves well enough to strongly endorse many personal attributes on self-esteem tests, which results in lower self-esteem scores.

Self-esteem can be construed in two primary ways: as a trait or a state. *Trait self-esteem* refers to the ongoing sense of confidence people possess regarding their abilities (athletic, assertive) and characteristics (friendliness, helpfulness). People's traits tend to stay with them and to remain constant; if one has high or low self-esteem in childhood, chances are one will have a similar level as an adult (Block & Robbins, 1993). In contrast, *state self-esteem* is dynamic and changeable, referring to how individuals feel about themselves in the moment (Heatherton & Polivy, 1991). Feedback from others, self-observation, one's point in the life span, moods, a temporary financial setback—all can lower one's current sense of self-worth. Those whose self-esteem fluctuates in response to daily experiences are highly sensitive to interactions and events that have potential relevance to their self-worth, and they may even mistakenly view irrelevant events as having significance (Kernis & Goldman, 2002). They always feel their self-worth is on the line.

FIGURE 6.3 | The structure of self-esteem

Self-esteem is a global evaluation that combines assessments of various aspects of one's self-concept, each of which is built up from many specific behaviors and experiences. (Adapted from Shavelson, Hubner, & Stanton, 1976)

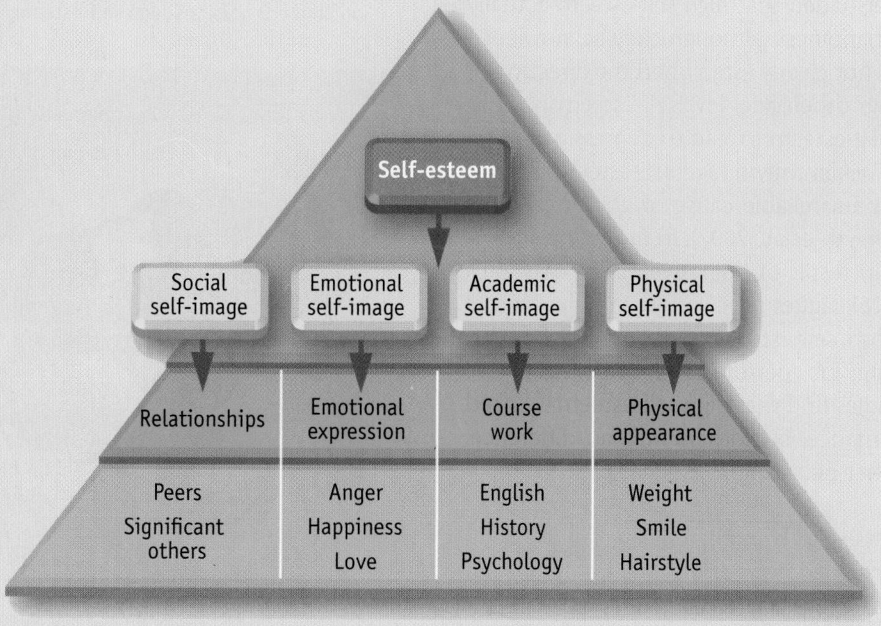

Investigating self-esteem is challenging for several reasons. For one thing, obtaining accurate measures of self-esteem is difficult. The problem is that researchers tend to rely on self-reports from subjects, which obviously may be biased. As you've seen, most individuals typically hold unrealistically positive views about themselves. Moreover, some people may choose not to disclose their actual self-esteem on a questionnaire. Second, in probing self-esteem it is often quite difficult to separate cause from effect. Thousands of correlational studies report that high and low self-esteem are associated with various behavioral characteristics. For instance, self-esteem is correlated with happiness. However, it is hard to tell whether high self-esteem causes happiness or vice versa. You should keep this problem in pinpointing causation in mind as we explore this fascinating topic.

6-2a THE IMPORTANCE OF SELF-ESTEEM

Popular wisdom holds that self-esteem is the key to a host of positive outcomes in life. In fact, its actual benefits are much fewer—but, we hasten to add, not unimportant (Krueger, Vohs, & Baumeister, 2009). A comprehensive review of research examined the purported and actual advantages of self-esteem (Baumeister et al., 2003). Let's look at the findings that relate to self-esteem and adjustment.

Self-Esteem and Adjustment

The clearest advantages of self-esteem are in the *emotional sphere*. Namely, self-esteem is strongly and consistently related to happiness. In fact, Baumeister and his colleagues are persuaded that high self-esteem actually leads to greater happiness, although they acknowledge that research has not clearly established the direction of causation. On the other side, low self-esteem is more likely than high self-esteem to lead to depression.

In the area of *achievement*, high self-esteem has not been shown to be a reliable cause of good academic performance (Forsyth et al., 2007). In fact, it may actually be the (weak) result of doing well in school. Baumeister and his colleagues speculate that other factors may underlie both self-esteem and academic performance. Regarding job performance, the results are mixed. Some studies find that high self-esteem is linked to better performance, but others find no difference. And it may be that occupational success leads to high self-esteem.

In the *interpersonal realm*, Baumeister and his colleagues report that people with high self-esteem claim to be more likable and attractive, to have better relationships, and to make better impressions on others than people with low self-esteem do. Interestingly, these advantages seem to exist mainly in the minds of the beholders, because objective data (ratings of peers) do not support these views. Regarding romantic relationships, those with low self-esteem are more likely to distrust their partners' expressions of love and support and to worry about rejection compared to high-self-esteem individuals. Still there is no evidence that self-esteem (high or low) is related to how quickly relationships end. When it comes to working in groups, high-self-esteem people are more likely to speak up and to criticize the group's approach. And they are perceived as contributing more to groups.

What about self-esteem and *coping*, a key aspect of adjustment? Individuals with low self-esteem *and* a self-blaming attributional style are definitely at a disadvantage here. For one thing, they become more demoralized after a failure than those with high self-esteem do. For them, failure contributes to depression and undermines their motivation to do better the next time. By contrast, individuals with high self-esteem persist longer in the face of failure. Second, as can be seen in Figure 6.4, individuals with low self-esteem often have

FIGURE 6.4 | **The vicious circle of low self-esteem and poor performance**

Low self-esteem is associated with low or negative expectations about performance. These low expectations often result in inadequate preparation and high anxiety, which heighten the likelihood of poor performance. Unsuccessful performance triggers self-blame, which feeds back to lower self-esteem.

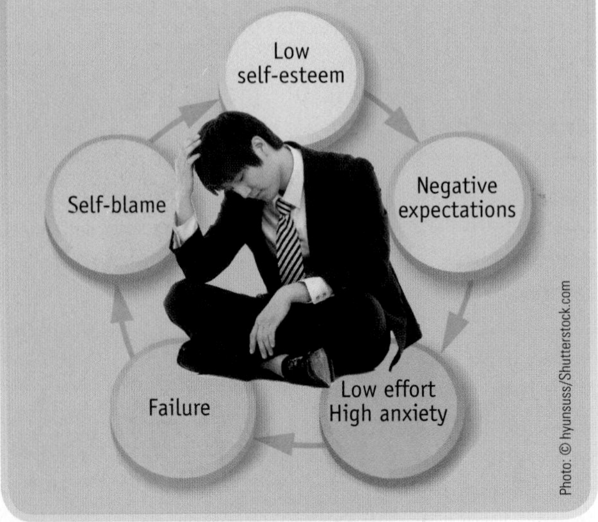

Source: Adapted from Brehm, S. S., & Kassin, S. M. (1996). *Social psychology.* (3rd ed.). Belmont, CA: Wadsworth. Reproduced by permission. www.cengage.com/permissions

negative expectations about their performance (in a social situation, at a job interview, on a test). Because self-esteem affects expectations, it operates in a self-perpetuating fashion. As a result, they feel anxious and may not prepare for the challenge. Then, if they blame themselves when they do poorly, they feel depressed and deliver one more blow to their already battered self-esteem. Of course, this cycle also works (in the opposite way) for those with high self-esteem. In either case, the important point is that self-esteem can affect not only the present, but also the future.

High Self-Esteem Versus Narcissism

Although feeling good about oneself is desirable, problems arise when people's self-views are inflated and unrealistic. Indeed, high self-esteem may not be all it's cracked up to be (Crocker & Park, 2004). As noted in Chapter 1, *narcissism* is the tendency to regard oneself as grandiosely self-important. Narcissistic individuals passionately want to think well of themselves and are highly sensitive to criticism (Twenge & Campbell, 2003). They are preoccupied with fantasies of success, believe that they deserve special treatment, and react aggressively when they experience threats to their self-views (ego threats). Those with fragile (unstable) self-esteem also respond in this manner (Kernis, 2003a). On the other hand, individuals whose positive self-appraisals are secure or realistic are not so susceptible to ego threats and are less likely to resort to hostility and aggression in the face of them.

Baumeister and his colleagues speculate that narcissists who experience ego threats have an elevated propensity to engage in aggression such as partner abuse, rape, gang violence, individual and group hate crimes, and political terrorism (Baumeister, 1999; Bushman et al., 2003). Is there any evidence to support this idea? In a series of studies, researchers gave participants the opportunity to aggress against someone who had either insulted or praised an essay they had written (Bushman & Baumeister, 1998). The narcissistic participants reacted to their "insultors" with exceptionally high levels of aggression (see Figure 6.5).

These findings have important practical implications (Baumeister, Smart, & Bolden, 1996). Most rehabilitation programs for spousal abusers, delinquents, and criminals are based on the faulty belief that these individuals suffer from low self-esteem. So far, there is little empirical evidence that low self-esteem leads to either direct (e.g., hitting someone) or indirect (e.g., giving someone a negative evaluation)

FIGURE 6.5 The path from narcissism to aggression

Individuals who score high on narcissism perceive negative evaluations by others to be extremely threatening. This experience of ego threat triggers strong hostile feelings and aggressive behavior toward the evaluator in retaliation for the perceived criticism. Those low in narcissism are less likely to perceive negative evaluations as threatening and, therefore, behave much less aggressively toward evaluators. (Adapted from Bushman & Baumeister, 1998)

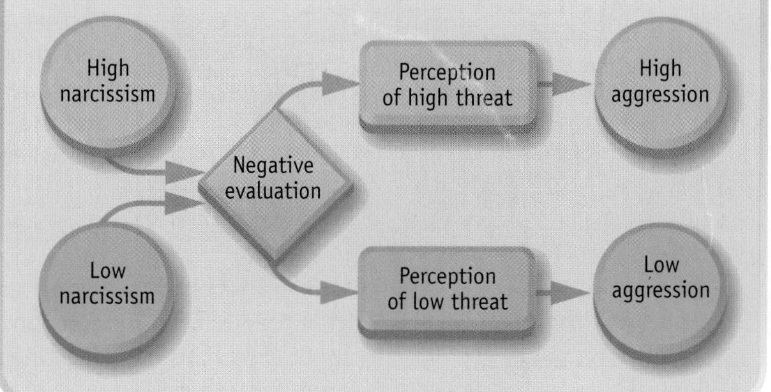

aggression (Bushman et al., 2009). Indeed, current research suggests that efforts to boost (already inflated) self-esteem are misguided. A better approach is to help such individuals develop more self-control and more realistic views of themselves.

6-2b THE DEVELOPMENT OF SELF-ESTEEM

Although people's sense of self-worth emerges in early childhood, individual differences in self-esteem begin to stand out in middle childhood and adolescence (Erol & Orth, 2011) and remain across the lifespan (Harter, 2006). The typical pattern found involves high self-esteem in childhood, an observed fall in adolescence (especially among girls), a gradual return and rise in adulthood, and a decline once more during old age (Robins & Trzesniewski, 2005). Because the foundations of self-esteem are laid early in life, psychologists have focused much of their attention on the role of parenting in self-esteem development. Indeed, there is ample evidence that parental involvement, acceptance, support, and exposure to clearly defined limits have a marked influence on children's self-esteem (Harter, 1998).

Two major dimensions underlie parenting behavior: acceptance and control (Maccoby & Martin, 1983). Diana Baumrind (1967) identified four distinct parenting styles as interactions between these two dimensions (see Figure 6.6). *Authoritative parenting* uses high emotional support and firm, but reasonable, limits (high acceptance, high control). *Authoritarian parenting* entails low emotional support with rigid limits (low acceptance, high control). *Permissive parenting* uses high emotional support with few limits (high acceptance, low control), and *neglectful parenting* involves low emotional support and few limits (low acceptance, low control). Baumrind and others have found correlations between these parenting styles and children's traits and behaviors, including self-esteem (Furnham & Cheng, 2000). Authoritative parenting is associated with the highest self-esteem scores, and this finding generally holds true across different ethnic groups (Wissink, Dekovic, & Meijer, 2006). In any case, all of these studies were correlational, so keep in mind they don't demonstrate that parenting style *causes* high or low self-esteem.

Parents, teachers, coaches, and other adults play a key role in shaping self-esteem.

FIGURE 6.6 Baumrind's parenting styles

Four parenting styles result from the interactions of parental acceptance and parental control, as theorized by Diana Baumrind (1971).

Parental control	Parental acceptance: Low	Parental acceptance: High
High	**Authoritarian** (low acceptance, high control)	**Authoritative** (high acceptance, high control)
Low	**Neglectful** (low acceptance, low control)	**Permissive** (high acceptance, low control)

Source: Adapted from Baumrind, D. (1971). Current patterns of parental authority [Monograph]. *Developmental Psychology, 4*(1, Part 2), 1–103. American Psychological Association. Reprinted with permission.

6-3 Self-Perception: Basic Principles

Now that you're familiar with some of the major aspects of the self, let's consider how people construct and maintain a coherent and positive view of the self. First we look at the basic cognitive processes involved and then at the fascinating area of self-attributions. Then we move on to discussions of explanatory style and the key motives guiding self-understanding, with a special emphasis on self-enhancement techniques.

6-3a COGNITIVE PROCESSES

People are faced with an inordinate number of decisions on a daily basis. How do they keep from being overwhelmed? The key lies in how people process information. According to Shelley Taylor (1981), people are "cognitive misers." In this model, cognitive resources (attention, memory, and so forth) are limited, so the mind works to "hoard" them by taking cognitive shortcuts. For example, you probably have the same morning routine—shower, drink coffee, read the paper as you eat breakfast, check email, and so forth. Because you do these things without a lot of thought, you can conserve your attentional, decision-making, and memory capacities for important cognitive tasks. This example illustrates the default mode of handling information: *automatic processing.* On the other hand, when important decisions arise or when you're trying to understand why you didn't get that job you wanted, you spend those precious cognitive resources. This mode is termed *controlled processing.* Ellen Langer (1989) describes these two states as *mindlessness* and *mindfulness*, respectively. Mindfulness promotes cognitive flexibility, which in turn can lead to self-acceptance and well-being (Langer, 2009) In contrast, mindlessness leads to rigid thinking in which details and important distinctions are lost.

People strive to understand themselves.

Another way that cognitive resources are protected is through *selective attention*, with high priority given to information pertaining to the self (Bargh, 1997). An example of this tendency is a phenomenon known as the "cocktail party effect"—the ability to pick out the mention of your name in a roomful of chattering people.

Another principle of self-cognition is that people strive to understand themselves. One way they do so, as you saw in our discussion of social comparison theory, is to compare themselves with others. Yet another is to engage in attributional thinking, our next topic.

6-3b SELF-ATTRIBUTIONS

Let's say that you win a critical match for your school's tennis team. To what do you attribute your success? Is your new practice schedule starting to pay off? Did you have the home court advantage? Was your opponent playing with a minor injury? This example from everyday life illustrates the nature of the self-attribution process. ***Self-attributions* are inferences that people draw about the causes of their own behavior and experiences.** People routinely make attributions to make sense out of what happens to them. These attributions involve inferences that ultimately represent guesswork on each person's part.

Fritz Heider (1958) was the first to assert that people tend to locate the cause of a behavior either within a person, attributing it to personal factors, or outside a person, attributing it to environmental factors. He thus established one of the crucial dimensions along which attributions are made: internal versus external. The other main dimension is stable-unstable. Let's discuss these two dimensions of attributions in greater detail.

Internal or external. Elaborating on Heider's insight, various theorists have agreed that explanations of behavior and events can be categorized as internal or external attributions (Jones & Davis, 1965). ***Internal attributions* ascribe the causes of behavior to personal dispositions, traits, abilities, and feelings. *External attributions* ascribe the causes of behavior to situational demands and environmental constraints.** For example, if you credit your poor statistics grade to your failure to prepare adequately for the test or to getting overly anxious during the test, you are making internal attributions. An external attribution could be that the course is simply too hard, that the teacher is unfair, or that the book is incomprehensible.

Whether one's self-attributions are internal or external can have a tremendous impact on one's personal adjustment. Studies suggest that people who attribute their setbacks to internal, personal causes while discounting external, situational explanations may be more prone to depression than people who display opposite tendencies (Riso et al., 2003).

Stable or unstable. According to Bernard Weiner (1986), a second dimension that people use in making causal attributions is the stability of the causes underlying behavior. A stable cause is one that is more or less permanent and unlikely to change over time. A sense of humor and intelligence are *stable internal* causes of behavior. *Stable external* causes of behavior include such things as laws and rules (speed limits, no-smoking areas). Unstable causes of behavior are variable or subject to change. *Unstable internal* causes of behavior include such things as mood (good or bad) and motivation (strong or weak). *Unstable external* causes could be the weather and the presence or absence of other people. In Weiner's model, the stable-unstable dimension in attribution cuts across the internal-external dimension, creating four types of attributions for success and failure, as shown in Figure 6.7.

Let's apply Weiner's model to a concrete event. Imagine that you are contemplating why you just landed the job you wanted. You might credit your situation to internal factors that are stable (excellent ability) or unstable (hard work on your attractive résumé). Or you might attribute the outcome to external factors that are stable (lack of top-flight competition) or unstable (luck). If you didn't get the job, your explanations would fall into the same four categories: internal-stable (lack of ability), internal-unstable (inadequate effort on your résumé), external-stable (too much competition in your field), and external-unstable (bad luck).

These two dimensions appear to be the central ones in the attribution process. Research has documented that self-attributions are motivational, guiding one toward or away from possible courses of action. Thus, one's self-beliefs can influence future expectations (success or failure) and emotions (pride, hopelessness, guilt), and these expectations and emotions can combine to influence subsequent performance (Weiner, 1986). Self-attributions, then, play a key role in one's feelings, motivational state, and behavior.

FIGURE 6.7 | Key dimensions of attributional thinking

Weiner's model assumes that people's explanations for success and failure emphasize internal versus external causes and stable versus unstable causes. For example, if you attribute an outcome to great effort or to lack of effort, you are citing causes that lie within the person. Because effort can vary over time, the causal factors at work are unstable. Other examples of causal factors that fit into each of the four cells in Weiner's model are shown in the diagram.

Internal-external dimension	Stability dimension: Unstable cause (temporary)	Stability dimension: Stable cause (permanent)
Internal cause	Effort Mood Fatigue	Ability Intelligence
External cause	Luck Chance Opportunity	Task difficulty

Source: From Weiner, B., Frieze, I., Kukla, A., Reed, L. & Rosenbaum, R. M. (1972). Perceiving the causes of success and failure. In E. E. Jones, D. E. Kanouse, H. H. Kelly, R. E. Nisbett, S. Valins, & B. Weiner (Eds.), *Perceiving causes of behavior.* Morristown, NJ: General Learning Press. Reprinted by permission of the author.

6-3c EXPLANATORY STYLE

Julio and Josh are freshmen who have just struck out trying to get their first college dates. After this disappointment, they reflect on the possible reasons for it. Julio speculates that his approach was too subtle. Looking back, he realizes that he wasn't very direct because he was nervous about asking the woman out. When she didn't reply, he didn't follow up for fear that she didn't really want to go out with him. On further reflection, he reasons that she probably didn't respond because she wasn't sure of his intentions. He vows to be more direct the next time. Josh, on the other hand, mopes, "I'll never have a relationship. I'm a total loser." On the basis of these comments, who do you think is likely to get a date in the future? If you guessed Julio, you are probably correct. Let's see why.

According to Martin Seligman (1991), people tend to exhibit, to varying degrees, an *optimistic explanatory style* or a *pessimistic explanatory style* (see Figure 6.8). ***Explanatory style* refers to the tendency to use similar causal attributions for a wide variety of events in one's life.** The person with an optimistic explanatory style usually attributes setbacks to external, unstable, and specific factors (Peterson & Steen, 2009). A person who failed to get a desired job, for example, might attribute this misfortune to factors in the interview situation ("The room was really hot") rather than to personal shortcomings. This style can be psychologically protective, helping people to discount their setbacks and thus maintain a favorable self-image (Gordon, 2008).

In contrast, people with a pessimistic explanatory style tend to attribute their setbacks to internal, stable, and global (or pervasive) factors. These attributions make them feel bad about themselves and doubtful about their ability to handle challenges in the future. As noted in Chapter 4, such a style can foster passive behavior and make people more vulnerable to *learned helplessness* and depression (Peterson, Maier, & Seligman, 1993).

6-3d MOTIVES GUIDING SELF-UNDERSTANDING

Whether people evaluate themselves by social comparisons, attributional thinking, or other means, they are highly motivated to pursue self-understanding. In seeking self-understanding, people are driven by four

FIGURE 6.8 | The effects of attributional style on expectations, emotions, and behavior

The pessimistic explanatory style is seen in the top row of boxes. This attributional style, which attributes setbacks to internal, stable, and global causes, tends to result in an expectation of lack of control over future events, depressed feelings, and passive behavior. A more adaptive, optimistic attributional style is shown in the bottom row of boxes.

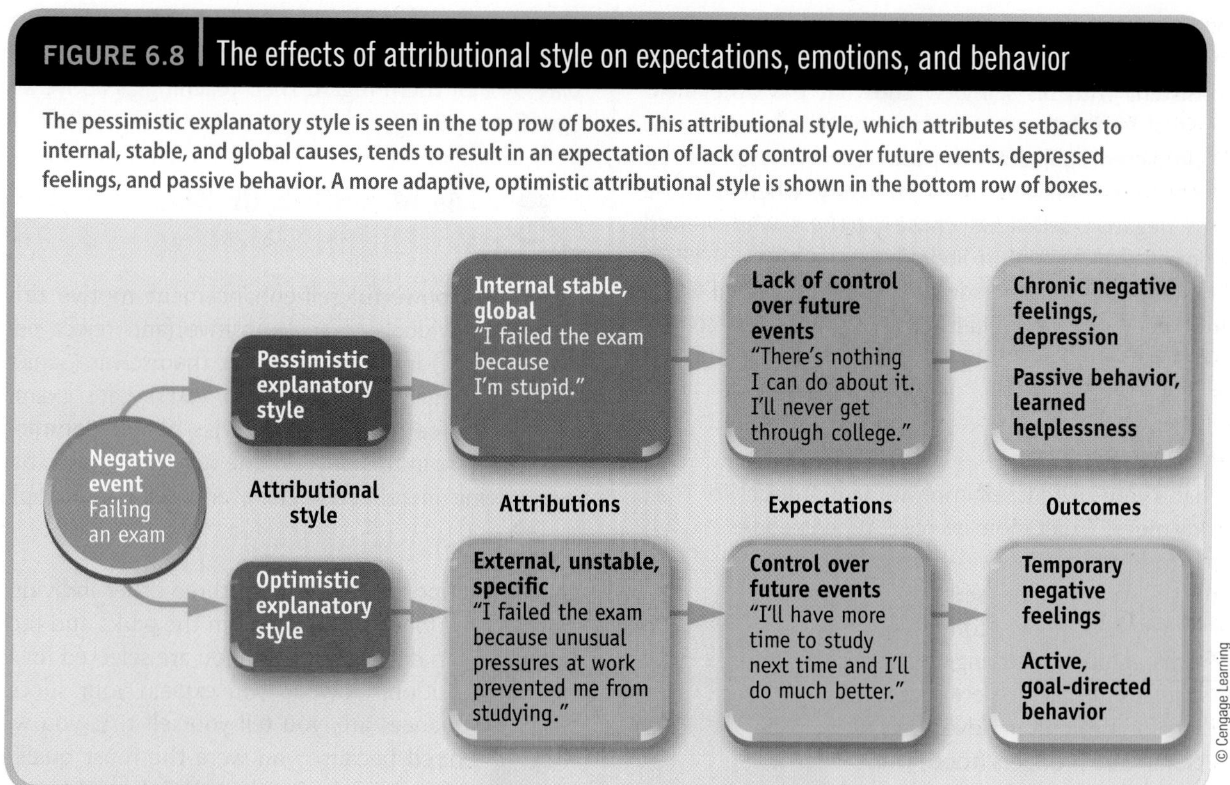

Negative event
Failing an exam
Pessimistic explanatory style
Optimistic explanatory style
Attributional style
Internal stable, global
"I failed the exam because I'm stupid."
External, unstable, specific
"I failed the exam because unusual pressures at work prevented me from studying."
Attributions
Lack of control over future events
"There's nothing I can do about it. I'll never get through college."
Control over future events
"I'll have more time to study next time and I'll do much better."
Expectations
Chronic negative feelings, depression
Passive behavior, learned helplessness
Temporary negative feelings
Active, goal-directed behavior
Outcomes
© Cengage Learning

major motives: assessment, verification, improvement, and enhancement.

Self-Assessment

The *self-assessment motive* is reflected in people's desire for truthful information about themselves (Trope, 1983). The problem is straightforward: Individuals don't know themselves all that well (Dunning, 2006). Unfortunately, many self-assessments are quite flawed; the only good news is that people are typically unaware of this fact, presumably because evaluating one's own abilities is a formidable challenge (Carter & Dunning, 2008). Still, there is some hope. Individuals do seek accurate feedback about many types of information, including their personal qualities, abilities, physical features, and so forth. It's obvious why people look for accurate information. After all, it helps them set realistic goals and behave in appropriate ways. Still, the bald truth is not always welcome. Accordingly, people are also motivated by other concerns.

Self-Verification

The *self-verification motive* drives people toward information that matches what they already believe about themselves, whether positive or negative (North & Swann, 2009a). This tendency to strive for a consistent self-image ensures that individuals' self-concepts are relatively stable. Individuals maintain consistent self-perceptions in a number of subtle ways and are often unaware of doing so (Schlenker & Pontari, 2000). For example, people maintain consistency between their past and present behavior by erasing past memories that conflict with present ones. To illustrate, people who were once shy and who later became outgoing have been shown to recall memories about themselves that indicate that they perceive themselves as always having been outgoing (Ross & Conway, 1986).

Another way people maintain self-consistency is by seeking out feedback and situations that will confirm their existing self-perceptions and by avoiding potentially disconfirming situations or feedback. Thus, self-verification processes are not only adaptive, they have other positive qualities as well (North & Swann, 2009b). According to ***self-verification theory*, people prefer to receive feedback from others that is consistent with their own self-views.** Thus, people with positive self-concepts should prefer positive feedback from others and those with negative self-concepts should prefer negative feedback. In one study, for example, college men were divided into positive and negative self-concept groups based on test scores. They were then asked to choose a partner for a subsequent 2- to 3-hour interaction. Participants were led to believe that one of the prospective partners held views of him that were consistent with his self-view and that the other held views of him that were inconsistent with his self-view. As predicted, subjects with positive self-views preferred partners who viewed them positively, whereas those with negative self-views chose partners who viewed them negatively (Swann, Stein-Seroussi, & Geisler, 1992). Among depressed persons, the persistent self-views predicted by self-verification processes may account for treatment setbacks or ongoing dejection (Petit & Joiner, 2006).

Self-Improvement

What is your current self-improvement project? To study more? To get more exercise? When people seek to better themselves, often after a failure or some other setback, the *self-improvement motive* comes into play (Kurman, 2006). In trying to improve, individuals typically look to successful others for inspiration. Advertisers of personal care products (tooth whiteners, exercise machines, and so forth) tap into this motive by showing before-and-after photographs of individuals who have used the products.

Self-Enhancement

Finally, people are motivated by the *self-enhancement motive*. ***Self-enhancement* is the tendency to maintain positive feelings about oneself.** One example of self-enhancement is the tendency to hold flattering views of one's personal qualities, a tendency termed the *better-than-average effect* (Alicke, 1985). You've already seen an example of this effect in our earlier report that 100% of students who took the SAT rated themselves above average in the ability to get along with others—a mathematical impossibility. Students can take perverse pleasure in knowing that faculty also succumb to this bias: 94% of them regard their teaching as above average (Cross, 1977)!

6-3e METHODS OF SELF-ENHANCEMENT

The powerful self-enhancement motive drives individuals to seek positive (and reject negative) information about themselves (Sanjuán, Magallares, & Gordillo, 2011). Let's examine three cognitive strategies people commonly use in this process: the self-serving bias, basking in reflected glory, and self-handicapping.

Self-Serving Bias

Suppose that you and three other individuals apply for a part-time job in the parks and recreation department and you are selected for the position. How do you explain your success? Chances are, you tell yourself that you were hired because you were the most qualified for the job. But how do the other three people interpret their negative outcome? Do they tell themselves that you got the job because you were the most able? Unlikely! Instead, they probably attribute their loss to "bad luck" or to not having had time to prepare for the interview. These different explanations for success and failure reflect **the *self-serving bias*, or the tendency to attribute one's successes to personal factors and one's failures to situational factors.**

One explanation for the self-serving bias is that unbiased self-judgments require a high degree of self-control, which is usually overridden by one's automatic drive toward self-enhancement (Krusemark, Campbell, & Clementz, 2008). For example, in one experiment,

PEANUTS

two strangers jointly took a test. They then received bogus success or failure feedback about their test performance and were asked to assign responsibility for the test results. Successful participants claimed credit, but those who failed blamed their partners (Campbell et al., 2000). Although the self-serving bias has been documented in a variety of cultures (Fletcher & Ward 1988), it seems to be particularly prevalent in individualistic, Western societies, where the emphasis on competition and high self-esteem motivates people to try to impress others, as well as themselves.

Basking in Reflected Glory

When your favorite sports team won the national championship last year, did you make a point of wearing the team cap? And when your best friend won that special award, do you remember how often you told others the good news about him? If you played a role in someone's success, it's understandable that you would want to share in the recognition; however, people often want to share recognition even when they are on the sidelines of an outstanding achievement. ***Basking in reflected glory* is the tendency to enhance one's image by publicly announcing one's association with those who are successful.**

Robert Cialdini and his colleagues (1976) studied this phenomenon at colleges with nationally ranked football teams. The researchers predicted that, when asked how their team had fared in a recent football game, students would be more likely to say, "We won" (in other words, to bask in reflected glory, or to "BIRG"—pronounced with a soft "g") when the home team had been successful than to respond "We lost" when it had been defeated. Indeed, the researchers found that students were more likely to use "we" in referring to their team when it won than when it lost. Also, subjects who believed that they had just failed a bogus test were more likely to use the words "We won" than those who believed they had performed well.

People frequently claim association with others who are successful (basking in the reflected glory) to maintain positive feelings about the self.

Photo: © Cal Sport Media via AP Images; Frame: © Picsfive/Shutterstock.com

A related self-enhancement strategy is "CORFing," or *cutting off reflected failure*. Because self-esteem is partly tied to an individual's associations with others, people often protect their self-esteem by distancing themselves from those who are unsuccessful (Cialdini et al., 1976). Thus, if your cousin is arrested for drunk driving, you may tell others that you don't really know him very well.

Self-Handicapping

When people fail at an important task, they need to save face. In such instances, individuals can usually come up with a face-saving excuse ("I had a terrible stomachache"). Curiously, some people actually behave in a way that sets them up to fail so that they have a readymade excuse for failure, should it occur. ***Self-handicapping* is the tendency to sabotage one's performance to provide an excuse for possible failure.** For example, when a big test is looming, they put off studying until the last minute or go out drinking the night before the test. If, as is likely, they don't do well on the exam, they explain their poor performance by saying they hadn't prepared. (After all, wouldn't you rather have others believe that your poor performance is due to inadequate preparation rather than to lack of ability?) People use a variety of other tactics for handicapping their performance: alcohol, drugs, procrastination, a bad mood, a distracting stimulus, anxiety, depression, and being overcommitted (Baumeister, 1998).

Self-handicapping should not be confused with *defensive pessimism*, a trait causing some people to mentally identify the worst possible outcome and to then subsequently work hard to make sure it never occurs (Norem, 1989). Although the two constructs appear similar, defensive pessimists are motivated to avoid bad outcomes, whereas self-handicappers undermine their own efforts (Elliot & Church, 2003). Imagine working on a huge end-of-term project for a class—one that will make or break your final course grade. Optimists cope with anxiety by anticipating they will do their best. Defensive pessimists will expect the worst and then get right to work, ending up pleasantly surprised when they do well. People engaging in self-handicapping, however, might procrastinate or do any number of things that, as we will see, can undermine their successful completion of the project.

Self-handicapping seems like a "win-win" strategy: If you fail, you have a face-saving excuse ready, and if you happen to succeed, you can claim that you are unusually gifted! However, it probably has not escaped your attention that self-handicapping is highly risky. By giving yourself an attributional "out" in case of failure, your self-defeating behavior will likely result in poor performance (Zuckerman, Kieffer, & Knee, 1998). Moreover, while self-handicapping may save you from negative self-attributions about your ability, it does not prevent others from making different negative attributions about you. Others may perceive you as lazy, inclined to drink too much, or highly anxious, depending on the means you use to self-handicap—perceptions that are sometimes accurate (Zuckerman & Tsai, 2005). Consequently, this self-enhancement tactic has serious drawbacks.

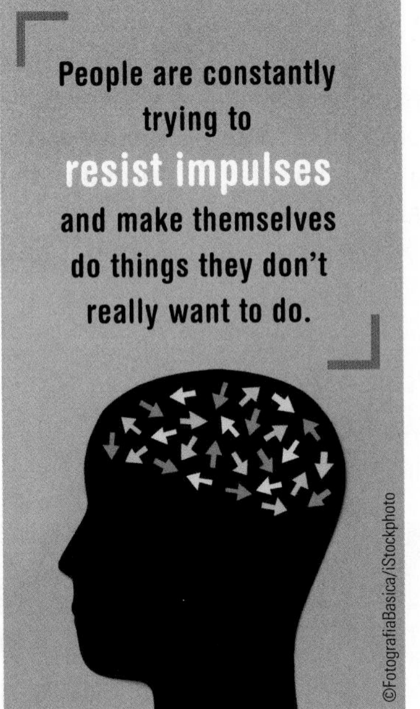
People are constantly trying to
resist impulses
and make themselves do things they don't really want to do.
©FotografiaBasica/iStockphoto

Potentially, anyone can engage in self-handicapping behavior (surely, you have come up with an excuse or two when things did not go your way), but research suggests that men self-handicap more than women, possibly because the latter place more importance on displaying effort (McCrea et al., 2008). High-status individuals are also likely to use self-handicapping as a social strategy (Lucas & Lovaglia, 2005). Why? Self-handicapping commonly occurs when self-esteem is threatened. Thus, high-status individuals will be more motivated to preserve their level of self-worth than people of a lower status.

6-4 Self-Regulation: The Challenge of Self-Control

"Should I have that hot fudge sundae or not?" "I guess I'd better get started on that English paper." "Would I better off checking Facebook one more time or going to bed?" People are constantly trying to resist impulses and make themselves do things they don't really want to do. ***Self-regulation* is the process of directing and controlling one's behavior.** Clearly, the ability to manage and direct what you think, how you feel, and how you behave is tied to your success at work, your relationships, and your mental and physical health (Vohs, Baumesiter, & Tice, 2008). Being able to forgo immediate gratification (studying instead of partying) and focus one's behavior on important, longer-range goals (graduating and getting a good job) is of paramount importance if one is to be successful in life.

One influential view is that people have a limited amount of self-control resources. If you tax these resources resisting temptation in a given situation, you may have a hard time resisting the next temptation or persisting at a new task. As a result, self-control can have a cost (Baumeister & Alquist, 2009). At least that's the idea behind the *ego depletion model of self-regulation* (Baumeister et al., 1998). To investigate this hypothesis, researchers asked college students to participate in a study of taste perception (the study was actually on self-control). Some participants were asked to eat two or three radishes in 5 minutes but not to touch the chocolate candy and chocolate chip cookies that were nearby. Others were asked to eat some candy or some cookies but were told not to eat any of the nearby radishes. A control group didn't participate in this part of the study. Then all subjects were asked to solve what were, unbeknownst-to-them, unsolvable puzzles while they supposedly waited for another part of the study. Researchers measured the subjects' self-control by the amount of time they persisted at the puzzles and the number of attempts they made. According to the ego depletion model, the radish eaters would use more self-control resources (resisting the chocolate) than the chocolate eaters (resisting the radishes) or the subjects in the no-food control group. Thus, this group should have the fewest self-control resources left to use for persisting at a difficult task. As you can see in Figure 6.9, the radish eaters gave up sooner and made fewer attempts on the puzzles than the chocolate eaters or the control group.

Self-regulation seems to develop early and remain relatively stable. One study reported that 4-year-olds who were better at delaying gratification did better in terms of both academic performance and social competence some ten years later (Shoda, Mischel, & Peake, 1990). Recent evidence suggests that self-regulation is

FIGURE 6.9 Persistence on unsolvable puzzles

Participants who were instructed to eat radishes and not to eat chocolate treats used more self-control resources than participants who were instructed to eat the chocolate and not touch the radishes or participants in the no-food control group. Because the radish eaters had relatively few self-control resources remaining to help them persist at a difficult task (unsolvable puzzles), they persisted for the shortest time and made the fewest attempts to solve the puzzles compared to the other two groups. (Adapted from Baumeister et al., 1998)

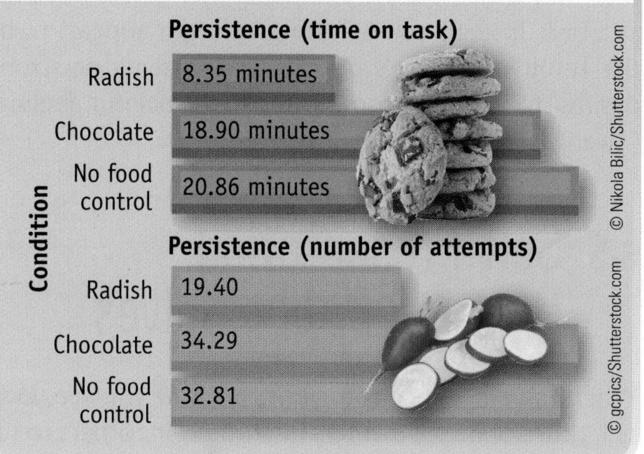

malleable and can be strengthened like a muscle, which means that with regular "exercise," people can become less vulnerable to ego depletion effects (Baumeister et al., 2006). Being in a good mood (Tice et al., 2007) and ingesting sugar, which fuels energy (Gailliot et al., 2007), can also restore people's self-control. In the next section, we examine self-efficacy, a key aspect of self-regulation, and then discuss self-defeating behavior, a case of self-control failure.

6-4a SELF-EFFICACY

***Self-efficacy* refers to one's belief about one's ability to perform behaviors that should lead to expected outcomes.** It represents people's conviction that they can achieve specific goals. According to Albert Bandura (1997), efficacy beliefs vary according to the person's skills. You may have high self-efficacy when it comes to making friends but low self-efficacy when it comes to speaking in front of a group. However, simply having a skill doesn't guarantee that you will be able to put it into practice. Like the Little Engine That Could, you must also *believe* that you are capable of doing so ("I *think* I can, I *think* I can . . ."). In other words, self-efficacy is concerned not with the skills you have, but with your *beliefs about what you can do* with these skills.

Correlates of Self-Efficacy

A number of studies have shown that self-efficacy affects individuals' commitments to goals, their performance on tasks, and their persistence toward goals in the face of obstacles. Self-efficacy is related to health promotion (Bandura, 2004), academic performance (Brady-Amoon & Fuertes, 2011), career choice (Betz & Klein, 1996), job performance (Stajkovic & Luthans, 1998), and coping with unemployment (Creed, Lehman, & Hood, 2009). Because of the importance of self-efficacy in psychological adjustment (Bandura, 2008), it is worth keeping in mind that self-efficacy is learned and can be changed. Research shows that increasing self-efficacy is an effective way to improve health (losing weight, stopping smoking) (Maddux & Gosselin, 2003) and to treat a variety of psychological problems, including test anxiety (Smith, 1989), fear of computer use (Wilfong, 2006), phobias (Williams, 1995), eating disorders (Goodrick et al., 1999), and substance abuse (Lozano, Stephens, & Roffman, 2006).

Developing Self-Efficacy

Self-efficacy is obviously a valuable quality. How does one acquire it? Bandura (2000) identifies four sources of self-efficacy: mastery experiences, vicarious experiences, persuasion/encouragement, and interpretation of emotional arousal.

1. *Mastery experiences.* The most effective path to self-efficacy is through mastering new skills. Sometimes new skills come easily—learning how to use the complicated copy machine in the library, for instance. Some things are harder to master, such as learning how to drive a stick-shift in a standard transmission car or how to play the piano. In acquiring more difficult skills, people usually make mistakes. If they persist through failure experiences to eventual success, they learn the lesson of self-efficacy: I *can* do it!

2. *Vicarious experiences.* Another way to improve self-efficacy is by watching others perform a skill you want to learn. For example, if you're shy about speaking up for yourself, observing someone who is good at doing so can help you develop the confidence to do it yourself.

3. *Persuasion and encouragement.* Although it is less effective than the first two approaches, a third way to develop self-efficacy is through the encouragement of others. For example, if you're having a hard time asking someone for a date, a friend's encouragement might give you just the push you need.

4. *Interpretation of emotional arousal.* The physiological responses that accompany feelings and one's interpretations of these responses are another source of self-efficacy. Let's say you're sitting in class waiting for your professor to distribute an exam. You notice that your palms are moist, your stomach feels a little queasy, and your heart is pounding. If you attribute these behaviors to fear, you can temporarily dampen your self-efficacy, thus decreasing your chances of doing well. Alternatively, if you attribute your sweaty palms and racing heart to the arousal everyone needs in order to perform well, you may be able to boost your self-efficacy and increase your chances of doing well. Of course, self-regulation doesn't always succeed. That's the case in self-defeating behavior, our next topic.

6-4b SELF-DEFEATING BEHAVIOR

People typically act in their own self-interest. But sometimes they knowingly do things that are bad for them—such as smoking, having unprotected sex, and completing important assignments at the last minute. ***Self-defeating behaviors* are seemingly intentional actions that thwart a person's self-interest.** According to Roy Baumeister (1997), there are three categories of intentional self-defeating behaviors: deliberate self-destruction, trade-offs, and counterproductive strategies. The key difference among these three behaviors lies in how intentional they are.

In *deliberate self-destruction,* people want to harm themselves and choose courses of action that will foreseeably lead to that result. Although this type of behavior may occur in individuals with psychological disorders, deliberate self-destruction appears to be infrequent in normal populations.

In *trade-offs,* people foresee the possibility of harming themselves but accept it as a necessary accompaniment to achieving a desirable goal. Overeating, smoking, and drinking to excess are examples that come readily to mind (recall Chapter 5). People engage in trade-offs because they bring immediate, positive, and reliable outcomes, not because they want to hurt themselves in the short or the long run.

© Marc Vaughn/Masterfile

Self-defeating behaviors come in many forms with many underlying motivations. Overeating is a matter of *trade-offs.* People realize that excessive eating may be harmful in the long run, but it is enjoyable at the time.

In *counterproductive strategies,* a person pursues a desirable outcome but misguidedly uses an approach that is bound to fail. Of course, you can't always know in advance if a strategy will pay off. Thus, people must *habitually* use this strategy for it to qualify as self-defeating. For example, some people tend to persist in unproductive endeavors, such as pursuing an unreachable career goal or an unrequited love. People persist in these behaviors because they erroneously believe they'll be successful, not because they are intent on self-defeat.

To conclude, although most people engage in self-defeating behavior at some time, there is little evidence that they deliberately try to harm themselves or to fail at a task. Instead, self-defeating behavior appears to be the result of people's distorted judgments or strong desires to escape from immediate, painful feelings (Twenge, Catanese, & Baumeister, 2002).

6-5 Self-Presentation: Crafting Public Selves

Whereas your self-concept involves how you see yourself, your public self involves how you want others to see you. **A *public self* is an image presented to others in social interactions.** This presentation of a public self may sound deceitful, but it is perfectly normal, and everyone does it (Schlenker, 2003). Many self-presentations (ritual greetings, for example) take place automatically and without awareness. But when it really counts (job interviews, for example), people consciously strive to make the best possible impression so they are perceived favorably.

Typically, individuals have a number of public selves that are tied to certain situations and certain people. For instance, you may have one public self for your parents

FIGURE 6.10 | Public selves and adjustment

Person 1 has divergent public selves with relatively little overlap among them. Person 2, whose public selves are more congruent with each other, is likely to be better adjusted than Person 1.

Public selves for
(a) spouse
(b) parents
(c) neighbors
(d) boss
(e) colleagues at work

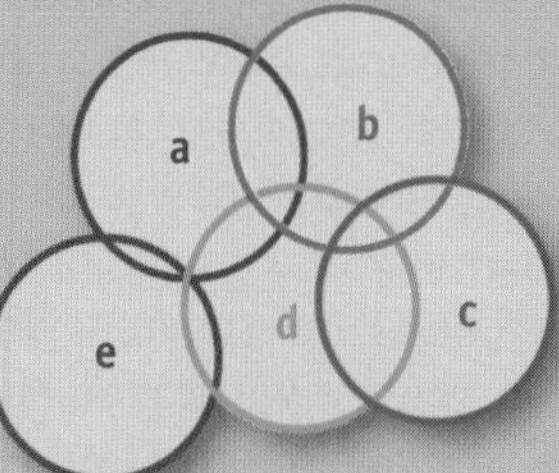

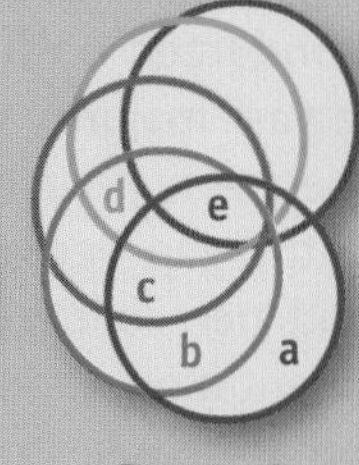

and another for your peers. You may have still others for your teachers, your boss, your co-workers, and so forth. Also, people differ in the degree of overlap or congruence among their various public selves (see Figure 6.10). Does it matter whether you perceive yourself to be essentially the same person in different situations? It seems so. People who see themselves as being similar across different social roles (with friends, at work, at school, with parents, with romantic partners) are better adjusted than those who perceive less integration in their self-views across these roles (Lutz & Ross, 2003).

6-5a IMPRESSION MANAGEMENT STRATEGIES

Interestingly, people think others notice and evaluate them more than is the actual case (Gilovich, Kruger, & Medvec, 2002). This common tendency is aptly termed *the spotlight effect*. In a related phenomenon, the *guilty by association effect*, people erroneously assume their social standing suffers as a result of embarrassing actions or blunders perpetrated

One reason people engage in impression management is to claim a particular identity.

by those they associate with ("My friend is making me look bad!") (Fortune & Newby-Clark, 2008). These two self-focused responses remind us that people normally strive to make a positive impression on others to be liked, respected, hired, and so forth. ***Impression management*** **refers to usually conscious efforts by people to influence how others think of them.**

One reason people engage in impression management is to claim a particular identity. Thus, you select a type of dress, hairstyle, and manner of speech to present a certain image of yourself. Tattoos and body piercings also create a specific image. A second motive for impression management is to gain liking and approval from others—by editing what you say about yourself and by using various nonverbal cues such as smiles, gestures, and eye contact. Because self-presentation is practiced so often, people usually do it automatically. At other times, however, impression management may be used intentionally—to get a job, a date, a promotion, and so forth. Some common self-presentation strategies include ingratiation, self-promotion, exemplification, intimidation, and supplication (Jones, 1990):

1. *Ingratiation.* Of all the self-presentation strategies, ingratiation is the most fundamental and most frequently used. ***Ingratiation*** **is behaving in ways to make oneself likable to others.** For example, *giving compliments* is effective, as long as you are sincere (people dislike insincerity and can often detect it). *Doing favors for others* is also a common tactic, as long as

your gestures aren't so spectacular they leave others feeling indebted.

2. *Self-promotion.* The motive behind self-promotion is earning respect. You do so by playing up your strong points so you will be perceived as competent. For instance, in a job interview, you might find ways to mention that you earned high honors at school and that you were president of the student body and a member of the soccer team.

3. *Exemplification.* Because most people try to project an honest image, you have to demonstrate exemplary behavior to claim special credit for integrity or character. Occupations fraught with danger, such as those in the military or law enforcement, provide obvious opportunities to exemplify moral virtue or to demonstrate courage.

4. *Intimidation.* This strategy sends the message, "Don't mess with me." Intimidation usually works only in nonvoluntary relationships—for instance, when it's hard for workers to find another employer or for an economically dependent spouse to leave a relationship. Obvious intimidation tactics include threats and the withholding of valuable resources (salary increases, promotions, sex). The other self-presentation strategies work by creating a favorable impression; intimidation usually generates dislike. Nonetheless, it can work.

5. *Supplication.* This is usually the tactic of last resort. To get favors from others, individuals try to present themselves as weak and dependent—as in the song, "Ain't Too Proud to Beg." Students may plead or break into tears in an instructor's office in an attempt to get a grade changed. Because of the social norm to help those in need, supplication may work. However, unless the supplicator has something to offer the potential benefactor, it's not an effective strategy.

© Piotr Marcinski/Shutterstock.com

6-5b PERSPECTIVES ON IMPRESSION MANAGEMENT

Curiously, almost all research on self-presentation has been conducted on first meetings between strangers, yet the vast majority of actual social interactions take place between people who already know each other. Noting the gap between reality and research, Dianne Tice and her colleagues (1995) investigated whether self-presentation varied in these two situations. They found that people strive to make positive impressions when they interact with strangers but shift toward modesty and neutral self-presentations when they are with friends. Why the difference? Because strangers don't know you, you want to give them positive information so they'll form a good impression of you. Besides, strangers have no way of knowing whether you are bending the truth. On the other hand, your friends already know your positive qualities. Thus, belaboring them is unnecessary and may make you seem boastful. The best approach to managing impressions may be a balanced one. Robinson, Johnson, and Shields (1995) found that people who presented themselves using a mix of self-promoting and self-deprecating comments were viewed as more genuine and likeable than those who relied exclusively on either type of descriptions.

In the upcoming Application, we redirect our attention to the critical issue of self-esteem and outline seven steps for boosting it.

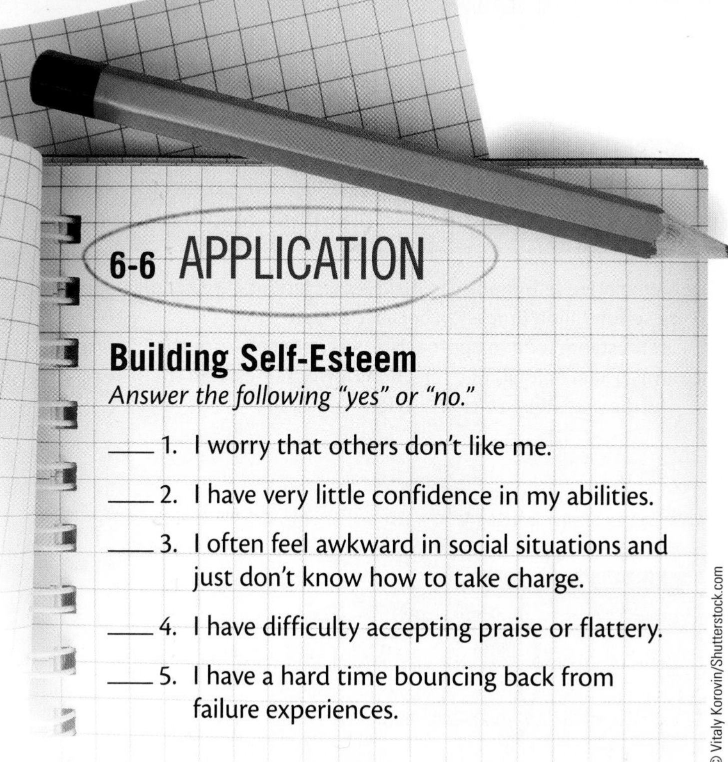

6-6 APPLICATION

Building Self-Esteem

Answer the following "yes" or "no."

___ 1. I worry that others don't like me.

___ 2. I have very little confidence in my abilities.

___ 3. I often feel awkward in social situations and just don't know how to take charge.

___ 4. I have difficulty accepting praise or flattery.

___ 5. I have a hard time bouncing back from failure experiences.

If you answered "yes" to most of these questions, you may suffer from low self-esteem. As we noted earlier, people with low self-esteem are less happy and more prone to depression, become demoralized after failures, and are anxious in relationships. Moreover, even people with high global self-esteem may have pockets of low self-esteem. For example, you may feel great about your "social self" but not so good about your "academic self." Thus, this Application can be useful to many people.

We have one caveat, however: It is possible for self-esteem to be too high—recall the earlier discussion about narcissism, ego threats, and violence. Better adjustment is associated with realistically high (and stable) self-esteem. Thus, our suggestions here are directed to those whose self-esteem could use a legitimate boost, not to those whose self-esteem is already inflated. The latter group can benefit from developing more realistic self-view.

As you saw in our discussion of self-efficacy, there is ample evidence that efforts at self-improvement can pay off by boosting self-esteem. Following are seven guidelines for building self-esteem. These suggestions are distilled from the advice of many experts, including Baumeister et al. (2003), McKay and Fanning (2000), Rogers (1977), and Zimbardo (1990).

1. Recognize That You Control Your Self-Image

The first thing you must do is recognize that *you* ultimately control how you see yourself. You *do* have the power to change your self-image. True, we have discussed at length how feedback from others influences your self-concept. Yes, social comparison theory suggests that people need such feedback and that it would be unwise to ignore it completely. However, the final choice about whether to accept or reject such feedback rests with you. Your self-image resides in your mind and is a product of your thinking. Although others may influence your self-concept, you are the final authority.

2. Learn More About Yourself

People with low self-esteem don't seem to know themselves in as much detail as those with high self-esteem. Accordingly, to boost your self-esteem, you need to take stock of yourself. To do so, review what you know about your physical appearance, personality characteristics, relations with others, school and job performance, intellectual functioning, and sexuality. By thinking through each area, you may discover that you're fuzzy about certain aspects of yourself. To get a clearer picture, pay careful attention to your thoughts, feelings, and behavior and utilize feedback from others.

3. Don't Let Others Set Your Goals

A common trap that many people fall into is letting others set the standards by which they evaluate themselves. Others are constantly telling you that you should do this or ought to do that. You may hear that you "should study accounting" or "ought to lose weight." Most of this advice is well intentioned and may contain good ideas. Still, it is important that you make your *own* decisions about what you will do and what you will believe in. Think about the source of and basis for your personal goals and standards. Do they really represent ideals that *you* value? Or are they beliefs that you have passively accepted from others without thinking?

4. Recognize Unrealistic Goals

Even if you truly value certain ideals and sincerely want to achieve certain goals, another question remains: Are your goals realistic? Many people demand too much of themselves. They want to always perform at their best, which is obviously impossible. For instance, you may have a burning desire to achieve national acclaim as an actress. However, the odds against such an achievement are enormous. It is important to recognize this reality so that you do not condemn yourself to failure. Some overly demanding people pervert the social comparison process by always comparing themselves to the *best* rather than to similar others. They assess their looks by comparing themselves with famous models, and they judge their finances by comparing themselves with the wealthiest people they know. Such comparisons are unrealistic and almost inevitably undermine self-esteem.

5. Modify Negative Self-Talk

How you think about your life influences how you see yourself (and vice versa). People who are low in self-esteem tend to engage in counterproductive modes of thinking. For example, when they succeed, they may attribute their success to good luck, and when they fail, they may blame themselves. Quite to the contrary, you should take credit for your successes and consider the possibility that your failures may not be your fault. As discussed in Chapter 4, Albert Ellis has pointed out that people often think irrationally and draw unwarranted negative conclusions about themselves. If someone breaks off a romantic relationship with you, do you think, "He doesn't love me. I must be a worthless, unlovable person?" The conclusion that you are a "worthless person" does *not* follow logically from the fact of the breakup. Such irrational thinking and negative self-talk breed poor self-esteem. Recognize the destructive potential of negative self-talk and bring it to a halt.

6. Emphasize Your Strengths

This advice may seem trite, but it has some merit. People with low self-esteem often derive little satisfaction from their accomplishments and virtues. They pay little heed to their good qualities while talking constantly about their defeats and frailties. The fact is that everyone has strengths and weaknesses. You should accept those personal shortcomings that you are powerless to change and work on those that are changeable, without becoming obsessed about it. At the same time, you should embrace your strengths and learn to appreciate them.

7. Approach Others with a Positive Outlook

Some people with low self-esteem try to cut others down to their (subjective) size through constant criticism. This fault finding and negative approach does not go over well. Instead, it leads to tension, antagonism, and rejection. This rejection lowers self-esteem still further (see Figure 6.11). You can boost your esteem-building efforts by recognizing and reversing this self-defeating tendency. Cultivate the habit of maintaining a positive, supportive outlook when you approach people. Doing so will promote rewarding interactions and help you earn others' acceptance. There is probably nothing that enhances self-esteem more than acceptance and genuine affection from others.

FIGURE 6.11 The vicious circle of low self-esteem and rejection

A negative self-image can make expectations of rejection a self-fulfilling prophecy, because people with low self-esteem tend to approach others in negative, hurtful ways. Real or imagined rejections lower self-esteem still further, creating a vicious circle.

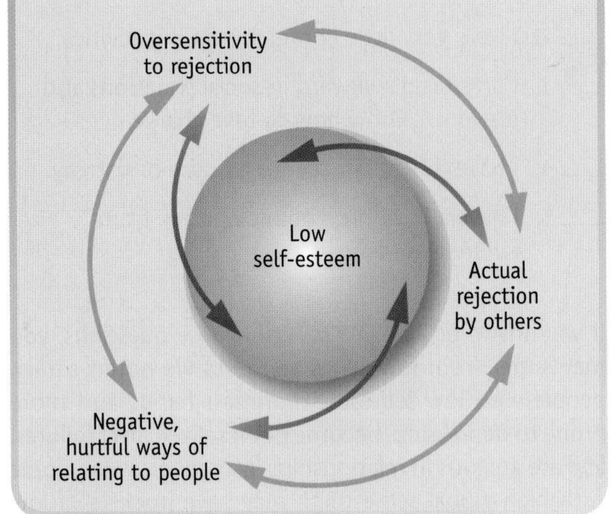

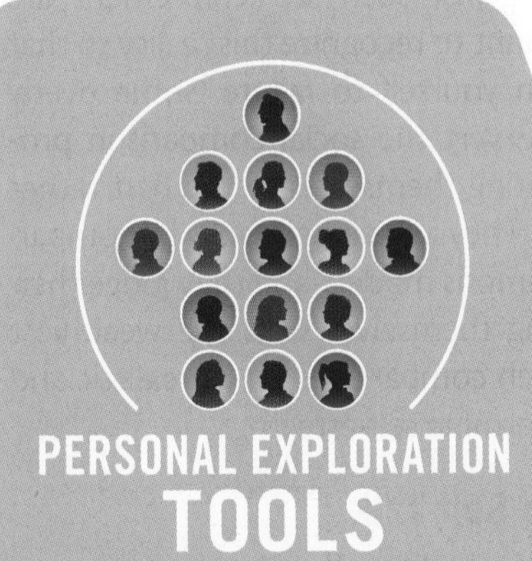

Curious about yourself? To learn more about how topics in this chapter relate to you, go online to CourseMate at www.cengagebrain.com where you can:

- Complete a **Self-Reflection** exercise that will help you think about your personal experiences in relation to topics in the chapter.
- Take a **Self-Assessment** scale that will show you how you score on a research instrument that measures personality traits or attitudes.
- Explore **Recommended Readings** that will provide brief overviews of useful self-help books.

STUDY TOOLS ▶ 6

Ready to study? In your book you can:

- **Test Yourself** with a multiple-choice quiz (below)
- Rip out the **Chapter Review card** (in the back of the book) to refresh yourself on the chapter's Key Ideas and Key Terms

Or you can go online to CourseMate at www.cengagebrain.com where you can:

- Take additional Practice Quizzes to prepare for your exam
- Review Key Terms with flash cards and a crossword puzzle
- View videos that expand on selected concepts

TEST YOURSELF

1. Which of the following statements is *not* true about the self-concept?

a. It is composed of one dominant belief about the self.
b. It is composed of many self-beliefs.
c. It is relatively stable over time.
d. It influences present as well as future behavior.

2. Andrew received a grade of C on his term paper. He was disappointed in his performance until he learned that his friend, Phil, earned a D on the same assignment. Andrew felt better because of

a. his reference group.
b. downward social comparison.
c. possible selves.
d. upward social comparison.

3. A person reared in a collectivist culture is likely to have a(n) ______ self-view, whereas a person reared in an individualistic culture is likely to have a(n) ______ self-view.

a. self-discrepant; self-consistent
b. self-consistent; self-discrepant
c. independent; interdependent
d. interdependent; independent

4. Low self-esteem is associated with

a. happiness.
b. high trust of others.
c. self-concept confusion.
d. recovering after failure experiences.

5. Aggression in response to self-esteem threats is more likely to occur in people who are

a. high in self-esteem.
b. low in self-esteem.
c. narcissistic.
d. self-defeating.

6. Which of the following is *not* a basic principle of self-perception?

a. People are "cognitive spenders."
b. People's explanatory style is related to adjustment.
c. People want to receive information that is consistent with their self-views.
d. People want to maintain positive feelings about the self.

7. After Keisha's favored political candidate lost the election in a landslide, she decides not to admit to her friends that she had actually voted for him. This is an example of

a. the self-serving bias.
b. basking in reflected glory.
c. cutting off reflected failure.
d. self-handicapping.

8. Which of the following statements about self-efficacy is true?

a. It can be developed by persevering through failure until one achieves success.
b. It is something that one is born with.
c. It essentially is the same as self-esteem.
d. It refers to conscious efforts to make a certain impression on others.

9. The self-presentation strategy of ingratiation involves trying to make others

a. respect you.
b. fear you.
c. feel sorry for you.
d. like you.

10. Which of the following will *not* help you build higher self-esteem?

a. Minimizing negative self-talk
b. Comparing yourself with those who are the best in a given area
c. Working to improve yourself
d. Approaching others with positive expectations.

Answers: 1. a, pages 115–116; 2. b, page 117; 3. d, page 118; 4. c, page 119; 5. c, pages 121–122; 6. a, page 123; 7. c, page 127; 8. a, page 129; 9. d, pages 131–132; 10. b, pages 133–134

© KL Services/Masterfile

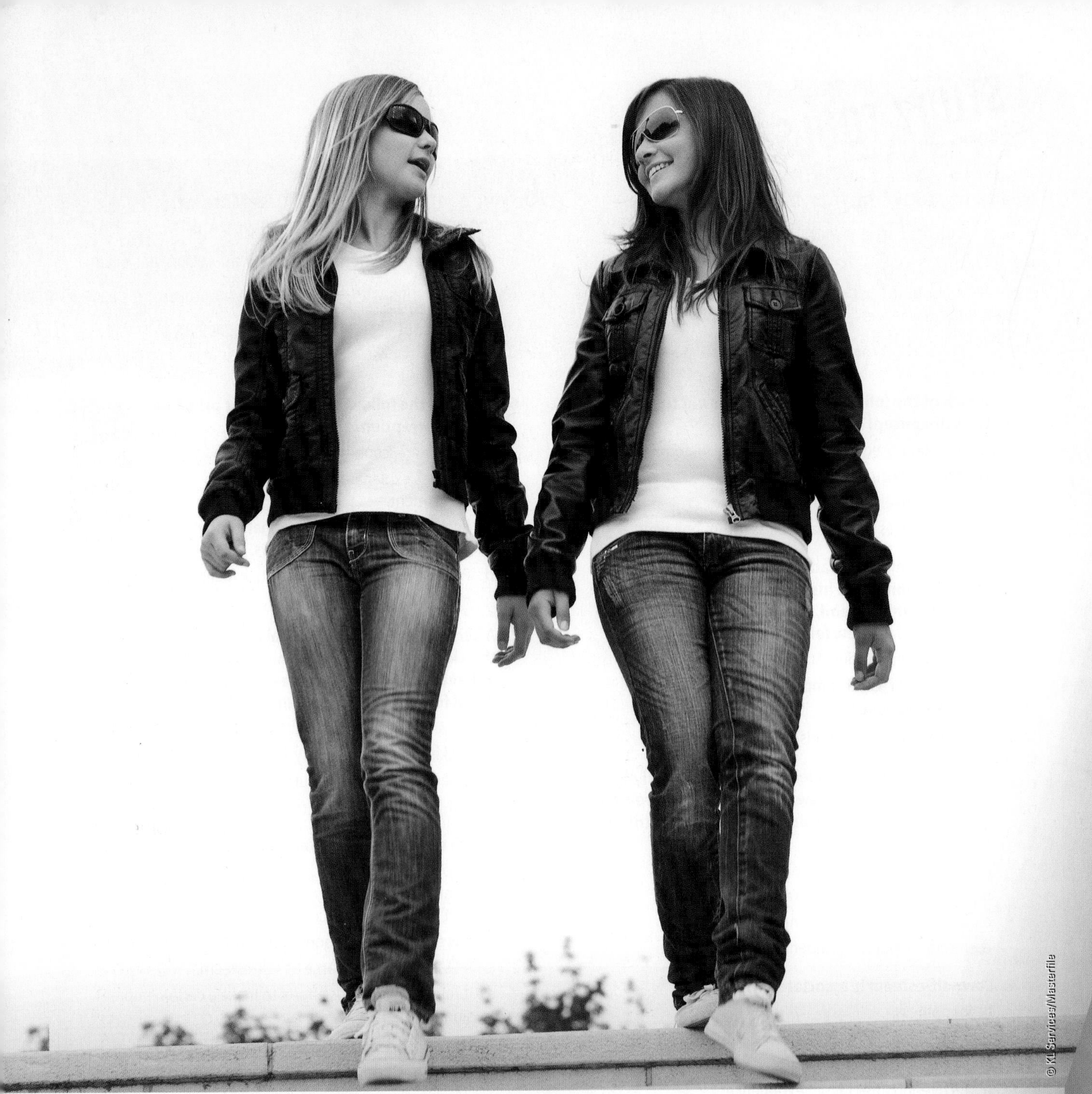

LEARNING OBJECTIVES

7-1 Understand the benefits and pitfalls of the psychological processes people use to form impressions of others.

7-2 Describe the nature and causes of prejudice and ways to reduce prejudice.

7-3 Review key elements in persuasive communications.

7-4 Summarize essential issues in understanding compliance, conformity, and obedience.

7-5 Recognize some typical compliance strategies found in everyday situations.

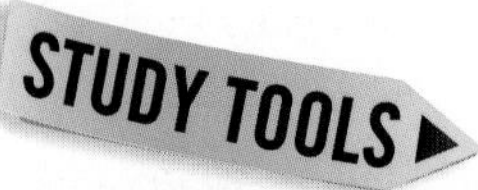

STUDY TOOLS ▸ After you have read the chapter, you can Test Yourself and learn about other Study Tools on page 159.

CHAPTER 7

Social Thinking and SOCIAL INFLUENCE

Your old boss was let go because of poor performance. Your new boss looks very serious. Unlike your old boss, who was friendly and joked around a lot, this fellow is very reserved. He rarely even says hello to you when your paths cross in the hall or out in the parking lot. You wonder whether he doesn't like you or happens to treat everyone that way. The new boss is also not much older than you—in fact, he might be your age. What if he thinks you are not working hard enough? Maybe he feels you should have advanced farther in the company, or that you are too nice. Could he be thinking about firing you?

This situation illustrates the process of person perception in everyday life. This chapter explores how people form impressions of others, as well as how and why such judgments can be incorrect. Our consideration of how people think about others then broadens to examine the problems posed by prejudice. We then look at how others try to influence one's beliefs and behavior. To do so, we explore the power of persuasive messages and the social pressures to conform and obey. As you will learn, social thinking and social influence play important roles in personal adjustment.

7-1 Forming Impressions of Others

Do you recall the first time you met your roommate? She seemed friendly but a little shy, and perhaps a bit on the neat side—so much so that you wondered whether you would get along. Happily, once you got to know her better, she warmed up to you and your clutter, and now you are close friends. As people interact with others, they constantly engage in ***person perception*, the process of forming impressions of others.** Because impression formation is usually such an automatic process, people are unaware that it is taking place. Nonetheless, the process is a complex one, involving perceivers, their social networks, and those who are perceived (Smith & Collins, 2009). Let's review some of its essential aspects.

7-1a KEY SOURCES OF INFORMATION

Because you can't read other people's minds, you are dependent on *observations* of others to determine what they are like. In forming impressions of others, people rely on five key sources of observational information: appearance, verbal behavior, actions, nonverbal messages, and situational cues.

1. *Appearance.* Despite the admonition "You can't judge a book by its cover," people frequently do exactly that. Physical features such as height, weight, skin color, race, and hair color are some of the cues used to "read" other people. Regardless of their accuracy, beliefs about physical features are used to form impressions of others (Hellström & Tekle, 1994). For example, Americans learn to associate the wearing of eyeglasses with studiousness.

2. *Verbal behavior.* Another obvious source of information about others is what they say. People form impressions based on what and how much others self-disclose, how often they give advice and ask questions, and how judgmental they are (Tardy & Dindia, 2006). If Tanisha speaks negatively about most of the people she knows, you will probably conclude that she is a critical person.

3. *Actions.* Because people don't always tell the truth, you have to rely on their behavior to provide insights about them. For instance, when you learn that Wade volunteers five hours a week at the local homeless

© SW Productions/Age fotostock

In forming impressions of others, people rely on cues such as appearance, actions, and verbal and nonverbal messages, as well as the nature of the situation.

shelter, you are likely to infer that he is a caring person. In impression formation, actions speak louder than words.

4. *Nonverbal messages.* As discussed in Chapter 8, a key source of information about others is nonverbal communication: facial expressions, eye contact, body language, and gestures (DePaulo & Friedman, 1998). These nonverbal cues provide information about people's emotional states and dispositions. For example, in our culture a bright smile and steady eye contact signal friendliness and openness, and a handshake can indicate extraversion (Bernieri & Petty, 2011).

5. *Situations.* The setting in which behavior occurs provides crucial information about how to interpret a person's behavior (Cooper & Withey, 2009). For instance, without situational cues (such as being at a wedding versus a funeral), it would be hard to know whether a person crying is happy or sad.

7-1b SNAP JUDGMENTS VERSUS SYSTEMATIC JUDGMENTS

In their interactions with others, people are bombarded with more information than they can possibly handle. To avoid being overwhelmed, they rely on alternative ways to process information (Kahneman, 2011). *Snap judgments* about others are those made quickly and based on only a few bits of information and preconceived notions. Thus, they may not be particularly accurate. Yet, as Susan Fiske (2004) puts it, "Good-enough accuracy in forming impressions allows us to navigate our social seas and not collide or run aground too often" (p. 132). Often, interactions with others are so fleeting or inconsequential that it makes little difference that such judgments are imprecise.

On the other hand, when it comes to selecting a friend, a mate, or an employee, it's essential that impressions be as accurate as possible. Thus, it's not surprising that people are motivated to take more care in these assessments. In forming impressions of those who can affect their welfare and happiness, people make *systematic judgments* rather than snap decisions (see Figure 7.1). That is, they take the time to observe the person in a variety of situations and to compare that person's behavior with that of others in similar situations.

In assessing what a significant individual is like, people are particularly interested in learning why the person behaves in a certain way. To determine the causes of others' behavior, people engage in the process of causal attribution.

7-1c ATTRIBUTIONS

As we have noted in earlier chapters, ***attributions* are inferences that people draw about the causes of their own behavior, others' behavior, and events.** In Chap-

FIGURE 7.1 | The process of person perception

In forming impressions of others, perceivers rely on various sources of observational information. When it's important to form accurate impressions of others, people are motivated to make systematic judgments, including attributions. When accuracy isn't a priority, people make snap judgments about others.

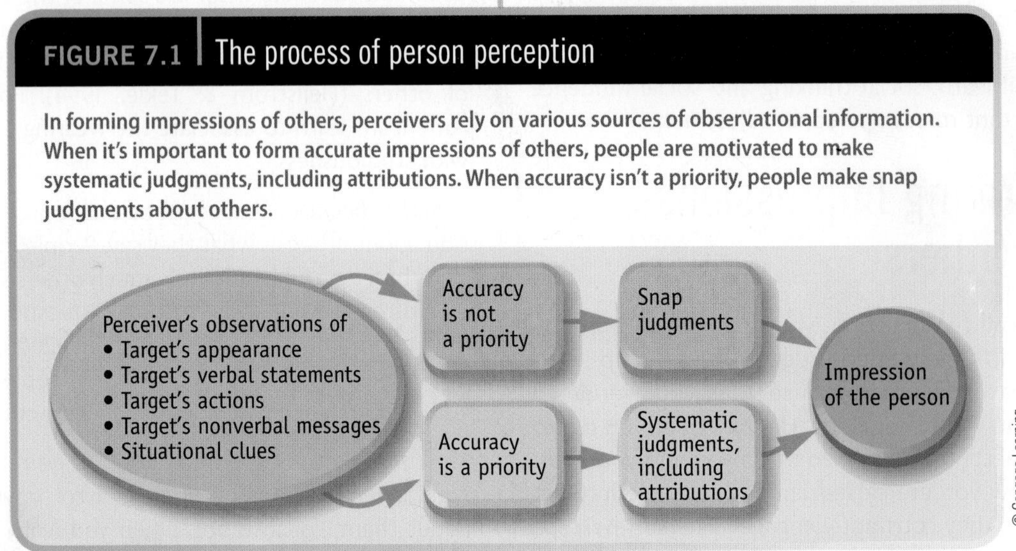

Source: From Brehm, S. S., & Kassin, S. M. (1996). *Social psychology*. Belmont, CA: Wadsworth/Cengage Learning. © Cengage Learning.

ter 6, we focused on self-attributions. Here, we'll apply attribution theory to the behavior of *other people*. In Chapter 6, we also noted that attributions have two key dimensions: internal versus external and stable versus unstable (Jones & Davis, 1965). For this discussion, we focus only on the internal/external dimension.

When people link the causes of someone's behavior to personal dispositions, traits, abilities, or feelings, they are making *internal* attributions. When they credit the causes of a person's behavior to situational demands and environmental constraints, they are making *external* attributions. For example, if a friend's business fails, you might attribute the failure to your friend's lack of business skills (an internal factor) or to negative trends in the economy (an external factor).

© Catalin Petolea/Shutterstock.com

Obviously, people don't make attributions about every person they meet. Research suggests that people are selective in this process (Jones, 1990). It seems they are most likely to make attributions (1) when others behave in unexpected or negative ways, (2) when events are personally relevant, and (3) when they are suspicious about another person's motives. For example, if Serena laughs loudly at the local student hangout, no one bats an eye. But if she does so in the middle of a serious lecture, it raises eyebrows and generates speculation about why she behaved this way. As we will see, situations do matter.

The Fundamental Attribution Error

When explaining the causes of others' behavior, people display a surprisingly strong tendency to make personal attributions while discounting the importance of situational factors. Although this tendency is not universal, it is strong enough that Lee Ross (1977) called it the "*fundamental* attribution error." **The *fundamental attribution error* refers to the tendency to explain other people's behavior as the result of personal, rather than situational, factors.** If Jeremy leaves class early, for example, you may be correct in inferring that he is inconsiderate, but he might also have had a previously scheduled job interview. Thus, a person's behavior at a given time may or may not reflect his or her personality or character—but observers tend to assume that it does.

Making attributions is a two-step process (Gilbert & Malone, 1995). As you can see in Figure 7.2, in the first step, which occurs automatically, observers make an

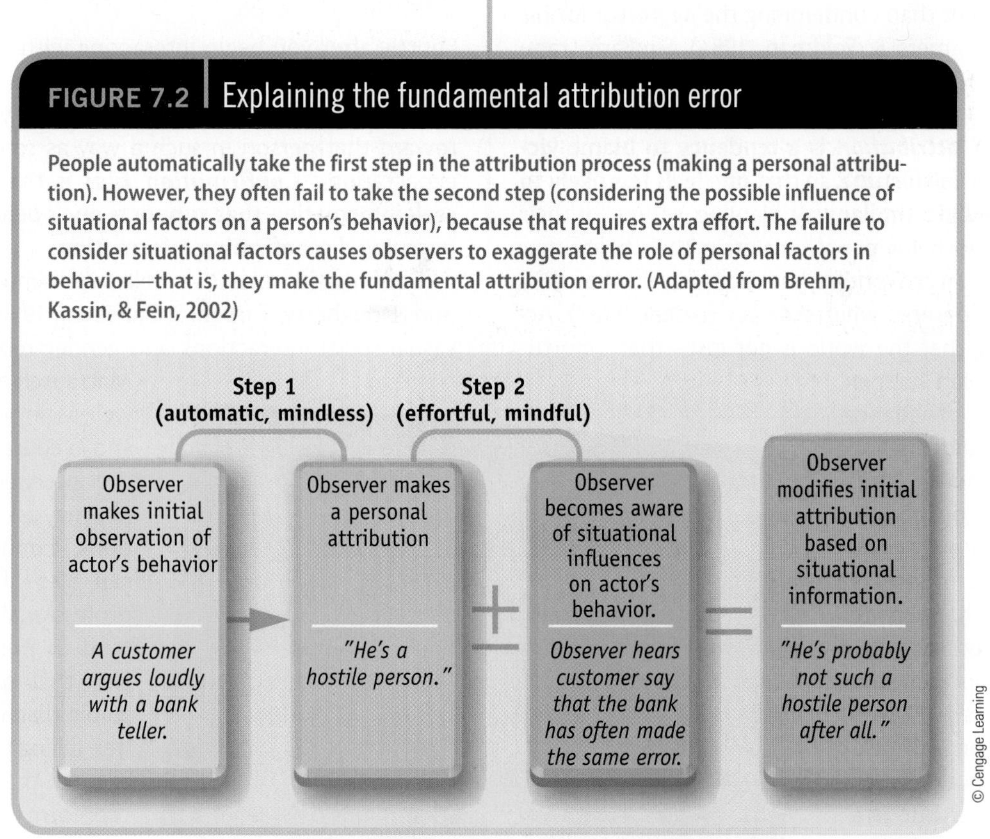

Step 1
(automatic, mindless)
Step 2
(effortful, mindful)
Observer makes initial observation of actor's behavior
A customer argues loudly with a bank teller.
Observer makes a personal attribution
"He's a hostile person."
+
−
Observer becomes aware of situational influences on actor's behavior.
Observer hears customer say that the bank has often made the same error.
=
Observer modifies initial attribution based on situational information.
"He's probably not such a hostile person after all."
© Cengage Learning

FIGURE 7.2 | Explaining the fundamental attribution error

People automatically take the first step in the attribution process (making a personal attribution). However, they often fail to take the second step (considering the possible influence of situational factors on a person's behavior), because that requires extra effort. The failure to consider situational factors causes observers to exaggerate the role of personal factors in behavior—that is, they make the fundamental attribution error. (Adapted from Brehm, Kassin, & Fein, 2002) internal attribution because they are focusing on the person rather than the situation. (At your bank, if you observe the man ahead of you yell at the teller, you might infer that he is a hostile person.) In the second step, observers weigh the impact of the situation on the target person's behavior and adjust their inference. (If you overhear the customer claim this is the third time in three weeks that the bank has made the same error in his account, you're likely to temper your initial judgment about his hostile tendencies.)

The first step in the attribution process occurs spontaneously, but the second step requires cognitive effort and attention. Thus, it is easy to stop after step one—especially if one is in a hurry or distracted. Failure to take the effortful second step can result in the fundamental attribution error. However, when people are motivated to form accurate impressions of others (Webster, 1993) or when they are suspicious about another's motives (Fein, 1996), they do expend the effort to complete the second step. In these cases, they are more likely to make accurate attributions.

Defensive Attribution

Observers are especially likely to make internal attributions in trying to explain the calamities and tragedies that befall other people. When a boyfriend or husband abuses a woman, for example, people frequently blame the victim by remarking how stupid she is to stay with the man, rather than condemning the aggressor for his behavior (Summers & Feldman, 1984). Similarly, rape victims are often judged to have "asked for it" (Abrams et al., 2003).

Defensive attribution **is a tendency to blame victims for their misfortune, so that one feels less likely to be victimized in a similar way.** Blaming victims for their calamities also helps people maintain their belief that they live in a "just world" where people get what they deserve and deserve what they get (Lerner, 1980). Acknowledging that the world is not just—that unfortunate events can happen as a result of chance factors—would mean having to admit the frightening possibility that the catastrophes that happen to others could also happen to oneself, especially when the victim is perceived to be like oneself (Correia, Vala, & Aguiar, 2007). Defensive attributions are a self-protective, but irrational, strategy that allows people to avoid such unnerving thoughts and helps them feel in control of their lives (Hafer, 2000). Unfortunately, when victims are blamed for their setbacks, people unfairly attribute undesirable traits to them, such as incompetence, foolishness, and laziness.

Some aspects of the attribution process are logical, of course, but observers often fail to notice the power situations have over people's behavior. As a result, observers often make snap judgments about people's personalities instead of considering situational explanations. Other sources of error also creep into the process of person perception, a topic we take up next.

7-1d PERCEIVER EXPECTATIONS

Remember Evan, that bully from the fourth grade? He made your life miserable—constantly looking for opportunities to poke fun at you and beat you up. Now when you meet someone named Evan, your initial reaction is negative, and it takes a while to warm up to him. Why? Your negative past experiences with an Evan have led you to expect the worst, whether or not it's warranted. This is just one example of how *perceiver expectations* can influence the perception of others. Let's look at two of the principles governing perceiver expectations: confirmation bias and self-fulfilling prophecy.

Confirmation Bias

Shortly after you begin interacting with someone, you start forming hypotheses about what the person is like. In turn, these hypotheses can influence your behavior toward that person in such a way as to confirm your expectations. ***Confirmation bias*** **is the tendency to seek information that supports one's beliefs while not pursuing disconfirming information.**

Confirmation bias is a well-documented phenomenon (Dougherty, Turban, & Callendar, 1994). It occurs in casual social interactions and gender relations (Traut-Mattausch et al., 2011), as well as in job interviews and in courtrooms, where the interviewer or attorney may ask leading questions. Confirmation bias can also affect medical professionals. Physicians tend to pursue information that supports their initial diagnosis while often failing to look for evidence that might disconform it (Tschan et al.,

DILBERT

2009). Likewise, when it comes to forming first impressions of others, the principle is not so much "seeing is believing" as "believing is seeing" (see Figure 7.3).

Confirmation bias also occurs because individuals selectively recall facts to fit their views of others. In one experiment, participants watched a videotape of a woman engaging in a variety of activities, including listening to classical music, drinking beer, and watching TV (Cohen, 1981). Half of them were told that the woman was a waitress and the other half were told that she was a librarian. When asked to recall the woman's actions on the videotape, participants tended to remember activities consistent with their stereotypes of waitresses and librarians. Thus, those who thought that the woman was a waitress recalled her drinking beer; those who thought she was a librarian recalled her listening to classical music.

FIGURE 7.3 | Confirmation bias

Confirmation bias is a two-pronged process in which people seek and remember information that supports their beliefs while discounting and forgetting information that is inconsistent with their beliefs. This common cognitive slant often distorts the process of person perception, leading to inaccurate impressions of people.

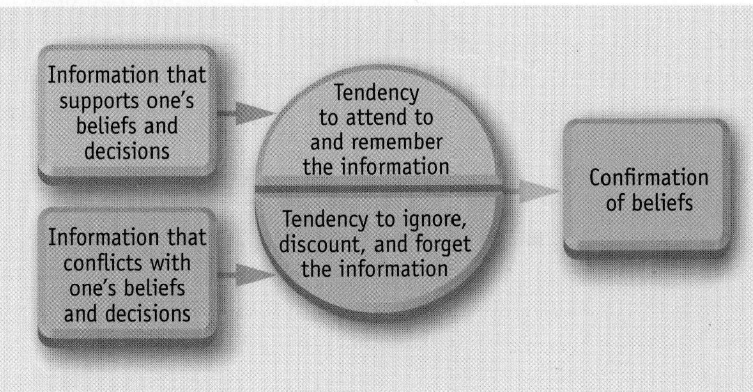

Self-Fulfilling Prophecies

Sometimes a perceiver's expectations can actually change another person's behavior (Madon et al., 2011). **A *self-fulfilling prophecy* occurs when expectations about a person cause him or her to behave in ways that confirm the expectations.** This term was originally coined by sociologist Robert Merton (1948) to explain phenomena such as "runs" on banks that occurred during the Depression. That is, when unfounded rumors would circulate that a bank couldn't cover its deposits, people would rush to the bank and withdraw their funds, thereby draining the deposits from the bank and making real what was initially untrue.

Figure 7.4 on the next page depicts the three steps in a self-fulfilling prophecy. First, the perceiver has an initial impression of someone. (A teacher believes that Jennifer is highly intelligent.) Then the perceiver behaves toward the target person according to his or her expectations. (He asks her interesting questions and praises her answers.) The third step occurs when the target person adjusts his or her behavior to the perceiver's actions, confirming the perceiver's hypothesis about the target person. (Jennifer works hard and performs well in class.) Note that both individuals are unaware that this process is operating. Also note that because perceivers are unaware of their expectations and of the effect they can have on others, they

FIGURE 7.4 The three steps of the self-fulfilling prophecy

Through a three-step process, your expectations about a person can cause that person to behave in ways that confirm those expectations. First, you form an impression of someone. Second, you behave toward that person in a way that is consistent with your impression. Third, the person exhibits the behavior that you encourage, which confirms your initial impression.

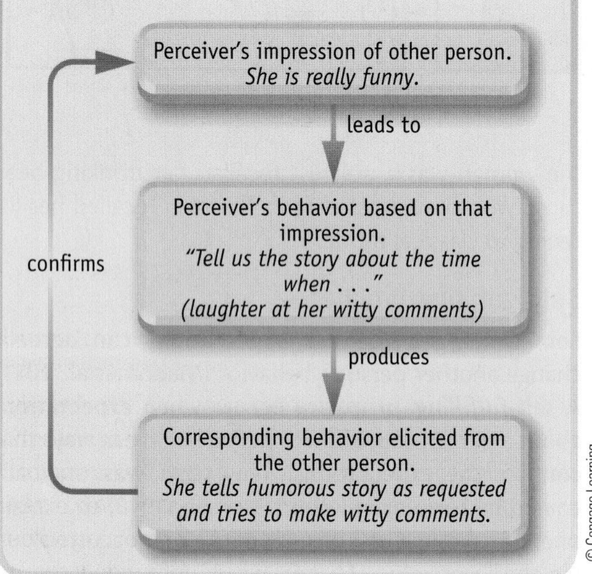

Perceiver's impression of other person.
She is really funny.
leads to
Perceiver's behavior based on that impression.
"Tell us the story about the time when . . ."
(laughter at her witty comments)
produces
Corresponding behavior elicited from the other person.
She tells humorous story as requested and tries to make witty comments.
confirms
© Cengage Learning

Source: Adapted from Smith, E. R., & Mackie, D. M. (2000). *Social psychology.* Philadelphia, PA: Psychology Press, p. 94. Copyright 2000. Reproduced with permission of Taylor & Francis Group, LLC.

mistakenly attribute the target person's behavior to an internal cause (Jennifer is smart), rather than an external one (their own expectations).

The best-known experiments on the self-fulfilling prophecy have been conducted in classroom settings, looking at the effect of teachers' expectations on students' academic performance (Rosenthal, 2002). A review of 400 studies of this phenomenon over a period of 30 years reported that teacher expectations significantly influenced student performance in 36% of the experiments.

7-1e COGNITIVE DISTORTIONS

Another source of error in person perception comes from distortions in the minds of perceivers. These errors in judgment are most likely to occur when a perceiver is in a hurry, is distracted, or is not motivated to pay careful attention to another person.

Social Categorization

One of the ways people efficiently process information is to classify objects (and people) according to their distinctive features (Fiske, 1998). Thus, people quite often categorize others on the basis of nationality, race, ethnicity, gender, age, religion, sexual orientation, and so forth. People frequently take the easy path of categorizing others to avoid expending the cognitive effort that would be necessary for a more accurate impression.

People classify those who are similar to them as members of their *ingroup* ("us") and those who are dissimilar to them as in the *outgroup* ("them"). Such categorizing has three important results. First, people usually have less favorable attitudes toward outgroup members than ingroup members, such that empathic reactions to those perceived to be in their ingroup are often exaggerated (Brown, Bradley, & Lang, 2006). Second, individuals usually see outgroup members as being much more alike than they really are, whereas they see members of their ingroup as unique individuals (Oakes, 2001). In other words, people frequently explain the behavior of outgroup members on the basis of the characteristic that sets them apart ("Those *Nerdians* are *all* drunks"), but attribute the same behavior by an ingroup member to individual personality traits ("*Brett* is a heavy drinker").

A third result of categorizing is that it heightens the visibility of outgroup members when there are only a few of them within a larger group. In other words, minority group status in a group makes more salient the quality that distinguishes the person—ethnicity, gender, whatever. When people are perceived as being unique or distinctive, they are also seen as gaining more

© olly/Shutterstock.com

attention in a group, and their good and bad qualities are given extra weight (Crocker & McGraw, 1984).

Stereotypes

***Stereotypes* are widely held beliefs that people have certain characteristics because of their membership in a particular group.** For example, many people assume that Jews are shrewd and ambitious, that African Americans have special athletic and musical abilities, and that Muslims are religious fanatics. Although a kernel of truth may underlie some stereotypes, it should be readily apparent that not all Jews, African Americans, Muslims, and so forth behave alike; there is eno[illegible]us diversity in behavior within any group.

Stereotypes may be based on physical a[illegible]ce. In particular, there is plenty [illegible]ce that physically attractiv[illegible] believed to have desirab[illegible]ality traits. This widespread pe[illegible]ception is termed the *"what-is-beautiful-is-good" stereotype* (Dion, Berscheid, & Walster, 1972). Specifically, attractive people are usually viewed as happier, more socially competent, more assertive, better adjusted, and more intellectually competent than those who are less attractive (Eagly et al., 1991). Yet most such perceptions have little basis in fact.

© Yuri Arcurs/Shutterstock.com

Stereotypes can be spontaneously triggered when people encounter members of commonly stereotyped groups, such as individuals from different racial groups, even in those who are not prejudiced (Devine, 1989). Worse still, racially based stereotypes can cause regrettable—and potentially dangerous—split-second decisions in which people see a weapon that isn't actually there (Payne, 2006). Because stereotyping is automatic, some psychologists are pessimistic about being able to control it, but others take a more optimistic view. For example, a recent study found less automatic race bias when men and women of different races (except blacks) were surreptitiously induced to smile while looking at photographs of blacks (Ito et al., 2006). If people put forth effort to respond in a friendly and open manner to individuals who are different from them on some important dimension (race, sexual orientation), perhaps the positive behaviors will lead to a reduction in automatic biases when reacting to others.

Why do stereotypes persist? For one thing, they are functional (Quinn, Macrae, & Bodenhausen, 2003). People have been characterized as "cognitive misers." Because people are deluged with much more information than they can process, they tend to reduce this complexity to simplicity. But, as we noted earlier, the tradeoff for simplification is inaccuracy. Stereotypes also endure because of confirmation bias. That is, when individuals encounter members of groups that they view with prejudice, they are likely to see what they expect to see. Self-fulfilling prophecy is a third reason stereotypes persist: Beliefs about another person may actually elicit the anticipated behavior and thus confirm biased expectations. The persistent influence of stereotypes can lead to prejudice, the topic of the next section.

7-2 The Problem of Prejudice

Let's begin our discussion by clarifying a couple of terms that are often confused. ***Prejudice* is a negative attitude toward members of a group; *discrimination* involves behaving differently, usually unfairly, toward the members of a group.** Prejudice and discrimination do tend to go together, but that is not always the case (see Figure 7.5). One classic social psychology study found almost no discriminatory behavior aimed at a Chinese couple traveling around the country with a white professor in the 1930s. Before making the trips, the professor anticipated that they would encounter some prejudice about where they could stay or dine, but the three were declined service only a few times. Months later, when the professor wrote to all the establishments they had visited to ask whether Chinese guests were welcome, however, the majority of the responses were prejudiced and uninviting, showing that, attitudes don't always predict behavior (LaPiere, 1934). Why can people respond in discriminatory ways sometimes but not always? It is possible that a restaurant owner would be prejudiced against Chinese individuals and yet treat them like anyone else because he needed their business. This is an example of prejudice without discrimination. Although it is probably less common, discrimination without prejudice may also occur. For example, an executive who has favorable attitudes toward blacks may not hire them because he thinks his boss would be upset.

FIGURE 7.5 Prejudice and discrimination

Prejudice and discrimination are highly correlated, but t[illegible] ily go hand in hand. As the examples in the blue cells sh[illegible] exist without discrimination and discrimination witho[illegible]

Discrimination	Prejudice: Absent	Prejudice: Pr[illegible]
Absent	No relevant behavior	A restaura[illegible] is bigo[illegible] Hispanics [illegible] hem fairly beca[illegible] she needs their business.
Present	An executive with favorable attitudes toward blacks doesn't hire them because he would get in trouble with his boss.	A professor who is hostile toward women grades his female students unfairly.

7-2a "OLD-FASHIONED" VERSUS MODERN DISCRIMINATION

Over the past 50 years, prejudice and discrimination against minority groups have diminished in the United States. Racial segregation is no longer legal, and discrimination based on race, ethnicity, gender, and religion is much less common than it was in the 1950s and 1960s. Thus, the good news is that overt, or *"old-fashioned," discrimination* against minority groups has declined. The bad news is that a more subtle form of prejudice and discrimination remains (Dovidio & Gaertner, 1996). That is, people may privately harbor racist or sexist attitudes but express them only when they feel such views are justified or when it's safe to do so. This new phenomenon has been termed *modern discrimination* (also called "modern racism"). Modern discrimination is also operating when people endorse equality as an abstract principle but oppose programs intended to promote equality on the grounds that discrimination against minority groups no longer exists (Wright & Taylor, 2003).

While modern racists do not wish to return to the days of segregation, they also feel that minority groups should not push too fast for advancement or receive special treatme[illegible] by the government. Individuals who endorse beliefs th[illegible] favor "modern" discrimination are much m[illegible]ote against a black political candidate[illegible]mative action, and to fa[illegible] tax law[illegible]es at the expense of [illegible] to [illegible] not endorse such [illegible] et al., 1[illegible]

One imp[illegible] the study of prejudice is the recogn[illegible]on that most white people consider the possibility that they might hold racist views to be very upsetting; indeed, they are conflicted about it. As a result, they avoid acting in any way that might be construed as racist by others or even by themselves. The upshot is that well-intentioned whites can engage in *aversive racism*, an indirect, subtle, ambiguous form of racism that occurs when their conscious endorsement of egalitarian ideals is in conflict with unconscious, negative reactions to minority group members (Dovidio et al., 2009). An aversive racist might act in a racist manner when a nonracist excuse is available ("I interviewed several qualified blacks for the job but I had to hire the best candidate, who happened to be white"). Fortunately, researchers are seeking ways to combat

© Bill Aaron/PhotoEdit
Which man looks guilty? If you picked the man on the right, you're wrong.
Wrong for judging people based on the color of their skin. Because if you
look closely, you'll see they're the same man. Unfortunately, racial stereotyping like this happens every day. On America's highways, police stop drivers
based on their skin color rather than for the way they are driving. For example,
in Florida 80% of those stopped and searched were black and Hispanic,
while they constituted only 5% of all drivers. These humiliating and illegal
searches are violations of th must be fought. Help us defend
your rights. Support t merican civil liberties union

This clever [illegible] sponsored by the American [illegible] Union, focuses a [illegible] on the sensitive issue of [illegible] profiling. Racial profiling, which is a manifestation of moder[illegible] influence of stereotyping. The phenomenon of rac[illegible] how simple, often automatic, cognitive distortions [illegible] nate consequences in everyday life.

such unintended but real bias toward others. When people cannot reconcile the conflict between their expressed attitudes and how they act, for example, their prejudice decreases (Son Hing, Li, & Zanna, 2002).

7-2b CAUSES OF PREJUDICE

Prejudice is obviously a complex issue and has multiple causes. Although we can't thoroughly examine all of the causes of prejudice, we'll examine some of the major psychological and social factors that contribute to this vexing problem.

Authoritarianism

In some of the earliest research on prejudice, Robert Adorno and his colleagues (1950) identified the *authoritarian personality*, a personality type characterized by prejudice toward *any* group perceived to be different from oneself. Over the past 50 years, both the definition and measurement of authoritarianism have evolved. The construct is now termed *right-wing authoritarianism* (RWA) (Altemeyer, 1988), and it is characterized by authoritarian submission (exaggerated deference to those in power), authoritarian aggression (hostility toward targets sanctioned by authorities), and conventionalism (strong adherence to values endorsed by authorities). Because authoritarians tend to support established authority, RWA is more commonly found among political conservatives than among political liberals (who are more likely to challenge the status quo). RWA has even been linked to the Big Five personality traits (recall Chapter 2) in that authoritarian individuals tend to score low on openness to experience and conscientiousness (Sibley & Duckitt, 2008).

Cognitive Distortions and Expectations

Much of prejudice is rooted in automatic cognitive processes that operate without conscious intent (Wright & Taylor, 2003). As already noted, *social categorization* predisposes people to divide the social world into ingroups and outgroups. This distinction can trigger negativity toward outgroup members.

Similarly, people are more likely to make the *fundamental attribution error* when evaluating targets of prejudice (Hewstone, 1990). Thomas Pettigrew (2001) suggests that perceiving negative characteristics as being dispositional (personality based) and due to group membership is the *ultimate attribution error*. Thus, when people take note of ethnic neighborhoods dominated by crime and poverty, they blame these problems on the residents (they're lazy and ignorant) and downplay or ignore situationally based explanations (job discrimination, poor police service, and so on). The old saying "They should pull themselves up by their own bootstraps" is a blanket dismissal of how situational factors may make it especially difficult for minorities to achieve upward mobility.

Defensive attributions, in which people unfairly blame victims of adversity to reassure themselves that the same thing won't happen to them, can also contribute to prejudice. For example, individuals who claim that people who contract AIDS deserve it may be trying to reassure themselves that they won't suffer a similar fate.

Expectations can also foster and maintain prejudice. You already know that once people have formed impressions, they are invested in maintaining them. For instance, people note and recall behavior that confirms their stereotypes better than they recall information that is inconsistent with their beliefs (Bodenhausen, 1988). Also, when an outgroup member's behavior contradicts a stereotype, people often "explain away" such behavior in order to leave their stereotype intact (Ickes et al., 1982). Unfortunately, the fact that social thinking is automatic, selective, and consistent means that people usually see what they expect to see when they look through prejudiced eyes (Vallone, Ross, & Lepper, 1985).

People usually see what they expect to see when they look with **prejudiced eyes.**

©FotografiaBasica/iStockphoto

Competition Between Groups

Back in 1954, Muzafer Sherif and his colleagues conducted a now-classic study at Robbers' Cave State Park in Oklahoma to look at competition and prejudice (Sherif et al., 1961). In this study, 11-year-old boys were invited to attend a three-week summer camp. What the boys didn't know was that they were participants in an experiment. The boys were randomly assigned to one of two groups. At camp, they went directly to their assigned campsites and had no knowledge of the other group's presence. During the first week, the boys got to know members of their own group through typical camp activities (hiking, swimming, and camping out). Each group also chose a name (the Rattlers and the Eagles).

In the second week, the Rattlers and Eagles were introduced to each other through intergroup competitions. Events included a football game, a treasure hunt, and a tug of war, with medals, trophies, and other desirable prizes for the winning team. Almost immediately after competitive games were introduced, hostile feelings erupted between the two groups and quickly escalated to highly aggressive behavior: Food fights broke out in the mess hall, cabins were ransacked, and group flags were burned. Thus, Sherif concluded that prejudice and hostility are a natural outgrowth of competition between groups for scarce resources.

This classic demonstration of the effects of competition on prejudice is often mirrored in the real world. For example, disputes over territory often provoke antagonism, as is the case in the Israeli-Palestinian conflict. The lack of jobs or other important resources can also create competition between social groups. Still, competition does not always breed prejudice. In fact, the *perception* of threats to one's ingroup (loss of status, for example) is much more likely to cause hostility between groups than actual threats to the ingroup are (Brown et al., 2001). Unfortunately, such perceptions are quite common, because ingroup members usually assume that outgroup members are competitive and will try to thwart the ingroup's success (Fiske & Ruscher, 1993). To conclude, then, there is ample evidence that conflict over actual and perceived resources can prejudice individuals toward outgroup members.

Threats to Social Identity

Although group membership provides individuals with a sense of identity and pride, it can also foster prejudice and discrimination, as we just noted. Members' individual identities become merged with the group and even societal processes (Turner & Reynolds, 2004). To explore a different facet of this idea, we turn to *social identity theory*, developed by Henri Tajfel (1982) and John Turner (1987). According to this theory, self-esteem is partly determined by one's *social identity*, or collective self, which is tied to one's group memberships (nationality, religion, gender, major, occupation, political party affiliation, and so forth). Whereas your personal self-esteem is elevated by individual accomplishments (you got an A on a history exam), your collective self-

© greenland/Shutterstock.com

esteem is boosted when your ingroup is successful (your team wins the football game, your party wins the election). Likewise, your self-esteem can be threatened on both the personal level (you didn't get called for that job interview) and the collective level (your football team loses the championship game, your party is defeated in an election).

Threats to both personal and social identity motivate individuals to restore self-esteem, but threats to social identity are more likely to provoke responses that foster prejudice and discrimination (Crocker & Luhtanen, 1990). When collective self-esteem is threatened, individuals react in two key ways to bolster it. The most common response is to show *ingroup favoritism*—for example, tapping an ingroup member for a job opening or rating the performance of an ingroup member higher than that of an outgroup member (Branscombe et al., 1993). The second way to deal with threats to social identity is to engage in *outgroup derogation*—in other words, to "trash" outgroups that are perceived as threatening. This latter tactic is especially likely to be used by individuals who identify strongly with an ingroup (Perreault & Bourhis, 1999). Figure 7.6 depicts the various elements of social identity theory. Significantly, it is "ingroup love," not "outgroup hate" that underlies most discrimination (Brewer, 1999). In other words, ingroups reward their own members and withhold rewards from outgroups, rather than deliberately blocking outgroups from desired resources (Fiske, 2002).

FIGURE 7.6 | Social identity theory

According to Tajfel (1982) and Turner (1987), individuals have both a personal identity (based on a unique sense of self) and a social identity (based on group memberships). When social identity is threatened, people are motivated to restore self-esteem either by showing favoritism to ingroup members or by derogating outgroup members. These tactics contribute to prejudice and discrimination.

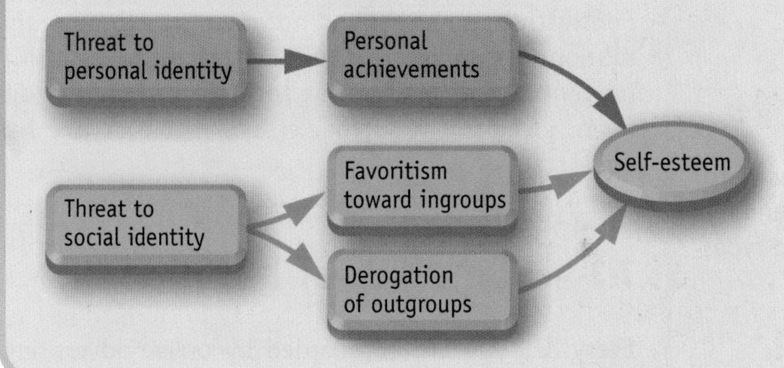

Source: Adapted from Brehm, S. S., & Kassin, S. M. (1996). *Social psychology.* Belmont, CA: Wadsworth. © Cengage Learning. Adapted with permission.

Stereotype Threat

Our discussion in this chapter has focused on stereotypes that are directed at others. What happens when individuals are the targets of a stereotype used by others to characterize the group they belong to? Is the stereotype ignored, or does the person internalize its impact?

Consider African Americans, for example. One pernicious stereotype is that African American students perform poorly on standardized tests compared to, say, white students. Steele (1992) suggests that while socioeconomic disadvantages can serve as an explanatory factor for the underperformance of blacks relative to whites on such tests, there may be other legitimate reasons. Steele argues that the availability and awareness of derogatory stereotypes connected to various stigmatized groups, including blacks, leads to *stereotype vulnerability,* otherwise known as *stereotype threat.* Feelings of stereotype vulnerability can undermine group members' performance on standardized tests, as well as other measures of academic achievement.

In one study by Steele and Aronson (1995), for example, black and white college students who scored well above average in academic ability were recruited (their comparable academic backgrounds ruled out cultural disadvantage as a factor in the research). All participants were asked to take a challenging 30-minute test of verbal ability composed of items drawn from the Graduate Record Exam (GRE). In one condition, stereotype vulnerability was made salient: The test was described as being an excellent index of a person's general verbal ability. In the other condition, the test was described as a means for researchers to analyze people's problem-solving strategies (thus, not as a measure of intellectual ability). What did Steele and Aronson find? When the African American students' stereotype vulnerability was not emphasized, the performances of black and white students did not differ (see the bars on the left side of Figure 7.7 on the next page). Yet when the same test was presented in a way that increased stereotype threat, the black students scored significantly lower than the white test takers (see the two bars on the right side of Figure 7.7).

Steele and his colleagues have demonstrated the stereotype threat can influence the performance of a variety of groups, not just minorities, suggesting its applicability to a variety of behavioral phenomena (Steele, 2011). Thus, for example, women have been shown to be vulnerable to stereo-

FIGURE 7.7 Stereotype vulnerability and test performance

Steele and Aronson (1995) compared the performance of African American and white students of equal ability on a 30-item verbal ability test constructed from difficult GRE questions. When the black students' stereotype vulnerability was not obvious, their performance did not differ from that of the white students; but when the threat of stereotype vulnerability was raised, the African American students performed significantly worse than the white students.

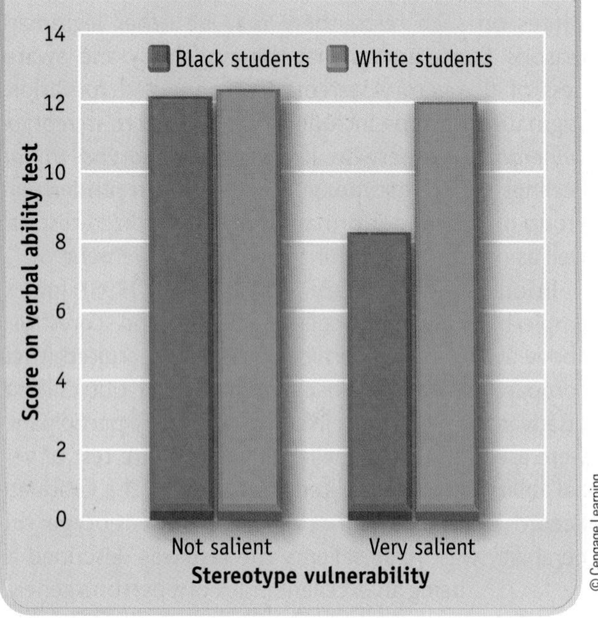

Source: Adapted from Steele, C. M., & Aronson, J. (1995). Stereotype threat and the intellectual test performance of African Americans. *Journal of Personality and Social Psychology, 69,* 797–811. Copyright © 1995 by the American Psychological Association. Adapted with permission.

type threat concerning the belief that men perform better on math-related tasks (Spencer, Steele, & Quinn, 1999). In turn, white men have been found to be "threatened" by the stereotype that men of Asian descent are superior when it comes to doing well at mathematics (Aronson et al., 1999).

7-2c REDUCING PREJUDICE

For decades, psychologists have searched for ways to reduce prejudice. Such a complicated problem requires solutions on a number of levels. Let's look at two types of interventions that have been shown to help.

Cognitive Strategies

Because stereotypes are part of the social air that people breathe, practically everyone learns stereotypes about various groups. This means that stereotyped thinking about others becomes a mindless habit—even for individuals who have been taught to be tolerant of those who are different from themselves (Devine, 1989). Although it's true that stereotypes kick in automatically, unintentionally, and unconsciously, individuals *can* override them—with some cognitive effort (Fiske, 2002). Thus, if you meet someone who speaks with an accent, your initial, automatic reaction might be negative. However, if you believe that prejudice is wrong and if you are aware that you are stereotyping, you can intentionally inhibit such thoughts.

Intergroup Contact

Let's return to the Robbers' Cave study. When we left them, the Rattlers and Eagles were engaged in food fights and flag burning. Understandably, the experimenters were eager to restore peace. First, they tried speaking with each group, talking up the other group's good points and minimizing their differences. They also made the Eagles and the Rattlers sit together at meals and "fun" events like movies. Unfortunately, these tactics fell flat.

Next, the experimenters designed intergroup activities based on the principle of *superordinate goals*—goals that require two or more groups to work together to achieve mutual ends. For example, each boy had to contribute in some way (building a fire, preparing the food) on a cookout so that all could eat. After the boys had participated in a variety of such activities, the hostility between the two groups was much reduced.

Researchers have identified four necessary ingredients in the recipe for reducing intergroup hostility (Brewer & Brown, 1998). First, groups must *work together for a common goal*—merely bringing hostile groups into contact is not effective in reducing intergroup antagonism and may in fact worsen it. Second, cooperative efforts must have *successful outcomes*—if groups fail at a cooperative task, they are likely to blame each other for the failure. Third, group members must have the opportunity to establish *meaningful connections* with one another and not merely go through the motions of interacting. The fourth factor of *equal status contact* requires bringing together members of different groups in ways that ensure that everyone has equal status.

7-3 The Power of Persuasion

Every day you are bombarded by online advertising, pop-up ads, and TV commercials—all attempts to alter your attitudes through persuasion. You may not even be out of bed before you start hearing radio advertisements that are meant to persuade you to buy specific toothpastes, cell phones, and athletic shoes. When you watch the morning news, you hear statements from numerous government officials, all of which have been carefully crafted to shape your opinions. On your way to school, you see billboards showing attractive models draped over cars in the hopes that they can induce positive feelings that will transfer to the vehicles. Walking to class, a friend tries to get you to vote for his candidate for student body president. "Does it ever let up?" you wonder.

When it comes to persuasion, the answer is "no." As Anthony Pratkanis and Elliot Aronson (2000) note, Americans live in the "age of propaganda." In light of this situation, let's examine some of the factors that determine whether persuasion works.

***Persuasion* involves the communication of arguments and information intended to change another person's attitudes.** What are attitudes? For the purposes of our discussion, we'll define ***attitudes* as beliefs and feelings about people, objects, and ideas.** Let's look more closely at two of the terms in this definition. We use the term *beliefs* to mean thoughts and judgments about people, objects, and ideas. For example, you may *believe* that equal pay for equal work is a fair policy or that capital punishment is not an effective deterrent to crime. The "feeling" component of attitudes refers to the positivity and negativity of one's feelings about an issue as well as how strongly one feels about it. For example, you may *strongly favor* equal pay for equal work but only *mildly disagree* with the idea that capital punishment reduces the crime rate. In any event, people's attitudes are often shaped by others' persuasive efforts. Let's look at some key factors in the process of persuasion.

© David McNew/Getty Images

People's attitudes are often shaped by others' **persuasive efforts.**

7-3a ELEMENTS OF THE PERSUASION PROCESS

The process of persuasion or attitude change includes four basic elements (Crano & Prislin, 2008), which are outlined in Figure 7.8 on the next page. **The *source* is the person who sends a communication, and the *receiver* is the person to whom the message is sent.** Thus, if you watched a presidential address on TV, the president would be the source, and you and millions of other viewers would be the receivers in this persuasive effort. **The *message* is the information transmitted by the source; the *channel* is the medium through which the message is sent.** In examining communication channels, investigators have often compared face-to-face interaction against appeals sent via mass media (such as television and radio). Although the research on communication channels is interesting, we'll confine our discussion to source, message, and receiver variables.

Source Factors

Persuasion tends to be more successful when the source has high *credibility* (Petty, Wegener, & Fabrigar, 1997). Two subfactors make a communicator credible: expertise and trustworthiness. People try to convey their *expertise* by mentioning their degrees, their training, and their experience or by showing an impressive grasp of the issue at hand (Wood & Kallgren, 1988). As to *trustworthiness*, whom would you believe if you were told that your state needs to reduce corporate taxes to stimulate its economy—the president of a huge corporation in your state or an economics professor from out of state? Probably the latter because the professor does not have a vested interest in the issue.

Likability is a second major source factor and includes a number of subfactors (Petty et al., 1997). Not surprisingly, a key consideration is a person's *physical attractiveness*. For example, one researcher found that attractive students were more successful than less attractive ones in obtaining signatures for a petition (Chaiken, 1979). People also respond better to sources who are *similar* to them in ways that are relevant to the issue at hand (Mackie, Worth, & Asuncion, 1990). Thus,

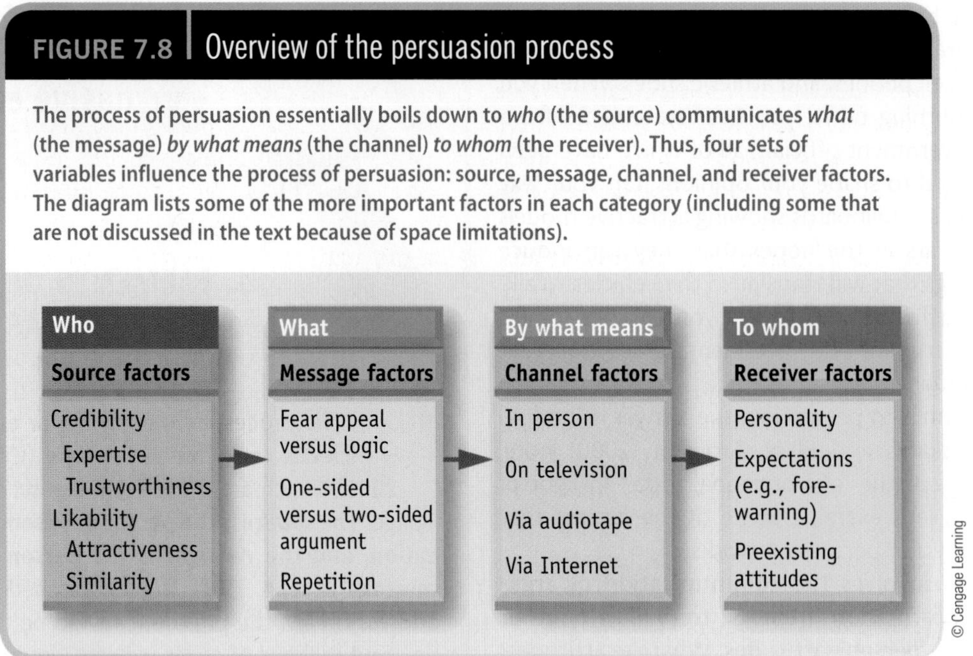

FIGURE 7.8 | Overview of the persuasion process

The process of persuasion essentially boils down to *who* (the source) communicates *what* (the message) *by what means* (the channel) *to whom* (the receiver). Thus, four sets of variables influence the process of persuasion: source, message, channel, and receiver factors. The diagram lists some of the more important factors in each category (including some that are not discussed in the text because of space limitations).

© Cengage Learning

Source: Lippa, R. A. *Introduction to Social Psychology*. Belmont, CA: Wadsworth Publishing. © 1994 Cengage Learning. Adapted with permission of the author.

politicians stress the values they and their constituents hold in common.

Source variables are used to great effect in advertising. Many companies spend a fortune to obtain a spokesperson such as George Clooney or Michael Jordan, who combine trustworthiness, likability, and a knack for connecting with people. Companies quickly abandon spokespersons whose likability declines. For example, many companies cancelled endorsement contracts with basketball star Kobe Bryant and golf legend Tiger Woods after they were implicated in tawdry sexual affairs. Thus, source variables are extremely important factors in persuasion.

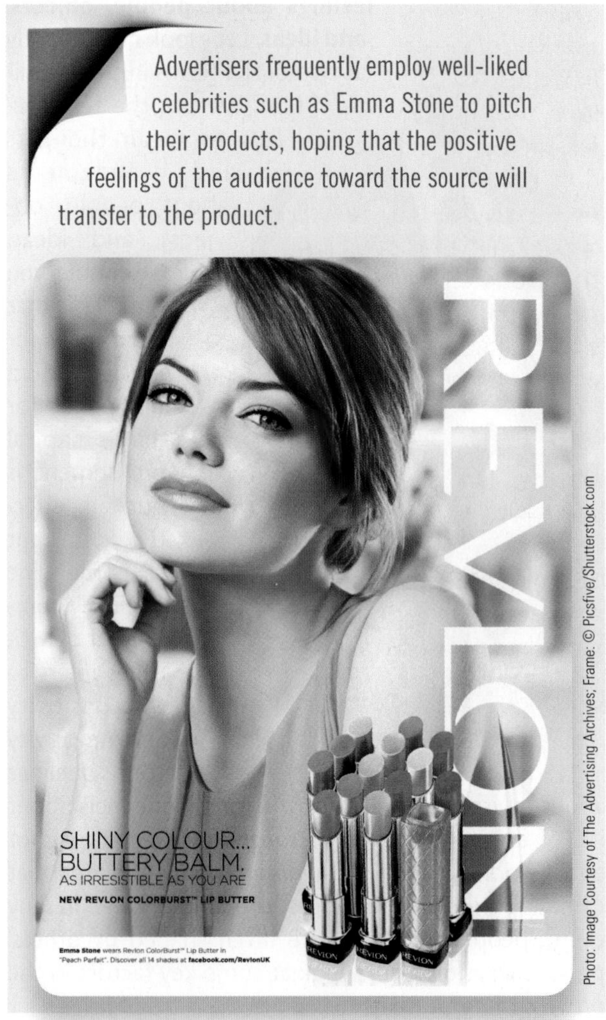

Advertisers frequently employ well-liked celebrities such as Emma Stone to pitch their products, hoping that the positive feelings of the audience toward the source will transfer to the product.

Photo: Image Courtesy of The Advertising Archives; Frame: © Picsfive/Shutterstock.com

Message Factors

Imagine that you are going to advocate the selection of a high-profile entertainer as the speaker at your commencement ceremony. In preparing your argument, you ponder the most effective way to structure your message. On the one hand, you're convinced that having a well-known entertainer on campus would be popular with students and would boost the image of your university in the community and among alumni. Still, you realize that this performer would cost a lot and that some people believe that an entertainer is not an appropriate commencement speaker. Should you present a *one-sided argument* that ignores the possible problems? Or should you present a *two-sided argument* that acknowledges concern about the problems and then downplays them?

In general, two-sided arguments seem to be more effective (Crowley & Hoyer, 1994). In fact, just mentioning that there are two sides to an issue can increase your credibility with an audience (Jones & Brehm, 1970). One-sided messages work only when your audience is uneducated about the issue or when they already favor your point of view.

Persuaders also use emotional appeals to shift attitudes. Insurance companies show scenes of homes on fire to arouse fear. Antismoking campaigns emphasize the threat of cancer. Deodorant ads prey on the fear of embarrassment. Does *fear arousal* work? Yes. Studies involving a wide range of issues (nuclear policy, auto safety, and dental hygiene among others) have shown that the arousal of fear often increases persuasion (Perloff, 1993). And fear appeals are influential if people feel susceptible to the threat (De Hoog, Stroebe, & De Wit, 2007).

Generating *positive feelings* is also an effective way to persuade people. Familiar examples of such tactics include the use of music and physically attractive actors in TV commercials, the use of laugh tracks in TV programs, and the practice of wining and dining prospective customers. People attend better to humorous messages than sober ones (Duncan & Nelson, 1985); later, they may recall that something was funny but forget what it was about (Cantor & Venus, 1980). Producing positive feelings to win people over *can* be effective—provided they don't care too much about the issue. If people do care about the topic, it takes more than good feelings to move them. For example, one study showed that the use of music in TV commercials was effective in persuading viewers, but only when the message concerned a trivial topic (Park & Young, 1986).

Receiver Factors

What about the receiver of the persuasive message? Are some people easier to persuade than others? Yes, but the answer is complicated. For instance, receptivity to a message can sometimes depend on people's *moods:* optimistic people process uplifting messages better than pessimists, who are drawn to counter-attitudinal communications, or those opposing their current views (Wegener & Petty, 1994). Other people want to think deeply about issues, having a so-called ***need for cognition*, the tendency to seek out and enjoy effortful thought, problem-solving activities, and in-depth analysis.** Such people, who truly relish intellectual give-and-take as well as debate, are more likely to be convinced by high-quality arguments than those who prefer more superficial analyses (Cacioppo et al., 1996). Moreover, they are more likely to be motivated to process complex messages more carefully (See et al., 2009).

Transient factors also matter in receptivity to persuasive messages. *Forewarning* the receiver about a persuasive effort and a receiver's initial position on an issue, for instance, seem to be more influential than a receiver's personality. When you shop for a new TV or a car, you expect salespeople to work at persuading you. To some extent, this forewarning reduces the impact of their arguments (Petty & Wegener, 1998). When receivers are forewarned about a persuasion attempt on a personally important topic, it is harder to persuade them than when they are not forewarned (Wood & Quinn, 2003).

7-4 The Power of Social Pressure

In the previous section, we showed you how others attempt to change your *attitudes*. Now you'll see how others attempt to change your *behavior*—by trying to get you to agree to their requests and demands.

7-4a CONFORMITY AND COMPLIANCE PRESSURES

If you extol the talent of Lady Gaga or keep a well-manicured lawn, are you exhibiting conformity? According to social psychologists, it depends on whether your behavior is freely chosen or the result of group pressure. ***Conformity* occurs when people yield to real or imagined social pressure.**

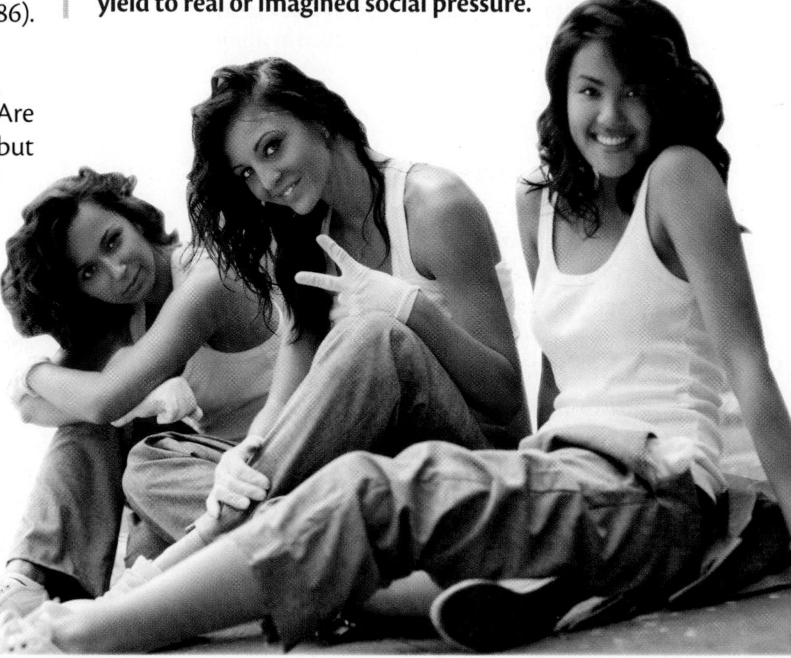
© chaoss/Shutterstock.com

For example, if you like Lady Gaga because you truly enjoy her music, that's not conformity. However, if you like her because it's "cool" and your friends would question your taste if you didn't, then you're conforming. Similarly, if you maintain a well-groomed lawn just to avoid complaints from your neighbors, you're yielding to social pressure. Interestingly, people are apt to explain the behavior of others as conforming but not think of their own actions this way (Pronin, Berger, & Moluki, 2007). As you read this section, remember that individuals often believe they are "alone in a crowd of sheep" because everyone else is conforming (Pronin et al., 2007).

The Dynamics of Conformity

To introduce this topic, we'll re-create a classic experiment devised by Solomon Asch (1955). The participants are male undergraduates recruited for a study of visual perception. A group of seven participants are shown a large card with a vertical line on it and asked to indicate which of three lines on a second card matches the original "standard line" in length (see Figure 7.9). All seven participants are given a turn at the task, and each announces his choice to the group. The subject in the sixth chair doesn't know it, but everyone else in the group is an accomplice of the experimenter.

The accomplices give accurate responses on the first two trials. On the third trial, line 2 clearly is the correct response, but the first five participants all say that line 3 matches the standard line. The genuine subject can't believe his ears. Over the course of the experiment, the accomplices all give the same incorrect response on 12 out of 18 trials. Asch wanted to see how the subject would respond in these situations. The line judgments are easy and unambiguous. Without group pressure, people make matching errors less than 1% of the time. So, if the subject consistently agrees with the accomplices, he isn't making honest mistakes—he is conforming. Will the subject stick to his guns, or will he go along with the group? Asch (1955) found that the men conformed (made mistakes) on 37% of the 12 trials. The subjects varied considerably in their tendency to conform, however. Of the 50 participants, 13 never caved in to the group, while 14 conformed on more than half the trials. One could argue that the results show that people confronting a unanimous majority generally tend to *resist* the pressure to conform. But given how clear and easy the line judgments were, most social scientists viewed the findings as a dramatic demonstration of humans' propensity to conform.

In subsequent studies, Asch (1956) determined that group size and group unanimity are key determinants of conformity. To examine group size, Asch repeated his procedure with groups that included one to fifteen accomplices. Little conformity was seen when a subject was pitted against just one accomplice. Conformity increased rapidly as group size went from two to four, peaked at a group size of seven, and then leveled off. Thus, Asch concluded that as group size increases, conformity increases—up to a point. Significantly, Asch found that group size made little difference if just one accomplice "broke" with the others, wrecking their unanimous agreement. The presence of another dissenter lowered conformity to about one-quarter of its peak, even when the dissenter made inaccurate judgments that happened to conflict with the majority view. Apparently, the participants just needed to hear a second person question the accuracy of the group's perplexing responses.

FIGURE 7.9 Stimuli used in Asch's conformity studies

Subjects were asked to match a standard line (top) with one of three other lines displayed on another card (bottom). The task was easy—until experimental accomplices started responding with obviously incorrect answers, creating a situation in which Asch evaluated subjects' conformity.

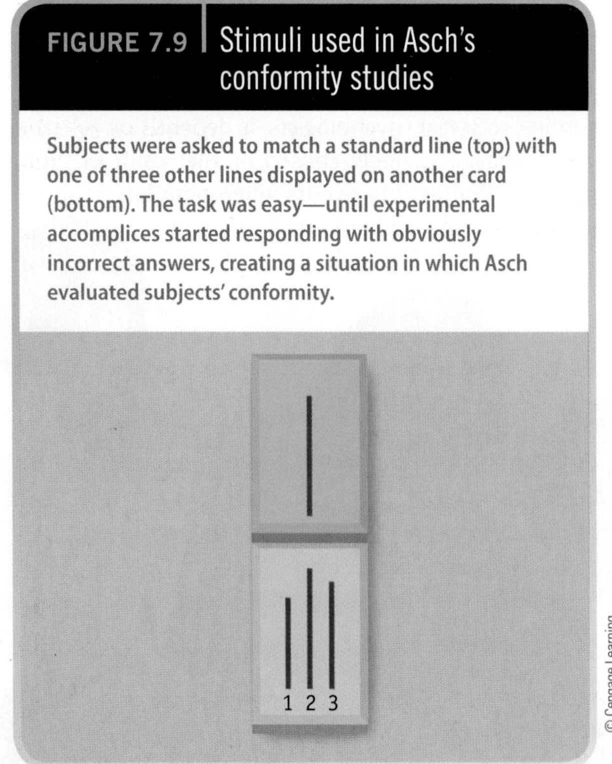

Source: Adapted from illustration on p. 35 by Sarah Love in Asch, S. (1955, November). Opinions and social pressure. *Scientific American, 193*(5), 31–35. Copyright © 1955 by Scientific American, Inc.

Conformity Versus Compliance

Did the conforming participants in Asch's study really change their beliefs in response to social pressure, or did they just pretend to change them? Subsequent studies asked participants to make their responses privately, instead of publicly (Deutsch & Gerard, 1955;

Insko et al., 1985). Conformity declined dramatically when participants wrote down their responses. Thus, it is likely that Asch's participants did not really change their beliefs. Based on this evidence, theorists concluded that Asch's experiments evoked a particular type of conformity, called compliance. ***Compliance* occurs when people yield to social pressure in their public behavior, even though their private beliefs have not changed.** For example, many people comply with modest group pressure daily—they "dress up" for work by wearing suits, ties, dresses, and so on—when they would prefer to wear more casual clothing.

The Whys of Conformity

People often conform or comply because they are afraid of being criticized or rejected. ***Normative influence* operates when people conform to social norms for fear of negative social consequences.** Compliance often results from subtle, implied pressure. For example, for fear of making a negative impression, you may remove your eyebrow ring for a job interview. However, compliance also occurs in response to explicit rules, requests, and commands. Thus, you'll probably follow your boss's instructions even when you think they're lousy ideas.

People often conform or comply because they are afraid of being criticized or rejected.

© desuza.communications/iStockphoto

People are also likely to conform when they are uncertain how to behave (Cialdini, 2001). Thus, if you're at a nice restaurant and don't know which fork to use, you may watch others to see what they're doing. ***Informational influence* operates when people look to others for how to behave in ambiguous situations.** In such cases, using others as a source of information about appropriate behavior is a good thing. But relying on others to know how to behave in unfamiliar situations can sometimes be problematic, as you'll see shortly.

Resisting Conformity Pressures

Sometimes conforming is just harmless fun—such as participating in Internet-generated "flash mobs." At other times, people conform on relatively trivial matters—such as dressing up to go to a dance or wedding. In this case, conformity and compliance minimize the confusion and anxiety people experience in unfamiliar situations. However, when individuals feel pressured to conform to antisocial norms, tragic consequences may result. Negative examples of "going along with the crowd" include drinking more than one knows one should because others say, "C'mon, have just one more" and driving at someone's urging when under the influence of alcohol or drugs. Other instances include refusing to socialize with someone simply because the person isn't liked by one's social group and failing to come to another's defense when it might make one unpopular.

The above examples all concern normative influence, but pressure can come from informational influence as well. A useful example concerns a paradox called **the *bystander effect*—the tendency for individuals to be less likely to provide help when others are present than when they are alone.** Numerous studies have confirmed that people are less helpful in

ZITS

ZITS © 2006 Zits Partnership, Dist. by King Features Syndicate

emergency situations when others are around (Latané and Nida, 1981). Thankfully, the bystander effect is less likely to occur when the need for help is very clear (Fischer, Greitemeyer, & Pollozek, 2006).

What accounts for the bystander effect? A number of factors are at work, and conformity is one of them. The bystander effect is most likely to occur in *ambiguous situations*, because people look around to see whether others are acting as if there's an emergency (Harrison & Wells, 1991). If everyone hesitates, this inaction (informational influence) suggests that help isn't needed. So the next time you witness what you think might be an emergency, don't automatically give in to the informational influence of inaction.

Obedience isn't good or bad; it depends on what one is being told to do.

7-4b PRESSURE FROM AUTHORITY FIGURES

***Obedience* is a form of compliance that occurs when people follow direct commands, usually from someone in a position of authority.** In itself, obedience isn't good or bad; it depends on what one is being told to do. For example, if the fire alarm goes off in your classroom building and your instructor "orders" you to leave, obedience is a good idea. On the other hand, if your boss asks you to engage in an unethical or illegal act, *disobedience* is probably in order.

The Dynamics of Obedience

Like many other people after World War II, social psychologist Stanley Milgram was troubled by how readily the citizens of Germany had followed the orders of dictator Adolf Hitler, even when the orders required morally repugnant actions, such as the slaughter of millions of Jews, as well as Russians, Poles, Gypsies, and homosexuals (Blass, 2004). This observation was Milgram's motivation to study the dynamics of obedience. Milgram's (1963) participants were a diverse collection of forty men from the local community who volunteered for a study on the effects of punishment on learning. When they arrived at the lab, they drew slips of paper from a hat to get their assignments. The drawing was rigged so that the subject always became the "teacher" and an experimental

Photo: © SuperStock/SuperStock; Frame: © Vitaly Korovin/Shutterstock.com

accomplice (a likable 47-year-old accountant) became the "learner."

The teacher watched while the learner was strapped into a chair and electrodes were attached to his arms (to be used to deliver shocks whenever he made a mistake on the task). The subject was then taken to an adjoining room that housed the shock generator that he would control in his role as the teacher. Although the apparatus looked and sounded realistic, it was a fake, and the learner was never shocked. The experimenter played the role of the authority figure who told the teacher what to do and who answered any questions that arose.

The experiment was designed such that the learner would make many mistakes, and the teacher was instructed to increase the shock level after each wrong answer. At 300 volts, the learner began to pound on the wall between the two rooms in protest and soon stopped responding to the teacher's questions. From this point forward, participants frequently turned to the experimenter for guidance. Whenever they did so, the experimenter (authority figure) firmly stated that the teacher should continue to give stronger and stronger shocks to the now-silent learner. Milgram wanted to know the maximum shock the teacher was willing to administer before refusing to cooperate.

In fact, 65% of the subjects administered all 30 levels of shock. Although they tended to obey the experimenter, many participants voiced and displayed considerable distress about harming the learner. They protested, groaned, bit their lips, trembled, and broke into a sweat—but they continued administering the shocks. Based on these findings, Milgram concluded that obedience to authority was even more common than he or others had anticipated. A recent replication by Burger (2009) suggests Milgram's conclusion still stands: Although participants were stopped at the 150-volt level for ethical reasons, 70% continued to shock the learner despite hearing cries of anguish.

The Causes of Obedience

After his initial demonstration, Milgram (1974) tried about twenty variations on his experimental procedure, looking for factors that influenced participants' obedience. For instance, he studied female participants to look at gender differences in obedience (he found no evidence of such differences). In another condition, two confederates played the role of teachers who defied the experimenter's demands to continue, one at 150 volts and one at 210 volts. In this condition, only 10% of the subjects shocked at the maximum level.

What caused the obedient behavior observed by Milgram? First, the demands on the participants (to shock the learner) escalated gradually so that very strong shocks were demanded only after the participant was well into the experiment. Second, participants were told that the authority figure, not the teacher, was responsible if anything happened to the learner. Third, subjects evaluated their actions in terms of how well they lived up to the authority figure's expectations, not by their harmful effects on the victim. Taken together, these findings suggest that human behavior is determined not so much by the *kind of person* one is as by the *kind of situation* one is in (Lewin, 1935). Applying this insight to Nazi war crimes and other atrocities, Milgram made a chilling assertion: Inhuman and evil visions may originate in the disturbed mind of an authority figure like Hitler, but it is only through the obedient actions of normal people that such ideas can be turned into frightening reality.

In the Application, we'll alert you to some social influence strategies that people use to get you and others to agree to their requests.

7-5 APPLICATION

Seeing Through Compliance Tactics

Which of the following statements is true?

____ 1. It's a good idea to ask for a small favor before soliciting the larger favor that you really want.

____ 2. It's a good idea to ask for a large favor before soliciting the smaller favor that you really want.

© Vitaly Korovin/Shutterstock.com

Would you believe that *both* of these conflicting statements are true? Although the two approaches work for different reasons, both can be effective ways to get people to do what you want. It pays to understand these and other social influence strategies because advertisers, salespeople, and fundraisers (not to mention friends and neighbors) use them frequently to influence people's behavior. So you can see the relevance of these strategies to your own life, we've grouped them by the principles that make them work. Much of our discussion is based on the work of Robert Cialdini (2007), a social psychologist who spent years observing social influence tactics used by compliance professionals.

7-5a THE CONSISTENCY PRINCIPLE

Once people agree to something, they tend to stick with their initial commitment (Cialdini, 2007). This tendency to prefer consistency in one's behavior is used to gain compliance in two ways. Both involve a person getting another individual to commit to an initial request and then changing the terms of the agreement to the requestor's advantage. Because people often stay with their initial commitments, the target will likely agree to the revised proposal, even though it may not be to his or her benefit.

FIGURE 7.10 The foot-in-the-door and door-in-the-face techniques

These two influence techniques are essentially the reverse of each other, but both can work. (a) In the foot-in-the-door technique, you begin with a small request and work up to a larger one. (b) In the door-in-the-face technique, you begin with a large request and work down to a smaller one.

(a) Foot-in-the-door technique
Small request first
"Would you donate some old clothes for one of our charity programs?"
If yes, then . . .
Larger request (the one desired in the first place)
"Would you donate $50 to our organization?"
© Blaj Gabriel/Shutterstock.com
(b) Door-in-the-face technique
Large request first
"Would you volunteer to run a weekly program for our youth group?"
If no, then . . .
Smaller request (the one desired in the first place)
"Would you donate $50 to our organization?"
© Blaj Gabriel/Shutterstock.com

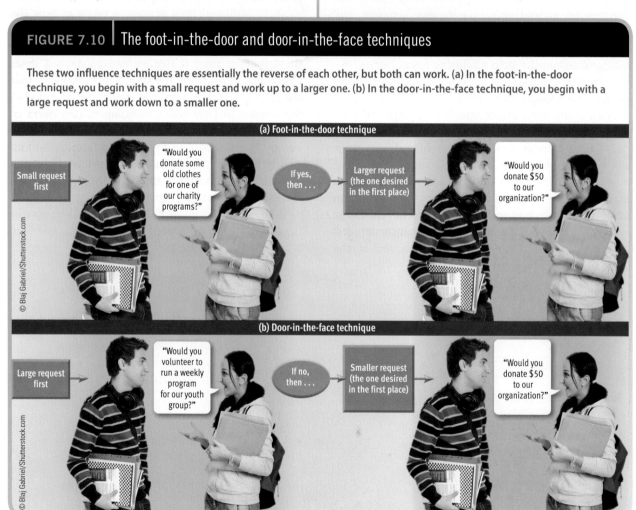

© Cengage Learning

For example, door-to-door salespeople have long recognized the importance of gaining a *little* cooperation from sales targets (getting a "foot in the door") before hitting them with the real sales pitch. **The *foot-in-the-door* (FITD) *technique* involves getting people to agree to a small request to increase the chances that they will agree to a larger request later** (see Figure 7.10a). This technique is widely used. For example, groups seeking donations often ask people to simply sign a petition first. Salespeople routinely ask individuals to try a product with "no obligations" before they launch their hard sell. In a similar vein, a wife might ask her husband to get her a cup of coffee, and when he gets up to fetch it say, "While you're up, would you fix me a peanut butter sandwich?"

© Thinkstock

The FITD technique was first investigated by Jonathon Freedman and his colleagues. In one study (Freedman & Fraser, 1966), the large request involved telephoning homemakers to ask whether a team of six men doing consumer research could come into their home to classify all their household products. Only 22% of the subjects in the control group agreed to this outlandish request. Subjects in the experimental group were contacted three days before the unreasonable request was made and were asked to answer a few questions about the soaps used in their home. When the large request was made three days later, 53% of the experimental group complied with that request.

Why does this strategy work? The best explanation is rooted in Daryl Bem's *self-perception theory*, or the idea that people sometimes infer their attitudes by observing their own behavior (Burger & Caldwell, 2003). When Joe agrees to sign a petition, he infers that he is a helpful person. So when he is confronted with a second, larger request to collect petition signatures, "helpful person" comes to mind, and Joe complies with the request.

A second commitment-based strategy is **the *lowball technique*, which involves getting someone to commit to an attractive proposition before its hidden costs are revealed.** The name for this technique derives from a common practice in automobile sales, in which a customer is offered a terrific bargain on a car. The bargain price gets the customer to commit to buying, but soon after, the dealer starts revealing some hidden costs. Typically, the customer discovers that options (e.g., floor mats) expected to be included in the original price are actually going to cost extra or that a promised low loan rate has "fallen through" leading to a higher car payment. Once they have committed to buying a car, however, most customers are unlikely to cancel the deal, so they end up paying the extra costs.

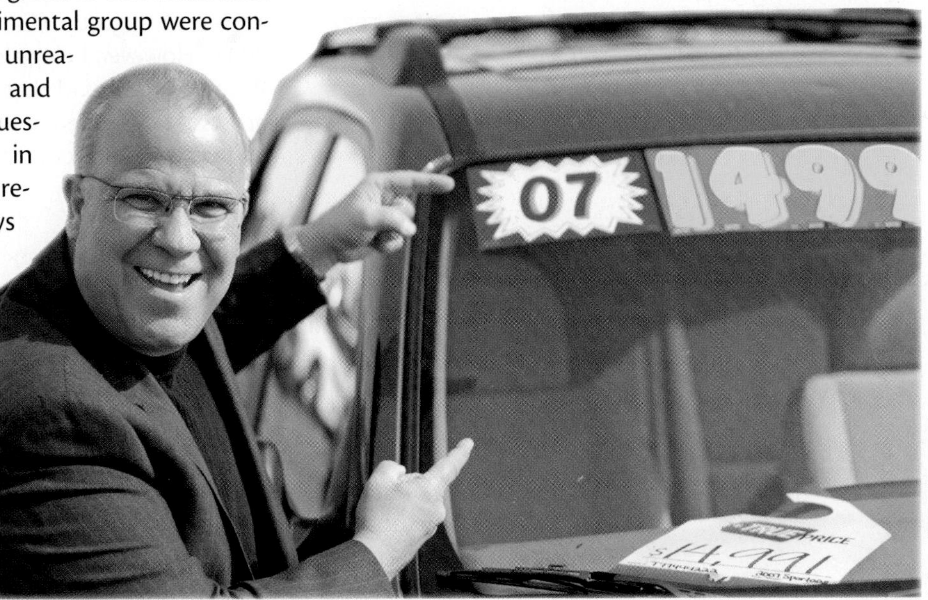

© Gunter Nezhoda/Shutterstock.com

People use a variety of methods to coax compliance from one another.
© Volodymyr Leus/Shutterstock.com

7-5b THE RECIPROCITY PRINCIPLE

Most people have been socialized to believe in **the *reciprocity principle*—the rule that one should pay back in kind what one receives from others.** Charities frequently make use of this principle. Groups seeking donations for the disabled, the homeless, and so forth routinely send "free" address labels, key rings, and other small gifts with their pleas for donations. The belief that people should reciprocate others' kindness is a powerful norm. Thus, people often feel obliged to reciprocate by making a donation in return for the gift. According to Cialdini (2007), the reciprocity norm is so powerful that it often works even when (1) the gift is uninvited, (2) the gift comes from someone you dislike, or (3) the gift results in an uneven exchange.

One influence strategy that takes advantage of the belief in reciprocity is the door-in-the-face technique, which reverses the sequence of requests used with the foot-in-the-door technique. **The *door-in-the-face (DITF) technique* involves making a large request that is likely to be turned down in order to increase the chances that people will agree to a smaller request later** (see Figure 7.10b). The name for this strategy is derived from the expectation that the initial request will be quickly rejected. For example, a wife who wants to coax her frugal husband into agreeing to buy a $30,000 sports car might begin by proposing that they purchase a $50,000 sports car. By the time he has talked his wife out of the more expensive car, the $30,000 price tag may look quite reasonable to him. And since she has made concessions (settling for a less expensive car), he may feel obligated to reciprocate with a concession (buying the car). For the DITF to work, there must be no delay between the two requests (O'Keefe & Hale, 2001).

7-5c THE SCARCITY PRINCIPLE

It's no secret that telling people they can't have something only makes them want it more. According to Cialdini (2007), this principle derives from two sources. First, people have learned that items that are hard to get are of better quality than items that are easy to get. From there, they often assume, erroneously, that anything that is scarce must be good. Second, when people's choices (of products, services, romantic partners, job candidates) are constrained in some way, they often want what they can't have even more (Brehm & Brehm, 1981).

Companies and advertisers frequently use the scarcity principle to drive up the demand for their products. Thus, you constantly see ads that scream "limited supply available," "for a limited time only," "while they last," and "time is running out." Perhaps the scarcity principle accounts for the reason so many antique and "vintage" items on eBay generate so much interest and auction dollars.

In summary, people use a variety of methods to coax compliance from one another. Despite the fact that many of these influence techniques are more or less dishonest, they're still widely used. There is no way to completely avoid being hoodwinked by influence strategies, and sometimes individuals may be more susceptible to such influence, as appears to be the case when someone feels ostracized and wants to get back in the good graces of a group (Carter-Sowell, Chen, & Williams, 2008). However, being alert to these techniques can reduce the likelihood that you'll be a victim of influence artists. As we noted in our discussion of persuasion, "to be forewarned is to be forearmed."

PERSONAL EXPLORATION
TOOLS

Curious about yourself? To learn more about how topics in this chapter relate to you, go online to CourseMate at www.cengagebrain.com where you can:

- Complete a **Self-Reflection** exercise that will help you think about your personal experiences in relation to topics in the chapter.
- Take a **Self-Assessment** scale that will show you how you score on a research instrument that measures personality traits or attitudes.
- Explore **Recommended Readings** that will provide brief overviews of useful self-help books.

© edge69/iStockphoto

STUDY TOOLS ▶ 7

Ready to study? In your book you can:

- **Test Yourself** with a multiple-choice quiz (below)
- Rip out the **Chapter Review card** (in the back of the book) to refresh yourself on the chapter's Key Ideas and Key Terms

Or you can go online to CourseMate at www.cengagebrain.com where you can:

- Take additional Practice Quizzes to prepare for your exam
- Review Key Terms with flash cards and a crossword puzzle
- View videos that expand on selected concepts

TEST YOURSELF

1. Inferences that people draw about the causes of events, their own behavior, and others' behavior are called

a. snap judgments.
b. self-fulfilling prophecies.
c. attributions.
d. attitudes.

2. When Jane attributes Bill's late arrival at work to laziness rather than slow freeway traffic, she may be exhibiting

a. The fundamental attribution error
b. The bystander effect
c. Stereotyping
d. Defensive attribution

3. Which of the following is *not* a potential source of cognitive distortion in perception?

a. Categorizing
b. The bystander effect
c. Stereotypes
d. Defensive attribution

4. "Old-fashioned" discrimination is ______________; modern discrimination is ______________.

a. blatant; subtle
b. legal; illegal
c. common; rare
d. race-based; gender-based

5. Which of the following is a cause of prejudice?

a. Mindfulness
b. Right-wing authoritarianism
c. Primacy effects
d. Activities based on superordinate goals

6. Receivers who are forewarned that someone will try to persuade them will most likely

a. be very open to persuasion.
b. listen intently but openly argue with the speaker.
c. be more resistant to persuasion.
d. heckle the persuader.

7. Within the persuasion process, the medium (radio, television, internet) through which a message is sent is called the

a. source
b. receiver
c. channel
d. perceiver

8. When people change their outward behavior but not their private beliefs, ______________ is operating.

a. conformity
b. persuasion
c. obedience
d. compliance

9. The results of Milgram's (1963) study imply that

a. situational factors can exert tremendous influence over behavior.
b. in the real world, most people resist pressures to act in harmful ways.
c. most people are willing to give obviously wrong answers on rigged perceptual tasks.
d. disobedience is far more common than obedience.

10. When charities send prospective donors free address labels and the like, which of the following social influence principles are they manipulating?

a. The consistency principle
b. The scarcity principle
c. The reciprocity principle
d. The foot-in-the-door principle

Answers: 1. c, page 138; 2. a, page 139; 3. b, pages 142–143; 4. a, pages 144–145; 5. b, page 145; 6. c, page 151; 7. c, page 149; 8. d, page 153; 9. a, page 155; 10. c, page 158

LEARNING OBJECTIVES

8-1 Describe the key aspects of the communication process.

8-2 Explain the significance of nonverbal communication for understanding and relating to others.

8-3 Learn to be an effective communicator when it comes to conversation, disclosure, and listening.

8-4 Recognize basic barriers that can undermine effective communication.

8-5 Discuss ways to constructively recognize and deal with conflict.

8-6 Outline the steps necessary for more-assertive communication.

After you have read the chapter, you can Test Yourself and learn about other Study Tools on page 180.

CHAPTER 8

Interpersonal COMMUNICATION

© Photo_Concepts/iStockphoto

Veronica, a high school senior, is getting ready for the prom. Her date, Javier, is waiting downstairs. As she fixes her hair, checks her makeup for what is probably the tenth time in the last hour, and smoothes the front of her new and costly dress, her 13-year-old sister, Amy, wanders into the room. As Veronica looks at her own reflection in a full-length mirror, she hears Amy snort, "*Nice* dress. Really *nice*." Amy's voice brims with the sort of sarcasm that is refined in middle-school hallways, but it is enough to shake Veronica's confidence. "What do you mean? What's wrong with this dress? It's beautiful—isn't it?" she says quickly, worry creeping into her voice. "*Oh, that* dress," grins Amy. "Why there's not a *thing* wrong with it, I am *so* sure Javier will just *love* it." Minutes later, her confidence still a bit rattled, Veronica descends the stairs. And then she hears Javier say, "Wow—that is a *really* nice dress. You look terrific, even amazing." She smiles at Javier and says, "Thanks, Javier, I think it's a nice dress, too."
A memorable night begins.

© Hannamariah/Shutterstock.com

Sometimes it's not so much what people say that matters but how they say it. The same word—like the word "nice"—can drip with sarcasm (as Amy demonstrated) or sincerity (as Javier showed). Learning to manage interpersonal communication in daily life is important. To understand other people, we need to be able to interpret their intentions accurately.

Communication skills are highly relevant to adjustment because they can be critical to happiness and success in life. In this chapter, we begin with an overview of the communication process and then turn to the important topic of nonverbal communication. Next, we discuss ways to communicate more effectively and examine common communication problems. Finally, we look at interpersonal conflict, including constructive ways to deal with it. In the Application, we consider ways to develop an assertive communication style.

8-1 The Process of Interpersonal Communication

Communication can be defined as the process of sending and receiving messages that have meaning. We define ***interpersonal communication* as an interactional process in which one person sends a message to another.** First, for communication to qualify as *interpersonal*, at least two people must be involved. Second, interpersonal communication is a *process* (Hargie, 2011). By this, we simply mean that it usually involves a series of actions: Kelli talks/Jason listens, Jason responds/Kelli listens, and so on. Third, this process is *interactional.* Effective communication is not a one-way street: Both participants send as well as receive information when they're interacting.

8-1a COMPONENTS AND FEATURES OF THE COMMUNICATION PROCESS

Let's take a look at the essential components of the interpersonal communication process. The key elements (most of which were introduced in Chapter 7) are (1) the sender, (2) the receiver, (3) the message, (4) the channel through which the message is sent, (5) noise or interference, and (6) the context in which the message is communicated. As we describe these components, refer to Figure 8.1 to see how they work together.

The *sender* is the person who initiates the message. In a typical two-way conversation, both people serve as senders (as well as receivers). Keep in mind that each person brings a unique set of expectations and understandings to each communication situation. **The *receiver* is the person to whom the message is targeted.**

The *message* refers to the information or meaning that is transmitted from the sender to the receiver. The message is the *content* of the communication—that is, the ideas and feelings conveyed to another person. Two important cognitive processes underlie the transmission of messages: Speakers *encode* or transform their ideas and feelings into symbols and organize them into a message; receivers *decode* or translate a speaker's message into their own ideas and feelings (see Figure 8.1).

The *channel* refers to the sensory means through which the message reaches the receiver. Typically, people receive information from multiple channels simultaneously. They not only hear what the other person says, they also see the person's facial expressions, observe his or her gestures, experience eye contact, and sometimes feel the person's touch. Note that the messages in the various channels may be consistent or inconsistent with each other, making their interpretation more or less difficult. Sometimes sound is the only channel available for receiving information—such as when you talk on the telephone.

Whenever two people interact, miscommunication can occur. ***Noise* refers to any stimulus that interferes with accurately expressing or understanding a message.** Sources of noise include environmental factors (street traffic, loud music, computer spam or pop-ups, crowded rooms), physical factors (poor hearing, poor vision), and physiological factors (hunger, headaches, medications). In addition, psychological factors such as defensiveness and anxiety can contribute to noise, as we'll see later in the chapter.

All social communication occurs in and is influenced by a ***context*, the environment in which communication takes place.** Context includes the *physical environment* (location, time of day, noise level) and how a conversation takes place (face to face, telephone call, on the Internet). Other important aspects of context include the nature of the participants' *relationship* (work associates, friends, family), their *history* (previous interactions), their current *mood* (happy, stressed), and their *cultural backgrounds* (Verderber et al., 2008).

FIGURE 8.1 A model of interpersonal communication

Interpersonal communication involves six elements: the sender, the receiver, the message, the channel through which the message is transmitted, distorting noise, and the context in which the message is sent. In conversations, both participants function as sender and receiver.

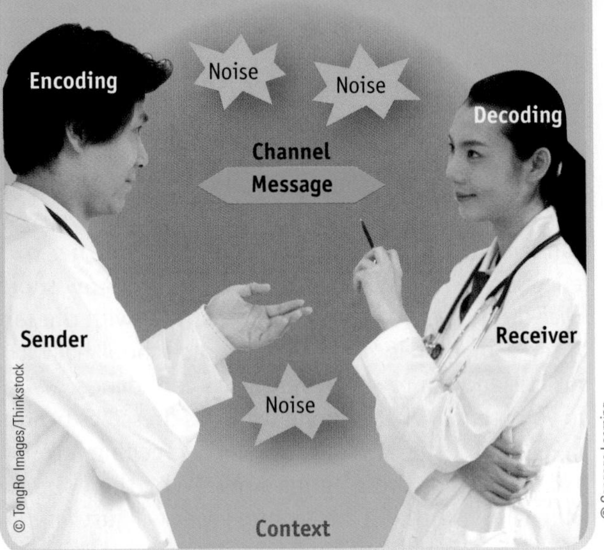

© Cengage Learning

Most person-to-person communications are characterized by common features. For example, you are probably not interested in engaging in intimate or private exchanges with everyone you meet. Instead, you are *selective* in initiating or responding to communications. Communications between people are not isolated events; rather, they have a *systemic* quality because of time, situation, social class, education, culture, personal histories, and other influences that are beyond individuals' control but that nonetheless affect how they interact with each other. Communications within a given relationship (such as those between you and a close friend) are also *unique*, having special patterns, vocabulary, even rhythms (Nicholson, 2006). When you become close to a given person, you may establish particular roles and rules for how you interact with each other that are distinct from the roles or rules used in your other relationships (Dainton, 2006). Finally, communications are part of a continuous and evolving *process* that becomes more personal as people interact with greater frequency (Wood, 2006).

8-1b TECHNOLOGY AND INTERPERSONAL COMMUNICATION

The recent explosion in electronic and wireless communication technology has revolutionized notions of interpersonal communication. Today, communication via email, mailing lists, text messaging, tweets, Facebook posts, blogs and vlogs, chat rooms, and videoconferencing must be considered along with face-to-face interactions. ***Electronically mediated communication* is interpersonal communication that takes place via technology** (including cell phones, computers, and hand-held devices).

Cell phones have both advantages and disadvantages. On the positive side, they are a convenient way to keep in touch with others, they provide a sense of security, and they can summon aid in an emergency. On the down side, they can tie people to their jobs, disrupt classrooms and public events, and bring private conversations into public places. Who hasn't been forced to listen to someone yelling his or her personal business into a cell phone in public? By now, most people are familiar with the basic rules of etiquette for cell phone use: (1) turn off your phone (or put it on "vibrate" mode) when the ringing will disturb others, (2) keep your calls short, and (3) make and receive calls unobtrusively or out of earshot from others.

Photo: © Blend_Images/iStockphoto; Frame: © Thomas Bethge/Shutterstock.com

8-1c SOCIAL NETWORKING SITES: PRIVACY AND SECURITY ISSUES

Do you take part in a social networking site (SNS) such as Facebook? The primary benefit of any SNS is being able to present yourself virtually to other people who may already know you, remember you from a shared past (high school, for example), or want to connect with you ("friend you," in Internet parlance) because of some common interest. In effect, an SNS allows you to express yourself and your personality (Carpernter et al., 2011) and to develop relationships with others who share similar attitudes, beliefs, interests, or backgrounds.

Does taking part in an SNS have any drawbacks? There can be, if you do not take appropriate steps to maintain your online privacy. Simply put, you never know who is reading your profile or what they are doing with the information you have shared (Lewis, Kaufman, & Christakis, 2008). Surely, you are already aware that you should be careful what financial information (such as PIN numbers) you share online and know that interfacing with a website is never a good idea unless you know it is a secure one (LaRose & Rifon, 2007).

Should you worry about the information you post on your SNS? Possibly yes. Consider the fact that Facebook has over 800 million active users. To presume that all of them are well intentioned seems somewhat foolhardy. There is also ample evidence that the content of student postings has been used by campus police to raid unsanctioned student parties (Hass, 2006) and to keep individuals from getting jobs (Finder, 2006). In short, private information of whatever type is not always so private. Is your SNS profile set so that it cannot be read, accessed, or searched by strangers? If not, perhaps you should adjust the privacy settings.

8-2 Nonverbal Communication

You're standing at the bar in your favorite hangout, gazing across a dimly lit room filled with people drinking, dancing, and talking. You signal to the bartender that you'd like another drink. Your companion comments on the loudness of the music, and you nod your head in agreement. You spot an attractive stranger across the bar; your eyes meet for a moment and you smile. In a matter of seconds, you have sent three messages without uttering a syllable. To put it another way, you have just sent three *nonverbal* messages. ***Nonverbal communication* is the transmission of meaning from one person to another through means or symbols other than words.** Communication at the nonverbal level takes place through a variety of behaviors: interpersonal distance, facial expression, eye contact, body posture and movement, gestures, physical touch, and tone of voice (Gifford, 2011).

8-2a GENERAL PRINCIPLES

Let's begin by examining some general principles of nonverbal communication.

1. *Nonverbal communication conveys emotions.* People can communicate their feelings without saying a word—for example, "a look that kills." Nonverbal demonstrations of positive feelings include sitting or standing close to those you care for, touching them often, and looking at them frequently.

2. *Nonverbal communication is multichanneled.* Nonverbal communication typically involves simultaneous messages sent through a number of channels. For instance, information may be transmitted through gestures, facial expressions, eye contact, and vocal tone at the same time.

3. *Nonverbal communication is ambiguous.* A shrug or a raised eyebrow can mean different things to different people. Moreover, receivers may have difficulty determining whether nonverbal messages are being sent intentionally.

4. *Nonverbal communication may contradict verbal messages.* How often have you seen people proclaim "I'm not angry" even though their bodies shout that they are positively furious? When you encounter such an inconsistency, which message should you believe? Because of their greater spontaneity, you're probably better off heeding the nonverbal signs. Research shows that when someone is instructed to tell a lie, deception is most readily detected through nonverbal signals (DePaulo, LeMay, & Epstein, 1991).

5. *Nonverbal communication is culture-bound.* Like language, nonverbal signals are different in different cultures (Weisbuch & Amady, 2008). Sometimes cultural differences can be quite dramatic. For example, in Tibet people greet their friends by sticking out their tongues (Ekman, 1975).

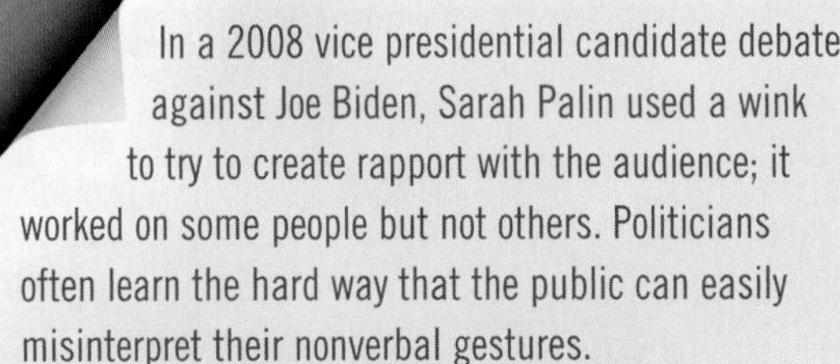

In a 2008 vice presidential candidate debate against Joe Biden, Sarah Palin used a wink to try to create rapport with the audience; it worked on some people but not others. Politicians often learn the hard way that the public can easily misinterpret their nonverbal gestures.

Photo: © AP Images/J. Scott Applewhite; Frame: © Picsfive/Shutterstock.com

8-2b ELEMENTS OF NONVERBAL COMMUNICATION

Nonverbal signals can provide a great deal of information in interpersonal interactions. As we discuss specific nonverbal behaviors, we will focus on what they communicate about interpersonal attraction and social status.

Personal Space

***Proxemics* is the study of people's use of interpersonal space. *Personal space* is a zone of space surrounding a person that is felt to "belong" to that person.** Personal space is like an invisible bubble you carry around with you in your social interactions. The size of this mobile zone is related to your cultural background, social status, personality, age, and gender.

The amount of interpersonal distance people prefer depends on the nature of the relationship and the situation (Hall, 2008). The appropriate distance between people is also regulated by social norms and varies by culture (Samovar, Porter, & McDaniel, 2007). For instance, people of Northern European heritage tend to engage in less physical contact and keep a greater distance between themselves than people of Latin or Middle Eastern heritage. The situation matters, too. Consider how much distance from others you want when using an ATM. Those waiting behind you in line know that you want your privacy in order to preserve the personal information you enter into the machine during a transaction (Li & Li, 2007). They, in turn, expect the same courtesy.

Anthropologist Edward T. Hall (1966) has described four interpersonal distance zones that are appropriate for middle-class encounters in American culture (see tion. Some representative results from this research are depicted in Figure 8.3 on the next page.

Each society has rules that govern whether and when it is appropriate to express one's feelings (Matsumoto, 2006). ***Display rules*** **are norms that govern the appropriate display of emotions in a culture.** In the United States, for instance, it is considered bad form to gloat over one's victories or to show envy or anger in defeat. Besides cultural differences, there are gender differences in facial expression. For example, unsuccessful contestants in beauty pageants are always seen smiling, while many are probably suppressing feelings of resentment, envy, or anger. In general, men show less facial expression than women do, a finding linked to social pressures for males to inhibit such displays (Kilmartin, 2007).

FIGURE 8.2 Interpersonal distance zones

According to Edward Hall (1966), people like to keep a certain amount of distance between themselves and others. The distance that makes one feel comfortable depends on whom one is interacting with and the nature of the situation.

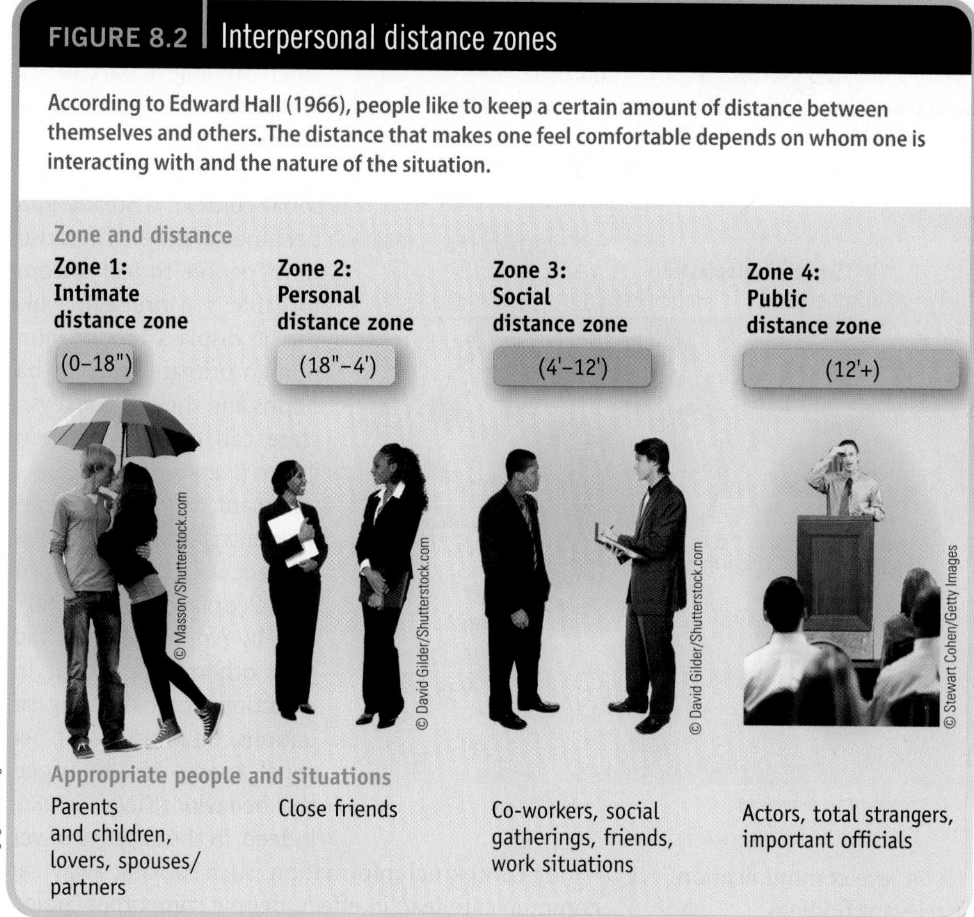

Figure 8.2). The general rule is that the more you like someone, the more comfortable you feel being physically close to that person. Of course, there are obvious exceptions, such as crowded subways and elevators, but these situations are often experienced as stressful. Invasions of personal space usually produce discomfort and stimulate attempts to restore your privacy zone. To illustrate, if someone stands too close, you may back up.

Facial Expression

More than anything else, facial expressions convey emotions (Hess & Thibault, 2009). Paul Ekman and Wallace Friesen have identified six distinctive facial expressions that correspond with six basic emotions: anger, disgust, fear, happiness, sadness, and surprise (Ekman & Friesen, 1984). Early research involving participants from many countries supported the idea that these six emotions are universally recognized (Ekman, 1972). In such studies, researchers showed photographs depicting different emotions to subjects from a variety of Western and non-Western cultures and asked them to match the photographs with an emo-

Eye Contact

Eye contact (also called *mutual gaze*) is another major channel of nonverbal communication. The duration of eye contact is its most meaningful aspect. Because

FIGURE 8.3 | **Facial expressions and emotions**

Ekman and Friesen (1984) found that people in highly disparate cultures showed fair agreement on the emotions portrayed in these photos. This consensus across cultures suggests that the facial expressions associated with certain emotions may have a biological basis.

Emotion displayed

Fear — Disgust — Happiness — Anger

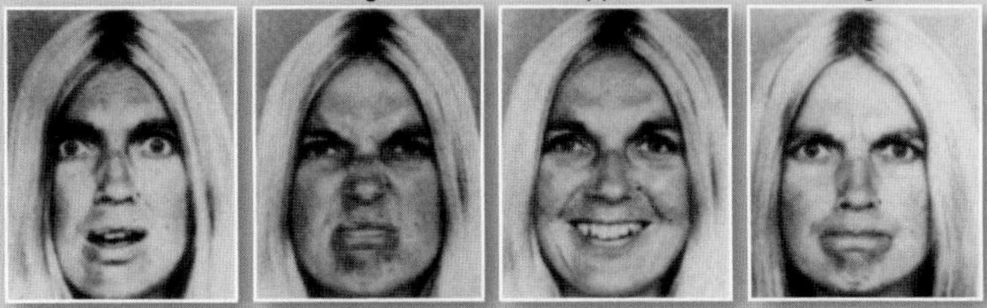

Country	**Agreement in judging photos (%)**			
	Fear	Disgust	Happiness	Anger
United States	85	92	97	67
Brazil	67	97	95	90
Chile	68	92	95	94
Argentina	54	92	98	90
Japan	66	90	100	90
New Guinea	54	44	82	50

Photos from *Unmasking the Face*, © 1975 by Paul Ekman, Ph.D./Paul Ekman Group, LLC

there is considerable research on "eye communication," we will summarize the most relevant findings.

Among European Americans, people who engage in high levels of eye contact are usually judged to have effective social skills and credibility. Similarly, speakers, interviewers, and experimenters receive higher ratings of competence when they maintain high rather than low eye contact with their audience. As a rule, people engage in more eye contact when they're listening than when they're talking (Bavelas, Coates, & Johnson, 2002).

There may be times when some types of communication either enhance or reduce eye contact. For example, researchers have long speculated that people are more likely to make eye contact with others when making sincere statements. Conversely, psychologists assumed that speakers making sarcastic or derisive comments become gaze averse—that is, they are more likely to break eye contact with listeners. A controlled study using speaker-listener pairs confirmed these expectations (Williams, Burns, & Harmon, 2009).

Gaze also communicates the *intensity* (but not the positivity or negativity) of feelings. For example, couples who say they are in love spend more time gazing at each other than other couples do (Patterson, 1988). Also, maintaining moderate (versus constant or no) eye contact with others typically generates positive feelings in them. When women make eye contact with men, a longer gaze can generate the latter's interest, sustaining it when smiling is part of the interaction (Guéguen et al., 2008).

In a negative interpersonal context, a steady gaze becomes a stare that causes most people to feel uncomfortable. Moreover, like threat displays among nonhuman primates such as baboons and rhesus monkeys, a stare can convey aggressive intent (Henley, 1986). Thus, if you want to avoid road rage incidents, avoid making eye contact with hostile motorists. People also communicate by *reducing* eye contact with others. Unpleasant interactions, embarrassing situations, or invasions of personal space usually trigger this behavior (Kleinke, 1986). Indeed, in the absence of verbal or contextual information, such looking away can communicate fear; in effect, people sometimes "point" to danger with their eyes (Hadjikhani et al., 2008).

In the United States, gender and racial differences have been found in eye contact. For instance, women tend to gaze at others more than men do (Briton & Hall, 1995). However, the patterning of eye contact also reflects status, and gender and status are often confounded. Higher-status individuals look at the other person more when speaking than when listening, while lower-status people behave just the opposite. Women usually show the lower-status visual pattern because they are typically accorded lower status than men. As you can see in Figure 8.4, when women are in high-power positions, they show the high-status visual pattern to the same extent that men do (Dovidio et al., 1988).

FIGURE 8.4 Visual dominance, status, and gender

Women typically show low visual dominance (see control condition) because they are usually accorded lower status than men (Dovidio et al. 1988). However, when researchers placed women in a high-power position and measured their visual behavior, women showed the high visual dominance pattern and men showed the low visual dominance pattern. When men were placed in the high-power position, the visual dominance patterns reversed. Thus, visual dominance seems to be more a function of status than of gender.

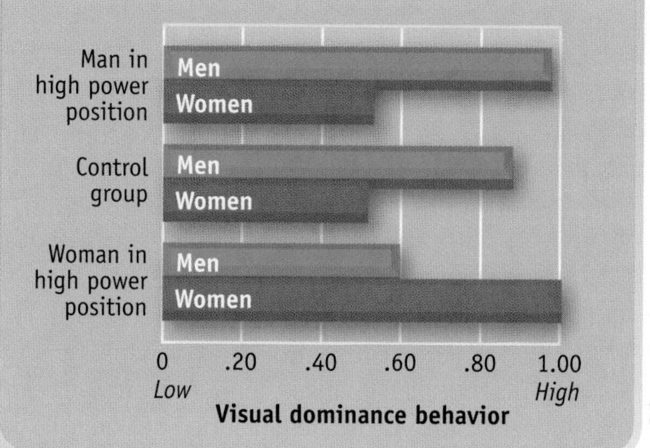

Body Language

Body movements—those of the head, trunk, hands, legs, and feet—also provide nonverbal avenues of communication. ***Kinesics* is the study of communication through body movements.** By noting a person's body movements, observers may be able to tell an individual's level of tension or relaxation. For instance, frequent touching of oneself or scratching suggests nervousness (Harrigan et al., 1991).

Posture also conveys information. Leaning back with arms or legs arranged in an asymmetrical or "open" position conveys a feeling of relaxation. Posture can also indicate someone's attitude toward you (McKay, Davis, & Fanning, 1995). A body leaning toward you typically indicates interest and a positive attitude. Conversely, a body angled away from you or crossed arms may indicate a negative attitude or defensiveness.

Posture can also convey status differences. Generally, a higher-status person will look more relaxed. By contrast, a lower-status person will tend to exhibit a more rigid body posture, often sitting up straight with feet together, flat on the floor, and arms close to the body (a "closed" position) (Hall, 1984). Again, status and gender differences are frequently parallel. That is, men are more likely to exhibit the high-status "open" posture and women the lower-status "closed" posture (Cashdan, 1998).

People use *hand gestures* to describe and emphasize the words they speak, as well as to help in persuasive efforts (Maricchiolo et al., 2009). To convey "no," you can extend the index finger of your dominant hand and wave it back and forth from left to right. Children know that when adults slide their right index finger up and down their left index finger, it means "shame on you." As travelers frequently discover, the meaning of gestures is not universal (Samovar et al., 2007). For instance, a circle made with the thumb and forefinger means that everything is "OK" to an American, but it is considered an obscene gesture in some countries.

Touch

Touch takes many forms and can express a variety of meanings, including support, consolation, and sexual intimacy. Touch can also convey messages of status and power. In the United States, people typically "touch downward"—in other words, higher-status individuals are freer to touch subordinates than vice versa (Henley & Freeman, 1995). Higher-status people who touch others while making requests ("I'm conducting a survey—will you answer some questions for me?") actually increase compliance rates (Guéguen, 2002). How people interpret the possible messages communicated by touch depends on the age and gender of the individuals involved, the setting in which the touching takes place, and the relationship between the toucher and recipient, among other things (Major, Schmidlin, & Williams, 1990). There are also gender differences related to status and touch: Adult women use touch to convey closeness or intimacy, whereas men use touch as a means to control or indicate their power in social situations (Hall, 2006a). Finally, there are strong norms about *where* on the body people are allowed to touch friends. These norms are quite different for same-gender as opposed to cross-gender interactions, as can be seen in Figure 8.5.

FIGURE 8.5 Where friends touch each other

Social norms govern where friends tend to touch each other. As these graphics show, the patterns of touching are different in same-gender as opposed to cross-gender interactions.

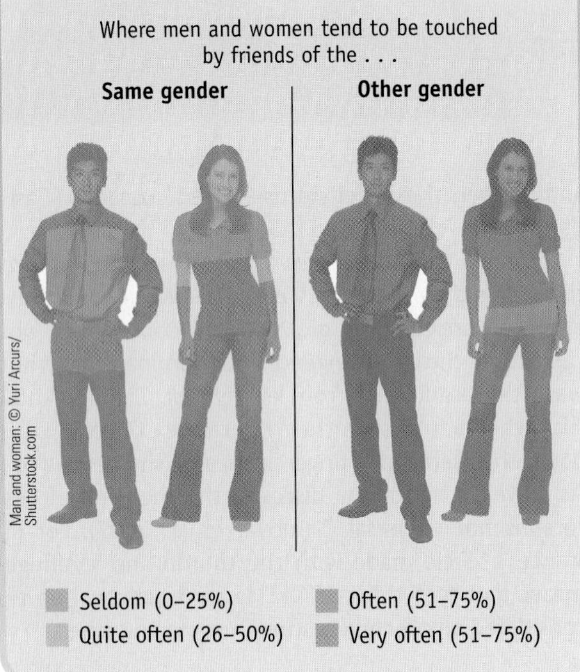

Source: Based on Marsh, P. (Ed.). (1988). *Eye to eye: How people interact.* ("Where friends touch each other"). Topsfield, MA: Salem House. Copyright © 1988 by Andromeda Oxford Ltd. and HarperCollins Publishers.

8-2c DETECTING DECEPTION

Like it or not, lying is a part of everyday life. People typically tell one to two lies a day (DePaulo et al., 1997). Most of these everyday lies are inconsequential "white lies," such as claiming to be better than one actually is or lying to avoid hurting someone's feelings. Of course, people tell more serious lies, too. When they do, such lies are used to gain some advantage—that is, to get what they want or to obtain something they feel entitled to, such as gaining credit for an idea (DePaulo et al., 2004). People tell such serious lies, too, when they want to avoid conflict or to protect or even harm other people ("That's right, I did the entire project myself; Bob and Susan were too busy to help me").

Is it possible to catch people in a lie? Yes, but it's difficult—even for experts (Bond & DePaulo, 2006). Some studies have found that professionals whose work involves detecting lies (police officers, FBI agents, and psychiatrists, for example) are more accurate judges of liars than nonexperts are (Ekman, O'Sullivan, & Frank, 1999), Still, even these individuals have accuracy rates around 57%—not much better than chance (50%). Moreover, recent meta-analyses found no significant differences in the accuracy rates of experts and nonexperts (Bond & DePaulo, 2008). Regardless, people overestimate their ability to detect liars (DePaulo et al., 1997).

The popular stereotypes about how liars give themselves away don't necessarily correspond to the actual clues related to dishonesty. For example, observers tend to focus on the face (the least revealing channel) and to ignore more useful information (Burgoon, 1994). Contrary to popular belief, for example, lying is *not* associated with slow talking, long pauses before speaking, excessive shifting of posture, reduced smiling, or lack of eye contact. Generally, liars say less, tell less-compelling stories, make a more negative impression, are more tense, and include less unusual content in their stories than truth tellers do (DePaulo et al., 2003).

So, how *do* liars give themselves away? Liars may blink less than usual while telling a lie because of cognitive demand—an overexpenditure of mental energy (Leal & Vrij, 2008). Eye blinks then accelerate once the lie has been told. Vocal cues include speaking with a higher pitch, giving relatively short answers, and excessive hesitations. Facial cues include dilation of the pupils. It's also helpful to look for inconsistencies between facial expressions and lower body movements. For example, a friendly smile accompanied by a nervous shuffling of feet could signal deception.

Bella DePaulo (1994), a noted researcher in this area, isn't too optimistic about the prospects of teaching people to spot lies, because the cues are usually subtle.

Starting in the Middle Ages, it was believed that if one told a lie with one's hand in the mouth of the sculpture (Mouth of Truth in Rome, Italy), it would be bitten off.

FIGURE 8.6 The polygraph measures emotional reactions

A lie detector measures the physiological arousal that most people experience when they tell a lie. After using nonthreatening questions to establish a baseline, a polygraph examiner looks for signs of arousal (such as the sharp change in GSR shown here) on incriminating questions.

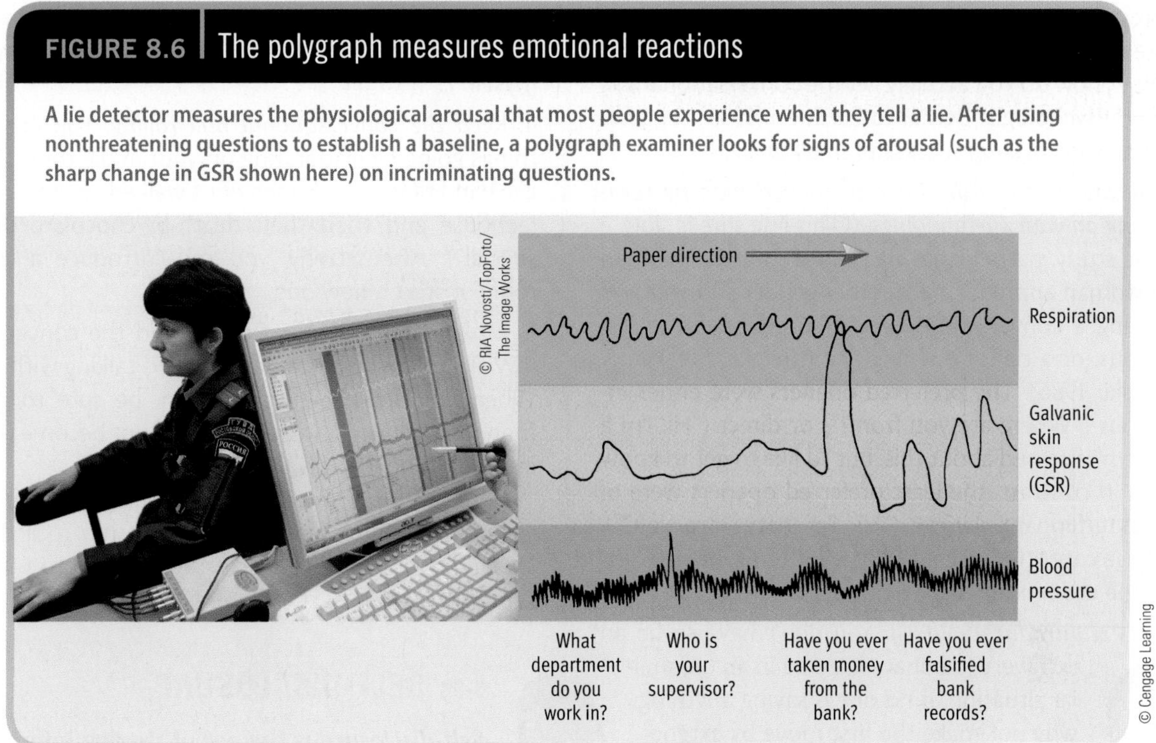

Paper direction
Respiration
Galvanic skin response (GSR)
Blood pressure
What department do you work in?
Who is your supervisor?
Have you ever taken money from the bank?
Have you ever falsified bank records?

If she's correct, perhaps *machines* can do better. **The *polygraph* is a device that records fluctuations in physiological arousal as a person answers questions.** Although called a "lie detector," it's really an emotion detector. The polygraph monitors key indicators of autonomic arousal such as heart rate, blood pressure, respiration rate, and perspiration, or galvanic skin response (GSR). The assumption is that when people lie, they experience emotion that produces noticeable changes in these physiological indicators (see Figure 8.6).

Polygraph experts claim that lie detector tests are 85%–90% accurate and that there is research support for the validity of polygraph testing (Honts, Raskin, & Kircher, 2002). These claims are clearly not supported by the evidence. Methodologically sound research on this question is surprisingly sparse (largely because the research is difficult to do), and the limited evidence available is not very impressive (Iacono, 2009). One problem is that when people respond to incriminating questions, they may experience emotional arousal even when they are telling the truth. Thus, polygraph tests often lead to accusations against the innocent. Another problem is that some people can lie without experiencing physiological arousal. Thus, because of high error rates, polygraph results are not admitted as evidence in most types of courtrooms (Iacono, 2008).

To summarize, deception is potentially detectable, but the nonverbal behaviors that accompany lying are subtle and difficult to spot.

8-3 Toward More Effective Communication

If you are like most people, you probably overestimate how effectively you communicate with others (Keysar & Henly, 2002). In this section, we turn to some practical issues that will help you become a more effective communicator with your family, friends, romantic partner, and co-workers. We'll review conversational skills, self-disclosure, and effective listening.

8-3a CONVERSATIONAL SKILLS

When it comes to meeting strangers, some people launch right into a conversation, while others break into a cold sweat as their minds go completely blank. If you fall into the second category, don't despair! The art of conversation is actually based on conversational *skills*. And these skills can be learned. To get you started, we'll offer a few general principles.

First, follow the Golden Rule. Give to others what you would like to receive from them. In other words, give others your attention and respect and let them know that you like them. Second, focus on the other person instead of yourself. Concentrate on what the person is saying, rather than on how you look, what you're going to say next, or winning the argument. Third, as we have noted, use nonverbal cues to communicate your interest in the other person. A welcoming smile can make a big difference in initial contacts.

Now, how do you actually get the conversational ball rolling? Psychologist Bernardo Carducci (1999) suggests five steps for making successful small talk:

1. *Indicate that you are open to conversation by commenting on your surroundings.* ("This line sure is slow.") In one study, participants viewed videotapes of a man or a woman approaching an other-gender stranger and initiating a conversation using a cute/flippant, an innocuous, or a direct opening line (Kleinke, Meeker, & Staneski, 1986). The preferred openers were either innocuous ("Where are you from?") or direct ("Hi, I'm a little embarrassed about this, but I'd like to get to know you"). In contrast, the least preferred openers were of the cute/flippant variety ("Hi, I'm easy—are you?"). Because cute lines often backfire, your best bet is probably the conventional approach.

2. *Introduce yourself.* You don't have to be an extravert to behave like one in an unfamiliar situation. If no one is saying anything, why not make the first move by extending your hand, looking the person in the eye, and introducing yourself. Do this early in the conversation and use specifics to give the other person information to help find common ground ("I'm Adam Weaver. I'm a psychology major at the university").

3. *Select a topic others can relate to.* Keep an eye out for similarities and differences between you and your conversational partner. Look for things you have in common—a tattoo, a class, a hometown—and build a conversation around that ("I heard a great band last night"). Alternatively, use your differences ("How did you get interested in science fiction? I'm a mystery fan myself").

4. *Keep the conversational ball rolling.* You can keep things going by elaborating on your initial topic ("After the band finished, a bunch of us walked to the new coffeehouse and tried their death-by-chocolate dessert special"). Alternatively, you can introduce a related topic or start a new one.

5. *Make a smooth exit.* Politely end the conversation ("Well, I've got to be going. I enjoyed talking with you"). When you see the person again, be sure to give a friendly smile and a wave. You need not become friends in order to be friendly.

After you've learned a little about another person, you may want to move the relationship to a deeper level. This is where self-disclosure comes into play, the topic we address next.

8-3b SELF-DISCLOSURE

***Self-disclosure* is the act of sharing information about yourself with another person.** In other words, self-disclosure involves opening up about yourself to others. The information you share doesn't have to be a deep, dark secret, but it may be. Conversations with strangers and acquaintances typically start with superficial self-disclosure—your opinion of the TV show you saw last night or your views on who will win the World Series. Typically, only when people have come to like and trust each other do they begin to share private information—such as self-consciousness about one's weight, one's health (Park et al., 2011), or jealousy of one's brother (Greene, Derlega, & Mathews, 2006). Figure 8.7 illustrates how self-disclosure varies according to the type of relationship.

DAVE

FIGURE 8.7 Breadth and depth of self-disclosure

Breadth of self-disclosure refers to how many topics one opens up about; depth refers to how far one goes in revealing private information. Both the breadth and depth of one's disclosures are greater with best friends as opposed to casual acquaintances or strangers. (Adapted from Altman & Taylor, 1973)

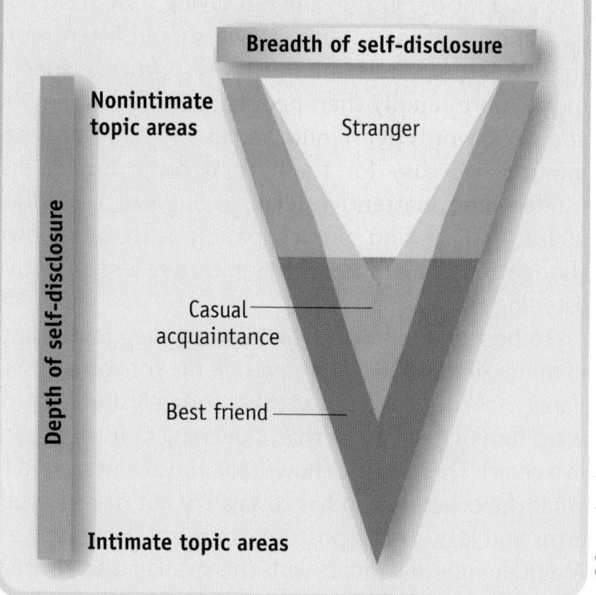

In discussing self-disclosure, the focus is usually on verbal communication—how people decide to share information with each other (Ignatius & Kokkonen, 2007). But keep in mind that *non*verbal communication plays an equally important role in self-disclosure (Laurenceau & Kleinman, 2006). Thus, if you tell a friend about a distressing experience and she signals her concern via sympathtic nonverbal cues (eye contact, leaning forward, intent facial expression), your feelings about the interaction will be positive. But if she conveys a lack of interest (looking around the room, bored facial expression), you will walk away with negative feelings.

Self-disclosure is critically important to adjustment for several reasons. First, sharing fears and problems (as well as good news) with others who are trustworthy and supportive plays a key role in mental health (Greene et al., 2006). And after mutual self-disclosures, people experience a boost in positive feelings (Vittengl & Holt, 2000). Second, self-disclosure is a way to build relationships with friends and co-workers (Tardy & Dindia, 2006). Third, emotional (but not factual) self-disclosures lead to feelings of closeness, as long as disclosers feel that listeners are understanding and accepting (Reis & Shaver, 1988). Fourth, self-disclosure in romantic relationships correlates positively with relationship satisfaction (Greene et al., 2006).

Self-Disclosure and Relationship Development

Earlier, we noted that self-disclosure leads to feelings of intimacy. Actually, the process is a little more complicated than that. Research suggests that only certain types of disclosures lead to feelings of closeness (Laurenceau, Barrett, & Rovine, 2005). For instance, emotional-evaluative self-disclosures (how you feel about your sister, for instance) do, but factual-descriptive self-disclosures (that you have three siblings, for example) do not. Moreover, for intimacy to develop in a relationship, a discloser must feel understood and cared for (Lin & Huang, 2006). In other words, self-disclosure alone doesn't lead to intimacy—how listeners respond matters, too (Maisel, Gable, & Strachman, 2008). Interestingly, people seem to feel strongly that their expressions of values and what they care about reveal a great deal to others about themselves. However, such self-disclosure is not necessarily viewed as revealing by observers (Pronin, Fleming, & Steffel, 2008).

Self-disclosure varies over the course of relationships. At the beginning of a relationship, high levels of mutual disclosure prevail (Taylor & Altman, 1987). Once a relationship is well established, the level of disclosure tapers off, although responsiveness remains high (Reis & Patrick, 1996). Also, in established relationships people are less likely to reciprocate disclosures in the same conversation. Thus, when a lover or a good friend reveals private information, you frequently respond with words of sympathy and understanding rather than a similar disclosure. This movement away from equal exchanges of self-disclosure appears to be based on twin needs that emerge as intimate relationships develop: (1) the need for connection (via openness) and (2) the need for

autonomy (via privacy) (Planalp, Fitness, & Fehr, 2006). By reciprocating support (versus information), individuals can strengthen relationships while maintaining a sense of privacy. In fact, successfully balancing these contradictory needs seems to be an important factor in relationship satisfaction.

When relationships are in distress, self-disclosure patterns change. For example, one or both individuals may decrease the breadth and depth of their self-disclosures, indicating that they are emotionally withdrawing (Baxter, 1988).

Culture, Gender, and Self-Disclosure

Americans generally assume that personal sharing is essential to close friendships and happy romantic partnerships. This view is consistent with an individualistic culture that emphasizes the individual and the expression of each person's unique feelings and experiences. In collectivist cultures such as China and Japan, on the other hand, people are open about their group memberships and status because these factors guide social interactions; however, sharing personal information is reserved for established relationships (Samovar et al., 2007).

In the United States, it has been found that females tend to be more openly self-disclosing than males, although the disparity seems smaller than once believed (Fehr, 2004). This gender difference is strongest in *same-gender* friendships, with female friends sharing more personal information than male friends (Reis, 1998). In *other-gender* relationships, self-disclosure is more equal, although men with traditional gender-role attitudes are less likely to self-disclose, because they view sharing personal information as a sign of weakness. Also, women share more personal information and feelings, whereas men share more nonpersonal information, both in conversations and in email messages (Kilmartin, 2007). That said, in the early stages of other-gender relationships, American men often disclose more than women do (Derlega et al., 1985). This finding is consistent with the traditional expectations that males should initiate relationships and females should encourage males to talk. Thus, it is an oversimplification to say that American women are always more open than men.

8-3c EFFECTIVE LISTENING

Listening and hearing are two distinct processes that are often confused. *Hearing* is a physiological process that occurs when sound waves come into contact with the eardrums. In contrast, ***listening* is a mindful activity and complex process that requires one to select and to organize information, interpret and respond to communications, and recall what one has heard.**

Effective listening is a vastly underappreciated skill. There's a lot of truth in the old saying, "We have two ears and only one mouth, so we should listen more than we speak." Because listeners process speech much more rapidly than people speak (between 500 and 1,000 words per minute versus 125–175 words per minute), it's easy for them to become bored, distracted, and inattentive (Hanna, Suggett, & Radtke, 2008). Fatigue and preoccupation with one's own thoughts are other factors that interfere with effective listening.

To be a good listener, you need to keep four points in mind. *First, signal your interest in the speaker by using nonverbal cues.* Face the speaker squarely and lean toward him or her (rather than slouching or leaning back in a chair). This posture shows that you are interested in what the other person has to say. Try not to cross your arms and legs, as this posture can signal defensiveness. Maintaining eye contact with the speaker also conveys your attentiveness. (You know how annoying it is to talk with someone whose eyes are roaming around the room.) Communicate your feelings about what the speaker is saying by nodding your head or raising your eyebrows.

Second, hear the other person out before you respond. Listeners often tune out or interrupt a conversational partner when (1) they know someone well (they believe they already know what the speaker will say), (2) a speaker has mannerisms listeners find frustrating (stuttering, mumbling, speaking in a monotone), and (3) a speaker discusses ideas (abortion, politics) that generate strong feelings or uses terms (*welfare cheat, redneck*) that push "hot buttons." Although it is challenging not to tune out a speaker or lob an insult in these situations, you'll be better able to formu-

© Robert Kneschke/Shutterstock.com

Being a good listener is an essential skill that contributes to success in relationships and on the job.

late an appropriate response if you allow the speaker to complete his or her thought.

Third, engage in active listening. Pay attention to what the speaker is saying and mindfully process the information. Active listening also involves the skills of clarifying and paraphrasing. Inevitably, a speaker will skip over an essential point or say something that is confusing. When this happens, you need to ask for clarification. "Was Bill her boyfriend or her brother?" Clarifying ensures that you have an accurate picture of the message and also tells the speaker that you are interested. Paraphrasing takes clarifying another step. To paraphrase means to state concisely what you believe the speaker said. You might say, "Let me see if I've got this right . . ." It's obviously silly to paraphrase every single thing the speaker says; you need to paraphrase only when the speaker says something important. Paraphrasing has a number of benefits. It reassures the speaker that you are "with" him or her, it derails misinterpretations, and it keeps you focused on the conversation.

Finally, pay attention to the other person's nonverbal signals. Listeners use a speaker's words to get the "objective" meaning of a message, but they rely on nonverbal cues for the emotional and interpersonal meanings of a message. Your knowledge of body language, tone of voice, and other nonverbal cues can give you deeper understanding of what others are communicating. Remember that these cues are available not only when the other person is speaking but also when you are talking. If you often get signals that your listener is drifting away, you might be going overboard on irrelevant details or, perhaps, hogging the conversation. The antidote is active listening.

8-4 Communication Problems

In this section, we focus on two aspects of communication that can interfere with effective communication: anxiety and communication barriers.

8-4a COMMUNICATION APPREHENSION

It's the first day of your child psychology class and you have just learned that 30-minute oral presentations are a course requirement. Do you welcome this requirement as an opportunity to polish your public speaking skills or, panic-stricken, do you race to the nearest computer station to drop the class? If you opted for the latter, you may suffer from ***communication apprehension*, or anxiety caused by having to talk with others.** Some people experience communication apprehension in all speaking situations (including one-on-one en-

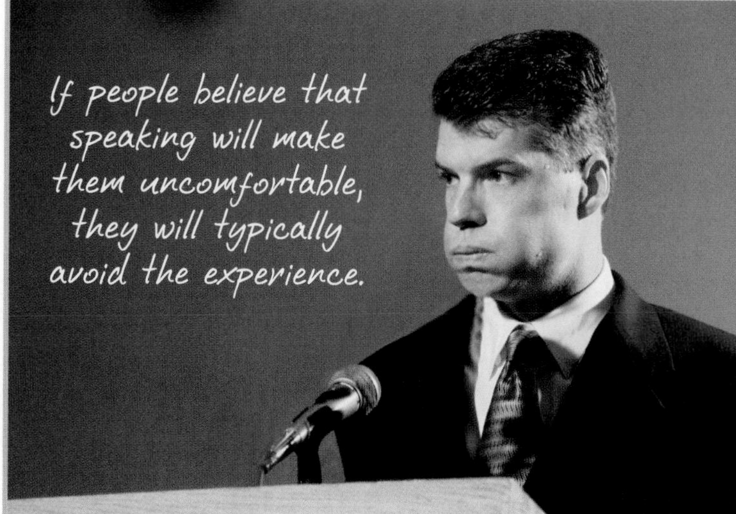
If people believe that speaking will make them uncomfortable, they will typically avoid the experience.
© Chuck Savage/CORBIS

counters), but most people who have the problem notice it only when they have to speak before groups. Communication apprehension is a concern for students as well as teachers because it can adversely affect general academic success as well as performance related to public speaking requirements in the classroom (Bourhis, Allen, & Bauman, 2006).

Bodily experiences associated with communication apprehension can range from "butterflies" in the stomach to cold hands, dry mouth, and a racing heart rate. These physiological effects are stress-induced "fight or flight" responses of the autonomic nervous system (see Chapter 3). The physiological responses themselves aren't the root of communication apprehension. Rather, the problem lies in the speaker's *interpretation* of these bodily responses. That is, high scorers on measures of communication apprehension frequently interpret the bodily changes they experience in public speaking situations as indications of fear. In contrast, low scorers often chalk up these reactions to the normal excitement in such a situation (Richmond & McCroskey, 1995).

Researchers have identified four responses to communication apprehension (Richmond & McCroskey, 1995). The most common is *avoidance*, or choosing not to participate when confronted with a voluntary communication opportunity. If people believe that speaking will make them uncomfortable, they will typically avoid the experience. *Withdrawal* occurs when people unexpectedly find themselves trapped in a communication situation they can't escape. In such cases, they may clam up entirely or say as little as possible. *Disruption* refers to the inability to make fluent oral presentations or to engage in appropriate verbal or nonverbal behavior. Of course, inadequate communication skills can produce this same behavioral effect, and it isn't always possible for

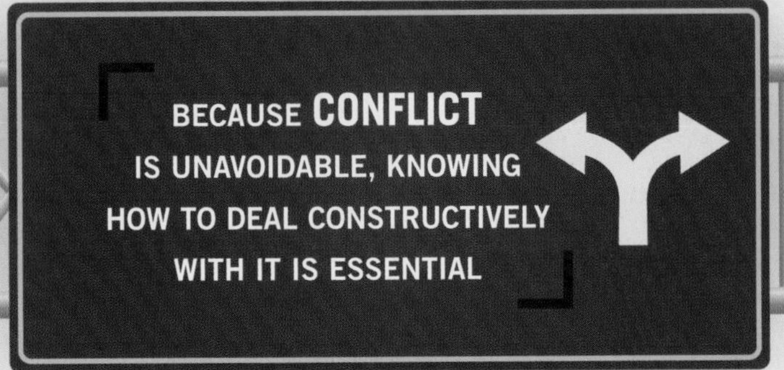
BECAUSE CONFLICT
IS UNAVOIDABLE, KNOWING
HOW TO DEAL CONSTRUCTIVELY
WITH IT IS ESSENTIAL

© Nelson Marques/Shutterstock.com

the average person to identify the actual cause of the problem. *Overcommunication*, or talking too much, is a relatively unusual response to high communication apprehension, but it does occur. Some people attempt to deal with social situations by talking nonstop. Although such individuals are seen as poor communicators, they are not usually perceived as having communication apprehension. That's because we expect to see this problem only in those who talk very little.

Obviously, avoidance and withdrawal tactics are merely short-term strategies for coping with communication apprehension. Because it is unlikely that you can go though life without having to speak in front of a group, it is important to learn to cope with this stressful event rather than avoid it time and again. Allowing the problem to get out of hand can result in self-limiting behavior, such as refusing a job promotion that entails public speaking.

Happily, there are effective ways to reduce speech anxiety. Using the technique of visualization, for example, you picture yourself successfully going through all of the steps involved in preparing for and making a presentation. Research shows that people who practice visualization have less anxiety and fewer negative thoughts when they actually speak when compared to prerevisualitization levels (Ayres, Hopf, & Ayres, 1994). Both *positive reinterpretation* (see Chapter 4) and *systematic desensitization* (Chapter 15) are also effective methods for dealing with this problem.

8-4b BARRIERS TO EFFECTIVE COMMUNICATION

Earlier in the chapter, we discussed the disruptive effects of noise and other physical factors on interpersonal communication. Now we want to check out some psychological factors that contribute to noise. These barriers to effective communication can reside in the sender, in the receiver, or sometimes in both. Common obstacles include defensiveness, ambushing, and self-preoccupation.

Defensiveness

Perhaps the most basic barrier to effective communication is *defensiveness*—an excessive concern with protecting oneself from being hurt. People usually react defensively when they feel threatened, such as when they believe that others are evaluating them or trying to control or manipulate them. Defensiveness is also triggered when others act in a superior manner. Thus, those who flaunt their status, wealth, brilliance, or power often put receivers on the defensive. Dogmatic people who project "I'm always right" also breed defensiveness. Strive to cultivate a communication style that minimizes defensiveness in others. At the same time, keep in mind that you don't have complete control over others' perceptions and reactions.

Ambushing

Some listeners are really just looking for the opportunity to attack a speaker. Although these "verbal bushwhackers" are really listening carefully and intently to what is being said, their purpose in doing so is simply to assail or harass the person talking (Wood, 2010). Understanding, discussing, or having an otherwise thoughtful exchange of ideas and opinions is not the point. People who engage in ambushing almost always arouse defensiveness from others, especially in those whom they attack. Sadly, ambushing can be an effective barrier to communication because few people relish being hassled or bullied in front of others.

Self-Preoccupation

Who hasn't experienced the frustration of trying to communicate with someone who is so self-focused as to make two-way conversation impossible? Self-preoccupied people are engaging in what is called *pseudolistening*, or pretending to listen while their minds are occupied with other topics that have captured their attention (O'Keefe, 2002). These annoying individuals seem to talk to hear themselves talk. If you try to slip in a word about *your* problems, they cut you off by proclaiming, "That's nothing. Listen to what happened to me!" Further, self-preoccupied people are poor listeners. When someone else is talking, they're mentally rehearsing their next comments. Because they are self-focused, these individuals are usually oblivious to their negative impact on others. No wonder people try to avoid these individuals if they can. If they can't, they usually respond only minimally to end the conversation quickly. Needless to say, you risk alienating others if you ignore the norm that conversations should involve a mutual sharing of information.

8-5 Interpersonal Conflict

People do not have to be enemies to be in conflict, and being in conflict does not make people enemies. ***Interpersonal conflict* exists whenever two or more people disagree.** By this definition, conflict occurs between friends and lovers as well as between competitors and enemies. Interpersonal conflict is present anytime people have disparate views, opposing perspectives, incompatible goals, and a desire to try to address and resolve their differences (Wilmot & Hocker, 2006). The discord may be caused by a simple misunderstanding, or it may be a product of clashing goals, values, attitudes, or beliefs. Because conflict is an unavoidable aspect of interactions, knowing how to deal constructively with it is essential.

8-5a STYLES OF MANAGING CONFLICT

How do you react to conflict? Most people have a habitual way or personal style of dealing with dissension. Studies have consistently revealed five distinct patterns of dealing with conflict: avoiding/withdrawing, accommodating, competing/forcing, compromising, and collaborating (Lulofs & Cahn, 2000). Two dimensions underlie these different styles: interest in satisfying one's own concerns and interest in satisfying others' concerns. You can see the location of these five styles on these two dimensions in Figure 8.8. As you read about these styles, try to determine where you fit.

- *Avoiding/withdrawing* (low concern for self and others). Some people simply find conflict extremely distasteful. When a conflict emerges, the avoider will change the subject, deflect discussion with humor, make a hasty exit, or pretend to be preoccupied with something else. Usually, people who prefer this style hope that ignoring a problem will make it go away. For minor problems, this tactic is often a good one—there's no need to react to every little annoyance. For bigger conflicts, avoiding/withdrawing is not a good strategy; it usually just delays the inevitable clash. Of course, in some cases it is good to postpone a discussion, especially if one or both individuals are tired or rushed or need time to cool off. Postponing qualifies as avoiding only if the promised discussion never takes place.
- *Accommodating* (low concern for self, high concern for others). Like the avoider, the accommodator feels uncomfortable with conflict. However, instead of ignoring the disagreement, this person brings the conflict to a quick end by giving in easily. People who are overly concerned about acceptance and approval from others commonly use this strategy of surrender. Habitual accommodating is a poor way of dealing with conflict because it does not generate creative thinking and effective solutions. Moreover, feelings of resentment (on both sides) may develop because the accommodator often likes to play the role of a martyr.

FIGURE 8.8 Five styles of handling interpersonal conflict

In dealing with discord, individuals typically prefer one of five styles. The two dimensions of *concern for self* and *concern for others* underlie each of the five styles.

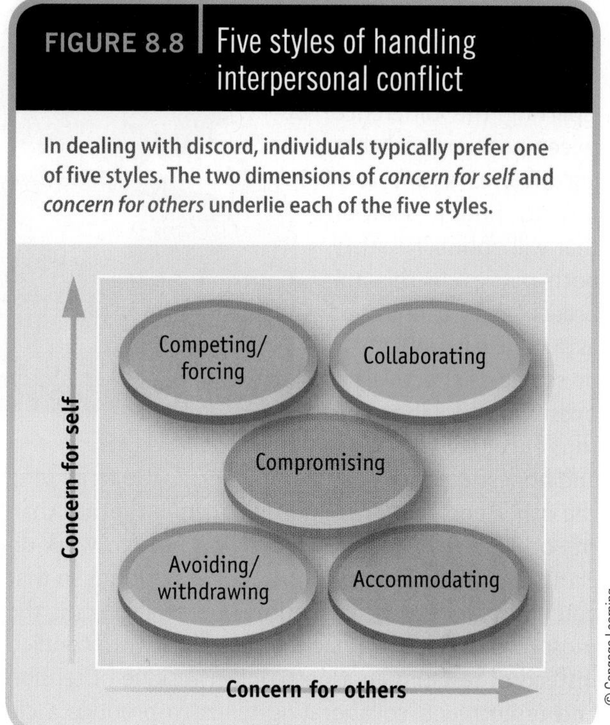

© Cengage Learning

- *Competing/forcing* (high concern for self, low concern for others). The competitor turns every conflict into a black-and-white, win-or-lose situation. Competitors will do virtually anything to emerge victorious from confrontations; thus, they can be deceitful and aggressive—including using verbal attacks and physical threats. They rigidly adhere to one position and will use threats and coercion to force the other party to submit. This style is undesirable because, like accommodation, it fails to generate creative solutions to problems. Moreover, this approach is especially likely to lead to postconflict tension, resentment, and hostility.
- *Compromising* (moderate concern for self and others). Compromising is a pragmatic approach to conflict that acknowledges the divergent needs of both parties. Compromisers are willing to negotiate and to meet the other person halfway. With this approach, each person gives up something so both can have partial satisfaction. Because both parties gain some satisfaction, compromising is a fairly constructive approach to conflict, especially when the issue is moderately important.

- *Collaborating* (high concern for self and others). Whereas compromising simply entails "splitting the difference" between positions, collaborating involves a sincere effort to find a solution that will optimally satisfy both parties. In this approach, conflict is viewed as a mutual problem to be solved as effectively as possible. Collaborating thus encourages openness and honesty. It also stresses the importance of criticizing the other person's *ideas* in a disagreement rather than the other *person*. To collaborate, you have to work on clarifying differences and similarities in positions so that you can build on the similarities. Generally, this is the most productive approach for dealing with conflict. Instead of resulting in a postconflict residue of tension and resentment, collaborating tends to produce a climate of trust.

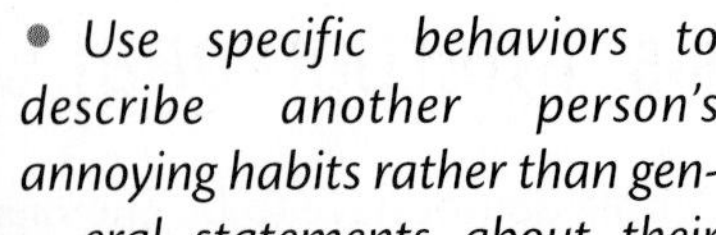

© Jason Stitt/Shutterstock.com

8-5b DEALING CONSTRUCTIVELY WITH CONFLICT

As you have seen, the most effective approach to conflict management is collaborating. To help you implement such an approach, we will offer some specific suggestions. But, before we get down to specifics, there are a few principles to keep in mind (Verderber et al., 2007). First, in a conflict situation, try to give the other person the benefit of the doubt; don't automatically assume that those who disagree with you are ignorant or mean-spirited. Show respect for their position, and do your best to empathize with, and fully understand, their frame of reference. Second, approach the other person as an equal. If you have a higher status or more power (parent, supervisor), try to set this difference aside. Third, define the conflict as a mutual problem to be solved cooperatively, rather than as a win-lose proposition. Fourth, choose a mutually acceptable time to sit down and work on resolving the conflict. It is not always best to tackle the conflict when and where it first arises. Finally, communicate your flexibility and willingness to modify your position.

Here are some specific guidelines for dealing effectively with interpersonal conflict (Alberti & Emmons, 2001):

- *Make communication honest and open.* Don't withhold information or misrepresent your position. Avoid deceit and manipulation.

- *Use specific behaviors to describe another person's annoying habits rather than general statements about their personality.* You'll probably get further with your roommate if you say something like, "Please throw your clothes in the hamper" rather than "You're such an inconsiderate slob." Remarks about specific actions are less threatening and are less likely to be taken personally. They also clarify what you hope will change.

- *Avoid "loaded" words.* Certain words are "loaded" in the sense that they tend to trigger negative emotional reactions in listeners. For example, you can discuss politics without using terms such as "right-winger" and "knee-jerk liberal."

- *Use a positive approach and help the other person save face.* Saying "I love it when we cook dinner together" will go over better than "You never help with dinner, and I resent it." Similarly, you can increase your chances of having a request accepted if you say, "I realize that you are very busy, but I'd really appreciate it if you would look at my paper again. I've marked the places I'd like you to reconsider."

- *Limit complaints to recent behavior and to the current situation.* Dredging up past grievances only rekindles old resentments and distracts you from the current problem. And avoid saying things like "You *always* say you're too busy" or "You *never* do your fair share of the housework." Such categorical statements are bound to put the other person on the defensive.

- *Assume responsibility for your own feelings and preferences.* Rather than "*You* make me mad," say "*I* am angry." Or, try "I'd appreciate it if you'd water the garden" instead of "Do you think the garden needs watering?"

- *Use an assertive (as opposed to submissive or aggressive) communication style.* This approach will make it easier to head off and deal constructively with conflict situations. In the upcoming Application, we elaborate on *assertive communication* and its usefulness in a wide variety of interpersonal situations, such as making acquaintances, developing relationships, and resolving conflicts.

8-6 APPLICATION

Developing an Assertive Communication Style

Answer the following questions "yes" or "no."

___ 1. When someone asks you for an unreasonable favor, is it difficult to say no?

___ 2. Do you feel timid about returning flawed merchandise?

___ 3. Do you have a hard time requesting even small favors from others?

___ 4. When a salesperson pressures you to buy something you don't want, is it hard for you to resist?

If you answered "yes" to several of these questions, you may need to increase your assertiveness.

8-6a THE NATURE OF ASSERTIVENESS

***Assertiveness* involves acting in one's own best interests by expressing one's thoughts and feelings directly and honestly.** Essentially, assertiveness involves standing up for your rights when someone else is about to infringe on them. To be assertive is to speak out rather than pull your punches.

The nature of assertive communication can best be clarified by contrasting it with other types of communication. *Submissive communication* is deferential, as it involves giving in to others on points of possible contention. Submissive people often let others take advantage of them. Typically, their biggest problem is that they cannot say no to unreasonable requests. A common example is the college student who can't tell her roommate not to borrow her clothes. Individuals who use this style often feel bad about themselves (for being "pushovers") and resentful of those they allow to take advantage of them. These feelings often lead the submissive individual to try to punish the other person by withdrawing, sulking, or crying (Bower & Bower, 2004. These manipulative attempts to get one's own way are sometimes referred to as "passive aggression" or "indirect aggression."

At the other end of the spectrum, *aggressive communication* focuses on saying and getting what one wants at the expense of others' feelings and rights. With assertive behavior, however, one strives to respect others' rights and defend one's own. Advocates of assertive communication argue that it is much more adaptive than either submissive or aggressive communication (Alberti & Emmons, 2001). The essential point with assertiveness is that you are able to state what you want clearly and directly. Being able to do so makes you feel good about yourself and will usually make others feel good about you, too. And, although being assertive doesn't guarantee your chances for getting what you want, it certainly enhances them.

> The essential point with assertiveness is that you are able to state what you want clearly and directly.

8-6b STEPS IN ASSERTIVENESS TRAINING

Most assertiveness training programs are based on behavioral principles. They generally emphasize gradual improvement and reinforcement of appropriate responses. The key steps in assertiveness training include the following.

1. Understand What Assertive Communication Is

To produce assertive behavior, you need to understand what it looks and sounds like. Thus, most programs begin by clarifying the nature of assertive communication. Assertiveness trainers often ask clients to imagine situations calling for assertiveness and compare hypothetical submissive (or passive), assertive, and aggressive responses. Let's consider one such comparison. In this example, a woman in assertiveness training is asking her roommate to cooperate in cleaning their apartment once a week. In this example, the roommate is playing the role of the antagonist—called a "downer" in the following scripts (excerpted from Bower & Bower, 2004, pp. 8, 9, 11).

The Passive Scene

SHE: *Uh, I was wondering if you would be willing to take time to decide about the housecleaning.*

DOWNER: *(listening to the music) Not now, I'm busy.*

SHE: *Oh, okay.*

The Aggressive Scene

SHE: *Listen, I've had it with you not even talking about cleaning this damn apartment. Are you going to help me?*

DOWNER: *(listening to the music) Not now, I'm busy.*

SHE: *Why can't you look at me when you turn me down? You don't give a damn about the housework or me! You only care about yourself!*

DOWNER: *That's not true.*

SHE: *You never pay any attention to the apartment or to me. I have to do everything around here!*

DOWNER: *Oh, shut up! You're just neurotic about cleaning all the time. Who are you, my mother?*

The Assertive Scene

SHE: *I know housework isn't the most fascinating subject, but it needs to be done. Let's plan when we'll do it.*

DOWNER: *(listening to music) Oh, c'mon—not now! I'm busy.*

SHE: *This won't take long. I feel that if we have a schedule, it will be easier to keep up with the chores.*

DOWNER: *I'm not sure I'll have time for all of them.*

SHE: *I've already drawn up a couple of rotating schedules for housework, so that each week we have an equal division of tasks. Will you look at them? I'd like to hear your decisions about them, say, tonight after supper?*

DOWNER: *[indignantly] I have to look at these now?*

SHE: *Is there some other time that's better for you?*

DOWNER: *Oh, I don't know.*

SHE: *Well, then let's discuss plans after supper for 15 minutes. Is that agreed?*

DOWNER: *I guess so.*

A helpful way to distinguish among the three types of communication is in terms of how people deal with their own rights and the rights of others. Submissive people sacrifice their own rights. Aggressive people tend to ignore the rights of others. Assertive people consider both their own rights *and* the rights of others.

2. Monitor Your Assertive Communication

Most people's assertiveness varies from one situation to another. In other words, they may be assertive in some social contexts and timid in others. Consequently, once you understand the nature of assertive communication, you should monitor yourself and identify when you are nonassertive. In particular, you should figure out *who* intimidates you, on *what topics*, and in *which situations*.

3. Observe a Model's Assertive Communication

Once you have identified the situations in which you are nonassertive, think of someone who communicates assertively in those situations and observe that person's behavior closely. In other words, find someone to model yourself after. This is an easy way to learn how to behave assertively in situations crucial to you. Your observations should also allow you to see how reward-

FIGURE 8.9 | Assertive responses to common put-downs

Having some assertive replies at the ready can increase your confidence in difficult social interactions.

ASSERTIVE RESPONSES TO SOME COMMON PUTDOWNS		
Nature of remark	**Put-down sentence**	**Suggested assertive reply**
Nagging about details	"Haven't you done this yet?"	"No, when did you want it done?" (Answer without hedging, and follow up with a question.)
Prying	"I know I maybe shouldn't ask, but . . ."	"If I don't want to answer, I'll let you know." (Indicate that you won't make yourself uncomfortable just to please this person.)
Putting you on the spot socially	"Are you busy Tuesday?"	"What do you have in mind?" (Answer the question with a question.)
Pigeonholing you	"That's a woman for you!"	"That's one woman, not *all* women." (Disagree—assert your individuality.)
Using insulting labels for your behavior	"That's a dumb way to . . ."	"I'll decide what to call my behavior." (Refuse to accept the label.)
Basing predictions on an amateur personality analysis	"You'll have a hard time. You're too shy."	"In what ways do you think I'm too shy?" (Ask for clarification of the analysis.)

Source: Adapted from Bower, S. A., & Bower, G. H. (1991). *Asserting yourself: A practical guide for positive change* (2nd ed.). Reading, MA: Addison-Wesley.

ing assertive communication can be, which should strengthen your assertive tendencies.

4. Practice Assertive Communication

The key to achieving assertive communication is to practice it and work toward gradual improvement. Your practice can take several forms. In *covert rehearsal,* you imagine a situation requiring assertion and the dialogue that you would engage in. In *role playing,* you ask a friend or therapist to play the role of an antagonist. Then practice communicating assertively in this artificial situation. Eventually, of course, you want to transfer your assertiveness skills to real-life situations.

5. Adopt an Assertive Attitude

Most assertiveness training programs have a behavioral orientation and focus on specific responses for specific situations (see Figure 8.9). However, it's obvious that real-life situations rarely match those portrayed in books. Thus, some experts maintain that acquiring a repertoire of verbal responses for certain situations is not as important as developing a new attitude that you're not going to let people push you around (or let yourself push others around, if you're the aggressive type) (Alberti & Emmons, 2001). Although most programs don't talk explicitly about attitudes, they do appear to instill a new attitude indirectly. A change in attitude is probably crucial to achieving flexible, assertive behavior.

PERSONAL EXPLORATION TOOLS

Curious about yourself? To learn more about how topics in this chapter relate to you, go online to CourseMate at www.cengagebrain.com where you can:

- Complete a **Self-Reflection** exercise that will help you think about your personal experiences in relation to topics in the chapter.
- Take a **Self-Assessment** scale that will show you how you score on a research instrument that measures personality traits or attitudes.
- Explore **Recommended Readings** that will provide brief overviews of useful self-help books.

STUDY TOOLS ▸ 8

Ready to study? In your book you can:

- **Test Yourself** with a multiple-choice quiz (below)
- Rip out the **Chapter Review card** (in the back of the book) to refresh yourself on the chapter's Key Ideas and Key Terms

Or you can go online to CourseMate at www.cengagebrain.com where you can:

- Take additional Practice Quizzes to prepare for your exam
- Review Key Terms with flash cards and a crossword puzzle
- View videos that expand on selected concepts

TEST YOURSELF

1. Which of the following is *not* a component of the interpersonal communication process?

a. The sender
b. The receiver
c. The channel
d. The monitor

2. Research shows that individuals from a variety of cultures

a. agree on the facial expressions that correspond with all emotions.
b. agree on the facial expressions that correspond with 15 basic emotions.
c. agree on the facial expressions that correspond with 6 basic emotions.
d. do not agree on the facial expressions that correspond with any emotions.

3. Which of the following is *not* an aspect of nonverbal communication?

a. Facial expressions
b. Laughter
c. Posture
d. Gestures

4. According to research, which of the following cues is associated with dishonesty?

a. Speaking with a higher-than-normal pitch
b. Speaking slowly
c. Giving relatively long answers to questions
d. Lack of eye contact

5. With regard to self-disclosure, which of the following is accurate?

a. Nonverbal communication is irrelevant to self-disclosure.
b. Self-disclosure inevitably leads to greater intimacy.
c. Self-disclosure varies over the course of relationships.
d. Females always disclose more than males.

6. Paraphrasing is an important aspect of

a. nonverbal communication.
b. active listening.
c. communication apprehension.
d. assertiveness.

7. When a listener is just looking for a way to attack a speaker, the listener is engaging in

a. assertiveness.
b. self-preoccupation.
c. ambushing.
d. defensiveness.

8. The conflict style that reflects low concern for self and low concern for others is

a. competing/forcing.
b. compromising.
c. accomodating.
d. avoiding/withdrawing.

9. Generally, the most productive style for managing conflict is

a. collaboration.
b. compromise.
c. accommodation.
d. avoidance.

10. Expressing your thoughts directly and honestly without trampling on other people is a description of which communication style?

a. Aggressive
b. Empathic
c. Submissive
d. Assertive

Answers: 1. d, page 162; 2. c, page 165; 3. b, pages 164–167; 4. a, page 168; 5. c, pages 171–172; 6. b, page 173; 7. c, page 174; 8. d, page 175; 9. a, page 176; 10. d, page 177

USE THE TOOLS.

- Rip out the Review Cards in the back of your book to study.

Or Visit CourseMate to:

- Read, search, highlight, and take notes in the Interactive eBook
- Review Flashcards (Print or Online) to master key terms
- Test yourself with Auto-Graded Quizzes
- Bring concepts to life with Games, Videos, and Animations!

Go to CourseMate for **ADJUST** to begin using these tools.
Access at **www.cengagebrain.com**

LEARNING OBJECTIVES

9-1 Identify some factors that influence initial attraction and getting acquainted, and describe some approaches to relationship maintenance.

9-2 Summarize gender and sexual orientation differences in friendship, and describe the friendship repair ritual.

9-3 Discuss sexual orientation and gender in relation to romantic love, describe contemporary theories of love and measures couples can take to help relationships last.

9-4 Understand how both culture and the Internet influence modern relationships.

9-5 Describe the types, roots, and correlates of loneliness, and list suggestions for conquering it.

STUDY TOOLS ▶ After you have read the chapter, you can Test Yourself and learn about other Study Tools on page 203.

CHAPTER 9

FRIENDSHIP and LOVE

© Photo_Concepts/iStockphoto

Antonio was so keyed up, he tossed and turned all night. When morning finally arrived, he was elated. In less than two hours, he would be meeting Sonia for coffee! In his first class that morning, thoughts and images of Sonia constantly distracted him from the lecture. When class was finally over, he had to force himself not to walk too fast to the Student Union, where they had agreed to meet. Sound familiar? Chances are that you recognize Antonio's behavior as that of someone falling in love.

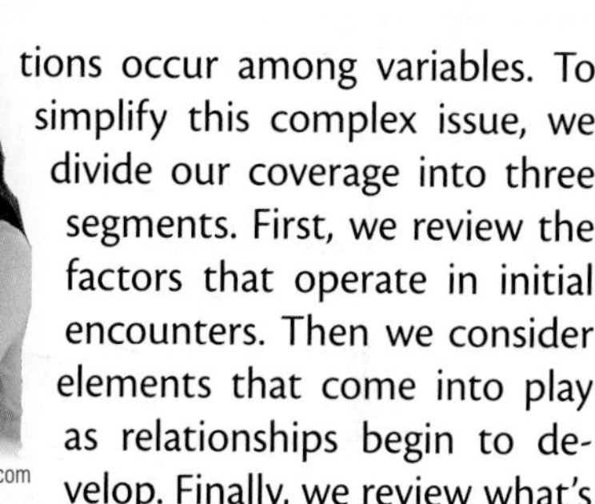
© Phase4Photography/Shutterstock.com

Friendship and love play a major role in psychological adjustment. ***Close relationships*** **are those that are important, interdependent, and long lasting.** In other words, people in close relationships spend a lot of time and energy maintaining the relationship, and what one person says and does affects the other. Close relationships are related to some of the best aspects of life (well-being, happiness, health), but they do have a dark side (abuse, deception, break-ups). This paradox makes friendship and love perennial interests for poets, philosophers, and psychologists alike.

We begin this chapter by considering why people are attracted to each other and how relationships are maintained. Then we probe more deeply into friendship and romantic love and discuss the issues of how culture and the Internet influence relationships. Finally, in the Application section, we focus on the painful problem of loneliness and how to overcome it.

9-1 Initial Attraction and Relationship Development

Attraction **is the initial desire to form a relationship.** Individuals use a multitude of factors to assess another person's appeal as a mate or a friend. Furthermore, because attraction is a two-way street, intricate interactions occur among variables. To simplify this complex issue, we divide our coverage into three segments. First, we review the factors that operate in initial encounters. Then we consider elements that come into play as relationships begin to develop. Finally, we review what's involved in maintaining relationships.

Our review of research in this section pertains to both friendships and romantic relationships. In some cases, a particular factor (such as physical attractiveness) may play a more influential role in love than in friendship, or vice versa. However, all the factors discussed in this section enter into both types of relationships. These factors also operate in the same way in both straight and gay friendships and romantic relationships. But we should note that homosexuals face three unique dating challenges (Peplau & Spaulding, 2003): They have a smaller pool of potential partners, they are often under pressure to conceal their sexual orientation, and they have limited ways to meet prospective partners.

9-1a INITIAL ENCOUNTERS

Sometimes initial encounters begin dramatically with two strangers' eyes locking across a room. More often, two people become aware of their mutual interest, usually triggered by each other's looks and early conversations. What draws two strangers together as either friends or lovers? Three factors stand out: proximity, familiarity, and physical attractiveness.

Proximity

Attraction usually depends on proximity: People have to be in the same place at the same time. ***Proximity*** **refers to geographic, residential, and other forms of spatial closeness.** Of course, proximity is not an issue in cyberspace interactions. But in everyday life people typically become attracted to, and acquainted with, someone who lives, works, shops, or plays nearby. Proximity effects may seem self-evident, but it is sobering to realize that your friendships and love interests are often shaped by seating charts, apartment availability, shift assignments, and office locations.

The importance of proximity was apparent in a study of Maryland state police trainees (Segal, 1974). At the training academy, both dormitory rooms and classroom seats were assigned on the basis of alphabetical order. Six months after their arrival, participants were asked to name their three closest friends among the group of trainees. Trainees whose last names were closer together in the alphabet were much more likely to be friends than trainees whose names were widely separated in the alphabet.

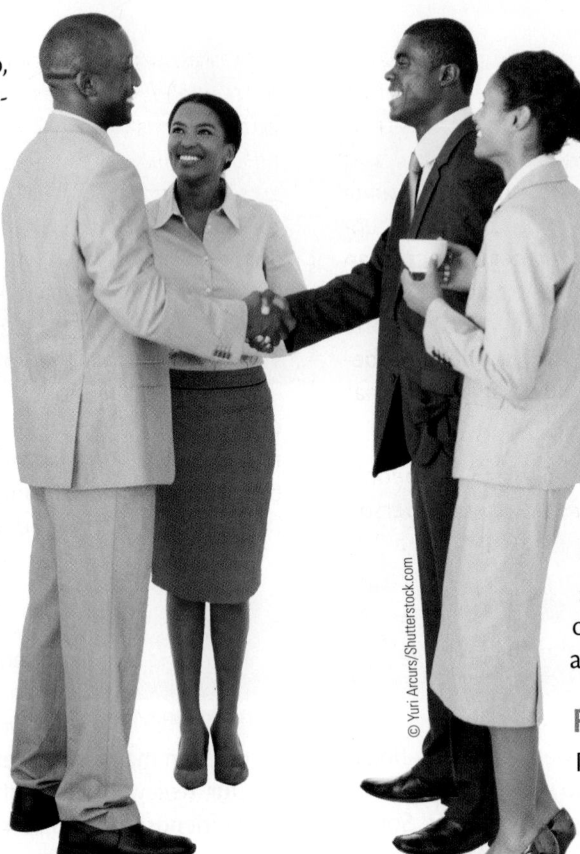
© Yuri Arcurs/Shutterstock.com

How does proximity increase attraction? Goodfriend (2009) asserts that first, people who are near each other are more likely to get acquainted and find out their similarities. Second, individuals who live or work close by may be seen as more convenient and less costly (in terms of time and energy) than those further away. Finally, people might develop attraction just because someone in close proximity becomes familiar to them.

Familiarity

You probably walk the same route to your classes several times a week. As the term progresses, you begin to recognize some familiar faces along the way. Have you also found yourself nodding or smiling at these people? If so, you've experienced the ***mere exposure effect*, or an increase in positive feelings toward a novel stimulus (person) based on frequent exposure to it** (Zajonc, 1968). Note that the positive feelings arise just on the basis of seeing someone frequently—not because of any interaction.

The implications of the mere exposure effect on initial attraction should be obvious. Generally, the more familiar someone is, the more you will like him or her (Le, 2009). Greater liking increases the probability that you will strike up a conversation and, possibly, develop a relationship with the person. Of course, people can be attracted to total strangers, so familiarity isn't the only factor involved in initial attraction.

Physical Attractiveness

Physical attractiveness plays a major role in initial face-to-face encounters. Among American college students, physical attractiveness in a dating partner has increased in importance over the past 50 years—for both sexes, but especially for men (Buss et al., 2001). As you might expect, the importance of physical appearance is different for a future spouse or life partner than for casual relationships. For a marriage partner, both male and female college students ranked the traits of honesty and trustworthiness as the highest (Regan & Berscheid, 1997). For a sexual partner, both men and women ranked "attractive appearance" the highest. Good looks play a role in friendships as well. People, especially males, prefer attractiveness in their same- and other-gender friends (Fehr, 2000).

> The importance of physical appearance is different for a future spouse or life partner than for casual relationships.

© stockcam/iStockphoto

Do gays and straights differ in the importance they place on the physical attractiveness of prospective dating partners? It seems not. In fact, researchers often find gender rather than sexual orientation to be the more important factor in partner preferences. For example, in the wording of gay and straight personal advertisements in newspapers, both heterosexual and homosexual men are more likely than heterosexual or homosexual women to request physically attractive partners (Deaux & Hanna, 1984).

The emphasis on beauty may not be quite as great as the evidence reviewed thus far suggests. In a 2005 Internet survey of over 200,000 participants, intelligence, humor, honesty, and kindness were ranked as the most important traits in a partner, with good looks coming in fifth. However, when results were separated by gender, attractiveness was still ranked higher by men than by women (Lippa, 2007). Figure 9.1 summarizes these findings. However, keep in mind that verbal reports don't always predict people's actual priorities and behavior, and some people might not be aware of what actually attracts them.

What makes someone attractive? Although people can hold different views about what makes a person attractive, they tend to agree on the key elements of good looks. Michael Cunningham (2009a), a pioneer in this area of research, identified four categories of qualities that cause someone to be seen as more or less attractive: neonate (baby-face) qualities, mature features, expressiveness, and grooming. Women who have *neonate qualities* such as large eyes, prominent cheekbones, a small nose, and full lips get high atttractiveness ratings. Although softer- and finer-featured male faces are also rated as attractive (Leonardo DiCaprio's, for example), neonate qualities contribute more to the attractiveness of females. Men who have *mature features* such as a strong jaw and a broad forehead get high ratings on attractiveness (George Clooney and Denzel Washington come to mind).

Expressive traits, such as a large smile and high-set eyebrows, are also related to perceptions of attractiveness. A broad smile is seen as more attractive, perhaps because it can indicate friendliness, and high-set eyebrows could be seen as a sign of interest and agreeableness. *Grooming qualities* are characteristics people use to enhance their other physical qualities, such as cosmetics, hairstyle, clothing, and accessories. Individuals will go to great lengths to enhance their physical attractiveness, as demonstrated by the increased rate of cosmetic surgery, especially among younger people. In 2008, over 10.2 million cosmetic procedures were performed (see Figure 9.2 on the next page), with breast augmentations and liposuction being the top two (American Society for Aesthetic Plastic Surgery, 2008).

Gay males also live in a subculture that emphasizes physical appearance. A study that experimentally induced self-objectification (wearing a swimsuit versus a turtleneck sweater) showed that gay males felt more body shame, had more body dissatisfaction, and ate less when given the opportunity than straight males did (Martins, Tiggermann, & Kirkbride, 2007). On average, both gay and heterosexual men desire to be thinner and more muscular, and this dissatisfaction increases with age (Tiggemann, Martins, & Kirkbride, 2007).

© Viorel Sima/Shutterstock.com

FIGURE 9.1 Rank order of most important traits in a partner

In a 2005 international Internet survey of over 200,000 participants (including heterosexuals and homosexuals, men and women), Lippa (2007) found that intelligence, humor, honesty, kindness, and good looks were ranked (in that order) as the most important traits in a partner for all participants. However, when the findings were separated by gender, good looks were still ranked higher by men than women.

IMPORTANT TRAITS IN ROMANTIC PARTNERS

Ranking	Men	Women
1	Intelligence	Humor
2	*Good looks*	Intelligence
3	Humor	Honesty
4	Honesty	Kindness
5	*Attractive face*	Values
6	Kindness	Communication skills
7	Values	Dependability
8	Communication skills	*Good looks*
9	Dependability	*Attractive face*
10	Age	Ambition

Source: Adapted from Lippa, R. A. (2007). The preferred traits of mates in a cross-national study of heterosexual and homosexual men and women: An examination of biological and cultural influences. *Archives of Sexual Behavior, 36*(2), 193–208. Reprinted by kind permission of Springer Science and Business Media.

Matching up on looks. Thankfully, people can enjoy rewarding social lives without being spectacularly good-looking. In the process of dating and mating, people apparently take into consideration their own level of attractiveness. **The *matching hypothesis* proposes that people of similar levels of physical**

FIGURE 9.2 Top five surgical cosmetic procedures in 2008

The number of cosmetic surgeries annually is on the rise. In 2008, over 10.2 million cosmetic procedures were performed.

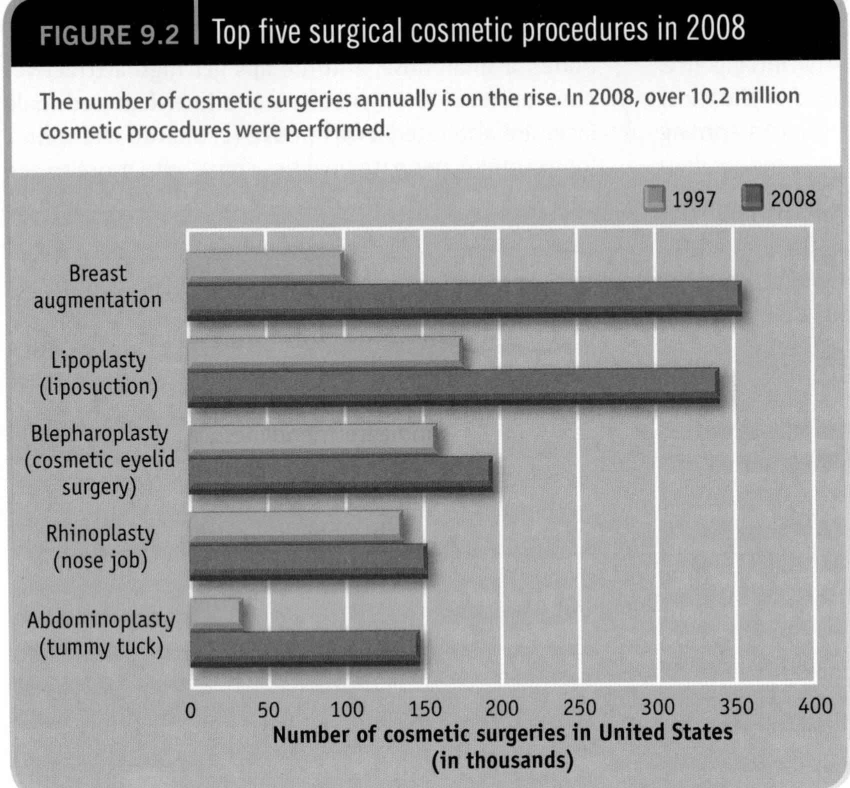

© Cengage Learning

Source: Retrieved from the American Society for Aesthetic Plastic Surgery, 2008, http://www.surgery.org/media/statistics.

attractiveness gravitate toward each other. That is, individuals tend to partner with others who are "in their same league." This hypothesis is supported by findings that both dating and married heterosexual couples tend to be similar in physical attractiveness. There is some debate, however, about whether people match up by their own choice. Some theorists maintain that physical attractiveness is a resource that partners bring to the relationship and that, in general, partners want to maintain an equitable balance (Hatfield & Sprecher, 2009).

Attractiveness and resource exchange. Although the matching hypothesis is often at work, physical attractiveness can be viewed as a resource that partners can exchange in relationships. A number of studies have shown that, in heterosexual dating, males "trade" their occupational status for youth and physical attractiveness in females, and vice versa (Fletcher, Overall, & Friesen, 2006). This finding also holds true in many other cultures. Men in most countries rate physical attractiveness in a prospective mate as more important than women do, whereas women rate "good financial prospects" and "ambitious and industrious" as more important characteristics than men do (Buss, 1989). In reviewing the content of personal ads in newspapers and magazines, Wiederman (1993) reported that female advertisers sought financial resources in prospective partners eleven times more often than the men did.

Photo: © Yuri Arcurs/Shutterstock.com; Frame: © L_amica/Shutterstock.com

According to the matching hypothesis, people tend to wind up with someone similar to themselves in attractiveness. However, other factors, such as personality, intelligence, and social status, also influence attraction.

Evolutionary social psychologists such as David Buss (1988) believe that these findings on age, status, and physical attractiveness reflect gender differences in inherited reproductive strategies that have been sculpted over thousands of generations by natural selection. Their thinking has been guided by ***parental investment theory,*** **which maintains that a species' mating patterns depend on what each gender has to invest—in the way of time, energy, and survival risk—to produce and nurture offspring.** Like many mammalian species, human males are required to invest little in the production of offspring beyond the act of copulation, so their reproductive potential is maximized by mating with as many females as possible. Also, males should prefer young and attractive females because these qualities are assumed to signal fertility, which should increase the chances of conception and passing genes on to the next generation. The situation for females is quite different. Females have to invest nine months in pregnancy, and our female ancestors typically had to devote at least several additional years to nourishing offspring through breastfeeding. These realities limit the number of offspring women can produce, regardless of how many males they mate with. Hence, females have

FIGURE 9.3 Parental investment theory and mating preferences

Parental investment theory suggests that basic differences between males and females in parental investment have great adaptive significance and lead to gender differences in mating propensities and preferences, as outlined here.

	Biological reality		Evolutionary significance		Behavioral outcomes
Males	Reproduction involves minimal investment of time, energy, and risk	→	Maximize reproductive success by seeking more sexual partners with high reproductive potential	→	More interest in uncommitted sex, greater number of sex partners over lifetime, look for youth and attractiveness in partners
Females	Reproduction involves substantial investment of time, energy, and risk	→	Maximize reproductive success by seeking partners willing to invest material resources in your offspring	→	Less interest in uncommitted sex, smaller number of sex partners over lifetime, look for income, status, and ambition in partners

© Cengage Learning

little or no incentive for mating with many males. Instead, females can optimize their reproductive potential by mating with reliable partners who have greater material resources. These preferences should increase the likelihood that a male partner will be committed to a long-term relationship and will be able to support the woman and their children, thus ensuring her genes will be passed on (see Figure 9.3).

Are there alternatives to the evolutionary explanation for patterns of mate selection and resource exchange in heterosexual relationships? Yes, sociocultural models can also provide plausible explanations that center on traditional gender-role socialization and men's greater economic power (Sprecher, Sullivan, & Hatfield, 1994). Some theorists argue that women have learned to value men's economic clout because their own economic potential has been severely limited in virtually all cultures by a long history of discrimination. Consistent with this hypothesis, it is women in countries with limited educational and career opportunities for females who show the strongest preferences for men with high incomes (Eagly & Wood, 1999). Moreover, when women's economic power increases, so does their preference for a physically attractive mate (Gangestad, 1993).

Evolutionary theory can explain why attractive young women often become romantically involved with much older men who happen to be wealthy.

© AP Images/Evan Agostini

9-1b GETTING ACQUAINTED

After several initial encounters, people typically begin the dance of getting to know each other. Is it possible to predict which budding relationships will flower and which will die on the vine? We'll examine two factors that can keep the ball rolling: reciprocal liking and perceived similarity.

BIZARRO

BIZARRO © 2000 Dan Piraro. Dist. by King Features Syndicate

Reciprocal Liking

An old adage advises, "If you want to *have* a friend, *be* a friend." This suggestion captures the idea of the reciprocity principle in relationships. ***Reciprocal liking*** **refers to liking those who show that they like you.** Many studies show that if you believe another person likes you, you will like him or her. Think about it. You respond positively when others sincerely flatter you, do favors for you, and use nonverbal behavior to signal their interest in you (eye contact, leaning forward). These interactions are enjoyable, validating, and positively reinforcing. As such, you usually reciprocate such behavior.

Once established, relationships require maintenance to remain intact.

© desuza.communications/iStockphoto

You can see a self-fulfilling prophecy at work here. If you believe that someone likes you, you behave in a friendly manner toward that person. Your behavior encourages him or her to respond positively, which confirms your initial expectation. A study by Rebecca Curtis and Kim Miller (1986) showed this self-fulfilling prophecy in action. College students who were strangers were divided into pairs for a 5-minute "get acquainted" conversation. Afterward, one member of each pair was led to believe that the other student either did or didn't like him or her. Then the pairs met again and talked about current events for 10 minutes. Raters, blind to the experimental condition of the participants, listened to tape recordings of the 10-minute interactions and rated the participants on a number of behaviors. As predicted, the participants who believed that they were liked were rated as disclosing more about themselves, behaving more warmly, disagreeing less, and having a more positive tone of voice and general attitude than those who believed that they were disliked.

Similarity

Do "birds of a feather flock together," or do "opposites attract"? Research offers far more support for the first adage than the second. Despite the increasing diversity in the United States, similarity continues to play a key role in attraction, and the similarity principle operates in both friendships and romantic relationships regardless of sexual orientation (Morry, 2009). In a longitudinal study of best friends, researchers found that similarity among friends in 1983 actually predicted their closeness in 2002—19 years later (Ledbetter, Griffin, & Sparks, 2007). We've already explored similarity in physical attractiveness (the matching hypothesis). Now, let's consider other similarities that contribute to attraction.

Heterosexual married and dating couples tend to be similar in *demographic characteristics* (age, race, religion, socioeconomic status, and education), *intelligence*, and *attitudes* (Watson et al., 2004). According to Donn Byrne's two-stage model, people first "sort" for dissimilarity, avoiding those who appear to be different. Then, from among the remaining group, they gravitate toward those who are most similar (Byrne, Clore, & Smeaton, 1986). Support for similarity in *personality* as a factor in attraction is weaker and mixed. Research findings indicate that perceived similarity in personality might be more important than actual similarity, at least in the early phases of getting aquatinted (Selfhout et al., 2009). Once people are in committed relationships, however, similarity in personality is associated with relationship satisfaction (Luo & Klohnen, 2005).

What is the appeal of similarity? For one thing, you assume that a similar person will probably like you. Second, when others share your beliefs, you feel validated. Finally, people who are similar are more likely to react to situations in the same way, thus reducing the chances for conflicts and stress.

9-1c ESTABLISHED RELATIONSHIPS

Over time, some acquaintanceships evolve into established relationships. Once established, relationships require maintenance to remain intact. ***Relationship maintenance*** **involves the actions and activities used to sustain the desired quality of a relationship.** In Figure 9.4, you can see a list of commonly used relationship maintenance behaviors. Often, these behaviors occur spontaneously (calling to check in, eating meals together); at other times, behaviors are more intentional and require more planning (traveling to visit family and friends). Obviously, strategies vary depending on the nature of a relationship (familial, friendship, romantic) and its stage of development (new, developing, mature).

Photo: © zubarev/Shutterstock.com; Frame: © Vitaly Korovin/Shutterstock.com

For example, married couples engage in more assurances and social networking than dating partners do (Stafford & Canary, 1991). Both spontaneous and intentional maintenance activities are correlated with relationship satisfaction and commitment (Canary & Dainton, 2006). Of the behaviors in Figure 9.4, the best predictors of marital satisfaction are positivity, assurances, and sharing tasks (Canary, Stafford, & Semic, 2002). Also, relationship satisfaction is higher when the frequency of one partner's maintenance activities is in line with the other's expectations or when maintenance contributions are equitable (Stafford & Canary, 2006). Gay and lesbian couples generally use the same maintenance behaviors as heterosexual couples.

Another approach to relationship maintenance is the use of "minding" (Harvey & Omarzu, 1997). *Minding* is an active and ongoing process of continuing mutual self-disclosure and maintaining relationship-enhancing beliefs and attributions about one's partner. To elaborate, a high degree of minding involves using good listening skills, having detailed knowledge about your partner's opinions, making generally positive attributions for your partner's behaviors, expressing feelings of trust and commitment, recognizing your partner's support and effort, and having an optimistic view of the future of the relationship. By contrast, a low degree of minding is characterized by a lack of interest in your partner's self-disclosures, generally negative attributions for your partner's behavior, dwelling on your partner's faults, and a pessimistic view of the future of the relationship. This model asserts that a high level of minding is associated with satisfying and intimate long-term relationships. Although the concept of minding was developed to shed light on the dynamics of committed romantic relationships, the model likely applies to family and friendship relationships as well (Omarzu, 2009).

We have examined relationship development from initial attraction to relationship maintenance. Now let's probe more deeply into two important types of close relationships: friendship and romantic partnerships.

FIGURE 9.4 Relationship maintenance strategies

College students were asked to describe how they maintained three different personal relationships over a college term. Their responses were grouped into eleven categories. You can see that, ironically, some people behave negatively in an attempt to enhance relationships. Openness was the most commonly nominated strategy. (Adapted from Canary & Stafford, 1994)

RELATIONSHIP MAINTENANCE STRATEGIES

Strategy	Behavioral example
Positivity	Try to act nice and cheerful
Openness	Encourage him/her to disclose thoughts and feelings to me
Assurances	Stress my commitment to him/her
Social networking	Show that I am willing to do things with his/her friends and family
Task sharing	Help equally with tasks that need to be done
Joint activities	Spend time hanging out
Mediated communication	Use e-mail to keep in touch
Avoidance	Respect each other's privacy and need to be alone
Antisocial behaviors	Act rude to him/her
Humor	Call him/her by a funny nickname
No flirting	Do not encourage overly familiar behavior (relevant in cross-gender friendships)

9-2 Friendship

It's hard to overestimate the importance of friends. They give help in times of need, advice in times of confusion, consolation in times of failure, and praise in times of achievement. Friends clearly are important to one's adjustment. In fact, friendship quality is predictive of overall happiness, in part because friends satisfy basic psychological needs (Demir & Özdemir, 2010). College students with strong friendships are more optimistic and deal better with stressful life events (Brissette, Scheir, & Carver, 2002). Intimate and stable friendships are associated with less stress in adulthood and less troublesome behavior in adolescence (Hartup & Stevens, 1999).

Exactly what makes someone a good friend? Researchers have identified three common themes that underlie friendships of all ages (de Vries, 1996). The first involves the emotional dimension of friendship (self-disclosure, expressing affection and support, and so forth). A second theme concerns the communal nature of friendship (participating in or supporting each other in mutually shared activities). The third dimension entails sociability and compatibility (friends are sources of fun and recreation). Studies show that the most important element of friendship is emotional support (Collins & Madsen, 2006).

9-2a GENDER AND SEXUAL ORIENTATION ISSUES

Men's and women's same-gender friendships have a lot in common; both sexes value intimacy, self-disclosure, and trust (Winstead, 2009). However, some interesting differences appear to be rooted in traditional gender roles and socialization. In the United States, women's friendships are more often emotionally based, whereas men's tend to be activity based (Fehr, 2004). Although some researchers have challenged this characterization, the current belief is that men's friendships are typically based on shared interests and doing things together, whereas women's friendships more often focus on talking—usually about personal matters. As a result, women's friendships tend to be closer and more satisfying because they involve more self-disclosure (Fehr, 2004).

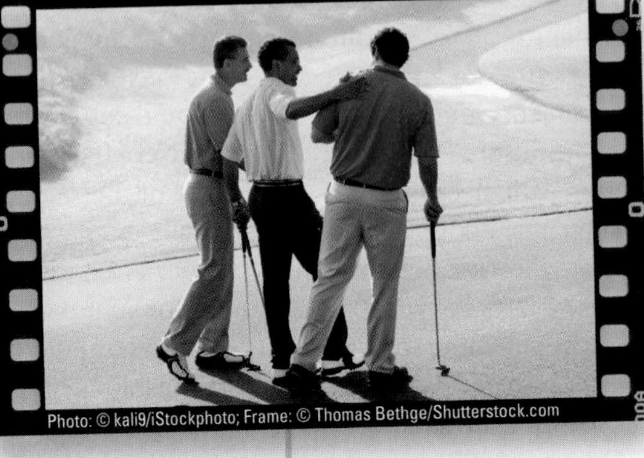
Photo: © kali9/iStockphoto; Frame: © Thomas Bethge/Shutterstock.com

The boundaries between the friendship and romantic or sexual relationships of gay men and lesbians appear to be more complex than those of heterosexuals. Many intimate relationships among lesbians begin as friendships and progress to romance and then to a sexual relationship. Obviously, discerning and negotiating these shifts can be difficult. Also, both lesbians and gay men are much more likely than heterosexuals to maintain social contacts with former sexual partners (Solomon, Rothblum, & Balsam, 2004). One possible explanation for this phenomenon is the fact that, compared to heterosexual couples, gay and lesbian couples have less support from families and societal institutions. So, maintaining close connections with friends and creating "safe spaces" through these connections is especially important (Goode-Cross & Good, 2008).

9-2b CONFLICT IN FRIENDSHIPS

Friends, especially long-term ones, are bound to experience conflicts. As with other types of relationships, conflicts can result from incompatible goals, mismatched expectations, or changes in individuals' interests over time. If the conflicts are great enough, they can result in the friendship ending. Alternatively, individuals can engage in behavior to preserve the relationship. Cahn (2009) describes three steps in friendship repair rituals. First, there is a *reproach*, in which the offended party acknowledges the problem and asks the offender for an explanation. Second, the offender offers a *remedy* by taking responsibility and offering a justification, a concession, an apology, or a combination of these three. Finally, in the *acknowledgment* stage, the offended party accepts the remedy and the friendship progresses. Of course at any point, either party can call off the ritual and dissolve the friendship. Ultimately, conflict is a reality in all relationships, whether platonic or romantic.

9-3 Romantic Love

Wander through a bookstore and you'll see an overwhelming array of titles such as *Men Who Can't Love, Women Who Love Too Much*, and *Getting the Love You Want*. Turn on your radio and you'll hear the refrains of "All You Need Is Love," "Crazy in Love," and "Love You Like a Love Song." Although there are other forms of love, such as parental love and platonic love, these books and songs are all about *romantic love*, a subject of consuming interest for almost everyone.

Love is difficult to define, difficult to measure, and frequently difficult to understand. Nonetheless, psychologists have conducted thousands of studies and developed a number of interesting theories about romantic love.

9-3a SEXUAL ORIENTATION AND LOVE

Sexual orientation **refers to a person's preference for emotional and sexual relationships with individuals of the same gender, the other gender, or either gender.** *Heterosexuals* seek emotional-sexual relationships with members of the other gender. *Homosexuals* seek emotional-sexual relationships with members of the same gender. *Bisexuals* seek emotional-sexual relationships with members of both genders. In recent years, the terms *gay* and *straight* have become widely used to refer to homosexuals and heterosexuals, respectively. *Gay* can refer to homosexuals of either gender, but most homosexual women prefer to call themselves *lesbians*. Chapter 12 goes into more details regarding sexual orientation.

Many studies of romantic love and relationships suffer from ***heterosexism*, or the assumption that all individuals and relationships are heterosexual.** For instance, most questionnaires on romantic love and romantic relationships fail to ask participants about their sexual orientation. Thus, when data are analyzed, there is no way to know whether subjects are referring to same- or other-gender romantic partners. Assuming that their subjects are all heterosexuals, some researchers proceed to describe their findings without any mention of homosexuals. Because most people identify themselves as heterosexual, heterosexism in research isn't likely to distort conclusions about heterosexuals; however, it renders homosexual relationships invisible. Further, research on same-sex relationships tends to focus on white, middle class Americans. Consequently, psychologists don't know as much about the range of homosexual relationships as they would like to. Researchers are now devoting much more attention to this issue.

We discuss gay and lesbian committed relationships more in Chapter 10, so we will just touch on the basics here. We *do* know that homosexual romances and relationships are essentially the same as those of heterosexuals. Both groups experience romantic and passionate love and make commitments to relationships (Peplau & Ghavami, 2009). Both gay and straight couples hold similar values about relationships, report similar levels of relationship satisfaction, perceive their relationships to be loving and satisfying, and say they want their partners to have characteristics similar to theirs (Peplau & Fingerhut, 2007). When relationship differences are found, they are much more likely to be rooted in gender than in sexual orientation.

The experience of romantic love seems to be the same regardless of a person's sexual orientation.

Photo: © Rikke/Shutterstock.com; Frame: © Picsfive/Shutterstock.com

9-3b GENDER DIFFERENCES

Stereotypes hold that women are more romantic than men. Nonetheless, research suggests just the opposite—that men are the more romantic gender. For example, men hold more romantic beliefs ("Love lasts forever" or "There is one perfect love in the world for everyone") (Peplau, Hill, & Rubin, 1993). In addition, men fall in love more easily than women, whereas women fall out of love more easily than men (Rubin, Peplau, & Hill, 1981).

In contrast, women are more likely to report physical symptoms associated with being in love—for instance, feeling as though they are "floating on a cloud" (Peplau & Gordon, 1985)—and they are somewhat more likely to verbalize and display tender emotions (Dindia & Allen, 1992). We should note, however, that men and women have more similarities than differences when it comes to relationships (Marshall, 2010). It appears that the notion that men and women are from different relational planets is somewhat of an exaggeration.

9-3c THEORIES OF LOVE

Can the experience of love be broken down into certain key components? How are romantic love relationships similar to other types of close relationships? These are the kinds of questions that two current theories of love address.

Triangular Theory of Love

Robert Sternberg's (1988) *triangular theory of love* posits that all love experiences are made up of three components: intimacy, passion, and commitment. Each of the components is represented as a point of a triangle, from which the theory derives its name (see Figure 9.5 on the next page).

***Intimacy* refers to warmth, closeness, and sharing in a relationship.** Signs of intimacy include giving and receiving emotional support, valuing the loved one, wanting to promote the welfare of the loved one, and sharing one's self and one's possessions with another. Self-disclosure is necessary to achieve and maintain feelings of intimacy in a relationship, whether platonic or romantic.

***Passion* refers to the intense feelings (both positive and negative) experienced in love relationships, including sexual desire.** Passion is related to drives that lead to romance, physical attraction, and sexual consummation. Although sexual needs may be dominant in many close relationships, other needs also figure in the experience of passion, including the needs for nurturance, self-esteem, dominance, submission, and self-actualization. For example, self-esteem is threatened when someone experiences jealousy. Passion obviously figures most prominently in romantic relationships.

***Commitment* involves the decision and intent to maintain a relationship in spite of the difficulties and costs that may arise.** According to Sternberg, commitment has both short-term and long-term aspects. The short-term aspect concerns the conscious decision to love someone. The long-term aspect reflects the determination to make a relationship endure. Although the decision to love someone usually comes before commitment, that is not always the case (in arranged marriages, for instance).

FIGURE 9.5 Sternberg's triangular theory of love

According to Robert Sternberg (1986), love includes three components: intimacy, passion, and commitment. These components are portrayed here as points on a triangle. The possible combinations of these three components yield the seven types of relationships mapped out here. The absence of all three components is called nonlove, which is not shown in the diagram.

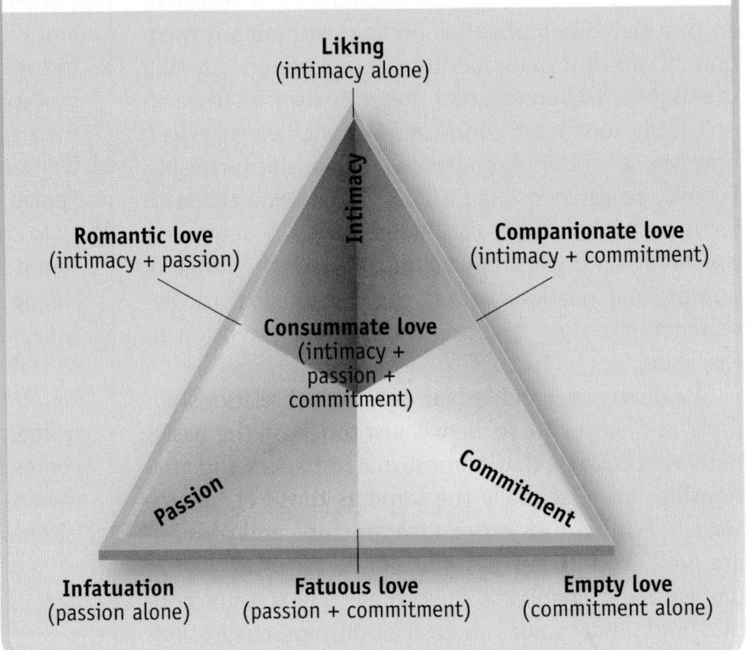

Source: From Sternberg, R. J. (1986). A triangular theory of love. *Psychological Review, 93,* 119–135. Copyright © 1986 by the American Psychological Association. Adapted with permission.

Sternberg has described eight types of relationships that can result from the presence or absence of each of the three components of love, as depicted in Figure 9.5. One of these relationship types, nonlove, is not pictured in the diagram because it is defined as the absence of any of the three components. Most casual interactions are of this type. When all three components are present, *consummate love* is said to exist.

Sternberg's model has generated considerable interest and research. All three components are positively related to satisfaction in dating relationships (Madey & Rodgers, 2009). Also, measures of commitment and intimacy were found to be among the best predictors of whether dating couples continued their relationships (Hendrick, Hendrick, & Adler, 1988). Another study looked at changes in passion, intimacy, and commitment scores over time (Lemieux & Hale, 2002). Participants ages 18 to 75 were classified as casually dating, exclusively dating, engaged, or married. Passion and intimacy scores were lower for casual daters, higher for engaged participants, and lower for married subjects, while commitment scores increased from casually dating participants to married participants.

The triangular theory alone doesn't fully capture the complexity of love. It seems that how people bond with others plays a role. Madey and Rodgers (2009) found that one's attachment style predicts intimacy and commitment levels, which in turns predicts relationship satisfaction. To see why that might be the case, let's turn our attention to attachment theory.

Romantic Love as Attachment

In a groundbreaking theory of love, Cindy Hazan and Phillip Shaver (1987) asserted that romantic love can be conceptualized as an attachment process, with similarities to the bond between infants and their caregivers. According to these theorists, adult romantic love and infant attachment share a number of features: intense fascination with the other person, distress at separation, and efforts to stay close and spend time together. Of course, there are also differences: Infant-caregiver relationships are one-sided, whereas caregiving in romantic relationships works both ways. A second difference is that romantic relationships usually have a sexual component, whereas infant-caregiver relationships do not.

Researchers who study attachment are keenly interested in the nature and development of ***attachment***

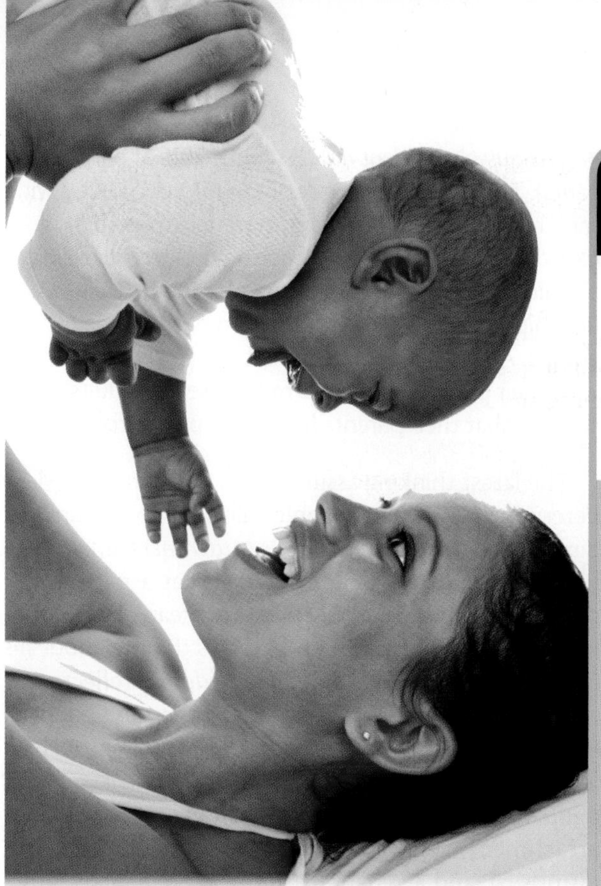

© Flashon Studio/Shutterstock.com

FIGURE 9.6 Infant attachment and romantic relationships

According to Hazan and Shaver (1987), romantic relationships in adulthood are similar in form to attachment patterns in infancy, which fall into three categories. The three attachment styles in adult intimate relationships identified by Hazan and Shaver are described here. (Based on Shaffer, 1989, and Hazan and Shaver, 1986, 1987)

Infant attachment		Adult attachment style
Secure attachment— An infant-caregiver bond in which the child welcomes contact with a close companion and uses this person as a secure base from which to explore the environment.	→	**Secure—**I find it relatively easy to get close to others and am comfortable depending on them and having them depend on me. I don't often worry about being abandoned or about someone getting too close to me.
Avoidant attachment— An insecure infant-caregiver bond, characterized by little separation protest and a tendency for the child to avoid or ignore the caregiver.	→	**Avoidant—**I am somewhat uncomfortable being close to others; I find it difficult to trust them, difficult to allow myself to depend on them. I am nervous when anyone gets too close, and often love partners want me to be more intimate than I feel comfortable being.
Anxious-ambivalent attachment—An insecure infant-caregiver bond, characterized by strong separation protest and a tendency of the child to resist contact initiated by the caregiver particularly after a separation.	→	**Anxious-ambivalent—** I find that others are reluctant to get as close as I would like. I often worry that my partner doesn't really love me or won't want to stay with me. I want to merge completely with another person, and this desire sometimes scares people away.

© Cengage Learning

***styles*, or typical ways of interacting in close relationships.** Their interest is fueled by the belief that attachment styles develop during the first year of life and strongly influence individuals' interpersonal interactions from then on.

Infant attachment. Hazan and Shaver's ideas build on earlier work in attachment theory by John Bowlby (1980) and Mary Ainsworth (Ainsworth et al., 1978). Based on actual observations of infants and their primary caregivers, they identified three attachment styles (see Figure 9.6). Over half of infants develop a *secure attachment style*. However, other infants develop insecure attachments. Some infants are very anxious when separated from their caretaker and show resistance at reunion, a response characterized as an *anxious-ambivalent attachment style*. A third group of infants never connect very well with their caretaker and are classified in the *avoidant attachment style*.

How do attachments in infancy develop? Three parenting styles have been identified as likely determinants of attachment quality. A *warm/responsive* approach seems to promote secure attachments, whereas a *cold/rejecting* style is associated with avoidant attachments. An *ambivalent/inconsistent* style seems to result in anxious-ambivalent attachments.

Adult attachment. What do these attachment styles look like in adulthood? To answer this question, we'll summarize the findings of a number of studies (Mickelson, Kessler, & Shaver, 1997; Shaver & Hazan, 1993).

You can also see capsule summaries of adult attachment styles in Figure 9.6.

- *Secure adults* (about 55% of participants). These people trust others, find it easy to get close to them, and are comfortable with mutual dependence. They rarely worry about being abandoned by their partner. Secure adults have the longest-lasting relationships and the fewest divorces. They describe their parents as behaving warmly toward them and toward each other.

- *Avoidant adults* (about 25% of participants). These individuals both fear and feel uncomfortable about getting close to others. They are reluctant to trust others and prefer to maintain emotional distance from others. They have the lowest incidence of positive relationship experiences of the three groups. Avoidant adults describe their parents as less warm than secure adults do and see their mothers as cold and rejecting.

- *Anxious-ambivalent adults* (about 20% of participants). These adults are obsessive and preoccupied with their relationships. They want more relationship closeness than their partners do and suffer extreme feelings of jealousy, based on fears of abandonment. Their relationships have the shortest duration of the three groups. Ambivalent adults describe their relationship with their parents as less warm than secure adults do and feel that their parents had unhappy marriages.

FIGURE 9.7 A revised approach to attachment styles

Contemporary research on attachment styles has led to the conclusion that it may be best to conceptualize them in terms of where people fall along two continuous dimensions: attachment avoidance and attachment anxiety (about abandonment). This system yields the four attachment styles described here, as opposed to the original three attachment styles. The preoccupied style is just a new name for the anxious-ambivalent style. The avoidant pattern is divided into two subtypes: avoidant-dismissing and avoidant-fearful (Based on Fraley & Shaver, 2000)

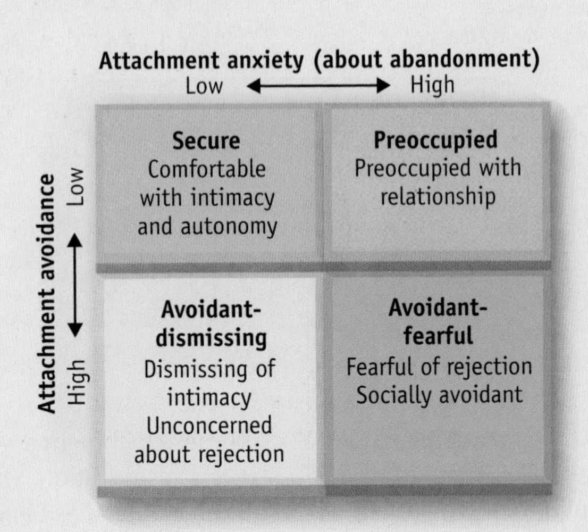

The latest thinking assumes that attachment style is determined by where people fall on two continuous dimensions (Mikulincer, 2006). *Attachment anxiety* reflects how much a person worries that a partner will not be available when needed. This fear of abandonment stems, in part, from a person's doubts about his or her lovability. *Attachment avoidance* reflects the degree to which a person distrusts a partner's goodwill and has tendencies to maintain emotional and behavioral distance from a partner. As shown in Figure 9.7, people's scores on these two dimensions yield four attachment styles: secure, preoccupied, avoidant-dismissing, and avoidant-fearful. You are already familiar with the secure style, and "preoccupied" is just a different label for the anxious-ambivalent style. The dismissing and fearful styles are two variations of the avoidant style.

Although it might appear from Figure 9.7 that the four attachment styles are distinctly different categories, that is not the case. Recall that the two underlying dimensions of anxiety and avoidance are distributed along a continuum (as indicated by the arrows in the figure) from low to high. This means that people are *more or less* anxious (or avoidant) versus totally consumed by anxiety or totally without anxiety.

Correlates of attachment styles. The idea of adult attachment styles has stimulated a huge body of research. Among other findings, studies consistently show that securely attached individuals have more committed, satisfying, interdependent, and well-adjusted relationships compared to those who are insecurely attached (Bartholomew, 2009). Also, having an anxious-ambivalent style is associated with not being in a relationship and with being in relationships of shorter duration, and an avoidant style is associated with shorter relationships (Shaver & Brennan, 1992).

When researchers subject couples to stress in order to study the connection between attachment style and relationship health, the findings generally support attachment theory predictions (Feeney, 2004). That is, securely attached individuals both seek out and provide support under stress. By contrast, avoidant people withdraw from their partners and may become angry either when they are asked for support or when they don't receive the support they want. Anxious individuals become fearful and sometimes exhibit hostility.

In terms of psychological adjustment, securely attached people typically have better mental health than insecurely attached people. Individuals who are insecurely attached are more vulnerable to a number of problems, including low self-esteem, low self-confidence, self-consciousness, anger, resentment, anxiety, loneliness, and depression (Mikulincer & Shaver, 2003). Further, attachment patterns exert influence far beyond romantic relationships. For instance, correlations have been found between attachment styles and gender roles (Schwartz, Waldo, & Higgins, 2004), religious beliefs (Kirkpatrick, 2005), sense of humor (Cann et al., 2008), death anxiety (Shaver & Mikulincer, 2007), and job satisfaction (Schirmer & Lopez, 2001).

Although attachment styles appear to be moderately stable over time, they are not set in stone. Consistent support (or lack thereof) from one's partner can either increase or decrease one's attachment anxiety (Shaver & Mikulincer, 2008). One study reported that a significant number of individuals (ages 26–64) in short-term psychotherapy shifted from an insecure to a secure attachment style (Travis et al., 2001). Thus, therapy may be a helpful option for those with attachment difficulties.

9-3d WHY ROMANTIC RELATIONSHIPS END

The question of why some relationships last while others end is a popular issue in relationship research. Nonetheless, the matter is complex, so easy answers have not been forthcoming. When it comes to break-ups, there are often differences in what people report publicly as the cause, what they actually think is the cause, and what the cause actually is.

In a landmark longitudinal study (Hill, Rubin, & Peplau, 1976), 200 couples (predominantly college students in Boston) were followed over two years. To participate, couples had to be "going steady" and believe that they were in love. If couples split, researchers asked them to give their reasons. The results of this and other studies (Buss, 1989; Powell & Fine, 2009; Sprecher, 1994) suggest that five prominent factors contribute to romantic break-ups:

1. *Premature commitment.* Virtually all the reasons for break-ups involved things that could only be known by

Many couples make romantic commitments without taking the time to get to know each other.

interacting over time. Hence, it seems that many couples make romantic commitments without taking the time to get to know each other. These individuals may find out later that they don't really like each other or that they have little in common. For these reasons, "whirlwind courtships" are risky. Intimacy needs to be combined with commitment if relationships are to survive. Additionally, perceiving that a partner's commitment is wavering predicts relationships ending, regardless of one's own commitment and satisfaction level (Arriaga et al., 2006b).

2. *Ineffective communication and conflict management skills.* All couples have disagreements. Not surprisingly, disagreements increase as couples learn more about each other and become more interdependent. Poor conflict management skills are a key factor in relationship distress and can lead to a break-up. Distressed couples tend to have more negativity in their communication, which can decrease problem solving and increase withdrawal. The solution to this problem is not to stifle disagreements, because conflict can be helpful to relationships. The key is to manage conflict constructively.

3. *Becoming bored with the relationship.* Couples who break up often rank "boredom with the relationship" high on the list of reasons for splitting. Novelty and arousal fade as people get to know each other, and boredom can set in. Individuals have needs for both novelty and predictability in close relationships. Balancing the two can be tricky for couples.

4. *Availability of a more attractive relationship.* Whether a deteriorating relationship actually ends depends, in great part, on the availability and awareness of a more attractive alternative. We all know of individuals who remained in unsatisfying relationships only until they met a more appealing prospect. Additionally, those without desirable alternatives experience more distress during break-ups than those who have desirable alternatives (Simpson, 1987).

5. *Low levels of satisfaction.* All of these factors can contribute to low levels of relationship satisfaction.

Becoming dissatisfied in a relationship can erode one's commitment and increase the chances of relationship dissolution. Obviously, many other factors play a role in relationship satisfaction, including one's expectations of a partner, attachment style, and stress level.

9-3e HELPING RELATIONSHIPS LAST

Close relationships are important to our health and happiness, so how can we increase the likelihood that they will last? Research supports the following suggestions:

1. *Take plenty of time to get to know the other person before you make a long-term commitment.* Research based on Sternberg's theory found that the best predictors of whether dating couples' relationships would continue were their levels of intimacy and of commitment (Hendrick et al., 1988). Regarding intimacy, we have already noted that self-disclosures that lead individuals to feel understood, cared for, and validated are crucial. Other advice comes from long-married couples who were asked why they thought their relationship had lasted (Lauer & Lauer, 1985). The most frequently cited responses of 351 couples who had been married for 15 years or more were (1) friendship ("I like my spouse as a person"); (2) commitment to the relationship ("I want the relationship to succeed"); (3) similarity in values and relationship issues ("We agree on how and how often to show affection"); and (4) positive feelings about each other ("My spouse has grown more interesting"). Thus, early attention to the intimacy foundations of a relationship and ongoing, mutual efforts to build a commitment can foster more enduring love.

2. *Emphasize the positive qualities in your partner and relationship.* It is essential to communicate more positive than negative feelings to your partner. Early in a relationship, this is easy to do, but it gets harder as relationships continue. Recall that in well-minded relationships, people explain their partner's behaviors in ways that enhance the relationship. Oddly, married couples generally make more negative and fewer positive statements to their spouse than to strangers (Fincham, 2001). Unfortunately, when one partner engages in this behavior, the other often responds in kind, which can set in motion a pattern of reciprocal negativity that makes things worse. Partners who see the best in each other, even in conflict, are more likely to stay together and experience greater satisfaction (Murray, Holmes, & Griffin, 1996). Hence, as the old song advises, it helps to "accentuate the positive."

3. *Find ways to bring novelty to long-term relationships.* As romantic partners learn more about each other and develop feelings of intimacy, they also become more predictable to each other. But, too much predictability can translate into loss of interest and, possibly, boredom. One way to keep things interesting is to engage in novel activities together. For example, one study reported that couples who participated in exciting activities together (versus just spending time together) showed increases in relationship satisfaction over a 10-week period (Reissman, Aron, & Bergen, 1993).

4. *Develop effective conflict management skills.* Conflicts arise in all relationships, so it's essential to handle them well. For one thing, it's helpful to distinguish between minor annoyances and significant problems. You need

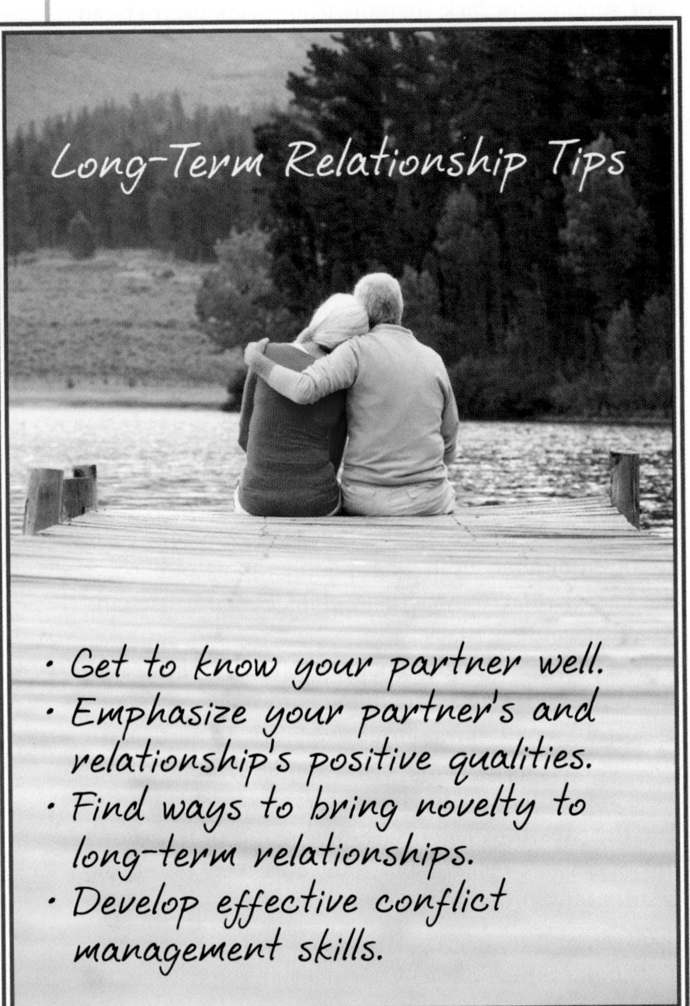
Long-Term Relationship Tips
• Get to know your partner well.
• Emphasize your partner's and relationship's positive qualities.
• Find ways to bring novelty to long-term relationships.
• Develop effective conflict management skills.

to learn to see minor irritations in perspective and recognize how little they matter. With big problems, however, it's usually best to avoid the temptation to sweep them under the rug in the hope that they'll disappear. An interaction pattern common to dissatisfied couples is "demand-withdraw" (Eldridge, 2009). Typically, this pattern involves the woman pressing the man to discuss a relationship problem and the man avoiding or withdrawing from the interaction. This pattern is associated with the "closeness versus separateness dilemma," in which one partner wants more intimacy and closeness and the other wants more privacy and independence (Sagrestano, Heavey, & Christensen, 2006). For more specific suggestions on handling conflict, refer to our discussion in Chapter 8.

9-4 Perspectives on Close Relationships

Now that we have explored friendships and romantic relationships, let's look at some perspectives on close relationships, including how culture shapes people's views of relationships and how the Internet affects relationships.

9-4a CULTURE AND CLOSE RELATIONSHIPS

Cross-cultural research on close relationships is largely limited to romantic relationships, so we'll focus on them. Although it appears that romantic love is experienced in all cultures, they do vary in their emphasis on romantic love as a prerequisite for marriage. Interestingly, love as the basis for marriage goes back only to the 18th century of Western culture (Stone, 1977). According to Elaine Hatfield and Richard Rapson (1993), "Marriage-for-love represents an ultimate expression of individualism" (p. 2). By contrast, marriages arranged by families and other go-betweens remain common in cultures high in collectivism.

Cultural views of love and marriage are linked to a country's values and to its economic health. In one study, researchers asked college students in eleven countries the following question: "If a man (woman) had all the other qualities you desired, would you marry this person if you were not in love with him (her)?" (Levine et al., 1995). Students in countries with more individualistic values and higher standards of living were significantly more likely to answer "no" to the question than were those in countries with more collectivist values and lower standards of living.

Marriages based on romantic love are the norm in Western cultures, whereas arranged marriages are more common in collectivist cultures.

Photo: © Exotica.im 2/Alamy; Frame: © Picsfive/Shutterstock.com

People from Western societies often hold a simplistic view of collectivist cultures' de-emphasis on romantic love and their penchant for arranged marriages, assuming that the modern conception of romantic love as the basis for marriage must result in better marital relationships than collectivist cultures' "antiquated" beliefs and practices. However, there is little empirical support for this ethnocentric view. Take, for example, a study of couples in India, which found that love grew over the years in arranged marriages, whereas it declined among couples who married for romantic love (Gupta & Singh, 1982). Another study found that Indian couples in arranged marriages living in the United States reported higher marital satisfaction than U.S. couples who married by choice (Madathil & Benshoff, 2008). Further, the expectation that marriage will fill diverse psychological needs places greater pressure on marital relationships in individualistic societies than on those in collectivist cultures; this expectation may be linked to the higher divorce rates in these societies. More cross-cultural research on love is needed, but it appears that common assumptions about the superiority of Western ways are misguided, given the high divorce rates.

9-4b THE INTERNET AND RELATIONSHIPS

The Internet has dramatically expanded opportunities for people to meet and develop relationships through social networking services (Facebook, Twitter), online dating services (eHarmony, Match.com), interactive virtual worlds (Second Life), online multiple player games, chat rooms, and blogs. Although critics are concerned that Internet relationships are superficial, studies suggest that virtual relationships can be just as intimate as face-to-face ones and are sometimes even closer (Bargh, McKenna, & Fitzsimons, 2002). Further, researchers find that romantic relationships that begin on the Internet seem to be just as stable over two years as traditional relationships (McKenna, Green, & Gleason, 2002).

KING

© Jerry King Cartoons, Inc.

"Your online profile stated that you were tall, dark and handsome. Have you ever considered a career in fiction writing?"

Because the Internet is shrouded in the cloak of anonymity, people can take greater risks in online self-disclosure. Thus, feelings of intimacy can develop more quickly. Anonymity also allows people to construct a virtual identity, increasing the likelihood of deception. The most common factors that online daters misrepresent are age, appearance, and marital status (Byrm & Lenton, 2001). In fact, one study found that the lower the online daters' attractiveness, the more likely they were to lie about their physical descriptors such as height, weight, and age (Toma & Hancock, 2010).

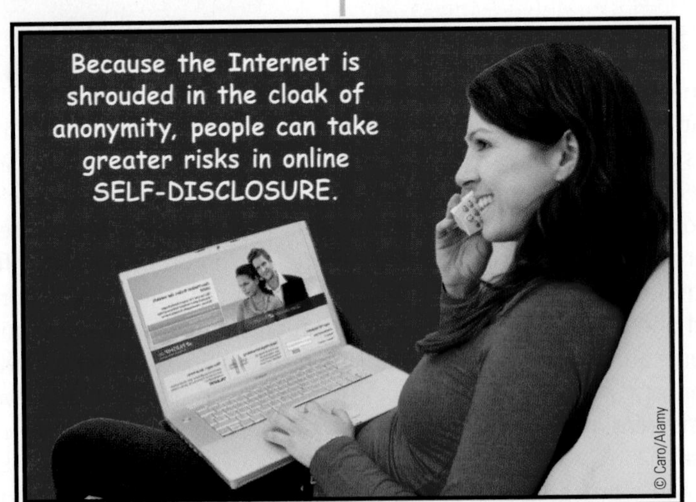
Because the Internet is shrouded in the cloak of anonymity, people can take greater risks in online SELF-DISCLOSURE.

© Caro/Alamy

Some people rationalize online deception because it has practical advantages: Men on dating sites who claim to earn high salaries receive more replies than those who say they earn less money (Epstein, 2007). Second, there are semantic misunderstandings: One person's "average" may be another person's "homely." Third, some people "stretch the truth" to work around frustrating constraints imposed by the technological design of dating websites (such as age cutoffs). Finally, creating an accurate online representation of oneself is a complex process: Individuals need to put their best self forward to attract potential dates, but they also need to present themselves authentically—especially if they expect to eventually meet the person face-to-face. One study found that online daters dealt with this tension by constructing profiles that reflected their *ideal* self rather than their *actual* self (Ellison, Heino, & Gibbs, 2006). Sprecher (2011) notes that these types of misrepresentations are typical in any early courtship; however, they are more common online because people are forced to provide comprehensive self- descriptions that ordinarily would come up gradually over time.

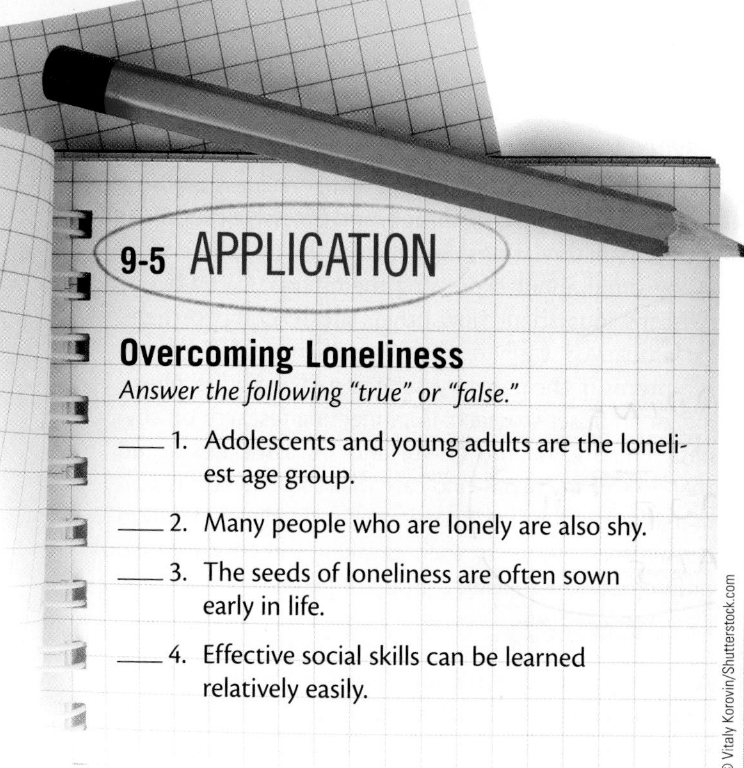

9-5 APPLICATION

Overcoming Loneliness

Answer the following "true" or "false."

____ 1. Adolescents and young adults are the loneliest age group.

____ 2. Many people who are lonely are also shy.

____ 3. The seeds of loneliness are often sown early in life.

____ 4. Effective social skills can be learned relatively easily.

© Vitaly Korovin/Shutterstock.com

All of the above are true, as you'll learn shortly. But let's start with a couple of general points. First, being alone doesn't necessarily produce feelings of loneliness. In these fast-paced times, solitude can provide needed down time to recharge your batteries. People need time alone to deepen self-understanding, wrestle with decisions, and contemplate important life issues. Second, people can feel lonely even when surrounded by others (at a party or concert, for instance). It's possible to have a large social network but not feel close to anyone in particular.

9-5a THE NATURE AND PREVALENCE OF LONELINESS

***Loneliness* occurs when a person has fewer interpersonal relationships than desired or when these relationships are not as satisfying as desired.** Of course, people vary in their needs for social connections. Thus, if you're not distressed by the quantity or quality of your social and emotional ties, you wouldn't be considered lonely.

We can think about loneliness in various ways. One approach is to look at the type of relationship deficit involved (Weiss, 1973). *Emotional loneliness* stems from the absence of an intimate attachment figure. For a child, this figure is typically a parent; for an adult, it is usually a spouse or partner or a best friend. *Social loneliness* results from the lack of a friendship network (typically provided in school, work, or church settings and in community groups). For example, a married couple who move to a new city will experience social loneliness until they make new social connections; however, because they have each other, they should not experience emotional loneliness.

A second way to look at loneliness is in terms of its duration (Young, 1982). *Transient loneliness* involves brief and sporadic feelings of loneliness, which many people may experience even when their social lives are reasonably adequate. *Transitional loneliness* occurs when people who have had satisfying social relationships in the past become lonely after experiencing a disruption in their social network (the death of a loved one or a move). *Chronic loneliness* is a condition that affects people who have been unable to develop a satisfactory interpersonal network over a period of years. Here we focus on chronic loneliness.

Anyone can experience loneliness. Many assume that the loneliest age group is the elderly, but this "distinction" actually belongs to adolescents and young adults (Snell & March, 2008). Gay and lesbian adolescents are particularly likely to be lonely (Westefeld et al., 2001). Another vulnerable group is beginning college students. One study reported that 75% of those in this group experienced loneliness in their first few weeks on campus (Cutrona, 1982). Women are found to be lonelier than men, but only on measures that use words such as "lonely" or "loneliness" (Borys & Perlman, 1985). Thus, it is likely that this apparent gender difference is really men's reluctance to admit to feeling lonely.

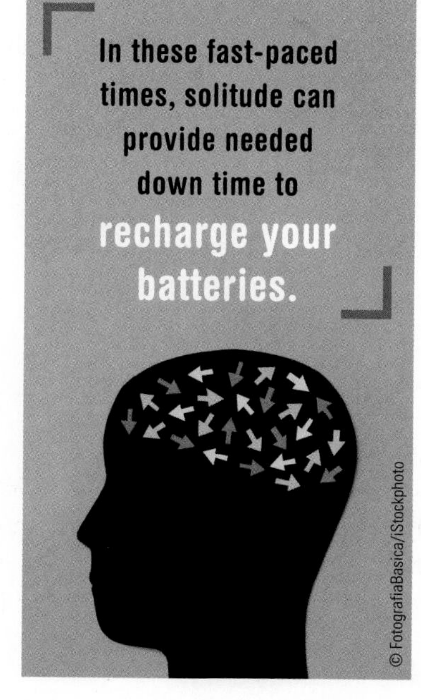
In these fast-paced times, solitude can provide needed down time to recharge your batteries.

© FotografiaBasica/iStockphoto

9-5b THE ROOTS OF LONELINESS

Any event that ruptures the social fabric of a person's life may lead to loneliness, so no one is immune. We'll consider the roles of early experience and social trends.

Early Experiences

A key problem in chronic loneliness seems to be early negative social behavior that leads to rejection by peers. Children who are aggressive or withdrawn are likely to suffer peer rejection even in preschool (Ray et al.,

1997). What prompts inappropriate social behavior in young children? One factor is an insecure attachment style. Because of difficult early parent-infant interactions, children often develop social behaviors (aggression, aloofness, competitiveness, overdependence) that "invite" rejection by adults and peers (Bartholomew, 1990). You can see how a vicious cycle gets set up. A child's inappropriate behavior prompts rejection, which in turn triggers negative expectations about social interactions in the child, which can lead to more negative behavior, and so on. To help break this self-defeating cycle (and head off the loneliness that can result), it is crucial to help children learn appropriate social skills early in life. Without intervention, this vicious cycle can continue and result in chronic loneliness.

Social Trends

Social isolation appears to be on the rise, according to a study based on national surveys in 1985 and 2004 (McPherson, Smith-Lovin, & Brashears, 2006). Among the troubling findings the researchers reported were that the number of people who said they had no one with whom to discuss important matters almost tripled during this period. In fact, 25% of the respondents in 2004 said that they had no one to confide in.

Some social scientists are concerned that recent trends are undermining social connections in our culture (McPherson et al., 2006). Parents (especially if they are single) may be so pressed for time that they have little time to cultivate adult relationships. Because of busy schedules, face-to-face interactions at home are reduced as family members eat on the run or in front of the TV without meaningful family conversation. While technology makes life easier in some respects and does provide opportunities for developing relationships, it has its down sides. For example, superficial social interactions become prevalent as people order meals and do their banking at drive-up windows.

9-5c CORRELATES OF LONELINESS

For people who are chronically lonely, painful feelings are a fact of life. Three factors that figure prominently in chronic loneliness are shyness, poor social skills, and a self-defeating attributional style. Of course, the link between these factors and loneliness could go either way. Feeling lonely might cause a person to make negative attributions about others, but making negative attributions can also lead to loneliness.

Shyness

Shyness is commonly associated with loneliness. ***Shyness* refers to discomfort, inhibition, and excessive caution in interpersonal relations.** Specifically, shy people tend to (1) be timid about expressing themselves, (2) be overly self-conscious about how others are reacting to them, (3) embarrass easily, and (4) experience physiological symptoms of their anxiety, such as a racing pulse, blushing, or an upset stomach. In pioneering research on shyness, Philip Zimbardo (1990) and his associates found that 60% of shy people indicate that their shyness is *situationally specific*. That is, their shyness is triggered only in certain social contexts, such as asking someone for help or interacting with a large group of people.

Poor Social Skills

A variety of problematic social skills are associated with loneliness. A common finding is that lonely people show lower responsiveness to their conversational partners and are more self-focused (Rook, 1998). Similarly, researchers report that lonely people are relatively inhibited and unassertive, speaking less than nonlonely people. They also seem to disclose less about themselves than those who are not lonely. This (often unconscious) tendency has the effect of keeping people at an emotional distance and limits interactions to a relatively superficial level.

Self-Defeating Attributional Style

Jeffrey Young (1982) points out that lonely people engage in *negative self-talk* that prevents them from pursuing intimacy in an active and positive manner. He has identified some clusters of ideas that foster loneliness. Figure 9.8 gives examples of typical thoughts from six of these clusters of cognitions and the overt behaviors that result. As you can see, several of the cognitions in Figure 9.8 are stable, internal self-attributions. This tendency to attribute loneliness to stable, internal causes constitutes a *self-defeating attributional style* (Anderson et al., 1994). That is, lonely people tell themselves that they're lonely because they're basically unlovable individuals. Not only is this a devastating belief, it is also self-defeating because it offers no way to change the situation. Happily, it *is* possible to reduce loneliness, as you'll see.

© Aspen Photo/Shutterstock.com

FIGURE 9.8 Patterns of thinking underlying loneliness

According to Young (1982), negative self-talk contributes to loneliness. Six clusters of irrational thoughts are illustrated here. Each cluster of cognitions leads to certain patterns of behavior (right) that promote loneliness.

CLUSTERS OF COGNITIONS TYPICAL OF LONELY PEOPLE

Clusters	Cognitions	Behaviors
A	1. I'm undesirable. 2. I'm dull and boring.	Avoidance of friendship
B	1. I can't communicate with other people. 2. My thoughts and feelings are bottled up inside.	Low self-disclosure
C	1. I'm not a good lover in bed. 2. I can't relax, be spontaneous, and enjoy sex.	Avoidance of sexual relationships
D	1. I can't seem to get what I want from this relationship. 2. I can't say how I feel, or he/she might leave me.	Lack of assertiveness in relationships
E	1. I won't risk being hurt again. 2. I'd screw up any relationship.	Avoidance of potentially intimate relationships
F	1. I don't know how to act in this situation. 2. I'll make a fool of myself.	Avoidance of other people

Source: From a paper presented at the annual convention of the American Psychological Association, 9/2/79. An expanded version of this paper appears in G. Emery, S. D. Hollan, & R. C. Bedrosian (Eds.) (1981), *New directions in cognitive therapy.* New York: Guilford Press; and in L. A. Peplau & D. Perlman (Eds.) (1982), *Loneliness: A sourcebook of current theory, research and therapy.* New York: Wiley; copyright © 1982 by John Wiley & Sons, Inc. and Jeffrey Young.

9-5d CONQUERING LONELINESS

The personal consequences associated with chronic loneliness can be painful and sometimes overwhelming: low self-esteem, hostility, depression, alcoholism, psychosomatic illness, and, possibly, suicide (McWhirter, 1990). Although there are no simple solutions to loneliness, there are some effective ones. Let's look at four useful strategies.

One option is to use the Internet to overcome loneliness, although this approach might be a double-edged sword. On the plus side, the Internet is advantageous for busy people, those with stigmatized social identities, and those who find physical mobility difficult (such as people with serious medical conditions). Moreover, shy people can interact without the anxiety involved in face-to-face communication. Among lonely persons, Internet use is associated with such benefits as reduced loneliness, improved social support, and formation of online friendships (Morahan-Martin & Schumacher, 2003). On the other hand, if lonely people spend a lot of time online, will they devote less time to face-to-face relationships? One study found that lonely individuals more often reported that Internet use caused disturbances in their daily functioning (Morahan-Martin & Schumacher, 2003), raising concerns about Internet addiction. This area awaits further research.

A second suggestion is to resist the temptation to withdraw from social situations. A study that asked people what they did when they felt lonely found the top responses to be "read" and "listen to music" (Rubenstein & Shaver, 1982). These days, playing computer games and using the Internet are also options. If used occasionally, these activities can be constructive ways of dealing with loneliness. However, as long-term strategies, they do nothing to help a lonely person acquire new "real-world" friends. The importance of staying active socially cannot be overemphasized. Recall that proximity is a powerful factor in the development of close relationships. To make friends, you have to be around people.

A third strategy is to break out of the habit of the self-defeating attributional style we discussed ("I'm lonely because I'm unlovable"). There are other attributions a lonely person could make, and these alternative explanations point to solutions (see Figure 9.9 on the next page). If someone says, "My conversational skills are weak" (unstable, internal cause), the solution would be: "I'll try to find out how to improve them." Or, if someone thinks, "It always takes time to meet people when

FIGURE 9.9 | Attributions and loneliness

Lonely people often have a self-defeating attributional style, in which they attribute their loneliness to stable, internal causes (see upper right quadrant). Learning to make alternative attributions (see other quadrants) can bring to light ways to deal with loneliness and facilitate active coping.

Internal-external dimension	Stability dimension: Unstable cause (temporary)	Stability dimension: Stable cause (permanent)
Internal cause	I'm lonely now, but won't be for long. I need to get out and meet some new people.	I'm lonely because I'm unlovable. I'll never be worth loving.
External cause	My lover and I just split up. I guess some relationships work and some don't. Maybe I'll be luckier next time.	The people here are cold and unfriendly. It's time to look for a new job.

Source: Based on Shaver, P., & Rubenstein, C. (1980). Childhood attachment experience and adult loneliness. In L. Wheeler (Ed.), *Review of Personality and Social Psychology* (Vol.1, pp. 42–73). Thousand Oaks, CA: Sage Publications. Adapted with permission of the Society for Personality and Social Psychology; permission conveyed through Copyright Clearance Center, Inc.

you move to a new location" (unstable, external cause), the solution might be to try harder to develop new relationships and give them time to develop. The attribution "I've really searched, but I just can't find enough compatible people at my workplace" (stable, external cause) may lead to the decision, "It's time to look for a new job." As you can see, the last three attributions lead to active modes of coping rather than the passivity fostered by a self-defeating attributional style.

Finally, to thwart loneliness, people need to cultivate their social skills. You'll find a wealth of information on this important topic in Chapter 8 (Interpersonal Communication). Lonely people, especially, should focus on attending to others' nonverbal signals, deepening the level of their self-disclosure, engaging in active listening, improving their conversational skills, and developing an assertive communication style.

Anyone who feels overwhelmed at the prospect of tackling loneliness on his or her own should consider seeing a counselor or therapist. Dealing with loneliness and shyness usually involves work on two fronts. First, counselors help people improve social skills through *social skills training*. In this program, individuals learn and practice the skills involved in initiating and maintaining relationships. Second, counselors use *cognitive behavioral therapy* (see Chapter 15) to help lonely individuals break the habit of automatic negative thoughts and self-defeating attributions (Hawkley & Cacioppo, 2010). Both of these approaches have high success rates, and they can pave the way to more positive social interactions that are critical to adjustment.

Curious about yourself? To learn more about how topics in this chapter relate to you, go online to CourseMate at www.cengagebrain.com where you can:

- Complete a **Self-Reflection** exercise that will help you think about your personal experiences in relation to topics in the chapter.
- Take a **Self-Assessment** scale that will show you how you score on a research instrument that measures personality traits or attitudes.
- Explore **Recommended Readings** that will provide brief overviews of useful self-help books.

STUDY TOOLS ▸ 9

Ready to study? In your book you can:

- **Test Yourself** with a multiple-choice quiz (below)
- Rip out the **Chapter Review card** (in the back of the book) to refresh yourself on the chapter's Key Ideas and Key Terms

Or you can go online to CourseMate at www.cengagebrain.com where you can:

- Take additional Practice Quizzes to prepare for your exam
- Review Key Terms with flash cards and a crossword puzzle
- View videos that expand on selected concepts

TEST YOURSELF

1. The *mere exposure effect* refers to an increase in positive feelings due to

a. seeing someone often.
b. interacting with someone.
c. communicating via e-mail often.
d. seeing someone once.

2. Jack and Liz have been dating for two years. They are a good example of the matching hypothesis. This means that they are matched on the basis of

a. religion.
b. personality.
c. socioeconomic status.
d. physical attractiveness.

3. A sociocultural explanation for the finding that women are more selective than men in choosing partners is that women

a. have better vision than men.
b. have less economic power than men.
c. are less superficial than men.
d. have to compensate for being more romantic than men.

4. Tracy is in a new relationship. He is experiencing intense feelings of desire. According to the triangular theory of love, Tracy's feelings represent which of the following components?

a. Arousal
b. Passion
c. Intimacy
d. Commitment

5. Women's same-gender friendships are typically based on ____; men's are typically based on ____.

a. shopping together; hunting together
b. shared activities; intimacy and self-disclosure
c. intimacy and self-disclosure; shared activities
d. there are no gender differences in the bases of friendships.

6. If a researcher fails to determine the sexual orientation of her research participants and reports her findings without any mention of homosexuals, her study suffers from

a. sexism.
b. homosexism.
c. heterosexism.
d. romantic bias.

7. Jenna tends to obsess about her boyfriend. She is prone to jealousy and worries constantly about losing her boyfriend. She would be classified in which of the following attachment styles?

a. Secure
b. Anxious-ambivalent
c. Avoidant
d. Cold-rejecting

8. Arranged marriages are most common in

a. individualistic cultures.
b. collectivist cultures.
c. unrequited cultures.
d. both individualistic and collectivist cultures.

9. Which of the following statements regarding self-disclosure in online communication is accurate?

a. Because online communication is anonymous, people take fewer risks in online self-disclosure.
b. Because online communication is anonymous, people take greater risks in online self-disclosure.
c. Because there is a potential record of one's online communication, people take fewer risks in online self-disclosure.
d. There is no difference in self-disclosure in online versus face-to-face communication.

10. A self-defeating attributional style associated with loneliness involves attributing loneliness to

a. internal, stable factors.
b. internal, unstable factors.
c. external, stable factors.
d. external, unstable factors.

Answers: 1. a, page 184; 2. d, pages 185–186; 3. b, page 187; 4. c, pages 191–192; 5. c, page 190; 6. c, page 191; 7. b, pages 193–194; 8. b, page 197; 9. b, page 198; 10. a, page 200

© Masterfile

LEARNING OBJECTIVES

10-1 Identify six recent social trends that are challenging the traditional concept of marriage.

10-2 Discuss factors surrounding the decision to marry, such as cultural influences, factors in mate selection, and predictors of a successful marriage.

10-3 Understand how discrepancies in role expectations, work issues, finances, and communication styles are vulnerable areas in a marriage.

10-4 Describe research on divorce rates, adjusting to divorce, how divorce affects children, and the success of remarriages.

10-5 Analyze gay relationships, cohabitation, and remaining single as alternatives to traditional marriage.

10-6 Compare and contrast partner abuse and date rape as two types of intimate partner violence.

STUDY TOOLS ▶ After you have read the chapter, you can Test Yourself and learn about other Study Tools on page 224.

MARRIAGE and INTIMATE RELATIONSHIPS

CHAPTER 10

"My hands are shaky. I want to call her again but I know it is no good. She'll only yell and scream. It makes me feel lousy. I have work to do but I can't do it. I can't concentrate. I want to call people up, go see them, but I'm afraid they'll see that I'm shaky. I just want to talk. I can't think about anything besides this trouble with Nina. I think I want to cry."—A recently separated man quoted in Marital Separation *(Weiss, 1975, p. 48)*

This man is describing his feelings a few days after he and his wife broke up. He feels overwhelmed by anxiety, remorse, and depression. He feels very alone and is scared at the prospect of remaining alone. His emotional distress is so great that he can't think straight or work effectively. His reaction to the loss of an intimate relationship is not all that unusual. Breakups are devastating for most people—a reality that illustrates the enormous importance of intimate relationships in people's lives.

In the previous chapter, we explored the important role of close relationships in personal adjustment. In this chapter we focus on marriage and committed intimate relationships. We discuss why people marry and how they progress toward the selection of a mate. To shed light on marital adjustment, we describe key vulnerable spots in marital relations and issues related to divorce. We also address alternative relationship lifestyles including gay partnerships, cohabitation, and singlehood. Finally, in the Application we examine the tragic problem of violence in intimate relationships. Let's begin by discussing recent challenges to the traditional concept of marriage.

10-1 Challenges to the Traditional Model of Marriage

***Marriage* is the legally and socially sanctioned union of sexually intimate adults.** Traditionally, the marital relationship has included economic interdependence, common residence, sexual fidelity, and shared responsibility for children. Although the institution of marriage remains popular, it sometimes seems to be under assault from shifting social trends, prompting many experts to ask whether marriage is in serious trouble. Although it appears that the institution of marriage will weather the storm, we should note some of the social trends that are shaking up the traditional model:

The institution of marriage remains popular, but sometimes seems to be under assault from shifting social trends.

1. *Increased acceptance of singlehood.* Remaining single is a trend that has been on the rise for several decades (Morris & DePaulo, 2009). In part, this trend reflects longer postponement of marriage than before. Figure 10.1 on the next page shows that the median age at which people marry has been increasing gradually since the mid-1960s. In 2010, the median age of first marriages was 26.1 years for women and 28.2 years for men (U.S. Bureau of the Census, 2011). Thus, remaining single is becoming a more acceptable lifestyle. Furthermore, the negative stereotype of people who remain single—lonely, frustrated, and unchosen—is gradually evaporating.

2. *Increased acceptance of cohabitation.* ***Cohabitation* is living together in a sexually intimate relationship without the legal bonds of marriage.** Although many people continue to disapprove of the practice, negative attitudes toward couples living together have clearly declined (Cherlin, 2004). The prevalence of cohabitation has grown dramatically in recent decades. Moreover, cohabiting relationships increasingly include children (Stanley & Rhoades, 2009).

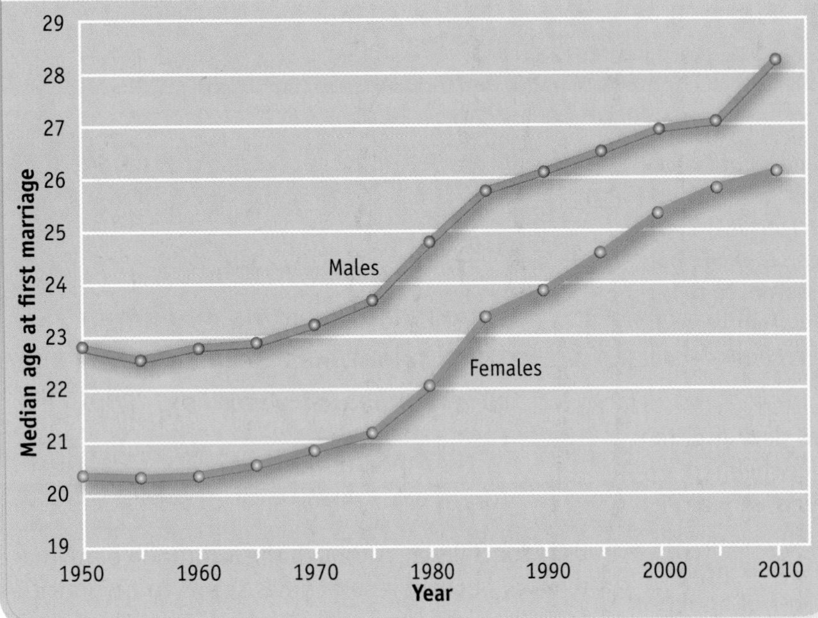

FIGURE 10.1 Median age at first marriage

The median age at which people in the United States marry for the first time has been creeping up for both males and females since the mid-1960s. This trend indicates that more people are postponing marriage. (Data from U.S. Bureau of the Census, 2011)

3. *Reduced premium on permanence.* Most people still view marriage as a permanent commitment, but an increasing number of people regard divorce as justifiable if their marriage fails to foster their interests as individuals. Accordingly, the social stigma associated with divorce has lessened, and divorce rates have climbed.

4. *Transitions in gender roles.* The traditional breadwinner and homemaker roles for the husband and wife are being discarded by many couples, as more and more married women enter the workforce (Halpern, 2005; see Figure 10.2). Role expectations for husbands and wives are becoming more varied, more flexible, and more ambiguous. Many people regard this trend as a step in the right direction. However, changing gender roles create new potential for conflict between marital partners.

5. *Increased voluntary childlessness.* In the past two decades, the percentage of women without children has climbed in all age groups as an increasing number of married couples have chosen not to have children or to delay having children. Researchers speculate that this trend is a result of new career opportunities for women, the tendency to marry at a later age, and changing attitudes (such as a desire for independence or concerns about overpopulation) (Hatch, 2009).

6. *Decline of the traditional nuclear family.* Thanks to endless reruns of television shows like *Happy Days, The Cosby Show,* and *Everybody Loves Raymond,* in the eyes of many American adults the ideal family should consist of a husband and wife married for the first time, rearing two or more children, with the man serving as the sole breadwinner. In reality, this image was never all that accurate, and today only a small minority of American families are estimated to match this ideal (Halpern, 2005). The increasing prevalence of single-parent households, stepfamilies, childless marriages, unwed parents, and working wives make the traditional nuclear family a highly deceptive mirage that does not reflect the diversity of family structures in America. Interestingly, this change is reflected in the fact that contemporary television shows often depict alternative family structures (for instance, *Two and a Half Men* and *Modern Family*).

In summary, the norms that mold marital and intimate relationships have been restructured in fundamental ways in recent decades. Thus, the institution of marriage is in a period of transition, creating new adjustment challenges for modern couples. Support for the concept of monogamy remains strong, but changes in society are altering the traditional model of marriage. The impact of these changes can be seen throughout this chapter as we discuss various facets of married life.

10-2 Deciding to Marry

"I'm ashamed of being single, I have to admit it. I have grown to hate the word. The worst thing someone can say is, 'How come you're still not married?' It's like saying, 'What's wrong with you?' I look at women who are frumpy and physically undesirable and they're monochromatic and uninteresting and they don't seem unselfish and giving and I wonder, 'How did they become such an integral part of a man's life that he wanted to marry them and spend his life with them?' I'm envious. They're married and I date."—A woman quoted in Tales from the Front *(Kavesh & Lavin, 1988, p. 91)*

© Pojoslaw/Shutterstock.com

FIGURE 10.2 | Women in the workforce

The percentage of women in the United States (over age 16) who work outside the home has been rising steadily, although it has leveled off in recent years. In the 25–54 age bracket, 75% of women are in the workforce. (Data from U.S. Bureau of Labor Statistics, 2011)

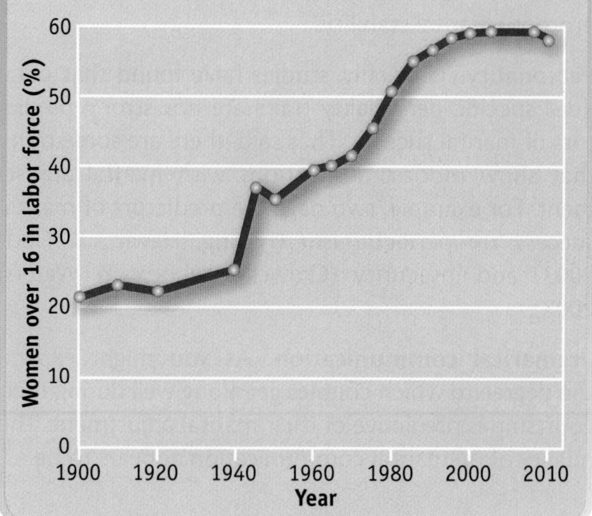

This woman desperately wants to be married. The intensity of her motivation for marriage may be a bit unusual, but otherwise she is fairly typical. Like most people, she has been socialized to believe that her life isn't complete until she finds a mate. Although alternatives to marriage are more viable than ever, experts project that over 90% of Americans will marry at least once (Cordova & Harp, 2009). Some will do it several times! But why? To address this questions, let's look at some of the factors that influence the decision to marry.

10-2a CULTURAL INFLUENCES ON MARRIAGE

Modern Western cultures are somewhat unusual in permitting free choice of one's marital partner. Many societies rely on parental arrangements, and often they severely restrict the range of acceptable partners along religious and class lines. Experts estimate that up to 80% of world cultures practice arranged marriage (Pasupathi, 2009). Marriages arranged by families and communities remain common in more collectivist cultures, although this practice is declining in some societies as a result of Westernization. Still, when couples in collectivist societies contemplate marriage, they strongly weigh the impact a relationship will have on their family rather than rely solely on what their heart says.

10-2b SELECTING A MATE

Mate selection in American culture is a gradual process that begins with dating and moves on to sometimes lengthy periods of courtship. Let's look at some of the factors that influence this important process.

Monogamy and Polygamy

***Monogamy* is the practice of having only one spouse at a time.** In our society, monogamous marital relationships are the norm and the law. In contrast, ***polygamy* is the practice of having more than one spouse at a time.** Polygamy is practiced worldwide and tends to be most common in societies where women have little independence, access to education, or political power (Cunningham, 2009b). Though many cultures practice polygamy, Westerners typically associate it with the Mormon religion, even though the Mormon Church officially denounced it in the late 19th century (Hatch, 2009).

Endogamy

***Endogamy* is the tendency for people to marry within their own social group.** Research demonstrates that people tend to marry others of the same race, religion, ethnic background, and social class (McPherson, Smith-Lovin, & Cook, 2001). Although endogamy is still the norm, it appears to be gradually declining along some dimensions. For example, in 2010 10% of all households reported an interracial marriage, up from 7% in 2000 (U.S. Bureau of the Census, 2012).

Homogamy

***Homogamy* is the tendency for people to marry others who have similar personal characteristics.** Among other things, marital partners tend to be similar in age and education (Jepsen & Jepsen, 2002), physical

People tend to marry others who are similar in race, religion, and social class—a phenomenon called endogamy.

Photo: © Thinkstock Images; Frame: © Vitaly Korovin/Shutterstock.com attractiveness (Feingold, 1988), attitudes and values (Luo & Klohnen, 2005), and marital history (Ono, 2006). Interestingly, homogamy *is* associated with longer-lasting and more satisfying marital relations (Gonzaga, 2009). These results should not be surprising, given that similarity fosters interpersonal attraction (see Chapter 9).

10-2c PREDICTORS OF MARITAL SUCCESS

Are there any factors that reliably predict marital success? A great deal of research has been devoted to this question. This effort has been plagued by one obvious problem: How do you measure "marital success"? Some researchers have simply compared divorced and intact couples in regard to premarital characteristics. The problem with this strategy is that it only assesses commitment and not satisfaction. Many intact couples obviously do not have happy or successful marriages. Other researchers have used elaborate questionnaires to measure couples' marital satisfaction. Unfortunately, these scales also have a number of problems. Among other things, they appear to measure complacency and lack of conflict more than satisfaction (Fowers et al., 1994). Although research shows some thought-provoking correlations between couples' premarital characteristics and marital adjustment, most of the correlations are relatively small. Thus, there are no foolproof predictors of marital success. Nevertheless, here are some of the factors that researchers have looked at in heterosexual couples.

Family background. The marital adjustment of partners is correlated with the marital satisfaction of their parents. People whose parents were divorced are more likely than others to experience divorce themselves. For a number of reasons, there appears to be an intergenerational "divorce cycle" (Wolfinger, 2005). Researchers speculate that this cycle may be due in part to how individuals learn to resolve conflicts. For better or worse, they often learn this behavior from their parents. Whitton and colleagues (2008) found that hostility levels of parents in family interactions predicted the marital hostility levels of their offspring 17 years later. This, in turn, was predictive of marital adjustment, especially for men.

Age. The ages of the bride and groom are also related to the likelihood of marriage success. Couples who marry young have higher divorce rates (Bramlett & Mosher, 2001), as Figure 10.3 shows. Perhaps people who marry later have more carefully selected their mate, or maybe they are less likely to undergo dramatic personal change that would render them incompatible with their partners.

Length of courtship. Longer periods of courtship are associated with a greater probability of marital success (Cate & Lloyd, 1988). Longer courtships may allow couples to evaluate their compatibility more accurately. Alternatively, people who are more cautious about marriage might have attitudes and values that promote marital stability.

Personality. Generally, studies have found that partners' specific personality traits are not strong predictors of marital success. That said, there are some traits that show modest correlations with marital adjustment. For example, two negative predictors of marital success are perfectionism (Haring, Hewitt, & Flett, 2003) and insecurity (Crowell, Treboux, & Waters, 2002).

Premarital communication. As you might expect, the degree to which couples get along well during their courtship is predictive of their marital adjustment. The quality of premarital communication appears to be es-

FIGURE 10.3 Age at marriage and probability of marital disruption in the first five years

Martin and Bumpass (1989) estimated the likelihood of marital disruption (either divorce or separation) within five years for various groups. The data summarized here show that the probability of marital disruption is substantially higher among those who marry young.

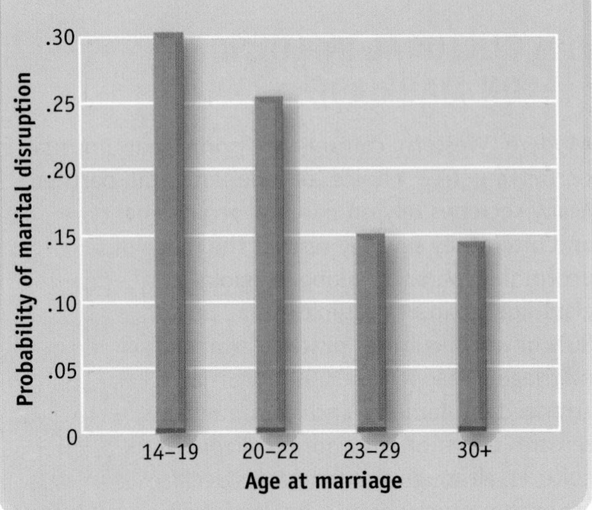

pecially crucial. For example, the more that prospective mates are negative, sarcastic, insulting, and unsupportive during courtship, the greater the likelihood of marital distress and divorce (Clements, Stanley, & Markman, 2004). Close relationships that include self-disclosure and acceptance of what is learned through disclosure are likely to be the most satisfying over long periods of time (Harvey & Omarzu, 1999).

Stressful events. So far we have talked about issues that individual partners bring to a marriage, but these relationships don't exist in a vacuum. Stressful situations surrounding a marriage (unemployment, financial difficulties, chronic illness, caregiving for an aging parent) can cause conflict, increase distress, and harm marital stability (Frame, Mattson, & Johnson, 2009). Research shows that the stress from work can spill over to affect mood at home, which ultimately can erode a marriage (Lavee & Ben-Ari, 2007).

© wavebreakmedia ltd /Shutterstock.com

10-3 Vulnerable Areas in Marital Adjustment

"When we first got married, the first six months of conflicts were all about getting him to take account of what I had planned for him at home. . . . He would come waltzing in an hour and a half late for dinner, or cancel an evening with friends, because he had to close a deal. . . . We would argue and argue . . . not because I didn't want him to make a living . . . but because I thought he had to be more considerate."—A wife quoted in American Couples *(Blumstein & Schwartz, 1983, p. 174)*

During courtship, couples tend to focus on pleasurable activities. But once couples are married, they deal with a variety of problems, such as arriving at acceptable role compromises, paying bills, and raising a family. Marital conflict is associated with several negative outcomes for partners and their family members, including increased depression, alcoholism, physical health problems, domestic violence, and divorce. All couples encounter problems, but successful marriages depend on couples' ability to handle those problems. In this section we analyze the major kinds of difficulties that are likely to emerge.

10-3a GAPS IN ROLE EXPECTATIONS

When individuals marry (heterosexual individuals, that is), they assume new roles—those of husband and wife. Each role comes with certain expectations that the partners hold about how wives and husbands should behave. The traditional role expectations for husbands and wives used to be fairly clear. A husband was supposed to act as the principal breadwinner, make the important decisions, and take care of certain household chores, such as car or yard maintenance. A wife was supposed to raise the children, cook, clean, and follow the leadership of her husband. In recent decades, however, the women's movement and other forces of social change have led to new expectations about marital roles. Thus, modern couples need to negotiate and renegotiate role responsibilities throughout a marriage.

Women may be especially vulnerable to ambivalence about shifting marital roles. More and more women are aspiring to demanding careers. Yet research shows that husbands' careers continue to take priority over their wives' ambitions (Haas, 1999). It is wives who are expected to interrupt their career to raise young children, stay home when children are sick, and abandon their jobs when husbands' careers require relocation. Moreover, even when both spouses are employed, many husbands maintain traditional role expectations about housework, child care, and decision making. Mothers, whether employed or not, are more bound to their child's schedule than fathers are (DeCaro & Worthman, 2007).

Although men's contribution to housework has increased noticeably since the 1960s (Calasanti & Harrison-Rexrod, 2009), wives are still doing the bulk of

© STOCK4B-RF/Age fotostock

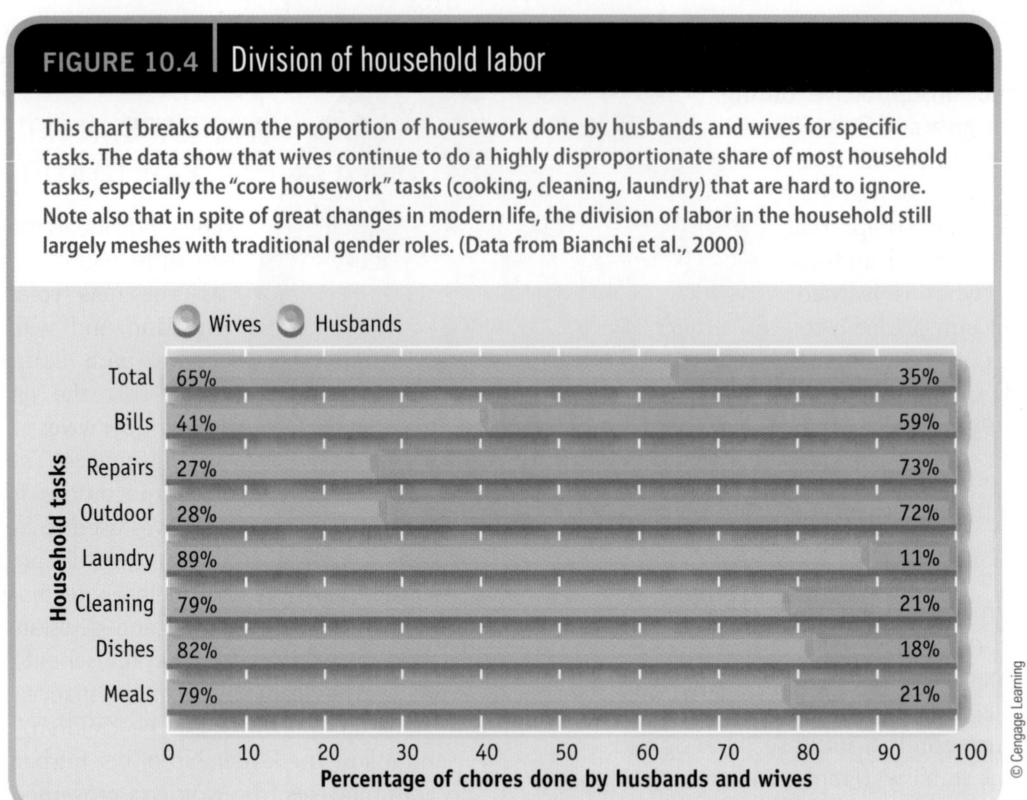

FIGURE 10.4 Division of household labor

This chart breaks down the proportion of housework done by husbands and wives for specific tasks. The data show that wives continue to do a highly disproportionate share of most household tasks, especially the "core housework" tasks (cooking, cleaning, laundry) that are hard to ignore. Note also that in spite of great changes in modern life, the division of labor in the household still largely meshes with traditional gender roles. (Data from Bianchi et al., 2000)

the household chores in America, even when they work outside the home (Sayer, 2005). For example, research indicates that wives take responsibility for about 65% of total housework (not including child care), while husbands do the remaining 35% (see Figure 10.4). Moreover, wives still account for 78% of the essential "core housework" such as cooking, cleaning, and laundry, while men continue to handle more discretionary, traditional "male chores," such as yard or auto maintenance (Bianchi et al., 2000).

Although married women perform the majority of all housework, only about one-third of wives characterize their division of labor as unfair, because most women don't expect a 50-50 split (Coltrane, 2001). These one-third of wives who perceive their division of labor as unfair constitute a sizable population of women for whom housework is a source of discontent. Research shows that women are more likely to perceive their share of housework as unfair when they have nontraditional attitudes about gender roles and when they work outside the home (Coltrane, 2001). As you might expect, wives who perceive their housework burden to be unfair tend to report lower levels of marital satisfaction (Haas, 1999).

In light of this reality, it is imperative that couples discuss role expectations in depth before marriage. If they discover that their views are divergent, they need to take the potential for problems seriously. Many people casually dismiss gender-role disagreements, thinking they can "straighten out" their partner later on. But assumptions about marital roles, whether traditional or not, may be deeply held and not easily changed.

10-3b WORK AND CAREER ISSUES

The possible interactions between one's occupation and one's marriage are numerous and complex. Although the data on the effect of income and employment on marital stability are inconsistent, individuals' job satisfaction and involvement can affect their own marital satisfaction, their partner's marital satisfaction, and their children's development.

Work and Marital Adjustment

Many studies have compared the marital adjustment of male-breadwinner versus dual-career couples. Typically, these studies simply categorize women as working or nonworking and evaluate couples' marital satisfaction. Most of these studies find little in the way of consistent differences in the marital adjustment of male-breadwinner versus dual-career couples, and there are often some benefits for dual-career couples, such as increased social contacts, self-esteem, and egalitarian attitudes (Steil, 2009). Although dual-career couples do face special problems in negotiating career priorities, child-care arrangements, and other practical matters, their marriage need not be negatively affected.

Other studies have investigated the relationship between spouses' job satisfaction and their marital adjustment. We could speculate that these two variables might be either positively or negatively related. On the one hand, if a spouse is highly committed to a satisfying career, he or she may have less time and energy to devote to marriage and family. On the other hand, the frustration and stress of an unsatisfying job might spill over to contaminate one's marriage.

The research on this question suggests that both scenarios are realistic possibilities. Both husbands and wives struggle to balance the demands of work and family, and for both, work-family conflict is associated with reduced life satisfaction and quality of marriage (Coursolle & Sweeney, 2009). When pressures at work increase, husbands and wives report more role conflicts and often feel overwhelmed by their multiple commitments (Crouter et al., 1999). Furthermore, studies find that spouses' stress at work can have a substantial negative effect on their marital and family interactions (Perry-Jenkins, Repetti, & Crouter, 2001). The stress associated with working night shifts appears to be especially tough on spouses and families (Presser, 2000), as does the experience of jobs that require travel (Zvonkovic et al., 2005).

Although the difficulties involved in juggling work and family roles can be challenging, some theorists have argued that in the long run multiple roles are beneficial to both men and women. Barnett and Hyde (2001) assert that negative effects of stress in one role can be buffered by success and satisfaction in another role. They also note that multiple roles can increase sources of social support and opportunities to experience success. Moreover, when both spouses work outside the home, income tends to be greater, and spouses often find they have more in common.

© Jaimie Duplass/Shutterstock.com

Parents' Work and Children's Development

Another issue of concern has been the potential impact of parents' employment on their children. Virtually all of the research in this area has focused on the effects of mothers' employment outside the home. What does the research on maternal employment show? Although many Americans seem to believe that maternal employment is detrimental to children's development, the vast majority of empirical studies have found little evidence that a mother's working is harmful to her children. For instance, studies generally have not found a link between mothers' employment status and the quality of infant-mother emotional attachment (NICHD Early Child Care Research Network, 1997) or children's achievement (Goldberg et al., 2008). In a longitudinal study spanning two decades, early maternal employment showed no "sleeper effects." That is, there were no negative outcomes that showed up later in life, leading researchers to conclude that the adverse outcomes of maternal employment are a "public myth" (Gottfried & Gottfried, 2008, p. 30).

In fact, maternal employment has been shown to have positive effects on children's development in some cases. Data from the Canadian National Longitudinal Survey of Children and Youth indicate that maternal employment is related to decreased hyperactivity, lower levels of anxiety, and increased prosocial behavior at age 4 (Nomaguchi, 2006). Further, while maternal employment doesn't eliminate poverty, it does mean that fewer children are raised in poverty. Children brought up in poverty exhibit poorer physical health, reduced mental health, lower academic performance, and increased delinquency in comparison to other children (Seccombe, 2001). However, experts are careful to note that any benefits of maternal employment might also come at the cost of fewer positive interactions between the mother and child (Nomaguchi, 2006).

10-3c FINANCIAL DIFFICULTIES

Neither financial stability nor wealth can ensure marital satisfaction. However, financial difficulties can cause stress in a marriage. Without money, families live in constant dread of financial drains such as illness, layoffs, or broken appliances. Spontaneity in communication may be impaired by an understandable reluctance to talk about financial concerns. Thus, it is not surprising that serious financial worries among couples are associated with increased hostility in husbands, increased depression in wives, and lower marital happiness in both husbands and wives (White & Rogers, 2001). Husbands' job insecurity is predictive of wives' reports of marital conflict and their thoughts of divorce (Fox & Chancey, 1998). Moreover, evidence consistently demonstrates that the risk of separation and divorce increases as husbands' income declines (Ono, 1998).

Even when financial resources are plentiful, money can be a source of marital strain. Quarrels about how to spend money are common and are potentially damaging at all income levels. For instance, studies have found that perceptions of financial problems (regardless of a family's actual income) are associated with decreased marital satisfaction (Dean, Carroll, & Yang, 2007). Further, newlywed couples who increase their consumer debt spend less time together and argue more about money than those who pay off their debt (Dew, 2008). In a study that examined how happily married couples handled their money in comparison to couples that eventually divorced, Schaninger and Buss (1986) found that the happy couples engaged in more joint decision making on finances. Thus, the best way to avoid troublesome battles over money is probably to engage in extensive planning of expenditures together; that is, to *communicate*.

10-3d INADEQUATE COMMUNICATION

Effective communication is crucial to the success of a marriage and is consistently associated with greater marital satisfaction. In a study of couples in the process of divorce, researchers found that communication difficulties were the most frequently cited problem among both husbands and wives (Cleek & Pearson, 1985).

EFFECTIVE COMMUNICATION IS CRUCIAL TO THE SUCCESS OF A MARRIAGE

Spouses' strategies for resolving conflicts may be particularly crucial to marital satisfaction. Because the ability to communicate emotions is associated with better marital adjustment, couples need to feel safe discussing conflict (Cordova, Gee, & Warren, 2005). Research supports the notion that marital adjustment depends not on whether there is conflict (conflict is virtually inevitable) but rather on how conflict is handled when it occurs (Driver et al., 2003). The marital communication–satisfaction link seems to be robust across cultures (Rehman & Holtzworth-Munroe, 2007).

The importance of marital communication was underscored in a widely cited study by John Gottman and his colleagues that attempted to predict the likelihood of divorce in a sample of fifty-two married couples (Buehlman, Gottman, & Katz, 1992). Each couple provided an oral history of their relationship and a 15-minute sample of their interaction style, during which they discussed two problem areas in their marriage. The investigators rated the spouses on a variety of factors that mostly reflected the subjects' ways of communicating with each other. Based on these ratings, they were able to predict which couples would divorce within three years with 94% accuracy!

Gottman, who is probably the world's foremost authority on marital communication, asserts that conflict and anger are normal in marital interactions and that they are not, in and of themselves, predictive of marital dissolution. Instead, Gottman (1994) identifies four other communication patterns, which he calls the "Four Horsemen of the Apocalypse," that are risk factors for divorce: contempt, criticism, defensiveness, and stonewalling. *Contempt* involves communicating insulting feelings that one's spouse is inferior. *Criticism* involves constantly expressing negative evaluations of one's partner. Criticism typically begins with the word *you* and involves sweeping negative statements. *Defensiveness* refers to responding to contempt and criticism by invalidating, refuting, or denying the partner's statements. This obstructive communication escalates marital conflict. *Stonewalling* is refusing to listen to one's partner, especially the partner's complaints. Gottman eventually added a fifth troublesome communication pattern, *belligerence*, which involves provocative, combative challenges to one's partner's power and authority (Gottman, Gottman, & DeClaire, 2006). Given the importance of good communication, many approaches to marital therapy emphasize the development of better communication skills in partners.

10-4 Divorce and Its Aftermath

"In the ten years that we were married I went from twenty-four to thirty-four and they were a very significant ten years. I started a career, started to succeed, bought my first house, had a child, you know, very significant years. And then all of a sudden, every goddamn thing, I'm back to zero. I have no house. I don't have a child. I don't have a wife. I don't have the same family. My economic position has been shattered. And nothing recoverable. All these goals which I had struggled for, every goddamn one of them, is gone."—A recently divorced man quoted in Marital Separation *(Weiss, 1975, p. 75)*

***Divorce* is the legal dissolution of a marriage.** It tends to be a painful and stressful event for most people, as this bitter quote illustrates. Any of the problems discussed in the previous section might lead a couple to consider divorce. However, people appear to vary in their threshold for divorce, just as they do in their threshold for marriage. Some couples will tolerate a great deal of disappointment and bickering without seriously considering divorce. Other couples are ready to call their attorney as soon as it becomes apparent

"We met, fell madly in love, got engaged, had a lovely wedding and honeymoon. Then things turned sour, we grew bitter, separated and divorced. It was quite a busy weekend!"

that their expectations for marital bliss were somewhat unrealistic. Typically, however, divorce is the culmination of a gradual disintegration of the relationship brought about by an accumulation of interrelated problems, which often date back to the beginning of a couple's relationship (Huston, Niehuis, & Smith, 2001).

10-4a DIVORCE RATES

Although relatively accurate statistics are available on divorce rates, it is still difficult to estimate the percentage of marriages that end in divorce. It is clear that divorce rates in the United states increased dramatically between the 1950s and 1980s, but they appear to have stabilized and even declined slightly since then (Teachman, 2009). When divorce rates were at their peak, the most widely cited estimates of future divorce risk were around 50%. However, the modest reductions in divorce rates in recent years appear to have lowered the risk of divorce to 40%–45% for today's couples (Whitehead & Popenoe, 2001). The decline in divorce rates is encouraging, but the chances of marital dissolution remain quite high. Although most people realize that divorce rates are high, they have a curious tendency to underestimate the likelihood that they will personally experience a divorce. On the average, people peg their probability of divorce at about 10%–11%, which is far below the actual probability for the population as a whole (Fowers et al., 2001).

FIGURE 10.5 Divorce rate as a function of years married

This graph shows the distribution of divorces in relation to how long couples have been married. As you can see, the vast majority of divorces occur in the early years, with divorce rates peaking between the fifth and tenth years of marriage. (Data from National Center for Health Statistics)

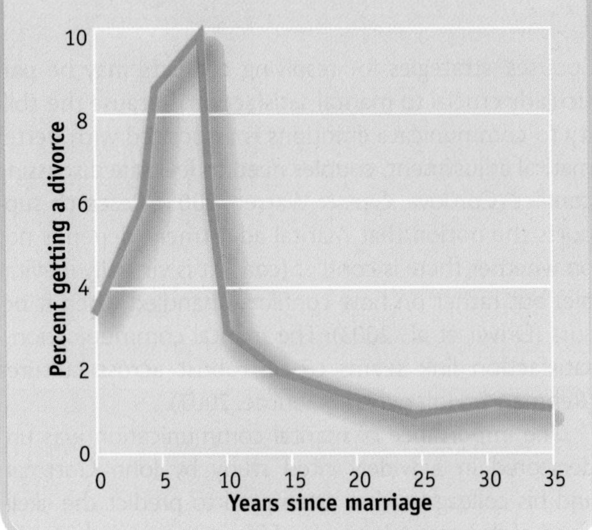

The high divorce rate has led to some novel ways of dealing with its worrisome legal aspects. Attorney Robert Nordyke discovered that the drive-up window at his new office—a former savings and loan branch in Salem, Oregon—was perfect for serving legal papers on his clients' spouses.

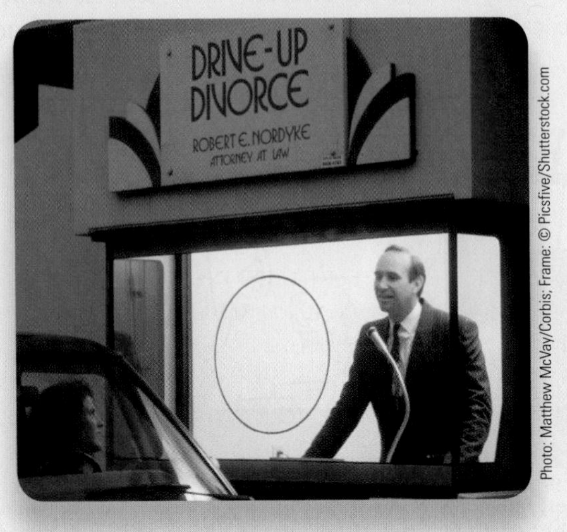

Photo: Matthew McVay/Corbis; Frame: © Picsfive/Shutterstock.com

Divorce rates are higher among blacks than whites or Hispanics, among lower-income couples, among couples who cohabitated, among couples who do not have children, among people who marry at a relatively young age, and among those whose parents divorced (Teachman, 2009). As Figure 10.5 shows, the vast majority of divorces occur during the first decade of a marriage.

A wide variety of social trends have probably contributed to increased divorce rates. The stigma attached to divorce has gradually eroded. Many religious denominations are becoming more tolerant of divorce, and marriage has thus lost some of its sacred quality. The shrinking of families probably makes divorce a more viable possibility. The entry of more women into the workforce has made many wives less financially dependent on the continuation of their marriage. New attitudes emphasizing individual fulfillment seem to have counterbalanced older attitudes that encouraged dissatisfied spouses to suffer in silence. Reflecting all these trends, the legal barriers to divorce have also diminished (Teachmen, 2009).

10-4b DECIDING ON A DIVORCE

Divorces are often postponed repeatedly, and they are rarely executed without a great deal of agonizing forethought. The decision to divorce is usually the outcome of a long series of smaller decisions or relationship stages that may take years to unfold, so divorce should be viewed as a process rather than a discrete event (Demo & Fine, 2009). Wives' judgments about the likelihood of their marriages ending in divorce tend to be more accurate than husbands' judgments (South, Bose, & Trent, 2004). This finding may be related to the fact that wives initiate two-thirds of divorce actions (Hetherington, 2003).

© Jupiterimages/Thinkstock Images

It is difficult to generalize about the relative merits of divorce as opposed to remaining in an unsatisfactory marriage. Extensive research clearly shows that people who are currently divorced suffer a higher incidence of both physical and psychological maladies and are less happy than those who are currently married (Trotter, 2009). Furthermore, the process of getting divorced is stressful for both spouses. As painful as marital dissolution may be, remaining in an unhappy marriage is also potentially detrimental. Research has shown that in comparison to divorced individuals, unhappily married people tend to show poorer physical health, lower levels of happiness, less life satisfaction, and lower self-esteem (Hawkins & Booth, 2005). Divorce can be related to higher rates of autonomy, self-awareness, and job success, especially when individuals have a stable financial situation and a strong social support network (Trotter, 2009), so the picture is not entirely negative.

10-4c ADJUSTING TO DIVORCE

Objectively speaking, divorce appears to be more difficult and disruptive for women than for men, especially in terms of finances. Women are more likely to assume the responsibility of raising the children, whereas men tend to reduce their contact with their children. Within the first year after divorce, half of fathers basically lose contact with their kids (Carter & McGoldrick, 1999). Another key consideration is that divorced women are less likely than their ex-husbands to have adequate income or a satisfying job. For example, one well-designed study found that custodial mothers experienced a 36% percent decrease in their standard of living, whereas noncustodial fathers experienced a 28% *increase* (Bianchi, Subaiya, & Kahn, 1999). The economic consequences of divorce clearly are more severe for women than for men, but in this era of two-income families, many men also experience a noticeable decline in their standard of living after going through a divorce (McManus & DiPrete, 2001).

Although divorce appears to impose greater financial stress on women than men, researchers do *not* find consistent gender differences in postdivorce adjustment. In the aggregate, the magnitude of the negative effects of divorce on individuals' psychological and physical well-being seems to be pretty similar for husbands and wives. Factors associated with favorable post-divorce adjustment include having higher income, getting remarried, having more positive attitudes about divorce, and being the partner who initiated the divorce (Wang & Amato, 2000). After a divorce, having social relationships, both in terms of one-to-one friendships and being part of a circle of friends, is important to adjustment (Krumrei et al., 2007). Forgiveness of the ex-spouse is also associated with increased well-being and lowered depression (Rye et al., 2004).

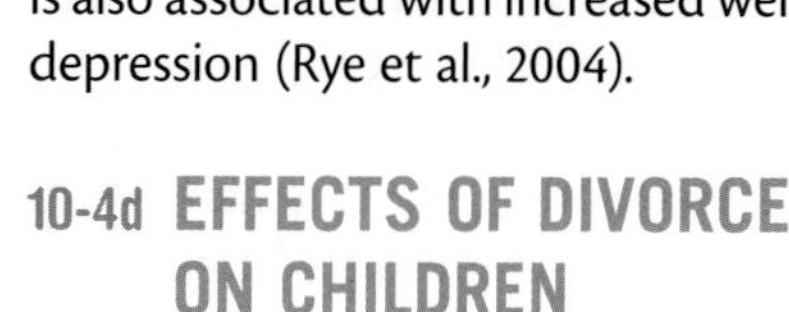

10-4d EFFECTS OF DIVORCE ON CHILDREN

When couples have children, decisions about divorce must take into account the potential impact on their offspring. Widely publicized research by Judith Wallerstein and her colleagues has painted a rather bleak picture of how divorce affects youngsters. In the early 1970s, the researcher began following a sample of 60 divorced couples and their 131 children. At the 10-year follow-up, almost half of the participants were characterized as "worried, underachieving, self-deprecating, and sometimes angry young men and women" (Wallerstein & Blakeslee, 1989, p. 299). Even 25 *years* after their parents' divorce, a majority of the participants were viewed as troubled adults who found it difficult to maintain stable and satisfying intimate relationships (Wallerstein, 2005).

Although the lengthy follow-up in Wallerstein's research is commendable, critics point out that her study suffers from a variety of flaws (Amato, 2003). It was based on a small sample of children from a wealthy area in California that clearly was not representative of the population at large. There was no comparison group, and conclusions were based on impressions from clinical interviews, in which it is easy for interviewers to see what they expect to see. Further, critics caution against drawing causal conclusions from correlational data.

Are Wallerstein's findings consistent with other research? Yes and no. The results of another long-running study by E. Mavis Hetherington (1999), which used a larger and more representative sample, a control group, and conventional statistical comparisons, suggest that Wallerstein's conclusions are unduly pessimistic. According to Hetherington, divorce can be traumatic for children, but a substantial majority adjust reasonably well after two to three years, and only about 25% show serious psychological or emotional problems in adulthood (versus 10% in the control group). That is, most children of divorce do not show long-term adjustment problems.

So what can we conclude about the effects of divorce on children? Overall, the weight of evidence suggests that divorce tends to have harmful effects on many children but can have beneficial effects for children if their parents' relationship was dominated by conflict (Amato, 2010). However, the latter assertion is based on the assumption that the parents' divorce brings their bickering to an end. Unfortunately, the conflicts between divorcing spouses often continue for many years after they part ways. It is also reasonable to conclude that divorces have highly varied effects on children that depend on a complex constellation of interacting factors. As Furstenberg and Kiernan (2001) put it, "Many researchers have become increasingly wary about public discussions of divorce that treat it as an undifferentiated and uniform occurrence resulting in similar outcomes for all children" (p. 446).

10-4e REMARRIAGE AND STEPFAMILIES

Evidence that adequate courtship opportunities exist for the divorced is provided by the statistics on remarriage: Roughly three-quarters of divorced people eventually remarry (Bramlett & Mosher, 2001). The mean length of time between divorce and remarriage is three to four years (Kreider, 2005).

How successful are second marriages? The answer depends on your standard of comparison. Divorce rates *are* higher for second than for first marriages, though the average duration for second marriages is about the same as for first, about eight to nine years (Kreider, 2005). However, this statistic may simply indicate that this group of people sees divorce as a reasonable alternative to an unsatisfactory marriage. Nonetheless, studies of marital adjustment suggest that second marriages are slightly less successful than first marriages, especially for women who bring children into the second marriage (Teachman, 2008). Of course, if you consider that in this pool of people *all* the first marriages ran into serious trouble, then the second marriages look rather good by comparison. As with first marriages, communication plays a major role in marital satisfaction for both spouses.

Another major issue related to remarriage is its effect on children. *Stepfamilies* or *blended families* (where both spouses bring in children from a previous relationship) are an established part of modern life, and adaptation to remarriage can be difficult for children (Bray, 2009). Wallerstein and Lewis (2007) argue that there is an inherent instability in parenting, as parents are caught between their desires to create a new intimate relationship and to maintain their parenting role. Evidence suggests that on the average, interaction in stepfamilies appears to be somewhat less cohesive and warm than interaction in first-marriage families, and stepparent-stepchild relations tend to be more negative and distant than parent-child relations in first marriages (Pasley & Moorefield, 2004), though it is important to

note that this doesn't mean that these relationships are necessarily problematic or dysfunctional.

Taken as a whole, the evidence suggests that children in stepfamilies are a little less well adjusted than children in first marriages and are roughly similar in adjustment to children in single-parent homes (Sweeney, Wang, & Videon, 2009). In an analysis of sixty-one studies, Jeynes (2006) found that children in stepfamilies tend to show lower academic achievement and psychological well-being than those from intact or single-parent families. However, the differences between stepfamilies and other types of families in the adjustment of their children tend to be modest.

Most homosexual men and nearly all heterosexual women prefer stable, long-term relationships.

© desuza.communications/iStockphoto

10-5 Alternative Relationship Lifestyles

So far we have been discussing the traditional model of marriage, which, as we noted at the beginning of the chapter, has been challenged by a variety of social trends. More and more people are experiencing alternative relationship lifestyles, including gay couples, cohabitating couples, and singles.

10-5a GAY RELATIONSHIPS

Up until this point, we have, for purposes of simplicity, focused our attention on *heterosexuals*, those who seek emotional-sexual relationships with members of the other gender. However, we have been ignoring a significant minority group: *homosexual* men and women, who seek committed, emotional-sexual relationships with members of the same gender. (In everyday language, the term *gay* is used to refer to homosexuals of both genders, although many homosexual women prefer the term *lesbian* for themselves.)

Popular stereotypes suggest that gays only rarely get involved in long-term intimate relationships. In reality, most homosexual men, and nearly all homosexual women, prefer stable, long-term relationships, and at any one time roughly 40%–60% of gay males and 45%–80% of lesbians are involved in committed relationships (Kurdek, 2004). Lesbian relationships are generally sexually exclusive. About half of committed homosexual male couples have "open" relationships, allowing for the possibility of sexual activity (but not affection) with outsiders.

Attitudes Toward Gay Couples

Although attitudes toward gays have become more favorable and accepting in recent decades, homophobia continues to be a common problem. ***Homophobia*** **(also called sexual prejudice) involves a pattern of prejudice, intolerance, and discrimination against homosexuals.** Unfortunately, sexual prejudice is common, and gay men and lesbians continue to be victims of employment and housing discrimination, not to mention verbal and physical abuse and hate crimes.

With rare exceptions, gay couples cannot choose to legally formalize their unions by getting married; they are therefore denied many economic benefits available to married couples. For example, they can't file joint tax returns, and gay individuals often can't obtain employer-provided health insurance for their partner. Thus, gay and lesbian rights have become a major political issue. Same-gender marriage is now a legal right in states such as Massachusetts, Connecticut, and New York, and civil unions and domestic partnerships are legally recognized in other states, such as New Jersey and California. However, many states have passed laws prohibiting same-gender marriages. Some argue that allowing gay marriages would erode traditional family values. A study using over a decade of data, however, does not bear this out. This research found no adverse effects on factors such as divorce, abortion rates, or single parenthood as result of allowing (or banning) gay marriage (Langbein & Yost, 2009).

© Allison Michael Orenstein/Getty Images/Digital Vision

Comparisons to Heterosexual Couples

Devoting a separate section to gay couples may seem to imply that the dynamics of their intimate relationships are different from those seen in heterosexual couples. However, research has documented that intimate relationships, gay or heterosexual, function in similar ways. Both types of couples report similar levels of love and commitment in their relationships, similar levels of overall satisfaction with their relationships, and similar levels of sexual satisfaction (Peplau & Ghavami, 2009). Similarity is also apparent when researchers study what gays and heterosexuals want out of their relationships (Peplau, 1988). Furthermore, homosexual and heterosexual couples are similar in terms of the factors that predict relationship satisfaction, the sources of conflict in their relationships, and their patterns of conflict resolution (Kurdek, 2004).

Given the lack of moral, social, legal, and economic support for gay relationships, are gay unions less stable than heterosexual unions? Researchers have not yet been able to collect adequate data on this question, but the limited data available suggest that gay couples' relationships *are* somewhat briefer and more prone to breakups than heterosexual marriages (Peplau, 1991). If that's the case, it might be because gay relationships face fewer barriers to dissolution—that is, fewer practical problems that make breakups difficult or costly.

Gay Parenting

Although research indicates striking similarities between homosexual and heterosexual relationships, basic misconceptions about the nature of gay relationships remain widespread. For example, lesbians and gay men tend to be thought of as individuals rather than as members of families. This thinking reflects a bias that homosexuality and family just don't mesh. In reality, gays are very much involved in families as sons and daughters, as parents and stepparents, and as aunts, uncles, and grandparents. According to the 2000 U.S. Census, 33% of female same-gender couples and 22% of male same-gender couples are rearing children. Many of these parental responsibilities are left over from previous marriages, as about 20%–30% of gays have been heterosexually married (Kurdek, 2004). But an increasing number of homosexuals are opting to have children in the context of their gay relationships (Gartrell et al., 1999).

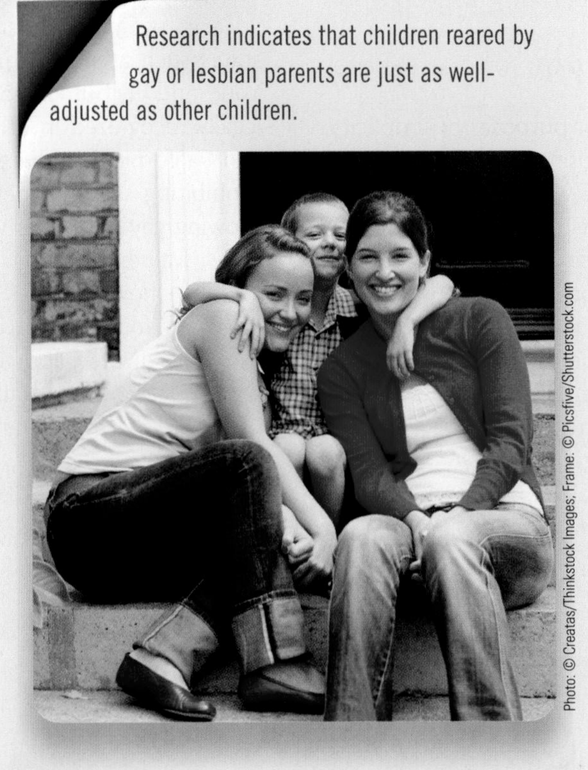

Research indicates that children reared by gay or lesbian parents are just as well-adjusted as other children.

Photo: © Creatas/Thinkstock Images; Frame: © Picsfive/Shutterstock.com

What do we know about gays and lesbians as parents? The evidence suggests that gays are similar to their heterosexual counterparts in their approaches to parenting and that their children are similar to the children of heterosexual parents in terms of personal development and peer relations (Patterson, 2009). The overall adjustment of children with gay parents appears similar in quality to that of children of heterosexual parents (Tasker, 2005). Moreover, the vast majority of children of gay parents grow up to identify themselves as heterosexual (Bailey & Dawood, 1998), and studies suggest that they are no more likely than others to become homosexual (Flaks et al., 1995). In sum, children reared by gay and lesbian parents do not appear to suffer any special ill effects and do not seem noticeably different from other children. Decades of research indicates that the quality of child-parent interactions is much more important to a child's development than parental sexual orientation.

10-5b COHABITATION

As we noted earlier in the chapter, *cohabitation* refers to living together in a sexually intimate relationship outside of marriage. Recent years have witnessed a tremendous increase in the number of cohabiting couples (see Figure 10.6). Although cohabitation is still illegal in a few states, it's estimated that 70% of couples live together before marriage (Stanley & Rhoades, 2009). Moreover, many cohabiting couples have children: About half of previously married cohabitants and 35% of never-married cohabitants have children in their household (Smock, 2000).

Although many people see cohabitation as a threat to the institution of marriage, many theorists see it as a new stage in the courtship process—a sort of trial marriage. Consistent with this view, about 30% of teenagers indicated that they would probably or definitely cohabit (Manning,

FIGURE 10.6 | Cohabitation in the United States

The number of unmarried couples living together has been increasing rapidly since 1970 (based on U.S. Census data). This increase shows no signs of leveling off.

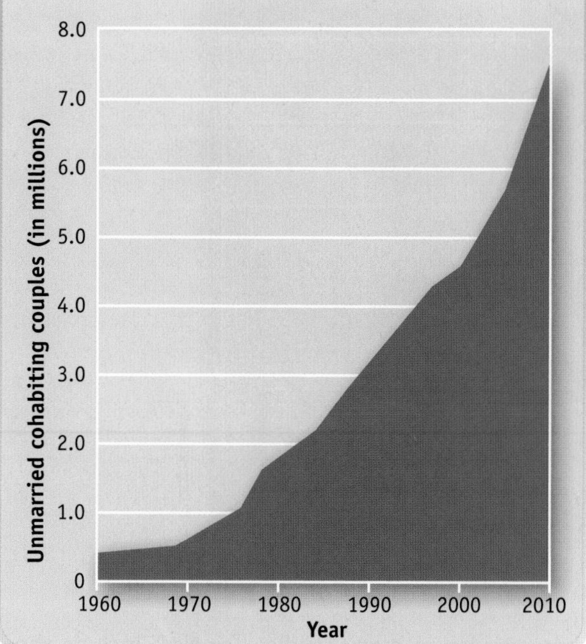

Longmore, & Giordano, 2007). Further, three-quarters of female cohabitants expect to marry their current partner (Lichter, Batson, & Brown, 2004). In spite of these expectations, however, cohabitants report that they are less satisfied with their relationships than married couples (Nock, 1995). Moreover, cohabitating relationships are notably less durable than marital relationships (Seltzer, 2004). Conceiving a child during cohabitation tends to increase couples' chances of staying together (Manning, 2004).

As a prelude to marriage, cohabitation should allow people to experiment with marital-like responsibilities and reduce the likelihood of entering marriage with unrealistic expectations, suggesting that couples who cohabit before they marry should go on to more successful marriages than those who do not. Although this analysis sounds plausible, researchers have *not* found that premarital cohabitation increases the likelihood of subsequent marital success. In fact, studies have consistently found an association between premarital cohabitation and *increased* marital discord and divorce rates (Teachman, 2003). This association, referred to as the *cohabitation effect*, has not decreased as cohabitation has become more accepted (Jose, O'Leary, & Moyer, 2010). Further, this effect holds true even for second marriages (Stanley et al., 2010).

What accounts for the cohabitation effect? Many theorists argue that this nontraditional lifestyle has historically attracted a more liberal and less conventional segment of the population with a weak commitment to the institution of marriage and relatively few qualms about getting divorced. This explanation has considerable empirical support (Smock, 2000), but some support also exists for the alternative explanation—that the experience of cohabitation changes people's attitudes, values, or habits in ways that somehow increase their vulnerability to divorce (Seltzer, 2001).

10-5c REMAINING SINGLE

The pressure to marry is still substantial in our society (Sharp & Ganong, 2011). People are socialized to believe that they are not complete until they have found their "other half" and have entered into a partnership for life. And reference is often made to people's "failure" to marry. In spite of this pressure, an increasing proportion of young adults are remaining single, as Figure 10.7 on the next page shows.

Does the greater number of single adults mean that people are turning away from the institution of marriage? Perhaps a little, but for the most part, no. A variety of factors have contributed to the growth of the single population. Much of this growth is a result of the higher median age at which people marry and the increased rate of divorce. The vast majority of single, never-married people do *hope* to marry eventually. In one study of never-married men and women, 87.4% of the 926 respondents ages 19 to 25 agreed with the statement "I would like to get married someday" (South, 1993).

Singles continue to be stigmatized and plagued by two disparate stereotypes. On the one hand, single people are sometimes portrayed as carefree swingers who are too busy enjoying the fruits of promiscuity to shoulder marital

FIGURE 10.7 The proportion of young people who remain single

This graph shows the percentage of single men and women ages 20–24 and 25–29 in 2010 as compared to 1960 (based on U.S. Census data). The proportion of people remaining single has increased substantially for both sexes, in both age brackets. Single men continue to outnumber single women in these age brackets.

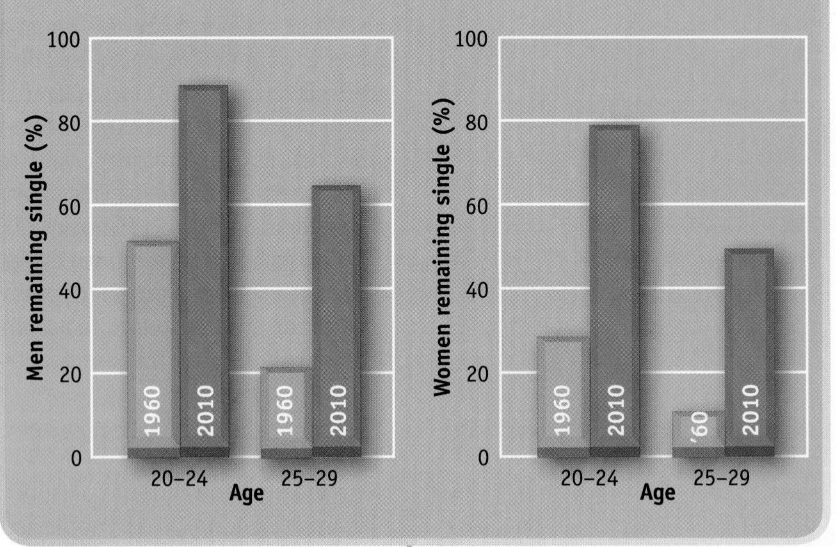

responsibilities. On the other hand, they are seen as losers who have not succeeded in snaring a mate and may be portrayed as socially inept, maladjusted, frustrated, lonely, and bitter. These stereotypes do a great injustice to the diversity that exists among those who are single. In fact, the negative stereotypes of singles have led some researchers to coin the term *singlism* to capture how single people can be victims of prejudice and discrimination (DePaulo & Morris, 2006).

The physical health benefits of being married appear to be greater for men than for women.

© stockcam/iStockphoto

Moving beyond stereotypes, what do scientists know about singlehood? It is true that single people exhibit poorer mental and physical health than married people (Waite, 1995), and they rate themselves as less happy than their married counterparts (Waite, 2000). However, we must use caution in interpreting these results; in many studies, "singles" include those who are divorced or widowed, which inflates this finding. Furthermore, the differences are modest, and the happiness gap has shrunk, especially among women. The physical health benefits of being married appear to be greater for men than for women. But most studies find that single women are more satisfied with their lives and less distressed than comparable single men, and various lines of evidence suggest that women get along without men better than men get along without women (Marker, 1996). When interviewing life-long single women between the ages of 65 and 77, Baumbusch (2004) found that these women expressed satisfaction with their decision to remain single and emphasized the importance of their independence.

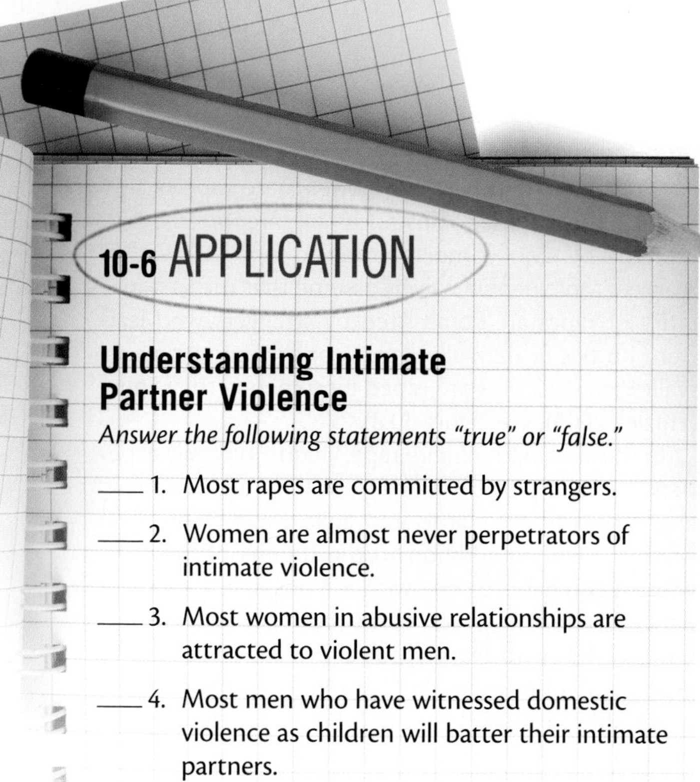

10-6 APPLICATION

Understanding Intimate Partner Violence

Answer the following statements "true" or "false."

____ 1. Most rapes are committed by strangers.

____ 2. Women are almost never perpetrators of intimate violence.

____ 3. Most women in abusive relationships are attracted to violent men.

____ 4. Most men who have witnessed domestic violence as children will batter their intimate partners.

All of the above statements are false, as you will see in this Application, which examines the darker side of marital and other intimate relationships. ***Intimate partner violence* is aggression toward those who are in close relationship to the aggressor.** Intimate partner violence takes many forms: psychological, physical, and sexual abuse. Tragically, this violence sometimes ends in homicide. In this Application, we'll focus on two serious social problems: partner abuse and date rape. Much of our discussion is based on the work of the Rape, Abuse, and Incest National Network (RAINN).

10-6a PARTNER ABUSE

Celebrity cases such as the one involving Chris Brown and Rihanna have dramatically heightened public awareness of partner violence, particularly battering. ***Battering* encompasses physical abuse, emotional abuse, and sexual abuse of an intimate partner**. Let's explore the research on physical abuse of partners.

Incidence and Consequences

As with other taboo topics, obtaining accurate estimates of physical abuse is difficult. Research suggests that about 25% of women and 7% of men have been physically assaulted by an intimate partner at some point in their lives (Tjaden & Thoennes, 2000). It is an oversimplification to assume that partner abuse involves only male aggression against women (Spitzberg, 2011). An estimated 2.78 million men in the U.S. have been victims of sexual assault or rape (National Institute of Justice, 1998). Further, men are victimized by women as well as men. That said, women are more likely to be victims of abuse. In 2010, females accounted for 91.9% of reported rapes and sexual assaults (Bureau of Justice Statistics, 2011). Further, a woman is the victim in 85% of nonfatal violent crimes committed by intimate partners and in 75% of murders by spouses (Rennison & Welchans, 2000). It is also inaccurate to assume that intimate violence is seen only in marital relationships—partner abuse is also a significant problem for cohabiting heterosexual couples and for gay couples.

The effects of battering reverberate beyond the obvious physical injuries. Victims of partner abuse tend to suffer from severe anxiety, depression, feelings of helplessness and humiliation, stress-induced physical illness, and symptoms of posttraumatic stress disorder (Lundberg-Love & Wilkerson, 2006). Children who witness marital violence also experience ill effects, such as anxiety, depression, reduced self-esteem, and increased delinquency (Johnson & Ferraro, 2001).

Characteristics of Batterers

Sexual assault perpetrators are a diverse group, so a single profile has not emerged. Some factors associated with an elevated risk for domestic violence include unemployment, drinking and drug problems, a tendency to anger easily, attitudes that condone aggression, and high stress (Stith et al., 2004). Studies indicate that men who were beaten as children or who witnessed their mothers being beaten are more likely to abuse their wives than other men are, although most men who grow up in these difficult circumstances do *not* become batterers themselves (Wareham, Boots, & Chavez, 2009). Batterers tend to be jealous in relationships, have unrealistic expectations of their partners, blame others for their own problems, and have their feelings hurt easily (Lundberg-Love & Wilkerson, 2006). Other relationship factors that are associated with domestic violence include having frequent disagreements, exhibiting a heated style of dealing with disagreements, and pairing a man holding traditional gender role attitudes with

a woman who has nontraditional views of gender roles (DeMaris et al., 2003).

Why Do Individuals Stay in Abusive Relationships?

Individuals leave abusive partners more often than popular stereotypes suggest, but people are still perplexed by the fact that many partners remain in abusive relationships that seem horrible and degrading. However, research shows that this phenomenon is not really that perplexing. A number of seemingly compelling reasons explain why many individuals feel that leaving is not a realistic option, and many of the reasons revolve around fear. Many lack financial independence and fear that they won't be able to survive financially without their partner. Many simply have no place to go and fear becoming homeless. Many feel guilty and ashamed about their failing relationship and don't want to face disapproval from family and friends, who are likely to fall into the trap of blaming the victim. Above all else, many fear that if they try to leave, they may precipitate more brutal violence and even murder. Unfortunately, this fear is not unrealistic, as many individuals have shown remarkable persistence in tracking down, stalking, threatening, beating, and killing their ex-partners.

10-6b DATE RAPE

Intimate violence is not limited to marital relations. Although date rape does not occur in the context of marriage, it is a serious issue and deserves some attention here. ***Date rape* refers to forced and unwanted intercourse in the context of dating.** Date rape, a type of acquaintance rape, can occur on a first date, with someone you've dated for a while, or with someone to whom you're engaged. Date rape occurs when a partner is coerced into sexual activity against his or her will. As such, the key factor in distinguishing this type of abuse is a partner's *consent*. There are two important considerations to keep in mind regarding consent. First, relationship status (either current or previous) and past acts of intimacy are *not* indicators of consent. Second, to ensure that activity is consensual, partners should seek consent with each sexual activity as the level of sexual intimacy increases (for instance when kissing, moving from kissing to petting, and from petting to oral sex).

© Catherine Yeulet/iStockphoto

Incidence and Consequences

It's difficult to estimate how often date rape occurs because the majority of instances go unreported. However, this behavior is much more common than widely realized. Most people naively assume that the vast majority of rapes are committed by strangers who leap from bushes or dark alleys to surprise their victims. In reality, most victims are raped by someone they know (Frazier, 2009) (see Figure 10.8).

In the aftermath of date rape, victims typically experience a variety of emotional reactions, including fear, anger, anxiety, self-blame, and guilt (Kahn & Andreoli Mathie, 1999). In addition to the trauma of the rape, women also have to cope with the possibilities of pregnancy. In addition, male victims (both gay and straight) have to deal with fears of social evaluation related to gender roles (for example, "I am less of a man for not being able to defend myself"). For either gender, the possibility of a sexually transmitted disease is a concern. Further, if the rape survivor presses charges against the attacker, he or she may have to deal with difficult legal proceedings, negative publicity, and social stigma.

Contributing Factors

To understand the phenomenon of date rape, it's essential to know something about the factors that contribute to this behavior. It probably comes as no surprise to learn that alcohol contributes to about half of sexually aggressive incidents (Abbey, 2009). Alcohol impairs judgment and reduces inhibitions, making individuals more willing to assert their power. Drinking also undermines one's ability to interpret ambiguous social cues, making one more likely to overestimate a date's interest in sex. The more intoxicated perpetrators are, the more aggressive they tend to be. Alcohol also increases one's vulnerability to sexual coercion. Drinking can cloud people's assessments of their risk and their ability to mount firm resistance or find a way to escape the situation.

So-called "date rape drugs" are also a cause for concern. Rohypnol ("roofies") and gamma hydroxybutyrate (GHB) are two drugs used to subdue dates. Although these drugs are colorless, odorless, and tasteless, their effects are anything but benign, and they can even be fatal. Victims typically pass out and have no recall of what happened while they were under the influence of the drug. To make it easier to spike a drink,

FIGURE 10.8 | Rape victim–offender relationships

Based on a national survey of 3,187 college women, Mary Koss and her colleagues (1988) identified a sample of 468 women who indicated that they had been a victim of rape and who provided information on their relationship to the offender. Contrary to the prevailing stereotype, only a small minority (11%) had been raped by a stranger. As you can see, over half of rapes occur in the context of dating relationships.

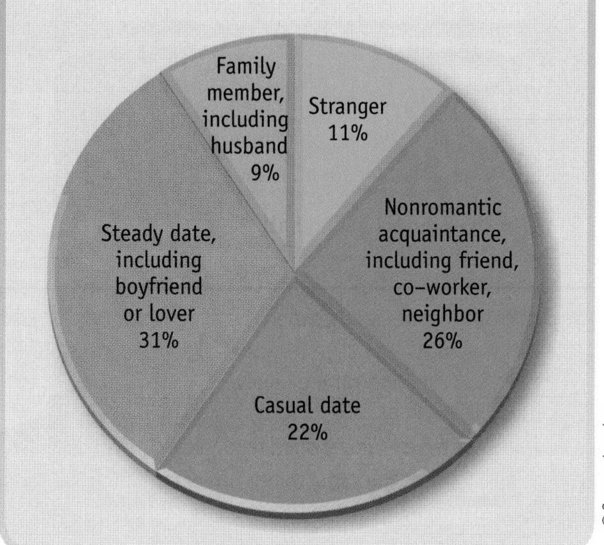

predators typically look for individuals who are already intoxicated.

Gender differences in sexual standards also contribute to date rape. Society still encourages a double standard for males and females. Men are encouraged to have sexual feelings, to act on them, and to "score," whereas women are socialized to be coy about their sexual desires. These social norms can encourage game playing, so dating partners may not always say what they mean or mean what they say. For instance, whereas the majority of women say "no" and mean it, some women may say "no" to sexual activity when they actually mean "maybe" or "yes." Studies surveying the extent of token resistance among college women report that approximately 38% of them have acted this way (Muehlenhard & McCoy, 1991; Shotland & Hunter, 1995). Unfortunately, this behavior can backfire. For men, it can cloud the issue of whether a woman has consented to sex.

Reducing the Incidence of Date Rape

In order to protect oneself, RAINN suggests that it is useful to understand the three stages of acquaintance rape. First, *intrusion* is when an offender violates the victim's personal space or level of comfort with unwelcome touches, stares, or sharing of information. *Desensitization*, the second stage, occurs when the victim gets used to the intrusive actions and sees them as less threatening. In this stage victims might still feel uncomfortable, but might convince themselves this feeling is unfounded. Finally, *isolation* occurs when the offender isolates the victims from others.

It is imperative to recognize date rape for what it is: an act of sexual aggression, and victims are never to blame for others' acts of aggression. There are steps one can take, however, to reduce one's likelihood of victimization. (1) Beware of excessive alcohol and drug use, which may undermine self-control and self-determination in sexual interactions. (2) Don't leave your drink unattended or accept drinks from people you don't know or trust. (3) When dating someone new, agree to go only to public places and always carry enough money for transportation back home. (4) Watch out for your friends and vice versa. (5) Finally, clearly and accurately communicate your feelings and expectations about sexual activity by engaging in appropriate self-disclosure.

PERSONAL EXPLORATION TOOLS

Curious about yourself? To learn more about how topics in this chapter relate to you, go online to CourseMate at www.cengagebrain.com where you can:

- Complete a **Self-Reflection** exercise that will help you think about your personal experiences in relation to topics in the chapter.
- Take a **Self-Assessment** scale that will show you how you score on a research instrument that measures personality traits or attitudes.
- Explore **Recommended Readings** that will provide brief overviews of useful self-help books.

STUDY TOOLS ▶ 10

Ready to study? In your book you can:

- **Test Yourself** with a multiple-choice quiz (below)
- Rip out the **Chapter Review card** (in the back of the book) to refresh yourself on the chapter's Key Ideas and Key Terms

Or you can go online to CourseMate at www.cengagebrain.com where you can:

- Take additional Practice Quizzes to prepare for your exam
- Review Key Terms with flash cards and a crossword puzzle
- View videos that expand on selected concepts

TEST YOURSELF

1. Which of the following is a recent social trend that is undermining the traditional model of marriage?

a. Decreased acceptance of singlehood
b. Less voluntary childlessness
c. Reduced acceptance of cohabitation
d. Reduced premium on permanence in marriage

2. Endogamy refers to

a. the tendency to marry within one's social group.
b. the tendency to marry someone with similar characteristics.
c. the final marriage in serial monogamy.
d. norms that promote marriage outside one's social unit.

3. Based on trends in the data, which of the following couples has the greatest likelihood of marital success?

a. Stephanie and David, whose parents are divorced
b. Jessica and Carlos, who are both perfectionists
c. Jenny and Ross, who had a long courtship
d. Carla and Turk, who married at a very young age

4. Although married women still perform the majority of all housework, only a minority of wives describe this division of labor as

a. fair. b. unfair.
c. satisfying. d. unsatisfying.

5. Which of the following characteristics in young children is related to maternal employment?

a. Insecure emotional attachment
b. Higher anxiety
c. Increased hyperactivity
d. Increased prosocial behavior

6. Truc and Hiroshi have plenty of financial resources. In their marriage, arguments about money

a. may still be quite common.
b. are highly unlikely to occur.
c. are a big problem only if the wife earns more than her husband.
d. are not likely to affect marital satisfaction.

7. The evidence suggests that the negative effects of divorce on former spouses' *psychological* well-being are

a. exaggerated for both sexes.
b. greater for men than women.
c. greater for women than men.
d. about the same for men and women.

8. Which of the following has been supported by research on intimate relationships among gay men and lesbians?

a. Gay couples rarely experience sexual prejudice.
b. Gays avoid becoming involved in long-term relationships.
c. Gays have impoverished family relations.
d. Gays want the same things out of intimate relationships that heterosexuals want.

9. Research on cohabitation indicates that

a. most cohabitants are just not interested in marriage.
b. most cohabitants would eventually like to marry.
c. cohabiting is declining.
d. cohabiting improves the chances that one's marriage will be successful.

10. Which of the following can a woman do to reduce the likelihood of being victimized by date rape?

a. Be coy about sexual desires and offer token resistance to sexual advances
b. Avoid communicating about sex altogether
c. Beware of excessive alcohol and drug use
d. Avoid acting aggressively if a partner continues unwanted advances

Answers: 1. d, pages 205–206; 2. a, page 207; 3. c, page 208; 4. b, page 210; 5. d, pages 211–212; 6. a, page 212; 7. d, page 215; 8. d, page 218; 9. b, pages 218–219; 10. c, page 223

WHY CHOOSE?

Every 4LTR Press solution comes complete with a visually engaging textbook in addition to an interactive eBook. Go to CourseMate for **ADJUST** to begin using the eBook. Access at **www.cengagebrain.com**

Complete the Speak Up survey in CourseMate at **www.cengagebrain.com**

Follow us at www.facebook.com/4ltrpress

© Bruno Ehrs/Corbis

LEARNING OBJECTIVES

11-1 Explain the nature of gender, gender stereotypes, and androcentrism.

11-2 Summarize the research on gender similarities and differences in cognitive abilities, personality and social behavior, and psychological disorders.

11-3 Describe how evolutionary processes, brain organization, and hormonal differences may contribute to gender differences in behavior.

11-4 Understand how parents, peers, schools, and the media influence gender-role socialization.

11-5 Describe gender-role expectations for males and females, and explain common problems associated with both.

11-6 Define gender-role identity and summarize the research on androgyny.

11-7 Evaluate the evidence for gender differences in communication style.

STUDY TOOLS ▸ After you have read the chapter, you can Test Yourself and learn about other Study Tools on page 248.

GENDER and BEHAVIOR

CHAPTER 11

© Photo_Concepts/iStockphoto

On January 14, 2005, the then-president of Harvard University Lawrence H. Summers spoke publically about Harvard's policies regarding diversity. Dr. Summers focused his remarks on the issue of women's underrepresentation in tenured positions in science and engineering at top universities. He offered three broad hypotheses about this gender disparity. The one that attracted the most media attention was what he called a "different availability of aptitude at the high end." While he acknowledged that there are differences in socialization and patterns of discrimination between men and women, he cited innate gender differences in mathematical and scientific ability as having greater "importance" in explaining the gender disparity (Harvard Crimson, 2005). Summers's remarks on this issue sparked a heated debate among academics, scientists, and the public. The war of words lingered for months and Summers eventually resigned as president of Harvard.

© nikkytok/Shutterstock.com

This incident demonstrates in a highly compelling way that gender research is relevant, important, and frequently divisive. Obviously, psychologists have a lot to offer in this area. In this chapter, we explore some intriguing and controversial questions: Are there genuine behavioral and cognitive differences between males and females? If so, what are their origins? Are traditional gender-role expectations healthy or unhealthy? What does the future hold for gender roles in our society? After addressing these questions, we explore gender and communication styles in the Application.

11-1 Gender Stereotypes

Let's begin by clarifying some terms. Some scholars prefer to use the term *gender* to refer to male-female differences that are learned and *sex* to designate biologically based differences between males and females. However, as respected authority Janet Shibley Hyde (2004) points out, making this sharp distinction between sex and gender fails to recognize that biology and culture interact. Following this reasoning, we'll use ***gender*** **to mean the state of being male or female.** (When we use the term *sex*, we're referring to sexual behavior.)

Obviously, males and females differ biologically—in their genitals and other aspects of anatomy, and in their physiological functioning. These readily apparent physical disparities between males and females lead people to expect other differences as well. Recall that *stereotypes* are widely held beliefs that people have certain characteristics simply because of their membership in a particular group. Thus, ***gender stereotypes*** **are widely shared beliefs about males' and females' abilities, personality traits, and social behavior.** The stereotyped attributes for males (active, ambitious, competitive, or independent, for instance) generally reflect the quality of ***instrumentality,*** **an orientation toward action and accomplishment.** In contrast, the stereotypes for females (such as considerate, sensitive, kind, or gentle) reflect the quality of ***expressiveness,*** **an orientation toward emotion and relationships.**

When it comes to stereotypes, there are some important points to keep in mind. First, despite the general agreement on a number of gender stereotypes, variability also occurs. Gender stereotypes represent the prototypic American male or female: white, middle-class, heterosexual, and Christian. But it is obvious that not everyone fits this set of characteristics. For example, the stereotypes for African American males and females are more similar on the dimensions of competence and expressiveness than those for white American males and females (Kane, 2000). Also, the stereotypes of white and Hispanic women are more positive than those for African American women (Niemann et al., 1994).

A second point about gender stereotypes is that since the 1980s, the boundaries between male and female stereotypes have become less rigid. Earlier, male and female stereotypes were seen as separate and distinct categories (for example, men are strong and women are weak). Now it seems that people perceive gender differences on a continuum as opposed to a dichotomy (Beall, Eagly, & Sternberg, 2004).

Since the 1980s, the boundaries between male and female stereotypes have become less rigid.

© stockcam/iStockphoto

A third consideration is that the traditional male stereotype is more complimentary than the conventional female stereotype, suggesting that men have virtually cornered the market on competence and rationality. This fact is related to ***androcentrism*****, or the belief that the male is the norm**. The implicit assumption, then, is that men are the "standard" from which women deviate.

11-2 Gender Similarities and Differences

Are men more aggressive than women? Do more women than men suffer from depression? Hundreds of studies have attempted to answer these and related questions about gender and behavior. Moreover, new evidence is pouring in constantly, and many researchers report conflicting findings. To add to the confusion, gender differences are not clear-cut; they are complex and often subtle. It is an oversimplification, for instance, to say that women are verbal and men are spatial.

Thus, it is an overwhelming task to keep up with the research in this area. Thankfully, a statistical technique called meta-analysis helps clarify this body of research. ***Meta-analysis*** **combines the statistical results of many studies of the same question, yielding an estimate of the size and consistency of a variable's effects.** This approach allows a researcher to assess the overall trends across all the previous studies of how gender is related to, say, math abilities or conformity. Meta-analysis has been a great boon to researchers, and quite a few meta-analyses on gender differences have now been conducted.

One such meta-analysis led Janet Shibley Hyde (2007b) to propose the *gender similarities hypothesis*. Based on the results of over forty-six meta-analyses, Hyde reports that that men and women are similar on most psychological variables and that most of the time when researchers report a difference, it is quite small. Critics of this hypothesis argue that Hyde omitted several important variables from her review and that methodological limitations led her to underestimate true gender differences. It will be interesting to see where this dispute leads in the future.

In addition, there is much debate on whether gender differences are largely attributable to environmental factors as opposed to biological factors, and there is evidence on both sides of the question. Before we examine the possible *causes* of gender differences, let's thread our way through the available research in three areas: cognitive abilities, personality traits and social behavior, and psychological disorders. Keep in mind

SIX CHIX

SIX CHIX © 2002 Margaret Shulock King Features Syndicate, Inc.

that our discussion focuses on modern Western societies; the story may be different in other cultures.

11-2a COGNITIVE ABILITIES

We should first point out that gender differences have *not* been found in *overall* intelligence (Hines, 2007). Of course, this fact shouldn't be surprising, because intelligence tests are intentionally designed to minimize differences between the scores of males and females. But what about gender differences in *specific* cognitive skills?

© Phaitoon Sutunyawatchai/Shutterstock.com

Verbal Abilities

Verbal abilities include a number of distinct skills, such as vocabulary, reading, writing, spelling, and grammar abilities. Girls and women generally have the edge in the verbal area, although the gender differences are small (Halpern, 2000). Among the findings worth noting are that girls usually start speaking a little earlier, have larger vocabularies and better reading scores in grade school, and are more verbally fluent (on tests of writing, for instance). Boys seem to fare better on verbal analogies. However, they are three to four times more likely to be stutterers (Skinner & Shelton, 1985) and five to ten times more likely than girls to be dyslexic (Vandenberg, 1987). It is important to remember that while gender differences in verbal abilities generally favor females, these differences are small. The overlap between males and females in verbal abilities is much greater than the gap between them.

Mathematical Abilities

Researchers have also looked at gender differences in *mathematical abilities*, including performing computations and solving word problems. Although it is conventional wisdom that males have greater mathematical abilities than females, a recent meta-analysis representing the data of over a million participants indicates otherwise (Lindberg et al., 2010). In support of the gender similarity hypothesis, these researchers found no reliable gender differences in mathematical performance.

In mathematical *problem solving*, boys start to slightly outperform girls when they reach high school. This difference is attributable in part to the fact that boys take more high school math courses (Halpern, 2000). Males also outperform females at the high end of the mathematical ability distribution (Dweck, 2007). For instance, when gifted seventh- and eighth-graders take the math subtest of the SAT (to identify mathematically precocious youth), boys outnumber girls 17 to 1 in the group scoring over 700 (Benbow, 1988).

Spatial Abilities

In the cognitive area, the most compelling evidence for gender differences is in *spatial abilities*, which include perceiving and mentally manipulating shapes and figures. Males typically outperform females in most spatial abilities, and gender differences favoring males are consistently found in the ability to perform mental rotations of a figure in three dimensions—a skill important in occupations such as engineering, chemistry, and the building trades (see Figure 11.1). This gender gap in the ability to handle mental rotations is relatively large and has been found repeatedly (Halpern, 2004). Further, by using creative methods, researchers have demonstrated this difference in infants as young as 5 months old (Moore & Johnson, 2008). However, experience and training can improve mental rotation in both girls and boys (Newcombe, 2007). In fact, playing action video games has been shown to improve mental rotation skills for both genders (Spence, Feng, & Marshman, 2009).

FIGURE 11.1 Mental rotation test

Spatial reasoning tasks can be divided into a variety of subtypes. Studies indicate that males perform slightly better than females on most, but not all, spatial tasks. The tasks on which males are superior often involve mentally rotating objects, such as in the problem shown here, for which the answer is no.

Can the set of blocks on the left be rotated to match the set at the right?

© Cengage Learning

Source: From Kalat, J. W. (2013). *Biological psychology* (11 ed.). Belmont, CA: Wadsworth. Reproduced by permission. www.cengage.com/permissions

11-2b PERSONALITY TRAITS AND SOCIAL BEHAVIOR

Turning to personality and social behavior, let's examine those factors for which gender differences are reasonably well documented.

Self-Esteem

Females typically score lower than males on tests of self-esteem, but the difference in scores is generally small, and Hyde (2005) argues that this difference has been exaggerated in the popular press. For example, a meta-analysis of several hundred studies that included respondents from 7 to 60 years of age found only a small difference in self-esteem that favored males (Kling et al., 1999). Other research consistently reports self-esteem differences between white men and women, but findings are mixed for other ethnic groups (Twenge & Crocker, 2002).

Obviously, the findings on self-esteem are complex. To add to the complexity, a recent meta-analysis of 115 studies examined gender differences in specific self-esteem domains (Gentile et al., 2009). The researchers found gender differences favoring males with regard to self-esteem domains of physical appearance, athleticism, and self-satisfaction, but they found differences in behavioral conduct and morality/ethics favoring females. Additionally, no gender differences were found for domains such as academics and social acceptance.

> Gender differences in aggression vary depending on the form aggression takes.

© desuza.communications/iStockphoto

Aggression

***Aggression* involves behavior that is intended to hurt someone, either physically or verbally.** Gender differences in aggression vary depending on the form aggression takes. A summary of cross-cultural meta-analyses reported that males consistently engage in more *physical aggression* than females (Archer, 2005). This difference is evident even in young children (Baillargeon et al., 2007). In the area of *verbal aggression* (insults, threats of harm), the findings are inconsistent. When it comes to *relational aggression,* such as giving someone the "silent treatment" to get one's way, talking behind another's back, or trying to get others to dislike someone, females are rated higher (Archer, 2005). *Indirect aggression* overlaps to some degree with relational aggression; it involves covert behaviors in which the target is not directly confronted—spreading rumors, for instance.

© Beth Van Trees/Shutterstock.com

In a study of 8-, 11-, and 15-year-olds from Finland, Israel, Italy, and Poland, researchers looked at gender differences in three types of aggression: physical, verbal, and indirect (Oesterman et al., 1998). Across nations, boys were equally likely to use physical and verbal aggression and less likely to use indirect aggression. Girls most often used indirect aggression, followed by verbal aggression, then physical aggression. Even in controlled laboratory settings where male and female participants are exposed to the same aggression-evoking stimulus, women are more likely than men to aggress indirectly (Gianciola et al., 2009).

However, when you consider extreme forms of aggression, there is no getting around the fact that men commit a grossly disproportionate share of violent crimes. The U.S. Department of Justice (2007) reports that only 7% of all federal inmates are women and, based on self-reports of victims, women make up 14% of violent offenders. Males are nine times more likely to commit murder than females (Cooper & Smith, 2011).

Emotional Expression

Conventional wisdom holds that women are more "emotional" than men. Does research support this belief? If being "emotional," means outwardly displaying one's emotions, the answer is yes. A number of studies have found that women express more emotion than men. Women are also better than men at recognizing emotions in others based on facial expressions or other nonverbal cues (Hampson, van Anders, & Mullin, 2006).

Do women actually *experience* more emotion? To answer this question, Ann Kring and Albert Gordon (1998) had college students view films selected to evoke sadness, happiness, and fear. The researchers videotaped the participants' facial expressions and asked them to describe their emotional experiences. As expected, the researchers found gender differences in the facial expression of emotion. However, they failed to find any gender differences in *experienced* emotions. Thus, gender differences in emotional functioning may be limited to the outward expression of feelings and could stem from the different rules parents teach their sons and daughters about displaying emotions (DeAngelis, 2001).

© leolintang/Shutterstock.com

Communication

Popular stereotypes suggest that females are much more talkative than males. In fact, the opposite seems to be true: Men talk more than women (Cameron, 2007). Men also tend to interrupt women more than women interrupt men, although this difference is small (Eckert & McConnell-Ginet, 2003). Yet when women have more power in work or personal relationships, women interrupt more (Aries, 1998). Thus, this supposed gender difference is probably better seen as a status difference. For more on gender and communication, see this chapter's Application.

11-2c PSYCHOLOGICAL DISORDERS

In terms of the *overall* incidence of mental disorders, only minimal gender differences have been found. When researchers assess the prevalence of *specific* disorders, however, they do find some rather consistent gender differences. Antisocial behavior, alcoholism, and other drug-related disorders are far more prevalent among men than among women. On the other hand, women are about twice as likely as men to suffer from depression and anxiety disorders (phobias, for example). Even when comparing opposite-sex fraternal twins, females have a higher rate of mood disorders than males (Kendler, Myers, & Prescott, 2005). Females also show higher rates of eating disorders. In addition, women *attempt* suicide more often than men, but men *complete* suicides (actually kill themselves) more frequently than women (Canetto, 2008). Throughout the lifespan, females are more likely to engage in deliberate self-harm than males (Hawton & Harriss, 2008).

11-2d PUTTING GENDER DIFFERENCES IN PERSPECTIVE

It pays to be cautious when interpreting gender differences. Although research has uncovered some genuine differences in behavior, remember that these are *group* differences. That is, they tell us nothing about individuals. Essentially, we are comparing the "average man" with the "average woman." Furthermore, as Hyde (2007b) argues, the differences between these groups are usually relatively small. Figure 11.2 shows how scores on a trait might be distributed for men and women. Although the group averages are detectably different, you can see that there is great variability within each group (gender) and huge overlap between the two group distributions. *Ultimately, the similarities between women and men greatly outweigh the differences.* Thus, a gender difference that shows up on the average does

FIGURE 11.2 The nature of group differences

Gender differences are group differences that tell us little about individuals because of the great overlap between the groups. For a given trait, one gender may score higher on the average, but there is far more variation within each gender than between the genders.

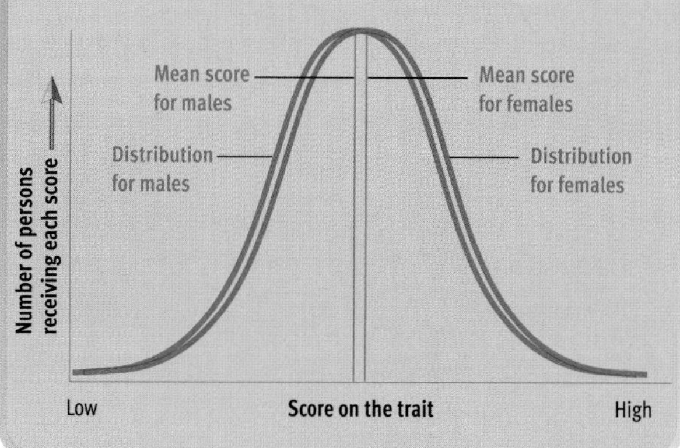

not by itself tell us anything about you or any other unique individual.

A second essential point is that gender accounts for only a minute proportion of the differences between individuals. Using complicated statistical procedures, it is possible to gauge the influence of gender (or other factors) on behavior. These tests often show that factors other than gender (for example, the social context in which behavior occurs) are far more important determinants of differences between individuals (Yoder & Kahn, 2003).

Another point to keep in mind is that when gender differences are found, they do not mean that one gender is better than the other. As Diane Halpern (1997) humorously notes, "It is about as meaningful to ask 'Which is the smarter sex?' . . . as it is to ask 'Which has the better genitals?'" (p. 1092). The problem is not with gender differences, but with how these differences are evaluated by the larger society.

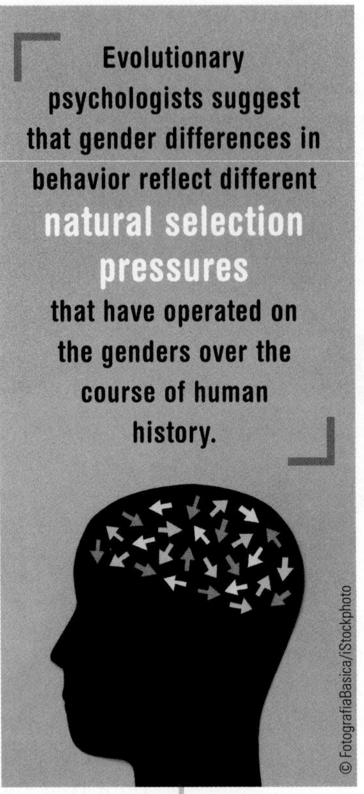
Evolutionary psychologists suggest that gender differences in behavior reflect different natural selection pressures that have operated on the genders over the course of human history.

© FotografiaBasica/iStockphoto

11-3 Biological Origins of Gender Differences

Are the gender differences that *do* exist biologically built in, or are they acquired through socialization? This is the age-old question of nature versus nurture. The "nature" theorists concentrate on how biological disparities between the genders contribute to differences in behavior. "Nurture" theorists, on the other hand, emphasize the role of learning and environmental influences. Although we will discuss biological and environmental influences separately, keep in mind that most contemporary researchers and theorists in this area recognize that biological and environmental factors interact. Let's first look at three biologically based lines of inquiry on this topic: evolutionary explanations, brain organization, and hormonal influences.

11-3a EVOLUTIONARY EXPLANATIONS

According to evolutionary theory, natural selection favors behaviors that maximize the chances of an organism passing on its genes to the next generation (reproductive success). Working from this assumption, evolutionary psychologists suggest that gender differences in behavior reflect different natural selection pressures that have operated on the genders over the course of human history.

To support their assertion that gender differences are rooted in biology, evolutionary psychologists look for gender differences that are consistent across cultures. Is there consistency across cultures for the better documented gender differences? Despite some fascinating exceptions, similar gender differences in cognitive abilities and aggression *are* found across many cultures (Halpern, 2000). According to evolutionary psychologists, these consistent differences have emerged because males and females have been confronted with different adaptive demands. For example, because females are more selective about mating than males are, males have to engage in more competition for sexual partners than females do. Therefore greater aggressiveness is thought to be adaptive for males in this competition for sexual access because it should foster social dominance over other males (Kenrick & Trost, 1993). However, it is important to remember that even in cross-cultural work, there are more differences *within* each gender than *between* the genders, especially when it comes to cognitive abilities.

Evolutionary analyses of gender differences are interesting, but controversial. While it is eminently plausible that evolutionary forces could have led to some divergence between males and females in typical behavior, evolutionary hypotheses are highly speculative and difficult to test empirically. In addition, evolutionary theory can be used to claim that the status quo in society is the inevitable outcome of evolutionary forces. Thus, if males have dominant status over females, natural selection must have favored this arrangement. The crux of the problem is that evolutionary analyses can be used to explain almost anything. For instance, if the situation regarding mental rotation were reversed—if females scored higher than males—evolutionary theorists might attribute females' superiority to the adaptive demands of gathering food, weaving baskets, and making clothes—and it would be difficult to prove otherwise.

11-3b BRAIN ORGANIZATION

Some theorists propose that male and female brains are organized differently, which might account for gender differences in some gender-specific abilities. As you may know, the human brain is divided into two halves. **The *cerebral hemispheres* are the right and left halves of the cerebrum, which is the convoluted outer layer of the brain.** The cerebrum, the largest and most complicated part of the human brain, is responsible for most complex mental activities. Some evidence suggests that the right and left cerebral hemispheres are specialized to handle different cognitive tasks. For example, it appears that the *left hemisphere* is more actively involved in *verbal and mathematical processing*, while the *right hemisphere* is specialized to handle *visual-spatial and other nonverbal processing.*

After these findings on hemispheric specialization surfaced, some researchers began looking for disparities between male and female brain organization as a way to explain the then-observed gender differences in verbal and spatial skills. Some thought-provoking findings have been reported. For instance, males exhibit more cerebral specialization than females (Hines, 1990). In other words, males tend to depend more heavily than females on the left hemisphere in verbal processing and on the right hemisphere in spatial processing. Gender differences have also been found in the size of the ***corpus callosum*, the band of fibers connecting the two hemispheres of the brain.** More specifically, some studies suggest that females tend to have a larger corpus callosum. This greater size might allow for better interhemispheric transfer of information, which in turn might underlie the more bilateral organization of female brains (Lippa, 2005). Thus, some theorists have argued that these differences in brain organization are responsible for gender differences in verbal and spatial ability (Clements et al. 2006).

Although this idea is intriguing, there are some important limitations in this line of reasoning. First, studies have not consistently found that males have more specialized brain organization than females (Kaiser et al., 2009), and the finding of a larger corpus callosum in females does not always show up (Fine, 2010). Second, because a significant amount of brain development occurs over the first five to ten years after birth, during which time males and females are socialized differently, it is possible that different life experiences may accumulate to produce slight differences in brain organization. In other words, the biological factors that supposedly cause gender differences in cognitive functioning may actually reflect the influence of environmental factors. Finally, it's important to remember that male and female brains are much more similar than they are different.

Studies have shown that the brain's cerebral hemispheres, shown here, are somewhat specialized in the kinds of cognitive tasks they handle and that such specialization is more pronounced in males than in females. Whether this difference bears any relation to gender differences in behavior is yet to be determined.

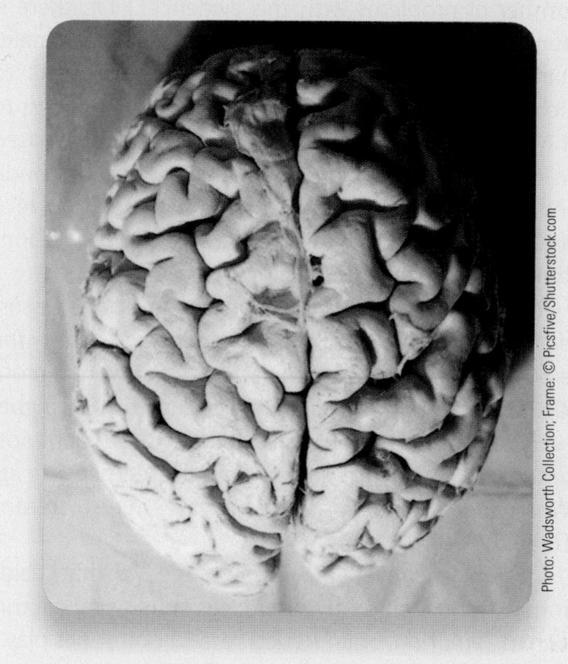

Photo: Wadsworth Collection; Frame: © Picsfive/Shutterstock.com

11-3c HORMONAL INFLUENCES

***Hormones* are chemical substances released into the bloodstream by the endocrine glands.** Although biological gender is determined at conception, both male and female embryos are essentially the same until about 8 to 12 weeks after conception. Around this time, male and female gonads (sex glands) begin to produce different hormonal secretions. The high level of *androgens* (male sex hormones such as testosterone) in males and the low level of androgens in females lead to the differentiation of male and female genital organs.

The influence of prenatal hormones on genitalia is clear; however, their influence on behavior is harder to establish and becomes apparent only when something interferes with normal prenatal hormonal secretions. Scientists have studied children born to mothers given an androgen-like drug to prevent miscarriage. Two trends have been noted in this research (Collaer & Hines, 1995). First, girls exposed prenatally to abnormally high levels of androgens exhibit more male-typical behavior than other girls do. Second, boys exposed prenatally to abnormally low levels of androgens exhibit more female-typical behavior than other boys.

These findings suggest that prenatal hormones shape gender differences in humans. But there are a number of problems with this evidence. First, there is much more and much stronger evidence for females than for males. Second, behavior is always subject to social factors after birth. Third, it's always dangerous to draw conclusions about the general population based on small samples of people who have abnormal conditions. Finally, most of the research is necessarily correlational, and it is always risky to draw causal conclusions from correlational data.

In adolescence and adulthood, the hormone testosterone plays an important role in *sexual desire and sexual activity* for both men and women (Bancroft, 2002a). Testosterone has also been linked with higher levels of *aggression* (impulsive and antisocial behavior) in humans, but the picture is complicated because aggressive behavior can produce increases in testosterone (Dabbs, 2000).

In sum, the overall evidence suggests that, aside from obvious physical differences, biological factors such as evolution, brain structure, and hormones play a relatively minor role in gender differences. In contrast, efforts to link gender differences to disparities in the way males and females are socialized have proven more fruitful.

11-4 Environmental Origins of Gender Differences

***Socialization* is the acquisition of the norms and roles expected of people in a particular society.** This process includes all the efforts made by a society to ensure that its members learn to behave in a manner that's considered appropriate. Teaching children about gender roles is an important aspect of the socialization process. ***Gender roles* are cultural expectations about what is appropriate behavior for each gender.** For example, in our culture women have been expected to rear children, cook meals, and clean house. On the other hand, men have been expected to be the family breadwinner, do yardwork, and tinker with cars.

Are gender roles in other cultures similar to those seen in our society? Generally, yes—but not necessarily. Despite a fair amount of cross-cultural consistency in gender roles, some dramatic variability occurs as well. For instance, anthropologist Margaret Mead (1950) conducted a now-classic study of three tribes in New Guinea. In one tribe, *both* genders followed our masculine role expectations (the Mundugumor); in another, *both* genders approximated our feminine role (the Arapesh). In a third tribe, the male and female roles were roughly the *reverse* of our own (the Tchambuli). Such remarkable discrepancies between cultures existing within 100 miles of one another demonstrate that gender roles are not a matter of biological destiny. Instead, like other roles, gender roles are acquired through socialization.

Four major sources of gender-role messages are parents, peers, schools, and the media. Keep in mind that gender-role socialization varies depending on one's culture. For example, black families typically make fewer distinctions between girls and boys compared to white families (Hill, 2002); as a result, gender roles are more flexible for black women (Littlefield, 2003). By contrast, gender roles are relatively rigidly defined in Asian and Hispanic families (Chia et al., 1994; Comas-Diaz, 1987). Also, gender roles are changing, so the generalizations that follow may say more about how *you* were socialized than about how your children will be.

11-4a THE INFLUENCE OF PARENTS

Although a meta-analysis of 172 studies of parental socialization practices suggests that parents don't treat girls and boys as differently as one might expect (Lytton & Romney, 1991), there are some important disparities. For one thing, there is a strong tendency for both mothers and fathers to emphasize and encourage *play activities* that are "gender appropriate." For example, studies show that parents encour-

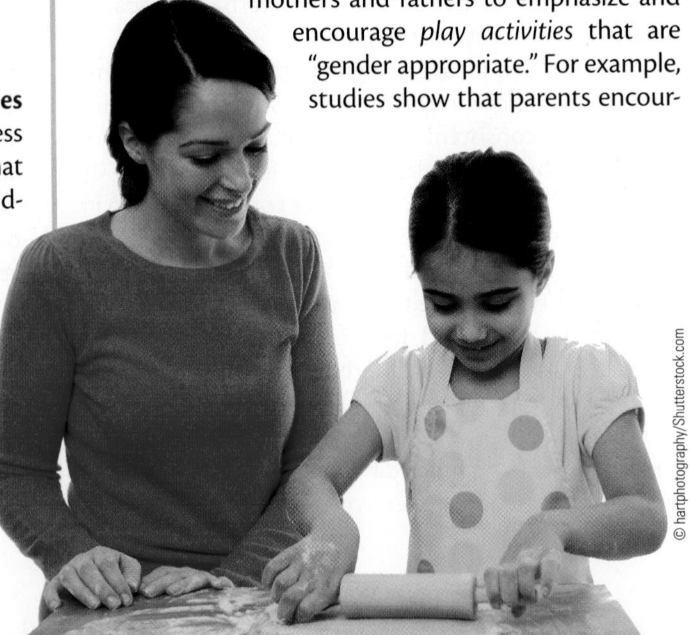
© hartphotography/Shutterstock.com

age boys and girls to play with different types of toys. Gender differences are found in toy preferences, and children as young as preschoolers have a clear definition of girl toys and boy toys (Freeman, 2007). Generally, boys have less leeway to play with "feminine" toys than girls do with "masculine" toys.

© Bubbles Photolibrary/Alamy

In addition, many of the picture books parents buy for their children depict characters engaging in gender-stereotypic activities. An analysis of 200 bestselling and award-winning children's books found nearly twice as many male as female main characters; also, the male characters were more likely to be in the illustrations, and the female characters were more nurturing and less likely to have an occupation (Hamilton et al., 2006). Even books that parents and teachers rate as "nonsexist" portray female characters with stereotypic personalities, chores, and leisure activities (Diekman & Murnen, 2004). Interestingly, this gender bias holds for representations of parents in these books as well. In a content analysis of 200 prominent children's picture books, Anderson and Hamilton (2005) found that fathers were underrepresented and, when they did appear, were withdrawn and ineffectual.

11-4b THE INFLUENCE OF PEERS

Peers form an important network for learning about gender-appropriate and gender-inappropriate behavior. Between the ages of 4 and 6, children tend to separate into same-gender groups, and these preferences appear to be child- rather than adult-driven (Fabes, Hanish, & Martin, 2003). From 6 to about age 12, boys and girls spend much more time with same-gender than other-gender peers. Moreover, according to Eleanor Maccoby (2002), over time boys' and girls' groups develop different "subcultures" (shared understandings and interests) that strongly shape youngsters' gender-role socialization.

Because both boys and girls are critical of peers who violate traditional gender norms, they perpetuate stereotypical behavior. Among children ages 3–11, boys are devalued more than girls for dressing like the other gender, whereas girls are evaluated more negatively than boys for playing like the other gender—for instance, loudly and roughly versus quietly and gently (Blakemore, 2003). Further, "gender atypical boys" more often report being a victim of bullying, more loneliness, and greater distress than their "typical" peers (Young & Sweeting, 2004). Associations between negative adjustment and gender atypical behavior, however, appear to be reduced with positive parenting styles (Alanko et al., 2008).

> Because both boys and girls are critical of peers who violate traditional gender norms, they perpetuate stereotypical behavior.

© stockcam/iStockphoto

11-4c THE INFLUENCE OF SCHOOLS

The school environment figures importantly in socializing gender roles. Like picture books, children's grade-school *textbooks* have often ignored or stereotyped girls and women (AAUW Educational Foundation, 1992). Although the depiction of stereotypical gender roles has declined considerably since the 1970s, researchers still find significant differences in how males and females are portrayed, even in supposedly nonsexist books (Diekman & Murnen, 2004). Many high school and college textbooks also contain gender bias. The most common problems are using generic masculine language ("policeman" versus "police officer" and so forth) and portraying males and females in stereotypic roles. In addition, subtle word choices can reinforce stereotypes, such as passivity in females (for example, women were *given* the right to vote) (Meece & Scantlebury, 2006).

Gender bias in schools also shows up in *teachers' treatment of boys and girls.* Preschool and grade-school teachers often reward gender-appropriate behavior in their pupils. Teachers also tend to pay greater attention to boys—helping them, praising them, and scolding them more than girls (Sadker & Sadker, 1994). By contrast, girls tend to be less visible in the classroom and to receive less encouragement for academic achievement from teachers. These findings have been replicated in other cultures as well (Best & Thomas, 2004). Additionally, many teachers and counselors encourage male students to pursue high-status careers in medicine or engineering while guiding female students toward less prestigious careers (Read, 1991). Overall, these teacher-student interactions reinforce the gender stereotype of male competence and dominance.

11-4d THE INFLUENCE OF THE MEDIA

American youngsters spend a lot of time watching TV. A 2006 Nielsen Media Research report found that TV viewing is at an all-time high, with the average household watching 8 hours, 14 minutes of TV per day! Approximately 35% of children are raised in homes where the TV is on "always" or "most of the time" (Vandewater et al., 2005).

An analysis of male and female characters on prime-time *television programs* showed that the number and variety of roles of female TV characters have increased over the past 30 years but that these shifts lag behind the actual changes in women's lives (Glascock, 2001). Compared to males, females appear less often, are less likely to be employed (especially in prestigious positions), are more likely to be younger, and are more likely to appear in secondary and comedy roles. As compared to female characters, males are still more likely to demonstrate competence-related behaviors such as reaching a goal, showing ingenuity, and answering questions (Aubrey & Harrison, 2004). In traditional children's adventure *cartoons* (as opposed to educational cartoons), male characters appear more often and engage in more physical aggression, whereas female characters are much more likely to show fear, act romantic, be polite, and act supportive (Leaper et al., 2002). These gender stereotypes are even more exaggerated on *television commercials* where women are frequently shown worrying about trivial matters such as laundry and cleaning products, whereas men appear as bold outdoorsmen or energetic sports fans (Lippa, 2005).

Photo: © Paco Gómez García/Age fotostock; Frame: © Thomas Bethge/Shutterstock.com

TV is not the only medium that perpetuates gender stereotypes; gender-role socialization is a multimedia event. Most *video games* push a hypermasculine stereotype featuring search-and-destroy missions, fighter pilot battles, and male sports (Lippa, 2005). Of the few video games directed at girls, the great majority are highly stereotypic (shopping and Barbie games). Similarly, in a content analysis of *educational software* for young children, most software programs had more male than female characters, portrayed males in more stereotypical ways, and focused more on gender-stereotypic appearance for females (Sheldon, 2004). Even daily *newspaper comics* follow these gender-stereotypic patterns (Glascock & Preston-Schreck, 2004).

Do the media actually influence children's views about gender? A meta-analysis reported a link between children's exposure to gender stereotyping in the media and the acquisition of gender-stereotyped beliefs (Oppliger, 2007). Admittedly, this research is correlational, so it is likely that other factors—such as parental values—come into play as well. Nonetheless, Greenwood and Lippman (2010) argue that our perceptions of gender differences might be an "artifact of the gender-stereotyped landscape of the mass media" (p. 662).

11-5 Gender-Role Expectations

Traditional gender roles are based on several unspoken assumptions: that all members of the same gender have basically the same traits, that the traits of one gender are very different from the traits of the other gender, and that masculine traits are more highly valued. In recent decades, many social critics and theorists in psychology and other fields have scrutinized gender roles, identifying the essential features and the ramifications of traditional roles. In this section, we review the research and theory in this area and note changes in gender roles over the past 30 to 40 years. We begin with the male role.

11-5a ROLE EXPECTATIONS FOR MALES

A number of psychologists have sought to pinpoint the essence of the traditional male role (Pleck, 1995). Many consider *anti-femininity* to be the central theme that runs through the male gender role. That is, "real men" shouldn't act in any way that might be perceived as feminine. For example, men should not publicly display vulnerable emotions, should avoid feminine occupations, and should not show obvious interest in relationships—especially homosexual ones. Five key attributes constitute the traditional male role (Brannon, 1976; Jansz, 2000):

1. *Achievement.* To prove their masculinity, men need to beat out other men at work and at sports. Having a high-status job, driving an expensive car, and making lots of money are aspects of this element.

2. *Aggression.* Men should be tough and fight for what they believe is right. They should aggressively defend themselves and those they love against threats.

3. *Autonomy.* Men should be self-reliant and not admit to being dependent on others.

4. *Sexuality.* Real men are heterosexual and are highly motivated to pursue sexual activities and conquests.

5. *Stoicism.* Men should not share their pain or express their "soft" feelings. They should be cool and calm under pressure.

Role Expectations for Males

1. Achievement
2. Aggression
3. Autonomy
4. Sexuality
5. Stoicism

© vgstudio/Shutterstock.com

According to Joseph Pleck (1995), who has written extensively on this issue, in the *traditional male role,* masculinity is validated by individual physical strength, aggressiveness, and emotional inexpressiveness. In the *modern male role,* however, masculinity is validated by economic achievement, organizational power, emotional control (even over anger), and emotional sensitivity and self-expression, but only with women. Thus, in modern societies, the traditional male role coexists with some new expectations. This flux in expectations means that males are experiencing role inconsistencies and pressures to behave in ways that conflict with traditional masculinity. Some psychologists believe that these pressures have shaken traditional masculine norms sufficiently enough that many men are experiencing a masculinity crisis and diminished pride in being a man (Levant, 2003). Brooks (2010) argues that distress over ever-changing gender roles fuels three major problems—violence, substance abuse, and sexual misconduct—as men channel their distress into these destructive behaviors.

11-5b PROBLEMS WITH THE MALE ROLE

It is often assumed that only females suffer from the constricting binds of traditional gender roles. Not so. Increasingly, the costs of the male role are a cause for concern. As we examine the relevant research, keep in mind that male gender roles "are not to be regarded as 'given,' neither psychological nor biologically, but rather as socially constructed" (Levant & Richmond, 2007, p. 141). Therefore, many researchers are calling for a closer examination of the influence of culture on gender-role stress.

Pressure to Succeed

Most men are socialized to be highly competitive and are taught that a man's masculinity is measured by the size of his paycheck and job status. As Christopher Kilmartin (2000) notes, "There is always another man who has more money, higher status, a more attractive partner, or a bigger house. The traditional man . . . must constantly work harder and faster " (p. 13).

The majority of men who have internalized the success ethic are unable to fully realize their dreams. How does this "failure" affect men? Although many are able to adjust to it, many are not. The men in this latter group are likely to suffer from shame and low self-esteem (Kilmartin, 2000). Men's emphasis on success also makes it more likely that they will spend long hours on the job. This pattern in turn decreases the amount of time families can spend together and increases the amount of time partners spend on housework and child care. This pattern might be changing however; a significantly smaller

Most men are socialized to be highly competitive and are taught that a man's masculinity is measured by the size of his paycheck and his job status. Experiences such as being laid off can lead to shame and low self-esteem.

© eva serrabassa/ iStockphoto

proportion of men between the ages of 18 and 37 are work focused (they want to spend more time with their families) compared to men age 38 and older (Families and Work Institute, 2004).

The Emotional Realm

Most young boys are trained to believe that men should be strong, tough, cool, and detached. Thus, they learn early to hide vulnerable emotions such as love, joy, and sadness because they believe that such feelings are feminine and imply weakness. Over time, some men become strangers to their own emotional lives. With the exception of anger, men with traditional views of masculinity are more likely to suppress outward emotions and to fear emotion, supposedly because having feelings may lead to a loss of composure (Jakupcak et al., 2003). Keep in mind, as with many gender gaps, differences in emotionality tend to be small, inconsistent, and dependent on the situation.

Males' difficulty with "tender" emotions has serious consequences. First, suppressed emotions can contribute to stress-related disorders. And worse, men are less likely than women to seek social support or help from health professionals (Lane & Addis, 2005). Second, men's emotional inexpressiveness can cause problems in their relationships with partners and children. For example, men who endorse traditional masculine norms report lower relationship satisfaction, as do their female partners (Burn & Ward, 2005). Further, children whose fathers are warm, loving, and accepting toward them have higher self-esteem and lower rates of aggression and behavior problems (Rohner & Veneziano, 2001). On a positive note, fathers are increasingly involving themselves with their children. And 30% of fathers report that they take at least as much responsibility for their children as their working wives do (Bond et al., 2003).

Sexual Problems

Men often experience sexual problems that derive partly from their gender-role socialization, which gives them a "macho" sexual image to live up to. Most men fear having a sexual encounter in which they are unable to achieve an erection. Unfortunately, these very fears often *cause* the dysfunction that men dread.

Another problem is that many men learn to confuse feelings of intimacy and sex. In other words, sex may be the only way some men can allow themselves to feel intimately connected to another. The confusion of intimacy and sex may underlie the tendency for men (compared to women) to perceive eye contact, a compliment, an innocent smile, a friendly remark, or a brush against the arm as a sexual invitation (Kowalski, 1993). Additionally, the sexualization of intimate feelings causes inappropriate anxiety when men feel affection for another man, thus promoting *homophobia* or sexual prejudice, *the intense intolerance of homosexuality.* Indeed, endorsement of traditional gender roles and hypermasculinity are both related to negative attitudes toward homosexuality (Parrott et al., 2008).

PEARLS BEFORE SWINE

11-5c ROLE EXPECTATIONS FOR FEMALES

In the past 40 years, the role expectations for American women have undergone dramatic changes, especially with regard to work. Prior to the 1970s, a woman was expected to be a housewife and a stay-at-home mother. Today, there are three major expectations for women:

1. *The marriage mandate.* Remaining single is a trend that has been on the increase for several decades; however, there is still a stigma attached to singlehood in a society where marriage is the norm (Gordon, 2003). Most women are socialized to feel incomplete until they find a mate.

2. *The motherhood mandate.* A major imperative of the female role is to have children. This expectation has been termed the "motherhood mandate" (Rice & Else-Quest, 2006). The prevailing ideology of today's motherhood mandate is that women should desire to have children, mothering should be wholly child-centered, and mothers should be self-sacrificing rather than persons who have their own needs and interests (Vandello et al., 2008).

3. *Work outside the home.* Most of today's young women, especially those who are college educated, expect to work outside the home, and they also want a satisfying family life. As you can see in Figure 11.3, the percentage of women in the labor force has risen considerably over the last 40 years.

11-5d PROBLEMS WITH THE FEMALE ROLE

Writers in the feminist movement generated some compelling analyses of the problems associated with the pre-1970s traditional role of wife and mother. Many criticized the assumption that women, unlike men, did not need an independent identity. Increasingly over the past 40 years, girls and women have been encouraged to develop and use their talents, and work opportunities for women have greatly expanded. Still, there are problems with female role expectations.

FIGURE 11.3 Increases in women's workforce participation

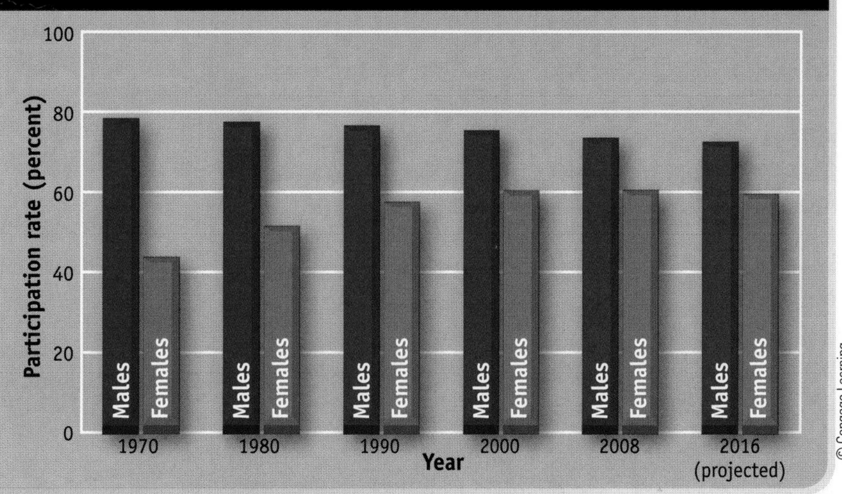

The percentage of women who work outside the home has increased steadily over the past century, especially since 1970, although it appears to be stabilizing at around 60%. (Data from the *Statistical Abstract of the United States*, 2010, Table 575)

Diminished Career Aspirations

Despite recent efforts to increase women's opportunities for achievement, young women continue to have lower career aspirations than young men with comparable backgrounds and abilities (Hakim, 2006). Also, they are more likely to underestimate their achievement than boys (who overestimate theirs), especially when estimating performance on "masculine" tasks such as science and math (Eccles, 2007). This is a problem because science and math are the foundations for many high-paying, high-status careers, and the lack of math background (as opposed to ability) often contributes to the inferior performance of some women (Dweck, 2007).

© Morgan Lane Photography/Shutterstock.com

The discrepancy between women's abilities and their level of achievement has been termed the *ability-achievement gap* (Hyde, 1996). The roots of this gap seem to lie in the conflict between achievement and femininity that is built into the traditional female role. The marriage and motherhood mandates fuel women's focus on *heterosexual success*—learning how to attract and interest males as prospective mates. The resulting emphasis on dating and marriage can lead some women away from a challenging career—they worry that they will be seen as unfeminine if they boldly strive for success. Of course, this is not a concern for all women. And, because younger men are more supportive of their wives' working than older men are, this conflict should ease for younger women.

Juggling Multiple Roles

Another problem with the female role is that societal institutions have not kept pace with the reality of women's lives, especially if women choose motherhood. In almost half of married couples, both the husband and wife work outside the home. Yet some workplaces (and many husbands and fathers) still operate as if all women were stay-at-home moms and as if there were no single-parent families. This gap between policies based on outdated assumptions and reality means that women who "want it all" experience burdens and conflicts that most men do not. That's because most men typically have *major* day-to-day responsibilities in only *one* role: worker. But most women have major day-to-day responsibilities in *three* roles: spouse, parent, and worker.

One way today's college-educated women deal with these conflicts is to postpone marriage and motherhood (and to have small families) in order to pursue more education or to launch their careers (Hoffnung, 2004). Additionally, they are more likely than men to disrupt their careers to focus on childrearing (Singer, Cassin, & Dobson, 2005). Given the three-role reality of their lives, they trade off the worker role and income for a slower pace and less stress to rear young children. Their strategy: "You can have it all, just not all at the same time" (Wallis, 2004, p. 53). Of course multiple roles, in themselves, are not inherently problematic. In fact, there is some evidence that multiple roles can be beneficial for mental health. Rather, the problem stems from the tensions among these roles and the unequal sharing of role responsibilities.

Ambivalence About Sexuality

Like men, women may have sexual problems that stem, in part, from their gender-role socialization. For many women, the problem is difficulty in enjoying sex. Why? For one thing, many girls are still taught to suppress or deny their sexual feelings. For another, they are told that a woman's role in sex is a passive one. In addition, girls are encouraged to focus on romance rather than on gaining sexual experience. As a result, many women feel uncomfortable (guilty, ashamed) with their sexual urges. Indeed, girls associate shame and guilt with sex more than boys do (Cuffee, Hallfors, & Waller, 2007). The experience of menstruation (and its association with blood and pain) and the fear of pregnancy add another dimension of negativity to sex. And females' concerns about sexual exploitation and rape also foster negative emotions. Thus, when it comes to sexuality, women are likely to have ambivalent feelings instead of the largely positive feelings that men have. Unfortunately, this ambivalence is often viewed as sexual "dysfunction" for women, as opposed to an attitude resulting from narrow gender roles and beliefs (Drew, 2003).

11-5e SEXISM: A SPECIAL PROBLEM FOR FEMALES

Intimately intertwined with the topic of gender roles is the issue of sexism. ***Sexism* is discrimination against**

people on the basis of their gender. Sexism usually refers to discrimination by men against women. However, sometimes *women* discriminate against other women and sometimes *men* are the victims of gender-based discrimination. Sexism is not limited to American culture; it is a cross-cultural phenomenon (Brandt, 2011). In this section, we'll discuss two specific problems: economic discrimination and aggression toward women.

Economic Discrimination

Women are victimized by two forms of economic discrimination: differential access to jobs and differential treatment once on the job. Concerning *job access*, the problem is that women still lack the same employment opportunities as men. For example, in 2008, men held 86% of architectural and engineering occupations and 73% of computer and mathematical occupations, while 74% of education and library occupations were held by women (U.S. Bureau of the Census, 2008). Ethnic minority women are even less likely than white women to work in high-status, male-dominated occupations. Across all economic sectors, men are more likely than women to hold positions with decision-making authority (Eagly & Sczesny, 2009). In contrast, women are overrepresented in "pink-collar ghetto" occupations, such as secretary and preschool and kindergarten teacher (see Figure 11.4).

The second aspect of economic discrimination is *differential treatment* on the job. For example, women typically earn lower salaries than men in the same jobs (see Figure 11.5 on the next page). And occupations that are male dominated typically pay more than those that are female dominated (Pratto & Walker, 2004). Further, when women demonstrate leadership qualities such as confidence, ambitiousness, and assertiveness, they are evaluated less favorably than men because this behavior contradicts the female gender stereotype (Lyness & Heilman, 2006). Thus, they are often penalized for their success. There appears to be a *glass ceiling* that prevents most women and ethnic minorities from being advanced to top-level profes-

FIGURE 11.4 Women in the world of work

Career opportunities for women have expanded dramatically in recent decades. Nonetheless, women remain underrepresented in many traditionally masculine occupations and overrepresented in many traditionally feminine occupations. (Data from U.S. Bureau of the Census, 2004)

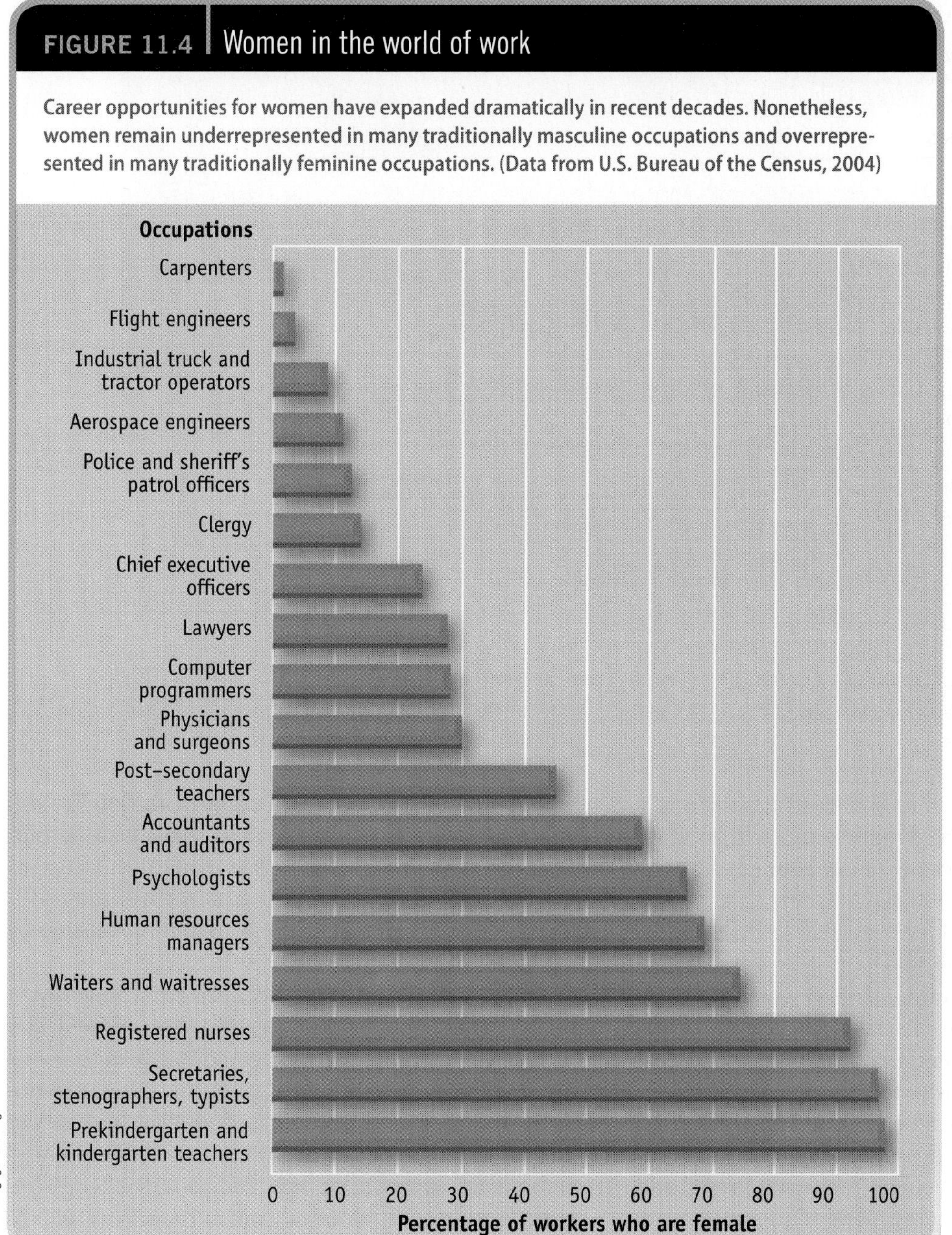

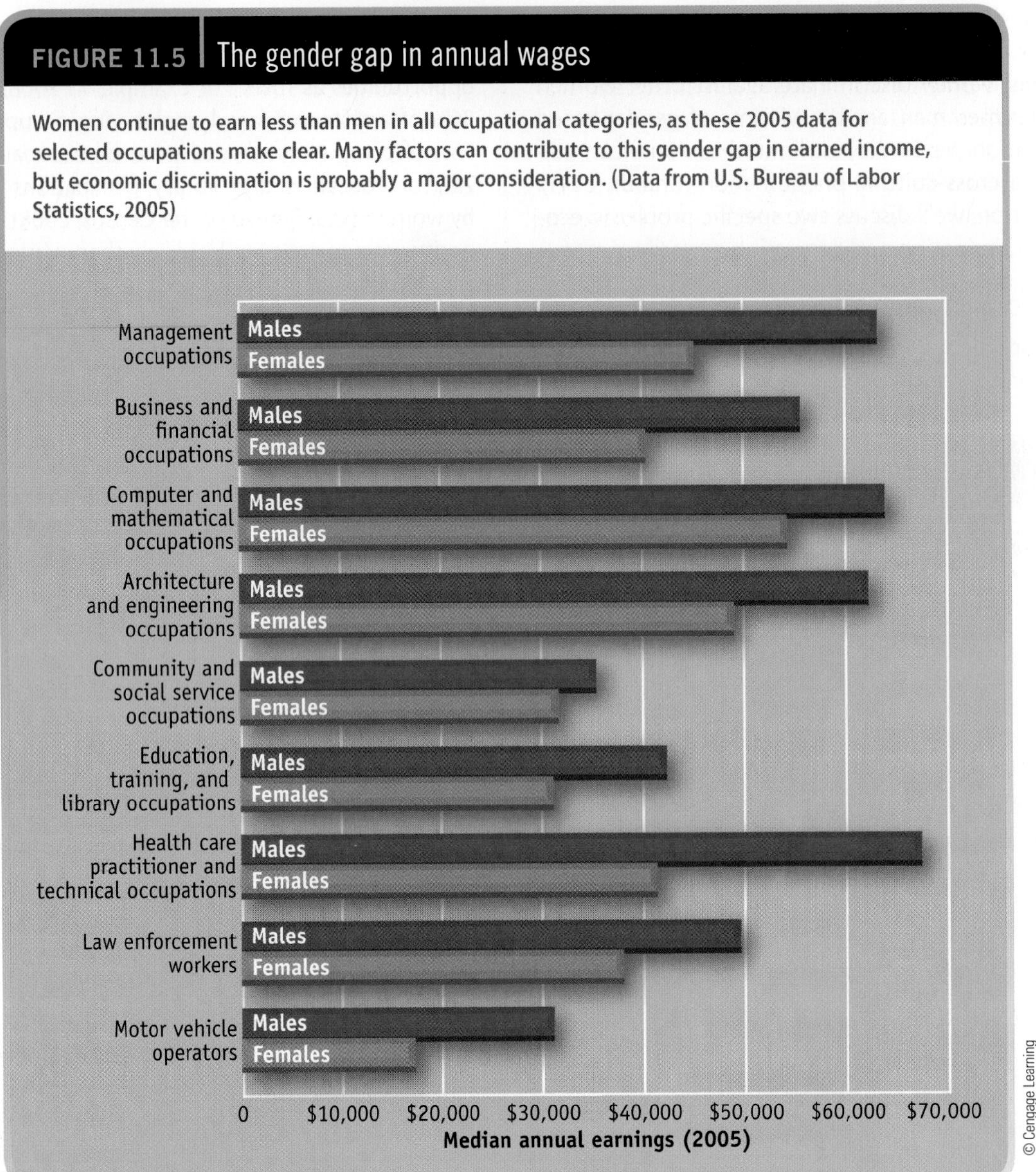

FIGURE 11.5 The gender gap in annual wages

Women continue to earn less than men in all occupational categories, as these 2005 data for selected occupations make clear. Many factors can contribute to this gender gap in earned income, but economic discrimination is probably a major consideration. (Data from U.S. Bureau of Labor Statistics, 2005)

sional positions. Ironically, men employed in traditionally female fields are promoted more quickly than their female counterparts, a phenomenon dubbed the *glass escalator* (Williams, 1998).

Aggression Toward Females

Forms of aggression toward girls and women include rape, intimate violence, sexual harassment, sexual abuse, incest, and violent pornography. We've discussed a number of these problems elsewhere, so we'll focus here on sexual harassment. ***Sexual harassment* is unwelcome conduct on the basis of gender.** It can include sexual advances, requests for sexual favors, and other verbal or physical harassment of a sexual nature. Sexual harassment has become recognized as a widespread problem that occurs not only on the job but also at home (obscene telephone calls), while walking outside (catcalls and whistles), and in medical and psychotherapy settings. It also takes place in schools and colleges. Sexual harassment is more about dominance and power than about desire.

Betz (2006) distinguishes between two categories of sexual harassment in the workplace. In *quid pro quo harassment* employees are expected to give in to sexual demands in exchange for employment, raises, promotions, and so forth. In *hostile environment harassment* employees are exposed to sexist or sexually oriented comments, cartoons, posters, and so forth. Recent research shows that minority women experience a form of "double jeopardy" when it comes to workplace harassment. When Berdahl and Moore (2006) surveyed employees from five ethnically diverse companies, they found that women experience more harassment than men, that minorities experience more harassment than whites, and that minority women experience more harassment than any other group. Given that harassment continues to be a major problem in the workplace and is related to poorer job outcomes (Settles et al., 2006), future researchers will no doubt continue to explore this issue.

11-6 Gender in the Past and in the Future

In Western society, gender roles are in a state of transition. As we have noted, sweeping changes in the female role have already occurred. It's hard to imagine today, but 100 years ago, women were not allowed to vote or to manage their own finances. It wasn't that long ago when it was virtually unheard of for a woman to initiate a date, manage a corporation, or run for public office. The future is likely to bring even more dramatic shifts in gender roles.

11-6a ALTERNATIVES TO TRADITIONAL GENDER ROLES

***Gender-role identity* is a person's identification with the qualities regarded as masculine or feminine.** Initially, gender-role identity was conceptualized as either "masculine" or "feminine." All males were expected to develop masculine role identities and females, feminine gender-role identities. Individuals who did not identify with the role expectations for their gender or who identified with the characteristics for the other gender were judged to have psychological problems.

In the 1970s, social scientists began to rethink their ideas about gender-role identity. One assumption that was called into question is that males should be "masculine" and females should be "feminine." For one thing, it appears that the serious strain that some people experience trying to conform to conventional roles is more common than widely assumed (Pleck, 1995). Research suggests that strong identification with traditional gender-role expectations is associated with a variety of negative outcomes. For example, high femininity in females is correlated with low self-esteem (Whitley, 1983) and increased psychological distress (Helgeson, 1994). High masculinity in males has been linked to chronic self-destructiveness (Van Volkom, 2008), greater sexual prejudice and homophobia (Barron et al., 2008), and vulnerability to certain types of psychopathology (Evans & Dinning, 1982). Furthermore, relationship satisfaction tends to be lower in heterosexual couples with traditional gender-role identities (Burn & Ward, 2005). Thus, contrary to earlier thinking, the evidence suggests that "masculine" males and "feminine" females may be less well adjusted, on the average, than those who are less traditional.

As people have become aware of the possible costs of traditional gender roles, there has been much debate about moving beyond them. A big question has been: What should we move toward? One idea that has received much attention is *androgyny*.

11-6b ANDROGYNY

Like masculinity and femininity, androgyny is a type of gender-role identity. ***Androgyny* refers to the coexistence of both masculine and feminine personality traits in a single person.** In other words, an androgynous person is one who scores above average on measures of *both* masculinity and femininity.

To help you fully appreciate the nature of androgyny, we need to briefly review other kinds of gender identity (see Figure 11.6). Males who score high on masculinity and low on femininity, and females who score high on femininity and low on masculinity, are said to be *gender-typed*. Males who score high on femininity but low on masculinity, and females who score high on masculinity but low on femininity, are said to be *cross-gender-typed*.

FIGURE 11.6 Possible gender-role identities

This diagram summarizes the relations between participants' scores on measures of masculinity and femininity and four possible gender identities.

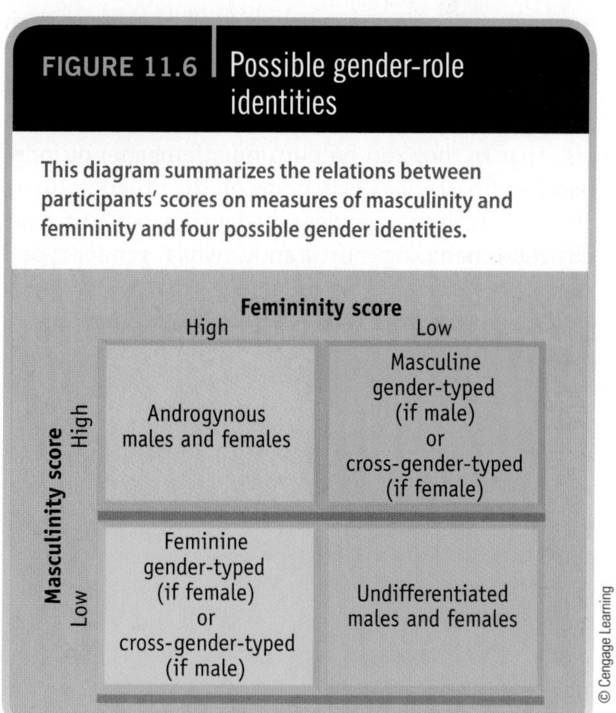

Femininity score
High
Low
Masculinity score
High
Low
Androgynous males and females
Masculine gender-typed (if male) or cross-gender-typed (if female)
Feminine gender-typed (if female) or cross-gender-typed (if male)
Undifferentiated males and females
© Cengage Learning

Finally, males and females who score low on both masculinity and femininity are characterized as *gender-role undifferentiated.*

Keep in mind that we are referring to individuals' descriptions of themselves in terms of personality traits traditionally associated with each gender (dominance, nurturance, and so on). People sometimes confuse gender-role identity with sexual orientation, but they are not the same. A person can be homosexual, heterosexual, or bisexual (sexual orientation) and be androgynous, gender-typed, cross-gender-typed, or gender-role undifferentiated (gender-role identity).

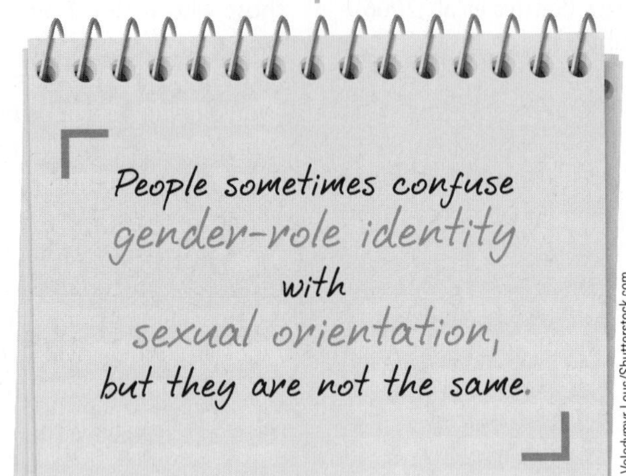
People sometimes confuse
gender-role identity
with
sexual orientation,
but they are not the same.
© Volodymyr Leus/Shutterstock.com

In groundbreaking research in the 1970s, Sandra Bem (1975) challenged the then-prevailing view that males who scored high in masculinity and females who scored high in femininity are better adjusted than "masculine" women and "feminine" men. She argued that traditionally masculine men and feminine women feel compelled to adhere to rigid and narrow gender roles that unnecessarily restrict their behavior. In contrast, androgynous individuals ought to be able to function more flexibly. She also advanced the idea that androgynous people are psychologically healthier than those who are gender-typed.

How have Bem's ideas played out over time? First, androgynous people do seem more flexible than others. That is, they can be nurturing (feminine) or independent (masculine), depending on the situation (Bem, 1975). In contrast, gender-typed males tend to have difficulty behaving nurturantly, while gender-typed females often have trouble with independence. Also, individuals whose partners are either androgynous or feminine (but not masculine or undifferentiated) report higher relationship satisfaction (Bradbury, Campbell, & Fincham, 1995). This finding holds for cohabiting heterosexuals, as well as for lesbian and gay couples (Kurdek & Schmitt, 1986b). Thus, in these areas, androgyny seems to be advantageous.

Bem's second assertion—that androgynous people are psychologically healthier than gender-typed individuals—requires a more complicated analysis. The findings depend on the *type* of masculine and feminine traits an androgynous person adopts. Obviously, there are both positive and negative masculine and feminine traits. Therefore someone who adopts predominantly positive traits for both would be *positively androgynous,* whereas someone who adopts predominantly negative traits for both would be *negatively androgynous.* In support of differentiating androgyny into these categories, Woodhill and Samuels (2003) found that positively androgynous individuals show higher levels of psychological health and well-being than those who were negatively androgynous.

However, researchers speculate that, due to changing gender roles, the traits Bem used to categorize gender identities are now outdated. Case in point—in a sample of college students, Auster and Ohm (2000) found that although 18 of the 20 feminine traits still qualified as feminine, only 8 of the 20 masculine traits were still perceived as strictly masculine.

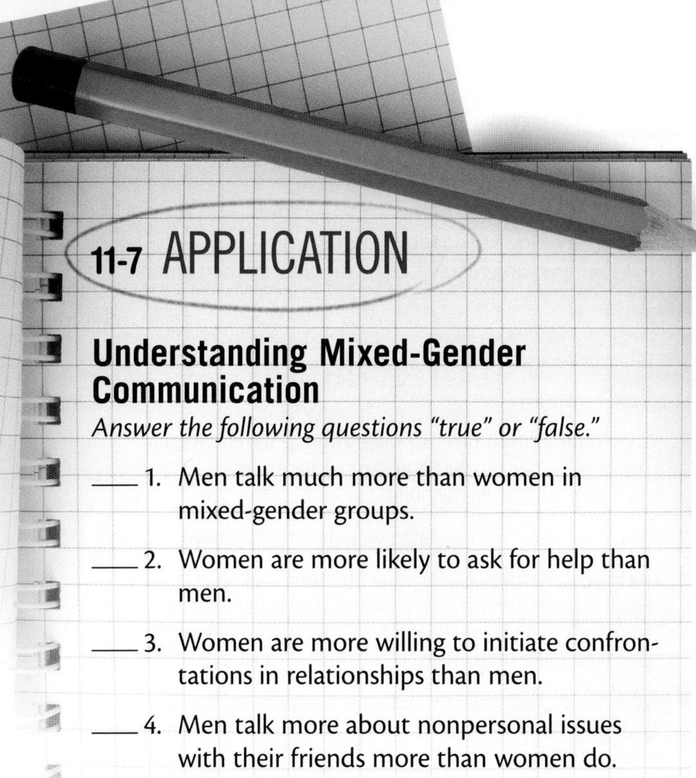

11-7 APPLICATION

Understanding Mixed-Gender Communication

Answer the following questions "true" or "false."

____ 1. Men talk much more than women in mixed-gender groups.

____ 2. Women are more likely to ask for help than men.

____ 3. Women are more willing to initiate confrontations in relationships than men.

____ 4. Men talk more about nonpersonal issues with their friends more than women do.

© Vitaly Korovin/Shutterstock.com

If you answered true to all of these statements, you were correct. They are just some of the observed differences in communication styles between males and females. While not characteristic of all men and women, or of all mixed-gender conversations, these style differences appear to be the source of many misunderstandings between males and females.

Before we go any further, it is important to remember that that gender differences in many areas, including communication, are exaggerated and that males and females are similar on most psychological variables (Hyde, 2005). As with many of the gender differences we have discussed in this chapter, differences in communication are often small and inconsistent (MacGeorge et al., 2004). In general, they are a matter of degree, not kind.

11-7a INSTRUMENTAL AND EXPRESSIVE STYLES

Some researchers posit that because of the differences in their socialization experiences, men are more likely to use an "instrumental" style of communication and women, an "expressive" style (Tannen, 1990). An *instrumental style* focuses on reaching practical goals and finding solutions to problems; an *expressive style* is characterized by being able to express tender emotions easily and being sensitive to the feelings of others. Of course, most individuals use both styles, depending on the situation.

© visi.stock/Shutterstock.com

11-7b NONVERBAL COMMUNICATION

Many studies indicate that women are more skilled than men in nonverbal communication—a key component of the expressive style. For example, they are better at reading and sending nonverbal messages (Hall & Matsumoto, 2004). But women engage in some "negative" expressive behaviors as well. For example, during relationship conflicts, women are more likely to (1) display strong negative emotions; (2) use psychologically coercive tactics, such as guilt manipulations, verbal attacks, and power plays; and (3) reject attempts at reconciliation (Barnes & Buss, 1985; Noller, 1987).

11-7c SPEAKING STYLES

Most studies have found that women speak more tentatively ("I may be wrong, but") than men, especially when discussing masculine topics in mixed-gender groups (Palomares, 2009). One explanation attributes women's greater use of tentative and polite language to gender-specific socialization (Athenstadt, Haas, & Schwab, 2004). Let's explore some theories about gender socialization specific to language and communication.

The Clash of Two "Cultures"

According to sociolinguist Deborah Tannen (1990), males and females are typically socialized in different "cultures." That is, males are likely to learn a language of "status and independence," while females learn a language of "connection and intimacy" (p. 42). Tannen likens male/female communications to other "cross-cultural" communications—full of opportunities for misunderstandings. For some hints on how to improve gender-based communication, see Figure 11.7 on the next page.

These differences in communication styles develop in childhood and are fostered by the socializing influences of parents, teachers, media, and childhood social inter-

FIGURE 11.7 Hints to improve communication between women and men

Productive personal and work relationships in today's world demand that people be knowledgeable about gender and communication styles. Both men and women may be able to benefit from the suggestions listed here. (Compiled by the authors based on insights from Tannen, 1990)

HINTS TO IMPROVE COMMUNICATION

Hints for men

1. Notice whether or not you have a tendency to interrupt women. If you do, work on breaking this habit. When you catch yourself interrupting, say, "I'm sorry, I interrupted you. Go ahead with what you were saying."
2. Avoid responding to a woman's questions in monosyllables ("Yep," "Nope," "Uh-huh"). Give her more details about what you did and explain why.
3. Learn the art of conversational give and take. Ask women questions about themselves. And listen carefully when they respond.
4. Don't order women around. For example, don't say, "Get me the newspaper." First, notice whether it might be an inconvenience for her to do something for you. If it isn't, say, "Would you mind giving me the newspaper?" or "Would you please give me the newspaper?"
5. Don't be a space hog. Be more aware of the space you take up when you sit with others (especially women). Watch that you don't make women feel crowded out.
6. Learn to open up about personal issues. Talk about your feelings, interests, hopes, and relationships. Talking about personal things helps others know who you are (and probably helps you clarify your self-perceptions, too).
7. Learn to convey enthusiasm about things in addition to the victories of your favorite sports teams.
8. Don't be afraid to ask for help if you need it.

Hints for women

1. When others interrupt you, politely but firmly redirect the conversation back to you. You can say, for example, "Excuse me. I haven't finished my point."
2. Look the person you're talking with directly in the eye.
3. A lower-pitched voice gets more attention and respect than a higher-pitched one, which is associated with little girls. Keeping your abdominal muscles firm as you speak will help keep your voice low.
4. Learn to be comfortable claiming more space (without becoming a space hog). If you want your presence to be noted, don't fold yourself up into an unobtrusive object.
5. Talk more about yourself and your accomplishments. This isn't offensive as long as others are doing the same and the circumstances are appropriate. If the conversation turns to photography and you know a lot about the topic, it's perfectly OK to share your expertise.
6. Make a point of being aware of current events so you'll be knowledgeable about what others are discussing and have an opinion to contribute.
7. Resist the impulse to be overly apologetic. Although many women say "I'm sorry" to convey sympathy or concern (not apology), these words are likely to be interpreted as an apology. Because apologizing puts one in a lower-power position, women who use apologetic words inappropriately put themselves at a disadvantage.

actions—usually with same-gender peers. Boys typically play in larger groups, usually outdoors, and farther away from home than girls (Feiring & Lewis, 1987). Thus, boys are less under the scrutiny of adults and are therefore more likely to engage in activities that encourage exploration and independence. Also, boys' groups are often structured in terms of high- and low-status roles. Boys achieve high status in their groups by engaging in dominant behavior (telling others what to do and enforcing compliance). The games that boys play often result in winners and losers, and boys frequently bid for dominance by interrupting each other, calling each other names, boasting to each other about their abilities, and refusing to cooperate with each other (Maccoby, 2002).

In contrast, girls usually play in small groups or in pairs, often indoors, and gain high status through popularity—the key to which is intimacy with peers. Many of the games girls play do not have winners or losers. And, while it is true that girls vary in abilities and skills, to call attention to oneself as better than others is frowned upon. Girls are likely to express their wishes as suggestions rather than as demands or orders (Maccoby, 2002). Dominance tends to be gained by verbal persuasion rather than by the direct bids for power characteristic of boys' social interactions (Charlesworth & Dzur, 1987). These two cultures shape the functions of speech in different ways. According to Eleanor Maccoby (1990), among boys, "speech serves largely egoistic functions and is used to establish and protect an individual's turf. Among girls, conversation is a more socially binding process" (p. 516).

Some Caveats

The idea that there are two cultures founded on gender-based communication styles has intuitive appeal because it confirms people's stereotypes and reduces complex issues to simple explanations. But there are some an important caveats here. First, as we have noted, status, power, and gender role expectations can lurk behind what seem to be gender differences. Second, many of Tannen's assertions are based on casual observation, and when put to the empirical test, the findings are mixed (McHugh & Hambaugh, 2010). Third, there are individual differences in preferred styles: Some women use the "male style" and some men use the "female style." Finally, the social context is a much stronger influence on behavior than gender, which means that many people use either style, depending on the situation. For example, one study found expected gender differences in willingness to initiate negotiations (women were less willing then men), but these differences disappeared when the negotiations were framed in terms of *asking* for something (as opposed to negotiating) (Small et al., 2007).

> Many scholars argue that we need to look at gender communications in more complex, less stereotypic ways.

© stockcam/iStockphoto

Therefore, we caution you to avoid reducing *all* communication problems between males and females to gender-based style differences. Many scholars argue that we need to look at gender communication in more complex, less stereotypic ways and that our current way of thinking has far-reaching implications for issues such as expectations for achievement, communication of sexual consent and date rape, and sexual harassment. It is simply not true that men and women come from different planets. In fact, MacGeorge et al. (2004) suggests that the idea of "different cultures is a myth that should be discarded" altogether (p. 143).

Curious about yourself? To learn more about how topics in this chapter relate to you, go online to CourseMate at www.cengagebrain.com where you can:

- Complete a **Self-Reflection** exercise that will help you think about your personal experiences in relation to topics in the chapter.
- Take a **Self-Assessment** scale that will show you how you score on a research instrument that measures personality traits or attitudes.
- Explore **Recommended Readings** that will provide brief overviews of useful self-help books.

© edge69/iStockphoto

STUDY TOOLS ▶ 11

Ready to study? In your book you can:

- **Test Yourself** with a multiple-choice quiz (below)
- Rip out the **Chapter Review card** (in the back of the book) to refresh yourself on the chapter's Key Ideas and Key Terms

Or you can go online to CourseMate at www.cengagebrain.com where you can:

- Take additional Practice Quizzes to prepare for your exam
- Review Key Terms with flash cards and a crossword puzzle
- View videos that expand on selected concepts

TEST YOURSELF

1. Taken as a whole, gender differences in verbal abilities are

a. small and favor females.
b. large and favor females.
c. nonexistent.
d. small and favor males.

2. Among the following traits, the largest gender differences are found in

a. verbal abilities.
b. mathematical abilities.
c. physical aggression.
d. conformity.

3. Which of the following statements about gender differences is true?

a. Females have higher self-esteem than males.
b. Females are more physically aggressive than males.
c. Men express more sadness than women.
d. Men talk more than women.

4. The finding that males exhibit more cerebral specialization than females supports which of the following biologically based explanations for gender differences?

a. Evolutionary theory
b. Brain organization
c. Hormones
d. Social constructionism

5. By learning that playing with trucks is appropriate behavior for boys, four-year-old Aaron is acquiring

a. a gender role.
b. gender differentiation.
c. androgyny.
d. androcentrism.

6. Parents tend to respond negatively to ____________ behavior, especially in ____________.

a. gender appropriate; boys
b. gender appropriate; girls
c. gender inappropriate; boys
d. gender inappropriate; girls

7. Which of the following statements about media influence is true?

a. Approximately 75% of children are raised in homes where the TV is on "always" or "most of the time."
b. In TV shows males appear less often and are less likely to be employed than females.
c. Television commercials show little evidence of gender stereotypes.
d. Most video games push a hypermasculine stereotype featuring search-and-destroy missions and male sports.

8. Which of the following is *not* a problem with the male role?

a. Pressure to succeed
b. Emotional inexpressiveness
c. Sexual problems
d. Androgyny

9. Which of the following is *not* a problem with the female role?

a. Poor nonverbal communication skills
b. Diminished aspirations
c. Juggling multiple roles
d. Ambivalence about sexuality

10. Sara exhibits both masculine and feminine personality traits. According to gender identity theory, she would be classified as

a. cross-gender-typed.
b. undifferentiated.
c. androcentric.
d. androgynous.

Answers: 1. a, page 229; 2. c, pages 229–230; 3. d, pages 230–231; 4. b, page 233; 5. a, page 234; 6. c, pages 234–235; 7. d, page 236; 8. d, pages 237–238; 9. a, pages 239–240; 10. d, page 243

© Dewayne Flowers/Shutterstock.com

LEARNING OBJECTIVES

12-1 Explain the factors involved in the development of sexual identity, including physiological and psychosocial influences, gender differences in socialization, and sexual orientation.

12-2 Describe the four phases of the human sexual response cycle, and discuss gender differences in patterns of orgasm.

12-3 Summarize six common ways people express themselves sexually.

12-4 Discuss typical patterns of sexual behavior both outside and inside of committed relationships.

12-5 Understand the significance of contraception and sexually transmitted diseases in sexual interactions.

12-6 Identify common sexual problems, and explain what couples can do to cope with them.

STUDY TOOLS ▸ After you have read the chapter, you can Test Yourself and learn about other Study Tools on page 271.

CHAPTER 12

Development and Expression of SEXUALITY

© Photo_Concepts/iStockphoto

Rachel and Marissa, both college seniors and new roommates, headed out to a local club on a Friday night. After a while, they were joined by Luis and Jim, whom they knew a little from one of their classes. As the evening progressed, they all got along well. After a couple of hours, Rachel took Marissa aside and asked if she would drive the car back to their apartment so Rachel could leave with Luis. Marissa agreed and went home. When she woke up the next morning, Marissa realized that Rachel hadn't come home yet. Questions raced through Marissa's mind. How could Rachel have spent the night with a guy she barely even knew? Was it being "prudish" to think that? Did Rachel or Luis have "protection"?

Photo: © Sergej Khakimullin/Shutterstock.com; Frame: © L_amica/Shutterstock.com

As this scenario illustrates, sexuality raises a lot of issues in people's lives. In this chapter we consider sexuality and adjustment. Specifically, we look at the development of sexuality and the interpersonal dynamics of sexual relationships. Then we discuss sexual arousal and the varieties of sexual expression. Next we consider patterns of sexual behavior both in and out of committed relationships. We also address the important topics of contraception and sexually transmitted diseases. In the Application, we offer some suggestions for enhancing sexual relationships.

12-1 Becoming a Sexual Person

People vary greatly in how they express their sexuality. While some eagerly reveal the intimate details of their sex lives, others can't even utter sexual words without embarrassment. To understand this diversity, we need to examine developmental influences on human sexual behavior.

Before beginning, we should note that sex research has some unique problems. Given the difficulties in conducting direct observation, sex researchers depend mostly on interviews and questionnaires. And people who are willing to volunteer information tend to be more liberal and more sexually experienced than the general population. In addition, respondents may shade the truth about their sex lives because of shame, embarrassment, boasting, or wishful thinking. Researchers also have difficulty getting representative samples, so most studies of American sexuality are overrepresented with white, middle-class volunteers. Thus, you need to evaluate the results of sex research with more than the usual caution.

12-1a KEY ASPECTS OF SEXUAL IDENTITY

Identity refers to a clear and stable sense of who one is in the larger society. We'll use the term ***sexual identity* to refer to the complex set of personal qualities, self-perceptions, attitudes, values, and preferences that guide one's sexual behavior.** In other words, your sexual identity is your sense of yourself as a sexual person. It includes two key features, sexual orientation and erotic preferences:

1. *Sexual orientation.* Sexual orientation is an individual's preference for emotional and sexual relationships with individuals of one gender or the other.

***Heterosexuals* seek emotional-sexual relationships with members of the other gender. *Homosexuals* seek emotional-sexual relationships with members of the same gender. *Bisexuals* seek emotional-sexual relationships with members of both genders.** However, sexual orientation is more complicated than these three categories make it appear.

In recent years, the terms *gay* and *straight* have become widely used to refer to homosexuals and heterosexuals, respectively. Male homosexuals are called *gay*, whereas female homosexuals prefer to be called *lesbians*. *Transgendered* individuals are those whose gender identity (sense of being a woman or man) does not match the gender they were assigned at birth. As such, transgendered individuals typically don't adhere to traditional gender roles in terms of physical appearance or sexual behaviors. Because the lesbian, gay male, bisexual, and transgendered communities often have intersecting interests, the term *LGBT* is used to refer to these groups.

2. *Erotic preferences*. Within the limits imposed by sexual orientation, people still differ in what they find enjoyable. One's erotic preferences encompass one's attitudes about self-stimulation, oral sex, intercourse, and other sexual activities. For instance, one study showed that although men and women were equally interested in erotic photos, they differed in terms of their preferences for the sexual activities depicted (Rupp & Wallen, 2009). Such preferences develop through a complex interplay of physiological and psychosocial influences—issues we take up next.

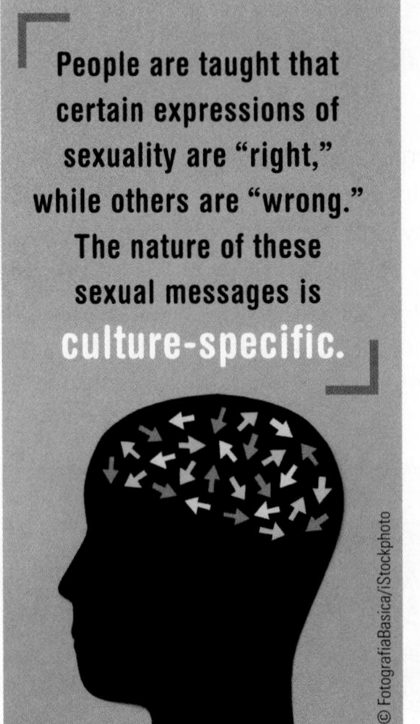
People are taught that certain expressions of sexuality are "right," while others are "wrong." The nature of these sexual messages is culture-specific.
© FotografiaBasica/iStockphoto

12-1b PHYSIOLOGICAL INFLUENCES

During the prenatal period, a number of biological developments result in a fetus that is male or female. Hormones play an important role in this process, which is termed *sexual differentiation*. Around the third month of prenatal development, different hormonal secretions begin to be produced by male and female ***gonads*—the sex glands.** In males, the testes produce ***androgens*, the principal class of male sex hormones.** Testosterone is the most important of the androgens. In females, the ovaries produce ***estrogens*, the principal class of female sex hormones.** Actually, both classes of hormones are present in both genders, but in different proportions. During prenatal development, the differentiation of the genitals depends primarily on the level of testosterone produced—high in males, low in females.

There are instances, though rare, in which sexual differentiation is incomplete and individuals are born with ambiguous genitals, sex organs, or sex chromosomes. These persons, called *intersex individuals* (previously called *hermaphrodites*), typically have both testicular and ovarian tissue. It is often difficult for these individuals to determine their "true" sexual identity (Gough et al., 2008).

At puberty, hormones reassert their influence on sexual development. In females, the onset of puberty is typically signaled by ***menarche*—the first occurrence of menstruation.** American girls typically reach menarche between ages 12 and 13, with further sexual maturation continuing until approximately age 16 (Susman, Dorn, & Schiefelbein, 2003). In males, there is no clear-cut marker of the onset of sexual maturity, although the capacity to ejaculate is used as an index of puberty. ***Spermarche*, or the first ejaculation,** usually occurs through masturbation. The average age of spermarche in American boys is around 13 (Archibald et al., 2003), with complete sexual maturation occurring at about 18 (Susman et al., 2003).

12-1c PSYCHOSOCIAL INFLUENCES

People are taught that certain expressions of sexuality are "right," while others are "wrong." The nature of these sexual messages is culture-specific. For example, the sexual double standard encourages sexual experimentation in males, but not females. Individuals are faced with the daunting task of sorting through these often-conflicting messages to develop their own sexual values and ethics. Similar to gender-role socialization, sexual identity is shaped by one's family, peers, schools, and religion, as well as the media.

Families

Parents and the home environment are significant influences on sexual identity in the early years. Before they reach school age, children usually display curiosity about sexual matters, asking questions such as "Where do babies come from?" Parents who stutter and squirm

I don't know what you've been hearing at the playground, but there's no such thing as sex.

when kids ask sexual questions convey the idea that sex is "dirty." As a result, children may begin to feel guilty about their sexual curiosity.

Many young people feel dissatisfied with the sexual information they receive from their parents, both in terms of quantity and quality. According to a 2003 Gallup Youth Survey, 63% of teenagers (ages 13 to 17) reported that their parents talked to them about sex, while 36% said that their parents mostly left this discussion up to the schools (Mazzuca, 2003). In another national survey of adolescents and young adults (ages 13 to 24), only 37% felt that they learned "a lot" of information about relationships and sexual health from their parents (Holt, Greene, & Davis, 2003). Parents who make sex a taboo topic reduce their influence on their kids' evolving sexual identity, as the children turn elsewhere for information.

Peers

Friends are a leading source of relationship and sexual health information. Unfortunately, peers can be a source of highly misleading information and often champion sexual behavior at odds with parents' views. While researchers acknowledge that the sexual socialization that comes from parents and peers is important for healthy sexual development, sexual education that comes from school-based programs is also significant.

Schools

Surveys show that the vast majority of parents and other adults support sex education programs in the schools, despite the media attention given to isolated, vocal protests (Eisenberg et al., 2008). Researchers who surveyed a nationally representative sample of American public, middle, junior, and senior high schools reported that 90% of schools offered *some* type of sex education (Kaiser Family Foundation, 2004). Among the surveyed schools, 30% offer "abstinence only" programs (no information about contraceptive methods), 47% offer "abstinence plus" programs (information about contraception and sexually transmitted diseases), and 20% offer comprehensive programs (information on such topics as contraception, abortion, sexually transmitted diseases, relationships, sexual orientation, and responsible decision making).

What is the effectiveness of these various programs? Research supports the effectiveness of comprehensive sexuality education (McCave, 2007). In fact, "abstinence only" programs do not deter adolescents from engaging in sex, do not delay first intercourse, and do not reduce the number of sexual partners (U.S. Department of Health and Human Services, 2007). In contrast, comprehensive programs result in a wide range of positive outcomes, including increased use of contraception, reduced pregnancies, and reduced high-risk sexual behavior (Schaalma et al., 2004). Further, these programs do not promote (and may delay) having early sex and do not increase (and may decrease) the number of sexual partners.

Religion

One's religious background (or lack thereof) can play a major role in the development of sexual identity. Religious teachings and traditions can dictate what is seen as sexually natural or unnatural. Using data from three national surveys, Regnerus (2007) found that the predominant message that teens receive about sex from their religious institutions is "Don't do it until you're married." This message is conveyed through church-based initiatives such as abstinence pledges, chastity vows, and purity rings. This message is largely ineffective, however. Teens who take these pledges tend to be just as sexually active (and less likely to use condoms or other forms of birth control) as their nonpledging peers. On the other hand, they *do* tend to feel more guilty about it (Rosenbaum, 2009).

Teens who take abstinence pledges or wear purity rings tend to be just as sexually active as their nonpledging peers.

The Media

Americans see thousands of sexual encounters a year on television, videos, DVDs, and computers. And the depiction of sexual content is on the rise (Kunkel et al., 2007). Television portrayals of sexual behavior can influence adolescents' beliefs about typical sexual practices as well as their sexual intentions and behavior. For adolescents, viewing sexual content is linked to increased sexual activity as well as intentions to engage in sexual behavior in the future (Fisher at al., 2009).

Books and magazines are another source of information about sex. Some 20% of adolescents and young adults reported that they had learned "a lot" about relationships and sexual health from magazines (Kaiser Family Foundation, 2003). Regrettably, sexual content in magazines often perpetuates gender stereotypes and sexual myths under the pretense of offering ideas for "improvement" (Johnson, 2007).

Turning to cyberspace, experts estimate that there were about 2.27 billion (32.7% of the total world population) Internet users worldwide in 2011 (Internet World Stats, 2011). Websites with sexually explicit images are extremely popular, especially among males. Parents are understandably alarmed about children having easy access to sexually explicit material online. Among 10- to 17-year-olds, 25% have encountered unwanted pornography, and 20% have been exposed to unwanted sexual solicitations (Finkelhor, Mitchell, & Wolak, 2000). On the bright side, the Internet provides easy and private access to useful information on a variety of sexual topics, including contraceptive methods and resources for the LGBT communities.

Note that any causal link between sexual behavior and sexual media viewing can go both ways. While those exposed to sex in the media are more sexually active, those who are more sexually active tend to view more sexual content (Bleakley et al., 2008). Although there are some advantages to sexual content in the media, scientists agree that media depictions of sexuality would have to change dramatically for consumption of sexual media to be considered a healthy part of sexual development (Hust, Brown, & L'Engle, 2008).

Photo: © Anton Oparin/Shutterstock.com; Frame: © Thomas Bethge/Shutterstock.com

12-1d GENDER DIFFERENCES IN SEXUAL SOCIALIZATION

To what degree are males and females socialized differently about sexual matters? Summarizing the research on gender differences in sexuality, Letitia Anne Peplau (2003), a major researcher on gender and relationships, concludes that there are five key differences and that all but one of them hold for both gay and straight people:

1. Men have more interest in sex than women (they think about and want to have sex more often).

2. The connection between sex and intimacy is more important for women than for men (women typically prefer sex in the context of a relationship).

3. Aggression is more often linked to sexuality for men than for women (coercive sex is more likely to be initiated by men).

4. Women's sexuality is more easily shaped by cultural and situational factors (their sexual attitudes are easier to change, and they are more likely to change their sexual orientation over time).

5. Among heterosexual couples, men typically take the lead in initiating sexual intimacy, while women serve as "gatekeepers," determining whether and when a couple engages in sexual activities.

Societal values and gender roles obviously come into play here. American males are encouraged to experiment sexually, to initiate sexual activities, and to enjoy sex without emotional involvement (Kilmartin, 2007). They also get the message to be conquest oriented regarding sex, typically desiring multiple partners (Fenigstein & Preston, 2007). Men are more likely than women to engage in sex activities for purely physical reasons (Meston & Ross, 2007). Thus, men may emphasize "sex for fun" in casual relationships and reserve "sex with love" for committed relationships.

Females are typically taught to view sex in the context of a loving relationship with one partner (Impett & Peplau, 2006). They learn about romance and the importance of physical attractiveness and catching a mate. Unlike males, they are not encouraged to experiment with sex or to have numerous sexual partners. Whereas social norms encourage males to be sexually active, these norms discourage such behavior in females—sexually active women may be looked on as "easy."

With differing views of sexuality and relationships, males and females can be out of sync with each other—particularly in adolescence and early adulthood. For instance, college men are more likely to believe that oral sex isn't sex, cybersex isn't cheating, and the frequency of intercourse decreases after marriage. College women, on the other hand, are likely to think exactly the opposite (Knox, Zusman, & McNeely, 2008). These gender differences mean that communication is essential for mutually satisfying sexual relationships.

Because both members of homosexual couples have been socialized similarly, they are less likely than straight couples to have problems with incompatible expectations. Like heterosexual women, lesbians typically experience emotional attraction to their partners before experiencing sexual feelings (Peplau & Fingerhut, 2007). By contrast, gay men (like heterosexual men) tend to place much more importance on physical appearance and sexual compatibility in selecting partners and to then develop emotional relationships out of sexual ones (Diamond, 2006).

12-1e SEXUAL ORIENTATION

Gay, straight, or in between? In this section, we'll explore the intriguing and controversial topic of sexual orientation.

Most people view heterosexuality and homosexuality as two distinct categories: you're either one or the other. However, many individuals who define themselves as heterosexuals have had homosexual experiences, and vice versa. Thus, it is more accurate to view heterosexuality and homosexuality as end points on a continuum. Indeed, Alfred Kinsey devised a seven-point scale, shown in Figure 12.1, to characterize sexual orientation.

Some researchers argue that even Kinsey's model is too simplistic. For instance, how would you categorize a person who was married for 10 years, has children, is divorced, and is now involved in a committed homosexual relationship? What about a woman who only dates men but who has homosexual fantasies and engages in same-gender sex on the Internet? And what about someone who self-identifies as straight but has had homosexual encounters in the past? Research supports a complex and malleable view of sexual orientation (Savin-Williams, 2009).

Origins

There is no consensus among researchers as to *why* some people are straight and others gay. A number of *environmental explanations* have been suggested as causes of sexual orientation. Freud believed that homosexuality originates from an unresolved Oedipus complex (see Chapter 2). That is, instead of coming to identify with the parent of the same gender, the child continues to identify with the parent of the other gender. Learning theorists assert that homosexuality results from early negative heterosexual encounters or early positive homosexual experiences. Sociologists propose that homosexuality develops because of poor relationships with same-gender peers or because being labeled a homosexual sets up a self-fulfilling prophecy. However, a comprehensive review of the causes of sexual orientation found no compelling support for *any* of these explanations of homosexuality (Bell, Weinberg, & Hammersmith, 1981).

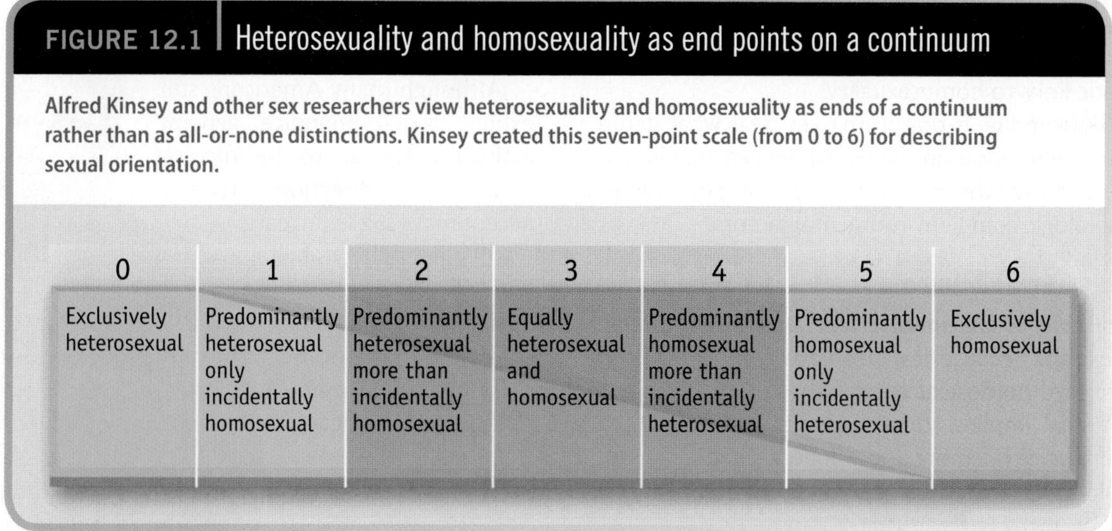

Similarly, there is no evidence that parents' sexual orientation is linked to that of their children (Patterson, 2003). That is, heterosexual parents are as likely to produce homosexual (or heterosexual) offspring as homosexual parents are. Children who grow up in gay or lesbian families are predominantly heterosexual.

Some theorists speculate that *biological factors* are involved in the development of homosexuality. Several lines of research suggest that hormonal secretions during prenatal development may shape sexual development, organize the brain in a lasting manner, and influence subsequent sexual orientation (Byne, 2007). Because of advances in technology that allow researchers to actually map the activity in the brain, we can begin to explore brain differences in sexual orientation. However, it is important to keep in mind that it is difficult to determine whether any brain differences are a cause or a consequence of sexual orientation.

Genetic factors are also of interest. In an important study, investigators identified gay and bisexual men who had a twin brother or an adopted brother (Bailey & Pillard, 1991). They found that 52% of the participants' identical twins were gay, 22% of their fraternal twins were gay, and only 11% of their adoptive brothers were gay. A companion study of lesbian women with twin or adopted sisters reported a similar pattern of results (Bailey et al., 1993; see Figure 12.2). More recent twin studies, with larger and more representative samples, have provided further support for the conclusion that heredity influences sexual orientation, although these studies have yielded smaller estimates of genetic influence (Bailey, Dunne, & Martin, 2000). Thus, there may be genetic links to homosexuality.

FIGURE 12.2 Genetics and sexual orientation

A concordance rate indicates the percentage of twin pairs or other pairs of relatives that exhibit the same characteristic. If relatives who share more genetic relatedness show higher concordance rates than relatives who share less genetic overlap, this evidence suggests a genetic predisposition to the characteristic. Recent studies of both gay men and lesbian women have found higher concordance rates among identical twins than fraternal twins, who, in turn, exhibit more concordance than adoptive siblings. These findings are consistent with the hypothesis that genetic factors influence sexual orientation. (Data from Bailey & Pillard, 1991; Bailey et. al., 1993)

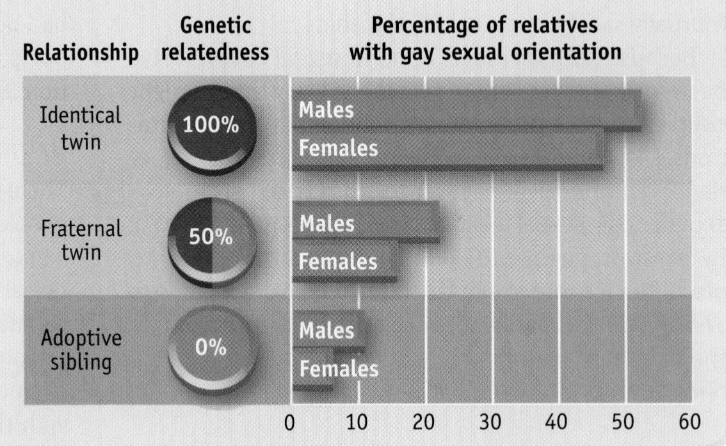

The bottom line is that it isn't yet clear what determines sexual orientation. The most we can conclude is that the explanations must lie in some complex interaction of biological and environmental factors.

Attitudes Toward Homosexuality

***Homophobia* is the intense fear and intolerance of homosexuals.** Because few people with negative attitudes toward homosexuals have the psychopathology that "phobia" implies, some psychologists believe that *sexual prejudice* is a more appropriate term. The lowest levels of sexual prejudice are found among individuals who personally know someone who is gay (Stotzer, 2009). Higher levels of sexual prejudice are associated with being older, male, less educated, and living in the South or Midwest and in rural areas (Herek & Capitanio, 1996). Unfortunately, negative attitudes sometimes translate into hate crimes. In a national survey, 23% of the LGB participants had been threatened with violence, and 49% reported verbal harassment. These percentages were even higher when just considering gay males (35% and 63% respectively; Herek, 2009a).

Although many Americans still exhibit sexual prejudice, general attitudes appear to be moving in a positive direction. Greater acceptance is due, in part, to the increasing visibility of lesbians and gays in society. For instance, homosexual content on television has increased dramatically over the past two decades, including hav-

ing more openly gay characters (*Glee*) and individuals (*Ellen*).

Perhaps we shouldn't be surprised that people's explanations of sexual orientation play a role in their attitudes. Viewing homosexuality as biological or genetic in origin (that is, uncontrollable) is associated with more favorable attitudes than attributing it to choice (Haider-Markel & Joslyn, 2008). Black Americans are more likely than white Americans to endorse choice as an explanation for sexual orientation (Jayaratne et al., 2009), which may explain some of the cultural differences in acceptance of homosexuality.

Adjustment

The mental health community initially classified homosexuality as a psychological disorder. But researchers demonstrated that view to be a myth; that is, gays and straights are indistinguishable in their general psychological processes and on measures of psychological health. As a result of research, changes in public attitudes, and political lobbying, homosexuality was deleted from the official list of psychological disorders in 1973. Since then, research continues to demonstrate that sexual orientation doesn't impair psychological adjustment in gay individuals, couples, and parents (Hancock & Greenspan, 2010). Similarly, there is no evidence of elevated psychopathology in nonclinical samples of bisexual men and women (Fox, 1996). However, there is evidence that exposure to sexual prejudice and discrimination can cause distress for some LGB individuals.

> Although many Americans still exhibit sexual prejudice, general attitudes appear to be moving in a positive direction.

© desuza.communications/iStockphoto

12-2 The Human Sexual Response

When people engage in sexual activity, exactly how does the body respond? Surprisingly, until William Masters and Virginia Johnson conducted their groundbreaking research in the 1960s, little was known about the physiology of the human sexual response. Masters and Johnson used physiological recording devices to monitor the bodily changes of volunteers engaging in sex. Their observations and interviews with their subjects yielded a detailed description of the human sexual response that won them widespread acclaim.

12-2a THE SEXUAL RESPONSE CYCLE

Masters and Johnson's (1966, 1970) description of the sexual response cycle is a general one, outlining typical rather than inevitable patterns—people vary considerably. Figure 12.3 on page 258 shows how the intensity of sexual arousal changes as women and men progress through the four phases of the sexual response cycle.

Excitement Phase

During the initial phase of excitement, the level of arousal usually escalates rapidly. In both sexes, muscle tension, respiration rate, heart rate, and blood pressure increase quickly. In males, ***vasocongestion*—engorgement of blood vessels**—produces penile erection, swollen testes, and the movement of the scrotum (the sac containing the testes) closer to the body. In females, vasocongestion leads to a swelling of the clitoris and vaginal lips, vaginal lubrication, and enlargement of the uterus. Most women also experience nipple erection and a swelling of the breasts.

Plateau Phase

The name given to the "plateau" stage is misleading because physiological arousal does not level off. Instead, it continues to build, but at a much slower pace. In women, further vasocongestion produces a tightening of the lower third of the vagina and a "ballooning" of the upper two-thirds, which lifts the uterus and cervix away from the end of the vagina. In men, the head of the penis may swell, and the testicles typically enlarge and move closer to the body. Many men secrete a bit of pre-ejaculatory fluid from the tip of the penis that may contain sperm.

Distractions during the plateau phase can delay or stop movement to the next stage. These include ill-timed interruptions like a telephone ringing or someone knocking—or not!—on the bedroom door. Equally distracting can be such things as physical discomfort, pain, guilt, frightening thoughts, feelings of insecurity or anger toward one's partner, and anxiety about not having an orgasm.

Orgasm Phase

***Orgasm* occurs when sexual arousal reaches its peak intensity and is discharged in a series of muscular contractions that pulsate through the pelvic area.** Heart rate, respiration rate, and blood pressure increase sharply during this exceedingly pleasant spasmodic

FIGURE 12.3 | The human sexual response cycle

There are similarities and differences between men and women in patterns of sexual arousal. Pattern A, which culminates in orgasm and resolution, is the most typical sequence for both sexes. Pattern B, which involves sexual arousal without orgasm followed by a slow resolution, is also seen in both genders, but it is more common among women. Pattern C, which involves multiple orgasms, is seen almost exclusively in women, as men go through a refractory period before they are capable of another orgasm. (Based on Masters & Johnson, 1966)

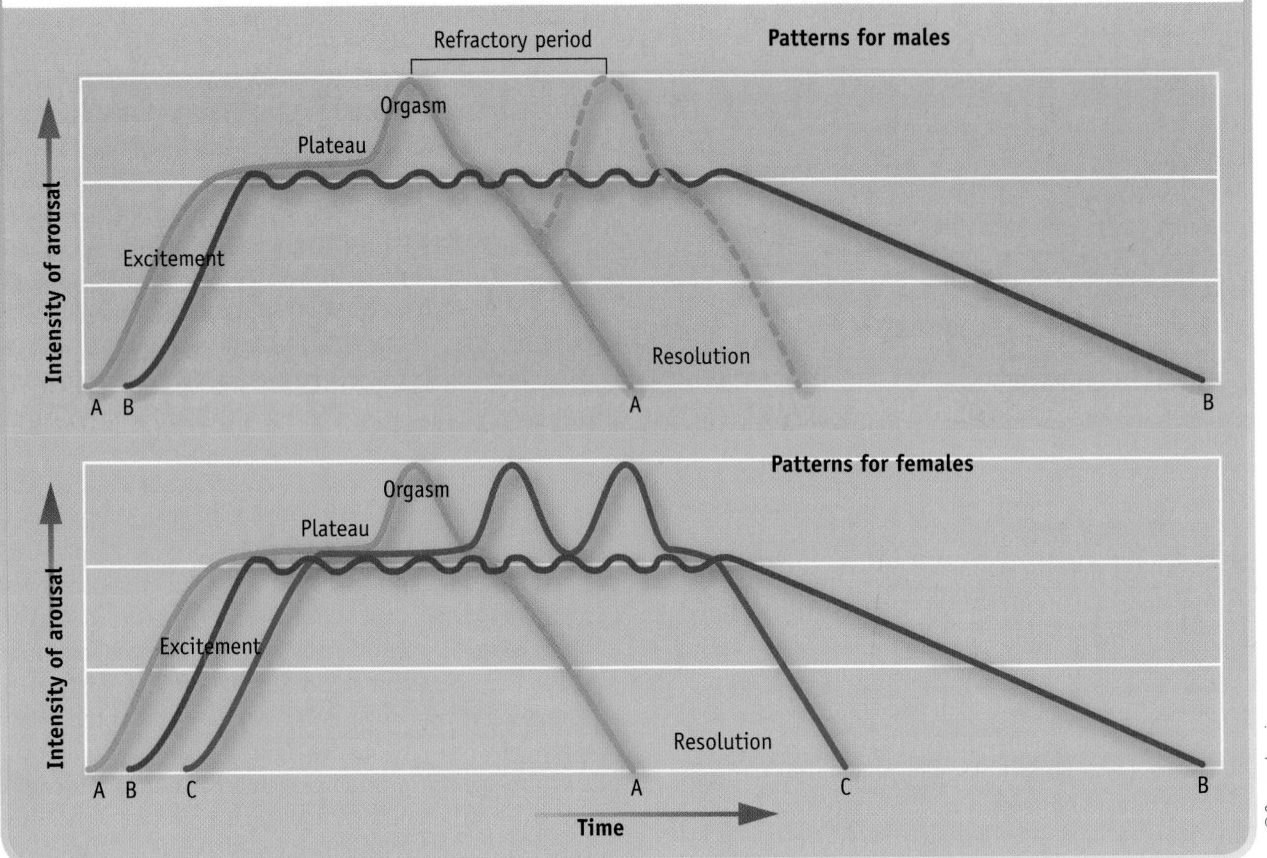

© Cengage Learning

response. The male orgasm is usually accompanied by ejaculation of seminal fluid. The subjective experience of orgasm appears to be essentially the same for men and women, although the relationship between subjective experience and physical response seems to be greater for men than for women (Suschinsky, Lalumiere, & Chivers, 2009). That is, there is a higher degree of agreement between men's physical response (erection) and their self-report of arousal than there is for women.

Resolution Phase

During the resolution phase, the physiological changes produced by sexual arousal subside. If one has not had an orgasm, the reduction in sexual tension may be relatively slow and sometimes unpleasant. After orgasm, men generally experience a ***refractory period,* a time following male orgasm during which males are largely unresponsive to further stimulation.** The refractory period varies from a few minutes to a few hours and increases with age.

12-2b GENDER DIFFERENCES IN PATTERNS OF ORGASM

As a whole, the sexual responses of women and men parallel each other fairly closely. Nonetheless, there are some interesting differences between the genders in their patterns of experiencing orgasm. During *intercourse,* women are less likely than men to reach orgasm (that is, they are more likely to follow pattern B in Figure 12.3). According to one survey of American sexual behavior (Laumann et al., 1994), about 29% of women reported that they *always* reached orgasm in their primary sexual relationships, compared to 75% of men (see Figure 12.4). However, 62% of partnered women reported that they were very satisfied with the frequency and consistency of their orgasms with their partners (Davis et al., 1996).

Women are more likely to orgasm when they engage in a variety of sexual behaviors such as oral sex whereas men are more likely to orgasm when sex includes intercourse. According to a national survey, 91% of men report having had an orgasm during their sexual activities in the past year compared to 64% of women (Herbenick et al., 2010).

How do we account for these disparities? First, although most women report that they enjoy intercourse, it is not the optimal mode of stimulation for them. This is because intercourse provides rather indirect stimulation to the clitoris, the most sexually sensitive genital area in most women. Thus, more lengthy *foreplay*, including manual or oral stimulation of the clitoris, is usually the key to enhancing women's sexual pleasure. Unfortunately, many couples are locked into the idea that orgasms should be achieved only through intercourse. Even the word *foreplay* suggests that any other form of sexual stimulation is merely preparation for the "main event."

Research suggests that lesbians have orgasms more often and more easily in sexual interactions than heterosexual women do (Diamond, 2006). Kinsey and colleagues (1953) attributed this difference to female partners' knowing more about women's sexuality and how to optimize women's sexual satisfaction than male partners do. Also, female partners are more likely to emphasize the emotional aspects of lovemaking than male partners (Peplau et al., 2004). Taken together, these facts support a socialization-based explanation of gender differences in orgasmic consistency.

Because women reach orgasm through intercourse less consistently than men, they are more likely than men to fake an orgasm. Surveys reveal that more than half of all adult women (straight and lesbian) have faked an orgasm (Elliott & Brantley, 1997). Men (straight and gay) also fake orgasms, but much less frequently. People typically do so to make their partner feel better or to bring sexual activity to an end when they're tired. Frequent faking is not a good idea, because it can become a vicious cycle and undermine communication about sex.

FIGURE 12.4 | Sexual satisfaction with primary partner

A major survey of American sexual behavior showed large gender differences in the consistency of orgasm, a physical measure of sexual satisfaction. Men's and women's subjective evaluations of physical and emotional sexual satisfaction are much more similar. These data indicate that not everyone who has an orgasm every time has a blissful sex life and that factors other than orgasm contribute to a satisfying sex life. (Based on Laumann et al., 1994)

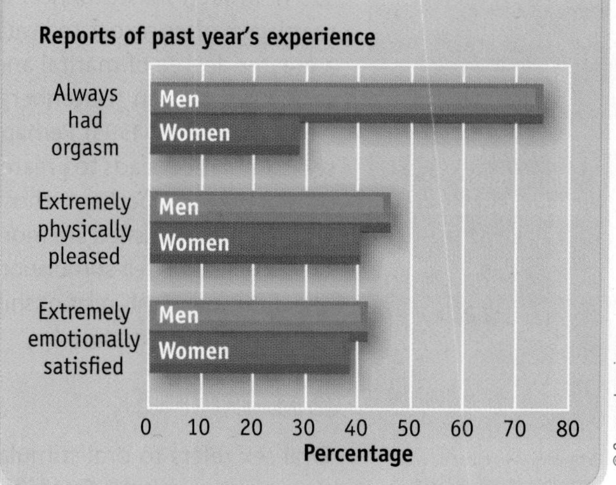

12-3 Sexual Expression

People experience and express sexuality in myriad ways. ***Erogenous zones*** **are areas of the body that are sexually sensitive or responsive.** The genitals and breasts usually come to mind when people think of erogenous zones, as these areas are particularly sensitive for most people. But it's worth noting that virtually any area of the body can function as an erogenous zone. And most long-term couples engage in a variety of sexual practices (see Figure 12.5 on the next page). In this section, we'll consider the most common forms of sexual expression.

12-3a FANTASY

The ultimate erogenous zone may be the mind. Skillful genital stimulation by a partner may have absolutely no impact if a person is not in the mood. Yet fantasy in the absence of any other stimulation can produce great arousal. Have you ever fantasized about having sex with someone other than your partner? If so, you've had one of the most commonly reported fantasies. In fact, a study of university students and employees reported that 98% of men and 80% of women had sexual fantasies involving someone other than their current partner (Hicks & Leitenberg, 2001). As you might expect, women's fantasies tend to be more romantic, while men's tend to contain more explicit imagery (Impett & Peplau, 2006). Most sex therapists view sexual fantasies as harmless ways to enhance sexual excitement and achieve orgasm either during masturbation or with a partner.

12-3b KISSING AND TOUCHING

Most two-person sexual activities begin with kissing and mutual caressing. In fact, there seems to be something special about kissing as a form of nonverbal communication. Floyd and colleagues (2009) randomly assigned heterosexual partners to either increase their romantic kissing frequency or not. After 6 weeks, they found that those who had increased kissing had less perceived stress levels and higher relationship satisfaction. These differences were still significant even after the researchers controlled for increased verbal affections and decreased conflict, two factors one might expect with increased romantic kissing.

© Jupiterimages/Goodshoot/Thinkstock

FIGURE 12.5 Percentages of sexual activities for heterosexual couples

Using data from the National Longitudinal Study of Adolescent Health, Kaestle and Halpern (2007) report the distribution percentages for young heterosexual adults who reported which sexual activities they had engaged in with their current partner (of at least three months). It is clear that young adults engage in a variety of sexual activities.

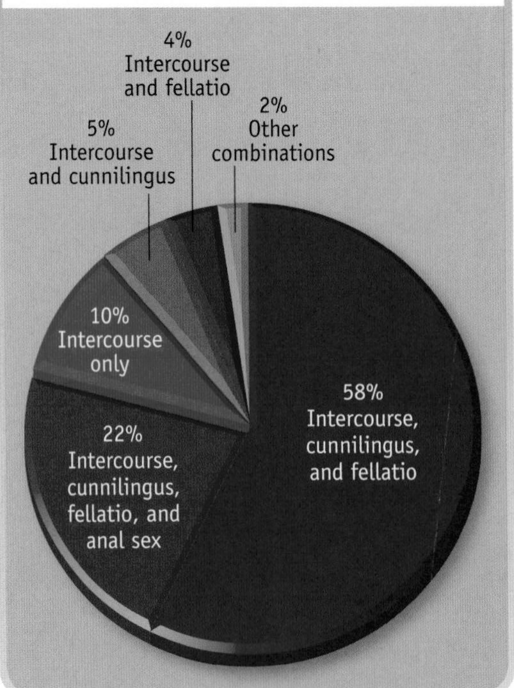

© Cengage Learning

Source: From Kaestle, C. E., & Halpern, C. T. (2007). What's love got to do with it? Sexual behaviors of opposite-sex couples through emerging adulthood. *Perspectives of Sexual and Reproductive Health, 39*(3), 134–140. Copyright © 2007 by the Guttmacher Institute.

12-3c SELF-STIMULATION

***Masturbation*, the stimulation of one's own genitals,** has historically been condemned as immoral because it is nonreproductive. Disapproval and suppression of masturbation were truly intense in the 19th and early 20th centuries, when people believed that the practice was harmful to physical and mental health. Because the term *masturbation* has acquired negative connotations, the preferred terminology is *self-stimulation* or *autoeroticism*.

Kinsey discovered over four decades ago that most people masturbate with no ill effects. Sexologists now recognize that self-stimulation is normal and healthy. In fact, sex therapists often prescribe masturbation to treat both male and female sexual problems (see this Chapter's Application). Nonetheless, many who engage in the practice feel guilty about it.

Self-stimulation is common in our society. In a national survey, 38% of women and 61% of men reported having engaged in self-stimulation in the past year (Das, 2007). African American males masturbate less than Asian, white, and Hispanic men (Laumann et al., 1994). Among married couples, 57% of husbands and 37% of wives report engaging in self-stimulation (Laumann et al., 1994). In fact, masturbation in marriage is often associated with a greater degree of marital and sexual satisfaction (Leitenberg, Detzer, & Srebnik, 1993). Perhaps self-stimulation leads to greater satisfaction, or perhaps those who are more satisfied are more likely to engage is self-stimulation. The direction of this relationship has yet to be determined.

12-3d ORAL SEX

Oral sex refers to oral stimulation of the genitals. ***Cunnilingus* is oral stimulation of the**

female genitals; *fellatio* is oral stimulation of the penis. Partners may stimulate each other simultaneously, or one partner may stimulate the other without immediate reciprocation. Oral sex is a major source of orgasms for many heterosexual couples, and it plays a central role in homosexual relationships. Both men and women perceive oral sex as less intimate than intercourse (Chambers, 2007).

A positive aspect of oral sex for some people is that it does not result in pregnancy. This fact partly accounts for the finding that younger teens are more likely to engage in oral sex than in intercourse (Halpern-Felsher et al., 2005). However, some sexually transmitted diseases, such as human immunodeficiency virus (HIV), can be contracted through mouth-genital stimulation, especially if there are small cracks in the mouth or if the mouth is exposed to semen. And a person with a cold sore can pass along the herpes virus during oral sex or kissing. Unfortunately, data suggest that up to 40% of sexually active teens either don't know that one can become infected with HIV through unprotected oral sex or are unsure about it (Centers for Disease Control, 2009a).

12-3e ANAL SEX

***Anal intercourse* involves insertion of the penis into a partner's anus and rectum.** Legally, it is termed *sodomy* (and is still considered illegal in some states). About 25% of men and women report that they have practiced anal sex at least once (Kaestle & Halpern, 2007). Anal intercourse is more popular among homosexual male couples than among heterosexual couples. However, even among gay men it ranks behind oral sex and mutual masturbation in prevalence. Anal sex is risky. Gay men who engage in anal sex without a condom (referred to as bareback sex) run a high risk for HIV infection because rectal tissues are easily torn, facilitating HIV transmission.

12-3f INTERCOURSE

Vaginal intercourse, known more technically as ***coitus*, involves inserting the penis into the vagina and (typically) pelvic thrusting.** It is the most widely endorsed and widely practiced sexual act in our society. In the American sex survey, 95% of heterosexual respondents said that they had practiced vaginal sex the last time they had sex (Laumann et al., 1994). Frequent intercourse is associated with greater sexual and relationship satisfaction, higher life satisfaction, and better mental health (Brody & Costa, 2009).

Couples use a variety of positions in intercourse and may use more than one position in a single encounter. The man-above, or "missionary," position is the most common, but the woman-above, side-by-side, and rear-entry positions are also common. Each position has its advantages and disadvantages. Although people are fascinated by the relative merits of various positions, specific positions may not be as important as the tempo, depth, and angle of movements in intercourse. As with other aspects of sexual relations, the crucial consideration is that partners communicate with each other about their preferences.

What kinds of sexual activities do homosexuals prefer in the absence of coitus (which is, by definition, a heterosexual act)? As is true with heterosexual couples, the preliminary activities of gay and lesbian couples include kissing, hugging, and caressing. Gay men also engage in fellatio, mutual masturbation, and anal intercourse, in that order of prevalence. Lesbians engage in cunnilingus, mutual masturbation, and *tribadism* (also known as humping or scissoring), in which partners rub their genitals together so that both receive genital stimulation at the same time.

12-4 Patterns of Sexual Behavior

The context of a sexual interaction influences the interaction itself. In this section we examine how the type of relationship one is in relates to sexual behavior.

12-4a SEX OUTSIDE OF COMMITTED RELATIONSHIPS

"Hooking up," a phenomenon that has increased since the late 1990s, involves two strangers or briefly acquainted people having a single sexual encounter. Hookups don't always involve intercourse (manual stimulation and oral sex are common). When looking at hookups that did include sexual intercourse, Eshbaugh and Gute (2008) found that 36% of sexually active women reported having had sex with someone only once and 29% reported having had sex with someone they had known less than 24 hours. Further, hookups that included sex were linked

to regret for women. Hookups typically result from flirting, drinking, and hanging out, and they typically end when one or both partners reach orgasm, or one person leaves or passes out (Paul, Wenzel, & Harvey, 2008).

It seems that college students wrongly believe that their peers are significantly more comfortable with hooking up than they themselves are (Lambert, Kahn, & Apple, 2003). Researchers speculate that these false perceptions might influence students to override their own comfort level and engage in sexual behavior to be in step with the *perceived* peer norm. Figure 12.6 depicts men's and women's comfort level with various hooking-up behaviors. Clearly, casual sex is risky: People don't always practice safe sex, and the risk of contracting sexually transmitted diseases increases with multiple partners.

"Friends-with-benefits" refers to friends who engage in sex but who don't label their relationship as romantic. This situation is different from hooking up because participants in a friend-with-benefits relationship anticipate maintaining their friendship. Surveys indicate that up to 60% of undergraduates have experienced this kind of relationship (Bisson & Levine, 2009). People who engage in a friends-with-benefits arrangement are more likely to be casual daters, to be nonromantics, and to hold more hedonistic (anything goes) sexual values (Puentes, Knox, & Zusman, 2008). Obviously, negotiating such relationships can be tricky. Friendships are jeopardized if unreciprocated desires for romantic commitment develop or if one person wants to end the sexual relationship.

12-4b SEX IN COMMITTED RELATIONSHIPS

Sex is a key aspect of most committed, romantic relationships. In this section, we examine patterns of sexual activity in dating couples, married couples, and gay couples.

Sex Between Dating Partners

At some point, couples confront the question of whether or when they should have sex. Some worry that sex might adversely affect the relationship; others fear that not having sex will cause trouble. Is there evidence to support either view? As it turns out, sexual intimacy is a positive predictor of relationship stability (Sprecher & Cate, 2004). However, gender and satisfaction are also part of this equation. For men, sexual (but not relationship) satisfaction is significantly correlated with relationship stability; for women, relationship (but not sexual) satisfaction is significantly associated with relationship stability (Sprecher, 2002).

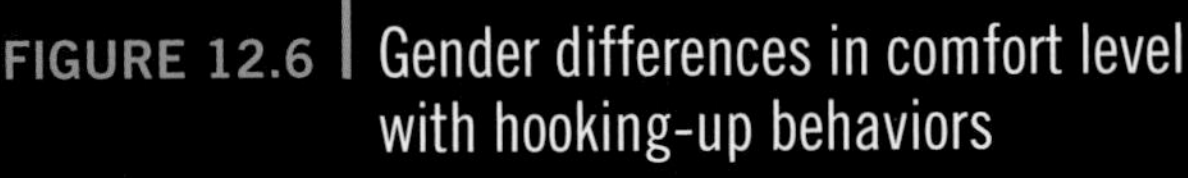

FIGURE 12.6 Gender differences in comfort level with hooking-up behaviors

College men and women were asked to rate their comfort level with four hooking-up behaviors. The ratings were made on an 11-point scale (11 = *Very comfortable*; 1 = *Not at all comfortable*). As you can see from the mean ratings shown here, men's comfort levels significantly exceeded women's for all four behaviors.

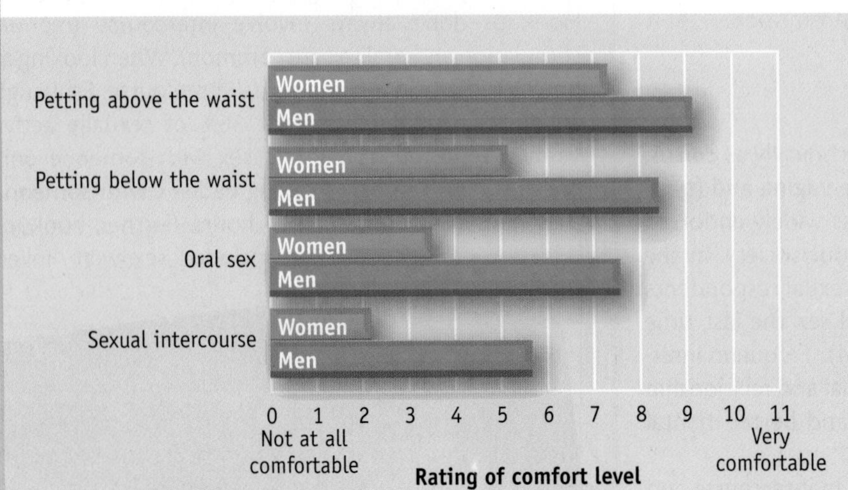

Source: From Lambert, T. A., Kahn, A. S., & Apple, K. J. (2003). Pluralistic ignorance and hooking up. *The Journal of Sex Research, 40*(2) 129–133. Copyright © 1979 Society for the Scientific Study of Sexuality. Reprinted by permission.

Marital Sex

Couples' overall marital satisfaction is strongly related to their satisfaction with their sexual relationship (Sprecher, Christopher, & Cate, 2006). Of course, it is difficult to know whether good sex promotes good marriages or good marriages promote good sex. In all probability, it's a two-way street. Relationship satisfaction is also correlated with satisfaction in other areas of a relationship (fairness in distribution of household labor, for example) (Impett & Peplau, 2006).

Married couples vary greatly in how often they have sex (see Figure 12.7). The frequency tends to decrease as the years pass (Hatfield & Rapson, 2008). Biological changes play some role in this trend, but social factors seem more compelling.

FIGURE 12.7 | Frequency of sex among married men and women

A well-sampled survey asked Americans, "How often have you had sex in the past 12 months?" Married individuals' responses to the question were wide ranging. The most frequent response was "a few times per month" followed by "2 to 3 times a week." (Based on Laumann et al., 1994)

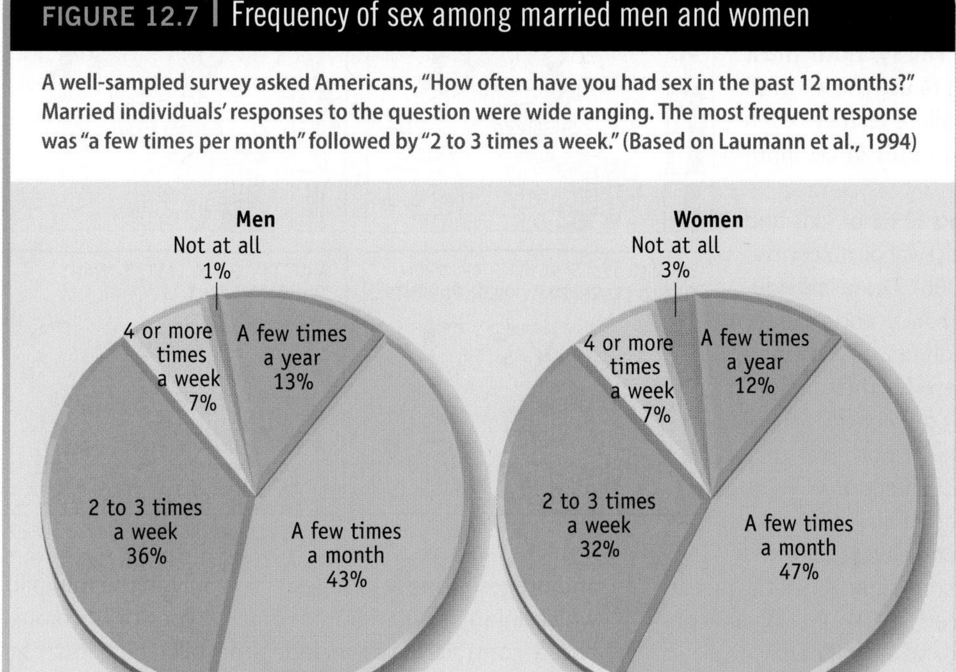

Most couples attribute this decline to increasing fatigue from work and childrearing and to growing familiarity with their sexual routine.

As men and women age, sexual arousal tends to build more slowly and orgasms tend to diminish in frequency and intensity. Males' refractory periods lengthen, and females' vaginal lubrication and elasticity decrease. Nevertheless, older people remain capable of rewarding sexual encounters. In a national survey of individuals ages 40 to 80, 79% of men and 69% of women reported having sex in the previous year (Laumann et al., 2009). In another study of participants 70 years or older, 18% of women and 41% of men were sexually active, with intercourse and masturbation being the most commonly reported sexual activities (Smith et al., 2007). Marrying for love, still being in love, and higher income are associated with sustained sexual activity in later adulthood (Papaharitou et al., 2008).

Sex in Homosexual Relationships

What about the frequency of sex among lesbian and gay couples? Peplau and her colleagues (2004) report three patterns. First, there is a general decline in the frequency of sexual behavior over time. Second, in the early stages of a relationship, gay males engage in sex more frequently than the other types of couples. For example, among couples who had been together for two years or less, 67% of gay men reported having sex three or more times a week, compared to 45% of married couples and 33% of lesbian couples (Blumstein & Schwartz, 1983). Third, lesbian couples have sex less often than other couples. Comparative studies find comparable levels of sexual satisfaction in gay, lesbian, and heterosexual couples (Kurdek, 2005). And for both lesbians and gay men, sexual satisfaction is correlated with overall relationship satisfaction.

12-5 Practical Issues in Sexual Activity

Regardless of the context of sexual activity, two practical issues are often matters of concern: contraception and sexually transmitted diseases. These topics are more properly in the domain of medicine than of psychology, but birth control and sex-related infections certainly do have their behavioral aspects.

12-5a CONTRACEPTION

Most people want to control whether and when they will conceive a child, so they need reliable contraception. Despite the availability of effective contraceptive methods, however, many people fail to exercise much control. In the United States, it is estimated that nearly half of pregnancies are unplanned (Finer & Henshaw, 2006).

Constraints on Effective Contraception

Effective contraception requires that intimate couples negotiate their way through a complex sequence of steps. First, both people must define themselves as sexually active. Second, both must have accurate knowledge about fertility and conception. Third, their chosen method of contraception must be readily accessible. Finally, both must have the motivation and skill to use the method correctly and consistently. Failure to meet even one of these conditions can result in an unintended pregnancy.

Many high school students (23% of girls and 16% of boys) use either withdrawal or no contraception at all (Santelli et al. 2006). These individuals are at high risk for pregnancy and sexually transmitted diseases. In addition, any couples who do not use condoms (even if they use another contraceptive method) can contract sexually transmitted diseases unless both partners have tested negatively for such infections.

Why do some individuals engage in risky sexual behavior? Researchers have identified various individual, interpersonal, and societal factors (Ayoola, Nettleman, & Brewer, 2007). Once again, conflicting norms about gender and sexual behavior play a role. Men are socialized to be the initiators of sexual activity, but when it comes to birth control, they often rely on women to take charge. It is hard for a woman to maintain an image of sexual naïveté and also be responsible for contraception. Telling her partner that she is "on the pill" or whipping out a condom could send an image of sexual eagerness. The mixed messages sent by some sexual education programs ("Use a condom but we can't supply you with one") add to the confusion. Finally, alcohol can undermine condom use.

Selecting a Contraceptive Method

How should an individual go about selecting a contraceptive method? A rational choice requires accurate knowledge of the effectiveness, benefits, costs, and risks of the various methods. The greater one's knowledge about birth control, the more likely one is to communicate with one's partner before sex (Ryan et al., 2007). Contraception is a joint responsibility. Hence, it's essential for partners to discuss their preferences, to decide what method(s) they are going to use, and to *act* on their decision. Let's look in more detail at two of the most widely used birth control methods in the Western world: hormone-based contraceptives and male condoms.

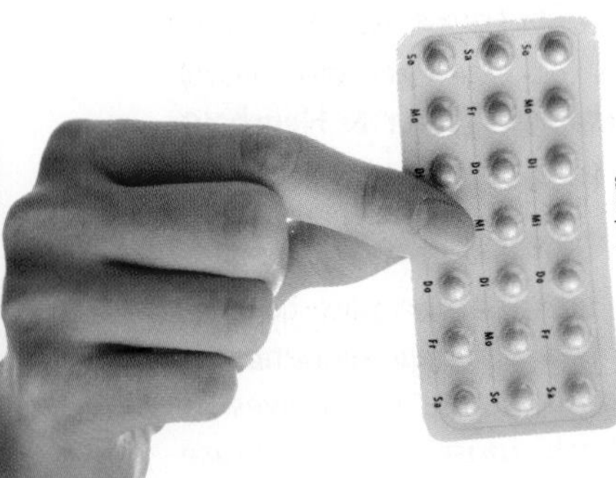

Hormone-based contraceptives contain synthetic forms of estrogen and progesterone (or progesterone only, in the minipill), which inhibit ovulation in women. Types of hormone-based contraceptives include "the pill," hormonal injectables (Depo-Provera), the transdermal patch (worn on the skin), the vaginal ring (inserted once a month), and contraceptive implants. Many couples prefer these birth control options because contraceptive use is not tied to the sex act. Only the interuterine device (IUD) permits a similar degree of sexual spontaneity. But these contraceptives do not protect against sexually transmitted diseases.

The *condom*, a barrier method of contraception, is a sheath worn over the penis during intercourse to collect ejaculated semen. The condom is the only widely available contraceptive device for use by males. A condom slightly reduces a man's sensitivity, but many men see this dulling as a plus because it can make sex last longer. Condoms can be purchased in any drugstore without a prescription. If used correctly, the condom is highly effective in preventing pregnancy and sexually transmitted diseases. It must be placed over the penis after erection but before any contact with the vagina, and space must be left at the tip to collect the ejaculate. The man should withdraw before completely losing his erection and firmly hold the rim of the condom during withdrawal to prevent any semen from spilling into the vagina. Other barrier methods include female condoms (which are inserted into the vagina), diaphragms, and spermicides.

Male condoms are made of polyurethane, latex rubber, or animal membranes ("skin"). Polyurethane condoms are thinner than latex condoms; however, they are more likely to break and to slip off than latex condoms. Using latex condoms definitely reduces the chances of contracting or passing on various sexually transmitted diseases. However, oil-based creams and lotions (petroleum jelly, massage oil, baby oil, and hand and body lotions, for example) should never be used with latex condoms (or diaphragms). Within 60 seconds, these products can make microscopic holes in the rubber membrane that are large enough to allow passage of HIV and organisms produced by other sexually transmitted diseases. Water-based lubricants such as Astroglide or K-Y Warming Liquid do not cause this problem. Polyurethane condoms are impervious to oils. Skin condoms do *not* offer protection against sexually transmitted diseases.

In closing, we should mention emergency contraception. Women may seek emergency contraception in cases of sexual assault, contraceptive failure, or unprotected sex. Progestin pills (also called "morning after" pills) are available from pharmacies without a prescription for women ages 18 and older (younger women must have a prescription) (Alan Guttmacher Institute, 2006). Morning after pills are 95% effective in preventing pregnancy if they are taken within 24 hours after intercourse (75% effective within 72 hours). The drug works like birth control pills, by preventing ovulation or fertilization and implantation of the fertilized egg into the uterine wall. If the fertilized egg is already implanted into the wall of the uterus, progestin will not harm it. By contrast, mifepristone (RU 486) is a drug that can induce a miscarriage in the first seven weeks of a pregnancy. Prescribed by a physician, mifepristone is typically administered in the form of two pills taken several days apart. Although no substitute for regular birth control, these drugs can be used after unprotected sex and are particularly helpful in cases of rape. They do not, however, provide any protection against sexually transmitted diseases.

Contraception is a joint responsibility.

© stockcam/iStockphoto

12-5b SEXUALLY TRANSMITTED DISEASES

A *sexually transmitted disease* (STD) is a disease or infection that is transmitted primarily through sexual contact. When people think of STDs (also referred to as sexually transmitted infections), they typically think of chlamydia and gonorrhea, but these diseases are only the tip of the iceberg. There are actually around 25 sexually transmitted diseases. Some of them—for instance, pubic lice—are minor nuisances that can readily be treated. Others, however, are severe afflictions that are difficult to treat. For instance, if it isn't detected early, syphilis can cause heart failure, blindness, and brain damage, and aquired immune deficiency syndrome (AIDS) is eventually fatal. Most of these infections are spread from one person to another through intercourse, oral-genital contact, or anal-genital contact.

Prevalence and Transmission

No one is immune to sexually transmitted diseases. Health authorities estimate that about 19 million new cases occur in the United States each year (Alan Guttmacher Institute, 2006). The highest incidence of STDs occurs in the under-25 age group (Cates, 2004). There are many types of sexually transmitted diseases. We will focus on HIV/AIDS and HPV.

An estimated 1.2 million people are living with HIV/AIDS (Centers for Disease Control, 2012b). The United States has seen a surge of HIV infections stemming from heterosexual transmission (Kaiser Family Foundation, 2006). And an estimated half of all new HIV infections occur in people under age 25. The rate of HIV infections is up among young gay and bisexual men, especially those of color (Kaiser Family Foundation, 2006). Unfortunately, the availability of new drug treatments for HIV seems to have increased risk taking among gay and bisexual men (Peterson & Bakeman, 2006).

AIDS is increasing more rapidly among women than among men, especially among blacks and Latinas (Kaiser Family Foundation, 2012a, 2012b). An increasing concern is that a woman's partner may be secretly having sex with other men and may deny that he is gay or bisexual (Kalb & Murr, 2006). This phenomenon, known as being on the "down low," is more common among black and Hispanic than white men, presumably because of cultural differences in attitudes toward homosexuality and bisexuality (Heath & Goggin, 2009). In one study, 22% of men on the down low had recently had both unprotected anal and vaginal sex (Siegel et al., 2008). Obviously, this lifestyle has serious implications for unknowing female partners in terms of increasing their risk for HIV infection or any STD.

© Elena Elisseeva/Shutterstock.com

Human papillomavirus (HPV) infections cause about half of STDs diagnosed among 15- to 24-year-olds (Alan Guttmacher Institute, 2006). HPV is increasingly common; it's estimated that 50% of sexually active men and women acquire genital HPV infections (Centers for Disease Control, 2012a). HPV tends to be more serious for women than men because certain types of HPV can lead to cervical cancer. In 2006, the U.S. Food and Drug Administration approved a vaccine (Gardisil) that will prevent infection with the types of HPV that lead to cervical cancer. The vaccination is recommended for both girls and boys, starting at age 11 (Alan Guttmacher Institute, 2012).

Prevention

Abstinence is obviously the best way to avoid acquiring STDs. Of course, for many people this is not an appealing or realistic option. Short of abstinence, the best strategy is to engage in sexual activity only in the context of a long-term relationship, where partners have an opportunity to know each other reasonably well.

Along with being judicious about sexual relations, you need to talk openly about safer sexual practices with your partner. But if you don't carry the process one step further and practice what you preach, you remain at risk.

We offer the following suggestions for safer sex:

- If you are not involved in a sexually exclusive relationship with someone free of disease, always use latex condoms with spermicides. They have a good track record of preventing STDs and offer effective protection against the AIDS virus. (And never use oil-based lubricants with latex condoms; use water-based lubricants instead.)
- If there is any possibility that you or your partner has an STD, abstain from sex, always use condoms, or use other types of sexual expression such as hand-genital stimulation.
- Don't have sex with lots of people. You increase your risk of contracting STDs.
- Don't have sex with someone who has had lots of previous partners. People won't always be honest about their sexual history, so it's important to know whether you can trust a prospective partner's word.
- Don't assume that the labels people attach to themselves (heterosexual or homosexual) accurately describe their actual sexual behavior. According to a study based on a nationally representative sample of individuals ages 15 to 44, 6% of males and 11% of females reported that they had had at least one same-gender sexual experience in their lives (Mosher, Chandra, & Jones, 2005).
- You should consider *any* activity that exposes you to blood (including menstrual blood), semen, vaginal secretions, urine, feces, or saliva as high-risk behavior *unless* you and your partner are in a mutual, sexually exclusive relationship and neither of you is infected.
- Because HIV is easily transmitted through anal intercourse, it's a good idea to avoid this type of sex. Rectal tissues are delicate and easily torn, thus letting the virus pass through the membrane. Always use a condom during anal sex.
- Oral-genital sex may also transmit HIV, particularly if semen is swallowed.
- Wash your genitals with mild soap and warm water before and after sexual contact.
- Urinate shortly after intercourse.
- Watch for sores, rashes, or discharge around the vulva or penis, or elsewhere on your body, especially the mouth. If you have cold sores, avoid kissing or oral sex.

If you have any reason to suspect that you have an STD, find a good health clinic and get tested *as soon as possible*. It's normal to be embarrassed or afraid of getting bad news, but don't delay. Health professionals are in the business of helping people, not judging them. To be really sure, get tested twice. If you have several sexual partners in a year, you should have regular STD checkups. You will have to ask for them, as most doctors and health clinics won't perform them otherwise.

Remember that the symptoms of some STDs disappear as the infection progresses. If your test results are positive, it's essential to get the proper treatment *right away*. Notify your sexual partner(s) so they can be tested immediately, too. And avoid sexual intercourse and oral sex until you and your partner are fully treated and a physician or clinic says you are no longer infectious.

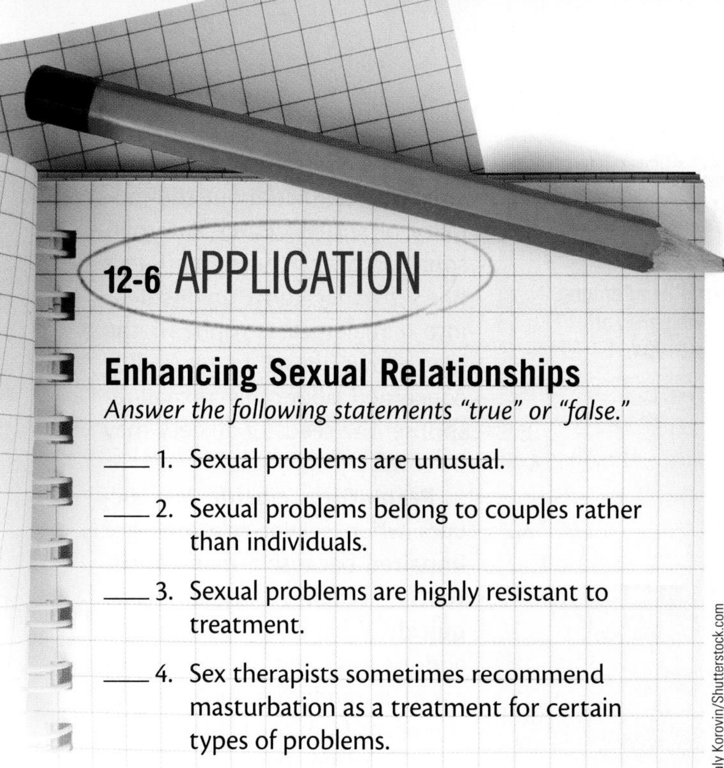

12-6 APPLICATION

Enhancing Sexual Relationships

Answer the following statements "true" or "false."

____ 1. Sexual problems are unusual.

____ 2. Sexual problems belong to couples rather than individuals.

____ 3. Sexual problems are highly resistant to treatment.

____ 4. Sex therapists sometimes recommend masturbation as a treatment for certain types of problems.

© Vitaly Korovin/Shutterstock.com

The answers are (1) false, (2) true, (3) false, and (4) true. If you missed several of these questions, you are by no means unusual. Misconceptions about sexuality are the norm rather than the exception. Fortunately, there is plenty of useful information on how to improve sexual relationships.

For the sake of simplicity, our advice is directed to heterosexual couples, but much of what we have to say is also relevant to same-gender couples. For advice aimed specifically at same-gender couples, we recommend *Permanent Partners: Building Gay and Lesbian Relationships That Last* by Betty Berzon (2004).

12-6a GENERAL SUGGESTIONS

Let's begin with some general ideas about how to enhance sexual relationships, drawn from several excellent books on sexuality (Carroll, 2007; Crooks & Baur, 2008; King, 2005). Even if you are satisfied with your sex life, these suggestions may be useful as "preventive medicine."

1. *Pursue adequate sex education.* The first step in promoting sexual satisfaction is to acquire accurate information about sex. The shelves of most bookstores are bulging with popular books on sex, but many of them are loaded with inaccuracies. A good bet is to pick up a college textbook or enroll in a course on human sexuality.

2. *Review your sexual values system.* Many sexual problems stem from a negative sexual values system that associates sex with immorality. The guilt feelings caused by such an orientation can interfere with sexual functioning. Thus, sex therapists often encourage adults to examine the sources and implications of their sexual values.

3. *Communicate about sex.* Good communication is essential in a sexual relationship. Many common problems—such as choosing an inconvenient time, too little erotic activity before intercourse, and too little tenderness afterward—are traceable largely to poor communication. Your partner is not a mindreader! You have to share your thoughts and feelings.

4. *Avoid goal setting.* Sexual encounters are not tests or races. Sexual experiences are usually best when people relax and enjoy themselves. People get overly concerned about orgasms or about both partners reaching orgasm simultaneously. It's better to adopt the philosophy that getting there is at least half the fun.

5. *Enjoy your sexual fantasies.* As we noted earlier, the mind is the ultimate erogenous zone. Research shows that sexual fantasies are most common among those who have the fewest sexual problems (Renaud & Byers, 2001). Men and women both report that their sexual fantasies increase their excitement. So don't be afraid to use fantasy to enhance your sexual arousal.

12-6b UNDERSTANDING SEXUAL DYSFUNCTION

Many people struggle with ***sexual dysfunctions*—impairments in sexual functioning that cause subjective distress.** Figure 12.8 on the next page shows the prevalence of some of the most common sexual problems (Laumann et al., 1994).

Let's examine the symptoms and causes of four common sexual dysfunctions: erectile difficulties, premature ejaculation, orgasmic difficulties, and low sexual desire.

***Erectile difficulties* occur when a man is persistently unable to achieve or maintain an erection adequate for intercourse.** (The traditional name for this

© Deklofenak/Shutterstock.com

FIGURE 12.8 Sexual dysfunction in normal couples

This graph shows the prevalence of various sexual dysfunctions during a year in a probability sample of American men and women. The most common problems among men are premature ejaculation and anxiety about performance; in women, they are lack of interest in sex and orgasmic difficulties. (Based on Laumann et al., 1994)

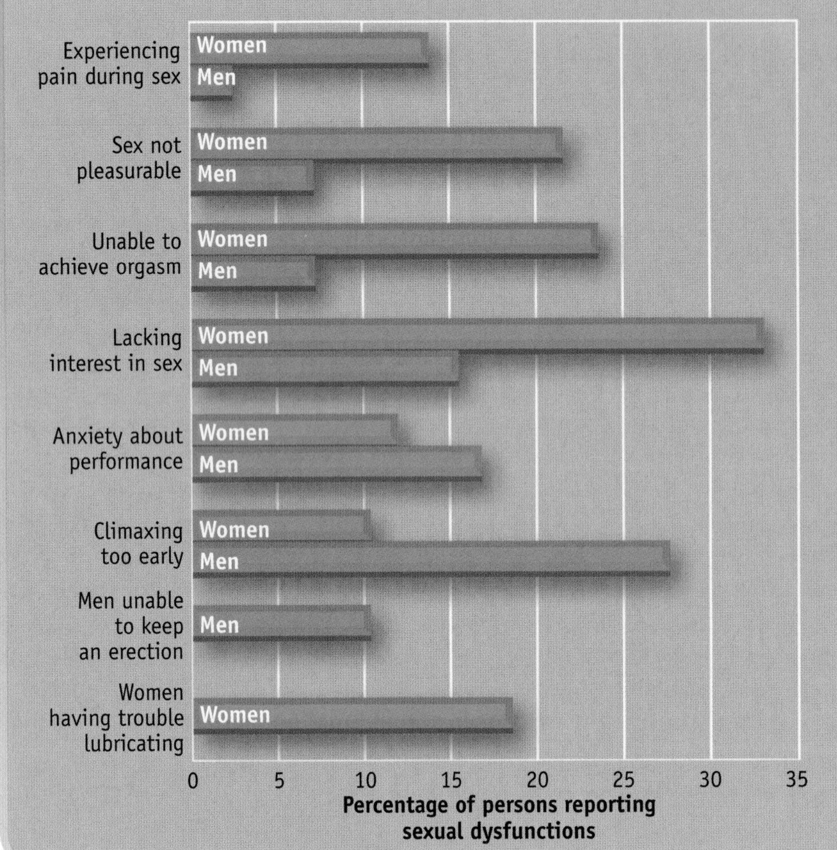

problem is *impotence*, but sex therapists have discarded the term because of its demeaning connotation.) In a recent international study of 27 countries, nearly half the men surveyed reported having erectile difficulties (Mulhall et al., 2008).

Physical factors can play a role in erectile dysfunction. For example, experts estimate that as many as 25% of all cases may be the result of side effects from medication (Miller, 2000). A host of common diseases (such as obesity, diabetes, heart disease, and high blood pressure) can produce erectile problems as a side effect. Many temporary conditions, such as fatigue, worry about work, an argument with one's partner, a depressed mood, or too much alcohol, can cause such incidents.

The most common psychological cause of erectile difficulties is anxiety about sexual performance. Anxiety may stem from doubts about virility or conflict about the morality of sexual desires. Interpersonal factors can have an effect if one's partner turns an incident into a major catastrophe. If the man allows himself to get unduly concerned about his sexual response, the seeds of anxiety may be sown.

Premature ejaculation **occurs when sexual relations are impaired because a man consistently reaches orgasm too quickly.** What is "too quickly"? To address this question, researchers asked a random sample of sex therapists from the United States and Canada for their expert opinions (Corty & Guardiani, 2008). They found that sustaining intercourse 3 to 13 minutes is not worthy of concern. Obviously, such time estimates, even from "experts," are arbitrary. The critical consideration is the subjective feelings of the partners. If either partner feels that the ejaculation is persistently too fast for sexual gratification, the couple have a problem. Approximately 29% of men repeatedly experience premature ejaculation (Laumann et al., 1994).

What causes this dysfunction? Some men who have a lifelong history of quick ejaculation may have a neurophysiological predisposition to the condition. Biological causes include hormones, thyroid problems, or inflammation of the prostate. Psychological causes can include stress, depression, or anger at one's partner. Some therapists believe that early sexual experiences in which a rapid climax was advantageous (or necessary to avoid being discovered) can establish a habit of rapid ejaculation.

Orgasmic difficulties **occur when people experience sexual arousal but have persistent problems in achieving orgasm.** When this problem occurs in men, it is often called *male orgasmic disorder.* The traditional name for this problem in women, *frigidity,* is no longer used because of its derogatory implications. Since this problem is much more common among women, we'll limit our discussion to them.

Physical causes of orgasmic difficulties are rare (although medications can be a problem). One of the leading psychological causes is a negative attitude toward sex. Women who have been taught that sex is dirty or sinful are likely to approach it with shame and guilt. These feelings can undermine arousal, inhibit sexual expression, and impair orgasmic responsiveness. Arousal may also be inhibited by fear of pregnancy or excessive concern about achieving orgasm.

***Hypoactive sexual desire,* or the lack of interest in sexual activity,** seems to be on the rise. Individuals with this problem rarely initiate sex or tend to avoid sexual activities with their partner. It occurs in both men and women, but it is more common among women (see Figure 12.8). Many attribute the recent increases in this problem to the fast pace of contemporary life and to couples' heavy workloads both at home and at work. In men, low sexual desire is often related to embarrassment about erectile dysfunction. In women, it is most often associated with relationship difficulties. Sometimes the problem arises when a person is trying to sort out his or her sexual orientation. Hypoactive desire tends to increase with age. In fact, low desire was the most commonly reported sexual problem for women in a national sample of adults ages 57 to 85 (Lindau et al., 2007).

12-6c COPING WITH SPECIFIC PROBLEMS

With the advent of modern sex therapy, sexual problems no longer have to be chronic sources of frustration and shame. ***Sex therapy* involves the professional treatment of sexual dysfunctions.** Masters and Johnson reported high success rates for their treatments of specific problems, and there is a consensus that sexual dysfunctions can be overcome with regularity. The advent of medications to treat sexual problems (such as Viagra) has resulted in an increased emphasis on medical and individual treatments over relationship interventions. Nonetheless, couple-based treatment approaches definitely have their place and are effective. If you're looking for a sex therapist, be sure to find someone who is qualified to work in this specialized field. One professional credential to look for is that provided by the American Association of Sex Educators, Counselors, and Therapists (AASECT).

© B BOISSONNET/Age fotostock

Erectile Difficulties

Viagra, the much-touted pill for treating erectile disorders, is about 80% effective. Still, it is not without its drawbacks—some of them life threatening. Cialis and Levitra are two similar pills that enhance erections. These drugs affect the muscles in the penis, allowing them to relax, which in turn increases the blood flow and results in an erection (Mayo Clinic, 2008).

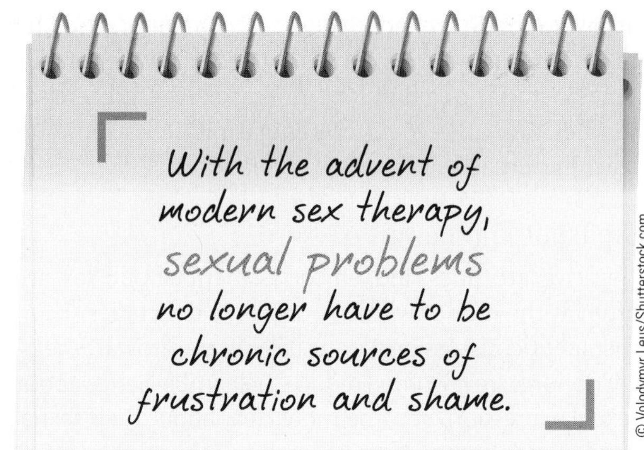
With the advent of
modern sex therapy,
sexual problems
no longer have to be
chronic sources of
frustration and shame.
© Volodymyr Leus/Shutterstock.com

The expectation that a pill alone will solve sexual problems that stem from relationship or psychological issues can set men up for additional sexual dysfunction. To overcome psychologically based erectile difficulties, the key is to decrease the man's performance anxiety. It is a good idea for a couple to discuss the problem openly. The woman should be reassured that the difficulty does not reflect lack of affection by her partner. Obviously, it is crucial for her to be emotionally supportive rather than hostile and demanding.

Premature Ejaculation

Men troubled by premature ejaculation range from those who climax almost instantly to those who cannot last the time that their partner requires. In the latter case, simply slowing down the tempo of intercourse may help. Sometimes the problem can be solved indirectly by discarding the traditional assumption that orgasms should come through intercourse. If the female partner enjoys oral or manual stimulation, these techniques can be used to provide her with an orgasm either before or after intercourse. This strategy can reduce the performance pressure for the male partner, and couples may find that intercourse starts to last longer.

For the problem of instant ejaculation, two treatments are effective: the *stop-start method* and the *squeeze technique*. With both, the woman brings the man to the verge of orgasm through manual stimulation. Then, she either stops stimulating him (stop-start technique) or squeezes the base or the end of his penis firmly for 3–5 seconds (squeeze technique) until he calms down. She repeats this procedure three or four times before bringing him to orgasm. These exercises can help a man recognize preorgasmic sensations and teach him that he can delay ejaculation.

Orgasmic Difficulties

Negative attitudes and embarrassment about sex are often at the root of women's orgasmic difficulties. Thus, therapeutic discussions are usually geared toward helping nonorgasmic women reduce their ambivalence about sexual expression, become more clear about their sexual needs, and become more assertive about them. Sex therapists often suggest that women who have never had an orgasm try to have one first through masturbation. Many women achieve orgasms with a partner after an initial breakthrough with self-stimulation. To make this transition, it is essential that the woman express her sexual wishes to her partner.

When a woman's orgasmic difficulties stem from not feeling close to her partner, treatment usually focuses on couples' relationship problems more than on sexual functioning per se. Therapists also focus on helping couples improve their communication skills.

Hypoactive Sexual Desire

Therapists consider reduced sexual desire the most challenging sexual problem to treat (Aubin & Heiman, 2004). This is because the problem usually has multiple causes, which can also be difficult to identify. If the problem is a result of fatigue from overwork, couples may be encouraged to allot more time to personal and relationship needs. Sometimes hypoactive sexual desire reflects relationship problems. Treatment for reduced sexual desire is usually more intensive than that for more specific sexual disorders, and it is usually multifaceted in order to deal with the multiple aspects of the problem.

Medications can be used for low sexual desire. For instance, some older men take supplemental testosterone to offset the age-related decline in this hormone. Hormonal therapies are also used for postmenopausal women. The medical and financial success of Viagra has encouraged pharmaceutical companies to develop drugs that will boost women's sexual desire. Still, drugs will not solve relationship problems. For these, couples therapy is needed. And as we have seen for most problematic issues in this chapter, communication between partners is crucial.

© Adam Gregor/Shutterstock.com

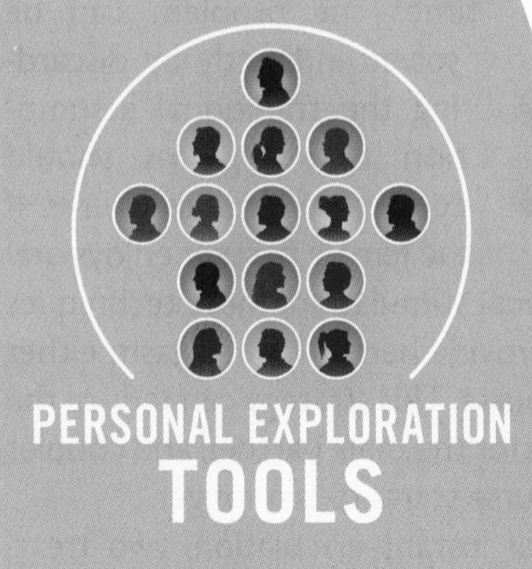

Curious about yourself? To learn more about how topics in this chapter relate to you, go online to CourseMate at www.cengagebrain.com where you can:

- Complete a **Self-Reflection** exercise that will help you think about your personal experiences in relation to topics in the chapter.
- Take a **Self-Assessment** scale that will show you how you score on a research instrument that measures personality traits or attitudes.
- Explore **Recommended Readings** that will provide brief overviews of useful self-help books.

© edge69/iStockphoto

STUDY TOOLS ▶ 12

Ready to study? In your book you can:

- **Test Yourself** with a multiple-choice quiz (below)
- Rip out the **Chapter Review card** (in the back of the book) to refresh yourself on the chapter's Key Ideas and Key Terms

Or you can go online to CourseMate at www.cengagebrain.com where you can:

- Take additional Practice Quizzes to prepare for your exam
- Review Key Terms with flash cards and a crossword puzzle
- View videos that expand on selected concepts

TEST YOURSELF

1. In rare cases, sexual differentiation during the prenatal period is incomplete and infants are born with ambiguous genitals. These individuals are referred to as

a. bisexual.
b. transsexual.
c. homosexual.
d. intersex.

2. Which of the following statements about sexual orientation is true?

a. Heterosexuality and homosexuality are best viewed as two distinct categories.
b. Sexual orientation is complex and malleable.
c. Biological factors alone probably determine sexual orientation.
d. Environmental factors alone probably determine sexual orientation.

3. Stacy is in the initial phase of sexual arousal. Her muscles are tense and her heart rate and blood pressure are elevated. She is in which phase of Masters and Johnson's sexual response cycle?

a. Foreplay
b. Orgasm
c. Excitement
d. Resolution

4. Sexual fantasies

a. are signs of abnormality.
b. are harmless ways to enhance sexual excitement.
c. rarely include having sex with someone other than one's partner.
d. are an excellent indication of what people want to experience in reality.

5. Which of the following is the technical term for vaginal intercourse?

a. Coitus
b. Tribadism
c. Cunnilingus
d. Fellatio

6. Regarding overall relationship satisfaction and sexual satisfaction in committed relationships, research indicates there is

a. a strong relationship.
b. a weak relationship.
c. no relationship.
d. a strong relationship, but only in the first year of marriage.

7. The frequency of sex tends to decrease as the years pass for which of the following couples?

a. Heterosexual couples
b. Heterosexual and gay male couples
c. Heterosexual and lesbian couples
d. Heterosexual, lesbian, and gay male couples

8. Which of the following statements about condoms is true?

a. It's okay to use oil-based lubricants with latex condoms.
b. Polyurethane condoms are thicker than latex condoms.
c. Skin condoms provide protection against STDs.
d. It's okay to use water-based lubricants with latex condoms.

9. Sexually transmitted diseases

a. are all very serious.
b. always cause symptoms right away.
c. are most common among people under age 25.
d. are most common among people between 26 and 40.

10. Which of the following is *not* one of the text's suggestions for enhancing your sexual relationships?

a. Pursue adequate sex education.
b. Review your sexual values system.
c. Communicate about sex.
d. Set clear goals for each sexual encounter.

Answers: 1. d, page 252; 2. b, page 255; 3. c, page 257; 4. b, page 260; 5. a, page 261; 6. a, page 262; 7. d, pages 262–263; 8. d, page 265; 9. c, page 265; 10. d, page 267

LEARNING OBJECTIVES

13-1 Understand some key factors that influence career interests and choices.

13-2 Identify some major changes and challenges occurring in the workplace.

13-3 Analyze the potential impact of job stress, sexual harassment, and unemployment.

13-4 Recognize the problems posed by workaholism and work-family conflicts.

13-5 Develop skills for writing an effective résumé and interviewing well for jobs.

After you have read the chapter, you can Test Yourself and learn about other Study Tools on page 293.

CHAPTER 13

CAREERS and WORK

Working is a defining characteristic in the lives of many people. Consider this: Do most of the people you know identify themselves by what they do in their careers? Do you introduce yourself by name and your major area of study, which is a way of alluding to your intended profession? When you meet someone new, isn't one of the first things you ask something like, "So, what do you do for a living?" How people reply to this question reveals information not only about their occupation, but also about their social status, educational background, lifestyle, personality, interests, and aptitudes. In Figure 13.1, you can see that how people view their jobs is strongly correlated with their income. In a very real sense, people *are* what they do at work. If that observation make sense to you, it should come as no surprise that being unemployed can have devastating consequences for people's sense of self and well-being.

Because work is such a significant aspect of life, psychologists take a great interest in it. ***Industrial/organizational (I/O) psychology*** **is the study of human behavior in the workplace.** I/O psychologists strive to increase the dignity and performance of workers and the organizations where they labor (Zedek, 2011). Among other issues, I/O psychologists study worker motivation and satisfaction, job performance, leadership, occupational hazards, personnel selection, and diversity in organizations. A recent concern is how individuals balance work and family life (Greenhaus & Powell, 2006). An imbalance between these two spheres can lead to what I/O psychologists call work-family conflict.

FIGURE 13.1 How workers view their jobs

The way workers view their jobs is strongly related to their income. Those who earn higher salaries are more likely to obtain a sense of identity from their work, whereas those who earn lower salaries typically see their jobs merely as a way to make a living. (Data from Moore, 2001)

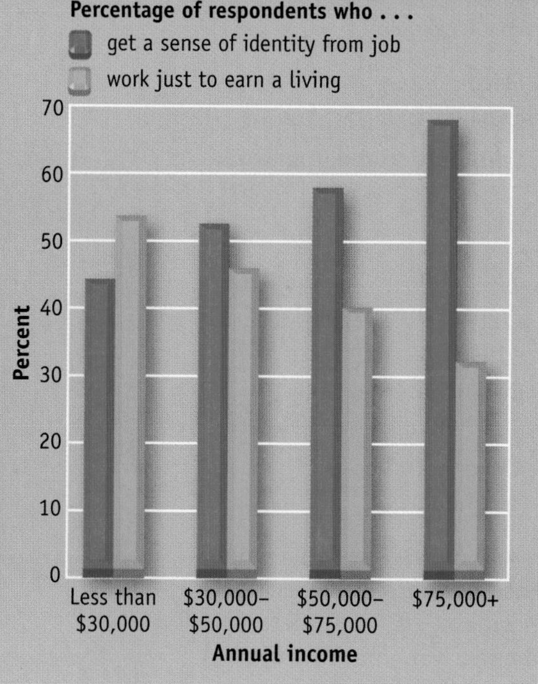

> **Aside from sleeping, most people spend more time working than in any other activity.**

We begin this chapter by reviewing some important considerations in choosing a career. Next, we examine how the workplace and workforce are changing and look at some occupational hazards such as job stress, sexual harassment, and unemployment. Finally, we address the important issues of balancing work, relationships, and leisure. In the Application, we offer some concrete suggestions for enhancing your chances of landing a desirable job.

© Angela Waye/Shutterstock.com

13-1 Choosing a Career

The average person works at least 8 hours a day, 5 days a week, 50 weeks a year, for 40 to 45 years. Some people work much more and, admittedly, some work considerably less. Still, such a time commitment—really, a lifetime commitment—implies that you should both enjoy and be proficient at what you do for a living. Imagine the dissatisfaction, if not drudgery, that people who neither like their careers nor are adept at them feel all the time. Aside from sleeping, most people spend more time working than in any other activity. Just consider a typical weekday:

Sleep
6–8 hours

Commute to and from work
1–2 hours

Work
8 hours

Prepare and eat meals
2 hours

TV and Internet time
1–3 hours

Other activities
1–2 hours

As you can see, the importance of your career decision is enormous. It may determine whether you are employed or unemployed, financially secure or insecure, happy or unhappy. In theory, what's involved in making a successful career choice is pretty straightforward. First, you need to have a clear grasp of your personal characteristics. Second, you need realistic information about potential careers. From there, it's just a matter of selecting an occupation that is a good match with your personal characteristics. In reality, however, the process is a lot more complicated than simply finding a match between these two elements. Let's take a closer look.

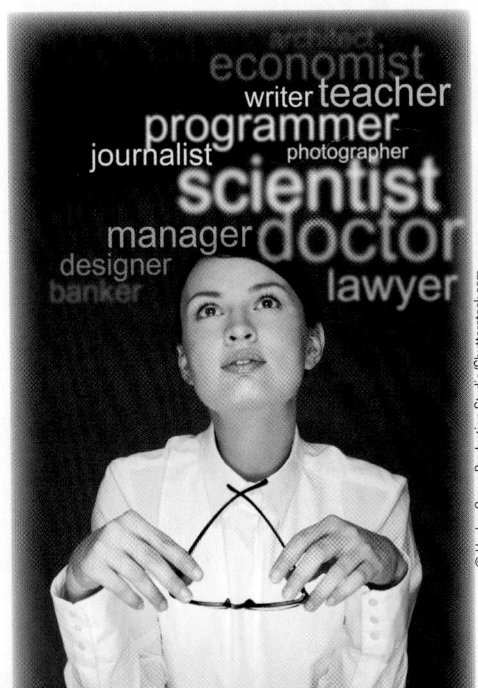

© Hasloo Group Production Studio/Shutterstock.com

13-1a EXAMINING PERSONAL CHARACTERISTICS AND FAMILY INFLUENCES

People with limited job skills and qualifications (education, training, experience) have limited job options. As a result, they often have to take whatever job is available rather than a job that is well suited for them. In fact, *choosing* a career is a luxury usually afforded to the middle and upper classes. For those who *are* able to select a career, personal qualities and family influences come into play.

Personal Characteristics

Making career decisions can be scary. What personal characteristics affect career choice? Although *intelligence* does not necessarily predict occupational success, it does predict the likelihood of entering particular occupations. That's because intelligence is related to academic success—the ticket required to enter certain fields. Professions such as law, medicine, and engineering are open only to those who can meet increasingly selective criteria as they advance from high school to college to graduate education and professional training.

In many occupations, special talents are more important than general intelligence. *Specific aptitudes* that might make a person well suited for certain occupations include creativity, artistic or musical talent, mechanical ability, clerical skill, mathematical ability, and persuasive talents. A particularly crucial characteristic is *social skills,* since teams are increasingly important in a wide variety of organizations (Kozlowski & Bell, 2003). A worker must be able not only to get along well with peers but also to counsel or supervise them.

As people travel through life, they acquire a variety of *interests.*

Are you intrigued by the business world? the academic world? international affairs? the outdoors? physical sciences? music? athletics? art and culture? human services? hospitality and recreation? The list of potential interests is virtually infinite. Because interests underlie your motivation for work and your job satisfaction, they should definitely be considered in your career planning. Finally, it is important to choose an occupation that is compatible with your *personality* (Swanson & D'Achiardi, 2005).

Family Influences

Individuals' career choices are strongly influenced by their family background (Whiston & Keller, 2004). That is, the jobs that appeal to people tend to be like those of their parents. For instance, people who grow up in middle-class homes are likely to aspire to high-paying professions in law, medicine, or engineering. On the other hand, individuals from low-income families often lean toward blue-collar jobs in construction work, office work, and food services.

Family background influences career choice for several reasons. For one thing, a key predictor of occupational status is the number of years of education an individual has completed (Arbona, 2005). And because parents and children often attain similar levels of education, they are likely to have similar jobs. Second, career attainment is related to socioeconomic status. The factors that mediate this relationship are educational aspirations and attainment during the school years (Schoon & Parsons, 2002). This means that parents and teachers can help boost children's career aspirations and opportunities by encouraging them to do well in school.

Finally, parenting practices come into play. Most children from middle-class homes are encouraged to be curious and independent, qualities that are essential to success in many high-status occupations. By contrast, children from lower-status families are often taught to conform and obey (Hochschild, 2003). As a result, they may have less opportunity to develop the qualities demanded in high-status jobs.

Career decisions are shaped by family background. For instance, many people pursue the same career as one of their parents.

Photo: © s_bukley/Shutterstock.com; Frame: © Picsfive/Shutterstock.com

13-1b RESEARCHING JOB CHARACTERISTICS

The second step in selecting an occupation is seeking out information about jobs. Because the sheer number of jobs is overwhelming, you have to narrow the scope of your search before you can start gathering information.

Sources of Career Information

Once you have selected some jobs that might interest you, the next question is: Where do you get information about them? A helpful place to start is the *Occupational Outlook Handbook*, available in most libraries and on the Internet. This government document, published every two years by the U.S. Bureau of Labor Statistics, is a comprehensive guide to occupations. It includes job descriptions, education and training requirements, salaries, and employment outlooks for over 800 occupations. In addition, it details numerous career information resources, including those geared toward the military, disabled persons, women, and minorities. You can also find tips on locating jobs and accepting salary offers in this useful resource.

If you want more detailed information on particular occupations, you can usually get it by doing some online searching. If you're interested in a career in psychology, you can obtain a number of pamphlets or books from the American Psychological Association (APA) or consult a book on bachelor's level careers in psychology by Eric Landrum (2009).

Essential Information About Occupations

When you examine occupational literature and interview people, what kinds of information should you seek? To some extent, the answer depends on your unique interests, values, and needs. However, some things are of concern to virtually anyone. Workers typically give high ratings to good health insurance, retirement plans, limited job stress, and recognition for performing well (Saad, 1999). Some key issues you need to know about include:

- *The nature of the work.* What would your duties and responsibilities be on a day-to-day basis?
- *Working conditions.* Is the work environment pleasant or unpleasant, low key or high pressure?
- *Job entry requirements.* What education and training are required to break into this occupational area?
- *Ongoing training or education.* Will you need to continue learning within or outside the workplace in order to remain proficient at your occupation?
- *Potential earnings.* What are entry-level salaries, and how much can you hope to earn if you're exceptionally successful? What does the average person earn? What are the fringe benefits?
- *Potential status.* What is the social status associated with this occupation? Is it personally satisfactory for you?
- *Opportunities for advancement.* How do you move up in this field? Are there adequate opportunities for promotion and advancement?
- *Intrinsic job satisfaction.* Apart from money and formal fringe benefits, what can you derive in the way of personal satisfaction from this job? Will it allow you to help people, have fun, be creative, or shoulder responsibility?
- *Future outlook.* What is the projected supply and demand for this occupational area?
- *Security.* Is the work apt to be stable, or can the job disappear if there is an economic downturn?

By the way, if you're wondering whether your college education will be worth the effort in terms of dollars and cents, the answer generally is yes. As we'll discuss shortly, the jobs that you can obtain with a college degree typically yield higher pay than those that require less education (Crosby & Moncarz, 2006). Educational attainment alone, however, does not predict who performs well in a given job setting. In other words, having a college degree is not as important as the grades you earn during college. Why? Higher grade point averages (GPAs) point to the ability to be trained, which in turn influences subsequent job performance (Roth et al., 1996), and salary level (Roth & Clarke, 1998). Still, experts agree that the future belongs to those who are better educated (Gordon, 2006).

13-1c USING PSYCHOLOGICAL TESTS FOR CAREER DECISIONS

If you are undecided about an occupation, you might consider taking some tests at your campus counseling center. ***Occupational interest inventories*** **measure your interests as they relate to various jobs or careers.** Two widely used tests of this type are the Strong Interest Inventory (SII) and the Self-Directed Search (SDS) (Brown, 2007).

Occupational interest inventories do not attempt to predict whether you would be successful in various occupations. Rather, they focus more on the likelihood of job *satisfaction* than job *success*. When you take an occupational interest inventory, you receive many scores indicating how similar your interests are to the typical interests of people in various occupations. For example, a high score on the accountant scale of a test means that your interests are similar to those of the average accountant. This correspondence in interests does not guarantee that you would enjoy a career in accounting, but it is a moderately good predictor of job satisfaction (Hansen, 2005).

Although interest inventories can be helpful in working through career decisions, several cautions are worth noting. First, you may score high on some occupations that you're sure you would hate. Given the sheer number of occupational scales on the tests, this can easily happen by chance. However, you shouldn't dismiss the remainder of the test results just because you're sure that a few specific scores are "wrong." Second, don't let the test make career decisions for you. Some students naively believe that they should pursue whatever occupation yields their highest score. That is not how the tests are meant to be used. They merely provide information for you to consider. Ultimately, you have to think things out for yourself.

Third, you should be aware that most occupational interest inventories have a lingering gender bias. Many of these scales were originally developed 30 to 40 years ago when outright discrimination or more subtle discouragement prevented women from entering many traditionally "male" occupations. Critics assert that interest inventories have helped channel women into gender-typed careers, such as nursing and teaching, while guiding them away from more prestigious "male" occupations, such as medicine and engineering. Undoubtedly, this was true in the past. Recently, progress has been made toward reducing gender bias in occupational tests, although it has not been eliminated (Hansen, 2005). Research suggests that ethnic bias on interest tests is less of a concern than gender bias (Worthington, Flores, & Navarro, 2005).

© Scott Eells/Bloomberg via Getty Images

People vary in their preferences for work environments. Some like high-pressure work; others prefer more low-key jobs.

13-1d TAKING IMPORTANT CONSIDERATIONS INTO ACCOUNT

As you contemplate your career options, here are some important points to keep in mind.

1. *You have the potential for success in a variety of occupations.* Career counselors stress that people have multiple potentials. Considering the huge variety of job opportunities, it's foolish to believe that only one career would be right for you.

2. *Be cautious about choosing a career solely on the basis of salary.* Because of the tremendous emphasis on material success in America, people are often tempted to choose a career solely on the basis of income or status. However, research suggests that meaning and purpose, rather than money, lead to happiness and well-being (Diener & Biswas-Diener, 2008). When people ignore personal characteristics in choosing a career, they risk being mismatched. Such job mismatching can result in boredom, frustration, and unhappiness with one's work, and these negative feelings can spill over into other spheres of life.

3. *There are limits on your career options.* Entry into a particular occupation is not simply a matter of choosing what you want to do. It's a two-way street. You get to make choices, but you also have to persuade schools and employers to choose you. Your career options will be limited to some extent by factors beyond your control, including fluctuations in the economy and the job market.

4. *Career choice is a developmental process that extends throughout life.* Occupational choice involves not a single decision but a series of decisions. Although this process was once believed to extend only from prepuberty to the early 20s, authorities now recognize that the process continues throughout life. Some experts predict that the average person will have ten jobs over the course of his or her working life (Levitt, 2006). Making occupational choices is not limited to one's youth.

5. *Some career decisions are not easily undone.* Although it's never too late to strike out in new career directions, it is important to recognize that many decisions are not readily reversed. Few middle-aged lawyers suddenly decide to attend medical school or become elementary school teachers, for example, but it does happen. Once you invest time, money, and effort in moving along a particular career path, it may not be easy to change paths.

In the next section, we explore changes in the nature of work and the workforce.

13-2 The Changing World of Work

Before you enter the working world, it's important to get your bearings. In this section we look at several important background issues: contemporary trends in the workplace, the relationship between education and earnings, and diversity in the workforce.

13-2a WORKPLACE TRENDS

Work **is an activity that produces something of value for others.** For some people, work is just a way to earn a living; for others, work is a way of life. For both types of workers, the nature of work is undergoing dramatic changes. Because such changes can affect your future job prospects, you need to be aware of seven important trends:

1. *Technology is changing the nature of work.* Computers and electronic equipment have dramatically transformed the workplace. These changes have both down

sides and up sides. On the negative side, computers automate many jobs that people perform, eliminating jobs. The digital workplace also demands that employees have more education and skills than were previously required (Cetron & Davies, 2003). On the positive side, technological advances allow employees to work at home and to communicate with others in distant offices and while traveling. Working at home while being electronically connected to the office is called *telecommuting* (Lautsch, Kossek, & Ernst, 2011), and approximately 47% of organizations use some form of it (SHRM, 2008). Telecommuting provides psychological as well as obvious practical benefits for workers, including lower levels of work-family life conflict and higher job satisfaction (Gajendran & Harrison, 2007).

2. *New work attitudes are required.* Yesterday's workers could usually count on job security. But today's workers have job security only as long as they can add value to a company. This situation means that workers must take a more active role in shaping their careers. In addition, they must develop a variety of valuable skills, be productive workers, and skillfully market themselves to prospective employers. In the new work environment, the keys to job success are self-direction, self-management, up-to-date knowledge and skills, flexibility, and mobility (Smith, 2000).

3. *Lifelong learning is a necessity.* Experts predict that today's jobs are changing so rapidly that in many cases, work skills will become obsolete over a 10- to 15-year period (Lock, 2005a). Thus, lifelong learning and training will become essential for employees. Every year, nearly one-third of American workers take courses to improve their job skills. Workers who know "how to learn" will be able to keep pace with the rapidly changing workplace and will be highly valued. Those who cannot may be left behind.

4. *Independent workers are increasing.* Corporations are downsizing and restructuring to cope with the changing economy and to be competitive globally. In doing so, they are slashing thousands of permanent jobs and doling out the work to temporary employees or to workers in other countries, a practice termed *outsourcing.* By reducing the number of regular workers, companies can chop their expenditures on payroll, health insurance, and pension plans, as temporary employees don't typically receive such benefits. According to Daniel Pink (2001), one way to survive in this new environment is to become a "free agent" and hire out your skills to one or more organizations on a contract basis. Many professionals thrive on contract work; they have freedom, flexibility, and high incomes. But for those who are short on skills and entrepreneurial spirit, this work can be stressful and risky. About a third of independent employees would prefer to work for someone else than to work for themselves (Bond et al., 2003).

5. *The boundaries between work and home are breaking down.* As already noted, today's technological advances allow people to work at home and stay in touch with the office via high-speed Internet, telephones, and fax machines. Working at home is convenient—workers save time (no commuting) and money (on gas, parking, clothes). Still, family members and friends may interrupt home-workers, necessitating setting rules to protect work time. With the advent of smart phones, expanding wireless networks, and handheld computers, employees can be contacted any time and any place, making some workers feel as though they are on an "electronic leash." Looking at the flip side, the availability of onsite day care in some large companies means that a traditional home function has moved to the office (Drago, 2007). This development is largely a response to increases in the number of single-parent families and ***dual-earner households,* in which both partners are employed.** Consider this fact: Over 40% of today's workers have children under the age of 18 (O'Toole & Ferry, 2002). Thus, quality onsite day care is a big draw to workers because it allows parents to interact with their children during the day.

© jo unruh/iStockphoto

6. *The highest job growth will occur in the professional and service occupations.* The United States, like many other industrialized nations, continues to shift from a manufacturing, or "goods-producing," economy to a service-producing one (U.S. Bureau of Labor Statistics, 2006). Whereas the bulk of yesterday's jobs were in manufacturing, construction, agriculture, and mining, the jobs of the next decade will be in the professional

(and related technical) occupations and service occupations. Among the professional occupations, jobs in the computer and health care industries are expected to expand dramatically. In psychology, jobs in health, clinical, counseling, and school psychology are expected to show strong growth. In the service occupations, strong job growth should occur in education, health services, social services, professional services, and business services.

7. *Job sharing is becoming more common.* Not everyone wants to work a 40-hour week or is able to do so. Having the opportunity to job share—that is, to share one job between two people—may be beneficial. Fewer than 20% of organizations currently provide this option (Burke, 2005). When sharing a job, each person usually works 20 hours per week at separate times. As you can imagine, job sharing is ideal for people who have small children or other family obligations, are enrolled in degree programs, want to work part time, or are considering gradually winding down their careers.

13-2b EDUCATION AND EARNINGS

Although many jobs exist for individuals without a college degree, these jobs usually offer the lowest pay and benefits. In fact, all but one (air traffic controller) of the fifty highest-paying occupations require a college degree or higher (U.S. Bureau of Labor Statistics, 2010). In Figure 13.2, you can see that the more you learn, the more you earn. Having a college degree is also associated with more career options, greater opportunities for professional advancement, and lower unemployment (Dohm & Wyatt, 2002). The link between learning and earning holds for both males and females, although, as you can see, men are paid approximately $12,000 to $35,000 more than women with the same educational credentials.

On the other hand, a college diploma is no guarantee of a great job. In fact, many college graduates are underemployed. ***Underemployment*** **is settling for a job that does not fully utilize one's skills, abilities, and training.** About 18% of college graduates take jobs that don't usually require a college degree (Lock, 2005a) and this percentage may increase in times of economic distress. And while it's true that the jobs you can obtain with a college degree pay more than those requiring less education, the higher-paying jobs go to college graduates with *college-level* reading, writing, and quantitative skills. College graduates without these skills more often end up in high-school-level jobs (Pryor & Schaffer, 1997).

Current employers are not very happy with the academic skills of many of their employees. According to a survey by the College Board's National Commission on Writing, a majority of U.S. employers say that about a third of their workers do not meet the writing requirements for their positions (College Entrance Examination Board, 2004). The ability to write clearly, concisely, and well is a skill that any savvy college graduate should tout to potential employers.

FIGURE 13.2 | Education and income

This graph shows the average incomes of year-round, full-time workers age 18 and over, by gender and educational attainment. As you can see, the more education people have, the higher their income tends to be. However, at all levels women earn less than men with comparable education. (Data from U.S. Bureau of the Census, 2006b)

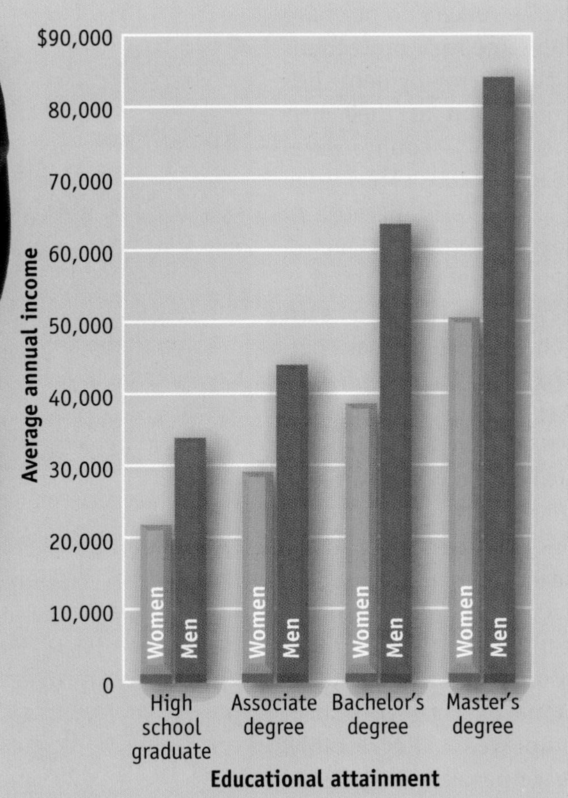

13-2c THE CHANGING WORKFORCE

The *labor force* consists of all those who are employed as well as those who are currently unemployed but are looking for work. In this section, we look at some of the changes affecting the labor force and consider how women and other minorities fare in the workplace.

Demographic Changes

The workforce is becoming increasingly diverse with regard to both gender and ethnicity. In 2005, 61% of married women worked, compared to 41% in 1970 (U.S. Bureau of the Census, 2006b). This percentage increase holds even for women with very young children. The workforce is also becoming more ethnically diversified (Tossi, 2009), as you can see in Figure 13.3. High school graduation rates for Asian Americans match those for European Americans, but college graduation rates for Asian Americans exceed those of European Americans. Both high school and college graduation rates of Hispanics and African Americans lag behind those of European Americans, although they have been improving in recent decades (Worthington et al., 2005). Consequently, both groups are at a disadvantage when it comes to competing for the better jobs.

Although gay, lesbian, and bisexual workers have been longstanding participants in the workplace, they are often "closeted" for fear of discrimination. Most of these workers do not have the same legal protections against employment discrimination as their heterosexual counterparts (Badgett, 2003). Thus, wage gaps can exist because of sexual orientation. One recent study suggests that gay men tend to earn somewhat less than heterosexual men, whereas lesbians may earn somewhat more than heterosexual women (Antecol, Jong, & Steinberger, 2008). Further, disclosing one's sexual orientation may cause a homophobic supervisor to fire, refuse to promote, or reduce the income of a gay or lesbian employee. Regrettably, wage penalties may be associated with disclosing one's sexual orientation (Cushing-Daniels & Tsz-Ying, 2009). Factors associated with the decision to disclose one's sexual orientation at work include employer policies and the perceived gay supportiveness of the employer (Griffith & Hebl, 2002). And in a survey of 534 gay and lesbian employees, more heterosexism—showing discriminatory favoritism for heterosexuals over homosexuals—was reported with male supervisors or male work teams (Ragins, Cornwell, & Miller, 2003).

John Browne, the long-time chief executive of British Petroleum and close associate of former British Prime Minister Tony Blair, had little choice but to resign after a judge cleared the way for a newspaper to publish allegations made by a former boyfriend. The exposé of Browne's private life ended his 41-year career at British Petroleum. The stunning demise of Browne's career demonstrates why many gay individuals choose to remain "closeted" in the workplace due to concern about recriminations.

Today's Workplace for Women and Minorities

Recent decades have seen a dramatic upsurge in the number of females and ethnic minorities in the workplace. Is today's workplace essentially the same for these groups as it is for white males? In many respects, the answer appears to be no. Although job discrimination on the basis of race and gender has been illegal for more than 40 years, women and minority group members continue to face obstacles to occupational success, as evidenced by relatively recent court decisions that found Wal-Mart and Morgan Stanley guilty of sex discrimination. Foremost among these obstacles is *job segregation*. Jobs are simultaneously typed by gender and by race. For example, skycaps are typically African American males, and most hotel maids are minority females. Most white women and minority workers tend to be concentrated in jobs where there is little opportunity for advancement or increase in salary (Equal Employment Opportunity Commission, 2007). Also, workers in female-dominated fields typically earn less than those in male-dominated fields, even when the jobs require similar levels of training, skill, and responsibility.

More women and ethnic minorities are entering higher-status occupations, but they still face discrimination because they are frequently *passed over for promotion* in favor of white men (Whitley & Kite, 2006). This seems to be a problem especially at higher levels of management. For example, in 2006, about 16% of corporate officer positions in Fortune 500 companies were held by women, and only about 1.5% were held

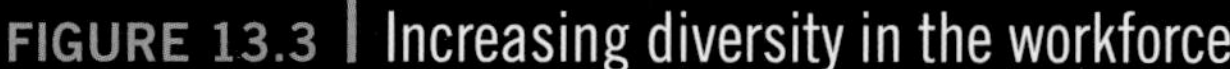

Women and minority group members are entering the workforce in greater numbers than before. This graph projects changes in the share of the labor force by gender and by ethnicity between 1990 and 2018. (Data from Tossi, 2009)

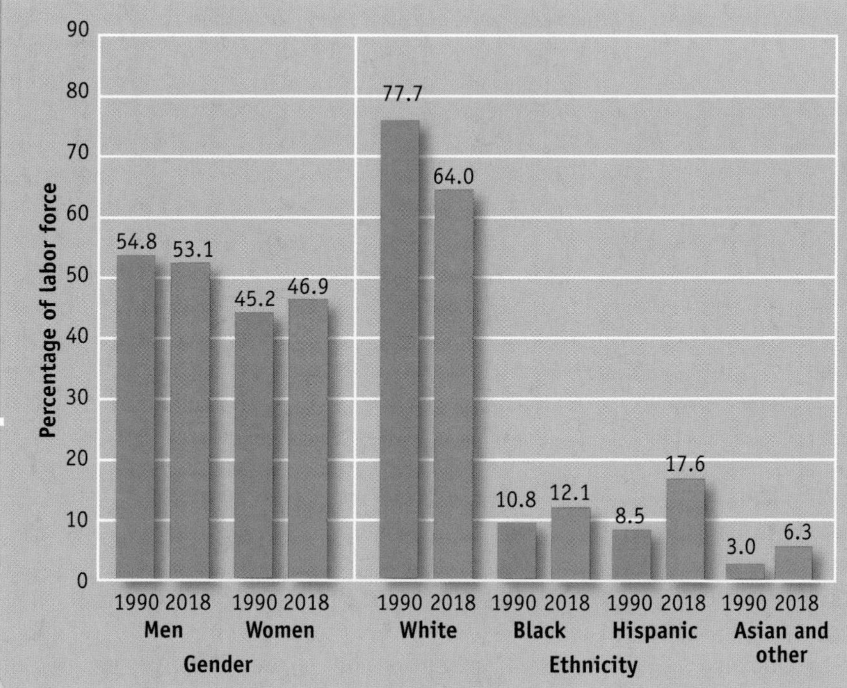

by women of color (Catalyst, 2007). There appears to be a ***glass ceiling,* or invisible barrier that prevents most women and ethnic minorities from advancing to the highest levels of occupations** (see Figure 13.4 on the next page). The fact that very few black women are in managerial positions has caused some to term the glass ceiling a "concrete wall" for women of color. Largely because of these reduced opportunities for career advancement, some female corporate managers are quitting their jobs and starting their own firms. In 2007 women owned 28.7% of nonfarm U.S. businesses (National Association of Women Business Owners, 2010). At the other end of the job spectrum, there seems to be a "sticky floor" that causes women and minorities to get stuck in low-paying occupations (Brannon, 2005).

When only one woman or minority person is employed in an office, that person becomes a ***token*—or a symbol of the members of that group.** Tokens are more distinctive or visible than members of the dominant majority. And, as we discussed in Chapter 7, distinctiveness makes a person's actions subject to intense scrutiny, stereotyping, and judgments. Thus, if a white male makes a mistake, it is explained as an *individual* problem. When a token woman or minority person makes a mistake, it is seen as evidence that *all* members of that group are incompetent. Hence, tokens experience a great deal of *performance pressure,* an added source of job stress (Thomas, 2005).

Another way the world of work is different for women, ethnic, and gay and lesbian minorities is that they have *less access to same-gender or same-group role models and mentors* (Murrell & James, 2001). Finally, *sexual harassment,* a topic we'll take up later, is much more likely to be a problem for working women than for working men. In sum, women and minority individuals must contend with discrimination on the job in a number of forms.

The Challenges of Change

The increasingly diverse workforce presents challenges to both organizations and workers. These challenges can occur within the workplace as well as within the community where workers reside (Pugh et al., 2008). Important cultural differences exist in managing time and people, in identifying with work, and in making decisions (Thomas, 2005). These differences can contribute to conflict. Not surprisingly, perhaps, members of majority groups (generally white males) do not perceive discrimination as often as the members of minority groups do (Avery, McKay, & Wilson, 2008). Another challenge is that some individuals feel that they are personally paying the price of prejudice in the workplace, and this perception causes resentment. Recognizing the problem, some corporations offer diversity training programs for their employees. Ironically, these programs can make the problem worse if they take a blaming stance toward white males or if they stir up workers' feelings but provide no ongoing support for dealing with them. Thus, it is essential that such programs be carefully designed (Ocon, 2006). The strong support of top management is also critical to their success.

Many who advocate abandoning affirmative action programs that are intended to promote access to jobs for women and minorities argue that these programs

FIGURE 13.4 | The glass ceiling for women and minorities

A longitudinal study looked at the chances of promotion to a managerial position in a sample of more than 26,000 adults over 30 years of career experience. This graph shows that promotion chances increased along with career experience for white men. By contrast, the promotion chances of white women and black men were much lower. As you can see, black women lagged far behind all groups. These trends are consistent with the existence of a glass ceiling for women and minorities.

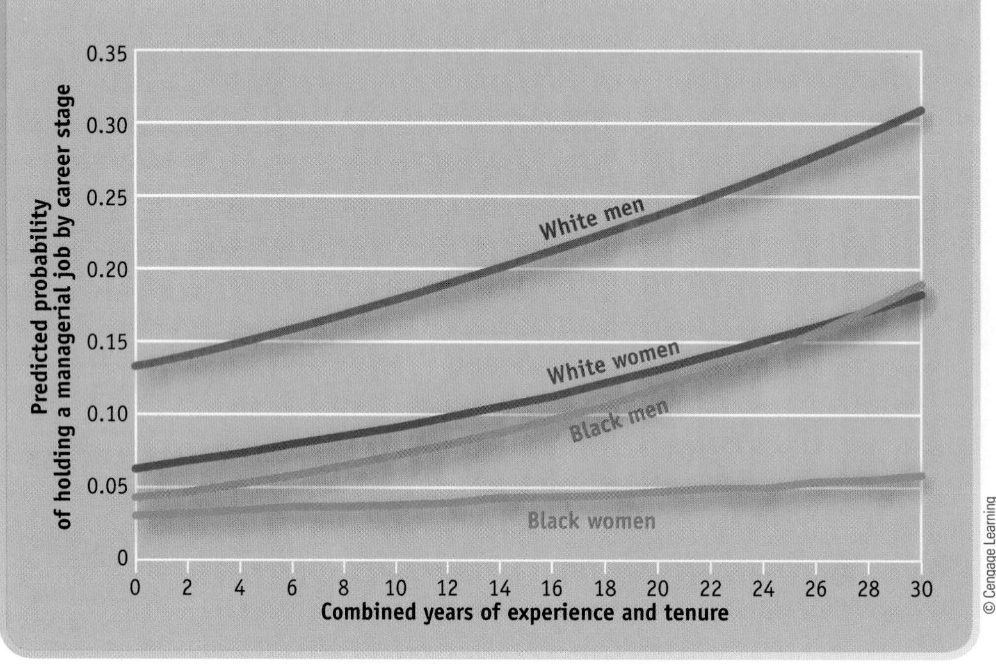

Source: From Maume, D. J. (2004). Is the glass ceiling a unique form of inequality? *Work and Occupations, 31*(2), 250–274. Copyright © 2004 by Sage Publications. Reprinted by permission of Sage Publications.

promote "reverse discrimination" through the use of unfair hiring and promotion practices. For some, this perception may reflect a sense of *privilege*, an unquestioned assumption that white males should be guaranteed a place in society and that others should compete for the remaining jobs (Jacques, 1997). Some also argue that affirmative action undercuts the role of merit in employment decisions and sets up (supposedly) underprepared workers for failure. Many laboratory studies show that individuals have negative feelings about employees who may have been hired under affirmative action (Crosby et al., 2003). However, studies conducted with actual workers have not found this situation (Taylor, 1995). Regardless, this potential negative effect can be counteracted when workers know that decisions are based on merit as well as on group membership.

To minimize conflict and to maintain worker productivity and satisfaction, companies can provide well-designed diversity programs, and managers can educate themselves about the varied values and needs of their workers (Ocon, 2006). Similarly, both majority and minority employees must be willing to learn to work comfortably with those who come from other backgrounds.

Let's close this section with some good news regarding diversity. According to one survey, 92% of human resources directors connect recruiting diverse employees to their organizations' strategic hiring plans (Koc, 2007). Within the contemporary world of work, diversity is here to stay.

13-3 Coping with Occupational Hazards

Work can bring people deep satisfaction; indeed, it can promote psychological health and well-being. Yet work can also be a source of frustration and conflict. In this section, we explore three occupational hazards for today's workers: job stress, sexual harassment, and unemployment.

13-3a JOB STRESS

You saw in Chapter 3 that stress can emerge from any corner of your life. However, many theorists suspect that the workplace is the primary source of stress in modern society. Consider this sobering statistic: Over 75% of the workers in the United States claim that their jobs are stressful (Smith, 2003).

Sources of Stress on the Job

Between 2001 and 2004, the number of Americans claiming to feel overworked rose from 28% to 44% (Galinsky et al., 2005). Estimates clock the average full-time workweek at 48 hours; in law and finance, 60-hour weeks are common (Hodge, 2002). Americans typically put in more time working than individuals from other countries. Also, among affluent nations, only the United States does not require a minimum number of sick days for workers (Heymann et al., 2004).

> The workplace is the primary source of stress in modern society.

© desuza.communications/iStockphoto

In addition to long hours, common job stressors include lack of privacy, high noise levels, unusual hours (such as rotating shifts), the pressure of deadlines, lack of control over one's work, inadequate resources to do a job, and perceived inequities at work (Fairbrother & Warn, 2003). Environmental conditions, such as workplace temperature (e.g., extreme heat in a steel mill, excessive cold in a meat packing plant), can affect physical, cognitive, and perceptual tasks (Pilcher, Nadler, & Busch, 2002). Fears of being downsized, concerns about health care benefits (losing them or paying increasingly higher premiums), and worries about losing pension plans also dog workers in today's economy. Office politics and conflict with supervisors, subordinates, and coworkers also make the list of job stressors. Having to adapt to changing technology and automated offices is another source of work stress. Firefighters, law enforcement officers, and coal miners face frequent threats to their physical safety. High-pressure jobs such as air traffic controller and surgeon demand virtually perfect performance, as errors can have disastrous consequences. Ironically, "underwork" (boring, repetitive tasks) can also be stressful.

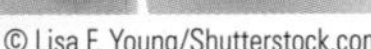

© Lisa F. Young/Shutterstock.com

Women may experience certain workplace stressors, such as sex discrimination and sexual harassment, at higher rates than men (Betz, 2005; Sulsky & Smith, 2005). African Americans and ethnic minorities must cope with racism and other types of discrimination on the job, which means members of minority groups may experience higher levels of stress than nonminorities (Sulsky & Smith, 2005). Discrimination is also a problem for gay and lesbian employees (Badgett, 2003). Workers from lower socioeconomic groups typically work in more dangerous jobs than workers from higher socioeconomic groups.

Why are American workers so stressed out? According to Keita and Hurrell (1994), four factors are the culprits:

1. *More workers are employed in service industries.* Although most customers are civil and easy to deal with, some are decidedly difficult. Nonetheless, even obnoxious and troublesome customers "are always right," so workers have to swallow their frustration and anger, and doing so is stressful. Such situations may contribute to residual stress, where strain and tension from work is carried over because workers have a hard time "letting go."

2. *The economy is unpredictable.* In the age of restructuring, downsizing, takeovers, and bankruptcies, even excellent workers aren't assured of keeping their jobs like workers in the past. Change in response to economic pressures often comes in the form of downsizing or restructuring (Robinson & Griffiths, 2005). Thus, the fear of job loss may lurk in the back of workers' minds. People may expend considerable time and emotional energy worrying about various "what if?" scenarios about their future, a future they cannot directly control.

3. *Rapid changes in computer technology tax workers' abilities to keep up.* Computers have taken over some jobs, forcing workers to develop new skills and to do so quickly. In other jobs, the stress comes from rapid and ongoing advances

in technology (software as well as hardware) that force workers to keep pace with the changes.

4. *The workplace is becoming more diverse.* As more women and minority group members enter the workplace, individuals from all groups must learn to interact more with people who are unfamiliar to them. Developing these skills takes time and may be stressful.

Taking a broader view, Robert Karasek contends that the two key factors in occupational stress are the *psychological demands* made on a worker and a worker's amount of *decision control* (Karasek & Theorell, 1990). Psychological demands are measured by asking employees questions such as "Is there excessive work?" and "Must you work fast (or hard)?" To measure decision control, employees are asked such questions as "Do you have a lot of say in your job?" and "Do you have freedom to make decisions?" In Karasek's demand-control model, *stress is greatest in jobs characterized by high psychological demands and low decision control.* Based on survey data obtained from workers, he has tentatively mapped out where various jobs fall on these two key dimensions of job stress, as shown in Figure 13.5. The jobs thought to be most stressful are those with heavy psychological demands and little control over decisions (see the lower right area of the figure).

Effects of Job Stress

As with other forms of stress, occupational stress is associated with numerous negative effects. In the work arena itself, job stress has been linked to an increased number of industrial accidents, increased absenteeism, poor job performance, and higher turnover rates (Colligan & Higgins, 2005). Experts estimate that stress-related reductions in workers' productivity may cost American industry hundreds of billions per year. Just under 3% of the workforce is absent on any given workday in the United States, and 13% of all employee absences can be chalked up to the impact of stress (Commerce Clearing House, 2007).

When job stress is temporary, as when important deadlines loom, workers usually suffer only minor and brief effects of stress, such as sleeplessness or anxiety. Prolonged high levels of stress are more problematic, as those who work in people-oriented jobs such as human services, education, and health care can attest. As we noted in Chapter 3, prolonged stress can lead to *burnout,* characterized by exhaustion, cynicism, and poor job performance (Maslach, 2005). The feelings of listlessness, detachment, and potential for depression among employees with burnout are linked with higher absenteeism rates, greater job turnover, and lowered worker performance (Parker & Kulik, 1995).

Of course, the negative effects of occupational stress extend beyond the workplace. Foremost among these adverse effects are those on employees' *physical health.* Work stress has been related to a variety of physical maladies, including heart disease, high blood

FIGURE 13.5 Karasek's model of occupational stress as related to specific jobs

Robert Karasek (1979) theorizes that occupational stress is greatest in jobs characterized by high psychological demands and low decision control. Based on survey data, this chart shows where various familiar jobs fall on these two dimensions. According to Karasek's model, the most stressful jobs are those shown in the shaded area on the lower right.

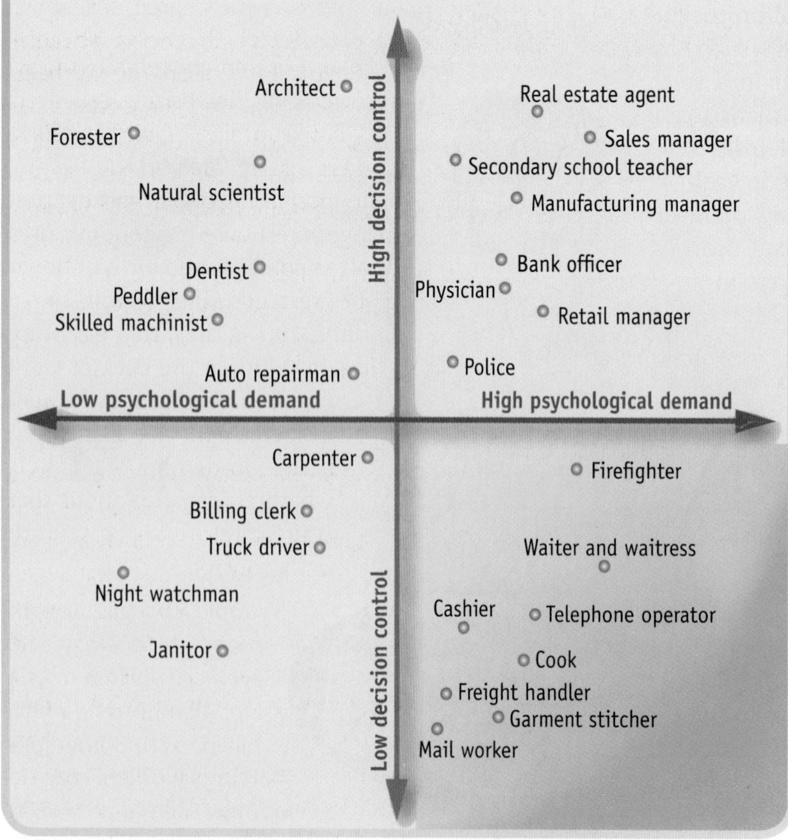

Source: Adapted from Landy, F. (1989). *Psychology of work behavior* (4th ed.). Pacific Grove, CA: Brooks/Cole. © 1989 Cengage Learning.

pressure, ulcers, arthritis, asthma, and cancer (Thomas, 2005). In a test of Karasek's model of work stress, symptoms of heart disease were more prevalent among Swedish men whose jobs were high in psychological demands and low in decision control (Karasek et al., 1981; see Figure 13.6). Job stress can also have a negative impact on workers' *psychological health.* Occupational stress has been related to emotional distress, anxiety, and depression (Blackmore et al., 2007).

Dealing with Job Stress

There are essentially three avenues of attack for dealing with occupational stress (Ivancevich et al., 1990). The first is to intervene at the *individual* level by modifying workers' ways of coping with job stress. The second is to intervene at the *organizational* level by redesigning the work environment itself. The third is to intervene at the *individual-organizational interface* by improving the fit between workers and their companies. Concrete suggestions for coping with stressors, including those found in the workplace, are discussed in Chapter 4.

FIGURE 13.6 | Job characteristics in Karasek's model and heart disease prevalence

Karasek et al. (1981) interviewed 1,621 Swedish men about their work and assessed their cardiovascular health. The vertical bars in this figure show the percentage of the men with symptoms of heart disease as a function of the characteristics of their jobs. The highest incidence of heart disease was found among men who had jobs high in psychological demands and low in decision control, just as Karasek's model of occupational stress predicts. (Based on Karasek et al., 1981)

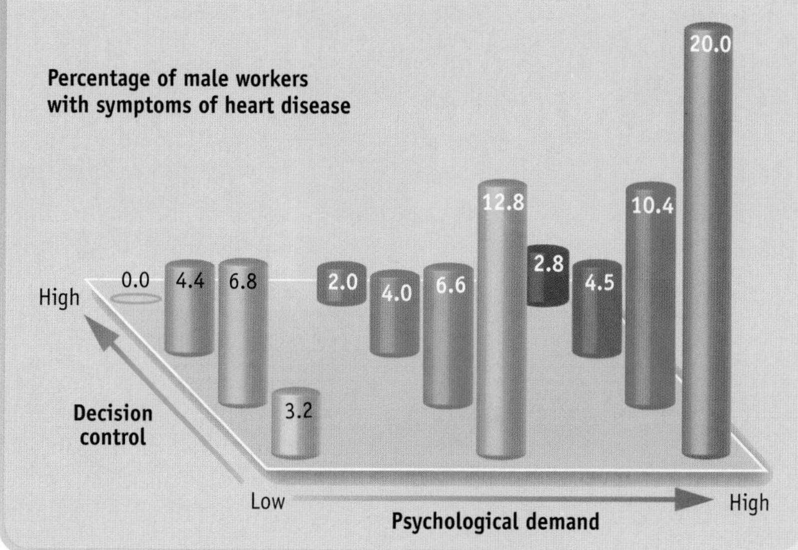

13-3b SEXUAL HARASSMENT

Sexual harassment burst into the American consciousness in 1991 during the televised confirmation hearings for the nomination of Clarence Thomas as a Justice of the U.S. Supreme Court. Although Justice Thomas survived the confirmation process, many would argue that his reputation was damaged by Anita Hill's public allegations of sexual harassment (while she was his assistant a decade earlier), and so was Hill's. Allegations of sexual harassment also caused serious problems for President Bill Clinton. These highly publicized examples of sexual harassment charges have served as a wake-up call to individuals and companies, as both can be sued for harassment. Although most workers recognize that they need to take the problem of sexual harassment seriously, many people remain relatively naive about what constitutes sexual harassment.

Sexual harassment **occurs when employees are subjected to unwelcome sexually oriented behavior.** According to law, there are two types of sexual harassment. The first is *quid pro quo* (from the Latin expression that translates as "something given or received in exchange for something else"). In the context of sexual harassment, quid pro quo involves making submission to unwanted sexual advances a condition of hiring, advancement (raise, promotion), or not being fired. In other words, the worker's survival on the job depends on agreeing to engage in unwanted sex. The second type of harassment is *hostile environment,* or any type of unwelcome sexual behavior that creates hostile work situations that can inflict psychological harm and interfere with job performance.

Sexual harassment can take a variety of forms: unsolicited and unwelcome flirting, sexual advances, or propositions; insulting comments about an employee's appearance, dress, or anatomy; unappreciated dirty jokes and sexual gestures; intrusive or sexual questions about an employee's personal life; explicit descriptions of the harasser's own sexual experiences; abuse of familiarities such as "honey" and "dear"; unnecessary and unwanted physical contact such as touching, hugging, pinching, or kissing; catcalls; exposure of genitals; physical or sexual assault; and rape.

Prevalence and Consequences

Sexual harassment in the workplace is more widespread than most people realize. A review of eighteen studies suggested that approximately 42% of female workers in the United States report having been sexually harassed (Gruber, 1990). A liberal estimate for male workers is 15% (Gutek, 1993). The typical female victim is young, divorced or separated, in a nonsenior position, and in a masculine-stereotyped field (Davidson & Fielden, 1999). A review of studies on women in the military reported rates of sexual harassment ranging from 55% to 79% (Goldzweig et al., 2006).

Experiencing sexual harassment can have negative effects on psychological and physical health (Norton, 2002). Problematic reactions include anger, reduced self-esteem, depression, and anxiety. Victims may also have difficulties in their personal relationships and in sexual adjustment (loss of desire, for example). Increased alcohol consumption, smoking, and dependence on drugs are also reported (Rospenda et al., 2008). In addition, sexual harassment can produce fallout on the job: Women who are harassed may be less productive, less satisfied with their jobs, and less committed to their work and employer (Kath et al., 2009; Woodzicka & LaFrance, 2005). Women who are sexually harassed also report lower job satisfaction and may withdraw from work as the result of physical and mental health problems. Some of these women are even found to display symptoms of posttraumatic stress disorder (Willness, Steel, & Lee, 2007).

Stopping Sexual Harassment

To predict the occurrence of sexual harassment, researchers have developed a two-factor model based on the person (prospective harasser) and the social situation (Pryor, Giedd, & Williams, 1995). According to this model, individuals vary in their proclivity for sexual harassment, and organizational norms regarding the acceptability of sexual harassment also vary. Sexual harassment is most likely to occur when individual proclivity is high and organizational norms are accepting. Thus, it follows that organizations can reduce the incidence of sexual harassment by promoting norms that are intolerant of it.

Acknowledging the prevalence and negative impact of sexual harassment, many organizations have taken steps to educate and protect their workers. Managers are publicly speaking out against sexual harassment, supporting programs designed to increase employees' awareness of the problem, issuing policies expressly forbidding harassment, and implementing formal grievance procedures for handling allegations of harassment.

13-3c UNEMPLOYMENT

A major consequence of recent economic upheavals is ***displaced workers*—individuals who are unemployed because their jobs have disappeared.** Losing one's job is difficult at best and devastating at worst. Given the high U.S. unemployment rate in recent years, many Americans have found themselves out of work and worried about their futures. Not only can unemployment cause economic distress, it can cause health problems and psychological difficulties, such as loss of self-esteem, depression, and anxiety (Bobek & Robbins, 2005). A recent meta-analysis found that the rate of psychological problems was more than doubled among unemployed persons compared to those who were working (Paul & Moser, 2009). Also, the rate of attempted and completed suicides is higher among those who are unemployed (Yang, Tsai, & Huang, 2011).

While losing a job at any age is highly stressful, those who are laid off in middle age seem to find the experience most difficult (Breslin & Mustard, 2003). For one thing, they typically have more financial responsibilities than those in other age groups. Second, if other family members aren't able to provide health insurance, the entire family's health

"The dip in sales seems to coincide with the decision to eliminate the sales staff."

and welfare is jeopardized. Third, older workers typically remain out of work longer than younger workers. Thus, economic hardship can be a real possibility and can threaten quality of life for the worker's family. Finally, middle-aged workers have been on the job for a number of years. Because they typically feel highly involved in their work, being cut off from this important source of life satisfaction is painful (Broomhall & Winefield, 1990).

For some practical suggestions for coping with job loss, we draw on the advice of career experts Michael Laskoff (2004) and Robert Lock (2005b):

- *Apply for unemployment benefits as soon as possible.* The average length of unemployment in 2011 was roughly 40 weeks. Thus, you need to look into unemployment benefits, which can help ease the financial pain created by unemployment. Contact the nearest office of your state's Employment Security Commission or Department of Labor.

- *Determine your income and expenses.* Determine precisely your sources of income (unemployment benefits, spouse or partner's income, savings) and how much you can count on per month. Itemize your monthly expenses. Set up a realistic budget and stick to it. Talk with your creditors if you need to.

- *Lower your expenses and think of ways to bring in extra income.* Cut out unnecessary expenses for now. Minimize your credit card purchases and pay off your credit card bills every month to avoid building up huge debt. For extra income, consider selling a car, having a garage sale, or putting items up for auction on eBay. Use your skills as a temporary worker.

- *Stay healthy.* To save money on medical expenses, eat well-balanced meals, maintain an exercise regimen, and get adequate sleep. Use relaxation techniques to manage your stress (see Chapter 4). Keep yourself in a positive frame of mind by recalling past successes and imagining future ones.

- *Reach out for support.* Although it is difficult to do, explain your job situation to your family and friends. You need their support, and they need to know how your unemployment will affect them. If you are having relationship problems, consult a counselor. Let your friends know that you are looking for work; they may have job leads.

- *Get organized and get going.* Start by setting aside time and space to work on your job search. Then consider your situation. Is your résumé up to date? Can you find the same type of job, or do you need to think about other options? Do you need to relocate? Do you need more education or retraining? Some people decide to go into business for themselves, so don't overlook this option. Expect to spend 15–25 hours a week on job-searching activities.

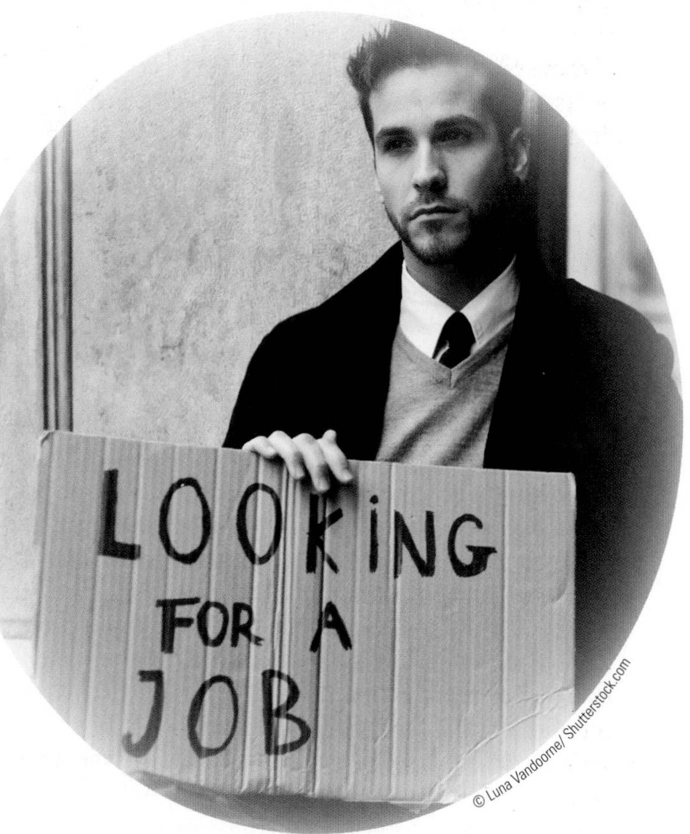

13-4 Balancing Work and Other Spheres of Life

A major challenge for individuals today is balancing work and family in ways that are personally satisfying (Major & Morganson, 2011). We noted earlier that dual-earner families are becoming increasingly common and that the traditional boundaries between family and paid work life are breaking down. These two developments are related. Historically, traditional gender roles assigned women's work to the home and men's work to outside the home. This division of labor created boundaries between family and work life. With more women entering the workforce, these boundaries have become blurred. Here we examine two issues related to balancing various life roles.

© Nelson Marques/Shutterstock.com

13-4a WORKAHOLISM

Most people cherish their leisure activities and relationships with their families and friends. However, *workaholics* devote nearly all their time and energy to their jobs; for them, work is addictive (Griffiths, 2011). They put in lots of overtime, take few vacations, regularly bring work home from the office, and think about work most of the time. They are energetic, intense, and ambitious.

Although workaholism has received considerable attention in the popular press, empirical research on the topic is relatively limited (Harpaz & Snir, 2003). A survey of 800 senior-level managers reported that nearly one in four considered themselves to be workaholics (Joyner, 1999). Psychologists are divided on the issue of whether workaholism is problematic. Should workaholics be praised for their dedication and encouraged in their single-minded pursuit of fulfillment through work (Burke, 2009)? Or is workaholism a form of addiction (Burke & Fiskenbaum, 2009), a sign that an individual is driven by compulsions he or she cannot control? In support of the former view is evidence that some workaholics tend to be highly satisfied with their jobs and with their lives (Bonebright, Clay, & Ankenmann, 2000). They work hard simply because work is the most meaningful activity they know. Yet other evidence suggests that workaholics may have poorer emotional and physical well-being than nonworkaholics (Bonebright et al., 2000). How can these conflicting findings be reconciled?

It seems that there are two types of workaholics (Aziz & Zickar, 2006). One type, the *enthusiastic workaholic*, works for the pure joy of it. Such people derive immense satisfaction from work and generally perform well in highly demanding jobs. These individuals may also qualify as being high in *work engagement*, an emerging positive and fulfilling construct linked to absorption in work (Bakker et al., 2008). The other type, the *nonenthusiastic workaholic*, feels driven to work but reports low job enjoyment. Moreover, these workaholics tend to report lower life satisfaction and less purpose in life than enthusiastic workaholics. Thus, it is not surprising that the nonenthusiastic group is more likely to develop *burnout* (Maslach, 2005).

Both types of workaholics experience an imbalance between work and personal time. Not surprisingly, this situation translates into a high degree of work-family conflict for both groups (Bakker, Demerouti, & Burke, 2009). Moreover, the families of both groups suffer (Robinson, Flowers, & Ng, 2006). A recent study found that students whose parents were workaholics tended to report lower levels of psychological well-being and self-acceptance and high numbers of physical health complaints (Chamberlin & Zhang, 2009). So, although enthusiastic workaholics really love their work, their devotion to their jobs has a price, one often paid by their families.

13-4b WORK AND FAMILY ROLES

One of the biggest recent changes in the labor force has been the emergence of dual-earner households, now the dominant family form in the United States (U.S. Bureau of the Census, 2006b). Dual-earner couples are struggling to discover better ways of balancing family life and the demands of work. These changes in work and family life have sparked the interest of researchers in many disciplines, including psychology.

DILBERT

An important fact of life for dual-earner couples is that they juggle *multiple roles:* spouse or partner and employee. TICKS (two-income couples with kids) add a third role: parent. Thus, today's working parents experience ***work-family conflict,*** **or the feeling of being pulled in multiple directions by competing demands from the job and the family.** In heterosexual dual-earner families, men are taking on more household chores and child care, but most wives still have greater responsibilities in these areas (Drago, 2007). In gay and lesbian dual-earner households, responsibilities are more evenly divided (Kurdek, 2005). Single parents are especially likely to have work-family conflicts.

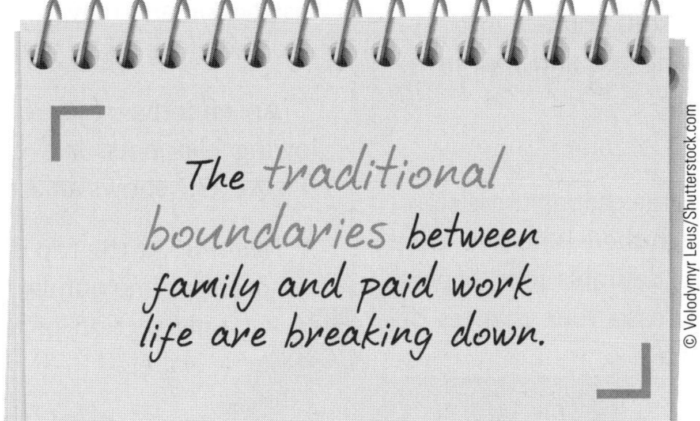

Although employers are reducing their contributions to employee benefits such as pension and retirement plans, health care benefits, and the like, they do not seem to be cutting back on flexible work schedules, family leave, and child and elder care support (Bond et al., 2005). A key reason employers are retaining these programs is that they help recruit and retain employees. Still, the fact is that most employees do not have access to such programs. Some believe that this situation is partly to blame for the downward drift in the percentage of mothers with infant children who are in the labor force. It makes sense that long work hours can spill over into time once reserved for family commitments, thereby introducing strain in family life (Hughes & Parkes, 2007). To gain more control over their lives, some women are temporarily opting out of the workforce; others are going into business for themselves.

Although today's working parents may feel stressed, researchers find that multiple roles are beneficial for both men's and women's mental, physical, and relationship health, at least in middle-class couples (Barnett, 2005). For women, the benefits of multiple roles are attributed primarily to the effects of the employee role. For men, family involvement is important, especially in the area of relationship health.

13-5 APPLICATION

Getting Ahead in the Job Game

Answer the following statements "true" or "false."

____ 1. The most common and effective job search method is answering classified ads.

____ 2. Your technical qualifications are the main factor in determining the success of your job search.

____ 3. Employment agencies are a good source of leads to high-level professional jobs.

____ 4. Your résumé should be very thorough and include everything you have ever done.

____ 5. It's a good idea to inject some humor into your job interviews to help you and your interviewer relax.

Most career counselors would agree that all these statements are generally false. Although there is no one "tried and true" method for obtaining desirable jobs, experts do have guidelines that can increase your chances of success. Their insights are summarized in this Application.

No matter what type of job you're looking for, successful searches have certain elements in common. First, you must prepare a résumé. Next, you need to target specific companies or organizations you would like to work for. Then, you must inform these companies of your interest in such a way as to get them interested in you.

The purpose of a résumé is not to get you a job, but to get get you an interview.

13-5a PUTTING TOGETHER A RÉSUMÉ

No matter what your job search strategy, an excellent résumé is a critical ingredient. The purpose of a résumé is not to get you a job, but to get you an interview. To be effective, your résumé must show that you have at least the minimum technical qualifications for the position, know the standard conventions of the work world, and are a person who is on the fast track to success. Furthermore, it must achieve these goals without being flashy or gimmicky.

Here are a few basic guidelines for a résumé that projects a positive, yet conservative image (Lock, 2005a):

1. Use high-quality white, ivory, or beige paper for hard copies.

2. Make sure the résumé contains not a single typographical error.

3. Keep it short. One side of an 8.5" × 11" sheet of paper will suffice for most college students; do not go over two pages.

4. Don't write in full sentences, and avoid using the word *I*. Instead, begin each statement with an "action" word that describes a specific achievement, such as "Supervised a staff of fifteen."

5. Avoid giving any personal information that is unrelated to the job. Such information is an unnecessary distraction and may give the reader cause to dislike you and therefore reject your application.

An effective résumé will generally contain the following elements, laid out in an easy-to-read format (Figure 13.7 shows an attractively prepared résumé):

- *Heading.* At the top of the page, give your name, address, phone number, and e-mail address. This is the only section of the résumé that is not given a label.
- *Objective.* State precisely and concisely the kind of position you are seeking. An example might be "Challenging, creative position in the communication field requiring extensive background in newspaper, radio, and television."
- *Education.* List any degrees you've earned, giving major field of study, date, and granting institution for each. You should list the highest degree you received first. If you have a college degree, you don't need to mention your high school diploma. If you have received any *academic* honors or awards, mention them in this section.
- *Experience.* This section should be organized chronologically, beginning with your most recent job and working backward. For each position, give the dates of employment and describe your responsibilities and your accomplishments. Be specific, and make sure your most recent position is the one with the greatest achievements. Don't list trivial attainments.

FIGURE 13.7 | Example of an attractively formatted résumé

The physical appearance of a résumé is very important. This example shows what a well-prepared résumé should look like. (Adapted from Lock, 2005b)

TERESA M. MORGAN

Campus Address	**Permanent Address**
1252 River St., Apt. 808	1111 W. Franklin
East Lansing, MI 48823	Jackson, MI 49203
(517)332-6086	(517)782-0819

OBJECTIVE	To pursue a career in interior design, or a related field, in which I can utilize my design training. Willing to relocate after June 2012.
EDUCATION Sept. 2010– June 2012	**Michigan State University,** East Lansing, MI 48825. Bachelor of Arts–Interior Design, with emphasis in Design Communication and Human Shelter. Courses include Lighting, Computers, Public Relations and History of Art. (F.I.D.E.R. accredited) 3.0 GPA (4.0 = A).
July 2011– Aug. 2011	**Michigan State University overseas study,** England and France, Decorative Arts and Architecture. 4.0 GPA (4.0 = A).
Sept. 2008– June 2010	**Jackson Community College,** Jackson, MI 49201. Associate's Degree. 3.5 GPA (4.0 = A).
EMPLOYMENT Dec. 2011– June 2012	**Food Service and Maintenance,** Owen Graduate Center, Michigan State University. • Prepared and served food. • Managed upkeep of adjacent Van Hoosen Residence Hall.
Sept. 2010– June 2011	**Food Service and Maintenance,** McDonel Residence Hall, Michigan State University. • Served food and cleaned facility. • Handled general building maintenance.
June 2007– Dec. 2007	**Waitress,** Charlie Wong's Restaurant, Jackson, MI. • Served food, dealt with a variety of people on a personal level. • Additional responsibilities: cashier, hostess, bartender, and employee trainer.
HONORS AND ACTIVITIES	• Community College Transfer scholarship from MSU. • American Society of Interior Design Publicity Chairman; Executive Board, MSU Chapter. • Sigma Chi Little Sisters. • Independent European travel, summer 2010. • Stage manager and performer in plays and musicals.
	REFERENCES and PORTFOLIO available upon request.

Technology is changing a number of aspects of the job search process, including the preparation and screening of résumés. Increasingly, companies are likely to electronically scan résumés for key words that match job specifications (Lock, 2005a). Thus, it's helpful to know how to create an electronic résumé in addition to the traditional paper version. You can get this information at your campus Career Services office. Also, many organizations post formatting instructions on their websites for people who want to submit electronic résumés.

13-5b FINDING COMPANIES YOU WANT TO WORK FOR

Initially, you need to determine what general type of organization will best suit your needs. Do you want to work in a school? a hospital? a small business? a large corporation? a government agency? a human services agency? To select an appropriate work environment, you need an accurate picture of your personal qualities and knowledge of various occupations and their characteristics. Job search manuals can provide you with helpful exercises in self-exploration. To learn about the characteristics of various occupations, check out relevant websites such as the *Occupational Outlook Handbook* or visit your Career Services office.

13-5c LANDING AN INTERVIEW

So, how do you get invited for an interview? If you are applying for an advertised vacancy, the traditional approach is to send a résumé with a cover letter to the hiring organization. If your letter and résumé stand out from the crowd, you may be invited for an interview. A good way to increase your chances is to persuade the prospective employer that you are interested enough in the company to have done some research on the organization (Pollak, 2007). By taking the time to learn something about a company, you should be able to make a convincing case about the ways in which your expertise will be particularly useful to the organization.

If you are approaching an organization in the absence of a known opening, your strategy may be somewhat different. You may still opt to send a résumé, along with a more detailed cover letter explaining why you have selected this particular company. Another option, suggested by Bolles (2007), is to introduce yourself (by phone or in person) directly to the person in charge of hiring and request an interview.

13-5d POLISHING YOUR INTERVIEW TECHNIQUE

The final, and most crucial, step in the process of securing a job is the face-to-face interview. If you've gotten this far, the employer already knows that you have the necessary training and experience to do the job. Your challenge is to convince the employer that you're the kind of person who would fit well in the organization. To create the right impression, you must come across as confident, enthusiastic, and ambitious. By the way, a firm (not wishy-washy or bone-crushing) handshake helps create a positive first impression, especially for women (Chaplin et al., 2000). Your demeanor should be somewhat formal and reserved, and you should avoid any attempts at humor—you never know what might offend your interviewer. Above all, never give more information than the interviewer requests, especially negative information. If asked directly what your weaknesses are—a common ploy—respond with a "flaw" that is really a positive, as in "I tend to work too hard at times." And don't interrupt or contradict your interviewer. Finally, don't ever blame or criticize anyone, especially previous employers, even if you feel that the criticism is justified (Lock, 2005b). A final word of advice: If possible, avoid any discussion of salary in an initial interview. The appropriate time for salary negotiation is *after* a firm offer of employment has been extended.

After you have an interview, you should follow up with a thank-you note and a résumé that will jog the prospective employer's memory about your training and talents.

© olly/Shutterstock.com

PERSONAL EXPLORATION TOOLS

Curious about yourself? To learn more about how topics in this chapter relate to you, go online to CourseMate at www.cengagebrain.com where you can:

- Complete a **Self-Reflection** exercise that will help you think about your personal experiences in relation to topics in the chapter.
- Take a **Self-Assessment** scale that will show you how you score on a research instrument that measures personality traits or attitudes.
- Explore **Recommended Readings** that will provide brief overviews of useful self-help books.

© edge69/iStockphoto

STUDY TOOLS ▶ 13

Ready to study? In your book you can:

- **Test Yourself** with a multiple-choice quiz (below)
- Rip out the **Chapter Review card** (in the back of the book) to refresh yourself on the chapter's Key Ideas and Key Terms

Or you can go online to CourseMate at www.cengagebrain.com where you can:

- Take additional Practice Quizzes to prepare for your exam
- Review Key Terms with flash cards and a crossword puzzle
- View videos that expand on selected concepts

TEST YOURSELF

1. Individuals' career choices are often

a. much higher in status than those of their parents.
b. similar to those of their parents.
c. much lower in status than those of their parents.
d. unrelated to their family background.

2. Findings on education and earnings show that

a. at all levels of education, men earn more than women.
b. at all levels of education, women earn more than men.
c. there are no gender differences in education and earnings.
d. there is no relationship between education and earnings.

3. Occupational interest inventories are designed to predict

a. how successful an individual is likely to be in a career.
b. how long a person will stay in a career.
c. how satisfied a person is likely to be in a career.
d. all of the above.

4. Which of the following is *not* an important consideration when thinking about career options?

a. Success can occur in a variety of occupations.
b. High income or high status leads to career satisfaction.
c. Career choice is a developmental process.
d. Some career decisions are not easily undone.

5. Which of the following is *not* a work-related trend?

a. Technology is changing the nature of work.
b. New work attitudes are required.
c. Most new jobs will be in the manufacturing sector.
d. Lifelong learning is a necessity.

6. When there is only one woman or minority person in a workplace setting, that person becomes a symbol of his or her group and is referred to as a

a. token.
b. scapegoat.
c. sex object.
d. protected species.

7. Job stress has been found to lead to all but which of the following negative effects?

a. Burnout
b. Bipolar disorder
c. Reduced productivity
d. Impaired physical health

8. According to law, the two types of sexual harassment are

a. quid pro quo and environmental.
b. legal and illegal.
c. caveat emptor and confrontational.
d. industrial and organizational.

9. Which of the following is a good tip for preparing an effective résumé?

a. Make your résumé as long as possible.
b. Use complete sentences.
c. Keep it short.
d. Provide a lot of personal information.

10. When you land a face-to-face interview, which of the following is an appropriate behavior to display?

a. An indifferent handshake
b. A confident attitude
c. Candor about your flaws
d. Critical assessment of past employers

Answers: 1. b, page 275; 2. a, page 279; 3. c, page 276; 4. b, page 277; 5. c, pages 278–279; 6. a, page 281; 7. b, pages 284–285; 8. a, page 285; 9. c, page 290; 10. b, page 292

© biffspandex/iStockphoto

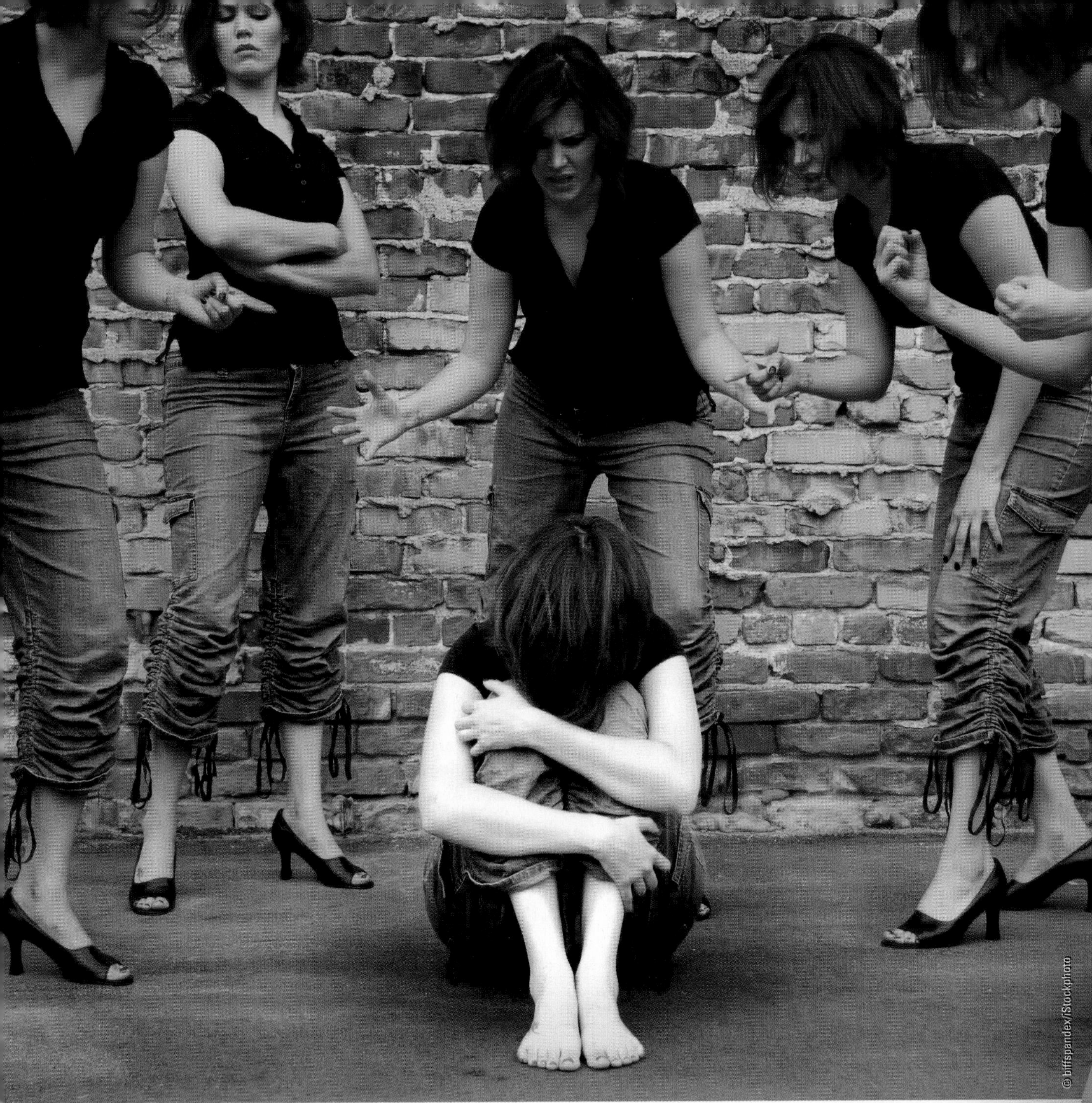

LEARNING OBJECTIVES

14-1 Discuss the medical model, the criteria of abnormality, and the modern diagnostic system.

14-2 Describe four anxiety disorders, and understand how genetics, conditioning, cognition, and stress contribute to their etiology.

14-3 Distinguish between two dissociative disorders, and summarize conflicting views regarding their causes.

14-4 Identify two mood disorders and clarify how genetic, neural, cognitive, interpersonal, and stress factors contribute to their etiology.

14-5 Describe the symptoms and subtypes of schizophrenia, and explain the role of genetics, neural factors, expressed emotion, and stress in their causation.

14-6 Describe the major types of eating disorders, and identify the key factors involved in their development.

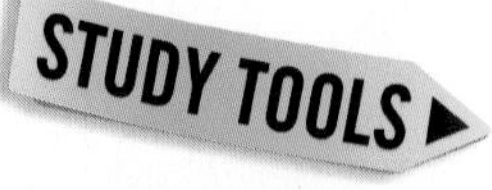

STUDY TOOLS ▶ After you have read the chapter, you can Test Yourself and learn about other Study Tools on page 316.

CHAPTER 14

Psychological DISORDERS

"The government of the United States was overthrown more than a year ago! I'm the president of the United States of America and Bob Dylan is vice president!" So said Ed, the author of a prominent book on journalism, who was speaking to a college journalism class, as a guest lecturer. Ed also informed the class that he had killed both John and Robert Kennedy, as well as Charles de Gaulle, the former president of France. He went on to tell the class that all rock music songs were written about him, that he was the greatest karate expert in the universe, and that he had been fighting "space wars" for 2000 years. The students in the class were mystified by Ed's bizarre, disjointed "lecture," but they assumed that he was putting on a show that would eventually lead to a sensible conclusion. However, their perplexed but expectant calm was shattered when Ed pulled a hatchet from the props he had brought with him and hurled the hatchet at the class! Fortunately, he didn't hit anyone, as the hatchet sailed over the students' heads. At that point, the professor for the class realized that Ed's irrational behavior was not a pretense. The professor evacuated the class quickly while Ed continued to rant and rave about his presidential administration, space wars, vampires, his romances with female rock stars, and his personal harem of 38 "chicks." (Adapted from Pearce, 1974)

Clearly, Ed's behavior was abnormal. Even *he* recognized that when he agreed later to be admitted to a mental hospital, signing himself in as the "President of the United States of America." What causes such abnormal behavior? Does Ed have a mental illness, or does he just behave strangely? What is the basis for judging behavior as normal versus abnormal? How common are such disorders? These are just a few of the questions we address in this chapter as we discuss psychological disorders and their complex causes.

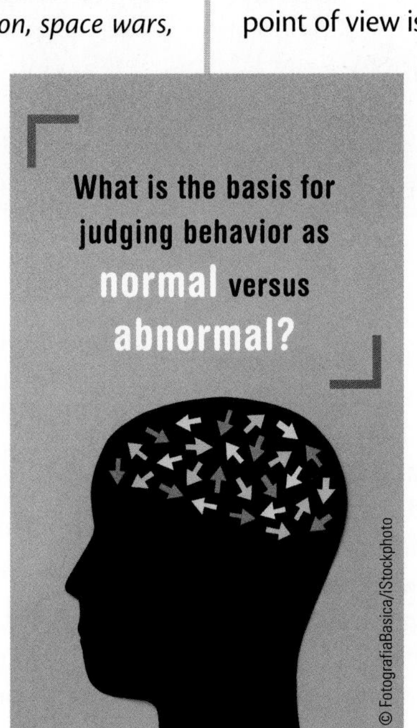
What is the basis for judging behavior as normal versus abnormal?

14-1 Abnormal Behavior: General Concepts

Misconceptions about abnormal behavior are common. We therefore need to clear up some preliminary issues before we describe the various types of psychological disorders. In this section, we discuss (1) the medical model of abnormal behavior, (2) the criteria of abnormal behavior, and (3) the classification of psychological disorders.

14-1a THE MEDICAL MODEL APPLIED TO ABNORMAL BEHAVIOR

In Ed's case, there's no question that his behavior was abnormal. But does it make sense to view his unusual and irrational behavior as an *illness*? This is a controversial question. **The *medical model* proposes that it is useful to think of abnormal behavior as a disease.** This point of view is the basis for many of the terms used to refer to abnormal behavior, including mental *illness*, psychological *disorder*, and psycho*pathology* (*pathology* refers to manifestations of disease). The medical model gradually became the conventional way of thinking about abnormal behavior during the 19th and 20th centuries. Its influence remains strong today.

The medical model clearly represented progress over earlier models of abnormal behavior. Prior to the 18th century, most conceptions of abnormal behavior were based on superstition. People who behaved strangely were thought to be possessed by demons, to be witches in league with the devil, or to be victims of God's punishment. Their disorders were "treated" with chants, rituals, exorcisms, and such. If the people's behavior was seen as threatening, they were candidates for chains, dungeons, torture, and death.

The rise of the medical model brought improvements in the treatment of those who exhibited abnormal behavior. As victims of an illness, they were viewed with more sympathy and less hatred and fear. Although living conditions in early asylums were often deplorable, gradual progress was made toward more humane care of the mentally ill.

However, in recent decades, some critics have suggested that the medical model may have outlived its usefulness (Boyle, 2007). A particularly vocal critic has been Thomas Szasz (1993). He asserts that "strictly speaking, disease or illness can affect only the body; hence there can be no mental illness. . . . Minds can be 'sick' only in the sense that jokes are 'sick' or economies are 'sick'" (1974, p. 267). He further argues that abnormal behavior usually involves a deviation from social norms rather than an illness. He contends that such deviations are "problems in living" rather than medical problems. According to Szasz, the medical model's disease analogy converts moral and social questions about what is acceptable behavior into medical questions.

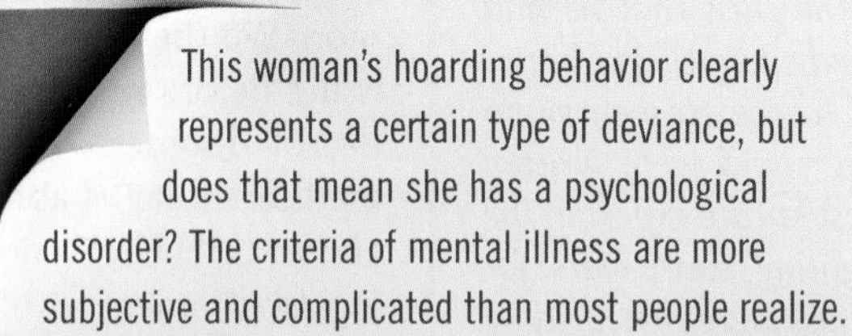

This woman's hoarding behavior clearly represents a certain type of deviance, but does that mean she has a psychological disorder? The criteria of mental illness are more subjective and complicated than most people realize.

Photo: © WR Publishing/Alamy; Frame: © Picsfive/Shutterstock.com

Although critics' analyses of the medical model have some merit, we'll take the position that the disease analogy continues to be useful, although you should keep in mind that it is *only* an analogy. Medical concepts such as *diagnosis*, *etiology*, and *prognosis* have proven valuable in the treatment and study of abnormality. ***Diagnosis*** **involves distinguishing one illness from another.** ***Etiology*** **refers to the apparent causation and developmental history of an illness. A** ***prognosis*** **is a forecast about the probable course of an illness.** These medically based concepts have widely shared meanings that permit clinicians, researchers, and the public to communicate more effectively in their discussions of abnormal behavior.

14-1b CRITERIA OF ABNORMAL BEHAVIOR

If your next-door neighbor scrubs his front porch twice every day and spends virtually all his time cleaning and recleaning his house, is he normal? If your sister-in-law goes to one physician after another seeking treatment for ailments that appear imaginary, is she psychologically healthy? How are we to judge what's normal and what's abnormal? Formal diagnoses of psychological disorders are made by mental health professionals. In making these diagnoses, clinicians rely on a variety of criteria, the foremost of which are the following:

1. *Deviance.* As Szasz has pointed out, people are often said to have a disorder because their behavior deviates from what their society considers acceptable. What constitutes normality varies somewhat from one culture to another, but all cultures have such norms. When people ignore these standards and expectations, they may be labeled mentally ill.

2. *Maladaptive behavior.* In many cases, people are judged to have a psychological disorder because their everyday adaptive behavior is impaired. This is the key criterion in the diagnosis of substance use (drug) disorders. When the use of cocaine, for instance, begins to interfere with a person's social or occupational functioning, a substance use disorder exists. In such cases, it is the maladaptive quality of the behavior that makes it disordered.

3. *Personal distress.* Frequently, the diagnosis of a psychological disorder is based on an individual's report of great personal distress. This is usually the criterion met by people who are troubled by depression or anxiety disorders. Such people are usually labeled as having a disorder when they describe their subjective pain and suffering to mental health professionals.

Although two or three criteria may apply in a particular case, people are often viewed as disordered when only one criterion is met. As you may have already noticed, diagnoses of psychological disorders involve *value judgments* about what represents normal or abnormal behavior (Sadler, 2005). The criteria of mental illness are not nearly as value-free as the criteria of physical illness. Judgments about mental illness reflect prevailing cultural values, social trends, and political forces, as well as scientific knowledge.

Antonyms such as *normal* versus *abnormal* and *mental health* versus *mental illness* imply that people can be divided neatly into two distinct groups: those who are normal and those who are not. In reality, it is often difficult to draw a line that clearly separates normality from abnormality. On occasion, everyone experiences personal distress. Everybody acts in deviant ways once in a while. And everyone displays some maladaptive behavior. People are judged to have psychological disorders only when their behavior becomes *extremely* deviant, maladaptive, or distressing. Thus, normality and abnormality exist on a continuum. It's a matter of degree, not an either-or proposition (see Figure 14.1).

14-1c PSYCHODIAGNOSIS: THE CLASSIFICATION OF DISORDERS

Obviously, we cannot lump all psychological disorders together without giving up all hope of understanding them better. A sound taxonomy of mental disorders can facilitate empirical research and enhance communication among scientists and clinicians. Hence, a great deal of effort has been invested in devising an elaborate system for classifying psychological disorders. This classification system, published by the American Psychiatric Association, is outlined in a book titled the *Diagnostic and Statistical Manual of Mental Disorders.* The fourth edition, referred to as DSM-IV, was released in 1994, and revised slightly in 2000.

DSM-IV used a *multiaxial* system of classification. It asked for judgments about individuals on five separate "axes." The diagnoses of disorders were made on Axes I and II. Clinicians recorded most types of disorders on Axis I; they used Axis II to list long-running personality disorders or intellectual disability (mental retardation). The remaining axes were used to record supplemental information. A patient's physical disorders were listed on Axis III (General Medical Conditions). On Axis IV (Psychosocial and Environmental Problems), the clinician made notations regarding the types of stress experienced by the individual in the past year. On Axis V (Global Assessment of Functioning), estimates were made of the individual's level of adaptive functioning (in social and occupational behavior, viewed as a whole).

Work has been under way for over a decade to formulate the next edition of the diagnostic system (e.g., Andrews et al., 2009; Regier et al., 2009), which will be identified as DSM-5 (instead of DSM-V), to facilitate incremental updates (such as DSM-5.1). It is tentatively scheduled for publication in 2013. Clinical researchers have been collecting data, holding conferences, and formulating arguments about whether various syndromes should be added, eliminated, redefined, or renamed. One major change in the preliminary draft for DSM-5 is that it appears that the multiaxial system will be retired. The distinction between Axis I and Axis II disorders will be discarded. Clinicians will still be encouraged to make notations about patients' medical conditions, stressors, and global functioning, but there will be no formal axes for this supplemental information. Many of the proposed revisions for DSM-5 have been highly controversial. Some prominent critics have argued vigorously that implementation of DSM-5 should be delayed pending further research, but at this point it appears that the American Psychiatric Association will proceed with

FIGURE 14.1 | Normality and abnormality as a continuum

No sharp boundary divides normal and abnormal behavior. Behavior is normal or abnormal in degree, depending on the extent to which it is deviant, personally distressing, or maladaptive.

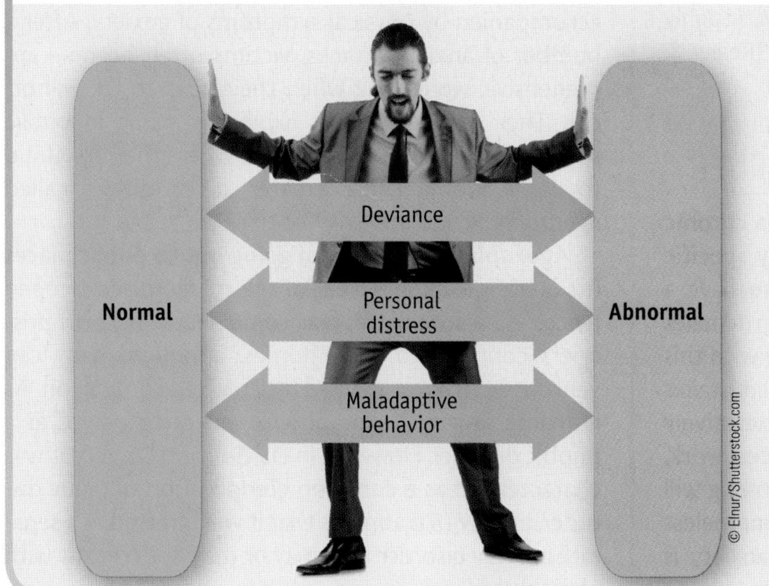

the publication of DSM-5 in 2013. Hence, we will mention some of the less contentious revisions that seem likely to make it into the final version.

We are now ready to start examining the specific types of psychological disorders. Obviously, we cannot cover all of the diverse disorders listed in the DSM system. However, we will introduce most of the major categories of disorders to give you an overview of the many forms abnormal behavior takes. In discussing each set of disorders, we begin with brief descriptions of the specific syndromes or subtypes that fall in the category. Then we focus on the *etiology* of the disorders in that category.

14-2 Anxiety Disorders

Everyone experiences anxiety from time to time. It is a natural and common reaction to many of life's difficulties. For some people, however, anxiety becomes a chronic problem. These people experience high levels of anxiety with disturbing regularity. ***Anxiety disorders*** **are a class of disorders marked by feelings of excessive apprehension and anxiety.** Major types of anxiety disorders include: generalized anxiety disorder, phobic disorder, obsessive-compulsive disorder, and panic disorder. However, the current proposal for DSM-5 would remove obsessive-compulsive disorder from the anxiety disorders category and put it in its own special category, called *obsessive-compulsive and related disorders*. Anxiety disorders are quite common. Over the course of their lives, roughly 19% of people experience an anxiety disorder (Regier & Burke, 2000).

Compulsions usually involve rituals that temporarily relieve anxiety.

© desuza.communications/iStockphoto

14-2a GENERALIZED ANXIETY DISORDER

Generalized anxiety disorder **is marked by a chronic high level of anxiety that is not tied to any specific threat.** Generalized anxiety disorder tends to have a gradual onset and is seen more frequently in females than males (Brown & Lawrence, 2009). People with this disorder worry constantly about yesterday's mistakes and tomorrow's problems. They worry excessively about minor matters related to family, finances, work, and personal illness. They hope that their worrying will help ward off negative events, but they nonetheless worry about how much they worry. Their anxiety is frequently accompanied by physical symptoms, such as muscle tension, diarrhea, dizziness, faintness, sweating, and heart palpitations.

14-2b PHOBIC DISORDER

In a phobic disorder, an individual's troublesome anxiety has a specific focus. **A *phobic disorder* is marked by a persistent and irrational fear of an object or situation that presents no realistic danger.** Although mild phobias are extremely common, people are said to have a phobic disorder only when their fears seriously interfere with their everyday behavior. Phobic reactions tend to be accompanied by physical symptoms of anxiety, such as trembling and palpitations.

People can develop phobic responses to virtually anything. Nonetheless, certain types of phobias are relatively common, including acrophobia (fear of heights), claustrophobia (fear of small, enclosed places), brontophobia (fear of storms), hydrophobia (fear of water), and various animal and insect phobias (McCabe & Antony, 2008). People troubled by phobias typically realize that their fears are irrational, but they still are unable to calm themselves when they encounter a phobic object.

14-2c PANIC DISORDER AND AGORAPHOBIA

A *panic disorder* is characterized by recurrent attacks of overwhelming anxiety that usually occur suddenly and unexpectedly. About two-thirds of people who suffer from panic disorder are female (Taylor, Cox, & Asmundson, 2009). Their paralyzing panic attacks are accompanied by physical symptoms of anxiety. After a number of anxiety attacks, victims often become apprehensive, wondering when their next attack will occur. Their concern about exhibiting panic in public sometimes escalates to the point where they are afraid to leave home. This creates a condition called *agoraphobia*.

Agoraphobia **is a fear of going out to public places** (its literal meaning is "fear of the marketplace or open places"). Because of this fear, some people become prisoners confined to their homes, although many can venture out if accompanied by a trusted companion. As its name suggests, agoraphobia was once viewed as a phobic disorder. However, in DSM-III and DSM-IV it was characterized as a common complication of panic disorder. In DSM-5 it appears that it will be listed as a separate anxiety disorder that may or may not co-exist with panic disorder.

14-2d OBSESSIVE-COMPULSIVE DISORDER

Obsessions are *thoughts* that repeatedly intrude on one's consciousness in a distressing way. Compulsions are *actions* that one feels forced to carry out. Thus, **an *obsessive-compulsive disorder (OCD)* is marked by persistent, uncontrollable intrusions of unwanted thoughts (obsessions) and urges to engage in senseless rituals (compulsions).**

Obsessions often center on fear of contamination, inflicting harm on others, suicide, or sexual acts. For example, comedian Howie Mandel has made it well-known that he has an intense fear of contamination that makes it impossible for him to shake hands with people. Compulsions usually involve rituals that temporarily relieve anxiety. Common examples include constant handwashing; repetitive cleaning of things that are already clean; endless rechecking of locks, faucets, and such; and excessive arranging, counting, and hoarding of things. Specific types of obsessions tend to be associated with specific types of compulsions. For instance, obsessions about contamination tend to be paired with cleaning compulsions, and obsessions about symmetry tend to be paired with ordering and arranging compulsions (Hollander & Simeon, 2008). The typical age of onset for OCD is late adolescence, with most cases (75%) emerging before the age of 30 (Kessler et al., 2005a). OCD can be a serious disorder, as it is often associated with severe social and occupational impairments.

14-2e ETIOLOGY OF ANXIETY DISORDERS

Like most psychological disorders, anxiety disorders develop out of complicated interactions among a variety of factors. Conditioning and learning appear especially important, but biological factors may also contribute.

Biological Factors

Recent studies suggest that there may be a weak to moderate genetic predisposition to anxiety disorders, depending on the specific type of disorder (Fyer, 2009). These findings are consistent with the idea that inherited differences in temperament might make some people vulnerable to anxiety disorders. Research suggests that an *inhibited temperament*, characterized by shyness, timidity, and wariness, is a risk factor for anxiety disorders (Coles, Schofield, & Pietrefesa, 2006).

Recent evidence suggests that a link may exist between anxiety disorders and neurochemical activity in the brain. ***Neurotransmitters* are chemicals that carry signals from one neuron to another.** Therapeutic drugs that reduce excessive anxiety (such as Valium) appear to alter activity at synapses for a neurotransmitter called GABA. This finding and other lines of evidence suggest that disturbances in the neural circuits using GABA may play a role in some types of anxiety disorders (Skolnick, 2003). Abnormalities in other neural circuits using the transmitter serotonin have been implicated in panic and obsessive-compulsive disorders (Stein & Hugo, 2004). Thus, scientists are beginning to unravel the neurochemical bases for anxiety disorders.

Conditioning and Learning

Many anxiety responses may be *acquired through classical conditioning* and *maintained through operant conditioning* (see Chapter 2). According to Mowrer (1947), an originally neutral stimulus (an elevator, for instance) may be paired with a frightening event (the elevator unexpectedly drops a few feet) so that it becomes a conditioned stimulus eliciting anxiety (see Figure 14.2 on the next page). Once a fear is acquired

FIGURE 14.2 Conditioning as an explanation for phobias

(1) Many phobias appear to be acquired through classical conditioning when a neutral stimulus is paired with an anxiety-arousing stimulus. (2) Once acquired, a phobia may be maintained through operant conditioning, because avoidance of the phobic stimulus leads to a reduction in anxiety, resulting in negative reinforcement.

through classical conditioning, the person may start avoiding the anxiety-producing stimulus. The avoidance response is *negatively reinforced* because it is followed by a reduction in anxiety. This process involves operant conditioning (also shown in Figure 14.2). Thus, separate conditioning processes may create and then sustain specific anxiety responses. Consistent with this view, studies find that a substantial portion of people suffering from phobias can identify a traumatic conditioning experience that probably contributed to their anxiety disorder (Mineka & Zinbarg, 2006).

The tendency to develop phobias of certain types of objects and situations may be explained by Martin Seligman's (1971) concept of *preparedness*. Like many theorists, Seligman believes that classical conditioning creates most phobic responses. *However, he suggests that people are biologically prepared by their evolutionary history to acquire some fears much more easily than others.* His theory would explain why people develop phobias of ancient sources of threat (such as snakes, spiders, and heights) much more readily than modern sources of threat (such as electrical outlets, hammers, or hot irons). Consistent with this view, researchers have found that phobic stimuli associated with evolutionary threats (snakes, spiders) tend to produce more rapid conditioning of fears and stronger fear responses than modern fear-relevant stimuli, such as guns and knives (Mineka & Öhman, 2002).

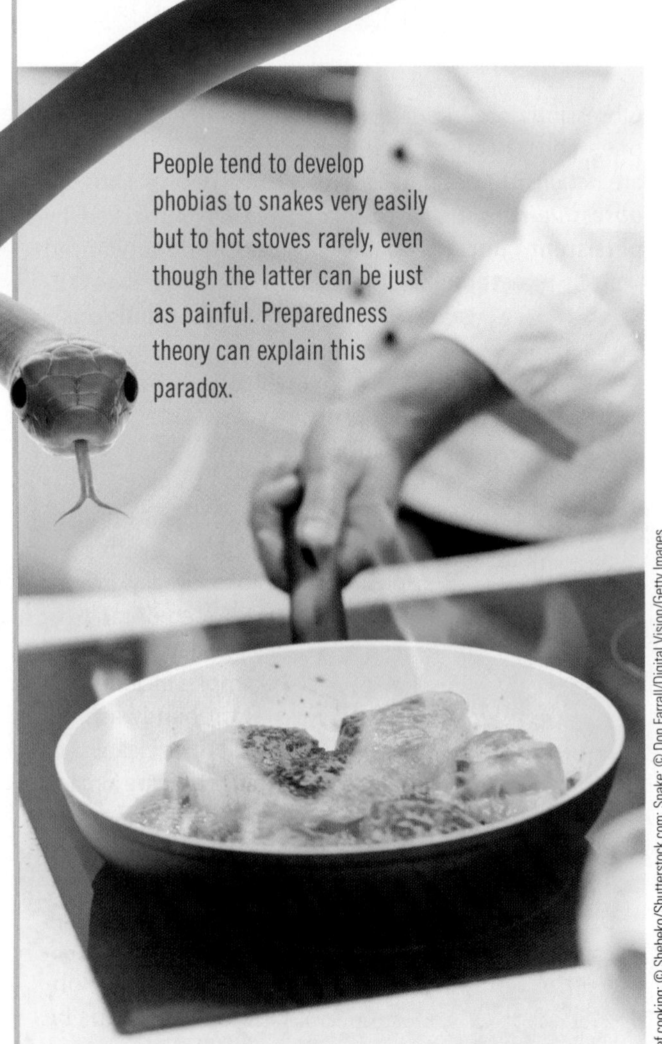

People tend to develop phobias to snakes very easily but to hot stoves rarely, even though the latter can be just as painful. Preparedness theory can explain this paradox.

Cognitive Factors

Cognitive theorists maintain that certain styles of thinking make some people particularly vulnerable to anxiety disorders (Craske & Waters, 2005). According to these theorists, some people are prone to suffer from problems with anxiety because they tend to (a) misinterpret harmless situations as threatening, (b) focus excessive attention on perceived threats, and (c) selectively recall information that seems threatening (Beck, 1997). In one intriguing test of the cognitive view, anxious and nonanxious subjects were asked to read thirty-two sentences that could be interpreted in either a threatening or a nonthreatening manner (Eysenck et al., 1991). For instance, one such sentence was "The doctor examined little Emma's growth," which could mean that the doctor checked her height or the growth of a tumor. The results showed that the anxious subjects interpreted the sentences in a threatening way more often than the nonanxious subjects did. Thus, the cognitive view holds that some people are prone to anxiety disorders because they see threat in every corner of their lives.

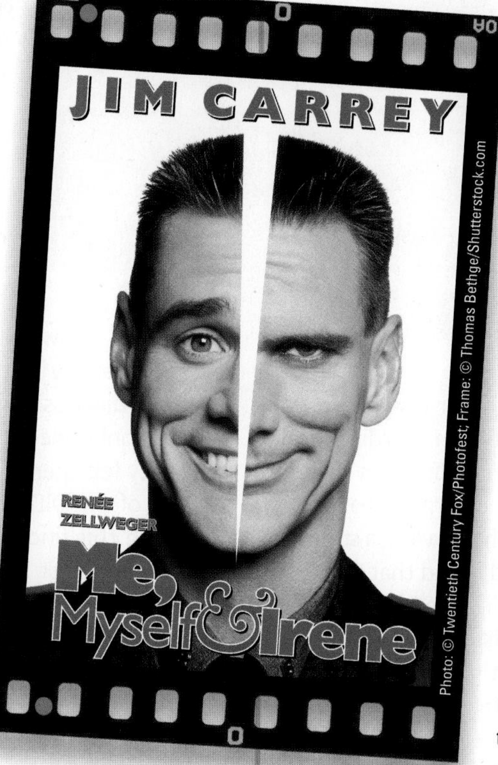

Photo: © Twentieth Century Fox/Photofest; Frame: © Thomas Bethge/Shutterstock.com

Stress

Finally, studies have supported the long-held suspicion that anxiety disorders are stress related (Beidel & Stipelman, 2007). For instance, Faravelli and Pallanti (1989) found that patients with panic disorder had experienced a dramatic increase in stress in the month prior to the onset of their disorder. In another study, Brown et al. (1998) found an association between stress and the development of social phobia. Thus, there is reason to believe that high stress often helps precipitate the onset of anxiety disorders.

14-3 Dissociative Disorders

Dissociative disorders are probably the most controversial set of disorders in the diagnostic system, sparking heated debate among normally subdued researchers and clinicians. ***Dissociative disorders* are a class of disorders in which people lose contact with portions of their consciousness or memory, resulting in disruptions in their sense of identity.** Here we describe two dissociative syndromes—dissociative amnesia and dissociative identity disorder—both of which are relatively uncommon.

14-3a DISSOCIATIVE AMNESIA

***Dissociative amnesia* is a sudden loss of memory for important personal information that is too extensive to be due to normal forgetting.** Memory losses may occur for a single traumatic event (such as an automobile accident or home fire) or for an extended period of time surrounding the event. Cases of amnesia have been observed after people have experienced disasters, accidents, combat stress, physical abuse, and rape, or after they have witnessed the violent death of a parent, among other things (Cardeña & Gleaves, 2007). In some cases, having forgotten their name, their family, where they live, and where they work, these people wander away from their home area. In spite of this wholesale forgetting, they remember matters unrelated to their identity, such as how to drive a car and how to do math.

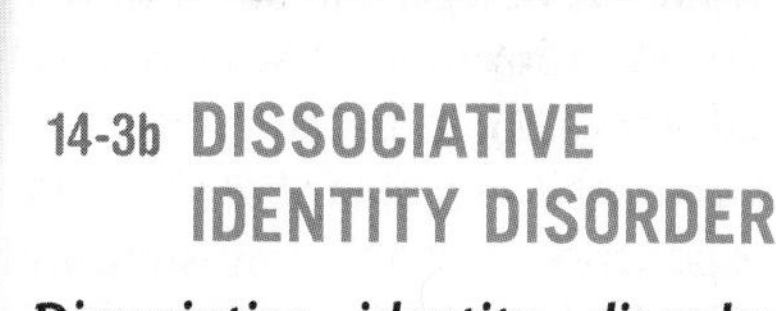

14-3b DISSOCIATIVE IDENTITY DISORDER

***Dissociative identity disorder (DID)* involves the coexistence in one person of two or more largely complete, and usually very different, personalities.** The name for this disorder used to be *multiple personality disorder,* which still enjoys informal usage. In dissociative identity disorder, the divergences in behavior go far beyond those that people normally display in adapting to different roles in life. People with "multiple personalities" feel that they have more than one identity. Each personality has his or her own name, memories, traits, and physical mannerisms. Although rare, this syndrome is frequently portrayed in novels, movies, and television shows, such as the satirical film *Me, Myself, and Irene,* a 2000 release starring Jim Carrey, and more recently, the Showtime series the *United States of Tara.* In popular media portrayals, the syndrome is often mistakenly called *schizophrenia.* As you will see later, schizophrenic disorders are entirely different and do not involve a "split personality."

In dissociative identity disorder, the various personalities generally report that they are unaware of each other. The alternate personalities commonly display traits that are quite foreign to the original personality. For instance, a shy, inhibited person might develop a flamboyant, extraverted alternate personality. Transitions between identities often occur suddenly. The disparities between identities can be bizarre, as personalities may assert that they are different in age, race, gender, or sexual orientation (Kluft, 1996). Dissociative identity disorder is seen more in women than men (Simeon & Loewenstein, 2009).

Starting in the 1970s, a dramatic increase occurred in the diagnosis of multiple-personality disorder (Kihlstrom, 2005). Only 79 well-documented cases had accumulated up through 1970, but by the late 1990s about 40,000 cases were estimated to have been reported (Lilienfeld & Lynn, 2003). Some theorists believe that these disorders used to be underdiagnosed—that is, that they often went undetected (Maldonado & Spiegel, 2008). However, other theorists argue that a handful of clinicians had begun overdiagnosing the condition and that some clinicians even *encouraged and contributed* to the emergence of DID (Powell & Gee, 1999). Consistent with this view, a survey of all the psychiatrists in Switzerland found that 90% of them had never seen a case of dissociative identity disorder, whereas 3 of the psychiatrists had each seen more than 20 DID patients (Modestin, 1992). The data from this study suggest that 6 psychiatrists (out of 655 surveyed) accounted for two-thirds of the dissociative identity disorder diagnoses in Switzerland.

Very little is known about the causes of dissociative identity disorder, which remains a controversial diagnosis.

14-3c ETIOLOGY OF DISSOCIATIVE DISORDERS

Dissociative amnesia is usually attributed to excessive stress. However, relatively little is known about why this extreme reaction occurs in a tiny minority of people but not in the vast majority who are subjected to similar stress.

The causes of dissociative identity disorder are particularly obscure. Some theorists (Lilienfeld et al., 1999; Spanos, 1996), believe that people with multiple personalities are engaging in intentional role playing to use mental illness as a face-saving excuse for their personal failings. They argue that a small minority of therapists help create multiple personalities in their patients by subtly encouraging the emergence of alternate personalities. According to this view, dissociative identity disorder is a creation of modern North American culture, much as demonic possession was a creation of early Christianity.

In spite of these concerns, many clinicians are convinced that DID is an authentic disorder (van der Hart & Nijenhuis, 2009). They argue that there is no incentive for either patients or therapists to manufacture cases of multiple personalities, which are often greeted with skepticism and outright hostility. They maintain that most cases of DID are rooted in severe emotional trauma that occurred during childhood (Maldonado & Spiegel, 2008). A substantial majority of people with DID report a history of disturbed home life, beatings and rejection from parents, and sexual abuse (Van der Hart & Nijenhuis, 2009). However, this link would not be unique to DID, as a history of child abuse elevates the likelihood of *many* disorders.

In the final analysis, very little is known about the causes of dissociative identity disorder, which remains a controversial diagnosis. In one survey of American psychiatrists, only one-fourth of the respondents indicated that they felt there was solid evidence for the scientific validity of the DID diagnosis (Pope et al., 1999). Consistent with this finding, a more recent study found that scientific interest in DID has dwindled since the mid-1990s (Pope et al., 2006).

14-4 Mood Disorders

What might Abraham Lincoln, Marilyn Monroe, Vincent Van Gogh, Ernest Hemingway, Winston Churchill, Virginia Woolf, Janis Joplin, Irving Berlin, Kurt Cobain, Francis Ford Coppola, Sting, Owen Wilson, Billy Joel, Larry Flynt, Catherine Zeta-Jones, Alec Baldwin, Jerry West, and Ben Stiller have in common? Yes, they all achieved great prominence, albeit in different ways at different times. But, more pertinent to our interest, they all suffered from mood disorders. Although mood disorders can be terribly debilitating, people with mood disorders may still achieve renown, because such disorders tend to be *episodic.* In other words, episodes of disturbance are interspersed among periods of normality.

Left and right: © Joe Seer/Shutterstock.com

Mood disorders are common and have afflicted many successful, well-known people, such as Catherine Zeta-Jones and Alec Baldwin.

Of course, we all have our ups and downs in terms of mood. Everyone experiences depression occasionally and has other days that bring an emotional high. Such emotional fluctuations are natural, but some people are prone to extreme distortions of mood. ***Mood disorders*** **are a class of disorders marked by emotional disturbances that may spill over to disrupt physical, perceptual, social, and thought processes.**

Mood disorders include two basic types: unipolar and bipolar (see Figure 14.3). People with *unipolar disorders* experience emotional extremes at just one end of the mood continuum—depression. People with *bipolar disorders* experience emotional extremes at both ends of the mood continuum, going through periods of both *depression* and *mania* (excitement and elation). The mood swings in bipolar disorders can be patterned in many ways. In DSM-5 it appears that depressive disorders and bipolar disorders may no longer be lumped together as mood disorders. The current proposal separates them into two distinct categories called *depressive disorders* and *bipolar and related disorders*.

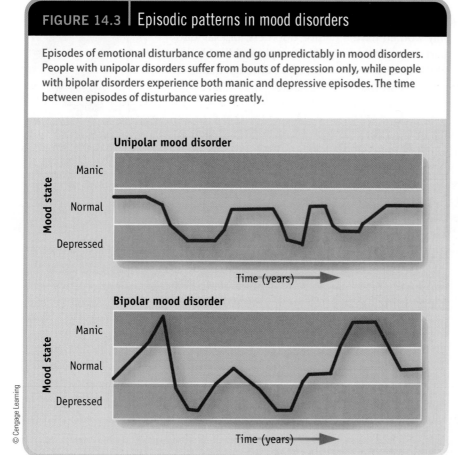

FIGURE 14.3 | Episodic patterns in mood disorders

Episodes of emotional disturbance come and go unpredictably in mood disorders. People with unipolar disorders suffer from bouts of depression only, while people with bipolar disorders experience both manic and depressive episodes. The time between episodes of disturbance varies greatly.

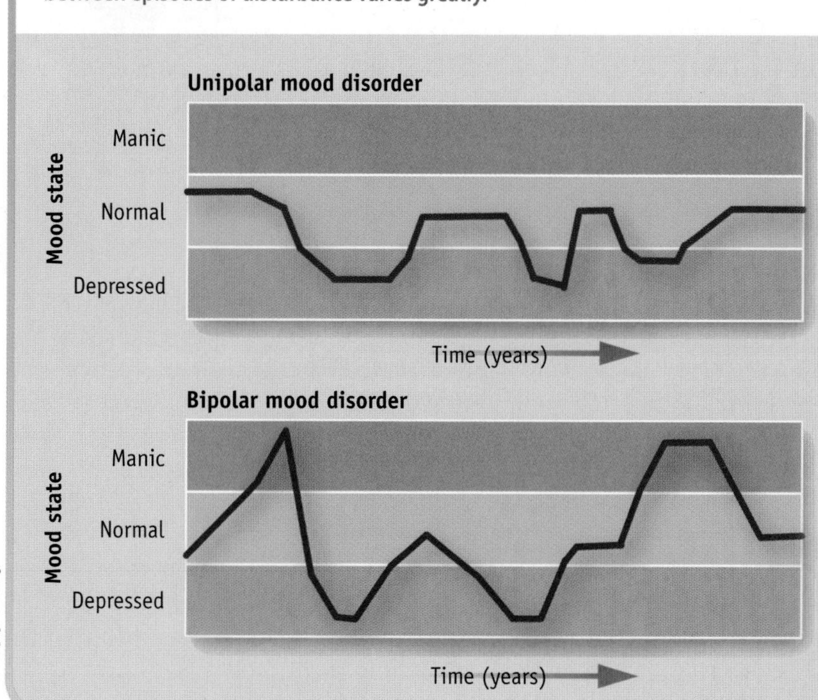

© Cengage Learning

14-4a MAJOR DEPRESSIVE DISORDER

The line between normal and abnormal depression can be difficult to draw. Ultimately, a subjective judgment is required. Crucial considerations in this judgment include the duration of the depression and its disruptive effects. When depression significantly impairs everyday adaptive behavior for more than a few weeks, there is reason for concern.

In *major depressive disorder* people show persistent feelings of sadness and despair and a loss of interest in previous sources of pleasure. Figure 14.4 on the next page summarizes the most common symptoms of depressive disorders and compares them to the symptoms of mania. Negative emotions form the heart of the depressive syndrome, but many other symptoms may appear. Depressed people often give up activities that they used to find enjoyable. For example, a depressed person might quit going bowling or give up a favorite hobby like photography. Reduced appetite and insomnia are common. People with depression often lack energy. They tend to move sluggishly and talk slowly. Anxiety, irritability, and brooding are frequently observed.

Self-esteem tends to sink as the depressed person begins to feel worthless. Depression plunges people into feelings of hopelessness, dejection, and boundless guilt. The severity of abnormal depression varies considerably.

Depressive disorders are very common. One large-scale study of a nationally representative sample found the lifetime prevalence of depressive disorder to be 16.2% (Kessler et al., 2003). That estimate suggests that over 30 million people in the United States will suffer from depression! The onset of unipolar disorder can occur at any point in the life span, but a substantial majority of cases emerge before age 40 (Hammen, 2003). Most people who suffer from depression experience more than one episode over the course of their lifetime. The average number of depressive episodes is five to six, and the average length of these episodes is about six months (Akiskal, 2009). Although depression tends to be episodic, some people suffer from chronic major depression that may persist for years (Klein, 2010).

Researchers also find that the prevalence of depression is about twice as high in women as it is in men (Rihmer & Angst, 2005). The many possible explanations for this gender gap are the subject of considerable debate. A small portion of the disparity may be a result of women's elevated vulnerability to depression at certain points in their reproductive life cycle (Nolen-Hoeksema & Hilt, 2009). Obviously, only women have to worry abut the phenomena of postpartum and post-menopausal depression. Susan Nolen-Hoeksema (2001) argues that women experience more depression than men because they are far more likely to be victims of sexual abuse and somewhat more likely to endure poverty, harassment, and role constraints. In other words, she attributes the higher prevalence of depression among women to their experience of greater stress and adversity. Nolen-Hoeksema also believes that women have a greater tendency than men to ruminate about setbacks and problems. Evidence suggests that this tendency to dwell on one's difficulties elevates vulnerability to depression, as we will discuss momentarily.

14-4b BIPOLAR DISORDER

***Bipolar disorder* is marked by the experience of both depressed and manic periods.** The symptoms seen in manic periods generally are the opposite of those seen in depression (see Figure 14.4 for a comparison). In a manic episode, a person's mood becomes elevated to the point of euphoria. Self-esteem skyrockets as the person bubbles over with optimism, energy, and extravagant plans. People become hyperactive and may go for days without sleep. They talk rapidly and shift topics wildly as their minds race at breakneck speed. Judgment is often impaired. Some people in manic periods gamble impulsively, spend money frantically, or become sexually reckless. Like depressive disorders, bipolar disorders vary considerably in severity. Although manic episodes may have

FIGURE 14.4 | Common symptoms in depressive and manic episodes

The emotional, behavioral, and cognitive symptoms exhibited in depressive and manic illnesses are largely the opposite of each other.

COMPARISON OF DEPRESSIVE AND MANIC SYMPTOMS

Symptoms	Depressive episode	Manic episode
Emotional symptoms	Dysphoric, gloomy mood Diminished ability to experience pleasure Sense of hopelessness	Euphoric, enthusiastic mood Excessive pursuit of pleasurable activities Unwarranted optimism
Behavioral symptoms	Fatigue, loss of energy Insomnia Slowed speech and movement Social withdrawal	Energetic, tireless, hyperactive Decreased need for sleep Rapid speech and agitation Increased sociability
Cognitive symptoms	Impaired ability to think and make decisions Slowed thought processes Excessive worry, rumination Guilt, self-blame, unrealistic negative evaluations of one's worth	Grandiose planning, indiscriminate decision making Racing thoughts, easily distracted Impulsive behavior Inflated self-esteem and self-confidence

"Those? Oh, just a few souvenirs from my bipolar-disorder days."

some positive aspects (increases in energy and optimism), bipolar disorder ultimately proves to be troublesome for most victims. Manic periods often have a paradoxical negative undertow of uneasiness and irritability (Goodwin & Jamison, 2007). Moreover, mild manic episodes often escalate to higher levels that become scary and disturbing.

Although not rare, bipolar disorder is much less common than unipolar depression. Bipolar disorder affects roughly about 1% of the population (Merikangas & Pato, 2009). Unlike depressive disorder, bipolar disorder is seen equally in men and women (Rihmer & Angst, 2009). As Figure 14.5 shows, the onset of bipolar disorder is age related. The typical age of onset is in the late teens or early twenties.

14-4c ETIOLOGY OF MOOD DISORDERS

We know quite a bit about the etiology of mood disorders, although the puzzle hasn't been assembled completely. There appear to be a number of routes into these disorders, involving intricate interactions between psychological and biological factors.

Genetic Vulnerability

The evidence strongly suggests that genetic factors influence the likelihood of developing major depression or a bipolar mood disorder (Lohoff & Berrettini, 2009). In studies that assess the impact of heredity on psychological disorders, investigators look at *concordance rates*. **A *concordance rate* indicates the percentage of twin pairs or other pairs of relatives that exhibit the same disorder.** If relatives who share more genetic similarity show higher concordance rates than relatives who share less genetic overlap, this finding supports the genetic hypothesis. Twin studies, which compare identical and fraternal twins (see Chapter 2), suggest that genetic factors *are* involved in mood disorders (Kelsoe, 2009). Concordance rates average around 65%–72% for identical twins but only 14%–19% for fraternal twins, who share less genetic similarity. Thus, evidence suggests that heredity can create a *predisposition* to mood disorders. Environmental factors probably determine whether this predisposition is converted into an actual disorder.

Neurochemical and Neuroanatomical Factors

Heredity may influence susceptibility to mood disorders by creating a predisposition toward certain types of neurochemical abnormalities in the brain. Correlations have been found between mood disorders and abnor-

FIGURE 14.5 | Age of onset for bipolar mood disorder

The onset of bipolar disorder typically occurs in adolescence or early adulthood. The data graphed here, which were combined from ten studies, show the distribution of age of onset for 1,304 bipolar patients. As you can see, bipolar disorder emerges most frequently during individuals' teenage years or their twenties.

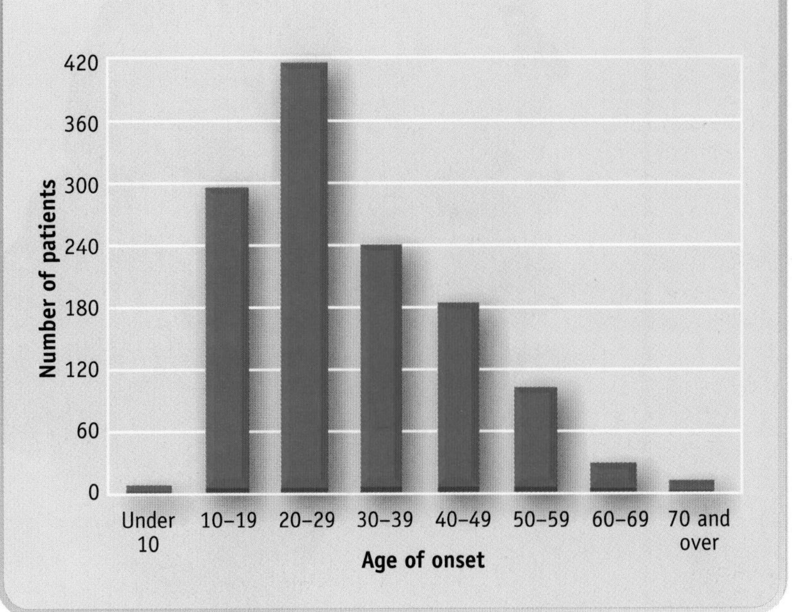

Source: From Goodwin, F. K., & Jamison, K. R. (1990). *Manic-depressive illness.* New York: Oxford University Press. Reprinted by permission from the Royal College of Psychiatrists.

mal levels of two neurotransmitters in the brain: norepinephrine and serotonin, although other neurotransmitter disturbances may also contribute (Dunlop, Garlow, & Nemeroff, 2009). The details remain elusive, but low levels of serotonin appear to be a crucial factor underlying many forms of depression (Johnson et al., 2009). A variety of drug therapies are fairly effective in the treatment of severe mood disorders. Most of these drugs are known to affect the availability (in the brain) of the neurotransmitters that have been related to mood disorders. Since this effect is unlikely to be a coincidence, it bolsters the plausibility of the idea that neurochemical changes produce mood disturbances.

Studies have also found some interesting correlations between mood disorders and a variety of structural abnormalities in the brain. Perhaps the best-documented correlation is the association between depression and *reduced hippocampal volume* (Davidson, Pizzagalli, & Nitschke, 2009). The *hippocampus*, which is known to play a major role in memory (see Figure 14.6), tends to be about 8%–10% smaller in depressed subjects than in normal subjects (Videbech & Ravnkilde, 2004).

A new theory of the biological bases of depression may be able to account for this finding. The springboard for this theory is the recent discovery that the human brain continues to generate new neurons in adulthood, especially in the hippocampal formation (Gage, 2002). This process is called *neurogenesis*. Evidence suggests that depression occurs when major life

FIGURE 14.6 | The hippocampus and depression

This graphic shows the hippocampus in blue. The photo inset shows a brain dissected to reveal the hippocampus in both the right and left hemispheres. It has long been known that the hippocampus plays a key role in memory, but its possible role in depression has only come to light in recent years. Research suggests that shrinkage of the hippocampal formation due to suppressed neurogenesis may be a key causal factor underlying depressive disorders.

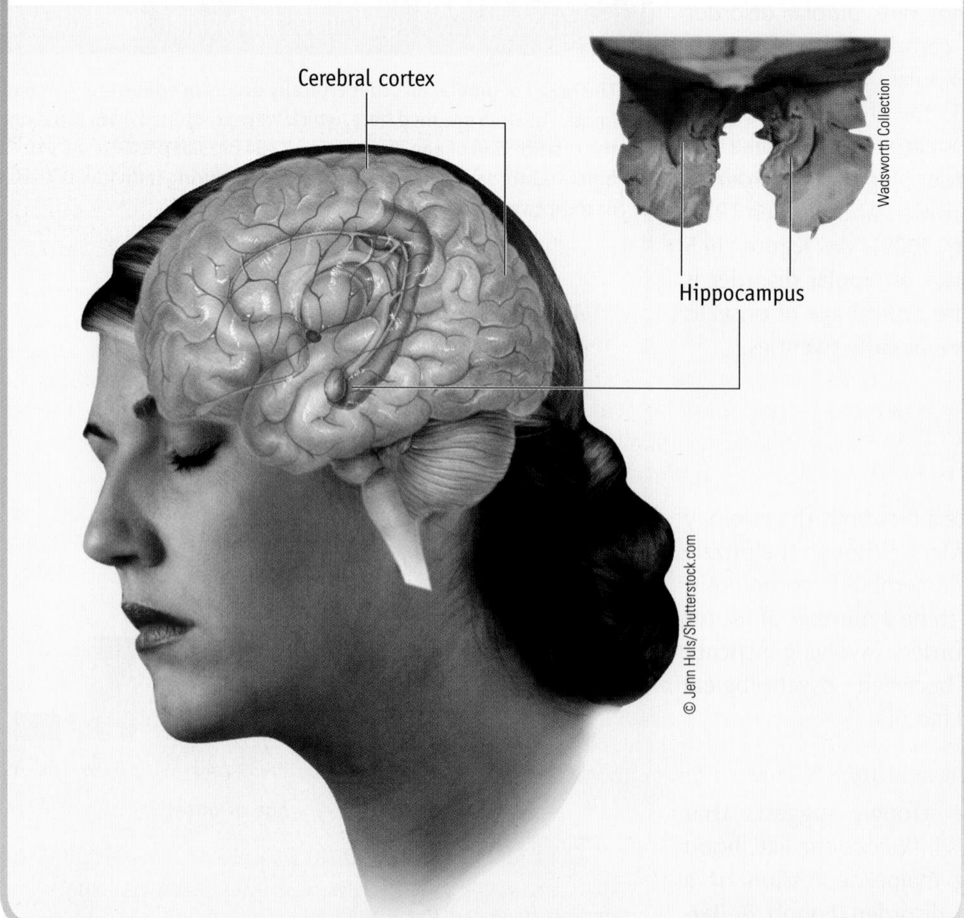

stress causes neurochemical reactions that suppress neurogenesis, resulting in reduced hippocampal volume (Warner-Schmidt & Duman, 2006). According to this view, the suppression of neurogenesis is the central cause of depression, and antidepressant drugs that relieve depression do so because they promote neurogenesis (Duman & Monteggia, 2006). A great deal of additional research will be required to fully test this innovative new model of the biological bases of depressive disorders.

Cognitive Factors

A variety of theories emphasize how cognitive factors contribute to depressive disorders. In this section, we examine Martin Seligman's *learned helplessness model* of depression. Based largely on animal research, Seligman (1974) proposed that depression is caused by *learned helplessness*—passive "giving up" behavior produced by exposure to unavoidable aversive events (such as uncontrollable shock in the laboratory). He originally considered learned helplessness to be a product of conditioning but eventually revised his theory, giving it a cognitive slant. The reformulated theory of learned helplessness postulates that the roots of depression lie in how people explain the setbacks and other negative events that they experience (Abramson, Seligman, & Teasdale, 1978). According to Seligman, people who exhibit a *pessimistic explanatory style* are especially vulnerable to depression. These people tend to attribute their setbacks to their personal flaws instead of to situational factors, and they tend to draw global, far-reaching conclusions about their personal inadequacies based on these setbacks.

In accord with cognitive models of depression, Susan Nolen-Hoeksema (2000) has found that people who *ruminate* about their problems and setbacks have elevated rates of depression and tend to remain depressed longer than those who do not ruminate. People who tend to ruminate repetitively focus their attention on their depressing feelings, thinking constantly about how sad, lethargic, and unmotivated they are. Excessive rumination tends to foster and amplify episodes of depression by increasing negative thinking, impairing problem solving, and undermining social support (Nolen-Hoeksema, Wisco, & Lyubomirsky, 2008). Nolen-Hoeksema believes that women have a greater tendency to ruminate than men and that this disparity may be a major reason that depression is more prevalent in women.

In sum, cognitive models of depression maintain that negative thinking is what leads to depression in many people. The principal problem with cognitive theories is their difficulty in separating cause from effect. Does negative thinking cause depression? Or does depression cause negative thinking (see Figure 14.7)? A *clear* demonstration of a causal link between negative thinking and depression is not possible because it would require manipulating people's explanatory style (which is not easy to change) in sufficient degree to produce full-fledged depressive disorders (which would not be ethical). However, a study by Lauren Alloy and her colleagues (1999) provided impressive evidence consistent with a causal link between negative thinking and depression. They assessed the explanatory style of a sample of first-year college students who were not depressed at the outset of the study. The students were characterized as being at high risk or low risk for depression based on whether they exhibited a negative cognitive style. The follow-up data over the ensuing two and a half years showed dramatic differences between the two groups in vulnerability to depression. During this relatively brief period, a major depressive disorder emerged in 17% of the high-risk students in comparison to only 1% of the low-risk students. These findings and other data from the study suggest that negative thinking makes people more vulnerable to depression.

FIGURE 14.7 Interpreting the correlation between negative thinking and depression

Cognitive theories of depression assert that consistent patterns of negative thinking cause depression. Although these theories are highly plausible, depression could cause negative thoughts, or both could be caused by a third factor, such as neurochemical changes in the brain.

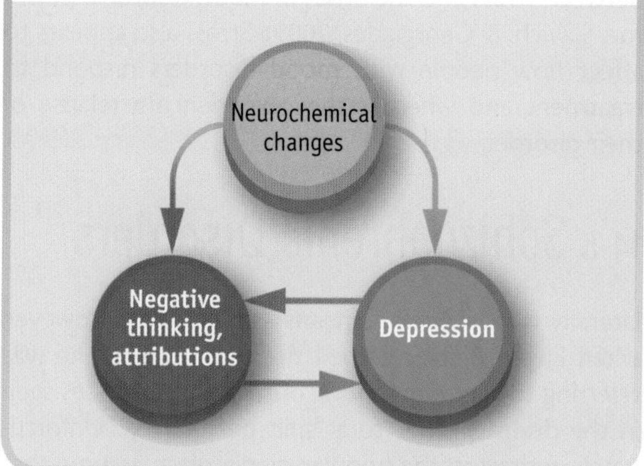

Interpersonal Roots

Some theorists suggest that inadequate social skills put people on the road to depressive disorders (Ingram, Scott, & Hamill, 2009). According to this notion, depression-prone people lack the social finesse needed to acquire many important kinds of reinforcers, such as good friends, top jobs, and desirable spouses. This paucity of reinforcers could understandably lead to negative emotions and depression (see Figure 14.8). Consistent with this theory, researchers have indeed found correlations between poor social skills and depression (Petty, Sachs-Ericsson, & Joiner, 2004).

FIGURE 14.8 Interpersonal factors in depression

Interpersonal theories about the etiology of depression emphasize how inadequate social skills may contribute to the development of the disorder. Recent studies suggest that excessive reassurance seeking may play a particularly critical role in the social dynamics promoting depression.

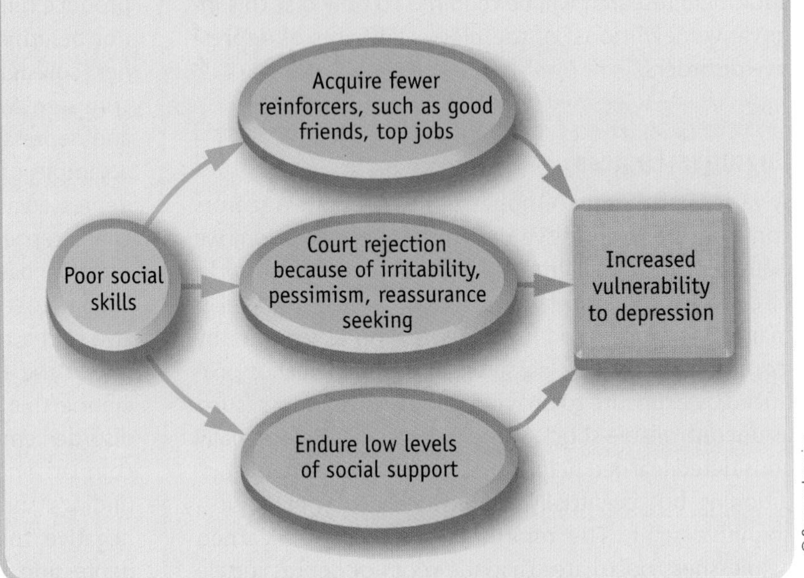

Another interpersonal factor is that depressed people tend to be depressing (Joiner & Timmons, 2009). Individuals suffering from depression often are irritable and pessimistic. They complain a lot and aren't particularly enjoyable companions. They also alienate people by constantly asking for reassurances about their relationships and their worth (Burns et al., 2006). As a consequence, depressed people tend to court rejection from those around them. This alienation of important sources of social support may contribute to their downward spiral into depression.

Precipitating Stress

Mood disorders sometimes appear mysteriously "out of the blue" in people who seem to be leading benign, nonstressful lives. For this reason, experts used to believe that mood disorders are relatively uninfluenced by stress. However, recent advances in the measurement of personal stress have altered this picture. The evidence available today suggests a moderately strong link between stress and the onset of mood disorders (Monroe, Slavich, & Georgiades, 2009). Stress also appears to affect how people with mood disorders respond to treatment and whether they experience a relapse of their disorder.

14-5 Schizophrenic Disorders

Literally, *schizophrenia* means "split mind." However, when Eugen Bleuler coined the term in 1911, he was referring to the fragmenting of thought processes seen in the disorder—not to a "split personality." Unfortunately, writers in the popular media often assume that the split-mind notion refers to the syndrome in which a person manifests two or more personalities. As you have already learned, this syndrome is actually called *dissociative identity disorder.* Schizophrenia is a much more common, and altogether different, type of disorder.

***Schizophrenic disorders* are a class of disorders marked by disturbances in thought that spill over to affect perceptual, social, and emotional processes.** How common is schizophrenia? Prevalence estimates suggest that about 1% of the population may suffer from schizophrenic disorders (Lauriello, Bustillo, & Keith, 2005). That may not sound like much, but it means that in North America alone there may be several million people troubled by schizophrenic disturbances. Moreover, schizophrenia is an extremely costly disorder for society, because it is a severe, debilitating illness that tends to have an early onset and often requires lengthy hospital care. Schizophrenic disorders typically emerge during adolescence or early adulthood. Those who develop schizophrenia usually have a long history of peculiar behavior and cognitive and social deficits, although most do not manifest a full-fledged psychological disorder during childhood. The emergence of schizophrenia may be sudden, but it usually is insidious and gradual.

14-5a GENERAL SYMPTOMS

Although there are a number of distinct schizophrenic syndromes, they share some general characteristics that we need to examine before looking at the subtypes. No single symptom is inevitably present, but the following symptoms are commonly seen in schizophrenia (Lewis, Escalona, & Keith, 2009).

Irrational thought. Cognitive deficits and disturbed thought processes are the central, defining feature of schizophrenic disorders (Heinrichs, 2005). Various kinds of delusions are common. ***Delusions* are false beliefs that are maintained even though they clearly are out of touch with reality.** For example, one patient's delusion that he was a tiger (with a deformed body) persisted for 15 years (Kulick, Pope, & Keck, 1990). More typically, affected persons believe that their private thoughts are being broadcast to other people, that thoughts are being injected into their mind against their will, or that their thoughts are being controlled by some external force. In *delusions of grandeur*, people maintain that they are extremely famous or important. For example, one patient insisted that she dictated the hobbit stories to Tolkien and that she was going to win the Nobel Prize for medicine. In addition to delusions, the schizophrenic person's train of thought deteriorates. Thinking becomes chaotic rather than logical and linear. There is a "loosening of associations" as the schizophrenic shifts topics in disjointed ways.

Deterioration of adaptive behavior. Schizophrenia involves a noticeable decline in the quality of the person's routine functioning in work, social relations, and personal care. Friends will often make remarks such as "Hal just isn't himself anymore." For example, personal hygiene habits may deteriorate.

Distorted perception. A variety of perceptual distortions may occur in schizophrenia, with the most common being auditory hallucinations, which are reported by about 75% of patients (Combs & Mueser, 2007). ***Hallucinations* are sensory perceptions that occur in the absence of a real external stimulus or that represent gross distortions of perceptual input.** Schizophrenics frequently report that they hear voices of nonexistent or absent people talking to them. These voices often provide an insulting running commentary on the person's behavior ("You're an idiot for shaking his hand"). The voices may be argumentative ("You don't need a bath"), and they may issue commands ("Prepare your home for visitors from outer space").

Disturbed emotion. Normal emotional tone can be disrupted in schizophrenia in a variety of ways. Although it may not be an accurate indicator of their underlying emotional experience, some victims show little emotional responsiveness, a symptom referred to as "blunted or flat affect." Others show inappropriate emotional responses that don't jell with the situation or with what they are saying. People with schizophrenia may also become emotionally volatile.

14-5b SUBTYPES

Four subtypes of schizophrenic disorders have traditionally been recognized: paranoid, catatonic, disorganized, and undifferentiated schizophrenia (Minzenberg, Yoon, & Carter, 2008). As its name implies, *paranoid schizophrenia* is dominated by delusions of persecution, along with delusions of grandeur. In this common form of schizophrenia, people come to believe that they have many enemies who want to harass and oppress them. *Catatonic schizophrenia* is marked by striking motor disturbances, ranging from muscular rigidity to random motor activity. Some catatonics go into an extreme form of withdrawal known as a catatonic stupor, while others may go into a state of catatonic excitement. In *disorganized schizophrenia*, a particularly severe deterioration of adaptive behavior is seen. Prominent symptoms include frequent incoherence and virtually complete social withdrawal. People who are clearly schizophrenic but who cannot be placed into any of the three previous categories are said to have *undifferentiated schizophrenia*, which is marked by idiosyncratic mixtures of schizophrenic symptoms.

However, it should be noted that one of the more radical proposals for DSM-5 is to discard these subtypes. Why? For many years researchers have pointed out that there aren't meaningful differences between the classic subtypes in etiology, prognosis, or response to treatment. The absence of such differences casts doubt on the value of distinguishing among the subtypes. Critics also noted that the catatonic and disorganized subtypes were rarely seen in contemporary clinical practice and that undifferentiated cases don't represent a subtype as much as a hodgepodge of "leftovers."

14-5c ETIOLOGY OF SCHIZOPHRENIA

Most of us can identify, at least to some extent, with people who suffer from mood disorders or anxiety disorders. You can probably imagine events that might leave you struggling with depression or grappling with anxiety. But what could possibly have led Ed to believe that he had been fighting space wars and vampires? What could lead someone to think that she had dictated the hobbit novels to Tolkien? As mystifying as these delusions may seem, you'll see that the etiology of schizophrenic disorders is not all that different from the etiology of other disorders.

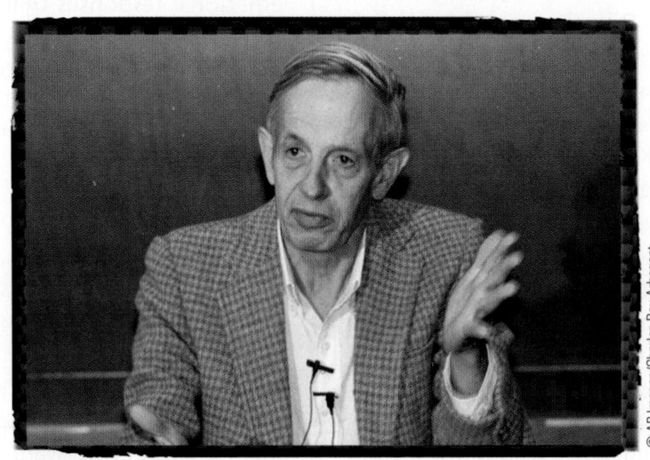
© AP Images/Charles Rex Arbogast

John Nash, the Nobel Prize-winning mathematician whose story was told in the film *A Beautiful Mind*, has struggled with paranoid schizophrenia since 1959.

Genetic Vulnerability

Evidence is plentiful that hereditary factors play a role in the development of schizophrenic disorders (Kirov & Owen, 2009). For instance, in twin studies, concordance rates for schizophrenia average around 48% for identical twins, in comparison to about 17% for fraternal twins (Gottesman, 2001). Studies also indicate that a child born to two schizophrenic parents has about a 46% probability of developing a schizophrenic disorder (as compared to the probability of about 1% for the population as a whole). These and other findings that demonstrate the genetic roots of schizophrenia are summarized in Figure 14.9. Overall, the picture is similar to that seen for mood disorders. Several converging lines of evidence indicate that people inherit a genetically transmitted *vulnerability* to schizophrenia. Some theorists suspect that genetic factors may account for as much as 80% of the variability in susceptibility to schizophrenia (Pogue-Geile & Yokley, 2010).

Neurochemical Factors

Like mood disorders, schizophrenic disorders appear to be accompanied by changes in the activity of one or more neurotransmitters in the brain. Excess *dopamine* activity has been implicated as a likely cause of schizophrenia (Javitt & Laruelle, 2006). This hypothesis makes sense because most of the drugs that are useful in the treatment of schizophrenia are known to dampen dopamine activity in the brain. However, the evidence linking schizophrenia to high dopamine levels is riddled with complexities and interpretive problems (Bobo et al., 2008), and in recent years the dopamine hypothesis has become more nuanced and complex. Researchers believe that dysregulation occurs in dopamine circuits and that the nature of this dysregulation may vary in different regions of the brain (Howes & Kapur, 2009).

Recent research has suggested that marijuana use during adolescence may help precipitate schizophrenia in young people who have a genetic vulnerability to the disorder (McGrath et al., 2010). This unexpected finding has generated considerable debate about whether and how cannabis might contribute to the emergence of schizophrenia (DeLisi, 2008). Some critics have suggested that schizophrenia might lead to cannabis use rather than the other way around. In other words, emerging psychotic symptoms may prompt young people to turn to marijuana to self-medicate. However, a carefully controlled, long-term study in Germany found no evidence to support the self-medication explanation (Kuepper et al., 2011).

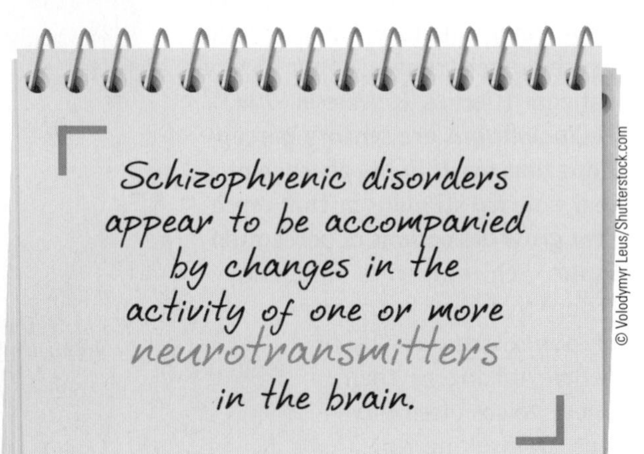
Schizophrenic disorders appear to be accompanied by changes in the activity of one or more neurotransmitters in the brain.
© Volodymyr Leus/Shutterstock.com

FIGURE 14.9 Genetic vulnerability to schizophrenic disorders

Relatives of schizophrenic patients have an elevated risk for schizophrenia. This risk is greater among closer relatives. Although environment also plays a role in the etiology of schizophrenia, the concordance rates shown here suggest that there must be a genetic vulnerability to the disorder. These concordance estimates are based on pooled data from 40 studies. (Based on Nicol & Gottesman, 1983; Gottesman, 1991)

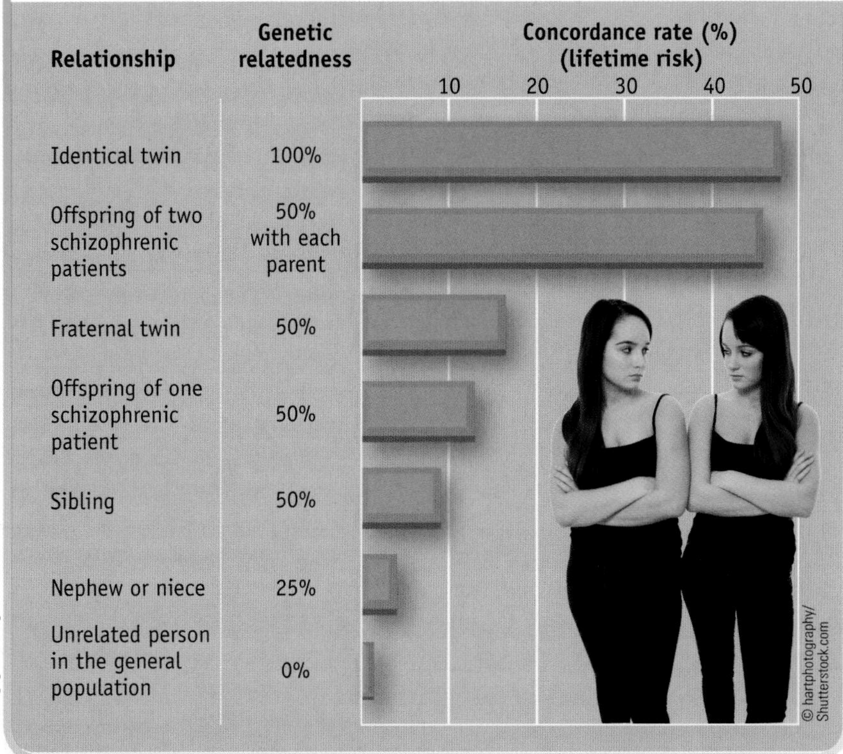

FIGURE 14.10 Schizophrenia and the ventricles of the brain

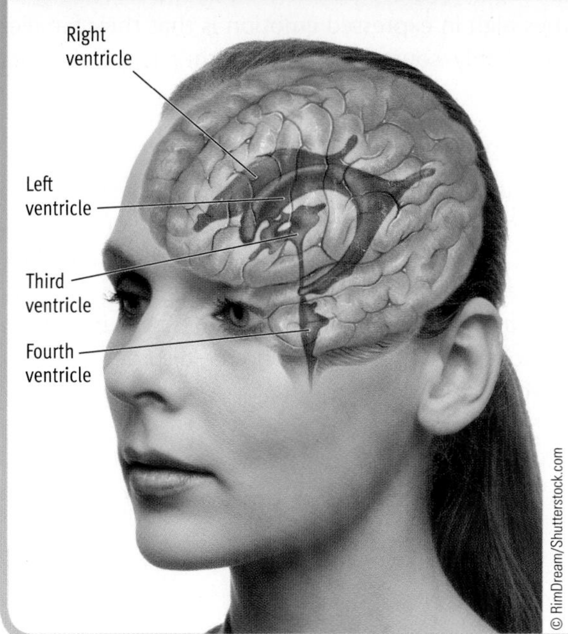

Cerebrospinal fluid (CSF) circulates around the brain and spinal cord. The hollow cavities in the brain filled with CSF are called *ventricles.* The four ventricles in the human brain are depicted here. Studies with modern brain-imaging techniques suggest that an association exists between enlarged ventricles in the brain and the occurrence of schizophrenic disturbance.

Structural Abnormalities in the Brain

For decades, studies have suggested that individuals with schizophrenia exhibit a variety of deficits in attention, perception, and information processing (Harvey, 2010). These cognitive deficits suggest that schizophrenic disorders may be caused by neurological defects. Until recent decades, however, this theory was based more on speculation than on actual research. However, advances in brain-imaging technology have yielded mountains of intriguing data since the mid-1980s. Research with various types of brain scans suggests an association between enlarged brain ventricles (the hollow, fluid-filled cavities in the brain depicted in Figure 14.10) and schizophrenic disturbance (Shenton & Kubicki, 2009). Enlarged ventricles are assumed to reflect either the degeneration or failure to develop of nearby brain tissue. The significance of enlarged ventricles is hotly debated, however. Structural deterioration in the brain could be a contributing *cause* or a *consequence* of schizophrenia.

The Neurodevelopmental Hypothesis

Several new lines of evidence have led to the emergence of the *neurodevelopmental hypothesis* of schizophrenia, which posits that schizophrenia is caused in part by various disruptions in the normal maturational processes of the brain before or at birth (Fatemi & Folsom, 2009). According to this hypothesis, insults to the brain during sensitive phases of prenatal development or during birth can cause subtle neurological damage that elevates individuals' vulnerability to schizophrenia years later in adolescence and early adulthood (see Figure 14.11 on the next page). What are

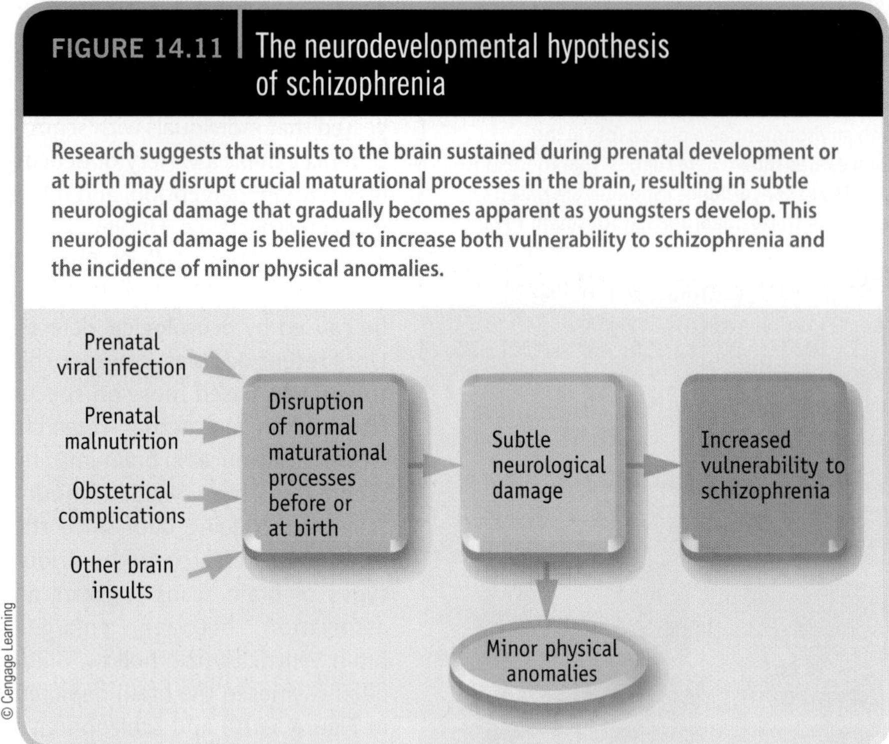

FIGURE 14.11 The neurodevelopmental hypothesis of schizophrenia

Research suggests that insults to the brain sustained during prenatal development or at birth may disrupt crucial maturational processes in the brain, resulting in subtle neurological damage that gradually becomes apparent as youngsters develop. This neurological damage is believed to increase both vulnerability to schizophrenia and the incidence of minor physical anomalies.

the sources of these early insults to the brain? Thus far, research has focused mainly on viral infections or malnutrition during prenatal development and on obstetrical complications during the birth process.

Quite a number of studies have found a link between exposure to influenza and other infections during prenatal development and an increased prevalence of schizophrenia (Brown & Derkits, 2010). Other research, which investigated the possible impact of prenatal malnutrition, found an elevated incidence of schizophrenia in a cohort of people who were prenatally exposed to a severe famine in 1944–45 because of a Nazi blockade of food deliveries in the Netherlands during World War II (Susser et al., 1996). Another line of study has shown that schizophrenic patients are more likely than control subjects to have a history of obstetrical complications (Murray & Bramon, 2005). Finally, research suggests that minor physical anomalies (slight anatomical defects of the head, hands, feet, and face) that would be consistent with prenatal neurological damage are more common in people with schizophrenia than in other people (Schiffman et al., 2002). Collectively, these diverse studies argue for a relationship between early neurological trauma and a predisposition to schizophrenia (King, St-Hilaire, & Heidkamp, 2010).

Expressed Emotion

Studies of expressed emotion have primarily focused on how this element of family dynamics influences the *course* of schizophrenic illness after the onset of the disorder. *Expressed emotion (EE)* reflects the degree to which a relative of a schizophrenic patient displays highly critical or emotionally overinvolved attitudes toward the patient. Audiotaped interviews of relatives' communication are carefully evaluated for critical comments, hostility toward the patient, and excessive emotional involvement (overprotective, overconcerned attitudes) (Hooley, 2004).

Studies show that a family's expressed emotion is a good predictor of the course of a schizophrenic patient's illness. After release from a hospital, patients who return to a family high in expressed emotion show relapse rates two to three times those of patients who return to a family low in expressed emotion (Hooley, 2009). Part of the problem for patients returning to homes high in expressed emotion is that their families are probably sources of *stress* rather than of *social support*.

Precipitating Stress

Many theories of schizophrenia assume that stress plays a role in triggering schizophrenic disorders (Walker & Tessner, 2008). According to this notion, various biological and psychological factors influence individuals' *vulnerability* to schizophrenia. High stress may then serve to precipitate a schizophrenic disorder in someone who is vulnerable.

14-6 APPLICATION

Understanding Eating Disorders

Answer the following "true" or "false."

____ 1. Although they have attracted attention only in recent years, eating disorders have a long history and have always been fairly common.

____ 2. People with anorexia nervosa are much more likely to recognize their eating behavior as pathological than people suffering from bulimia nervosa.

____ 3. The prevalence of eating disorders is twice as high in women as it is in men.

____ 4. The binge-and-purge syndrome seen in bulimia nervosa is not common in anorexia nervosa.

All of these statements are false, as you will see in this Application. The psychological disorders that we discussed in the main body of the chapter have largely been recognized for centuries and generally are found in one form or another in all cultures and societies. Eating disorders, however, present a sharp contrast to this picture: They have only been recognized in recent decades, and initially they were largely confined to affluent, Westernized cultures. In spite of these fascinating differences, eating disorders have much in common with traditional forms of pathology.

14-6a TYPES OF EATING DISORDERS

Although most people don't seem to take eating disorders as seriously as other types of psychological disorders, you will see that they are dangerous and debilitating. No class of psychological disorders is associated with a greater elevation in mortality (Striegel-Moore & Bulik, 2007). ***Eating disorders*** **are severe disturbances in eating behavior characterized by preoccupation with weight and unhealthy efforts to control weight.** The two principal types of eating disorders are *anorexia nervosa* and *bulimia nervosa.* A third syndrome, called *binge-eating disorder,* is likely to be included in DSM-5. In this Application we will mainly focus on anorexia and bulimia, but we will briefly outline the symptoms of this new disorder.

Anorexia Nervosa

Anorexia nervosa **involves intense fear of gaining weight, disturbed body image, refusal to maintain normal weight, and dangerous measures to lose weight.** Two subtypes have been distinguished. In *restricting type anorexia nervosa,* people drastically reduce their intake of food, sometimes literally starving themselves. In *binge-eating/purging type anorexia nervosa,* victims attempt to lose weight by forcing themselves to vomit after meals, by misusing laxatives and diuretics, and by engaging in excessive exercise.

Both types entail a disturbed body image. No matter how frail and emaciated the victims become, they insist that they are too fat. Their morbid fear of obesity means that they are never satisfied with their weight. If they gain a pound or two, they panic. The only thing that makes them happy is to lose more weight. The common result is a relentless decline in body weight—in fact, patients entering treatment for anorexia nervosa are typically 25%–30% below their normal weight. Because of their disturbed body image, people suffering from anorexia generally do *not* appreciate the maladaptive quality of their behavior and rarely seek treatment on their own. They are typically coaxed or coerced into treatment by friends or family members who are alarmed by their appearance. Anorexia nervosa eventually leads to a cascade of medical problems (Halmi, 2008). Anorexia is a debilitating illness that leads to death in 5%–10% of patients.

Bulimia Nervosa

Bulimia nervosa **involves habitually engaging in out-of-control overeating followed by unhealthy compensatory efforts, such as self-induced vomiting, fasting, abuse of laxatives and diuretics,**

Eating disorders have become distressingly common among young women in Western cultures. No matter how frail they become, people suffering from anorexia insist that they are too fat.

and excessive exercise. The eating binges are usually carried out in secret and are followed by intense guilt and concern about gaining weight. These feelings motivate ill-advised strategies to undo the effects of the overeating. However, vomiting prevents the absorption of only about half of recently consumed food, and laxatives and diuretics have negligible impact on caloric intake, so people suffering from bulimia nervosa typically maintain a reasonably normal weight.

Obviously, bulimia nervosa shares many features with anorexia nervosa, such as a morbid fear of becoming obese, preoccupation with food, and rigid, maladaptive approaches to controlling weight that are grounded in naive all-or-none thinking. However, the syndromes also differ in crucial ways. First and foremost, bulimia is a less-life-threatening condition. Second, although their weight and appearance usually is more "normal" than that seen in anorexia, people with bulimia are much more likely to recognize that their eating behavior is pathological and are more prone to recognize their need for treatment.

Binge-Eating Disorder

***Binge-eating disorder* involves distress-inducing eating binges that are not accompanied by the purging, fasting, and excessive exercise seen in bulimia.** Obviously, this syndrome resembles bulimia, but it is less severe. Still, this disorder creates great distress, as binge eaters tend to be disgusted by their bodies and distraught about their overeating. People with binge-eating disorder are frequently overweight. Their excessive eating is often triggered by stress. Research suggests that this comparatively mild syndrome may be more common than anorexia or bulimia (Hudson et al., 2007).

14-6b HISTORY AND PREVALENCE

Historians have been able to track down descriptions of anorexia nervosa that date back centuries, so the disorder is not entirely new, but anorexia did not become a *common* affliction until the middle of the 20th century (Vandereycken, 2002). Although binging and purging have a long history in some cultures, they were not part of a pathological effort to control weight, and bulimia nervosa appears to be a new syndrome that emerged gradually in the middle of the 20th century and was first recognized in the 1970s (Steiger & Bruce, 2009).

Both disorders are products of modern, affluent Western culture, where food is generally plentiful and the desirability of being thin is widely endorsed. Until recently, these problems were not seen outside of Western cultures. However, advances in communication have exported Western culture to farflung corners of the globe, and eating disorders have started showing up in many non-Western societies, especially affluent Asian countries (Becker & Fay, 2006).

A huge gender gap exists in the likelihood of developing eating disorders.

© stockcam/iStockphoto

A huge gender gap exists in the likelihood of developing eating disorders. About 90%–95% of individuals who are treated for anorexia nervosa and bulimia nervosa are female (Thompson & Kinder, 2003). This staggering discrepancy appears to be a result of cultural pressures rather than biological factors. Western standards of attractiveness emphasize being slender more for females than for males, and women generally experience heavier pressure to be physically attractive than men do (Strahan et al., 2008). Eating disorders mostly afflict *young* women. The typical age of onset for anorexia is 14–18, and for bulimia it is 15–21 (see Figure 14.12).

How common are eating disorders in Western societies? Studies of young women suggest that about 1% develop anorexia nervosa and about 2%–3% develop bulimia nervosa (Anderson & Yager, 2005). In some respects, these figures may only scratch the surface of the problem. Evidence suggests that as many as 20% of female college students may struggle with transient bulimic symptoms (Anderson & Yager, 2005).

14-6c ETIOLOGY OF EATING DISORDERS

Like other types of psychological disorders, eating disorders are caused by multiple determinants that work interactively.

Genetic Vulnerability

The evidence is not nearly as strong or complete for eating disorders as it is for many other types of psychopathology (such as anxiety, mood, and schizophrenic disorders), but some people may inherit a genetic vulnerability to these problems (Thornton, Mazzeo, & Bulik, 2011). Twin studies of females report higher concordance rates for identical twins than fraternal twins, suggesting that a genetic predisposition may be at work (Steiger, Bruce, & Israël, 2003).

Personality Factors

Certain personality traits may increase vulnerability to eating disorders. Although there are innumerable exceptions, victims of anorexia nervosa tend to be obsessive, rigid, neurotic, and emotionally restrained, whereas

FIGURE 14.12 Age of onset for anorexia nervosa

Eating disorders emerge primarily during adolescence, as these data for anorexia nervosa show. This graph depicts how age of onset was distributed in a sample of 166 female patients from Minnesota. As you can see, over half experienced the onset of their illness before the age of 20, with vulnerability clearly peaking between the ages of 15 and 19. (Data from Lucas et al., 1991)

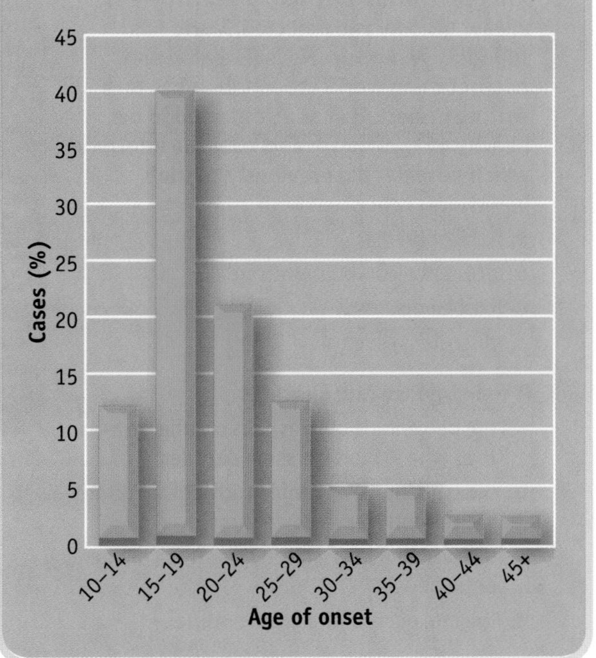

victims of bulimia nervosa tend to be impulsive, overly sensitive, and low in self-esteem (Wonderlich, 2002). Recent research also suggests that perfectionism is a risk factor for anorexia (Steiger & Bruce, 2009).

Cultural Values

The contribution of cultural values to the increased prevalence of eating disorders can hardly be overestimated. In Western society, young women are socialized to believe that they must be attractive and that to be attractive they must be as thin as the actresses and fashion models that dominate the media. Thanks to this cultural milieu, many young women are dissatisfied with their weight because the societal ideals promoted by the media are unattainable for most of them (Thompson & Stice, 2001). Unfortunately, in a small portion of these women, the pressure to be thin, in combination with genetic vulnerability, family pathology, and other factors, leads to unhealthy efforts to control weight.

The Role of the Family

Many theorists emphasize how family dynamics can contribute to the development of anorexia nervosa and bulimia nervosa in young women. The principal issue appears to be that some mothers contribute to eating disorders simply by endorsing society's message that "you can never be too thin" and by modeling unhealthy dieting behaviors of their own (Francis & Birch, 2005). In conjunction with media pressures, this role modeling leads many daughters to internalize the idea that the thinner you are, the more attractive you are.

Cognitive Factors

Many theorists emphasize the role of disturbed thinking in the etiology of eating disorders (Williamson et al., 2001). For example, anorexic patients' typical belief that they are fat when they are really wasting away is a dramatic illustration of how thinking goes awry. Patients with eating disorders display rigid, all-or-none thinking and many maladaptive beliefs, such as "I must be thin to be accepted," "If I am not in complete control, I will lose all control," and "If I gain one pound, I'll go on to gain enormous weight." Additional research is needed to determine whether distorted thinking is a *cause* or merely a *symptom* of eating disorders.

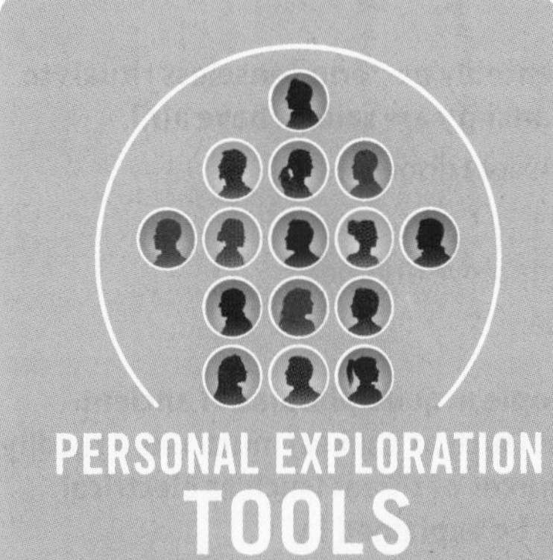

Curious about yourself? To learn more about how topics in this chapter relate to you, go online to CourseMate at www.cengagebrain.com where you can:

- Complete a **Self-Reflection** exercise that will help you think about your personal experiences in relation to topics in the chapter.
- Take a **Self-Assessment** scale that will show you how you score on a research instrument that measures personality traits or attitudes.
- Explore **Recommended Readings** that will provide brief overviews of useful self-help books.

STUDY TOOLS ▸ 14

Ready to study? In your book you can:

- **Test Yourself** with a multiple-choice quiz (below)
- Rip out the **Chapter Review card** (in the back of the book) to refresh yourself on the chapter's Key Ideas and Key Terms

Or you can go online to CourseMate at www.cengagebrain.com where you can:

- Take additional Practice Quizzes to prepare for your exam
- Review Key Terms with flash cards and a crossword puzzle
- View videos that expand on selected concepts

TEST YOURSELF

1. Sergio has just entered treatment for bipolar disorder, and he is informed that most patients respond to drug treatment within a month. This information represents

a. a prognosis.
b. an etiology.
c. a histology.
d. a concordance.

2. Although Sue always feels high levels of dread, worry, and anxiety, she still meets her daily responsibilities. Sue's behavior

a. should not be considered abnormal, since her adaptive functioning is not impaired.
b. should not be considered abnormal, since everyone sometimes experiences worry and anxiety.
c. can still be considered abnormal, since she feels great personal distress.
d. both a and b.

3. People who repeatedly perform senseless rituals to overcome their anxiety are said to have a(n)

a. generalized anxiety disorder.
b. manic disorder.
c. obsessive-compulsive disorder.
d. phobic disorder.

4. The fact that people acquire phobias of ancient sources of threat (such as snakes) much more readily than modern sources of threat (such as electrical outlets) can best be explained by

a. classical conditioning.
b. operant conditioning.
c. observational learning.
d. preparedness.

5. Which of the following statements about dissociative identity disorder is true?

a. The original personality is always aware of the alternate personalities.
b. The transitions between personalities are usually very gradual.
c. The personalities are typically all quite similar to one another.
d. Starting in the 1970s, a dramatic increase occurred in the diagnosis of dissociative identity disorder.

6. After several months during which he was always gloomy and dejected, Mario has suddenly perked up. He feels elated and energetic and works around the clock on a writing project. He has also started to bet heavily on sporting events over the Internet, which he never did previously. Mario's behavior is consistent with

a. schizophrenia.
b. obsessive-compulsive disorder.
c. bipolar disorder.
d. dissociative identity disorder.

7. A concordance rate indicates

a. the percentage of twin pairs or other relatives who exhibit the same disorder.
b. the percentage of people with a given disorder who are currently receiving treatment.
c. the prevalence of a given disorder in the general population.
d. the rate of cure for a given disorder.

8. Which of the following is *not* a common symptom of schizophrenia?

a. Auditory hallucinations
b. Irrational thought
c. Coexistence of two or more very different personalities
d. Deterioration of adaptive behavior

9. Which of the following has *not* been implicated in the etiology of schizophrenia?

a. Classical conditioning of psychotic responses
b. Genetic vulnerability
c. Excess or dysregulated dopamine activity in the brain
d. Disruptions in the normal maturational processes of the brain before or at birth

10. About ________ % of patients with eating disorders are female.

a. 40
b. 50–60
c. 75
d. 90–95

Answers: 1. a, page 296; 2. c, pages 296–297; 3. c, page 299; 4. d, page 300; 5. d, pages 301–302; 6. c, pages 304–305; 7. a, page 305; 8. c, page 309; 9. a, pages 310–312; 10. d, page 314

LEARNING OBJECTIVES

15-1 Identify the basic elements of the treatment process.

15-2 Describe psychoanalysis, client-centered therapy, and group therapy, and assess their efficacy.

15-3 Understand how systematic desensitization, aversion therapy, social skills training, and cognitive-behavioral treatments can solve behavioral problems.

15-4 Outline the benefits and risks associated with drug therapies and electroconvulsive therapy.

15-5 Discuss the merits of blending approaches to therapy and efforts to enhance cultural sensitivity in treatment.

15-6 Learn how to find a good therapist.

After you have read the chapter, you can Test Yourself and learn about other Study Tools on page 340.

CHAPTER 15

PSYCHOTHERAPY

© Photo_Concepts/iStockphoto

What do you picture when you hear the term *psychotherapy*? If you're like most people, you probably envision a troubled patient lying on a couch in a therapist's office, with the therapist asking penetrating questions and providing sage advice. Typically, people believe that psychotherapy is only for those who are "sick" and that therapists have special powers that allow them to "see through" their clients. It is also widely believed that therapy requires years of deep probing into a client's innermost secrets. Many people further assume that therapists routinely tell their patients how to lead their lives. Like most stereotypes, this picture of psychotherapy is a mixture of fact and fiction, as you'll see in the upcoming pages.

In this chapter, we take a down-to-earth look at the process of *psychotherapy*, using the term in its broadest sense to refer to all the diverse approaches to the treatment of psychological problems. We start by discussing some general questions about the provision of treatment. Who seeks therapy? What kinds of professionals provide treatment? How many types of therapy are there? After considering these general issues, we examine some of the more widely used approaches to treating psychological maladies, analyzing their goals, techniques, and effectiveness. The Application at the end of the chapter focuses on practical issues involved in finding a therapist, in case you ever have to advise someone about seeking help.

15-1 The Elements of the Treatment Process

Today people have a bewildering array of psychotherapy approaches to choose from. In fact, the immense diversity of therapeutic treatments makes defining the concept of *psychotherapy* difficult. All psychotherapies involve a helping relationship (the treatment) between a professional with special training (the therapist) and another person in need of help (the client).

15-1a TREATMENTS: HOW MANY TYPES ARE THERE?

In their efforts to help people, mental health professionals use many methods of treatment, including discussion, emotional support, persuasion, conditioning procedures, relaxation training, role playing, drug therapy, biofeedback, and group therapy. Some therapists also use a variety of less-conventional procedures, such as rebirthing, poetry therapy, and primal therapy. No one knows exactly how many approaches to treatment there are. One expert (Kazdin, 1994) estimates that there may be over 400 distinct types of psychotherapy! As varied as therapists' procedures are, approaches to treatment can be classified into three major categories:

1. *Insight therapies*. Insight therapy is "talk therapy" in the tradition of Freud's psychoanalysis. This is probably the approach to treatment you envision when you

All psychotherapies involve a helping relationship (the treatment) between a professional with special training (the therapist) and another person in need of help (the client).

© Paula Connelly/iStockphoto

think of psychotherapy, where clients (individually or in a group) engage in complex verbal interactions with their therapists.

2. *Behavior therapies.* Behavior therapies are based on the principles of learning and conditioning, which were introduced in Chapter 2. Instead of emphasizing personal insights, behavior therapists make direct efforts to change clients' problematic responses (phobic behaviors, for instance) and maladaptive habits (drug use, for instance).

3. *Biomedical therapies.* Biomedical approaches to therapy involve interventions into a person's physiological functioning. The most widely used procedures are drug therapy and electroconvulsive therapy.

In this chapter we examine approaches to therapy that fall into each of these three categories.

15-1b CLIENTS: WHO SEEKS THERAPY?

According to the 1999 U.S. Surgeon General's report on mental health (U.S. Department of Health and Human Services, 1999), about 15% of the U.S. population use mental health services in a given year. These people come to therapy with a full range of human problems, but the two most common presenting problems are excessive anxiety and depression (Olfson & Marcus, 2010). A client in treatment does *not* necessarily have an identifiable psychological disorder. Some people seek professional help for everyday problems (career decisions, for instance) or vague feelings of discontent.

People vary considerably in their willingness to seek psychotherapy. One study found that even when people perceive a need for professional assistance, only 59% actually seek professional help (Mojtabai, Olfson, & Mechanic, 2002). As you can see in Figure 15.1, women are more likely than men to receive treatment, and whites are more likely than blacks or Hispanics to obtain therapy. Treatment is also more likely when people have medical insurance and when they have more education (Wang, Lane et al., 2005). *Unfortunately, it appears that many people who need therapy don't receive it* (Kessler et al., 2005b). Lack of health insurance and cost concerns appear to be major barriers to obtaining needed care for many people. Unfortunately, many people equate seeking therapy with admitting personal weakness.

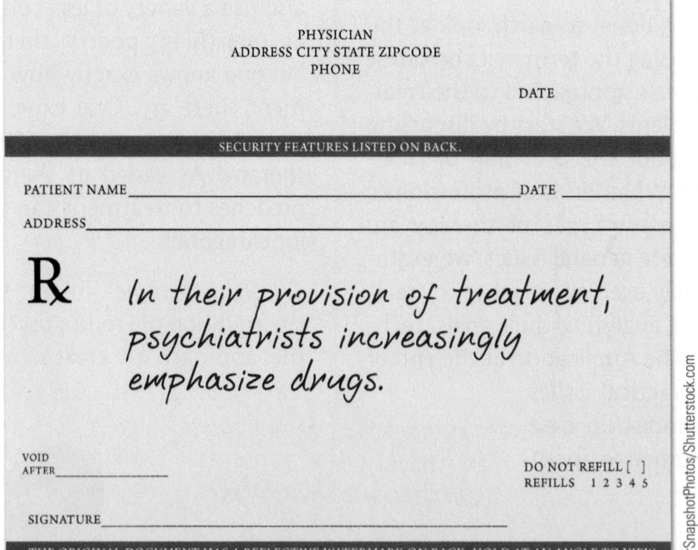

15-1c THERAPISTS: WHO PROVIDES PROFESSIONAL TREATMENT?

Psychotherapy refers to *professional* treatment by someone with special training. Psychology and psychiatry are the principal professions involved in psychotherapy, providing the lion's share of mental health care. However, therapy is also provided by social workers, psychiatric nurses, and counselors.

Psychologists

***Clinical psychologists* and *counseling psychologists* specialize in the diagnosis and treatment of psychological disorders and everyday behavioral problems.** In theory, the training of clinical psychologists emphasizes treatment of full-fledged disorders, whereas the training of counseling psychologists is slanted toward treatment of everyday adjustment problems in normal people. In practice, however, there is great overlap between clinical and counseling psychologists in training, in skills, and in the clientele they serve (Morgan & Cohen, 2008).

Both types of psychologists must earn a doctoral degree (Ph.D., Psy.D., or Ed.D.). The process of gaining admission to a Ph.D. program in clinical psychology is highly competitive (about as competitive as for medical school). Psychologists receive most of their training on university campuses, although they also serve a one- to two-year internship in a clinical setting, such as a hospital.

In providing therapy, psychologists use either insight or behavioral approaches. In comparison to psychiatrists, they are more likely to use behavioral techniques and less likely to use psychoanalytic methods. Clinical and counseling psychologists do psychological testing as well as psychotherapy, and many also conduct research.

FIGURE 15.1 Therapy utilization rates

Olfson and Marcus (2010) analyzed data on the use of outpatient mental health services in the United States in relation to various demographic variables. In regard to marital status, utilization rates are particularly high among those who are divorced or not married. The use of therapy is also greater among those who have more education. Females are more likely to pursue therapy than males are, but utilization rates are relatively low among ethnic minorities and those who lack health insurance.

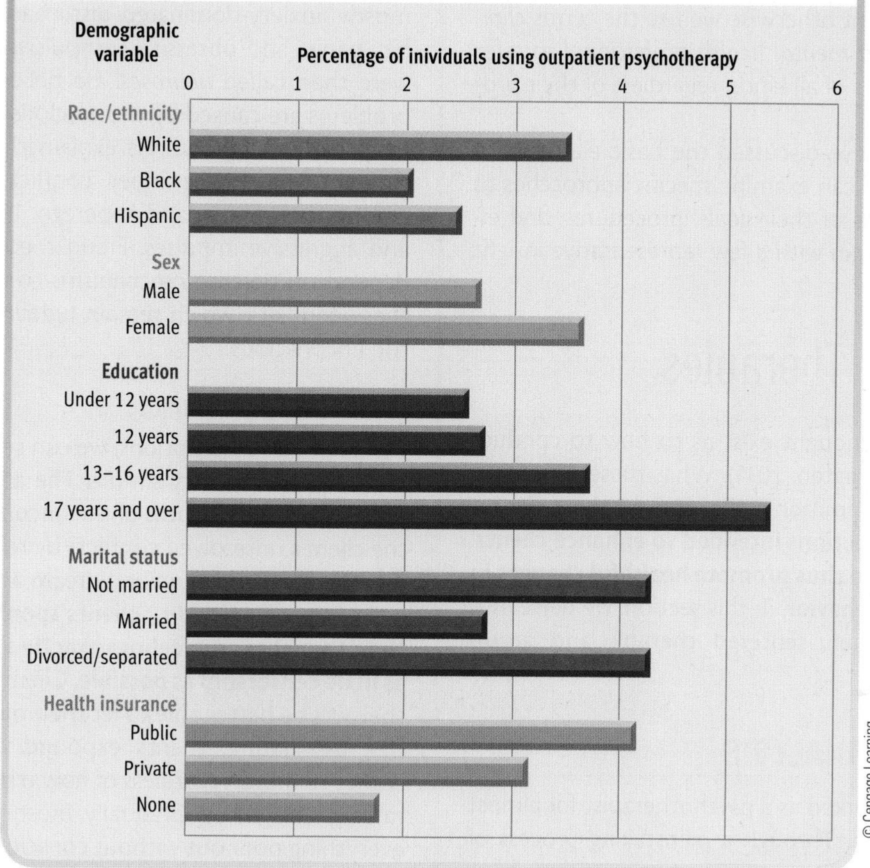

Psychiatrists

***Psychiatrists* are physicians who specialize in the treatment of psychological disorders.** Compared to psychologists, psychiatrists devote more time to relatively severe disorders (schizophrenia, mood disorders) and less time to everyday marital, family, job, and school problems. Psychiatrists have an M.D. degree. Their psychotherapy training occurs during their medical residency, as the required course work in medical school is essentially the same for all students, whether they are going into surgery, pediatrics, or psychiatry.

In their provision of treatment, psychiatrists increasingly emphasize drugs. Indeed, in one recent study of over 14,000 visits to psychiatrists, only 29% of the visits involved the provision of some therapy other than the prescription and management of medications (Mojtabai & Olfson, 2008). Less than a decade earlier that figure was 44% of visits, so psychiatrists clearly are abandoning talk therapies and behavioral interventions in favor of drug treatments.

Other Mental Health Professionals

In hospitals and other institutions, *psychiatric social workers* and *psychiatric nurses* often work as part of a treatment team with a psychologist or psychiatrist. Psychiatric nurses, who may have a bachelor's or master's degree in their field, play a large role in hospital inpatient treatment. Psychiatric social workers generally have a master's degree and typically work with patients and their families to ease the patient's integration back into the community.

Many kinds of *counselors* also provide therapeutic services. Counselors are usually found working in schools, colleges, and human services agencies (youth centers, geriatric centers, family planning centers, and so forth). Counselors typically have a master's degree. They often specialize in particular types of problems, such as vocational counseling, marital counseling, rehabilitation counseling, and drug counseling.

In this chapter, we refer to psychologists or psychiatrists as needed, but otherwise we use the terms *clinician, therapist,* and *mental health professional* to refer to psychotherapists of all kinds, regardless of their professional degree.

Now that we have discussed the basic elements in psychotherapy, we can examine specific approaches to treatment in terms of their goals, procedures, and effectiveness. We begin with a few representative insight therapies.

15-2 Insight Therapies

Many schools of thought exist as to how to conduct insight therapy (Braaten, 2011). What these varied approaches have in common is that ***insight therapies* involve verbal interactions intended to enhance clients' self-knowledge and thus promote healthful changes in personality and behavior.** In this section, we delve into psychoanalysis, client-centered therapy, and group therapy.

15-2a PSYCHOANALYSIS

Sigmund Freud worked as a psychotherapist for almost 50 years in Vienna. Through a painstaking process of trial and error, he developed innovative techniques for the treatment of psychological disorders and distress. His system of *psychoanalysis* dominated psychiatry for more than half a century. Although this dominance has eroded in recent decades, a diverse array of psychoanalytic approaches continue to evolve and remain influential today (Luborsky, O'Reilly-Landry, & Arlow, 2011; Ursano, Sonnenberg, & Lazar, 2008).

© Photos 12/Alamy

***Psychoanalysis* is an insight therapy that emphasizes the recovery of unconscious conflicts, motives, and defenses through techniques such as free association, dream analysis, and transference.** Freud treated mostly anxiety-dominated disturbances, such as phobic, panic, and obsessive-compulsive disorders, which were then called *neuroses*. He believed that neurotic problems are caused by unconscious conflicts left over from early childhood. As explained in Chapter 2, he thought that these inner conflicts involve battles among the id, ego, and superego, usually over sexual and aggressive impulses. Freud theorized that people depend on defense mechanisms to avoid confronting these conflicts, which remain hidden in the depths of the unconscious.

Probing the Unconscious

Given Freud's assumptions, we can see that the logic of psychoanalysis is very simple. The analyst attempts to probe the murky depths of the unconscious to discover the client's unresolved conflicts by relying on two techniques: free association and dream analysis.

In ***free association,* clients spontaneously express their thoughts and feelings exactly as they occur, with as little censorship as possible.** Clients lie on a couch so they will be better able to let their minds drift freely. In free associating, clients expound on anything that comes to mind, regardless of how trivial, silly, or embarrassing it might be. Gradually, most clients begin to let everything pour out without conscious censorship. The analyst studies these free associations for clues about what is going on in the unconscious.

In ***dream analysis,* the therapist interprets the symbolic meaning of the client's dreams.** For Freud, dreams were the "royal road to the unconscious," the most direct means of access to patients' innermost conflicts, wishes, and impulses. Clients are encouraged and trained to remember their dreams, which they describe in therapy. The therapist then analyzes the symbolism in these dreams to interpret their meaning.

To better illustrate these matters, let's look at an actual case treated through psychoanalysis (adapted from Greenson, 1967, pp. 40–41). Mr. N claimed to love his wife, but he preferred sexual relations with prostitutes. Mr. N reported that his parents also endured lifelong marital difficulties. His childhood conflicts about their relationship appeared to be related to his problems. Both dream analysis and free association can be seen in the following description of a session in Mr. N's treatment:

> *Mr. N reports a fragment of a dream. All that he can remember is that he is waiting for a red traffic light to change when he feels that someone has bumped into him from behind. . . . The associations led to Mr. N's love of cars, especially sports cars. He loved the sensation, in particular, of whizzing by those fat, old, expensive cars. . . . His father always hinted that he had been a great athlete, but he never substantiated it. . . . Mr. N doubted whether his father could really perform. His father would flirt with a waitress in a cafe or make sexual remarks about women passing by, but he seemed to be showing off. If he were really sexual, he wouldn't resort to that.*

As is characteristic of free association, Mr. N's train of thought meandered about with little direction. What did Mr. N's therapist extract from this session? The therapist saw sexual overtones in the dream fragment, where Mr. N was bumped from behind. The therapist also inferred that Mr. N had a competitive orientation toward his father, based on the free association about whizzing by fat, old, expensive cars. As you can see, analysts must *interpret* their clients' dreams and free associations.

Interpretation

***Interpretation* involves the therapist's attempts to explain the inner significance of the client's thoughts, feelings, memories, and behaviors.** Contrary to popular belief, analysts do not interpret everything, and they generally don't try to dazzle clients with startling revelations. Instead, analysts move forward inch by inch, offering interpretations that should be just out of the client's own reach (Samberg & Marcus, 2005). Mr. N's therapist eventually offered the following interpretations to his client:

> *I said to Mr. N near the end of the hour that I felt he was struggling with his feelings about his father's sexual life. He seemed to be saying that his father was sexually not a very potent man. . . . He also recalls that he once found a packet of condoms under his father's pillow when he was an adolescent and he thought "My father must be going to prostitutes." I then intervened and pointed out that the condoms under his father's pillow seemed to indicate more obviously that his father used the condoms with his mother, who slept in the same bed. However, Mr. N wanted to believe his wish-fulfilling fantasy: mother doesn't want sex with father and father is not very potent.*

As you may already have guessed, the therapist concluded that Mr. N's difficulties were rooted in an Oedipal complex (see Chapter 2). Mr. N had unresolved sexual feelings toward his mother and hostile feelings about his father. These unconscious conflicts, rooted in his childhood, were distorting his intimate relations as an adult.

Analysts move forward inch by inch, offering interpretations that should be just ouf of the client's own reach.

Resistance

How would you expect Mr. N to respond to his therapist's suggestion that he was in competition with his father for the sexual attention of his mother? Obviously, most clients would have great difficulty accepting such an interpretation. Freud fully expected clients to display some resistance to therapeutic efforts. ***Resistance* involves largely unconscious defensive maneuvers intended to hinder the progress of therapy.** Resistance is assumed to be an inevitable part of the psychoanalytic process (Samberg & Marcus, 2005). Clients try to resist the helping process because they don't want to face up to the painful, disturbing conflicts that they have buried in their unconscious.

Resistance may take many forms. Patients may show up late for their sessions, merely pretend to engage in free association, or express hostility toward the therapist. For instance, Mr. N's therapist noted that after the session just described, "The next day he began by telling me that he was furious with me." Often, a key consideration is the handling of *transference*.

Transference

***Transference* occurs when clients start relating to their therapist in ways that mimic critical relationships in their lives.** Thus, a client might start relating to a therapist as if the therapist were an overprotective mother, rejecting brother, or passive spouse. In a sense, the client *transfers* conflicting feelings about important people onto the therapist (Høglend et al., 2011). For instance, Mr. N transferred some of the competitive hostility he felt toward his father onto his analyst. Psychoanalysts often encourage transference so that clients begin to reenact relations with crucial people in the context of therapy. These reenactments can help bring repressed feelings and conflicts to the surface, allowing the client to work through them.

Psychoanalysis tends to be a lengthy process because patients need time to gradually work through their problems and genuinely accept unnerving revelations

(Williams, 2005). Ultimately, if resistance and transference can be handled effectively, the therapist's interpretations should lead the client to profound insights. For instance, Mr. N eventually admitted, "The old boy is probably right, it does tickle me to imagine that my mother preferred me and I could beat out my father. Later, I wondered whether this had something to do with my own screwed-up sex life with my wife." According to Freud, once clients recognize the unconscious sources of their conflicts, they can resolve these conflicts and discard their neurotic defenses.

Although still available, classical psychoanalysis as done by Freud is not widely practiced anymore (Kay & Kay, 2008). Many variations on Freud's original approach to psychoanalysis have developed over the years and are collectively known as *psychodynamic approaches* to therapy. Recent reviews of these approaches suggest that interpretation, resistance, and transference continue to play key roles in therapeutic efforts (Høglend et al., 2008) and that psychodynamic approaches can be helpful in the treatment of a diverse array of disorders, including depression, anxiety disorders, personality disorders, and substance abuse (Gibbons, Crits-Christoph, & Hearon, 2008).

15-2b CLIENT-CENTERED THERAPY

You may have heard of people going into therapy to "find themselves" or to "get in touch with their real feelings." These now-popular phrases emerged out of the human potential movement, which was stimulated in part by the work of Carl Rogers (1951). Taking a humanistic perspective, Rogers devised *client-centered therapy* (also known as *person-centered therapy*; Cooper & McLeod, 2011) in the 1940s and 1950s. ***Client-centered therapy*** **is an insight therapy that emphasizes providing a supportive emotional climate for clients, who play a major role in determining the pace and direction of their therapy.** You may wonder why the troubled, untrained client is put in charge of the pace and direction of the therapy. Rogers (1961) provides a compelling justification:

> *It is the client who knows what hurts, what directions to go, what problems are crucial, what experiences have been deeply buried. It began to occur to me that unless I had a need to demonstrate my own cleverness and learning, I would do better to rely upon the client for the direction of movement in the process. (pp. 11–12)*

Rogers maintained that most personal distress is due to inconsistency, or "incongruence," between a person's self-concept and reality (see Figure 15.2). Incongruence makes people prone to feel threatened by realistic feedback about themselves from others. For example, if you inaccurately viewed yourself as a hardworking, dependable person, you would feel threatened by contradictory feedback from friends or co-workers. According to Rogers, anxiety about such feedback often leads to reliance on defense mechanisms, distortions of reality, and stifled personal growth. Excessive incongruence is thought to be rooted in clients' overdependence on others for approval and acceptance. Client-centered therapists help clients realize that they do not have to worry constantly about pleasing others and winning acceptance. Ultimately, they try to foster self-acceptance and personal growth.

Therapeutic Climate

In client-centered therapy, the *process* of therapy is not as important as the emotional *climate* in which the therapy takes place. According to Rogers, it is critical for

FIGURE 15.2 | Rogers's view of the roots of disorders

Carl Rogers's theory posits that anxiety and self-defeating behavior are rooted in an incongruent self-concept that makes one prone to recurrent anxiety, which triggers defensive behavior, which fuels more incongruence.

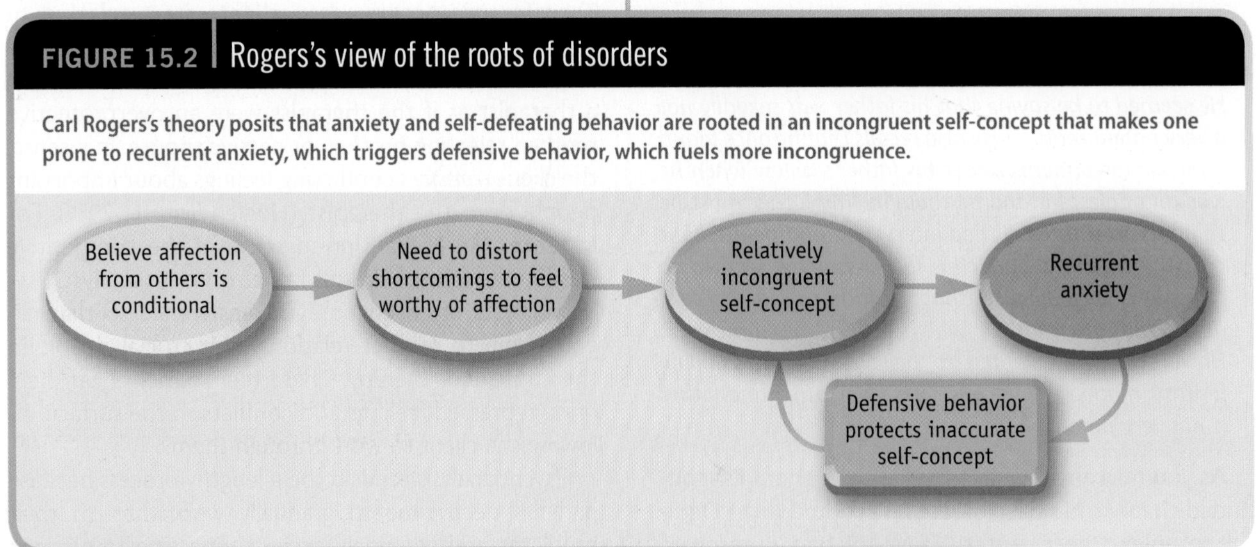

the therapist to provide a warm, supportive, accepting climate in which clients can confront their shortcomings without feeling threatened. To create this atmosphere of emotional support, Rogers believed that client-centered therapists must provide three conditions:

1. *Genuineness.* The therapist must be genuine with the client, communicating in an honest and spontaneous manner. The therapist should not be phony or defensive.

2. *Unconditional positive regard.* The therapist must also show complete, nonjudgmental acceptance of the client as a person. The therapist should provide warmth and caring for the client with no strings attached. This mandate does not mean that the therapist has to approve of everything that the client says or does.

3. *Empathy.* Finally, the therapist must provide accurate empathy for the client. This means that the therapist must understand the client's world from the client's point of view.

Rogers firmly believed that a supportive emotional climate is the major force that promotes healthy changes in therapy. However, some client-centered therapists place more emphasis on the therapeutic process (Rice & Greenberg, 1992).

Therapeutic Process

In client-centered therapy, the client and therapist work together almost as equals. The therapist provides relatively little guidance and keeps interpretation and advice to a minimum. The therapist's key task is *clarification.* Client-centered therapists try to function like a human mirror, reflecting statements back to their clients, but with enhanced clarity. They help clients become more aware of their true feelings by highlighting themes that may be obscure in the clients' rambling discourse. In particular, they try to help clients become more aware of and comfortable about their genuine selves. Obviously, these are ambitious goals. Client-centered therapy resembles psychoanalysis in that both seek to achieve a major reconstruction of a client's personality.

15-2c GROUP THERAPY

Although it dates back to the early part of the 20th century, group therapy came of age during World War II and its aftermath in the 1950s (Rosenbaum, Lakin, & Roback, 1992). ***Group therapy* is the simultaneous treatment of several or more clients in a group.** Most major insight therapies have been adapted for use with groups. Although group therapy can be conducted in a variety of ways, we can provide a general overview of the process as it usually unfolds.

Participants' Roles

A therapy group typically consists of four to twelve people, with six to eight participants regarded as an ideal number (Cox, Vinogradov, & Yalom, 2008). The therapist usually screens the participants, excluding anyone who seems likely to be disruptive. There is some debate about whether it is better to have a homogeneous group (people who are similar in age, gender, and presenting problem) than a heterogeneous one. Practical necessities usually dictate that groups be at least somewhat diversified.

In group treatment the therapist's responsibilities include selecting participants, setting goals for the group, initiating and maintaining the therapeutic process, and protecting clients from harm. The therapist always retains a special status, but the therapist and clients are on much more equal footing in group therapy than in individual therapy. The leader in group therapy expresses emotions, shares feelings, and copes with challenges from group members (Burlingame & McClendon, 2008).

In group therapy, participants essentially function as therapists for one another (Schachter, 2011). Group members describe their problems, trade viewpoints, share experiences, discuss coping strategies, and provide acceptance and emotional support for each other. In this supportive atmosphere, group members work at peeling away the social masks that cover their insecurities. As members come to value one another's opinions, they work hard to display healthy changes to win the group's approval.

Advantages of the Group Experience

For many types of patients and problems, group therapy can be just as effective as individual treatment (Knauss, 2005). Moreover, group therapy has unique strengths of its own, including the following (Yalom, 1995):

1. *In group therapy, participants often come to realize that their misery is not*

unique. In the group situation, they quickly see that their problems and burdens are not unique, that many other people have similar or even worse problems.

2. *Group therapy provides an opportunity for participants to work on their social skills in a safe environment.* Group therapy can provide a workshop for improving interpersonal skills that cannot be matched by individual therapy.

3. *Certain kinds of problems are especially well suited to group treatment.* In peer self-help groups, for example, people who have a problem in common get together regularly to help one another out. The original peer self-help group was Alcoholics Anonymous, and today similar groups are made up of former psychiatric patients, single parents, drug addicts, and so forth.

Are insight therapies worth the investment? Let's look at the research evidence on the efficacy of insight therapies.

15-2d EVALUATING INSIGHT THERAPIES

Evaluating treatment results for insight therapies is complicated (Aveline, Strauss, & Stiles, 2005). Various schools of therapy pursue entirely different goals. And clients' ratings of their progress are likely to be slanted toward a favorable evaluation because they want to justify their effort, their heartache, their expense, and their time. Even evaluations by professional therapists can be highly subjective (Luborsky, Singer, & Luborsky, 1999). Moreover, people enter therapy with diverse problems of varied severity, creating huge confounds in efforts to assess the effectiveness of therapeutic interventions.

Despite these difficulties, thousands of outcome studies have been conducted to evaluate the effectiveness of insight therapy. These studies consistently indicate that insight therapy *is* superior to no treatment or to placebo treatment and that the effects of therapy are reasonably durable (Lambert, 2011; Torres & Saunders, 2009). And when insight therapies are compared head to head against drug therapies, they usually show roughly equal efficacy (Arkowitz & Lilienfeld, 2007). Studies generally find the greatest improvement early in treatment (the first thirteen to eighteen weekly sessions), with further gains gradually diminishing over time. Overall, about 50% of patients show a clinically meaningful recovery within about twenty sessions, and another 25% of patients achieve this goal after about forty-five sessions (Lambert & Ogles, 2004) (see Figure 15.3).

15-2e THERAPY AND THE RECOVERED MEMORIES CONTROVERSY

While debate about the efficacy of insight therapy has simmered for many decades, the 1990s brought an entirely new controversy to rock the psychotherapy profession like never before. This emotionally charged debate was sparked by a spate of reports of people recovering repressed memories of sexual abuse and other childhood trauma through therapy. Such recovered memories have led to a rash of lawsuits in which adult plaintiffs have sued their parents, teachers, neighbors, pastors, and so forth for alleged child abuse 20 or 30 years earlier. For the most part, those accused have denied the allegations. Many of them have seemed genuinely baffled by the accusations, which have torn apart some previously happy families (McHugh et al., 2004). In an effort to make sense of the charges, many accused parents have argued that their children's recollections are false memories created inadvertently by well-intentioned therapists through the power of suggestion. Recovered recollections of sexual abuse have become so common, a support group has been formed for accused people who feel that they have been victimized by "false memory syndrome."

Group therapies have proven particularly helpful when members share similar problems, such as alcoholism, drug abuse, overeating, or depression.

FIGURE 15.3 Recovery as a function of number of therapy sessions

Based on a national sample of over 6,000 patients, Lambert, Hansen, and Finch (2001) mapped out the relationship between recovery and the duration of treatment. These data show that about half of the patients had experienced a clinically significant recovery after twenty weekly sessions of therapy. After forty-five therapy sessions, about 70% had recovered.

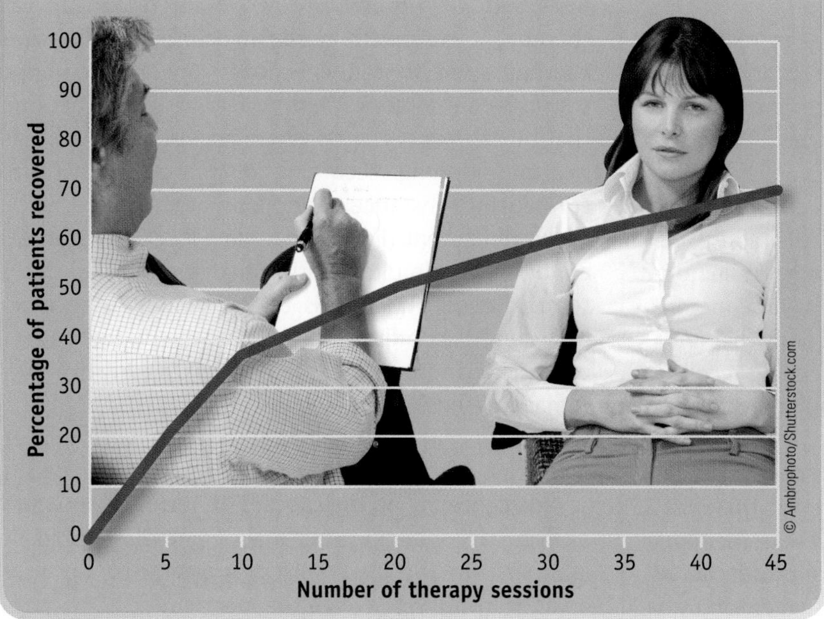

Source: Adapted from Lambert, M. J., Hansen, N. B., & Finch, A. E. (2001). Patient-focused research: Using patient outcome data to enhance treatment effects. *Journal of Consulting and Clinical Psychology, 69,* 159–172. Copyright © 2001 by the American Psychological Association. Adapted with permission..

Psychologists are sharply divided on the issue of recovered memories, leaving the public understandably confused. Many psychologists, especially therapists in clinical practice, accept most recovered memories at face value (Gleaves & Smith, 2004; Legault & Laurence, 2007). They assert that it is common for patients to bury traumatic incidents in their unconscious (Wilsnack et al., 2002). Citing evidence that sexual abuse in childhood is far more widespread than most people realize (MacMillan et al., 1997), they argue that most repressed memories of abuse are probably genuine.

In contrast, many other psychologists, especially memory researchers, have expressed skepticism about the recovered memories phenomenon (Loftus, 2003; McNally, 2007). They maintain that some suggestible, confused people struggling to understand profound personal problems have been convinced by persuasive therapists that their emotional problems must be the result of abuse that occurred years before. Critics blame a small minority of therapists who presumably have good intentions but operate under the dubious assumption that virtually all psychological problems are attributable to childhood sexual abuse (Loftus & Davis, 2006). Using hypnosis, dream interpretation, and leading questions, they supposedly prod and probe patients until they inadvertently create the memories of abuse that they are searching for (Thayer & Lynn, 2006).

DOONESBURY

Psychologists who doubt the authenticity of repressed memories support their analysis by pointing to recanted and discredited cases of recovered memories. For example, with the help of a church counselor, one woman recovered memories of how her minister father had repeatedly raped her, got her pregnant, and then aborted the pregnancy with a coat hanger. However, subsequent evidence revealed that the woman was still a virgin and that her father had had a vasectomy years before (Brainerd & Reyna, 2005).

Of course, psychologists who believe in recovered memories have mounted rebuttals to these arguments. For example, Kluft (1999) argues that a recantation of a recovered memory of abuse does not prove that the memory was false. Gleaves (1994) points out that individuals with a history of sexual abuse often vacillate between denying and accepting that the abuse occurred. Harvey (1999) argues that laboratory demonstrations showing how easy it is to create false memories have involved trivial memory distortions that are a far cry from the vivid, emotionally wrenching recollections of sexual abuse that have generated the recovered memories controversy.

So, what can we conclude about the recovered memories controversy? It seems pretty clear that therapists can unknowingly create false memories in their patients and that a significant portion of recovered memories of abuse are the product of suggestion (McNally & Geraerts, 2009). But it also seems likely that some cases of recovered memories are authentic (Smith & Gleaves, 2007). At this point, we don't have adequate data to estimate what proportion of recovered memories of abuse fall in each category. Thus, the matter needs to be addressed with great caution.

15-3 Behavior Therapies

Insight therapists treat pathological symptoms as signs of an underlying problem. In contrast, behavior therapists think that the symptoms *are* the problem. Thus, ***behavior therapies* involve the application of the principles of learning to direct efforts to change clients' maladaptive behaviors.**

Behavior therapies are based on two main assumptions (Stanley & Beidel, 2009). *First, it is assumed that behavior is a product of learning.* No matter how self-defeating or pathological a client's behavior might be, the behavioral therapist believes the behavior is the result of past conditioning. *Second, it is assumed that what has been learned can be unlearned.* The same learning principles that explain how the maladaptive behavior was acquired can be used to get rid of it. Thus, behavior therapists attempt to change clients' behavior by applying the principles of classical conditioning, operant conditioning, and observational learning.

15-3a SYSTEMATIC DESENSITIZATION

Devised by Joseph Wolpe (1987), systematic desensitization revolutionized psychotherapy by giving therapists their first useful alternative to traditional "talk therapy." ***Systematic desensitization* is a behavior therapy used to reduce clients' anxiety responses through counterconditioning.** The treatment assumes that most anxiety responses are acquired through classical conditioning. According to this model, a harmless stimulus (for instance, a bridge) may be paired with a frightening event (lightning striking it), so it becomes a conditioned stimulus eliciting anxiety. The goal of systematic desensitization is to weaken the association between the conditioned stimulus (the bridge) and the conditioned response of anxiety (see Figure 15.4). Systematic desensitization involves three steps.

First, the therapist helps the client build an anxiety hierarchy. The hierarchy is a list of anxiety-arousing stimuli centering on the specific source of anxiety, such as flying, academic tests, or snakes. The client ranks the stimuli from the least anxiety arousing to the most anxiety arousing to create the hierarchy.

The second step involves training the client in deep muscle relaxation. This second phase may begin during

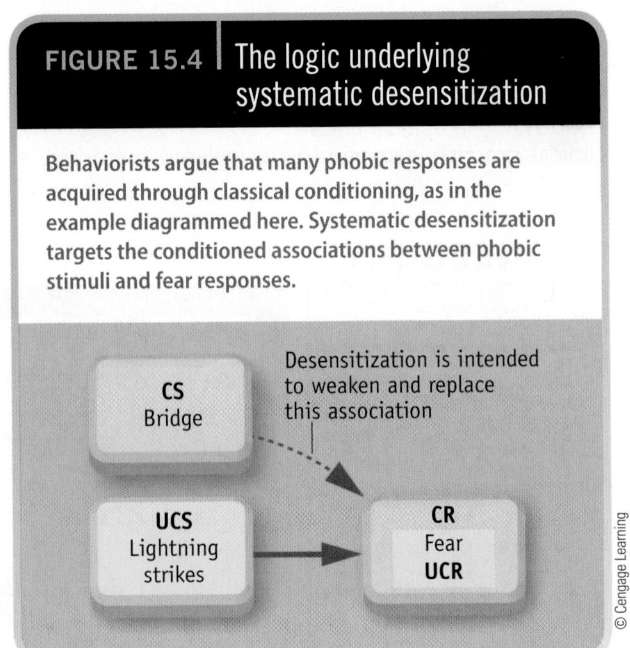

FIGURE 15.4 The logic underlying systematic desensitization

Behaviorists argue that many phobic responses are acquired through classical conditioning, as in the example diagrammed here. Systematic desensitization targets the conditioned associations between phobic stimuli and fear responses.

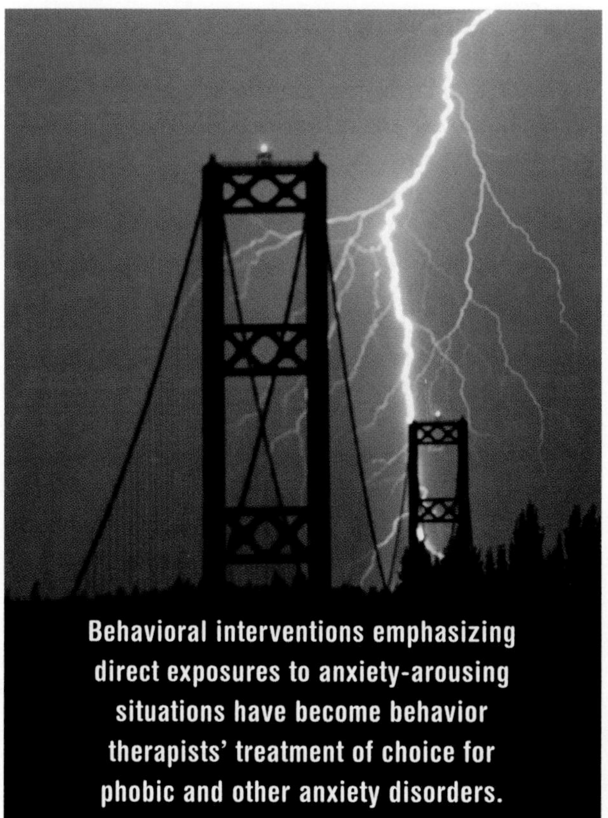

Behavioral interventions emphasizing direct exposures to anxiety-arousing situations have become behavior therapists' treatment of choice for phobic and other anxiety disorders.

© Chris Boswell/Alamy

early sessions while the therapist and client are still constructing the anxiety hierarchy. Whatever training procedures are used, the client must learn to engage in deep and thorough relaxation on command from the therapist.

In the third step, the client tries to work through the hierarchy (from least to most arousing), learning to remain relaxed while imagining each stimulus. If the client experiences strong anxiety, he or she drops the imaginary scene and concentrates on relaxation. The client keeps repeating this process until he or she can imagine a scene with little or no anxiety. Gradually, over a number of therapy sessions, the client progresses through the hierarchy, unlearning troublesome anxiety responses.

Although desensitization to imagined stimuli *can* be effective by itself, contemporary behavior therapists usually follow it up with direct exposures to the real anxiety-arousing stimuli (Emmelkamp, 2004). Indeed, behavioral interventions emphasizing direct exposures to anxiety-arousing situations have become behavior therapists' treatment of choice for phobic and other anxiety disorders (Rachman, 2009). Usually, these real-life confrontations prove harmless, and individuals' anxiety responses decline.

15-3b AVERSION THERAPY

Aversion therapy is far and away the most controversial of the behavior therapies. What's so terrible about aversion therapy? The client has to endure decidedly unpleasant stimuli, such as shocks or drug-induced nausea.

***Aversion therapy* is a behavior therapy in which an aversive stimulus is paired with a stimulus that elicits an undesirable response.** For example, alcoholics have had drug-induced nausea paired with their favorite drinks during therapy sessions (Landabaso et al., 1999). By pairing an *emetic drug* (one that causes vomiting) with alcohol, the therapist hopes to create a conditioned aversion to alcohol (see Figure 15.5).

Aversion therapy takes advantage of the automatic nature of responses produced through classical conditioning. Admittedly, alcoholics treated with aversion therapy know that they won't be given an emetic outside of their therapy sessions. However, their reflex response to the stimulus of alcohol may be changed so that they respond to it with nausea and distaste. Obviously, this response should make it much easier to resist the urge to drink.

© Patrick Steel/Alamy

Aversion therapy is not a widely used technique, and when it is used it is usually

FIGURE 15.5 | Aversion therapy

Aversion therapy uses classical conditioning to create an aversion to a stimulus that has elicited problematic behavior. For example, in the treatment of drinking problems, alcohol may be paired with a nausea-inducing drug to create a conditioned aversion to alcohol.

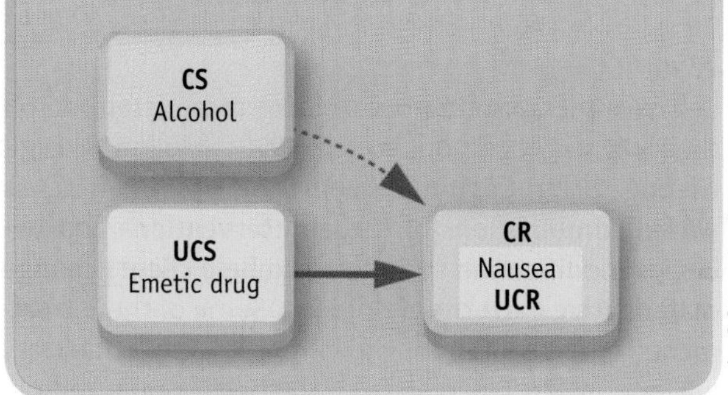

Art: © Cengage Learning

only one element in a larger treatment program. Troublesome behaviors treated successfully with aversion therapy have included drug and alcohol abuse, sexual deviance, gambling, shoplifting, stuttering, cigarette smoking, and overeating (Bordnick et al., 2004; Emmelkamp, 1994).

15-3c SOCIAL SKILLS TRAINING

Behavior therapists point out that humans are not born with social finesse. People acquire their social skills through learning. Unfortunately, some people have not learned how to be friendly, how to make conversation, how to express anger appropriately, and so forth. Such social ineptitude can contribute to anxiety, feelings of inferiority, and various kinds of disorders. Therapists are increasingly using social skills training in efforts to improve clients' social abilities, yielding promising results in the treatment of social anxiety (Herbert et al., 2005), autism (Cappadocia & Weiss, 2010), attention deficit disorder (Monastra, 2008), and schizophrenia and other psychotic disorders (Horan et al., 2011).

***Social skills training* is a behavior therapy designed to improve interpersonal skills that emphasizes modeling, behavioral rehearsal, and shaping.** Social skills training depends on the principles of operant conditioning and observational learning. The therapist makes use of *modeling* by encouraging clients to watch socially skilled friends and colleagues, so that the clients can acquire responses (eye contact, active listening, and so on) through observation.

In *behavioral rehearsal*, the client tries to practice social techniques in structured role-playing exercises. The therapist provides corrective feedback and uses approval to reinforce progress. Eventually, clients try their newly acquired skills in real-world interactions. *Shaping* is used in that clients are gradually asked to handle more complicated and delicate social situations.

15-3d COGNITIVE-BEHAVIORAL TREATMENTS

Behavior therapists started to focus more attention on their clients' cognitions in the 1970s (Hollon & Digiuseppe, 2011). ***Cognitive-behavioral treatments* use varied combinations of verbal interventions and behavior modification techniques to help clients change maladaptive patterns of thinking.** Some of these treatments emerged out of an insight therapy tradition, whereas others emerged from the behavioral tradition. Here we focus on Aaron Beck's system of cognitive therapy (Newman & Beck, 2009).

***Cognitive therapy* uses specific strategies to correct habitual thinking errors that underlie various types of disorders.** Cognitive therapy was originally devised as a treatment for depression, but in recent years it has been applied fruitfully to a wide range of disorders (Wright, Thase, & Beck, 2008), and it has proven particularly valuable as a therapy for anxiety disorders (Rachman, 2009). According to cognitive therapists, depression is caused by "errors" in thinking. They assert that depression-prone people tend to (1) blame their setbacks on personal inadequacies without considering circumstantial explanations, (2) focus selectively on negative events while ignoring positive ones, (3) make unduly pessimistic projections about the future, and (4) draw negative conclusions about their worth as a person based on insignificant events. For instance, imagine that you got a low grade on a minor quiz in a class. If you made the kinds of errors in thinking just described, you might blame the grade on your woeful stupidity, dismiss comments from a classmate that it was an unfair test, gloomily predict that you will surely flunk the course, and conclude that you are not genuine college material.

The goal of cognitive therapy is to change clients' negative thoughts and maladaptive beliefs (Kellogg & Young, 2008). To begin, clients are taught to detect their automatic negative thoughts, the sorts of self-defeating statements that people are prone to make when analyzing problems (e.g., "I'm just not smart enough," "No one really likes me"). The therapist helps them see how unrealistically negative the thoughts are.

Cognitive therapy uses a variety of behavioral techniques, including modeling, systematic monitoring of one's behavior, and behavioral rehearsal (Beck & Weishaar, 2011). Clients are given "homework assignments" that focus on changing their overt behaviors. They may be instructed to engage in overt responses on their own, outside of the clinician's office.

15-3e EVALUATING BEHAVIOR THERAPIES

There is ample research on the effectiveness of behavior therapy (Stanley & Beidel, 2009). How does its effectiveness compare to that of insight therapy? In direct comparisons, the differences between the therapies are usually small. For our purposes, it is sufficient to note that there is favorable evidence on the efficacy of most of the widely used behavioral interventions (Zinbarg & Griffith, 2008). Behavior therapies can make significant contributions to the treatment of depression, anxiety problems, phobias, obsessive-compulsive disorders, sexual dysfunction, schizophrenia, drug-related problems, eating disorders, hyperactivity, autism, and mental retardation (Hollon & Dimidjian, 2009; Wilson, 2011).

15-4 Biomedical Therapies

Today, biomedical therapies, such as drug treatment, lie at the core of psychiatric practice. ***Biomedical therapies* are physiological interventions intended to reduce symptoms associated with psychological disorders.** These therapies assume that psychological disorders are caused, at least in part, by biological malfunctions. We will discuss two biomedical approaches to psychotherapy: drug therapy and electroconvulsive therapy.

15-4a TREATMENT WITH DRUGS

***Psychopharmacotherapy* is the treatment of mental disorders with medication.** We will refer to this kind of treatment more simply as *drug therapy*. Therapeutic drugs for psychological problems fall into four major groups: antianxiety drugs, antipsychotic drugs, antidepressant drugs, and mood stabilizers.

Antianxiety Drugs

Most of us know someone who pops pills to relieve anxiety. The drugs involved in this common coping strategy are ***antianxiety drugs*, which relieve tension, apprehension, and nervousness.** The most popular of these drugs are Valium and Xanax. These and other drugs in the benzodiazepine family are often called *tranquilizers*. Such drugs are routinely prescribed for people diagnosed with anxiety disorders and are also given to millions of people who simply suffer from chronic nervous tension.

Antianxiety drugs exert their effects almost immediately, and they can be fairly effective in alleviating feelings of anxiety (Dubovsky, 2009). However, the effects are measured in hours, so their impact is relatively short-lived. Common side effects of antianxiety drugs include drowsiness, depression, nausea, and confusion. These drugs also have some potential for abuse, dependency, and overdose, although the prevalence of these problems has been exaggerated (Martinez, Marangell & Martinez, 2008). Another drawback is that patients who have been on antianxiety drugs for a while often experience withdrawal symptoms when their drug treatment is stopped.

Antipsychotic Drugs

Antipsychotic drugs, such as Thorazine, Mellaril, and Haldol, are used primarily in the treatment of schizophrenia. They are also given to people with severe mood disorders who become delusional. ***Antipsychotic drugs* are used to gradually reduce psychotic symptoms, including hyperactivity, mental confusion, hallucinations, and delusions.** Studies suggest that antipsychotics reduce symptoms in about 70% of patients, albeit in varied degrees (Kane, Stroup, & Marder, 2009). When antipsychotic drugs are effective, they work their magic gradually, as shown in Figure 15.6. Patients usually begin to respond within one to three weeks, but considerable variability in responsiveness is seen. Further improvement may occur for several months. Many schizophrenic patients are placed on antipsychotics indefinitely because these drugs can reduce the likelihood of a relapse into an active schizophrenic episode (van Kammen, Hurford, & Marder, 2009).

FIGURE 15.6 The time course of antipsychotic drug effects

Antipsychotic drugs reduce psychotic symptoms gradually, over a span of weeks, as graphed here. In contrast, patients given placebo pills show little improvement.

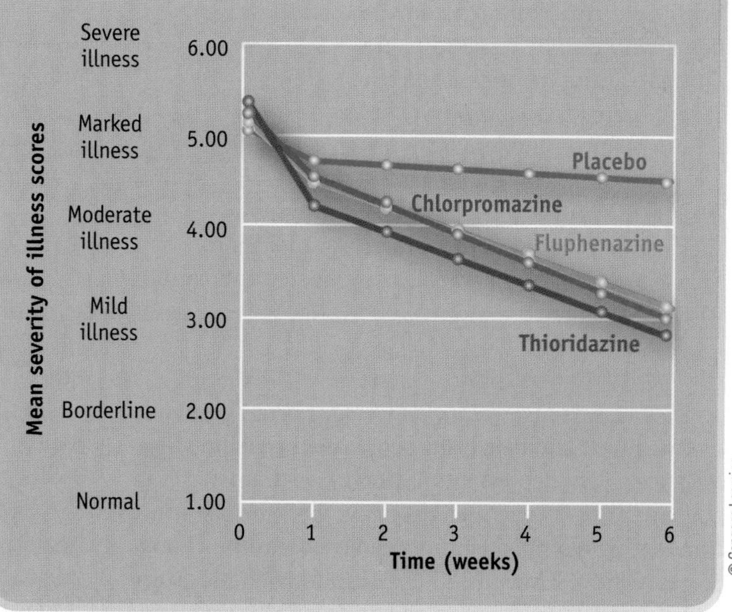

Source: From Cole, J. O., Goldberg, S. C., & Davis, J. M. (1966). Drugs in the treatment of psychosis. In P. Solomon (Ed.), *Psychiatric drugs*. New York: Grune & Stratton. From data in the NIMH-PSC Collaborative Study I. Reprinted by permission of J. M. Davis.

Antipsychotic drugs undeniably make a major contribution to the treatment of severe mental disorders, but they are not without problems. They have many unpleasant side effects (Dolder, 2008). Drowsiness, constipation, and cotton mouth are common. Patients may also experience tremors, muscular rigidity, and impaired coordination. After being released from a hospital, many schizophrenic patients, supposedly placed on antipsychotics indefinitely, discontinue their drug regimen because of the disagreeable side effects. Unfortunately, after patients stop taking antipsychotic medication, about 70% relapse within a year (van Kammen et al., 2009). In addition to minor side effects, antipsychotics may cause a severe and lasting problem called *tardive dyskinesia*, which is seen in about 20%–30% of patients who receive long-term treatment with traditional antipsychotics (Kane et al., 2009). ***Tardive dyskinesia* is a neurological disorder marked by chronic tremors and involuntary spastic movements.** Once this debilitating syndrome emerges, there is no cure, although spontaneous remission sometimes occurs after the discontinuation of antipsychotic medication.

Psychiatrists are currently enthusiastic about a newer class of antipsychotic agents called *atypical* or *second-generation antipsychotic drugs*. These drugs appear to be roughly similar to the first-generation antipsychotics in therapeutic effectiveness, but they offer some advantages over the older drugs (Meltzer & Bobo, 2009). For instance, they can help some treatment-resistant patients who do not respond to traditional antipsychotics. And the second-generation antipsychotics produce fewer unpleasant side effects and carry less risk for tardive dyskinesia. Of course, like all powerful drugs, they carry some risks. This drug class appears to increase patients' vulnerability to diabetes and cardiovascular problems.

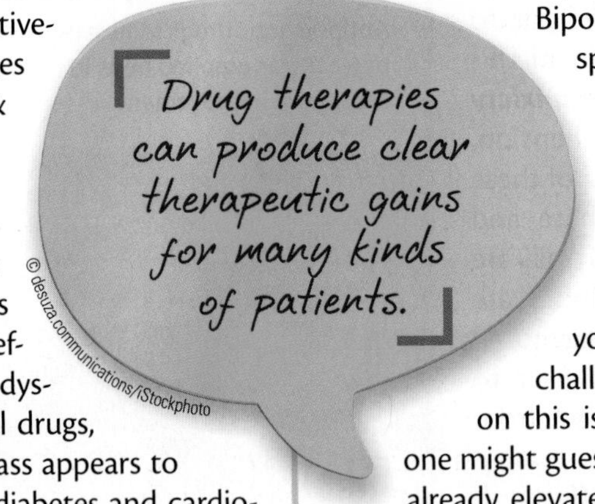

Drug therapies can produce clear therapeutic gains for many kinds of patients.

© desuza.communications/iStockphoto

Antidepressant Drugs

As their name suggests, ***antidepressant drugs* gradually elevate mood and help bring people out of a depression.** Reliance on antidepressants has increased dramatically in the last 10 to 15 years, as they have become the most frequently prescribed class of medication in the United States (Olfson & Marcus, 2009). Like antipsychotic drugs, antidepressants exert their effects gradually over a period of weeks, but about 60% of improvement tends to occur in the first two weeks (Gitlin, 2009).

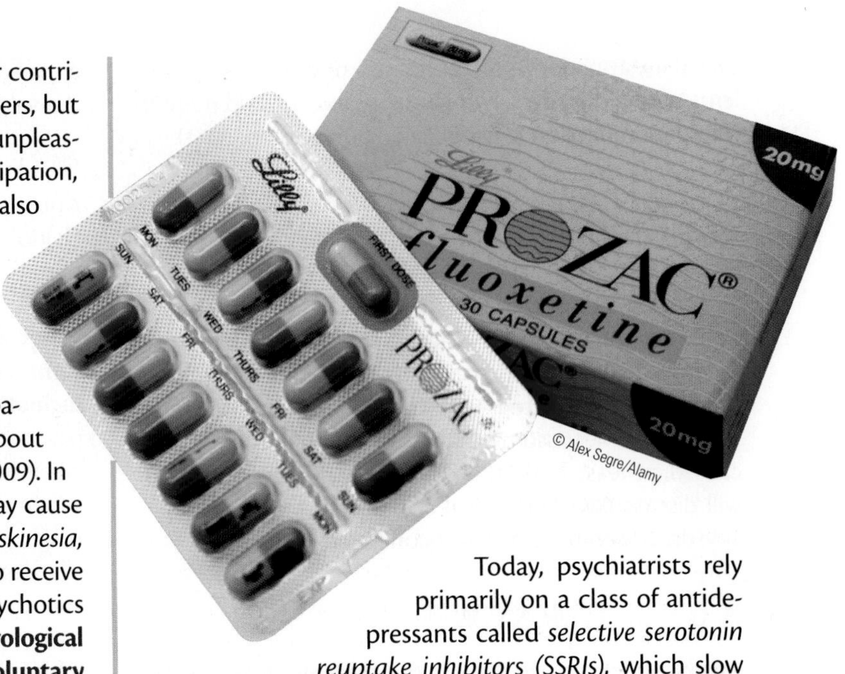

© Alex Segre/Alamy

Today, psychiatrists rely primarily on a class of antidepressants called *selective serotonin reuptake inhibitors (SSRIs)*, which slow the reuptake process at serotonin synapses. SSRIs have proven valuable in the treatment of depression, obsessive-compulsive disorders, panic disorders, and other anxiety disorders (Mathew, Hoffman, & Charney, 2009). However, there is some doubt about how effective the SSRIs (and other antidepressants) are in relieving episodes of depression among patients suffering from bipolar disorder (Berman et al., 2009). Bipolar patients do not seem to respond as well as those who suffer from depression only.

A major concern in recent years has been evidence from a number of studies that SSRIs may increase the risk for suicide, primarily among adolescents and young adults (Holden, 2004). The challenge of collecting definitive data on this issue is much more daunting than one might guess, in part because suicide rates are already elevated among people who exhibit the disorders for which SSRIs are prescribed (Berman, 2009). Some researchers have collected data suggesting that suicide rates have *declined* slightly because of widespread prescription of SSRIs (Baldessarini et al., 2007), while others have found no association between SSRIs and suicide (Simon et al., 2006).

Overall, however, when antidepressants are compared to placebo treatment, the data suggest that antidepressants lead to a slight elevation in the risk of suicidal behavior, from roughly 2% to 4% (Bridge et al., 2007). Elevated suicide risk appears to be a problem mainly among a small minority of children and adolescents in the first month after starting antidepressants, especially the first nine days (Jick, Kaye, & Jick, 2004). Regulatory warnings from the U.S. Food and Drug Administration (FDA) have led to a decline in the prescription of SSRIs for adolescents (Nemeroff et al., 2007). This trend has prompted concern that increases in suicide may occur among untreated individuals. This concern seems legitimate in that suicide risk clearly peaks in the month prior to people beginning treatment for depression, whether that treatment involves SSRIs or psychotherapy (Simon & Savarino, 2007). This pattern presumably occurs because the escalating agony of depression finally prompts people to seek treatment, but it also suggests that getting treatment with drugs or therapy reduces suicidal risk. In the final analysis, this is a complex issue, but the one thing experts seem to agree on is that adolescents starting on SSRIs should be monitored closely.

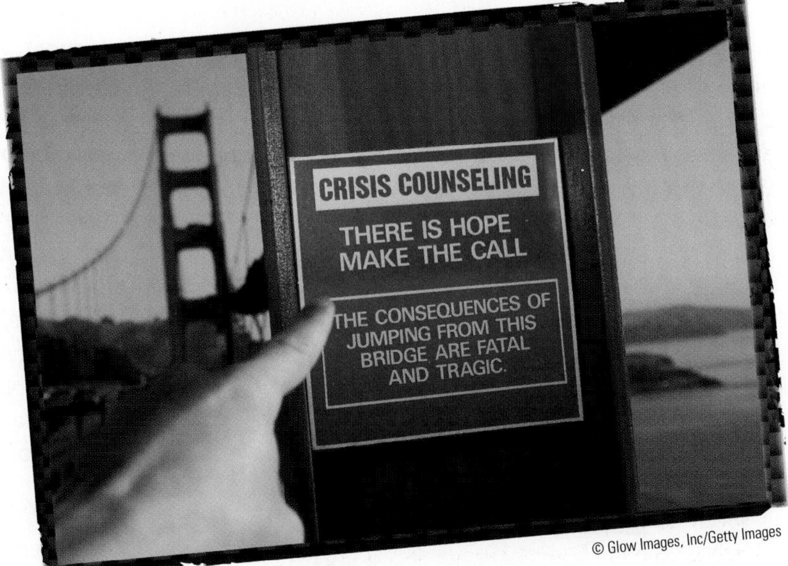

© Glow Images, Inc/Getty Images

Mood Stabilizers

***Mood stabilizers* are drugs used to control mood swings in patients with bipolar mood disorders.** For many years, lithium was the only effective drug in this category. Lithium has proven valuable in preventing *future* episodes of both mania and depression in patients with bipolar illness (Post & Altshuler, 2009). Lithium can also be used in efforts to bring patients with bipolar illness out of *current* manic or depressive episodes (Keck & McElroy, 2006), although antipsychotics and antidepressants are also used for these purposes. On the negative side of the ledger, lithium does have some dangerous side effects if its use isn't managed skillfully (Jefferson & Greist, 2009). Lithium levels in the patient's blood must be monitored carefully, because high concentrations can be toxic and even fatal.

In recent years a number of alternatives to lithium have been developed. The most popular is an anticonvulsant agent called *valproate,* which has become more widely used than lithium in the treatment of bipolar disorders (Thase & Denko, 2008). Valproate appears to be roughly as effective as lithium in efforts to treat current manic episodes and to prevent future affective disturbances (Moseman et al., 2003). The advantage provided by valproate is that it is better tolerated by patients. In some cases, a combination of valproate and lithium may be used in treatment (Post & Altshuler, 2009).

Evaluating Drug Therapies

Drug therapies can produce clear therapeutic gains for many kinds of patients, yet critics of drug therapy have raised a number of issues (Breggin & Cohen, 2007; Greenberg & Fisher, 1997). First, some argue that drug therapies often produce superficial curative effects, such as temporary relief from an unpleasant symptom. Second, critics charge that many drugs are overprescribed and many patients overmedicated. Third, some critics charge that the side effects of therapeutic drugs are worse than the illnesses the drugs are supposed to cure. Citing problems such as tardive dyskinesia, lithium toxicity, and addiction to antianxiety agents, these critics argue that the risks of therapeutic drugs aren't worth the benefits. Finally, critics maintain that the negative effects of psychiatric drugs are not fully appreciated because the pharmaceutical industry has managed to gain undue influence over the research enterprise as it relates to drug testing (Insel, 2010; Weber, 2006). Today, most researchers who investigate the benefits and risks of medications and write treatment guidelines have lucrative financial

© Lisa S./Shutterstock.com

© Barbara Smaller/The New Yorker Collection/www.cartoonbank.com

I think the dosage needs adjusting. I'm not nearly as happy as the people in the ads.

arrangements with the pharmaceutical industry, which they often fail to disclose (Lurie et al., 2006). Unfortunately, these financial ties appear to undermine the objectivity required in scientific research, as studies funded by pharmaceutical and other biomedical companies are far more likely to report favorable results than nonprofit-funded studies (Perlis et al., 2005).

Obviously, drug therapies have stirred up some debate. However, drug therapy controversies pale in comparison to the furious debates inspired by electroconvulsive (shock) therapy (ECT). What makes ECT so controversial? You'll see in the next section.

15-4b ELECTROCONVULSIVE THERAPY (ECT)

***Electroconvulsive therapy (ECT)* is a biomedical treatment in which electric shock is used to produce a cortical seizure accompanied by convulsions.** In ECT, electrodes are attached to the skull over one or both temporal lobes of the brain. A light anesthesia is induced, and the patient is given a variety of drugs to minimize the likelihood of complications, such as spinal fractures. An electric current is then applied for about a second. The current should trigger a brief (5–20 seconds) convulsive seizure, during which the patient usually loses consciousness. Patients normally awaken in an hour or two. People typically receive between six and twelve treatments over a period of about a month (Glass, 2001).

ECT is *not* a rare form of therapy. Although only about 8% of psychiatrists administer ECT (Hermann et al., 1998), estimates suggest that about 100,000 people receive ECT treatments each year in the United States (Hermann et al., 1995). Some critics argue that ECT is overused because it is a lucrative procedure that boosts psychiatrists' income while consuming relatively little of their time in comparison to insight therapy (Frank, 1990). Conversely, some advocates argue that ECT is underutilized because the public harbors many misconceptions about its risks and side effects (McDonald et al., 2004). Although ECT was once considered appropriate for a wide range of disorders, in recent decades it has primarily been recommended for the treatment of depression.

Effectiveness of ECT

Proponents of ECT maintain that it is a remarkably effective treatment for major depression (Prudic, 2009). Many patients who do not benefit from antidepressant medication improve in response to ECT (Nobler & Sackeim, 2006). However, opponents of ECT argue that the available studies are flawed and inconclusive and that ECT is probably no more effective than a placebo (Rose et al., 2003). Overall, enough favorable evidence seems to exist to justify *conservative* use of ECT in treating severe mood disorders in patients who have not responded to medication (Carney & Geddes, 2003). Unfortunately, over 50% of patients relapse within 6 to 12 months, although relapse rates can be reduced by giving ECT patients antidepressant drugs (Sackeim et al., 2001).

This patient is being prepared for electroconvulsive therapy. The mouthpiece keeps the patient from biting her tongue during the electrically induced seizures.

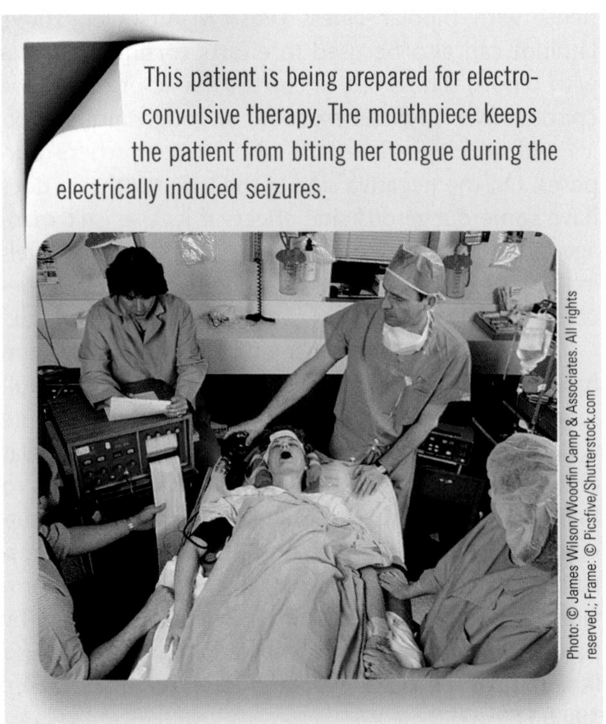

Photo: © James Wilson/Woodfin Camp & Associates. All rights reserved.; Frame: © Picsfive/Shutterstock.com

The debate about whether ECT works does *not* make ECT unique among approaches to the treatment of psychological disorders. Controversies exist regarding the effectiveness of most therapies. However, this controversy is especially problematic because ECT carries some risks.

Risks Associated with ECT

Even ECT proponents acknowledge that memory loss, impaired attention, and other cognitive deficits are common short-term side effects of electroconvulsive therapy (Nobler & Sackeim, 2006). However, they assert that these deficits are mild and usually disappear within a month or two (Glass, 2001). An American Psychiatric Association (2001) task force concluded that there is no objective evidence that ECT causes structural damage in the brain or that it has any lasting negative effects on the ability to learn and remember information. In contrast, ECT critics maintain that ECT-induced cognitive deficits are often significant and sometimes permanent (Rose et al., 2003), although their evidence seems to be largely anecdotal. Given the concerns about the risks of ECT and the doubts about its efficacy, it appears that the use of ECT will remain controversial for some time to come.

15-5 Current Trends and Issues in Treatment

As we saw in our discussion of insight, behavioral, and drug therapy, recent decades have brought many changes in the world of mental health care. In this section, we'll discuss two trends that are not tied to a specific mode of treatment. Specifically, we'll look at the trend toward blending various approaches to therapy and efforts to respond more effectively to increasing cultural diversity in Western societies.

15-5a BLENDING APPROACHES TO TREATMENT

There is no rule that a client must be treated with just one approach to therapy. For example, a depressed person might receive group therapy (an insight therapy), social skills training (a behavior therapy), and antidepressant medication (a biomedical therapy). Multiple approaches are particularly likely when a treatment *team* provides therapy.

The value of multiple approaches may explain why a significant trend seems to have crept into the field of psychotherapy: a movement away from strong loyalty to individual schools of thought and a corresponding move toward integrating various approaches to therapy (Castonguay et al., 2003). Most clinicians used to depend exclusively on one system of therapy while rejecting the utility of all others. This era of fragmentation may be drawing to a close. One survey of psychologists' theoretical orientations, which is summarized in Figure 15.7, found that 36% of the respondents described themselves as *eclectic* in approach (Norcross, Hedges, & Castle, 2002). *Eclecticism* involves drawing ideas from two or more systems of therapy, instead of committing to just one system, while tailoring the intervention strategy to the unique needs of each client. Advocates of eclecticism, such as Arnold Lazarus (2008), maintain that therapists should ask themselves, "What is the best approach for this specific client, problem, and situation?" and then adjust their strategy accordingly.

15-5b INCREASING MULTICULTURAL SENSITIVITY IN TREATMENT

Research on how cultural factors influence the process and outcome of psychotherapy has burgeoned in recent years, motivated in part by the need to improve mental health services for ethnic minority groups in American society (Worthington, Soth-McNett, &

FIGURE 15.7 The leading approaches to therapy among psychologists

These data, from a survey of 531 psychologists who belong to the American Psychological Association's Division of Psychotherapy, provide some indication of how common an eclectic approach to therapy has become. The findings suggest that the most widely used approaches to therapy are eclectic, psychodynamic, and cognitive-behavioral treatments. (Based on data from Norcross, Hedges, & Castle, 2002)

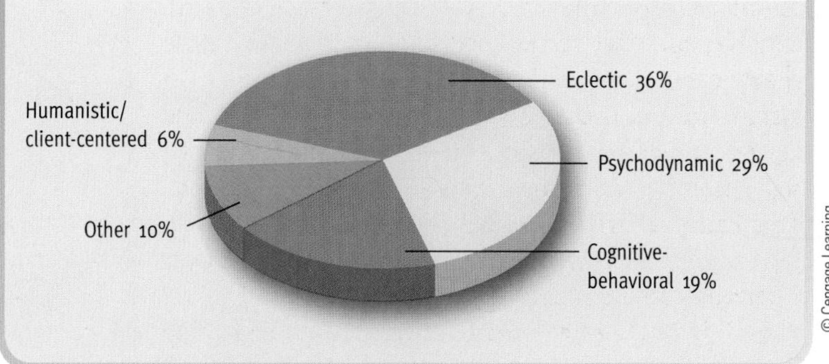

Moreno, 2007). The data are ambiguous for a couple of ethnic groups, but studies suggest that American minority groups generally underutilize therapeutic services (Bender et al., 2007). A variety of barriers appear to contribute to this problem, including the following (Snowden & Yamada, 2005; Zane et al., 2004):

1. *Cultural barriers.* In times of psychological distress, some cultural groups are reluctant to turn to formal, professional sources of assistance. Given their socialization, they prefer to rely on informal assistance from family members, the clergy, respected elders, herbalists, acupuncturists, and so forth, who share their cultural heritage.

2. *Language barriers.* Effective communication is crucial to the provision of psychotherapy, yet most hospitals and mental health agencies are not adequately staffed with therapists who speak the languages used by minority groups in their service areas. The resulting communication problems make it awkward and difficult for many minority group members to explain their problems and obtain the type of help they need.

3. *Institutional barriers.* The vast majority of therapists have been trained almost exclusively in the treatment of middle-class white Americans and are not familiar with the cultural backgrounds and unique characteristics of various ethnic groups. This culture gap often leads to misunderstandings, ill-advised treatment strategies, and reduced rapport.

What can be done to improve mental health services for American minority groups? Discussions of possible solutions usually begin with the need to recruit and train more ethnic minority therapists, as ethnic minorities are more likely to go to mental health facilities that are staffed by a higher proportion of people who share their ethnic background (Snowden & Hu, 1996). Individual therapists have been urged to work harder at building a vigorous *therapeutic alliance* (a strong supportive bond) with their ethnic clients (Bender et al., 2007). Finally, most authorities urge further investigation of how traditional approaches to therapy can be modified and tailored to be more compatible with specific cultural groups' attitudes, values, norms, and traditions (Hwang, 2006).

15-6 APPLICATION

Looking for a Therapist

Answer the following "true" or "false."

___ 1. Psychotherapy is an art as well as a science.

___ 2. The type of professional degree that a therapist holds is relatively unimportant.

___ 3. Psychotherapy does not have to be expensive.

All of these statements are true. Do any of them surprise you? If so, you're in good company. Many people know relatively little about the practicalities of selecting a therapist. The task of finding an appropriate therapist is no less complex than shopping for any other major service. Should you see a psychologist or a psychiatrist? Should you opt for individual therapy or group therapy? Should you see a client-centered therapist or a behavior therapist? The unfortunate part of this daunting situation is that people seeking psychotherapy often feel overwhelmed by personal problems. The last thing they need is to be confronted by yet another complex problem.

Nonetheless, the importance of finding a good therapist cannot be overestimated. In this Application, we present some information that should be helpful if you ever have to look for a therapist for yourself or for a friend or family member (based on Beutler, Bongar, & Shurkin, 2001; Ehrenberg & Ehrenberg, 1994; Pittman, 1994).

15-6a WHERE DO YOU FIND THERAPEUTIC SERVICES?

Psychotherapy can be found in a variety of settings. Contrary to general belief, most therapists are not in private practice. Many work in institutional settings such as community mental health centers, hospitals, and human services agencies. The principal sources of therapeutic services are described in Figure 15.8. The exact configuration of therapeutic services available will vary from one community to another. To find out what your community has to offer, it is a good idea to consult your friends, your local phone book, the Internet, or your local community mental health center.

15-6b IS THE THERAPIST'S PROFESSION OR SEX IMPORTANT?

Psychotherapists may be trained in psychology, psychiatry, social work, counseling, psychiatric nursing, or marriage and family therapy. Researchers have *not* found any reliable associations between therapists'

FIGURE 15.8 | Sources of therapeutic services

Therapists work in a variety of organizational settings. Foremost among them are the five described here.

PRINCIPAL SOURCES OF THERAPEUTIC SERVICES

Source	Comments
Private practitioners	Self-employed therapists are listed in the Yellow Pages under their professional category, such as psychologists or psychiatrists. Private practitioners tend to be relatively expensive, but they also tend to be highly experienced therapists.
Community mental health centers	Community mental health centers have salaried psychologists, psychiatrists, and social workers on staff. The centers provide a variety of services and often have staff available on weekends and at night to deal with emergencies.
Hospitals	Several kinds of hospitals provide therapeutic services. There are both public and private mental hospitals that specialize in the care of people with psychological disorders. Many general hospitals have a psychiatric ward, and those that do not will usually have psychiatrists and psychologists on staff and on call. Although hospitals tend to concentrate on inpatient treatment, many provide outpatient therapy as well.
Human service agencies	Various social service agencies employ therapists to provide short-term counseling. Depending on your community, you may find agencies that deal with family problems, juvenile problems, drug problems, and so forth.
Schools and workplaces	Most high schools and colleges have counseling centers where students can get help with personal problems. Similarly, some large businesses offer in-house counseling to their employees.

INSIDE WOODY ALLEN

INSIDE WOODY ALLEN © 1977 King Features Syndicate, World Rights Reserved

professional background and therapeutic efficacy (Beutler et al., 2004), probably because many talented therapists can be found in all of these professions. Thus, the kind of degree that a therapist holds doesn't need to be a crucial consideration in your selection process.

Whether a therapist's sex is important depends on your attitude (Nadelson, Notman, & McCarthy, 2005). If *you* feel that the therapist's sex is important, then for you it is. The therapeutic relationship must be characterized by trust and rapport. Feeling uncomfortable with a therapist of one sex or the other could inhibit the therapeutic process. Hence, you should feel free to look for a male or female therapist if you prefer to do so. This point is probably most relevant to female clients whose troubles may be related to the extensive sexism in our society (Kaplan, 1985). It is entirely reasonable for women to seek a therapist with a feminist perspective if that would make them feel more comfortable.

15-6c IS THERAPY ALWAYS EXPENSIVE?

Psychotherapy does not have to be prohibitively expensive. Private practitioners tend to be the most expensive, charging between $75 and $150 per (50-minute) hour. These fees may seem high, but they are in line with those of similar professionals, such as dentists and attorneys. Community mental health centers and social service agencies are usually supported by tax dollars. Hence, they can charge lower fees than most therapists in private practice. Many of these organizations use a sliding scale, so that clients are charged according to how much they can afford. Thus, most communities have inexpensive opportunities for psychotherapy. Moreover, many health insurance plans provide at least partial reimbursement for the cost of treatment.

15-6d IS THE THERAPIST'S THEORETICAL APPROACH IMPORTANT?

Logically, you might expect that the diverse approaches to therapy ought to vary in effectiveness. For the most part, that is *not* what researchers find, however. After reviewing the evidence, Jerome Frank (1961) and Lester Luborsky and his colleagues (1975) both quote the dodo bird who has just judged a race in *Alice in Wonderland:* "Everybody has won, and *all* must have prizes." Improvement rates for various theoretical orientations usually come out pretty close in most studies (Lambert & Ogles, 2004). In their landmark review of outcome studies, Smith and Glass (1977) estimated the effectiveness of many major approaches to therapy. As Figure 15.9 shows, the estimates cluster together closely.

However, these findings are a little misleading, as they have been averaged across many types of patients and many types of problems. Most experts seem to think that *for certain types of problems, some approaches to therapy are more effective than others.* For example, Martin Seligman (1995) asserts that panic disorders respond best to cognitive therapy, that specific phobias are most amenable to treatment with systematic desensitization, and that obsessive-compulsive disorders are best treated with behavior therapy or medication. Thus, for a specific type of problem, a therapist's theoretical approach *may* make a difference.

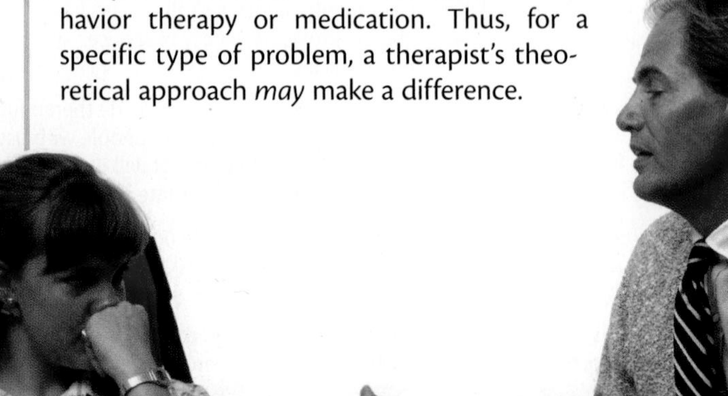

© Will & Deni McIntyre/Getty Images

FIGURE 15.9 | Efficacy of various approaches to therapy

Smith and Glass (1977) reviewed nearly 400 studies in which clients who were treated with a specific type of therapy were compared with a control group made up of people with similar problems who went untreated. The bars indicate the percentile rank (on outcome measures) attained by the average client treated with each type of therapy when compared to control subjects. The higher the percentile, the more effective the therapy was. As you can see, the approaches were fairly close in their apparent effectiveness.

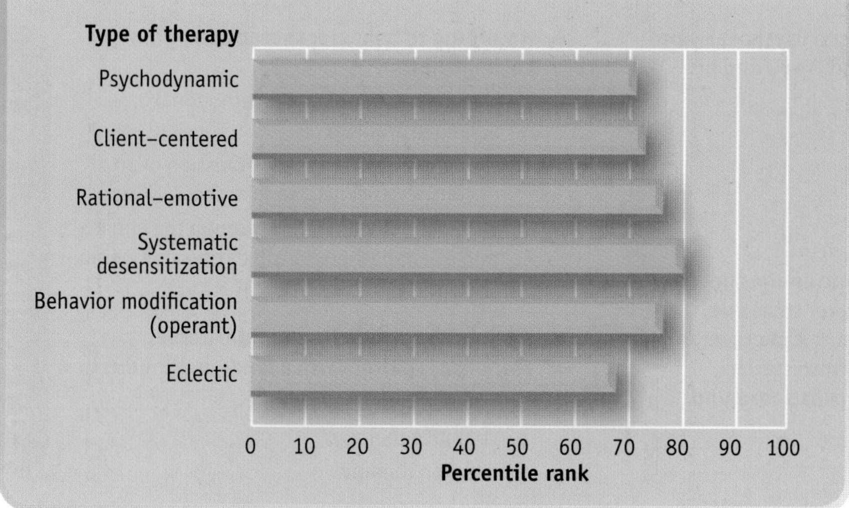

Source: Smith, M. L., & Glass, G. V. (1977). Meta-analysis of psychotherapy outcome series. *American Psychologist, 32,* 752–760. Copyright © 1977 by the American Psychological Association. Adapted by permission.

It is also important to point out that the finding that various approaches to therapy are roughly equal in overall efficacy does not mean that all *therapists* are created equal. Some therapists unquestionably are more effective than others. However, these variations in effectiveness appear to depend on individual therapists' personal skills rather than on their theoretical orientation (Beutler et al., 2004). Good, bad, and mediocre therapists are found within each school of thought. Indeed, the tremendous variation among individual therapists in skills may be one of the main reasons why it is hard to find efficacy differences between theoretical approaches to therapy (Staines, 2008).

The key point is that effective therapy requires skill and creativity. Arnold Lazarus (1989), who devised an approach to treatment called *multimodal therapy,* emphasizes that therapists "straddle the fence between science and art." Therapy is scientific in that interventions are based on extensive theory and empirical research (Forsyth & Strong, 1986). Ultimately, though, each client is a unique human being, and the therapist has to creatively fashion a treatment program that will help that individual.

15-6e WHAT IS THERAPY LIKE?

It is important to have realistic expectations about therapy, or you may be unnecessarily disappointed. Some people expect miracles. They expect to turn their life around quickly with little effort. Others expect their therapist to run their lives for them. These are unrealistic expectations.

Therapy is usually a slow process. Your problems are not likely to melt away quickly. Moreover, therapy is hard work, and your therapist is only a facilitator. Ultimately, *you* have to confront the challenge of changing your behavior, your feelings, or your personality. This process may not be pleasant. You may have to face up to some painful truths about yourself. As Ehrenberg and Ehrenberg (1994) point out, psychotherapy takes time, effort, and courage.

PERSONAL EXPLORATION TOOLS

Curious about yourself? To learn more about how topics in this chapter relate to you, go online to CourseMate at www.cengagebrain.com where you can:

- Complete a **Self-Reflection** exercise that will help you think about your personal experiences in relation to topics in the chapter.
- Take a **Self-Assessment** scale that will show you how you score on a research instrument that measures personality traits or attitudes.
- Explore **Recommended Readings** that will provide brief overviews of useful self-help books.

© edge69/iStockphoto

STUDY TOOLS ▶ 15

Ready to study? In your book you can:

- **Test Yourself** with a multiple-choice quiz (below)
- Rip out the **Chapter Review card** (in the back of the book) to refresh yourself on the chapter's Key Ideas and Key Terms

Or you can go online to CourseMate at www.cengagebrain.com where you can:

- Take additional Practice Quizzes to prepare for your exam
- Review Key Terms with flash cards and a crossword puzzle
- View videos that expand on selected concepts

TEST YOURSELF

1. Which of the following approaches to psychotherapy is based on the theories of Sigmund Freud and his followers?

a. Behavior therapies
b. Client-centered therapy
c. Biomedical therapies
d. Psychoanalytic therapy

2. Miriam is seeing a therapist who encourages her to let her mind ramble and say whatever comes up, regardless of how trivial or irrelevant it may seem. The therapist explains that she is interested in probing the depths of Miriam's unconscious mind. This therapist appears to practice ____________ and the technique in use is ____________.

a. psychoanalysis; transference
b. psychoanalysis; free association
c. cognitive therapy; free association
d. client-centered therapy; clarification

3. Because Suzanne has an unconscious sexual attraction to her father, she behaves seductively toward her therapist. Suzanne's behavior is most likely a form of

a. resistance.
b. transference.
c. misinterpretation.
d. spontaneous remission.

4. Client-centered therapy emphasizes

a. interpretation.
b. probing the unconscious.
c. clarification.
d. all of the above.

5. With regard to studies of the efficacy of various treatments, research suggests

a. insight therapy is superior to no treatment or placebo treatment.
b. individual insight therapy is effective, but group therapy is not.
c. group therapy is effective, but individual insight therapy rarely works.
d. insight therapy is effective, but only if patients remain in therapy for at least three years.

6. According to behavior therapists, pathological behaviors

a. are signs of an underlying emotional or cognitive problem.
b. should be viewed as the expression of an unconscious sexual or aggressive conflict.
c. can be modified directly through the application of established principles of conditioning.
d. both a and b.

7. A stimulus that elicits an undesirable response is paired with a noxious stimulus in

a. systematic desensitization.
b. cognitive therapy.
c. aversion therapy.
d. psychoanalysis.

8. Bryce's psychiatrist has prescribed both an antidepressant and a mood stabilizer for him. Bryce's diagnosis is probably

a. schizophrenia.
b. obsessive-compulsive disorder.
c. bipolar disorder.
d. dissociative disorder.

9. Drug therapies have been criticized on the grounds that

a. they are ineffective in most patients.
b. they temporarily relieve symptoms without addressing the real problem.
c. many drugs are overprescribed and many patients are overmedicated.
d. both b and c.

10. A therapist's theoretical approach is not nearly as important as his or her

a. age.
b. appearance.
c. personal characteristics and skills.
d. type of professional training.

Answers: 1. d, page 322; 2. b, page 322; 3. b, pages 323–324; 4. c, page 325; 5. a, page 326; 6. c, page 328; 7. c, page 329; 8. c, page 333; 9. d, pages 333–334; 10. c, pages 338–339

REFERENCES

AAUW Educational Foundation (1992). *How schools shortchange girls.* Washington, DC: AAUW.

Abbey, A. (2009). Alcohol and sexual assault. In H. T. Reis & S. Sprecher (Eds.), *Encyclopedia of human relationships* (Vol. 1). Los Angeles, CA: Sage Reference Publication.

Abrams, D., Viki, G. T., Masser, B., & Bohner, G. (2003). Perceptions of stranger acquaintance rape: The role of benevolent and hostile sexism in victim blame and rape proclivity. *Journal of Personality and Social Psychology, 84,* 111–125.

Abramson, L. Y., Seligman, M. E. P., & Teasdale, J. D. (1978). Learned helplessness in humans: Critique and reformulation. *Journal of Abnormal Psychology, 87,* 49–74.

Adler, A. (1927). *Practice and theory of individual psychology.* New York, NY: Harcourt, Brace & World.

Adorno, T. W., Frenkel-Brunswik, E., Levinson, D. J., & Sanford, B. W. (1950). *The authoritarian personality.* New York, NY: Harper & Row.

Ai, A. L., Santangelo, L. K., & Cascio, T. (2006). The traumatic impact of the September 11, 2001, terrorist attacks and the potential protection of optimism. *Journal of Interpersonal Violence, 21,* 689–700.

Ainsworth, M. D. S., Blehar, M. C., Waters, E., & Wall, S. (1978). *Patterns of attachment: A psychological study of the strange situation.* Hillsdale, NJ: Erlbaum.

Akerstedt, T., Kecklund, G., & Axelsson, J. (2007). Impaired sleep after bedtime stress and worries. *Biological Psychology, 76*(3), 170–173.

Akiskal, H. S. (2009). Mood disorders: Clinical features. In B. J. Sadock, V. A. Sadock, & P. Ruiz (Eds.), *Kaplan & Sadock's comprehensive textbook of psychiatry* (pp. 1693–1733). Philadelphia, PA: Lippincott Williams & Wilkins.

Alan Guttmacher Institute. (2006). *Plan B decision by FDA a victory for common sense.* Retrieved from http://guttmacher.org/media/inthenews/2006/08/27/index.html.

Alan Guttmacher Institute. (2012). *Facts on American teens' sexual and reproductive health.* Retrieved from http://www.guttmacher.org/pubs/FB-ATSRH.html

Alanko, K., Santtila, P., Harlaar, N., Witting, K., Varjonen, M., Jern, P., Johansson, A., von der Pahlen, B., & Sandnabba, N. K. (2008). The association between childhood gender atypical behavior and adult psychiatric symptoms is moderated by parenting style. *Sex Roles, 58,* 837–847.

Alberti, R. E., & Emmons, M. L. (2001). *Your perfect right.* San Luis Obispo, CA: Impact Publishers.

Aldwin, C. M. (2007). *Stress, coping, and development: An integrative perspective.* New York, NY: Guilford.

Alexander, C. N., Robinson, P., Orme-Johnson, D. W., Schneider, R. H., et al. (1994). The effects of transcendental meditation compared with other methods of relaxation and meditation in reducing risk factors, morbidity, and mortality. *Homeostasis in Health & Disease, 35,* 243–263.

Alicke, M. D. (1985). Global self-evaluation as determined by the desirability and controllability of trait adjectives. *Journal of Personality and Social Psychology, 49*(6), 1621–1630.

Allan, R. (2011). Type A behavior pattern. In R. Allen & J. Fisher (Eds.), *Heart and mind: The practice of cardiac psychology* (2nd ed., pp. 287–290). Washington, DC: American Psychological Association.

Allgood, W. P., Risko, V. J., Alvarez, M. C., & Fairbanks, M. M. (2000). Factors that influence study. In R. F. Flippo & D. C. Caverly (Eds.), *Handbook of college reading and study strategy research.* Mahwah, NJ: Erlbaum.

Alloy, L. B., Abramson, L. Y., Whitehouse, W. G., Hogan, M. E., Tashman, N. A., Steinberg, D. L., Rose, D. T., & Donovan, P. (1999). Depressogenic cognitive styles: Predictive validity, information processing and personality characteristics, and developmental origins. *Behavioral Research and Therapy, 37,* 503–531.

Altemeyer, B. (1998). The other "authoritarian personality." *Advances in Experimental Social Psychology, 30,* 47–92.

Altman, I., & Taylor, D. A. (1983). *Social penetration: The development of interpersonal relationships.* New York, NY: Irvington.

Amato, P. R. (2003). Reconciling divergent perspectives: Judith Wallerstein, quantitative family research, and children of divorce. *Family Relations: Interdisciplinary Journal of Applied Family Studies, 52*(4), 332–339.

Amato, P. R. (2004a). Divorce in social and historical context: Changing scientific perspectives on children and marital dissolution. In M. Coleman & L. H. Ganong (Eds.), *Handbook of contemporary families: Considering the past, contemplating the future.* Thousand Oaks, CA: Sage.

Amato, P. R. (2004b). Tension between institutional and individual views of marriage. *Journal of Marriage and Family, 66,* 959–965.

Amato, P. R. (2010). Research on divorce: Continuing trends and new developments. *Journal of Marriage and Family,* 72(3), 650–666. doi:10.1111/j.1741-3737.2010.00723.x

American Psychiatric Association. (1994). *Diagnostic and statistical manual of mental disorders* (4th ed.). Washington, DC: Author.

American Psychiatric Association Task Force on Electroconvulsive Therapy. (2001). *The practice of electroconvulsive therapy: Recommendations for treatment* (2nd ed.). Washington, DC: American Psychiatric Association.

American Psychological Association. (2010). *Stress in America Findings.* Washington, DC: APA.

American Society for Aesthetic Plastic Surgery. (2008). Surgical and nonsurgical procedures: 12-year Comparison, 1997–2008. Retrieved from http://www.surgy.org.media/statistics

Anderson, A. E., & Yager, J. (2005). Eating disorders. In B. J. Sadock & V. A. Sadock (Eds.), *Kaplan & Sadock's comprehensive textbook of psychiatry.* Philadelphia, PA: Lippincott Williams & Wilkins.

Anderson, C. A., & Bushman, B. J. (2001). Effects of violent video games on aggressive behavior, aggressive cognition, aggressive affect, physiological arousal, and prosocial behavior: A meta-analytic review of the scientific literature. *Psychological Science, 12,* 353–359.

Anderson, C. A., Miller, R. S., Riger, A. L., Dill, J. C., & Sedikides, C. (1994). Behavioral and characterological attributional styles as predictors of depression and loneliness: Review, refinement, and test. *Journal of Personality and Social Psychology, 66,* 549–558.

Anderson, D. A., & Hamilton, M. (2005). Gender role stereotyping of parents in children's picture books: The invisible father. *Sex Roles, 52*(3–4), 145–151.

Andreasen, N. C. (2009). Schizophrenia: A conceptual history. In M. C. Gelder, N. C. Andreasen, J. J. López-Ibor, Jr., & J. R. Geddes (Eds.). *New Oxford textbook of psychiatry,* Vol. 1 (2nd ed.). New York, NY: Oxford University Press.

Andrews, B., & Hejdenberg, J. (2007). Stress in university students. In G. Fink (Ed.), *Encyclopedia of stress: Vols. 1–4* (2nd ed., pp. 612–614). San Diego, CA: Elsevier Academic Press.

Andrews, G., Charney, D., Sirovatka, P., & Regier, D. (Eds.) (2009). *Stress-induced and fear circuitry disorders: Advancing the research agenda for DSM-V.* Arlington, VA: American Psychiatric Publishing.

Anson, K., & Ponsford, J. (2006). Coping and emotional adjustment following traumatic brain injury. *Journal of Head Trauma Rehabilitation, 21,* 248–259.

Antecol, H., Jong, A., & Steinberger, M. (2008). The sexual orientation wage gap: The role of occupational sorting and human capital. *Industrial & Labor Relations Review, 61,* 518–543.

Anthony, I. C., & Bell, J. E. (2008). The neuropathology of HIV/AIDS. *International Review of Psychiatry, 20*(1), 15–24.

Arbona, C. (2005). Promoting the career development and academic achievement of at-risk youth: College access programs. In S. D. Brown & R. W. Lent (Eds.), *Career development and counseling: Putting theory and research to work.* New York, NY: Wiley.

Archibald, A. B., Graber, J. A., & Brooks-Gunn, J. (2003). Pubertal processes and physiological growth in adolescence. In G. R. Adams & M. D. Berzonsky (Eds.), *Blackwell handbook of adolescence.* Malden, MA: Blackwell Publishing.

Archer, J. (2005). Are women or men the more aggressive sex? In S. Fein, G. R. Goethals, & M. J. Sandstrom (Eds.), *Gender and aggression: Interdisciplinary perspectives.* Mahwah, NJ: Erlbaum.

Argyle, M. (1999). Causes and correlates of happiness. In D. Kahneman, E. Diener, & N. Schwarz (Eds.), *Well-being: The foundations of hedonic psychology.* New York, NY: Sage.

Argyle, M. (2001). *The psychology of happiness* (2nd ed.). New York, NY: Routledge.

Aries, E. (1998). Gender differences in interaction: A reexamination. In D. J. Canary & K. Dindia (Eds.), *Sex differences and similarities in communication: Critical essays and empirical investigations of sex and gender in interaction.* Mahwah, NJ: Erlbaum.

Arkowitz, H., & Lilienfeld, S. O. (2006). Do self-help books help? *Scientific American Mind, 17*(5), 78–79.

Arkowitz, H., & Lilienfeld, S. O. (2007). The best medicine? How drugs stack up against talk therapy for the treatment of depression. *Scientific American Mind, 18*(5), 80–83.

Aronson, J., Lustina, M. J., Good, C., Keough, K., Steele, C. M., & Brown, J. (1999). White men can't do math: Necessary and sufficient factors in stereotype threat. *Journal of Experimental Social Psychology, 35*(1), 29–46.

Arriaga, P., Esteves, F., Carneiro, P., & Monteiro, M. B. (2006a). Violent computer games and their effects on state hostility and physiological arousal. *Aggressive Behavior, 32,* 358–371.

Arriaga, X. B., Reed, J. T., Goodfriend, W., & Agnew, C. R. (2006b). Relationship perceptions and persistence: Do fluctuations in perceived commitment undermine dating relationships? *Journal of Personality and Social Psychology, 91,* 1045–1065.

Asch, S. E. (1955). Opinions and social pressures. *Scientific American, 193*(5), 31–35.

Asch, S. E. (1956). Studies of independence and conformity: A minority of one against a unanimous majority. *Psychological Monographs, 70* (9, Whole No. 416).

Aspinwall, L. G., & Taylor, S. E. (1993). Effects of social comparison direction, threat, and self-esteem on affect, evaluation, and expected success. *Journal of Personality and Social Psychology, 64,* 708–722.

Associated Press. (2005, October 22). How many survivors does it take to tell a joke? MSNBC. Retrieved from http://www.msnbc.msn.com/id/9783819/ns/us/us_news-katrina_the_long_road_back/

Athenstaedt, U., Haas, E., & Schwab, S. (2004). Gender role self-concept and gender-typed communication behavior in mixed-sex and same-sex dyads. *Sex Roles, 50*(1/2), 37–52.

Aubin, S., & Heiman, J. R. (2004). Sexual dysfunction from a relationship perspective. In J. H. Harvey, A. Wenzel, & S. Sprecher (Eds.), *The handbook of sexuality in close relationships.* Mahwah, NJ: Lawrence Erlbaum.

Aubrey, J. S., & Harrison, K. (2004). The gender-role content of children's favorite television programs and its links to their gender-related perceptions. *Media Psychology, 6,* 11–146.

Auster, C. J., & Ohm, S. C. (2000). Masculinity and femininity in contemporary American society: A reevaluation using the Bem Sex-Role Inventory. *Sex Roles, 43,* 499–528.

Aveline, M., Strauss, B., & Stiles, W. B. (2005). Psychotherapy research. In G. O. Gabbard, J. S. Beck, & J. Holmes (Eds.), *Oxford textbook of psychotherapy.* New York, NY: Oxford University Press.

Avery, D., McKay, P., & Wilson, D. (2008). What are the odds? How demographic similarity affects the prevalence of perceived employment discrimination. *Journal of Applied Psychology, 93*(2), 235–249.

Ayar, A. A. (2006). Road Rage: Recognizing a psychological disorder. *Journal of Psychiatry & Law, 34,* 123–143.

Ayoola, A. B., Nettleman, M., & Brewer, J. (2007). Reasons for unprotected intercourse in adult women. *Journal of Women's Health, 16,* 302–310.

Ayres, J., Hopf, T., & Ayres, D. M. (1994). An examination of whether imaging ability enhances the effectiveness of an intervention designed to reduce speech anxiety. *Communication Education, 43*(3), 252–258.

Aziz, S., & Zickar, M. J. (2006). A cluster analysis investigation of workaholism as a syndrome. *Journal of Occupational Health Psychology, 11*(1), 52–62.

Badgett, M. V. L. (2003). Employment and sexual orientation: Disclosure and discrimination in the workplace. In L. D. Garnets & D. C. Kimmel (Eds.), *Psychological perspectives on lesbian, gay, and bisexual experiences* (2nd ed,). New York, NY: Columbia University Press.

Bailey, J. M., & Dawood, K. (1998). Behavior genetics, sexual orientation, and the family. In C. J. Patterson & A. R. D'Augelli (Eds.), *Lesbian, gay and bisexual identities in families: Psychological perspectives.* New York, NY: Oxford University Press.

Bailey, J. M., Kim, P. Y., Hills, A., & Linsenmeier, J. A. W. (1997). Butch, femme, or straight acting? Partner preferences of gay men and lesbians. *Journal of Personality and Social Psychology, 73*(5), 960–973.

Bailey, J. M., & Pillard, R. C. (1991). A genetic study of male sexual orientation. *Archives of General Psychiatry, 48,* 1089–1096.

Bailey, J. M., Pillard, R. C., Neale, M. C., & Agyei, Y. (1993). Heritable factors influence sexual orientation in women. *Archives of General Psychiatry, 50,* 217–223.

Baillargeon, R. H., Zoccolillo, M., Keenan, K., Cote, S., Persusse, D., Wu, H., Boivin, M., & Tremblay, R. E. (2007). Gender differences in physical aggression: A prospective population-based survey of children before and after 2 years of age. *Developmental Psychology, 43,* 13–26.

Baker, F., Ainsworth, S. R., Dye, J. T., Crammer, C., Thun, M. J., Hoffmann, D., Repace, J. L., Henningfield, J. E., Slade, J., Pinney, J., Shanks, T., Burns, D. M., Connolly, G. N., & Shopland, D. R. (2000). Health risks associated with cigar smoking. *Journal of the American Medical Association, 284,* 735–740.

Bakker, A. B., Demerouti, E., & Burke, R. (2009). Workaholism and relationship quality: A spillover-crossover perspective. *Journal of Occupational Health Psychology, 14*(1), 23–33.

Bakker, A. B., Schaufeli, W. B., Leiter, M. P., & Taris, T. W. (2008). Work engagement: An emerging concept in occupational health psychology. *Work & Stress, 22*(3), 187–200.

Baldessarini, R. J., Tondo, L., Strombom, I. M., Dominguez, S., Fawcett, J., Licinio, J., Oquendo, M. A., Tollefson, G. D., Valuck, R. J., & Tohen, M. (2007). Ecological studies of antidepressant treatment and suicidal risks. *Harvard Review of Psychiatry, 15,* 133–145.

Balsam, K. F., Beauchaine, T. P., Mickey, R. M., & Rothblum, E. D. (2005). Mental health of lesbian, gay, bisexual, and heterosexual siblings: Effects of gender, sexual orientation, and family. *Journal of Abnormal Psychology, 114,* 471–476.

Bancroft, J. (2002a). Biological factors in human sexuality. *The Journal of Sex Research, 39*(1), 15–21.

Bancroft, J. (2002b). The medicalization of female sexual dysfunction: The need for caution. *Archives of Sexual Behavior, 31*(5), 451–455.

Bandura, A. (1986). *Social foundations of thought and action: A social-cognitive theory.* Englewood Cliffs, NJ: Prentice-Hall.

Bandura, A. (1997). *Self-efficacy: The exercise of control.* New York, NY: W. H. Freeman.

Bandura, A. (1999). Social cognitive theory of personality. In L. A. Pervin & O. P. John (Eds.), *Handbook of personality: Theory and research* (2nd ed.). New York, NY: Guilford Press.

Bandura, A. (2000). Social cognitive theory: An agentic perspective. *Annual Review of Psychology, 52,* 1–26.

Bandura, A. (2004). Health promotion by social cognitive means. *Health Education & Behavior, 31*(2), 143–164.

Bandura, A. (2008). An agentic perspective on positive psychology. In S. J. Lopez (Ed.), *Positive psychology: Exploring the best in people* (pp. 167–196). Westport, CT: Praeger.

Bargh, J. A., & McKenna, K. Y. A. (2004). The Internet and social life. *Annual Review of Psychology, 55,* 573–590.

Bargh, J. A., McKenna, K. Y. A., & Fitzsimons, G. M. (2002). Can you see the real me? Activation and expression of the "true self" on the Internet. *Journal of Social Issues, 58*(1), 33–48.

Barnes, M. L., & Buss, D. M. (1985). Sex differences in the interpersonal behavior of married couples. *Journal of Personality and Social Psychology, 48,* 654–661.

Barnes, V. A., Treiber, F., & Davis, H. (2001). The impact of Transcendental Meditation on cardiovascular function at rest and during acute stress in adolescents with high norspeed in old age. *Current Directions in Psychological Science, 6,* 163–169.

Barnett, R. C. (2005). Dual-earner couples: Good/bad for her and/or him? In D. F. Halpern & S. E. Murphy (Eds.), *From work-family balance to work-family interaction: Changing the metaphor.* Mahwah, NJ: Erlbaum.

Barnett, R. C., & Hyde, J. S. (2001). Women, men, work, and family: An expansionist theory. *American Psychologist, 56*(10), 781–796.

Barron, J. M., Struckman-Johnson, C., Quevillon, R., & Banka, S. R. (2008). Heterosexual men's attitudes toward gay men: A hierarchical model including masculinity, openness, and theoretical explanations. *Psychology of Men & Masculinity, 9,* 154–166.

Barsky, A. J. (1988). The paradox of health. *New England Journal of Medicine, 318,* 414–418.

Bartholomew, K. (1990). Avoidance of intimacy: An attachment perspective. *Journal of Social and Personal Relationships, 7,* 47–178.

Bartholomew, K. (2009). Adult attachment, individual differences. In H. T. Reis & S. Sprecher (Eds.), *Encyclopedia of human relationships: Vol. 1* (pp. 34–39). Los Angeles, CA: Sage Reference Publication.

Bartone, P., Roland, R., Picano, J., & Williams, T. (2008). Psychological hardiness predicts success in U.S. Army Special Forces candidates. *International Journal of Selections and Assessment, 16*(1), 78–81.

Baum, A., Trevino, L. A., & Dougall, A. L. (2011). Stress and the cancers. In R. J. Contrada,& A. Baum (Eds.), *The handbook of stress: Biology, psychology, and health* (pp. 411–423). New York, NY: Springer.

Baumbusch, J. L. (2004). Unclaimed treasures: Older women's reflections on lifelong singlehood. *Journal of Women & Aging, 16,* 105–121.

Baumeister, R. F. (1984). Choking under pressure: Self-consciousness and paradoxical effects of incentives on skillful performance. *Journal of Personality and Social Psychology, 46,* 610–620.

Baumeister, R. F. (1989). The optimal margin of illusion. *Journal of Social and Clinical Psychology, 8,* 176–189.

Baumeister, R. F. (1995). Disputing the effects of championship pressures and home audiences. *Journal of Personality and Social Psychology, 68,* 644–648.

Baumeister, R. F. (1997). Esteem threat, self-regulatory breakdown, and emotional distress as factors in self-defeating behavior. *Review of General Psychology, 1,* 145–174.

Baumeister, R. F. (1998). The self. In D. T. Gilbert, S. T. Fiske, & G. Lindzey (Eds.), *The handbook of social psychology.* Boston, MA: Mcgraw-Hill.

Baumeister, R. F. (1999). The nature and structure of the self: An overview. In R. F. Baumeister (Ed.), *The self in social psychology.* Ann Arbor, MI: Edwards Bros.

Baumeister, R. F., & Alquist, J. L. (2009). Is there a downside to good self-control? *Self and Identity, 8*(2–3), 115–130.

Baumeister, R. F., Bratslavsky, E., Muraven, M., & Tice, D. M. (1998). Ego depletion: Is the active self a limited resource? *Journal of Personality and Social Psychology, 74*(5), 1252–1265.

Baumeister, R. F., Campbell, J. D., Krueger, J. I., & Vohs, K. D. (2003). Does high self-esteem cause better performance, interpersonal success, happiness, or healthier lifestyles? *Psychological Science in the Public Interest, 4*(1), 1–44.

Baumeister, R. F., Gailliot, M., DeWall, M., & Oaten, M. (2006). Self-regulation and personality: How interventions increase regulatory success, and how depletion moderates the effects of traits on behavior. *Journal of Personality, 74,* 1773–1801.

Baumeister, R. F., Smart, L., & Boden, J. M. (1996). Relation of threatened egotism to violence and aggression: The dark side of high self-esteem. *Psychological Review,* 103, 5–33.

Baumeister, R. F., & Twenge, J. M. (2003). The social self. In T. Millon & M. J. Lerner (Eds.) *Handbook of psychology: Vol. 5. Personality and social psychology.* New York, NY: Wiley.

Baumrind, D. (1967). Child care practices anteceding three patterns of preschool behavior. *Genetic Psychology Monographs, 75,* 43–88.

Baumrind, D. (1971). Current patterns of parental authority. *Developmental Psychology Monographs, 4* (1, Part 2).

Bavelas, J. B., Coates, L., & Johnson, T. (2002). Listener responses as a collaborative process: The role of gaze. *Journal of Communication, 52*(3), 566–580.

Baxter, L. A. (1988). A dialectical perspective on communication strategies in relationship development. In S. Duck (Ed.), *Handbook of personal relationships.* New York, NY: Wiley.

Beall, A. E., Eagly, A. H., & Sternberg, R. J. (2004). Introduction. In A. H. Eagly, A. E. Beall, & R. J. Sternberg (Eds.), *The psychology of gender.* New York, NY: Guilford Press.

Beck, A. T., & Weishaar, M. E. (2011). Cognitive therapy. In R. J. Corsini & D. Wedding (Eds.), *Current psychotherapies* (9th ed.). Belmont, CA: Brooks/Cole.

Becker, A., & Fay, K. (2006). Sociocultural issues and eating disorders. In S. Wonderlich, J. Mitchell, M. de Zwaan, & H. Steiger (Eds.), *Annual review of eating disorders.* Oxon, England: Radcliffe.

Becker, E. (1997). *The denial of death.* New York, NY: Free Press.

Beckman, H., Regier, N., & Young, J. (2007). Effect of workplace laughter groups on personal efficacy beliefs. *The Journal of Primary Prevention, 28*(2), 167–182.

Behar, R. (1991, May 6). The thriving cult of greed and power. *Time,* pp. 50–77.

Beidel, D. C., & Stipelman, B. (2007). Anxiety disorders. In M. Hersen, S. M. Turner, & D. C. Beidel (Eds.), *Adult psychopathology and diagnosis.* New York, NY: Wiley.

Beilock, S. L., Kulp, C. A., Holt, L. E., & Carr, T. H. (2004). More on the fragility of performance: Choking under pressure in mathematical problem solving. *Journal of Experimental Psychology, 133,* 584–600.

Bell, A. P., Weinberg, M. S., & Hammersmith, K. S. (1981). *Sexual preference—Its development in men and women.* Bloomington: Indiana University Press.

Belsky, J. (2006). Early child care and early child development: Major findings of the NICHD study of Early Child Care. *European Journal of Developmental Psychology, 3,* 95–110.

Bem, S. L. (1975, September). Androgyny vs. the tight little lives of fluffy women and chesty men. *Psychology Today,* pp. 58–62.

Benbow, C. P. (1988). Sex differences in mathematical reasoning ability in intellectually talented preadolescents: Their nature, effects, and possible causes. *Behavioral and Brain Sciences, 11,* 169–232.

Bender, D. S., Skodol, A. E., Dyck, I. R., Markowitz, J. C., Shea, M. T., Yen, S., et al. (2007). Ethnicity and mental health treatment utilization by patients with personality disorders. *Journal of Consulting and Clinical Psychology, 75,* 992–999.

Berdahl, J. L., & Moore, C. (2006). Workplace harassment: Double jeopardy for minority women. *Journal of Applied Psychology, 91,* 426–436.

Berman, A. L. (2009). Depression and suicide. In I. H. Gotlib & C. L. Hammen (Eds.), *Handbook of depression* (2nd ed.). New York, NY: Guilford Press.

Berman, R. M., Sporn, J., Charney, D. S., & Mathew, S. J. (2009). Principles of the pharmacotherapy of depression. In D. S. Charney & E. J. Nestler (Eds.), *Neurobiology of mental illness* (pp. 491–515). New York, NY: Guilford.

Bernieri, F. J., & Petty, K. N. (2011). The influence of handshakes on first impression accuracy. *Social Influence, 6*(2), 78–87. doi: 10.1080/15534510.2011.566706

Berthoud, H., & Morrison, C. (2008). The brain, appetite, and obesity. *Annual Review of Psychology, 59,* 55–92.

Berzon, B. (2004). *Permanent partners: Building gay and lesbian relationships that last.* New York, NY: The Penguin Group.

Best, D. L., & Thomas, J. J. (2004). Cultural diversity and cross-cultural perspectives. In A. H. Eagly, A. E. Beall, & R. J. Sternberg (Eds.), *The psychology of gender.* New York, NY: Guilford Press.

Betz, N. E. (2005). Women's career development. In S. D. Brown & R. W. Lent (Eds.), *Career development and counseling: Putting theory and research to work.* New York, NY: Wiley.

Betz, N. E. (2006). Women's career development. In J. Worell & C. D. Goodheart (Eds.), *Handbook of girls' and women's psychological health.* New York, NY: Oxford University Press.

Betz, N. E., & Klein, K. L. (1996). Relationships among measures of career self-efficacy, generalized self-efficacy, and global self-esteem. *Journal of Career Assessment, 4*(3), 285–298.

Beutler, L. E., Bongar, B., & Shurkin, J. N. (2001). *A consumers guide to psychotherapy.* New York, NY: Oxford University Press.

Bianchi, S., Milkie, M. A., Sayer, L. C., & Robinson, J. P. (2000). Is anyone doing the housework? Trends in the gender division of household labor. *Social Forces, 79*(1), 191–228.

Bianchi, S., Subaiya, L., & Kahn, J. R. (1999). The gender gap in the economic well-being of nonresident fathers and custodial mothers. *Demography, 36,* 195–203.

Bisson, M. A., & Levine, T. R. (2009). Negotiating a friend with benefits relationship. *Archives of Sexual Behavior, 38,* 66–73.

Blackmore, E. R., Stansfield, S. A., Weller, L., Munce, S., Zagorski, B. M., & Stewart, D. E. (2007). Major depressive episodes and work stress: Results from a national population survey. *American Journal of Public Health, 97,* 2088–2093.

Blair, S. N., Cheng, Y., & Holder, J. S. (2001). Is physical activity or physical fitness more important in defining health benefits? *Medicine and Science in Sports and Exercise, 33,* S379–S399.

Blair, S. N., Kohl, H. W., Paffenbarger, R. S., Clark, D. G., Cooper, K. H., & Gibbons, L. W. (1989). Physical fitness and all-cause mortality: A prospective study of healthy men and women. *Journal of the American Medical Association, 262,* 2395–2401.

Blakemore, J. E. O. (2003). Children's beliefs about violating gender norms: Boys shouldn't look like girls, and girls shouldn't act like boys. *Sex Roles, 48*(9/10), 411–419.

Blanchard, E. B., & Keefer, L. (2003). Irritable bowel syndrome. In A. M. Nezu, C. M. Nezu, & P. A. Geller (Eds.), *Handbook of psychology: Vol. 9. Health psychology.* New York, NY: Wiley.

Blanton, H., Buunk, B. P., Gibbons, F. X., & Kuyper, H. (1999). When better-than-others compare upward: Choice of comparison and comparative evaluation as independent predictors of academic performance. *Journal of Personality and Social Psychology, 76,* 420–430.

Blass, T. (1999). The Milgram paradigm after 35 years: Some things we now know about obedience to authority. *Journal of Applied Social Psychology, 29*(5), 955–978.

Blass, T. (2004). *The man who shocked the world: The life and legacy of Stanley Milgram.* New York, NY: Basic Books.

Bleakley, A., Hennessy, M., Fishbein, M, & Jordan, A. (2008). It works both ways: The relationship between exposure to sexual content in the media and adolescent sexual behavior. *Media Psychology, 11,* 443–461.

Block, J., & Robbins, R. W. (1993). A longitudinal study of consistency and change in self-esteem from early adolescence to early adulthood. *Child Development, 64,* 909–923.

Blumstein, P., & Schwartz, P. (1983). *American couples: Money, work, sex.* New York, NY: Morrow.

Bobek, B. L., & Robbins, S. B. (2005). Counseling for career transition: Career pathing, job loss, and reentry. In S. D. Brown & R. W. Lent (Eds.), *Career development and counseling: Putting theory and research to work.* New York, NY: Wiley.

Bobo, W. V., Rapoport, J. L., Abi-Dargham, A., Fatemi, H., & Meltzer, H. Y. (2008). The neurobiology of schizophrenia. In A. Tasman, J. Kay, J. A. Lieberman, M. B. First, & M. Maj (Eds.), *Psychiatry* (3rd ed.). New York, NY: Wiley-Blackwell.

Bodenhausen, G. V. (1988). Stereotypic biases in social decision making and memory: Testing process models of stereotype use. *Journal of Personality and Social Psychology, 55,* 726–737.

Bolles, R. N. (2007). *The 2007 what color is your parachute? A practical manual for job-hunters and career-changers.* Berkeley, CA: Ten Speed Press.

Bond, C. F., Jr., & DePaulo, B. M. (2006). Accuracy of deception judgments. *Personality and Social Psychology Review, 10*(3), 214–234.

Bond, C. F., Jr., & DePaulo, B. M. (2008). Individual differences in judging deception: Accuracy and bias. *Psychological Bulletin, 134,* 477–492.

Bond, J. T., Galinsky, E., Kim, S. S., & Brownfield, E. (2005). *The 2005 national study of employers.* New York, NY: Families and Work Institute.

Bond, J. T., Thompson, C., Galinsky, E., & Prottas, D. (2003). *The 2002 national study of the changing workforce.* New York, NY: Families and Work Institute.

Bonebright, C. A., Clay, D. L., & Ankenmann, R. D. (2000). The relationship of workaholism with work-life conflict, life satisfaction, and purpose in life. *Journal of Counseling Psychology, 47,* 469–477.

Bordnick, P. S., Elkins, R. L., Orr, T. E., Walters, P., & Thyer, B. A. (2004). Evaluating the relative effectiveness of three aversion therapies designed to reduce craving among cocaine abusers. *Behavioral Interventions, 19*(1), 1–24.

Borys, S., & Perlman, D. (1985). Gender differences in loneliness. *Personality and Social Psychology Bulletin, 11,* 63–74.

Bourhis, J., Allen, M., & Bauman, I. (2006). Communication apprehension: Issues to consider in the classroom. In B. M. Gayle, R. W. Preiss, N. Burrell, & M. Allen (Eds.), *Classroom communication and instructional processes: Advances through meta-analysis* (pp. 211–227). Mahwah, NJ: Erlbaum.

Bower, G. H. (1970). Organizational factors in memory. *Cognitive Psychology, 1,* 18–46.

Bower, S. A., & Bower, G. H. (1991). *Asserting yourself: A practical guide for positive change* (2nd ed.). Reading, MA: Addison-Wesley.

Bower, S. A., & Bower, G. H. (2004). *Asserting yourself: A practical guide for positive change* (updated ed.). Cambridge, MA: Da Capo Press/Perseus.

Bowins, B. (2004). Psychological defense mechanisms: A new perspective. *American Journal of Psychoanalysis, 64*(1), 1–26.

Bowlby, J. (1980). *Attachment and loss: Vol. 3. Loss: Sadness and depression.* New York, NY: Basic Books.

Boyce, C. J., Brown, G. A., & Moore, S. C. (2010). Money and happiness: Rank of income, not income, affects life satisfaction. *Psychological Science, 21*(4), 471–475.

Boyle, M. (2007). The problem with diagnosis. *The Psychologist, 20,* 290–292.

Braaten, E. B. (2011). Psychotherapy: Interpersonal and insight-oriented approaches. In E. B. Braaten (Ed.), *How to find mental health care for your child* (pp. 171–183). Washington, DC: American Psychological Association.

Bradbury, T. N., Campbell, S. M., & Fincham, F. D. (1995). Longitudinal and behavioral analysis of masculinity and femininity in marriage. *Journal of Personality and Social Psychology, 68*(2), 328–341.

Brady-Amoon, P., & Fuertes, J. N. (2011). Self-efficacy, self-rated abilities, adjustment, and academic performance. *Journal of Counseling & Development, 89*(4), 431–438.

Brainerd, C. J., & Reyna, V. F. (2005). *The science of false memory.* New York, NY: Oxford University Press.

Bramlett, M. D., & Mosher, W. D. (2001). *First marriage dissolution, divorce, and remarriage: United States. Advance data from vital and health statistics, No. 323.* Hyattsville, MD: National Center for Health Statistics.

Brandes, D., Ben-Schachar, G., Gilboa, A., Bonne, O., Freedman, & S., Shalev, A. Y. (2002). PTSD symptoms and cognitive performance in recent trauma survivors. *Psychiatry Research, 110,* 231–238.

Brandt, M. J. (2011). Sexism and gender inequality across 57 societies. *Psychological Science, 22*(11), 1413–1418. doi:10.1177/0956797611420445

Brannon, L. (2005). *Gender: Psychological perspectives.* Boston, MA: Allyn & Bacon.

Brannon, R. (1976). The male sex role: Our culture's blueprint of manhood, and what it's done for us lately. In D. David & R. Brannon (Eds.), *The forty-nine percent majority.* Reading, MA: Addison-Wesley.

Branscombe, N. R., Wann, D. L., Noel, J. G., & Coleman, J. (1993). In-group or out-group extremity: Importance of the threatened social identity. *Personality and Social Psychology Bulletin, 19,* 381–388.

Bray, J. H. (2009). Remarriage. In H. T. Reis & S. Sprecher (Eds.), *Encyclopedia of human relationships: Vol. 3* (pp. 1359–1363). Los Angeles, CA: Sage Reference Publication.

Breggin, P. R., & Cohen, D. (2007). *Your drug may be your problem: How and why to stop taking psychiatric medications.* New York, NY: Da Capo Lifelong Books.

Brehm, S. S., & Brehm, J. W. (1981). *Psychological reactance.* New York, NY: Academic Press.

Brehm, S. S., & Kassin, S. M. (1993). *Social psychology.* Boston, MA: Houghton Mifflin.

Brehm, S. S., Kassin, S. M., & Fein, S. (2002). *Social psychology.* Boston, MA: Houghton Mifflin.

Breslin, F. C., & Mustard, C. (2003). Factors influencing the impact of unemployment on mental health among young and older adults in a longitudinal, population-based survey. *Scandinavian Journal of Work, Environment & Health, 29*(1), 5–14.

Brewer, M. B. (1999). The psychology of prejudice: Ingroup love or outgroup hate? *Journal of Social Issues, 55,* 429–444.

Brewer, M. B., & Brown, R. J. (1998). Inter-group relations. In D. T. Gilbert, S. T. Fiske, & G. Lindzey (Eds.), *The handbook of social psychology* (4th ed., Vol. 2). New York, NY: McGraw-Hill.

Bridge, J. A., Iyengar, S., Salary, C. B., Barbe, R. P., Birmaher, B., Pincus, H. A., et al. (2007). Clinical response and risk for reported suicidal ideation and suicide attempts in pediatric antidepressant treatment: A meta-analysis of randomized controlled trials. *Journal of the American Medical Association, 297,* 1683–1969.

Bridges, K. R., & Roig, M. (1997). Academic procrastination and irrational thinking: A re-examination with context controlled. *Personality & Individual Differences, 22,* 941–944.

Brissette, I., Scheier, M. F., & Carver, C. S. (2002). The role of optimism in social network development, coping, and psychological adjustment during a life transition. *Journal of Personality and Social Psychology, 82*(1), 102–111.

Briton, N. J., & Hall, J. A. (1995). Beliefs about female and male nonverbal c ommunication. *Sex Roles, 32*(1-2), 79–90.

Britton, B. K., & Tesser, A. (1991). Effects of time-management practices on college grades. *Journal of Educational Psychology, 83,* 405–410.

Brody, S., & Costa, R. M. (2009). Satisfaction (sexual, life, relationship, and mental health) is associated directly with penile and vaginal intercourse, but inversely with other sexual behavior frequencies. *Journal of Sexual Medicine, 6,* 1947–1954.

Bromage, B. K., & Mayer, R. E. (1986). Quantitative and qualitative effects of repetition on learning from technical text. *Journal of Educational Psychology, 78,* 271–278.

Brondolo, E., ver Halen, N. B., Libby, D. & Pencille, M. (2011). Racism as a psychosocial stressor. In R.J. Contrada & A. Baum (Eds.). *The Handbook of stress science: Biology, psychology, and health* (pp. 167–184). New York, NY: Springer Publishing Company.

Brooks, G. R. (2010). The crisis of masculinity. In G. R. Brooks (Ed.), *Beyond the crisis of masculinity: A transtheoretical model for male-friendly therapy* (pp. 13–32). Washington, DC: American Psychological Association. doi:10.1037/12073-001

Broomhall, H. S., & Winefield, A. H. (1990). A comparison of the affective well-being of young and middle-aged unemployed men matched for length of employment. *British Journal of Medical Psychology, 63,* 43–52.

Brown, A. S., & Derkits, E. J. (2010). Prenatal infection and schizophrenia: A review of epidemiologic and translational studies. *American Journal of Psychiatry, 167*(3), 261–280. doi:10.1176/appi.ajp.2009.09030361

Brown, D. (2007). *Career information, career counseling, and career development.* Boston, MA: Allyn & Bacon.

Brown, E. J., Juster, H. R., Heimberg, R. G., & Winning, C. D. (1998). Stressful life events and personality styles: Relation to impairment and treatment outcome in patients with social phobia. *Journal of Anxiety Disorders, 12*(3), 233–251.

Brown, L. M., Bradley, M. M., & Lang, P. J. (2006). Affective reactions to pictures of ingroup and outgroup members. *Biological Psychology, 71,* 303–311.

Brown, R. D., Goldstein, E., & Bjorklund, D. F. (2000). The history and zeitgeist of the repressed–false memory debate: Scientific and sociological perspectives on suggestibility and childhood memory. In D. F. Bjorklund (Ed.), *False-memory creation in children and adults.* Mahwah, NJ: Erlbaum.

Brown, S. L., Nesse, R. M., Vinokur, A. D., & Smith, D. M. (2003). Providing social support may be more beneficial than receiving it: Results from a prospective study of mortality. *Psychological Science, 14*(4), 320–327.

Brown, T. A., & Lawrence, A. E. (2009). Generalized anxiety disorders and obsessive-compulsive disorder. In P. H. Blaney & T. Millon (Eds.), *Oxford textbook of psychopathology* (pp.146–175). New York, NY: Oxford University Press.

Brownell, K. D., & Wadden, T. A. (2000). Obesity. In B. J. Sadock, & V. A. Sadock (Eds.), *Kaplan and Sadock's comprehensive textbook of psychiatry* (7th ed.). Philadelphia, PA: Lippincott/Williams & Wilkins.

Buehlman, K. T., Gottman, J. M., & Katz, L. F. (1992). How a couple views their past predicts their future: Predicting divorce from an oral history interview. *Journal of Family Psychology, 5,* 295–318.

Bureau of Justice Statistics. (2011). *Criminal victimization, 2010.* Washington, DC: U. S. Department of Justice. Table 1, http://bjs.ojp.usdoj.gov/content/pub/pdf/ cv10.pdf (accessed September 28, 2011).

Burger, J. M. (2008). *Personality* (7th ed.). Belmont, CA: Wadsworth.

Burger, J. M. (2009). Replicating Milgram: Would people still obey today? *American Psychologist, 64*(1), 1–11.

Burger, J. M., & Caldwell, D. F. (2003). The effects of monetary incentives and labelling on the foot-in-the-door effect: Evidence for a self-perception process. *Basic and Applied Social Psychology, 25*(3), 235–241.

Burgoon, J. K. (1994). Nonverbal signals. In M. L. Knapp & G. R. Miller (Eds.), *Handbook of interpersonal communication* (2nd ed.). Thousand Oaks, CA: Sage.

Burhans, K. K., & Dweck, C. S. (1995). Helplessness in early childhood: The role of contingent worth. *Child Development, 66,* 1719–1738.

Burke, M. E. (2005). *2004 reference and background checking survey report.* Alexandria, VA: Society for Human Resource Management.

Burke, R. J. (2009). Working to live or living to work: Should individuals and organizations care? *Journal of Business Ethics, 84*(Suppl2), 167–172.

Burke, R. J., & Fiskenbaum, L. (2009). Work motivations, work outcome, and health: Passion versus addiction. *Journal of Business Ethics, 84*(Suppl2), 257–263.

Burlingame, G. M., & McClendon, D. T. (2008). Group therapy. In J. L. Lebow (Ed.), *Twenty-first century psychotherapies: Contemporary approaches to theory and practice.* New York, NY: Wiley.

Burn, S. M., & Ward, A. Z. (2005). Men's conformity to traditional masculinity and relationship satisfaction. *Psychology of Men and Masculinity, 6,* 254–263.

Burns, A. B., Brown, J. S., Plant, E. A., Sachs-Ericsson, N., & Joiner, T. E. Jr. (2006). On the specific depressotypic nature of excessive reassurance-seeking. *Personality and Individual Differences, 40*(1), 135–145.

Bushman, B. J. (2002). Does venting anger feed or extinguish the flame? Catharsis, rumination, distraction, anger, and aggressive responding. *Personality and Social Psychology Bulletin, 28,* 724–731.

Bushman, B. J., & Anderson, C. A. (2001). Media violence and the American public. *American Psychologist, 56,* 477–489.

Bushman, B. J., & Baumeister, R. F. (1998). Threatened egotism, narcissism, self-esteem, and direct and displaced aggression: Does self-love or self-hate lead to violence? *Journal of Personality and Social Psychology, 75*(1), 219–229.

Bushman, B. J., Baumeister, R. F., Thomaes, S., Ryu, E., Begeer, S., & West, S. G. (2009). Looking again, and harder, for a link between self-esteem and aggression. *Journal of Personality, 77*(2), 427–446.

Bushman, B. J., Bonacci, A. M., van Dijk, M., & Baumeister, R. F. (2003). Narcissism, sexual refusal, and aggression: Testing a narcissistic reactance model of sexual coercion. *Journal of Personality and Social Psychology, 84,* 1027–1040.

Buss, D. M. (1988). The evolution of human intrasexual competition: Tactics of mate attraction. *Journal of Personality and Social Psychology, 54,* 616–628.

Buss, D. M. (1989). Sex differences in human mate preferences: Evolutionary hypotheses tested in 37 cultures. *Behavioral and Brain Sciences, 12,* 1–14.

Buss, D. M. (1991). Evolutionary personality psychology. *Annual Review of Psychology, 42,* 459–491.

Buss, D. M. (1997). Evolutionary foundation of personality. In R. Hogan, J. Johnson, & S. Briggs (Eds.), *Handbook of personality psychology.* San Diego, CA: Academic Press.

Buss, D. M., & Schmitt, D. P. (1993). Sexual strategies theory: A contextual evolutionary analysis of human mating. *Psychological Review, 100,* 204–232.

Buss, D. M., Shackelford, T. K., Kirkpatrick, L. A., & Larsen, R. J. (2001). A half century of mate preferences: The cultural evolution of values. *Journal of Marriage and Family, 63,* 491–503.

Butler, J. L., & Baumeister, R. F. (1998). The trouble with friendly faces: Skilled performance with a supportive audience. *Journal of Personality and Social Psychology, 75*(5), 1213–1230.

Byne, W. (2007). Biology and sexual minority status. In I. L. Meyer & M. E. Northridge (Eds.), *The health of sexual minorities: Public health perspectives on lesbian, gay, bisexual, and transgender populations* (pp. 65–90). New York, NY: Springer Science and Business Media.

Byrm, R. J., & Lenton, R. L. (2001). *Love online: A report on digital dating in Canada.* Retrieved from http://www.nelson.com/nelson/harcourt/sociology/newsociety3e/loveonline.pdf.

Byrne, D., Clore, G. L., & Smeaton, G. (1986). The attraction hypothesis: Do similar attitudes affect anything? *Journal of Personality and Social Psychology, 51,* 1167–1170.

Byrne, R. (2006). *The secret.* New York, NY: Atria Books.

Cacioppo, J. T., Petty, R. E., Feinstein, J., & Jarvis, B. (1996). Individual differences in cognitive motivation: The life and times of people varying in need for cognition. *Psychological Bulletin, 119,* 197–253.

Cahn, D. D. (2009). Friendship, conflict and dissolution. In H. T. Reis & S. Sprecher (Eds.), *Encyclopedia of human relationships: Vol. 1* (pp. 703–706). Los Angeles, CA: Sage Reference Publication.

Calasanti, T., & Harrison-Rexrode, J. (2009). Gender roles in relationships. In H. T. Reis & S. Sprecher (Eds.), *Encyclopedia of human relationships: Vol. 1* (pp. 754–757). Los Angeles, CA: Sage Reference Publication.

Cameron, D. (2007). *The myth of Mars and Venus: Do men and women really speak different languages?* Oxford, UK: Oxford University Press.

Cameron, L., Leventhal, E. A., & Leventhal, H. (1993). Symptom representations and affect as determinants of care seeking in a community-dwelling, adult sample population. *Health Psychology, 12,* 171–179.

Campbell, J. D. (1990). Self-esteem and clarity of the self-concept. *Journal of Personality and Social Psychology, 59,* 538–549.

Campbell, J. D., & Lavallee, L. F. (1993). Who am I? The role of self-concept confusion in understanding the behavior of people with low self-esteem. In R. Baumeister (Ed.), *Self-esteem: The puzzle of low self-regard.* New York, NY: Plenum.

Campbell, L. F., & Smith, T. P. (2003). Integrating self-help books into psychotherapy. *Journal of Clinical Psychology, 59*(2), 177–186.

Campbell, W. K., Sedikides, C., Reeder, G. D., & Elliot A. J. (2000). Among friends? An examination of friendship and the self-serving bias. *British Journal of Social Psychology, 39*(2), 229–239.

Canary, D. J., & Dainton, M. (2006). Maintaining relationships. In A. L. Vangelisti & D. Perlman (Eds.), *The Cambridge handbook of personal relationships.* New York, NY: Cambridge University Press.

Canary, D. J., & Stafford, L. (1994). Maintaining relationships through strategic and routine interaction. In D. J. Canary & L. Stafford (Eds.), *Communication and relationship maintenance* (pp. 3–22). San Diego: Academic Press.

Canary, D. J., Stafford, L., & Semic, B. A. (2002). A panel study of the associations between maintenance strategies and relational characteristics. *Journal of Marriage and Family, 64,* 395–406.

Canetto, S. S. (2008). Women and suicidal behavior: A cultural analysis. *American Journal of Orthopsychiatry, 78,* 259–266.

Cann, A., Norman, M. A., Welbourne, J. L., & Calhoun, L. G. (2008). Attachments styles, conflict styles and humour styles: Interrelationships and associations with relationship satisfaction. *European Journal of Personality, 22,* 131–146.

Cannon, W. B. (1929). *Bodily changes in pain, hunger, fear, and rage.* Oxford, England: Appleton.

Cannon, W. B. (1932). *The wisdom of the body.* New York, NY: Norton.

Cantor, J. R., & Venus, P. (1980). The effects of humor on recall of a radio advertisement. *Journal of Broadcasting, 24,* 13–22.

Cappadocia, M., & Weiss, J. A. (2011). Review of social skills training groups for youth with Asperger syndrome and high functioning autism. *Research in Autism Spectrum Disorders, 5*(1), 70–78. doi:10.1016/j.rasd.2010.04.001

Cardeña, E., & Gleaves, D. H. (2007). Dissociative disorders. In M. Hersen, S. M. Turner, & D. C. Beidel (Eds.), *Adult* *psychopathology and diagnosis*. New York, NY: Wiley.

Carducci, B. J. (1999). *The pocket guide to making successful small talk*. New Albany, IN: Pocket Guide Publications.

Carey, M. P., & Vanable, P. A. (2003). AIDS/HIV. In A. M. Nezu, C. M. Nezu, & P. A. Geller (Eds.), *Handbook of psychology: Vol. 9. Health psychology*. New York, NY: Wiley.

Carlson, R. (1997). *Don't sweat the small stuff . . . and it's all small stuff: Simple ways to keep the little things from taking over your life*. New York, NY: Hyperion.

Carney, S., & Geddes, J. (2003). Electroconvulsive therapy. *British Medical Journal, 326*, 1343–1344.

Carpenter, J. M., Greem M. C., & LaFlam, J. (2011). People or profiles: Individual differences in online social networking use. *Personality and Individual Differences, 50*(5), 538–541. doi: 10.1016/j.paid.2010.11.006

Carroll, J. L. (2007). *Sexuality now: Embracing diversity*. Belmont, CA: Wadsworth.

Carter, B., & McGoldrick, M. (1999). Overview: The expanded family life cycle: Individual, family, and social perspectives. In B. Carter & M. McGoldrick (Eds.), *The expanded family life cycle: Individual, family, and social perspectives* (3rd ed.). Boston, MA: Allyn & Bacon.

Carter, T. J., & Dunning, D. (2008). Faulty self-assessment: Why evaluating one's own competence is an intrinsically difficult task. *Social and Personality Psychology Compass, 2*(1), 346–360.

Carter-Sowell, A. R., Chen, Z., & Williams, K. D. (2008). Ostracism increases social susceptibility. *Social Influence, 3*(3),143–153.

Carver, C. S. (2007). Stress, coping, and health. In H. S. Friedman & R. C. Silver (Eds.), *Foundations of health psychology*. New York, NY: Oxford University Press.

Carver, C. S. (2011). Coping. In R.J. Contrada & A. Baum (Eds.). *The handbook of stress science: Biology, psychology, and health* (pp. 221–229). New York, NY: Springer Publishing Company.

Carver, C. S., Pozo, C., Harris, S. D., Noriega, V., Scheier, M. F., Robinson, D. S., Ketcham, A. S., Moffat, F. L., Jr., & Clark, K. C. (1993). How coping mediates the effect of optimism on distress: A study of women with early-stage breast cancer. *Journal of Personality and Social Psychology, 65*, 375–390.

Carver, C. S., & Scheier, M. F. (2002). Optimism. In C. R. Snyder & S. J. Lopez (Eds.), *Handbook of positive psychology*. New York, NY: Oxford University Press.

Cashdan, E. (1998). Smiles, speech, and body posture: How women and men display sociometric status and power. *Journal of Nonverbal Behavior, 22*, 209–228.

Castonguay, L. G., Reid Jr., J. J., Halperin, G. S., & Goldfried, M. R. (2003). Psychotherapy integration. In G. Stricker, & T. A. Widiger (Eds.), *Handbook of psychology: Vol. 8. Clinical psychology*. New York, NY: Wiley.

Castro Martin, T. & Bumpass, L. (1989). Recent trends in marital disruption. *Demography, 26*(1), 37–51.

Catalyst. (2007). *Catalyst releases 2006 census of women in Fortune 500 corporate officer and board positions*. Retrieved from http://www.catalyst.org/pressroom/press_releases/2006_Census_Release.pdf.

Cate, R. M., & Lloyd, S. A. (1988). Courtship. In S. Duck (Ed.), *Handbook of personal relationships*. New York, NY: Wiley.

Cates, W., Jr. (2004). Reproductive tract infections. In R. A. Hatcher, J. Trussell, F. H. Stewart, A. L. Nelson, W. Cates Jr., F. Guest, & D. Kowal (Eds.), *Contraceptive technology*. New York, NY: Ardent Media.

Caverly, D. C., Orlando, V. P., & Mullen, J. L. (2000). Textbook study reading. In R. F. Flippo & D. C. Caverly (Eds.), *Handbook of college reading and study strategy research*. Mahwah, NJ: Erlbaum.

Centers for Disease Control. (2009). *Oral sex and HIV risk*. Retrieved from http:www.cdc.gov/hiv

Centers for Disease Control. (2012a). *Genital HPV infection—fact sheet*. Retrieved from http://www.cdc.gov/std/HPV/STDFact-HPV.htm

Centers for Disease Control. (2012b). *HIV in the United States*. Retrieved from http://www.cdc.gov/hiv/resources/factsheets/us.htm

Cetron, M. J., & Davies, O. (2003, March–April). Trends shaping the future: Technological, workplace, management, and institutional trends. *The Futurist*, pp. 30–43.

Chaiken, S. (1979). Communicator's physical attractiveness and persuasion. *Journal of Personality and Social Psychology, 37*, 1387–1397.

Chamberlin, C. M., & Zhang, N. (2009). Workaholism, health, and self-acceptance. *Journal of Counseling & Development, 87*(2), 159–169.

Chambers, W. C. (2007). Oral sex: Varied behaviors and perceptions in a college population. *Journal of Sex Research, 44*, 28–42.

Chang, R. Y., & Kelly, P. K. (1993). *Step-by-step problem solving: A practical guide to ensure problems get (and stay) solved*. Irvine, CA: Richard Chang Associates.

Chaplin, W. F., Phillips, J. B., Brown, J. D., Clanton, N. R., & Stein, J. L. (2000). Handshaking, gender, personality, and first impressions. *Journal of Personality and Social Psychology, 79*(1), 110–117.

Charlesworth, W. R., & Dzur, C. (1987). Gender comparisons of preschoolers' behavior and resource utilization in group problem-solving. *Child Development, 58*, 191–200.

Chen E., & Miller, G. E. (2007). Stress and inflammation in exacerbation of asthma. *Brain, Behavior, and Immunity, 21*, 993–999.

Chen, G., & Martin, R. A. (2007). A comparison of humor styles, coping humor, and mental health between Chinese and Canadian university students. *Humor, 20*, 215–234.

Chen, Y. Y., Gilligan, S., & Coups, E. J. (2005). Hostility and perceived social support: Interactive effects on cardiovascular reactivity to laboratory stressors. *Annals of Behavioral Medicine, 29*, 37–43.

Cherlin, A. J. (2004). The deinstitutionalization of American marriage. *Journal of Marriage and Family, 66*, 848–861.

Chia, R. C., Moore, J. L., Lam, K. N., Chuang, C. J., & Cheng, B. S. (1994). Cultural differences in gender role attitudes between Chinese and American students. *Sex Roles, 31*, 23–29.

Chida, Y., Hamer, M., Wardle, J., & Steptoe, A. (2008). Do stress-related psychosocial factors contribute to cancer incidence and survival? *Nature Clinical Practice Oncology, 5*(8), 466–475.

Chiu, C.-Y., Kim, Y. -H., & Wan, W. W. N. (2008). Personality: Cross-cultural perspectives. In G. J. Boyle, G. Matthews, D. H. Saklofske (Eds.), *The Sage handbook of personality theory and assessment* (pp. 124–144). Los Angeles, CA: Sage.

Christensen, A. J., & Johnson, J. A. (2002). Patient adherence with medical treatment regimens: An interactive approach. *Current Directions in Psychological Science, 11*(3), 94–97.

Church, A. (2010). Current perspectives in the study of personality across cultures. *Perspectives on Psychological Science, 5*(4), 441–449. doi:10.1177/1745691610375559

Cialdini, R. B. (2001). *Influence: Science and practice* (4th ed.). Boston, MA: Allyn & Bacon.

Cialdini, R. B. (2007). *Influence: Science and practice* (5th ed.). New York, NY: HarperCollins.

Clarke, V. A., Lovegrove, H., Williams, A., & Machperson, M. (2000). Unrealistic optimism and the health belief model. *Journal of Behavioral Medicine, 23*, 367–376.

Cleek, M. G., & Pearson, T. A. (1985). Perceived causes of divorce: An analysis of interrelationships. *Journal of Marriage and the Family, 47*, 179–183.

Clements, A. M., Rimrodt, S. L., Abel, J. R., Blankner, J. G., Mostofsky, S. H., Pekar, J. J., et al. (2006). Sex differences in cerebral laterality of language and visuospatial processing. *Brain and Language, 98*(2), 150–158.

Clements, M. L., Stanley, S. M., & Markman, H. J. (2004). Before they said "I do": Discriminating among marital outcomes over 13 years. *Journal of Marriage and Family, 66*, 613–626.

Clifford, S., Barber, N., & Horne, R. (2008). Understanding different beliefs held by adherers, unintentional nonadherers, and intentional nonadherers: Application of the Necessity-Concerns Framework. *Journal of Psychosomatic Research, 64,* 41–46.

Cohen, C. E. (1981). Person categories and social perception: Testing some boundaries of the processing effects of prior knowledge. *Journal of Personality and Social Psychology, 40,* 441–452.

Cohen, S. (2005). Keynote presentation at the eighth International Congress of Behavioral Medicine. *International Journal of Behavioral Medicine, 12*(3), 123–131.

Cohen, S., Evans, G. W., Krantz, D. S., & Stokols, D. (1980). Physiological, motivational, and cognitive effects of aircraft noise on children: Moving from the laboratory to the field. *American Psychologist, 35,* 231–243.

Cohen, S., Frank, E., Doyle, W. J., Skoner, D. P., Rabin, B. S., & Gwaltney, J. M., Jr. (1998). Types of stressors that increase susceptibility to the common cold in healthy adults. *Health Psychology, 17,* 214–223.

Cohen, S., Kessler, R. C., & Gordon, L. U. (1995). Strategies for measuring stress in studies of psychiatric and physical disorders. In S. Cohen, R. C. Kessler, & L. U. Gordon (Eds.), *Measuring stress: A guide for health and social scientists.* New York, NY: Oxford University Press.

Cohen, S., Lichtenstein, E., Prochaska, J. O., Rossi, J. S., Gritz, E. R., Carr, C. R., Orleans, C. T., Schoenbach, V. J., Biener, L., Abrams, D., DiClemente, C., Curry, S., Marlatt, G. A., Cummings, K. M., Emont, S. L., Giovino, A., & Ossip-Klein, D. (1989). Debunking myths about self-quitting: Evidence from 10 prospective studies of persons who attempt to quit smoking by themselves. *American Psychologist, 44,* 1355–1365.

Colder, C. R. (2001). Life stress, physiological and subjective indexes of negative emotionality and coping reasons for drinking: Is there evidence for a self-medication model of alcohol use? *Psychology of Addictive Behaviors, 15*(3), 237–245.

Coles, M. E., Schofield, C. A., & Pietrefesa, A. S. (2006). Behavioral inhibition and obsessive-compulsive disorder. *Journal of Anxiety Disorders, 20,* 1118–1132.

Collaer, M. L., & Hines, M. (1995). Human behavioral sex differences: A role for gonadal hormones during early development? *Psychological Bulletin, 118,* 55–107.

College Entrance Examination Board. (2004). *Writing a Ticket to Work . . . Or a Ticket Out: A Survey of Business Leaders.* Retrieved from www.writingcommission.org/prod_downloads/writingcom/writing-ticket-to-work.pdf

Colligan, T. W., & Higgins, E. M. (2005). Workplace stress: Etiology and consequences. *Journal of Workplace Behavioral Health, 21*(2), 89–97.

Collins, W. A., & Madsen, S. D. (2006). Personal relationships in adolescence and early adulthood. In A. L. Vangelisti & D. Perlman (Eds.), *The Cambridge handbook of personal relationships.* New York, NY: Cambridge University Press.

Coltrane, S. (2001). Marketing the marriage "solution": Misplaced simplicity in the politics of fatherhood. *Sociological Perspectives, 44*(4), 387–418.

Comas-Diaz, L. (1987). Feminist therapy with mainland Puerto Rican women. *Psychology of Women Quarterly, 11,* 461–474.

Combs, D. R., & Mueser, K. T. (2007). Schizophrenia. In M. Hersen, S. M. Turner, & D. C. Beidel (Eds.), *Adult psychopathology and diagnosis.* New York, NY: Wiley.

Commerce Clearing House. (2007). *2007 CCH unscheduled absenteeism survey.* Riverwoods, IL: Commerce Clearning House.

Compton, M. T., Goulding, S. M., & Walker, E. F. (2007). Cannabis use, first-episode psychosis, and schizotypy: A summary and synthesis of recent literature. *Current Psychiatry Reviews, 3,* 161–171.

Cooper, A., & Smith, E. (2011). *Homicide trends in the United States, 1980–2008.* Retrieved from http://bjs.ojp.usdoj.gov/index.cfm?ty=pbdetail&iid=2221

Cooper, C. L., & Dewe, P. (2004). *Stress: A brief history.* Malden, MA: Blackwell Publishing.

Cooper, M., & McLeod, J. (2011). Person-centered therapy: A pluralistic perspective. *Person-Centered And Experiential Psychotherapies, 10*(3), 210–223. doi:10.1080/14779757.2011.599517

Cooper, P. J. (1995). Eating disorders and their relationship to mood and anxiety disorders. In K. D. Brownell & C. G. Fairburn (Eds.), *Eating disorders and obesity: A comprehensive handbook.* New York, NY: Guilford Press.

Cooper, W. H., & Withey, M. J. (2009). The strong situation hypothesis. *Personality and Social Psychology Review, 13*(1), 62–72.

Cordova, J. V., & Harp, A. G. (2009). Deteriorating relationships. In H. T. Reis & S. Sprecher (Eds.), *Encyclopedia of human relationships: Vol. 2* (pp. 402–407). Los Angeles, CA: Sage Reference Publication.

Cordova, J. V., Gee, C. B., & Warren, L. Z. (2005). Emotional skillfulness in marriage: Intimacy as a mediator of the relationship between emotional skillfulness and marital satisfaction. *Journal of Social and Clinical Psychology, 24,* 218–235.

Cornell, D. G. (1997). Post hoc explanation is not prediction. *American Psychologist, 52,* 1380.

Correia, I., Vala, J., & Aguiar, P. (2007). Victim's innocence, social categorization, and the threat to the belief in a just world. *Journal of Experimental Social Psychology, 43,* 31–38.

Corty, E. W., & Guardiani, J. M. (2008). Canadian and American sex therapists' perceptions of normal and abnormal ejaculatory latencies: How long should intercourse last? *Journal of Sexual Medicine, 5,* 1251–1256.

Costa, P. T., Jr., & McCrae, R. R. (1992). *Revised NEO Personality Inventory: NEO PI and NEO Five-Factor Inventory (Professional Manual).* Odessa, FL: Psychological Assessment Resources.

Costa, P. T., Jr., & McCrae, R. R. (2008). The revised NEO Personality Inventory (NEO-PI-R). In G. J. Boyle, G. Matthews, & D. H. Saklofske (Eds.), *The Sage handbook of personality theory and assessment* (Vol. 2, pp.179–198). Los Angeles, CA: Sage.

Coursolle, K. M., & Sweeney, M. M. (2009). Work-family conflict. In H. T. Reis & S. Sprecher (Eds.), *Encyclopedia of human relationships: Vol. 3* (pp. 1691–1694). Los Angeles, CA: Sage Reference Publication.

Covey, S. R. (1989). *The seven habits of highly effective people.* New York, NY: Simon & Schuster.

Cox, P. D., Vinogradov, S., & Yalom, I. D. (2008). Group therapy. In R. E. Hales, S. C. Yudofsky, & G. O. Gabbard (Eds.), *The American psychiatric publishing textbook of psychiatry* (pp. 1329–1376). Washington, DC: American Psychiatric Publishing, Inc.

Crano, W. D., & Prislin, R. (Eds.). (2008). *Attitudes and attitude change.* New York, NY: Psychology Press.

Craske, M. G., & Waters, A. M. (2005). Panic disorders, phobias, and generalized anxiety disorder. *Annual Review of Clinical Psychology, 1,* 197–225.

Creed, P., Lehmann, K., & Hood, M. (2009). The relationship between core self-evaluations, employment commitment, and well-being in the unemployed. *Personality and Individual Differences, 47*(4), 310–315.

Crews, F. (2006). *Follies of the wise: Dissenting essays.* Emeryville, CA: Shoemaker Hoard.

Crocker, J., & Luhtanen, R. (1990). Collective self-esteem and ingroup bias. *Journal of Personality and Social Psychology, 58,* 60–67.

Crocker, J., & McGraw, K. M. (1984). What's good for the goose is not good for the gander: Solo status as an obstacle to occupational achievement for males and females. *American Behavioral Scientist, 27,* 357–370.

Crocker, J., & Park, L. E. (2004). The costly pursuit of self-esteem. *Psychological Bulletin, 130,* 392–414.

Crooks, R., & Baur, K. (2008). *Our sexuality.* Belmont, CA: Wadsworth.

Crosby, O., & Moncarz, R. (2006, Fall). The 2004–14 job outlook for college graduates. *Occupational Outlook Quarterly,* pp. 42–57.

Crosby, O., Iyer, A., Clayton, S., & Downing, R. A. (2003). Affirmative action: Psychological data and the policy debates. *American Psychologist, 58*(1), 93–115.

Cross, P. (1977). Not can but will college teaching be improved? *New Directions for Higher Education, 17,* 1–15.

Cross, S. E., & Gore, J. S. (2003). Cultural models of the self. In M.R. Leary & J. P. Tangney (Eds.), *Handbook of self and identity.* New York, NY: Guilford.

Cross, S. E., & Madson, L. (1997). Models of the self: Self-construal and gender. *Psychological Bulletin, 122*(1), 5–37.

Crouter, A. C., Bumpus, M. F., Maguire, M. C., & McHale, S. M. (1999). Linking parents' work pressure and adolescents' well-being: Insights into dynamics in dual-earner families. *Developmental Psychology, 35,* 1453–1461.

Crowell, J. A., Treboux, D., & Waters, E. (2002). Stability of attachment representations: The transition to marriage. *Developmental Psychology, 38,* 467–479.

Crowley, A. E., & Hoyer, W. D. (1994). An integrative framework for understanding two-sided persuasion. *Journal of Consumer Research, 20,* 561–574.

Cuffee, J. J., Hallfors, D. D., & Waller, M. W. (2007). Racial and gender differences in adolescent sexual attitudes and longitudinal associations with coital debut. *Journal of Adolescent Health Care, 41,* 19–26.

Cunningham, M. R. (2009a). Physical attractiveness, defining characteristics. In H. T. Reis & S. Sprecher (Eds.), *Encyclopedia of human relationships: Vol. 3* (pp. 1237–1242). Los Angeles, CA: Sage Reference Publication.

Cunningham, M. R. (2009b). Polygamy. In H. T. Reis & S. Sprecher (Eds.), *Encyclopedia of human relationships: Vol. 3* (pp. 1256–1259). Los Angeles, CA: Sage Reference Publication.

Curioni, C. C., & Lourenco, P. M. (2005). Long-term weight loss after diet and exercise: A systematic review. *International Journal of Obesity, 29,* 1168–1174.

Curtis, R. C., & Miller, K. (1986). Believing another likes or dislikes you: Behaviors making the beliefs come true. *Journal of Personality and Social Psychology, 51,* 284–290.

Cushing-Daniels, B., & Tsz-Ying, Y. (2009). Wage penalties and sexual orientation: An update using the general social survey. *Contemporary Economic Policy, 27*(2), 164–175.

Cutrona, C. E. (1982). Transition to college: Loneliness and the process of social adjustment. In L. A. Peplau & D. Perlman (Eds.), *Loneliness: A sourcebook of current theory, research, and therapy.* New York, NY: Wiley.

Dabbs, J. M., with Dabbs, M. G. (2000). *Heroes, rogues, and lovers: Testosterone and behavior.* New York, NY: McGraw-Hill.

Dainton, M. (2006). Cat walk conversations: Everyday communication in dating relationships. In J. T. Wood & S. W. Duck (Eds.), *Composing relationships: Communication in everyday life* (pp. 36–45). Belmont, CA: Thompson/Wadsworth.

Das, A. (2007). Masturbation in the United States. *Journal of Sex & Marital Therapy, 33,* 301–317.

De Hoog, N., Stroebe, W., & De Wit, J. B. F. (2007). The impact of vulnerability to and severity of a health risk on processing and acceptance of fear-arousing communications: A meta-analysis. *Review of General Psychology, 11*(3), 258–285.

de Vries, B. (1996). The understanding of friendship: An adult life course perspective. In C. Magai & S. H. McFadden (Eds), *Handbook of emotion, adult development, and aging.* San Diego, CA: Academic Press.

Dean, L. R., Carroll, J. S., & Yang, C. (2007). Materialism, perceived financial problems, and marital satisfaction. *Family and Consumer Sciences Research Journal, 35,* 260–281.

DeAngelis, T. (2001, December). Are men emotional mummies? *Monitor on Psychology,* pp. 40–41.

DeAngelis, T. (2004). What's to blame for the surge in super-size Americans? *Monitor on Psychology, 35*(1), 46, 62.

Deaux, K., & Hanna, R. (1984). Courtship in the personals column: The influence of gender and sexual orientation. *Sex Roles, 11,* 363–375.

DeCaro, J. A., & Worthman, C. M. (2007). Cultural models, parent behavior, and young child experience in working American families. *Parenting: Science and Practice, 7,* 177–203.

DeLisi, L. E. (2008). The effect of cannabis on the brain: Can it cause brain anomalies that lead to increased risk for schizophrenia? *Current Opinion in Psychiatry, 21,* 140–150.

DeMaris, A., Benson, M. L., Fox, G. L., Hill, T., & Van Wyk, J. (2003). Distal and proximal factors in domestic violence: A test of an integrated model. *Journal of Marriage and Family, 65,* 652–667.

Demir, M., & Özdemir, M. (2010). Friendship, need satisfaction and happiness. *Journal of Happiness Studies, 11*(2), 243–259. doi:10.1007/s10902-009-9138-5

Demo, D. H. (1992). Parent-child relations: Assessing recent changes. *Journal of Marriage and the Family, 54,* 104–117.

Demo, D. H., & Fine, M. A. (2009). Children and divorce. In H. T. Reis & S. Sprecher (Eds.), *Encyclopedia of human relationships: Vol. 2* (pp. 453–458). Los Angeles, CA: Sage Reference Publication.

DePaulo, B. M. (1994). Spotting lies: Can humans learn to do better? *Current Directions in Psychological Science, 3(3),* 83–86.

DePaulo, B. M., Ansfield, M. E., Kirkendol, S. E., & Boden, J. M. (2004). Serious lies. *Basic and Applied Social Psychology, 6,* 147–167.

DePaulo, B. M., Charlton, K., Cooper, H., Lindsay, J. J., & Muhlenbruck, L. (1997). The accuracy-confidence correlation in the detection of deception. *Personality and Social Psychology Review, 1*(4), 346–357.

DePaulo, B. M., & Friedman, H. (1998). Nonverbal communication. In D. T. Gilbert, S. T. Fiske, & G. Lindzey (Eds.), *The handbook of social psychology* (Vol. 2). Boston, MA: McGraw-Hill.

DePaulo, B. M., LeMay, C. S., & Epstein, J. A. (1991). Effects of importance of success and expectations for success on effectiveness at deceiving. *Personality and Social Psychology Bulletin, 17,* 14–24.

DePaulo, B. M., Lindsay, J. J., Malone, B. E., Muhlenbruck, L., Charlton, K., & Cooper, H. (2003). Cues to deception. *Psychological Bulletin, 129*(1), 74–118.

DePaulo, B. M., & Morris, W. L. (2006). The unrecognized stereotyping and discrimination against singles. *Current Directions in Psychological Science, 15,* 251–254.

Derlega, V. J., Winstead, B. A., Wong, P. T. P., & Hunter, S. (1985). Gender effects in an initial encounter: A case where men exceed women in disclosure. *Journal of Social and Personal Relationships, 2,* 25–44.

Deutsch, M., & Gerard, H. B. (1955). A study of normative and informational social influences upon individual judgment. *Journal of Abnormal and Social Psychology, 51,* 629–636.

Devine, P. G. (1989). Stereotypes and prejudice: Their automatic and controlled components. *Journal of Personality and Social Psychology, 56,* 5–18.

Dew, J. (2008). Debt change and marital satisfaction change in recently married couples. *Family Relations, 57,* 60–71.

Dew, M. A., Bromet, E. J., & Switzer, G. E. (2000). Epidemiology. In M. Hersen & A. S. Bellack (Eds.), *Psychopathology in adulthood.* Boston, MA: Allyn & Bacon.

Dhabhar, F. S. (2011). Effects of stress on immune function: Implications for immunoprotection and immunopathology. In R. J. Contrada & A. Baum (Eds.). *The handbook of stress science: Biology, psychology, and health* (pp. 47–64). New York, NY: Springer Publishing Company.

Diamond, L. M. (2006). The intimate same-sex relationships of sexual minorities. In A. L. Vangelisti & D. Perlman (Eds.), *The Cambridge handbook of personal relationships.* New York, NY: Cambridge University Press.

Diekman, A. B., & Murnen, S. K. (2004). Learning to be little women and little men: The inequitable gender equality of nonsexist children's literature. *Sex Roles, 50*(5/6), 373–385.

Diener, E., & Biswas-Diener, R. (2008). *Happiness: Unlocking the mysteries of psychological wealth* London, England: Wiley-Blackwell.

Diener, E., Gohm, C. L., Suh, E., & Oishi, S. (2000). Similarity of the relations between marital status and subjective well-being across cultures. *Journal of Cross-Cultural Psychology, 31,* 419–436.

Diener, E., Kesebir, P., & Tov, W. (2009). Happiness. In M. R. Leary & R. H. Hoyle (Eds.), Handbook of individual differences in social behavior (pp. 147–160). New York, NY: Guilford.

Diener, E., & Seligman, M. E. P. (2004). Beyond money: Toward an economy of well-being. *Psychological Science in the Public Interest, 5*(1), 1–31.

Diener, E., Wolsic, B., & Fujita, F. (1995). Physical attractiveness and subjective well-being. *Journal of Personality and Social Psychology, 69,* 120–129.

Dijkstra, P., Gibbons, F. X., & Buunk, A. P. (2010). Social comparison theory. In J. E. Maddux & J. P. Tangney (Eds.), *Social psychological foundations of clinical psychology* (pp. 195–211). New York, NY: Guilford.

Dillard, A. J., McCaul, K. D., & Klein, W. M. P. (2006). Unrealistic optimism in smokers: Implications for smoking myth endorsement and self-protective motivation. *Journal of Health Communication, 11,* 93–102.

DiMatteo, M. R. (2004). Variations in patients' adherence to medical recommendations: A quantitative review of 50 years of research. *Medical Care, 42*(3), 200–209.

Dindia, K., & Allen, M. (1992). Sex differences in self-disclosure: A meta-analysis. *Psychological Bulletin, 112,* 106–124.

Dion, K. K., Berscheid, E., & Walster, E. (1972). What is beautiful is good. *Journal of Personality and Social Psychology, 24,* 285–290.

Dishotsky, N. I., Loughman, W. D., Mogar, R. E., & Lipscomb, W. R. (1971). LSD and genetic damage: Is LSD chromosome damaging, carcinogenic, mutagenic, or teratogenic? *Science, 172,* 431–440.

Dohm, A., & Wyatt, I. (2002). College at work: Outlook and earnings for college graduates, 2000-10. *Occupational Outlook Quarterly, 46*(3), 3–15.

Dolder, C. R. (2008). Side effects of antipsychotics. In K. T. Mueser & D. V. Jeste (Eds.), *Clinical handbook of schizophrenia* (pp. 168–177). New York, NY: Guilford.

Donovan, R. L., & Jackson, B. L. (1990). Deciding to divorce: A process guided by social exchange, attachment and cognitive dissonance theories. *Journal of Divorce, 13,* 23–35.

Dougall, A. L., & Baum, A. (2001). Stress, health, and illness. In A. Baum, T. A. Revenson, & J. E. Singer (Eds.), *Handbook of health psychology.* Mahwah, NJ: Erlbaum.

Dougherty, J. (2009, October 22). For some seeking rebirth, Sweat Lodge was end. *The New York Times.* Retrieved from http://www.nytimes.com/2009/10/22/us/22sewat.html

Dougherty, T. W., Turban, D. B., & Callender, J. C. (1994). Confirming first impressions in the employment interview: A field study of interview behavior. *Journal of Applied Psychology, 79*(5), 659–665.

Dovidio, J. F., Ellyson, S. L., Keating, C. F., Heltman, K., & Brown, C. E. (1988). The relationship of social power to visual display of dominance between men and women. *Journal of Personality and Social Psychology, 54,* 233–242.

Dovidio, J. F., & Gaertner, S. L. (1996). Affirmative action, unintentional racial biases, and intergroup relations. *Journal of Social Issues, 52,* 51–75.

Dovidio, J. F., Gaertner, S. L., Esses, V. M., & Brewer, M. B. (2003). Social conflict, harmony, and integration. In T. Millon & M. J. Lerner (Eds.) *Handbook of psychology: Vol. 5. Personality and social psychology.* New York, NY: Wiley.

Dovidio, J. F., Gaertner, S. L., Penner, L. A., Pearson, A. R., Norton, W. E. (2009). Aversive racism—how unconscious bias influences behavior: Implications for legal, employment, and health care contexts. In J. L. Chin (Ed.), *Diversity in mind and in action, Vol. 3: Social justice matters* (pp. 21–35). Santa Barbara, CA: Praeger/ABC-CLIO.

Drago, R. W. (2007). *Striking a balance: Work, family, life.* Boston, MA: Dollars & Sense.

Drew, J. (2003). The myth of female sexual dysfunction and its medicalization. *Sexualities, Evolution and Gender, 5*(2), 89–96.

Driver, J., Tabares, A., Shapiro, A., Nahm, E. Y., & Gottman, J. M. (2003). Interactional patterns in marital success and failure: Gottman laboratory studies. In F. Walsh (Ed.), *Normal family processes: Growing diversity and complexity.* New York, NY: Guilford.

Dubbert, P. M., King, A. C., Marcus, B. H., & Sallis, J. F. (2004). Promotion of physical activity through the life span. In J. M. Raczynski & L. C. Leviton (Eds.), *Handbook of clinical health psychology: Vol. 2. Disorders of behavior and health.* Washington, DC: American Psychological Association.

Dubovsky, S. L. (2009). Benzodiazepine receptor agonists and antagonists. In B. J. Sadock, V. A. Sadock, & P. Ruiz (Eds.), *Kaplan & Sadock's comprehensive textbook of psychiatry* (pp. 3044–3055). Philadelphia, PA: Lippincott Williams & Wilkins.

Duman, R. S., & Monteggia, L. M. (2006). A neurotrophic model for stress–related mood disorders. *Biological Psychiatry, 59,* 1116–1127.

Duncan, C. P., & Nelson, J. E. (1985). Effects of humor in a radio advertising experiment. *Journal of Advertising, 14,* 33–40, 64.

Dunlop, B. W., Garlow, S. J., & Nemeroff, C. B. The neurochemistry of depressive disorders: Clinical studies. In D. S. Charney & E. J. Nestler (Eds.), *Neurobiology of mental illness* (pp. 435–460). New York, NY: Oxford University Press.

Dunn, A. L., Trivedi, M. H., & O'Neal, H. A. (2001). Physical activity dose-response effects on outomes of depression and anxiety. *Medicine and Science in Sports and Exercise, 33,* S587–S597.

Dunning, D. (2006). Strangers to ourselves? *The Psychologist, 19*(10), 600–603.

Dweck, C. S. (2007). Is math a gift? Beliefs that put females at risk. In S. J. Ceci & W. M. Williams (Eds.), *Why aren't more women in science?* (pp. 47–56). Washington, DC: American Psychological Association.

Eagly, A. H., Ashmore, R. D., Makhijani, M. G., & Longo, L. C. (1991). What is beautiful is good, but . . . : A meta-analytic review of research on the physical attractiveness stereotype. *Psychology Bulletin, 110,* 107–128.

Eagly, A. H., & Sczesny, S. (2009). Stereotypes about women, men, and leaders: Have times changed? In M. Barreto, M. K. Ryan, & M. T. Schmitt (Eds.), *The glass ceiling in the 21st century: Understanding barriers to gender equality* (pp. 21–47). Washington, DC: American Psychological Association.

Eagly, A. H., & Wood, W. (1999). The origins of sex differences in human behavior: Evolved dispositions versus social roles. *American Psychologist, 54*(6), 408–423.

Easterlin, B. L., & Cardena, E. (1999). Cognitive and emotional differences between short- and long-term Vipassana meditators. *Imagination, Cognition and Personality, 18*(1), 68–81.

Ebbinghaus, H. (1885/1964). *Memory: A contribution to experimental psychology.* (H. A. Ruger & E. R. Bussemius, Trans.). New York, NY: Dover. (Original work published 1885)

Eccles, J. S. (2007). Where are all the women? Gender differences in participation in physical science and engineering. In S. J. Ceci & W. M. Williams (Eds.), *Why aren't more women in science?* (pp. 199–210). Washington, DC: American Psychological Association.

Eckert, P., & McConnell-Ginet, S. (2003). *Language and gender.* Cambridge, UK: Cambridge University Press.

Ehrenberg, O., & Ehrenberg, M. (1994). *The psychotherapy maze: A consumer's guide to getting in and out of therapy.* Northvale, NJ: Jason Aronson.

Einstein, G. O., & McDaniel, M. A. (2004). *Memory fitness: A guide for successful aging.* New Haven, CT: Yale University Press.

Eisenberg, M. E., Bernat, D. H., Bearinger, L. H., & Resnick, M. D. (2008). Support for comprehensive sexuality education: Perspectives from parents of school-age youth. *Journal of Adolescent Heath, 42,* 352–359.

Ekman, P. (1972). Universals and cultural differences in facial expressions of emotion. In J. Cole (Ed.), *Nebraska symposium on motivation, 1971*. Lincoln, NE: University of Nebraska Press.

Ekman, P. (1975, September). The universal smile: Face muscles talk every language. *Psychology Today,* pp. 35–39.

Ekman, P., & Friesen, W. V. (1974). Detecting deception from the body or face. *Journal of Personality and Social Psychology, 29*(3), 288–298.

Ekman, P., & Friesen, W. V. (1984). *Unmasking the face*. Palo Alto, CA: Consulting Psychologists Press.

Ekman, P., O'Sullivan, M., & Frank, M. G. (1999). A few can catch a liar. *Psychological Science, 10*(3), 263–266.

Eldridge, K. A. (2009). Conflict patterns. In H. T. Reis & S. Sprecher (Eds.), *Encyclopedia of human relationships: Vol. 1* (pp. 307–310). Los Angeles, CA: Sage Reference Publication.

Elliot, A. J., & Church, M. A. (2003). A motivational analysis of defensive pessimism and self-handicapping. *Journal of Personality, 71,* 369–393.

Elliot, L., & Brantley, C. (1997). *Sex on campus*. New York, NY: Random House.

Ellis, A. (1973). *Humanistic psychotherapy: The rational-emotive approach*. New York, NY: Julian Press.

Ellis, A. (1995). Thinking processes involved in irrational beliefs and their disturbed consequences. *Journal of Cognitive Psychotherapy, 9,* 105–116.

Ellison, N., Heino, R., & Gibbs, J. (2006). Managing impressions online: Self-presentation processes in the online dating environment. *Journal of Computer-Mediated Communication, 11,* 415–441.

Emanuel, H. M. (1987). Put time on your side. In A. D. Timpe (Ed.), *The management of time*. New York, NY: Facts On File.

Emavardhana, T., & Tori, C. D. (1997). Changes in self-concept, ego defense mechanisms, and religiosity following seven-day Vipassana meditation retreats. *Journal for the Scientific Study of Religion, 36,* 194–206.

Emmelkamp, P. M. G. (1994). Behavior therapy with adults. In A. E. Bergin & S. L. Garfield (Eds.), *Handbook of psychotherapy and behavior change* (4th ed.). New York, NY: Wiley.

Emmelkamp, P. M. G. (2004). In M. J. Lambert (Ed.), *Bergin and Garfield's handbook of psychotherapy and behavior change*. New York, NY: Wiley.

Epstein, R. (2007, February–March). The truth about online dating. *Scientific American Mind, 18,* pp. 28–35.

Equal Employment Opportunity Commission. (2007). *Occupational employment in private industry by race/ethnic group/sex, and by industry, United States, 2005*. Retrieved from http://www.eeoc.gov/stats/jobpat/2005/national.html.

Erdelyi, M. H. (2001). Defense processes can be conscious or unconscious. *American Psychologist, 56*(9), 761–762.

Erikson, E. H. (1963). *Childhood and society*. New York, NY: Norton.

Erikson, E. H. (1968). *Identity: Youth and crisis*. New York, NY: Norton.

Erol, R. Y., & Orth, U. (2011). Self-esteem development from age 14 to 30 years: A longitudinal study. *Journal of Personality and Social Psychology, 101* (3), 607–619. doi: 10.1037/a0024299

Eschleman, K. J., Bowling, N. A., & Alarcon, G. M. (2010). A meta-analytic examination of hardiness. *International Journal of Stress Management, 17*(4), 277–307. doi:10.1037/a0020476

Eshbaugh, E. M., & Gute, G. (2008). Hookups and sexual regret among college women. *Journal of Social Psychology, 148,* 77–89.

Esterling, B. A., Kiecolt-Glaser, J. K., Bodnar, J. D., & Glaser, R. (1994). Chronic stress, social support, and persistent alterations in the natural killer cell response to cytokines in older adults. *Health Psychology, 13,* 291–298.

Evans, G. W. (2001). Environmental stress and health. In A. Baum, T. A. Revenson, & J. E. Singer (Eds.), *Handbook of health psychology*. Mahwah, NJ: Erlbaum.

Evans, G. W., & Wener, R. E. (2007). Crowding and personal space invasion on the train: Please don't make me sit in the middle. *Journal of Environmental Psychology, 27,* 90–94.

Evans, R. G., & Dinning, W. D. (1982). MMPI correlates of the Bem Sex Role Inventory and Extended Personal Attributes Questionnaire in a male psychiatric sample. *Journal of Clinical Psychology, 38,* 811–815.

Everson, S. A., Kauhanen, J., Kaplan, G. A., Goldberg, D. E., Julkunen, J., Tuomilehto, J., & Salonen, J. T. (1997). Hostility and increased risk of mortality and acute myocardial infarction: The mediating role of behavioral risk factors. *American Journal of Epidemiology, 146*(2), 142–152.

Eysenck, H. J. (1967). *The biological basis of personality*. Springfield, IL: Charles C Thomas.

Eysenck, H. J. (1982). *Personality, genetics and behavior: Selected papers*. New York, NY: Praeger.

Eysenck, M. W., Mogg, K., May, J., Richards, A., & Mathews, A. (1991). Bias in interpretation of ambiguous sentences related to threat in anxiety. *Journal of Abnormal Psychology, 100,* 144–150.

Fabes, R. A., Hanish, L. D., & Martin, C.L. (2003). Children at play: The role of peers in understanding the effects of child care. *Child Development, 74,* 1039–1043.

Fairbrother, K., & Warn, J. (2003). Workplace dimensions, stress, and job satisfaction. *Journal of Managerial Psychology, 18*(1), 8–21.

Falsetti, S. A., & Ballenger, J. C. (1998). Stress and anxiety disorders. In J. R. Hubbard & E. A. Workman (Eds.), *Handbook of stress medicine: An organ system approach*. New York, NY: CRC Press.

Families and Work Institute. (2004). *Generation and gender in the workplace*. New York, NY: Families and Work Institute.

Fang, C., Miller, S., Bovbjerg, D., Bergman, C., Edelson, M., Rosenblum, N., et al. (2008). Perceived stress is associated with impaired T-cell response to HPV 16 in women with cervical dysplasia. *Annals of Behavioral Medicine, 35*(1), 87–96.

Faravelli, C., & Pallanti, S. (1989). Recent life events and panic disorders. *American Journal of Psychiatry, 146,* 622–626.

Fatemi, S., & Folsom, T. D. (2009). The neurodevelopmental hypothesis of schizophrenia, revisited. *Schizophrenia Bulletin, 35*(3), 528–548. doi:10.1093/schbul/sbn187

Feeney, J. A. (2004). Adult attachment and relationship functioning under stressful conditions: Understanding partners' responses to conflict and challenge. In W. S. Rholes & J. A. Simpson (Eds.), *Adult attachment: Theory, research, and clinical implications*. New York, NY: Guilford.

Feeny, N. C., Stines, L. R., & Foa, E. B. (2007). Posttraumatic stress disorder-clinical. In G. Fink (Ed.), *Encyclopedia of stress: Vols. 1–4* (2nd ed., pp. 135–139). San Diego, CA: Elsevier Academic Press.

Fehr, B. (2000). The life cycle of friendship. In C. Hendrick & S. S. Hendrick (Eds.), *Close relationships: A sourcebook*. Thousand Oaks, CA: Sage.

Fehr, B. (2004). Intimacy expectations in same-sex friendships: A prototype interaction-pattern model. *Journal of Personality and Social Psychology, 86*(2), 265–284.

Fein, S. (1996). Effects of suspicion on attributional thinking and the correspondence bias. *Journal of Personality and Social Psychology, 70,* 1164–1184.

Feingold, A. (1988). Matching for attractiveness in romantic partners and same-sex friends: A meta-analysis and theoretical critique. *Psychological Bulletin, 104,* 226–235.

Feiring, C., & Lewis, M. (1987). The child's social network: Sex differences from three to six years. *Sex Roles, 17,* 621–636.

Feldman, P. J., Cohen, S., Doyle, W. J., Skoner, D. P., & Gwaltney, J. M., Jr. (1999). The impact of personality on the reporting of unfounded symptoms and illness. *Journal of Personality and Social Psychology, 77*(2), 370–378.

Felson, R. B. (1992). Coming to see ourselves: Social sources of self-appraisals. *Advances in Group Processes, 9,* 185–205.

Fenigstein, A, & Preston, M. (2007). The desired number of sexual partners as a function of gender, sexual risks, and the meaning of "ideal." *Journal of Sex Research, 44,* 89–95.

Ferrari, J. R. (1992). Psychometric validation of two adult measures of procrastination: Arousal and avoidance measures. *Journal of Psychopathology & Behavioral Assessment, 14,* 97–100.

Ferrari, J. R. (2001). Getting things done on time: Conquering procrastination. In C. R. Snyder (Ed.), *Coping with stress: Effective people and processes.* New York, NY: Oxford University Press.

Ferrari, J. R., Diaz-Morales, J. F., O'Callaghan, J., Diaz, K., & Argumedo, D. (2007). Frequent behavioral delay tendencies by adults: International prevalence rates of chronic procrastination. *Journal of Cross-Cultural Psychology, 38,* 458–464.

Ferrari, J. R., Johnson, J. L., & McCown, W. G. (1995). *Procrastination and task avoidance: Theory research and treatment.* New York, NY: Plenum Press.

Festinger, L. (1954). A theory of social comparison processes. *Human Relations, 7,* 117–140.

Figueredo, A. J., Gladden, P., Vásquez, G., Wolf, P. S. A., & Jones, D. N. (2009). Evolutionary theories of personality. In P. J. Corr & G. Matthews (Eds.), *The Cambridge handbook of personality psychology* (pp. 265–274). New York, NY: Cambridge University Press.

Finan, P. H., Zautra, A. J., & Wershba, R. (2011). The dynamics of emotion on adaptation to stress. In S. Folkman (Ed.). *The Oxford handbook of stress, health, & coping.* (pp. 209–220). New York, NY: NY: Oxford University Press.

Fincham, F. D. (2001). Attributions in close relationships: From Balkanization to integration. In G. J. O. Fletcher, & M. S. Clark (Eds.), *Blackwell handbook of social psychology: Vol. 2. Interpersonal processes.* Oxford: Blackwell.

Finder, A. (2006, June 11). For some, online persona undermines a resume. *New York Times.* Retrieved from http://www.nytimes.com/2006/06/11/us/11recruit.html

Fine, C. (2010). From scanner to sound bite: Issues in interpreting and reporting sex differences in the brain. *Current Directions in Psychological Science, 19*(5), 280–283. doi:10.1177/0963721410383248

Finer, L. B., & Henshaw, S. K. (2006). Disparities in rates of unintended pregnancy in the United States, 1994 and 2001. *Perspectives on Sexual Reproductive Health, 38,* 90–96.

Finkelhor, D., Mitchell, K., & Wolak, J. (2000). *Online victimization: A report on the nation's youth.* Washington, DC: National Center for Missing and Exploited Children.

Fischer, P., Greitemeyer, T., & Pollozek, F. (2006). The unresponsive bystander: Are bystanders more responsive in dangerous emergencies? *European Journal of Social Psychology, 36,* 267–278.

Fischer, R., Ferreira, M. C., Assmar, E., Redford, P., Harb, C., Glazer, S., Cheng, B.-S., Jiang, D.-Y., Wong, C. C., Kumar, N., Kärtner, J., Hofer, J., & Achoui, M. (2009). Individualism-collectivism as descriptive norms: Development of a subjective norm approach to cultural measurement. *Journal of Cross-Cultural Psychology, 40*(2), 187–213.

Fisher, D. A., Hill, D. L., Grube, J. W., Bersamine, M. M., Walker, S., & Gruber, E. L. (2009). Televised sexual content and parental mediation: Influences on adolescent sexuality. *Media Psychology, 12,* 121–147.

Fiske, S. T. (1998). Stereotyping, prejudice, and discrimination. In D. T. Gilbert, S. T. Fiske, & G. Lindzey (Eds.), *The handbook of social psychology.* New York, NY: McGraw-Hill.

Fiske, S. T. (2002). What we know now about bias and intergroup conflict, the problem of the century. *Current Directions in Psychological Science, 11*(4), 123–128.

Fiske, S. T. (2004). *Social beings: A core motives approach to social psychology.* New York, NY: Wiley.

Fiske, S. T., & Ruscher, J. B. (1993). Negative interdependence and prejudice: Whence the affect? In D. M. Mackie & D. L. Hamilton (Eds.), *Affect, cognition, and stereotyping: Interactive processes in group perception.* New York, NY: Academic.

Flaks, D. K., Ficher, I., Masterpasqua, M., & Joseph, G. (1995). Lesbians choosing motherhood: A comparative study of lesbians and heterosexual parents and their children. *Developmental Psychology, 31,* 105–114.

Fleeson, W. (2004). Moving personality beyond the person-situation debate: The challenge and the opportunity of within-person variability. *Current Directions in Psychological Science, 13*(2), 83–87.

Fletcher, G. J. O., Overall, N. C., & Friesen, M. D. (2006). Social cognition in intimate relationships. In A. L. Vangelisti & D. Perlman (Eds.), *The Cambridge handbook of personal relationships.* New York, NY: Cambridge University Press.

Fletcher, G. J. O., & Ward, C. (1988). Attribution theory and processes: A cross-cultural perspective. In M. H. Bond (Ed.), *The cross-cultural challenge to social psychology.* Newbury Park, CA: Sage.

Floyd, K., Boren, J. P., Hannawa, A. F., Hesse, C., McEwan, B., & Veksler, A. E. (2009). Kissing in marital and cohabiting relationships: Effects on blood lipids, stress, and relationship satisfaction. *Western Journal of Communication, 73,* 113–133.

Flynn, F. J. (2005). Having an open mind: The impact of openness to experience on interracial attitudes and impression formation. *Journal of Personality and Social Psychology, 88,* 816–826.

Foa, E. B. (1998). Rape and posttraumatic stress disorder. In E. A. Blechman & K. D. Brownell (Eds.), *Behavioral medicine and women: A comprehensive handbook.* New York, NY: Guilford Press.

Folkman, S. (2008). The case for positive emotions in the stress process. *Anxiety, Stress, Coping, 21,* 3–14.

Folkman, S., Moskowitz, J. T., Ozer, E. M., & Park, C. L. (1997). Positive meaningful events and coping in the context of HIV/AIDS. In B. H. Gottlieb (Ed.), *Coping with chronic stress.* New York, NY: Plenum.

Forsyth, D. R., Lawrence, N. K., Burnette, J. L., & Baumeister, R. F. (2007). Attempting to improve the academic performance of struggling college students by bolstering self-esteem: An intervention that backfired. *Journal of Social and Clinical Psychology, 26,* 447–459.

Forsyth, D. R., & Strong, S. R. (1986). The scientific study of counseling and psychotherapy: A unificationist view. *American Psychologist, 41,* 113–119.

Fortune, J. L., & Newby-Clark, I. R. (2008). My friend is embarrassing me: Exploring the guilty by association effect. *Journal of Personality and Social Psychology, 95*(6), 1440–1449.

Fowers, B. J., Applegate, B., Olson, D. H., & Pomerantz, B. (1994). Marital conventionalization as a measure of marital satisfaction: A confirmatory factor analysis. *Journal of Family Psychology, 8,* 98–103.

Fowers, B. J., Lyons, E., Montel, K. H., & Shaked, N. (2001). Positive illusions about marriage among married and single individuals. *Journal of Family Psychology, 15*(1), 95–109.

Fox, G. L., & Chancey, D. (1998). Sources of economic distress: Individual and family outcomes. *Journal of Family Issues, 19,* 725–749.

Fox, R. (1996). Bisexuality in perspective: A review of theory and research. In B. Firestein (Ed.), *Bisexuality: The psychology and politics of an invisible minority.* Thousand Oaks, CA: Sage.

Fraley, R. C., & Shaver, P. R. (2000). Adult romantic attachment: Theoretical developments, emerging controversies, and unanswered questions. *Review of General Psychology, 4,* 132–154.

Frame, L. E., Mattson, R. E., & Johnson, M. D. (2009). Predicting success or failure of marital relationships. In H. T. Reis & S. Sprecher (Eds.), *Encyclopedia of human relationships: Vol. 3* (pp. 1275–1279). Los Angeles, CA: Sage Reference Publication.

Francis, L. A., & Birch, L. L. (2005). Maternal influences on daughters' restrained eating behavior. *Health Psychology, 24,* 548–554.

Frank, J. D. (1961). *Persuasion and healing.* Baltimore, MD: John Hopkins University Press.

Frank, L. R. (1990). Electroshock: Death, brain damage, memory loss, and brain-

washing. *The Journal of Mind and Behavior, 11,* 489–512.
Frazier, P. A. (2009). Rape. In H. T. Reis & S. Sprecher (Eds.), *Encyclopedia of human relationships: Vol. 3* (pp. 1325–1328). Los Angeles, CA: Sage Reference Publication.
Frederick, S., & Loewenstein, G. (1999). Hedonic adaptation. In D. Kahneman, E. Diener, & N. Schwarz (Eds.), *Well-being: The foundations of hedonic psychology.* New York, NY: Sage.
Fredrickson, B. L., & Branigan, C. (2005). Positive emotions broaden the scope of attention and thought-action repertoires. *Cognition and Emotion, 19,* 313–332.
Fredrickson, B. L., Tugade, M. M., Waugh, C. E., & Larkin, G. R. (2003). What good are positive emotions in crises? A prospective study of resilience and emotions following the terrorist attacks on the United States on September 11th, 2001. *Journal of Personality and Social Psychology, 84*(2), 365–376.
Freedman, J. L., & Fraser, S. C. (1966). Compliance without pressure: The foot-in-the-door technique. *Journal of Personality and Social Psychology, 4,* 195–202.
Freeman, N. K. (2007). Preschoolers' perceptions of gender appropriate toys and their parents' beliefs about genderized behaviors: Miscommunication, mixed messages, or hidden truths? *Early Childhood Education Journal, 34,* 357–366.
Freud, S. (1901/1960). *The psychopathology of everyday life* (Standard ed., Vol. 6.) London, England: Hogarth. (Original work published 1901)
Freud, S. (1920/1924). *A general introduction to psychoanalysis.* New York, NY: Boni and Liveright. (Original work published 1920)
Frewen, P. A., Brinker, J., Martin, R. A., & Dozois, D. J. A. (2008). Humor styles and personality-vulnerability to depression. *Humor, 21,* 179–195.
Friedman, H. S. (1991). *The self-healing personality: Why some people achieve health and others succumb to illness.* New York, NY: Holt.
Friedman, H. S. (2007). Personality, disease, and self-healing. In H. S. Friedman & R. C. Silver (Eds.), *Foundations of health psychology.* New York, NY: Oxford University Press.
Friedman, M., & Rosenman, R. F. (1974). *Type A behavior and your heart.* New York, NY: Knopf.
Fromm, E. (1981). *Sane society.* New York, NY: Fawcett.
Funder, D. C. (2001). Personality. *Annual Review of Psychology, 52,* 197–221.
Furnham, A., & Cheng, H. (2000). Perceived parental behavior, self-esteem and happiness. *Social Psychiatry and Psychiatric Epidemiology, 35*(10), 463–470.
Furstenberg, F. F., Jr., & Kiernan, K. E. (2001). Delayed parental divorce: How much do children benefit? *Journal of Marriage and Family, 63,* 446–457.
Fyer, A. J. (2009). Anxiety disorders: Genetics. In B. J. Sadock, V. A. Sadock, & P. Ruiz (Eds.), *Kaplan & Sadock's comprehensive textbook of psychiatry* (pp. 1898–1905). Philadelphia, PA: Lippincott Williams & Wilkins.

Gabriel, S., & Gardner, W. L. (1999). Are there "his" and "hers" types of interdependence? The implications of gender differences in collective versus relational interdependence for affect, behavior, and cognition. *Journal of Personality and Social Psychology, 77*(3), 642–655.
Gage, F. H. (2002). Neurogenesis in the adult brain. *Journal of Neuroscience, 22,* 612–613.
Gailliot, M. T., Baumeister, R. F., DeWall, C. N., Maner, J. K., Plant, E. A., Tice, D. M., Brewer, L. E., & Schmeichel, B. J. (2007). Self-control relies on glucose as a limited energy source: Willpower is more than a metaphor. *Journal of Personality and Social Psychology, 92*(2), 325–336.
Gaines, S. O., Jr. (2009). Interracial and interethnic relationships. In H. T. Reis & S. Sprecher (Eds.), *Encyclopedia of human relationships: Vol. 1* (pp. 905–907). Los Angeles, CA: Sage Reference Publication.
Gajendran, R. S., & Harrison, D. A. (2007). The good, the bad, and the unknown about telecommuting: Meta-analysis of psychological mediators and individual consequences. *Journal of Applied Psychology, 92*(6), 1524–1541.
Galdas, P. M., Cheater, F., & Marshall, P. (2005). Men and health-seeking behavior: Literature review. *Journal of Advanced Nursing, 49,* 616–623.
Galinsky, E., Bond, J. T., Kim, S. S., Backon, L., Brownfield, E., & Sakai, K. (2005). *Overwork in America.* New York, NY: Families and Work Institute.
Gangestad, S. W. (1993). Sexual selection and physical attractiveness: Implications for mating dynamics. *Human Nature, 4,* 205–235.
Gartrell, N., Banks, A., Hamilton, J., Reed, N., Bishop, H., & Rodas, C. (1999). The national lesbian family study: Interviews with mothers of toddlers. *American Journal of Orthopsychiatry, 69,* 362–369.
Gentile, B., Grabe, S., Dolan-Pascoe, B., Twenge, J. M., Wells, B. E., & Maitino, A. (2009). Gender differences in domain-specific self-esteem: A meta-analysis. *Review of General Psychology, 13*(1), 34–45.
Giancola, P. R., Levinson, C. A., Corman, M. D., Godlaski, A. J., Morris, D. H., Philips, J. P., & Holt, J. C. D. (2009). Men and women, alcohol and aggression. *Experimental and Clinical Psychopharmacology, 17,* 154–164.
Giannoglou, G., Chatzizisis, Y., Zamboulis, C., Parcharidis, G., Mikhailidis, D., & Louridas, G. (2008). Elevated heart rate and atherosclerosis: An overview of the pathogenic mechanisms. *International Journal of Cardiology, 126*(3), 302–312.
Gibbons, M. B. C., Crits-Christoph, P., & Hearon, B. (2008). The empirical status of psychodynamic therapies. *Annual Review of Clinical Psychology, 4,* 93–108.
Gifford, R. (2011). The role of nonverbal communication in interpersonal relations. In L. M. Horowitz & S. Strack (Eds.), *Handbook of interpersonal psychology: Theory, research, assessment, and therapeutic interventions* (pp. 171–190). Hoboken, NJ: Wiley.
Gilbert, D. T., & Malone, P. S. (1995). The correspondence bias. *Psychological Bulletin, 117,* 21–38.
Gillham, J. E., & Reivich, K. (2007). Cultivating optimism in childhood and adolescence. In A. Monat, R. S. Lazarus, & G. Reevy (Eds.), *The Praeger handbook on stress and coping* (pp. 309–326). Westport, CT: Praeger Publishers.
Gillham, J. E., Shatté, A. J., Reivich, K. J., & Seligman, M. E. P. (2001). Optimism, pessimism, and explanatory style. In E. C. Chang (Ed.), *Optimism & pessimism: Implications for theory, research, and practice.* Washington, DC: American Psychological Association.
Gilovich, T., Kruger, J., & Medvec, V. H. (2002). The spotlight effect revisited: Overestimating the manifest variability of our actions and appearance. *Journal of Experimental Social Psychology, 38,* 93–99.
Gitlin, M. (2009). Pharmacotherapy and other somatic treatments for depression. In I. H. Gotlib & C. L. Hammen (eds.), *Handbook of depression* (pp. 554–585). New York, NY: The Guilford Press.
Glascock, J. (2001). Gender roles on prime-time network television: Demograhics and behaviors. *Journal of Broadcasting and Electronic Media, 45*(4), 656–669.
Glascock, J., & Preston-Schreck, C. (2004). Gender and racial stereotypes in daily newspaper comics: A time-honored tradition. *Sex Roles, 51,* 423–431.
Glass, R. M. (2001). Electroconvulsive therapy. *Journal of the American Medical Association, 285*(10), 1346–1348.
Gleaves, D. H. (1994). On "the reality of repressed memories." *American Psychologist, 49,* 440–441.
Gleaves, D. H., & Smith, S. M. (2004). False and recovered memories in the laboratory and clinic: A review of experimental and clinical evidence. *Clinical Psychology: Science and Practice, 11*(1), 2–28.
Gmel, G., & Rehm, J. (2003). Harmful alcohol use. *Alcohol Research & Health, 27,* 52–62.
Goeders, N. E. (2004). Stress, motivation, and drug addiction. *Current Directions in Psychological Science, 13*(1), 33–35.

Gold, M. S., & Jacobs, W. S. (2005). Cocaine and crack: Clinical aspects. In J. H. Lowinson, P. Ruiz, R. B. Millman, & J. G. Langrod (Eds.), *Substance abuse: A comprehensive textbook.* Philadelphia, PA: Lippincott/Williams & Wilkins.

Gold, R. (2008). Unrealistic optimism and event threat. *Psychology, Health, and Medicine, 13,* 193–201.

Goldberg, W. A., Prause, J., Lucas-Thompsom, R., & Himsel, A. (2008). Maternal employment and children's achievement in context: A meta-analysis of four decades of research. *Psychological Bulletin, 134,* 77–108.

Goldzweig, C. L., Balekian, T. M., Rolon, C., Yano, E. M., & Shekelle, P. G. (2006). The state of women veterans' health research: Results of a systematic literature review. *Journal of General Internal Medicine, 21*(Suppl 3), S82–S92.

Gonzaga, G. C. (2009). Similarity in ongoing relationships. In H. T. Reis & S. Sprecher (Eds.), *Encyclopedia of human relationships: Vol. 3* (pp. 1496–1499). Los Angeles, CA: Sage Reference Publication.

Goode-Cross, D. T., Good, G. E. (2008). African American men who have sex with men: Creating safe spaces through relationships. *Psychology of Men & Masculinity, 9,* 221–234.

Goodfriend, W. (2009). Proximity and attraction. In H. T. Reis & S. Sprecher (Eds.), *Encyclopedia of human relationships: Vol. 3* (pp. 1297–1299). Los Angeles, CA: Sage Reference Publication.

Goodrick, G. K., Pendleton, V. R., Kimball, K. T., Poston, W. S., Carlos, R., Rebecca, S., & Foreyt, J. P. (1999). Binge eating severity, self-concept, dieting self-efficacy and social support during treatment of binge eating disorder. *International Journal of Eating Disorders, 26*(3), 295–300.

Goodwin, F. K. & Jamison, K. R. (2007). *Manic-depressive illness: Bipolar disorders and recurrent depression.* New York, NY: Oxford University Press.

Gordon, P. A. (2003). The decision to remain single: Implications for women across cultures. *Journal of Mental Health Counseling, 25*(1), 33–44.

Gordon, R. A. (2008). Attributional style and athletic performance: Strategic optimism and defensive pessimism. *Psychology of Sport and Exercise, 9*(3), 336–350.

Gordon, V. M. (2006). *Career advising: An academic advisor's guide.* San Francisco, CA: Jossey-Bass.

Gornter, E., Rude, S. S., & Pennebaker, J. W. (2006). Benefits of expressive writing in lowering rumination and depressive symptoms. *Behavior Therapy, 37,* 292–303.

Gottdiener, J. S., Krantz, D. S., & Howell, R. H., Hecht, G. M., Klein, J., Falconer, J. J., & Rozanski, A. (1994). Induction of silent myocardial ischemia with mental stress testing: Relationship to the triggers of ischemia during daily life activities and to ischemic functional severity. *Journal of the American College of Cardiology, 24,* 1645–1651.

Gottesman, I. I. (1991) *Schizophrenia genesis: The origins of madness.* New York, NY: Free Press.

Gottesman, I. I. (2001). Psychopathology through a life span–genetic prism. *American Psychologist, 56,* 867–878.

Gottfried, A. E., & Gottfried, A. W. (2008). The upside of maternal and dual-earner employment: A focus on positive family adaptations, home environments, and child development in the Fullerton longitudinal study. In A. Marcus-Newhall, D. F. Halpern, & S. J. Tan (Eds.), *The changing realities of work and family* (pp. 25–42). Malden, MA: Wiley-Blackwell.

Gottman, J. M. (1994). *What predicts divorce?* Hillsdale, NJ: Erlbaum.

Gottman, J. M., Gottman, J. S., & Declaire, J. (2006). *Ten lessons to transform your marriage: America's love lab experts share their strategies for strengthening your relationship.* New York, NY: Crown Publishing.

Gough, B., Weyman, N., Alderson, J., Butler, G., & Stoner, M. (2008). "They did not have a word": The parental quest to locate a "true sex" for their intersex children. *Psychology and Health, 23,* 493–507.

Gourevitch, M. N., & Arnsten, J. H. (2005). Medical complications of drug use. In J. H. Lowinson, P. Ruiz, R. B. Millman, & J. G. Langrod (Eds.), *Substance abuse: A comprehensive textbook.* Philadelphia, PA: Lippincott/Williams & Wilkins.

Graham, J. E., Christian, L. M., & Kiecolt-Glaser, J. K. (2006). Stress, age, and immune function: Toward a lifespan approach. *Journal of Behavioral Medicine, 29,* 389–400.

Graziano, W. G. & Tobin, R. M. (2009). Agreeableness. In M. R. Leary & R. H. Hoyle (Eds.), *Handbook of individual differences in social behavior* (pp. 46–61). New York, NY: Guilford.

Green, J. D., Sedikides, C., Pinter, B., & Van Tongeren, D. R. (2009). Two sides to self-protection: Self-improvement strivings and feedback from close relationships eliminate mnemic neglect. *Self and Identity, 8*(2–3), 233–250.

Greenberg, R. P., & Fisher, S. (1997). Mood-mending medicines: Probing drug, psychotherapy and placebo solutions. In S. Fisher & R. P. Greenberg (Eds.), *From placebo to panacea: Putting psychiatric drugs to the test.* New York, NY: Wiley.

Greene, K., Derlega, V. J., & Mathews, A. (2006). Self-disclosure in personal relationships. In A. L. Vangelisti & D. Perlman (Eds.), *The Cambridge handbook of personal relationships.* New York, NY: Cambridge University Press.

Greene, K., Derlega, V., & Mathews, A. (2006). Self-disclosure in personal relationships. In: A. L. Vangelisti & D. Perlman (Eds.). *Cambridge handbook of personal relationships.* Cambridge: Cambridge University Press.

Greenhaus, J. H. (2003). Career dynamics. In W. C. Borman, D. R. Ilgen, & R. J. Klimoski (Eds.), *Handbook of psychology: Vol. 12. Industrial and organizational psychology.* New York, NY: Wiley.

Greenhaus, J. H., & Powell, G. N. (2006). When work and family are allies: A theory of work-family enrichment. *Academy of Management Review, 31*(1), 72–92.

Greenland, P., Knoll, M. D., Stamler, J., Neaton, J. D., Dyer, A. R., Garside, D. B., & Wilson, P. W. (2003). Major risk factors as antecedents of fatal and nonfatal coronary heart disease events. *Journal of the American Medical Association, 290,* 891–897.

Greenson, R. R. (1967). *The technique and practice of psychoanalysis* (Vol. 1). New York, NY: International Universities Press.

Greenwood, D. N., & Lippman, J. R. (2010). Gender and media: Content, uses, and impact. In J. C. Chrisler & D. R. McCreary (Eds.), *Handbook of gender research in psychology* (Vol. 2, pp. 643–669). New York, NY: Springer Publishing Company.

Griffith, K. H., & Hebl, M. R. (2002). The disclosure dilemma for gay men and lesbians: "Coming out" at work. *Journal of Applied Psychology, 87*(6), 1191–1199.

Griffiths, M. (2011). Workaholism—a 21st-century addiction. *The Psychologist, 24* (10), 740–744.

Grinspoon, L., Bakalar, J. B., & Russo, E. (2005). Marihuana: Clinical aspects. In J. H. Lowinson, P. Ruiz, R. B. Millman, & J. G. Langrod (Eds.), *Substance abuse: A comprehensive textbook.* Philadelphia, PA: Lippincott/Williams & Wilkins.

Gross, J. J. (2001). Emotion regulation in adulthood: Timing is everything. *Current Directions in Psychological Science, 10,* 214–219.

Gruber, J. E. (1990). Methodological problems and policy implication in sexual harassment research. *Population Research and Policy Review, 9,* 235–254.

Grunberg, N. E., Faraday, M. M., & Rahman, M. A. (2001). The psychobiology of nicotine self-administration. In A. Baum, T. A. Revenson, & Singer, J. E. (Eds.), *Handbook of health psychology* (pp. 249–261). Mahwah, NJ: Erlbaum.

Grzywacz, J. G., Almeida, D. M., Neupert, S. D., & Ettner, S. L. (2004). Socioeconomic status and health: A micro-level analysis of exposure and vulnerability to daily stressors. *Journal of Health and Social Behavior, 45,* 1–16.

Guéguen, N. (2002). Status, apparel and touch: Their joint effects on compliance to a request. *North American Journal of Psychology, 4*(2), 279–286.

Guéguen, N., Fischer-Lokou, J., Lefebvre, L., & Lamy, L. (2008). Women's eye contact and men's later interest: Two field experiments. *Perceptual and Motor Skills, 106*(1), 63–66.

Gupta, U., & Singh, P. (1982). Exploratory study of love and liking type of marriages. Indian *Journal of Applied Psychology, 19,* 92–97.

Gutek, B. A. (1993). Responses to sexual harassment. In S. Oskamp & M. Costanzo (Eds.), *Gender issues in contemporary society.* Newbury Park, CA: Sage.

Haas, L. (1999). Families and work. In M. B. Sussman, S. K. Steinmetz, & G. W. Peterson *Handbook of marriage and the family.* New York, NY: Plenum Press.

Hadjikhani, N., Hoge, R., Snyder, J., & de Gelder, B. (2008). Pointing with the eyes: The role of gaze in communicating danger. *Brain and Cognition, 68*(1), 1–8.

Hafer, C. L. (2000). Do innocent victims threaten the belief in a just world? Evidence from a modified Stroop task. *Journal of Personality and Social Psychology, 79*(2), 165–173.

Haider-Markel, D. P., & Joslyn, M. R. (2008). Beliefs about the origins of homosexuality and support for gay rights: An empirical test of attribution theory. *Public Opinion Quarterly, 72,* 291–310.

Hakim, C. (2006). Women, careers, and work-life preferences. *British Journal of Guidance & Counselling, 34,* 279–294.

Hall, E. T. (1966) *The hidden dimension.* Garden City, NY: Doubleday.

Hall, E. T. (2008). Adumbration as a feature of intercultural communication. In C. D. Mortensen (Ed.), *Communication theory* (2nd ed., pp. 420–432). New Brunswick, NJ: Transaction Publishers.

Hall, J. A. (1984). *Nonverbal sex differences: Communication accuracy and expressive style.* Baltimore, MD: Johns Hopkins University Press.

Hall, J. A. (2006a). How big are nonverbal sex differences? The case of smiling and nonverbal sensitivity. In K. Dindia & D. Canary (Eds.), *Sex differences and similarities in communication* (pp. 59–81). Mahwah, NJ: Erlbaum.

Hall, J. A. (2006b). Women's and men's nonverbal communication: Similarities, differences, stereotypes, and origins. In V. Manusov & M. L. Patterson (Eds.), *The Sage handbook of nonverbal communication* (pp. 201–218). Thousand Oaks, CA: Sage.

Hall, J. A., & Matsumoto, D. (2004). Gender differences in judgments of multiple emotions from facial expressions. *Emotion, 4*(2), 201–206.

Halmi, K. A. (2008). Eating disorders: Anorexia nervosa, bulimia nervosa, and obesity. In R. E. Hales, S. C. Yudofsky, & G. O. Gabbard (Eds.), *The American psychiatric publishing textbook of psychiatry* (pp. 971–998). Washington, DC: American Psychiatric Publishing.

Halpern, D. F. (1997). Sex differences in intelligence: Implications for education. *American Psychologist, 52,* 1091–1102.

Halpern, D. F. (2000). *Sex differences in cognitive abilities* (3rd ed.). Mahwah, NJ: Erlbaum.

Halpern, D. F. (2004). A cognitive-process taxonomy for sex differences in cognitive abilities. *Current Directions in Psychological Science, 13*(4), 135–139.

Halpern, D. F. (2005). Psychology at the intersection of work and family: Recommendations for employers, working families, and policymakers. *American Psychologist, 60,* 397–409.

Halpern-Felsher, B. L., Cornell, J. L., Kropp, R. Y., & Tschann, J. M. (2005). Oral versus vaginal sex among adolescents: Perceptions, attitudes, and behavior. *Pediatrics, 115,* 845–851.

Hamilton, M. C., Anderson, D., Broaddus, M., & Young, K. (2006), Gender stereotyping and underrepresentation of female characters in 200 popular children's picture books: A twenty-first century update. *Sex Roles, 55,* 757–765.

Hammen, C. (2003). Mood disorders. In G. Stricker & T. A. Widiger (Eds.), *Handbook of psychology: Vol. 8. Clinical psychology.* New York, NY: Wiley.

Hampson, E., van Anders, S. M., & Mullin, L. I. (2006). A female advantage in the recognition of emotional facial expressions: Test of an evolutionary hypothesis. *Evolution and Human Behavior, 27,* 401–416.

Hancock, K. A., & Greenspan, K. (2010). Emergence and development of the psychological study of lesbian, gay, bisexual, and transgender issues. In J. C. Chrisler & D. R. McCreary (Eds.). *Handbook of gender research in psychology* (Vol. 1, pp. 59–78). New York, NY: Springer Publishing Company.

Hansen, J. C. (2005). Assessment of Interests. In S. D. Brown & R. W. Lent (Eds.), *Career development and counseling: Putting theory and research to work.* Hoboken, NJ: Wiley.

Harber, K. D., Zimbardo, P. G., & Boyd, J. N. (2003). Participant self-selection bias as a function of individual differences in time perspective. *Basic and Applied Social Psychology, 25,* 255–264.

Hargie, O. (2011). *Skilled interpersonal communication: Research, theory, and practice* (5th ed.). New York, NY: Routedge/Taylor & Francis.

Haring, M., Hewitt, P. L., & Flett, G. L. (2003). Perfectionism, coping, and quality of intimate relationships. *Journal of Marriage & Family, 65*(1), 143–158.

Harpaz, I., & Snir, R. (2003). Workaholism: Its definition and nature. *Human Relations, 56*(3), 291–319.

Harrigan, J. A., Lucic, K. S., Kay, D., McLaney, A., & Rosenthal, R. (1991). Effect of expresser role and type of self-touching on observers' perceptions. *Journal of Applied Psychology, 21,* 585–609.

Harris, C. & Wagner, D. (2009, October 23). Business has grown for sweat-lodge guru: Cracks form in motivational mogul's empire. *The Arizona Republic.* Retrieved from http://www.azcentral.com/12news/news/articles/2009/10/23/20091023rayprofile1023-CP.html

Harris, J. B., Schwartz, S. M., & Thompson, B.(2008). Characteristics associated with self-identification as a regular smoker and desire to quit among college students who smoke cigarettes. *Nicotine and Tobacco Research, 10,* 69–76.

Harris, T. (1967). *I'm OK—You're OK.* New York, NY: HarperCollins.

Harrison, J. A., & Wells, R. B. (1991). Bystander effects on male helping behavior: Social comparison and diffusion of responsibility. *Representative Research in Social Psychology, 19*(1), 53–63.

Harter, S. (1998). The development of self-representations. In N. Eisenberg (Ed.), *Handbook of child psychology: Vol. 3. Social, emotional, and personality development.* New York, NY: Wiley.

Harter, S. (2003). The development of self-representations during childhood and adolescence. In M. R. Leary & J. P. Tangney (Eds.), *Handbook of self and identity.* New York, NY: Guilford.

Harter, S. (2006). Developmental and individual difference perspectives on self-esteem. In D. K. Mroczek & T. D. Little (Eds.), *Handbook of personality development.* Mahwah, NJ: Erlbaum.

Hartup, W. W., & Stevens, N. (1999). Friendships and adaptation across the life span. *Current Directions in Psychological Science, 8*(3), 76–79.

Harvard Crimson. (2005, January 14). Full transcript: President Summers' remarks at the National Bureau of Economic Research. *Harvard Crimson,* Retrieved from http://www.thecrimson.com/article.aspx?ref=505844.

Harvey, J. H., & Omarzu, J. (1997). Minding the close relationship. *Personality and Social Psychology Review, 1*(3), 224–240.

Harvey, J. H., & Omarzu, J. (1999). *Minding the close relationship: A theory of relationship enhancement.* New York, NY: Cambridge University Press.

Harvey, M. H. (1999). Memory research and clinical practice: A critique of three paradigms and a framework for psychotherapy with trauma survivors. In L. M. Williams, & V. L. Banyard (Eds.), *Trauma & memory.* Thousand Oaks, CA: Sage.

Harvey, P. D. (2010). Cognitive functioning and disability in schizophrenia. *Current Directions in Psychological Science, 19*(4), 249254. doi:10.1177/0963721410378033

Hass, N. (2006, January). In your Facebook.com. *The New York Times,* pp. A4, A30.

Hatch, A. (2009). Alternative relationship lifestyles. In H. T. Reis & S. Sprecher (Eds.), *Encyclopedia of human relationships: Vol. 2* (pp. 85–88). Los Angeles, CA: Sage Reference Publication.

Hatfield, E., & Rapson, R. L. (1993). *Love, sex, and intimacy: Their psychology, biology, and history.* New York, NY: HarperCollins.

Hatfield, E., & Rapson, R. L. (2008). Passionate love and sexual desire: Multidisciplinary perspectives. In J. P. Forgas & J. Fitness (Eds.), *Social Relationships* (pp. 21–38). New York, NY: Taylor & Francis.

Hatfield, E., & Sprecher, S. (2009). Matching hypothesis. In H. T. Reis & S. Sprecher (Eds.), *Encyclopedia of human relationships: Vol. 2* (pp. 1065–1067). Los Angeles, CA: Sage Reference Publication.

Hawkins, D. N., & Booth, A. (2005). Unhappily ever after: Effects of long-term, low-quality marriages on well-being. *Social Forces, 84,* 451–471.

Hawkley, L. C., & Cacioppo, J. T. (2009). Loneliness. In H. T. Reis & S. Sprecher (Eds.), *Encyclopedia of human relationships: Vol. 2* (pp. 985–990). Los Angeles, CA: Sage Reference Publication.

Hawkley, L. C., & Cacioppo, J. T. (2010). Loneliness matters: A theoretical and empirical review of consequences and mechanisms. *Annals Of Behavioral Medicine, 40*(2), 218–227. doi:10.1007/s12160-010-9210-8

Hawton, K., & Harriss, L. (2008). The changing gender ratio in occurrence of deliberate self-harm across the life cycle. *Crisis, 29,* 4–10.

Hazan, C., & Shaver, P. (1986). *Parental caregiving style questionnaire.* Unpublished questionnaire.

Hazan, C., & Shaver, P. (1987). Romantic love conceptualized as an attachment process. *Journal of Personality and Social Psychology, 52,* 511–524.

Heath, J., & Goggin, K. (2009). Attitudes towards male homosexuality, bisexbuality, and the down low lifestyle: Demographic differences and HIV implications. *Journal of Bisexuality, 9,* 17–31.

Heatherton, T. F., & Polivy, J. (1991). Development and validation of a scale for measuring state self-esteem. *Journal of Personality and Social Psychology, 60,* 895–910.

Heider, F. (1958). *The psychology of interpersonal relations.* New York, NY: Wiley.

Heine, S. J., Buchtel, E. E., & Norenzayan, A. (2008). What do cross-national comparisons of personality traits tell us? The case of conscientiousness. *Psychological Science, 19*(4), 309–313.

Heinrichs, R. W. (2005). The primacy of cognition in schizophrenia. *American Psychologist, 60,* 229–242.

Helgeson, V. S. (1994). Relation of agency and communion to well-being: Evidence and potential explanations. *Psychological Bulletin, 116,* 412–428.

Hellström, A., & Tekle, J. (1994). Person perception through facial photographs: Effects of glasses, hair, and beard on judgments of occupation and personal qualities. *European Journal of Social Psychology, 24*(6), 693–705.

Hendrick, S. S., Hendrick, C., & Adler, N. L. (1988). Romantic relationships: Love, satisfaction, and staying together. *Journal of Personality and Social Psychology, 54,* 980–988.

Henley, N. M. (1986). *Body politics: Power, sex, and nonverbal communication* (2nd ed.). New York, NY: Simon & Schuster.

Henley, N. M., & Freeman, J. (1995). The sexual politics of interpersonal behavior. In J. Freeman (Ed.), *Women: A feminist perspective* (5th ed.). Mountain View, CA: Mayfield.

Henman, L. D. (2001). Humor as a coping mechanism: Lessons from POWs. *Humor, 14,* 83–94.

Henriksson, M. M., Aro, H. M., Marttunen, M. J., Heikkinen, M. E., Isometsa, E. T., Kuoppasalmi, K. I., & Lonnqvist, J. K. (1993). Mental disorders and commorbidity of suicide. *American Journal of Psychiatry, 150,* 935–940.

Heppner, P. P., & Lee, D. (2005). Problem-solving appraisal and psychological adjustment. In C. R. Snyder & S. J. Lopez (Eds.), *Handbook of positive psychology.* New York, NY: Oxford University Press.

Herbenick, D., Reece, M., Schick, V., Sanders, S. A., Dodge, B., & Fortenberry, J. D. (2010). Sexual behavior in the United States: Results from a national probability sample of men and women ages 14–94. *Journal of Sexual Medicine, 7*(5), 255–265.

Herbert, J. D., Gaudiano, B. A., Rheingold, A. A., Myers, V. H., Dalrymple, K., & Nolan, E. M. (2005). Social skills training augments the effectiveness of cognitive behavioral group therapy for social anxiety disorder. *Behavior Therapy, 36,* 125–138.

Herek, G. M. (2009a). Hate crimes and stigma-related experiences among sexual minority adults in the United States: Prevalence estimates from a national probability sample. *Journal of Interpersonal Violence, 24,* 54–74.

Herek, G. M. (2009b). Sexual prejudice. In T. D. Nelson (Ed.), *Handbook of prejudice, stereotyping, and discrimination* (pp. 441–467). New York, NY: Psychology Press.

Herek, G. M., & Capitanio, J. (1996). "Some of my best friends": Intergroup contact concealable stigma, and heterosexuals' attitudes toward gay men and lesbians. *Personality and Social Psychology Bulletin, 22,* 412–424.

Hermann, R. C., Dorwart, R. A., Hoover, C. W., & Brody, J. (1995). Variation in ECT use in the United States. *American Journal of Psychiatry, 152,* 869–875.

Hermann, R. C., Ettner, S. L., Dorwart, R. A., Hoover, C. W., & Yeung, E. (1998). Characteristics of psychiatrists who perform ECT. *American Journal of Psychiatry, 155,* 889–894.

Hess, U., & Thibault, P. (2009). Darwin and emotion expression. *American Psychologist, 64,* 120–128.

Hetherington, E. M. (1999). Should we stay together for the sake of the children? In E. M. Hetherington (Ed.), *Coping with divorce, single parenting, and remarriage: A risk and resiliency perspective.* Mahwah, NJ: Erlbaum.

Hetherington, E. M. (2003). Intimate pathways: Changing patterns in close personal relationships across time. *Family Relations: Interdisciplinary Journal of Applied Family Studies, 52*(4), 318–331.

Hewstone, M. (1990). The ultimate attribution error? A review of the literature on intergroup causal attribution. *European Journal of Social Psychology, 20,* 311–335.

Heymann, J., Earle, A., Simmons, S., Breslow, S., & Kuehnhoff, A. (2004). *The work, family, and equity index: Where does the United States stand globally?* Boston, MA: Harvard School of Public Health.

Hicks, T. V., & Leitenberg, H. (2001). Sexual fantasies about one's partner versus someone else: Gender differences in incidence and frequency. *Journal of Sex Research, 38*(1), 43–50.

Hill, A. J. (2002). Prevalence and demographics of dieting. In C. G. Fairburn & K. D. Brownell (Eds.), *Eating disorders and obesity: A comprehensive handbook.* New York, NY: Guilford.

Hill, C. T., Rubin, Z., & Peplau, L. A. (1976). Breakups before marriage: The end of 103 affairs. *Journal of Social Issues, 32,* 147–168.

Hill, J. O., & Wyatt, H. R. (2005). Role of physical activity in preventing and treating obesity. *Journal of Applied Physiology, 99,* 765–770.

Hines, M. (1990). Gonadal hormones and human cognitive development. In J. Balthazart (Ed.), *Hormones, brain and behavior in vertebrates: 1. Sexual differentiation, neuroanatomical aspects, neurotransmitters and neuropeptides.* Basel: Karger.

Hines, M. (2007). Do sex differences in cognition cause the shortage of women in science? In S. J. Ceci & W. M. Williams (Eds.), *Why aren't more women in science?* (pp. 101–112).

Hiroto, D. S., & Seligman, M. E. P. (1975). Generality of learned helplessness in man. *Journal of Personality and Social Psychology, 31,* 311–327.

Hochschild, A. R. (2003). *The managed heart: Commercialization of human feeling.* Berkeley, CA: University of California Press.

Hodge, B. (2002, March). PCs and the healthy office. *Smart Computing,* pp. 64–67.

Hoffnung, M. (2004). Wanting it all: Career, marriage, and motherhood during college-educated women's 20s. *Sex Roles, 50*(9/10), 711–723.

Høglend, P., Bøgwald, K.-P., Amlo, S., Marble, A., Ulberg, R., Sjaastad, M. C., et al. (2008). Transference interpretations in dynamic psychotherapy: Do they really yield sustained effects? *American Journal of Psychiatry, 165,* 763–771.

Høglend, P., Hersoug, A., Bøgwald, K., Amlo, S., Marble, A., Sørbye, Ø., & Crits-Christoph, P. (2011). Effects of transference work in the context of therapeutic alliance and quality of object relations. *Journal Of Consulting And Clinical Psychology, 79*(5), 697–706. doi:10.1037/a0024863

Holden, C. (2004). FDA weighs suicide risk in children on antidepressants. *Science, 303,* 745.

Hollander, E. & Simeon, D. (2008). Anxiety disorders. In R. E. Hales, S. C. Yudofsky, & G. O. Gabbard (Eds.), *The American psychiatric publishing textbook of psychiatry* (pp. 505–608). Washington, DC: American Psychiatric Publishing.

Hollon, S. D., & DiGiuseppe, R. (2011). Cognitive theories of psychotherapy. In J. C. Norcross, G. R. Vandenbos, & D. K. Freedheim (Eds.), *History of psychotherapy: Continuity and change* (2nd ed.). Washington, DC: American Psychological Association.

Hollon, S. D., & Dimidjian, S. (2009). Cognitive and behavioral treatment of depression. In I. H. Gotlib & C. L. Hammen (Eds.), *Handbook of depression* (pp. 586–603). New York, NY: Guilford Press.

Holmes, T. H., & Rahe, R. H. (1967). The Social Readjustment Rating Scale. *Journal of Psychosomatic Research, 11,* 213–218.

Holt, T., Greene, L., & Davis, J. (2003). *National survey of adolescents and young adults: Sexual health knowledge, attitudes, and experience.* Menlo Park, CA: Henry J. Kaiser Family Foundation.

Honts, C. R., Raskin, D. C., & Kircher, J. C. (2002). The scientific status of research on polygraph testing. In D. L. Faigman, D. H. Kaye, M. J. Saks, & J. Sanders (Eds.), *Modern scientific evidence: The law and science of expert testimony* (Vol. 2). St. Paul, MN: West Publishing.

Hoobler, J. M., & Brass, D. J. (2006). Abusive supervision and family undermining as displaced aggression. *Journal of Applied Psychology, 91,* 1125–1133.

Hooley, J. M. (2004). Do psychiatric patients do better clinically if they live with certain kinds of families? *Current Directions in Psychological Science, 13*(5), 202–205.

Hooley, J. M. (2009). Schizophrenia: Interpersonal functioning. In P. H. Blaney & T. Millon (Eds.), *Oxford textbook of psychopathology* (pp. 333–360). New York, NY: Oxford University Press.

Horan, W. P., Kern, R. S., Tripp, C., Hellemann, G., Wynn, J. K., Bell, M., & Green, M. F. (2011). Efficacy and specificity of Social Cognitive Skills Training for outpatients with psychotic disorders. *Journal Of Psychiatric Research, 45*(8), 1113–1122. doi:10.1016/j.jpsychires.2011.01.015

Hovanesian, S., Isakov, I., & Cervellione, K. L. (2009). Defense mechanisms and suicide risk in major depression. *Archives of Suicide Research, 13,* 74–86.

Howes, O. D., & Kapur, S. (2009). The dopamine hypothesis of schizophrenia: Version III—The final common pathway. *Schizophrenia Bulletin, 35*(3), 549–562. doi:10.1093/schbul/sbp006

Hudson, J. I., Hiripi, E., Pope, H. G., & Kessler, R. C. (2007). The prevalence and correlates of eating disorders in the national comorbidity survey replication. *Biological Psychiatry, 61,* 348–358.

Hughes, E., & Parkes, K. (2007). Work hours and well-being: The roles of work-time control and work-family interference. *Work & Stress, 21*(3), 264–278.

Hust, S. J. T., Brown, J. D., & L'Engle, K. L. (2008). Boys will be boys and girls better be prepared: An analysis of the rare sexual health messages in young adolescents' media. *Mass Communication & Society, 11,* 3–23.

Huston, T. L., Niehuis, S., & Smith, S. E. (2001). The early marital roots of conjugal distress and divorce. *Current Directions in Psychological Science, 10*(4), 116–119.

Hyde, J. S. (1996). Where are the gender differences? Where are the gender similarities? In D.M. Buss & N. M. Malamuth (Eds.), *Sex, power, conflict: Evolutionary and feminist perspectives.* New York, NY: Oxford University Press.

Hyde, J. S. (2004). *Half the human experience: The psychology of women.* Boston, MA: Houghton Mifflin.

Hyde, J. S. (2005). The gender similarities hypothesis. *American Psychologist, 60,* 581–592.

Hyde, J. S. (2007a) Women in science: Gender similarities in abilities and sociocultural forces. In S. J. Ceci & W. M. Williams (Eds.), *Why aren't more women in science?* (pp. 131–146). Washington, DC: American Psychological Association.

Hyde, J. S. (2007b). New directions in the study of gender similarities and differences. *Current Directions in Psychological Science, 16,* 259–263.

Iacono, W. G. (2008). Accuracy of polygraph techniques: Problems using confessions to determine the truth. *Physiology & Behavior, 95*(1–2), 24–26.

Iacono, W. G. (2009). Psychophysiological detection of deception and guilty knowledge. In K. S. Douglas, J. L. Skeem, & S. O. Lilienfeld (Eds.), *Psychological science in the courtroom: Consensus and controversy* (pp. 224–241). New York, NY: Guilford.

Ickes, W., Patterson, M. L., Rajecki, D. W., & Tanford, S. (1982). Behavioral and cognitive consequences of reciprocal versus compensatory responses to preinteraction expectancies. *Social Cognition, 1,* 160–190.

Ignatius, E., & Kokkonen, M. (2007). Factors contributing to verbal self-disclosure. *Nordic Psychology, 59*(4), 362–391.

Impett, E. A., & Peplau, L. A. (2006). "His" and "her" relationships? A review of the empirical evidence. In A. L. Vangelisti & D. Perlman (Eds.), *The Cambridge handbook of personal relationships.* New York, NY: Cambridge University Press.

Impett, E. A., Peplau, L. A., & Gable, S. L. (2005). Approach and avoidance sexual motives: Implications for personal and interpersonal well-being. *Personal Relationships, 12,* 465–482.

Infante, J. R., Torres-Avisbal, M., Pinel, P., Vallejo. J. A., Peran, F., Gonzalez, F., Contreras, P., Pacheco, C., Roldan, A., & Latre, J. M. (2001). Catecholamine levels in practitioners of the transcendental meditation technique. *Physiology & Behavior, 72*(1-2), 141–146.

Ingram, R. E., Scott, W. D., & Hamill, S. (2009). Depression: Social and cognitive aspects. In P. H. Blaney & T. Millon (Eds.), *Oxford textbook of psychopathology* (pp. 230–252). New York, NY: Oxford University Press.

Insel, T. R. (2010). Psychiatrists' relationships with pharmaceutical companies: Part of the problem or part of the solution? *Journal of the American Medical Association, 303*(12), 1192–1193. doi:10.1001/jama.2010.317

Insko, C. A., Smith, R. H., Alicke, M. D., Wade, J., & Taylor, S. (1985). Conformity and group size: The concern with being right and the concern with being liked. *Personality and Social Psychology Bulletin, 11,* 41–50.

Internet World Stats. (2011). *Internet usage statistics—the Internet big picture.* Retrieved from http://www.internetworldstats.com/stats.htm

Isometsa, E. T., Heikkinen, M. E., Marttunen, M. J., Henriksson, M. M., Aro, H. M., & Lonnqvist, J. K. (1995). The last appointment before suicide: Is suicide intent communicated? *American Journal of Psychiatry, 152,* 919–922.

Ito, T. A., Chiao, K. W., Devine, P. G., Lorig, T., & Cacioppo, J. T. (2006). The influence of facial feedback on race bias. *Psychological Science, 17,* 256–261.

Ivancevich, J. M., Matteson, M. T., Freedman, S. M., & Phillips, J. S. (1990). Worksite stress management interventions. *American Psychologist, 45,* 252–261.

Izard, C. E. (1994). Innate and universal facial expressions: Evidence from developmental and cross-cultural research. *Psychological Bulletin, 115,* 288–299.

Izard, C. E., Fine, S., Schultz, D., Mostow, A., Ackerman, B., & Youngstrom, E. (2001). Emotion knowledge as a predictor of social behavior and academic competence in children at risk. *Psychological Science, 12*(1), 18–23.

Jacques, R. (1997). The unbearable whiteness of being: Reflections of a pale, stale male. In P. Prasad, A. Mills, M. Elmes, & A. Prasad (Eds.), *Managing the organizational melting pot: Dilemmas of workplace diversity.* Thousand Oaks, CA: Sage.

Jain, S., Shapiro, S. L., Swanick, S., Roesch, S. C., Mills, P. J., Bell, I., & Schwartz, G. E. R. (2007). A randomized controlled trial of mindfulness meditation versus relaxation training: Effects on distress, positive states of mind, rumination, and distraction. *Annals of Behavioral Medicine, 33,* 11–21.

Jakicic, J. M., & Gallagher, K. I. (2002). Physical activity considerations for management of body weight. In D. H. Bessesen, & R. Kushner (Eds.), *Evaluation & Management of Obesity.* Philadelphia, PA: Hanley & Belfus.

Jakupcak, M., Salters, K., Gratz, K. L., & Roemer, L. (2003). Masculinity and emotionality: An investigation of men's primary and secondary emotional responding. *Sex Roles, 49*(3/4), 111–120.

Janis, I. L. (1958). *Psychological stress.* New York, NY: Wiley.

Janis, I. L. (1993). Decision making under stress. In L. Goldberger & S. Breznitz (Eds.), *Handbook of stress: Theoretical and clinical aspects* (2nd ed.). New York, NY: Free Press.

Jansz, J. (2000). Masculine identity and restrictive emotionality. In A. H. Fischer (Ed.), *Gender and emotion: Social psychological perspectives.* Cambridge, UK: Cambridge University Press.

Javitt, D. C., & Laruelle, M. (2006). Neurochemical theories. In J. A. Liberman, T. S. Stroup, & D. O. Perkins (Eds.), *Textbook of schizophrenia.* Washington, DC: American Psychiatric Publishing.

Jayaratne, T. E., Gelman, S. A., Feldbaum, M., Sheldon, J. P., Petty, E. M., & Kardia, S. L. R. (2009). The perennial debate: Nature, nurture, or choice? Black and white Americans' explanations for individual differences. *Review of General Psychology, 13,* 24–33.

Jefferson, J. W. & Greist, J. H. (2009). Lithium. In B. J. Sadock, V. A. Sadock, & P. Ruiz (Eds.), *Kaplan & Sadock's comprehensive textbook of psychiatry* (pp. 3132–3144). Philadelphia, PA: Lippincott Williams & Wilkins.

Jeffery, R. W., Epstein, L. H., Wilson, G. T., Drewnowski, A., Stunkard, A. J., Wing, R. R., & Hill, D. R. (2000). Long-term maintenance of weight loss: Current status. *Health Psychology, 19*(1), 5–16.

Jemmott, J. B., III, & Magloire, K. (1988). Academic stress, social support, and secretory Immunoglobin A. *Journal of Personality and Social Psychology, 55,* 803–810.

Jepsen, L. K., & Jepsen, C. A. (2002). An empirical analysis of the matching patterns of same-sex and opposite-sex couples. *Demography, 39,* 435–453.

Jeynes, W. H. (2006). The impact of parental remarriage on children: A meta-analysis. *Marriage & Family Review, 40,* 75–102.

Jick, H., Kaye, J. A., & Jick, S. S. (2004). Antidepressants and the risk of suicidal behaviors. *Journal of the American Medical Association, 292*(3), 338–343.

Johnson, A. J., Haigh, M. M., Becker, J. A. H., Craig, E. A., & Wigley, S. (2008). College students' use of relational management strategies in email in long-distance and geographically close relationships. *Journal of Computer-Mediated Communication, 13,* 381–404.

Johnson, B. A., & Ait-Daoud, N. (2005). Alcohol: Clinical aspects. In J. H. Lowinson, P. Ruiz, R. B. Millman, & J. G. Langrod (Eds.), *Substance abuse: A comprehensive textbook.* Philadelphia, PA: Lippincott/Williams & Wilkins.

Johnson, M. P., & Ferraro, K. J. (2001). Research on domestic violence in the 1990's: Making distinctions. In R. M. Milardo (Ed.), *Understanding families into the new millennium: A decade in review.* Minneapolis, MN: National Council on Family Relations.

Johnson, S. (2007). Promoting easy sex without genuine intimacy: *Maxim* and *Cosmopolitan* cover lines and cover images. In M. Galician, & D. L. Merskin (Eds.), *Critical thinking about sex, love, and romance in the mass media* (pp. 55–74). Mahwah, NJ: Erlbaum.

Johnson, S. B., & Carlson, D. N. (2004). Medical regimen adherence: Concepts, assessment, and interventions. In J. M. Raczynski, & L. C. Leviton (Eds.), *Handbook of clinical health psychology: Vol. 2. Disorders of behavior and health.* Washington, DC: American Psychological Association.

Johnson, S. L., Joormann, J., Lemoult, J., & Miller, C. (2009). Mood disorders: Biological bases. In P. H. Blaney & T. Millon (Eds.), *Oxford textbook of psychopathology* (pp. 198–229). New York, NY: Oxford University Press.

Johnson, W. (2010). Understanding the genetics of intelligence: Can height help? Can corn oil? *Current Directions in Psychological Science, 19*(3), 177–182. doi:10.1177/0963721410370136

Johnson, W., & Krueger, R. F. (2006). How money buys happiness: Genetic and environmental processes linking finances and life satisfaction. *Journal of Personality and Social Psychology, 90,* 680–691.

Johnston, L. D., O'Malley, P. M., Bachman, J. G., & Schulenberg, J. E. (2009). *Monitoring the future: National survey on drug use, 1975–2008: Volume II, College students and adults ages 19–50* (NIH Publication No. 09-7403). Bethesda, MD: National Institute on Drug Abuse.

Johnston, L. D., O'Malley, P. M., Bachman, J. G., & Schulenberg, J. E. (2008). *Monitoring the future: National results on adolescent drug use: Overview of key findings* (NIH Publication No. 08–6418). Bethesda, MD: National Institute on Drug Abuse.

Joiner, T. E., & Timmons, K. A. (2009). Depression in its interpersonal context. In I. H. Gotlib & C. L. Hammen (Eds.), *Handbook of depression* (pp. 322–339). New York, NY: Guilford.

Jones, E. E. (1990). *Interpersonal perception.* New York, NY: Freeman.

Jones, E. E., & Davis, K. (1965). From acts to dispositions: The attribution process in person perception. In L. Berkowitz (Ed.), *Advances in experimental social psychology* (Vol. 2). New York, NY: Academic Press.

Jones, R. A., & Brehm, J. W. (1970). Persuasiveness of one- and two-sided communications as a function of awareness there are two sides. *Journal of Experimental Social Psychology, 6,* 47–56.

Jorgensen, R. S., & Kolodziej, M. E. (2007). Suppressed anger, evaluative threat, and cardiovascular reactivity: A tripartite profile approach. *International Journal of Psychophysiology, 66,* 102–108.

Jorgensen, R. S., Johnson, B. T., Kolodziej, M. E., & Schreer, G. E. (1996). Elevated blood pressure and personality: A meta-analytic review. *Psychological Bulletin, 120,* 293–320.

Jose, A., Daniel O'Leary, K. K., & Moyer, A. (2010). Does premarital cohabitation predict subsequent marital stability and marital quality? A meta-analysis. *Journal of Marriage & the Family, 72*(1), 105–116. doi:10.1111/j.1741-3737.2009.00686.x

Joyner, T. (1999, November 14). All-work is American way: Atlanta poll finds 21 percent work 50-plus hours a week. *The Atlanta Journal-Constitution,* pp. R1, R5.

Judge, T. A., & Klinger, R. (2008). Job satisfaction: Subjective well-being at work. In M. Eid & R. J. Larsen (Eds.), *The science of subjective well-being* (pp. 393–413). New York, NY: Guilford.

Julien, R. M. (2008). *A primer of drug action* (11th ed.). New York, NY: Worth.

Jung, C. G. (1933). *Modern man in search of a soul.* New York, NY: Harcourt, Brace & World.

Justman, S. (2005). *Fool's paradise: The unreal world of pop psychology.* Chicago: Ivan R. Dee.

Kaestle, C. E., & Halpern, C. T. (2007). What's love got to do with it? Sexual behaviors of opposite-sex couples through emerging adulthood. *Perspectives on Sexual and Reproductive Health, 39,* 134–140.

Kahn, A. S., & Andreoli Mathie, V. (1999). Sexuality, society, and feminism: Psychological perspectives on women. In C. B. Travis & J. W. White (Eds.), *Sexuality, society, and feminism: Psychological perspectives on women.* Washington, DC: American Psychological Association.

Kahneman, D. (1999). Objective happiness. In D. Kahneman, E. Diener, & N. Schwarz (Eds.), *Well-being: The*

foundations of hedonic psychology. New York, NY: Sage.

Kahneman, D. (2011). *Thinking, fast and slow.* New York, NY: Farrar, Straus, & Giroux.

Kahneman, D., & Deaton, A. (2010). High income improves evaluation of life but not emotional well-being. *Proceedings of the National Academy of Sciences of the United States of America, 107*(38), 16489–16493. doi:10.1073/pnas.1011492107

Kahneman, D., Krueger, A. B., Schkade, D., Schwarz, N., & Stone, A. A. (2006). Would you be happier if you were richer? A focusing illusion. *Science, 312,* 1908–1910.

Kaiser, A., Haller, S., Schmitz, S., & Nitsch, C. (2009). On sex/gender related similarities and differences in fMRI language research. *Brain Research Reviews, 61,* 49–59.

Kaiser Family Foundation. (2004). *Sex education in America: Principals' survey.* Menlo Park, CA: Henry J. Kaiser Family Foundation.

Kaiser Family Foundation. (2006). *HIV/AIDS policy fact sheet.* Retrieved from http://www.kff.org/hivaids/us.cfm.

Kaiser Family Foundation. (2012a). *HIV/AIDS policy fact sheet: Black Americans and HIV/AIDS.* Retrieved from http://www.kff.org/hivaids/6007.cfm

Kaiser Family Foundation. (2012b). *HIV/AIDS policy fact sheet: Latinos and HIV/AIDS.* Retrieved from http://www.kff.org/hivaids/6007.cfm

Kaiser Family Foundation, Holt, T., Greene, L., & Davis, J. (2003). *National Survey of adolescents and young adults: Sexual health knowledge, attitudes, and experiences.* Menlo Park, CA: Henry J. Kaiser Family Foundation.

Kalant, H. (2004). Adverse effects of cannabis on health: An update of the literature since 1966. *Progress in Neuro-Psychopharmocology and Biological Psychiatry, 28,* 849–863.

Kalb, C., & Murr, A. (2006, May 16). Battling a black epidemic. *Newsweek,* pp. 42–48.

Kalichman, S. C., Roffman, R. A., Picciano, J. F., & Bolan, M. (1998). Risk for HIV infection among bisexual men seeking HIV-prevention services and risks posed to their female partners. *Health Psychology, 17,* 320–327.

Kandell, J. J. (1998). Internet addiction on campus: The vulnerability of college students. *CyberPsychology and Behavior, 1*(1), 11–17.

Kane, E. W. (2000). Racial and ethnic variations in gender-related attitudes. *Annual review of sociology, 26,* 419–439.

Kane, J. M., Stroup, T. S., & Marder, S. R. (2009). Schizophrenia: Pharmacological treatment. In B. J. Sadock, V. A. Sadock, & P. Ruiz (Eds.), *Kaplan & Sadock's comprehensive textbook of psychiatry* (pp. 1547–1555). Philadelphia, PA: Lippincott Williams & Wilkins.

Kanner, A. D., Coyne, J. C., Schaefer, C., & Lazarus, R. S. (1981). Comparison of two modes of stress measurement: Daily hassles and uplifts versus major life events. *Journal Of Behavioral Medicine, 4*(1), 1–39. doi:10.1007/BF00844845

Kaplan, A. G. (1985). Female or male therapists for women patients: New formulations. *Psychiatry, 48,* 111–121.

Karasek, R. A., Jr. (1979). Job demands, job decision latitude, and mental strain: Implications for job redesign. *Administrative Science Quarterly, 24,* 285–308.

Karasek, R. A., Jr., & Theorell, T. (1990). *Healthy work: Stress, productivity, and the reconstruction of working life.* New York, NY: Basic Books.

Karasek, R. A., Jr., Baker, D., Marxer, F., Ahlbom, A., & Theorell, T. (1981). Job decision latitude, job demands, and cardiovascular disease: A prospective study of Swedish men. *American Journal of Public Health, 71,* 694–705.

Karpicke, J. D., & Roediger, H. L., III. (2008). The critical importance of retrieval for learning. *Science, 319*(5865), 966–968. doi:10.1126/science.1152408

Kasser, T. (2002). *The high prices of materialism.* Cambridge, MA: MIT Press.

Kasser, T., Ryan, R. M., Couchman, C. E., & Sheldon, K. M. (2004). Materialistic values: Their causes and consequences. In T. Kasser & A. D. Kanner (Eds.), *Psychology and consumer culture: The struggle for a good life in a materialistic world.* Washington, DC: American Psychological Association.

Kath, L., Swody, C., Magley, V., Bunk, J., & Gallus, J. (2009). Cross-level, three-way interactions among work-group climate, gender, and frequency of harassment on morale and withdrawal outcomes of sexual harassment. *Journal of Occupational & Organizational Psychology, 82*(1), 159–182.

Kavesh, L., & Lavin, C. (1988). *Tales from the front.* New York, NY: Doubleday.

Kay, J., & Kay, R. L. (2003). Individual psychoanalytic psychotherapy. In A. Tasman, J. Kay, & J. A. Lieberman (Eds.), *Psychiatry.* New York, NY: Wiley.

Kay, J., & Kay, R. L. (2008). Individual psychoanalytic psychotherapy. In A. Tasman, J. Kay, J. A. Lieberman, M. B. First, & M. Maj (Eds.), *Psychiatry* (3rd ed.). New York, NY: Wiley-Blackwell.

Kazdin, A. E. (1994). Methodology, design, and evaluation in psychotherapy research. In A. E. Bergin & S. L. Garfield (Eds.), *Handbook of psychotherapy and behavior change* (4th ed.). New York, NY: Wiley.

Keck, P. E., Jr., & McElroy, S. L. (2006). Lithium and mood stabilizers. In D. J. Stein, D. J. Kupfer, & A. F. Schatzberg (Eds.), *Textbook of mood disorders.* Washington, DC: American Psychiatric Publishing.

Keesey, R. E. (1993). Physiological regulation of body energy: Implications for obesity. In A. J. Stunkard & T. A. Wadden (Eds.), *Obesity: Theory and therapy.* New York, NY: Raven Press.

Keinan, G. (1987). Decision making under stress: Scanning of alternatives under controllable and uncontrollable threats. *Journal of Personality and Social Psychology, 52,* 639–644.

Kellogg, S. H., & Young, J. E. (2008). Cognitive therapy. In J. L. Lebow (Ed.), *Twenty-first century psychotherapies: Contemporary approaches to theory and practice.* New York, NY: Wiley.

Kelsoe, J. R. (2009). Mood disorders: Genetics. In B. J. Sadock, V. A. Sadock, & P. Ruiz (Eds.), *Kaplan & Sadock's comprehensive textbook of psychiatry* (pp. 1653–1663). Philadelphia, PA: Lippincott Williams & Wilkins.

Kendler, K. S., Myers, J., & Prescott, C. A. (2005). Sex differences in the relationship between social support and risk for major depression: A longitudinal study of opposite-sex twin pairs. *American Journal of Psychiatry, 162,* 250–256.

Kenfield, S. A., Stampfer, M. J., Rosner, B. A., & Colditz, G. A. (2008). Smoking and smoking cessation in relation to mortality in women. *Journal of the American Medical Association, 299,* 2037–2047.

Kenrick, D. T., & Trost, M. R. (1993). The evolutionary perspective. In A. E. Beall & R. J. Sternberg (Eds.), *The psychology of gender.* New York, NY: Guilford Press.

Kernis, M. H. (2003a). Optimal self-esteem and authenticity: Separating fantasy from reality. *Psychological Inquiry, 14*(1), 83–89.

Kernis, M. H. (2003b). Toward a conceptualization of optimal self-esteem. *Psychological Inquiry, 14*(1), 1–26.

Kernis, M. H., & Goldman, B. M. (2002). Stability and variability in self-concept and self-esteem. In M. R. Leary and J. P. Tangney (Eds.), *Handbook of self and identity.* New York, NY: Guilford.

Kessler, R. C., Berglund, P., Demler, O., Jin, R., & Walters, E. E. (2005a). Lilfetime prevalence and age-of-onset distributions of DSM-IV disorders in the national comorbidity survey replication. *Archives of General Psychiatry, 62,* 593–602.

Kessler, R. C., Berglund, P., Demler, O., Jin, R., Koretz, D., Merikangas, K. R., Rush, A. J., Walters, E. E., & Wang, P. S. (2003). The epidemiology of major depressive disorder: Results from the national comorbidity survey replication (NCS-R). *The Journal of the American Medical Association, 289*(23), 3095–3105.

Kessler, R. C., Demier, O., Frank, R. G., Olfson, M., Pincus, H. A., Walters, E. E., Wang, P., Wells, K. B., & Zaslavsky, A. M. (2005b). Prevalence and treatment of mental disorders. 1990–2003. *New England Journal of Medicine, 352,* 2515–2523.

Keysar, B., & Henly, A. S. (2002). Speakers' overestimation of their effectiveness. *Psychological Science, 13,* 207–212.

Kiecolt-Glaser, J. K., Garner, W., Speicher, C., Penn, G. M., Holliday, J., & Glaser, R. (1984). Psychosocial modifiers of immunocompetence in medical students. *Psychosomatic Medicine, 46,* 7–14.

Kieffer, K. M., Cronin, C., & Gawet, D. L. (2006). Test and study worry and emotionality in the prediction of college students' reason for drinking: An exploratory investigation. *Journal of Alcohol and Drug Addiction, 50*(1), 57–81.

Kihlstrom, J. F. (2005). Dissociative disorders. *Annual Review of Clinical Psychology, 1,* 227–253.

Kilmartin, C. T. (2000). *The masculine self* (2nd ed.). Boston, MA: McGraw-Hill.

Kilmartin, C. T. (2007). *The masculine self.* Cornwall-on-Hudson, NY: Sloan Publishing.

Kim, H. S., Sherman, D. K., Ko, D., & Taylor, S. E. (2006). Pursuit of comfort and pursuit of harmony: Culture, relationships, and social support seeking. *Personality and Social Psychology Bulletin, 32,*1595–1607.

Kim, H. S., Sherman, D. K., & Taylor, S. E. (2008). Culture and social support. *American Psychologist, 63,* 518–526.

King, B. M. (2005). *Human sexuality today.* Upper Saddle River, NJ: Pearson Prentice Hall.

King, L. A., & Emmons, R. A. (1990). Conflict over emotional expression: Psychological and physical correlates. *Journal of Personality and Social Psychology, 58,* 864–877.

King, L. A., King, D. W., Fairbank, J. A., Keane, T. M., & Adams, G. A. (1998). Resilience-recovery factors in post-traumatic stress disorder among female and male Vietnam veterans: Hardiness, postwar social support, and additional stressful life events. *Journal of Personality and Social Psychology, 74,* 420–434.

King, S., St-Hilaire, A., & Heidkamp, D. (2010). Prenatal factors in schizophrenia. *Current Directions in Psychological Science, 19*(4), 209–213. doi:10.1177/0963721410378360

Kinsey, A. C., Pomeroy, W. B., Martin, C. E., & Gebhard, P. H. (1953). *Sexual behavior in the human female.* Philadelphia, PA: Saunders.

Kirkpatrick, L. A. (2005). *Attachment, evolution, and the psychology of religion.* New York, NY: Guilford.

Kirov, G. & Owen, M. J. (2009). Genetics of schizophrenia. In B. J. Sadock, V. A. Sadock, & P. Ruiz (Eds.), *Kaplan & Sadock's comprehensive textbook of psychiatry* (pp. 1462–1474). Philadelphia, PA: Lippincott Williams & Wilkins.

Klassen, M. (1987). How to get the most out of your time. In A. D. Timpe (Ed.), *The management of time.* New York, NY: Facts on File.

Klein, D. N. (2010). Chronic depression: Diagnosis and classification. *Current Directions in Psychological Science, 19*(2), 96–100. doi:10.1177/0963721410366007

Klein, T. W., Friedman, H., & Specter, S. (1998). Marijauna, immunity and infection. *Journal of Neuroimmunology, 83,* 102–115.

Kleinke, C. L. (1986). Gaze and eye contact: A research review. *Psychological Bulletin, 100,* 78–100.

Kleinke, C. L. (2007). What does it mean to cope? In A. Monat, R. S. Lazarus, & G. Reevy (Eds.), *The Praeger handbook on stress and coping* (pp. 289–308). Westport, CT: Praeger Publishers.

Kleinke, C. L., Meeker, F. B., & Staneski, R. A. (1986). Preference for opening lines: Comparing ratings by men and women. *Sex Roles, 15,* 585–600.

Kline, P. (1995). A critical review of the measurement of personality and intelligence. In D. H. Saklofske & M. Zeidner (Eds.), *International handbook of personality and intelligence.* New York, NY: Plenum Press.

Kling, K. C., Hyde, J. S., Showers, C. J., & Buswell, B. N. (1999). Gender differences in self-esteem: A meta-analysis. *Psychological Bulletin, 125*(4), 470–500.

Klonoff, E. A., & Landrine, H. (1999). Cross-validation of the schedule of racist events. *Journal of Black Psychology, 25*(2), 231–254.

Kluft, R. P. (1996). Dissociative identity disorder. In L. K. Michelson & W. J. Ray (Eds.), *Handbook of dissociation: Theoretical, empirical, and clinical perspectives.* New York, NY: Plenum.

Kluft, R. P. (1999). True lies, false truths, and naturalistic raw data: Applying clinical research findings to the false memory debate. In L. M. Williams & V. L. Banyard (Eds.), *Trauma & memory.* Thousand Oaks, CA: Sage.

Knauss, W. (2005). Group psychotherapy. In G. O. Gabbard, J. S. Beck, & J. Holmes (Eds.), *Oxford textbook of psychotherapy*. New York, NY: Oxford University Press.

Knox, D., Zusman, M., & McNeely, A. (2008). University student beliefs about sex: Men vs. women. *College Student Journal, 42,* 181–185.

Kobasa, S. C. (1979). Stressful life events, personality, and health: An inquiry into hardiness. *Journal of Personality and Social Psychology, 37,* 1–11.

Kobasa, S. C. (1984, September). How much stress can you survive? *American Health,* pp. 64–77.

Koopman, C., Classen, C., & Spiegel, D. (1994). Predictors of posttraumatic stress symptoms among survivors of the Oakland/Berkeley, Calif., firestorm. *American Journal of Psychiatry, 151,* 888–894.

Koss, M. P. (1988). Hidden rape: Sexual aggression and victimization in the national sample of students in higher education. In M. A. Pirog-Good & J. E. Stets (Eds.)., *Violence in dating relationships: Emerging social issues* (pp. 145–168). New York, NY: Praeger.

Koss, M. P., Gidycz, C. A., & Wisniewski, N. (1988). The scope of rape: Incidence and prevalence of sexual aggression and victimization in a national sample of higher education students. *Journal of Consulting and Clinical Psychology, 55,* 162–170.

Kowalski, R. M. (1993). Inferring sexual interest from behavioral cues: Effects of gender and sexually relevant attitudes. *Sex Roles, 29,* 13–36.

Kozlowski, S. W. J., & Bell, B. S. (2003). Work groups and teams in organizations. In W. C. Borman, D. R. Ilgen, & R. J. Klimoski (Eds.), *Handbook of psychology: Vol. 12. Industrial and organizational psychology.* New York, NY: Wiley.

Kraft, S. (2009, October 22). Sweat lodge deaths a new test for self-help guru. *LA Times.* Retrieved from http://www.latimes.com/news/nationworld/nation/la-na-guru22-2009oct22,0,6180058.story

Kramer, P. D. (2006). *Freud: Inventor of the modern mind.* New York, NY: HarperCollins.

Kreider, R. M. (2005). *Number, timing, and duration of marriages and divorces: 2001. U.S. Census Bureau, Household Economic Studies.* Washington DC: Department of Commerce.

Kring, A. M., & Gordon, A. H. (1998). Sex differences in emotion: Expression, experience, and physiology. *Journal of Personality and Social Psychology, 74*(3), 686–703.

Krueger, J. I., Vohs, K. D., & Baumeister, R. F. (2009). Is the allure of self-esteem a mirage after all? *American Psychologist, 63,* 64–65.

Krueger, R. F. & Johnson, W. (2008). Behavioral genetics and personality: A new look at the integration of nature and nurture. In O. P. John, R. W. Robins, & L. A. Pervin (Eds.), *Handbook of personality: Theory and research* (pp. 287–310). New York, NY: Guilford.

Krumrei, E, Coit, C., Martin, S., Fogo, W., & Mahoney, A. (2007). Post-divorce adjustment and social relationships: A meta-analytic review. *Journal of Divorce & Remarriage, 46,* 145–166.

Krusemark, E. A., Campbell, W. K., & Clementz, B. A. (2008). Attributions, deception, and event related potentials: An investigation of the self-serving bias. *Psychophysiology, 45*(4), 511–515.

Kuepper, R., van Os, J., Lieb, R., Wittchen, H., Höfler, M., & Henquet, C. (2011). Continued cannabis use and risk of incidence and persistence of psychotic symptoms: 10-year follow-up cohort study. *BMJ: British Medical Journal, 342*(7796). Retrieved from http://www.bmj.com/content/342/bmj.d738.full

Kuiper, N., Martin, R, & Olinger, L. J. (1993). Coping humour, stress, and cognitive appraisals. *Canadian Journal of Behavioural Science, 25,* 81–96.

Kulick, A. R., Pope, H. G., & Keck, P. E. (1990). Lycanthropy and self-identification. *Journal of Nervous and Mental Disease, 178,* 134–137.

Kunkel, D., Farrar, K. M., Eyal, K., Biely, E., Donnerstein, E., & Rideout, V. (2007). Sexual socialization messages on entertainment television: Comparing content trends, 1997–2002. *Media Psychology, 10,* 595–622.

Kurdek, L. A. (2004). Gay men and lesbians: The family context. In M. Coleman & L. H. Ganong (Eds.), *Handbook of contemporary families: Considering the past, contemplating the future.* Thousand Oaks, CA: Sage.

Kurdek, L. A. (2005). What do we know about gay and lesbian couples? *Current Directions in Psychological Science, 14*(5), 251–254.

Kurdek, L. A., & Schmitt, J. P. (1986a). Early development of relationship quality in heterosexual married, heterosexual cohabiting, gay, and lesbian couples. *Developmental Psychology, 22,* 305–309.

Kurdek, L. A., & Schmitt, J. P. (1986b). Interaction of sex role self-concept with relationship quality and relationship beliefs in married, heterosexual cohabiting, gay, and lesbian couples. *Journal of Personality and Social Psychology, 51,* 365–370.

Kurman, J. (2006). Self-enhancement, self-regulation, and self-improvement following failures. *British Journal of Social Psychology, 45*(2), 339–356.

La Greca, A. M. (2007). Posttraumatic stress disorder in children. In G. Fink (Ed.), *Encyclopedia of stress: Vols. 1–4* (2nd ed., pp. 145–149). San Diego, CA: Elsevier Academic Press.

Lakein, A. (1996). *How to get control of your time and your life.* New York, NY: New American Library.

Lambert, M. J. (2011). Psychotherapy research and its achievements. In J. C. Norcross, G. R. Vandenbos, & D. K. Freedheim (Eds.), *History of psychotherapy: Continuity and change* (2nd ed.). Washington, DC: American Psychological Association.

Lambert, M. J., Hansen, N. B., & Finch, A. E. (2001). Patient-focused research: Using patient outcome data to enhance treatment effects. *Journal of Consulting and Clinical Psychology, 69,* 159–172.

Lambert, M. J., & Ogles, B. M. (2004). The efficacy and effectiveness of psychotherapy. In M. J. Lambert (Ed.), *Bergin and Garfield's handbook of psychotherapy and behavior change.* New York, NY: Wiley.

Lambert, T. A., Kahn, A. S., & Apple, K. J. (2003). Pluralistic ignorance and hooking up. *Journal of Sex Research, 40*(2), 129–133.

Lampe, A., Soellner, W., Krismer, M., Rumpold, G., Kantner-Rumplmair, W., Ogon, M., & Rathner, G. (1998). The impact of stressful life events on exacerbation of chronic low-back pain. *Journal of Psychosomatic Research, 44*(5), 555–563.

Landabaso, M. A., Iraurgi, I., Sanz, J., Calle, R., Ruiz de Apodaka, J., Jimenez-Lerma, J. M., & Gutierrez-Fraile, M. (1999). Naltrexone in the treatment of alcoholism. Two-year follow up results. *European Journal of Psychiatry, 13,* 97–105.

Landrum, R. E. (2009). *Finding jobs with a psychology bachelor's degree: Expert advice for launching your career.* Washington, DC: American Psychological Association.

Lane, J. M., & Addis, M. E. (2005). Male gender role conflict and patterns of help seeking in Costa Rica and the United States. *Psychology of Men & Masculinity, 6,* 155–168.

Langbein, L., & Yost, M. A. (2009). Same-sex marriage and negative externalities. *Social Science Quarterly, 90,* 292–308.

Langer, E. J. (1989). *Mindfulness.* New York, NY: Addison-Wesley.

Langer, E. J. (2009). Mindfulness. In S. J. Lopez (Ed.), *The encyclopedia of positive psychology* (Vol. II, pp. 618–622). Malden, MA: Wiley-Blackwell.

LaPiere, R. T. (1934). Attitudes vs. actions. *Social Forces, 13,* 230–237.

LaRose, R., & Rifon, N. A. (2007). Promoting *i*-safety: Effects of privacy warnings and privacy seals on risk assessment and online privacy behavior. *The Journal of Consumer Affairs, 41*(1), 127–149.

Laskoff, M. B. (2004). *Landing on the right side of your ass: A survival guide for the recently unemployed.* New York, NY: Three Rivers Press.

Latané, B., & Nida, S. A. (1981). Ten years of research on group size and helping. *Psychological Bulletin, 89,* 308–324.

Lauer, J., & Lauer, R. (1985, June). Marriages made to last. *Psychology Today,* pp. 22–26.

Laumann, E. O., Gagnon, J. H., Michael, R. T., & Michaels, S. (1994). *The social organization of sexuality: Sexual practices in the United States.* Chicago: University of Chicago Press.

Laumann, E. O., Glasser, D. B., Neves, R. C. S., & Moreira, E. D. (2009). A population-based survey of sexual activity, sexual problems and associated help-seeking behavior patterns in mature adults in the United States of America. *International Journal of Impotence Research, 21,* 171–178.

Laurenceau, J., P. Barrett, L. F., & Rovine, M. J. (2005). The interpersonal process model of intimacy in marriage: A daily-diary and multilevel modeling approach. *Journal of Family Psychology, 19,* 314–323.

Laurenceau, J. P., & Kleinman, B. M. (2006). Intimacy in personal relationships. In A. L. Vangelisti & D. Perlman (Eds.), *The Cambridge handbook of personal relationships.* New York, NY: Cambridge University Press.

Lauriello, J., Bustillo, J. R., & Keith, S. J. (2005). Schizophrenia: Scope of the problem. In B. J. Sadock & V. A. Sadock (Eds.), *Kaplan & Sadock's comprehensive textbook of psychiatry.* Philadelphia, PA: Lippincott Williams & Wilkins.

Lautsch, B. A., Kossek, B. A., & Ernst, E. (2011). Managing a blended workforce: Telecommuters and non-telecommuters. *Organizational Dynamics, 40* (1), 10–17. doi: 10.1016/j.orgdyn.2010.10.005

Lavee, Y., & Ben-Ari, A. (2007). Relationship of dyadic closeness with work-related stress: A daily diary study. *Journal of Marriage and Family, 69,* 1021–1035.

Lazarus, A. A. (1989). Multimodal therapy. In R. J. Corsini & D. Wedding (Eds.), *Current psychotherapies.* Itasca, IL: F. E. Peacock.

Lazarus, A. A. (2008). Technical eclecticism and multimodal therapy. In J. L. Lebow (Ed.), *Twenty-first century psychotherapies: Contemporary approaches to theory and practice.* New York, NY: Wiley.

Lazarus, R. S. (1993). Why we should think of stress as a subset of emotion. In L. Goldberger & S. Breznitz (Eds.), *Handbook of stress: Theoretical and clinical aspects* (2nd ed.). New York, NY: Free Press.

Lazarus, R. S., & Folkman, S. (1984). *Stress, appraisal and coping.* New York, NY: Springer.

Le, B. (2009). Familiarity principle of attraction. In H. T. Reis & S. Sprecher (Eds.), *Encyclopedia of human relationships: Vol. 1* (pp. 596–597). Los Angeles, CA: Sage Reference Publication.

Leal, S., & Vrij, A. (2008). Blinking during and after lying. *Journal of Nonverbal Behavior, 32,* pp. 187–194.

Leaper, C. R., Breed, L., Hoffman, L., & Perlman, C. A. (2002). Variations in the gender-stereotyped content of children's television cartoons across genres. *Journal of Applied Social Psychology, 32,* 1653–1662.

Leavitt, F. (1995). *Drugs and behavior* (3rd ed.). Thousand Oaks, CA: Sage.

Lechner, S. C., Tennen, H., & Affleck G. (2009). Benefit-finding and growth. In S. J. Lopez & C. R. Snyder (Eds.), *Oxford handbook of positive psychology* (2nd ed., pp. 633–640). New York, NY: Oxford.

Ledbetter, A. M., Griffin, E., & Sparks, G. G. (2007). Forecasting "friends forever": A longitudinal investigation of sustained closeness between best friends. *Personal Relationships, 14,* 343–350.

Lee, I.-M., & Skerrett, P. J. (2001). Physical activity and all-cause mortality. What is the dose-response relation? *Medicine and Science in Sports and Exercise, 33,* S459–S471.

Lee, S., & Oyserman, D. (2009). Expecting to work, fearing homelessness: The possible selves of low-income mothers. *Journal of Applied Social Psychology, 39*(6), 1334–1355.

Lefcourt, H. M., Davidson, K., Shepherd, R., Phillips, M., Prkachin, K., & Mills, D. (1995). Perspective-taking humor: Accounting for stress moderation. *Journal of Social and Clinical Psychology, 14,* 373–391.

Legault, E., & Laurence, J.-R. (2007). Recovered memories of childhood sexual abuse: Social worker, psychologist, and psychiatrist reports of beliefs, practices, and cases. *Australian Journal of Clinical & Experimental Hypnosis, 35,* 111–133.

Leibel, R. L., Rosenbaum, M., & Hirsch, J. (1995). Changes in energy expenditure resulting from altered body weight. *New England Journal of Medicine, 332,* 621–629.

Leitenberg, H., Detzer, M. J., & Srebnik, D. (1993). Gender differences in masturbation and the relation of masturbation experience in preadolescence and/or early adolescence to sexual behavior and sexual adjustment in young adulthood. *Archives of Sexual Behavior, 22,* 87–98.

Leiter, M. P., & Maslach, C. (2001). Burnout and health. In A. Baum, T. A. Revenson, & J. E. Singer (Eds.), *Handbook of health psychology* (pp. 415–426). Mahwah, NJ: Erlbaum.

Lemieux, R., & Hale, J. L. (2002). Cross-sectional analysis of intimacy, passion, and commitment: Testing the assumptions of the triangular theory of love. *Psychological Reports, 90,* 1009–1014.

Lengua, L. J., Long, A. C., & Meltzoff, A. N. (2006). Pre-attack stress-load, appraisals, and coping in children's responses to the 9/11 terrorist attacks. *Journal of Child Psychology and Psychiatry, 47,* 1219–1227.

Lerner, M. J. (1980). *The belief in a just world: A fundamental decision.* New York, NY: Plenum.

Lett, H. S., Blumenthal, J. A., Babyak, M. A., Sherwood, A., Strauman, T., Robins, C., & Newman, M. F. (2004). Depression as a risk factor for coronary artery disease: Evidence, mechanisms, and treatment. *Psychosomatic Medicine, 66*(3), 305–315.

Levant, R. F. (2003, Fall). Why study boys and men? *Nova Southeastern University Center for Psychological Studies Newsletter,* pp. 12–13.

Levant, R. F., & Richmond, K. (2007). A review of research on masculinity ideologies using the Male Role Norms Inventory. *The Journal of Men's Studies, 15,* 130–146.

Levenstein, S. (2002). Psychosocial factors in peptic ulcer and inflammatory bowel disease. *Journal of Consulting & Clinical Psychology, 70*(3), 739–750.

Levine, R. V., Sato, S., Hashimoto, T., & Verma, J. (1995). Love and marriage in eleven cultures. *Journal of Cross-Cultural Psychology, 26*(5), 554–571.

Levinthal, C. F. (2008). *Drugs, behavior, and modern society.* Boston, MA: Pearson.

Lewin, K. (1935). *A dynamic theory of personality.* New York, NY: McGraw-Hill.

Lewis, K., Kaufman, J., & Christakis, N. (2008). The taste for privacy: An analysis of college student privacy settings in an online social network. *Journal of Computer-Mediated Communication, 14,* 79–100.

Lewis, S., Escalona, P. R., & Keith, S. J. (2009). Phenomenology of schizophrenia. In B. J. Sadock, V. A. Sadock, & P. Ruiz (Eds.), *Kaplan & Sadock's comprehensive textbook of psychiatry* (pp. 1433–1450). Philadelphia, PA: Lippincott Williams & Wilkins.

Li, S., & Li, Y-M. (2007). How far is enough? A measure of information privacy in terms of interpersonal distance. *Environment and Behavior, 39,* 317–331.

Lichter, D. T., Batson, C. D., & Brown, J. B. (2004). Welfare reform and marriage promotion: The marital expectations and desires of single and cohabiting mothers. *Social Service Review, 78*(1), 2–25.

Lichter, D. T., & Crowley, M. L. (2004). Welfare reform and child poverty: Effects of maternal employment, marriage, and cohabitation. *Social Science Research, 33,* 385–408.

Liewer, L., Mains, D., Lykens, K., & René, A. (2008). Barriers to women's cardiovascular risk knowledge. *Health Care for Women International, 29*(1), 23–38.

Lilienfeld, S. O., & Lynn, S. J. (2003). Dissociative identity disorder: Multiple personalities, multiple controversies. In S. O. Lilienfeld, S. Lynn, S. Jay, & J. M. Lohr (Eds.), *Science and pseudoscience in clinical psychology.* New York, NY: Guilford Press.

Lilienfeld, S. O., Lynn, S. J., Kirsch, I., Chaves, J. F., Sarbin, T. R., Ganaway, G. K., & Powell, R. A. (1999). Dissociative identity disorder and the sociocognitive model: Recalling the lessons of the past. *Psychological Bulletin, 125*(5), 507–523.

Lilienfeld, S. O., Wood, J. M., & Garb, H. N. (2000). The scientific status of projective tests. *Psychological Science in the Public Interest, 1*(2), 27–66.

Lin, Y., & Huang, C. (2006). The process of transforming daily social interactions to relationship intimacy: A longitudinal study. *Chinese Journal of Psychology, 48*(1), 35–52.

Lindau, S. T., Schumm, L. P., Laumann, E. O., Levinson, W., O'Muircheartaigh, C. A., & Waite, L. J. (2007). A study of sexuality and health among older adults in the United States. *The New England Journal of Medicine, 357,* 762–775.

Lindberg, S. M., Hyde, J., Petersen, J. L., & Linn, M. C. (2010). New trends in gender and mathematics performance: A meta-analysis. *Psychological Bulletin, 136*(6), 1123–1135. doi:10.1037/a0021276

Lindgren, H. C. (1969). *The psychology of college success: A dynamic approach.* New York, NY: Wiley.

Lippa, R. A. (2005). *Gender, nature, and nurture.* Mahwah, NJ: Erlbaum.

Lippa, R. A. (2007). The preferred traits of mates in a cross-national study of heterosexual and homosexual men and women: An examination of biological and cultural influences. *Archives of Sexual Behavior 36,* 193–208.

Littlefield, M. B. (2003). Gender role identity and stress in African American women. *Journal of Human Behavior in the Social Environment, 8*(4), 93–104.

Llorca, P. (2008). Monitoring patients to improve physical health and treatment outcome. *European Neuropsychopharmacology, 18,* S140–S145.

Lock, R. D. (2005a). *Taking charge of your career direction: Career planning guide, Book 1.* Belmont, CA: Wadsworth.

Lock, R. D. (2005b). *Job Search: Career Planning Guide, Book 2.* Belmont, CA: Wadsworth.

Loftus, E. F. (2003). Make believe memories. *American Psychologist, 58,* 864–873.

Loftus, E. F., & Davis, D. (2006). Recovered memories. *Annual Review of Clinical Psychology, 2,* 469–498.

Lohoff, F. W. & Berrettini, W. H. Genetics of mood disorders. In D. S. Charney & E. J. Nestler (Eds.), *Neurobiology of mental illness* (pp. 360–377). New York, NY: Oxford University Press.

Longman, D. G., & Atkinson, R. H. (2006). *Class: College learning and study skills.* Belmont, CA: Wadsworth.

Lonsdale, A. J., & North, A. C. (2009). Musical taste and ingroup favouritism. *Group Processes & Intergroup Relations, 12*(3), 319–327.

Lowinson, J. H., Ruiz, P., Millman, R. B., & Langrod, J. G. (2005). *Substance abuse: A comprehensive textbook.* Philadelphia, PA: Lippincott/Williams & Wilkins.

Lozano, B. E., Stephens, R. S., & Roffman, R. A. (2006). Abstinence and moderate use goals in the treatment of marijuana dependence. *Addiction, 101,* 1589–1597.

Luborsky, E. B., O'Reilly-Landry, M., & Arlow, J. A. (2011). Psychoanalysis. In R. J. Corsini & D. Wedding (Eds.), *Current psychotherapies* (9th ed.). Belmont, CA: Brooks/Cole.

Luborsky, L., Singer, B., & Luborsky, L. (1975). Comparative studies of psychotherapies: Is it true that everyone has won and all must have prizes? *Archives of General Psychiatry, 32,* 995–1008.

Lucas, A. R., Beard, C. M., O'Fallon, W. M., & Kurland, L. T. (1991). 50-year trends in the incidence of anorexia nervosa in Rochester, Minn.: A population-based study. *American Journal of Psychiatry, 148,* 917–922.

Lucas, J. W., & Lovaglia, M. J. (2005). Self-handicapping: Gender, race, and status. *Current Research in Social Psychology, 10*(16), [electronic journal].

Lucas, R. E. (2007). Adaptation and the set-point model of subjective well-being: Does happiness change after major life events? *Current Directions in Psychological Science, 16,* 75–79.

Lucas, R. E. (2008). Personality and subjective well-being. In M. Eid & R. J. Larsen (Eds.), *The science of subjective well-being* (pp. 171–194). New York, NY: Guilford.

Lucas, R. E., Clark, A. E., Georgellis, Y., & Diener, E. (2004). Unemployment alters the set point for life satisfaction. *Psychological Science, 15*(1), 8–13.

Lucas, R. E., & Diener, E. (2008). Personality and subjective well-being. In O. P. John, R. W. Robins, & L. A. Pervin (Eds.), *Handbook of personality: Theory and research* (pp. 795–814). New York, NY: Guilford.

Lulofs, R. S. (1994). *Conflict: From theory to action.* Scottsdale, AZ: Gorsuch Scarisbuck Publishers.

Lulofs, R. S., & Cahn, D. D. (2000). *Conflict: From theory to action* (2nd ed.). Boston, MA: Allyn & Bacon.

Lund, O. C. H., Tamnes, C. K., Moestue, C., Buss, D. M., & Vollrath, M. (2007). Tactics of hierarchy negotiation. *Journal of Research in Personality, 41,* 25–44.

Lundberg-Love, P. K., & Wilkerson, D. K. (2006). Battered women. In P. K. Lundberg-Love & S. L. Marmion (Eds.), *"Intimate" violence against women: When spouses, partners, or lovers attack.* Westport, CT: Praeger.

Luo, S., & Klohnen, E. C. (2005). Assortative mating and marital quality in newlyweds: A couple-centered approach. *Journal of Personality and Social Psychology, 88,* 304–326.

Lurie, P., Almeida, C. M., Stine, N., Stine, A. R., & Wolfe, S. M. (2006). Financial conflict of interest disclosure and voting patterns at food and drug administration drug advisory committee meetings. *JAMA, 295,* 1921–1928.

Lutz, C. J., & Ross, S. R. (2003). Elaboration versus fragmentation: Distinguishing between self-complexity and self-concept differentiation. *Journal of Social and Clinical Psychology, 22(5),* 537–559.

Lyness, K. S., & Heilman, M. E. (2006). When fit is fundamental: Performance evaluations and promotions of upper-level female and male managers. *Journal of Applied Psychology, 91,* 777–785.

Lytton, H., & Romney, D. M. (1991). Parents' differential socialization of boys and girls: A meta-analysis. *Psychological Bulletin, 109,* 267–296.

Lyubomirsky, S., Sheldon, K. M., & Schkade, D. (2005). Pursuing happiness: The architecture of sustainable change. *Review of General Psychology,* 9(2), 111–131.

Maatta, S., Nurmi, J., & Stattin, H. (2007). Achievement orientations, school adjustment, and well-being: A longitudinal study. *Journal of Research on Adolescence, 17,* 789–812.

Maccoby, E. E. (1990). Gender and relationships: A developmental account. *American Psychologist, 45,* 513–520.

Maccoby, E. E. (2002). Gender and group processes: A developmental perspective. *Current Direction in Psychological Science, 11*(2), 54–58.

Maccoby, E. E., & Martin, J. A. (1983). Socialization in the context of the family: Parent-child interaction. In P. H. Mussen (Series Ed.) & E. M. Hetherington (Vol. Ed.), *Handbook of child psychology: Vol. 4. Socialization, personality, and social development.* New York, NY: Wiley.

MacGeorge, E. L., Graves, A. R., Feng, B., Gillihan, S. J., & Burleson, B. R. (2004). The myth of gender cultures: Similarities outweigh differences in men's and women's provision of and responses to supportive communication. *Sex Roles, 50*(3/4), 143–175.

Mack, A. H., Franklin Jr., J. E., & Frances, R. J. (2003). Substance use disorders. In R. E. Hales & S. C. Yudofsky (Eds.), *Textbook of clinical psychiatry.* Washington, DC: American Psychiatric Publishing.

Mackenzie, R. A. (1997). *The time trap.* New York, NY: AMACOM.

Mackie, D. M., Worth, L. T., & Asuncion, A. G. (1990). Processing of persuasive in-group messages. *Journal of Personality and Social Psychology, 58,* 812–822.

MacMillian, H. L., Fleming, J. E., Trocme, N., Boyle, M. H., Wong, M., Racine, Y. A., Beardslee, W. R., & Offord, D. R. (1997). Prevalence of child physical and sexual abuse in the community: Results from the Ontario health supplement. *Journal of the American Medical Association, 278,* 131–135.

Madathil, J., & Benshoff, J. M. (2008). Importance of marital characteristics and marital satisfaction: A comparison of Asian Indians in arranged marriages and Americans in marriages of choice. *The Family Journal, 16,* 222–230.

Maddi, S. R. (2007). The story of hardiness: Twenty years of theorizing, research, and practice. In A. Monat, R. S. Lazarus, & G. Reevy (Eds.), *The Praeger handbook on stress and coping* (pp. 327–340). Westport, CT: Praeger Publishers.

Maddux, J. E., & Gosselin, J. T. (2003). Self-efficacy. In M. R. Leary & J. P. Tangney (Eds.), *Handbook of self and identity.* New York, NY: Guilford.

Madey, S. F., & Rodgers L. (2009). The effect of attachment and Sternberg's triangular theory of love on relationship satisfaction. *Individual Differences Research, 7,* 76–84.

Madon, S., Willard, J., Guyll, M., & Scherr, K. C. (2011). Self-fulfilling prophecies: Mechanisms, power, and links to social problems. *Social and Personality Psychology Compass, 5*(8), 578–590. doi: 10.1111/j.1751-9004.2011.00375.x

Mahoney, M. J. (1979). *Self-change: Strategies for solving personal problems.* New York, NY: Norton.

Maisel, N. C., Gable, S. L., & Strachman, A. (2008). Responsive behaviors in good times and in bad. *Personal Relationships, 15,* 317–338.

Major, B., Schmidlin, A. M., & Williams, L. (1990). Gender patterns in social touch: The impact of setting and age. *Journal of Personality and Social Psychology, 58,* 634–643.

Major, D. A., & Morganson, V. J. (2011). Applying industrial-organizational psychology to help organizations and individuals balance work and family life. *Industrial and Organizational Psychology: Science and Practice, 4* (3), 398–401. doi: 10.1111/j.1754-9434.2011.01360.x

Maldonado, J. R. & Spiegel, D. (2008). Dissociative disorders. In R. E. Hales, S. C. Yudofsky, & G. O. Gabbard (Eds.), *The American psychiatric publishing textbook of psychiatry* (pp. 665–710). Washington, DC: American Psychiatric Publishing.

Mandler, G. (1993). Thought, memory, and learning: Effects of emotional stress. In L. Goldberger & S. Breznitz (Eds.), *Handbook of stress: Theoretical and clinical aspects* (2nd ed.). New York, NY: Free Press.

Manning, W. D. (2004). Children and the stability of cohabiting couples. *Journal of Mariage and Family, 66,* 674–689.

Manning, W. D., Longmore, M. A., & Giordano, P. C. (2007). The changing institution of marriage: Adolescents' expectations to cohabit and to marry. *Journal of Marriage and Family, 69,* 559–575.

Marcenes, W. G., & Sheiham, A. (1992). The relationship between work stress and oral health status. *Social Science and Medicine, 35,* 1511.

Maricchiolo, F., Gnisci, A., Bonaiuto, M., & Ficca, G. (2009). Effects of different types of hand gestures in persuasive speech on receivers' evaluations. *Language and Cognitive Processes, 24*(2), 239–266.

Marker, N. F. (1996). Flying solo at midlife: Gender, marital status, and psychological well-being. *Journal of Marriage and the Family, 58,* 917–932.

Marsh, P. (Ed.). (1988). *Eye to eye: How people interact.* Topsfield, MA: Salem House.

Marshall, T. C. (2010). Gender, peer relations, and intimate romantic relationships. In J. C. Chrisler & D. R. McCreary (Eds.). *Handbook of gender research in psychology* (Vol 2, pp. 281–310). New York, NY: Springer.

Martin, L. R., Friedman, H. S., & Schwartz, J. E. (2007). Personality and mortality risk across the life span: The importance of conscientiousness as a biopsychosocial attribute. *Health Psychology, 26,* 428–436.

Martin, L. R., Haskard-Zolnierek, K. B., & DiMatteo, M. R. (2010). *Health behavior change and treatment adherence: Evidence-based guidelines for improving healthcare.* New York, NY: Oxford University Press.

Martin, R., Rothrock, N., Leventhal, H., & Leventhal, E. (2003). Common sense models of illness: Implications for symptom perception and health-related behaviors. In J. Suls & K. A. Wallston (Eds.), *Social psychological foundations of health and illness.* Malden, MA: Blackwell Publishing.

Martin, R. A., & Lefcourt, H. M. (1983). Sense of humor as a moderator of the relation between stressors and moods. *Journal of Personality and Social Psychology, 45,* 1313–1324.

Martin, T. C., & Bumpass, L. L. (1989). Recent trends in marital disruption. *Demography, 26,* 37–51.

Martinez, E. (2009, October 27). James Ray gives "laughable" 50 percent refund to Sweat Lodge victim's family. *CBS News*, Retrieved from http://www.cbsnews.com/blogs/2009/08/28/crimesider/entry5271390.shtml

Martinez, M., Marangell, L. B., & Martinez, J. M. (2008). Psychopharmacology. In R. E. Hales, S. C. Yudofsky, & G. O. Gabbard (Eds.), *The American psychiatric publishing textbook of psychiatry* (pp. 1053–1132). Washington, DC: American Psychiatric Publishing, Inc.

Martins, Y., Tiggemann, M., & Kirkbride, A. (2007). Those speedos become them: The role of self-objectification in gay and heterosexual men's body image. *Personality and Social Psychology Bulletin, 33*, 634–647.

Maslach, C. (2005). Understanding burnout: Work and family issues. In D. F. Halpern & S. E. Murphy (Eds.), *From work-family balance to work-family interaction: Changing the metaphor*. Mahwah, NJ: Erlbaum.

Maslach, C., & Leiter, M. P. (2007). *Burnout*. In G. Fink (Ed.), *Encyclopedia of stress: Vols. 1–4* (2nd ed., pp. 368–371). San Diego, CA: Elsevier Academic Press.

Maslow, A. H. (1968). *Toward a psychology of being*. New York, NY: Van Nostrand.

Maslow, A. H. (1970). *Motivation and personality*. New York, NY: Harper & Row.

Masters, W. H., & Johnson, V. E. (1966). *Human sexual response*. Boston, MA: Little, Brown.

Masters, W. H., & Johnson, V. E. (1970). *Human sexual inadequacy*. Boston, MA: Little, Brown.

Mathew, S. J., Hoffman, E. J., Charney, D. S. (2009). Pharmacotherapy of anxiety disorders. In D. S. Charney & E. J. Nestler (Eds.), *Neurobiology of mental illness* (p. 731). New York, NY: Guilford.

Matsumoto, D. (2006). Culture and nonverbal behavior. In V. Manusov & M. L. Patterson (Ed.), *The Sage handbook of nonverbal communication* (pp. 219–235). Thousand Oaks, CA: Sage.

Matsumoto, D., & Willingham, B. (2009). Spontaneous facial expressions of emotion of congenitally and noncongenitally blind individuals. *Journal of Personality and Social Psychology, 96*(1), 1–10.

Mattar, C., Harharahm, L., Su, L., Agarwal, A., Wong, P., & Choolani, M. (2008). Menopause, hormone therapy and cardiovascular and cerebrovascular disease. *Annals of the Academy of Medicine Singapore, 37*(1), 54–62.

Matthews, G., Emo, A. K., Funke, G., Zeidner, M., Roberts, R. D., Costa Jr., P. T., & Schulze, R. (2006). Emotional intelligence, personality, and task-induced stress. *Journal of Experimental Psychology: Applied, 12*, 96–107.

Mayo Clinic. (2008). *Erectile dysfunction*. Retrieved from http:/www.mayoclinic.com/health/erectile-dysfunction/DS00162

Mazzuca, J. (2003, March 25). *Open dialogue: Parents talk to teens about sex*. Retrieved from http://www.Gallup.Com/Poll/Content/?Ci=8047.

McCabe, R. E., & Antony, M. M. (2008). Anxiety disorders: Social and specific phobias. In A. Tasman, J. Kay, J. A. Lieberman, M. B. First, & M. Maj (Eds.), *Psychiatry* (3rd ed.). New York, NY: Wiley-Blackwell.

McCave, E. L. (2007). Comprehensive sexuality education vs. abstinence-only sexuality education: The need for evidence-based research and practice. *School Social Work Journal, 32*, 14–28.

McClernon, F. J., & Gilbert, D. G. (2007). Smoking and stress. In G. Fink (Ed.), *Encyclopedia of stress: Vols. 1–4* (2nd ed., pp. 515–520). San Diego, CA: Elsevier Academic Press.

McCrae, R. R. (1984). Situational determinants of coping responses: Loss, threat and challenge. *Journal of Personality and Social Psychology, 46*, 919–928.

McCrae, R. R., & Costa, P. T., Jr. (1987). Validation of the five-factor model of personality across instruments and observers. *Journal of Personality and Social Psychology, 52*, 81–90.

McCrae, R. R., & Costa, P. T., Jr. (1997). Personality trait structure as a human universal. *American Psychologist, 52*, 509–516.

McCrae, R. R., & Costa, P. T., Jr. (2003). *Personality in adulthood: A five-factor theory perspective*. New York, NY: Guilford.

McCrae, R. R., & Costa, P. T., Jr. (2008a). Empirical and theoretical status of the five-factor model of personality traits. In G. J. Boyle, G. Matthews, D. H. Saklofske (Eds.), *The Sage handbook of personality theory and assessment* (pp. 273–294). Los Angeles, CA: Sage.

McCrae, R. R., & Costa, P. T., Jr. (2008b). The five-factor theory of personality. In O. P. John, R. W. Robins, & L. A. Pervin (Eds.), *Handbook of personality: Theory and research* (pp. 159–181). New York, NY: Guilford.

McCrae, R. R., & Sutin, A. R. (2009). Openness to experience. In M. R. Leary & R. H. Hoyle (Eds.), *Handbook of individual differences in social* behavior (pp. 257–274). New York, NY: Guilford.

McCrae, R. R., & Terracciano, A. (2006). National character and personality. *Current Direction in Psychological Science, 15*(4), 156–161.

McCrae, R. R., Terracciano, A., & 78 members of the Personality Profiles of Cultures Project. (2005). Universal features of personality traits from the observer's perspective: Data from 50 cultures. *Journal of Personality and Social Psychology, 88*, 547–561.

McCrea, S. M., Hirt, E. R., Hendrix, K. L., Milner, B. J., Steele, N. L.(2008). The worker scale: Developing a measure to explain gender differences in behavioral self-handicapping. *Journal of Research in Personality, 42*(4), 949–970.

McCullough, M. E. (2001). Forgiving. In C. R. Snyder (Ed.), *Coping with stress: Effective people and processes*. New York, NY: Oxford University Press.

McCullough, M. E., & Witvliet, C. V. (2005). The psychology of forgiveness. In C. R. Snyder & S. J. Lopez (Eds.), *Handbook of positive psychology*. New York, NY: Oxford University Press.

McDonald, W. M., Thompson, T. R., McCall W. V., & Zormuski, C. F. (2004). In A. F. Schatzberg, & C. B. Nemeroff (Eds.), *Textbook of psychopharmacology*. Washington, DC: American Psychiatric Publishing.

McDougle, L. G. (1987). Time management: Making every minute count. In A. D. Timpe (Ed.), *The management of time*. New York, NY: Facts on File.

McElwee, R. O., & Haugh, J. A. (2010). Thinking clearly versus frequently about the future self: Exploring this distinction and its relation to possible selves. *Self and Identity, 9*(3), 298–321. doi: 10.1080/15298860903054290

McGlashan, T. H., & Hoffman, R. E. (2000). Schizophrenia: Psychodynamic to neurodynamic theories. In B. J. Sadock & V. A. Sadock (Eds.), *Kaplan and Sadock's comprehensive textbook of psychiatry* (7th ed., Vol. 1). Philadelphia, PA: Lippincott/Williams & Wilkins.

McGrath, J., Welham, J., Scott, J., Varghese, D., Degenhardt, L., Hayatbakhsh, M., et al. (2010). Association between cannabis use and psychosis-related outcomes using sibling pair analysis in a cohort of young adults. *Archives of General Psychiatry, 67*(5), 440–447. doi:10.1001/archgenpsychiatry.2010.6

McHugh, M. C., & Hambaugh, J. (2010.) She said, he said: Gender, language and power. In J. C. Chrisler & D. R. McCreary (Eds.). *Handbook of gender research in psychology* (Vol. 2, pp. 379–410). New York, NY: Springer.

McHugh, P. R., Lief, H. I., Freyd, P. P., & Fetkewicz, J. M. (2004). From refusal to reconciliation: Family relationships after an accusation based on recovered memories. *Journal of Nervous and Mental Disease, 192*, 525–531.

McKay, M., Davis, M., & Fanning, P. (1995). *Messages: The communication skills book*. Oakland, CA: New Harbinger.

McKay, M., & Fanning, P. (2000). *Self-esteem* (3rd ed.). Oakland, CA: New Harbinger.

McKenna, K. Y. A., Green, A., & Gleason, M. (2002). Relationship formation on the Internet: What's the big attraction? *Journal of Social Issues, 58*, 9–31.

McManus, P. A., & DiPrete, T. (2001). Losers and winners: Financial consequences of separation and divorce for men. *American Sociological Review, 66*, 246–268.

McNally, R. J. (2007). Betrayal trauma theory: A critical appraisal. *Memory, 15*, 280–294.

McNally, R. J., & Geraerts, E. (2009). A new solution to the recovered memory debate. *Perspectives on Psychological Science, 4*(2), 126–134.

McNulty, J. K. (2011). The dark side of forgiveness: The tendency to forgive predicts continued psychological and physical aggression in marriage. *Personality and Social Psychology Bulletin, 37*(6), 770–783. doi:10.1177/0146167211407077

McPherson, M., Smith-Lovin, L., & Brashears, M. E. (2006). Social isolation in America: Changes in core discussion networks over two decades. *American Sociological Review, 71,* 353–375.

McPherson, Smith-Lovin, L., and Cook, J. M. (2001). Birds of a feather: Homophily in social networks. *Annual Review of Sociology, 27,* 415–444.

McWhirter, B. T. (1990). Loneliness: A review of current literature, with implications for counseling and research. *Journal of Counseling and Development, 68,* 417–422.

McWhorter, K. T. (2007). *College reading & study skills.* New York, NY: Pearson Longman.

Mead, M. (1950). *Sex and temperament in three primitive societies.* New York, NY: Mentor Books.

Meece, J. L., & Scantlebury, K. (2006). Gender and schooling: Progress and persistent barriers. In J. Worrell & C. D. Goodheart (Eds.), *Handbook of girls' and women's psychological health.* New York, NY: Oxford University Press.

Mehl, M. R., Vazire, S., Holleran, S. E., & Clark, C. (2010). Eavesdropping on happiness: Well-being is related to having less small talk and more substantive conversations. *Psychological Science, 21*(4), 539–541.

Meichenbaum, D. (1993). Stress inoculation training: A 20-year update. In P. M. Lehrer & R. L. Woolfolk (Eds.), *Principles and practice of stress management* (2nd ed.). New York, NY: Guilford Press.

Meltzer, H. Y., & Bobo, W. V. (2009). Antipsychotic and anticholinergic drugs. In M. C. Gelder, N. C. Andreasen, J. J. López-Ibor, Jr., & J. R. Geddes (Eds.), *New Oxford textbook of psychiatry* (2nd ed., Vol. 1). New York, NY: Oxford University Press.

Merikangas, K. R., & Kalaydjian, A. E. (2009). Epidemiology of anxiety disorders. In B. J. Sadock, V. A. Sadock, & P. Ruiz (Eds.), *Kaplan & Sadock's comprehensive textbook of psychiatry* (pp. 1856–1863). Philadelphia, PA: Lippincott Williams & Wilkins.

Merikangas, K. R., & Pato, M. (2009). Recent developments in the epidemiology of bipolar disorder in adults and children: Magnitude, correlates, and future directions. *Clinical Psychology: Science and Practice, 16*(2), 121–133. doi:10.1111/j.1468-2850.2009.01152.x

Merton, R. (1948). The self-fulfilling prophecy. *Antioch Review, 8,* 193–210.

Meston, C. M., & Buss, D. (2007). Why humans have sex. *Archives of Sexual Behavior, 36,* 477–507.

Mickelson, K. D., Kessler, R. C., & Shaver, P. R. (1997). Adult attachment in a nationally representative sample. *Journal of Personality and Social Psychology, 73,* 1092–1106.

Mikulincer, M. (2006). Attachment, caregiving, and sex within romantic relationships: A behavioral systems perspective. In M. Mikulincer & G. S. Goodman (Eds.), *Dynamics of romantic love: Attachment, caregiving, and sex.* New York, NY: The Guilford Press.

Mikulincer, M., & Shaver, P. R. (2003). The attachment behavioral system in adulthood: Activation, psychodynamics, and interpersonal processes. In Mark P. Zanna (Ed.), *Advances in Experimental Social Psychology* (Vol. 35). San Diego, CA: Academic Press.

Milgram, S. (1963). Behavioral study of obedience. *Journal of Abnormal and Social Psychology, 67,* 371–378.

Milgram, S. (1974). *Obedience to authority.* New York, NY: Harper & Row.

Miller Burke, J., & Attridge, M. (2011). Pathways to career and leadership success: Part 1—A psychosocial profile of $100k professionals. *Journal of Workplace Behavioral Health,* 26(3), 175–206. doi:10.1080/15555240.2011.589718

Miller, G. P. (1978). *Life choices: How to make the critical decisions—about your education, career, marriage, family, life style.* New York, NY: Thomas Y. Crowell.

Miller, L. C., Berg, J. H., & Archer, R. L. (1983). Openers: Individuals who elicit intimate self-disclosure. *Journal of Personality and Social Psychology, 44,* 1234–1244.

Miller, T. (2000). Diagnostic evaluation of erectile dysfunction. *American Family Physician, 61,* 95–104.

Mineka, S., & Öhman, A. (2002). Phobias and preparedness: The selective, automatic and encapsulated nature of fear. *Biological Psychiatry, 52,* 927–937.

Mineka, S., & Zinbarg, S. (2006). A contemporary learning theory perspective on the etiology of anxiety disorders: It's not what you thought it was. *American Psychologist, 61,* 10–26.

Mino, I., Profit, W. E., & Pierce, C. M. (2000). Minorities and stress. In G. Fink (Ed.), *Encyclopedia of stress* (Vol. 1). San Diego, CA: Academic Press.

Minzenberg, M. J., Yoon, J. H., & Carter, C. S. (2008). Schizophrenia. In R. E. Hales, S. C. Yudofsky, & G. O. Gabbard (Eds.), *The American psychiatric publishing textbook of psychiatry* (pp. 407-456). Washington, DC: American Psychiatric Publishing.

Mischel, W. (1990). Personality dispositions revisited and revised: A view after three decades. In L. A. Pervin (Ed.), *Handbook of personality: Theory and research.* New York, NY: Guilford Press.

Mischel, W., & Morf, C. C. (2003). The self as a psycho-social dynamic processing system: A meta-perspective on a century of the self in psychology. In M. R. Leary & J. P. Tangney (Eds.), *Handbook of self and identity.* New York, NY: Guilford.

Misra, R., & Castillo, L. G. (2001). Academic stress among college students: Comparison of American and international students. *International Journal of Stress Management, 11*(2), 132–148.

Mitchell, V. F. (1987). Rx for improving staff effectiveness. In A. D. Timpe (Ed.), *The management of time.* New York, NY: Facts on File.

Modestin, J. (1992). Multiple personality disorder in Switzerland. *American Journal of Psychiatry, 149,* 88–92.

Mojtabai, R., & Olfson, M. (2008). National trends in psychotherapy by office-based psychiatrists. *Archives of General Psychiatry, 65,* 962–970.

Mojtabai, R., Olfson, M., & Mechanic, D. (2002). Perceived need and help-seeking in adults with mood, anxiety, or substance use disorder. *Archives of General Psychiatry, 59,* 77–84.

Mokdad, A. H., Marks, J. S., Stroup, D. F., & Gerberding, J. L. (2004). Actual causes of death in the United States, 2000. *Journal of the American Medical Association, 291,* 1238–1245.

Monastra, V. J. (2008). Social skills training for children and teens with ADHD: The neuroeducational life skills program. In V. J. Monastra (Ed.), *Unlocking the potential of patients with ADHD: A model for clinical practice.* Washington, DC: American Psychological Association.

Monroe, S. M., & McQuaid, J. R. (1994). Measuring life stress and assessing its impact on mental health. In W. R. Avison & I. H. Gotlib (Eds.), *Stress and mental health: Contemporary issues and prospects for the future.* New York, NY: Plenum.

Monroe, S. M., Slavich, G. M., & Georgiades, K. (2009).The social environment and life stress in depression. In I. H. Gotlib & C. L. Hammen (Eds.), *Handbook of depression* (pp. 340–360). New York, NY: Guilford.

Moore, D. S., & Johnson, S. P. (2008). Mental rotation in human infants. *Psychological Science, 19,* 1063–1066.

Moore, D. W. (2001, August 31). Most American workers satisfied with their job: One-third would be happier in another job. [On-line]. The Gallup Organization. Retrieved from www.gallup.com/poll/releases/pr010831.asp

Moos, R. H., & Billings, A. G. (1982). Conceptualizing and measuring coping resources and processes. In L. Goldberger & S. Breznitz (Eds.), *Handbook of stress: Theoretical and clinical aspects.* New York, NY: Free Press.

Morahan-Martin, J., & Schumacher, P. (2003). Loneliness and social uses of the Internet. *Computers in Human Behavior, 19*(6), 659–671.

Morgan, R. D., & Cohen, L. M. (2008). Clinical and counseling psychology: Can differences be gleaned from printed recruiting materials? *Training and Education in Professional Psychology, 2*(3), 156–164.

Morgenstern, J. (2000). *Time management from the inside out.* New York, NY: Holt.

Morris, W. L., & DePaulo, B. M. (2009). Singlehood. In H. T. Reis & S. Sprecher (Eds.), *Encyclopedia of human relationships: Vol. 3* (pp. 1504–1507). Los Angeles, CA: Sage Reference Publication.

Morry, M. M. (2009). Similarity principle of attraction. In H. T. Reis & S. Sprecher (Eds.), *Encyclopedia of human relationships: Vol. 3* (pp. 1500–1504). Los Angeles, CA: Sage Reference Publication.

Mortenson, S. T. (2006). Cultural differences and similarities in seeking support as a response to academic failure: A comparison of American and Chinese college students. *Communication Education, 55*(2), 127–146.

Moseman, S. E., Freeman, M. P., Misiaszek, J., & Gelenberg, A. J. (2003). Mood stabilizers. In A. Tasman, J. Kay, & J. A. Lieberman (Eds.), *Psychiatry.* New York, NY: Wiley.

Mosher, W. D., Chandra, A., & Jones, J. (2005). *Sexual behavior and selected health measures: Men and women 15–44 years of age, United States, 2002.* Hyattsville, MD: National Center for Health Statistics.

Mowrer, O. H. (1947). On the dual nature of learning: A reinterpretaton of "conditioning" and "problem-solving." *Harvard Educational Review, 17,* 102–150.

Muehlenhard, C. L., & McCoy, M. L. (1991). Double standard/double bind: The sexual double standard and women's communication about sex. *Psychology of Women Quarterly, 15,* 447–461.

Mulhall, J., King, R., Glina, S., & Hvidsten, K. (2008). Importance of and satisfaction with sex among men and women worldwide: Results of the Global Better Sex Survey. *Journal of Sexual Medicine, 5,* 788–795.

Munck, A. (2000). Corticosteroids and stress. In G. Fink (Ed.), *Encyclopedia of stress* (Vol. 1). San Diego, CA: Academic Press.

Murray, R. M., & Bramon, E. (2005). Developmental model of schizophrenia. In B. J. Sadock & V. A. Sadock (Eds.), *Kaplan & Sadock's comprehensive textbook of psychiatry.* Philadelphia, PA: Lippincott Williams & Wilkins.

Murray, S. L., Holmes, J. G., & Griffin, D. W. (1996). The self-fulfilling nature of positive illusions in romantic relationships: Love is not blind, but prescient. *Journal of Personality and Social Psychology, 71,* 1155–1180.

Murrell, A. J., & James, E. H. (2001). Gender and diversity in organizations: Past, present, and future directions. *Sex Roles, 45*(5/6), 243–257.

Murrell, A. J., Dietz-Uhler, B. L., Dovidio, J. F., Gaertner, S. L., & Drout, E. (1994). Aversive racism and resistance to affirmative action: Perceptions of justice are not necessarily color blind. *Basic and Applied Social Psychology, 17*(1–2), 71–86.

Myers, D. G. (1980). *Inflated self: Human illusions and the biblical call to hope.* New York, NY: Seabury Press.

Myers, D. G. (1992). *The pursuit of happiness: Who is happy—and why.* New York, NY: Morrow.

Myers, D. G. (2008). Religion and human flourishing. In M. Eid & R. J. Larsen (Eds.), *The science of subjective well-being* (pp. 323–346). New York, NY: Guilford.

Myers, D. G., & Diener, E. (1997). The pursuit of happiness. *Scientific American, Special Issue 7,* 40–43.

Nadelson, C. C., Notman, M. T., & McCarthy, M. K. (2005). Gender issues in psychotherapy. In G. O. Gabbard, J. S. Beck, & J. Holmes (Eds.), *Oxford textbook of psychotherapy.* New York, NY: Oxford University Press.

National Association of Women Business Owners. (2010). New census data reinforces the economic power of women owned businesses in the U.S. says NAWBO. Retrieved from http://http://nawbo.org/content_11800.cfm

National Institute of Justice & Centers for Disease Control & Prevention. (1998). *Prevalence, incidence and consequences of violence against women survey.*

Nelson, E. L., Wenzel, L., Osann, K., Dogan-Ates, A., Chantana, N., Reina-Patton, A., et al. (2008). Stress, immunity, and cervical cancer: biobehavioral outcomes of a randomized clinical trial. *Clinical Cancer Research, 14,* 2111–2118.

Nemeroff, C. B., Kalali, A., Keller, M. B., Charney, D. S., Lenderts, S. E., Cascade, E. F., et al. (2007). Impact of publicity concerning pediatric suicidality data on physician practice patterns in the United States. *Archives of General Psychiatry, 64,* 466–472.

Newcombe, N. S. (2007). Taking science seriously: Straight thinking about spatial sex differences. In S. J. Ceci & W. M. Williams (Eds.), *Why aren't more women in science?* (pp. 69–78). Washington, DC: American Psychological Association.

Newman, C. F. & Beck, A. T. (2009). Cognitive therapy. In B. J. Sadock, V. A. Sadock, & P. Ruiz (Eds.), *Kaplan & Sadock's comprehensive textbook of psychiatry* (pp. 2857–2872). Philadelphia, PA: Lippincott Williams & Wilkins.

Nezu, A. M., Nezu, C. M., Felgoise, S. H., & Zwick, M. L. (2003). Psychosocial oncology. In A. M. Nezu, C. M. Nezu, & P. A. Geller (Eds.), *Handbook of psychology: Vol. 9. Health psychology.* New York, NY: Wiley.

Niaura, R., & Abrams, D. B. (2002). Smoking cessation: Progress, priorities, and prospectus. *Journal of Consulting & Clinical Psychology, 70*(3), 494–509.

NICHD Early Child Care Research Network. (1997). The effects of infant child care on infant-mother attachment security: Results of the NICHD Study of Early Child Care. *Child Development, 68,* 860–879.

Nicholson, C. (2006). Freedom and choice, culture, and class. *APS Observer, 19*(8), 31, 45.

Nickerson, C., Schwarz, N., Diener, E., & Kahneman, D. (2003). Zeroing in on the dark side of the American dream: A closer look at the negative consequences of the goal for financial success. *Psychological Science, 14*(6), 531–536.

Nicol, S. E. & Gottesman, I. I. (1983). Clues to the genetics and neurobiology of schizophrenia. *American Scientist, 71,* 398–404.

Niederhoffer, K. G., & Pennebaker, J. W. (2005). Sharing one's story: On the benefits of writing or talking about emotional experience. In C. R. Snyder & S. J. Lopez (Eds.), *Handbook of positive psychology.* New York, NY: Oxford University Press.

Niemann, Y. F., Jennings, L., Rozelle, R. M., Baxter, J. C., & Sullivan, E. (1994). Use of free responses and cluster analysis to determine stereotypes of eight groups. *Personality and Social Psychology Bulletin, 20,* 379–390.

Nobler, M. S., & Sackeim, H. A. (2006). Electroconvulsive therapy and transcranial magnetic stimulation. In D. J. Stein, D. J. Kupfer, & A. F. Schatzberg (Eds.), *Textbook of mood disorders.* Washington, DC: American Psychiatric Publishing.

Nock, S. L. (1995). A comparison of marriages and cohabitating relationships. *Journal of Family Issues, 13,* 53–76.

Nolen-Hoeksema, S. (2000). The role of rumination in depressive disorders and mixed anxiety/depressive symptoms. *Journal of Abnormal Psychology, 109*(3), 504–511.

Nolen-Hoeksema, S. (2001). Gender differences in depression. *Current Directions in Psychological Science, 10,*173–176.

Nolen-Hoeksema, S., & Hilt, L. M. (2009). Gender differences in depression. In I. H. Gotlib & C. L. Hammen (Eds.), *Handbook of depression* (pp. 386–404). New York, NY: Guilford.

Nolen-Hoeksema, S., Wisco, B. E., & Lybomirsky, S. (2008). Rethinking rumination. *Perspectives on Psychological Science, 3,* 400–424.

Noller, P. (1987). Nonverbal communication in marriage. In D. Perlman & S. Duck (Eds.), *Intimate relationships: Development, dynamics, and deterioration.* Newbury Park, CA: Sage.

Nomaguchi, K. M. (2006). Maternal employment, nonparental care, mother-child interactions and child outcomes during preschool years. *Journal of Marriage and Family, 68,* 1341–1369.

Norcross, J. C., Hedges, M., & Castle, P. H. (2002). Psychologists conducting psychotherapy in 2001: A study of the Division 29 membership. *Psychotherapy: Theory, Research, Practice, Training, 39*, 97–102.

Norem, J. K. (1989). Cognitive strategies as personality: Effectiveness, specificity, flexibility, and chance. In D. M. Buss & N. Cantor (Eds.), *Personality psychology: Recent trends and emerging directions.* New York : Springer-Verlag.

North, R. J., & Swann, W. B. Jr. (2009a). Self-verification 360°: Illuminating the light and dark sides. *Self and Identity, 8*(2–3), 131–146.

North, R. J., & Swann, W. B. Jr. (2009b). What's positive about self-verification? In S. J. Lopez & C. R. Snyder (Eds.), *Oxford handbook of positive psychology* (2nd ed., pp. 464–474). New York, NY: Oxford University Press.

Norton, S. (2002). Women exposed: Sexual harrassment and female vulnerability. In L. Diamant & J. Lee (Eds.), *The psychology of sex, gender, and jobs.* Westport, CT: Praeger.

Oakes, P. (2001). The root of all evil in intergroup relations? Unearthing the categorization process. In R. Brown & S. L. Gaertner (Eds.), *Blackwell handbook of social psychology: Intergroup processes.* London, England: Blackwell.

Ocon, R. (2006). *Issues on gender and diversity in management.* Lanham, MD: University Press of America.

Oesterman, K., Bjoerkqvist, K., Lagerspetz, K. M. J., Kaukiainen, A., Landau, S. F., Fraczek, A., & Caprara, G. V. (1998). Cross-cultural evidence of female indirect aggression. *Aggressive Behavior, 24*(1), 1–80.

Ogden, C. L., Carroll, M. D., & Flegal, K. M. (2008). High body mass index for age among US children and adolescents, 2003–2006. *Journal of the American Medical Association, 299*, 2401–2405.

O'Keefe, D. (2002). *Persuasion: Theory and research* (2nd ed.). Newbury Park, CA: Sage.

O'Keefe, D. J., & Hale, S. L. (2001). An odds-ratio based meta-analysis of research on the door-in-the-face influence strategy. *Communication Reports, 14*(1), 31–38.

Olfson, M., & Marcus, S. C. (2010). National trends in outpatient psychotherapy. *The American Journal of Psychiatry, 167*(12), 1456–1463. doi:10.1176/appi.ajp.2010.10040570

Olfson, M., Marcus, S. C., Druss, B., & Pincus, H. A. (2002). National trends in the use of outpatient psychotherapy. *American Journal of Psychiatry, 159*, 1914–1920.

Omarzu, J. (2009). Minding the relationship. In H. T. Reis & S. Sprecher (Eds.), *Encyclopedia of human relationships: Vol. 2* (pp. 1107–1108). Los Angeles, CA: Sage Reference Publication.

Ono, H. (1998). Husbands' and wives' resources and marital dissolution. *Journal of Marriage and the Family, 60*, 674–689.

Ono, H. (2006). Homogamy among the divorced and never married on marital history in recent decades: Evidence from vital statistics data. *Social Science Research, 35*, 356–383.

Oppliger, P. A. (2007). Effects of gender stereotyping on socialization. In R. W. Preiss, B. M. Gayle, N. Burrell, M. Allen, & J. Bryant (Eds.), *Mass media effects research: Advances through meta-analysis* (pp. 199–214). Mahwah, NJ: Erlbaum.

Osteen, J. (2009). *Become a better you: 7 keys to improving your life every day.* New York, NY: Free Press.

O'Toole, R. E., & Ferry, J. L. (2002). The growing importance of elder care benefits for an aging workforce. *Compensation & Benefits Management, 18*(1), 40–44.

Ozer, E. J., & Weiss, D. S. (2004). Who develops posttraumatic stress disorder? *Current Directions in Psychological Science, 13*, 169–172.

Palomares, N. A. (2009). Women are sort of more tentative than men, aren't they? How men and women use tentative language differently, similarly, and counterstereotypically as a function of gender salience. *Communication Research, 36*, 538–560.

Papaharitou, S., Nakopoulou, E., Kirana, P., Giaglis, G., Moraitou, M., & Hatzichristou, D. (2008). Factors associated with sexuality in later life: An exploratory study in a group of Greek married older adults. *Archives of Gerontology and Geriatrics, 46*, 191–201.

Park, C. L., Bharadwaj, A. K., & Blank, T. O. (2011). Illness centrality, disclosure, and well-being in younger and middle-aged adult cancer survivors. *British Journal of Health Psychology, 16*(4), 880–889. doi: 10.1111/j.2044-8287.2011.02024.x

Park, C. W., & Young, S. M. (1986). Consumer response to television commercials: The impact of involvement and background music on brand attitude formation. *Journal of Marketing Research, 23* 11–24.

Parker, P. A., & Kulik, J. A. (1995). Burnout, self- and supervisor-related job performance and absenteeism among nurses. *Journal of Behavioral Medicine, 18*, 581–599.

Parker, R. (2000). Health literacy: A challenge for American patients and their health care providers. *Health Promotion International, 15*, 277–283.

Parrott, D. J., Peterson, J. L., Vincent, W., & Bakeman, R. (2008). Correlates of anger in response to gay men: Effects of male gender role beliefs, sexual prejudice, and masculine gender role stress. *Psychology of Men & Masculinity, 9*, 167–178.

Pashang, B, & Singh, M. (2008). Emotional intelligence and use of coping strategies. *Psychological Studies, 53*, 81–82.

Pasley, K., & Moorefield, B. S. (2004). Stepfamilies: Changes and challenges. In M. Coleman, & L. H. Ganong (Eds.), *Handbook of contemporary families: Considering the past, contemplating the future.* Thousand Oaks, CA: Sage.

Pasupathi, M., McLean, K. C., & Weeks, T. (2009). To tell or not to tell: Disclosure and the narrative self. *Journal of Personality, 77*, 89–124.

Patterson, C. J. (2003). Children of lesbian and gay parents. In L. D. Garnets & D. C. Kimmel (Eds.), *Psychological perspectives on lesbian, gay, and bisexual experiences.* New York, NY: Columbia University Press.

Patterson, C. J. (2009). Lesbian and gay parents and their children: A social science perspective. In D. A. Hope (Ed.), *Contemporary perspectives on lesbian, gay, and bisexual identities* (pp. 141–182). New York, NY: Springer Science and Business Media.

Patterson, M. L. (1988). Functions of nonverbal behavior in close relationships. In S. Duck (Ed.), *Handbook of personal relationships: Theory, research, and interventions.* New York, NY: Wiley.

Paul, A. M. (2001). Self-help: Shattering the myths. *Psychology Today, 34*(2), 60.

Paul, E. L., Wenzel, A., & Harvey J. (2008). Hookups: A facilitator or a barrier to relationship initiation and intimacy development? In S. Sprecher, A. Wenzel, & J. Harvey (Eds.), *Handbook of Relationship Initiation* (pp. 375–388). New York, NY: Psychology Press.

Paul, K. I., & Moser, K. (2009). Unemployment impairs mental health: Meta-analyses. *Journal of Vocational Behavior, 74*(3), 264–282.

Pavlov, I. P. (1906). The scientific investigation of psychical faculties or processes in the higher animals. *Science, 24*, 613–619.

Payne, B. K. (2006). Weapon bias: Split-second decisions and unintended sterotyping. *Current Directions in Psychological Science, 15*, 287–291.

Pearce, L. (1974). Duck! It's the new journalism. *New Times, 2*, 40–41.

Pechnick, R. N., & Ungerleider, T. J. (2005). Hallucinogens. In J. H. Lowinson, P. Ruiz, R. B. Millman, & J. G. Langrod (Eds.), *Substance abuse: A comprehensive textbook.* Philadelphia, PA: Lippincott/Williams & Wilkins.

Pennebaker, J. W., Colder, M., & Sharp, L. K. (1990). Accelerating the coping process. *Journal of Personality and Social Psychology, 58*, 528–537.

Peplau, L. A. (1988). Research on homosexual couples: An overview. In J. P. De Cecco (Ed.), *Gay relationships.* New York, NY: Harrington Park Press.

Peplau, L. A. (1991). Lesbian and gay relationships. In J. C. Gonsiorek & J. D. Weinrich (Eds.), *Homosexuality: Research implications for public policy.* Newbury Park, CA: Sage.

Peplau, L. A. (2003). Human sexuality: How do men and women differ? *Current Directions in Psychological Science, 12*(2), 37–40.

Peplau, L. A., & Fingerhut, A. W. (2007). The close relationships of lesbians and gay men. *Annual Review of Psychology, 58,* 405–424.

Peplau, L. A., Fingerhut, A., & Beals, K. P. (2004). Sexuality in the relationships of lesbians and gay men. In J. H. Harvey, A. Wenzel, & S. Sprecher (Eds.), *The handbook of sexuality in close relationships.* Mahwah, NJ: Lawrence Erlbaum.

Peplau, L. A., & Ghavami, N. (2009). Gay, lesbian, and bisexual relationships. In H. T. Reis & S. Sprecher (Eds.), *Encyclopedia of human relationships: Vol. 1* (pp. 746–751). Los Angeles, CA: Sage Reference Publication.

Peplau, L. A., & Gordon, S. L. (1985). Women and men in love: Gender differences in close heterosexual relationships. In V. E. O'Leary, R. K. Unger, & B. S. Wallston (Eds.), *Women, gender, and social psychology.* Hillsdale, NJ: Erlbaum.

Peplau, L. A., Hill, C. T., & Rubin, Z. (1993). Sex role attitudes in dating and marriage: A 15-year follow-up of the Boston couples study. *Journal of Social Issues, 49,* 31–52.

Peplau, L. A., & Spalding, L. R. (2003). The close relationships of lesbians, gay men, and bisexuals. In L. D. Garnets & D. C. Kimmel (Eds.), *Psychological perspectives on lesbian, gay, and bisexual experiences.* New York, NY: Columbia University Press.

Perlis, R. H., Perlis, C. S., Wu, Y., Hwang, C., Joseph, M., & Nierenberg, A. A. (2005). Industry sponsorship and financial conflict of interest in the reporting of clinical trials in psychiatry. *American Journal of Psychiatry, 162,* 1957–1960.

Perloff, R. M. (1993). *The dynamics of persuasion.* Hillsdale, NJ: Erlbaum.

Perry-Jenkins, M., Repetti, R. L., & Crouter, A. C. (2001). Work and family in the 1990s. In R. M. Milardo (Ed.), *Understanding families into the new millennium: A decade in review.* Minneapolis, MN: National Council on Family Relations.

Pervin, L. A., & John, O. P. (2001). *Personality: Theory and research.* New York, NY: Wiley.

Peterson, C., Maier, S. F., & Seligman, M. E. P. (1993). *Learned helplessness: A theory for the age of personal control.* New York, NY: Oxford University Press.

Peterson, C., & Park, N. (2010). What happened to self-actualization? Commentary on Kenrick et al. (2010). *Perspectives on Psychological Science, 5*(3), 320–322. doi:10.1177/1745691610369471

Peterson, C., & Seligman, M. E. P. (2004). *Character strengths and virtues: A handbook and classification.* New York, NY: Oxford University Press/Washington, DC: American Psychological Association.

Peterson, C., & Steen, T. A. (2009). Optimistic explanatory style. In S. J. Lopez & C. R. Snyder (Eds.), *Oxford handbook of positive psychology* (2nd ed., pp. 313–321). New York, NY: Oxford University Press.

Peterson, J. L., & Bakeman, R. (2006). Impact of beliefs about HIV treatment and peer condom norms on risky sexual behavior among gay and bisexual men. *Journal of Community Psychology, 34*(1), 37–46.

Petit, J. W., & Joiner, T. E. (2006). *Chronic depression: Interpersonal sources, therapeutic solutions.* Washington, DC: American Psychological Association.

Petrill, S. A. (2005). Behavioral genetics and intelligence. In O. Wilhelm & R. W. Engle (Eds.), *Handbook of understanding and measuring intelligence.* Thousand Oaks, CA: Sage Publications.

Petry, N. M. (2010). Pathological gambling and the DSM-V. *International Gambling Studies, 10*(2), 113–115. doi:10.1080/14459795.2010.501086

Petty, R. E., & Wegener, D. T. (1998). Attitude change: Multiple roles for persuasion variables. In D. T. Gilbert, S. T. Fiske, & G. Lindzey (Eds.), *The handbook of social psychology* (4th ed., Vol. 1). New York, NY: McGraw-Hill.

Petty, R. E., Wegener, D. T., & Fabrigar, L. R. (1997). Attitudes and attitude change. *Annual Review of Psychology, 48,* 609–647.

Petty, S. C., Sachs-Ericsson, N., & Joiner, T. E., Jr. (2004). Interpersonal functioning deficits: Temporary or stable characteristics of depressed individuals. *Journal of Affective Disorders, 81*(2), 115–122.

Pilcher, J. J., Nadler, E., & Busch, C. (2002). Effects of hot and cold temperature exposure on performance: A meta-analysis. *Ergonomics, 45,* 682–698.

Pinel, J. P. J., Assanand, S., & Lehman, D. R. (2000). Hunger, eating, and ill health. *American Psychologist, 55,* 1105–1116.

Pink, D. H. (2001). *Free agent nation: The future of working for yourself.* New York, NY: Warner Business Books.

Pittman, F., III. (1994, January/February). A buyer's guide to psychotherapy. *Psychology Today,* pp. 50–53, 74–81.

Planalp, S., Fitness, J., & Fehr, B. (2006). Emotion in theories of close relationships. In A. L. Vangelisti & D. Perlman (Eds.), *The Cambridge handbook of personal relationships.* New York, NY: Cambridge University Press.

Plante, T. G. (2005). *Contemporary clinical psychology.* New York, NY: Wiley.

Plante, T. G., Caputo, D., & Chizmar, L. (2000). Perceived fitness and responses to laboratory induced stress. *International Journal of Stress Management, 7*(1), 61–73.

Pleck, J. H. (1995). The gender role strain paradigm: An update. In R. F. Levant & W. S. Pollack (Eds.), *A new psychology of men.* New York, NY: Basic Books.

Plomin, R., DeFries, J. C., McClearn, G. E., & McGuffin, P. (2008). *Behavioral genetics.* New York, NY: Worth.

Pogue-Geile, M. F., & Yokley, J. L. (2010). Current research on the genetic contributors to schizophrenia. *Current Directions in Psychological Science, 19*(4), 214–219. doi:10.1177/0963721410378490

Pollak, L. (2007). *Getting from college to career: 90 things to do before you join the real world.* New York, NY: HarperCollins.

Pope, H. G., Barry, S., Bodkin, A., & Hudson, J. I. (2006). Tracking scientific interest in the dissociative disorders: A study of scientific publication output 1984–2003. *Psychotherapy and Psychosomatics, 75,* 19–24.

Pope, H. G., Gruber, A. J., & Yurgelun-Todd, D. (2001). Residual neuropsychologic effects of cannabis. *Current Psychiatry Report, 3,* 507–512.

Pope, H. G., Oliva, P. S., Hudson, J. I., Bodkin, J. A., & Gruber, A. J. (1999). Attitudes toward DSM-IV dissociative disorders diagnoses among board-certified American psychiatrists. *American Journal of Psychiatry, 156*(2), 321–323.

Porcerelli, J. H., Cogan, R., Kamoo, R., & Miller, K. (2010). Convergent validity of the Defense Mechanisms Manual and the Defensive Functioning Scale. *Journal of Personality Assessment, 92*(5), 432–438. doi:10.1080/00223891.2010.497421

Post, R. M. & Altshuler, L. L. (2009). Mood disorders: Treatment of bipolar disorders. In B. J. Sadock, V. A. Sadock, & P. Ruiz (Eds.), *Kaplan & Sadock's comprehensive textbook of psychiatry* (pp. 1743–1812). Philadelphia, PA: Lippincott Williams & Wilkins.

Powell, D. E., & Fine, M. A. (2009). Dissolution of relationships, causes. In H. T. Reis & S. Sprecher (Eds.), *Encyclopedia of human relationships: Vol. 1* (pp. 436–440). Los Angeles, CA: Sage Reference Publication.

Powell, R. A., & Gee, T. L. (1999). The effects of hypnosis on dissociative identity disorder: A reexamination of the evidence. *Canadian Journal of Psychiatry, 44,* 914–916.

Prati, G., & Pietrantoni, L. (2009). Optimism, social support, and coping strategies as factors contributing to posttraumatic growth: A meta-analysis. *Journal of Loss and Trauma, 1,* 364–388.

Pratkanis, A. R., & Aronson, E. (2000). *Age of propaganda: The everyday use and abuse of persuasion.* New York, NY: Freeman.

Pratt, L. A., Ford, D. E., Crum, R. M., Armenian, H. K., Gallo, J. J., & Eaton, W. W. (1996). Depression, psychotropic medication, and risk of myocardial infarction: Prospective data from the Baltimore ECA follow-up. *Archives of Internal Medicine, 94,* 3123–3129.

Pratto, F., Sidanius, J., Stallworth, L. M., & Malle, B. F. (1994). Social dominance orientation: A personality variable predicting social and political attitudes. *Journal of Personality and Social Psychology, 67,* 741–763.

Presser, H. B. (2000). Nonstandard work schedules and marital instability. *Journal of Marriage and the Family, 62,* 93–110.

Pressman, S. (1993). *Outrageous betrayal: The real story of Werner Erhard, EST and the Forum.* New York, NY: St. Martin's Press.

Preston, P. (2006). Marijuana use of coping response to psychological strain: Racial, ethnic, and gender differences among young adults. *Deviant Behavior, 27,* 397–421.

Pronin, E., Berger, J., & Moluki, S. (2007). Alone in a crowd of sheep: Asymmetric perceptions of conformity and their roots in an introspection illusion. *Journal of Personality and Social Psychology, 92,* 585–595.

Pronin, E., Fleming, J. J., & Steffel, M. (2008). Value revelations: Disclosure is in the eye of the beholder. *Journal of Personality and Social Psychology, 95,* 795–809.

Proulx, C. M., Helms, H. M., & Cheryl, B. (2007). Marital quality and personal well-being: A meta-analysis. *Journal of Marriage and Family, 69,* 576–593.

Prudic, J. (2009). Electroconvulsive therapy. In B. J. Sadock, V. A. Sadock, & P. Ruiz (Eds.), *Kaplan & Sadock's comprehensive textbook of psychiatry* (pp. 3285–3300). Philadelphia, PA: Lippincott Williams & Wilkins.

Pryor, F. L., & Schaffer, D. (1997, July). Wages and the university educated: A paradox resolved. *Monthly Labor Review,* 3–14.

Pryor, J. B., Giedd, J. L., & Williams, K. B. (1995). A social psychological model for predicting sexual harassment. *Journal of Social Issues, 51,* 69–84.

Puentes, J., Knox, D., & Zusman, M. E. (2008). Participants in "friends with benefits" relationships. *College Student Journal, 42,* 176–180.

Pugh, S., Dietz, J., Brief, A., & Wiley, J. (2008). Looking inside and out: The impact of employee and community demographic composition on organizational diversity climate. *Journal of Applied Psychology, 93,* 1422–1428.

Quinn, K. A., Macrae, C. N., & Bodenhausen, G. V. (2003). Stereotyping and impression formation: How categorical thinking shapes person perception. In M. A. Hogg & J. Cooper (Eds.), *The Sage handbook of social psychology.* Thousand Oaks, CA: Sage Publications.

Quoidbach, J., Dunn, E. W., Petrides, K. V., & Mikolajczak, M. (2010). Money giveth, money taketh away: The dual effect of wealth on happiness. *Psychological Science, 21*(6), 759–763.

Rachman, S. J. (2009). Psychological treatment of anxiety: The evolution of behavior therapy and cognitive behavior therapy. *Annual Review of Clinical Psychology, 5,* 97–119.

Ragins, B. R., Cornwell, J. M., & Miller, J. S. (2003). Heterosexism in the workplace: Do race and gender matter? *Group & Organization Management, 28*(1), 45–74.

Rahe, R. H., Veach, T. L., Tolles, R. L., & Murakami, K. (2000). The stress and coping inventory: An educational and research instrument. *Stress Medicine, 16,* 199–208.

Ramaekers, J. G., Robbe, H. W. J., & O'Hanlon, J. F. (2000). Marijuana, alcohol and actual driving performance. *Human Psychopharmacology Clinical & Experimental, 15*(7), 551–558.

Raphael, B., & Dobson, M. (2000). Effects of public disasters. In G. Fink (Ed.), *Encyclopedia of stress* (Vol. 1). San Diego, CA: Academic Press.

Ray, G. E., Cohen, R., Secrist, M. E., & Duncan, M. K. (1997). Relating aggressive and victimization behaviors to children's sociometric status and friendships. *Journal of Social and Personal Relationships, 14*(1), 95–108.

Read, C. R. (1991). Achievement and career choices: Comparisons of males and females. *Roeper Review, 13* 188–193.

Rees, C. J., & Metcalfe, B. (2003). The faking of personality questionnaire results: Who's kidding whom. *Journal of Managerial Psychology, 18,* 156–165.

Regan, P. C., & Berscheid, E. (1997). Gender differences in characteristics desired in potential sexual and marriage partners. *Journal of Psychology and Human Sexuality, 9*(1), 25–37.

Regier, D. A., & Burke, J. D. (2000). Epidemiology. In B. J. Sadock & V. A. Sadock (Eds.), *Kaplan and Sadock's comprehensive textbook of psychiatry.* Philadelphia, PA: Lippincott/Williams & Wilkins.

Regier, D. A., Narrow, W. E., Kuhl, E. A., & Kupfer, D. J. (2009). The conceptual development of DSM-V. *American Journal of Psychiatry, 166*(6), 645–650. doi:10.1176/appi.ajp.2009.09020279

Regnerus, M. D. (2007). *Forbidden fruit: Sex and religion in the lives of American teenagers.* New York, NY: Oxford Press.

Rehm, L. P., Wagner, A., & Ivens-Tyndal, Co. (2001). Mood disorders: Unipolar and bipolar. In P. B. Sutker & H. E. Adams (Eds.), *Comprehensive handbook of psychopathology* (3rd ed.). New York, NY: Kluwer Academic/Plenum.

Rehman, U. S., & Holtzworth-Munroe, A. (2007). A cross-cultural examination of the relation of marital communication behavior to marital satisfaction. *Journal of Family Psychology, 21,* 759–763.

Reibel, D. K., Greeson, J. M., Brainard, G. C., & Rosenzweig, S. (2001). Mindfulness-based stress reduction and health-related quality of life in a heterogeneous patient population. *General Hospital Psychiatry, 23*(4), 183–192.

Reich, M., Lesur, A., & Perdrizet-Chevallier, C. (2008). Depression, quality of life and breast cancer: A review of the literature. *Breast Cancer Research and Treatment, 110*(1), 9–17.

Reis, H. T. (1998). Gender differences in intimacy and related behaviors: Context and processes. In D. Canary & K. Dindia (Eds.), *Sex and gender in communication: Similarities and differences.* Mahwah, NJ: Erlbaum.

Reis, H. T., & Patrick. B. C. (1996). Attachment and intimacy: Component processes. In E. T. Higgins & A. Kruglanski (Eds.), *Social psychology: Handbook of basic principles.* New York, NY: Guilford.

Reis, H. T., & Shaver, P. (1988). Intimacy as an interpersonal process. In S. W. Duck (Ed.), *Handbook of personal relationships.* New York, NY: Wiley.

Reissman, C., Aron, A., & Bergen, M. R. (1993). Shared activities and marital satisfaction: Causal direction and self-expansion versus boredom. *Journal of Social and Personal Relationships, 10,* 243–254.

Renaud, C. A., & Byers, E. S. (2001). Positive and negative sexual cognitions: Subjective experience and relationships to sexual adjustment. *Journal of Sex Research, 38*(3), 252–262.

Rennison, C. M., & Welchans, S. (2000). *Intimate partner violence.* Washington, DC: U.S. Department of Justice, Office of Justice Programs, Bureau of Justice Statistics.

Repetto, M., & Gold, M. S. (2005). Cocaine and crack: Neurobiology. In J. H. Lowinson, P. Ruiz, R. B. Millman, & J. G. Langrod (Eds.), *Substance abuse: A comprehensive textbook.* Philadelphia, PA: Lippincott/Williams & Wilkins.

Riccardi, N. (2011, June 22). Self-help guru convicted in Arizona sweat lodge deaths. *Los Angeles Times,* retrieved from http://articles.latimes.com/2011/jun/22/nation/la-na-sweat-lodge-trial-20110623

Rice, J. K., & Else-Quest, N. (2006). The mixed messages of motherhood. In J. Worrell & C. D. Goodheart (Eds.), *Handbook of girls' and women's psychological health.* New York, NY: Oxford University Press.

Rice, L. N., & Greenberg, L. S. (1992). Humanistic approaches to psychotherapy. In D. K. Freedheim (Ed.), *History of psychotherapy: A century of change.* Washington, DC: American Psychological Association.

Richardson, C. R., Kriska, A. M., Lantz, P. M., & Hayword, R. A. (2004). Physical activity and mortality across cardiovascular disease risk groups. *Medicine and Science in Sports and Exercise, 36*(11), 1923–1929.

Richmond, V. P., & McCroskey, J. C. (1995). *Communication: Apprehension, avoidance, and effectiveness* (5th ed.). Boston, MA: Allyn & Bacon.

Rihmer, Z., & Angst, J. (2005). Mood disorders: Epidemiology. In B. J. Sadock & V. A. Sadock (Eds.), *Kaplan & Sadock's comprehensive textbook of psychiatry.* Philadelphia, PA: Lippicott Williams & Wilkins.

Rihmer, Z., & Angst, J. (2009). Mood disorders: Epidemiology. In B. J. Sadock, V. A. Sadock, & P. Ruiz (Eds.), *Kaplan & Sadock's comprehensive textbook of psychiatry* (pp. 1645–1652). Philadelphia, PA: Lippincott Williams & Wilkins.

Riis, J., Loewenstein, G., Baron, J., Jepson, C., Fagerlin, A., & Ubel, P. A. (2005). Ignorance of hedonic adaptation to hemodialysis: A study using ecological momentary assessment. *Journal of Experimental Psychology: General, 134,* 3–9.

Ringström, G., Abrahamsson, H., Strid, H., & Simrén, M. (2007). Why do subjects with irritable bowel syndrome seek health care for their symptoms? *Scandinavian Journal of Gastroenterology, 42,* 1194–1203.

Riso, L. P., du Toit, P. L., Blandino, J. A., Penna, S., Dacey, S., Duin, J. S., Pacoe, E. M., Grant, M. M., & Ulmer, C. S. (2003). Cognitive aspects of chronic depression. *Journal of Abnormal Psychology, 112*(1), 72–80.

Roberts, B. W., Caspi, A., & Moffitt, T. (2003). Work experiences and personality development in young adulthood. *Journal of Personality and Social Psychology, 84,* 582–593.

Roberts, B. W., Jackson, J. J., Fayard, J. V., Edmonds, G., & Meints, J. (2009). Conscientiousness. In M. R. Leary & R. H. Hoyle (Eds.), *Handbook of individual differences in social* behavior (pp. 369–381). New York, NY: Guilford.

Roberts, B. W., Kuncel, N. R., Shiner, R., Caspi, A., & Goldberg, L. R. (2007). The power of personality: The comparative validity of personality traits, socioeconomic status, and cognitive ability for predicting important life outcomes. *Perspectives on Psychological Science, 2,* 313–345.

Robins, R. W., & Trzesniewski, K. H. (2005). Self-esteem development across the lifespan. *Current Direction in Psychological Science, 14,* 158–162.

Robinson, B., Frye, E. M., & Bradley, L. J. (1997). Cult affiliation and disaffiliation: Implications for counseling. *Counseling and Values, 41,* 166–173.

Robinson, B. E., Flowers, C., & Ng, K. (2006). The relationship between workaholism and marital disaffection: Husband's perspective. *Family Journal: Counseling and Therapy for Couples and Families, 14,* 213–220.

Robinson, M. D., Johnson, J. T., & Shields, S. A. (1995). On the advantages of modesty: The benefits of a balanced self-presentation. *Communication Research, 22,* 575–591.

Robinson, O., & Griffiths, A. (2005). Coping with the stress of transformational change in a government department. *Journal of Applied Behavioral Science, 41*(2), 203–221.

Rodin, J., Schank, D., & Striegel-Moore, R. H. (1989). Psychological features of obesity. *Medical Clinics of North America, 73* 47–66.

Rogers, C. J., Colbert, L. H., Greiner, J. W., Perkins, S. N., & Hursting, S. D. (2008). Physical activity and cancer prevention: Pathways and targets for intervention. *Sports Medicine, 38,* 271–296.

Rogers, C. R. (1951). *Client-centered therapy: Its current practice, implications, and theory.* Boston, MA: Houghton Mifflin.

Rogers, C. R. (1961). *On becoming a person: A therapist's view of psychotherapy.* Boston, MA: Houghton Mifflin.

Rogers, C. R. (1977). *Carl Rogers on personal power.* New York, NY: Delacorte.

Rohner, R. P., & Veneziano, R. A. (2001). The importance of father love: History and contemporary evidence. *Review of General Psychology, 5*(4), 382–405.

Rohrer, D., & Taylor, K. (2006). The effects of overlearning and distributed practice on the retention of mathematics knowledge. *Applied Cognitive Psychology, 20,* 1209–1224.

Rook, K. S. (1998). Investigating the positive and negative sides of personal relationships: Through a lens darkly? In B. H. Spitzberg & W. R. Cupach (Eds.), *The dark side of close relationships.* Mahwah, NJ: Lawrence Erlbaum.

Rook, K. S., August, K. J., & Sorkin, D. H. (2011). Social network functions and health. In R. J. Contrada & A. Baum (Eds.), *The handbook of stress science: Biology, psychology, and health* (pp. 123–135). New York, NY: Springer Publishing Company.

Rose, D., Wykes, T., Leese, M., Bindman, J., & Fleischmann, P. (2003). Patient's perspectives on electroconvulsive therapy: Systematic review. *British Medical Journal, 326,* 1363–1365.

Rosen, G. M. (1993). Self-help or hype? Comments on psychology's failure to advance self-care. *Professional Psychology: Research and Practice, 24,* 340–345.

Rosen, G. M., Glasgow, R. E., & Moore, T. E. (2003). Self-help therapy: The science and business of giving psychology away. In S. O. Lilienfeld, S. J. Lynn, & J. M. Lohr (Eds.), *Science and pseudoscience in clinical psychology.* New York, NY: Guilford Press.

Rosen, R. D. (1977). *Psychobabble.* New York, NY: Atheneum.

Rosenbaum, J. E. (2009). Patient teenagers? A comparison of the sexual behavior of virginity pledgers and matched nonpledgers. *Pediatrics, 123,* 110–120.

Rosenbaum, M., Lakin, M., & Roback, H. B. (1992). Psychotherapy in groups. In D. K. Freedheim (Ed.), *History of psychotherapy: A century of change.* Washington, DC: American Psychological Association.

Rosenthal, R. (2002). The Pygmalion effect and its mediating mechanisms. In J. Aronson (Ed.), *Improving academic achievement: Impact of psychological factors on education* (pp. 25–36). San Diego, CA: Academic Press.

Rospenda, K. M., Fujishiro, K., Shannon, C. A., & Richman, J. A. (2008). Workplace harassment, stress, and drinking behavior over time: Gender differences in a national sample. *Addictive Behaviors, 33*(7), 964–967.

Ross, L. D. (1977). The intuitive psychologist and his shortcomings: Distortions in the attribution process. In L. Berkowitz (Ed.), *Advances in experimental social psychology* (Vol. 10). New York, NY: Academic Press.

Ross, M., & Conway, M. (1986). Remembering one's own past: The construction of personal histories. In R. M. Sorrentino & E. T. Higgins (Eds.), *Handbook of motivation and cognition: Foundations of social behavior.* New York, NY: Guilford Press.

Roth, P. L., & Clarke, R. L. (1998). Meta-analyzing the relationship between grades and salary. *Journal of Vocational Behavior, 53,* 386–400.

Roth, P. L., BeVier, C. A., Switzer, F. S., & Schippmann, J. S. (1996). Meta-analyzing the relationship between grades and job performance. *Journal of Applied Psychology, 81*(5), 548–556.

Rubenstein, C. M., & Shaver, P. (1982). The experience of loneliness. In L. A. Peplau & D. Perlman (Eds.), *Loneliness: A sourcebook of current theory, research and therapy.* New York, NY: Wiley.

Rubin, Z., Peplau, L. A., & Hill, C. T. (1981). Loving and leaving: Sex differences in romantic attachments. *Sex Roles, 7,* 821–835.

Rupp, H. A., & Wallen, K. (2009). Sex-specific content preferences for visual sexual stimuli. *Archives of Sexual Behavior, 38,* 417–426.

Rutter, M. (2007). Gene-environment interdependence. *Developmental Science, 10,* 12–18.

Ryan, S., Franzettta, K., Manlove, J., & Holcombe, E. (2007). Adolescents' discussions about contraception or STDs with partners before first sex. *Perspectives on Sexual and Reproductive Health, 39,* 149–157.

Rye, M. S., Folck, C. D., Heim, T. A., Olszewski, B. T., & Traina, E. (2004). Forgiveness of an ex-spouse: How does it relate to mental health following a divorce? *Journal of Divorce and Remarriage, 41,* 31–51.

Saad, L. (1999, September 3). *American workers generally satisfied, but indicate their jobs leave much to be desired.* Princeton, NJ: Gallup News Service.

Sabatelli, R. M. (2009). Social exchange theory. In H. T. Reis & S. Sprecher (Eds.), *Encyclopedia of human relationships: Vol. 3* (pp. 1521–1524). Los Angeles, CA: Sage Reference Publication.

Sackeim, H. A., Haskett, R. F., Mulsant, B. H., Thase, M. E., Mann, J. J., Pettinati, H. M., Greenberg, R. M., Crowe, R. R., Cooper, T. B., & Prudic, J. (2001). Continuation pharmacotherapy in the prevention of relapse following electroconvulsive therapy: A randomized controlled trial. *Journal of the American Medical Association, 285*(10), 1299–1307.

Sadker, M., & Sadker, D. (1994). *Failing at fair-ness: How America's schools cheat girls.* New York, NY: Scribners.

Sadler, J. Z. (2005). *Values and psychiatric diagnosis.* New York, NY: Oxford University Press.

Sagrestano, L. M., Heavey, C. L., & Christensen, A. (2006). Individual differences versus social structural approaches to explaining demand-withdraw and social influence behaviors. In K. Dindia, & D. J. Canary (Eds.), *Sex differences and similarities in communication.* Mahwah, NJ: Erlbaum.

Salerno, S. (2005). *Sham: How the self-help movement made America helpless.* New York, NY: Crown Publishers.

Salovey, P., & Mayer, J. D. (1990). Emotional intelligence. *Imagination, Cognition, and Personality, 9,* 185–211.

Salovey, P., Mayer, J. D., & Caruso, D. (2005). The positive psychology of emotional intelligence. In C. R. Snyder & S. J. Lopez (Eds.), *Handbook of positive psychology.* New York, NY: Oxford University Press.

Samberg, E., & Marcus, E. R. (2005). Process, resistance, and interpretation. In E. S. Person, A. M. Cooper, & G. O. Gabbard (Eds.), *Textbook of psychoanalysis.* Washington, DC: American Psychiatric Publishing.

Samovar, L. A., Porter, R. E., & McDaniel, E. R. (2007). *Communication between cultures.* Belmont, CA: Wadsworth.

Sanjuán, P., Magallares, A., & Gordillo, R. (2011). Self-serving attributional bias and hedonic and eudaimonic aspects of well-being. In I. Brdar (Ed.), *The human pursuit of well-being: A cultural approach* (pp. 15–26). New York, NY: Springer.

Santelli, J. S., Morrow, B., Anderson, J. E., & Lindberg, L. D. (2006). Contraceptive use and pregnancy risk among U. S. high school students, 1991–2003. *Perspectives on Sexual and Reproductive Health, 38*(2), 106–111.

Sapolsky, R. M. (2004). *Why zebras don't get ulcers: The acclaimed guide to stress, stress-related diseases, and coping.* New York, NY: Holt.

Sarason, I. G., Pierce, G. R., & Sarason, B. R. (1994). General and specific perceptions of social support. In W. R. Avison & I. H. Gotlib (Eds.), *Stress and mental health: Contemporary issues and prospects for the future.* New York, NY: Plenum.

Sarwer, D. B., Foster, G. D., & Wadden, T. A. (2004). Treatment of obesity I: Adult obesity. In J. K. Thompson (Ed.), *Handbook of eating disorders and obesity.* New York, NY: Wiley.

Savin-Williams, R. C. (2009). How many gays are there? It depends. In D. A. Hope (Ed.), *Contemporary perspectives on lesbian, gay, and bisexual identities* (pp. 5–42). New York, NY: Springer Science and Business Media.

Sayer, L. C. (2005). Gender, time, and inequality: Trends in women's and men's paid work, unpaid work, and free time. *Social Forces, 84,* 285–303.

Schaalma, H. P., Abraham, C., Gillmore, M. R., & Kok, G. (2004). Sex education as health promotion: What does it take? *Archives of Sexual Behavior, 33,* 259–269.

Schachter, R. (2011). Using the group in cognitive group therapy. *Group, 35*(2), 135–149.

Schachter, S. (1959). *The psychology of affiliation.* Stanford, CA: Stanford University Press.

Schaninger, C. M., & Buss, W. C. (1986). A longitudinal comparison of consumption and finance handling between happily married and divorced couples. *Journal of Marriage and the Family, 48,* 129–136.

Scheier, M. F., & Carver, C. S. (1985). Optimism, coping, and health: Assessment and implications of generalized outcome expectancies. *Health Psychology, 4,* 219–247.

Scheier, M. F., Matthews, K. A., Owens, J. F., Magovern, G. J., Sr., Lefebvre, R. C., Abbott, R. A., & Carver, C. S. (1989). Dispositional optimism and recovery from coronary artery bypass surgery: The beneficial effects on physical and psychological well-being. *Journal of Personality and Social Psychology, 57,* 1024–1040.

Schiffman, J., Ekstrom, M., LaBrie, J., Schulsinger, F., Sorenson, H., & Mednick, S. (2002). Minor physical anomalies and schizophrenia spectrum disorders: A prospective investigation. *American Journal of Psychiatry, 159,* 238–243.

Schilit, W. K. (1987). Thinking about managing your time. In A. D. Timpe (Ed.), *The management of time.* New York, NY: Facts On File.

Schirmer, L. L., & Lopez, F. G. (2001). Probing the social support and work strain relationship among adult workers: Contributions of adult attachment orientations. *Journal of Vocational Behavior, 59*(1), 17–33.

Schlenger, W. E., Kulka, R. A., Fairbank, J. A., Hough, R. L., et al. (1992). The prevalence of post-traumatic stress disorder in the Vietnam generation: A multimethod, multisource assessment of psychiatric disorder. *Journal of Traumatic Stress, 5,* 333–363.

Schlenker, B. R. (2003). Self-presentation. In M. R. Leary & J. P. Tangney (Eds.), *Handbook of self and identity.* New York, NY: Guilford.

Schlenker, B. R., & Pontari, B. A. (2000). The strategic control of information: Impression management and self-presentation in daily life. In A. Tesser, R. B. Felson, & J. M. Suls (Eds.), *Psychological perspectives on self and identity.* Washington, DC: American Psychological Association.

Schlicht, W., Kanning, M., & Bös, K. (2007). Psychosocial interventions to influence physical inactivity as a risk factor: Theoretical models and practical evidence. In J. Dordan, B. Bardé, & A. M. Zeiher, (Eds.), *Contributions toward evidence-based psychocardiology: A systematic review of the literature* (pp. 107–123). Washington, DC: American Psychological Association.

Schmitt, D. P., et al. (2003). Universal sex differences in the desire for sexual variety: Tests from 52 nations, 6 continents, and 13 islands. *Journal of Personality and Social Psychology, 85*(1), 85–104.

Schmitz, J. M., & DeLaune, K. A. (2005). Nicotine. In J. H. Lowinson, P. Ruiz, R. B. Millman, & J. G. Langrod (Eds.), *Substance abuse: A comprehensive textbook.* Philadelphia, PA: Lippincott/Williams & Wilkins.

Schoon, I., & Parsons, S. (2002). Teenage aspirations for future careers and occupational outcomes. *Journal of Vocational Behavior, 60*(2), 262–288.

Schraw, G., Wadkins, T., & Olafson, L. (2007). Doing the things we do: A grounded theory of academic procrastination. *Journal of Educational Psychology, 99*(1), 12–25.

Schuckit, M. A. (2000). Alcohol-related disorders. In B. J. Sadock & V. A. Sadock (Eds.), *Kaplan and Sadock's comprehensive textbook of psychiatry* (7th ed.). Philadelphia, PA: Lippincott/Williams & Wilkins.

Schwartz, J. P., Waldo, M., & Higgins, A. J. (2004). Attachment styles: Relationship to masculine gender role conflict in college men. *Psychology of Men & Masculinity, 5*(2), 143–146.

Schwartz, P., & Young, L. (2009). Sexual satisfaction in committed relationships. *Sexuality Research & Social Policy: A Journal of the NSRC, 6*(1), 1–17.

Schwarzer, R., & Schulz, U. (2003). Stressful life events. In A. M. Nezu, C. M. Nezu, & P. A. Geller (Eds.), *Handbook of psychology: Vol. 9. Health psychology.* New York, NY: Wiley.

Seccombe, K. (2001). Families in poverty in the 1990s: Trends, causes, consequences, and lessons learned. In R. M. Milardo (Ed.), *Understanding families into the new millennium: A decade in review.* Minneapolis: National Council on Family Relations.

See, Y. H. M., Petty, R. E., Evans, L. M. (2009). The impact of perceived message complexity and need for cognition on information processing and attitudes. *Journal of Research in Personality, 43*(5), 880–889.

Segal, M. W. (1974). Alphabet and attraction: An unobtrusive measure of the effect of propinquity in a field setting. *Journal of Personality and Social Psychology, 30,* 654–657.

Segerstrom, S. C., & Miller, G. E. (2004). Psychological stress and the human immune system: A meta-analytic study of 30 years of inquiry. *Psychological Bulletin, 130,* 601–630.

Selfhout, M., Denissen, J., Branje, S., & Meeus, W. (2009). In the eye of the beholder: Perceived, actual, and peer-rated similarity in personality, communication, and friendship intensity during the acquaintanceship process. *Journal of Personality and Social Psychology, 96,* 1152–1165.

Seligman, M. E. P. (1971). Phobias and preparedness. *Behavior Therapy, 2,* 307–321.

Seligman, M. E. P. (1974). Depression and learned helplessness. In R. J. Friedman & M. M. Katz (Eds.), *The psychology of depression: Contemporary theory and research.* New York, NY: Wiley.

Seligman, M. E. P. (1990). *Learned optimism: How to change your mind and your life.* New York, NY: Pocket Books.

Seligman, M. E. P. (1991). *Learned optimism.* New York, NY: Alfred A. Knopf.

Seligman, M. E. P. (1992). *Helplessness: On depression, development, and death.* New York, NY: Freeman.

Seligman, M. E. P. (1995). The effectiveness of psychotherapy. *American Psychologist, 50,* 965–974.

Seltzer, J. A. (2001). Families formed outside of marriage. In R. M. Milardo (Ed.), *Understanding families into the new millennium: A decade in review.* Minneapolis: National Council on Family Relations.

Seltzer, J. A. (2004). Cohabitation and family change. In M. Coleman & L. H. Ganong (Eds.), *Handbook of contemporary families: Considering the past, contemplating the future.* Thousand Oaks, CA: Sage.

Selye, H. (1936). A syndrome produced by diverse nocuous agents. *Nature, 138,* 32.

Selye, H. (1956). *The stress of life.* New York, NY: McGraw-Hill.

Senecal, C., Lavoie, K., & Koestner, R. (1997). Trait and situational factors in procrastination: An interactional model. *Journal of Social Behavior and Personality, 12,* 889–903.

Seta, J. J., Seta, C. E., & McElroy, T. (2002). Strategies for reducing the stress of negative life experiences: An averaging/summation analysis. *Personality and Social Psychology Bulletin, 28*(11), 1574–1585.

Shaffer, D. R. (1989). *Developmental psychology.* Pacific Grove, CA: Brooks/Cole.

Shapiro, S. L., Astin, J. A., Bishop, S. R., & Cordova, M. (2005). Mindfulness-based stress reduction for health care professionals: Results from a randomized trial. *International Journal of Stress Management, 12,* 164–176.

Sharp, E. A., & Ganong, L. (2011). "I'm a loser, I'm not married, let's just all look at me": Ever-single women's perceptions of their social environment. *Journal of Family Issues, 32*(7), 956–980. doi:10.1177/0192513X10392537

Shavelson, R. J., Hubner, J. J., & Stanton, G. C. (1976). Self-concept: Validation of construct interpretations. *Review of Educational Research, 46,* 407–411.

Shaver, P. R., & Brennan, K. A. (1992). Attachment styles and the "Big Five" personality traits: Their connections with each other and with romantic relationship outcomes. *Personality and Social Psychology Bulletin, 18,* 536–545.

Shaver, P. R., & Hazan, C. (1993). Adult attachment: Theory and research. In W. Jones & D. Perlman (Eds.), *Advances in personal relationships* (Vol. 4). London, England: Jessica Kingsley.

Shaver, P. R., & Mikulincer, M. (2007). Adult attachment strategies and the regulation of emotion. In J. J. Gross (Ed.), *Handbook of emotion regulation* (pp. 446–465). New York, NY: Guilford.

Shaver, P. R., & Mikulincer, M. (2008). Augmenting the sense of security in romantic, leader-follower, therapeutic, and group relationships: A relational model of psychological change. In J. P. Forgas & J. Fitness (Eds.) *Social relationships: Cognitive, affective, and motivational processes* (pp. 55–74). New York, NY: Psychology Press.

Sheldon, J. P. (2004). Gender stereotypes in educational software for young children. *Sex Roles, 51,* 433–444.

Shenton, M. E., & Kubicki, M. (2009). Structural brain imaging in schizophrenia. In B. J. Sadock, V. A. Sadock, & P. Ruiz (Eds.), *Kaplan & Sadock's comprehensive textbook of psychiatry* (pp. 1494–1506). Philadelphia, PA: Lippincott Williams & Wilkins.

Sherif, M., Harvey, O., White, B., Hood, W., & Sherif, C. (1961). *Intergroup conflict and cooperation: The Robber's Cave experiment.* Norman: University of Oklahoma, Institute of Group Behavior.

Shoda, Y., Mischel, W., & Peake, P. K. (1990). Predicting adolescent cognitive and self-regulatory competencies from preschool delay of gratification: Identifying diagnostic conditions. *Developmental Psychology, 26,* 978–986.

Shotland, R. L., & Hunter, B. A. (1995). Women's "token resistant" and compliant sexual behaviors are related to uncertain sexual intentions and rape. *Personality and Social Psychology Bulletin, 21,* 226–236.

SHRM. (2008). *2008 Employee benefits: How competitive is your organization?* Alexandria, VA: Society for Human Resource Management.

Sibley, C. G., & Duckitt, J. (2008). Personality and prejudice: A meta-analytic and theoretical review. *Personality and Social Psychology Review, 12*(3), 248–279.

Siegel, K., Schrimshaw, E. W., Lekas, H., & Parsons, J. T. (2008). Sexual behaviors of non-gay identified non-disclosing men who have sex with men and women. *Archives of Sexual Behavior, 37,* 720–735.

Siegman, A. W. (1994). From Type A to hostility to anger: Reflections on the history of coronary-prone behavior. In A. W. Siegman & T. W. Smith (Eds.), *Anger, hostility, and the heart* (pp. 1–21). Hillsdale, NJ: Erlbaum.

Simeon, D. & Loewenstein, R. J. (2009). Dissociative disorders. In B. J. Sadock, V. A. Sadock, & P. Ruiz (Eds.), *Kaplan & Sadock's comprehensive textbook of psychiatry* (pp. 1965–2026). Philadelphia, PA: Lippincott Williams & Wilkins.

Simon, G. E., & Savarino, J. (2007). Suicide attempts among patients starting depression treatment with medications or psychotherapy. *American Journal of Psychiatry, 164,* 1029–1034.

Simon, G. E., Savarino, J., Operskalski, B., & Wang, P. S. (2006). Suicide risk during antidepressant treatment. *American Journal of Psychiatry, 163,* 41–47.

Simpson, J. A. (1987). The dissolution of romantic relationships: Factors involved in relationship stability and emotional distress. *Journal of Personality and Social Psychology, 53,* 683–692.

Singer, A. R., Cassin, S. E., & Dobson, K. S. (2005). The role of gender in the career aspirations of professional psychology graduates: Are there more similarities than differences? *Canadian Psychology, 46*(4), 215–222.

Singer, M. T. (2003). *Cults in our midst.* San Francisco, CA: Jossey-Bass.

Skinner, B. F. (1953). *Science and human behavior.* New York, NY: Macmillan.

Skinner, B. F. (1974). *About behaviorism.* New York, NY: Knopf.

Skinner, P. H., & Shelton, R. L. (1985). *Speech, language, and hearing: Normal processes and disorders* (2nd ed.). New York, NY: Wiley.

Skolnick, P. (2003). Psychiatric pathophysiology: Anxiety disorders. In A. Tasman, J. Kay, & J. A. Lieberman (Eds.), *Psychiatry.* New York, NY: Wiley.

Slashinki, M. J., Coker, A. L., & Davis, K. E. (2003). Physical aggression, forced sex, and stalking victimization by a dating partner: An analysis of the National Violence Against Women Survey. *Violence & Victims, 18*(6), 595–617.

Slowinski, J. (2007). Sexual problems and dysfunctions in men. In A. F. Owens & M. S. Tepper (Eds.), *Sexual Health: Vol. 4. State-of-the-art treatments and research* (pp. 1–14). Westport, CT: Praeger Publishers/Greenwood Publishing Group.

Small, D. A., Gelfand, M., Babcock, L., & Gettman, H. (2007). Who goes to the bargaining table? The influence of gender and framing on the initiation of negotiation. *Journal of Personality and Social Psychology, 93,* 600–613.

Smith, A. K. (2000, November 6). Charting your own course. *U.S. News & World Report,* 56–60, 62, 64–65.

Smith, E. R., & Collins, E. C. (2009). Contextualizing person perception: Distributed social cognition. *Psychological Review, 116*(2), 343–364.

Smith, L. J., Mulhall, J. P., Deveci, S., Monaghan, N., & Reid, M. (2007). Sex after seventy: A pilot study of sexual function in older persons. *Journal of Sexual Medicine, 4,* 1247–1253.

Smith, M. (2003, January). Employee health affects more than the bottom line. *IPMA News,* pp. 8–10.

Smith, M. L., & Glass, G. V. (1977). Meta-analysis of psychotherapy outcome studies. *American Psychologist, 32,* 752–760.

Smith, R. E. (1989). Effects of coping skills training on generalized self-efficacy and locus of control. *Journal of Personality and Social Psychology, 56,* 228–233.

Smith, S. M., & Gleaves, D. H. (2007). Recovered memories. In M. P. Toglia, J. D. Read, D. F. Ross, & R. C. L. Lindsay (Eds.), *Handbook of eyewitness psychology: Volume 1. Memory for events.* Mahwah, NJ: Erlbaum.

Smith, T. W. (2006). Personality as risk and resilience in physical health. *Current Directions in Psychological Science, 15,* 227–231.

Smith, T. W., & Gallo, L. C. (1999). Hostility and cardiovascular reactivity during marital interaction. *Psychosomatic Medicine, 61,* 436–445.

Smith, T. W., & Gallo, L. C. (2001). Personality traits as risk factors for physical illness. In A. Baum, T. A. Revenson, & J. E. Singer (Eds.), *Handbook of health psychology.* Mahwah, NJ: Erlbaum.

Smith, T. W., Pope, M. K., Sanders, J. D., Allred, K. D., & O'Keefe, J. L. (1988). Cynical hostility at home and work: Psychosocial vulnerability across domains. *Journal of Research in Personality, 22,* 525–548.

Smith, W. P., Compton, W. C., & West, W. B. (1995). Meditation as an adjunct to a happiness enhancement program. *Journal of Clinical Psychology, 51,* 269–273.

Smock, P. J. (2000). Cohabitation in the United States: An appraisal of research themes, findings, and implications. *Annual Review of Sociology, 26,* 1–20.

Smyth, J., Litcher, L., Hurewitz, A., & Stone, A. (2001). Relaxation training and cortisol secretion in adult asthmatics. *Journal of Health Psychology, 6*(2), 217–227.

Smyth, J. M., & Pennebaker, J. W. (2001). What are the health effects of disclosure? In A. Baum, T. A. Revenson, & J. E. Singer (Eds.), *Handbook of health psychology.* Mahwah, NJ: Erlbaum.

Snell, J. C., & Marsh, M. (2008). Life cycle loneliness curve. *Psychology and Education: An Interdisciplinary Journal, 45,* 26–28.

Snowden, L. R., & Hu, T. W. (1996). Outpatient service use in minority-serving mental health programs. *Administration and Policy in Mental Health, 24,* 149–159.

Snowden, L. R., & Yamada, A. (2005). Cultural differences in access to care. *Annual Review of Clinical Psychology, 1,* 143–166.

Solomon, S. E., Rothblum, E. D., & Balsam, K. F. (2004). Pioneers in partnership: Lesbian and gay male couples in civil unions compared with those not in civil unions and married heterosexual siblings. *Journal of Family Psychology, 18,* 275–286.

Solowij, N., Stephens, R. S., Roffman, R. A., Babor, T., Kadden, R., Miller, M., Christiansen. K., McRee, B., & Vendetti, J. (2002). Cognitive functioning of long-term heavy cannabis users seeking treatment. *Journal of the American Medical Association, 287,* 1123–1131.

Son Hing, L. S., Bobocel, D. R., & Zanna, M. P. (2007). Authoritarian dynamics and unethical decision making: High social dominance orientation leaders and high right wing authoritarianism followers. *Journal of Personality and Social Psychology, 92,* 67–81.

South, S. J. (1993). Racial and ethnic differences in the desire to marry. *Journal of Marriage and the Family, 55,* 357–370.

South, S. J., Bose, S., & Trent, K. (2004). Anticipating divorce: Spousal agreement, predictive accuracy, and effects on labor supply and fertility. *Journal of Divorce and Remarriage, 40*(3–4), 1–22.

Souza, R., Bernatsky, S., Reyes, R., & de Jong, K. (2007). Mental health status of vulnerable tsunami-affected communities: A survey in Aceh Province, Indonesia. *Journal of Traumatic Stress, 20,* 263–269.

Spanos, N. P. (1996). *Multiple identities and false memories.* Washington, DC: American Psychological Association.

Spence, I., Yu, J. J., Feng, J., & Marshman, J. (2009). Women match men when learning a spatial skill. *Journal of Experimental Psychology, 35,* 1097–1103.

Spitzberg, B. H. (2011). Intimate partner violence and aggression: Seeing the light in a dark place. In W. R. Cupach & B. H. Spitzberg (Eds.). *The dark side of close relationships II* (pp. 327–380).). New York, NY: NY: Routledge.

Sprecher, S. (1994). Two sides to the breakup of dating relationships. *Personal Relationships, 1,* 199–222.

Sprecher, S. (2002). Sexual satisfaction in premarital relationships: Associations with satisfaction, love, commitment, and stability. *The Journal of Sex Research, 39*(3), 190–196.

Sprecher, S. (2011). Internet matching services: The good, the bad, and the ugly (disguised as attractive). In W. R. Cupach & B. H. Spitzberg (Eds.). *The dark side of close relationships II* (pp. 119–143). New York, NY: Routledge.

Sprecher, S., & Cate, R. M. (2004). Sexual satisfaction and sexual expression as predictors of relationship satisfaction and stability. In J. H. Harvey, A. Wenzel, & S. Sprecher (Eds.), *The handbook of sexuality and close relationships.* Mahwah, NJ: Lawrence Erlbaum.

Sprecher, S., Christopher, F. S., & Cate, R. (2006). Sexuality in close relationships. In A. L. Vangelisti & D. Perlman (Eds.), *The Cambridge handbook of personal relationships.* New York, NY: Cambridge University Press.

Sprecher, S., Sullivan, Q., & Hatfield, E. (1994). Mate selection preferences: Gender differences examined in a national sample. *Journal of Personality and Social Psychology, 66,* 1074–1080.

Stafford, L., & Canary, D. J. (2006). Equity and interdependence as predictors of relational maintenance strategies. *The Journal of Family Communication, 6,* 227–254.

Staines, G. L. (2008). The relative efficacy of psychotherapy: Reassessing the methods-based paradigm. *Review of General Psychology, 12*(4), 330–343.

Stajkovic, A. D., & Luthans, F. (1998). Self-efficacy and work-related performance: A meta-analysis. *Psychological Bulletin, 124*(2), 240–261.

Stanley, M. A. & Beidel, D. C. (2009). Behavior therapy. In B. J. Sadock, V. A. Sadock, & P. Ruiz (Eds.), *Kaplan & Sadock's comprehensive textbook of psychiatry* (pp. 2781–2803). Philadelphia, PA: Lippincott Williams & Wilkins.

Stanley, S. M., & Rhoades, G. K. (2009). Cohabitation. In H. T. Reis & S. Sprecher (Eds.), *Encyclopedia of human relationships: Vol. 2* (pp. 229–231). Los Angeles, CA: Sage Reference Publication.

Stanley, S. M., Rhoades, G. K., Amato, P. R., Markman, H. J., & Johnson, C. A. (2010). The timing of cohabitation and engagement: Impact on first and second marriages. *Journal Of Marriage And Family, 72*(4), 906–918. doi:10.1111/j.1741-3737.2010.00738.x

Stanton, A. L. (2011). Regulating emotions during stressful experiences: The adaptive utility of coping through emotional approach. In S. Folkman (Ed.). *The Oxford Handbook of stress, health, & coping* (pp. 369–386). New York, NY: NY: Oxford University Press.

Starker, S. (1990). Self-help books: Ubiquitous agents of health care. *Medical Psychotherapy: An International Journal, 3* 187–194.

Steel, P. (2007). The nature of procrastination: A meta-analytic and theoretical review of quintessential self-regulatory failure. *Psychological Bulletin, 133*(1), 65–94.

Steele, C. M. (1992, April). Race and the schooling of black Americans. *The Atlantic Monthly,* 68–78.

Steele, C. M. (2011). *Whistling Vivaldi: How stereotypes affect us and what we can do.* New York, NY: Norton.

Steele, C. M., & Aronson, J. (1995). Stereotype threat and the intellectual test performance of African Americans. *Journal of Personality and Social Psychology, 69,* 797–811.

Steiger, H., & Bruce, K. R. (2009). Eating disorders. In P. H. Blaney & T. Millon (Eds.), *Oxford textbook of psychopathology* (pp. 431–451). New York, NY: Oxford University Press.

Steiger, H., Bruce, K. R., & Israël, M. (2003). Eating disorders. In G. Stricker & T. A. Widiger (Eds.), *Handbook of psychology: Vol. 8. Clinical psychology.* New York, NY: Wiley.

Steil, J. M. (2009). Dual-earner couples. In H. T. Reis & S. Sprecher (Eds.), *Encyclopedia of human relationships: Vol. 2* (pp. 469–471). Los Angeles, CA: Sage Reference Publication.

Stein, D. J., & Hugo, F. J. (2004). Neuropsychiatric aspects of anxiety disorders. In S. C. Yudofsky & R. E. Hales (Eds.), *Essentials of neuropsychiatry and clinical neurosciences*. Washington, DC: American Psychiatric Publishing.

Sternberg, R. J. (1986). A triangular theory of love. *Psychological Review, 93* 119–135.

Sternberg, R. J. (1988). Triangulating love. In R. J. Sternberg & M. L. Barnes (Eds.), *The psychology of love.* New Haven, CT: Yale University Press.

Stith, S. M., Smith, D. B., Penn, C. E., Ward, D. B., & Tritt, D. (2004). Intimate partner physical abuse perpetration and victimization risk factors: A meta-analytic review. *Aggression and Violent Behavior, 10,* 65–98.

Stone, L. (1977). *The family, sex and marriage in England 1500–1800.* New York, NY: Harper & Row.

Stotzer, R. L. (2009). Straight allies: Supportive attitudes towards lesbians, gay men, and bisexuals in a college sample. *Sex Roles, 60,* 67–80.

Strahan, E. J., Lafrance, A., Wilson, A. E., Ethier, N., Spencer, S. J., & Zanna, M. P. (2008). Victoria's dirty secret: How sociocultural norms influence adolescent girls and women. *Personality and Social Psychology Bulletin, 34*(2), 288–301.

Striegel-Moore, R. H., & Bulik, C. M. (2007). Risk factors for eating disorders. *American Psychologist, 62,* 181–198.

Stunkard, A. J., Allison, K. C., Geliebter, A., Lundgren, J. D., Gluck, M. E., O'Reardon, J. P. (2009). Development of criteria for a diagnosis: Lessons from the night eating syndrome. *Comprehensive Psychiatry, 50*(5), 391–399.

Sulsky, L., & Smith, C. (2005). *Work stress.* Belmont, CA: Wadsworth.

Sulsky, L., & Smith, C. (2007). Work stress: Macro-level work stressors. In A. Monat, R. S. Lazarus, & G. Reevy (Eds.), *The Praeger handbook on stress and coping* (pp. 53–86). Westport, CT: Praeger Publishers.

Summers, G., & Feldman, N. S. (1984). Blaming the perpetrator: An attributional analysis of spouse abuse. *Journal of Social and Clinical Psychology, 2,* 339–347.

Suschinsky, K. D., Lalumiere, M. L. & Chivers, M. L. (2009). Sex differences in patterns of genital sexual arousal: Measurement artifacts of true phenomena? *Archives of Sexual Behavior, 38,* 559–574.

Susman, E. J., Dorn, L. D., & Schiefelbein, V. L. (2003). Puberty, sexuality, and health. In R. M. Lerner, M.A. Easterbrooks, & J. Mistry (Eds.), *Handbook of psychology: Vol. 6. Developmental psychology.* New York, NY: Wiley.

Susser, E., Neugebauer, R., Hoek, H. W., Brown, A. S., Lin, S., Labovitz, D., & Gorman, J. M. (1996). Schizophrenia after prenatal famine: Further evidence. *Archives of General Psychiatry, 53,* 25–31.

Sutherland, V. J. (2000). Understimulation/boredom. In G. Fink (Ed.), *Encyclopedia of stress* (Vol. 3). San Diego, CA: Academic Press.

Sutin, A. R., Ferrucci, L., Zonderman, A. B., & Terracciano, A. (2011). Personality and obesity across the adult life span. *Journal of Personality and Social Psychology, 101*(3), 579–592.

Swan, G. E., Hudmon, K. S., & Khroyan, T. V. (2003). Tobacco dependence. In A. M. Nezu, C. M. Nezu, & P. A. Geller (Eds.), *Handbook of psychology: Vol. 9. Health psychology.* New York, NY: Wiley.

Swann, W. B., Jr., Stein-Seroussi, A., & McNulty, S. E. (1992). Outcasts in a white-lie society: The enigmatic worlds of people with negative self-conceptions. *Journal of Personality and Social Psychology, 62,* 618–624.

Swanson, J. L., & D'Achiardi, C. (2005). Beyond interests, needs/values, and abilities: Assessing other important career constructs over the life span. In S. D. Brown & R. W. Lent (Eds.), *Career development and counseling: Putting theory and research to work.* New York, NY: Wiley.

Sweeney, M. M., Wang, H., & Videon, T. M. (2009). Reconsidering the association between stepfather families and adolescent well-being. In H. E. Peters & C. M. K. Dush (Eds.), *Marriage and family: Perspectives and complexities* (pp. 177–225). New York, NY: Columbia University Press.

Szasz, T. S. (1974). *The myth of mental illness.* New York, NY: HarperCollins.

Szasz, T. S. (1993). *A lexicon of lunacy: Metaphoric malady, moral responsibility, and psychiatry.* New Brunswick, NJ: Transaction.

Tajfel, H. (1982). *Social identity and intergroup relations.* London, England: Cambridge University Press.

Tannen, D. (1990). *You just don't understand: Women and men in conversation.* New York, NY: Ballantine.

Tannen, D. (2002). *You just don't understand: Women and men in conversation.* New York, NY: Ballantine.

Tardy, C. H., & Dindia, K. (2006). Self-disclosure: Strategic revelation of information in personal and professional relationships. In O. Hargie (Ed.), *The handbook of communication skills* (3rd ed., pp. 229–266). New York, NY: Routledge.

Tasker, F. (2005). Lesbian mothers, gay fathers, and their children: A review. *Journal of Developmental & Behavioral Pediatrics, 26,* 224–240.

Tavris, C. (1982). *Anger: The misunderstood emotion.* New York, NY: Simon & Schuster.

Taylor, D. A., & Altman, I. (1987). Communication in interpersonal relationships: Social penetration processes. In M. E. Roloff & G. R. Miller (Eds.), *Interpersonal processes: New directions in communication research.* Newbury Park, CA: Sage.

Taylor, M. C. (1995). White backlash to workplace affirmative action: Peril or myth? *Social Forces, 73,* 1385–1414.

Taylor, S., Cox, B. J., & Asmundson, J. G. (2009). Anxiety disorders: Panic and phobias. In P. H. Blaney & T. Millon (Eds.), *Oxford textbook of psychopathology* (pp. 119–145). New York, NY: Oxford University Press.

Taylor, S. E. (1981). The interface of cognitive and social psychology. In J. Harvey (Ed.), *Cognition, social behavior, and the environment* (pp. 189–211). Hillsdale, NJ: Lawrence Erlbaum.

Taylor, S. E. (2007). Social support. In H. S. Friedman & R. C. Silver (Eds.), *Foundations of health psychology.* New York, NY: Oxford University Press.

Taylor, S. E., & Brown, J. D. (1988). Illusion and well-being: A social psychological perspective on mental health. *Psychological Bulletin, 103,* 193–210.

Taylor, S. E., & Brown, J. D. (1994). Positive illusions and well-being revisited: Separating fact from fiction. *Psychological Bulletin, 116,* 21–27.

Taylor, S. E., Sherman, D. K., Kim, H. S., Jarcho, J., Takagi, K., & Dunagan, M. S. (2004). Culture and social support: Who seeks it and why? *Journal of Personality, 87,* 354–362.

Teachman, J. D. (2003). Premarital sex, premarital cohabitation, and the risk of subsequent marital dissolution among women. *Journal of Marriage and Family, 65,* 444–445.

Teachman, J. D. (2008). Complex life course patterns and the risk of divorce in second marriages. *Journal of Marriage and Family, 70,* 294–305.

Teachman, J. D. (2009). Divorce, prevalence and trends. In H. T. Reis & S. Sprecher (Eds.), *Encyclopedia of human relationships: Vol. 2* (pp. 461–464). Los Angeles, CA: Sage Reference Publication.

Tedeschi, R. G., & Calhoun, L. G. (1996). The traumatic growth inventory: Measuring the positive legacy of trauma. *Journal of Traumatic Stress, 9,* 455–471.

Tedeschi, R. G., & Calhoun, L. G. (2004). Posttraumatic growth: Conceptual foundations and empirical evidence. *Psychological Inquiry, 15*(1), 1–18.

Terracciano, A., Abdel-Khalak, A. M., Adam, N., Adamovova, L., Ahn, C. K., Ahn, H. N., et al. (2005). National character does not reflect mean personality trait levels in 49 cultures. *Science, 310,* 96–100.

Tez, M., & Tez, S. (2008). Is cancer an adaptation mechanism to stress? *Cell Biology International, 32*(6), 713.

Thase, M. E., & Denko, T. (2008). Pharmacotherapy of mood disorders. *Annual Review of Clinical Psychology, 4,* 53–91.

Thayer, A., & Lynn, S. J. (2006). Guided imagery and recovered memory therapy: Considerations and cautions.

Journal of Forensic Psychology Practice, 6, 63–73.

Thobaben, M. (2005). Defense mechanisms and defense levels. *Home Health Care Management & Practice, 17,* 330–332.

Thomas, K. M. (2005). *Diversity dynamics in the workplace.* Belmont, CA: Wadsworth.

Thompson, J. K., & Kinder, B. (2003). Easting disorders. In M. Hersen & S. Turner (Eds.), *Handbook of adult psychopathology.* New York, NY: Plenum Press.

Thompson, J. K., & Stice, E. (2001). Thin-ideal internalization: Mounting evidence for a new risk factor for body-image disturbance and eating pathology. *Current Directions in Psychological Science, 10*(5), 181–183.

Thornton, L. M., Mazzeo, S. E., & Bulik, C. M. (2011). The heritability of eating disorders: Methods and current findings. In R. H. Adan & W. H. Kaye (Eds.), *Behavioral neurobiology of eating disorders* (pp. 141–156). New York, NY: Springer-Verlag.

Thune, I., & Furberg, A. (2001). Physical activity and cancer risk: Dose-response and cancer, all sites and site specific. *Medicine and Science in Sports and Exercise, 33*(6), S530–S550.

Tice, D. M., & Baumeister, R. F. (1997). Longitudinal study of procrastination, performance, stress, and health: The cost and benefits of dawdling. *Psychological Science, 8,* 454–458.

Tice, D. M., Baumeister, R. F., Shmueli, D., & Muraven, M. (2007). Restoring the self: Positive affect helps improve self-regulation following ego depletion. *Journal of Experimental Social Psychology, 43*(3), 379–384.

Tice, D. M., Bratslavsky, E., & Baumeister, R. F. (2001). Emotional distress regulation takes precedence over impulse control: If you feel bad, do it! *Journal of Personality and Social Psychology, 80*(1), 53–67.

Tice, D. M., Butler, J. L., Muraven M. B., & Stillwell A. M. (1995). When modesty prevails: Differential favorability of self-presentation to friends and strangers. *Journal of Personality and Social Psychology, 69,* 1120–1138.

Tiggemann, M., Martins, Y., & Kirkbride, A. (2007). Oh to be lean and muscular: Body image ideals in gay and heterosexual men. *Psychology of Men & Masculinity, 8,* 15–24.

Titsworth, B. S., & Kiewra, K. A. (2004). Spoken organizational lecture cues and student notetaking as facilitators of student learning. *Contemporary Educational Psychology, 29,* 447–461.

Tjaden, P., & Thoennes, N. (2000). Prevalence and consequences of male-to-female and female-to-male intimate partner violence as measured by the National Violence Against Women Survey. *Violence Against Women, 6,* 142–161.

Toffler, A. (1980). *The third wave.* New York, NY: Bantam Books.

Toma, C. L., & Hancock, J. T. (2010). Looks and lies: The role of physical attractiveness in online dating self-presentation and deception. *Communication Research, 37*(3), 335–351. doi:10.1177/0093650209356437

Torres, L., & Saunders, S. M. (2009). Evaluation of psychotherapy. In B. J. Sadock, V. A. Sadock, & P. Ruiz (Eds.), *Kaplan & Sadock's comprehensive textbook of psychiatry* (9th ed.). Philadelphia, PA: Lippincott, Williams & Wilkins.

Torrey, E. F. (1992). *Freudian fraud: The malignant effect of Freud's theory on American thought and culture.* New York, NY: Harper Perennial.

Tossi, M. (2009, November). Labor force projections to 2018: Older workers staying more active. *Monthly Labor Review,* 30–51. U.S. Bureau of Labor Statistics.

Tov, W., & Diener, E. (2007). Culture and subjective well-being. In S. Kitayama & D. Cohen (Eds.), *Handbook of cultural psychology* (pp. 691–713). New York, NY: Guilford.

Traut-Mattausch, E., Jones, E., Frey, D., & Zanna, M. P. (2011). Are there "his" and "her" types of decisions? Exploring gender differences in the confirmation bias. *Sex Roles, 65,* 223–233. doi: 10.1007/s11199-011-0009-2

Travis, L. A., Bliwise, N. G., Binder, J. L., & Horne-Moyer, H. L. (2001). Changes in clients' attachment style over the course of time-limited dynamic psychotherapy. *Psychotherapy: Theory, Research, Practice, Training, 38*(2), 149–159.

Triandis, H. C. (2001). Individualism-collectivism and personality. *Journal of Personality, 69*(6), 907–924.

Trope, Y. (1983). Self-assessment in achievement behavior. In J. Suls & A. Greenwald (Eds.), *Psychological perspectives* (Vol. 2). Hillsdale, NJ: Erlbaum.

Trotter, P. B. (2009). Divorce, effects on adults. In H. T. Reis & S. Sprecher (Eds.), *Encyclopedia of human relationships: Vol. 2* (pp. 458–461). Los Angeles, CA: Sage Reference Publication.

Tschan, F., Semmer, N. K., Gurtner, A., Bizzari, L., Spychiger, M., Breuer, M., & Marsch, S. U. (2009). Explicit reasoning, confirmation bias, and illusory transactive memory: A simulation study of group medical decision making. *Small Group Research, 40*(3), 271–300.

Tucker, O. N., Szomstein, S., & Rosenthal, R. J. (2007). Nutritional consequences of weight loss surgery. *Medical Clinics of North America, 91,* 499–513.

Turner, J. C. (1987). *Rediscovering the social group: A self-categorization theory.* Oxford, England: Basil Blackwell.

Turner, J. C., & Reynolds, K. J. (2004). The social identity perspective in intergroup relations: Theories, themes, and controversies. In M. B. Brewer & M. Hewstone (Eds.), *Self and social identity.* Malden, MA: Blackwell.

Turner, J. R., & Wheaton, B. (1995). Checklist measurement of stressful life events. In S. Cohen, R. C. Kessler, & L. U. Gordon (Eds.), *Measuring stress: A guide for health and social scientists.* New York, NY: Oxford University Press.

Twenge, J. M. (2000). The age of anxiety? Birth cohort change in anxiety and neuroticism, 1952–1993. *Journal of Personality and Social Psychology, 79*(6), 1007–1021.

Twenge, J. M., & Campbell W. K. (2003). Isn't it fun to get the respect that we're going to deserve? Narcissism, social rejection, and aggression. *Personality and Social Psychology, 29*(2), 261–272.

Twenge, J. M., & Campbell, W. K. (2009). *The narcissism epidemic: Living in the age of entitlement.* New York, NY: Free Press.

Twenge, J. M., Catanese, K. R., & Baumeister, R. F. (2002). Social exclusion causes self-defeating behavior. *Journal of Personality and Social Psychology, 83*(3), 606–615.

Twenge, J. M., & Crocker, J. (2002). Race and self-esteem: Meta-analyses comparing whites, blacks, Hispanics, Asians, and American Indians and comment on Gray-Little and Hafdahl (2000). *Psychological Bulletin, 128*(3), 371–408.

Uhlmann, E., & Swanson, J. (2004). Exposure to violent video games increases automatic aggressiveness. *Journal of Adolescence, 27,* 41–52.

Ullman, S. E. (2004). Sexual assualt victimization and suicidal behavior in women: A review of the literature. *Aggression and Violent Behavior, 9*(4), 331–351.

Ullman, S. E., Filipas, H. H., Townsend, S. M., & Starzynski, L. L. (2007). Psychosocial correlates of PTSD symptom severity in sexual assault survivors. *Journal of Traumatic Stress, 20,* 821–831.

Ursano, R. J., Sonnenberg, S. M., & Lazar, S. G. (2008). Psychodynamic psychotherapy. In R. E. Hales, S. C. Yudofsky, & G. O. Gabbard (Eds.), *The American psychiatric publishing textbook of psychiatry* (pp. 1171–1190). Washington, DC: American Psychiatric Publishing.

U.S. Bureau of Labor Statistics. (2004). *Occupational outlook handbook: 2004–2005.* Washington, DC: U.S. Government Printing Office.

U.S. Bureau of Labor Statistics. (2006). *Occupational outlook handbook, 2006–2007 edition.* Washington, D.C.: U. S. Government Printing Office.

U.S. Bureau of Labor Statistics. (2011). *Women in the workforce: A databook.* Report 1034. December, 2011.

U.S. Bureau of the Census. (2004). *Statistical abstract of the United States: 2004–2005.* Washington, DC: U.S. Government Printing Office.

U.S. **Bureau of the Census.** (2006a). *Americans marrying older, living alone more, see households shrinking, Census Bureau reports* (CB06-83). Retrieved from http://www.census.gov/Press-Release/www/releases/archives/families_households/006840.html.

U.S. Bureau of the Census. (2006b). *Statistical abstract of the United States: 2007.* Washington, DC: U.S. Government Printing Office.

U.S. Bureau of the Census. (2008). *Occupation by sex and median earnings in the past 12 months (in 2008 inflation-adjusted dollars) for the civilian unemployed population 16 years and over.* Retrieved from http://factfinder.census.gov/servlet/STTable?_bm+y&-geo_id=

U.S. Bureau of the Census. (2011). *Current population survey.* March and Annual Social and Economic Supplements.

U.S. Bureau of the Census. (2012). Retrieved from http://www.census.gov/newsroom/releases/archives/2010_census/cb12-68.html

U.S. Department of Health and Human Services. (1999). *Mental health: A report of the Surgeon General.* Washington, DC: U.S. Government Printing Office.

U.S. Department of Health and Human Services. (2004). *The health consequences of smoking: A report of the Surgeon General.* Atlanta, GA: DHHS.

U.S. Department of Health and Human Services. (2007). *Impacts of four Title V, Section 510 abstinence education programs, final report.* Retrieved from http://aspe.hhs.gov/hsp/abstinence07/index.htm

U.S. Department of Justice. (2007). *Criminal offenders statistics.* Retrieved from http://www.ojp.usdoj.gov/bjs/crimoff.htm

U.S. Small Business Administration. (2006). *Women in business, 2006: A demographic review of women's business ownership.* Retrieved from http://www.sba.gov/advo/research/rs280tot.pdf

Vallone, R. P., Ross, L., & Lepper, M. R. (1985). The hostile media phenomenon: Biased perception and perceptions of bias in coverage of the Beirut massacre. *Journal of Personality and Social Psychology, 50,* 482–491.

Van Blerkom, D. L. (2006). *College study skills: Becoming a strategic learner.* Belmont, CA: Wadsworth.

Van Boven, L. (2005). Experientialism, materialism, and the pursuit of happiness. *Review of General Psychology,* 9(2), 132–142.

Van der Hart, O. & Nijenhuis, E. R. S. (2009). Dissociative disorders. In P. H. Blaney & T. Millon (Eds.), *Oxford textbook of psychopathology* (pp. 452–481). New York, NY: Oxford University Press.

van Kammen, D. P., & Marder, S. R. (2005). Serotonin-dopamine antagonists (atypical or second-generation antipsychotics). In B. J. Sadock & V. A. Sadock (Eds.), *Kaplan and Sadock's comprehensive textbook of psychiatry.* Philadelphia, PA: Lippincott Williams & Wilkins.

Van Kammen, D. P., Hurford, I., & Marder, S. R. (2009). First-generation antipsychotics. In B. J. Sadock, V. A. Sadock, & P. Ruiz (Eds.), *Kaplan & Sadock's comprehensive textbook of psychiatry* (pp. 3105–3126). Philadelphia, PA: Lippincott Williams & Wilkins.

Van Volkmon, M. (2008). Attitudes toward cigarette smoking among college students. *College Student Journal, 42,* 294–304.

Vandello, J. A., Bosson, J. K., Cohen, D., Burnaford, R. M., & Weaver, J. R. (2008). Precarious manhood. *Journal of Personality and Social Psychology, 95,* 1325–1339.

Vandenberg, S. G. (1987). Sex differences in mental retardation and their implications for sex differences in ability. In J. M. Reinisch, L. A. Rosenblum, & S. A. Sanders (Eds.), *Masculinity/Femininity: Basic perspectives.* New York, NY: Oxford University Press.

Vandereycken, W. (2002). History of anorexia nervosa and bulimia nervosa. In C. G. Fairburn & K. D. Brownell (Eds.), *Eating disorders and obesity.* New York, NY: Guilford Press.

Vazquez, C., Cervellon, P., Perez-Sales, P., Vidales, D., & Gaborit, M. (2005). Positive emotions in earthquake survivors in El Salvador (2001). *Journal of Anxiety Disorders, 19,* 313–328.

Veenhoven, R. (2008). Healthy happiness: Effects of happiness on physical health and the consequences for preventive care. *Journal of Happiness Studies,* 9(3), 449–469.

Veenstra, M. Y., Lemmens, P. H. H. M., Friesema, I. H. M., Tan, F. E. S., Garrentsen, H. F. L., Knottnerus, J. A., & Zwietering, P. J. (2007). Coping style mediates impact of stress on alcohol use: A prospective population-based study. *Addiction, 102,* 1890–1898.

Verderber, R. F., Verderber, K. S., & Berryman-Fink, C. (2008). *Communicate.* Belmont, CA: Wadsworth.

Videbech, P., & Ravnkilde, B. (2004). Hippocampal volume and depression: A meta-analysis of MRI studies. *American Journal of Psychiatry, 161,* 1957–1966.

Viglione, D. J., & Rivera, B. (2003). Assessing personality and psychopathology with projective methods. In J. R. Graham, & J. A. Naglieri (Eds.), *Handbook of psychology: Vol. 10. Assessment psychology.* New York, NY: Wiley.

Vittengl, J. R., & Holt, C. S. (2000). Getting acquainted: The relationship of self-disclosure and social attraction to positive affect. *Journal of Social and Personal Relationships,* 17(1), 53–56.

Voas, R. B., Roman, T. E., Tippetts, A. S., & Durr-Holden, C. (2006). Drinking status and fatal crashes: Which drinkers contribute most to the problem? *Journal of Studies on Alcohol, 67,* 722–729.

Vohs, K. D., Baumeister, R. F., & Tice, D. M. (2008). Self-regulation: Goals, consumption, choices. In C. P. Haugtvedt, P. M. Herr, & F. R. Kardes (Eds.), *Handbook of consumer psychology* (pp. 349–366). New York, NY: Taylor & Francis Group/Lawrence Erlbaum Associates.

Waite, L. J. (1995). Does marriage matter? *Demography, 32,* 483–507.

Waite, L. J. (2000). Trends in men's and women's well-being in marriage. In L. J. Waite (Ed.), *The ties that bind.* New York, NY: Aldine de Gruyter.

Walker, E., & Tessner, K. (2008). Schizophrenia. *Perspectives on Psychological Science, 3,* 30–37.

Wallerstein, J. S. (2005). Growing up in the divorced family. *Clinical Social Work Journal, 33,* 401–418.

Wallerstein, J. S., & Blakeslee, S. (1989). *Second chances: Men, women, and children a decade after divorce.* Boston, MA: Houghton Mifflin.

Wallerstein, J. S., & Lewis, J. M. (2007). Sibling outcomes and disparate parenting and stepparenting after divorce: Report from a 10-year longitudinal study. *Psychoanalytic Psychology, 24,* 445–458.

Wallis, C. (2004, March 22). The case for staying home. *Time,* pp. 51–59.

Wang, H., & Amato, P. R. (2000). Predictors of divorce adjustment: Stressors, resources, and definitions. *Journal of Marriage and the Family, 62,* 655–668.

Wang, P. S., Lane, M., Olfson, M., Pincus, H. A., Wells, K. B., & Kessler, R. C. (2005). Twelve-month use of mental health services in the United States: Results from the National Comorbidity Survey Replication. *Archives of General Psychiatry, 62,* 629–640.

Wardle, J., & Gibson, E. L. (2007). Diet and stress, non-psychiatric. In G. Fink (Ed.), *Encyclopedia of stress: Vols. 1–4* (2nd ed., pp. 797–805). San Diego, CA: Elsevier Academic Press.

Wareham, J., Boots, D. P., & Chavez, J. M. (2009). A test of social learning and intergenerational transmission among batterers. *Journal of Criminal Justice, 37,* 163–173.

Warner-Schmidt, J. L., & Duman, R. S. (2006). Hippocampal neurogenesis: Opposing effects of stress and antidepressant treatment. *Hippocampus, 16,* 239–249.

Warren, R. (2002). *The purpose driven life: What on Earth am I here for?* Grand Rapids, MI: Zondervan.

Waters, E. A., Klein, W. M. P., Moser, R. P., Yu, M., Waldron, W. R., McNeel, T. S., & Freedman, A. N. (2011). Correlates of unrealistic optimism in a nationally representative sample. *Journal of Behavioral Medicine,* 34(3), 225–235.

Watson, D., Klohnen, E. C., Casillas, A., Nus Simms, E., Haig, J., & Berry, D. S. (2004). Match makers and deal breakers: Analyses of assortative mating in newlywed couples. *Journal of Personality, 72,* 1029–1068.

Watson, D. L., & Tharp, R. G. (2007). *Self-directed behavior: Self-modification for personal adjustment.* Belmont, CA: Wadsworth.

Watson, J. B. (1913). Psychology as the behaviorist views it. *Psychological Review, 20,* 158–177.

Weber, L. J. (2006). *Profits before people?* Bloomington, IN: Indiana University Press.

Webster, D. M. (1993). Motivated augmentation and reduction of the overattribution bias. *Journal of Personality and Social Psychology, 65,* 261–271.

Wechsler, H., Lee, J. E., Kuo, M., Seibring, M., Nelson, T. F., & Lee, H. (2002). Trends in college binge drinking during a period of increased prevention efforts. *Journal of American College Health, 50*(5), 203–217.

Wegener, D. T., & Petty, R. E. (1994). Mood management across affective states: The hedonic contingency hypothesis. *Journal of Personality and Social Psychology, 66,* 1034–1048.

Weinberger, D. A. (1990). The construct validity of the repressive coping style. In J. L. Singer (Ed.), *Repression and dissociation.* Chicago: University of Chicago Press.

Weiner, B. (1986). *An attribution theory of emotion and motivation.* New York, NY: Springer-Verlag.

Weinstein, N. D. (2003). Exploring the links between risk perceptions and preventive health behavior. In J. Suls & K. A. Wallston (Eds.), *Social psychological foundations of health and illness.* Malden, MA: Blackwell Publishing.

Weinstein, N. D., Slovic, P., & Gibson, G. (2004). Accuracy and optimism in smokers' beliefs about quitting. *Nicotine & Tobacco Research, 6*(Suppl3), 375–380.

Weisbuch, M., & Ambady, N. (2008). Nonconscious routes to building culture: Nonverbal components of socialization. *Journal of Consciousness Studies, 15,* 159–183.

Weiss, R. S. (1973). *Loneliness: The experience of emotional and social isolation.* Cambridge, MA: MIT Press.

Weiss, R. S. (1975). *Marital separation.* New York, NY: Basic Books.

Weiten, W. (1998). Pressure, major life events, and psychological symptoms. *Journal of Social Behavior and Personality, 13,* 51–68.

Wesson, D. R., Smith, D. E., Ling, W., & Seymour, R. B. (2005). Sedatives-hypnotics. In J. H. Lowinson, P. Ruiz, R. B. Millman, & J. G. Langrod (Eds.), *Substance abuse: A comprehensive textbook,* Philadelphia, PA: Lippincott/Williams & Wilkins.

Westefeld, J. S., Maples, M. R., Buford, B., & Taylor, S. (2001). Gay, lesbian, and bisexual college students: The relationship between sexual orientation and depression, loneliness and suicide. *Journal of College Student Psychotherapy, 15*(3), 71–82.

Westen, D., Gabbard, G. O., & Ortigo, K. M. (2008). Psychoanalytic approaches to personality. In O. P. John, R. W. Robins, & L. A. Pervin (Eds.), *Handbook of personality: Theory and research* (pp. 61–113). New York, NY: The Guilford Press.

Wheeler, L., & Suls, J. (2005). Social comparison and self-evaluations of competence. In A. J. Elliot & C. S. Dweck (Eds.), *Handbook of competence and motivation.* New York, NY: Guilford.

Whelan, C. B. (2009, October 25). For these "spiritual warriors," the casualties were real. *The Washington Post.* Retrieved from http://www.washigtonpost.com/wp-dyn/content/article/2009/10/23//AR2009102302411.html

Whiston, S. C., & Keller, B. K. (2004). The influences of the family of origin on career development: A review and analysis. *Counseling Psychologist, 32*(4), 493–568.

White, L. K., & Rogers, S. J. (1997). Strong support but uneasy relationships: Coresident and adult children's relationships with their parents. *Journal of Marriage and the Family, 59,* 62–76.

Whitehead, B. D., & Popenoe, D. (2001). *The state of our unions: The social health of marriage in America, 2001.* Piscataway, NJ: The National Marriage Project.

Whitehouse, W. G., Orne, E. C., & Orne, M. T. (2007). Relaxation techniques. In G. Fink (Ed.), *Encyclopedia of stress: Vols. 1–4* (2nd ed., pp. 345–350). San Diego, CA: Elsevier Academic Press.

Whitley, B. E. (1983). Sex role orientation and self-esteem: A critical meta-analytic review. *Journal of Personality and Social Psychology, 44,* 765–778.

Whitley, B. E., & Kite, M. E. (2006). *The psychology of prejudice and discrimination.* Belmont, CA: Wadsworth.

Whitton, S. W., Waldinger, R. J., Schulz, M. S., Allen, J. P., Crowell, J. A., & Hauser, S. T. (2008). Prospective associations from family-of-origin interactions to adult marital interactions and relationship adjustment. *Journal of Family Psychology, 22,* 274–286.

Widiger, T. A. (2009). Neuroticism. In M. R. Leary & R. H. Hoyle (Eds.), *Handbook of individual differences in social* behavior (pp. 129–146). New York, NY: The Guilford Press.

Wiederman, M. W. (1993). Evolved gender differences in mate preferences: Evidence from personal advertisements. *Ethology and Sociobiology, 14,* 331–352.

Wilfong, J. D. (2006). Computer anxiety and anger: The impact of computer use, computer experience, and self–efficacy beliefs. *Computers in Human Behavior, 22,* 1001–1011.

Williams, C. L. (1998). The glass escalator: Hidden advantages for men in the female professions. In M. S. Kimmel & M. A. Messner (Eds.), *Men's lives.* Boston, MA: Allyn & Bacon.

Williams, J. A., Burns, E. L., & Harmon, E. A. (2009). Insincere utterances and gaze: Eye contact during sarcastic statements. *Perceptual and Motor Skills, 108*(2), 565–572.

Williams, J. E., Paton, C. C., Siegler, I. C., Eigenbrodt, M. L., Neito, F. J., & Tyroler, H. A. (2000). Anger proneness predicts coronary heart disease risk. *Circulation, 101,* 2034–2039.

Williams, P. (2005). What is psychoanalysis? What is a psychoanalyst? In E. S. Person, A. M. Cooper, & G. O. Gabbard (Eds.), *Textbook of psychoanalysis.* Washington, DC: American Psychiatric Publishing.

Williams, R. B. (1996). Hostility and the heart. In D. Goleman & J. Gurin (Eds.), *Mind-body medicine: How to use your mind for better health.* Yonkers, NY: Consumer Reports Books.

Williams, R. B., & Williams, V. P. (1993). *Anger kills: Seventeen strategies for controlling the hostility that can harm your health.* New York, NY: Times Books/Random House.

Williams, S. L. (1995). Self-efficacy, anxiety, and phobic disorders. In J. E. Maddux (Ed.), *Self-efficacy, adaptation, and adjustment: Theory, research, and application.* New York, NY: Plenum Press.

Williamson, D. A., Zucker, N. L., Martin, C. K., & Smeets, M. A. M. (2001). Etiology and management of eating disorders. In P. B. Sutker & H. E. Adams (Eds.), *Comprehensive handbook of psychopathology* (3rd ed.). New York, NY: Kluwer Academic/Plenum.

Williamson, I., & Gonzales, M. H. (2007). The subjective experience of forgiveness: Positive construals of the forgiveness experience. *Journal of Social and Clinical Psychology, 26,* 407–446.

Willness, C. R., Steel, P., & Lee, K. (2007). A meta-analysis of antecedents and consequences of workplace sexual harassment. *Personnel Psychology, 60*(1), 127–162.

Wills, T. A. (1986). Stress and coping in early adolescence: Relationships to substance use in urban school samples. *Health Psychology, 5,* 503–529.

Wills, T. A., & Sandy, J. M. (2001). Comparing favorably: A cognitive approach to coping through comparison with other persons. In C. R. Snyder (Ed.), *Coping with stress: Effective people and processes* (pp. 154–177). New York, NY: Oxford University Press.

Wilmot, W., & Hocker, J. (2006). *Interpersonal conflict* (7th ed.). New York, NY: McGraw-Hill.

Wilsnack, S. C., Wonderlich, S. A., Kristjanson, A. F., Vogeltanz-Holm, N. D., & Wilsnack, R. W. (2002). Self-reports of forgetting and remembering childhood sexual abuse in a nationally representative sample of U.S. women. *Child Abuse and Neglect, 26*(2), 139–147.

Wilson, G. T. (2011). Behavior therapy. In R. J. Corsini & D. Wedding (Eds.), *Current psychotherapies* (9th ed.). Belmont, CA: Brooks/Cole.

Wilson, T. D., & Gilbert, D. T. (2005). Affective forecasting: Knowing what to want. *Current Directions in Psychological Science, 14*(3), 131–134.

Wilt, J. & Revelle, W. (2009). Extraversion. In M. R. Leary & R. H. Hoyle (Eds.), *Handbook of individual differences in social* behavior (pp. 27–45). New York, NY: Guilford.

Wing, J. F., Schutte, N. S., & Byrne, B. (2006). The effect of positive writing on emotional intelligence and life satisfaction. *Journal of Clinical Psychology, 62,* 1291–1302.

Wing, R. R., & Polley, B. A. (2001). Obesity. In A. Baum, T. A. Revenson, & J. E. Singer (Eds.), *Handbook of health psychology*. Mahwah, NJ: Erlbaum.

Winick, C., & Norman, R. L. (2005). Epidemiology. In J. H. Lowinson, P. Ruiz, R. B. Millman, & J. G. Langrod (Eds.), *Substance abuse: A comprehensive textbook*. Philadelphia, PA: Lippincott/Williams & Wilkins.

Winstead, Z. A. (2009). Friendships, sex differences and similarities. In H. T. Reis & S. Sprecher (Eds.), *Encyclopedia of human relationships: Vol. 2* (pp. 713–716). Los Angeles, CA: Sage Reference Publication.

Wissink, I. B., Dekovic, M., & Meijer, A. M. (2006). Parenting behavior, quality of the parent-adolescent functioning in four ethnic groups. *Journal of Early Adolescence, 26,* 133–159.

Wolfinger, N. H. (2005). *Understanding the divorce cycle: The children of divorce in their own marriages*. New York, NY: Cambridge University Press.

Wolpe, J. (1987). The promotion of scientific therapy: A long voyage. In J. K. Zeig (Ed.), *The evolution of psychotherapy.* New York, NY: Brunner/Mazel.

Wonderlich, S. A. (2002). Personality and eating disorders. In C. G. Fairburn & K. D. Brownell (Eds.), *Eating disorders and obesity: A comprehensive handbook*. New York, NY: Guilford.

Wong, P. T. P. (2006). Existential and humanistic theories. In J. C. Thomas & D. L. Segal (Eds.), *Comprehensive handbook of personality and psychopathology*. New York, NY: Wiley.

Wood, J. T. (2006) Chopping the carrots: Creating intimacy moment by moment. In J. T. Wood & S. W. Duck(Eds.), *Composing relationships: Communication in everyday life* (pp. 24–35). Belmont, CA: Thompson/Wadsworth.

Wood, J. T. (2010). *Interpersonal communication: Everyday encounters* (6th ed.). Belmont, CA: Wadsworth/ Cengage.

Wood, R. T. A., & Griffiths, M. D. (2007). A qualitative investigation of problem gambling as an escape-based coping strategy. *Psychology and Psychotherapy: Theory, Research, and Practice, 80,* 107–125.

Wood, W., & Kallgren, C. A. (1988). Communicator attributes and persuasion: Recipients' access to attitude-relevant information in memory. *Personality and Social Psychology Bulletin, 14,* 172–182.

Wood, W., & Quinn, J. M. (2003). Forewarned and forearmed? Two meta-analytic syntheses of forewarnings of influence appeals. *Psychological Bulletin, 129*(1), 119–138.

Woodzicka, J. A., & LaFrance, M. (2005). The effects of subtle sexual harassment on women's performance in a job interview. *Sex Roles, 53,* 67–77.

Worthington E. L., Jr., Witvliet, C. V. O., Pietrini, P., & Miller, A. J. (2007). Forgiveness, health, and well-being: A review of evidence for emotional versus decisional forgiveness, dispositional forgivingness, and reduced unforgiveness. *Journal of Behavioral Medicine, 30,* 291–302.

Worthington, R. L., Flores, L. Y., & Navarro, R. L. (2005). Career development in context: Research with people of color. In S. D. Brown & R. W. Lent (Eds.), *Career development and counseling: Putting theory and research to work*. New York, NY: Wiley.

Worthington, R. L., Soth-McNett, A. M., & Moreno, M. V. (2007). Multicultural counseling competencies research: A 20-year content analysis. *Journal of Counseling Psychology, 54,* 351–361.

Wright, J. H., Thase, M. E., & Beck, A. T. (2008). Cognitive therapy. In R. E. Hales, S. C. Yudofsky, & G. O. Gabbard (Eds.), *The American psychiatric publishing textbook of psychiatry* (pp. 2111–1256). Washington, DC: American Psychiatric Publishing.

Wright, S. C., & Taylor, D. M. (2003). The social psychology of cultural diversity: Social stereotyping, prejudice, and discrimination. In M. A. Hogg & J. Cooper (Eds.), *The Sage handbook of social psychology.* Thousand Oaks, CA: Sage Publications.

Xie, J. (2011). Relationship between emotional intelligence, job burnout and job satisfaction. *Chinese Journal of Clinical Psychology, 19*(3), 372–373.

Yalom, I. D. (1995). *The theory and practice of group psychotherapy* (4th ed.). New York, NY: Basic Books.

Yang, A. C., Tsai, S.-J., & Huang, N. E. (2011). Decomposing the association of completed suicide with air pollution, weather, and unemployment data at different time scales. *Journal of Affective Disorders, 129* (1–3), 275–281. doi:10.1016/j.jad.2010.08.010

Yehuda, R. (2003). Changes in the concept of PTSD and trauma. *Psychiatric Times, 20*(4), 35–40.

Yi, H., Stinson, F. S., Williams, G. D., & Dufour, M. C. (1999). *Surveillance report #53: Trends in alcohol-related fatal traffic crashes, United States, 1977–1998*. Rockville, MD: National Institute on Alcohol Abuse and Alcoholism.

Ying, Y., & Han, M. (2006). The contribution of personality, acculturative stressors, and social affiliation to adjustment: A longitudinal study of Taiwanese students in the United States. *International Journal of Intercultural Relations, 30,* 623–635.

Yoder, J. D., & Kahn, A. S. (2003). Making gender comparisons more meaningful: A call for more attention to social context. *Psychology of Women Quarterly, 27,* 281–290.

Young, J. E. (1982). Loneliness, depression and cognitive therapy: Theory and application. In L. A. Peplau & D. Perlman (Eds.), *Loneliness: A sourcebook of current theory, research and therapy.* New York, NY: Wiley.

Young, R., & Sweeting, H. (2004). Adolescent bullying, relationships, psychological well-being, and gender-atypical behavior: A gender diagnosticity approach. *Sex Roles, 50,* 525–537.

Zajonc, R. B. (1968). Attitudinal effects of mere exposure. *Journal of Personality and Social Psychology, 9,* 1–27.

Zane, N., Hall, G. C. N., Sue, S., Young, K., & Nunez, J. (2004). Research on psychotherapy with culturally diverse populations. In M. J. Lambert (Ed.), *Bergin and Garfield's handbook of psychotherapy and behavior change.* New York, NY: Wiley.

Zautra, A. J., & Reich, J. W. (2011). Resilience: The meanings, methods, and measures of a fundamental characteristic of human adaptation. In S. Folkman (Ed.). *The Oxford Handbook of stress, health, & coping.* (pp. 173–185). New York, NY: NY: Oxford University Press.

Zautra, A. J., & Smith, B. W. (2001). Depression and reactivity to stress in older women with rheumatoid arthritis and osteoarthritis. *Psychosomatic Medicine, 63*(4), 687–696.

Zedek, S. (Ed.). (2011). *APA handbook of industrial and organizational psychology* (2 vols.). Washington, DC: American Psychological Association.

Zimbardo, P. G. (1990). *Shyness.* Reading, MA: Addison-Wesley.

Zimbardo, P. G. (1992). Cults in everyday life: Dependency and power. *Contemporary Psychology, 37,* 1187–1189.

Zinbarg, R. E., & Griffith, J. W. (2008). Behavior therapy. In J. L. Lebow (Ed.), *Twenty-first century psychotherapies: Contemporary approaches to theory and practice*. New York, NY: Wiley.

Zuckerman, M., Kieffer, S. C., & Knee, C. R. (1998). Consequences of self-handicapping: Effects of coping, academic performance, and adjustment. *Journal of Personality and Social Psychology, 74*(6), 1619–1628.

Zuckerman, M., & Tsai, F. (2005). Costs of self-handicapping. *Journal of Social Psychology, 73,* 411–442.

Zvonkovic, A. M., Solomon, C. R., Humble, A. M., & Monoogian, M. (2005). Family work and relationships: Lessons from families of men whose jobs require travel. *Family Relations, 54,* 411–422.

NAME INDEX

M

N

O

P

Q

R

S

X

Y

Z

SUBJECT INDEX

A

B

C

F

G

H

I

N

O

P

T

U

V

W

XYZ

CHAPTER REVIEW 1

KEY TERMS

1-1

narcissism The tendency to regard oneself as grandiosely self-important.

1-2

psychology The science that studies behavior and the physiological and mental processes that underlie it and the profession that applies the accumulated knowledge of this science to practical problems.

behavior Any overt (observable) response or activity by an organism.

clinical psychology The branch of psychology concerned with the diagnosis and treatment of psychological problems and disorders.

adjustment The psychological processes through which people manage or cope with the demands and challenges of everyday life.

1-3

empiricism The premise that knowledge should be acquired through observation.

experiment A research method in which the investigator manipulates an (independent) variable under carefully controlled conditions and observes whether there are changes in a second (dependent) variable as a result.

independent variable In an experiment, a condition or event that an experimenter varies in order to see its impact on another variable.

dependent variable In an experiment, the variable that is thought to be affected by manipulations of the independent variable.

experimental group The subjects in an experiment who receive some special treatment in regard to the independent variable.

control group Subjects in an experiment who do not receive the special treatment given to the experimental group.

correlation coefficient A numerical index of the degree of relationship that exists between two variables.

naturalistic observation An approach to research in which the researcher engages in careful observation of behavior without intervening directly with the subjects.

case study An in-depth investigation of an individual subject.

surveys Structured questionnaires designed to solicit information about specific aspects of participants' behavior.

KEY IDEAS

1-1 Provide examples of people's search for direction in their lives, and analyze the value of self-help books.

- According to many theorists, the basic challenge of modern life has become the search for a sense of direction and meaning. This search has many manifestations, including the appeal of self-help gurus, self-realization programs, and religious cults.
- The enormous popularity of self-help books is an interesting manifestation of people's struggle to find a sense of direction. Some self-help books offer worthwhile advice, but most are dominated by psychobabble and are not based on scientific research. Many also lack explicit advice on how to change behavior and some encourage a self-centered, narcissistic approach to interpersonal interactions.
- Although this text deals with many of the same issues as self-realization programs, self-help books, and other types of pop psychology, its philosophy and approach are quite different. This text is based on the premise that accurate knowledge about the principles of psychology can be of value in everyday life.

1-2 Describe the two key facets of psychology, and explain the concept of adjustment.

- Psychology is both a science and a profession that focuses on behavior and related mental and physiological processes. Adjustment is a broad area of study in psychology concerned with how people adapt effectively or ineffectively to the demands and pressures of everyday life.

1-3 Explain the nature of experimental and correlational research, and evaluate the advantages of each approach.

- The scientific approach to understanding behavior is empirical. Psychologists base their conclusions on systematic observations that allow them to test their hypotheses.
- Experimental research involves manipulating an independent variable to discover its effects on a dependent variable. The experimenter usually does so by comparing experimental and control groups, which must be alike except for the variation created by the manipulation of the independent variable. Experiments permit conclusions about cause-effect relationships between variables, but this method isn't usable for the study of many questions.
- Psychologists conduct correlational research when they are unable to exert experimental control over the variables they want to study. The correlation coefficient is a numerical index of the degree of relationship between two variables. Correlational research methods include naturalistic observation, case studies, and surveys. Correlational research facilitates the investigation of many issues that are not open to experimental study, but it cannot demonstrate that two variables are causally related.

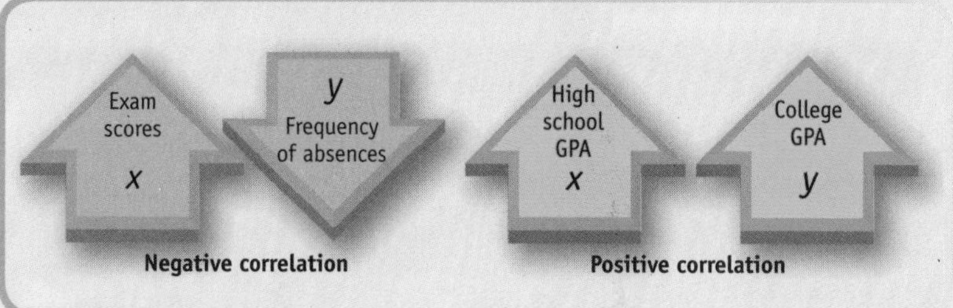

KEY TERMS *continued*

1-4

subjective well-being Individuals' personal assessments of their overall happiness or life satisfaction.

affective forecasting Efforts to predict one's emotional reactions to future events.

hedonic adaptation The phenomenon that occurs when the mental scale that people use to judge the pleasantness and unpleasantness of their experiences shifts so that their neutral point, or baseline for comparison, is changed.

KEY IDEAS *continued*

1-4 Review information on the factors that are and are not predictive of subjective well-being.

- A scientific analysis of happiness reveals that many commonsense notions about the roots of happiness appear to be incorrect, including the notion that most people are unhappy. Factors such as money, age, parenthood, intelligence, and attractiveness are not correlated with subjective well-being.
- Physical health, social relationships, and religious faith appear to have a modest impact on feelings of happiness. The only factors that are clearly and strongly related to happiness are love and marriage, work satisfaction, and personality, which probably reflects the influence of heredity.
- Happiness is a relative concept mediated by people's highly subjective assessments of their lives. Research on affective forecasting shows that people are surprisingly bad at predicting what will make them happy. Individuals adapt to both positive and negative events in their lives, which creates a hedonic treadmill effect.

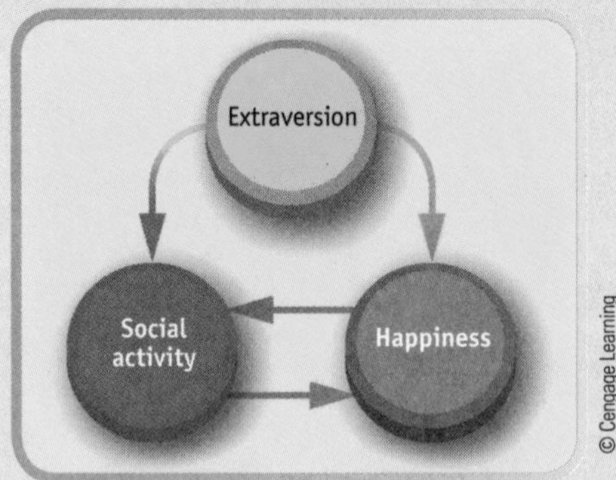

1-5 Discuss some strategies for improving study habits, note taking, reading comprehension, and memory.

- To foster sound study habits, you should devise a written study schedule and reward yourself for following it. You should also try to find places for studying that are relatively free of distractions.
- You should use active reading techniques to select the most important ideas from the material you read. Highlighting textbook material *is* a useful strategy—if you're reasonably effective in focusing on the main ideas in the material and subsequently review what you have highlighted. Good note taking can help you get more out of lectures. It's important to use active listening techniques and to record lecturers' ideas in your own words.
- Repeatedly reviewing information facilitates retention. Distributed practice and deeper processing tend to improve memory. Evidence also suggests that organization facilitates retention, so outlining reading assignments can be valuable. The process of being tested on material seems to enhance retention of that material.

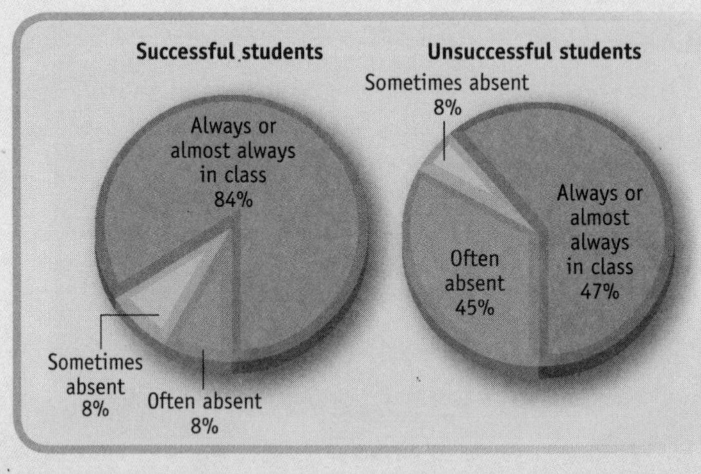

Theories of Personality

CHAPTER REVIEW 2

KEY TERMS

2-1

personality trait A durable disposition to behave in a particular way in a variety of situations.

2-2

id In Freud's theory, the primitive, instinctive component of personality that operates according to the pleasure principle.

ego According to Freud, the decision-making component of personality that operates according to the reality principle.

superego According to Freud, the moral component of personality that incorporates social standards about what represents right and wrong.

conscious According to Freud, whatever one is aware of at a particular point in time.

preconscious According to Freud, material just beneath the surface of awareness that can be easily retrieved.

unconscious According to Freud, thoughts, memories, and desires that are well below the surface of conscious awareness but that nonetheless exert great influence on one's behavior.

defense mechanisms Largely unconscious reactions that protect a person from unpleasant emotions such as anxiety and guilt.

rationalization Creating false but plausible excuses to justify unacceptable behavior.

repression Keeping distressing thoughts and feelings buried in the unconscious.

projection Attributing one's own thoughts, feelings, or motives to another person.

displacement Diverting emotional feelings (usually anger) from their original source to a substitute target.

reaction formation Behaving in a way that is the opposite of one's true feelings.

regression A reversion to immature patterns of behavior.

identification Bolstering self-esteem by forming an imaginary or real alliance with some person or group.

psychosexual stages In Freud's theory, developmental periods with a characteristic sexual focus that leave their mark on adult personality.

collective unconscious According to Jung, a storehouse of latent memory traces inherited from people's ancestral past that is shared with the entire human race.

compensation According to Adler, efforts to overcome imagined or real inferiorities by developing one's abilities.

KEY IDEAS

2-1 Explain the concept of personality traits, and describe the five-factor model of personality.

- The concept of personality explains the consistency in individuals' behavior over time and situations while also explaining their distinctiveness. Personality traits are dispositions to behave in certain ways.
- According to the five-factor model, the complexity of personality can be reduced to just five basic traits: extraversion, neuroticism, openness to experience, agreeableness, and conscientiousness. The Big Five traits predict important life outcomes, such as occupational attainment, divorce, health, and mortality.

2-2 Outline Freud's theory of personality and psychosexual development.

- Freud's psychoanalytic theory emphasizes the importance of the unconscious. Freud described personality structure in terms of three components (id, ego, and superego), operating at three levels of awareness, that are involved in internal conflicts, which generate anxiety.

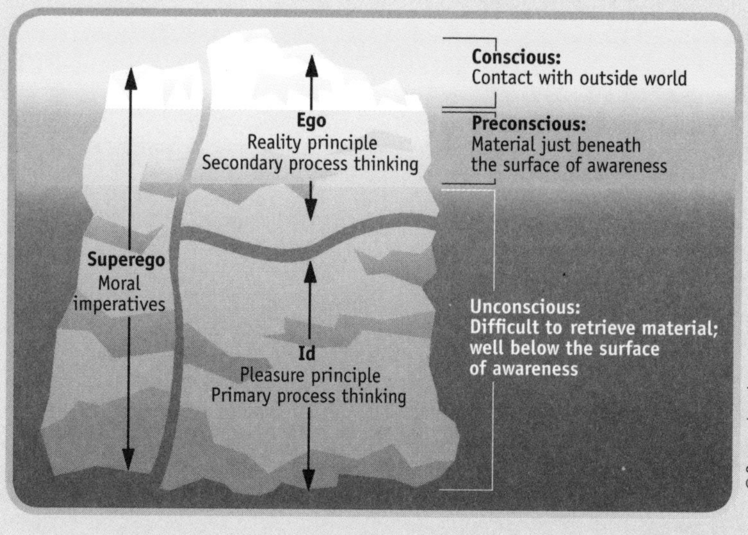

- According to Freud, people often ward off anxiety and other unpleasant emotions with defense mechanisms, which work through self-deception. Freud believed that the first five years of life are extremely influential in shaping adult personality. He described five psychosexual stages that children undergo in their personality development: the oral, anal, phallic, latency, and genital stages.
- Jung's analytical psychology stresses the importance of the collective unconscious. Adler's individual psychology emphasizes how people strive for superiority to compensate for feelings of inferiority.

2-3 Understand how classical conditioning, operant conditioning, and observational learning help shape personality.

- Behavioral theories view personality as a collection of response tendencies shaped through learning. Pavlov's classical conditioning can explain how people acquire emotional responses.
- Skinner's model of operant conditioning shows how consequences such as reinforcement, extinction, and punishment strengthen and weaken various response tendencies that represent charcteristic behavior. Bandura's social cognitive theory shows how people can be conditioned indirectly through observation.

KEY TERMS *continued*

2-3

classical conditioning A type of learning in which a neutral stimulus acquires the capacity to evoke a response that was originally evoked by another stimulus.

extinction The gradual weakening and disappearance of a conditioned response tendency.

operant conditioning A form of learning in which voluntary responses come to be controlled by their consequences.

positive reinforcement The strengthening of a response because it is followed by the arrival of a (presumably) pleasant stimulus.

negative reinforcement The strengthening of a response because it is followed by the removal of a (presumably) unpleasant stimulus.

punishment The weakening (decrease in frequency) of a response because it is followed by the arrival of a (presumably) unpleasant stimulus.

observational learning Learning that occurs when an organism's responding is influenced by observing others, who are called models.

2-4

self-concept A collection of beliefs about one's basic nature, unique qualities, and typical behavior.

incongruence The disparity between one's self-concept and one's actual experience.

hierarchy of needs A systematic arrangement of needs, according to priority, in which basic needs must be met before less basic needs are aroused.

need for self-actualization The need to fulfill one's potential; the highest need in Maslow's motivational hierarchy.

2-5

twin studies A research method in which researchers assess hereditary influence by comparing the resemblance of identical twins and fraternal twins on a trait.

heritability ratio An estimate of the proportion of trait variability in a population that is determined by variations in genetic inheritance.

2-7

standardization The uniform procedures used to administer and score a test.

test norms Statistics that provide information about where a score on a psychological test ranks in relation to other scores on that test.

reliability The measurement consistency of a test.

validity The ability of a test to measure what it was designed to measure.

KEY IDEAS *continued*

2-4 Describe Rogers's views on self-concept development and Maslow's hierarchy of needs.

- Humanistic theories take an optimistic view of people's conscious, rational ability to chart their own courses of action. Rogers focused on the self-concept as the critical aspect of personality. He maintained that incongruence between one's self-concept and reality creates anxiety and leads to defensive behavior.

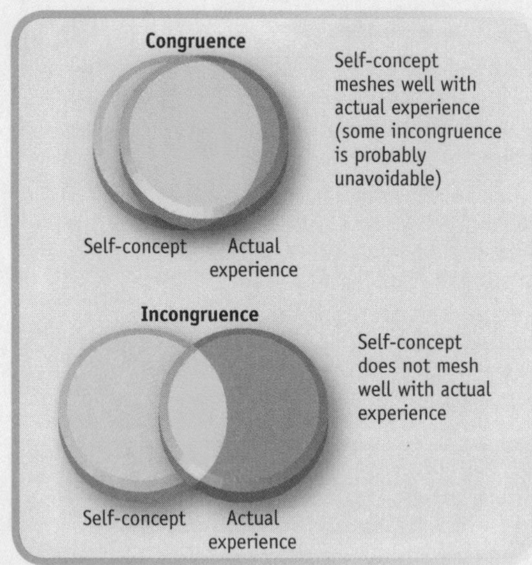

- Maslow theorized that needs are arranged hierarchically so that satisfaction of lower needs activates needs at higher levels. He asserted that psychological health depends on self-actualization, which is the need to fulfill one's potential.

2-5 Discuss the genetic and evolutionary roots of personality.

- Eysenck believes that inherited individual differences in physiological functioning affect conditioning and thus influence personality. Recent twin studies have provided impressive evidence that genetic factors shape personality. Behavioral genetics research suggests that the heritability of each of the Big Five traits is around 50%.
- The basic premise of evolutionary psychology is that natural selection favors behaviors that enhance organisms' reproductive success. Evolutionary psychologists maintain that natural selection has favored the emergence of the Big Five traits as crucial dimensions of personality.

2-6 Explain how researchers have found both cross-cultural similarities and differences in personality.

- Research suggests that the basic trait structure of personality may be much the same across cultures, as the Big Five traits usually emerge in cross-cultural studies. Cultural variations have been found in average trait scores on the Big Five traits, but the differences are modest. People's perceptions of national character appear to be remarkably inaccurate.

2-7 Describe the nature, value, and limitations of personality tests.

- Psychological tests are standardized measures of behavior. Test norms indicate what represents a high or low score. Psychological tests should produce consistent results upon retesting, a quality called reliability. Validity refers to the degree to which a test measures what it was designed to measure.
- Self-report inventories, such as the 16PF and NEO Personality Inventory, ask respondents to describe themselves. Self-report inventories can provide a better snapshot of personality than casual observations, but they are vulnerable to deception and social desirability bias.
- Projective tests, such as the Rorschach and TAT, assume that people's responses to ambiguous stimuli reveal something about their personality. Projective tests' reliability and validity appear to be disturbingly low.

Stress and Its Effects

CHAPTER REVIEW 3

KEY TERMS

3-1

stress Any circumstances that threaten or are perceived to threaten one's well-being and thereby tax one's coping abilities.

primary appraisal An initial evaluation of whether an event is (1) irrelevant to one, (2) relevant but not threatening, or (3) stressful.

secondary appraisal An evaluation of one's coping resources and options for dealing with stress.

ambient stress Chronic environmental conditions that, although not urgent, are negatively valued and place adaptive demands on people.

acculturation Changing to adapt to a new culture.

3-2

acute stressors Threatening events that have a relatively short duration and a clear end point.

chronic stressors Threatening events that have a relatively long duration and no readily apparent time limit.

frustration The feelings that occur in any situation in which the pursuit of some goal is thwarted.

internal conflict The struggle that occurs when two or more incompatible motivations or behavioral impulses compete for expression.

life changes Any noticeable alterations in one's living circumstances that require readjustment.

pressure Expectations or demands that one behave in a certain way.

3-3

emotions Powerful, largely uncontrollable feelings, accompanied by physiological changes.

fight-or-flight response A physiological reaction to threat that mobilizes an organism for attacking (fight) or fleeing (flight) an enemy.

autonomic nervous system (ANS) That portion of the peripheral nervous system made up of the nerves that connect to the heart, blood vessels, smooth muscles, and glands.

general adaptation syndrome A model of the body's stress response, consisting of three stages: alarm, resistance, and exhaustion.

endocrine system Glands that secrete chemicals called hormones into the bloodstream.

coping Active efforts to master, reduce, or tolerate the demands created by stress.

KEY IDEAS

3-1 Understand how one's appraisals, environment, and culture can influence the experience of stress.

- Stress involves transactions with the environment that are perceived to be threatening. To a large degree, stress lies in the eye of the beholder. According to Lazarus and Folkman, primary appraisal determines whether events appear threatening, while secondary appraisal assesses whether one has the resources to cope with challenges.

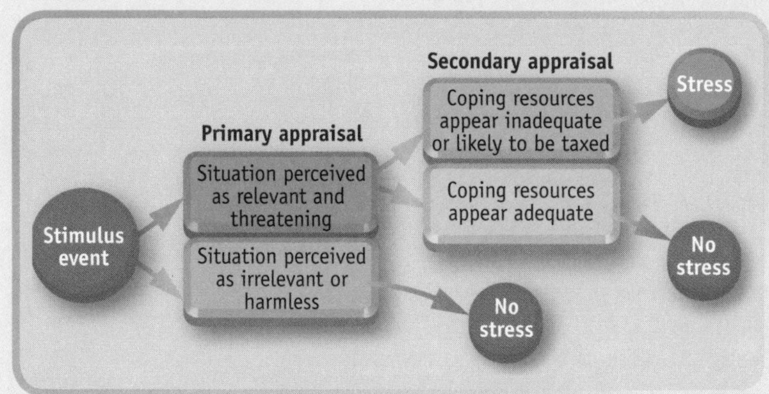

- Some of the stress that people experience comes from their environment, such as excessive noise, crowding, and urban decay. Stress can vary with culture. Within Western culture, discrimination and acculturation can be sources of stress.

3-2 Describe the four major sources of stress in modern life.

- Major sources of stress include frustration, conflict, change, and pressure. Frustration occurs when an obstacle prevents one from attaining some goal. Internal conflict occurs when one experiences two or more incompatible motivations or behavioral impulses.
- A large number of studies with the SRRS suggest that change is stressful. Although that may be true, it is now clear that the SRRS is a measure of general stress rather than just change-related stress. Pressure (to perform and to conform) also appears to be stressful. Often this pressure is self-imposed.

3-3 Discuss some of the typical emotional, physiological, and behavioral responses to stress.

- Emotional reactions to stress typically involve anger, fear, or sadness. However, people also experience positive emotions while under stress, and these positive emotions may promote resilience. Emotional arousal may interfere with functioning. As tasks get more complex, the optimal level of arousal declines.
- Physiological arousal in response to stress was originally called the fight-or-flight response by Cannon. Selye's general adaptation syndrome describes three stages in the physiological reaction to stress: alarm, resistance, and exhaustion. Diseases of adaptation may appear during the exhaustion stage.
- In response to stress, the brain sends signals along two major pathways to the endocrine system. Actions along these paths release two sets of hormones into the bloodstream, catecholamines and corticosteroids. These stress hormones appear to contribute to suppression of the immune response.
- Behavioral responses to stress involve coping, which may be healthy or maladaptive. If people cope effectively with stress, they can short-circuit potentially harmful emotional and physical responses.

KEY TERMS *continued*

3-4
burnout Physical, mental, and emotional exhaustion that is attributable to work-related stress.

posttraumatic stress disorder (PTSD) Disturbed behavior that emerges sometime after a major stressful event is over.

3-5
social support Aid and succor provided by members of one's social networks.

hardiness A personality characteristic marked by commitment, challenge, and control that is associated with strong stress resistance.

optimism A general tendency to expect good outcomes.

3-6
behavior modification A systematic approach to changing behavior through the application of the principles of conditioning.

antecedents In behavior modification, events that typically precede a target response.

shaping Modifying behavior by reinforcing closer and closer approximations of a desired response.

behavioral contract A written agreement outlining a promise to adhere to the contingencies of a behavior modification program.

KEY IDEAS *continued*

3-4 Describe some of the potential effects of stress, both positive and negative.

- Common negative effects of stress include impaired task performance, disruption of attention and other cognitive processes, and pervasive emotional exhaustion known as burnout. Other effects include a host of everyday psychological problems, full-fledged psychological disorders including posttraumatic stress disorder, and varied types of damage to physical health.

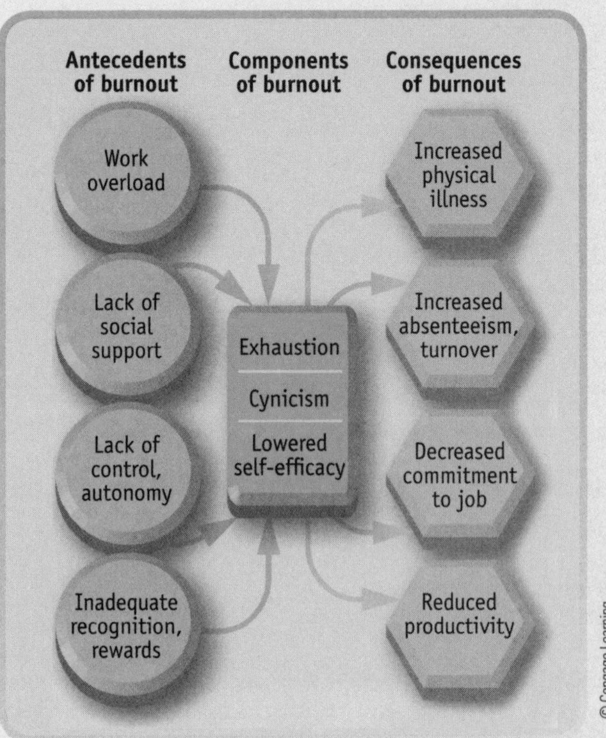

- Stress can also have positive effects. It can lead to personal growth and self-improvement, can fulfill a basic human need for challenge, and can have an inoculation effect, preparing the person for the next stressful event.

3-5 Identify three moderating variables that influence one's stress tolerance.

- People differ in how much stress they can tolerate without experiencing ill effects. A person's social support can be a key consideration in buffering the effects of stress. The personality factors associated with hardiness—commitment, challenge, and control—may increase stress tolerance. People high in optimism also have advantages in coping with stress, although unrealistic optimism can be problematic.

3-6 Explain how one might reduce stress through behavior modification.

- Stress often results from a lack of self-discipline. Behavior modification techniques can be used to increase one's self-control. In behavior modification, the principles of learning are used to change behavior directly. The first step in self-modification is to specify the overt target behavior to be increased or decreased.
- The second step is to gather baseline data about the initial rate of the target response and identify any typical antecedents and consequences associated with the behavior. The third step is to design a program. If you are trying to increase the strength of a response, you'll depend on positive reinforcement. A number of strategies can be used to decrease the strength of a response, including control of antecedents, punishment, and indirectly, reinforcement.
- The fourth step is to execute and evaluate the program. Self-modification programs often require some fine-tuning. The final step is to determine how and when you will phase out your program.

Coping Processes
CHAPTER REVIEW 4

KEY TERMS

coping Active efforts to master, reduce, or tolerate the demands created by stress.

4-1

learned helplessness Passive behavior produced by exposure to unavoidable aversive events.

aggression Any behavior intended to hurt someone, either physically or verbally.

catharsis The release of emotional tension.

defense mechanisms Largely unconscious reactions that protect a person from unpleasant emotions such as anxiety and guilt.

4-2

constructive coping Efforts to deal with stressful events that are judged to be relatively healthful.

4-3

rational-emotive therapy An approach to therapy that focuses on altering clients' patterns of irrational thinking to reduce maladaptive emotions and behavior.

catastrophic thinking Unrealistic appraisals of stress that exaggerate the magnitude of one's problems.

KEY IDEAS

4-1 Identify some common responses to stress that tend to be maladaptive.

- Giving up, possibly best understood in terms of learned helplessness, is a common coping pattern that tends to be of limited value. Another is engaging in aggressive behavior. Frequently caused by frustration, aggression tends to be counterproductive because it often creates new sources of stress.
- Indulging oneself is a common coping strategy that is not inherently unhealthy, but it is frequently taken to excess and thus becomes maladaptive, especially when it involves excessive eating, drinking, smoking, or drug use. Blaming yourself with negative self-talk is associated with increased distress and depression.
- Defensive coping is common and may involve any of a number of defense mechanisms. Defense mechanisms shield people from emotional discomfort through self-deception. The adaptive value of defensive coping tends to be less than optimal because avoidance and wishful thinking are rarely helpful. Although some illusions may be healthful, extreme forms of self-deception are maladaptive.

4-2 Describe the characteristics of constructive coping, and distinguish among the three categories of coping techniques.

- Constructive coping involves efforts to deal with stress that are judged as relatively healthful. Constructive coping is rational, realistic, and action oriented. It involves self-control. Constructive coping techniques can be divided into three broad categories: appraisal-focused coping, problem-focused coping, and emotion-focused coping.

4-3 Understand the merits of appraisal-focused constructive coping strategies, including rational thinking, humor, and positive reinterpretation.

- Appraisal-focused constructive coping depends on altering appraisals of threatening events. Ellis maintains that catastrophic thinking causes problematic emotional reactions. He asserts that catastrophic thinking can be reduced by digging out the irrational assumptions that cause it. Rational appraisals of the stressors in one's life can foster healthier adjustment.
- Evidence indicates that the use of humor can reduce the negative effects of stress through a variety of mechanisms. Among other things, humor can increase positive emotions and social support. Positive reinterpretation and benefit finding are also valuable strategies for dealing with some types of stress.

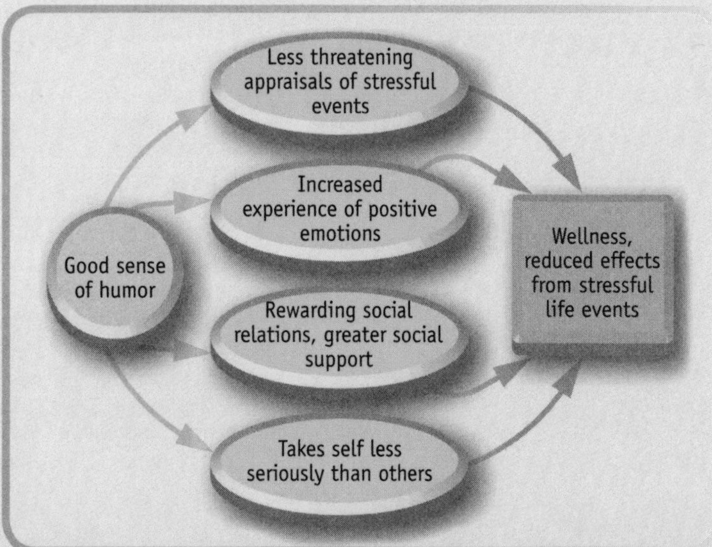

KEY TERMS *continued*

4-4

brainstorming Generating as many ideas as possible while withholding criticism and evaluation.

4-5

emotional intelligence The ability to monitor, assess, express, or regulate one's emotions; the capacity to identify, interpret, and understand others' emotions; and the ability to use this information to guide one's thinking and actions.

forgiveness Counteracting the natural tendencies to seek vengeance or avoid an offender, thereby releasing this person from further liability for his or her transgression.

meditation A family of mental exercises in which a conscious attempt is made to focus attention in a nonanalytical way.

4-6

procrastination The tendency to delay tackling tasks until the last minute.

KEY IDEAS *continued*

4-4 Discuss the adaptive value of problem-focused coping strategies, including systematic problem solving, seeking help, and improving time management.

- Systematic problem solving has been linked to better psychological adjustment. Systematic problem solving can be facilitated by following a four-step process: (1) clarify the problem, (2) generate alternative courses of action, (3) evaluate your alternatives and select a course of action, and (4) take action while maintaining flexibility.
- A problem-focused coping tactic with potential value is seeking social support. There appear to be cultural differences regarding who seeks social support, as Asian Americans are less likely to seek social support in times of stress than European Americans are. Improving time management can also aid problem-focused coping.

4-5 Summarize evidence on the merits of emotion-focused coping techniques, such as cultivating emotional intelligence, expressing emotions, managing hostility, forgiving others, and meditating.

- Emotional intelligence consists of the ability to perceive and express emotion, use emotions to facilitate thought, understand and reason with emotion, and regulate emotion. Emotional intelligence may help people to be more resilient in the face of stress. Inhibition of emotions appears to be associated with increased health problems. Thus, it appears that appropriate emotional expression is adaptive. In particular, talking or writing about stressful personal issues can have beneficial effects.
- Research suggests that it is wise for people to learn how to manage their feelings of hostility. New evidence also suggests that forgiving people for their offenses is healthier than nursing grudges.
- Meditation can be valuable in soothing emotional turmoil. Meditation is associated with lower levels of stress hormones, improved mental health, and other indicators of wellness. Some of these benefits may also be attained through systematic relaxation procedures.

4-6 Identify the causes of wasted time and procrastination, and describe strategies for managing time effectively.

- There are many causes of wasted time including the inabilities to stick with priorities, say no, delegate, throw things away, and accept anything less that perfection. Procrastination is a problem for many people, especially those who are perfectionists. Procrastination is fueled by a desire to minimize time on a task, a desire for optimal efficiency, and close proximity to reward.
- Engaging in sound time-management techniques can reduce time-related stress. Effective time management is facilitated by monitoring your use of time, clarifying your goals, planning your schedule, protecting your prime time, and increasing your efficiency.

Psychology and Physical Health

CHAPTER REVIEW 5

KEY TERMS

biopsychosocial model The idea that physical illness is caused by a complex interaction of biological, psychological, and sociocultural factors.

health psychology The subfield of psychology concerned with the relation of psychosocial factors to the promotion and maintenance of health, and with the causation, prevention, and treatment of illness.

5-1

coronary heart disease A chronic disease characterized by a reduction in blood flow from the coronary arteries, which supply the heart with blood

atherosclerosis A disease characterized by gradual narrowing of the coronary arteries.

Type A personality A personality style marked by a competitive orientation, impatience and urgency, and anger and hostility.

Type B personality A personality style marked by relatively relaxed, patient, easygoing, amicable behavior.

hostility A persistent negative attitude marked by cynical, mistrusting thoughts, feelings of anger, and overtly aggressive actions.

cancer Malignant cell growth, which may occur in many organ systems in the body.

immune response The body's defensive reaction to invasion by bacteria, viral agents, or other foreign substances.

5-2

unrealistic optimism Awareness that certain health-related behaviors are dangerous but erroneously viewing those dangers as risks for others rather than oneself.

alcohol dependence A chronic, progressive disorder marked by a growing compulsion to drink and impaired control over drinking that eventually interfere with health and social behavior.

KEY IDEAS

5-1 Explain how stressful events and certain personality traits can promote either health or disease.

- The biopsychosocial model holds that physical health is influenced by a complex network of biological, psychological, and sociocultural factors. Stress is one of the psychological factors that can affect physical health. In particular, cynical hostility has been implicated as a contributing cause of coronary heart disease. A number of mechanisms may contribute to this connection.
- Emotional reactions may also influence susceptibility to heart disease. Recent research has suggested that transient mental stress and the negative emotions that result may tax the heart. Yet another line of research has identified the emotional dysfunction of depression as a risk factor for heart disease.
- The findings are complicated, but stress and personality do appear to be related to both the onset and the course of many types of cancer. Researchers have also found associations between stress and the onset of a variety of other diseases. Stress may play a role in a variety of diseases because it can temporarily suppress immune functioning. While there's little doubt that stress can contribute to the development of physical illness, the link between stress and illness is modest.

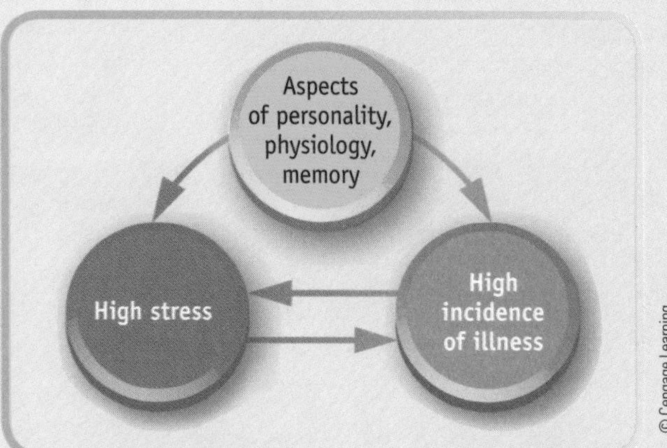

5-2 Describe ways that people's good habits can foster well-being and bad habits can compromise health.

- People commonly engage in health-impairing habits and lifestyles. These habits creep up slowly, and their risks are easy to ignore because the dangers often lie in the distant future. People also have a tendency to underestimate the risks associated with their own health-impairing habits while viewing the risks associated with others' self-destructive behaviors much more accurately.
- Smokers have much higher mortality rates than nonsmokers because they are more vulnerable to a variety of diseases, especially cardiovascular diseases and some types of cancer. Giving up smoking can reduce one's health risks, but doing so is difficult and relapse rates are high.
- Drinking rivals smoking as a source of health problems. In the short term, drinking can impair driving, cause various types of accidents, and increase the likelihood of aggressive interactions or reckless sexual behavior. In the long term, chronic, excessive alcohol consumption increases one's risk for numerous health problems, including cirrhosis of the liver, heart disease, hypertension, stroke, and cancer.
- Obesity elevates one's risk for many health problems. Body weight is influenced by genetic endowment, eating and exercise habits, and one's set point. Weight loss is best accomplished by decreasing caloric consumption while increasing exercise. Self-modification techniques can be helpful. Surgical options can be effective as a last resort among those who are extremely obese.

KEY TERMS *continued*

body mass index (BMI) Weight (in kilograms) divided by height (in meters) squared (kg/m^2).

acquired immune deficiency syndrome (AIDS) A disorder in which the immune system is gradually weakened and eventually disabled by the human immunodeficiency virus (HIV).

5-3

tolerance A progressive decrease in responsiveness to a drug with continued use.

physical dependence The need to continue to take a drug to avoid withdrawal illness.

psychological dependence The need to continue to take a drug to satisfy intense mental and emotional craving for it.

overdose An excessive dose of a drug that can seriously threaten one's life.

narcotics (opiates) Drugs derived from opium that are capable of relieving pain.

sedatives Sleep-inducing drugs that tend to decrease central nervous system and behavioral activity.

stimulants Drugs that tend to increase central nervous system and behavioral activity.

hallucinogens A diverse group of drugs that have powerful effects on mental and emotional functioning, marked most prominently by distortions in sensory and perceptual experience.

cannabis The hemp plant from which marijuana, hashish, and THC are derived.

KEY IDEAS *continued*

- Lack of exercise is associated with elevated mortality rates. Regular exercise can reduce one's risk for cardiovascular disease, cancer, and obesity-related diseases. Exercise can also buffer the effects of stress, enhance mental health, and lead to desirable personality changes.

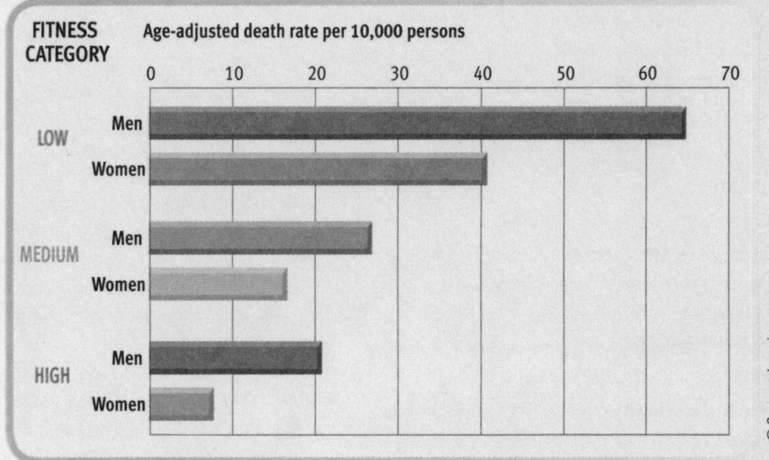

- Although misconceptions abound, HIV is transmitted almost exclusively by sexual contact and the sharing of needles by intravenous drug users. One's risk for HIV infection can be reduced by avoiding IV drug use, having fewer sexual partners, using condoms, and curtailing certain sexual practices.

5-3 Discuss the distinct psychological effects of various recreational drugs, as well as their physical and psychological risks.

- Recreational drugs vary in their potential for tolerance effects, psychological dependence, physical dependence, and overdose. The risks associated with narcotics use include both types of dependence, overdose, and the acquisition of infectious diseases.
- Sedatives can also produce both types of dependence, are subject to overdoses, and elevate the user's risk for accidental injuries. Stimulant use can lead to psychological dependence, overdose, psychosis, and a deterioration in physical health. Cocaine overdoses have increased greatly in recent years.
- Hallucinogens can contribute to accidents, suicides, and psychological disorders, and they can cause flashbacks. The risks of marijuana use include psychological dependence, impaired driving, respiratory and pulmonary diseases, and increased vulnerability to schizophrenia. Recent studies suggest that marijuana use may have some long-term negative effects on cognitive processes.

5-4 Identify factors influencing decisions to seek medical treatment, the quality of doctor-patient communication, and compliance with medical recommendations.

- Variations in seeking treatment are influenced by the severity, duration, and disruptiveness of one's symptoms and by the reactions of friends and family. The biggest problem is the tendency of many people to delay needed medical treatment.
- Good communication is crucial to effective health services, but many factors undermine communication between patients and health providers, such as short visits, overuse of medical jargon, and patients' reluctance to ask questions.
- Noncompliance with medical advice is a major problem, which appears to occur 30%–50% of the time. The likelihood of nonadherence is greater when instructions are difficult to understand, when recommendations are difficult to follow, and when patients are unhappy with their doctor.

CHAPTER REVIEW 6

KEY TERMS

6-1

self-concept A collection of beliefs about one's basic nature, unique qualities, and typical behavior.

possible selves One's conceptions about the kind of person one might become in the future.

social comparison theory The idea that people need to compare themselves with others in order to gain insight into their own behavior.

reference group A set of people who are used as a gauge in making social comparisons.

individualism Putting personal goals ahead of group goals and defining one's identity in terms of personal attributes rather than group memberships.

collectivism Putting group goals ahead of personal goals and defining one's identity in terms of the groups to which one belongs.

6-2

self-esteem One's overall assessment of one's worth as a person; the evaluative component of the self-concept.

6-3

self-attributions Inferences that people draw about the causes of their own behavior.

internal attributions Ascribing the causes of behavior to personal dispositions, traits, abilities, and feelings rather than to external events.

external attributions Ascribing the causes of behavior to situational demands and environmental constraints.

KEY IDEAS

6-1 Describe the nature of the self-concept and factors that shape it.

- The self-concept is composed of a number of beliefs about what one is like, and it is not easily changed. It governs both present and future behavior. Self-concepts tend to be stable over time, but they are not set in concrete. The self-concept is shaped by several factors, including individuals' observations of their own behavior, which often involve social comparisons with others. Self-observations tend to be biased in a positive direction.
- In addition, feedback from others shapes the self-concept; this information is also filtered to some extent. Cultural guidelines also affect the way people see themselves. Members of individualistic cultures usually have an independent view of the self, whereas those in collectivist cultures often have an interdependent view of the self.

6-2 Explain the importance of self-esteem, its relation to adjustment, and how it develops.

- Self-esteem is a person's global evaluation of his or her worth. Like the self-concept, it tends to be stable, but it can fluctuate in response to daily ups and downs. Self-esteem is important in that it is associated with a variety of positive outcomes in life, although fewer than most people assume. Theorists distinguish between trait self-esteem, which is stable, and state self-esteem, which is dynamic and changeable.

From Brehm, *Social Psychology* 3/e. © Cengage Learning.

- Compared to those with high self-esteem, individuals with low self-esteem are less happy, are more likely to be depressed, are more likely to give up after failure, and are less trusting of others. Narcissistic individuals are prone to aggression when their self-esteem is threatened. Self-esteem develops through interactions with significant others. Parenting styles may play a key role. Authoritative parenting is the optimal style for promoting self-esteem.

6-3 Discuss self-attributions, motives for self-understanding, and the process of self-enhancement.

- To avoid being overwhelmed with information, people tend to use automatic processing, but for important decisions, they shift to controlled processing. *Self-attributions* are inferences that people draw about the causes of their own behavior and experiences. Generally, people attribute their behavior to internal or external factors and to stable or unstable factors.

KEY TERMS *continued*

explanatory style The tendency to use similar causal attributions for a wide variety of events in one's life.

self-verification theory The idea that people prefer to receive feedback from others that is consistent with their own self-views.

self-enhancement The tendency to maintain positive views of oneself.

self-serving bias The tendency to attribute one's successes to personal factors and one's failures to situational factors.

basking in reflected glory The tendency to enhance one's image by publicly announcing one's association with those who are successful.

self-handicapping The tendency to sabotage one's performance to provide an excuse for possible failure.

6-4

self-regulation Directing and controlling one's behavior.

self-efficacy One's belief about one's ability to perform behaviors that should lead to expected outcomes.

self-defeating behaviors Seemingly intentional acts that thwart a person's self-interest.

6-5

public self An image presented to others in social interactions.

impression management Usually conscious efforts to influence the way others think of one.

ingratiation Efforts to make oneself likable to others.

KEY IDEAS *continued*

- In making attributions, people tend to use either an optimistic explanatory style or a pessimistic explanatory style to understand various events that occur in their lives. These attributional styles are related to psychological adjustment, with an optimistic style being much healthier.
- People are guided by four distinct motives in seeking to understand themselves. The self-assessment motive directs people toward accurate feedback about the self. The self-verification motive drives people toward information that matches their current self-views, even though doing so may involve some distortion of reality. The self-improvement motive underlies people's attempts to better themselves. The self-enhancement motive enables people to maintain positive views of themselves.
- Common self-enhancement strategies include attributing successes to personal factors and failures to external factors (the self-serving bias), basking in the reflected glory of others who are successful, and sabotaging one's performance to provide an excuse for possible failure (self-handicapping).

6-4 Define self-regulation, its psychological benefits, and its challenges.

- Self-regulation involves setting goals and directing behavior to meet those goals. It is crucial to achieving long-term goals and success in various aspects of life. According to the ego depletion model of self-regulation, engaging in self-control can temporarily deplete what appears to be a limited underlying resource. A key aspect of self-regulation is self-efficacy—an individual's belief that he or she can achieve specific goals. Self-efficacy plays a key role in adjustment and can be learned through mastery experiences, vicarious experiences, persuasion, and positive interpretations of emotional arousal.
- Self-regulation can be difficult. Self-defeating behaviors are seemingly intentional actions that thwart a person's self-interest. These self-defeating actions fall into three categories: deliberate self-destruction, tradeoffs, and counterproductive strategies.

6-5 Discuss why and how people engage in impression management, and describe strategies for creating favorable impressions.

- Public selves are the various images that individuals project to others. Typically, individuals have a number of public selves that are tied to certain situations and certain people, which may not be well integrated. People engage in impression management to claim a particular identity or to gain liking and approval. People try to manage the impressions they make by using a variety of strategies, including ingratiation, self-promotion, exemplification, intimidation, and supplication.

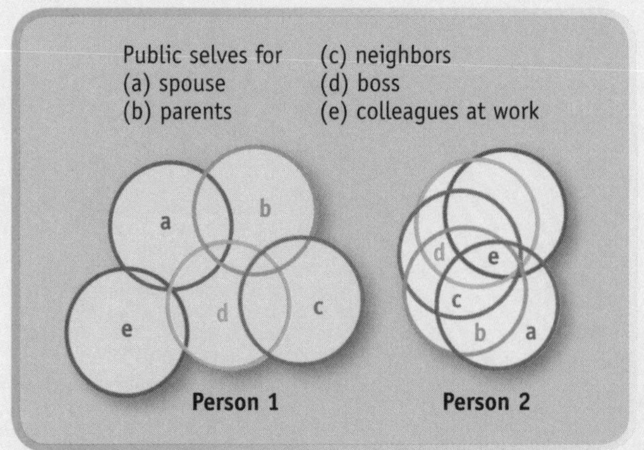

6-6 List seven ways to build self-esteem.

- The seven building blocks to higher self-esteem are (1) recognizing that you control your self-image, (2) learning more about yourself, (3) not letting others set your goals, (4) recognizing unrealistic goals, (5) modifying negative self-talk, (6) emphasizing your strengths, and (7) approaching others with a positive outlook.

Social Thinking and Social Influence

CHAPTER REVIEW 7

KEY TERMS

7-1

person perception The process of forming impressions of others.

attributions Inferences that people draw about the causes of events, others' behavior, and their own behavior.

fundamental attribution error The tendency to explain others' behavior as a result of personal rather than situational factors.

defensive attribution The tendency to blame victims for their misfortune, so that one feels less likely to be victimized in a similar way.

confirmation bias The tendency to behave toward others in ways that confirm your expectations about them.

self-fulfilling prophecy The process whereby expectations about a person cause the person to behave in ways that confirm the expectations.

stereotypes Widely held beliefs that people have certain characteristics simply because of their membership in a particular group.

7-2

prejudice A negative attitude toward members of a group.

discrimination Behaving differently, usually unfairly, toward members of a group.

KEY IDEAS

7-1 Understand the benefits and pitfalls of the psychological processes people use to form impressions of others.

- In forming impressions of other people, individuals rely on appearance, verbal behavior, actions, nonverbal messages, and situational cues. Individuals usually make snap judgments about others unless accurate impressions are important. To explain the causes of other people's behavior, individuals make attributions (either internal or external).
- When people make the fundamental attribution error, they discount situational factors and explain others' behavior in terms of internal attributions. Defensive attribution often leads people to blame victims for their misfortunes.
- People often try to confirm their expectations about what others are like, which can result in biased impressions. Self-fulfilling prophecies can actually change a target person's behavior in the direction of a perceiver's expectations.

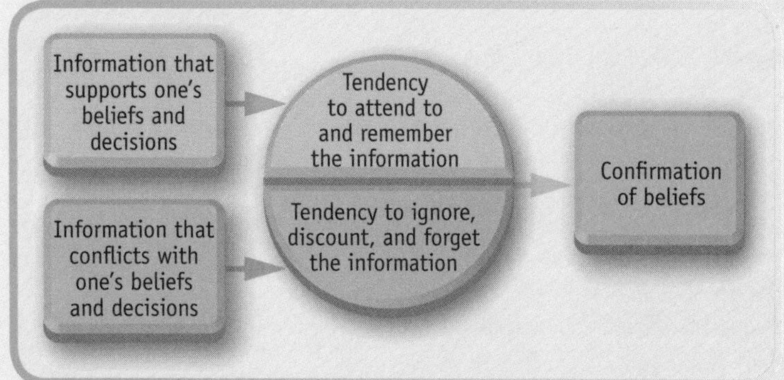

- Categorization of people into ingroups and outgroups can slant social perceptions. Stereotypes, which are widely held beliefs about the typical characteristics of various groups, can distort one's perceptions of others.

7-2 Describe the nature and causes of prejudice and ways to reduce prejudice.

- Prejudice is a particularly unfortunate outcome of the tendency to view others inaccurately. Blatant ("old-fashioned") discrimination occurs relatively infrequently today, but subtle expressions of prejudice and discrimination ("modern discrimination," aversive racism) have become more common.
- Common causes of prejudice include the personality trait of right-wing authoritarianism, cognitive distortions due to stereotyping and attributional errors, competition between groups, and threats to one's social identity. Stereotype threat can undermine group members' academic performance. Strategies for reducing prejudice include efforts to override automatic, unconscious reactions and collaborative intergroup contact.

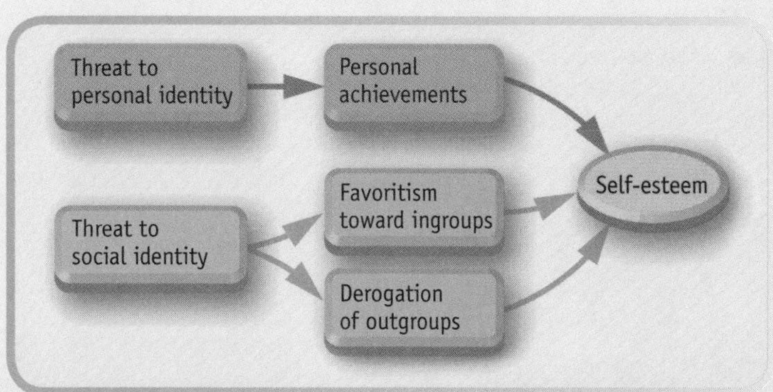

KEY TERMS *continued*

7-3

persuasion The communication of arguments and information intended to change another person's attitudes.

attitudes Beliefs and feelings about people, objects, and ideas.

source The person who initiates, or sends, a message.

receiver The person to whom a message is targeted.

message The information or meaning that is transmitted from one person to another.

channel The medium through which a message reaches the receiver.

need for cognition The tendency to seek out and enjoy effortful thought, problem-solving activities, and in-depth analysis.

7-4

conformity Yielding to real or imagined social pressure.

compliance Yielding to social pressure in one's public behavior, even though one's private beliefs have not changed.

normative influence Pressure to conform that operates when people conform to social norms for fear of negative social consequences.

informational influence Pressure to conform that operates when people look to others for how to behave in ambiguous situations.

bystander effect The social phenomenon in which individuals are less likely to provide needed help when others are present than when they are alone.

obedience A form of compliance that occurs when people follow direct commands, usually from someone in a position of authority.

7-5

foot-in-the-door technique Getting people to agree to a small request to increase the chances that they will agree to a larger request later.

lowball technique Getting people to commit themselves to an attractive proposition before its hidden costs are revealed.

reciprocity principle The rule that one should pay back in kind what one receives from others.

door-in-the-face technique Making a very large request that is likely to be turned down to increase the chance that people will agree to a smaller request later.

KEY IDEAS *continued*

7-3 Review key elements in persuasive communications.

- The success of persuasive efforts depends on several factors. A source of persuasion who is expert, trustworthy, likable, physically attractive, and similar to the receiver tends to be relatively effective. Although there are some limitations, two-sided arguments, arousal of fear, and generation of positive feelings are effective elements in persuasive messages. Persuasion is enhanced when people are in good moods or are drawn to detailed arguments, but it is undermined when receivers are forewarned about the position being advocated.

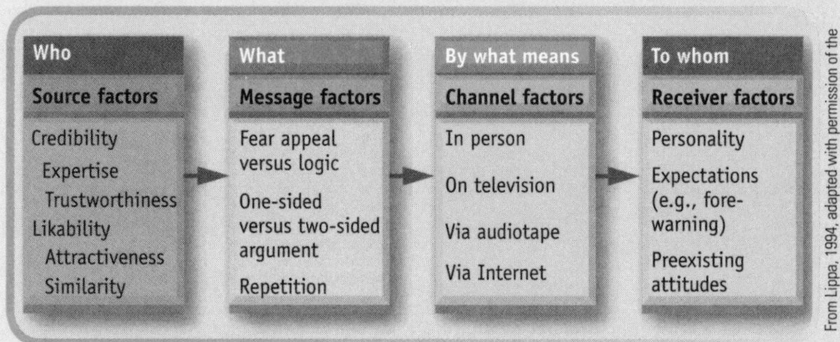

From Lippa, 1994, adapted with permission of the author. © Cengage Learning.

7-4 Summarize essential issues in understanding compliance, conformity, and obedience.

- Asch found that subjects often conform to the group, even when the group reports inaccurate judgments. Asch's experiments may have produced public compliance while subjects' private beliefs remained unchanged. Both normative and informational influence can produce conformity. In some cases, conformity can lead to unfortunate consequences.
- In Milgram's landmark study of obedience to authority, subjects showed a remarkable tendency to follow orders to shock an innocent stranger. Milgram's findings highlight the influence of situational pressures on behavior. Although people often obey authority figures, sometimes they are disobedient, usually because they have support from others.

7-5 Recognize some typical compliance strategies found in everyday situations.

- Although they work for different reasons, all compliance tactics have the same goal: getting people to agree to requests. The foot-in-the-door and the lowball technique are based on the fact that people prefer consistency in their behavior.
- The door-in-the-face technique and the tactic of offering "giveaway" items are manipulations of the principle of reciprocity, the rule that one should pay back in kind what one receives from others. When advertisers suggest that products are in short supply, they are taking advantage of the scarcity principle. Understanding these strategies can make you less vulnerable to manipulation.

CHAPTER REVIEW 8

KEY TERMS

8-1

interpersonal communication An interactional process whereby one person sends a message to another.

sender The person who initiates a message.

receiver The person to whom a message is targeted.

message The information or meaning that is transmitted from one person to another.

channel The medium through which a message reaches the receiver.

noise Any stimulus that interferes with accurately expressing or understanding a message.

context The environment in which communication takes place.

electronically mediated communication Interpersonal communication that takes place via technology.

8-2

nonverbal communication The transmission of meaning from one person to another through means or symbols other than words.

proxemics The study of people's use of interpersonal space.

display rules Norms that govern the appropriate display of emotions.

kinesics The study of communication through body movements.

polygraph A device that records fluctuations in physiological arousal as a person answers questions.

KEY IDEAS

8-1 Describe the key aspects of the communication process.

- Interpersonal communication is the interactional process that occurs when one person sends a message to another. Communication takes place when a sender transmits a message to a receiver either verbally or nonverbally. The message is the meaning that is communicated and the chanel is the sensory means through which the message is transmitted. Noise refers to anything that interferes with accurate transmission of messages. The widespread use of electronic communication devices has raised new issues, including privacy and security, in interpersonal communication.

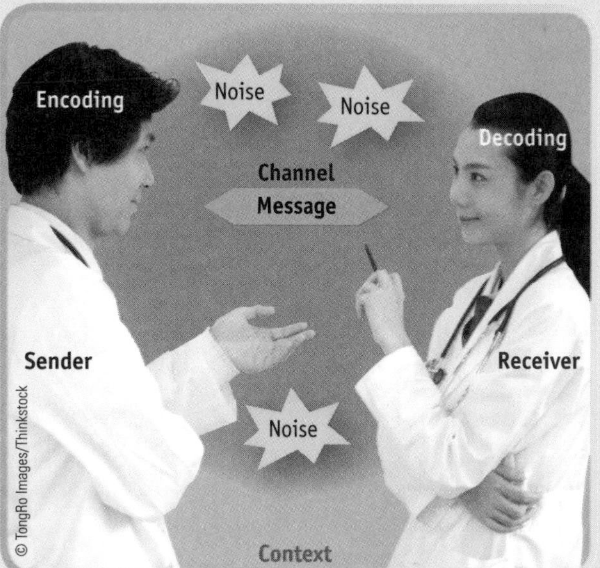

8-2 Explain the significance of nonverbal communication for understanding and relating to others.

- Nonverbal communication conveys emotions, above all. It tends to be more spontaneous than verbal communication, and it is more ambiguous. Sometimes it contradicts what is communicated verbally. It is often multichanneled and is culturally bound.
- The amount of personal space that people prefer depends on culture, gender, social status, and situational factors. Facial expressions can convey a great deal of information about people's emotions. Variations in eye contact can influence nonverbal communication in a host of ways.
- Body postures can hint at interest in communication, and they often reflect status differences. Touch can communicate support, consolation, intimacy, status, and power.
- Certain nonverbal cues are associated with deception, but many of these cues do not correspond to popular beliefs about how liars give themselves away. Discrepancies between facial expressions and other nonverbal signals may suggest dishonesty. The vocal and visual cues associated with lying are so subtle, however, that the detection of deception is difficult. Machines used to detect deception (polygraphs) are not particularly accurate.

KEY TERMS *continued*

8-3

self-disclosure The voluntary act of verbally communicating private information about oneself to another person.

listening A mindful activity and complex process that requires one to select and to organize information, interpret, and respond to communications, and recall what one has heard.

8-4

communication apprehension The anxiety caused by having to talk with others.

8-5

interpersonal conflict Disagreement among two or more people.

8-6

assertiveness Acting in one's own best interest by expressing one's feelings and thoughts honestly and directly.

KEY IDEAS *continued*

8-3 Learn to be an effective communicator when it comes to conversation, disclosure, and listening.

- To be an effective communicator, it's important to develop good conversational skills, including knowing how to make small talk with strangers. It helps to give others your attention and respect and let them know that you like them.
- Self-disclosure—opening up to others—is associated with good mental health, happiness, and satisfying relationships. Self-disclosure can foster emotional intimacy in relationships. Emotional-evaluative self-disclosures lead to feelings of closeness, but factual-descriptive disclosures do not. The level of self-disclosure varies over the course of relationships. Cultures vary in their preferred level of self-disclosure. American women tend to disclose more than men, but this disparity is not as large as it once was.
- Effective listening is an essential aspect of interpersonal communication.To foster effective listening one should signal interest, hear the other person out, engage in active listening, and pay attention to nonverbal signals.

8-4 Recognize basic barriers that can undermine effective communication.

- A number of problems can arise that interfere with effective communication. Individuals who become overly anxious when they talk with others suffer from communication apprehension. This difficulty can cause problems in relationships and in work and educational settings. Visualization and other strategies can be used to reduce communication apprehension. Psychological factors can contribute to noise in interpersonal communication. Barriers to effective communication include defensiveness, ambushing, and self-preoccupation.

8-5 Discuss ways to constructively recognize and deal with conflict.

- Dealing constructively with interpersonal conflict is an important aspect of effective communication. In dealing with conflict, most people have a preferred style: avoiding/withdrawing, accommodating, competing, compromising, or collaborating. Two dimensions underlie these different styles: interest in satisfying one's own concerns and interest in satisfying others' concerns. Collaborating is the most effective style in managing conflict. Constructive approaches to conflict depend on being honest, avoiding disparaging personality attributions, not using loaded words, taking a positive approach, and using an assertive communication style.

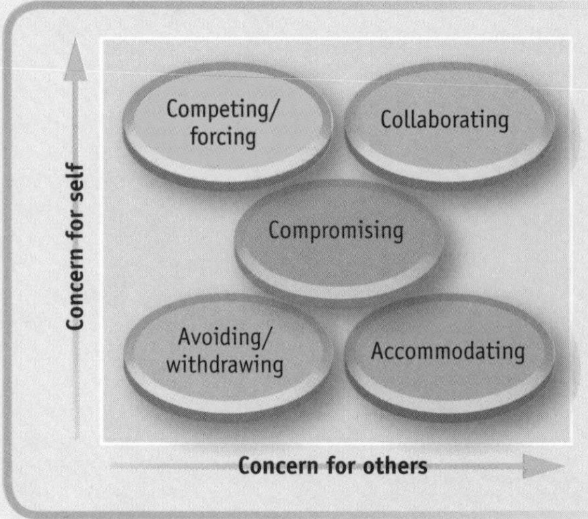

8-6 Outline the steps necessary for more-assertive communication.

- Assertiveness enables individuals to stand up for themselves while respecting the rights of others. To become more assertive, individuals need to understand what assertive communication is, monitor assertive communication, observe a model's assertive communication, practice being assertive, and adopt an assertive attitude.

Friendship and Love

CHAPTER REVIEW 9

KEY TERMS

close relationships Interpersonal relationships that are important, interdependent, and long lasting.

9-1

attraction The initial desire to form a relationship.

proximity Geographic, residential, and other forms of spatial closeness.

mere exposure effect An increase in positive feelings toward a novel stimulus (such as a person) based on frequent exposure to it.

matching hypothesis The idea that people of similar levels of physical attractiveness gravitate toward each other.

parental investment theory The idea that a species' mating patterns depend on what each gender has to invest—in the way of time, energy, and survival risk—to produce and nurture offspring.

reciprocal liking Liking those who show they like you.

relationship maintenance The actions and activities used to sustain the desired quality of a relationship.

9-3

sexual orientation A person's preference for emotional and sexual relationships with individuals of the same gender, the other gender, or either gender.

heterosexism The assumption that all individuals and relationships are heterosexual.

KEY IDEAS

9-1 Identify some factors that influence initial attraction and getting acquainted, and describe some approaches to relationship maintenance.

- People are initially drawn to others who are nearby, who are seen often, and who are physically attractive. Although physical attractiveness plays a key role in initial attraction, people also seek other desirable characteristics, such as kindness, intelligence, dependable character, and maturity. Perceptions of physical attractiveness are influenced by neonate (baby-face) qualities, mature features, expressiveness, and grooming. People often match up on looks, but sometimes men trade status for physical attractiveness in women, and vice versa. Parental investment theory assserts that males and females seek to maximize their reproductive success in different ways.

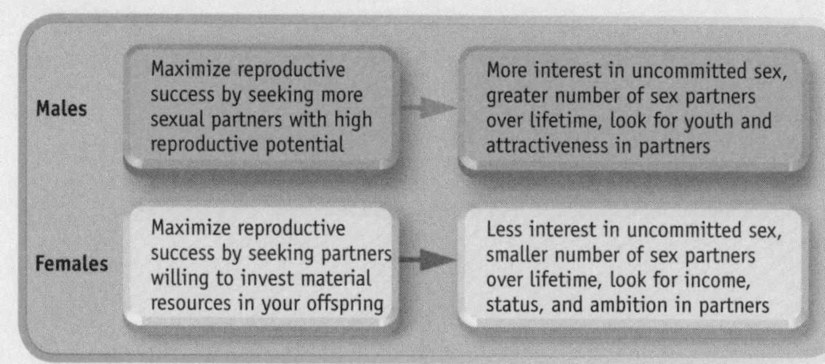

Males
Maximize reproductive success by seeking more sexual partners with high reproductive potential
More interest in uncommitted sex, greater number of sex partners over lifetime, look for youth and attractiveness in partners
Females
Maximize reproductive success by seeking partners willing to invest material resources in your offspring
Less interest in uncommitted sex, smaller number of sex partners over lifetime, look for income, status, and ambition in partners
© Cengage Learning

- As people get acquainted, they prefer others who like them and who are similar to them in various ways. Couples tend to be similar in age, race, religion, education, and attitudes. Once relationships are established, people engage in various maintenance behaviors and actions to sustain them. Mutual self-disclosure and relationship-enhancing beliefs are associated with satisfying long-term relationships. A high level of minding may be associated with satisfying relationships.

9-2 Summarize gender and sexual orientation differences in friendship, and describe the friendship repair ritual.

- Women's same-gender friendships are usually characterized by self-disclosure and intimacy, whereas men's same-gender friendships typically involve doing things together. Some friendship issues are more complex for homosexuals than heterosexuals, in part because gay and lesbian friendships have less support from families and societal institutions. In dealing with conflict, friends often go through a friendship repair ritual, marked by reproach, offering a remedy, and acknowledgement of the remedy.

9-3 Discuss sexual orientation and gender in relation to romantic love, contemporary theories of love, and measures couples can take to help relationships last.

- In spite of issues with heterosexism, research indicates that the experience of romantic love is essentially the same for heterosexual and homosexual individuals. Contrary to stereotypes, men may be more romantic in some ways than women. However, men and women have more similarities than differences when it come to relationships.

KEY TERMS *continued*

intimacy Warmth, closeness, and sharing in a relationship.

passion The intense feelings (both positive and negative) experienced in love relationships, including sexual desire.

commitment The decision and intent to maintain a relationship in spite of the difficulties and costs that may arise.

attachment styles Typical ways of interacting in close relationships.

9-5

loneliness The emotional state that occurs when a person has fewer interpersonal relationships than desired or when these relationships are not as satisfying as desired.

shyness Discomfort, inhibition, and excessive caution in interpersonal relations.

KEY IDEAS *continued*

- Sternberg's triangular theory of love proposes that passion, intimacy, and commitment combine into eight types of love. All three components of love are related to satisfaction in intimate relationships, albeit in complex ways. Hazan and Shaver theorize that love relationships follow the form of attachments in infancy. They described three attachment styles: secure, anxious-ambivalent, and avoidant. Securely attached individuals tend to have more committed, satisfying relationships Researchers subsequently expanded the number of attachment styles from three to four: secure, preoccupied, avoidant-dismissing, and avoidant-fearful. Although attachment styles show stability over time, it is possible for them to change.

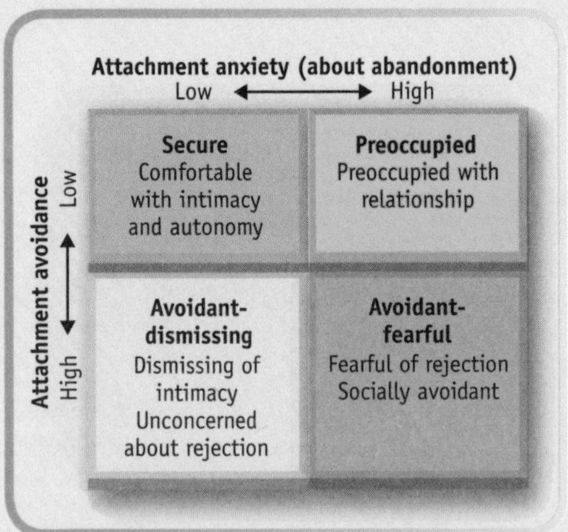

- The chief causes of relationship failure are the tendency to make premature commitments, ineffective conflict management skills, boredom with the relationship, the availability of a more attractive relationship, and low levels of satisfaction. To help relationships last, couples should take the time to know each other very well, emphasize the positive qualities in their partner and relationship, engage in novel activities together, and develop effective conflict management skills.

9-4 Understand how both culture and the Internet influence modern relationships.

- People in individualistic cultures believe that romantic love is a prerequisite for marriage, whereas those in collectivist cultures are accustomed to arranged marriages. People from Western societies tend to assume that collectivist cultures' deemphasis on romantic love must lead to less successful relationships. However, there is little empirical support for the belief that marriages based on romantic love are more successful.
- The Internet offers many new vehicles for meeting others and developing relationships. Although critics are concerned that Internet relationships are superficial, studies suggest that virtual relationships can be just as intimate as face-to-face ones. Because the Internet is anonymous, there are more opportunities for deception.

9-5 Describe the types, roots, and correlates of loneliness, and list suggestions for conquering it.

- Loneliness involves discontent with the extent and quality of one's interpersonal network. Emotional loneliness stems from the absence of an intimate attachment figure, whereas social loneliness results from the lack of a friendship network. Chronic loneliness affects people who have been unable to develop a satisfactory interpersonal network over a period of years. The age groups most affected by loneliness contradict stereotypes.
- The origins of chronic loneliness can often be traced to early negative behavior that triggers rejection by peers and teachers. Social trends may also promote loneliness. Loneliness is associated with shyness, poor social skills, and self-defeating attributions.
- The keys to overcoming loneliness include using the Internet to connect with others, resisting the temptation to withdraw from social situations, avoiding self-defeating attributions, and working on one's social skills.

CHAPTER REVIEW 10

KEY TERMS

10-1

marriage The legally and socially sanctioned union of sexually intimate adults.

cohabitation Living together in a sexually intimate relationship without the legal bonds of marriage.

10-2

monogamy The practice of having only one spouse at a time.

polygamy Having more than one spouse at one time.

endogamy The tendency of people to marry within their own social group.

homogamy The tendency of people to marry others who have similar personal characteristics.

KEY IDEAS

10-1 Identify six recent social trends that are challenging the traditional concept of marriage.

- The traditional model of marriage is being challenged by the increasing acceptability of singlehood, the greater popularity of cohabitation, the reduced premium on permanence, changes in gender roles, the increasing prevalence of voluntary childlessness, and the decline of the traditional nuclear family. Nonetheless, marriage remains quite popular.

10-2 Discuss factors surrounding the decision to marry, such as cultural influences, factors in mate selection, and predictors of a successful marriage.

- A multitude of factors influence an individual's decision to marry, including one's culture. The norm for our society is to select a mate and engage in a monogamous marriage. However, arranged marriages and polygamy are normative in many cultures. Mate selection is influenced by endogamy (the tendency to marry within one's social groups) and homogamy (the tendency to marry those who have similar characteristics).
- There are some premarital predictors of marital success. In terms of family background, people whose parents were divorced are more likely than others to experience divorce. A younger age at marriage and a shorter courtship are correlated with a reduced probability of marital success. Personality traits are only weak predictors of marital success. The nature of a couple's premarital communication is a better predictor of marital adjustment. Stressful events surrounding the marriage influence marital stability.

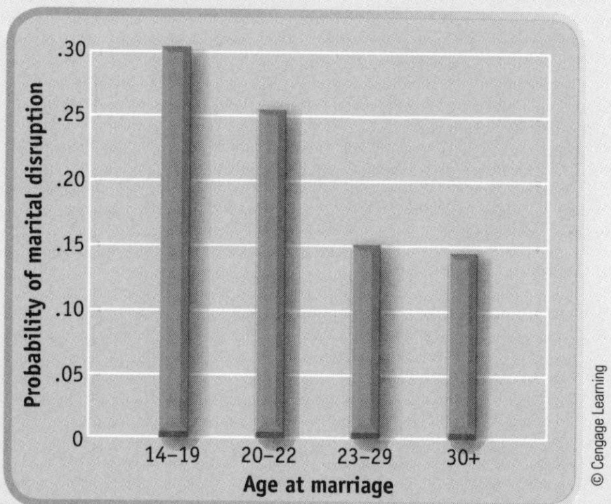

10-3 Understand how discrepancies in role expectations, work issues, finances, and communication styles are vulnerable areas in a marriage.

- Gaps in expectations about marital roles may create marital stress. Disparities in expectations about gender roles and the distribution of housework may be especially common and problematic. Overall, minimal differences are found between dual-career couples and traditional couples in marital adjustment. However, work concerns can clearly spill over to influence marital functioning. The links between parents' employment and children's adjustment are complex, but there is little evidence that a mother's working is harmful to her children.
- Wealth does not ensure marital happiness, but a lack of money can produce marital problems. Money can be a source of conflict even in couples who are well off. Inadequate communication is a commonly reported marital problem, which is predictive of divorce. According to Gottman, contempt, criticism, defensiveness, stonewalling, and belligerence create serious problems in marital communication.

KEY TERMS *continued*

10-4

divorce The legal dissolution of a marriage.

10-5

homophobia The intense fear and intolerance of homosexuality (also called sexual prejudice).

10-6

intimate partner violence Aggression toward those who are in close relationships to the aggressor.

battering Physical abuse, emotional abuse, and sexual abuse, especially in marriage or relationships.

date rape Forced and unwanted intercourse with someone in the context of dating.

KEY IDEAS *continued*

10-4 Describe research on divorce rates, adjusting to divorce, how divorce affects children, and the success of remarriages.

- Divorce rates have increased dramatically in recent decades, but they appear to be stabilizing at around 40%–45% of couples. The vast majority of divorces occur during the first decade of a marriage. Deciding on a divorce tends to be a gradual process marred by indecision. Unpleasant as divorce may be, the evidence suggests that toughing it out in an unhappy marriage can often be worse. Although divorce appears to impose greater financial stress on women than men, researchers do not find consistent gender differences in postdivorce adjustment.

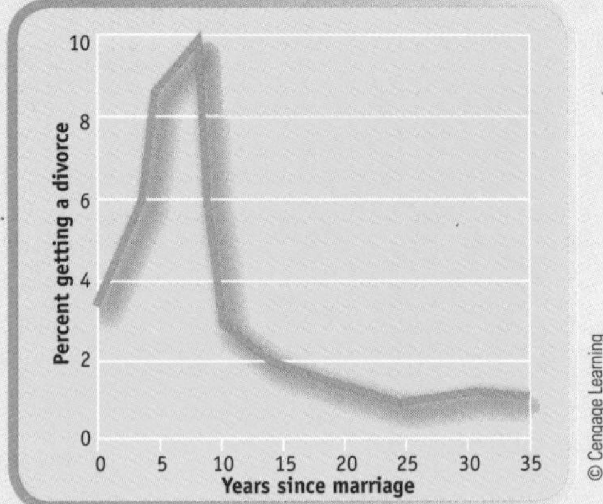

- Wallerstein's research suggests that divorce tends to have extremely negative effects on children. Hetherington's research suggests that most children recover from divorce after a few years. The effects of divorce on children vary, but negative effects can be long-lasting.
- Roughly three-quarters of divorced people remarry. These second marriages have a somewhat lower probability of success than first marriages. The adjustment of children in stepfamilies appears to be somewhat lower that for other families, but differences are modest.

10-5 Analyze gay relationships, cohabitation, and remaining single as alternatives to traditional marriage.

- Contrary to stereotypes, most homosexuals desire long-term intimate relationships. Nonetheless, many Americans hold negative attitudes toward gay couples. Studies have found that heterosexual and homosexual couples are largely similar in commitment, satisfaction, and what they want out of their relationships. Children raised by gay parents do not show poorer adjustment than other children and are no more likely to be gay than others.
- The prevalence of cohabitation has increased dramatically. Logically, one might expect cohabitation to facilitate marital success, but research has consistently found an association between cohabitation and marital instability.
- An increasing proportion of the young population are remaining single, but this fact does not mean that people are turning away from marriage. Although singles generally have the same adjustment problems as married couples, evidence suggests that singles tend to be somewhat less happy and less healthy.

10-6 Compare and contrast partner abuse and date rape as two types of intimate partner violence.

- Research suggests that about 25% of women and 7% of men have been victims of partner abuse. Women are the principal victims of serious, dangerous abuse. Men who batter their partners are diverse, but they tend to anger easily, be jealous, and have unrealistic expectations of their partner. Women stay in abusive relationships for a variety of compelling, practical reasons, including economic realities.
- The majority of rapes are committed by someone the victim knows. Rape is a traumatic experience that has many serious consequences. Alcohol abuse, drug use, and gender-based sexual standards all contribute to date rape. Miscommunication about token resistance is particularly problematic. There are several steps a woman can take to reduce the incidence of date rape.

Gender and Behavior

CHAPTER REVIEW 11

KEY TERMS

11-1

gender The state of being male or female.

gender stereotypes Widely shared beliefs about males' and females' abilities, personality traits, and social behavior.

instrumentality A style of communication that focuses on reaching practical goals and finding solutions to problems.

expressiveness A style of communication characterized by the ability to express tender emotions easily and to be sensitive to the feelings of others.

androcentrism The belief that the male is the norm.

11-2

meta-analysis A statistical technique that evaluates the results of many studies on the same question.

aggression Any behavior intended to hurt someone, either physically or verbally.

11-3

cerebral hemispheres The right and left halves of the cerebrum, which is the convoluted outer layer of the brain.

corpus callosum The band of fibers connecting the two hemispheres of the brain.

KEY IDEAS

11-1 Explain the nature of gender, gender stereotypes, and androcentrism.

- Gender is the state of being male or female. Gender stereotypes are widely shared beliefs about males' and females' abilities, personality traits, and social behavior. Gender stereotypes may vary depending on ethnicity, and they typically favor males. Androcentrism refers to the belief that the male is the norm.

11-2 Summarize the research on gender similarities and differences in cognitive abilities, personality and social behavior, and psychological disorders.

- Some contemporary researchers have adopted the gender similarities hypothesis, emphasizing the fact that males and females are more similar than different on most psychological variables. There are no gender differences in general intelligence. When it comes to verbal abilities, gender differences are small, and generally favor females. Gender differences in mathematical abilities are typically small as well, and they favor males. Males perform much better than females on the spatial ability of mental rotation; however, this skill can be improved through practice.
- Research shows that males typically are somewhat higher in self-esteem, although the findings are complex. Males tend to exhibit far more physical aggression than females; however, females are higher in relational aggression. Males and females are similar in the experience of emotions, but females are more likely to outwardly display emotions and are better at recognizing others' emotions. Gender differences in communication might be better explained by status differences. The genders are similar in overall mental health, but they differ in prevalence rates for specific psychological disorders. Overall, gender accounts for only a small proportion of the differences among individuals.

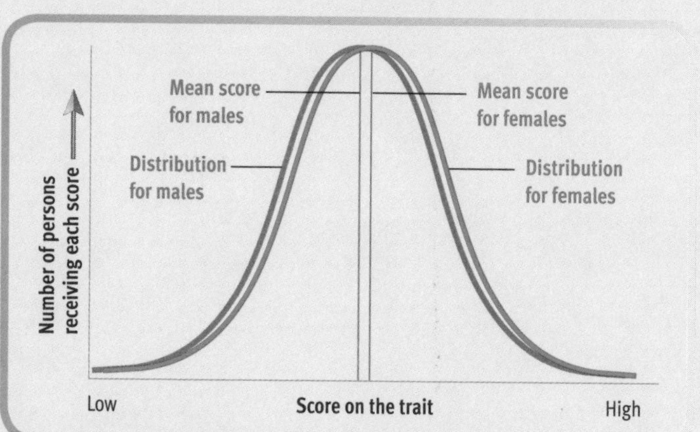

11-3 Describe how evolutionary processes, brain organization, and hormonal differences may contribute to gender differences in behavior.

- Evolutionary psychologists explain gender differences on the basis of their purported adaptive value in ancestral environments. These psychologists suggest that gender differences in behavior reflect different natural selection pressures that have operated on males and females over the course of human history. These analyses are speculative and difficult to test empirically.
- Regarding brain organization, some studies suggest that males exhibit more cerebral specialization than females and that females tend to have a larger corpus callosum. However, linking these findings to gender differences in cognitive abilities is questionable for a number of reasons.

KEY TERMS *continued*

hormones Chemical substances released into the bloodstream by the endocrine glands.

11-4

socialization The process by which individuals acquire the norms and roles expected of people in a particular society.

gender roles Cultural expectations about what is appropriate behavior for each gender.

11-5

sexism Discrimination against people on the basis of their sex.

sexual harassment The subjection of individuals to unwelcome sexually oriented behavior.

11-6

gender-role identity A person's identification with the traits regarded as masculine or feminine.

androgyny The coexistence of both masculine and feminine personality traits in an individual.

KEY IDEAS *continued*

- Girls exposed prenatally to abnormally high levels of androgens exhibit more male-typical behavior than other girls do. Similarly, boys exposed prenatally to abnormally low levels of androgens exhibit more female-typical behavior than other boys. However, aside from physical characteristics, efforts to tie hormone levels to gender differences have been troubled by interpretive problems. Nonetheless, there probably is some hormonal basis for gender differences in aggression and in some aspects of sexual behavior.

11-4 Understand how parents, peers, schools, and the media influence gender-role socialization.

- Gender roles are cultural expectations about what is appropriate behavior for each gender. They are learned through socialization. There is a strong tendency for parents to encourage play activities that are "gender appropriate." Peers form an important network for learning about gender-appropriate behavior. Textbooks that contain gender bias and teacher-student interactions that reinforce gender stereotypes contribute to gender-role socialization. Television shows, commercials, video games, and other forms of media entertainment often perpetuate gender stereotypes.

11-5 Describe gender-role expectations for males and females, and explain common problems associated with both.

- Five key attributes of the traditional male role include achievement, aggression, autonomy, sexuality, and stoicism. The theme of anti-femininity cuts across these dimensions. Problems associated with the traditional male role include excessive pressure to succeed, difficulty in dealing with emotions, and sexual problems. Homophobia is a particular problem for men.
- Role expectations for females include the marriage mandate, the motherhood mandate, and working outside the home. Among the principal costs of the female role are diminished aspirations, juggling of multiple roles, and ambivalence about sexuality. In addition to these psychological problems, women also face sexist hurdles in the economic domain and may be victims of sexual harassment.

© Morgan Lane Photography/Shutterstock.com

11-6 Define gender-role identity, and summarize the research on androgyny.

- Gender roles are in transition. Gender-role identity is a person's identification with the qualities regarded as masculine or feminine. Androgyny refers to the coexistence of both masculine and feminine personality traits in a single person. Bem's assertion that androgynous people are psychologically healthier than gender-typed individuals has garnered some support, but the evidence is complicated.

11-7 Evaluate the evidence for gender differences in communication style.

- Because of different socialization experiences, many males and females learn different communication styles. Men are more likely to use an "instrumental" style of communication and women an "expressive" style. These differences, however, appear to be a matter of degree. Women appear to be more skilled at nonverbal communication than men and tend to use more tentative language.
- Although the idea of gender-based communication styles has intuitive appeal, the research is mixed. Other factors besides gender play an important role in these differences. In addition, men and women can alter their communication styles to fit the situation. Scholars suggest we explore mixed-gender communication in less stereotypic ways.

Development and Expression of Sexuality

CHAPTER REVIEW 12

KEY TERMS

12-1

sexual identity The complex of personal qualities, self-perceptions, attitudes, values, and preferences that guide one's sexual behavior.

heterosexuals People who seek emotional/sexual relationships with members of the other gender.

homosexuals People who seek emotional/sexual relationships with members of the same gender.

bisexuals People who seek emotional/sexual relationships with members of both genders.

gonads The sex glands.

androgens The principal class of male sex hormones.

estrogens The principal class of female sex hormones.

menarche The first occurrence of menstruation.

spermarche An adolescent male's first ejaculation.

homophobia The intense fear and intolerance of homosexuality.

12-2

vasocongestion Engorgement of blood vessels.

orgasm The release that occurs when sexual arousal reaches its peak intensity and is discharged in a series of muscular contractions that pulsate through the pelvic area.

refractory period A time after orgasm during which males are largely unresponsive to further stimulation.

12-3

erogenous zones Areas of the body that are sexually sensitive or responsive.

masturbation The stimulation of one's own genitals

cunnilingus The oral stimulation of the female genitals.

KEY IDEAS

12-1 Explain the factors involved in the development of sexual identity, including physiological and psychosocial influences, gender differences in socialization, and sexual orientation.

- One's sexual identity includes sexual orientation and erotic preferences. Physiological factors such as hormones influence sexual differentiation and anatomy. Psychosocial factors appear to have more impact on sexual behavior. Sexual identity is shaped by families, peers, schools, religion, and the media. Because of differences in sexual socialization, sexuality usually has different meanings for males and females.
- Experts believe that sexual orientation is complex and should be viewed as a continuum. The determinants of sexual orientation are not yet known but appear to be a complex interaction of biological and environmental factors. Genetic factors and hormonal secretions during prenatal development may shape sexual orientation.
- General attitudes toward homosexuals are often negative but appear to be moving in a positive direction. Research continues to demonstrate that gay individuals, couples, and parents do not show elevated levels of psychological maladjustment. However, distress can result from exposure to sexual prejudice.

12-2 Describe the four phases of the human sexual response cycle, and discuss gender differences in patterns of orgasm.

- The physiology of the human sexual response was described by Masters and Johnson. They analyzed the sexual response cycle into four phases: excitement, plateau, orgasm, and resolution. However, people vary considerably in their sexual responses.
- Women reach orgasm in intercourse less consistently than men, usually because foreplay and intercourse are too brief and because of gender differences in sexual socialization. Lesbians have orgasms more often and more easily in sexual interactions than heterosexual women do.

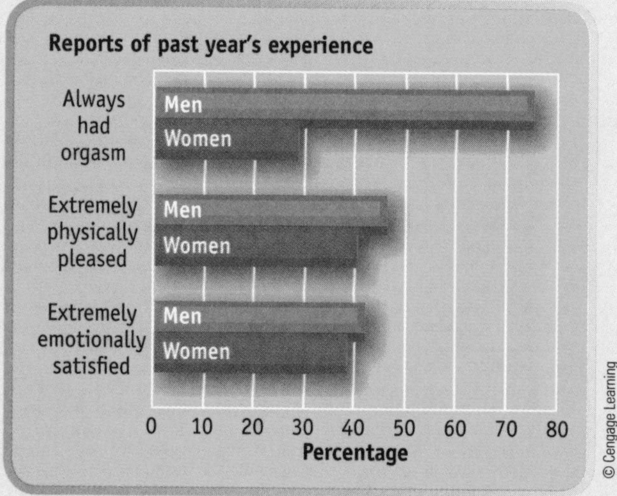

12-3 Summarize six common ways people express themselves sexually.

- Sexual fantasies are normal and are an important aspect of sexual expression. Kissing and touching are important erotic activities, but their importance is often underestimated by heterosexual males. Despite the negative attitudes about masturbation that are traditional in our society, self-stimulation is quite common, even among married people. Oral-genital sex has become a common element in most couples' sexual repertoires. Anal sex is less common than other types of sex for both gay and heterosexual couples.

KEY TERMS *continued*

fellatio The oral stimulation of the penis.

anal intercourse The insertion of the penis into a partner's anus and rectum.

coitus The insertion of the penis into the vagina and (typically) pelvic thrusting.

12-5

sexually transmitted disease (STD) A disease or infection that is transmitted primarily through sexual contact.

12-6

sexual dysfunction An impairments in sexual functioning that causes subjective distress.

erectile difficulties The male sexual dysfunction characterized by the persistent inability to achieve or maintain an erection adequate for intercourse.

premature ejaculation Impaired sexual relations because a man consistently reaches orgasm too quickly.

orgasmic difficulties Sexual disorders characterized by an ability to experience sexual arousal but persistent problems in achieving orgasm.

hypoactive sexual desire Lack of interest in sexual activity.

sex therapy The professional treatment of sexual dysfunctions.

KEY IDEAS *continued*

- Coitus is the most widely practiced sexual act in our society. Frequent intercourse is associated with greater sexual and relationship satisfaction, and higher life satisfaction. Sexual activities between gay males include mutual masturbation, fellatio, and, less often, anal intercourse. Lesbians engage in mutual masturbation, cunnilingus, and tribadism.

12-4 Discuss typical patterns of sexual behavior both outside and inside of committed relationships.

- Hooking up, a phenomenon that has been on the rise since the 1990s, is a common practice for young adults. College students tend to wrongly believe that their peers are significantly more comfortable with hooking up than they themselves are. The casual sex associated with hookups is risky. Many young adults also engage in friends-with-benefits arrangements. These relationships can be tricky to negotiate.

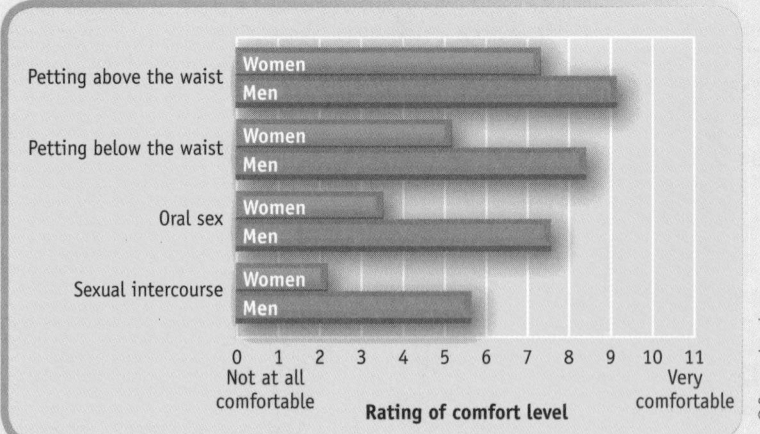

Source: From Lambert, T. A., Kahn, A. S., & Apple, K. J. (2003). Pluralistic ignorance and hooking up. *The Journal of Sex Research, 40*(2) 129–133. Copyright © 1979 Society for the Scientific Study of Sexuality. Reprinted by permission.

- In committed relationships, satisfaction with sex is correlated with overall relationship satisfaction in both gay and straight couples. Younger married couples tend to have sex about two or three times a week. This frequency declines with age in both heterosexual and same-gender couples, though sexual activity in late adulthood is common.

12-5 Understand the significance of contraception and sexually transmitted diseases in sexual interactions.

- Contraception and sexually transmitted diseases are two practical issues that concern many sexually active individuals. Individuals engage in risky sexual behavior for a variety of reasons. Hormone-based contraceptives and condoms are two of the most common birth control methods. Each have advantages and disadvantages.
- STDs are increasing in prevalence, especially among those under 25. The danger of contracting STDs is higher among those who have had more sexual partners. In the United States, the rates of HIV infections stemming from heterosexual sex are on the rise, particularly among women. HIV rates are also up among young gay and bisexual men. HPV is also increasingly common among sexually active individuals. Using condoms decreases the risk of contracting STDs. Early treatment of STDs is important.

12-6 Identify common sexual problems, and explain what couples can do to cope with them.

- To enhance their sexual relationships, individuals need to have adequate sex education and positive values about sex. They also need to be able to communicate with their partners about sex, avoid goal setting in sexual encounters, and enjoy sexual fantasies.
- Common sexual dysfunctions include erectile difficulties, premature ejaculation, orgasmic difficulties, and hypoactive sexual desire. To overcome psychologically based erectile difficulties and premature ejaculation, the key is often to decrease the man's performance anxiety. Therapy for nonorgasmic women typically strives to reduce their ambivalence about sexual expression. Treatments for low sexual desire are less effective than those for more specific sexual problems. Sex therapy can be useful.

CHAPTER REVIEW 13

KEY TERMS

industrial/organizational (I/O) psychology The study of human behavior in the workplace.

13-1

occupational interest inventories Tests that measure one's interests as they relate to various jobs or careers.

13-2

work An activity that produces something of value for others.

dual-earner households Households in which both partners are employed.

underemployment Settling for a job that does not fully utilize one's skills, abilities, and training.

KEY IDEAS

13-1 Understand some key factors that influence career interests and choices.

- Ideally, people look for jobs that are compatible with their personal characteristics. Thus, individuals need to have a sense of their own abilities, interests, and personality. Family background also influences career choices.
- There are abundant resources for those who want to learn about possible career options. In researching prospective careers, it is important to find out about the nature of the work, working conditions, entry requirements, potential earnings, potential status, opportunities for advancement, intrinsic satisfactions, and the future outlook for jobs.
- Some individuals may find it helpful to take an occupational interest inventory to identify occupations that may be compatible with their interests. People have the potential for success in a variety of occupations, although there are limits on career options. One should be cautious about overemphasizing salary and remember that some career decisions are not easily undone.

13-2 Identify some major changes and challenges occurring in the workplace.

- A number of contemporary trends, such as increased reliance on technology, reduced job security, and the need for lifelong learning, are changing the world of work. Other trends include increased dependence on independent workers, blurring of the borders between work and home, high growth in professional and service occupations, and more job sharing. Generally, the more education that individuals obtain, the higher their salaries will be.

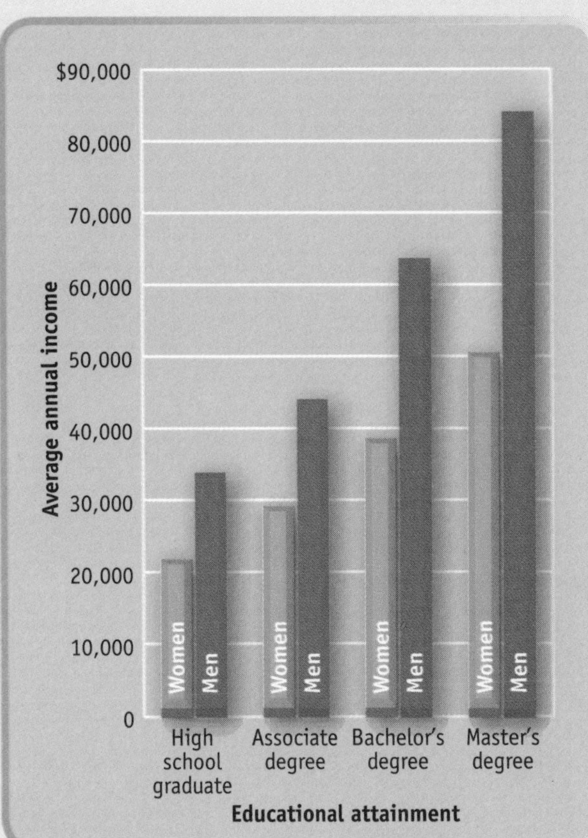

KEY TERMS *continued*

labor force All people who are employed as well as those who are currently unemployed but are looking for work.

glass ceiling An invisible barrier that prevents most women and ethnic minorities from advancing to the highest levels of an occupation.

token A symbol of all the members of a group.

13-3

sexual harassment The subjection of individuals to unwelcome sexually oriented behavior.

displaced workers Individuals who are unemployed because their jobs have disappeared.

13-4

work-family conflict The feeling of being pulled in multiple directions by competing demands from job and family.

KEY IDEAS *continued*

- In the future, more women and minorities will join the labor force. Although women and minorities participate in the workforce at all occupational levels, they tend to be concentrated in lower-paying and lower-status positions. Furthermore, women and minorities face discrimination in a number of areas. Increasing diversity in the workforce presents challenges to both organizations and workers.

13-3 Analyze the potential impact of job stress, sexual harassment, and unemployment.

- A great many employees find their jobs highly stressful, in part because of their long work hours. According to Karasek, stress is greatest in jobs characterized by high psychological demands and low decision control. Occupational stress is associated with numerous negative effects. Interventions to manage stress in the workplace can be made at the individual level, the organizational level, and the individual-organizational interface.
- Sexual harassment may involve forced quid pro quo transactions or the creation of a hostile environment. Victims of sexual harassment often develop physical and psychological symptoms of stress that can lead to decreased work motivation and productivity. Many organizations are educating their workers about this problem. Organizations can reduce the incidence of sexual harassment by promoting norms that are intolerant of it.
- Because of dramatic changes in the economy, unemployment is a problem for both skilled and unskilled workers. Job loss is highly stressful. Middle-aged workers are most distressed by the experience. There are practical steps for coping with unemployment, including remembering that social support is critical.

© Lisa S./Shutterstock.com

13-4 Recognize the problems posed by workaholism and work-family conflicts.

- A major challenge for workers today is balancing work and family in ways that are personally satisfying. Workaholism may be based on positive or negative motives, but it still creates work-family conflict for workaholics and their families.
- As dual-earner families have become the family norm, juggling multiple roles has emerged as a challenge, especially for women. At the organizational level, flexible work schedules, family leave, and child and elder care support can reduce work-family conflicts. Although today's working parents may feel stressed, researchers find that multiple roles generally are beneficial for both men's and women's mental, physical, and relationship health.

13-5 Develop skills for writing an effective résumé and interviewing well for jobs.

- Résumés should be brief and project a positive, yet conservative image. To locate prospective employers, it is good to use a variety of strategies. In interviews you should try to appear confident and enthusiastic. Try to avoid salary discussions in your initial interview.
- The essential elements of a successful job search include (1) determining the type of organization that will best suit one's needs, (2) constructing an effective résumé, (3) getting a job interview, and (4) developing an effective interview technique.

Psychological Disorders

CHAPTER REVIEW 14

KEY TERMS

14-1

medical model The idea that it is useful to think of abnormal behavior as a disease.

diagnosis Distinguishing one illness from another.

etiology The apparent causation and developmental history of an illness.

prognosis A forecast about the probable course of an illness.

14-2

anxiety disorders A class of psychological disorders marked by feelings of excessive apprehension and anxiety.

generalized anxiety disorder A psychological disorder marked by a chronic high level of anxiety that is not tied to any specific threat.

phobic disorders Anxiety disorders marked by a persistent and irrational fear of an object or situation that presents no realistic danger.

panic disorder Recurrent attacks of overwhelming anxiety that usually occur suddenly and unexpectedly.

agoraphobia A fear of going out to public places.

obsessive-compulsive disorder (OCD) A psychological disorder marked by persistent uncontrollable intrusions of unwanted thoughts (obsessions) and by urges to engage in senseless rituals (compulsions).

neurotransmitters Chemicals that carry signals from one neuron to another.

14-3

dissociative disorders A class of psychological disorders characterized by loss of contact with portions of one's consciousness or memory, resulting in disruptions in one's sense of identity.

dissociative amnesia A sudden loss of memory for important personal information that is too extensive to be due to normal forgetting.

dissociative identity disorder Dissociative disorder involving the coexistence in one person of two or more largely complete, and usually very different, personalities. Also called multiple-personality disorder.

14-4

mood disorders A class of disorders marked by emotional disturbances that may spill over to disrupt physical, perceptual, social, and thought processes.

major depressive disorder Psychological disorder characterized by persistent feelings of sadness and despair and a loss of interest in previous sources of pleasure.

KEY IDEAS

14-1 Discuss the medical model, the criteria of abnormality, and the modern diagnostic system.

- The medical model views abnormal behavior as a disease. There are some problems with the medical model, but the disease analogy is useful and medical concepts such as *diagnosis, etiology,* and *prognosis* have proven valuable. Three criteria are used in deciding whether people suffer from psychological disorders: deviance, personal distress, and maladaptive behavior. Often, it is difficult to draw a clear line between normality and abnormality, which exist on a continuum.
- DSM-IV is the official psychodiagnostic classification system in the United States, although the next edition (DSM-5) is tentatively scheduled for publication in 2013. The DSM-IV system asks for information about patients on five axes. However, it appears that this multiaxial system will be discarded in DSM-5.

14-2 Describe four anxiety disorders, and understand how genetics, conditioning, cognition, and stress contribute to their etiology.

- Generalized anxiety disorder is marked by a chronic high level of anxiety that is not tied to any specific threat. A phobic disorder is marked by a persistent and irrational fear of an object or situation that presents no realistic danger. Panic disorders are characterized by recurrent attacks of overwhelming anxiety that usually occur suddenly and unexpectedly. An obsessive-compulsive disorder (OCD) is marked by persistent, uncontrollable intrusions of unwanted thoughts (obsessions) and urges to engage in senseless rituals (compulsions).
- These disorders may be linked to a mild genetic predisposition and neurochemical abnormalities in the brain. Many anxiety responses, especially phobias, may be caused by classical conditioning and maintained by operant conditioning. Cognitive theorists maintain that some people are vulnerable to anxiety disorders because they see threat everywhere. Stress appears to contribute to the onset of these disorders.

14-3 Distinguish between two dissociative disorders, and summarize conflicting views regarding their causes.

- Dissociative amnesia is a sudden loss of memory for important personal information that is too extensive to be due to normal forgetting. Dissociative identity disorder (DID) involves the coexistence in one person of two or more largely complete, and usually very different, personalities.
- Dissociative amnesia is usually attributed to excessive stress. Some theorists believe that people with dissociative identity disorder are engaging in intentional role playing to use mental illness as a face-saving excuse for their personal failings. Other theorists assert that most cases of DID are authentic and rooted in severe emotional trauma that occurred during childhood. DID is a controversial diagnosis.

14-4 Identify two mood disorders, and clarify how genetic, neural, cognitive, interpersonal, and stress factors contribute to their etiology.

- In major depressive disorder people show persistent feelings of sadness and despair, a loss of interest in previous sources of pleasure, low self-esteem, and a sluggish lack of energy. Bipolar disorder is marked by the experience of both depressed and manic periods. Manic episodes are characterized by feelings of euphoria, racing thoughts, impulsive behavior, and hyperactivity.
- People vary in their genetic vulnerability to mood disorders, which are accompanied by changes in neurochemical activity in the brain. Reduced hippocampal volume caused by suppressed neurogenesis may be key factors in depression. Cognitive models posit that a pessimistic explanatory style, rumination, and other types of negative thinking contribute to depression. Depression is often rooted in interpersonal inadequacies, as people who lack social finesse often have difficulty acquiring life's reinforcers. Mood disorders are sometimes stress related.

KEY TERMS *continued*

bipolar disorders Psychological disorders marked by the experience of both depressed and manic periods.

concordance rate A statistic indicating the percentage of twin pairs or other pairs of relatives that exhibit the same disorder.

14-5

schizophrenic disorders A class of disorders marked by disturbances in thought that spill over to affect perceptual, social, and emotional processes.

delusions False beliefs that are maintained even though they clearly are out of touch with reality.

hallucinations Sensory perceptions that occur in the absence of a real external stimulus or that represent gross distortions of perceptual input.

14-6

eating disorders Severe disturbances in eating behavior characterized by preoccupation with weight and unhealthy efforts to control weight.

anorexia nervosa An eating disorder characterized by intense fear of gaining weight, disturbed body image, refusal to maintain normal weight, and use of dangerous methods to lose weight.

bulimia nervosa An eating disorder characterized by habitual out-of-control overeating followed by unhealthy compensatory efforts, such as self-induced vomiting, fasting, abuse of laxatives and diuretics, and excessive exercise.

binge-eating disorder An eating disorder that involves distress-inducing eating binges that are not accompanied by the purging, fasting, and excessive exercise seen in bulimia.

KEY IDEAS *continued*

14-5 Describe the symptoms and subtypes of schizophrenia, and explain the role of genetics, neural factors, expressed emotion, and stress in their causation.

- Schizophrenic disorders are characterized by deterioration of adaptive behavior, irrational thought including delusions, distorted perception including auditory hallucinations, and disturbed mood. Schizophrenic disorders have traditionally been classified as paranoid, catatonic, disorganized, or undifferentiated. However, these subtypes are likely to be discarded in DSM-5.
- People appear to vary in their genetic vulnerability to schizophrenia. Excess dopamine activity in the brain has been implicated as a likely cause of schizophrenia. Enlarged ventricles in the brain are associated with schizophrenic disturbance. The neurodevelopmental hypothesis attributes schizophrenia to disruptions of normal maturational processes in the brain before or at birth. Patients who return to homes high in expressed emotion tend to have elevated relapse rates. Precipitating stress may also contribute to the emergence of schizophrenia.

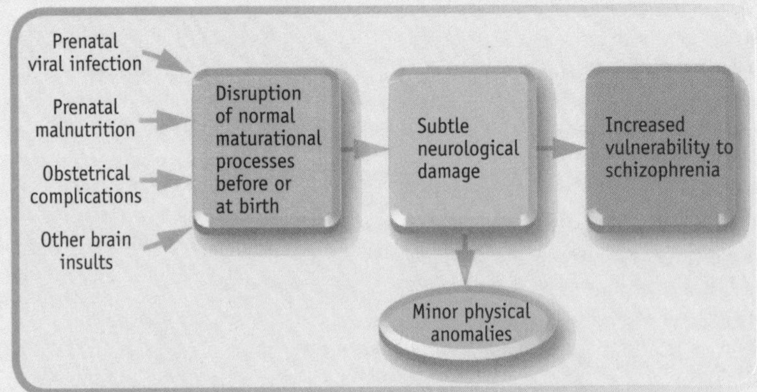

14-6 Describe the major types of eating disorders, and identify the key factors involved in their development.

- Anorexia nervosa involves intense fear of gaining weight, disturbed body image, refusal to maintain normal weight, and dangerous measures to lose weight. Bulimia nervosa involves habitually engaging in out-of-control overeating followed by unhealthy compensatory efforts, such as self-induced vomiting and fasting. Binge-eating disorder involves distress-inducing eating binges that are not accompanied by the purging, fasting, and excessive exercise seen in bulimia. Eating disorders appear to be a product of modern, affluent, Westernized culture. Females account for 90%–95% of eating disorders. The typical age of onset is roughly 15 to 20.
- There appears to be a genetic vulnerability to eating disorders, which may be mediated by heritable personality traits. Cultural pressures on young women to be thin clearly help foster eating disorders. Some theorists emphasize how family dynamics can contribute to the development of eating disorders. Other theorists emphasize the role of disturbed, rigid thinking in the etiology of eating disorders.

Psychotherapy

CHAPTER REVIEW 15

KEY TERMS

15-1

clinical psychologists Psychologists who specialize in the diagnosis and treatment of psychological disorders and everyday behavioral problems.

counseling psychologists Psychologists who specialize in the treatment of everyday behavioral problems.

psychiatrists Physicians who specialize in the treatment of psychological disorders.

15-2

insight therapies A group of psychotherapies in which verbal interactions are intended to enhance clients' self-knowledge and thus promote healthful changes in personality and behavior.

psychoanalysis An insight therapy that emphasizes the recovery of unconscious conflicts, motives, and defenses through techniques such as free association, dream analysis, and transference.

free association A psychotherapeutic technique in which clients spontaneously express their thoughts and feelings exactly as they occur, with as little censorship as possible.

dream analysis A psychotherapeutic technique in which the therapist interprets the symbolic meaning of the client's dreams.

interpretation A therapist's attempts to explain the inner significance of the client's thoughts, feelings, memories, and behaviors.

resistance Largely unconscious defensive maneuvers intended to hinder the progress of therapy.

transference A phenomenon that occurs when clients start relating to their therapist in ways that mimic critical relationships in their lives.

client-centered therapy An insight therapy that emphasizes providing a supportive emotional climate for clients, who play a major role in determining the pace and direction of their therapy.

group therapy The simultaneous treatment of several or more clients in a group.

15-3

behavior therapies The application of the principles of learning to direct efforts to change clients' maladaptive behaviors.

systematic desensitization A behavior therapy used to reduce clients' anxiety responses through counterconditioning.

KEY IDEAS

15-1 Identify the basic elements of the treatment process.

- Psychotherapy involves three elements: treatments, clients, and therapists. Approaches to treatment are diverse, but they can be grouped into three categories: insight therapies, behavior therapies, and biomedical therapies. People vary considerably in their willingness to seek psychotherapy, and many people who need therapy do not receive it.
- Therapists come from a variety of professional backgrounds. Clinical and counseling psychologists earn a doctoral degree and tend to depend on insight or behavioral treatments. Psychiatrists earn an M.D. degree and tend to rely on biomedical treatments, primarily drug therapies. Social workers, psychiatric nurses, and counselors also provide therapeutic services.

15-2 Describe psychoanalysis, client-centered therapy, and group therapy, and assess their efficacy.

- Insight therapies involve verbal interactions intended to enhance self-knowledge. In psychoanalysis, free association and dream analysis are used to explore the unconscious. When an analyst's probing hits sensitive areas, resistance can be expected. The transference relationship may be used to overcome this resistance. Classical psychoanalysis is not widely practiced anymore, but Freud's legacy lives on in a rich diversity of modern psychodynamic therapies.
- Rogers pioneered client-centered therapy, which is intended to provide a supportive climate in which clients can restructure their self-concepts. This therapy emphasizes clarification of the client's feelings and self-acceptance. Most theoretical approaches to insight therapy have been adapted for use with groups. Group therapy has its own unique strengths and is not merely a cheap substitute for individual therapy.
- Research consistently indicates that insight therapy is superior to no treatment or to placebo treatment and that the effects of therapy are reasonably durable. Studies generally find the greatest improvement early in treatment. Repressed memories of childhood sexual abuse recovered through therapy are a new source of controversy in the mental health field. Although many recovered memories of abuse may be the product of suggestion, some probably are authentic.

15-3 Understand how systematic desensitization, aversion therapy, social skills training, and cognitive-behavioral treatments can solve behavioral problems.

- Behavior therapies use the principles of learning in direct efforts to change specific aspects of behavior. Wolpe's systematic desensitization is a treatment for phobias. It involves the construction of an anxiety hierarchy, relaxation training, and step-by-step movement through the hierarchy.

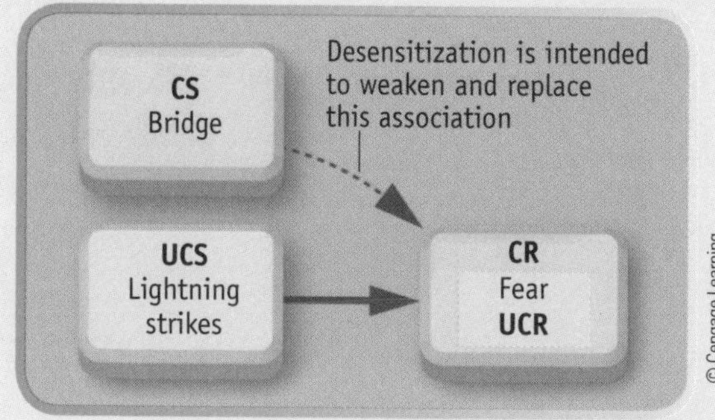

KEY TERMS *continued*

aversion therapy A behavior therapy in which an aversive stimulus is paired with a stimulus that elicits an undesirable response.

social skills training A behavior therapy designed to improve interpersonal skills that emphasizes shaping, modeling, and behavioral rehearsal.

cognitive-behavioral treatments Therapy approach that uses varied combinations of verbal interventions and behavior modification techniques to help clients change maladaptive patterns of thinking.

cognitive therapy An insight therapy that emphasizes recognizing and changing negative thoughts and maladaptive beliefs.

15-4

biomedical therapies Physiological interventions intended to reduce symptoms associated with psychological disorders.

psychopharmacotherapy The treatment of mental disorders with medication.

antianxiety drugs Drugs that relieve tension, apprehension, and nervousness.

antipsychotic drugs Drugs used to gradually reduce psychotic symptoms, including hyperactivity, mental confusion, hallucinations, and delusions.

tardive dyskinesia A neurological disorder marked by chronic tremors and involuntary spastic movements.

antidepressant drugs Drugs that gradually elevate mood and help to bring people out of a depression.

mood stabilizers Drugs used to control mood swings in patients with bipolar mood disorders.

electroconvulsive therapy (ECT) A biomedical treatment in which electric shock is used to produce a cortical seizure accompanied by convulsions.

KEY IDEAS *continued*

- In aversion therapy, a stimulus associated with an unwanted response is paired with an unpleasant stimulus in an effort to eliminate the maladaptive response. Social skills training can improve clients' interpersonal skills through shaping, modeling, and behavioral rehearsal. Beck's cognitive therapy concentrates on changing the way clients think about events in their lives. Ample evidence shows that behavior therapies are effective.

15-4 Outline the benefits and risks associated with drug therapies and electroconvulsive therapy.

- Biomedical therapies involve physiological interventions for psychological problems. A great variety of disorders are treated with drugs. Antianxiety drugs are used to relieve tension and nervousness. Antipsychotic drugs gradually reduce psychotic symptoms, such as hyperactivity, hallucinations, and delusions. Antidepressant drugs gradually help bring people out of episodes of depression. Mood stabilizers can control mood swings in people with bipolar disorders.
- Drug therapies can be effective, but they have their pitfalls. Many drugs produce problematic side effects, and some are overprescribed. Critics are also concerned that the pharmaceutical industry has gained too much influence over drug testing research.
- Electroconvulsive therapy (ECT) is used to trigger a cortical seizure that is believed to have therapeutic value for depression. There is contradictory evidence and heated debate about the effectiveness of ECT and about possible risks associated with its use, such as memory losses.

15-5 Discuss the merits of blending approaches to therapy and efforts to enhance cultural sensitivity in treatment.

- Combinations of insight, behavioral, and biomedical therapies are often used fruitfully in the treatment of psychological disorders. Many modern therapists are eclectic, using ideas and techniques gleaned from a number of theoretical approaches.

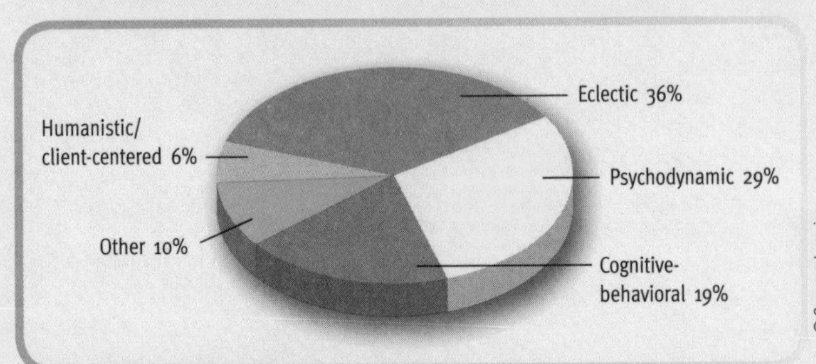

- Because of cultural, language, and access barriers, therapeutic services are underutilized by ethnic minorities in America. Possible solutions include recruiting and training more ethnic minority therapists, building better therapeutic alliances, and tailoring treatments for specific cultural groups.

15-6 Learn how to find a good therapist.

- Therapeutic services are available in many settings, and such services do not have to be expensive. Excellent and mediocre therapists can be found in all of the mental health professions. Thus, therapists' personal skills are more important than their professional degree. In selecting a therapist, it is reasonable to insist on a therapist of one gender or the other.
- The various theoretical approaches to treatment appear to be fairly similar in overall effectiveness. However, for certain types of problems, some approaches to therapy may be more effective than others, and individual therapists vary in their effectiveness. Therapy requires time, hard work, and the courage to confront your problems.